HANDBOOKS

D0094155

WASHINGTON

ERICKA CHICKOWSKI

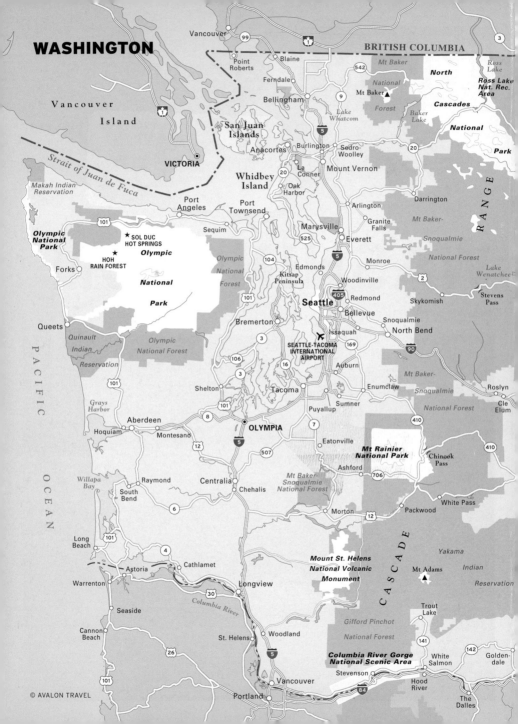

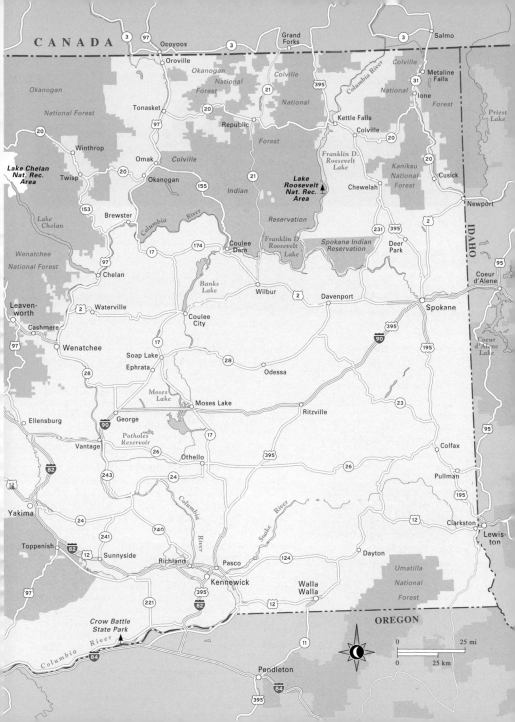

Contents

Discover Washington

Washington engages the senses — all of them.

Catch a whiff of bracing salt air along the wild and scenic coast, or the fragrant aroma of blackberries along the Puget Sound.

Feel the ice tickle your eyelashes through the flurries of the Northern Cascades, or the sweat trickle down your back under the hot sun in the high desert of Eastern Washington.

Experience the joy of seeing Mount Rainier rise over Lake Washington on a brilliant summer day, or watching raindrops break the foam of a perfect cappuccino when the drizzle sets in.

Listen for the mournful, deep booming of train horns through the Columbia Gorge, or the quiet swishing of skis on the backcountry trails of the Cascades.

Or try tasting Washington — the sweetness of wild blueberries in August, the smoky richness of freshly caught and grilled salmon, the robust complexities of a Columbia River cabernet sauvignon — they're all here waiting to be experienced.

Tromp through rain forests, raft on rivers, and clamber up rocky outcroppings long enough and you'll be won over by the natural charms of the state. During Washington's long summer days, an after-work hike is de rigeur for the locals, with a striking and well-maintained trail never far away. Turquoise-colored alpine lakes beckon fly-fishing anglers in their

peaceful art. Miles of bike-friendly roads and trails await those of the two-wheeled persuasion, while horse lovers can take their four-footed companions far from the madding crowd.

But these aren't the state's only draws – Washington is also a hub of art and culture, engineering and history. The region is home to historic lighthouses, impressive skyscrapers, and great works of art, such as the outdoor designs at the Seattle Olympic Sculpture Park. You're likely to be equally impressed by the dizzying heights of Seattle's Columbia Center tower and Mount Rainier.

The Evergreen State isn't just a destination for the body and mind, but for the soul, too. If you don't try too hard, the secret zen of this place just might open up to you. It might come standing atop mountain peaks hewn over thousands of years, under trees that took root before the birth of Columbus, or maybe amid the rolling solitude of golden wheat fields planted last spring. Wherever you are, be ready for it. Washington has a way of rewarding those who come ready to embrace it.

Planning Your Trip

▶ WHERE TO GO

Seattle

Washington's largest city and cultural center-piece, Seattle is known as the Emerald City for good reason. The city is awash in green spaces and parks such as the Washington Arboretum and Discovery Park, which balance well with the sleekly engineered Space Needle and city high-rises like the Columbia Tower. Seattle is surrounded by water, so don't forget your boat shoes. Enjoy Lake Union by kayak or floatplane, Elliott Bay by ferry, or Lake Washington by canoe.

taking it easy at Lake Union Park in Seattle

IF YOU HAVE . . .

- **A WEEKEND:** Visit Seattle, the Eastside, and the Puget Sound.

- **A WEEK:** Add a trip to Mount Rainier and Mount St. Helens.

- **TWO WEEKS:** Drive the Olympic Peninsula and the coast, then drive the Columbia River Gorge.

- **A MONTH:** Add a trip to Eastern Washington's wine country, stopping in Spokane and the Grand Coulee Dam. Drive the North Cascades Highway. Spend a weekend in the San Juan Islands.

The Eastside

Seattle's tony bedroom communities lie east of Lake Washington in an expanse that is part rural, part subdivision, and part outdoor park. Sip a little vino at the boutique wineries in Woodinville, take a sailing lesson at the Kirkland marina, hike to the top of the Issaquah Alps, or enjoy a good meal and some upscale shopping in Bellevue.

North Puget Sound

North of Seattle, cities line up along the Sound until development gives way first to suburb, then to country. See where Boeing builds its jumbo-liners in Everett. Or for some solitude, pedal the farm roads past the loamy soil of Skagit County. Motor along Chuckanut Drive, which careens by coves and bays along the wooded edge of the Sound until you reach historic Fairhaven in Bellingham. Northernmost along I-5 is

San Juan Island

Washington's portal to Canada, Blaine, home to the symbolic Peace Arch at the border.

South Puget Sound

The southern stretch of the Puget Sound is a craggy puzzle of inlets, islands, and peninsulas. Explore the industrial center turned cultural mecca of Tacoma, with its well-preserved historic brick buildings and an amazing collection of art and history museums. Travel even farther south to Olympia, home of the state's Capitol Campus, with its whitewashed legislative building, gardens, and parks. In between them, a curious traveler can find nature preserves and historic parks galore.

San Juan Islands

Puget Sound's prominent archipelago lies east of Anacortes. At low tide there are more than 786 islands, but the four serviced by Washington State Ferries are San Juan Island, Orcas Island, Lopez Island, and Shaw Island. The largest of the four, San Juan offers the widest variety of historic sites,

restaurants, and lodging. Orcas features the most rugged landscapes and the best trails. Lopez is a favorite for bicycling and Shaw is the most pastoral.

Olympic Peninsula and the Coast

Surf-pounded sea stacks, steaming hot springs, and crystal clear rivers all greet the traveler out in the Olympic Peninsula and Washington's coast. Crowning the interior of the peninsula are the majestic Olympic Mountains, reachable only by foot. At the

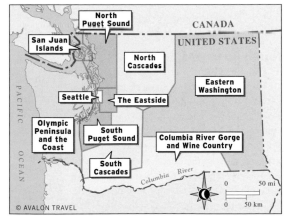

the Bavarian-themed town of Leavenworth

southernmost point, at the mouth of the Columbia River, lies Long Beach peninsula, the longest stretch of sandy beach in the state, which protects Willapa Bay, known for its oysters.

Columbia River Gorge and Wine Country

East of Vancouver, road-trippers will find a stretch of road seemingly made just for Sunday afternoons. Ramble alongside the deep gorge cut by the mighty Columbia River. Peer over craggy cliffs plunging down to the swift river waters, often dotted with windsurfers and kiteboarders, then make your way to the wineries along the Columbia River Highway.

North Cascades

The northern spires of the Cascades reach all the way up to the Canadian border in a network of glacial lakes, trout-filled rivers, alpine meadows, and wooded trails. The highlight is the pristine North Cascades National Park. Nearby is the miles-long Lake Chelan, a summer destination for all Washingtonians. Also in the region is the Bavarian lookalike town of Leavenworth, a favorite among hikers in summer and skiers when the snow flies.

South Cascades

From the state line all the way up to the I-90 corridor, rolling through Snoqualmie Pass, the Cascade mountains cut a wide swath across the middle of the state. Most notable among them is the tallest mountain in the continental United States, Mount Rainier. Contrast the tall and complete snowcaps on Rainier to the craggy, gaping hole left in Mount St. Helens. The oft-overlooked but rugged Mount Adams is surrounded by public forest land, just waiting to be explored.

windsurfing on the Columbia River

Eastern Washington

Wind your way up and over any one of Washington's passes from the Puget Sound and you're likely to find Seattle's precious commodity in abundant supply: sunshine. Enjoy the weather at giant reservoirs out here, including the granddaddy of them all, Lake Roosevelt, formed by the massive Grand Coulee Dam. If all the rural, arid, rocky landscape gets too lonely for you, get a taste of city life in Spokane, home of one of the nicest city parks in the state, Riverfront Park.

► WHEN TO GO

There's no doubt about it, there is nothing so sublime as late summer in Washington, particularly the month of August. During this time, visitors have the best chance of catching sunshine throughout the state, even in rainy Puget Sound. All of the snow has usually melted from mountain trails by then, replaced by blossoms kissing the alpine meadows. And hot Eastern Washington beckons sun lizards looking to hang out by its innumerable lakes under the late afternoon light.

Of course, other times of year bring their own joys. In spring, the tulips burst forth in the Skagit Valley and hearty rhododendron blossoms explode from seemingly every streetside bush in the Puget Sound.

In much of Washington, fall is harvest time. Take a drive along the back roads of the Palouse hills in Eastern Washington to see farmers working away at the golden sea of wheat or tour wine country during the grape harvest to see what it takes to perfect those vintages. This is also one of the most dramatic times to watch the surf pound the ocean along the coast or revel in the water dripping off the Olympic rain forest leaves.

And though the drizzle descends pretty unceasingly onto the Puget Sound in winter, the season is far from gloomy to those willing to strap on skis or snowshoes. The Cascade Mountain range is painted white each year, easily reachable in as little as a half hour from Seattle. If that isn't your thing, this is also the perfect time to huddle up in a Seattle coffee shop and enjoy the museums around the region.

Nothing beats a hike in the North Cascades during the height of wildflower season.

Explore Washington

► THE BEST OF WASHINGTON

Washington is filled with mountain vistas, remote beaches, country roads, and urban hideaways. Enjoy the very best the state has to offer on this whirlwind tour.

Day 1

From Seattle, take a meandering drive up to Mount Rainier, soaking up the views from the lovely flower-filled meadows at aptly named Paradise and then from the stunning alpine ridges high up at Sunrise. On the way back from Sunrise, stop in for a short hike to the towering ancient trees at Grove of the Patriarchs. Settle in for a soak in the hot tub and maybe even a massage at Wellspring in Ashford.

Day 2

Today is an early day. Head to Castle Rock, gateway to the Mount St. Helens National Volcanic Monument. You'll wind your way up the Spirit Lake Memorial Highway, past areas once ravaged by the mountain's explosive force. At the end of the road lies the Johnston Ridge Observatory, the closest viewpoint reachable by car, with vistas of the mountain and of log-strewn Spirit Lake. Stay the night at Eco Park at Mount St. Helens, the only lodging within the mountain's blast zone.

Day 3

Motor south on I-5 to Vancouver, sister city to Portland, Oregon, just across the mighty Columbia. Spend the day exploring the orderly barracks, officers' rows, and marching grounds at Fort Vancouver National Historic Reserve before catching a late lunch at Officer's Row. Then check out the rebuilt wooden stockades and grounds at old Fort Vancouver and the prop-driven relics at Pearson Air Museum, both also on the reserve.

Day 4

Put on the driving gloves again for a leisurely drive along the dramatic banks of the

the high altitude views at Sunrise near Mount Rainier

Spokane's Riverfront Park

Columbia. Take the time to climb up to the top of Beacon Rock, and imagine the thrill Lewis and Clark felt navigating the river below. Continue on to Maryhill Winery for a glass of wine, and enjoy the sunset as you look over the Gorge and Mount Hood. Then continue up to Goldendale Observatory for a nighttime star show through the observatory's telescopes.

Day 5

Drive up and over the Cascade foothills to reach the heart of wine country, the Yakima Valley. Start with a quick stop in Toppenish, a genuine western town known for its amazing murals. Then take a drive around the wineries in the Rattlesnake Hills. Finally, cruise by the apple and fruit orchards around Wapato. Settle down for the evening in Yakima.

Day 6

Take the scenic route up to I-90 along the Yakima River on Highway 821. Then blast over the asphalt eastward toward Spokane. Take a long break along the way, stopping to check out the trees made of stone at Ginkgo Petrified Forest State Park. Finish the day with a relaxing spa treatment at the luxurious Davenport Hotel, your home for the evening.

Day 7

Start the day off with a gondola ride over Spokane Falls at Riverfront Park, enjoying a leisurely lunch at nearby Clinkerdagger's Restaurant. Then hop in the car up to Grand Coulee Dam for a late-afternoon tour of the grounds. Stay the night here so you can enjoy the laser light show at the dam later in the evening.

Day 8

Travel to the marvelously sunny Methow Valley and explore the faux-Western town of Winthrop, being sure to stop off at Sheri's Sweet Shop for treats. Rent a mountain bike and explore the valley's trails, hike Hart's Pass, or just stick around town and visit Shafer Museum.

Day 9

Experience the breathtaking North Cascades Highway, rambling right by the glaciated spires and turquoise lakes of North Cascades National Park. Stop for vistas at the Washington Pass Viewpoint, Ross

Ross Lake Overlook

you'll stay in a restored 1914 farmhouse at Benson's Farmstead.

Day 12

Today you have a choice. You'll be making the short drive south to Deception Pass, over the arching green-trussed Deception Pass Bridge and onto Whidbey Island. You can spend the day exploring the numerous trails and lakes in Deception Pass State Park and even catch a boat under the bridge. Or you can continue south and enjoy the rolling pastoral land in Ebey's Landing National Historical Reserve, examine museum artifacts and a blockhouse in Coupeville, and enjoy a slice of loganberry pie and pet the llamas at Greenbank Farm. Either way, end the day with a ferry ride to Mukilteo and stay the night in Seattle.

Day 13

Enjoy a quintessential day in Seattle. Pick through the wares at Pike Place Market and

Lake Overlook and Diablo Lake Overlook. In Diablo, catch the speedboat to unique floating cabins at Ross Lake Resort for a couple nights of rest and relaxation.

Day 10

Time to take it easy. Relax dockside with a book or rent a boat and fish Ross Lake for rainbow trout. If you're really feeling ambitious, hike the nearly seven-mile trail to the top of Desolation Peak, where writer Jack Kerouac once stood watch at the fire lookout that still stands there today.

Day 11

Catch the ferry and hit the North Cascades Highway eastward again. Stop in Marblemount, grab a paddle and life vest, and climb aboard a guided rafting trip down the Skagit River. Once you've had your fun, continue on the highway until the landscape opens up into the wide open fields of the Skagit Valley and head north to Bow, where

Pike Place Market

WINES OF WASHINGTON

Located at the same latitude as some of the most famed wine-growing regions in France, Washington has certainly taken advantage of its geographical windfall. The number of wineries in the state has increased fourfold in the last decade, and the state has become home to 11 different American Viticultural Areas (AVA) wine appellations, each with its own characteristic varietals based on the climate of the region. Here are some of the highlights of the most famous growing regions:

COLUMBIA VALLEY

This "macro" AVA runs across much of central and eastern Washington, across the entire Columbia River plateau. As growers have learned more about microclimates, various regions have been broken into sub-appellations. Best reds: merlot, cabernet sauvignon. Best whites: Semillon, sauvignon blanc, Riesling.

COLUMBIA RIVER GORGE

Including both the Washington and Oregon sides of the Gorge, this AVA is known to grow a huge variety of grapes due to the area's contrast of rainy and dry climate depending on how far east along the Gorge you go. You'll find a great selection of funky blends here as

a result. Best reds: Syrah, pinot noir, zinfandel. Best whites: Riesling, chardonnay.

YAKIMA VALLEY

The longest-lived AVA in the state, Yakima Valley's storied winemaking history dates back to a vineyard planting by a French immigrant back in 1869. It's known for a more temperate climate than the rest of the Columbia Valley, making for better chardonnay. Best reds: cabernet sauvignon, merlot, Syrah. Best whites: chardonnay, Riesling.

WALLA WALLA VALLEY

The same loamy soil that lends itself well to Walla Walla's famous sweet onions and its bountiful wheat production also combines with the warm weather to produce particularly complex red varietals. Best reds: cabernet sauvignon, Sangiovese, Tempranillo.

PUGET SOUND

The only appellation in Washington located east of the Cascades, the Puget Sound is a less common place to grow, producing only about one percent of the state's grapes. The cool, wet climate lends itself mostly to whites. Best reds: pinot noir. Best whites: Madeleine Angevine, Muller-Thurgau, pinot gris.

fruit of the vine in Washington wine country

watch the fish fly. Then travel up to Ballard to see the fishies in their own environment, making their way up the fish ladder at Hiram M. Chittenden Locks. Cap off the touring with an elevator ride to the top of the Space Needle for a 360-degree view of the city. Finally, finish off your last evening in Seattle with a dinner downtown or in Belltown. If you haven't had Northwest salmon yet, now's your chance.

Day 14

Grab your camera and explore the state's capitol in Olympia. Visit the grand dome of Washington, the Legislative Building, then watch the kids run through the dancing waters of Heritage Fountain at Heritage Park. Enjoy lunch by Tumwater Falls at Falls Terrace Restaurant on the south end of Capitol Lake. Then drive north to Tacoma and check into the swanky Hotel Murano, home to a kaleidoscope of one-of-a-kind glass art.

Day 15

From your downtown digs, walk to Tacoma's museum row and start by touring the

Washington capitol dome

interactive exhibits at one of the state's finest, the Washington State History Museum. Cross native son Dale Chihuly's Bridge of Glass to the fascinating Museum of Glass and watch glassmaking demonstrations in its hot shop before heading home.

The Museum of Glass in Tacoma offers live glassblowing demonstrations.

► WEEKEND GETAWAYS

The state has so much to offer visitors and residents alike that it is really most fun to explore in small chunks. Here are a few weekend itineraries to get you started.

Jet City

Seattle has enough sights to keep the curious occupied for weeks. The following trip highlights the very best the city has to offer.

DAY 1

Take a little drive to the southern part of the city and start the day at the Museum of Flight with a tour of the aviation industry that first put Seattle on the map. Then park your car in the hotel garage for the rest of the weekend—you'll be able to walk or take alternative means of transportation after that. Grab a camera and take a ride on the monorail from Westlake Center to Seattle Center and spend some time atop the Space Needle. Bundle up—it gets cold on that observation deck!

DAY 2

The weekends are the best time of the week to visit Pike Place Market, which absolutely teems with activity on these days. Try an Asian pear or some fresh honeycomb, listen to street buskers croon, and pet Rachel, the bronze pig. Then take the stairs all the way down the Pike Street Hill Climb to the Waterfront. Enjoy the octopus, sea urchins, and sea mammals at the Seattle Aquarium. Check out Sylvester, the mummy, at Ye Olde Curiosity Shop. Enjoy some fish and chips from restaurant stalls lined up by the piers. And then, if you've still got some life in you, walk it all off with a long stroll all the way down to Olympic Sculpture Park.

DAY 3

Take the Elliot Bay Water Taxi over to West Seattle and enjoy one of the best Sunday brunches in the state at Salty's on Alki, feasting on crab legs, prime rib, and dainty

Seattle's Waterfront

little desserts. Then relax by the water with a walk along Alki Beach, taking in the Seattle view from a distance. Give yourself enough time in the afternoon to head back downtown to learn about the exploding toilets, the seedy houses of ill repute, and the Great Fire at the lively Seattle Underground tour. Once aboveground again, check out the Klondike Gold Rush National Historic Park and the brick facades of historic Pioneer Square. Spend the evening enjoying a performance by the symphony at Benaroya Hall or the impressive Seattle Opera.

DAY 4

Enjoy your last morning on the water. Take the Lake Union Trolley down to South Lake Union and then trek a mile up Westlake Avenue, or take bus 17 over to NorthWest Outdoor Center. Hop in a kayak for a close-up look at the houseboats made famous by the film *Sleepless in Seattle.* Check out the giant structures at Gasworks Park and watch the seaplanes zip over the water.

Gorgeous Gorge

Take in the natural wonders of the Columbia River Gorge National Scenic Area from both sides of the mighty river in a long weekend loop tour that'll make you think you're in a car commercial.

DAY 1

Sure, this is a guidebook about Washington, but the Gorge is a bi-state region, so you'll want to start your trip in Oregon. Drive from Portland on I-84 until you hit the turnoff for the Historic Columbia River Highway. Break out your wide-angle lens from the overlook at Vista House at Crown Point and continue east to take in the Gorge Waterfalls along the highway. Stop off for lunch at the Multnomah Lodge under the towering Multnomah Falls. Stop at the Bonneville Fish Hatchery to check out Herman the Sturgeon, a 10-foot, 70-year-old white sturgeon. Finish the day off with a dinner cruise aboard the Sternwheeler Columbia Gorge from the town of Cascade Locks.

Oregon's Multnomah Falls is a great place to start your Washington vacation.

the White Salmon River

DAY 2

A stay in either Cascade Locks or nearby Hood River the night before will have put you in perfect position to seize the day early with a morning kiteboarding or windsurfing lesson at Kite Beach, just west of the Hood River Bridge. Dry off and share lunch with the fellow recreation enthusiasts in Hood River before taking it easy. Spend a leisurely afternoon visiting the farms, orchards, wineries, and alpaca farms scattered along the bucolic Fruit Loop north of town.

DAY 3

Cross the Hood River Bridge over to the Washington side of the Gorge and start the day with a thrilling rafting trip down the White Salmon River. Then take a drive east along the golden grasses of the dry side of the Gorge to visit Maryhill Museum. Backtrack west a little along State Route 14 to finish the day with a mineral spa treatment at the historic Carson Hot Springs Resort.

DAY 4

An early hike to the top of Beacon Rock will get your circulation flowing and give you one last stupendous look at the cavernous beauty of the Gorge from a great vantage point. Time to head back west for a flight out of Portland.

Island Hopper

Escape city life on a trip to the Puget Sound's premier weekend destination, the San Juan Islands. This trip can also be taken by car and ferry, departing from Anacortes.

DAY 1

Make your getaway from Seattle to the San Juan Islands aboard a floatplane. Have the pilot touch down near Friday Harbor on San Juan Island. Rent a moped to explore the back roads of the island. Stop for a wine-tasting at San Juan Vineyard, pet the alpacas and buy a sweater at Krystal Acres, and wander the fragrant flower fields at Pelindaba Lavender Farm. Be sure to also check out

Moran State Park on Orcas Island

American Camp and English Camp on opposite sides of the island, both a part of the San Juan Islands National Historic Park, which memorializes an international scuffle started over a pig.

DAY 2

Spend the morning whale-watching, either on a motorboat or on a kayak tour, in search of breaching and spyhopping killer whales. Then jump aboard the ferry to Orcas Island and take the shuttle bus to Moran State Park. Set up camp for the night, or stay at the park's guesthouse, then explore. Ply the park's lakes for fish, or hike up to the rumbling Cascades Falls.

DAY 3

Moran State Park is home to the island chain's highest peak, Mount Constitution. Wake early and trek four miles up to the top for an unbeatable view of the Sound. Then pack up and head out for a ferry over to the flat, bike-friendly terrain of Lopez Island.

Arrange for Lopez Bicycle Works to bring you bike rentals and tour the island on two wheels. Stay the night on Lopez and hitch a floatplane back to Seattle in the morning.

Over the River and Through the Woods

You don't have to drive hours from Seattle to experience the great outdoors. There are loads of natural wonders right out the doorstep from the Puget Sound.

DAY 1

Drive up to the thundering water of Snoqualmie Falls, the waterfall made famous as the backdrop for the TV series *Twin Peaks*. Take a short hike down to the bottom of the falls and then splurge on a gourmet meal in the Salish Lodge overlooking the scenery here.

DAY 2

Enjoy the Issaquah Alps today, with a nice hike up to the top of Tiger Mountain for fantastic views of Seattle and the Eastside. Then drive over to the unique Cougar Mountain Zoo and visit the menagerie of endangered animals there.

DAY 3

Take a drive to Kanasket-Palmer State Park and put-in with a guided rafting trip over the white water of the Green River. Experience class IV rapids with quirky names like the Nozzle and the Ledge Drop as you float by the hanging gardens along the river until you reach Flaming Geyser State Park.

▶ THE OLYMPIAD

Take a rugged tour around the Olympic Peninsula's U.S. 101 loop and visit Olympic National Park.

Day 1

Start the Highway 101 loop heading north between the Olympic mountains and Hood Canal. If you've got dive experience, rent equipment from Mike's Dive Resort and search the murky depths for a giant octopus. Or just take a short hike at Dosewallips State Park. Enjoy a lunch of Hood Canal oysters in Hoodsport, and take it easy for the night in Port Townsend.

Day 2

Enjoy the history in Port Townsend with a visit to Fort Worden State Park. Then head east to Sequim for a brisk hike along the longest natural sand spit in the United States, Dungeness Spit. Head west on 101 to Port Angeles. Learn about the wilderness on the peninsula at the Olympic National Park Visitors Center and find a local bed-and-breakfast to rest for the evening.

Day 3

Start the morning by taking a drive to one of the best viewpoints in Washington,

Dosewallips State Park

Hurricane Ridge. Then continue east to the Sol Duc River Valley. Take a hike up to Sol Duc Falls and soak in the hot spring waters at Sol Duc Hot Springs Resort, where you'll rest for the evening.

by the neon blue waters of Lake Crescent. Stop for an interpretive hike at Barnes Point by the lakeshore. Stay the night in La Push and enjoy a walk along the log-strewn beach here.

Day 4

Continue east on 101, and you'll be greeted

Day 5

Get back on 101 going south, until you reach

WASHINGTON'S FIVE CORNERS

Gas up the car and head deep into this oddly shaped state's five corners. You'll discover some hidden gems that are well worth the drive.

BLAINE
You'll get the chance to put one foot in Canada and the other in the United States on the lawn of **Peace Arch State Park,** a lovely park right on the border with British Columbia. The giant white arch here symbolizes the friendship between Americans and Canadians.

NEAH BAY
The blustery tip of land at **Cape Flattery** in Neah Bay is the northwesternmost point in the continental United States and a deliciously remote spot to explore. Hike around the Cape and then head south to **Shi Shi Beach,** one of the most peaceful stretches of sand along the entire Washington coast.

CAPE DISAPPOINTMENT
Get a glimpse of the Pacific Ocean from the same vantage point as Lewis and Clark had more than 200 years ago. Where the Columbia River meets the ocean is home to the popular **Cape Disappointment State Park,** which offers an old military fort, scenic beaches and lighthouses, trails for exploration, and an interpretive center about America's favorite transcontinental explorers.

PALOUSE COUNTRY
The undulating golden wheat hillsides of the Palouse greet travelers to the lonely rural countryside of the southeast corner of the state. Road-trippers are rewarded with his-

Peace Arch State Park

toric sites and classy vineyards in **Walla Walla,** as well as the thundering waters of the state's mightiest cataract, **Palouse Falls.**

PEND OREILLE
Enjoy the satisfying crunch of pine needles and cones underfoot in the quiet backcountry of the state's northeastern corner. This is a land of solitude, blessed with still mountain lakes, serene campgrounds, and miles of trails. It is also home to the **Pend Oreille River,** the only river in the States to flow north, looping up into Canada until it reaches the Columbia River.

Hoh Rain Forest

Upper Hoh Road. This will take you east along the Hoh River, deep into the lush Hoh Rain Forest. Pick one of the many trails to tramp between the towering pines drooped with moss here. Then continue on to the bluffs of Kalaloch for a look at the rugged Washington coast.

Day 6

Today you'll explore Lake Quinault, less than an hour south of Kalaloch along Highway 101. Take the 30-mile loop around the lake—numerous trails butt up against the road if you're eager to stretch your legs. Take it easy by the lake at Lake Quinault Resort.

Day 7

From Lake Quinault, sneak back over to the coast on Moclips-Quinault Road, and take a leisurely scenic drive down Highway 109. Stop at Pacific Beach State Park or Griffiths-Priday State Park to fly a kite or cast a fishing line. Then keep driving south until you hit Ocean Shores, to enjoy the last hours of sunlight riding horseback along the beach.

▶ INTO THE WILD CASCADES

The Cascade Range is a recreational playground that offers a full spectrum of outdoor adventures, no matter your preference.

Hiking

Hikers will find most passes open after the Fourth of July, making this a prime time for epic backpacking trips on the Wonderland Trail around Mount Rainier or Chelan Lakeshore Trail to Stehekin in the North Cascades. Or just opt for a day hike up to Heather Meadows near Mount Baker, the Big Four Ice Caves on the Mountain Loop Highway, or the dramatic Kendall Katwalk along the longer Pacific Crest Trail.

Mountain Biking

Advanced mountain bikers will want to put

Wenatchee River just outside of Leavenworth

the trails at Crystal Mountain on their bucket list. A number of grueling ascents will net you an amazing view from 7,000 feet of Rainier, Adams, and St. Helens, plus a one-way ticket to bomb down some amazing stretches of downhill. Beginner and intermediate riders can also opt for the incredible mountain biking trail through the Plains of Abraham, which leads you straight through the Mount St. Helens blast zone. It's an area that looks more like the moon than a mountain range on planet Earth.

Boating and Fishing

Come summertime, water rats can go gangbusters whizzing a speedboat up Lake Chelan, a great spot for fishing, boating, and waterskiing. Or get your heart pumping with a whitewater trip down the Wenatchee River near Leavenworth. In the fall, try your artistry with a fly rod outside of Cle Elum on the Yakima River. Once the snow hits the mountains and the lakes freeze up, bring a thermos and an auger to catch those lunkers by ice fishing Lost Lake near Snoqualmie Pass. For ever-so-slightly warmer winter

waters, try the Skykomish River to hook a hard-fighting steelhead.

Skiing

Downhill skiers have a full spectrum of resorts and ski areas to choose from within the Cascades. Most convenient to Seattle is Snoqualmie Pass, less than an hour away from the city, with a decent range of runs. Better yet, travel just a bit farther up to Stevens Pass for one of the best all-around ski areas in the state.

Hardcore skiers will do well to make the trek up north to Mount Baker, down south to Crystal Mountain, or toward Mission Ridge for the most challenging runs, even if they are a bit out of the way.

Those who prefer to ski on level ground can also sweat it out on the miles of cross-country trails offered by the Methow Valley Sport Trails Association, near Winthrop, which offers small camping huts along the trail for a multiday adventure. Similar hut-to-hut skiing can be found along the Mount Tahoma Trails Association network of trails near Mount Rainier.

SEATTLE

Newcomers to Seattle are inevitably impressed by this big but still friendly home to 560,000 people, where the various monikers that have been applied—America's Most Livable City, Emerald City, Latte Land, and City of Niceness—all seem to fit. The obvious charms of Seattle and the Puget Sound region draw more tourists each year, many of whom come back to stay.

Seattle's appeal comes from its beautiful setting, its friendly and creative people, and the way the city has grown up along the shores of Puget Sound and Lake Washington. Oddly shaped towers and preserved historical districts stand alongside modern skyscrapers and the busy waterfront in jaunty disharmony. Every major event in the city's short life span, from Yesler's 1850s sawmill to the 1962 World's Fair

to the 1990s high-tech boom (and subsequent bust) has left its legacy; the resulting mishmash of periods gives the city a flavor absent in showpieces of urban renewal.

History doesn't make a city livable, though, and no one event or attraction can ever take that credit. Rather, it's a thousand incidents, enjoyed daily: dining at the waterfront, watching the sun set behind the Olympics as sailboats head home; reading the paper on your early-morning ferry commute, accompanied by a lively porpoise escort service; listening to a free outdoor lunchtime concert in the heart of downtown; stopping for fresh vegetables or fish at Pike Place Market; cleansing your lungs with fresh, rain-rinsed air as you dodge slugs and puddles on your morning run; attending a summertime party on a harbor tour boat;

© ERICKA CHICKOWSKI

HIGHLIGHTS

◖ Seattle Underground: Learn Seattle's colorful history on this tour of the underground formed when Seattle was rebuilt after the Great Fire of 1889 (page 35).

◖ Seattle Art Museum: Explore a world of artwork that ranges from Renaissance masterpieces to delicate painted porcelain to tribal ritual art (page 35).

◖ Pike Place Market: Experience the buzz of farmers hawking their produce, flying fish, and scrumptious treats at the oldest continually operating market in the country (page 36).

◖ Seattle Aquarium: Explore the depths of the Puget Sound without even getting wet (page 37).

◖ Space Needle: Seattle's iconic landmark, this tower offers stellar views from the observation deck (page 40).

◖ Experience Music Project: Check out the guitars, the concert jumpsuits, the street flyers, and all sorts of ephemera from the rock 'n' roll age (page 41).

◖ Discovery Park: This is Seattle's largest park, a big slice of nature sitting on a bluff overlooking the Sound (page 45).

◖ Chittenden Locks: See the boats navigate from the Puget Sound to the Lake Washington Ship Canal, watch the fish push up the salmon ladder from the viewing windows, and take in the flowers in the gardens at this Ballard favorite (page 46).

◖ University of Washington Park Arboretum and Japanese Garden: Green thumbs and garden lovers will admire the foliage and plant diversity at Seattle's premier botanic reserve (page 50).

◖ Museum of Flight: Follow the history of flight and aviation and learn about Seattle's contribution to the skies at this extremely well-curated museum (page 51).

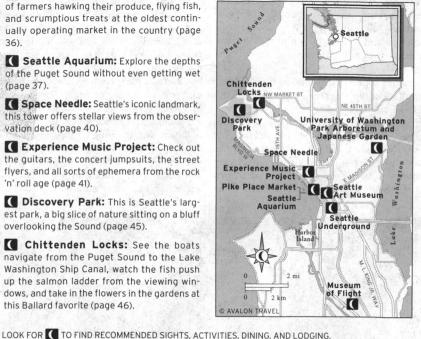

LOOK FOR ◖ TO FIND RECOMMENDED SIGHTS, ACTIVITIES, DINING, AND LODGING.

and being surprised by a clear view of bashful Mount Rainier from the highway or the University of Washington campus.

Seattle maintains a justified reputation for kindness and open-mindedness. It's the little things that immediately impress visitors: drivers waiting for other cars to pull out ahead of them, the almost total lack of horn-honking, the easy acceptance of long lines at an espresso bar, the friendly bus drivers who don't charge for a short ride, and the pedestrians waiting for the Walk sign before crossing a deserted street. Sometimes this laid-back nature approaches the annoying stage—such as the times clerks stop to chat with a customer about her kids while a long queue waits patiently—but Seattleites take

it all in stride. Maybe it's the Northwest heritage of acceptance and community; maybe it's the on-again, off-again rain that teaches patience… or maybe it's something they put in the coffee.

HISTORY

Long before skyscrapers or even brick Victorian buildings popped up along Elliott Bay, Seattle was a magnet for Native Americans who gravitated around the plentiful salmon and lush edible landscape here. Chief Si'ahl, the famous Duwamish leader, ended up the namesake of the city that first took shape in 1851. It was around that time that the first city elders came here in hopes to establish "the New York of the Pacific Coast." As with many city founders of the West, they faced plenty of mishaps along the way that would influence the identity of Seattle.

Their first blunder was building on the exposed Alki Point. It didn't take long out there in the blustery Seattle weather to drive them to the much more sheltered area now known as Pioneer Square.

The second site posed its own unique problems. The new location was on the mudflats of the Duwamish River and flooding was an annual event. More regularly, toilets and sewers tended to back up during high tides.

It was a disgusting mess that could only be solved by a burning pot of glue that tipped over

in a cabinet shop one afternoon in 1889. It sparked one of the gravest calamities in Seattle's history: a 58-block blaze that razed the city. While the Great Fire certainly turned the fortunes of many early Seattleites, it also provided city organizers the opportunity to regrade by literally building on top of the rubble. Streets and sidewalks were raised, leaving existing storefronts below ground and forcing shop owners to cut doorways in what used to be their second story. As you walk through downtown, look out for purple squares of glass in the sidewalk—these are essentially skylights into the "Seattle Underground" that was created as a result.

The Great Fire could have easily sunk Seattle were it not for two strokes of good luck at the end of the 19th century.

First, in 1893 the Great Northern Line railroad added Seattle as a terminus, giving boost to the economically significant lumber and coal businesses that initially had to send all of their wares back East by boat all the way around Cape Horn.

But maybe even more important was the news in 1896 that a few intrepid explorers had discovered gold deep in Canada's Yukon on a creek that fed into the Klondike River. As the frenzy of the Klondike Gold Rush began, fathers left their families, workmen left their jobs, and even Seattle's mayor quit to go seek

CHIEF SI'AHL OF THE DUWAMISH

Chief Si'ahl ruled the Duwamish people in the Puget Sound during the first white settlement in the 1850s. A noted warrior and powerful speaker, Si'ahl befriended the early settlers. He and the Duwamish people offered the settlers invaluable advice and assistance in exchange for their help holding back the Patkanim people, who were trying to push Si'ahl and his tribe off of their land.

Si'ahl is also famous for a speech he gave in 1854, proclaiming the brotherhood of man and that "what befalls the earth befalls all the sons of the earth." While stirring, the speech

was given in the Lushootseed language, which was then translated into Chinook, and finally into English. The version we have today didn't appear until several years after the speech. While Chief Si'ahl was by all accounts well-spoken, and the speech's message resonates, it was probably the product of some latter-day polishing.

Today a bronze sculpture of Chief Si'ahl stands at the corner of 5th and Denny Way. His burial site is marked with an elaborate marble monument at a peaceful Suquamish cemetery that overlooks his namesake's skyline.

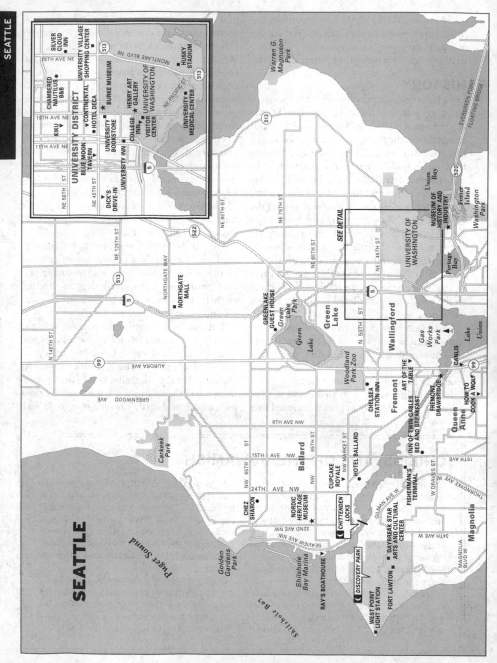

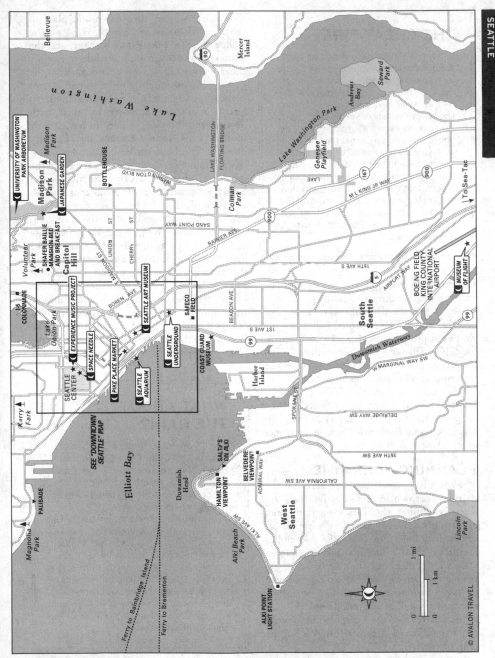

Bellevue

90

Mercer Island

Seward Park

Lake Washington

UNIVERSITY OF WASHINGTON PARK ARBORETUM

Madison Park

LAKE WASHINGTON FLOATING BRIDGE

Andrews Bay

Lake Washington Park

BOTHHOUSE

Madison Park

JAPANESE GARDEN

WASHINGTON BLVD

Genesee Playfield

167

900

SAND POINT WAY

Colman Park

RAINIER AVE

M L KING JR WAY

LAKE

To Sea-Tac

Volunteer Park

SHAFER BAILLIE MANSION BED AND BREAKFAST

19TH ST

UNION ST

CHERRY

900

15TH AVE S

5

BOEING FIELD KING COUNTY INTERNATIONAL AIRPORT

AIRPLAT WAY

MUSEUM OF FLIGHT

Capitol Hill

E MADISON ST

BOREN AVE

SEATTLE ART MUSEUM

I-5 COLONNADE

EXPERIENCE MUSIC PROJECT

BEACON AVE

South Seattle

99

Lake Union Park

SPACE NEEDLE

SAFECO FIELD

1ST AVE S

SEATTLE CENTER

PIKE PLACE MARKET

SEATTLE UNDERGROUND

99

Duwamish Waterway

W MARGINAL WAY SW

Kerry Park

SEATTLE AQUARIUM

COAST GUARD MUSEUM

Harbor Island

SPOKANE ST

PALISADE

SEE "DOWNTOWN SEATTLE" MAP

DELRIDGE WAY SW

Magnolia Park

Elliott Bay

Duwamish Head

SALTY'S ON ALKI

BELVEDERE VIEWPOINT

35TH AVE SW

HAMILTON VIEWPOINT

CALIFORNIA AVE SW

ALKI AVE SW

ADMIRAL WAY

CALIFORNIA AVE SW

West Seattle

Lincoln Park

Alki Beach Park

Ferry to Bainbridge Island

Ferry to Bremerton

ALKI POINT LIGHT STATION

1 mi

1 km

0

0

© AVALON TRAVEL

THE GREAT FIRE

In the mid-19th-century American West, fortunes could go up in smoke quickly. Hastily constructed wooden buildings, narrow streets, poor water pipes, and a reckless spirit destroyed dozens of fledgling towns. On June 6, Seattle nearly went the same way when a burning pot of glue tipped over inside a cabinet shop. All available citizens were enlisted to fight the fire and by 8:30 that night, the fire was at least under control. A traumatized public agreed that they must rebuild, and they must do so in brick. Today, several of the eclectic post-fire buildings still stand, and many are still in use, especially in today's Pioneer Square.

his fortune in the Klondike. But the real gold vein ran straight through Seattle.

The trip to the Klondike was a rough one, and the North West Mounted Police required that each prospector carry a year's supply of food, plus necessary tools and clothing. As the closest city to the gold fields, it only made sense for prospectors to stock up in Seattle.

It's said that half the $200 million in Klondike gold ended up in Seattle. More than any other event in the city's history, the Klondike Gold Rush made Seattle the biggest city in America's Northwest corner.

PLANNING YOUR TIME

The sparkling, clear summers make all that drizzle worthwhile. Between late July and early September, the thirsty emerald greenery that gives the city her name is usually offset by deep blue, cloudless skies and endless mountain vistas. Humidity stays low, temperatures range between the 70s and 80s, and people wonder why anyone would ever want to live anywhere else. Be sure to book hotel reservations well in advance during this time as the weather and the Alaska cruise ship traffic that spikes in summer brings a bumper crop of tourists.

If you're staying downtown and plan on mostly sticking to the Seattle staples—the **Space Needle, Pike Place Market,** and the **Underground Tour**—it's possible to explore the city unrushed in a day or two. If this is the game plan, you might also be able to conveniently forgo a rental car. Spread out and hilly, Seattle is still a walkable city in spurts, with downtown pretty convenient to navigate by foot and cab. **Pioneer Square** and the entry down to the Underground Tour are a few blocks from most downtown hotels. From the downtown shopping district, the Market and **Seattle Aquarium** at the waterfront are also an easy walk. The slog back from the waterline can be a huff-and-puff uphill affair, though, but it isn't something that a short taxi ride can't fix. To get to the **Seattle Center,** the Space Needle, and the **Experience Music Project** from downtown, step on the **Monorail** from Westlake Center Station for a convenient lift and a chance to cross that iconic space-age train from your to-do list. Westlake Center is also the departure point of the **South Lake Union Seattle Street Car,** which will take you to the sparkling waters along South Lake

WHAT ABOUT THE RAIN?

Yes, it's true. In 1898, a boy actually drowned on a downtown Seattle street. He was trying to cross an enormous sinkhole on a raft, fell off, and couldn't swim. But contrary to the story, there's really no rea...n to pack your snorkel.

The city actually gets less annual rainfall than New York City, it just falls more slowly here. Gray and drizzly skies are standard fare from October-May and when it does rain, it's usually a who-needs-an-umbrella sprinkle. One of Seattle's oddest facts is that more pairs of sunglasses are sold there per capita than any other American city, but umbrella and raincoat sales are no higher than average.

Union Park, the forest of masts at the **Center for Wooden Boats** and the newly relocated **Museum of History and Industry.**

If you hope to explore further afield, you'll need to add more time to the itinerary and consider your transportation options more carefully. Water-lovers hoping to appreciate the Puget Sound from the city shoreline should consider setting aside either a full day or at least an afternoon to explore **Alki Beach** in West Seattle or **Golden Gardens Park** in Ballard. Alki can be reached by the West Seattle Water Taxi from downtown, but Golden Gardens requires a car or some close examination of the Metro bus timetables.

Those with a soft spot for animals will want to put time in the schedule to spend a morning visiting the **Woodland Park Zoo** in Green Lake, perhaps following it up in the afternoon with a short jaunt over to Ballard to watch the fish jump the salmon ladder at the famous **Chittenden Locks.** If you have a free afternoon or morning and prefer flora over fauna, the **University of Washington Park Arboretum** adjacent to the U-District displays a diverse collection of plants and trees in a pastoral park along Lake Washington. Green thumbs looking for respite from the cold on drearier days will also appreciate the collection of orchids and palms at **Volunteer Park Conservatory,** a steamy retreat from the rain. A car is best to check out a lot of these last few sights when time is crunched, but those with more forgiving schedules will find Ballard, the U District, and Capitol Hill well served by public transportation.

ORIENTATION

The city's street-numbering system takes a little time to understand, but makes sense after a while. Avenues run north and south and streets run east and west, but street names get more complex than this. Example: NE 63rd Street is in the Ravenna District east of 1st Avenue NE, and 63 blocks north of Yesler Way; 63rd Avenue SW is in West Seattle, south of Yesler Way and 63 blocks west of the Duwamish Waterway.

Sights

Seattle is big enough to keep an intrepid visitor busy with weeks of explorations, and even residents who have spent years here still have not ventured into all its nooks and crannies. Like most large American cities, Seattle is a conglomeration of neighborhoods, each with an individual character that reflects both its inhabitants and its history.

CityPass

Seven of Seattle's most popular attractions—the Space Needle, Pacific Science Center, Experience Music Project, Seattle Aquarium, the Museum of Flight, Argosy harbor cruise, and Woodland Park Zoo—have gotten together to offer a discount CityPass ($59 adults, $39 ages 4–12) that provides entrance to six of these seven attractions. Passes are valid for nine days and can be purchased at any of the six attractions. This is an excellent deal for travelers, and it beats waiting in lines for tickets at each venue.

DOWNTOWN

Downtown Seattle is a busy, almost frenetic place, with the expected mix of stuffed shirts, confused tourists, and pierced and tattooed hipsters. Pack comfortable walking shoes. Seattle's sloping streets rival those of San Francisco in steepness.

Skyscrapers and Architectural Highlights
COLUMBIA CENTER
The striking onyx Columbia Center (701 5th Ave., 206/386-5151, 8:30 A.M.–4:30 P.M. Mon.–Fri., $5 adults, $3 seniors and kids) climbs 76 stories above the city, dwarfing every other building in town. A glassed-in viewing deck on the 73rd floor provides a panorama of

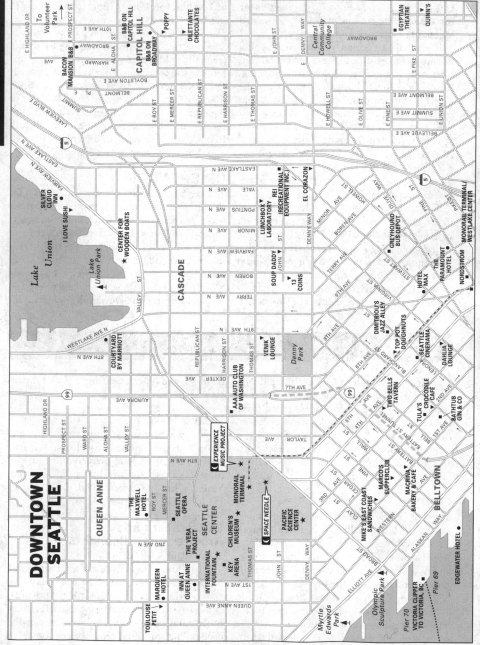

DOWNTOWN SEATTLE

QUEEN ANNE

CASCADE

CAPITOL HILL

BELLTOWN

Lake Union

Lake Union Park

To Volunteer Park

Myrtle Edwards Park

Olympic Sculpture Park

Denny Park

Central Community College

Hotels / B&Bs
- SILVER CLOUD INN
- THE MAXWELL HOTEL
- MARQUEEN HOTEL
- INN AT QUEEN ANNE
- COURTYARD BY MARRIOTT
- BACON MANSION B&B
- B&B ON CAPITOL HILL
- B&B ON BROADWAY
- HOTEL MAX
- THE PARAMOUNT HOTEL
- EDGEWATER HOTEL

Attractions / Landmarks
- CENTER FOR WOODEN BOATS
- EXPERIENCE MUSIC PROJECT
- SEATTLE OPERA
- THE VERA PROJECT
- CHILDREN'S MUSEUM
- SEATTLE CENTER
- INTERNATIONAL FOUNTAIN
- KEY ARENA
- MONORAIL TERMINAL
- SPACE NEEDLE
- PACIFIC SCIENCE CENTER
- REI (RECREATIONAL EQUIPMENT INC.)
- NORDSTROM
- MONORAIL TERMINAL/WESTLAKE CENTER
- GREYHOUND BUS DEPOT
- SEATTLE CINERAMA
- EGYPTIAN THEATRE

Food / Drink
- I LOVE SUSHI
- TOULOUSE PETIT
- SOUP DADDY
- LUNCHBOX LABORATORY
- PONTUS
- EL CORAZON
- VENIK LOUNGE
- AAA AUTO CLUB OF WASHINGTON
- 13 COINS
- MIKE'S EAST COAST SANDWICHES
- MARCO'S SUPPERCLUB
- MACRINA BAKERY & CAFE
- TWO BELLS TAVERN
- TULA'S
- CROCODILE CAFE
- BATHTUB GIN & CO
- DAHLIA LOUNGE
- TOP POT DOUGHNUTS
- DIMITRIOU'S JAZZ ALLEY
- POPPY
- DILETTANTE CHOCOLATES
- QUINN'S

Piers
- Pier 70
- Pier 69
- VICTORIA CLIPPER TO VICTORIA, BC

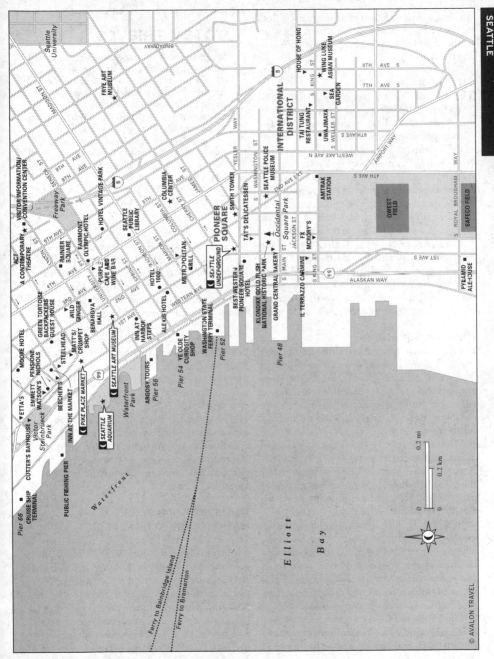

Seattle University

Broadway

Seattle University

FRYE ART MUSEUM ★

Freeway Park

VISITOR INFORMATION/ CONVENTION CENTER ★

ACT A CONTEMPORARY THEATRE ★

HOTEL VINTAGE HOTEL ★

FAIRMONT OLYMPIC HOTEL ▲

RAINIER SQUARE ★

SEATTLE PUBLIC LIBRARY ★

COLUMBIA CENTER ★

PURPLE CAFE AND WINE BAR ●

SMITH TOWER ★

METROPOLITAN GRILL ●

HOTEL 1000 ▲

PIONEER SQUARE

SEATTLE UNDERGROUND ★

TAT'S DELICATESSEN ●

SEATTLE POLICE MUSEUM ★

Occidental Square Park

BEST WESTERN PIONEER SQUARE HOTEL ▲

KLONDIKE GOLD RUSH NATIONAL HISTORIC PARK ★

GRAND CENTRAL BAKERY ●

FX McRORY'S ●

IL TERRAZZO CARMINE ●

INTERNATIONAL DISTRICT

HOUSE OF HONG ●

WING LUKE ASIAN MUSEUM ★

TAI TUNG RESTAURANT ●

UWAJIMAYA ★

SEA GARDEN ●

8TH AVE S

7TH AVE S

6TH AVE S

WESTLAKE AVE N

AIRPORT WAY

AMTRAK STATION ■

QWEST FIELD

SAFECO FIELD

4TH AVE S

1ST AVE S

S ROYAL BROUGHAM WAY

ALASKAN WAY

PYRAMID ALE HOUSE ■

Smith Tower

YESLER WAY

WASHINGTON ST

S WASHINGTON ST

S MAIN ST

S JACKSON ST

S KING ST

S WELLER ST

S KING ST

BENAROYA HALL ★

MATT'S CRUMPET SHOP ●

WILD GINGER ●

GREEN TORTOISE BACKPACKERS GUEST HOUSE ▲

STEELHEAD ●

BEECHER'S ●

PENSIONE NICHOLS ▲

EMMETT WATSON'S ●

MOORE HOTEL ▲

ETTA'S ●

CUTTER'S BAYHOUSE ●

Victor Steinbrueck Park

INN AT THE MARKET ▲

PIKE PLACE MARKET ★

SEATTLE ART MUSEUM ★

SEATTLE AQUARIUM ★

INN AT HARBOR STEPS ▲

ALEXIS HOTEL ▲

YE OLDE CURIOSITY SHOP ★

WASHINGTON STATE FERRY TERMINAL ★

Waterfront Park

ARGOSY TOURS ★

Pier 56

Pier 54

Pier 52

Pier 48

Pier 66

CRUISE SHIP TERMINAL ■

PUBLIC FISHING PIER ■

Waterfront

Elliott Bay

Ferry to Bainbridge Island

Ferry to Bremerton

0   0.2 mi

0   0.2 km

© AVALON TRAVEL

the entire region. Ask at the information desk in the lobby for access. With a view like this, it's hard to imagine a better locale to watch the traffic.

SMITH TOWER

The 42-story Smith Tower (Yesler Way and 2nd Ave., 206/622-4004, www.smithtower.com) was the tallest building west of the Mississippi when completed in 1914, and it remained Seattle's highest for several decades. Now dwarfed by neighboring skyscrapers, it is still an interesting place, with elevator rides—run by some of the last elevator operators on the West Coast—to a 35th-floor outdoor observation deck (10 A.M.–4 P.M. Sat.–Sun. Nov.–Mar., 10 A.M.–5 P.M. daily Apr. and Oct., 10 A.M.–8:30 P.M. daily May–Jul., 10 A.M.–8 P.M. daily Aug., 10 A.M.–7:30 P.M. daily Sept., $7.50 adults, $6 seniors and students, free kids five and under). Also on this floor is the ornately furnished Chinese Room, a popular place for meetings and wedding receptions.

Pioneer Square

Pioneer Square offers a striking clash of cultures. High-end art galleries, Oriental-carpet stores, and sidewalk cafés are nestled between corner missions, while executives in tailored suits and young couples out for a night on the town pass Occidental Park's homeless residents.

Pioneer Square is the oldest section of Seattle, although the center of activity has long since migrated north a half mile or so. After the great fire of 1889, the area was rebuilt in magnificent brick buildings, many of which are still standing.

In spite of frequent complaints about the aggressiveness of the transients who reside in the alleys or nearby shelters, the 20-block restored historical district along 1st Avenue, Yesler Way, and S. Main Street, south of downtown, is also home to upscale boutique hotels, fine restaurants, galleries, and a busy nightlife.

The center of Pioneer Square activity—for better and worse—is at **Occidental Square Park** (Occidental Ave. S. and S. Main St.), a

---

TOTEM THIEVES

When you walk around Pioneer Square, be sure to take a gander at the towering **Tlingit totem** in the middle of it all. This is a replica of an unlucky pole destroyed by an arsonist in 1938. The original pole was stolen on a fateful night in 1890 from Southeast Alaska's Tongass Island by a group of Seattle's leaders who believed the village to be deserted. Legend holds that after the original was burned, the city sent a check for $5,000 to carve a new one; the Tlingits cashed the check, and then sent a note saying, "Thanks for finally paying for the first one. A new pole will cost another $5,000."

---

cobblestone space with several totem poles and park benches shared by tourists waiting for the Underground Tour, suited people noshing on lunch, cooing pigeons, and a rotating crew of street musicians and homeless folk.

The neighborhood is also home to one of Seattle's most tranquil urban parks, **Waterfall Garden** (2nd Ave. S. and S. Main St.). Tucked away between several buildings, visitors find a secret cascade of water that provides a break from the street noise.

The southern edge of the Pioneer Square area abuts the International District and the sports stadiums; to the north are the downtown skyscrapers. Get to Pioneer Square from town center by riding one of the free buses along 1st Avenue.

KLONDIKE GOLD RUSH
NATIONAL HISTORICAL PARK

Housed in the historic Cadillac Hotel Building (319 2nd Ave. S., 206/553-7220, www.nps.gov/klse, 9 A.M.–5 P.M. daily, free), this is Seattle's portion of a two-part national historical park commemorating the Klondike Gold Rush; the primary section is in Skagway, Alaska. The center traces Seattle's role in the 1897 gold rush with films on the event—including Charlie Chaplin's *The Gold*

Rush—informative exhibits, wonderful old photos, and gold rush and natural history books. During the summer, there's usually something going on: ranger talks, gold-panning demonstrations, films, and guided walks. Free one-hour walking tours typically depart at 10 A.M. daily from mid-June–Labor Day. Be sure to pick up the interesting gold rush map and brochure that includes descriptions of historic Pioneer Square buildings.

Parks

At 6th Avenue and Seneca *over* I-5, the aptly named **Freeway Park** is a solution to the blight of a freeway roaring through the heart of a city. Located just outside of the Washington State Convention Center, the park was built on a lid over part of that freeway. Venture to this surprising sanctuary to find greenery, waterfalls, fountains, and free summertime lunch concerts.

Right across the street from Westlake Center and plopped down right in the middle of Seattle's best shopping, the plaza at **Westlake Park** can make a good stop to rest those retail-weary legs a little. Studded with trees and benches and lined with a waterfall fountain, the park is usually teaming with folks toting parcels, cooing pigeons, and colorful street performers.

Seattle Underground

Bill Speidel's Underground Tour (1st Ave. and James St., 206/682-1646 or 888/608-6337, www.undergroundtour.com, $16 adults, $13 seniors, $8 ages 7–12, challenging for younger children) is one of the city's most distinctive tours. From Doc Maynard's Public House you roam the Pioneer Square area above and below with a guide who provides humorous anecdotes about local history. You'll learn about the speakeasies, gambling parlors, illegal lotteries, and opium dens that once occupied this section under the streets. You'll also hear how the city's tidewater location created all sorts of problems for early residents—particularly those who tried to flush toilets on an incoming tide—and how the "seamstress tax" was applied to single women working out of the Sweet Home Boarding House in the red-light district. The tour ends shamelessly in a museum/gift shop where you're encouraged to purchase such practical items as deluxe rubber rats and cockroaches. These very popular 1.5-hour tours leave several times daily. Reservations are recommended, particularly in the summer.

Museums
SEATTLE ART MUSEUM
The first thing you see in a visit to the Seattle Art Museum (1300 1st Ave., 206/654-3100, www.seattleartmuseum.org, 10 A.M.–5 P.M. Sat.–Wed., 10 A.M.–9 P.M. Thurs.–Fri., closed Mon.–Tues., $15 adults, $12 seniors, $9 students, free kids under 12) is Jonathan Borofsky's 48-foot-high *Hammering Man* sculpture, pounding relentlessly away on the corner of University Street and 1st Avenue. Step inside the dramatically modern building to find three stories of gallery space, a large auditorium and lecture hall, a gift shop, and a café. The permanent collection is filled with works from Asia, Africa, and Native American cultures.

© ERICKA CHICKOWSKI

Hammering Man sculpture by Jonathan Borofsky, outside the Seattle Art Museum

You're also guaranteed a look at well-known American and European art, including one room with avant-garde works that range from the frivolously fun to the freakishly foolish.

Your ticket gets you into both the Seattle Art Museum and the Seattle Asian Art Museum in Volunteer Park. The first Thursday of every month admission is just $3 per person, and first Saturdays are free. Free docent-led tours of SAM are offered daily; see the information board in the lobby for the next tour.

SEATTLE POLICE MUSEUM
The largest privately owned museum of its type in the U.S., the Seattle Police Museum (317 3rd Ave. S., 206/748-9991, 11 A.M.–4 P.M. Tues.–Sat., $4 adults, $4 kids) features badges, uniforms, antique firearms, and other artifacts from as far back as the 1860s.

BELLTOWN, PIKE PLACE MARKET, AND WATERFRONT
◖ Pike Place Market
The Space Needle might be Seattle's iconographic symbol, but Pike Place Market (www .pikeplacemarket.org, 9 A.M.–6 P.M. Mon.–Sat., 11 A.M.–5 P.M. Sun.) is the true heart and soul of the city, a sensory and social statement of why Seattle is such a livable place. Mingle with the locals here to buy the freshest fish and produce in town, listen to colorful street musicians, enjoy the parade of humanity, and explore a myriad of shops. It's hard not to love it.

Initial appearances can be deceiving in Pike Place Market. It's much larger than you might think, spreading over three levels in the Main Arcade, and up several blocks to include half a dozen other large buildings, each filled with additional shops. All told, the market contains more than 250 businesses covering nine acres. Early risers have the advantage; things are pretty slow early in the morning, giving you more time to explore without having to fight your way through the crowds.

The main focal point is beneath the famous "Public Market Center" neon sign and clock. Enter here to meet **Rachel,** the fat bronze charity piggy bank that has been here since 1986. Follow the throngs of tourists to **Pike**

Pike Place Market

© ERICKA CHICKOWSKI

Place Fish (www.pikeplacefish.com), right behind Rachel. You can't miss the famous flying fish (watch your head!), the raucous repartee, and the clowning around. It helps to be part showman to work here. Despite a competitor's complaint that "I can't see how throwing fish makes them taste any better," everything here is fresh.

INFORMATION AND TOURS

For a market map and newsletter, head to the tiny **Pike Place Information Booth** (10 A.M.–6 P.M. daily) near the market entrance on the corner of Pike Street and 1st Avenue; you can also purchase half-price tickets here for concerts and plays on the day of the show.

In-depth **Pike Place Market Heritage Tours** (206/682-7453, www.pikeplacemarket foundation.org, $10 adults, $7 seniors and kids) are offered Wednesday–Sunday. These three-hour traipses blend history with quirky anecdotes, led by knowledgeable insiders.

Along the Waterfront

Generally a sightseer's first waterfront stop, Elliott Bay's Piers 48–70 represent the main waterfront: fish-and-chip eateries, gift shops, museums, the aquarium, and harbor-tour departure points. Washington State Ferries (206/464-6400, 888/808-7977, or 800/843-3779 for automated info, www.wsdot.wa.gov/ferries) depart Pier 52 for Bainbridge Island and Bremerton across the sound.

MINERS LANDING AND PIER 54

With touristy restaurants and shops, an indoor carousel ($1.50) popular with young children, and a plethora of video games for the older ones, Miners Landing at Pier 57 is worth a stop during your waterfront ambles. Outside, watch local anglers ply the waters of Elliot Bay at **Waterfront Park** and see the ferries chug away toward the outer reaches of Bainbridge Island and beyond.

Even if you aren't a souvenir shopper at heart, don't miss **Ye Olde Curiosity Shop** (206/682-5844, www.yeoldecuriosityshop .com) next door at Pier 54. This combination museum/gift shop specializes in the bizarre: tucked away at the back of the store you'll find exhibits with shrunken heads and the mummified bodies of "Sylvester" and "Sylvia," two of Seattle's most desiccated attractions.

◖ SEATTLE AQUARIUM

A visit to Pier 59's Seattle Aquarium (206/386-4320, www.seattleaquarium.org, 9:30 A.M.–5 P.M. daily, $15 adults, $10 ages 4–12, free ages 3 and under) will give you an appreciation for the incredible diversity of sea life swimming right below your feet. The traditional part of the aquarium leads you past a "touch tank" filled with various tide-pool creatures, and aquariums containing everything from an octopus to an electric eel. The real treat is outside, where you'll find large tanks containing harbor seals, sea otters, and northern fur seals, along with a salmon ladder and hatchery. Check the board for the next feeding time for the sea mammals and diving birds. Ducks and shorebirds occupy another noisy section, but the star feature is an underwater dome where you sit surrounded by fish from the Sound. It's as if the tables have been turned and the humans are in a giant fishbowl

THE DENNY REGRADE

One of the prominent features of Seattle is its steep hills, which make walking and driving difficult. Many schemes have been hatched to eliminate them, but only one ever came to fruition: the Denny Regrade project. Beginning in 1902, the city engineer directed high-pressure hoses that pumped water from Lake Union onto the steep slopes of Denny Hill in an area now called Belltown, washing the soil into Elliott Bay and creating the waterfront of today. It took eight years to complete the project, but this is now one of the few relatively level parts of this otherwise hilly city.

©ERICKA CHICKOWSKI

Seattle Aquarium

looking outward at salmon, skates, halibut, rockfish, and other creatures.

COAST GUARD MUSEUM
On the south end of the waterfront, Pier 36 hosts the Coast Guard Museum (206/217-6993, 9 A.M.–3 P.M. Mon., Wed., and Fri., free) with nautical artifacts, models of Coast Guard cutters, historic photographs, and a 15-minute slide show. The Coast Guard home-ports three 400-foot icebreakers and two 378-foot cutters at Pier 36.

OLYMPIC SCULPTURE PARK
Settled on a grassy hillside overlooking the water and the distant peaks of the Olympic Mountains, this gorgeous park's real treasure is its stunning sculpted artwork. Sponsored by the Seattle Art Museum, this open air gallery (30 minutes before sunrise–30 minutes after sunset daily, free) sits right where Alaskan Way takes a hard right turn to become Broad Street at the north end of the waterfront. Many of the permanent exhibits, like the park's signature red painted steel swooping structure called *The Eagle*, are big, colorful,

and pretty hard to miss. But other temporary exhibits are often designed to blend into the native vegetation of the landscaping, offering those willing to put the wide-angle lens down for a moment a few delightful surprises during their ramble through the park.

Be sure to stop by the giant steel-and-glass PACCAR Pavilion, which usually houses some of the best visiting exhibits in the park.

MYRTLE EDWARDS PARK
Right where the Sculpture Park meets the waterfront, if you take the path that hugs the shoreline, it will take you right through Myrtle Edwards Park, a picturesque piece of shoreline with beautiful rocky beaches strewn with bleached driftwood. The paved path that runs through the 1.25-mile long property is sandwiched by green grass in many places, so there are more than a few spots to throw out a blanket and enjoy the views.

INTERNATIONAL DISTRICT
This part of Seattle has long been home to people from all over Asia, including those

of Japanese, Korean, Chinese, Filipino, and Vietnamese ancestry. The International District is easy to reach; just catch one of the free buses and ride through the tunnel to the International District bus tunnel station, where outsized origami pieces decorate the walls.

All roads lead to **Hing Hay Park,** a small

THE SOUND OF BUSINESS BEING DONE

Today, the Seattle area is known for its individuality and entrepreneurship, supported by such major corporations as Starbucks, Boeing, Microsoft, Costco, and Weyerhaeuser. But the city is also home to thousands of other businesses, some of which are listed below.

• Alaska Air
• Amazon.com
• Bartell Drugs
• Classmates.com
• Corbis
• Costco
• Cutter & Buck
• Eddie Bauer
• Expedia
• Fisher Communications
• Getty Images
• Jones Soda
• Mike's Hard Lemonade
  Nintendo of America
• Nordstrom
• PACCAR
• PEMCO
• Premera Blue Cross
• Redhook Ale
• Safeco Insurance
• Sub Pop Records
• T-Mobile USA
• Tully's Coffee
• Union Bay
• Uwajimaya
• Weyerhaeuser
• Zillow.com

city park with a colorful pagoda-style Chinese pavilion donated by the city of Taipei. Watch out for the hundreds of pigeons that get fed here and coat the pavilion with their droppings.

The **Wing Luke Asian Museum** (719 South King St., 206/623-5124, www.wingluke.org, 10 A.M.–5 P.M. Tues.–Sun., $12.95 adults, $9.95 seniors and students, $8.95 ages 5–12, free kids under 5) has artifacts from early Asian businesses, memorabilia of all types, hand-painted kites, a 35-foot Chinese dragon, plus many historic photos. The museum also displays changing exhibits of Asian art and history. Admission is free on the first Thursday and third Saturday of the month, when the museum is open 10 A.M.–8 P.M.

King Street is the heart of the district, with Chinese shops lining both sides. The International District lacks the crowded intensity of San Francisco's Chinatown, but the streets are bordered with hole-in-the-wall restaurants, shops selling imported goods, and Asian grocers (some of the biggest are up the hill near the corner of S. Jackson Street and 12th Avenue). You can easily find a filling lunch for $8. **Kobe Terrace Park,** a community garden, follows the hillside above the International District; it is capped by a concrete lantern given to Seattle by its sister city of Kobe, Japan.

Chinese-American Vi Mar leads interesting **Chinatown Discovery Tours** (425/885-3085, www.seattlechinatowntour.com) of the International District. A variety of walking tours are offered, including one with lunch at a dim sum restaurant.

SEATTLE CENTER AND QUEEN ANNE

In 1962, the city of Seattle decided to show off its success to the rest of the world and throw itself a party in the process. "Century 21" was a World's Fair without peer. Drawing almost 10 million people, the event not only made Seattle an international destination, but also left behind Seattle Center (206/684-7200, www.seattlecenter.com), sandwiched between

Belltown to the south and the Queen Anne neighborhood to the north.

Crowning the tallest hill in Seattle, Queen Anne's great for commanding vistas. Which is why captains of industry built mansions here at the turn of the 20th century. Many of these spacious and grand old homes are still here, along with a few cobblestone streets, but alongside are other, less ostentatious homes that give Queen Anne a comfortable atmosphere.

Seattle Center

Seattle Center is in the first stages of a decades-long redevelopment project, so the rickety amusement park rides that once surrounded the Center House have been dismantled and are making way for more green spaces. To celebrate the Center's 50-year anniversary, visitors in 2012 and beyond can expect to see a new **Chihuly Gardens,** a glass and vegetative landscape designed by Dale Chihuly, and a newly renovated Center House.

Seattle's lasting icon, the Space Needle

© ERICKA CHICKOWSKI

SEATTLE MONORAIL

The best way to venture into this space-age world is aboard the kitschy Monorail (206/441-6038, www.seattlemonorail.com, 7:30 A.M.–11 P.M. Mon.–Fri., 8:30 A.M.–11 P.M. Sat.–Sun, $2 each way), the elevated train that connects trendy Westlake Center at 5th and Pine with passé Seattle Center. This strange contraption was considered a model for transportation in its day but never really caught on. The 90-second ride departs every 15 minutes.

€ SPACE NEEDLE

The Space Needle (400 Broad St., 206/443-2111 or 800/937-9582, www.spaceneedle .com, 9 A.M.–midnight daily, $18 adults, $16 for seniors and military, $12 for ages 4–12, free for younger kids) is one of Seattle's trademarks, a 605-foot tower topped by a flying saucer viewing deck and restaurant. Elevators levitate you to the top, where you can walk out on the observation deck for a 360-degree view of downtown Seattle, of planes flying by, and of the Cascades, Mount Rainier, and the Olympics on a clear day. On a rainy day you may be able to make out downtown. Detailed signboards describe the buildings and other surrounding features in the distance.

Even for those who dislike the trappings of touristy venues, the spectacular view is worth at least one trip up the zippy bronze elevators. And if you have restaurant reservations, the ride is free.

PACIFIC SCIENCE CENTER

After half a century of use, the Pacific Science Center (206/443-2001 or 866/414-1912, www .pacsci.org, 10 A.M.–6 P.M. daily mid-June through Labor Day, 10 A.M.–5 P.M. Mon.–Fri., 10 A.M.–6 P.M. Sat.–Sun. the rest of the year, $17 adults, $15 seniors, $13 ages 6–12, $11 kids 3–5, free under age 3) is showing its age a bit gracelessly. The dated architecture stands in marked contrast to the glitzy, high-tech Experience Music Project just a short walk away. Despite this, the Science Center is a wonderful place to take kids for a day of learning and fun. Distinctive white concrete arches rise over pools and fountains at this hugely popular family museum that attracts almost two million visitors annually. The five buildings are filled with hands-on exhibits: virtual reality voyages, a planetarium, a menagerie of mechanized Mesozoic dinosaurs, a tropical butterfly house, a colony of naked mole rats, plus fun and educational exhibits of all types. The fountains outside are filled with water toys that blast jets of water at all sorts of objects; there's even a spinning two-ton granite ball. Two big **IMAX screens** ($9 adults) here create unforgettably dramatic first-run movies; one even shows high-tech 3-D IMAX films.

◖ EXPERIENCE MUSIC PROJECT

With a wildly curvy exterior of multicolored aluminum—said to mimic the shape of an electric guitar—it's pretty hard to miss this outlandish building plunked on the edge of Seattle Center (5th Ave. and Harrison St., 206/367-5483 or 877/367-5483, www.empsfm .org, 10 A.M.–7 P.M. daily Memorial Day–Labor Day weekend, 10 A.M.–5 P.M. Labor Day–Memorial Day weekend, $18 adults, $15 for seniors and military, $12 students, add $2 on weekends, free under age 4). Experience Music Project (EMP) is the brainchild of Microsoft billionaire Paul Allen, whose fascination with Seattle-born Jimi Hendrix led him to bankroll much of this massive homage to rock.

Visitors are treated to an amazing array of displays and interactive exhibits on musicians and their music, including oral histories from all sorts of rockers representing every genre from rockabilly to hip-hop. Some of the best parts are the displays of obscure memorabilia, including the Fender Stratocaster that Hendrix used to play "The Star-Spangled Banner" at Woodstock. Kurt Cobain's handwritten song lyrics, Paul Revere and the Raiders' stage uniforms and instruments, Elvis Presley's black leather jacket, and a pink feather boa worn by Janis Joplin.

EMP is also home to the Science Fiction Museum and Hall of Fame, which shares the

---

EMP RADIO

Experience Music Project even has its own radio station. **KEXP** (FM 90.3, www.kexp .org) is a great local radio station with an amazing mix of music and no ads. Although owned by the University of Washington, it is connected to the EMP.

---

building with a collection of memorabilia that even music geeks see as a little nerdy. But sci-fi enthusiasts will love it for its assortment of props and costumes from the sets of famous shows and movies such as *Star Trek, Planet of the Apes,* and *Blade Runner,* as well as the interpretive exhibits that explore the origins of sci-fi and examine the innate human desire to explain the unknown and prognosticate the future. The hours are the same as EMP and admission gets you into both.

CENTER HOUSE

The Center House started life as an armory, but was reborn as a shopping and food mall for the 1962 World's Fair. In 2012 it was reinvented yet again with a facelift that installed huge glass ceilings with views of the Needle and an improved food court meant to feature local and organic foods.

The House is still home to the delightful **Seattle Children's Museum** (305 Harrison St., 206/441-1768, www.thechildrens museum.org, 10 A.M.–5 P.M. Mon.–Fri. and 10 A.M.–6 P.M. Sat.–Sun., $7.50 for adults and children over age 1, $6.50 for grandparents and military), which is filled with wacky and fun exhibits that manage to educate children. For years, droves of kids have dragged their parents through the museum's expansive play space. The exhibits change all the time, but there's always something fun to do here, including hands-on workshops. Kids love this place— the average stay is three hours (try getting any child to do anything for three hours!). The gift shop sells educational toys. Adults must accompany children under 12.

INTERNATIONAL FOUNTAIN

The deceptively simple International Fountain (6–11 P.M. Mon.–Fri. and 2–11 P.M. Sat.–Sun.) never ceases to delight kids trying to escape the random jets of water and amuse adults when the inevitable happens. The fountain erupts in an on-the-hour frenzy of action complete with music pumped through loudspeakers.

Kerry Park

Mount Rainier, downtown Seattle, the Olympics, and the harbor can all be seen from tiny Kerry Park (W. Highland Dr. and 2nd Ave. W.) on the south slope of Queen Anne Hill. It's especially popular with photographers in search of picture-postcard shots of Seattle and the Space Needle.

SOUTH LAKE UNION

A natural lake that was transformed early in this century when canals were dug linking it to Lake Washington and Puget Sound, Lake Union was once treated mostly as an industrial area that floated. Decades later, the factories and Navy base are gone and the southern end of the lake is a hub of attractive green parks, trendy restaurants, gorgeous historic boats, and one of Seattle's nicest museums.

Lake Union Park

Picked up by the city from the Navy in 2000, Lake Union Park (860 Terry Ave. N., www.at lakeunionpark.org) has developed into one of Seattle's prettiest waterfront spots, with plenty of grassy areas to loll about and watch kayakers paddle, sailboats tack, and seaplanes swoop over Lake Union. The park is great fun for kids, who will love the model boat pond, the 300-foot-long water fountain, and the park's unique **Historic Ships Wharf,** which docks the steamer *Virginia V,* the tugboat *Arthur Foss,* the fireboat *Duwamish,* and the lightship *Swiftsure.* The park is home to both the Center for Wooden Boats and the Museum of History and Industry. It also makes for an ideal embarkation point to explore the city's new six-mile **Cheshiahud Lake Union Loop,** which offers a stretch of paved trail all the way around the lake.

CENTER FOR WOODEN BOATS

Run by volunteers, the Center for Wooden Boats (1010 Valley St., 206/382-2628, www.cwb .org, 10 A.M.–5 P.M. Tues.–Sun. Nov.–mid-Mar., 10 A.M.–6 P.M. daily mid-Mar.–early May and Sept.–Nov., 10 A.M.–8 P.M. daily early May–Aug., free) restores and maintains a fleet

view of Lake Union from the Space Needle's observation deck

THE KING IS DEAD. LONG LIVE THE KING!

Consult any county website and you'll quickly find that King County was named after Atlanta civil-rights leader Martin Luther King Jr. Which was perhaps a bit forward-looking for the county fathers who named the county roughly 80 years before the Nobel laureate was born.

The original Mr. King was William Rufus King, a moderate Senator from Alabama and short-lived vice president under President Franklin Pierce. He is chiefly remembered for helping to draft the Compromise of 1850 and also for his very, very close relationship with bachelor President James Buchanan. The county was named during the very short period between King's inauguration as vice president and his 1853 death from tuberculosis.

The county's name was altered by a bipartisan, biracial faction in the King County Council, and signed into state law in 2007.

of historic rowboats and sailboats. Take a class here to learn about wooden boat building, or rent one of its boats to sail or row around the lake for an afternoon. Right next door is the small **Maritime Heritage Center** (206/447-9800, www.nwseaport.org), with vintage wooden boats and programs detailing maritime restoration.

MUSEUM OF HISTORY AND INDUSTRY

After a half a century hidden away behind the Montlake Bridge, MOHAI moved to resplendent new digs in 2012, making its home inside of the retrofitted and restored old Naval Reserve Building right at South Lake Union Park (860 Terry Ave. N., 206/324-1126, www.seattlehistory.org, 10 A.M.–5 P.M. daily, $8 adults, $7 seniors, students, and military, $6 ages 5–17, and free for kids under 5, free to all on Tuesday). The city's most respected

historical museum, MOHAI had to make room for the State Route 520 floating bridge expansion, but it ended up gaining more space and a boatload of relocation funds from the state. A moving campaign also netted additional expansion funds from donors, including a cool $10 million from Amazon.com founder Jeff Bezos. So expect to see a wide spectrum of exhibits on the city's more than 160-year history, from salmon processors all the way up to computer chip processors.

CAPITOL HILL

Capitol Hill is a study in sharp contrasts. The hill itself is one of the most prestigious old neighborhoods in Seattle, with countless mansions and stately older homes, quite a few of which are now elaborate bed-and-breakfast inns. At one time local politicians dreamed of making this the location for Washington's capitol building—hence the name. At the same time, Capitol Hill is at the epicenter of Seattle's countercultural movement, a haven for disaffected twenty- and thirty-somethings. Today the campuses of Seattle Central Community College and Seattle University mark the southern edge of the neighborhood, while two commercial centers attract visitors: a small, fairly quiet strip along 15th Avenue East, and the frenetic Broadway Avenue East stretch.

Broadway Avenue

Broadway Avenue's vibrant gay and lesbian community opens the neighborhood to comparison with San Francisco's Castro District, but the hipsters and hippies of the area flavor it into something that could just as easily be measured against Greenwich Village in New York. It's a great place to people-watch and catch up on the latest fashion statements from the art-school crowd. You're guaranteed to see more skinny jeans paired with '80s retro tees, frenzied fluorescent green hair, tattoos, nose rings, and pink triangles here than anywhere else in Seattle. Walk down the street in either direction and you'll discover artist Jack Mackie's amusing *Dancers Series: Steps,* bronze footprints of various dances embedded in the sidewalk. You'd be surprised at how many of those too-cool-for-school types take a stab at following along with the dance steps.

Volunteer Park

This Capitol Hill park (enter from 14th or 15th Ave. E, 206/684-4743, www.ci.seattle .wa.us/parks, 10 A.M.–4 P.M. daily Oct.–Apr., 10 A.M.–7 P.M. daily May–mid-Sept.) has 44 acres of lawn, a concrete reservoir, and a number of interesting attractions. Completed in 1912, the park is one of many famous sites—including New York's Central Park and the University of Washington campus—designed by the famed Olmsted Brothers landscape architectural firm. Climb the long spiral staircase up the 75-foot brick **water tower** for a grand view across the city. On the other side of the park is the glass **conservatory,** built in 1912 and filled with colorful plants of all kinds. One room houses cacti; others contain ferns, bromeliads, and seasonal displays. The central space features a gorgeous collection of orchids, along with a banana palm and fig tree. There's always something in bloom at the Conservatory, making this a great, steamy place to visit on a rainy winter day.

Museums

FRYE ART MUSEUM

Connoisseurs are well rewarded by visiting this museum (704 Terry Ave., 206/622-9250, www.fryeart.org, 10 A.M.–5 P.M. Tues.–Sun., 11 A.M.–7 P.M. Thurs., closed Mon., free admission), which features significant 19th-century German artists from the Munich School. Interestingly, the emphasis on these works came by happenstance—the founding collection and museum itself was endowed by Charles and Emma Frye, who made some of their millions selling lard to the Germans after World War I and taking oil paintings as partial payment. Today, this collection of melodramatic oils in gilded frames may well be a relief to traditionalists weary of the contemporary conceptual art scene. Among the museum's well-regarded collection is Alexander Max Koester's *Ducks.* Other galleries at the recently

expanded Frye contain changing exhibits, and a café offers light meals.

SEATTLE ASIAN ART MUSEUM

The centerpiece of Volunteer Park is the Seattle Asian Art Museum (1400 E. Prospect St., 206/654-3100, www.seattleartmuseum.org, 10 A.M.–5 P.M. Wed.–Sun., 10 A.M.–9 P.M. Thurs., closed Mon.–Tues., $7 adults, $5 seniors and students, free kids under 12), a 1933 art-deco building. Exhibits cover two spacious wings, including rooms with Japanese folk art, Native American Mughal art, Qing dynasty Chinese art, and Korean art. Of particular interest are the beautiful Japanese screens, the bronze Buddhist sculptures, and the collection of intricate Chinese snuff bottles.

Admission gets you in to both the Asian Art Museum and the Seattle Art Museum downtown on the same day. The first Thursday of every month is free, and first Saturdays are free for families.

Lakeview Cemetery

Just north of Volunteer Park is Lakeview Cemetery (1554 15th Ave. E., 206/322-1582, www.lakeviewcemeteryassociation.com, 9 A.M.–dusk daily), where many of the city's early residents are buried, including Doc Maynard (the doctor who named Seattle after Chief Si'ahl) and the daughter of Chief Si'ahl. Most folks come here, however, to visit the grave of martial artist and actor Bruce Lee, who died in 1973. His son, Brandon Lee, also a martial artist and actor, is buried here as well. He was accidentally killed in 1993 while filming *The Crow.*

BALLARD AND MAGNOLIA

Ballard and nearby Shilshole Bay were the Nordic section of Seattle when immigration from Norway and Sweden peaked from 1890–1910. Ballard still retains a trace of its Scandinavian heritage, although with the influx of new condos and other developments the ethnic lines have blurred considerably.

Just south of Ballard and west of Queen Anne is the quiet Magnolia neighborhood,

© ERICKA CHICKOWSKI

Ballard, one of Seattle's many neighborhoods

home to a wonderful shoreside route (Magnolia Drive) along the north edge of Elliott Bay and to one of Seattle's most serene parks.

⟨ Discovery Park

Set on a point looking out toward Bainbridge Island, Seattle's largest park (3801 Discovery Park Blvd., 6 A.M.–11 P.M daily) plays host to a slice of secluded urban wilderness unmatched in the entire city. Here nature fans can explore forests and meadows that run up to some dramatic waterfront cliffs, or clamber down to sandy beaches and tide pools when the tide is out. The park's West Point is one of Seattle's best bird-watching spots. Birders frequently catch sight of loons, grebes, cormorants, and terns among the 150 species of birds known to fly here. Once the grounds of Fort Lawton, a military outpost in place between the 1890s all the way through World War II, Discovery's 535 acres have been open to exploration for 40 years. Quite a few of the fort's structures remain, including more than a dozen from the earliest days. An interesting walking tour booklet detailing the fort and its history is available at the park's visitors center (8:30 A.M.–5 P.M. daily).

Visitors to Discovery may also enjoy the small collection of Native American art located at the **Daybreak Star Arts and Cultural Center** (206/285-4425), which acts as a community center for the Seattle-area tribal community.

Magnolia Park

Perched upon a high bluff along Magnolia Drive, Magnolia Park (1461 Magnolia Blvd. W., 4 A.M.–11:30 P.M. daily), is a great place for views of Puget Sound and the Olympics and a favorite spot to grill some dogs or burgers and watch the sun set over a picnic. The park's trademark trees are in fact madrona and not magnolia—the misnomer came from a U.S. Coastal Survey lieutenant misidentifying the trees from a ship in the mid-19th century.

Downtown Ballard

In spite of the gentrification of downtown

Ballard, the area still flies Norwegian and Swedish flags along Market Street, and you'll still find plenty of remnants of its Nordic past in the neighborhood, including **Olsen's Scandinavian Foods** (2248 NW Market St., 206/783-8288), where you can still swing by to pick up some lutefisk. Ballard's **Syttende Mai Parade** takes place on May 17, Norwegian Constitution Day; this is the largest Syttende Mai parade outside Norway.

Nordic Heritage Museum

An early 1900s red-brick grade school has been transformed into the Nordic Heritage Museum (3014 NW 67th St., 206/789-5707, www.nordic museum.org, 10 A.M.–4 P.M. Tues.–Sat., noon–4 P.M. Sun., $6 adults, $5 seniors and students, $4 ages 6–16 years, and free for kids under 6), the only museum of its kind in America. The first floor opens with a lengthy and educational Dream of America exhibit, including the factors that pushed people to emigrate here in the 19th century. Upper levels cover the new life—in tenement slums, logging camps, and aboard fishing boats—with more exhibits on explorations by the Vikings, changing art and craft displays, and a gift shop with books on the homeland. The third floor has individual spaces for each of the Nordic countries: Norway, Sweden, Finland, Denmark, and Iceland. The museum is also home to Norwegian rosemaling classes; music, theater, and children's programs; a research library; and the **Scandinavian Language Institute** (www .sliseattle.com), where you can join classes in Danish, Norwegian, or Swedish. The museum is free on the first Tuesday of each month.

Come to the museum on the weekend after the 4th of July for the **Tivoli Festival,** with a pancake breakfast, food and craft booths, entertainment, and a beer garden. Return on the weekend after Thanksgiving for **Yulefest,** with traditional carols, Nordic crafts, and food.

◖ Chittenden Locks

At the west end of Ballard, Hiram M. Chittenden Locks (NW 54th St., 206/783-7059, www.nws.usace.army.mil, 7 A.M.–9 P.M.

daily) connect saltwater Puget Sound with freshwater Lake Washington via Lake Union. Also known as the Ballard Locks, they serve as a passageway for ships, a way to prevent saltwater intrusion into the lakes, and as a fish ladder.

Come to watch container ships, tugs, and pleasure craft navigate the locks and stay to see salmon return home to spawn through the ladder that's viewable through big underwater windows. The best time to look for the salmon is late June–early September, but the ships stream by all year long. You'll be able to watch educational videos on the locks at the **visitors center** (10 A.M.–6 P.M. daily May 1–Sept. 30., and 10 A.M.–4 P.M. Thurs.– Mon. rest of the year) or learn more during free hour-long guided tours that leave from the center every day at 1 P.M. and 3 P.M. in the summer, and on Saturday and Sunday at 2 P.M. in the winter months.

You can cap your explorations off with a stroll on the bank overlooking the locks, where the **Carl S. English Jr. Botanical Gardens** maintains more than 500 species of plants collected from around the world, plus plenty of native Northwest species.

Golden Gardens Park

North of downtown Ballard, the enormously popular Golden Gardens Park (8498 Seaview Pl. NW, 6 A.M.–11:30 P.M.) stands as one of the city's preeminent stretches of shoreline, home to nearly every type of beach the Sound offers. The park is perhaps best known for a sandy beach rare for these parts, making it a favorite among the volleyball and sandcastle-building crowd. But you'll also have the opportunity to amble about more rugged coast, and hike through wetland and forest trails here. The park also hosts an off-leash area for dogs in its northern corner, plus a pier and a boat launch jutting into the Sound.

FREMONT, WALLINGFORD, AND GREEN LAKE

Long known as Seattle's most eccentric neighborhood, the character of the "Republic of Fremont" is best summed up by its official motto emblazoned on the iconic Cold War-era rocket fuselage that towers over the neighborhood: *De Libertas Quirkas.* That's right, folks, people exercise their "freedom to be peculiar" in Fremont every day.

Fremont blends into the decidedly less quirky neighborhoods of Wallingford and Green Lake, to the east and north, respectively. In either neighborhood you'll drive by pretty tree-lined streets filled with well-kept Craftsman homes. A sort of buffer zone just west of the University District, Wallingford's quiet streets are close enough to the university to have a strong student flavor, but far enough away to mix in a more upscale atmosphere. Meanwhile, Green Lake is a center for recreation in the area. On the south side of the neighborhood's eponymous lake you'll find the Woodland Park Zoo.

Fremont Drawbridge

Arrive in Fremont in style by reaching it from downtown across the Fremont Drawbridge, the world's most active drawbridge according to the *Guinness World Records* book. Be ready to wait; on busy summer weekends it often opens every 10 minutes or so to let through boat traffic moving through the Chittenden Locks in Ballard.

Public Art

Once you cross the bridge, you'll come across one of Seattle's most famous pieces of public art, **Waiting for the Interurban.** Richard Beyer's life-size group of commuters and a dog are often decked out in used hats, balloons, or umbrellas contributed by passersby.

Head one block east and turn up the road beneath the Aurora Bridge that towers above you. Two blocks uphill you'll meet the locally famous **Aurora Bridge Troll** in the act of devouring a VW bug. The sculpture has become so entwined in Seattle culture over the decades that the city renamed the road it sits on Troll Avenue North.

From here, walk to the official "Center of the Universe" at the corner of N. 35th Street and Evanston Avenue, where the 53-foot-high **Fremont Rocket** stands ready to blast off from its "launch pad." Nearby stands **Lenin** in heroic pose. This statue originally stood in Slovakia until the 1989 revolution, when it was toppled and sold to capitalists. Old Vlad would be shocked to hear that his monument was made available to the first American with $150,000 to spend.

Gasworks Park

Built on the site of a former gas plant, Gasworks Park (2101 N. Northlake Way, 6 A.M.–10 P.M.) is the world's only industrial site–conversion park. Much of the original rusting gas equipment was incorporated into the park's landscaping, including a play barn that kids love. Enjoy the views of Seattle and Lake Union from the water's banks and fly a kite from the hills here. The paved and very popular **Burke-Gilman Trail** begins west of Gasworks, skirts Lake Washington, connects to the Sammamish River Trail, and ends in Redmond's Marymoor Park, 24 miles away.

Woodland Park Zoo

Ranked among the nation's best, the Woodland Park Zoo (601 N. 59th St., 206/684-4800, www.zoo.org, 9:30 A.M.–4 P.M. daily Oct.–Apr., 9:30 A.M.–6 P.M. daily May–Sept., $17.50 adults, $15.50 seniors, $11.50 ages 3–12, free 2 and under, parking $5.25) has re-created wildlife habitats from around the world. Also included are a tropical Asian habitat and elephant forest where you can watch daily elephant logging demonstrations during the summer, and a Northern Trail section that leads past brown bears, river otters, bald eagles, mountain goats, gray wolves, and snowy owls, all in a relatively realistic setting (even the plants are native to Alaska). Bug World reveals the secret lives of singing katydids, Brazilian cockroaches, New Guinea walking sticks, and assassin bugs. Raptor demonstrations are given on summer weekends, and the big field in the middle is a good place for a lunch break. The newest zoo exhibit is African village, where you enjoy music, dancing, and storytelling while watching animals from the African savanna.

Next to the zoo is the **Woodland Park Rose Garden,** with hundreds of rose varieties spread over two acres.

Green Lake Park

An extremely popular three-mile paved bicycle, jogging, and skating loop—watch out for errant skateboards—hugs Green Lake (7201 E. Green Lake Dr. N.), where you can also sail and swim or rent a paddleboat, canoe, kayak, sailboard, or rowboat. A kids-only fishing pier is at the east end of the lake. Crocodile hunting was popular here in 1986, when assorted reports of a lake creature took on the proportions of a Loch Ness Monster. The "monster" turned out to be a three-pound, 28-inch caiman, which was shipped to a private breeder in Kansas City; the lake is now believed crocodile-free.

UNIVERSITY DISTRICT AND MADISON PARK

The University District (better known as "the U District") is a somewhat gritty center for student activity near the University of Washington's campus. The U District covers several blocks near the intersection of University Way NE ("the Ave") and NE 45th Street, with inexpensive restaurants, used CD and book stores, pizza joints, copy centers, Internet cafés, coffeehouses, and other student-oriented places. This is probably the best place in Seattle to get a quick lunch or an ethnic dinner for just a few bucks. To find the best spots, follow your nose and the students. If it's packed, it's probably tasty—or it serves cheap beer. Either way, you're golden.

University of Washington

With tall brick buildings, springtime cherry blossoms, gushing fountains, views of Lake Washington, and beautifully landscaped grounds, the University of Washington (www.washington.edu) isn't just a well-respected institution of learning, it's a darned nice place to ramble, too.

For a taste of the good life, head to Red Square on a sunny spring day and join the throngs of sun-seekers, skateboarders, Frisbee players, musicians, and brown-baggers as they

the University District's Montlake Bridge

© ERICKA CHICKOWSKI

U-DUB

Outsiders may scratch their heads in wonder when a local refers to some place called "U-Dub." This is just a tender shortening of the already shortened acronym for University of Washington.

Even though the nickname may be informal, UW takes learning very seriously. This is the state's biggest and best school – a major center for research in the fields of Asian languages, zoology, astronomy, cell biology, forestry, fisheries, physics, and many other areas of study. UW's medical school and teaching hospital frequently rank in the nation's top 10. Three UW faculty members have won Nobel Prizes in physics and medicine, and five others have been awarded the MacArthur Foundation "genius grants." The school is highly competitive and the graduate programs are widely acknowledged as some of the strongest in America. The UW library system contains 5.5 million volumes spread over two dozen campus libraries, making it one of the largest in the nation. The university's football and basketball teams often rank in the nation's top 20. Walk down University Way on the day of a football game, and you'll quickly learn that the team colors are purple and gold, and the mascot for the Huskies is an Alaskan malamute. By the way, the shorthand term for the Huskies is "Dawg" – never "Dog."

information about the school, bus schedules, or upcoming events, you can also stop by the **UW Visitors Information Center** (4014 University Way NE, 206/543-9198, 8 A.M.–5 P.M. Mon.–Fri.). Ninety-minute campus tours depart the visitors center at 10:30 A.M. Monday–Friday. You can also pick up a self-guided walking tour brochure at the visitors center if you want to head out on your own.

BURKE MUSEUM

The Burke Museum (NE 45th St. and 17th Ave., 206/543-5590, www.washington.edu/burkemuseum, 10 A.M.–5 P.M. daily, $10 adults, $8 seniors, $7.50 students and ages 5–18, and free to kids under 6 and UW students and staff) stands just inside the north entrance to the campus and features an extraordinary collection of anthropological and natural-history displays. As you enter the museum you face a "treasures case" with Tlingit potlatch masks, a feathered Pomo basket, and even a ceramic horse from China's Wei dynasty. Permanent exhibits focus on Washington's geological, paleontological, and biological history, and on various Pacific cultures. The museum also features outstanding changing exhibitions, a gift shop, and totem poles out front.

HENRY ART GALLERY

A blend of red-brick collegiate Gothic combined with a contemporary collage of glass, cast stone, and textured stainless steel, the architecture of Henry Art Gallery (206/543-2280, www.henryart.org, 11 A.M.–4 P.M. Wed. and Sat.–Sun, 11 A.M.–9 P.M. Thurs. and Fri., closed Mon.–Tues., $10 adults, $6 seniors, free students and under 14, free to all on Thursday) mirrors the diverse art inside, itself a reflection of the tradition and experimentation at the college campus it sits on. When it opened in 1927 it was the first public art gallery in the state; today it continues to innovate with a robust revolving schedule of exhibitions that can include anything from Polaroids taken by Warhol to sculpture by breakout artists.

check out Mount Rainier from this prime vantage point. History buffs might also find **Denny Hall** interesting. The oldest building on campus, it was completed in 1895 around the time that the then 34-year-old UW was moved from downtown Seattle to make way for a growing city.

The center of campus amenities can be found at the appropriately named HUB, or **Husky Union Building** for the uninitiated. Go bowling, play pool, watch a show, or grab a bite to eat here if you're so inclined. If you're in town to consider attending or just want some more

Warren G. Magnuson Park

Settled into a giant piece of property that once housed the Sand Point Naval Air Station, Warren G. Magnuson Park occupies a prime spot on Lake Washington just northeast of the University of Washington. Many of the former naval buildings have been repurposed for recreation and the park is a hub of sporting activity, with tons of ball fields and even an indoor facility for beach volleyball. Magnuson also offers trails to meander and one of the biggest off-leash dog parks in the city. What's more, the kids' playground is one of the most inventive in all of Seattle's parks, with climbing walls, swings, slides, and a sand box that are all designed and themed to pay tribute to its placement at the former site of the control tower of the naval air station.

◖ University of Washington Park Arboretum and Japanese Garden

Trees and shrubs from all over the world thrive at the 267-acre University of Washington Park Arboretum (Lake Washington Blvd., www .depts.washington.edu/uwbg, dawn–dusk daily, free). A half-mile trail leads visitors past lodgepole pine, Oregon crabapple, huckleberry, Pacific dogwood, madrona, and more than 5,500 other varieties of plants. The 0.75-mile Azalea Way path winds through cherry, Japanese maple, azalea, dogwood, and rhododendron trees and bushes; it's a gorgeous place in the spring when everything is in bloom. In the off-season, head to the Joseph A. Witt Winter Garden.

Pick up a nature guide at the west end or at the arboretum visitors center. Stop by the **Graham Visitors Center** (206/543-8800, 9 A.M.–5 P.M. daily) on weekends for free 90-minute guided tours or shop at the center for gardening books and knickknacks or plants propagated from the arboretum collection.

The petite Japanese Tea Garden (206/684-4725, opens at 10 A.M. daily Mar.–Nov., closes at varying times depending upon the season and weather, $6 adults, $4 kids and seniors,

BRIDGES TO NOWHERE

Anyone who's ever paddled a canoe or taken a walk near where the Aboretum meets Lake Washington has probably taken note of a curious sight. Two huge freeway appendages hanging off of Highway 520 appear to be bridges to nowhere. These two offshoots were the start of the R. H. Thomson Expressway, a freeway meant to link the I-90 and Highway 520 routes. After realizing what the expressway would do to the Arboretum and their quiet neighborhoods, citizens rose up to put the kibosh on the project, but not before the interchanges were built. Today, these bridges are popular spots for thrill-seeking bridge jumpers who like to get their kicks cannonballing into Lake Washington from the edge.

kids under 6 free) sits at the south end of the arboretum with manicured ornamental trees, a secluded pond, and an authentic teahouse given to Seattle by its sister city, Kobe, in the 1960s. A popular tea ceremony takes place at 1:30 P.M. on the third Saturday of each month.

WEST SEATTLE

A high bridge spans the **Duwamish Waterway,** which separates industrial South Seattle's docks, warehouses, factories, and train tracks from quiet West Seattle. Once over the bridge you'll discover a neighborhood of simple homes and apartments with views across Puget Sound. Several shore-side parks provide places to ride bikes, walk the beaches, and enjoy the view.

Alki Beach Park

For a leisurely scenic drive, head along the water on Harbor Avenue Southwest to Duwamish Head, then west on Alki Avenue Southwest to Alki Beach Park a long, narrow, sandy stretch that's Seattle's official beach getaway when the sun shines down. In warm weather a whole beach culture emerges here, complete with pickup volleyball, the comforting aroma of suntan lotion, and bonfires galore. The atmosphere is sometimes even enough to convince a few brave souls to take the plunge in the water, which only rarely rises above 55°F. Keep going on Alki Avenue to the **Alki Point Lighthouse** (206/286-5423). Tours of the station are available weekdays by reservation.

Other Parks

Traveling south on Beach Drive SW, you'll reach the wonderful Lincoln Park, where you'll find great trails, playgrounds, and a long beach facing Puget Sound. A bike path follows the same scenic route. Just south of here is the **Fauntleroy** state ferry dock, with connections to Vashon Island and Southworth.

For photography buffs, **Hamilton Viewpoint Park** (1531 California Way SW) offers a panoramic view of Seattle's skyline, the Cascades, and Elliott Bay, as does **Belvedere Park** (SW Admiral Way and 36th Ave. SW).

SOUTH SEATTLE

The south end of Seattle is dominated by industrial developments, especially an enormous Boeing plant. The area is not especially attractive, but does feature one of Seattle's most enjoyable sights, the fabulous Museum of Flight.

€ Museum of Flight

This world-class museum (9404 E. Marginal Way S., 206/764-5720, www.museumofflight .org, 10 A.M.–5 P.M. daily, $16 adults, $14 seniors, $9 kids ages 5–17, kids under 5 free) is one of Seattle's premier attractions, and the largest air and space museum on the West Coast. The main focal point is a dramatic steel-and-glass **Great Gallery** packed with more than 50 planes, many of which appear to be flying in formation. You can gape upward at such gleaming beauties as a Douglas DC-3, a replica of the Wright Brothers' glider, and a human-powered Gossamer Albatross II among the many aircraft suspended overhead. Or walk among the dozens more planes on the replica tarmac below, including a Russian MiG-21,

---

SEATTLE, JET CITY

It's hard to believe that a rich guy with a little bit of flight experience and a lot of lumber could make metropolitan Seattle an economic powerhouse. But that's exactly what William E. Boeing did in 1910, after deciding that he could slap together a better seaplane than Curtiss. Utilizing the cheap spruce wood of the Northwest, Boeing rolled out so many Model C seaplanes for the U.S. Navy that he was able to create a solid brand and compete successfully for future government contracts.

Things were slow between wars, but the success of Boeing's B-17 Flying Fortress bumped employment up from a modest 4,000 to a whopping 50,000. An inevitable slump came after VJ Day. Boeing was starting to realize that a sustainable company had to do more than quietly wait for the next armed conflict.

While it was already in the commercial aircraft market and competing primarily against the Douglas DC-3, the introduction of the 707 in the 1950s was something special. The jet airliner was fast, efficient, and carried over 100 passengers. The Boeing Company had officially ushered in the Jet Age, bringing rainy little Seattle to the national eye as an aviation leader.

Since those glory days, the Boeing Company has continued to improve on the success of the 707 with its 737 and 747 aircraft. While Chicago wooed Boeing corporate headquarters away from the Puget Sound in 2001, as long as Renton keeps turning out 737s, Everett the 787 Dreamliner, and three shifts show up to rivet, paint, and polish, Seattle will always have a claim to the title "Jet City."

an F4C Phantom II, and the famous M/D-21 Blackbird, officially the fastest plane ever to fly. Outside, visitors can walk through the first **Air Force One,** used by Presidents Eisenhower, Kennedy, Johnson, and Nixon.

Don't pass up the chance to check out the **Red Barn,** Boeing Company's original manufacturing plant and now home to one of the best-curated exhibits at the museum, which traces the history of flight over two floors. Some highlights include a restored 1917 Curtiss Jenny biplane and a replica of the Wright Brothers' wind tunnel.

Visitors can also listen in on air traffic from busy Boeing Field at the full-size control tower exhibit here, and kids can pretend to pilot their own miniature aircraft at a special hands-on area.

Entertainment and Events

As the biggest city in a state known for producing full-flavored microbrews and complex wines, Seattle is grand central for imbibing in a wide range of tasty adult beverages. However, don't expect to go too wild here. With closing time at a very early 2 A.M. and denizens usually preferring Birkenstocks over stilettos, the Emerald City is hardly what you'd call a clubbing town.

Its citizens *do* know a thing or two about good music, though. In the early 1990s Seattle gained a reputation as a center for grunge music, with local bands such as Nirvana, Pearl Jam, and Alice in Chains achieving an international following. Twenty years later, the scene here continues to evolve. Seattle bands to gain national notoriety over the last few years include The Moondogies, Grand Archives, and The Maldives.

Seattle doesn't disappoint when it comes to the finer performance arts, either. Nobody is quite sure why—maybe it really is the weather—but film and artsy live performances have always done very well in Seattle and you'll always have a wide choice of art films, plays, and musicals to check out.

NIGHTLIFE
Bars
BREWERIES AND PUBS
The Northwest has long been a center for high-quality handcrafted ales. Though many folks still swill down Rainier or Budweiser, microbrewed specialty beers are as de rigueur here as fleece jackets and sandals with socks.

Right off the Burke-Gilman Trail and plopped down between Fremont and Ballard **Hale's Ales Brewery** (4301 Leary Way NW, 206/706-1544, www.halesales .com, 11:30 A.M.–10 P.M. Mon.–Thurs., 11:30 A.M.–11 P.M. Fri., 9:30 A.M.–11 P.M. Sat., 9:30 A.M.–10 P.M. Sun.) cranks out seven different draft-only beers and serves meals in its cozy pub or outside on its small deck. There are no scheduled tours, but the staff will describe the brewing process to you and the brewery frequently holds tastings.

Not far away in Ballard, **Jolly Roger Taproom** (1111 NW Ballard Way, 206/782-6181, http://maritimebrewery.ypguides.net, 11 A.M.–11 P.M. Mon.–Thurs., 11 A.M.–midnight Fri.–Sat., noon–9 P.M. Sun.) is named after Maritime Pacific Brewing Company's best known holiday ale. Slurp down a pint of Jolly Roger, Bosun's Black Porter, Portage Bay Pilsner, or one of another close to a dozen beers on tap and pair it with one of many dishes featuring Maritime brews as the secret ingredient. For true barley-and-hops enthusiasts, the real treasure at this nautically themed pub is the rotating selection of three different cask-conditioned ales pumped through English beer engines.

Before the first pitch is tossed out at Safeco Field, the crowds gather across the street at **Pyramid Alehouse** (1201 First Ave. S., 206/682-3377, www.pyramidbrew.com, 11 A.M.–10 Mon.–Thurs., 11 A.M.–11 P.M. Fri.–Sat., 11 A.M.–9 P.M. Sun.), a huge brewhouse known for its expansive outdoor beer garden patio. Pyramid is perhaps best known for its textured, wheaty ales. Fans of flavored beer will surely dig Pyramid's Apricot Ale and on a summer's day the smooth Curveball Blonde Ale hits it out of the park about as well as an Ichiro walk-off homer. If you can't make up your mind, the alehouse offers a sampler tray so you can taste a number of different beers without impairing your ability to catch those foul balls at the game later on.

Cap off a fun day at the market or downtown with a visit to **Pike Brewing Company** (1415 1st Ave., 206/622-6044, www.pike brewing.com, 11 A.M.–2 A.M.), a popular and friendly alehouse with some of the best micros in town. A quiet locals joint this is not. Its location—smack dab in the middle of Pike Place Market—makes for a party atmosphere that caters to happy vacationers. Whether that frenetic energy is your thing or not, the drinks are sure to please. Beer snobs should give it a go with the XXXXX Stout for the best shot at brewery bliss. The brash but silky English-style ale offers hints of chocolate and espresso intertwined with its malty flavor.

Out in the U District, **Big Time Brewery and Alehouse** (4133 University Way NE, 206/545-4509, www.bigtimebrewery.com) features several house-brewed ales on tap and an antique back bar where you can enjoy the passing scene on "the Ave" through the big front windows. Nearby, with its fireplace, comfy sofas, and vintage pinball machine, **College Inn Pub** (4006 University Way NE, 206/634-2307, www.collegeinnpub.com, 11:30 A.M.–2 A.M. Mon–Fri., 2 P.M.–2 A.M. Sat., 2 P.M.–1 A.M. Sun.) is another favorite place to catch a beer with the grad students and profs around UW. Chill out at the bar or compete with the locals in a rousing game of pool or darts at this wood-paneled classic.

MARTINI LOUNGES

About as close to being a classic speak-easy without hopping into a time machine, **Bathtub Gin & Co** (2205 2nd Ave. between Blanchard St. and Bell St., 206/728-6069, www.bathtubginseattle.com, 5 P.M.–2 A.M. daily) lies hidden away in a Belltown alley behind an inconspicuous lacquered wood door. A small, cursive-script metal placard on a windowless brick wall lets you know you found the spot—inside you'll be rewarded for your search with stiff, well-balanced cocktails made by a staff of veteran barkeeps who especially know a thing or two about juniper berries. Set inside a former boiler room, the two-story lounge keeps its lighting low to complete the saucily illicit atmosphere. Head down the stairs for a little more space and some comfortable couches to enjoy your drinks.

If vodka's your passion, then saunter over to South Lake Union's **Venik Lounge** (227 9th Ave. N. #A, 206/223-3734, www.veniklounge.com, 4–10 P.M. Mon., 4–11 P.M. Tues.–Fri.), a classy but relaxed spot known for seasonal vodka infusions and house-made bitters. Its most unique specialty drink is the Dirty Pickle, a cocktail composed of infused garlic vodka mixed with pickle juice.

WINE BARS AND TASTING ROOMS

Just south of Madison Park in the Madrona neighborhood, **Bottlehouse** (1416 34th Ave., 206/708-7164, http://bottlehouseseattle.com, noon–11 P.M. Tues.–Thurs., noon–midnight Fri.–Sat.) offers everything one would expect from a quality wine bar. Romantic lighting, tasty small bites with an emphasis on cheese and charcuterie, an amazing selection of vino, and a staff well-versed enough in wine to serve it well. With a special emphasis on Northwest wines and an option to try most of them in a two-ounce pour, Bottlehouse makes a perfect stop for oenophiles who don't have time to make the journey out to Washington's wine country.

For wine and cheese a little closer to your downtown hotel, try **Purple Cafe and Wine Bar** (1225 4th Ave., 206/829-2280, www.the purplecafe.com, 11 A.M.–11 P.M. Mon.–Thurs., 11 A.M.–midnight Fri., noon–midnight Sat., noon–11 P.M. Sun.). Slide into a chair at the giant semicircle bar and gape upward at two-story columnar tower of wine bottles that fuels a dizzying list of varietals there for the tasting. The carefully designed cheese and appetizer menu offers pairing suggestions for everything and Purple's impressive wine flight selection can educate beginner wine aficionados with a decent lesson in one night.

DIVE BARS

In keeping with Seattle's informal nature, the best joints in town to throw back a few drinks are the hidden, hole-in-the-wall bars that would never make you look bad for your choice to go out on the town in T-shirt and jeans.

The U District's **Blue Moon Tavern** (712 NE 45th St., 206/675-9116, http://bluemoon seattle.wordpress.com, 2 P.M. Mon–Fri.) is one of the most famous old-time hangouts in Seattle, the sort of place that once attracted the likes of Allen Ginsberg, Jack Kerouac, and Tom Robbins. It still brings in the Deadheads on Sunday nights for a jukebox jam. Monday is opera night, and the first Wednesday of every month is poetry night.

Grab a handful of peanuts from the endless free bowls at **Hooverville Bar** (1721 1st Ave. S., 206/264-2428, www.hooverville seattle.com, 2 P.M.–2 A.M. daily) and don't worry about the shells—just throw 'em on the ground. Situated near the stadiums, this lovable bar borders on the edge of poseur, maybe just slightly too conscious of its divey-ness. But, hey, there's Pabst Blue Ribbon on tap and pinball machines waiting for a new high score. Who can argue with that?

The view of Elliott Bay is great at **Alki Tavern** (1321 Harbor Ave. SW, 206/932-9970, www.thealkitavern.com, 10:45 A.M.–1:45 A.M.), as long as you look out the open doors—the windows are pretty grimy and tiny, a symbol of this place's dive status. The drinks are plentiful and cheap and the barkeeps are friendly, making this place a keeper. Visit on Tuesday night for $1 burgers.

The unpretentious **Nite Lite** (1926 2nd Ave., 206/443-0899, www.thenitelite.com, 4 P.M.–2 A.M. daily) serves drinks strong enough to put a little kink in a writer's step. This dark den is right downtown next to the Moore

Theatre, a secret favorite among comics and other artists who like to visit after their shows.

GAY AND LESBIAN BARS

Check out the *Seattle Gay News* (www.sgn .org), a free weekly newspaper, for the latest in events and music. Otherwise, direct yourself to **Neighbours** (1509 Broadway, 206/324-5358, www.neighboursnightclub .com, 9 P.M.–2 A.M. Tues.–Wed., 9 P.M.–3 A.M. Thurs., 7:30 P.M.–4 A.M. Fri., 9 P.M.–4 A.M. Sat., 10 P.M.–2 A.M. Sun.) on Capitol Hill, Seattle's definitive gay bar, complete with sharp young men, drag queens, and straights who love them all. It's loud, crowded, and perfect for an all-night dance party. Thursday night brings out the crowd with "Rock Lobster" and other 1980s tunes. You can also get your groove on at **Re-Bar** (1114 E. Howell St., 206/233-9873), a predominately gay dance club with DJs spinning disco, hip-hop, house, and techno music Friday–Sunday (and sometimes shows or other types of music on other nights).

Partiers looking for a wild time on the town line up around the corner some nights to get into **The Cuff Complex** (1533 13th Ave., 206/323-1525, www.cuffcomplex.com, 2 P.M.–2 A.M. Mon.–Thurs., 2 P.M.–3 A.M. Fri.–Sat.), a decades-old establishment known for a clientele with a predilection for leather. Taking up an entire city block, this place offers a sprawling dance floor and draws in top DJs on the weekends and throughout Pride Week.

For something a little lower key—read: no dance floor—check out **The Elite** (1520 E. Olive Way, 206/860-0999, noon–2 A.M. daily), a friendly neighborhood hangout in Capitol Hill. With friendly servers, good brew on tap, and darts and pool to play, this joint has the makings for a chill night out.

Lesbians (and some hopeful dudes) head to **The Wild Rose** (1021 E. Pike St., 206/324-9210, www.thewildrosebar.com, 5 P.M.–midnight Mon., 3 P.M.–1 A.M. Tues.–Thurs., 3 P.M.–2 A.M. Fri.–Sat., 3 P.M.–midnight Sun.) with its dartboards, pool tables, jukebox, and karaoke on Wednesday night; there's DJ dance music on Saturday night.

Live Music
HEADLINERS AND LOCAL ACTS

The city's most elaborate music venue, **Sky Church** (325 5th Ave. N., 206/770-2777, www.empsfm.org), sits inside Experience Music Project. Well-known performers often come here, though space for the audience is limited—meaning there's barely room to stand. You also can't carry drinks into the performance area. But the enormous high-tech video screen is an attraction in its own right.

You'll also find a lot of national acts at the **Showbox** (1426 1st Ave., 206/628-3151), near Pike Place Market. This decades-old venue has such a rep for good performances that it had to open an annex in Pioneer Square (1700 1st Ave. S.) to satisfy Seattle's thirst for rockin' shows.

The Belltown area north of downtown keeps the beats alive at several popular clubs, including **Crocodile Café** (2200 2nd Ave., 206/441-5611, www.thecrocodile.com), a club that acted as the alternative scene's incubator for years, went bust for a couple and came back better than ever. It's a good place to look for rock stars passing through town.

After operating for 90 years as a single screen

SMELLS LIKE SEATTLE BANDS

The city of Seattle has a long and storied musical history, with legendary artists and genres that include:

- **Grunge music:** The Seattle area is still most closely associated with the "grunge" movement of the early 1990s. Characterized by distorted electric instrumentation, a fashion sense borrowed from local lumberjacks, and angsty, lamenting lyrics, grunge is undeniably Northwestern. The dean of all grunge acts, Nirvana, was formed by two Aberdeen locals, Kurt Cobain and Krist Novoselic. It was in the Lake Washington area of Seattle that Cobain killed himself in 1994. Pearl Jam, Alice in Chains, and Screaming Trees are all Seattle bands, as is Soundgarden, whose breakthrough hit "Spoonman" was written about a street performer who once frequented Pike Place Market.

- **Sub Pop and Kill Rock Stars:** These two legendary labels are based in Washington, the former in Seattle and the latter in Olympia.

- **Harvey Danger:** This band was best known for its late-1990s post-grunge anthem "Flagpole Sitta."

- **Heart:** Ann and Nancy Wilson, the founding sisters of this iconic rock group, are both from Seattle.

- **Jimi Hendrix:** The guitar virtuoso was born in Seattle and learned to play his instrument here, belonging to various local bands in his youth. Hendrix left the area in 1961 and never lived here again, although he is buried at Greenwood Memorial Park in Renton.

- **Kenny G:** The mellow saxophonist was born in Seattle and is a graduate of the University of Washington.

- **Modest Mouse and Death Cab for Cutie:** Both of these emo superbands played the local club circuit for years before hitting the big time.

- **Murder City Devils:** These hard-edge punk rockers were the yin to grunge's yang in the 1990s and are just now seeing a resurgence in the national club scene.

- **Queensrÿche:** This Bellevue progressive-metal band experienced some celebrity in 1990 with locally themed hit "Jet City Woman."

- **Quincy Jones:** Producer, singer, composer, musician, the legendary Quincy Jones lived in Seattle through much of his childhood.

- **Sir Mix-a-Lot:** The man behind "Posse on Broadway" and "Baby Got Back" was born in Seattle and still calls the city home. The reference to Broadway is actually the street in Seattle's Capitol Hill area, not the better known one in New York.

cinema, the historic **Neptune Theatre** in the U District was rehabbed and retrofitted to start a new life in late 2011 as a multiuse venue that will host concerts in a range of genres, as well as spoken-word, comedy, and even DJ performances. The same company that operates Neptune also runs **Paramount Theatre** (911 Pine St., 206/467-5510, http://stgpresents.org/paramount) and **Moore Theatre** (1932 2nd Ave., 206/467-5510, http://stgpresents.org/moore), two more converted historic cinemas with storied histories whose stages host headliner performances. The largest of the three, Paramount was bankrolled by Paramount Pictures, which poured a whopping $3 million into its construction during the roaring '20s.

ALL AGES
Old and young flock to **El Corazon** (109 Eastlake Ave. E., 206/381-3094, www.elcorazonseattle.com), which dishes up some of the area's hottest bands in a mixed setting that gives the under-21 set a chance to get a taste of the music scene. This has been the city's best all-ages venue for years now, albeit under a spate of different names.

Run by a corps of dedicated volunteers, **The Vera Project** (Warren Ave. and Republican St., 206/956-8372, www.theveraproject.org) at Seattle Center was opened to cultivate interest in music and arts among the city's 14- to 24-year-old contingent. In addition to all-ages shows from up-and-coming and established bands, Vera also holds classes in audio engineering, event production, and even silkscreen printing.

JAZZ AND BLUES
The most popular place for Seattle jazz buffs is **Dimitriou's Jazz Alley** (2033 6th Ave., 206/441-9729, www.jazzalley.com, sets at 7:30 Tues., Wed., Thurs. and 7:30 & 9:30 Thurs., Fri., and Sat.) where big-time national acts and up-and-coming talent can be heard. This is an elegant, dress-up place. More authentic is my favorite, **Tulas Jazz Club** (2214 2nd Ave., 206/443-4221, www.tulas.com, 3 P.M.–midnight Sun.–Thurs., 3 P.M.–1 A.M. Fri.–Sat.), an old-fashioned cabaret that is only missing

the bouncer asking for a code word. Quarters are cramped, service is surly, and the music is like honey. That's the way it's supposed to be, you dig?

Find more live jazz at the **Seattle Art Museum** (206/654-3100, www.seattleartmuseum.org) on the second Thursday of the month, January through June starting at 5:30 P.M.

In Pioneer Square, there are a number of places to find live tunes. **New Orleans Creole Restaurant** (114 1st St., 206/622-2563, www.neworleanscreolerestaurant.com) serves up spicy Creole meals plus live Dixieland jazz, blues, and zydeco every night but Sunday. Seattle's oldest bar, **Central Saloon** (207 1st Ave., 206/622-0209, http://centralsaloon.com) offers great blues, jazz, funk, and reggae bands Thursday–Saturday.

FOLK AND COUNTRY
The unpretentious **Owl 'n' Thistle Irish Pub** (808 Post Ave., 206/621-7777, www.ownthistle.com) is Seattle's most famous Irish pub, with world-class Celtic tunes from the house band on weekends, and a wide range of other styles the rest of the week—from blues to jazz to rock. There's no cover charge, and the back room has pool and darts. Needless to say, Guinness is the drink of choice.

Head north for nightclubs that attract big alt-country and honky-tonk acts. Click those boots on over to the **Tractor Tavern** (5213 Ballard Ave., 206/789-3599, www.tractortavern.com) in Ballard or **Little Red Hen** (7115 Woodlawn Ave. NE, 206/522-1168, www.littleredhen.com) in Greenlake.

Nightclubs
It is no Miami Beach, but Seattle does have a healthy mix of dance clubs for those looking to get their groove on. Perhaps the best place for some booty-shakin', bump-and-grindin' action is over in Pioneer Square.

The aptly named **Trinity** (111 Yesler Way, 206/447-4140, trinitynightclub.com, 6 P.M.–2 A.M. Tues.–Sat.) spreads the music vibes over three levels, offering different jams on each floor. For some truly high-class partying, round up your peeps and head to **Heaven** (172 S. Washington St., 206/622-1863, www.heavenseattle.com, 6 P.M.–11 P.M. Tues.–Wed., 6 P.M.–2 A.M. Thurs.–Sat., 10 P.M.–2 A.M. Sun.), a swank Pioneer Square club with VIP tables and bottle service at the ready.

The just-turned-21 partiers congregate nearby at **Last Supper Club** (124 S. Washington St., 206/748-9975, www.lastsupperclub.com, 6 P.M.–2 A.M. Wed.–Sun.) one of the town's place-to-be-seen spots, featuring techno on the main floor and hip-hop down on the dance floor in the basement.

Trying to bring a bit of the Las Vegas glitter and swagger to downtown, **PNK Ultra Lounge** (600 Pine St., 206/623-2222, www.pnkultralounge.com, 4 P.M.–2 A.M. daily) draws in the young professional types looking to let loose a little in their sleekest dresses and slightly unbuttoned clubbing shirts. The setting is certainly glamorous, but you'll also get the same expensive drinks and aloof attitude from the staff that you would in Sin City. But, hey, the bartenders fill out their black outfits nicely, so that should count for something.

On a completely different note, the **Century Ballroom** (915 E. Pine St., 206/324-7263, www.centuryballroom.com) on Capitol Hill is a snazzy spot for swing and salsa dance enthusiasts, boasting one of the largest dance floors in the state.

Comedy Clubs

Seattle's biggest comedy club, **Comedy Underground** (222 S. Main St., 206/622-4550, www.comedyunderground.com) in Pioneer Square is one of the top West Coast destinations for national comedy acts. Expect capacity crowds in a crowded setting when attending headliner acts.

Check out theater sports and improv acts at one of two venues. Near Pike Place Market, **Unexpected Productions** (1428 Post Alley, 206/587-2414) offers quirky competitions between quick-thinking thespians à la *Whose Line Is it Anyway?* and in the U District, **Jet City Improv** (5031 University Way NE, 206/781-

3879, www.jetcityimprov.com) performs from-the-hip sketches and bits on Friday and Saturday nights.

THE ARTS

After Ticket/Ticket shut down a few years ago, Seattle was left without a decent kiosk in town to buy bargain day-of event tickets. However, a quick search online at www.goldstar.com or www.halfpriceshows.com will usually snag you some half-off tickets if you're not choosy.

Live Theater

Much of the on-stage performance action takes place at Seattle Center's theaters. America's largest—and perhaps most talent-packed—kids theater, the **Seattle Children's Theater** (206/441-3322, www.sct.org) is housed within the impressive Charlotte Martin Theatre at Seattle Center. Productions and classes include both the silly and the serious. Other Center House productions can be found at **Seattle Repertory Theatre** (206/443-2210, www.seattlerep.org), which puts on classic and contemporary productions October through May and **Book-It Repertory Theatre** (206/216-0833, www.book-it.org), which puts on year-round performances of literary classics by everyone from Jane Austen to James Purdy. The Intiman Theatre Company also produces classic dramatic productions May–November at Seattle Center's **Intiman Theatre** (201 Mercer St., 206/269 1901, www.intiman.org).

Downtown, A Contemporary Theatre, or **ACT** (700 Union St., 206/292-7676, www.acttheatre.org), rounds out the theater season with more gutsy experimental contemporary plays, while the **Seattle Public Theater** (7312 W. Greenlake Dr. N., 206/524-1300, www.seattlepublictheater.org) presents a wide range of plays at the refurbished bathhouse along Green Lake. Also of note is **On the Boards** (100 W. Roy St., 206/217-9888, www.ontheboards.org) in Queen Anne.

Finally, Broadway musical fans would be remiss in failing to check for shows at either the **5th Avenue Theatre** (1308 5th Ave., 206/625-1418, www.5thavenuetheatre.org) or the beautifully restored, historic **Paramount Theater** (Pine St. near 9th Ave., 206/292-2787, www.theparamount.com), both of which do a bang-up job of producing larger shows.

Music and Dance

Just uphill from the Seattle Art Museum, the marvelous Benaroya Hall is home to the **Seattle Symphony** (2nd Ave. and University St., 206/215-4747 www.seattlesymphony.org). The largest employer of artists in the Pacific Northwest, the symphony earns international attention under conductor Gerard Schwartz, with more than a dozen compact discs and at least 10 Grammy nominations. Performances take place in the state-of-the-art auditorium September–June, with more than 100 concerts a year. On Sunday afternoons, the Musically Speaking series mixes the classics with commentary about the music and the composers. Tours are available. Also performing frequently at Benaroya, **Seattle Youth Symphony** (206/362-2300, www.syso.org) offers music enthusiasts a glimpse at the up-and-coming orchestral talent the city has to offer. Benaroya Hall is open 10 A.M.–6 P.M. weekdays, with one-hour tours starting at noon.

Marion Oliver McCaw Hall at Seattle Center hosts the **Seattle Opera** (206/389-7676, www.seattleopera.org), whose September–May regular season almost always sells out. It presents five productions annually, plus Richard Wagner's famous four-opera *Ring* cycle every four years—the next one's scheduled in 2013. The **Pacific Northwest Ballet** (206/628-0888, www.pnb.org), whose season is October–May, is best known for the traditional *Nutcracker* production it holds each Christmas.

Film

Seattle has earned an international reputation among filmmakers as having one of the most discriminating audiences in America. Movies are often tested on this urban market before being released, and Seattle viewers have often had a hand at making little-known films winners.

For the ultimate movie experience, join the crowds at downtown's **Cinerama Theatre** (2100 4th Ave., 206/441-3080, www.cinerama.com) where billionaire Paul Allen's money is once again in evidence. This 800-seat remodeled classic is *the* place to see a flick in Seattle. The screen is enormous, the sound and projection systems are state-of-the-art, and the first-run blockbuster movies are just plain fun.

Off-the-beaten-path cinemas showing arthouse films include **Grand Illusion Cinema** (NE 50th St. and University Way NE, 206/523-3935, www.grandillusioncinema.com) and **Varsity Theatre** (4329 University Way NE, 206/632-3131) in the U District, **Guild 45th** (2115 N. 45th St., 206/781-5755) in Wallingford, and **Egyptian Theatre** (801 E. Pine, 206/323-4978) on Capitol Hill. Looking for a cheap flick? Head out to the **Crest Cinema Center** (16505 5th Ave. NE, 206/363-6338) in North Seattle, where all shows are only $3.

For a throwback to Hollywood's silent era, head through the filigreed arches of **Paramount Theatre** (911 Pine St., 206/467-5510, http://stgpresents.org/paramount) for Silent Movie Mondays, when the venue presents films in the way it was built to show them, accompanied by the antique tunes piping through its Mighty Wurlitzer Organ.

FESTIVALS AND EVENTS
January–February

Start off the year with a plunge into fitness and some really, really cold water down at Magnuson Park at the **Resolution Run and Polar Bear Dive** (7400 Sand Point Way NE, 206/729-9972, www.promotionevents.com/resorun). Held on January 1, this 5k run followed by a dip in Lake Washington provides partiers a good way to shake off those New Year's Day hangovers.

In late January or early February, the International District comes alive with parades, kimonos, and colorful papier-mâché displays to celebrate **Chinese New Year** (206/382-1197, www.cidbia.org). The highlight is usually the lion and dragon dancing, complemented by Taiko drumming and martial arts performances.

Mardi Gras revelers tend to congregate in Pioneer Square during the weeklong celebration that typically hits in February. All the clubs in the neighborhood pitch into to throw an extended party that features jazz and Cajun music, arts and crafts, and a parade.

March-April

The green beer and shamrocks spilleth over at the Seattle Center the weekend closest to St. Patrick's Day, where Seattle's **Irish Festival** (www.irishclub.org) whoops it up ginger-style. For 25 consecutive years the Irish Heritage Club of Seattle has run the event in concert with the annual St. Patrick's Day Parade, which starts at Jefferson and 4th, running past Westlake Park and ending at the Seattle Center on the Saturday of the festival.

A two-week kiddie extravaganza, **Seattle Center Whirligig!** turns Seattle's prime event grounds into a giant bounce house for the 12-and-under set. Coinciding with Seattle schools' spring break, this late-March–early-April event takes over the Center House with bright decorations, inflatable rides, clowns, face painting, and hands-on arts-and-crafts booths.

May-June

If you are in town in May and June, be sure to take in a flick at the outstanding **Seattle International Film Festival** (206/324-9997, www.siff.net). It's the largest of its kind in America, attracting more than 100,000 filmgoers.

On a smaller scale, the **Fremont Outdoor Cinema** (N. 34th St. and Phinney Ave. N., 206/781-4230, www.fremontoutdoormovies .com, $5) is held on summer Saturday nights in Seattle's quirkiest neighborhood. Bring your lawn chair to join in the fun of watching old B movies and cult classics.

The first Saturday of May brings the **opening day of boating season** (206/527-3801, www.seattleyachtclub.org) with a big parade of boats and the **Windermere Cup Races** (www.huskycrew.com), where top university rowing teams from around the world compete on the Montlake Cut. This is the top event

of its kind in the nation and fans pack in the sidewalks underneath the Montlake Bridge to cheer the crew teams on.

On the third weekend of May, the **University District Street Fair** (206/547-4417, www.udistrictchamber.org) attracts hundreds of artists who display their wares on University Way Northeast—also known as the Ave. Also here are food booths and live music. More than 6,000 musicians, dancers, and craftspeople display their talents while enormous amounts of food are consumed at the **Northwest Folklife Festival** (206/684-7300, www.nwfolklife.org), held at Seattle Center on Memorial Day weekend. In late May, the **Pike Place Market Festival** (206/587-0351, www.pikeplacemarket.com) has free entertainment and music, a beer garden, chalk art, and a kids' area.

In June the **Pioneer Square Fire Festival** (206/622-6235, www.lastresortfd.org) recalls Seattle's Great Fire of 1889 (any excuse for a party, right?) with free activities in Occidental Square Park, a parade of classic firefighting equipment, contests, and entertainment.

In late June, the funky "Republic of Fremont" holds the **Summer Solstice Parade and Fair** (206/547-7440, www.fremontfair .com) with booths, live music, ethnic food and drink, and assorted street performers and residents from the fringe. These are not your standard productions, but instead visual and performance works from new artists that push the envelope. The events could be bizarre, disconcerting, funny, psychedelic, and haunting all at the same time. A handful of nude participants are always there for a bit of spice.

July

The 4th of July brings twin fireworks displays, one over Gasworks Park on Lake Union and the other at Myrtle Edwards Park on Elliott Bay. The latter is said to be one of the largest in America. The downtown fun begins with **4th of Jul-Ivar's** (206/587-6500, www .ivarsrestaurants.com), a celebration featuring food booths and entertainment, including a fly-over by acrobatic aerial performers piloting

SEAFAIR

Held over the whole month of July, Seafair is the annual celebration of all things Seattle. Events include a marathon, a triathlon, a fun run, hydroplane races, fireworks, and a traditional performance by the Navy's precision flyers, the Blue Angels.

The festival begins with the Seafair Pirates' Landing, in which many city leaders, dressed as pirates and acting the role to the hilt, "sack" Seattle and are handed the keys to the city by the mayor. The fair's centerpiece is the signature Torchlight Parade, held at the end of the month. This long-running event brings upwards of 300,000 onlookers to watch the clowning pirates as well as local drill teams, equestrians, floats, and bands as they march through the streets of downtown.

Most events are extremely family-friendly and do a fantastic job of conveying the flavor of this unique city.

during the Bite, more than half a million foodies and their families come out to sample small bites served by dozens of restaurants from throughout the city. Across the way in Ballard, **Seafoodfest** (206/784-9705, www.ballard chamber.com) breaks out the shell crackers and filet knives in late July for an annual street festival highlighted by a salmon barbecue, crafts booths, beer garden, and children's games.

One of Seattle's biggest musical festivals outside of Bumbershoot, the **Capitol Hill Block Party** (http://capitolhillblockparty.com) cordons off the streets of Capitol Hill to host dozens of bands on open-air stages over the course of three days. The event is a bonanza for indie music lovers, who crowd the streets rain or shine to jam to an eclectic blend of music.

Seattle's biggest fair of the year, **Seafair** (206/728-0123, www.seafair.com) starts on the 4th of July and packs in a month of festivities, crafts, more than a dozen parades, along with triathlons, ethnic festivals, live music, a milk-carton boat race, ship tours, and demonstrations by the Navy's Blue Angels.

both antique and modern aircraft. Also in early July, the **Lake Union Wooden Boat Festival** (206/382-2628, www.cwb.org) takes place at the south end of Lake Union, where you'll see some of the most beautiful boats on Puget Sound.

Thousands of cyclists take to the back roads of Washington each year in mid-July to participate in the **Seattle to Portland Bicycle Classic** (http://shop.cascade.org), or STP, as it is affectionately referred to by the helmet and saddle crowd. The 200-mile event is one of the premier cycling events in the country, with a fully supported and monitored route that takes cyclists through some of the most scenic rural roads of Western Washington and Oregon. The event typically starts out of the University of Washington's main parking lot on Montlake Boulevard.

In mid-July the sizzle and tantalizing aromas of great comestibles take over Seattle Center during the **Bite of Seattle** (206/232-2982, www.biteofseattle.com). For three days

August

In early August Seafair culminates with the roaring of the iconic thunderboats competing in Seattle's renowned **General Motors Cup Hydroplane Races** held atop the waters of Lake Washington. The races are best viewed from south of I-90 at Lake Washington Boulevard Park and Stan Sayres Memorial Park (3808 Lake Washington Blvd.), which is grand central for the boat pits and event booths. Come ready to get pumped, and don't forget the earplugs for your kiddos.

Seattle music fans have a long-standing date on August Friday evenings at the **Seattle Center Mural Amphitheatre** (www.seattle center.com), which has hosted free concerts for decades in the late Seattle summer light. In fact, Pearl Jam played its first outdoor show over 20 years ago at one of these free concerts. Also in August, the **Seattle Music Fest** (206/664-1000, www.seattlemusicfest.org) brings 20 or so bands to Alki Beach.

Professional bubble blowers create bubbles

in every imaginable shape during the **Bubble Festival** (206/443-2001, www.pacsci.org), held in mid-August at the Pacific Science Center.

When a group of Seattle bike messengers raced pell-mell down a Belltown hill from one dive bar to another back in 1996, they probably had no inkling that they'd be the pacesetters for one of Seattle's most storied annual bicycle events. Now held over in West Seattle's Georgetown neighborhood, **Dead Baby Downhill** still sends participants down a different steep hill every year. They crash down hell-bent-for-leather and skid to a halt at a raucous after-party that features plenty of libations, tall-bike jousting, and more than a few racers sporting charlie horses and raspberries from their efforts.

September-December

A Labor Day weekend arts extravaganza, **Bumbershoot** (206/281-7788, www.bumber shoot.org) brings together top-billed musicians, writers, and craftspeople for a huge end-of-summer blowout at Seattle Center. Bumbershoot attracts more than a quarter million visitors annually and features internationally known musicians, along with local talents. All told, more than 2,500 artists perform! Find the full schedule at http://bumbershoot.org/lineup, available in the spring prior to the festival.

The "Center of the Known Universe" is also the focal point of the city's most entertaining fall festival, **Fremont Oktoberfest** (www.fremontoktoberfest.com), held the last weekend of September. Yes, there are plenty of big steins to go around and the beer garden is always the main attraction, but when push comes to shove this is a family event with loads of oompa music, pumpkin carving, and a 5K and street scramble to round out the festivities. Lederhosen and dirndls are optional, but certainly not frowned upon.

Long-distance runners tackle Seattle hills and the chilly November air at the **Amica Insurance Seattle Marathon and Half Marathon** (www.seattlemarathon.com), one of the top endurance footraces in the country. Runners are routed through scenic lakefront parks, the Arboretum, and Seattle Center.

The festival atmosphere of the holidays washes over Seattle Center during **Winterfest,** a five-week holiday celebration with decorations, children's entertainers, choirs, an ice rink, and a holiday lighting ceremony. It all culminates with the annual New Year's Eve celebration underneath the Space Needle. Hang out at the Needle or find a hilly overlook somewhere in the city to watch the fireworks that go kaboom here at the stroke of midnight.

The last festival of the year is the multiday **Christmas Ships Parade** (206/461-5840), a lighted flotilla that cruises Lake Washington in mid-December.

Shopping

SHOPPING CENTERS
Westlake Center

The undisputed hub of downtown Seattle shopping, Westlake Center (400 Pine St., 206/467-1600 www.westlakecenter.com, 10 A.M.–8 P.M. Mon.–Thurs., 10 A.M.–9 P.M. Fri.–Sat., 11 A.M.–6 P.M. Sun.) serves as the southern hub of the Monorail from Seattle Center and the above-ground Westlake Station there leads down to Seattle's bus terminal. The distinctive and airy window-paneled shopping center hosts four stories of shopping, plus a food-court that hits the spot when there's no time to visit one of the sit-down restaurants downtown. Shopping options here vary from the touristy—pick up gifts for relatives back home at the **Made in Washington** store—to the chic—buy apparel at Jessica McClintock or Caché.

Other Downtown Centers and Department Stores

Seattle's downtown shopping scene radiates

© ERICKA CHICKOWSKI

Westlake Center

outward from the Westlake Center, with the best choices centered in a cluster of blocks bounded by Olive Way and University Street to the north and south and 2nd and 7th Avenues to the west and east. Westlake itself is sandwiched between two icons of downtown department store shopping. To the west you'll find the old Bon Marché building, now owned by and operated as Macy's. To the east lies the flagship store for Seattle-based Nordstrom (6th Ave. between Olive and Pine St., www.nordstrom.com), which itself synchs up on its eastern side with a skywalk over to **Pacific Place** (600 Pine St., 206/405-2655 www.pacificplaceseattle.com), a retail and entertainment center with five levels of shops, three restaurants, and a multiplex movie theater. This complex is home to **Eddie Bauer,** another store founded in Seattle that went national.

Somewhat of a hidden gem, the underground mall at **Rainier Square** (1333 5th Ave., 206/373-7119, www.rainier-square.com) offers shoppers an upscale selection of boutique clothing, jewelry, and dining just a few blocks away from Westlake Center.

Northgate Shopping Mall

No-nonsense shoppers should flee downtown and motor seven miles north on I-5 to Northgate Shopping Mall (401 NE Northgate Way, 206/362-4778, 10 A.M.–9 P.M. Mon.–Sat., 11 A.M.–7 P.M. Sun.). With ample free parking and no downtown shopping price premiums, this mall is anchored by Target, Macy's, Nordstrom, and JCPenney and can help any travelers caught off-guard by unseasonable weather to pick out the right clothes or gear as quickly as possible and be on their way.

University Village Mall

The attractive University Village Mall (25th Ave. NE) near campus down NE 45th St. is another good neighborhood mall, with numerous boutiques, a Barnes and Noble, loads of restaurants, and a grocery store.

Pike Place Market

Pike Place Market is loaded with tiny wine shops, boutiques, and craft stores, not to mention the colorful farm and craft stands it's best known for. Many market rookies make the mistake of watching the suspendered fishmongers toss a few fish under the clock, sauntering by a few of the stalls along the Main Arcade, and figuring they've pretty much covered Pike Place. But there's so much more to the market than that.

MAIN ARCADE AND NORTH ARCADE
First of all, you haven't really "done" the market until you've at least followed the upper level Main Arcade from end-to-end and browsed through all of the vendors back in the recesses of the North Arcade. Even after visiting more than once, the routine bears repeating, as the vendors who frequent the temporary day stalls come on different days and are not always in the same booth location each time. So your experience will change from trip to trip. During your exploration, keep on the lookout for intricately carved woodcraft, supple leather accessories, unique jewelry, and a whole host of other handicrafts.

CORNER MARKET AND SANITARY MARKET
Across from the clock on the northwest corner of 1st Avenue and Pike Street, the Corner Market and Sanitary Market play host to several cute shops. Pick out men's or women's vintage clothes from the 1950s and 1960s at **Old Duffers Stuff,** which also offers plenty of smart hats and belts to complete the outfits. Women with more modern tastes can also peruse the unique inventory of **Earth, Wind and Fire Boutique,** which sells fashions featuring exotic silks and textiles, unique jewelry from dozens of different designers, and a great scarf selection.

Also in the mix, **Metsker Maps** gives vagabonds and travel nuts the opportunity to geek out over a truly exceptional stock of maps from around the world.

ECONOMY MARKET
You'll find Economy Market just southeast of the flying fish, where the information booth sits. If you've ever yearned for playthings of yesteryear, your best shot at satisfying the

nostalgia is at **The Great Wind Up,** a store that specializes in antique wind-up toys. Hello, Mr. Monkey Playing a Set of Symbols, where have you been all my life?

Meanwhile, mystics and homeopathy fans will dig the vibe at **Tenzing Momo,** a purveyor of tarot cards, herbs, tinctures, incense, and lots of intricate Buddhist statues and carvings.

NORTH END AND POST ALLEY
Whether flowery and dainty British pots or funky Asian cartoon character tea sets are your kind of thing, the kettles, cozies, and strainers at **Perennial Tea Room** are sure to please. With a robust selection of loose leaf teas, there's also plenty to put inside that sparkling new equipment.

Also down this stretch of the Market, the seductive cookware and kitchen accessories at **Sur La Table** are enough to lure just about any otherwise sensible traveler to buy enough goodies to surely put their baggage over the weight limit at the airline check-in.

DOWNUNDER ARCADE
A rabbit's warren of quirky shops, the Downunder Arcade is home to some of my favorite Pike Place shops. The above-ground sign that says "More Shops Below" will point you right down to them and straight back to your youth, as there's a strong concentration of shops that cater to the Peter Pan inside of all of us. If you ever wanted to learn how to pull a rabbit out of a hat, or just how to prank someone really effectively with a whoopee cushion or squirting flowers, talk to the experts over at **Market Magic Shop.** Or pick up that extra special rookie card or Buffalo nickel to complete your childhood collection at **Market Coins.** While down there, don't forget to leave time for the jam-packed, sometimes chaotic and always amusing aisles of **Golden Age Collectables.** Featuring old movie memorabilia and posters, wacky toys, and racks and racks of comics, Golden Age is a treasure trove of pop culture sure to satisfy anyone who considers a trip to Comic-Con a lifelong dream.

SKID ROW

Seattle has the dubious distinction of coining the term "skid row." The phrase started out innocently enough. Local loggers used it to refer to the corduroy road they built along Yesler Way using rows of timber. It was set up that way so they could skid logs from the top of First Hill down to Henry Yesler's sawmill on the waterfront.

As time went on, many of the city's well-to-do denizens migrated to other parts of the city, and the timber industry dried up somewhat. The fortunes of Pioneer Square began to slide as surely as the timber once did, and Yesler Way grew into a seedy part of town.

The term became synonymous with a neighborhood down on its luck early in the 20th century, when teetotaling local preacher Rev. Mathews proclaimed: "Yesler Way was once a skid road down which logs were pushed to Henry Yesler's sawmill on the waterfront. Today it is a skid road down which human souls go sliding to hell!"

PIKE STREET HILLCLIMB

Leading down, down, down to the waterfront from the steep embankment on which the market is perched, the wide steps of the Hillclimb are lined with boutiques and restaurants galore. Print and literary nerds will get a kick out of the antique printing press **Pike Street Press** uses to put out classy business cards, invitations, and other paper products. And the creamy and aromatic soaps and lotions at **Black Creek Botanicals** make a perfect alternative to the harsh stuff your maid puts in the hotel bathroom every morning.

Fashionistas also must visit **Simone and Sylvia** to consider adding some custom clothing to their closets. In addition to unique ready-to-wear styles on the racks here, the shop offers a selection of fabrics and patterns and will take your measurements to create one-of-a-kind items to suit your style and build.

GALLERIES

Several galleries fill a pedestrian-only stretch of Occidental Street and along 1st Avenue S. in Pioneer Square. Join the Pioneer Square throngs on the **first Thursday** of each month, when the galleries all stage opening receptions. It has become a big event and is a good opportunity to mingle with artists and art connoisseurs; bargain hunters appreciate the free munchies and drinks. Make an evening of it: the Seattle Art Museum is also open late that night with free admission.

For a taste of folk or experimental art, plus a dose of creativity from breakout artists, wander a little farther afield from downtown to Capitol Hill, Fremont, and Ballard, all of which host their fair share of studio collectives and other alternatives to the establishment scene. In Fremont, check out the monthly **First Friday Art Walk,** which showcases artists at work and is one of the neighborhood's many attractions for art lovers.

For the latest fine arts exhibitions throughout Puget Sound, pick up a copy of **Art Access** (www.artaccess.com) from a local gallery.

Contemporary

Set in a striking space featuring brick interior walls and buffed wood floors that complement a rotating mix of painting, sculpture, and glasswork by artists from the Pacific Northwest and abroad, **Artforte** (307 Occidental Ave S., 206/748-0187, 10:30 A.M.–6 P.M. Mon.–Sat., noon–5 P.M.) is a particularly worthwhile stop along the Pioneer Square walkways. While you're in the neighborhood, be sure to check out **Greg Kucera Gallery** (212 3rd Ave. S., 206/624-0770, www.gregkucera.com, 10:30 A.M.–5:30 P.M. Tues.–Sat.) a wide open and airy space with an ironic-chic exposed industrial ceiling and artwork from a range of respected artists. Meander over to the gallery's unique outdoor patio to check out its collection of sculptures.

If the array of handicrafts and other folksy pieces sold along the Pike Place Market arcade don't do it for you, tramp upstairs to the loft at **Lisa Harris Gallery** (1922 Pike Pl.,

206/443-3315, www.lisaharrisgallery.com, 10:30 A.M.–5 P.M. Mon.–Sat., 11 A.M.–4 P.M. Sun.), which primarily represents West Coast artists, particularly those with ties to the Pacific Northwest. The art battles it out for visual superiority with the sweeping views of the Puget Sound seen through the gallery's windows.

Meanwhile, the art speaks for itself alone at **Francine Seders Gallery** (6701 Greenwood Ave N., 206/782-0355, 11 A.M.–5 P.M. Tues.–Sat., 1–5 P.M. Sun.) near Green Lake, a 45-year-old institution that's shown pieces by some of the greatest artists the Emerald City has had ties to over the years, including Jacob Lawrence and George Tsutakawa. Set within an old house in a quiet area away from the pretension of downtown, the gallery primarily reps established artists, so the quality of work is universally good.

Folk and Experimental

Pick up folk art and fine crafts from around the world at **La Tienda Folk Art Gallery** (2050 NW Market St., 206/297-3605, www .latienda-folkart.com, 10:30–6 P.M. Mon.–Fri., 10 A.M.–6 P.M. Sat., noon–4:30 P.M. Sun.) in Ballard. Open now for just about half a century, this shop offers particularly impressive pottery, sculpture, and wood crafts from Latin America and Southeast Asia.

Frank and Dunya (3418 Fremont Ave. N., 206/547-6760, www.frankanddunya.com, 11 A.M.–7 P.M. Mon.–Wed. and Fri.–Sun., 11 A.M.–8 P.M. Thurs.) captures the spirit of Fremont with its collection of "fun and functional" pieces by Washington artists. One part gift shop, one part gallery, Frank and Dunya displays and sells from a diverse and rotating collection that includes everything from jewelry created from recycled soda cans to plein air landscapes.

Can furniture be art? You bet your sweet block sander it can. Visit the showroom at **Northwest Gallery of Fine Woodworking** (101 S. Jackson St., 206/625-0542, www .nwfinewoodworking.com, 10:30 A.M.–5:30 P.M. Tues.–Sat., noon–5 P.M. Sun.) to see how woodworking artisans can make timber come alive with their creative and sumptuous furnishings.

An artist-owned space known for holding some pretty rockin' show openings—with trendy DJs and all—the **Greenwood Collective** (8537 Greenwood Ave N., 206/708-7281, www.greenwoodcollective.com, noon–6 P.M. Wed.–Fri.) features a solid mix of work from emerging Pacific Northwest urban artists. From wacky to profound, the style here seems to be a cross between street art, the best in advertising graphic design, and something from Diego Rivera.

Glasswork and Sculpture

Feel the heat of the furnace and watch students blow luminescent glasswork at the **Edge of Glass Gallery** (513 N. 36th St., 206/632-7807, www.edgeofglass.com, 11 A.M.–6 P.M. Wed.–Sun.), a teaching studio and gallery in Fremont that offers particularly stunning lamps, chandeliers, and other hanging lights. The oldest glassblowing studio in the Northwest, **Glasshouse Studio** (311 Occidental Ave. S., 206/682-9939, www.glasshouse-studio.com, 10 A.M.–5 P.M. Mon.–Sat., 11 A.M.–4 P.M. Sun.) in Pioneer Square was founded just as Dale Chihuly's Pilchuck Glass School and the Northwest Glass Movement first grew legs in the early 1970s. Featuring weird and fantastical shapes, a swirling mix of color and perfectly placed lighting to highlight the creativity, the work featured here comes from some of the best blowers in the city.

Settled into the second floor of a restored, century-old warehouse that's located across the street from the Seattle Art Museum, **Traver Gallery** (110 Union St., 206/587-6501, www.traver.com, 10 A.M.–6 P.M. Tues.–Fri., 10 A.M.–5 P.M. Sat., noon–5 P.M. Sun.) shows a wide range of contemporary art but is perhaps best known for its glass, sculpture, and mixed-media art.

BOOKS AND MAGAZINES

Seattleites spend more money on books per capita than any other American city—almost twice the national average. Given this, you can be assured that the city has lots of choices when it comes to buying books. With more than 150,000 titles on the shelves, a comfortable atmosphere, knowledgeable staff, and a café and almost nightly readings by acclaimed authors and poets, the **Elliott Bay Book Company** (1521 10th Ave., 206/624-6600, www.elliottbaybook.com) is a local legend. This Pioneer Square bookstore is *the* quintessential place for Seattle bibliophiles. Pick up its quarterly *Elliott Bay Booknotes* for detailed book reviews and articles about the craft of writing.

The **University Bookstore** (4326 University Way NE, 206/634-3400 or 800/335-7323, www.bookstore.washington.edu) competes with Harvard's book shop for the nation's largest university bookstore, carrying an impressive array of titles, plus office supplies, "go Huskies" clothing, cameras, CDs, and more. Just down the block, **Bulldog News** (4208 University Way NE, 206/632-6397, http://bulldognewsstand.blogspot.com) maintains the best magazine and newspaper store in town, with over 2,000 titles, including quite a few foreign magazines. Almost any night you're bound to find several dozen folks scanning the issues (and doing quite a bit of reading).

Over in Capitol Hill, the funky collection of used books at **Twice Sold Tales** (4501 University Way NE, 206/545-4226, www.twice-sold-tales.biz, 10 A.M.–9 P.M. Mon.–Thurs., 10 A.M.–10 P.M. Fri.–Sat.) sits inside a grand old brick building. The literary finds are complemented by an even more comforting collection of store cats who skitter about the place just waiting for a scritch on the neck.

For a great selection of travel books, visit **Wide World Books and Maps** (1911 N. 45th Ave., 206/634-3453, www.wideworldtravels.com, 10 A.M.–9 P.M. Mon.–Sat., 11 A.M.–6 P.M. Sun.) in Wallingford. Established in 1976, it was the first travel-only bookshop in America. The tea shop next door is a fine place to read about Asia while sipping Chinese tea.

Unrepentant leftists, socialists, and radicals love **Left Bank Books** (206/322-2868, www.leftbankbooks.com, 10 A.M.–7 P.M. Mon.–Sat., 11 A.M.–6 P.M. Sun.) at Pike Place Market.

East West Book Shop (1032 NE 65th St., 206/523-3726, www.eastwest.com) is the place for the crystal, channeling, and pyramid-power crowd. For something more down to earth (literally), be sure to visit **Flora and Fauna** (121 1st Ave., 206/623-4727, www.ffbooks.com), the biggest purveyor of natural history volumes in the West.

PHOTOGRAPHY

Casual photographers can stock up on simple supplies at **Cameras West** (1908 4th Ave., 206/622-0066). Professionals and serious amateurs usually prefer **Glazer's Camera Supply** (430 8th Ave. N., 206/624-1100 or 888/531-3232, www.glazerscamera.com), where the shelves are crammed with lighting gear, tripods, and other supplies. Also of note is **PhotoTronics** (513 Dexter Ave. N., 206/682-2646), which offers quick camera repair. It is the only place downtown that will clean a digital sensor within a day.

OUTDOOR GEAR

In business since 1938, **REI** (222 Yale Ave., 206/223-1944 or 800/426-4840, www.rei.com) got its start in Seattle. Its enormous flagship store is best recognized as the home of the world's tallest indoor climbing wall. Give it your best shot on the wall, test hiking boots or mountain bikes on the loop trail outside, enjoy an espresso next to the waterfall, try out Gore-Tex jackets in the rain room, plan trips with the help of Park Service or Forest Service personnel at the in-store Outdoor Recreation Information Center, or simply wander through the clothing and gear. REI also rents all sorts of outdoor equipment, including backpacks, climbing shoes, tents, sleeping bags, ice axes, and skis. The store features an auditorium where you can watch outdoor presentations and clinics most evenings. Below the store are three levels of free underground parking.

Sports and Recreation

BOATING

Rent wooden rowboats and sailboats and learn about building these classics at the **Center for Wooden Boats** (1010 Valley St., 206/382-2628, www.cwb.org), on the south end of Lake Union. Or rent sea kayaks from the **Northwest Outdoor Center** (2100 Westlake Ave. N., 206/281-9694 or 800/683-0637, www.nwoc.com) on the southwest side of the lake. This is an outstanding place to learn about sea kayaking from the experts, with classes at all levels. It also sells kayaks and provides guided tours. Also on the south end of Lake Union, **Moss Bay Rowing & Kayak Center** (1001 Fairview N., 206/682-2031, www.mossbay.net) offers kayak rentals and lessons, plus sculling lessons and teams.

Rent sailboards, surfboards, and in-line skates from **Urban Surf** (2100 N. Northlake Way, 206/545-9463, www.urbansurf.com). Washington's largest rafting store, **Swiftwater** (206/547-3377) sells and rents rafts and non-motorized inflatable boats of all types.

In the summer you can rent kayaks, rowboats, pedalboats, sailboards, and canoes to play around the warm waters of Green Lake from **Green Lake Boat Rentals** (7351 E. Green Lake Dr., 206/527-0171).

Over on Lake Washington, head to **University of Washington Waterfront Activities Center** (just east of the Montlake Bridge, 206/543-9433) for canoe or rowboat rentals. You can also take rowing, sailing, canoeing, or kayaking lessons on Lake Washington from **Mount Baker Rowing and Sailing Center** (3800 Lake Washington Blvd., 206/386-1913).

WALKING AND RUNNING

As one of Seattle's largest sanctuaries of green space, **Discovery Park** is an ideal park to stretch out your legs no matter how fast your pace. The park sports more than 11 miles of trails through forest and meadow, with access to 2 miles of Puget Sound beaches.

North beyond this is **Carkeek Park** (NW

© ERICKA CHICKOWSKI

Jogging is a popular activity at many of Seattle's parks.

110th St.), where you'll find a beautiful picnic area and playground, enjoyable hiking trails, and walks and talks at the **Environmental Education Center** (206/684-0877). A scenic walking beach along Puget Sound is accessible via a footbridge over the railroad tracks. Just be aware that if the tide's in, chances are the beach here will be out.

All but hidden from view in a ravine under the 15th Avenue Northeast bridge, **Ravenna Park** is made up of 52 acres of woodlands and a babbling brook, accessible via a series of beautiful trails, plus a children's play area and soccer field, all in a most unlikely location. Douglas fir, Pacific madrona, western red cedar, bigleaf maple, and English and Pacific yew line the nature trail. It's a wonderful place for a morning jog.

The **University of Washington Park Arboretum** also makes for great jogs or strolls. For something longer than the short interpretive trails here, try the Waterfront Trail, a 1.5-mile round-trip through wooded islands and Union Bay's shores at the north end of the arboretum, passing through the largest remaining wetland in Seattle (duck sightings guaranteed). The woodchip and boardwalk trail is level, with numerous benches for resting.

Jutting into Lake Washington on a forested peninsula, **Seward Park** (Lake Washington Blvd. S. and S. Juneau Street) features trails, picnic areas, fishing, swimming, and Mount Rainier views. A one-mile loop trail takes you past Douglas firs six feet in diameter, madronas, bigleaf maples, and the shores of Lake Washington.

CYCLING AND MOUNTAIN BIKING

Bikes are a favorite way to get around Seattle, even on rainy winter days. For an easy and level ride, walk, run, or skate, join the throngs at **Green Lake,** where a 2.8-mile paved path circles the duck-filled lake. On sunny spring weekends you're likely to meet hundreds if not thousands of other folks out for fun in the sun.

One of Seattle's most popular bike/running

paths is an old railroad route, the **Burke-Gilman Trail.** This 14-mile-long paved path begins in Fremont at 8th Ave. NW, cuts through Gasworks Park on the north shore of Lake Union, and follows along Lake Washington all the way to the north end in Kenmore. From here, the 10-mile-long **Sammamish River Trail** continues to Marymoor Park in Redmond for a total of 24 miles of bike riding, in-line skating, running, or walking pleasure.

Another favorite ride is the six-mile **Alki Trail,** which follows the shore of Puget Sound at Alki Point. It begins at the intersection of Harbor Avenue SW and SW Florida Street and curves around the north tip and then west to Alki Point Lighthouse.

Lake Washington Boulevard through the Arboretum and south along Lake Washington to Madrona Park makes for a scenic cycle, but traffic can get heavy, so it pays to ride defensively and be extra cautious when the asphalt is slick. Other popular cycling paths include Seward Park (in south Lake Washington), and Elliott Bay Trail (just northwest of downtown off Alaskan Way).

For a city overflowing with green space in a region known for fat tire tracks, Seattle stands surprisingly bereft of mountain biking trails within city limits. One bright spot keeps enthusiasts pedaling when the mountains are socked in with snow, though. Set up as an urban sanctum for shredding, **Colonnade Park** (800 Lakeview Blvd. E., http://evergreenmtb .org/colonnade, 4 A.M.–11:30 P.M.) runs incongruously under I-5 between Capitol Hill and Eastlake. Featuring cross-country tracks with log rides, progressive drops, and rock chutes galore, plus a flow track and BMX, the park offers good practice for novices but also enough challenges to give veterans a good workout.

Bike Rentals

Tougher insurance regulations have really put a dent in the number of city shops that offer bike rentals these days. Your best bet is one of two shops in the U District. Budget riders should check out **Recycled Cycles** (1007 NE Boat St., 206/547-4491, 10 A.M.–8 P.M. Mon.–Fri.,

© ERICKA CHICKOWSKI

Shred the obstacles under the freeway at Colonnade Park.

10 A.M.–6 P.M. Sat., 10 A.M.–6 P.M. Sun., $40 per day), which rents decent road bikes, mountain bikes, comfort bikes, and trailers. Bike snobs might be happier at **Montlake Bicycle Shop** (2223 24th Ave. E., 206/329-7333, 10 A.M.–7 P.M. Mon.–Fri., 9 A.M.–5 P.M. Sat., 10 A.M.–4 P.M. Sun., $35–90 per day), which offers a fuller range of rentals, including some of the top mountain and road bikes around.

If you are looking to ride along Alki Beach for the afternoon, **Alki Kayak Tours** (1660 Harbor Ave. SW, 206/953-0237, http://kayakalki.com, 10 A.M.–5:30 P.M. daily with rentals back by 7 P.M.) offers simple steeds for a very reasonable $10 per hour.

SWIMMING

The very popular outdoor **Colman Pool** (8603 Fauntleroy Way SW, 206/684-7494) is open in the summer for saltwater bathing. Meanwhile, **Green Lake** is a favorite natural summertime swimming hole, but the water gets a bit rank by the end of the season with algae. Fortunately, that's when it is usually warm enough to brave

the waters of Lake Washington. Beaches with lifeguards in the summer include Madison Park, Madrona Park, Magnuson Park, Matthews Beach, Mount Baker Park, Pritchard Beach, and Seward Park.

MOUNTAINEERING AND CLIMBING

Backcountry enthusiasts should contact the **Washington Alpine Club** (206/467-3042, www.washingtonalpineclub.org), in existence since 1916. Monthly meetings include slide shows and discussions, and the group also offers climbing and skiing classes. **Mountain Madness** (4218 SW Alaska St., 206/937-8389 800/328-5925, www.mountainmadness.com) offers courses in rock climbing, mountaineering, and ski mountaineering, and staff leads technical climbs up several North Cascades peaks.

Practice rock climbing at the 65-foot artificial pinnacle at the REI store (222 Yale Ave., 206/223-1944 or 800/426-4840, www.rei.com). Several other indoor climbing facilities are available, including America's original indoor climbing gym—**Vertical World** (2123 W. Elmore St., 206/283-4497, www.verticalworld.com) in Magnolia. More climbing is available at **The Stone Gardens** (2839 NW Market St., 206/781-9828, www.stonegardens.com) in Ballard.

SPECTATOR SPORTS

The **Seattle Mariners** (206/346-4001 or 800/696-2746, www.mariners.mlb.com) play Major League Baseball at the striking **Safeco Field** (1250 1st Ave. S.), located just south of Pioneer Square. Sports fans will appreciate the retractable roof, real grass, state-of-the-art video board, excellent sight lines, family barbecue area, kids zone, and the 47,000 made-for-baseball seats. Hour-long ballpark tours (206/622-4487, $3) are given daily in the summer or Tues.–Sun. in winter.

The NFL's **Seattle Seahawks** (206/628-0888, www.seahawks.com) play right next door at the equally popular **CenturyLink Field** (800 Occidental Ave. S., 206/381-7848), an open-air gridiron stadium that also hosts the **Seattle**

Sounders FC (206/622-3415, www.seattle sounders.net), a professional soccer team that has quickly grown a following that throngs in a sell-out crowd on game days.

Seattle basketball fans are still mourning the loss of their beloved SuperSonics to a very controversial move to the Midwest. The only professional basketball action in town these days is the championship-winning (2004) **Seattle Storm** (206/217-9622, www.storm.wnba .com) women's professional team, which plays in Key Arena during the summer months. The **Seattle Thunderbirds** (206/448-7825, www .seattle-thunderbirds.com) also play at Key Arena. The team competes in minor-league hockey October through May for the Western Hockey League.

College sports are big here, particularly the University of Washington's **Husky football** (206/543-2200, www.gohuskies.com) and men's and women's **basketball teams** (206/543-2200, www.gohuskies.com).

Accommodations

Anyone willing to spend $150 or more will find a wide range of options close to the heart of the action, including many of the large chain hotels. Remember, though, that you are paying dearly for the location. The same room 15 miles north or south usually costs half as much.

Run by the Seattle-King County Convention and Visitors Bureau, the Super Saver hotel booking program (206/461-5882 or 800/535-7071, www.visitseattle.org) offers a best price guarantee on rates at more than 80 Seattle-area properties. It's a good one-stop place to find a room in your price range and requires no booking fees, no prepayments and no cancellation fees up to 24 hours before check-in.

DOWNTOWN
Under $100
A well-run historic place close to Pike Place Market, **Moore Hotel** (1926 2nd Ave., 206/448-4851 or 800/421-5508, www.moore hotel.com, $59 s or $71 d shared bath, $74 s or $97 d private bath) offers bath-down-the-hall rooms, but it also has rooms with private baths; all contain TVs and phones. Parking is available in local lots for $12 per day.

Seattle's only private hostel, **(Green Tortoise Backpacker's Guest House** (1525 2nd Ave., 206/340-1222, www.greentortoise .com, $32–36 pp, $90 d private room) has 38 rooms right in the center of town. It's near Pike

Place, but the neighborhood also can be a little dodgy. The hostel itself is clean, well managed, and friendly. The hostel has storage lockers, a full kitchen, free Internet access, and daily walking tours. There is no curfew, and alcohol is permitted; there is even free beer on Fridays! Parking is available in local parking garages for around $14 per day. As with other Seattle lodging places, the Green Tortoise fills up quickly in the summer; call ahead for reservations.

Green Tortoise Backpacker's Guest House

For longer-term lodging, Green Tortoise offers **Backpackers Garden Apartments** (715 2nd Ave. N., 206/340-1222), where you can stay in four-bed dorms for $300 a month; it's a popular place for young folks relocating to Seattle. The hostel is connected with the Green Tortoise Adventure Travel (415/956-7500 or 800/867-8647, www.greentortoise.com/adventure.travel.html), a great and inexpensive way to explore the country. Trips run all over the continent, even north to Alaska or south to Central America.

$100-150

The renovated and historic **Best Western Pioneer Square Hotel** (77 Yesler Way, 206/340-1234 or 800/800-5514, www.pioneersquare.com, $160–350 s or d, parking $20) features tastefully appointed rooms and continental breakfast, plus convenient shopping in nearby art galleries or the chance to see a Seattle Mariners ball game, whose stadium is just a few blocks away.

$200-250

A couple of posh Seattle hotels well worth investigating include **The Paramount Hotel** (724 Pine St., 206/292-9500 or 800/426-0670, www.westcoasthotels.com, $199–239 d) near the famed theater and downtown's **Hotel Vintage Park** (1100 5th Ave., 206/624-8000 or 800/853-3914, www.kimptonhotels.com, $189–239 d), a boutique hotel that's serious about wine.

Over $250

Ask for a room with a view at **◖ Alexis Hotel** (1007 1st Ave., 206/624-4844 or 800/264-8482, www.alexishotel.com, $335–395 d, suites $510–825 d) and watch the sun set over the Puget Sound. The sumptuous rooms here feature 300-thread-count linens, flat-screen TVs, and plush furnishings. The themed decor revolves around the arts, and each room is decorated with unique work, as are public areas such as the lobby, where you can sit and sip a cup of complimentary coffee in the morning. Guests can also enjoy complimentary wine-tasting each afternoon downstairs

at the acclaimed Library Bistro, which serves Northwest fare in its bookshelf-paneled nooks, as well as one of the better breakfasts on 1st Avenue. The property has a full spa, fitness center, and steam room. It is also pet-friendly—the front desk will even watch your pooch for you while you explore downtown or grab a bite to eat. Valet parking costs $30.

Fairmont Olympic Hotel (411 University St., 206/621-1700 or 800/821-8106 in Washington, 800/223-8772 outside Washington, www.fairmont.com/seattle, $269 d, $330–875 suites) is one of Seattle's grande dames of hospitality, erected in 1924 and still a center of luxury. The service is tops, and features include two upscale restaurants (Shuckers and The Georgian), an indoor pool, hot tub, saunas, health club, and self-parking ($35).

Classy but not stuffy, **◖ Hotel 1000** (1000 First Ave., 206/957-1000, www.hotel1000.com, $449 d, $649 suite, $39 parking) is one of downtown's finest upscale lodging establishments. Decor is modern, but not uncomfortably so, with muted, dark furnishings accented by colorful lighting and art. Rooms are well appointed, the highlights being the large marbled bathrooms featuring waterfall showerheads. The hotel features all of the business amenities you'd expect of a hotel of this caliber, plus a spa and a unique virtual "golf course" just steps away from the lobby that allows you to unwind with a driver without ever putting on your golf shoes.

As soon as you walk into the lobby and see the giant photo mural of a model in the nude it becomes pretty clear that the boutique **Hotel Max** (620 Stewart St., 206/728-6299, www.hotelmaxseattle.com, $269 d, $30 parking) is not your mom and dad's luxury hotel. This artsy hotel offers modern furnishings and edgy photos and paintings in the public spaces and in rooms, a spiritual menu of holy books that far surpass that lonely Gideon Bible in most hotel drawers, and a pillow menu for choosy sleepers. It's also pet friendly—tell them you're checking in with your pooch and they'll leave you a dog bed, some treats, and even doggie bottled water.

SEATTLE

BELLTOWN, PIKE MARKET, AND WATERFRONT

$100-150

In the heart of Pike Place Market, (**Pensione Nichols B&B** (1923 1st Ave., 206/441-7125 or 800/440-7125, www.pensionenichols.com, $110 s or $140 d, $16 parking) is a European-style place with 10 antique-furnished guest rooms with shared baths, plus two suites ($225 for four people). The B&B has great views across Puget Sound. A continental breakfast is served, and kids are welcome in the suites. Pets welcome, too.

$200-250

Inn at Harbor Steps (1221 1st Ave., 206/748-0973 or 888/728-8910, www.innatharbor steps.com, $225–275 s or d, $18 parking) is an elegant 28-room urban inn popular with corporate travelers who appreciate the indoor lap pool, hot tub, sauna, fitness facility, fireplaces, wet bars, fridges, full breakfasts, and hors d'oeuvres.

Over $250

Seattle's only waterfront lodging on Elliot Bay, the modern 233-room (**Edgewater Hotel** (2411 Alaskan Way, 206/728-7000 or 800/624-0670, www.edgewaterhotel.com, $343–377, $559 suites, $34 parking d) sits on Pier 67. Decorated in a mountain-lodge style

```
FINDING THE
PERFECT B&B

Seattle has a number of homey B&Bs,
particularly among the historic mansions
in the Capitol Hill neighborhood. If you
want to simplify your search, contact a
reservation service. Two good ones are
the Seattle Bed and Breakfast Associa-
tion (206/547-1020 or 800/348-5630,
www.seattlebandbs.com) and A Pacific
Reservation Service (206/439-7677
or 800/684-2932, www.seattlebedand
breakfast.com).
```

with in-room fireplaces and pine furniture, the hotel fronts Elliott Bay and the Olympic Mountains, so be sure to ask for a waterside room. Valet parking is $26.

If you want to be in the heart of the action, it's hard to beat the elegant **Inn at the Market** (86 Pine St., 206/443-3600 or 800/446-4484, www.innatthemarket.com, $29 parking), just a few steps from bustling Pike Place Market. The 70 beautifully appointed rooms start at $255 d, spiraling up to a $625 parlor suite. Amenities include a complimentary shuttle, concierge, twice-daily maid service, and robes.

SEATTLE CENTER AND QUEEN ANNE

$100-150

The (**Inn at Queen Anne** (505 1st Ave. N., 206/282-7357 or 800/952-5043, www.inn atqueenanne.com, $129 d) features charming downtown studios and suites, all with kitchens and continental breakfasts. The great location near Seattle Center, moderate rates, and apartment-style units make Inn at Queen Anne popular with families. Book well ahead for the summer. Parking is $10 daily.

Inn of Twin Gables (3258 14th Ave. W., 206/284-3979 or 866/466-3979, www.inn oftwingables.com, $185 d, $250 suites) is a classic Craftsman home built in 1915. Inside, you will find an enclosed sun porch, plus a cozy living room with fireplace and overstuffed furniture. One room has its own bath, and the other two share the master bath. Rates include a substantial gourmet breakfast. No children are allowed here.

$150-200

Built in 1918 and beautifully restored eight decades later, the 53-room **MarQueen Hotel** (600 Queen Ave. N., 206/282-7407 or 888/445-3076, www.marqueen.com, $189 d, $280 suites, $25 parking) is close to Seattle Center. The spacious rooms feature period-style furnishings, hardwood floors, Internet ports, elegant artwork, and full kitchens.

Colorful and funky, the boutique rooms at **The Maxwell Hotel** (300 Roy St., 206/286-

0629 or 866/866-7977, www.themaxwellhotel.com, $185–245) come decked out in furnishings that give a nod to mod squad design while still offering contemporary touches like black marble bathroom countertops and large flat screen TVs. You can see the Space Needle from the window of many rooms and the property offers perks like free wireless and parking, an indoor pool, and complimentary use of bicycles. For a fee, the hotel also accommodates guests of the four-legged persuasion.

SOUTH LAKE UNION
$150-200
Over in South Lake Union, **Courtyard by Marriott-Lake Union** (925 Westlake Ave. N., 206/213-0100 or 800/321-2211, www.courtyard.com, $159 d, $20 parking) is a good bet, convenient to the lake, the freeway, and Seattle Center. Rooms are what you would expect from this chain, complemented by amenities including an outdoor pool, hot tub, and exercise room.

$200-250
One of the most affordable places to perch your noggin for the night in South Lake Union, **Silver Cloud Inn-Seattle Downtown Lake Union** (1150 Fairview Ave. N., 206/447 9500 or 800/551-7207, www.scinns.com, $179–199 d) features free breakfast, parking, and Internet, plus a free shuttle downtown. The well-appointed rooms come equipped with plush beds and plasma-screen TVs.

CAPITOL HILL
The quiet residential streets of Capitol Hill are home to nearly a dozen classic bed-and-breakfasts, set inside the neighborhood's stately Victorian and Craftsman homes.

Under $100
Bed and Breakfast on Capitol Hill (739 Broadway E., 206/325-0320, $75–125 s or d) has three guest rooms with shared or private baths; rooms include a self-serve "continental plus" breakfast. The Foursquare home was built in 1903 and contains family antiques. No

kids under 16 are permitted and a two-night minimum is required.

$100-150
Bed & Breakfast on Broadway (722 Broadway E., 206/329-8933 or 888/329-8933, www.bbonbroadway.com, $135–175 d) is a 1906 home with the original stained glass windows, oriental rugs, a fireplace, and a grand piano. The three guest rooms have private baths. A continental breakfast is served, and no children under 16 are allowed.

Housed in a historic 1905 home, **Gaslight Inn** (1727 15th Ave., 206/325-3654, www.gaslight-inn.com, $98–168 s or d) is one of the larger B&Bs in Seattle, with eight rooms, a library, and heated outdoor pool. A continental breakfast is served on the sideboard in an elegant wood-paneled dining room.

Thankfully for B&B-loving families, several places do welcome the little ones. One of the most impressive is **Bacon Mansion B&B** (959 Broadway E., 206/329-1864 or 800/240-1864, www.baconmansion.com, $99–234 s or d). This superb 1909 Tudor mansion sprawls over four levels, with an adjacent carriage house. Inside the mansion you'll find marble fireplaces, a crystal chandelier, grand piano, and 11 guest rooms, 9 with private baths. An expanded continental breakfast is served.

Built in 1890, **Mildred's B&B** (1202 15th Ave. E., 206/325-6072 or 800/889-2110, www.mildredsbnb.com, $90–165 s or d) is an attractive Capitol Hill Victorian with a wraparound porch facing Volunteer Park. It has four guest rooms with private baths, and the living room contains a grand piano and fireplace. Guests also have fun on the little putting green on the front lawn. Kids are also welcome here.

$150-200
Settled inside a 1914 English manor-style home, **❰ Shafer-Baillie Mansion Guest House** (907 14th Ave. E., 206/322-4654 or 800/922-4654, www.sbmansion.com, $149 d, $174–219 suites) sits along "Millionaire's Row" just south of Volunteer Park in Capitol Hill. The innkeepers lay out an expanded continental buffet

that includes delights such as smoked salmon, hard boiled eggs, and prosciutto throughout the morning to accommodate late and early risers, and children are welcome to stay.

BALLARD AND MAGNOLIA
$100-150
Chez Sharon B&B (8068 26th Ave. NW, 206/789-6660, www.chezsharoninseattle.com, $105 d) lets out a single, quiet Ballard-district suite facing a flower-filled garden. A continental breakfast is served. This is an adults-only establishment.

The only hotel in downtown Ballard, the brand new **Hotel Ballard** (530 Ballard Ave. NW, 206/789-5011, www.hotelballard.com, $99–159) is an affordable, chic choice easy stumbling distance from the area's watering holes. Set in a historic 1902 building, this intimate inn does it up European style with shared bathrooms and somewhat cozy rooms.

FREMONT, WALLINGFORD, AND GREEN LAKE
Two of the city's best bed-and-breakfast inns can be found along the quiet streets of Fremont and Green Lake.

$150-200
Sitting literally across the street from the Woodland Park Zoo and Rose Garden, **Chelsea Station Inn** (4915 Linden Ave. N., 206/547-6077, www.chelseastationinn.com, $195) offers four spacious suites within an impressive 1920s-era brick home. Rooms are well appointed but cleanly designed, perfect for a new generation of B&B lovers who're turned off by the cluttered antique and lace that so many older inns favor. Each room features a double walk-in shower, living room with queen-size pullout, a dining room, and fully-stocked kitchenette. Guests can expect a gourmet hot breakfast served to their room each morning.

Over in Green Lake, with a view of the water, **Greenlake Guest House** (7630 E. Green Lake Dr. N., 206/729-8700, $144–214) is nestled inside a 1920s Craftsman home. Every room features a private bath, with most featuring a jetted tub or fireplace. There's even one room with two beds perfect for kids or a girlfriend getaway. The inn supplies fresh fruit, tea, coffee, and cookies throughout the day and serves a made-to-order hot breakfast in the morning that includes dishes like brie and apple stuffed French toast and feta omelets.

UNIVERSITY DISTRICT
Under $100
College Inn (4000 University Way NE, 206/633-4441, www.collegeinnseattle.com, $55–95 d) is a historic 1909 University District hotel with down-the-hall baths and a European feeling. The owners are friendly. A generous continental breakfast is included, but there are no elevators in this four-story building, so pack light. You'll also need to find a nearby lot to park your car overnight.

University Motel (4731 12th Ave. NE, 206/522-4724 or 800/522-4720, $96–128 d) has dated motel accommodations that will do just fine for visiting students. All rooms contain full kitchens—a real plus for travelers—and parking is free, but there is no elevator at this three-story motel.

Eastlake Inn (2215 Eastlake Ave., 206/322-7726, $80 s or d, $100–120 suites for up to six people) is a little family-run motel just five minutes by car south of the University, near Lake Union. The decor is rather plain in this older motel, but all rooms contain kitchenettes.

$100-150
University Inn (4140 Roosevelt Way NE, 206/632-5055 or 800/733-3855, www.universityinnseattle.com, $105–129 s or $115–139 d) is just a five-minute walk from the campus. The property has an outdoor pool, hot tub, fitness room, continental breakfast, and free parking. Some rooms contain fridges and microwaves; all are nonsmoking.

(**Hotel Deca** (4507 Brooklyn Ave. NE, 206/634-2000 or 800/899-0251, www.universitytowerhotel.com, $255 d, $12 parking) is the swankiest spot to sleep in the U District, and one of the best bargains in the city. This 15-story luxury hotel is the product of a $2 million renovation that installed art deco decor with a colorful modern flair. The tower is within easy walking distance of all campus sights and restaurants; amenities include a complimentary breakfast and newspaper, exercise room, and free parking.

$150-200

The modern **Silver Cloud Inn-University Village** (5036 25th Ave. NE, 206/526-5200 or 800/205-6940, www.scinns.com, $199 d) is just a short distance from University Village Mall, one of the nicer local places to shop. The campus is a few uphill blocks away, though the steepness makes it less than an ideal walk. Guests enjoy the use of an indoor pool, hot tub, exercise room, continental breakfast, and free parking.

The Chambered Nautilus B&B (5005 22nd Ave. NE, 206/522-2536 or 800/545-8459, www.chamberednautilus.com, $139–204 s or d) offers Cascade views on a hill just four blocks north of the university. This Georgian Colonial home was built in 1915 and is the only B&B close to campus. There's a library and pleasant sun porch, and the six large guest rooms all have private baths, TVs, and phones. The Chambered Nautilus fills fast, so book early. Kids over eight are accepted. Next to the B&B, the owners have a newer four-plex building called **University Suites** with one- and two-bedroom apartments—all with full kitchens ($189 one-bedroom or $214 two-bedroom). Guests at Chambered Nautilus and University Suites are served a gourmet three-course breakfast.

Food

The options listed herein are only a minuscule sampling of Seattle's food and drink establishments. If you are serious about your meals out, take a gander at a specific guide to Seattle dining.

DOWNTOWN
Cafés and Delis

A classy restaurant based out of the Alexis Hotel, **Library Bistro** (92 Madison St., 206/624-3646, www.librarybistro.com, 7–10:30 A.M. and 11:30 A.M.–2 P.M. Mon.–Fri., 8 A.M.–1 P.M. Sat.–Sun., $15) features breakfasts, brunches, and lunches that favor Northwest cuisine with a flair. Kids and kids-at-heart will love the book-filled shelving and the butcher-paper and crayons at each table.

Stop by **13 Coins** (125 Boren Ave. N., 206/682-2513, www.13coins.com, $20), Seattle's classic 24-hour restaurant and gathering place for both the famous and the infamous. It offers more than 130 menu items.

Those with bigger appetites will rave over the cheesesteaks at **Tat's Delicatessen**

Seattle's coffee scene is alive and well.

© ERICKA CHICKOWSKI

COFFEEHOUSES

If you can't find an espresso café within a block of any Seattle shopping district, your eyes are closed and you've lost your sense of smell. It's hard to know where to begin when it comes to coffee in this place where coffee consumption tops that of any other American city. The most famous, of course, is **Starbucks** (www.star bucks.com), with dozens of shops scattered across the city. The original shop is in the Pike Place Market and sports a somewhat more risqué logo than all the other stores. Starbucks is considered by many the godfather of quality coffee in the Northwest. That first store opened in 1971, offering dark-roasted beans and a commitment to quality.

Tully's Coffee (www.tullys.com) and **Seattle's Best Coffee** (www.seattlesbest.com), have a dozen or so Seattle shops. Seattle's Best Coffee is, sneakily enough, a wholly owned subsidiary of Starbucks. Even when you think they don't have ya, they do . . .

Roasteria (321 Broadway E., Capitol Hill, 206/860-5869, www.espressovivace.com, 6:30 A.M.-11 P.M. daily) is a great little walk-up spot for espresso in the heart of Capitol Hill. It also has a second, larger shop downtown (901 E. Denny Way, 206/860-5869, same hours).

Caffe Ladro (600 Queen Anne Ave. N., 206/282-1549, www.caffeladro.com, 5:30 A.M.-11 P.M. daily) has over a dozen locations around town, including two in Queen Anne. **Diva Espresso Bar** (7916 Greenwood Ave. N., 206/781-1213, 7 A.M.-10 P.M. Mon.-Sat., 8 A.M.-8 P.M. Sun.) and **Caffè Umbria** (320 Occidental Ave. S., 206/624-5847, www .caffeumbria.com) is in Pioneer Square.

Another old favorite – it opened in 1975 – is just a few blocks down. **Cafe Allegro** (4214½ University Way NE, facing the alley on 15th St., 206/633-3030, www.cafeallegro.com, 6 A.M.-10:30 P.M. Mon.-Fri., 7 A.M.-10:30 P.M. Sat., 7:30 A.M.-10:30 P.M. Sun.) is a popular sit-down-and-stay-awhile espresso house with three rooms spread over two floors.

Pair that perfect cappuccino with something sweet.

© ERICKA CHICKOWSKI

(115 Occidental Ave. S., 206/264-8287, www.tatsdeli.com, 8 A.M.–7 P.M. Mon.–Fri., 11 A.M.–7 P.M. Sat., until kickoff on Sun. when the Seahawks play, $10). These sandwiches "wit Whiz" are the closest you're gonna get to Philly around these parts.

Contemporary Northwest

Sitting in the Fairmont Olympic Hotel, the **Georgian Room** (411 University St., 206/621-7889, www.fairmont.com/seattle, 6 A.M.–2:30 P.M. and 5:30–10 P.M. Tues.–Sat., $40) is an elegant dining room with a Renaissance look and Northwest cuisine. The food is very expensive but much lighter than what you might expect in a luxury hotel. The salmon, sturgeon, rabbit, lamb, veal, and steaks are cooked to a creative perfection, and the menu also includes a five-course vegetarian dinner that has garnered national praise. Expect to pay at least $150 for a dinner for two with wine and dessert.

Steak and Seafood

€ **Metropolitan Grill** (820 2nd Ave., 206/624-3287, www.themetropolitangrill .com, 11 A.M.–10 P.M. Mon.–Thurs., 11 A.M.–10:30 P.M. Fri., 4–11 P.M. Sat., 4–9 P.M. Sun., $50) is one of the best places in town for steak, and it fills up with business folk at lunch. Seafood (including great clam chowder), pork, lamb, and pastas are also on the menu.

Located a short stroll from Safeco Field and Qwest Field, **F.X. McRory's Steak, Chop & Oyster House** (419 Occidental Ave. S., 206/623-4800, www.fxmcrorys .com, 11:30 A.M.–9 P.M. Mon.–Thurs., 11:30 A.M.–10 P.M. Fri., noon–10 P.M. Sat., closed Sun. except stadium event days, $18) is the ideal place for a post-game party with friends. The fun-loving young crowd is loud, and the menu includes prime rib and salmon, along with six types of raw oysters on the half-shell. Beer isn't brewed here, but more than two dozen different Northwest microbrews are on tap.

Asian

Pan-Asian fare has a strong following in Seattle, and trendy noodle houses are as plentiful as coffee beans and Gore-Tex. One of the best of the bunch, **Wild Ginger** (1401 3rd Ave., 206/623-4450, www.wildginger .net, 11:30 A.M.–3 P.M. and 5–11 P.M. Mon.–Fri., 11:30 A.M.–3 P.M. and 4:30–11 P.M. Sat., 4–9 P.M. Sun., $18), jumps all over Asia: Vietnamese, Thai, Indonesian, and Szechuan Chinese dishes all come out of this creative kitchen. Wild Ginger is best known for its *satay* bar, which features skewered and grilled seafood, chicken, pork, and vegetables, but it also offers delicious curries, soups, and crab. The menu changes seasonally.

Italian

Il Terrazzo Carmine (411 1st Ave. S., 206/467-7797, www.ilterrazzocarmine.com, 11:30 A.M.–4 P.M. and 5–10 P.M. Mon.–Fri.,

5–10 P.M. Sat., closed Sun., $30) is a delightful Pioneer Square restaurant perfect for a romantic dinner. Choose from homemade pastas, creamy risottos, and fantastic meat dishes, including a fall-off-the-bone osso bucco.

Bakeries

Pick up a big, chewy bagel slathered in house-made whipped cream cheese at **Seattle Bagel** (804 Howell St., 206/667-9327, www.seattle bestbagel.com, $4), which offers a range of bagel and schmear flavors. It also serves up lots of bagel sandwich choices come lunchtime.

The suits love to tuck the napkins into their shirts at **Grand Central Bakery** (214 1st Ave. S., 206/622-3644, www.grandcentralbakery .com, 7 A.M.–5 P.M. Mon.–Fri., 8 A.M.–4 P.M. Sat., $8), which offers ample choices of soups, salads, and healthy sandwiches at lunch and some tasty breakfast plates to boot.

Markets

The tiny brick **Esquin Wine Merchants** (2700 4th Ave., 206/682-7374, www.esquin .com, 9:30 A.M.–7 P.M. Mon.–Fri., 9:30 A.M.–5:30 P.M. Sat. 11 A.M.–5 P.M. Sun.) shop is big on Italian wines but also carries Northwest varieties and offers tastings, classes, and reasonable prices.

BELLTOWN, PIKE MARKET, AND WATERFRONT
Cafés and Diners

Foodies love € **Steelhead Diner** (95 Pine St., 206/625-0129, www.steelheaddiner.com, 11 A.M.–10 P.M. daily, $20) for its inventive take on counter-and-stool roadhouse fare. Nosh on delicious eggs served with andouille sausage and potato latkes, veggie "meat" loaf, delectable roast chicken with wilted spinach, and dozens more dishes that will make your eyes roll back in your head. Don't skip this one.

You won't find a traditional grinder on a hoagie here, so I can't say it's *completely* authentic, but **Mike's East Coast Sandwiches** (113 Cedar St., 206/818-1744, www.mikeseast coast.com, 11 A.M.–1:30 P.M. Mon.–Fri., closed weekends, $6) does serve a darned good reuben on rye, plus unique creations. Try the meat and potato sandwich, which puts potato salad right in there with the meat and other sandwich fillings. Nutella fanatics will also dig the Nutella fluffernutter, served with the cocoa and hazelnut spread, marshmallow fluff, and peanut butter.

Artists, wannabe artists, folks on the fringe, and even the button-down set jam the counter at **Two Bells Tavern** (2313 4th Ave., 206/441-3050, www.thetwobells.com, 11 A.M.–10 P.M. daily, $10). They all come here for some of the best and biggest burgers in Seattle, served on sourdough rolls and topped with fried onions. The menu expands to include tasty soups, salads, and other well-prepared pub grub.

Contemporary Northwest

OK, so you've just strolled the market's main arcade and taken in the sights and smells whirling about the kaleidoscope of fresh food. You'd love to taste it, too, but you just don't have a kitchen or the inclination to cook with the market's bounty, right? Get thee immediately to **(Matt's in the Market** (94 Pike St., Ste. 32, 206/467-7909, www.mattsinthemarket .com, 11:30 A.M.–2:30 P.M. and 5:30–10 P.M. Mon.–Sat., closed Sun., $30), a charming bistro whose staff crafts the menu each day based on what's freshest in the stalls. Trust them to be your culinary guides. From your perch in this second story eatery you can watch the crowds bustle below and enjoy your meal 'neath the glow of the market's iconic clock display.

Marco's Supperclub (2510 1st Ave., 206/441-7801, www.marcossupperclub.com, 5–10 P.M. Mon.–Sat., $20) is a bright and arty Belltown place with a menu that bumps from grilled salmon to Jamaican jerk chicken to fried sage-leaf appetizers (far better than it sounds). The food is always creative, and the atmosphere is relaxed.

A trendy eatery with widely varied and spicy fare created by famed chef/owner Tom Douglas, **Dahlia Lounge** (2001 4th Ave., 206/682-4142, www.tomdouglas.com, 11:30 A.M.–2:30 P.M. and 5–10 P.M. Mon.–Thurs., 11:30 A.M.–2:30 P.M. and 5–11 P.M. Fri., 9 A.M.–2 P.M.

and 5–11 P.M. Sat., 9 A.M.–2 P.M. and 5–9 P.M. Sun., $28) has been serving farm-to-table fare to loyal fans for upwards of two decades now.

Seafood

Given its waterfront location, it should come as no surprise that Seattle's specialty is fresh seafood of all types. The city is jammed with fishy restaurants, from takeout fish-and-chips joints to luxury dining that will set you back $60 per person and more.

With five species of oysters grown in Puget Sound waters—including the native Olympia oyster—Seattle has a reputation as one of the best places to slurp fresh oysters on the half-shell. **Emmett Watson's Oyster Bar** (1916 Pike Pl., 206/448-7721, 11:30 A.M.–7 P.M. Mon.–Thurs., 11:30 A.M.–8 P.M. Fri.–Sat., 11:30 A.M.–6 P.M. Sun., $12) is one of the best of these, a relaxed little place in the Soames-Dunn Building at Pike Place Market, with reasonable prices and ultra-fresh oysters, plus great salmon soup or fish and chips. **Elliott's Oyster House & Seafood Restaurant** (Pier 56, 206/623-4340, www.elliottsoysterhouse.com, 11 A.M.–10 P.M. Sun.–Thurs., 11 A.M.–11 P.M. Fri.–Sat., $28) is one of the better waterfront seafood restaurants, with crab, clams, and freshly shucked oysters. Expensive, but it's a fantastic location.

You will not go wrong at **Etta's Seafood** (2020 Western Ave., 206/443-6000, www .tomdouglas.com, 11:30 A.M.–9:30 P.M. Mon.–Thurs., 11:30 A.M.–10 P.M. Fri., 9 A.M.–3 P.M. and 4–10 P.M. Sat., 9 A.M.–3 P.M. and 4–9 P.M.Sun., $26–34) in Pike Place Market. The mixed drinks are great.

The food is beautifully presented and the atmosphere is raucous at Belltown's **Flying Fish** (2234 1st Ave., 206/728-8595, www.fly ingfishrestaurant.com, 11:30 A.M.–2 P.M. and 5–11 P.M. Mon.–Fri., 5–11 P.M. Sat.–Sun., $28). Take a seat in the bar to survey the crowd below.

Ivar's Acres of Clams (on the waterfront at Pier 54, 206/624-6852, www.ivars.com, 11 A.M.–10 P.M. Mon.–Sat., 3–10 P.M. Sun., $22) was folk singer Ivar Haglund's original

© ERICKA CHICKOWSKI

Ivar's Acres of Clams

restaurant (open since 1938). The restaurant is an unpretentious, quality seafood restaurant that often surprises diners who only know Ivar's for the tourist-friendly takeout bar out front ($7.50 for four-piece cod and chips).

Just up the street from Pike Place Market, **Cutter's Bayhouse** (2001 Western Ave., 206/448-4884, www.cuttersbayhouse.com, 11 A.M.–10 P.M. Mon.–Thurs., 11 A.M.– midnight Fri., 10 A.M.–midnight Sat., 10 A.M.–10 P.M. Sun., $30) has a lively bar with a long list of hors d'oeuvres; its specialties— fresh fish, pasta, and prime rib dishes—are accompanied by an extensive wine-by-the-glass list. Sunsets over the Olympics are even more notable than the food.

French

Impress your sweetheart and secure a table upstairs at **Place Pigalle** (81 Pike St., 206/624-1756, www.placepigalle-seattle.com, 11:30 A.M.–3 P.M. and 5:30–9:30 P.M. Mon.– Thurs., 11:30 A.M.–3 P.M. 5:30–10 P.M. Fri.– Sat., 11:30 A.M.–3 P.M. Sun., $27), a cozy bistro

with a certain *je ne sais quoi*. Its entrance is hidden in a market nook just between the flying fish. Come during happy hour, when the menu is really affordable and tasty and you can watch the sun sink down behind the Olympics from the bank of windows looking out over the Sound.

Right in Pike Place Market is **Cafe Campagne** (1600 Post Alley, 206/728-2233, www.campagnerestaurant.com, 11 A.M.–10 P.M. Mon.–Fri., 5:30 A.M.–10 P.M. Sat.–Sun., $22), the downstairs neighbor of the more upscale Campagne. The café serves all three meals, but its breakfasts are a relative bargain. Try the Provençal eggs at breakfast and at dinner go for the French 101, a three-course prix fixe for $33.

Another classic Pike Place restaurant with French inspirations is **Maximilien in the Market** (81A Pike St., 206/682-7270, www.maximilienrestaurant.com, 11:30 A.M.–10 P.M. Mon.–Thurs., 11 A.M.–10 P.M. Fri.–Sat., 11 A.M.–9 P.M. Sun., $35) with stunning views across Elliott Bay and lamb, fish, veal, and beef entrées.

If you're trying to impress your date without breaking the bank, try **Le Pichet** (1933 1st Ave., 206/256-1499, www.lepichetseattle.com, 8 A.M.–midnight daily, $18), an ideal Belltown spot near Pike Place Market with a fun atmosphere, exquisite French meals, a fine wine selection, and reasonable prices.

Bakeries

In the land of latte, the lowly doughnut has fallen out of favor among epicurean elitists. However, there still remains a place where fried dough in the round reigns supreme. Located at several strategic spots about town, **Top Pot Doughnuts** (2124 5th Ave., 206/728-1966, www.toppotdoughnuts.com, 6 A.M.–7 P.M. Mon.–Fri., 7 A.M.–7 P.M. Sat.–Sun., $3) is most easily found in its spacious two-story Belltown castle. Choose between 40 types of doughnuts including cake doughnuts, bear claws, and Boston crème pies.

A comfy place to hang out Seattle-style, **Macrina Bakery and Café** (2408 1st Ave.,

206/448-4032, www.macrinabakery.com, 7 A.M.–6 P.M. daily, $10) provides ample opportunities for guests to lounge outside on the sidewalk or in the cozy café confines over a repast of delicious breads, light lunches, and perfect lattes. A cross between a croissant and a cinnamon bun, Macrina's special roly-poly pastry is a great guilty pleasure pick during breakfast hours.

For a taste of old England, don't miss ◖ **The Crumpet Shop** (1503 1st Ave., 206/682-1598, www.thecrumpetshop.com, 7 A.M.–5 P.M. Mon.–Fri., 7:30 A.M.–5 P.M. Sat.–Sun., $5) in the Sanitary Market building, where you can get delicious fresh crumpets and a steaming pot of tea. Don't miss the fluffy scones, either. They'll make you forever swear off those lumpy rocks most coffee shops masquerade as scones these days.

Some hungers, though, just can't be satisfied with scones and crumpets alone. If you're looking for something a little more substantial, stop in for a piping hot meat pastry at **Piroshky Piroshky** (1908 Pike Pl., 206/441-6068, www .piroshkybakery.com, 7:30 A.M.–6:30 P.M. Mon.–Fri., 7:30 A.M.–7 P.M. Sat.–Sun. in summer, 8 A.M.–6:00 P.M. daily in fall–spring, $5). This is a long-time personal favorite, a little food stand with just a table or two in front of its displays packed full with its namesake pastry, an Eastern European pocket of cheeses, veggies, meats, and delicious spices.

Markets

The stalls and shops at **Pike Place Market** (www.pikeplacemarket.org) are the place to go for fresh fruit, veggies, nuts, and even jalapeño jelly. Pick up some flowers for your honey while you're at it—and maybe even some honey, too! Those big bears full of the golden stuff sold at the day stalls in the North Arcade will make you swear off grocery store honey forever. Most of the following vendors are open during the market's peak hours of 10 A.M.–6 P.M. Monday through Saturday and 11 A.M.–5 P.M. Sunday.

MAIN AND NORTH ARCADES

You can find the pepper jelly at **Mick's Peppouri** (1531 Pike Pl., 206/233-0128, www .micks.com) a permanent fixture in the Main Arcade that mixes up unique blends featuring horseradish, lime, garlic, and more. It might sound a little weird to the uninitiated, but wander over here for a taste—they've always got samples out—and you'll likely be hooked for life!

Pick a pinch of penne at **Pappardelle's Pasta of Pike Place Market** (1519 Pike Pl., Ste. 8, 206/340-4114, www.pappardellespasta .com), right in the Main Arcade. With dozens of lusciously fresh pastas on hand at all times, this place is a must when looking for a starchy accompaniment for seafood snagged at the market.

Even though Pike Place is best associated with the flying fish guys over at **Pike Place Fish** (86 Pike Pl., 206/682-7181, www.pike placefish.com), that's far from the only quality fishmonger at the market. Try **Pure Food Fish** (1511 Pike Pl., 206/622-5765, www.freshsea food.com) for cheaper prices and some of the best shellfish at the market.

© ERICKA CHICKOWSKI

making the signature item at The Crumpet Shop

TEAHOUSES

Although Seattle is best known for its lattes, the city also has a number of quality tea shops. **Seattle Best Tea** (504 S. King St., 206/749-9855, http://seattlebesttea.com) is a little shop across from Uwajimaya in the International District with an excellent selection of Asian teas. The **Teacup** (2128 Queen Anne N., 206/283-5931, http://seattleteacup.com) in Queen Anne sells 150 varieties of black, green, and herb teas from all over the globe and always has something interesting to taste. The Chinese-style **Teahouse Kuan Yin** (1911 N. 45th St., 206/632-2055, www.teahousekuanyin.com, 9 A.M.–11 P.M. daily) is connected to Wide World Books and offers a taste of Asian teas, along with light meals. Also visit the **Japanese Tea Garden** (206/684-4725, 10 A.M.–7 P.M. daily) at the University of Washington Arboretum.

The best place for a formal afternoon high tea is at **Queen Mary Tea Room** (2912 NE 55th St., 206/527-2770, www.queenmarytearoom.com, 9 A.M.–4 P.M. daily).

At **Market Spice,** gourmands and tea fanatics will swoon over the rows and rows of bulk spice jars, identified with neatly handwritten labels over clear glass that shows off the exotic contents within. The 100-year-old shop is most famous for its spicy and sweet house-made tea blend with hints of orange and cinnamon, a particular favorite during the holiday months.

CORNER MARKET AND SANITARY MARKET

The owner of **Pike Place Market Creamery** (1514 Pike Pl. Ste. 3, 206/622-5029, 9 A.M.–6 P.M. Mon.–Sat., 10 A.M.–5 P.M. Sun.) is so passionate about fresh eggs, butter, and cream that she legally changed her name to Nancy Nipples the Milkmaid. 'Nuff said, doncha think?

Meanwhile, just across the street from the Main Arcade, **Oriental Mart's** (1506 Pike Place Market, 206/622-8488, 10 A.M.–5 P.M. daily) lunch counter Filipino food is the stuff of legends, but definitely not the only draw. You can also pick up a wide range of specialty grocery items from all over Asia here.

NORTH END AND POST ALLEY

The cheese is out of this world and so are the prices at ◖ **Beechers Handmade Cheese** (1600 Pike Pl., 206/956-1964, www.beechershandmadecheese.com), where it is not impossible to plunk down $25 or more for a little wedge. But I'm telling you, it is worth it, particularly if you're already spending a mint on some good Washington wine. The specialty is the Flagship cheese, aged one year. While you pick up some cheese to go, save room for the house specialty mac and cheese or grilled cheese sandwich, served up hot at the café attached to the store.

Right where Pike Place funnels out to Western Avenue, **Pike and Western Wine Merchants** (1934 Pike Pl., 206/441-1307, www.pikeandwestern.com, 9:30 A.M.–6:30 P.M. Mon.–Fri., 9:30 A.M.–6 P.M. Sat., 11 A.M.–5 P.M. Sun.) sells an impressive selection of wines from around the world, including

If you really want to walk on the wild side, why not pair up those mussels you just bought with some artisan-crafted andouille? You'll find the best sausage in the shop right next to Pure Food at **Uli's Famous Sausage** (1511 Pike Pl., 206/839-1100, www.ulisfamoussausage.com), a market fixture and a favorite among award-winning chefs around the city.

ECONOMY MARKET AND LASALLE BUILDING

If you're facing the clock, veer left to reach the Economy Market and La Salle Building to further your taste-sploration of the market. You can fill up a picnic basket or hiking backpack with goodies from **DeLaurenti Market** (1435 1st Ave., 206/622-0141, www.delaurenti.com, 9 A.M.–6 P.M. Mon.–Sat., 10 A.M.–5 P.M. Sun.), jammed with gourmet imported groceries and wines from Europe.

a diverse choice of local wines at some of the best prices around the market and downtown, so there's no excuse to leave that delicious Beecher's cheese unpaired.

INTERNATIONAL DISTRICT
Chinese

As you might guess, the International District is laden with Chinese restaurants. Among the best is **(House of Hong** (409 8th Ave. S., 206/622-7997, www.houseofhong.com, 9:30 A.M.–11 P.M. Sun.–Thurs., 9:30 A.M.–11 P.M. Fri.–Sat., $10) with dim sum, seafood, chicken, and Hong Kong barbecue. Morning through afternoon the clattering dim sum carts will spur adventurous eaters into grabbing for more bites, while at night the boisterous and crowded dining room makes for a good meeting spot for family affairs.

Founded in 1937, **Tai Tung** (655 S. King St., 206/622-7372, 10 A.M.–11 P.M. Sun.–Thurs., 10 A.M.–1:30 A.M. Fri.–Sun., $9) stands as the oldest Chinese restaurant in Seattle. It's real deal, packed with local Asians who consistently rate it an International District favorite.

Sea Garden Restaurant (509 7th Ave. S., 206/623-2100, 11 A.M.–2 A.M. Mon.–Thurs., 11 A.M.–3 A.M. Fri.–Sat., 11 A.M.–1 A.M. Sun., $12) serves Cantonese meals, but the food isn't the bland chow mein you might expect. Instead, the menu offers a wide range of soups, seafood specialties, and perfectly cooked vegetables.

Vietnamese

Pho Bac (415 7th Ave. S., 206/323-4387, 8 A.M.–9 P.M. daily) is a haven for those of us who love the Vietnamese staple, a flavorful soup called *pho*. It's all they serve, so you know they do it right here! The setting is budget, and so are the prices—$6.50 for a large bowl.

If *pho* isn't your game, don't give up on Vietnamese food! Try the delicious *bahn mi,* or Vietnamese sandwiches, at **Saigon Vietnam Deli** (1200 S. Jackson St., 206/328-2357, 7 A.M.–8 P.M. daily) for something completely different. Consisting of soft baguettes, crispy veggies, and meats such as shredded pork, ham, and

pâté, these make for a cheap and filling meal—most sandwiches clock in at a minuscule $2.25.

Markets

The International District has quite a few small markets selling Asian groceries, but none compare to the sprawling **Uwajimaya** (600 5th Ave., 206/624-6248, www.uwajimaya .com, 8 A.M.–10 P.M. Mon.–Sat., 9 A.M.–9 P.M. Sun.). The largest Asian supermarket in the Northwest, it sells everything from high-quality groceries to Japanese furniture. Step inside for an eye-opening venture across the Pacific, plus excellent light meals in the Japanese deli.

Snag the tastiest—and sometimes funniest—fortune cookies at **Tsue Chong Co. Inc.** (800 S. Weller St., 206/623-0801, 9:30 A.M.–5:30 P.M. Mon.–Fri., 10 A.M.–2 P.M. Sat., closed Sun.), where you can buy bags of uniquely flavored fortune cookies, witty "misfortune" cookies stuffed with predictions unseen in most Chinese desserts, as well as the standard fare. Tsue Chong also sells scrumptious egg noodles.

SEATTLE CENTER AND QUEEN ANNE
Cafés and Diners

Queen Anne's **5 Spot** (1502 Queen Anne Ave. N., 206/285-7768, www.chowfoods .com/five, 8:30 A.M.–midnight Mon.–Fri., 8:30 A.M.–3 P.M. and 5 P.M.–midnight Sat.–Sun., $14). The 5 Spot emphasizes all-American comfort food. You will not go wrong here, but be ready for a mob scene if you wake up after 9 A.M. on Sunday morning. All of these also offer down-home American cooking for lunch and dinner. Highly recommended.

Everything is so delicious at the New Orleans-inspired **Toulouse Petit** that it would be very easy to pass up dessert. But that would be a mistake. In addition to a scrumptious selection of gumbos, po' boys, jambalayas, and other Cajun and Creole fare, Toulouse serves some of the best desserts in town, including Big Easy favorites like beignets, Bananas Foster, and pecan pie. But the bees knees is the ice cream and Valhrona brownie sundae, featuring pear caramel, lightly caramelized bananas, and candied pecans.

Contemporary Northwest

Specializing in small-plate, Northwest-with-an-Italian-twist fare, **(How to Cook a Wolf** (2208 Queen Anne Ave. N., 206/838-8090, www.howtocookawolf.com, 5–10 P.M. Sun.–Mon., 5 P.M.–midnight Fri.–Sat., $35) is a fantastic choice for those who enjoy the simple pleasure of fresh and innovative dishes but who are turned off by the eccentricities of many fine dining establishments. Unpretentious and extremely attentive, the servers here are generously scattered in a high wait staff-to-table ratio. Diners are seated first come, first served—no reservations taken here. And, best of all, the kitchen lets the delicious Northwest ingredients speak for themselves.

A long-time Seattle favorite perched high above Lake Union, **Canlis** (2576 Aurora Ave. N., www.canlis.com, 5:30 P.M.–midnight Mon.–Sat., $45) is where the hip still go to dig into juicy steaks and a tasty house salad that has had patrons raving for 50 years. The pastry chef here is one of the tops in the city, so do not skip that last course. But be sure to plan ahead—reservations are highly recommended.

Located atop the Space Needle, **SkyCity Restaurant** (206/443-2111, www.spaceneedle.com, 11:30 A.M.–2:45 P.M. and 5–9:45 P.M. Mon.–Fri., 9:30 A.M.–2:45 P.M. and 5–9:45 P.M. Sat.–Sun., $45) is a top-of-the-world dining experience at 500 feet, very popular with tourists, visiting relatives, and teens on prom night. The food is mediocre and pricey, but the view is unsurpassed, as the revolving restaurant completes a 360-degree turn by the time your dessert arrives.

Asian

Take your pick: **Orrapin Thai Cuisine** (10 Boston St. in Queen Anne, 206/283-7118, www.orrapin.com, 11 A.M.–10 P.M. daily, $11) and **Bahn Thai** (409 Roy St., 206/283-0444, www.bahnthaimenu.com, 11:30 A.M.–9:30 P.M. Mon.–Thurs., 11:30 A.M.–10 P.M.

Fri., noon–10 P.M. Sat., noon–9:30 P.M. Sun., $11) are inexpensive and both offer fantastic Thai specials. Orrapin offers better Tom Kah and curries, and Bahn better noodle dishes such as Phad See Ew.

For Asian fusion try **Asian Breeze** (366 Roy St., 206/285-6713, www.asianbreezedelivery.com, 11 A.M.–2 P.M. and 5–10 P.M. Tue.–Fri., 5–10 P.M. Sat.–Sun., closed Mon., $14) where the food is always packed with garlic, and the portions are enormous. It's excellent and reasonably priced.

Owned by one of Seattle's most revered sushi chefs, Shiro Kashiba, **Shiro's** (2401 2nd Ave., 206/443-9844, www.shiros.com, 5–10 P.M. daily, $20) serves some of the most flavorful sushi in town. Sushi lovers won't go wrong by ordering the *omakase* here, letting the chefs take them through a culinary tour through the freshest seafood in stock.

SOUTH LAKE UNION
Cafés and Delis

There's no Soup Nazi at **(Soup Daddy** (211 Fairview Ave. N., 206/682-7202, www.soupdaddysoups.com, 7 A.M.–4 P.M. Mon.–Fri., $7), and thank goodness for that, because I would have a meltdown if I were ever denied its stunning soup selection. Set in the hip South Lake Union neighborhood, the eatery ladles five or so different soups each day. Pair it with a bread bowl, sandwich, or salad to make the perfect midday meal. And it doesn't limit itself to breakfast, either. Daddy done added an expanded breakfast menu, too.

If Dr. Frankenstein had opened up a restaurant, it very well may have looked a lot like **Lunchbox Laboratory** (1253 Thomas St., 206/621-1090, www.lunchboxlaboratory.com, 11 A.M.–11 P.M. daily, $17), a haven for monstrously sized burgers custom designed by diners. Pick between a choice of meats such as prime rib, buffalo, lamb, and even "dork," a duck-pork combo. Then add on a range of cheeses, rolls, veggies, and sauces to make a creation of your very own. Just be prepared; science is not cheap and the Lab isn't either. Once you've picked out all those add-ons, it is possible to have created a $20 burger. And that's without fries.

Seafood

Chandler's Crabhouse (901 Fairview Ave. N., 206/223-2722, 11 A.M.–3 P.M. and 4–9 P.M. Sun.–Thurs., 4–10 P.M. Fri.–Sat., $40) is on the south shore of Lake Union with views north across the lake. The specialties here are crab dishes of all sorts, including a flavorful whiskey crab bisque. This is dependably good seafood in a busy waterfront setting. It's a great place to watch the seaplanes landing and taking off.

Japanese

My favorite sushi counter is in South Lake Union at **I Love Sushi** (1001 Fairview Ave. N., 206/625-9604, www.ilovesushi.com, 11:30 A.M.–2 P.M. and 4–10 P.M. Mon.–Fri., noon–2:30 P.M. and 5–10:30 P.M. Sat., noon–9:30 P.M. Sun., $25), where the experienced chefs will do well by you if you bring some cash and just ask them to make whatever they think you will like until you're full. I never go wrong with soft-shell crab spider rolls here, and the *unagi*—or freshwater eel for the uniniti-ated—is the perfect blend of sweet and salty, crispy and velvety.

CAPITOL HILL
Cafés and Delis

No place fills the morning urge for hearty grub more than **Coastal Kitchen** (429 15th Ave. E., 206/322-1145, www.seattle-eats.com, 8 A.M.–10 P.M. Mon.–Thurs., 8 A.M.–11 P.M. Fri., 8 A.M.–3 P.M. and 5–11 P.M. Sat., 8 A.M.–3 P.M. and 5–10 P.M. Sun., $9). Among the highlights are out-of-this-world pancakes. Or try **Glo's** (1621 E. Olive Way, 206/324-2577, 7 A.M.–3 P.M. Mon.–Fri., noon–4 P.M. Sat.–Sun., $10), a fun little place that whips up particularly tasty eggs Benedict and Belgian waffles in the morning hours.

For a light dinner or an indulgent week-end brunch, try Capitol Hill's **Table 219** (219 Broadway Ave. E., 206/328-4604, www .table219.com, 4:30–10 P.M. Tues.–Thurs., 9 A.M.–10 P.M. Fri.–Sat., 9 A.M.–3 P.M. Sun.,

$10), which serves inventive dishes such as andouille corndogs, bread salad, and a sand-wich made with roasted garlic, gorgonzola, and sherry shallot marmalade.

When it comes to chocolates, it is pretty hard to beat **Dilettante Chocolates** (538 Broadway E., 206/329-6463, www.dilettante .com, 5–11 P.M. Mon.–Thurs., 5 P.M.–1 A.M. Fri., 10 A.M.–1 A.M. Sat., 10 A.M.–11 P.M. Sun., $10), where you'll also find a light menu of soups, salads, and sandwiches. Dilettante has three other shops scattered around Seattle.

Contemporary Northwest

Imbued with the quiet bustle of a European bis-tro, **Lark** (926 12th Ave., 206/323-5275, www .larkseattle.com, 5 P.M.–10:30 P.M. Tues.–Sun., $30) invites languorous meals underneath its exposed-beam ceilings and soft lighting. The menu is made for grazing, with generous selec-tions of cheese, charcuteries, and small plates carefully crafted by the eatery's James Beard Award-winning chef.

Established by some of the gastronomic geniuses behind the renowned Herb Farm in Woodinville, **Poppy** (622 Broadway E., 206/324-1108, www.poppyseattle.com, 5:30–10 P.M. Sun.–Thurs., 5:30–11 P.M. Fri.–Sat.) draws in diners with the prospect of its eclectic "thali" plates. For $32, these dinner collections consist of about 10 different petite dishes, some no larger than what other restau-rants serve as *amuse-bouche,* but all packing in plenty of creativity and flavor.

Asian

Set in a post-modern great room, **Boom Noodle** (1121 E. Pike St., 206/701-9130, www.boom noodle.com, 11:30 A.M.–9 P.M. Mon.–Wed., 11:30 A.M.–10 P.M. Thurs., 11:30 A.M.–11 P.M. Fri., noon–11 P.M. Sat., noon–9 P.M. Sun., $15) offers a trendy take on cafeteria-style seating, minus the buffet line or the mus-tached lunch lady. Sit at one of the banks of long communal tables in the boisterously loud dining room to partake in stylishly presented Asian fusion, including a dizzying array of ramen, soba, and udon.

Try the sumptuous Vietnamese-fusion at **Monsoon** (615 19th Ave. E., 206/325-2111, http://monsoonrestaurants.com, noon–10 P.M. Mon.–Fri., 10 A.M.–10 P.M. Sat.–Sun., $18) to taste a thoughtful collision of East-meets-West cuisine. The banana-leaf wrapped halibut is a particular favorite here.

Fill up on *bento* box lunches, salmon teriyaki, sushi, sashimi, tempura, and other simple Japanese meals at **Hana Restaurant** (219 Broadway Ave. E., 206/328-1187, 11 A.M.–10 P.M. Mon.–Sat., 4–10 P.M. Sun., $15), a popular spot for the after-work gang. It can get jammed during peak hours, so if negotiating a crowd isn't your thing, consider getting takeout and strolling over to nearby Cal Anderson park for a picnic.

Pub Grub

Seattle has embraced the gastropub movement with open, albeit pint-holding, arms. No establishment in the genre garners better reception than **Quinn's** (1001 E. Pike St., 206/325-7711, www.quinnspubseattle.com, 5 P.M.–midnight Mon.–Thurs., 5 P.M.–1 A.M. Fri.–Sat., 5–10 P.M. Sun., $16), a hideaway on the hill that revels in good beer and the food that makes you thirst for it. The menu is awash in a sea of tantalizingly exotic choices designed for the most hearty food explorers ready to set sail toward a new horizon of taste. Find beef tongue hash, fried frog legs, and even wild boar sloppy joes.

If you're looking for a fun saloon serving up the more traditional bar-food standard bearers, opt instead for **The Buck** (1506 E. Olive Way, 206/329-2493, 5 P.M.–2 A.M. daily, $9). Somewhere halfway between an old hunting lodge and a country honky-tonk, this raucous canteen offers delicious pizzas and tasty nacho skillets on the cheap.

BALLARD AND MAGNOLIA

Cafés

The crowds line up around the corner on weekend mornings at **The Dish** (4358 Leary Way NW, 206/782-9985, www.thedishseattle.com, 7 A.M.–1:45 P.M. Tue.–Sat., 8 A.M.–1:45 P.M. Sun., $12) for good reason. This tiny little diner

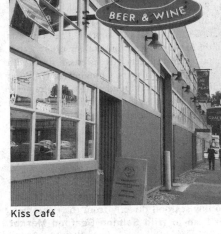

Kiss Café

© ERICKA CHICKOWSKI

griddles up the best breakfasts in town. The place is cramped, so if you're serious about your morning meal, stop in during the weekdays.

When the wait is too long at Dish, walk down the block to **Vera's** (5417 22nd Ave. NW, 206/782-9966, 7 A.M.–2:30 P.M. Mon.– Fri., 8 A.M.–2:30 P.M. Sat., 8 A.M.–2 P.M. Sun., $12), a classic stool-and-counter diner that's been flipping flapjacks for locals since the name Sven was more common than John 'round these parts. Just be prepared with some of the green stuff—this place is so old-school that it still works on the cash-only model.

A home-away-from-home kind of neighborhood joint, **Kiss Café** (2817 NW Market St., 206/789-5477, www.ballardkisscafe.com, 11 A.M.–11 P.M. Sun. and Mon.–Thurs., 11 A.M.– midnight Fri.–Sat., $8) offers up a slate of sandwiches, salads, and comfortable café faves in a spot equally perfect for sipping coffee or beer.

Contemporary Northwest

One of my favorite special-event restaurants in the city is hidden away in Magnolia over the Elliott Bay Marina. With a Southern Seas–type decor and incredibly tasty steaks, seafood, and Northwest cuisine touched with a bit of Polynesia, **⟨ Palisade** (2601 West Marina Pl., 206/285-1000, www.palisaderestaurant .com, 9:30 A.M.–2 P.M. and 4–9 P.M. Sun., 11:30 A.M.–2 P.M. and 5–9 P.M. Mon.–Thurs., 11:30 A.M.–2 P.M. and 5–10 P.M. Fri., 4–10 P.M. Sat., $40) never fails to impress. The best parts of the menu bookend your entrées: the appetizer pupu platters and delicious desserts. If you're with a group, don't miss the Captain's Tower Pupu with seared teriyaki tenderloins, tiger prawns, and Dungeness crab. And finish the meal off with the trio of flavored crème brûlées. Yum.

Seafood

Across the Ballard Bridge in Salmon Bay is the **Fishermen's Terminal,** a bustling marina— largest in the Northwest—packed with some 700 commercial fishing boats. Ask around to buy seafood directly from the fishermen, or head to **Wild Salmon Seafood Market** (1900 W. Nickerson St., 206/283-3366, 8:30 A.M.–6 P.M. daily) on the water's edge.

West of the Chittenden Locks, Seaview Avenue curves north along the shore past Shilshole Bay, with several popular seafood restaurants—most notably Ray's Boathouse and Anthony's HomePort.

Some of Seattle's finest seafood is supped at **Ray's Boathouse** (6049 Seaview Ave. W., 206/789-3770, www.rays.com, 5–9:30 P.M. daily, $28). North of the Ship Canal along Shilshole Bay, with outstanding views over Puget Sound at sunset (be sure to reserve a window table) and perfectly prepared oysters, fish, and other fresh seafood, this large and attractive place has a nautical design with wooden floors and beams like an old boat shed. It is a bit expensive (expect a bill of $35 per person), but the seafood is great. Reservations are a must. You can save money and avoid the crowds by arriving weeknights 5–6 P.M. Upstairs is a spacious and equally popular café serving a lighter menu that includes oysters and fish and chips.

Pub Grub

Anyone bestowed with a healthy appetite and a fast metabolism will appreciate the honkin' servings of chili doled out at **Mike's Chili Parlour** (1447 NW Ballard Way, 206/782-2808, www.mikeschiliparlor.com, 11 A.M.–11 P.M. Mon.–Thurs., 11 A.M.–midnight Fri.–Sat., noon–8 P.M. Sun., $5), a Ballard classic that's been ladling chili over dogs, fries, spaghetti, and more for decades. The stout of heart can dig into the satellite dish-size Big Ass Bowl for $10.

Bakeries

Eating cake in small bites doesn't count for as many calories, right? Whatever your cupcake philosophy, **⟨ Cupcake Royale** (2052 NW Market St., 206/782-9557, www.cupcakeroyale.com, 6:30 A.M.–10 P.M. Mon.–Thurs., 6:30 A.M.–11 P.M. Fri.–Sat., 7:30 A.M.–10 P.M. Sun.) in Ballard is there to fulfill the snacking urge with moist little creations topped with a heavenly buttercream whip. Pair that with a smooth cappuccino to combat that inevitable sugar crash about 15 minutes later.

Or you can lose the guilt altogether and instead visit **Tall Grass Bakery** (5907 24th St. NW, 206/706-0991, http://tallgrassbakery. com, 9 A.M.–7 P.M. daily), which emphasizes hearty, organic breads. Find everything from well-crafted baguettes to spongy sourdough to dark rye.

FREMONT, WALLINGFORD, AND GREEN LAKE
Cafés and Diners

A cozy eatery with a penchant for cow kitsch, **Mae's Phinney Ridge Café** (6412 Phinney Ave. N., 206/782-1222, www.maescafe.com, 8 A.M.–2 P.M. Mon.–Fri., 8 A.M.–3 P.M. Sat.–Sun., $8) plays up its theme with a "Moo Room" for milk shakes and displays of cartoon cow paraphernalia. But it doesn't depend on a schtick for the rave reviews. Food is all made from scratch and includes big, sticky cinnamon rolls and scrumptious hash browns. Bring the family in tow on the weekends and fear not the stray giggles or cries—the boisterous crowd will drown it out.

Another great place where you'll have to fend off the weekend brunch crowd is **Julia's** (4401 Wallingford Ave., 206/633-1175, www.juliasrestaurantseattle.com, 7 A.M.–3 P.M. Mon, 7 A.M.–9 P.M. Tue.–Sat., 7:30 A.M.–9 P.M., $17). The food is tasty, with lots of vegetarian items and a lively atmosphere.

Fans of good old-fashioned American breakfast won't go unsatisfied at **Beth's Café** (7311 Aurora Ave. N., 206/782-5588, www.bethscafe.com, 24 hours daily, $9). A Green Lake establishment since 1957, Beth's keeps the locals coming back with its honkin' huge omelettes, greasy hash browns, loud jukebox music, and no-nonsense waitresses. The reasonable prices don't hurt the appeal, either.

You'll have to grin-and-bear it through the surly New York–style service at **Bagel Oasis** (2112 NE 65th St., 206/526-0525; and 462 N. 36th St., 206/633-2676, 6 A.M.–5 P.M. Mon.–Fri., 6 A.M.–4 P.M. Sat.–Sun., $5) in order to get your mitts on the best New York–style bagels in the Northwest.

Looking for the best burger in Seattle? The argument rages, but the public votes with their feet (and mouths) for **Dick's Drive-In** (111 NE 45th St., 206/632-5125, www.ddir.com, 10:30 A.M.–2 A.M. daily, $5). The food at this straight-from-the-1950s joint consists of marvelously greasy fries, juicy burgers, and wonderful chocolate milk shakes. The Wallingford drive-in is Seattle's oldest continuously operating fast food restaurant, but you can find other Dick's locations throughout the city and the rest of the Northwest.

Contemporary Northwest
The food at ☾ **Art of the Table** (1054 N. 39th St., 206/282-0942, www.artofthetable.net) is a celebration of the earth, Seattle's seminal tribute to the farm-to-table movement. Chef Dustin Ronspies establishes convivial bonhomie amongst his diners at the Weekend Supper Club, regularly walking and talking with eager participants who sit for his prix fixe four-course meals (7 P.M., $55) fashioned with ingredients hand-plucked from weekend markets around the city. For something a little less formal, stop by for a small-bites, evening-long happy hour on Mondays or Thursdays (5–10 P.M.) with no reservations required.

The rotating list of mouthwatering dishes at **Tilth** (1411 N. 45th St., 206/633-0801, www.tilthrestaurant.com, 10 A.M.–2 P.M. Sat.–Sun. and 5–10 P.M. Sun.–Thurs., 5–10:30 P.M. Fri.–Sat., $26) prominently feature organic fresh fruits, veggies, meats, and seafood grown in the Northwest, a seasonal tour of the state served tableside.

International
Musashi's Sushi & Grill (1400 N. 45th St., 206/633-0212, 11:30 A.M.–2:30 P.M. and 5–9 P.M. Tues.–Thurs., 11:30 A.M.–2:30 P.M. and 5–10 P.M. Fri., 5–9:30 P.M. Sat., closed Sun., $15) is an always-crowded, friendly little place with inexpensive fresh sushi (the main attraction), chicken teriyaki, and *bento* box lunches.

For something from the Near East, **Kabul** (2301 N. 45th St., 206/545-9000, www.kabulrestaurant.com, 5–11 P.M. daily, $18) creates reasonably priced Afghan cuisine, which offers a sort of blend between Indian and Mediterranean dishes. Kabul dishes out quite a few vegetarian dishes such as sautéed eggplant with a tomato, yogurt, and mint sauce and the basmati rice spiced with saffron and pepper and topped with raisins and nuts is a treat all by itself.

Fremont's **El Camino Restaurant** (607 N. 35th St., 206/632-7303, www.elcaminorestaurant.com, 5–10 P.M. Mon.–Fri., noon–3 P.M. and 5–10 P.M. Sat.–Sun., $15) is a great little nouvelle Mexican place that serves chiles rellenos, baby back ribs, and fantastic margaritas.

Vegetarian
Check out **Carmelita** (7314 Greenwood Ave. N., 206/706-7703, www.carmelita.net, 5–9 P.M. Tues.–Thurs. and Sun., 5–10 P.M. Fri.–Sat., $18), a hip little Green Lake vegetarian dinner spot. Even carnivores will go away impressed at flavorful dishes such as the carrot-mascarpone gnocci or the artisanal polenta cake. Try the lemon pound cake for dessert.

Seafood

Cap off a nice day at Gasworks Park at nearby **Ivar's Salmon House** (401 NE Northlake Way, 206/632-7223, 11 A.M.–9:30 P.M. Mon.–Thurs., 11 A.M.–10 P.M. Fri.–Sat., 9:30 A.M.–2 P.M. and 3:30–9:30 P.M. Sun., $22) on Lake Union. Set in a reproduction Native American cedar longhouse, the Salmon House plays up the area's Northwest heritage with historic photos, Tlingit carvings on the walls, and dugout canoes hanging from the rafters. The deck is a pleasant place to watch the sailboats glide by the downtown Seattle vista ahead during summer. If you're only looking for nibbles, stop by the restaurant's Whale Maker Lounge and check out the rather intimidating (for men at least) killer whale "whalemakers." The lounge serves free hors d'oeuvres during happy hour (4–6:30 P.M. Mon.–Fri.) and you're more likely to get a window seat there than in the restaurant.

Bakeries

Bar none, Seattle's most unusual bakery is in Fremont, where you'll find X-rated cakes, pastries, and other goodies rising from the oven at **The Erotic Bakery** (2323 N. 45th St., 206/545-6969, http://theeroticbakery.com, 10 A.M.–7 P.M. Mon.–Sat.). This is a favorite among not-so-PC co-workers, maids of honor, and anyone else looking to shock and titillate their friends.

For more traditionally shaped goodies, **The Urban Bakery** (7850 E. Greenlake Dr. N., 206/524-7951, 7 A.M.–6 P.M. Mon.–Sat., 8 A.M.–5 P.M. Sun.) is a great spot for fresh-from-the-oven baked treats, including scrumptious chocolate cakes, cheesecakes, and pies. The espresso bar is a favorite stopping place for the Green Lake post-jogging crowd.

Markets

As might be expected, Seattle has quite a few natural and organic grocers. The oldest is **Puget Consumers' Co-op Natural Markets,** aka PCC, with seven stores around Seattle offering bulk foods, organic produce, and other healthy edibles. You don't have to be a member to shop here, though prices are a bit lower if you join. Several of the markets—notably the one in Fremont (716 N. 34th St., 206/632-6811, www.pccnaturalmarkets.com, 6 A.M.–midnight daily)—have fine delis with both vegetarian and meat dishes.

Fremont Sunday Market (www.fremontmarket.com) brings a farmers market, jewelry, flea market, and live music to N. 34th Street in Fremont between late April and Christmas. During the winter months it moves inside a parking garage at 400 N. 34th Street. It takes place 10 A.M.–4 P.M. Sunday.

UNIVERSITY DISTRICT AND MADISON PARK

Cafés

Tucked into a vibrant blue Victorian house built in 1904, **Hi Spot Café** (1410 34th Ave., 206/325-7905, www.hispotcafe.com, 8–11:30 A.M. Mon.–Fri., 8 A.M.–2:30 P.M. Sat.–Sun., $12) is best known for its breakfast and brunch. Settle down in front of a giant cinnamon roll or the house special French brioche toast with almond butter and pure maple syrup and you'll be ready to walk it off afterward. Lucky for you, Madrona Park is only a couple of blocks away.

Chinese

The U District has a big cluster of cheap student-oriented places with heaping helpings of Asian comestibles. Just walk up the Ave to see what looks good. A personal favorite is **Mandarin Chef** (5022 University Way NE, 206/528-7596, www.mandarinchef.com, 11 A.M.–10 P.M. Mon.–Sat., closed Sun., $8) with homemade noodles and dumplings for practically nothing. Tasty mu shu dishes, too.

For Chinese food with a difference, head to the always-crowded **Black Pearl** (7347 35th Ave. NE, 206/283-9030, www.blackpearlchinesecuisine.com, 11 A.M.–9:30 P.M. Mon.–Thurs., 11 A.M.–10 P.M. Fri.–Sat., 4–9:30 P.M. Sun., $10) just north of the U District in Wedgwood. Watch the busy cooks in the open kitchen, and enjoy the friendly service and distinctive dishes such as a batter-fried eggplant with vegetables, or green onion and smoked salmon pancakes. But be ready for a wait most evenings. Save time and order out; there's free delivery to the north end of town (including the U District).

Japanese

One of the most popular student eateries in the U District, **Kiku Tempura House** (5018 University Way NE, 206/524-1125, 11 A.M.–10 P.M. daily, $8) whips up tempura and teriyaki that's quick, delicious, and served up in huge portions. Great for a quick lunch or evening meal; order at the counter and wait for them to call your number.

For the ultimate in sushi—even diehard fans from Tokyo are impressed—be sure to make reservations for a meal at **Nishino** (3130 E. Madison St., 206/322-5800, www.nishino restaurant.com, 5:30–10:30 P.M. Mon.–Sat., 10:30 A.M.–9:30 P.M. Sun., $25). It's a busy and sometimes-noisy place, but the food is impeccable and perfectly prepared. For a real treat, request the chef's menu (a fixed-price six-course meal, $60) when you reserve a table. Nishino is expensive, but worth every dollar.

Thai and Vietnamese

A notable U District place for inexpensive and tasty Vietnamese lunches is **My's Restaurant** (4220 University Way NE, 206/634-3526, 11 A.M.–10 P.M. daily, $8) This immensely popular student eatery dishes up huge portions of *pho* and fried noodles, including several vegetarian specialties.

Indian

Neelam Authentic Indian Cuisine (4735 University Way NE, 206-523-6830, 11 A.M.–10 P.M. daily, $15) lives up to its name with outstanding and very spicy East Indian meals. It has tandoori and vegetarian specialties, plus wonderful curries. The onion *kulcha* bread is hard to beat.

Another extremely popular and reasonable UW hangout is **Tandoor Indian Restaurant** (5024 University Way NE, 206/523-7477, www.tandoor-india.com, 4:30–10 P.M. Mon.–Thurs., 11 A.M.–2:30 A.M. and 4:30–10 P.M.

Mon.–Fri., 11 A.M.–3 P.M. and 4:30–10 P.M. Sat.–Sun., $12), which offers decent dishes at slightly more student-friendly prices.

Mediterranean

An excellent southern Italian eatery, **Salvatore Ristorante Italiano** (6100 Roosevelt Way NE, 206/527-9301, www.salvatoreristoranteitaliano .com, 5–10 P.M. Tues.–Thurs., 5–10:30 P.M. Fri.–Sat., 5–9:30 P.M. Sun., closed Mon., $18) in Ravenna dishes up favorites such as veal, linguine with clams, and pasta with red hot peppers, tomatoes, capers, anchovies, and olives. There's also a satisfying selection of antipasti and Italian wines. No reservations are accepted, so be prepared to wait if you come late.

Continental Restaurant (4549 University Way NE, 206/632-4700, http://the-continental.bite2go.com, 7 A.M.–11 P.M. Mon.–Fri., 8 A.M.–11 P.M. Sat.–Sun., $12) on the Ave is a longtime favorite of mine for inexpensive Greek meals and friendly service. Go there often enough and they'll treat you like family. If you come in the morning, any omelette with feta will satisfy. Visit later and be sure to finish the meal off with some of the best baklava on the planet. There's also a deli here.

For impressive French cuisine, you will not go wrong at Madison Park's **Rover's** (2808 E. Madison St., 206/325-7442, www.rovers-seattle .com, 6–10 P.M. Tues.–Thurs., noon–1:30 P.M. and 5:30–10 P.M. Fri., 5:30–10 P.M. Sat., 5–10 P.M. Sun., $22), where the food, service, and setting win uniform praise. The outstanding wine list is a nice accompaniment. Many people regard this as Seattle's finest restaurant. Complete tasting menus typically run $59–135 per person.

Mexican

Over by the Arboretum, **Cactus** (4220 E. Madison St., 206/324-4140, www.cactus restaurants.com, 11:30 A.M.–10 P.M. Mon.–Thurs., 11:30 A.M.–11 P.M. Fri.–Sat., $15) blend of Spanish and Southwest dishes. You'll find a fun tapas bar, a comfortable patio that looks out onto a quiet neighborhood and a menu featuring Indian fry bread, fajitas, enchiladas, and lots of unusual dishes. A personal fave is the grilled jalapeños, stuffed with goat cheese and wrapped in bacon.

Pizza

Seattle's best quick pizza place is **Pizzeria Pagliacci** (www.pagliacci.com), with three sit-down locations around town, including one on the Ave (4529 University Way NE, 206/632-0421, 11 A.M.–11 P.M. Sun.–Thurs., 11 A.M.–midnight Fri.–Sat.). This is about as close as you can get to real New York–style pizzas: perfect thin crusts and distinctive toppings. Several types of pizzas are always available by the slice at this location, along with calzones and lasagna.

Northlake Tavern & Pizza House (660 NE Northlake Way, 206/633-5317, 11 A.M.–10 P.M. Sun.–Thurs., 11 A.M.–11 P.M. Fri., 11 A.M.–midnight Sat.) mixes three American favorites: great pizza, beer, and sports on the television. The place is a favorite haunt of University of Washington sports fans, but be aware that in order to eat in this bar's dining room you'll need to be 21.

Vegetarian

Cash-poor students absolutely flock to **Flowers** (4247 University Way NE, 206/633-1903, 11 A.M.–2 A.M. daily) on the Ave, a once-upon-a-time floral shop that now serves an impressive lunchtime vegetarian buffet and stays open late to serve stiff cocktails to boot. The unlimited feast of veggies during the day can be had for around $8 during the week and $10 on the weekends. Just be prepared to invest a little time to reap the benefits of cheap food—the service is notoriously slow here.

If you prefer a more grown-up dining experience, **Café Flora** (2901 E. Madison St., 206/325-9100, www.cafeflora.com, 9 A.M.–10 P.M. Mon.–Fri., 9 A.M.–2 P.M. and 5–10 P.M. Sat.–Sun., $15) in Madison Park is one of the city's best-loved vegetarian restaurants. The rustic polenta is especially notable, and it also offers offbeat pizzas and portobello Wellington (grilled portobello mushrooms) on the ever-changing menu. The kitchen can get noisy at times, and service may be uneven.

© ERICKA CHICKOWSKI

Grab an economical vegetarian meal at Flowers' lunch buffet.

WEST SEATTLE
Cafés

Pies aren't just for dessert at **Shoofly Pie Company** (4444 California Ave. SW, 206/938-0680, www.shooflypiecompany.com, 10 A.M.–8 P.M. Wed.–Thurs., 10 A.M.–9 P.M. Fri.–Sat., 10 A.M.–4 P.M. Sun., closed Mon.–Tues., $5), which specializes in everything from sweet to savory. Dig into slices of cheesy quiches, caramelized onion galettes, creamy pot pies, and sublime tarts. Don't forget to try the namesake, a classic Pennsylvania Dutch molasses pie that's sweet enough to put the dentist on call.

Contemporary Northwest

Escape the pretension of downtown's fine dining scene at **Spring Hill** (4437 California Ave. SW, 206/935-1075, www.springhill northwest.com, 10 A.M.–2 P.M. Sat.–Sun. and 5:45–10 P.M. Mon.–Sat., $25) a chic little place tucked away in West Seattle where you can order high-brow meals minus the self-absorbed attitude. You'll find a warm and friendly atmosphere in this dining room bedecked with modern light woods, glazed cement flooring, and plenty of light streaming in through the floor-to-ceiling windows up front. The food's the real star, though. The menu allows you to go as casual or fancy as you like—order anything along the spectrum from the gigantic and juicy burgers to the roasted duck with quinoa waffle.

Steak and Seafood

Undoubtedly the best view of the Seattle skyline is from a window-side seat in **❰ Salty's on Alki** (1936 Harbor Ave. SW, 206/937-1600, www.saltys.com, 11:30 A.M.–3 P.M. and 5–9 P.M. Mon.–Fri., 9 A.M.–1 P.M. and 4–9 P.M. Sat.–Sun., $30). Situated on West Seattle's Alki Point, this offers the choicest glimpse of the glimmering lights reflected off Elliott Bay. Best of all, the food is worthy of the view, with plenty of seafood offerings and a few decent cuts of meat thrown in for good measure. On Saturday and Sunday, Salty's lays out the best brunch buffet in Seattle, with unlimited platters of shellfish, prime rib, and pastries all served up with your choice of mimosas or Bloody Marys. Be sure to set brunch reservations in advance. Reservations fill up fast here.

If that all sounds a little extravagant to you, then try another West Seattle classic, **Spud Fish and Chips** (2666 Alki Ave. SW, 206/938-0606, 11 A.M.–10 P.M. daily), which has been frying up fishies by Alki Beach since 1935.

Asian

Extremely popular—and justifiably so—are a couple of Asian offerings: **Pailin Thai Cuisine** (2223 California Ave. SW, 206/937-8807, www.palinthai.com, 11:30 A.M.–10 P.M. Mon.–Fri., 5–10 P.M. Sat.–Sun.) and **Mashiko Japanese Restaurant** (4725 California Ave. SW, 206/935-4339, 5–9:30 P.M. Sun.–Thurs., 5–11 P.M. Fri.–Sat.).

Information and Services

INFORMATION CENTERS

For information on Seattle attractions and events, plus maps and other assistance, contact the **Seattle/King County Convention and Visitors Bureau** (800 Convention Place, www.seeseattle.org, 8:30 A.M.–5 P.M. Mon.–Fri., 10 A.M.–4 P.M. Sat.–Sun. April–Oct.; 8:30 A.M.–5 P.M. Mon.–Fri. the rest of the year), located in the Washington State Convention and Trade Center on the Galleria level. At Sea-Tac Airport, the **Visitor Information Booth** (9:30 A.M.–7:30 P.M. daily in the summer; brochures available at other times) also doles out local information and brochures.

Set up inside the flagship REI store, the **Outdoor Recreation Information Center** (222 Yale Ave. N., 206/470-4060, www .nps.gov/ccso, 10:30 A.M.–7 P.M. Tues.–Fri., 9 A.M.–7 P.M. Sat., and 11 A.M.–6 P.M. Sun., closed Mon.) delivers the straight skinny on outdoorsy adventures throughout the state. Stop here to ask about hiking trails, campgrounds, and backcountry access, and pick up public land recreation permits while you're at it.

If you're a member, the **AAA Travel Store** (1523 15th Ave. W., 206/218-1222, www .aaawa.com, 8:30 A.M.–5:30 P.M. Mon.–Fri.) is a good source of free maps and area information plus travel guidebooks, luggage, and other travel-related accessories.

FOREIGN CURRENCY EXCHANGE

Thomas Cook (206/248-0401 or 800/287-7362, www.us.thomascook.com) runs currency exchange booths at the airport and Westlake Center (4th and Pine). You can also change money at **Travelex Currency Exchange** (400 Pine St., 206/682-4525) downtown.

LIBRARIES AND INTERNET ACCESS

The main branch of the **Seattle Public Library** (1000 4th Ave., 206/386-4636, www.spl.org) is perhaps the coolest downtown library in the entire country, a giant glass-and-steel masterpiece well worth a couple of hours of exploration on a rainy day. Another 23 neighborhood libraries are scattered around Seattle.

The University of Washington has collections totaling more than five million volumes in its various campus libraries, the majority of which are housed in the sprawling **Suzzallo and Allen Libraries** (206/543-0242 for details, www.lib.washington.edu), both on Red Square.

Some good Internet cafés (free if you buy a coffee) are **Bulldog News** (4208 University Way NE, 206/632-6397), **Cafe Allegro** (4214 University Way NE, 206/633-3030), **Alibi Room** (85 Pike St., Pike Place Market, 206/623-3180), and **Speakeasy Café** (2304 2nd Ave., Belltown, 206/728-9770).

PERIODICALS

Since 2009 Seattle has operated as a one-newspaper town, when the last edition of the *Seattle Post-Intelligencer* (www.seattlep-i.com) rolled off the presses and the publication became the largest daily paper to operate completely on the Internet. Now the *Seattle Times* (www.seattletimes.com) rules the roost in the printed arena, but the two still duke it out for online supremacy. The *Seattle Weekly* (www.seattleweekly.com) and the *Stranger* (www.thestranger.com) offer some of the best entertainment guides, plus opinionated articles on politics and Seattle goings-on—not to mention phone sex and singles ads. And the swanky *Seattle Met* (www.seattlemet.com) puts out a glossy monthly publication chock-full of well written articles on local politics, entertainment, and personalities, all of which is complemented by sleek photography and design.

Getting There

BY AIR

Seattle's airport is 12 miles south of town and midway between Seattle and Tacoma, hence the name **Sea-Tac Airport** (206/431-4444 or 800/544-1965, www.portseattle.org). All the major domestic and many international airlines fly into Sea-Tac. Foreign travelers can change money at the Thomas Cook booth in the main terminal. Storage lockers are scattered around the airport, but you'll need to pass through security first. Another option is **Ken's Baggage and Frozen Food Storage** (located near the baggage claim area, 206/433-5333, open 5:30 A.M.–12:30 A.M. daily).

Getting to and from the Airport
LIGHT RAIL AND BUSES

The sparkling new **Sound Transit Link** (www.soundtransit.com, $2.00–2.75) light rail trains are the cheapest and most convenient means to reach downtown if you're going without a car

during the trip. Operating between 5 A.M. and midnight Monday through Saturday and 6 A.M. through 11 P.M. Sunday, the trains leave at most every 15 minutes, with shorter intervals during peak times. They take approximately 40 minutes to reach their final terminus at Westlake Center, with nearly a dozen other stops in the city along the way. The least expensive way to reach Seattle from the airport is aboard a **Metro Transit** (206/447-4800 or 800/542-7876; http://metro.kingcounty.gov, one-way $2.25 off-peak or $3 peak) bus. Route 124 runs between Sea-Tac and downtown Seattle about every half hour. Buses leave from outside the lower-level baggage claim area of the domestic terminal (turn right as you exit), or catch them downtown if you're headed out. It takes approximately 50 minutes to reach downtown from Sea-Tac. Metro buses travel along the Pacific Highway and provide the cheapest access for the many motels close to the airport.

TAXI AND SHUTTLE SERVICES

For door-to-door service, the easiest way downtown from the airport is to grab a cab on the airport's second level. Taxis cost a flat rate of $32 between the downtown hotel district and Sea-Tac. Outside the flat-rate zone, the drop is $2.50, plus $2.50 per mile, with a $1 airport tax.

Shuttle Express (206/622-1424 or 800/942-7433, www.shuttleexpress.com) runs door-to-door van service between Sea-Tac and Seattle ($36), as well as Bellevue and points north to Everett and south to Tacoma. Reserve ahead for a pickup. It also offers scheduled service to hotels in Seattle and Bellevue.

CAR RENTAL

The big operators run desks near baggage claim at Sea-Tac Airport, with some of the discount chains providing free shuttle service from the pick-up zone on the third floor of the parking garage to their offsite lots just a few blocks away. The best rates are often from locations away from the airport such as Bellevue; sometimes the company will provide a shuttle van to its office. For wheelchair-friendly van rentals, contact **Wheelchair Getaways** (425/788-7318 or 888/376-1500, www.wheelchairgetaways.com).

BY TRAIN

Amtrak serves Seattle from its historic **King Street Station** (3rd Ave. S. and S. King St., 206/464-1930 or 800/872-7245, www.amtrak.com), recognizable in the Seattle skyline by the tall Venetian-style clock tower

that rises above it. The *Coast Starlight* leaves four times a day, connecting Seattle with Tacoma, Olympia, Centralia, Kelso-Longview, Vancouver, Portland, and south to Oakland and Los Angeles. The *Empire Builder* provides daily service from Seattle to Edmonds, Everett, Wenatchee, Ephrata, and Spokane, and continuing eastward to Minneapolis and Chicago. The futuristic-looking *Cascades* provides daily train connections to Vancouver, B.C., via Edmonds, Everett, Mount Vernon, and Bellingham; it continues south as far as Eugene, Oregon.

BY BUS

Greyhound (9th Ave. and Stewart St., 206/628-5508 or 800/231-2222, www.greyhound.com) has daily bus service throughout the lower 48 and to Vancouver, B.C., from its bus terminal downtown. **Northwest Trailways** (206/728-5955 or 800/366-3830, www.nwadv.com/northw) operates from both the Greyhound station and the Amtrak depot, with service to Everett, Tacoma, Spokane, Pullman, and points between.

Pierce Transit (253/581-8000 or 800/562-8109, www.piercetransit.org) operates southern Puget Sound public bus service connecting downtown Seattle with Tacoma and **Community Transit** (800/562-1375, www.commtrans.org) provides commuter bus service connecting Everett, Edmonds, and other Snohomish County cities with downtown Seattle and the University District.

Getting Around

BY BUS

Getting around downtown is easy—all King County **Metro** (206/553-3000 or 800/542-7876, http://transit.metrokc.gov) buses here are free every day between the hours of 6 A.M. and 7 P.M. The boundaries for this free area are S. Jackson Street, I-5, Pine Street, Battery Street, and Alaskan Way. A bus tunnel runs through the center of the city, with downtown

stops at Convention Place (9th and Pine St.), Westlake Center (4th and Pine), University Street (3rd and University), Pioneer Square, and the International District (5th Ave. and S. Jackson St.). Metro buses also connect the rest of the city and the Eastside on routes that run 6 A.M.–1 A.M. every day. Fares cost $2.25 off-peak anywhere, $2.50 peak within the city or $3 beyond Seattle city limits. All Metro buses carry bikes at no extra charge, but bikes are not carried within the Ride Free area of downtown.

BY FERRY OR WATER TAXI
Washington State Ferries

One of the best ways to see Seattle is from the water. Washington State Ferries (206/464-6400, 888/808-7977, or 800/843-3779 for automated info, www.wsdot.wa.gov/ferries) operate almost continuously from before sunrise to after 1 A.M. daily, leaving from the main terminal at Pier 52 for Bainbridge Island and Bremerton. To either destination, summertime car-and-driver fares are $15.20 each way; passengers and walk-ons pay only $7.10 round-trip. A passenger-only **Seattle-Vashon Island** ferry ($4.55 round-trip) runs daily departures from Pier 50 in the summer, with Mon.–Sat. departures in the winter.

The Fauntleroy ferry dock in West Seattle serves Southworth on the Kitsap Peninsula and Vashon Island about every 20–50 minutes daily. Summertime car-and-driver fares are $19.45 one-way; passengers and walk-ons pay just $4.55 round-trip. The crossing to Southworth takes approximately 35 minutes, while the **Fauntleroy-Vashon Island** takes 15 minutes. Get to the Fauntleroy dock by

© ERICKA CHICKOWSKI

No trip to Seattle is complete without a ride aboard the ferry.

heading south on I-5 to exit 163; follow the signs from there.

There is a $1 surcharge to carry bikes on all these ferry runs. Fares for vehicles are lower in the off-season (mid-October–mid-May), and discounts are available for seniors, children, and people with disabilities. If you're going to be traveling a lot on the ferries, ask about frequent-user coupon books. There are no state ferry connections from Seattle to the San Juan Islands; you must leave from Anacortes or Sidney, B.C., or take the *Victoria Clipper.*

Victoria and San Juan Islands Ferries

For a day-long excursion to Canada, take the passenger-only *Victoria Clipper* (206/448-5000 or 800/888-2535, www.victoriaclipper .com, $137) from Pier 63 to Ogden Point in Victoria. Reservations are required for this high-speed catamaran cruise, and it takes two hours to reach Victoria. The round-trip cruise can be completed in one day (8:30 A.M. departure and 9:30 P.M. return) while allowing a brief stay in Olde English Victoria. For variety, take the *Clipper* to Victoria and fly back on Kenmore Air (206/486-1257 or 800/543-9595, www.kenmoreair.com). The *Clipper* also offers optional one- or two-night stays in Victoria, a "triple play" that includes a night each in Victoria and Vancouver, and a wide range of other tours into British Columbia. In addition, it has service between Seattle and the San Juan Islands, and between Victoria and the San Juans ($80–120).

BY CAR

According to one recent study, Seattle's traffic was the third worst in the United States; the average Seattleite spends over 44 hours per year stuck in traffic jams! If possible, try to stay on public transit, both for your own sanity and for the environment. By all means avoid the 3–7 P.M. weekday rush hour, when I-5 and the I-90 and Highway 520 floating bridges are often virtual parking lots.

One of the more difficult aspects of Seattle city driving isn't getting there, but getting back: finding an I-5 entrance ramp can be frustrating, especially after you zigzag over and under the highway a few times. One sure cure: head down 5th Avenue, because entrances to both north- and southbound traffic are along it. Another good, although very busy, way to approach the freeway is on Mercer Street; get in the right lanes for southbound, left lanes for northbound.

Parking

As in any metropolitan center, parking in downtown Seattle isn't always easy or cheap. However, one big bonus is that you probably don't have to fumble for coins for most on-street parking. Over the last decade the city has replaced nearly all of its meters with pay stations that accept credit cards and dole out stickers to indicate how much time you've bought. Parking downtown, by the waterfront, in Belltown, and the International district is $2.50 per hour with a two-, three-, or four-hour limit depending on the neighborhood. In South Lake Union, Capitol Hill, Ballard, and the University District the cost is $2 per hour, with some longer-term parking slots available for $1.25 per hour. And in Fremont, Wallingford, and Green Lake, the cost is $1.50 per hour with some longer-term spots available for $0.75 per hour. Most on-street parking is free between 6 P.M. and 8 A.M. Monday through Saturday and all day on Sunday and holidays. The Commercial Core, Belltown, Chinatown/International District, Pike-Pine, Capitol Hill, Uptown, and University Districts follow the same hours as above, except free parking doesn't begin until 8 P.M. Tempting fate can be costly—parking tickets are usually around $42.

During peak times or for all-day excursions, you may want to also consider the numerous pay lots throughout downtown, which range from $24–35 per day. One of the best garage deals in town is at the **Public Market Garage** (1531 Western Ave., 206/774-5242, $4 per hour, $20 per day), which offers an early bird special that charges only $10 if you arrive before 9:30 A.M. and leave by 9:30 P.M. Accessible

from Western Avenue or Alaskan Way, parking is also free here after 5 P.M. with validation at some Pike Place Market restaurants.

TOURS

When it comes to tours, Seattle has every possible option, from the standard drive-'em-around-in-the-bus types to the goofy, tongue-planted-firmly-in-cheek versions.

Flightseeing Tours

To see the city from about 1,500 feet, try one of **Seattle Seaplanes'** (206/329-9638 or 800/637-5553, www.seattleseaplanes.com, $87.50 pp, two-person minimum) 20-minute scenic floatplane rides over Seattle. Longer flights are available to Mount St. Helens, Mount Rainier, or the San Juan Islands. Flights take off and land at Lake Union.

In business since 1946, **Kenmore Air** (206/486-1257 or 800/543-9595, www.kenmore air.com) flies year-round scheduled floatplane flights from Lake Union or the north shore of Lake Washington. Destinations include the San Juan Islands (approx. $225 round-trip), Gulf Islands, Victoria (approx $250), and onward to several Vancouver Island destinations. A 24-pound baggage weight limit is in effect for these flights, with excess baggage charged at $1 per pound. In addition, Kenmore offers more standard flight-seeing trips over Seattle at $89 per person for up to three people on a quick 20-minute flight.

The most distinctive way to see Seattle is aboard a classic biplane from **Olde Thyme Aviation** (206/730-1412, www.oldethyme aviation.com). Flights start at $135 for two people on a 20-minute trip. They operate from the Museum of Flight at Boeing Field throughout the spring and summer, and passengers suit up in old-fashioned barnstorming regalia.

Bus and Van Tours

Gray Line of Seattle (206/626-5208 or 800/426-7532, www.graylineofseattle.com) offers a variety of Puget Sound tours. Its 3.5-hour city tour ($45) highlights Ballard Locks, the University of Washington, and Pioneer

Square. The Double Decker tour ($35) includes eight stops around downtown and Seattle Center. Riders are given a narrated tour and can get off and on at any of the stops. Or save your money by riding the free Metro buses around downtown and let the landscape narrate for itself. Gray Line has several other sightseeing trips, including Everett's Boeing plant ($55) and day trips to Mount Rainier ($65–85).

Several other companies offer more specialized tours. At **Private Eye Tours** (206/622-0590, www.privateeyetours.com), a semiretired private detective takes you on a murder and mystery exploration of Seattle. **Scenic Bound Tours** (206/433-6907 or 888/293-1404, www.seattlecitytours.com, $79) takes you on all-day van trips to the wild places around Puget Sound, including both Mount St. Helens and Mount Rainier.

Kids usually love **Ride the Ducks** (206/441-3825 or 800/817-1116, www.seattleducktours.net), which cruises through town—and into Lake Union—in a restored World War II landing craft, especially once they get their hands on the Wacky Quacker noisemakers provided to quack loudly at passersby.

Boat Tours

A number of boat tours and ferry services depart from Seattle's waterfront, providing a relaxing, scenic change of pace for the foot-weary traveler. The most popular ones are offered year-round by **Argosy Cruises** (206/623-4252 or 206/623-1445, www.argosycruises.com, $22.50–40.25), which operates a fleet of a dozen cruise vessels.

One of Argosy's most popular tours takes you from Elliott Bay through the Chittenden Locks into Lake Union, and then back by bus. The *Royal Argosy,* the company's flagship, offers lunch and dinner cruises ($49 lunch, $80–89 dinner). Argosy also offers cruises to Tillicum Village, jetboat trips, and special event cruises throughout the year.

Let's Go Sailing (206/624-3931, www.sailingseattle.com) offers 1.5-hour sails during the day ($30), and 2.5-hour sunset sailing

trips ($48) aboard two 70-foot sloops. Trips depart Pier 54 several times a day during the summer.

Classic boat fans will appreciate the tour of Lake Union aboard **Queen of Seattle** (departs from Lake Union Park, 425/898-2701, http://queenofseattle.com, $32) the largest steam powered paddle wheeler west of the Mississippi. Employees get in the act, dressing in Gold Rush–era costumes and performing the Live Klondike Cabaret Show during the two-hour tour.

Romantic paddle fans can take one of the guided sunset or moonlight sea kayak tours of Lake Union and Ballard Locks offered periodically in the summer by **Northwest Outdoor Center** (2100 Westlake Ave. N., 206/281-9694 or 800/683-0637, www.nwoc.com). **Outdoor Odysseys** (206/361-0717 or 200/647-4621, www.outdoorodysseys.com) also offers sea kayak tours around various parts of the Sound and to the San Juan Islands.

Walking and Biking Tours

Several notable walking tours are described under *Sights* in this chapter: the Park Service's free gold rush historical walks around Pioneer Square; the three-hour walking tours of Pike Place Market; the walking/eating tours of International District offered by Chinatown Discovery Tours; and Bill Speidel's Underground Tours. All are interesting and educational, but the last of these is particularly popular; guides cover the Pioneer Square area, providing humorous anecdotes, along with dollops of local history.

Several private companies lead guided walking tours of Seattle on a daily basis, including **The World's Greatest Seattle Walking Tour** (206/885-3173, www.theseattlewalkingtour.com, $15) and **See Seattle Walking Tours** (425/226-7641, www.see-seattle.com, $20).

Excellent **Viewpoints Discover Tours** (206/667-9186, www.seattlearchitecture.org, $15) take place throughout the year, focusing on Seattle's architectural heritage. These last two hours and are led by members of the Seattle Architectural Foundation.

THE EASTSIDE

Head east across the glistening waters of Lake Washington on either of Seattle's famous floating bridges and you'll stumble across what locals refer to as "the Eastside." This chain of suburban cousins to the Emerald City is where you'll find Microsoft millionaires tap-tap-tapping on their laptops at coffeehouse hot spots and see their husbands schlepping the kids off to soccer practice in BMW minivans. Look hard enough, though, and you'll also discover outdoors nuts enjoying some of the finest urban trails in the country, wine aficionados sipping reds and whites in area tasting rooms, equestrians enjoying open pastures on horseback, and cyclists spinning along stream-lined bike paths and lazy waterfront roads.

The Eastside may not be as exciting as Seattle to some travelers, but it is hardly the one-dimensional enclave it is often painted to be by certain city dwellers across the lake.

Sure, there are McMansions and high-tech business parks galore. And shopping does seem to be a favorite activity among the locals, who love to roam the upscale malls and kitschy little boutiques out here. But really, if there is something suburbanites and tourists have in common, it's a mutual love of browsing wares.

And between all of these stereotypical Eastside trappings, the curious traveler will discover plenty of unexpected sights. Here you'll find everything from pastoral farmlands to lakeshore beaches to lowland forests. There's an art museum touted as one of the region's best and a lesser-known pair of quirky little zoos. And when the sun is shining, the Eastside shines even brighter, with its enviable collection

© ERICKA CHICKOWSKI

HIGHLIGHTS

◖ **Bellevue Arts Museum:** This unique gallery focuses on the arts of craft and design (page 100).

◖ **Bellevue Botanical Garden:** Stop and smell the rhododendrons, the dahlias, and all the flowers in between at this colorful park (page 100).

◖ **Downtown Kirkland Waterfront:** Spend an afternoon window shopping, strolling the grassy lakeside parks, and maybe even taking a sail from Kirkland's charming village center (page 109).

◖ **Saint Edward State Park:** Once home to a Catholic seminary, this wooded retreat still offers plenty of space along its waterfront and its trails for thoughtful contemplation and recreational healing (page 110).

◖ **Marymoor Park:** Tucked away on the northern end of Lake Sammamish, this green space is made for activity. It features an enormous off-leash dog park, an acclaimed velodrome, tennis courts, a radio-controlled aircraft field, playgrounds, and more (page 116).

◖ **Cougar Mountain Zoo:** This small zoo offers a much more intimate animal experience than at your typical city zoo (page 121).

◖ **Bothell Landing:** Set along the Sammamish River Trail, this spot is a hub for recreation, shopping, and relaxation (page 126).

◖ **Chateau Ste. Michelle Winery:** Washington's oldest winery and Puget Sound's finest, this elegant destination offers cellar tours and barrel tasting (page 126).

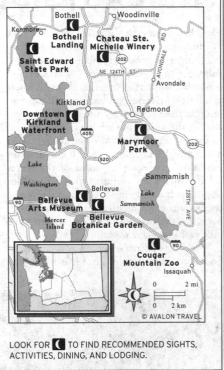

© AVALON TRAVEL

LOOK FOR ◖ TO FIND RECOMMENDED SIGHTS, ACTIVITIES, DINING, AND LODGING.

of eclectic parks for picnickers, dog walkers, swimmers, lollygaggers, and everyone in between. So don't let the clichés hold you back—those bridges really are worth crossing.

PLANNING YOUR TIME

Reachable just across Lake Washington from Seattle, the Eastside is easily explored from a base of operations set up at one of Seattle's hotels and vice versa. Bus service does run throughout cities like Redmond, Kirkland, and Bellevue

over to Seattle's transportation hubs. But like most suburbs, these towns are best explored with a car. Each of the floating bridges (I-5 and I-90) take only 20–30 minutes to cross when traffic is light, which is just about never. With commuters traveling in both directions at odd hours throughout the week (hey, this is a tech region that runs on computer geek workweeks!), plan on at least 45 minutes to get over the bridges in either direction during most of the week. During peak traffic times, make it an hour to be safe.

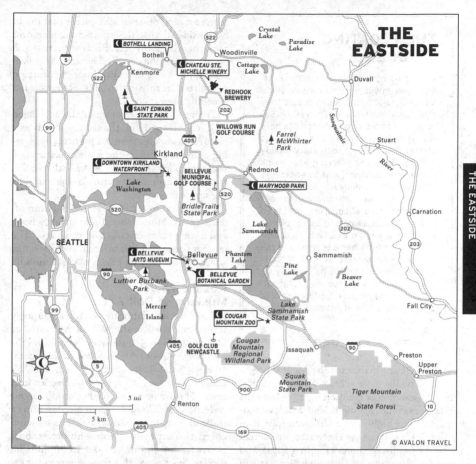

Bellevue and Mercer Island

Directly across Lake Washington, Bellevue has certainly grown up from the sleepy Seattle suburb it used to be. When the city was incorporated in 1953, the surrounding land was primarily strawberry fields, and Bellevue's streets were simple gravel roads. These days visitors are likely to see more towering construction cranes here than in downtown Seattle. As the home to many rapidly expanding high-tech industries, Bellevue now has its own high-rise downtown, with a well-respected art museum, crowded nightspots, and one of the fanciest shopping malls in the Northwest.

It is here and in the nearby bedroom community of Mercer Island that the stereotype of hoity-toity Eastsiders blossomed. Teenagers drive around Bellevue in brand-new luxury cars, and a little fixer-upper of a home can go for well over $1 million. Here is where you'll find Bill Gates's $125 million digs. He lives just

THE FLOATING BRIDGES

When passing from Seattle to the East-side, you might notice how low-slung both I-90 and 520 bridges are as they cross Lake Washington. The reason Se-attle hasn't built an elevated bridge here is simple: this glacial lake sinks to depths of more than 200 feet, with a silty, muddy bottom. There's no practical way to sink pillars that far down, and so engineers came up with a unique solution. The cur-rent bridges are built on floating seg-mented squares of concrete, anchored with enormous weights. It seems utterly improbable, but it works. Well, except for the time in 1990 when a big chunk of the I-90 bridge broke loose and sank. Nobody was hurt and the bridge was quickly re-paired. On the whole, you are far, far bet-ter off worrying about the crippling traffic crossing the bridge at just about any time of day or night.

west of Bellevue in the exclusive Medina neighborhood on the shore of Lake Washington. His 20,000-square-foot mansion is visible from the Evergreen Point Floating Bridge. Microsoft co-founder and high-profile philanthropist Paul Allen lives just across the water on Mercer Island's southwest shore. Hop in a kayak and you can check out his floating helicopter pad bobbing in the lake.

SIGHTS
◖ Bellevue Arts Museum
You won't find classical paintings at the Bellevue Arts Museum (510 Bellevue Way NE, 425/519-0770, www.bellevuearts.org, 10 A.M.–5 P.M. Tues., Wed., Fri., and Sat., 10 A.M.–8 P.M. Thurs., noon–5 P.M. Sun., closed Mon., $6 adults, $4 seniors and students, free for kids under 6). This organization eschews the traditional with its constant rotation of exhibits dedicated to the arts of crafts and design. Sculpture, carvings, glasswork,

fabric art, and other unique pieces that might be considered novelties at other art museums are rather the norm here. Because there are no permanent exhibits on display here, the collection can be hit or miss. But since the museum revitalized its mission in 2005, curation has generally been spot on.

Designed by the internationally acclaimed architect Steven Holl, the facility stands as a piece of artwork itself, with a particularly pleasing outdoor court on the rooftop featuring a wall that follows the curve of the 48th parallel. It perfectly captures the sun's movement during summer solstice.

In addition to exhibitions, the museum offers an artist-in-residence studio, an art school, and a wide range of talks and programs. The museum extends hours to 9 P.M. and offers free admission on the first Friday of every month.

Rosalie Whyel Museum of Doll Art
Housed in an elaborate Victorian fantasy structure, the Rosalie Whyel Museum of Doll Art (1116 108th Ave. NE, 425/455-1116 or 800/440-3655, www.dollart.com, 10 A.M.–5 P.M. Mon.–Sat., 1–5 P.M. Sun., $7 adults, $6 seniors, $5 ages 5–17, free for kids under 5) is home to one of the world's largest collections of dolls and is guaranteed to bring a smile to every four-year-old girl. The museum covers two expansive floors with professional presentations and more than 1,000 dolls on display. Start out with a five-minute video explaining the history of doll making, then head upstairs to check out the diverse collection that includes thumbnail-sized Egyptian tomb dolls and other antique dolls. Downstairs are 20th-century dolls, including mechanical dolls, authentically detailed dollhouses, Barbies, G.I. Joes, teddy bears, and even Elvis figures. Also downstairs is a gift shop filled with dolls and doll paraphernalia. The museum is especially popular with the over-60 set, and busloads roll in from senior centers all over the state.

◖ Bellevue Botanical Garden
Stroll the grounds at Bellevue Botanical

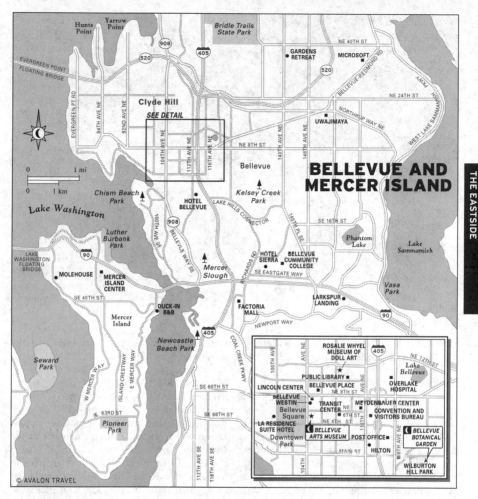

THE EASTSIDE

Garden (12001 Main St., 425/462-2750, www.bellevuebotanical.org, dawn–dusk daily, free) to take in over 53 acres of floral displays and native greenery. Garden highlights include an alpine rock garden with high elevation varietals, a tranquil Japanese garden, and a 19-acre botanical reserve featuring forest, wetlands, and meadowland. An army of enthusiastic volunteers helps run the visitors center (10 A.M.–6 P.M. daily May–Sept., 10 A.M.–4 P.M. daily Oct.–Apr.) on the grounds. Tours can be caught here at 2 P.M. on Saturday and Sunday April–October.

The garden is beautiful year-round, but its dahlia bloom in summer is the marquee draw. Over 40 varieties surround the historic Sharp Cabin in a kaleidoscopic display. Park volunteers also take advantage of the short days of winter each year to put on a display of Christmas lights fashioned as flowers during its Garden d'Lights festival. From the end of November through the beginning of January

© ERICKA CHICKOWSKI

Bellevue Botanical Garden

the park is open until 9:30 P.M. each night for visitors to admire the sparkling spectacle.

Bellevue Parks

The 79-acre **Kelsey Creek Farm and Park** (13204 SE 8th Pl., 425/455-7688, 7 A.M.–6 P.M. daily, free) is a choice destination for animal-lovin' youngsters. The main attraction here is a welcoming petting zoo with cows, rabbits, sheep, pigs, and ponies galore.

The property offers primo opportunities for the enthusiastic shutterbug. On premises, visitors can aim a lens at two enormous hip-roofed barns, an 1888 pioneer log cabin, a Japanese garden, a rustic farmhouse, and, of course, the animals.

Mercer Slough covers 320 acres of marsh habitat just south of downtown Bellevue. Here you'll discover 10 miles of trails, as well as four miles of waterways perfect for exploring in a canoe or kayak. It's a fine place to watch for deer, muskrats, ducks, herons, and other critters. This entire area was underwater until 1917, when Seattle's Chittenden Locks were completed, lowering the level of Lake Washington by nine feet.

Mercer Island Parks

Mercer Island's postage-stamp 10 square miles is dominated by nearly 500 acres of parks and green spaces just ripe for exploration. Most prized among them is **Luther Burbank Park** (2040 84th Ave. SE). This is the island's best waterfront park, featuring nearly a mile of shoreline, public boat docks, a roped-in swimming beach, and plenty of spots to plunk down a lure. Visitors can dip their toes in the chilly waters or just stroll the shore to work up an appetite before grilling up some dogs in the barbecue area. There's also a fun playground and swings to let the shoulder monkeys loose, and even an off-leash dog park.

Those who seek a little solitude should wander into **Pioneer Park.** This undeveloped park is an homage to the island's wilder days, before sprawling estates and $5 lattes. It features over six miles of multiuse trails that wander through stands of old-growth cedar, Douglas fir, bigleaf maple, and alder.

One of the most novel parks on the island, **The Park on the Lid** is a slice of greenery known less for what is on park grounds than for what the park grounds are on—namely, the I-90 tunnel lid. Check out the big white stovepipe-looking tubes set amid the well-manicured picnic lawns. These are the vents that filter out fumes from the freeway below.

ENTERTAINMENT AND EVENTS
Nightlife

As downtown Bellevue grows up, so does the surrounding nightlife. Though it doesn't rival Seattle's scene, Bellevue's collection of nightspots offers enough variety to keep most people happy for an evening or two.

Besides, happy hour is so much happier when you don't have to contend with traffic over the bridges. Bellevue has some particularly attractive spots come happy hour, including **Taphouse Grill** (550 106th Avenue NE, 425/467-1730, www.taphousegrill.com, 11 A.M.–10 P.M. Sun.–Thurs., 11 A.M.–11 P.M. Fri.–Sat.) in the Galleria shopping center. This upscale brewhouse has more than 160 beers on tap; during happy hour drinkers can nosh on a number of finger foods for under $5 a plate. During peak weekend evenings, this is a very popular gathering spot for the flirty twenty-something crowd.

Just a few blocks west, the **520 Bar and Grill** (10138 Main St., 425/450-0520, www.520barandgrill.com) is another favorite happy-hour hangout, particularly among the well-heeled middle-aged set. The trick is to get there early, as happy hour runs 2–5:20 P.M.; specials are also good all day on Sunday. Set slightly away from the Bellevue Square rush, this bar prides itself on its uniqueness. Happy hour appetizers are distinctive, and there isn't a whiff of chain-bar flair—just classy walnut columns and oak floors, handmade furniture, and a genuine public-house vibe.

Those looking to impress a date should look to the Bellevue skies for help. Set atop

the 989 Elements High Rise, **Vertigo Lounge and Grill** (989 112th Ave. NE, 425/467-6767, www.vertigobellevue.com) is a big-city-style establishment with sleek modern furnishings and plenty of jet-setters to fill them. Vertigo is best known for its jazz lineup, generally putting on shows Wednesday through Saturday night each week.

Finally, Bellevue also has options for the restless types who prefer doing something while they drink. Lincoln Center plays host to a pair of fun sporting nightspots. **The Parlor** (700 Bellevue Way NE Ste. 300, 425/289-7000, www.parlorbilliards.com, 11 A.M.–2 A.M. Mon.–Sat., 11 A.M.–midnight Sun., tables $10–18 per hour) is an upscale pool hall where the players come dressed to impress. **Lucky Strike Lanes** (700 Bellevue Way NE, Ste. 250, 425/453-5137, www.bowlluckystrike.com, noon–midnight Mon.–Thurs., noon–2 A.M. Fri., 11 A.M.–2 A.M. Sat., 11 A.M.–midnight Sun.) is a posh bowling alley. Its chic decor pays homage to the mid-20th-century stylings popular during bowling's heyday, without the gross 50-year-old bowling shoes.

The Arts

You won't find anything approaching the Seattle music scene in Bellevue, but **Crossroads Shopping Center** (15600 NE 8th Ave., 425/644-1111, www.crossroadsbellevue.com) does put on free concerts of all types on Friday and Saturday nights.

The **Bellevue Philharmonic Orchestra** (425/455-4171, www.bellevuephilharmonic.com) performs classical and pop concerts at various local venues, including the state-of-the-art **Meydenbauer Center** (112th Ave. NE and NE 6th St., www.meydenbauer.com). The Meydenbauer also hosts theatrical and musical productions from a variety of Eastside companies, including the **Bellevue Chamber Chorus** (425/881-0445, www.bellevuechamberchorus.net), a group of 30 singers who perform October–May. The **Bellevue Civic Theatre** (4038 Factoria Blvd. #165, 425/235-5087, www.bellevuecivic.org) is the city's professional acting company.

Festivals and Events

Bellevue Arts Museum sponsors the annual **Bellevue Arts Fair** (425/519-0742 or www .bellevuearts.org), held on the last full weekend of July. One of the state's largest art fairs, this one has been going on since 1947 and usually features more than 300 booths. The juried show and crowds that top 300,000 have helped many artists' careers along.

SHOPPING

Bellevue's motto might be best expressed by a bumper sticker seen on local cars: "When the going gets tough, the tough go shopping."

Shopping Centers

Bellevue is a town known for its high-ticket shopping scene. The beating heart of it all is centrally located **Bellevue Square** (NE 8th St. and Bellevue Way NE, 9:30 A.M.–9:30 P.M. Mon.–Sat., 11 A.M.–7 P.M. Sun.). It has been around the longest among Bellevue's shopping meccas, and it still reigns as the king of 'em all. High-class customers are drawn to over 180 stores and restaurants like Ruth's Chris Steakhouse and Cheesecake Factory. So what if there's a JCPenney here? It's also got a Tiffany and Co., Bose, Coach, and Lush. There's even a branch of a national financial planner tucked away to help you sort out the wreckage you may have just caused. The mall puts on couture events throughout the year, and yes, of course there's valet parking here.

Just across the street, **Lincoln Square** (700 Bellevue Way NE, 425/450-9100, www.lin colnsquare.com) expands on "Belle Square's" shopping range with more stores, including Ex Officio, Henredon, and Paper Source. It also houses a billiards parlor, bowling alley, luxury cinema, and a spa. A convenient footbridge connects Bellevue and Lincoln Squares together, and both are open the same hours.

Shoppers who prefer to save a buck or two might want to run over to **Crossroads Mall** (15600 NE 8th St., 425/644-1111, www.cross roadsbellevue.com, 10 A.M.–9 P.M. Mon.–Sat., 11 A.M.–6:00 P.M. Sun.), about 10 minutes away from the hotsy-totsy downtown area.

GEARING UP

Heading from Seattle, Eastside cities are often the last stop in civilization before driving into the wilderness for a bit of outdoor fun. Here are some of the best shops around the area to buy or rent gear and grab trail food and the like on your way to the woods or the slopes.

Marmot Mountain Works (827 Bellevue Way NE, Bellevue, 425/453-1515, www.mar motmountain.com, 10 A.M.–8 P.M. Mon, Thurs., Fri., 10 A.M.–6 P.M. Tues., Wed., Sat., noon–6 P.M. Sun.) specializes in hard-to-find climbing, skiing, and backpacking gear and parts, as well as apparel, outerwear, and maps. Its rental shop offers climbing, camping, and skiing gear.

Gerk's Alpine Hut (7875 Leary Way, Redmond, 425/883-7544, www.gerksalpinehut .com, 10 A.M.–7 P.M. Mon.-Fri., 10 A.M.–5 P.M. Sat., noon–5 P.M. Sun.) is a small, local shop with mountain biking, cycling, and ski gear. Daily, weekly, and seasonal ski rentals are available.

REI (7500 166th Ave. NE, Redmond, 425/882-1158, 10 A.M.–9 P.M. Mon.-Fri., 10 A.M.–8 P.M. Sat., 11 A.M.–6 P.M. Sun.) offers two stories of all nature of outdoor gear. The larger of two REI stores on the Eastside, the Redmond outpost has a rental shop with camping, climbing, mountaineering, and snow sports gear. **REI** (735 NW Gilman Blvd., Issaquah, 425/313-1660, 9 A.M.–9 P.M. Mon.-Fri., 9 A.M.–8 P.M. Sat., 10 A.M.–6 P.M. Sun.) in Issaquah is smaller than the Redmond store but closer to Snoqualmie Pass. The rental shop here only offers snowshoes.

Montlake Bike Shop (208 Kirkland Ave., Kirkland, 425/828-3800, 10 A.M.–7 P.M. Mon.-Fri., 9 A.M.–5 P.M. Sat., 10 A.M.–4 P.M. Sun.) is one of the best bike shops on the Eastside, offering a full range of bike rentals on a daily and weekly basis.

This shopping complex has an Old Navy, Sports Authority, Petco, and Bed, Bath and Beyond, among others. It also has an extensive food court that serves up delicious international food from around the world.

Old Bellevue Boutiques

Shoppers who prefer those one-of-a-kind items that make friends ask enviously, "Where'd you find *that?*" should skip the mall and trek a few blocks to Old Bellevue's restored business district on Main Street between 100th and Bellevue Way.

Far East importers **Ming's Asian Gallery** (10217 Main St., 425/462-4008, mingsgallery. com, 10 A.M.–6 P.M. Mon.–Sat., noon–5 P.M. Sun.,) carries a staggeringly diverse lineup of art, from furnishings to jade to Chinese Communist propaganda posters.

Fashionistas will love this stretch as well. Ladies looking for sleek designer apparel and accessories should make it a point to hit **La Ree** (11 103rd Ave. NE, 425/453-7868, www .lareeboutique.com, 10 A.M.–7 P.M. Mon.–Fri., 11 A.M.–6 P.M. Sat., 11 A.M.–5 P.M.), a New York-style specialty shop that loads up on lines such as Alexander Wang, Mint, and Proportion of Blue.

You'll have endless options for matching pumps, sandals, or flats at **Gotta Have Shoes** (10047 Main St. #101, 425/460-8316, 10 A.M.–6 P.M. Mon.–Sat., 11 A.M.–5 P.M. Sun.).

Bookstores

Bellevue also is home to several bookstores offering a wide selection of reading material. **Barnes and Noble** (626 106th Ave. NE, 425/451-8463, www.bn.com) has plenty of little isolated spots to test-drive books before you buy, and **University Book Store** (990 102nd Ave. NE, 425/462-4500, www.bookstore .washington.edu), a branch of the University of Washington that sells lots more than just textbooks.

SPORTS AND RECREATION
Bridle Trails State Park

As the name attests, Bridle Trails State Park (116th Ave. NE, www.parks.wa.gov, no camping) is an urban retreat for equestrian lovers. Settled in a wooded plot resting between Bellevue and Kirkland, the park offers 28 miles of equestrian and hiking trails, as well as a riding arena that hosts regular shows and competitions during the summer months. Riders and hikers can also extend their exploration over the **Bridle Crest Trail,** which continues on to Redmond's Marymoor Park.

Walking and Running

Bellevue's **Lake Hills Greenbelt** (off 156th Ave. SE) features five miles of trails through 100 acres of wetlands and pines in the heart of the city. Open to joggers, cyclists, wheelchairs, and hikers, the greenbelt trail links Larsen and Phantom Lakes. A ranger station has information on the area's natural history.

If that isn't enough land to roam, take to the **Lake to Lake Parkway Trail,** a paved cycling and running path connecting Lake Sammamish with Lake Washington.

Water Sports

Cascade Canoe & Kayak Center (425/637-8838, www.canoe-kayak.com) offers sea kayak tours, lessons, and rentals on Lake Washington at **Enatai Beach Park** (108th Ave. SE at 35th Ave.). It is affiliated with REI.

Located along Lake Washington, both **Chism Beach Park** (off 100th Ave. SE) and **Newcastle Beach Park** (off Lake Washington Blvd. SE) have picnic areas, trails, and swimming beaches with summertime lifeguards.

Golf

Just south of Bellevue in the onetime coal-mining settlement of Newcastle, **The Golf Club at Newcastle** (15500 Six Penny Lane, 425/793-5566, www.newcastlegolf.com) has been called one of the top 10 courses in America. Short of the peaks of the Issaquah Alps, the greens and fairways here offer the most stunning Eastside vistas of Seattle and the Cascades on a clear day.

ACCOMMODATIONS

As Bellevue continues to gentrify, the city's budget lodging options have dwindled considerably. Those travelers wishing to stay close to the city in cheap lodging under $100 should motor south on I-405 for the most options. Renton and its environs are only a few minutes away and will have a number of chain hotels that fetch a much more modest price than comparable digs within Bellevue's high-demand zip codes.

$100-150

That's not to say that the Bellevue area doesn't have a few lodging deals waiting to be snagged. For example, right downtown on the west side of Bellevue Square, **La Residence Suite Hotel** (475 100th Ave. NE, 425/455-1475, www.belle vuelodging.com, $125 one bedroom, $165 two bedroom) offers guests who stay for at least seven days a super rate of $105 per night in its one-room suites. The rooms here are converted condos, so every room comes complete with full kitchen, dining room, and living room. The furnishings are a bit tired, but for the price and the location it is a steal.

Both Bellevue and Mercer Island play host to a few surprisingly reasonable B&Bs. Just 10 minutes from the heart of downtown Bellevue's high-rises and shopping centers, **Gardens Retreat** (3444 140th Ave. NE, 206/370-2484, www.gardensretreat.com, $95–110 s, $110–135 d) is cozied up near the little pastures and barns of Bellevue's quaint Bridle Trails neighborhood. The inn has two rooms, one with private bathroom, a lovely backyard garden, and a cozy library for lounging. Full breakfast is served each morning. Both rooms have wireless Internet, and there is a printer and fax in the library for business travelers.

In Mercer Island, **Molehouse** (3308 West Mercer Way, 206/232-1611, www.bedbreak fasthome.com/molehouse, $99 s or d) has a winsome private suite perched atop the innkeeper's three-story home. Guests can gaze out to Lake Washington from the private balcony here. Breakfast is do-it-yourself, with all the necessary accoutrements stocked in the suite's refrigerator and pantry.

For just a few dollars more than the Molehouse, the **Duck-In B&B** (4118 100th Ave.

SE, 206/232-2554, www.seattlebestbandb.com/ duckin, $135 d) in Mercer Island is probably the best B&B deal in the area. This romantic, two-bedroom, 1920s-era cottage is settled right on the shore of Lake Washington, with a big grassy lawn leading out to the water. A continental breakfast is provided, and kids are welcome.

$150-200

Conveniently located just off of I-90 in Bellevue's Eastgate neighborhood, **Larkspur Landing** (15805 SE 37th St., 425/373-1212, www.larkspurlanding.com, $103–169 s or d) is a new hotel built in pleasing Craftsman-style architecture. This is a great spot for those who mix long business trips with pleasure—all rooms come with fully equipped kitchens, deliciously comfy feather-top beds, large desks, and high-speed Internet. The place is kid- and pet-friendly, laundry facilities are free to use, and continental breakfast is served each morning. Plus, there's a pool and a well-appointed gym. Best of all, freshly baked cookies are served every afternoon.

Hotel Sierra (3244 139th Ave. SE, 425/747-2705, www.hotel-sierra.com, s or d $179) is another of Bellevue's newly renovated hotels, gussied up to accommodate travelers expecting luxurious digs. Rooms feature plush furniture and plasma TVs, and there's an indoor pool and fitness center on premises. Stay comes with complimentary breakfast in the morning, including a made-to-order omelette bar, and an evening wine hour with appetizers.

Over $250

Because Bellevue accommodates so many business travelers, many luxury room-rate schedules are the reverse of a typical tourist resort—weekdays are the most expensive days to stay. Some of downtown's nicest hotels are nearly half the rack rate on weekend nights.

This is true of the **Bellevue Westin** (600 Bellevue Way NE, 425/638-1000, www.westin .com, $159–419 s or d), arguably downtown's nicest luxury chain hotel. The rooms are impeccable here, and one can stay for as little as $159 on some weekends. Try to get a room above the sixth floor, as many below that have obstructed views.

The city's classiest lodging is **Hotel Bellevue** (11200 SE 6th St., 425/454-4424 or 800/579-1110, www.thehotelbellevue.com, $180–650 s or d), where you'll find all the amenities: indoor pool, sauna, hot tub, racquetball courts, tennis courts, a complete athletic facility, twice-daily housekeeping, and private minibars.

Camping

Although the nearest public campground is many miles away in the Cascades, Bellevue does have tent and vehicle spaces at two private RV parks: **Trailers Inn RV Park** (exit 11 west from I-90, 15531 SE 37th St., 425/747-9181 or 800/659-4684, www.trailerinnsrv.com/ seattle, open year-round, $22–48) and **Vasa Park Resort** (2560 W. Lake Sammamish Rd. SE, 425/746-3260, www.vasaparkresort.com, mid-May–Sept., $32 full hookups). Vasa is right along Lake Sammamish and features a fun dock and slide that dumps kids right into the lake, and a boat launch.

FOOD
Cafés and Diners

Burger-lovers are in for a singular treat in Bellevue. **Wibbley's Gourmet Hamburgers** (2255 140th Ave NE in Bellevue, 425/747-7818, 11 A.M.–8 P.M. Mon.–Fri., 11 A.M.–4 P.M. Sat.) grills up a delectable straightforward burger, a burger with green chile, and one slathered in teriyaki sauce. Their Wibbley's dressing is delicious, the staff is friendly, and the inside has comforting dark wood paneling. Before you rush off and order up, prepare more than your appetite: they only take cash.

Steak and Seafood

Located 21 floors up in the Bank of America Building at Bellevue Place, **Daniel's Broiler** (10500 NE 8th St., 425/462-4662, www .schwartzbros.com/daniels, 5 P.M.–10 P.M. Sun.–Thurs., 5 P.M.–11 P.M. Fri.–Sat., $50) has good seafood chowder and steaks, and extraordinary views. The lounge serves wines by the glass, oysters on the half-shell, and a variety of light meals and desserts, plus jazz or piano music nightly.

Asian

Thai Ginger (3717 Factoria Blvd. SE, 425/641-4008, www.thaiginger.com, 11 A.M.–9:30 P.M. Mon.–Fri, $10) is a super place for Thai food, prepared in the open kitchen. Try the garlic prawns or chicken satay.

The best local Chinese restaurant is **Yeas Wok** (6969 Coal Creek Parkway SE, 425/644-5546, http://yeaswok.com, 11 A.M.–9:30 P.M. Tues.–Thurs., 11 A.M.–10:30 P.M. Fri., 10:30 A.M.–10:30 P.M. Sat., 11 A.M.–9:30 P.M. Sun., $11) in Newcastle, where specialties include Hunan, Szechuan, and Mandarin dishes, notably the crispy shrimp. It's in a strip mall, but don't let that put you off; the food is authentic and the menu vast. **Noble Court** (1644 140th Ave. NE, 425/641-6011, www.the noblecourt.com, 11 A.M.–9:30 P.M. Mon.–Thurs., 11 A.M.–10:30 P.M. Fri., 10 A.M.–10:30 P.M. Sat., 10 A.M.–5 P.M. Sun., $9) has the tastiest dim sum on the Eastside, along with many unusual offerings.

Nigiri lovers would do well to swing by **I Love Sushi** (11818 NE 8th St., 425/454-5706, www.ilovesushi.com, 11:30 A.M.–2 P.M. Mon.–Sat. and 5 P.M.–10 P.M. Mon.–Thurs., 5 P.M.–9:30 P.M. Fri.–Sat., $15), an excellent Japanese restaurant and sushi bar with some of the best knife-wielding chefs this side of Lake Washington.

Mercer Island's best-known Thai restaurant, **Pon Preom Restaurant** (3039 78th Ave. SE, 206/236-8424, 11:30 A.M.–3 P.M. and 5 P.M.–9:30 P.M. Mon.–Thurs., 5–10 P.M. Fri.–Sat., 5–9 P.M. Sun., $11) is worth a visit. Its friendly, polite staff serves up delicious noodles or spring rolls. And its refreshing Thai iced tea is perfect after a day in the sun at Luther Burbank Park.

Uwajimaya (699 120th Ave. NE 425/747-9012, www.uwajimaya.com, 8 A.M.–10 P.M. Mon.–Sat., 9 A.M.–9 P.M. Sun.) is the local outpost of the Asian grocery chain, featuring fresh seafood, high-quality produce, a deli with sushi, and other many Asian specialties, plus Japanese books and gifts.

THE EASTSIDE

Continental and Mediterranean

BIS on Main (10213 Main St., 425/455-2033, www.bisonmain.com, 11:30 A.M.–11 P.M. Mon.–Thurs., 11:30 A.M.–midnight Fri., 5:30 P.M.–midnight Sat., 5–9 P.M. Sun., $38), is *the* place to be seen in downtown Bellevue, with a great service and wonderful continental cuisine and seafood. It's where locals go to impress business clients. Try the whipped potatoes with wasabi or the savory fish soup.

Pogacha (119 106th Ave. NE, 425/455-5670, www.pogacha.com, 11:30 A.M.–2:30 P.M. Mon.–Fri. and 5–8:30 P.M. Sun.–Mon., 5–9 P.M. Tues.–Thurs., 5–10 P.M. Fri., 5–9:30 P.M. Sat., $15) is certainly one of the more unusual Bellevue restaurants, with flavorful toppings on Croatian-style pizzas and delightfully crunchy breads.

Spazzo (10655 NE 4th St., 425/454-8255, www.schwartzbros.com/spazzo, 11:30 A.M.–3 P.M. and 4–9 P.M. daily, $21) offers impressive vistas from the top of the Key Bank Building. The Mediterranean menu includes well-prepared food from North Africa, Turkey, and Greece.

Tucked away into an unassuming strip mall in Overlake, **Tosoni's** (14320 NE 20th St., 425/644-1668, 5–10 P.M. Tues.–Sat., closed Sun.–Mon., $25) is actually one of the nicest eateries on the Eastside. Step inside and you're greeted by a cozy romantic bistro with white tablecloths, flickering candles, and a window into the kitchen. The rosy-cheeked chef often comes out to greet guests after he cooks his heart out, serving creative and hearty servings of Italian and Eastern European fare. The wait staff is very knowledgeable, so you can always trust in them to find a great wine pairing for your meal from the amply stocked reserve.

If you're on Mercer Island and craving wholesome food with a bit of French and Italian flair, **Bennett's Pure Food Bistro** (7650 SE 27th St., Mercer 206/232-2759, www.bennettsbistro.com, 11:30 A.M.–2 P.M. Mon.–Fri., 10 A.M.–3 P.M. Sat.–Sun. and 4–9:30 P.M. Sun.–Thurs., 4–10 P.M. Fri.–Sat., $22) serves only fresh, local foods with an emphasis on whole foods and handmade artisan meats, cheeses, and breads. Cheese fans will be happy to note that this well-regarded restaurant is a sister establishment to Pike Place icon Beecher's Handmade Cheese.

Brunch

The luxurious **Calcutta Grill** (15500 Six Penny Lane, 425/793-4646, www.newcastlegolf.com, 11 A.M.–10 P.M. Mon.–Thurs., 11 A.M.–11 P.M. Fri., 9:30 A.M.–11 P.M. Sat., 9:30 A.M.–10 P.M. Sun., $32), located in The Golf Club at Newcastle, is known for its popular Sunday brunch spread. Come for the gourmet omelettes, prime rib, and desserts, and stay for the sweeping vistas of the Seattle skyline. It's also open for lunch and dinner daily. Reservations are highly recommended at any time of day.

INFORMATION AND SERVICES

For additional information on Bellevue and the surrounding area, contact the helpful **Visit Bellevue Washington** (11100 NE 6th St., 425/450-3777, www.visitbellevuewashington.com) visitors bureau.

The modern **Bellevue Public Library** (11501 Main, 425/455-6889, www.kcls.org) is the largest in King County and offers visitors a place to log on to free Wi-Fi or use a computer for a spell.

Visit **Mercer Island Chamber of Commerce** (7601 SE 27th St., 206/232-3404, www.mercerislandchamber.com) in the island's "downtown" district for local information. The main annual event is **Summer Celebration,** held in mid-July, with a street fair, fireworks, concerts, and more fun.

GETTING THERE AND AROUND

The eastern ends of both of Lake Washington's floating bridges land in Bellevue. Downtown Bellevue is closer to Highway 520 by a hair, and generally it is a toss-up between routes from Seattle. Sometimes, though, one bridge will definitely have the traffic advantage over another. Check the state Department of Transportation website (www.wsdot.wa.gov/traffic/seattle) for a color-coded traffic map and web cams to help you make up your mind. The only way to drive to Mercer Island is to take I-90 over the Lake Washington Floating Bridge. Mercer's small business district is located on the north end of the island and just off I-90.

Metro Transit (800/542-7876, http://metro .kingcounty.gov) has several buses serving Bellevue and Mercer Island from Seattle, plus numerous local routes. The main stop is the Bellevue Transit Center on NE 6th Street downtown.

Kirkland

The oldest city on the east side of Lake Washington, Kirkland's gentrified neighborhoods may never have been what they are today if the town's namesake had his way. Back around 1886, Peter Kirk hoped to turn the town into the "Pittsburgh of the West" with a giant steel mill along Lake Washington. Plans changed and lucky for Kirkland, because the town's centerpiece is its well-manicured waterfront. Many area boutiques, art galleries, cafés, parks, and houses line the lake, and downtown directly abuts its lapping water.

SIGHTS
◖ Downtown Kirkland Waterfront
Kirkland's charms are particularly evident along

Lake Street, in the city's villagelike downtown. Just a skipped stone away from the shores of Lake Washington, this quaint commercial district is a fun place to do some window shopping, grab a bite to eat, or sit down with a cup of joe for an afternoon of people-watching.

Much of Kirkland's waterfront activity centers on **Marina Park** (25 Lakeshore Plaza Dr., 425/587-3342, 7 A.M.–11 P.M. daily), a welcoming shore-side haven that features a sandy beach and ample grass for lounging while checking out the views of downtown Seattle and the Olympic Mountains. In the summer it seems as if the rigging of nearby docked boats ping against their masts in time with the music from the park's regularly held community concerts.

THE EASTSIDE

© ERICKA CHICKOWSKI

Kirkland's waterfront

THE EASTSIDE

◖ Saint Edward State Park

Head farther north on NE 145th Street to Saint Edward State Park (425/296-2970, www.parks .wa.gov, 8 A.M.–dusk daily, $10 day use), a 316-acre retreat from civilization. This quiet piece of property was part of a Catholic seminary until 1977. When the seminary closed, the diocese sold the land to the state and the park opened the following summer. Saint Edward boasts almost a mile of forested, undeveloped Lake Washington shoreline, and five miles of hiking and mountain biking trails, plus picnic areas and a gymnasium.

Other Parks

Condos and lakefront homes line Kirkland's curvy Lake Washington shoreline, but the stretch is also studded with plenty of city parks so that everyone can enjoy the water. Right downtown, **Waverly Beach Park** (633 Waverly Way, 425/587-3300, 8 A.M.–10 P.M. daily) has a lovely swimming area and a great across-the-lake views. Keep driving north and you'll eventually hit upon **Juanita Bay Park** (2201 Market St., 425/587-3300, 8 A.M.–10 P.M.), an old golf course now transformed with scenic hiking trails and guided walks in the summer, and **Juanita Beach Park** (9703 NE Juanita Dr., 425/587-3300, 8 A.M.–10 P.M.), with an impressively long pier, picnic tables, and one of the area's best swimming beaches. Northwest of Juanita, **O.O. Denny Park** (12400 Holmes Point Dr. NE, 425/587-3300, 8 A.M.–10 P.M.), has a small beach, picnic area, and hiking trail leading to King County's largest Douglas fir. Standing 255 feet high and 8 feet in diameter, the tree is estimated to be 600 years old.

ENTERTAINMENT AND EVENTS
Nightlife

Proving that conventional wisdom is wrong and that the Eastside does, in fact, have a sense of humor, **Laughs Comedy Spot** (12099 124th Ave., 425/823-6306) draws a combination of nationally known and up-and-coming comedians to its intimate club. And you needn't have your belly-laughs on an empty belly. There's a full restaurant and a liquor bar at Laughs, too.

The dimly lit divey crowd should cruise by the **Central Tavern** (124 Kirkland Ave., 425/827-0808). Live music, cheap drinks, and sticky floors will take you back to your early 20s. Unless you're in your early 20s, in which case you'll find the Tavern just the thing. Many Microsofties love it—in an ironic, hipster way, of course.

Should you prefer your wine from a bottle instead of a box, **The Purple Café and Wine Bar** (323 Park Place Center, 425/828-3772, www .thepurplecafe.com, 11 A.M.–10 P.M. Mon.–Thurs., 11 A.M.–11 P.M. Fri.–Sat., noon–9 P.M. Sun.) should have more than enough elegance to please. The café cooks up some very special dishes that mix Northwest ingredients with haute cuisine preparations and presentations.

The Arts

Downtown Kirkland is sprinkled with fun public sculptures, including *Cow and the Coyote* on Central Way. **Kirkland Arts Center** (620 Market St., 425/822-7161, www.kirk landartscenter.org) presents exhibits and classes in the historic Peter Kirk Building, built in 1891. The second Thursday of each month, Kirkland galleries open for **Art Walk** (425/889-8212, 6–9 P.M.), featuring artist receptions and shows.

The modern and spacious **Kirkland Performance Center** (350 Kirkland Ave., 425/893-9900, www.kpcenter.org) is home to theater, dance, classical, and pop music concerts, and family programs.

Festivals and Events

Kirkland's big day out is July's **Kirkland Uncorked** (25 Lakeshore Plaza, 206/633-0422, http://kirklanduncorked.com), a celebration of sophisticated pleasures. Wine and beer tastings complement the extensive art show and heighten one's appreciation of the signature Dog Modeling Contest.

Summerfest (425/822-7161), on the second weekend in July, attracts crowds of people for local arts and crafts. **Kirkland Farmers Market** (425/893-8766) fills Park Lane East between 3rd Street and Main with vegetables, flowers, sweets, and crafts 1–7 P.M. on summertime Wednesdays.

SHOPPING

If you are on the Eastside and are at all serious about shopping, you're going to find a very good friend in downtown Kirkland. The city itself is small, so "downtown" is really more of the waterfront area. But don't let the layout lull you into hesitation. Specialty shops address just about any interest from highbrow to somewhat pedestrian. Between the enchanting Lake Washington setting and the depth of options, this is the perfect day out for the right sort of person.

Shopping Malls

If you get fed up with hunting for parking only to shop one-note boutiques, drive out to **Totem Lakes Mall** (12601 120th Ave.). The smaller shopping center was already a bit obsolete when the bottom dropped out of the economy, so don't expect a world-class experience. In fact, it's a bit of a depressing collection of vacant storefronts broken by Big 5 Sporting Goods, Denny's Pet World, Mark's Hallmark, a Ross, Guitar Center, and Trader Joe's grocery. A former Circuit City storefront completes the tone of a gothic/romantic urban ruin.

Boutiques

Bikini Beach (92 Kirkland Ave., 425/893-9542) is right where you need it when the weather gets sunny and the water starts to look inviting. It's open for the other 11 months of the year, too. The Beach carries swimwear for men and women with bathing suits sized for just about any gal.

Barkz (115 Lake St. S, 425/822-0292, www.barkz.com) has got hot gear for dogs from lhasas to labs. Not only does it offer food, treats, and furniture, but there's an indoor off-leash area where prescreened pooches can get some social time. Call well in advance to schedule an evaluation and bring proof of inoculation. Hey, dogs need exclusive clubs, too.

Toy Stores

Kirkland is generally considered a playground, but only for kids over 30 or so. True to form, the toy stores tend to cater to an older crowd, but aren't so mean as to keep the little ones out completely. **Eastside Trains** (217 Central Way, 425/828-4098, www.eastsidetrains.com) is a surprisingly large shop where forty-something men play with model trains and pretend that the trains they buy are for their kids. The excitingly named **Amazing Heroes** (11232 120th Ave. NE #108, 425/889-5999, noon–6 P.M. Mon.–Fri., 11 A.M.–5 P.M. Sat.) specializes in video games and collectables spanning back to the '70s. They buy and sell G.I. Joes, Transformers, and old video games and systems dating back to the Atari 2600.

Galleries

There must be something about the aura around Central Way NE and Park Lane in downtown Kirkland. It attracts art galleries almost as if by magic. The museumlike space at **Howard/Mandville Gallery** is quite large and comfortable. While you'll find the usual assortment of local artists, the owners bring in regionally and nationally known artists to keep the scene from becoming too inbred. The **Parklane Gallery** (130 Park Ln., 425/827-1462) is a little different than your usual co-op art gallery. Artists unusually remain members of only a short while—anywhere from six months to a few years. New artists must be voted in by the standing members. It's a process that results in fresh blood, and sometimes some cutting-edge art the likes of which you won't see anywhere else.

Lakeshore Gallery (107 Park Ln., 425/827-0606) fits in nicely and hangs original watercolors, acrylics, and oils right alongside fine woodworking, pottery, and blown glass.

SPORTS AND RECREATION
Boating

Kirkland is a natural jumping-off point for Lake Washington boaters hoping to get a closer look at area estates and wetland parks along the lake's perimeter. The **Kirkland Marina** is

THE EASTSIDE

the only public dock with overnight moorage available; the nearby boat launch is a popular spot to ease craft into the water. A $10 permit is required to access the launch. Permits can be picked up at the Kirkland Parks and Community Services office (505 Market St.) 8 A.M.–5 P.M., Monday–Friday. The office is closed on weekends and holidays, so plan ahead.

Nearby, Yarrow Bay Marina is a convenient place to fuel up vessels from the water. It is also a good spot to quell a little bit of boat envy. Yarrow rents 19- to 21-foot runabouts for $75 per two hours. For paddles with attitude, talk to the folks at **Northwest Paddle Surfers** (Kirkland Marina, 206/1787, http://northwestpaddlesurfers.com, 10 A.M.–7 P.M. Wed.–Sat.), who will set you up with a stand-up paddleboard with accessories for $20 per hour. Or dump the paddles and let the wind spread your sails with **Island Sailing Charters** (2nd Avenue Dock, 200 Lake St. S., 800/303-2470, www.islandsailingclub.com, 10 A.M.–5 P.M. Thurs.–Mon.). If you have basic ASA certification, you can try out their fleet of 22-foot sailboats for half a day ($70–160) or a full day ($105–370) or you can take classes at a variety of levels, offered on weekends.

Cycling and Mountain Biking

Mountain bikers and cyclists love Kirkland for its endless spaghetti bowl of quiet surface streets and its cornucopia of fat tire–friendly trails. Most popular among roadies is a curvy 15-mile out-and-back along Lake Washington. To take this route, park at St. Edward State Park and ride south along Juanita Drive Northeast. The road will curve to the northeast and eventually you'll need to turn right to head south on 98th Avenue Northeast, which turns into Market Street. From there, continue south on Lake Street, which turns into Lake Washington Boulevard and takes you to the doorsteps of Carillon Point, your turnaround spot. This commercial plaza is a good lunch spot, either in its bistros or sack-lunch style in its central plaza. Listen for the six ringing carillon bells that toll every half hour. Saint Edward

sailboats at Kirkland Marina

© ERICKA CHICKOWSKI

is also a popular stop among mountain bikers, who zigzag and bunny-hop along the wooded trails here.

If your bike is hung up in the garage back home, or if you'd simply like to give these routes a go on something other than an old beater, try **Montlake Bicycle Shop** (208 Kirkland Ave., 425/828-3800, www.montlakebike.com, 10 A.M.–7 P.M. Mon.–Fri., 9 A.M.–5 P.M. Sat., 10 A.M.–4 P.M. Sun.). It offers a range of premium road and mountain bikes for $25–125 per day.

ACCOMMODATIONS
$100-150

Kirkland's most affordable lodging is in Totem Lake. Though they might not be fancy, the motels around here are safe, close to I-405, and are usually reasonably priced. One of the better deals can be found at **Baymont Inn and Suites** (12223 NE 116th St., 425/229-6668, www.baymontinns.com, $135 s or d), which has clean rooms, an indoor spa, and continental breakfast served each morning. It is right next to the freeway, so come with earplugs or be prepared to imagine there's a very loud river nearby.

$150-200

A step up from most Totem Lake motels, the **Carlton Inn** (12233 NE Totem Lake Way, 425/821-2202, $149–169 s or d) has a much nicer interior than its worn exterior might suggest. This comfortable budget-to-midrange hotel's rooms can sometimes be had for around $100 during off-peak times. Amenities include an outdoor heated pool, indoor spa, and fitness center. Plus, it's got interior entry halls, a safety feature that many motels, such as the Baymont, lack.

Over $250

Arguably the Eastside's nicest hotel, the **Heathman Hotel** (220 Kirkland Ave., 425/284-5800 or 800/551-0011 or, www .heathmankirkland.com, $239–899 s or d) gets all of the details right. There's no front desk here because staff greets guests at the front

doorstep and personally walk them through check-in at small kiosks before whisking them away to their rooms. Not only is there a pillow menu, there's a mattress menu here as well—there are different kinds of mattresses on each floor, giving the guest a comfortable number of options. The new hotel was built ecofriendly from the ground up; smart rooms automatically switch vents off when windows are opened and turn lights off after you've left the room. If money is no object, the suites are big enough to spend a whole vacation in without darkening the doorstep—some even have jetted tubs on private patios.

The somewhat staid **Woodmark Hotel** (1200 Carillon Pt., 425/822-3700 or 800/822-3700, www.thewoodmark.com, $255–1,800 s or d), keeps an amazing secret under its red-brick and glass exterior. Inside, you'll find one of the cushiest lodging options in the area. From the grand piano in the lobby to stocked minibars, terrycloth robes, a full breakfast, Lake Washington views, and yes—TVs in the bathroom as a final touch of class. This is the only hotel on the shores of the lake, so expect to pay for what you get.

FOOD

Kirkland is blessed with a mix of quick eateries and renowned restaurants, many of which are right downtown.

Cafés and Diners

Puget Sound coffeeshops are known for taking a great deal of pride in every last single tiny piece of their operation, no matter how seemingly minute. The goal is pleasing their customers, so it's generally best to just let them have their fun. Case study: The **urban COFFEE lounge** (9744 NE 119th Way, 425/820-7788, 6 A.M.–9 P.M. Mon., 6 A.M.–10 P.M. Tues.–Sat., 7 A.M.–9 P.M. Sun.) Baristas do extensive training, all ingredients are single-sourced and the crisp pop-post-industrial decor might make you wonder if a caffeine-induced trance has lead you back to the 1960s.

Just steps away from Marina Park, **Coffee & Cone** (1 Lake Shore Plaza, 425/827-7098) is ideal for those craving a simple cup of drip coffee. It is also a great place to grab some ice cream before lounging by the lake.

Downtown's best bet for breakfast is **Hector's Restaurant** (112 Lake St., 425/827-4811, www .hectorskirkland.com, 7:30 A.M.–4 P.M. Mon.– Fri., 8 A.M.–4 P.M. Sat.–Sun. and 5–10 P.M. Mon.–Thurs., 5–11 P.M. Fri.–Sat., 5–9 P.M. Sun., $25), with an array of unique home-style breakfasts. Try the Hobo Scramble ($10.50) with potatoes, caramelized onions, mushrooms, and tomatoes. The restaurant also has a tasty lobster bisque at lunch.

Brown Bag Café (12217 NE 116th St., 425/822-9462, www.brownbagcafes.com, 6:30 A.M.–3 P.M. daily, $10) is another favorite breakfast spot, particularly good if you're staying in a nearby Totem Lake motel whose continental breakfast won't satisfy the growling tummy. Servings are substantial, and all the usual favorites are here, along with such specialties as cinnamon roll French toast and shrimp omelettes. Be prepared to wait on the weekend, when crowds throng to eat here. For a restaurant that takes great pride in their deep-fryer, visit **Juanita Spud Fish and Chips** (9702 NE Juanita Dr., 425/823-0607, http:// spudfishandchips.com, 11 A.M.–9 P.M. Sun.– Thurs., 11 A.M.–9 P.M. Fri.–Sat.). This long-time favorite serves up blue-ribbon fish and chips. Wash it down with a thick, delicious milkshake.

Contemporary Northwest

It's not unusual for a chef to be passionate about his food, but not many go through the trouble of growing it for themselves like the executive chef at **Trellis** at the Heathman Hotel (220 Kirkland Ave., 425/284-5900, www .heathmankirkland.com, hours vary, reservations recommended). Fresh organic ingredients and hundreds of wines make the experience completely worthwhile.

For another elegant option with windows on scenic Lake Washington, visit **bin on the lake** (1270 Carillon Point, 425/803-5595, binonthelake.com, 4–10 P.M. nightly $32),which takes a great deal of pride in their food and wine pairings. Let the competent wait staff help you choose the perfect vino to go with decadent dishes featuring black cod, swordfish, diver scallops, and more.

Asian

Izumi (Totem Lake West Shopping Center, 12539 116th Ave. NE, www.izumikirkland .com, 425/821-1959, 11:30 A.M.–1:30 P.M. Tues.–Fri. and 5–9 P.M. Tues.–Sun., $20) serves tasty Japanese sushi, tempura, teriyaki, and other specialties. Reasonable prices, too.

Another treat is the extremely popular **Shamiana Restaurant** (10724 NE 68th St., http://shamianarestaurant.com, 425/827-4902, 11 A.M.–2:30 P.M. Mon.–Fri. and 5–9:30 P.M. Sun.–Thurs., 5–10 P.M. Fri.–Sat., $15), a great place for Indian and Pakistani food, including a number of vegetarian specials. Lunch is an especially good deal, and there's live sitar music on Sunday and Monday evenings.

The Thin Pan (170 Lake St., 425/827-4000, 11:30 A.M.–10:00 P.M. Mon.–Thurs., 11:30 A.M.–10:30 P.M. Fri.–Sat., noon–9:30 P.M. Sun., $12) is the place to go if you can't quite make it to Thailand in time for dinner. Choose between spicy curries and tangy noodle dishes including the tasty specialty, Thin Pan Noodles, which features a thick rice noodle stir-fried with veggies and your choice of meat. The location is right in Kirkland's downtown district.

Italian

Ristorante Paradiso (120 A Park Lane, 425/889-8601, www.ristoranteparadiso.com, 11 A.M.–10:30 P.M. Mon.–Fri., 3–10:30 P.M. Sat.–Sun., $18) offers outstanding nouvelle cuisine with an Italian twist, including fresh seafood, lamb chops, and veal.

Also of interest is **Cafe Juanita** (9702 NE 120th Pl., 425/823-1505, www.cafejuanita .com, 5–10 P.M. Tues.–Sat., 5–9 P.M. Sun., $28), which offers up highly innovative fresh pastas in a scenic setting along Lake Washington just north of Kirkland. The food is dependably great, and the selection of Italian wines is noteworthy.

INFORMATION

For maps and a limited amount of other information, drop by the **Kirkland Chamber of Commerce** (upstairs in Parkplace Mall, 425/822-7066, www.kirklandchamber.org, 9 A.M.–5 P.M. Mon.–Fri.).

GETTING THERE AND AROUND
By Bus

Metro Transit (425/447-4800 or 800/542-7876, http://metro.kingcounty.gov) provides daily bus service to Kirkland from Seattle and other points in King County.

Boat Tours

Argosy Cruises (425/623-1445 or 800/642-7816, www.argosycruises.com, $30.50 adults, $27 seniors, $10.75 kids, free kids under 5) offers scenic 1.5-hour boat tours of Lake Washington, departing from Kirkland's Marina Park daily May–September, up to three tours a day July–September. These feature the lake and surrounding sights, including homes of the rich and famous.

Redmond

Redmond began as a boat landing along the Sammamish Slough, the slow-moving stream that links Lake Washington and Lake Sammamish. Today the city moves more quickly, serving as the de facto epicenter of the state's technology industry. The city is home to a number of tech companies, including Nintendo of America and—most famously—software giant Microsoft. The Microsoft campus now encompasses more than eight million square feet of office space in Redmond and has additional facilities in nearby Eastside cities and in Seattle.

SIGHTS
Museums and Churches

The **Microsoft Visitor Center** (4420 148th Ave. NE., 425/703-6214, www.microsoft.com/about/companyinformation/visitorcenter/en/us/default.aspx, 9 A.M.–7 P.M. Mon.–Fri., free) houses a few items from the company's quarter century of history, along with some signature high-tech exhibits. You can even play computer games or check your email. It's housed on the company's sprawling main campus.

Smack dab in the heart of tech country lies one of the largest Buddhist temples in the state, and you'd probably never find it if you weren't looking. **Ling Shen Ching Tze Temple** (17012 NE 40th Ct., 425/882-0916, www.tbsseattle.org/english, 9:30 A.M.–6 P.M. Mon.–Sat.) lies hidden away on an unassuming neighborhood street just a few blocks from Microsoft's main campus. Guests are invited to check out the temple and experience meditations at 8 P.M. on Saturdays.

MICROSOFT HQ

One of the largest employers in the region, Microsoft has done a lot to shape the Eastside. Nearly everyone knows of some Microsoft millionaire who made it big when the company went gangbusters in the 1990s. Nowadays it is much harder to make a million as a Microsoftie, but the company still pours a lot of wealth into Eastside communities: the sheer number of German luxury vehicles up and down State Route 520 can attest to that.

MICROSOFT FAST FACTS

- Founded: 1975
- Moved to Puget Sound: 1979
- Redmond Headquarters Established: 1986
- Puget Sound Sites: 120
- Puget Sound Employees: 40,454
- Net Income in 2008: $18.76 billion

◖ Marymoor Park

Redmond is home to King County's Marymoor Park (6046 W. Lake Sammamish Pkwy. NE, 206/205-3661), the most beautiful and varied municipal park on the Eastside. The park preserves the north end of pretty Lake Sammamish in its natural state, but also provides over 500 acres of soccer, cricket, and baseball fields, picnic grounds, a climbing wall, tennis courts, an amphitheater, and food concessions. The park has one of the largest and nicest fenced off-leash dog parks in the state. It can be fun to come here and watch the radio-controlled airplane enthusiasts perform acrobatics in the section designated just for them. Every summer, the amphitheater draws musicians of both national and local stripe for its Concerts at Marymoor series. Marymoor Park is known for its **Velodrome** (425/389-5825), a banked 400-meter bike-racing track that draws competitors from across the United States. Bike races are held Friday evenings April–November.

© ERICKA CHICKOWSKI

rock climbing wall at Marymoor Park

Other Parks

South of Marymoor Park along the west shore of Lake Sammamish, **Idylwood Park** (3650 West Lake Sammamish Pkwy. NE) is a neighborhood secret, a waterfront park treasured by the locals for quiet grassy picnics, a lazy game of catch, or a dip in the lake's chilly waters.

Kids love the 68-acre **Farrel-McWhirter Park** (10400 192nd Ave. NE) for its barnyard zoo and horse arena. The park makes for a great family afternoon with its many equestrian and hiking trails. "Charlotte's Trail" is a paved path circling the park and makes the perfect spot to test out the little one's first bike, streamers and all.

ENTERTAINMENT AND EVENTS
Nightlife

For such a small city, Redmond has a surprising number of fun watering holes. Perhaps it is the Microsoft influence—many early-retiring Microsofties tend to get their kicks opening up places they would like to enjoy themselves.

That was the case for **Celtic Bayou** (7281 W. Lake Sammamish Pkwy. NE, 425/869-5933, www.celticbayou.com), opened by an enterprising tech millionaire who thought it would be cool to marry an Irish pub with Cajun cookin'. The bizarre combo works, as the place is thronged most every weekend and on some weeknights, too.

Just down Leary Way, **Matador Restaurant and Tequila Bar** (7824 Leary Way NE, 425/883-2855, www.matadorseattle.com) offers a safer Tex-Mex menu to pair with its cocktails. Happy hour is peak time at this bar, which is set within Redmond's historic brick Brown Building. Legend has it the building's second story was the town's house of ill repute back in the 19th century. Nowadays the crowd is a little more law abiding, but the place does have an ornate saloon bar worthy of its historic surroundings.

If wine is your thing, then saunter over to **Jerzy's Wine Bar** (16727 Redmond Way, 425/702-8575, www.jerzyswinebar.com). Located in a cute two-story house on the fringe of downtown Redmond's central core,

© ERICKA CHICKOWSKI

THE EASTSIDE

Find Tex-Mex repast and plenty of libations at the trendy Matador Restaurant and Tequila Bar.

this place has a cozy atmosphere, if a somewhat limited wine list for a bar that specializes in vino. The interior is swathed in tapestries and accented with lots of wrought-iron furniture, plush barstools, and artistic blown-glass light fixtures.

Live Music
Marymoor Amphitheatre (206/205-3661, www.concertsatmarymoor.com), a relative newcomer to Seattle's cadre of outdoor music venues, has quickly established itself as one of the best. Set next to the grassy area near Clise Mansion, this stage is frequently trod by A-list acts such as Sheryl Crow, the Doobie Brothers, Erykah Badu, G-Love and Special Sauce, and Willie Nelson. During the summer it is also the venue for a series of free movie nights.

Festivals and Events
Head to Marymoor Park on the 4th of July weekend for the very popular **Heritage Festival** (425/296-2964) with arts and crafts, music, ethnic dancing, and food booths.

The **Redmond Bicycle Derby Days** (425/885-4014, http://redmondderbydays.com)

in mid-July is a major cycling event with street criterion bike races, a carnival, an antique car show, parades, arts and crafts, and plenty of food. It has been going on since 1939.

The **Redmond Saturday Market** (7730 Leary Way, 425/556-0636, www.redmond saturdaymarket.org, 9 A.M.–3 P.M. Sat. May–Oct.) brings fresh veggies, flowers, crafts, fruit, honey, and more downtown.

The **Evergreen Classic Horse Show** (www.evergreenclassic.com)—one of the top 10 equestrian shows in the nation—takes place at Marymoor Park each August.

SHOPPING
Redmond's shopping centerpiece is **Redmond Town Center** (16495 NE 74th St., 425/867-0808, www.redmondtowncenter.com), an outdoor mall with 110 stores. Most shops are smaller boutiques, with only a couple of large anchors, including Macy's, REI, and Aeropostale.

SPORTS AND RECREATION
Sammamish River Trail
The paved 13-mile Sammamish River Trail

begins in Marymoor Park and follows the river through Redmond, Woodinville, and on to Kenmore. There it connects with Seattle's Burke-Gilman Trail, which continues all the way to Fremont, a total distance of approximately 27 miles. This immensely popular path provides Mount Rainier and Lake Washington views and passes the Chateau Ste. Michelle and Columbia wineries, favorite stopping places. The **Puget Power-Redmond Trail** is a three-mile gravel path (great for mountain bikes) that connects the Sammamish River Trail to Farrel-McWhirter Park.

Cycling

As the self-professed Bicycle Capital of the Northwest, Redmond is home to a number of bike shops, but only one of them rents bikes. **Redmond Cycle** (16205 Redmond Way, 425/885-6363, www.redmondcycle.com) rents adult hybrids for $10 per hour or $30 per day. It also has a good selection of steeds for sale, along with a repair shop, parts, and tools. Washington-based **REI** (7500 166th Ave. N, 425/882-1158, 10 A.M.–9 P.M. Mon.–Fri., 10 A.M.–8 P.M. Sat., 11 A.M.–7 P.M. Sun.) has a store in the centrally located Redmond Town Center. It sells top-end cycles and can perform anything from a tire-inflation to the most complicated bike repair at their full-service cycle shop.

If you don't see the accessories or other bike-related miscellanea your pedaling little heart desires, then check out **Sammamish Valley Cycle** (8451 164th Ave. NE, 425/881-8442, www.sammamishcycle.com) or **Gerk's Alpine Hut** (7875 Leary Way, 425/883-7544, www.gerksalpinehut.com). All three are within an easy five-minute ride of one another.

Golf

Known as one of the Eastside's best public links, **Willows Run** (10402 Willows Rd. NE, 425/883-1200, www.willowsrun.com) is a first-class facility with a little something for every type of golfer. The grounds are home to two challenging 18-hole courses with tall grass and water hazards lurking around every

dogleg. There's also a shorter, nine-hole, family pitch-and-putt course, as well as a fun putting course that puts the average miniature golf course to shame.

If tee-times are in short supply at Willows, give **The Golf Club at Redmond Ridge** (11825 Trilogy Pkwy. NE, 425/836-1510,) a try. Situated within a quiet suburban setting, The Golf Club's par-70 course is well known for its meticulously groomed greens and fairways.

Hot-Air Ballooning

The Balloon Depot (16138 NE 87th St., 425/881-9699 or 877/881-9699, www.balloondepot.com) lifts off with hot-air balloon rides most mornings and evenings. Morning flights are $189 per person daily. Evening flights are $210 and include a buffet dinner.

ACCOMMODATIONS

Cottage Creek Inn B&B (425/881-5606, www.cottagecreekinn.com, $120–165 s or d) is a Tudor-style manor home in a beautiful country setting with an attractive garden and hot tub. The four guest rooms include private baths and a full breakfast each morning.

Redmond Inn (15304 NE 21st St., 425/883-4900 or 800/634-8080, www.redmondinn.com, $103–129 s or d) features an outdoor pool and hot tub. Rates include a continental breakfast.

Surrounded by the stores and restaurants of Redmond Town Center, **Redmond Marriott Town Center** (7401 164th Ave. NE, 425/498-4000, $239 d) is a favorite among business travelers working with Microsoft, which means weekenders can usually sneak in with some pretty amazing rates (as low as $100 a night). The business-class amenities can be a nice change of pace for those used to humbler digs. Rooms come with huge bathrooms, oversized flat-screen TVs, and fluffy quilted-top beds. There's a fee for Internet, but for around $14 you'll get unlimited local long distance and local calls, plus wired or wireless connectivity. Downstairs, saunter past the fireplace lobby and enjoy wine and appetizers at the wine bar.

There's also a fitness center and business center on premises.

FOOD
Cafés and Delis

Redmond has a great selection of coffee shops above and beyond the Starbucks stores that you will literally find one across the street from another. Camouflaged as a New Age bookstore, **Soulfood Books** (15748 Redmond Way, 425/881-5309, www.soulfoodbooks.com, 9 A.M.–6 P.M. Sun.–Tues., 9 A.M.–9 P.M. Wed.–Thurs., 9 A.M.–10 P.M. Fri.–Sat.) is actually a pleasant little coffee shop to boot. The coffee is good, if a little pricy, and, of course, organic. They've got live music, usually focused on mellow guitar jams and hypnotizing drums. If you're more interested in a crema-topped espresso and less about joining a tribal community, order up at **Sorrento Coffee** (22310 NE Marketplace Dr., 425/898-9787, http://sorrentoscoffee.com, 5 A.M.–7 P.M. Mon.–Fri., 6 A.M.–6 P.M. Sat.–Sun.). They make all the standards plus enough sweet flavored coffee drinks to fill a diabetic's nightmares. They welcome dogs, as well, even if they're muddy from a romp at Marymoor. **Victor's Coffee** (7993 Gilman St., 425/881-6451, www.victorscelticcoffee.com, 5:30 A.M.–7 P.M. Mon.–Fri., 7 A.M.–7 P.M. Sat., 8 A.M.–6 P.M. Sun.) is one of the best coffee joints on the Eastside. Here, they won't chase you off right after your cup has run dry, even offering board games and paperbacks in case you're in no hurry to get back into the cold drizzle outside.

Redmond Way and roundabout is also packed so tightly with the major chains—Starbucks, Peet's and Tully's—that if you can't find one on your own, then your needs might be greater than caffeine and a guide-book.

For a delicious, if busy, Sunday brunch, try **Village Square Café** (16150 NE 85th, 425/885-7287, 6 A.M.–3 P.M. Mon.–Sat., 7 A.M.–3 P.M. Sun., $11). **Mikie's Brooklyn Bagel Deli** (16640 Redmond Way, 425/881-3344, www.mikiesbagel.com, 6:30 A.M.–4 P.M.

Mon.–Fri., 7:30 A.M.–3:30 P.M. Sat., closed Sun., $6) has fresh-baked breads and deli meats from New York; locals call the bagels here the most authentic on the Eastside.

Asian

Microsoft and other tech companies have brought an influx of Indian and Pakistani workers into Redmond on temporary work visas. That's good news for foodies hankering for a good curry or tandoori chicken, as numerous Indian places have cropped up in recent years to satisfy demand. Perhaps the best Indian place on the Eastside, if not the entire Seattle area, is **Kanishka** (16651 Redmond Way, 425/869-9182, www.kanishkaofredmond.com, buffet is 11 A.M.–2:30 P.M. Mon.–Fri., 11:30 A.M.–3 P.M. Sat.–Sun. and 5–10 P.M. daily, $12) in downtown Redmond. Flavors are evocative and complex, ingredients are fresh, and the steady procession of Indians through the door attest to the fact that the genuine article is served here.

Kikuya (8105 161st Ave. NE, 425/881-8771, 11:30 A.M.–2 P.M. and 5–9 P.M. daily, $16) is a wonderful small Japanese restaurant with friendly service and high-quality food. But don't come here on a weekend evening unless you're ready to wait. No need to dress up to sup on Redmond's best teriyaki. **Yummy Teriyaki** (17218 Redmond Way, 425/861-1010, 10:30 A.M.–9 P.M. Mon.–Sat., $8) is a nice and comfy jeans-and-T-shirt kind of place where you order up front and take a plastic number to your table. Dishes are huge, so come with an appetite or a partner to share your plate.

Italian

Don't let the strip mall location at **Tropea Ristorante Italiano** (8042 161st Ave. NE, 425/867-1082, www.ristorantetropea.com, 11 A.M.–2 P.M. Mon.–Fri. and 4:30–10 P.M. Sat.–Sun., 4:30–10 P.M. Fri.–Sat., $18) fool you. Inside, just past the cultivated bushes grown by the door as a screen, there is a charming grotto serving up Southwestern Italian fare.

The seafood pastas are especially scrumptious. Portions are huge, so be sure to take some of your dinner home to save room for dessert. The homemade fruit sorbets are to die for and beautifully presented in the flavor's corresponding fruit rind.

INFORMATION

The **Greater Redmond Chamber of Commerce** (16210 NE 80th St., 425/885-4014, www.redmondchamber.org, 9 A.M.–5 P.M. Mon.–Fri.) has local information, including a "visitor's packet."

GETTING THERE AND AROUND

Metro Transit (800/542-7876, http://metro .kingcounty.gov/) has daily bus service around Redmond, on to Seattle and Bellevue, and throughout King County.

Issaquah

Settled between the foot of an impressive set of Cascade foothills and the southern tip of Lake Sammamish, Issaquah (ISS-a-kwa) offers an escape to country-fresh air in a fast-growing town loaded with history. Native Americans fished the lake and picked berries on nearby hillsides well into the 19th century. These first inhabitants called this place "Squak," a native term meaning "the sound of birds." To white settlers, the Native American word sounded something like "Issaquah." Later, coal mining on nearby Cougar and Squak mountains fueled an economic boom in the area, lasting a few decades before the mines became depleted. Some signs of turn-of-the-century mining can still be found along the hiking trails on these mountains.

From coal-mining to logging to suburban development, the impressive Issaquah Alps remain unblemished, preserved in their forested state for all to enjoy. These very old, glacial-worn mountains are at an elevation low enough to keep them hikeably snow-free virtually year-round.

The town itself is a pleasant place to enjoy the blend of old and new. Historic buildings are next to shiny new office complexes. You can even find traces of Issaquah's farming legacy at the Darigold creamery, which still produces all of the company's yogurt sold in the Northwest.

CARRYING COALS TO NEWCASTLE

When people think of American coal mining, they usually imagine the bluegrass hills of Kentucky, Pennsylvania, and West Virginia. Even some locals don't realize that the Eastside cities of Issaquah and Newcastle once had their own coal boom beginning in 1890. Over a brief 20 years or so, the mountains east of the Puget Sound produced tens of thousands of tons of coal. Underground mines burrowed all over the region, with the richest veins located on Squak and Cougar Mountains. When the coal market took a hit just after the turn of the century, unsentimental miners packed up and headed for other mines elsewhere.

Fans of enormous holes and rusting metal can see plenty of both along the 36-mile trail system that ribbons its way though Cougar Mountain. Several interpretive markers provide useful background, and the remaining machinery and building foundations provide some perspective of how tough it must have been to dig and transport coal among the hills, black bears, and mountain lions.

HISTORICAL ISSAQUAH

The Issaquah coal mines may have shut down over 120 years ago, but there's still plenty left to visit. Some buildings, such as the miner's homes, are still in use today. Drive down Newport Way to Park Boulevard and turn right onto Wildwood for a look. A depression in the ground at the end of the block marks the entrance to the mine's first shaft. To the right is the concrete bulkhead used to anchor the mine's hauling machinery.

Actual rusting coal-mining equipment, dangling steel cables, grated mineshafts, and other trappings of coal mining can be seen on **Tiger Mountain** along the Red Town Trail. They seem to be right where the miners abandoned them while leaving the site.

Quaint little downtown Issaquah still has an **Odd Fellows Hall,** built in 1888. The 1903 **Grand Central Hotel** now houses offices and apartments. And if you follow the tracks to Sunset Way, you'll find the **Railroad Depot,** built in 1889, as Washington was on the verge of statehood but still known as Washington Territory, hence the "W.T." symbol on the facade.

SIGHTS
Museums

The **Gilman Town Hall Museum** (165 SE Andrews, 425/392-3500, www.issaquahhistory.org, 11 A.M.–3 P.M. Thurs., Fri., and Sat., $2 adults and $1 children) building, built in the 1890s, served as the original town hall, back when Issaquah was known as Gilman. Railroad tools, children's toys, a pioneer kitchen and grocery store, artifacts, and many historical photographs are on display inside. Don't miss the old two-cell town jail around back.

Issaquah Train Depot Museum (Front and Sunset Sts., 425/392-2322, www.issaquahhistory.org, 11 A.M.–3 P.M. Fri.–Sun., $2 adults, $1 children) in the restored 1889 train depot offers a collection of historical photos and artifacts. Of course, the vintage caboose and other railcars on display outside the station completely steal the show.

Boehm's Candies

Candy lovers, try to visit the Swiss-style building that houses Boehm's Candies (255 NE Gilman Blvd., 425/392-6652, www.boehms.com, 9 A.M.–3 P.M. Mon.–Fri.). Free candy factory tours are offered July–mid-September by appointment. If you can't get on a tour, just walk outside and peek in the side windows. Adjacent to the chocolate factory is a shady garden with a replica of a Swiss chapel.

◖ Cougar Mountain Zoo

Issaquah's very own zoo (19525 SE 54th St., 425/391-5508, www.cougarmountainzoo.org, 9:30 A.M.–5 P.M. Wed.–Sun. Jan.–Nov., 10 A.M.–4:30 P.M. daily Dec. 1–23, 11 A.M.–3 P.M. daily Dec. 26–30, $11 adults, $10.50 seniors, $9 ages 2–12, free under 2) is one of the more unusual in Washington, emphasizing threatened or endangered animals from around the globe, including the Formosa Sika elk and hyacinthine macaw. The real attraction, though, is the cougars. If you looked them eye-to-eye this closely on a nearby trail, you'd probably need to change your pants. But here, it's an encounter all in the name of entertainment. Visitors to the zoo are treated to highly informative tours by the helpful docents and staff.

Issaquah State Salmon Hatchery

The Issaquah State Salmon Hatchery (125 W. Sunset Way, 425/392-3180, www.issaquahfish.org, daylight hours daily, 8 A.M.–4 P.M. daily for indoor exhibits) raises five million chinook and one million coho salmon annually for release into Issaquah Creek. Built in 1936, the hatchery is a good place to learn about the life cycle of salmon and how they are raised. The grounds are open dawn–dusk daily, with tours in late summer.

ENTERTAINMENT AND EVENTS
The Arts

The semiprofessional **Village Theatre** (303 Front St. N, 425/392-2202, www.villagetheatre.org) puts on first-rate productions in its modern 488-seat theater (complete with a soundproof room for screaming babies). Theatrical productions are generally on the light side, with a heavy dose of musical favorites.

Festivals and Events

Issaquah's **Down Home 4th of July Parade** is fun for everyone, with all the usual events. Every fall, salmon return to their birthplace at the state salmon hatchery, and Issaquah doesn't miss the opportunity for a celebration. The two-day **Issaquah Salmon Days** (206/270-2532, www.salmondays.org) comes around the first weekend in October with a parade, kids fair, 350 arts and crafts booths, live music, a pancake feed, fun run, and hatchery tours. More than 200,000 people crowd downtown Issaquah for the somewhat untraditional festival. The **Issaquah Reindeer Festival** (425/391-5508, www.cougarmountainzoo.org) takes place at Cougar Mountain Zoo in December, with thousands of twinkling lights, plus Santa and his herd of real live Siberian reindeer.

SHOPPING

Issaquah's **Gilman Village** (317 NW Gilman Blvd., 425/392-6802, www.gilmanvillage.com) is the fruit of the labor of Marvin and Ruth Mohl, who in 1972 decided it would be too much of a shame for several dilapidated 19th century Issaquah homes to meet the bulldozer, making room for new construction. They began the process that would result in a cute shopping center with dozens of boutiques and specialty shops. Now you'll find jewelry, clothing, spas, health studios, and plenty of interesting stuff to browse on a lazy day. Local fashion diva **Lizzie Parker** (317 NW Gilman Blvd. Ste. 22, 425/427-0708, www.lizzieparker.com) works with a small team to create original fashions that have received a good deal of national attention. She concentrates on using the most ecofriendly materials and methods available. She releases four lines per year, for sale only in her boutique or online. Make time for **Aubrey's Clock Gallery** (317 NW Gilman Blvd., 425/392-5200, 10 A.M.–6 P.M. Mon.–Sat., noon–5 P.M. Sun.) Their cuckoo collection runs the gamut from grandfather clocks to designer wristwatches. For your art needs, drop by **Revolution** (317 NW Gilman Blvd. #26, Gillman Village, 425/392-4982, www.revolutiongallery.com/), a gallery committed to supporting local artists and featuring less common media like fused art glass, fine woodworking, and mosaics.

SPORTS AND RECREATION
The Issaquah Alps

As "Trailhead City," Issaquah takes pride in the Issaquah Alps, a chain of nearby mountains older than the Cascades. Just two exits east of Renton on I-90, these venerable foothills are within an easy half-hour drive of Seattle or Tacoma.

You can start exploring on your own or with help from the **Issaquah Alps Trails Club** (425/328-0480, www.issaquahalps.org), which organizes hikes every Saturday and Sunday, and some during the week, to points of interest along 200 miles of trails. No membership or previous registration is necessary.

The crown jewel of the Alps is **Tiger Mountain State Forest,** which covers 13,500 acres of forested lands that easily make up the state's most popular hiking area, attracting hundreds of hikers and mountain bikers on sunny summer days. Try bagging the peak of 3,004-foot tall **East Tiger Mountain** to soak up Tiger's views of Issaquah and beyond. To reach the trailhead, take I-90 exit 25; go right onto Highway 18 and drive three miles to a dirt road on the right; proceed to the power line and park. Start your seven-mile hike on the uphill road under the power line.

Cougar Mountain Regional Wildland Park (www.kingcounty.gov/recreation/parks) encompasses second-growth forests surrounding this 1,595-foot peak, with well-marked trails

NIKE MISSILE BASES

In the early days of the Cold War, the heightened fear that the Soviets would "just do it" and bomb the daylights out of America's West Coast led to a novel program. The U.S. Army established a series of hilltop bases equipped with so-called Nike missiles. The idea was to blast the heavy Soviet bombers out of the sky before they could drop fiery death on U.S. cities. By the mid-1960s, intercontinental ballistic missiles made these bases seem quaint at best. Most were decommissioned, demilitarized, and turned over to civilian authorities to be demolished and developed or turned into parks. Today, you can still see quite a few of these relics around the state of Washington.

Site S-20 is at the end of a short hike to the peak of Issaquah's Cougar Mountain. While there are no interpretive displays, it's fun to tromp around atop the steel-plate former silos or wait out the rain in the now-mossy guard shack. Nearby Redmond is home to **Sites S-13** and **S-14,** which are now, respectively, school buildings and a nice grassy park, aptly named Nike Park. Even on swanky Vashon Island, you can visit **Site S-61,** the outbuildings of which now house a variety of local businesses and the field of which has been transformed into a horse park.

winding through deep, damp woods past long stretches of solitude or up to relics of an old U.S. Air Force missile site near the peak. While there are absolutely cougars (aka mountain lions) here, the park is busy enough to keep them back in the darker recesses. To get just a taste of the mountain, try the one-mile Red Town Trail that wanders alongside abandoned coal mining equipment and the titular town, although the latter is burned, grown over, and completely reabsorbed into the forest. Headed east on I-90, you'll want to take exit 13—West Lake Sammamish/SE Newport Way. Turn right onto Lakemont Boulevard SE and follow for just over three miles. You'll see the parking lot on the left marked "Cougar Mountain Regional Wildland Park." The trailhead is exceptionally well-marked.

Squak Mountain State Park gets less attention from the locals, but it can still make for a nice day of hiking. Many of the trails are coal-mining and logging roads that are slowly returning to nature. The West Side Trail is definitely the best entry-level hike on the mountain. It leads up to a stone fireplace and chimney—the only remains of an old burned-out cabin. From there, a little leg and lung power will get you to a vantage point overlooking Issaquah and Renton, and maybe even the mountains. If you're heading east on I-90 toward Issaquah, take exit 15. It will take you to State Route 900, which leads to a little parking lot on your left near mile-marker 19. If there's no parking in the lot, shoulder parking is allowed on State Route 900. Squak Mountain is a little less formally organized. The trail is sometimes called the West Access Trail, the West Side Trail, or the Bullitt Chimney Trail. You can absolutely get lost in the woods here, so bring water, snacks, a map and compass if possible, and plenty of awareness. You can learn more at www.parks.wa.gov or www.wta.org.

Paragliding

There are more exhilarating ways of seeing Tiger Mountain than huffing it in hiking boots. On any warm summer afternoon you're bound to see the brightly colored paragliders gently drift across the deep blue sky on their way from peak to parking lot. Why just watch when you can take your own flight with **Seattle Paragliding** (11206 Issaquah Hobart Rd. SE, 206/387-3477, www.seattleparagliding.com)? You can go through instruction and become a certified pilot for around $1,800, but more than likely, a hit-the-ground-running tandem flight with one of its pilots would serve you best at $175 weekdays or $195 weekends. Also, when you hit the ground, be sure that you are running.

RAINDROPS ARE FALLIN' ON MY SKIN

If you think the chilly drizzle is tough enough with a fleece jacket and mittens, take a moment to offer respect to the brave, naked souls at Tiger Mountain's **Fraternity Snoqualmie Nudist Park** (425/392-NUDE). The park is virtually invisible to all but those intrepid individuals who know it's there. The 40-acre family-friendly spread sponsors events throughout the year like the clothing-optional Bare Buns Fun Run and the summer music festival **Nudestock.**

Horseback Riding

Even if you've had no prior experience, riding a horse along wooded trails can be a relaxing, enjoyable way to view the scenery. **Tiger Mountain Stables** (132nd Ave., 425/392-5090) offers guided three-hour trips in Tiger Mountain State Forest. **High Country Outfitters** (23836 SE 24th, 888/235-0111, www.campwahoo.com) leads trail rides and overnight trips into the Cascades.

Water Sports

Just over 1.5 miles northwest of Issaquah, **Lake Sammamish State Park** (425/455-7010, www.parks.wa.gov, no camping) is one of the more popular Puget Sound area parks. Facilities include a big sandy beach for sunbathing and swimming, a swimming float, boat ramps, picnic tables, hiking trails, and a concession stand selling fast food. The smooth lake with views of trees and mountains is a worldwide destination for wakeboarders who strap in to an aquatic snowboard and carve the waves behind a fast-moving boat. Unfortunately, the only way to take part is to bring your own boat and board or be charismatic enough to make fast friends with someone who will take you out. **Issaquah Paddle Sports** (425/891-5039 or 206/527-1825, http://issaquahpaddlesports .com) offers sea kayak tours, lessons, and summertime rentals on Lake Sammamish.

Owners of smaller motorboats, canoes, and rafts may prefer **Pine Lake** (off 228th Ave. SE), a nearby county park with a five-mph speed limit on its lake and lots of fish willing to rise for bait.

ACCOMMODATIONS
Under $100

There are two motels available on the east side of Issaquah. Standard, inexpensive motel rooms can be found at **Motel 6** (1885 15th Pl. NW at I-90 exit 15, 425/392-8405 or 800/466-8356, www.motel6.com, $60 s or $66 d), including an outdoor pool. You'll find more refined accommodations at **Issaquah Holiday Inn** (1801 12th Ave. NW, 425/392-6421 or 800/465-4329, www.hi.com, $120–107 s or d). Amenities include a salmon-shaped outdoor pool, sauna, and hot tub.

$150-200

Lakehouse Bed & Breakfast (415 E. Lake Sammamish Pkwy., 425/868-7536, www.lake housebb.net, $120–200 d, additional $10 fee for a one-night stay) is beside Lake Sammamish. Two of the rooms have fetching polished hardwood floors. Innkeepers emphasize organic and in-season ingredients in their breakfast dishes, and guests are encouraged to take advantage of the property's row boat to work it all off after indulging. There are three rooms here, the best of which features French doors opening up directly out to the lake. Quite a few innkeepers claim that their property is "unique," but **Treehouse Point** (6922 Preston-Fall City Rd. SE, 425/441-8087, www.treehousepoint .com, $140–215) makes all the rest look like conformists. True to its name, the four cabins are literally posted in tall trees. Styles range from a smaller unit with a shed-style roof to a two-story treehouse that seems inspired by ultramodern minimalist architecture. It's worth seeing even if you don't spend the night.

Camping

Although there are no public campgrounds near Issaquah, you can camp in comfort at the 120-acre **Issaquah Highlands Camping Club**

(10610 Renton-Issaquah Rd. SE, 425/392-2351). It's far enough out of town to get that woodsy feeling. The park works to maintain a family atmosphere and is proud of the level of security it is able to provide. There's a nice library if you get bored with hiking the trails abutting the campground. **Issaquah Village RV Park** (50 1st Ave. NE, 425/392-9233 or 800/258-9233, $47) is one of the best campgrounds close to Seattle. It's close to the highway, with both the good and bad that brings. The Issaquah Village has some pull-through sites and clean showers and laundry facilities. **Blue Sky RV Park** (9002 302nd Ave. SE in Preston, 425/222-7910, www.bluesky preston.com, $35) Unlike genuine Seattle blue sky, this campground butting up against Tiger Mountain is always there for you. All the pads are paved and there is a gazebo for guests' use.

FOOD

Issaquah has a surprising diversity of restaurants serving everything from fast food to gourmet fare. Several of the best are in **Gilman Village** (317 NW Gilman Blvd.), where the historic buildings add to the ambience. Despite appearances, the restaurants here are far from the tea and cucumber-sandwich variety. Instead, they are mostly focused around an international palate and sometimes quite exotic. If you've never tried Afghani and Persian food, treat yourself at **Bamiyan** (317 NW Gilman Blvd. Ste. 91D, 425/391-8081). They serve lamb and chicken with eastern spices. **Tantalus Restaurant** (425/391-6090, http://tantalusrestaurant.com, 11:15 A.M.–9 P.M. daily, $14), featuring Greek specialties, and **Ristorante Nicolino Italiano** (425/391-8077, 11:30 A.M.–2 P.M. Mon.–Fri., 5–9 P.M. Sun.–Thurs., 5–10 P.M. Fri.–Sat., $16), with deliciously authentic southern Italian dinners.

Don't just limit yourself to Gilman Village, though. Housed in the Village Theatre building, **Fins Bistro Seafood Restaurant** (303 Front St. N., 425/392-0109, http://fins-bistro.net, 11 A.M.–9 P.M. Tues.–Thurs., 9 A.M.–10 P.M. Fri., 4–8 P.M. Sun, closed Mon.,

$19) is an elegant café with fresh-from-the-sea specials.

The Chinese food is tasty at **Mandarin Garden** (40 E. Sunset Way, 425/392-9476, http://mandaringardenissaquah.com, 10 A.M.–9:30 P.M. Sun.–Thurs., 11 A.M.–10 P.M. Fri.–Sat., $9).

Home of Bullfrog Ale, **Issaquah Brewhouse** (35 W. Sunset Way, 425/557-1911, www.rogue.com 11:30 A.M.–10:30 P.M. daily, $12) boasts up to a dozen beers on tap, all brewed on-site. Beyond the specialty beers, expect a surprisingly diverse menu ranging from Kurobuta Kurizo tacos to towering burgers, all the way down to deep-fried frog's legs.

XXX Rootbeer Drive-In (98 NE Holly St., 425/392-1266, www.triplexrootbeer.com, 11 A.M.–9 P.M. daily, $6) is a double-barrel explosion of nostalgia, with burgers, shakes, and the best root beer around. On summer weekends, the parking lot overflows with dozens of vintage cars. For greater historical realism, the XXX does not accept credit or debit cards.

Don't even think of having a burger without a float at XXX Rootbeer Drive-In.

THE EASTSIDE

© ERICKA CHICKOWSKI

The **Issaquah Farmers Market** (425/837-3321, 9 A.M.–2 P.M. Sat. mid-Apr.–Oct.), located in the Pickering Barn off 10th Avenue, features all sorts of handicrafts, fresh produce, food vendors, and mini-concerts.

Get quality cuts of meat and fresh smoked salmon at **Fischer's Meats and Seafoods** (85 Front St. N, 425/392-3131, www.fischermeatsnw.com), serving discerning carnivores since 1910.

INFORMATION

For maps and information, contact the **Issaquah Visitor Information Center** (155 NW Gilman Blvd., 425/392-7024, www.issaquah.org, 9 A.M.–5 P.M. daily). It's housed in the beautiful historic Alexander house surrounded by rose bushes.

The impressive, modern **Issaquah Library** (Front St. and Sunset Way, 425/392-5430, www.kcls.org) is located in the heart of downtown.

GETTING THERE AND AROUND

You can get to and from Seattle, Bellevue, and other points in King County via **Metro Transit** (425/447-4800 or 800/542-7876, http://metro.kingcounty.gov).

Woodinville and Bothell

Two cities side by side on the fringes of the Eastside have plenty in common. Both towns started out in the late 1800s as farming and logging communities. Both got a big boost during WWII, and both sort of languished for many years after. In fact, the two are so generally similar in nature that Bothell tried its best to officially annex its neighbor in the 1990s, but different enough that Woodinville fought tooth-and-nail and retained its independence. Today, Bothell and Woodinville have gained a huge economic benefit from Microsoft, as more and more current and former executives build grand (if bland) homes on former pasture land. The country feel is far from gone, too. Drive around Woodinville and you're sure to see horses in front-yard dirt rings, maybe even at farmhouses with a Hummer in the driveway. Deer dash out into roads connecting multimillion-dollar homes. And an unguarded silky terrier in the yard could very well become a snack for a marauding mountain lion or sharp-eyed eagle. In recent years, Bothell has pulled ahead of sleepy Woodinville economically, enticing biotech, computer, engineering, and media companies to set up shop. But Woodinville has her parks, bike trails, and wineries still, not too concerned with any comparison you make.

SIGHTS
◖ Bothell Landing

The featured attraction in Bothell is Bothell Landing (18120 NE Bothell Way), where a park and a small shopping complex mark the original steamboat berth along the Sammamish Slough. The museum is housed in the 1893 William Hannan cabin. Cross the footbridge behind the museum to pick up the **Sammamish River Trail** and follow it east to Marymoor Park in Redmond, or head west on the **Burke-Gilman Trail** to Seattle.

◖ Chateau Ste. Michelle Winery

Surrounded by 87 acres of manicured grounds that include experimental vineyards, an arboretum, and trout ponds, Chateau Ste. Michelle (14111 NE 145th St., 425/415-3300, www.ste-michelle.com) in Woodinville is one of the state's largest and oldest wineries. Established shortly after the end of Prohibition, the winery has come to represent the Washington wine industry to the rest of the country, if not the world. Though the wine grapes are grown (and most of the wine is produced) in eastern Washington, this winery is among the nicest to visit in the state.

The winery's iconic chateau was built in 1912 and offers informative cellar tours and

© ERICKA CHICKOWSKI

Chateau Ste. Michelle

free tastings every half-hour 10 A.M.–4:30 P.M. daily, except Christmas and New Year's Day. Weekends can get pretty hectic, so try to plan your visit on a Monday or Tuesday. The tour includes a tasting of four different wines, but you're free to sample more even if you don't take the tour.

The grounds are also home to an amphitheater that hosts **Summer Festival on the Green,** a full summer of music and arts events with picnics on the lawn.

Columbia Winery

Directly across the road from Chateau Ste. Michelle you'll find the pretty faux-Victorian home of the Columbia Winery (425/488-2776 or 800/488-2347, www.columbiawinery.com, www.columbiawinery.com, 11 A.M.–6 P.M. Sun.–Thurs., 11 A.M.–7 P.M. Wed.–Sat, 11 A.M.–8 P.M. Thurs. during summer, closed holidays). Founded in 1962 by a group of University of Washington professors, Columbia produces award-winning chardonnay, semillon, cabernet sauvignon, and merlot, among others.

Sample five wines for $5 per person, which includes guidance and educational remarks provided by staff experts. The tasting is offered 11 A.M.–6 P.M., Sunday through Thursday and 11 A.M. through 6 P.M. Wednesday through Saturday. The best time to visit is during the grape crush in September and October.

Other Winery Tours

Woodinville is home to literally dozens of vintners, all with their unique take on the fruit of the vine. Perhaps taking the term "wine flight" a bit too seriously, **Airfield Estates** (14450 Woodinville-Redmond Rd., 425/877-1006, www.airfieldwines.com, noon–5 P.M. weekdays, 11 A.M.–6 P.M. weekends Apr.–Oct., noon–5 P.M. Mon.–Thurs., noon–6 P.M. Fri.–Sun. Nov.–Mar., $15) themes its winery around military aviation, especially of the WWII era. Its extensive offerings aim to satisfy both the hoary wine snob and the new recruit. Two small wineries are also located in Woodinville. **Silver Lake Winery** (15029-A Woodinville-Redmond Rd., 425/485-2437,

www.silverlakewinery.com, 11 A.M.–5 P.M.
Mon.–Sat., noon–5 P.M. Sun.) is the largest customer-owned winery in Washington
and offers the Glen Fiona and Hoodsport
labels as well. Little **Facelli Winery** (16120
Woodinville-Redmond Rd., 425/488-1020,
www.facelliwinery.com, noon–4 P.M. Sat.–
Sun.), a small family operation, produces a
mere 2,500 cases annually focused on varietal
wines. Rather than a stately chalet, their tasting room is in a Woodinville business park,
but don't let that make you think they don't
absolutely love their wines.

Butler Seattle (206/233-9233, www
.butlerseattle.com/wine-tours) can arrange
custom tours including time at Chateau Ste.
Michelle, Columbia Winery, and Silver Lake
Winery, plus a lunch and wine-tasting.

Redhook Ale Brewery

Woodinville is more than fine wine. The
Columbia Winery is practically within dart-
throwing range of the Redhook Ale Brewery
(14300 NE 145th St., 425/483-3232, www
.redhook.com). This large brewery is one of
two operated by Redhook. The brewery's
bustling pub, **Forecasters Public House**
(11 A.M.–10 P.M. Mon.–Thurs., 11 A.M.–midnight Fri.–Sat., 11 A.M.–8 P.M. Sun., open one
hour later on Sundays between Memorial Day
and Labor Day) has all of Redhook's beers on
tap and the best burgers around. On the weekend, you're likely to find the patio full of cyclists from the adjacent Burke-Gilman Trail.

FESTIVALS AND EVENTS

In Woodinville, local events include late
March's madcap **All Fool's Day Parade** (www
.woodinvillechamber.org/All-Fools-2011.aspx)
full of costumed revelry and even, on occa-
sion, antics. The very popular **Woodinville
Wine Festival** is held in September. Chateau
Ste. Michelle hosts **Summer Concerts on the
Green** on their premises. Tickets are available
from Ticketmaster (206/628-0888, www
.ticketmaster.com). In addition, free **Summer
Concerts** take place at noon on Thursday in
DeYoung Park in downtown Woodinville and

evening concerts (425/398-9327) are held on
Sundays at City Hall Plaza.

The **Woodinville Farmers Market** (13209
NE 175th, 425/485-1042, 9 A.M.–5 P.M. Sat.) is
held in downtown Woodinville, in support of
local farmers, whose products are featured exclusively. The market runs April–mid-October.

Bothell's **4th of July** celebration is a fun
event, with both a children's parade and a
grand parade through town. Also popular is
the free **Music in the Park** series on Friday
evenings in July and August.

SPORTS AND RECREATION

For a bit of fresh Woodinville air try the **Tolt
Pipeline Trail,** an 11-mile hiking and horse
trail that passes through town and extends
to Snoqualmie Valley near Duvall. Find the
trailhead just around the corner from Chateau
Ste. Michelle. The paved **Sammamish River
Trail** passes through on the other side of Ste.
Michelle on its way north and west to Bothell
and Seattle, or south to Redmond.

Hot-air ballooning is a popular attraction in
Woodinville. Flights leave Woodinville twice

Sammamish River Trail

© ERICKA CHICKOWSKI

daily from mid-June through mid-September. Contact **Over the Rainbow Balloon Flights** (425/861-8611, www.letsgoballooning.com) for details.

ACCOMMODATIONS

Willows Lodge (425/424-3900 or 877/424-3930, www.willowslodge.com, $220–290 d, $350–750 suites) is a fashionable hotel directly across from the Herbfarm and Barking Frog restaurants, and just a short walk from the Chateau Ste. Michelle and Columbia wineries. The rooms are nicely appointed and include all the amenities that well-heeled business travelers may want, including Australian lamb's-wool mattress pads, private patios, 40-inch HDTVs, robes, and free Wi-Fi. Its spa is open to the public as well, offering massage, facials, and much more. Plus, they are pet friendly.

For those of us who have to look at the check before we sign it, there is **SpringHill Suites by Marriott** (3850 Monte Villa Pkwy., 425/398-9700 or 888/287-9400, www.springhillsuites.com, $130–109 s or d), with an indoor pool, hot tub, fitness room, and suites containing microwaves and fridges, not to mention free wireless in-room and a hot breakfast served daily at no additional charge.

Camping can be found at **Lake Pleasant RV Park** (24025 Bothell-Everett Hwy., 425/483-9436, year-round, $18–28 per family), offering full hookup RV sites and campsites situated around two small lakes. You can also park an RV at **Twin Cedars RV Park** (17826 Hwy. 99, 425/742-5540 or 800/878-9304, $32), although the spaces can be a bit tight.

FOOD
Woodinville

Just up the road from Chateau Ste. Michelle Winery, Redhook Brewery, and Columbia Winery is the **Herbfarm** (206/784-2222, www.theherbfarm.com, by reservation), one of the Northwest's most famous restaurants. The setting is eye-poppingly Victorian and the meal is an elaborate nine-course affair that includes paired wines. This isn't a place for those with threadbare wallets; prix fixe menus are

an equally eye-popping $189–195 per person. The Herbfarm books up months ahead of time. Fortunately, you can get on the waiting list, as there are often cancellations. Many herbs used at the restaurant are grown on a one-acre farm just down the road.

A few steps from Herbfarm is **Barking Frog** (425/424-2999, 6 A.M.–2:30 P.M. and 5–10 P.M. daily, $35), part of the luxurious Willows Lodge. Another high-end gourmet restaurant, the menu includes such specialties as roasted venison and grilled beef tenderloin. The wine selection is impressive and the dining room cozy at this artistic bistro.

Not every Woodinville eatery is so spendy. **Forecasters Public House** (14300 NE 145th St., 425/483-3232, www.redhook.com) at Redhook Ale Brewery appeals to more plebeian tastes.

Chan's Place (14203 NE Woodinville-Duvall Rd., 425/483-2223, www.chansplaces.com, 11:15 A.M.–9:15 P.M. Sun.–Thurs., 11:15 A.M.–10:15 P.M. Fri.–Sat., $12), is a little Chinese restaurant with food as good as their neon façade is dazzling. **Italianissimo** (17650 140th Ave. NE, 425/485-6888, www.italianissimoristorante.com, 11 A.M.–9:30 P.M. Mon.–Thurs., 11 A.M.–10 Fri., 5–10 P.M. Sat., 5–9:30 P.M. Sun., $20) is a delightful place where the pasta is homemade and veal is the house specialty. Vegetarians love the eggplant parmigiana.

Out in Maltby (approximately five miles northeast of Woodinville on Highway 522) is **Maltby Café** (425/483-3123, http://maltbycafe.com, 7 A.M.–3 P.M. daily, $10), where the outstanding breakfasts and lunches are well worth the drive. The cinnamon rolls here are blissful and big enough to feed a battalion of bigfoots.

Bothell

Bothell has its share of decent restaurants, generally seeming to trend to the Asian side. But for pure Americana on a bun with drive-up service, go to **Burgermaster** (18626 Bothell Everett Hwy., 425/486-8980). This is one of four locations in the area, but no matter which one you visit, their grilled hot-dog sandwich may well change your life. At **Elizabeth & Alexander** (23808 Bothell Everett Hwy., 425/489-9210, www.elizabethandalexander .com, 9 A.M.–3 P.M. Mon.–Fri., 8 A.M.–4 P.M. Sat., 10 A.M.–3 P.M. Sun.) the only thing that would make the atmosphere more British is a visit from Her Royal Majesty herself. Serving breakfast, lunch, and high tea, the simple offerings (including quiche, chicken, and greens) will keep you feeling right healthy for no more than a few quid. The **Main St. Alehouse & Eatery** (10111 Main St., 425/485-2972, www .alehousebothell.com 11 A.M.–10 P.M. Mon.– Thurs. and Sat., 11 A.M.–11 P.M. Fri., closed Sun., $13) has an old-timey feeling, and not without reason. There have been taverns on this spot since McKinley was president. Enjoy craft brews and creative takes on old favorites, like Thai-spiced buffalo wings and spicy cod pitas.

You might already know it, but if not, the Northwest is heaven for teriyaki lovers. You won't find more and better teriyaki in any other English-speaking region anywhere. And a great representative of that tradition is **Osaka Grill Teriyaki** (18001 Bothell Everett Hwy. Ste. S., 425/415-6211). The mouthwatering, inexpensive food is something you'll long remember. Just as soon as you start to think that Bothell is nothing but burgers and chicken katsu, the **Preservation Kitchen** (17121 Bothell Way NE, 425/408-1306, www.preservationkitchen .com, 11 A.M.–2 P.M. and 4–10 P.M. Tues.–Sun., 9 A.M.–2 P.M. Sat.–Sun.) comes along to shatter that opinion. The charmer of a Northwest-style

brick building provides an intimate venue for a memorable meal. Start with the prosciutto and duck egg appetizer, move on to a Waldorf salad, savor a tender filet mignon, and finish with something off of an ever-changing menu of fresh desserts. The bar has a full selection of absinthe cocktails for the bohemian in you.

INFORMATION

Get local information from the **Woodinville Chamber of Commerce** (13205 NE 175th St., 425/481-8300, www.woodinvillechamber.org, 9 A.M.–5 P.M. Mon.–Fri.) inside the old city hall or at Bothell's **Greater Bothell Chamber of Commerce** (10017 NE 185 St., 425/485-4353 www.bothellchamber.biz, 10 A.M.–2 P.M. Mon.–Fri.).

GETTING THERE AND AROUND

Metro Transit (800/542-7876, http://metro. kingcounty.gov/) has daily bus service between Seattle and the neighborhoods of Woodinville and Bothell. Once in Bothell you can travel to Lynnwood, Edmonds, or Everett on **Community Transit** (800/562-1375, www .commtrans.org).

Shuttle Express (800/487-7433, www .shuttleexpress.com) provides frequent direct service from Bothell to Sea-Tac Airport.

Kenmore Air (206/486-1257 or 800/543-9595, www.kenmoreair.com) has daily floatplane flights from the nearby town of Kenmore on the north end of Lake Washington to Victoria, B.C., and the San Juan Islands.

NORTH PUGET SOUND

Outdoor enthusiasts can find a whole lot to do once they break the Seattle northern city limits. The Puget Sound region in this direction is awash in marine parks, dramatic beaches, scenic drives, colorful flower fields, and quiet marina towns. Pedal the rolling hills of historic Ebey's Landing on Whidbey Island or cast a fly on one of the lakes at Deception Pass State Park. Slip on some flippers and a scuba tank and immerse yourself in the Edmonds Water Park or pedal along the trails at Japanese Gulch in Mukilteo. Whatever your predilections, there's plenty to get the ol' ticker pounding while enjoying the scenery along the way.

And if it's something a little calmer that really sets your heart aflutter, no worries: Try window shopping antique towns like La Conner or Snohomish. Lay a picnic blanket under the Peace Arch at the Canadian border. Or tour the giant jumbo-jet production line in Everett. Any way you shake it, the northern reaches of the Sound have got enough afternoon excursions to keep you busy for quite some time.

PLANNING YOUR TIME

With fertile farmlands sitting on scenic river flood plains, picturesque cliff sides overlooking the inky depths of the Puget Sound and mountain foothills just waiting to be explored, the North Puget Sound is a road-tripper's delight. The region remains glued together by the north-south spine of I-5, so nothing is so far from the freeway to cause much inconvenience. And yet this corner of the state still manages to feel "out of the way" in all the right ways.

© MATT RAGEN/123RF.COM

HIGHLIGHTS

◖ Ebey's Landing National Historical Reserve: Tour the undulating agrarian hillsides, the pebbly beaches, and the blast-from-the-past seaport of Coupeville at this historic treasure (page 146).

◖ Future of Flight Center and Boeing Tour: Come see the engineers and assembly-line crew at work on the next generation of jumbo jets on this landmark tour (page 156).

◖ Skagit Valley Tulip Festival: During the month of April, the valley erupts into a rainbow quilt of color (page 168).

◖ Chuckanut Drive: The nicest back-road tour in all of the Puget Sound, this one tracks along marshland, bluff sides, and wooded parkland (page 176).

◖ Fairhaven: This is Bellingham's storied historic district, home to boutique shopping and scads of cute restaurants (page 178).

◖ Peace Arch: The giant white arch marks the entrance to Canada and symbolizes the friendly relations of American and Canadian people (page 191).

LOOK FOR ◖ TO FIND RECOMMENDED SIGHTS, ACTIVITIES, DINING, AND LODGING.

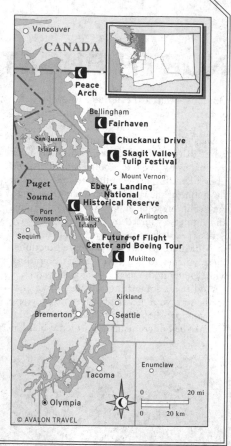

Driven straight through, the jaunt from Seattle up to the Canadian border in Blaine takes a little less than two hours. Without too many detours, a visit to northern destinations such as the **Peace Arch,** the **Boeing Museum of Flight,** the Dutch-themed town of **Lynden,** or the historic **Fairhaven** district in Bellingham can be made in a long day trip from Seattle. The direct route up the freeway takes you through the pastoral acreage of Skagit Valley, which in spring erupts in a riot of colors during the celebrated **Skagit Valley Tulip Festival.**

But with hundreds of miles of country back roads and ferry-serviced islands to explore, some of the best sights are meant to be seen during a weekend getaway or longer. Take your time through **Whidbey Island** and **Deception Pass,** drive the winding **Chuckanut Drive** or explore Snohomish County's mountain foothills leisurely with a stop at one of many bed-and-breakfasts along those routes. It's worth the extra time.

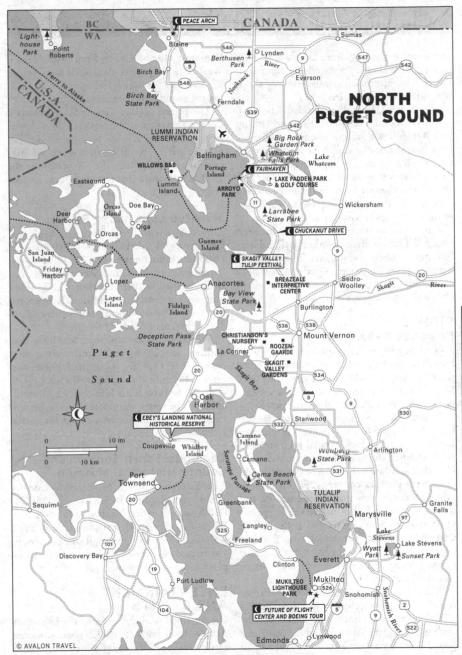

© AVALON TRAVEL

Edmonds and Mukilteo

Motor north along I-5 from Seattle and you'll soon stumble along two waterfront communities ripe for afternoon strolls, window shopping, and leisurely dinners.

First comes Edmonds, a pleasant little town centered around a scenic marina and fishing pier. Art galleries, antique shops, and friendly little bistros line the well-tended, pedestrian-friendly streets here. The biggest draw, though, isn't by the water—it's *in* the water. Just offshore from the ferry terminal and Brackett's Landing lies Edmonds Underwater Park, one of the most popular dive sites in the sound.

One town north of Edmonds, Mukilteo (muck-il-TEE-o) offers another idyllic shoreline spot to circle the wagons. The highlight here is a postcard-perfect lighthouse set on a scenic little state park with windswept vistas of Whidbey Island in the distance.

SIGHTS
Edmonds Waterfront

A good way to see Edmonds is to begin with a stroll on the half-mile-long **Sunset Avenue** with its Victorian homes and views of Puget Sound and the Olympic Mountains. If the tide is out, you can walk back along the beach.

The marine sanctuary at **Olympic Beach** (200 W. Dayton St.) is an excellent place to take youngsters to look at tidal creatures and shellfish when the tide is low. From Memorial Day through Labor Day come on the weekends to the **visitors center** (425/775-1344) to talk with docents about local marine life and see the aquarium full of native species swimming around. Also on premises is the lighted **Edmonds Fishing Pier,** which runs 950 feet over the Sound. Try your hand at fishing or just watch anglers cast for salmon and bottom fish and jig for squid.

Walkers and joggers like the boardwalk that runs 0.25 mile along the Port of Edmonds marina. The marina is home to 1,000 boats, including the largest charter fishing fleet on Puget Sound. It is only a short walk down to the small

Edmonds Marina Beach Park (498 Admiral Way). This is a perfect place to fly kites, cook a dinner over a beach fire, and watch ferries crossing the sound into the sunset.

The prized park of Edmonds, **Brackett's Landing Park** envelops the ferry dock downtown. Here you can see picnicking families mingle with wet-suited diving enthusiasts gearing up to slip into the water to tour the 27-acre **Edmonds Underwater Park,** located just offshore.

Mukilteo Lighthouse Park

Adjacent to the ferry terminal, Mukilteo Lighthouse Park is home to the scenic **Mukilteo Lighthouse** (425/355-9602, www.parks.wa.gov). Built in 1905, this red-and-white beauty is still functional and, along with its restored outbuildings, is open for tours noon–5 P.M. Saturday and Sunday April–September, for a token $1 donation.

The park also has a popular beach for sunbathing, launching boats, and casting lines from shore into the bountiful Possession Sound. Because of consistent winds, the park is also a favorite with kite flyers and windsurfers. The water around here is treacherous, though, so it isn't recommended for casual swimmers.

Edmonds-South Snohomish County Historical Museum

The Edmonds-South Snohomish County Historical Museum (118 5th Ave. N, 425/774-0900, www.historicedmonds.org, 1–4 P.M. Wed.–Fri., 1 P.M.–4 P.M. Sun., free) has a working shingle mill model, historical photos, a marine room, model trains, and other displays depicting Edmonds's past.

ENTERTAINMENT AND EVENTS

On the third weekend of June, the **Edmonds Art Festival** (425/771-6412, www.edmonds artsfestival.com) includes a juried art show,

© ERICKA CHICKOWSKI

Mukilteo Lighthouse

artists in action, arts and crafts booths, and live music. The **Taste of Edmonds Festival** (425/670-9112) on the second weekend of August is a popular street fair with ethnic foods, a carnival, music, and beer garden.

Held at the base of the city's pride and joy, the mid-August **Mukilteo Lighthouse Festival** (www.mukilteolighthousefesti val.com) features a pancake breakfast, parade, salmon barbecue, fishing derby, arts and crafts display, and country music and dancing.

SHOPPING
Shopping Malls

East of Mukilteo find the enormous **Alderwood Mall** (3000 184th St. SW, Lynnwood, www .alderwoodmall.com, 10 A.M.–9:30 P.M. Mon.–Thurs., 10 A.M.–10 P.M. Fri.–Sat., 11 A.M.–7 P.M. Sun.), which hosts Macy's, Nordstrom, JCPenney, Sears, and many smaller stores; the mall is surrounded by smaller shopping plazas and is conveniently right at the junction of I-5 and I-405.

Antiques and Galleries

Edmonds has several large antique and collectibles stores, including the **Waterfront Antique Mall** (190 Sunset Ave. S, 425/670-0770, 10 A.M.–6 P.M. Mon.–Sat., noon–6 P.M. Sun.) inside an antique Safeway building, which offers a good mix of art deco, midcentury, and Victorian pieces.

Edmonds has a vibrant art scene, with numerous galleries popping up all over downtown. One of the best is **Gallery North** (508 Main St., 425/779-0946, www.gallery-north .com) an artists' cooperative that has been going strong for over 40 years.

Get a good overview of the local gallery scene each third Thursday of the month during the **Edmonds Art Walk,** which focuses on a rotating list of participants. For a list of activities and a map, visit www.edmondswa.com/ Events/ArtWalk.

Rick Steves' Europe Through the Back Door

Rick Steves' Europe Through the Back Door

(130 4th Ave., 425/771-8303, www.ricksteves .com) is headquarters for the large operation directed by the well-known travel author and TV host. The staff sets up guided tours of Europe, and the center is a great stop for anyone planning a trip to the Continent. In addition to a large travel library, the center puts on free travel workshops twice a week in the summer, along with free Saturday lectures.

SPORTS AND RECREATION

Gear up in Lynnwood, which has an **REI** (4200 194th St. SW, 425/774-1300, www.rei .com) with all sorts of outdoor gear.

Diving

Edmonds is home to one of the premier diving sites within the Seattle metropolitan area. Just offshore from Brackett's Landing and the ferry terminal lies the very first underwater park ever established in Washington, **Edmonds Underwater Park.** The artificial reef was created in 1935 when municipal leaders sank a 300-foot DeLion dry dock to act as a breakwater. Since then, the marine environment has claimed the DeLion and the companion ships dropped next to it as the reef has been built up over the years.

Today, divers can explore the underwater, rope-lined "streets" that have been developed over the years to help navigate the park. Observant divers should be able to find dozens of species of fish, crustaceans, and marine vegetation that thrive here.

You can fill your tanks, rent diving equipment, learn to dive, or find a dive buddy at **Underwater Sports** (264 Railroad Ave., 425/771-6322, www.underwatersports.com), two blocks south across the street from the Amtrak depot.

Walking and Running

Just two blocks from downtown is the **Edmonds Marsh,** a haven for wildlife of all kinds. It's an amazing little piece of the natural world where blackbirds, herons, ducks, and crows feed in an enclave hidden from the suburban development that surrounds it. A boardwalk overlooks the marsh and provides an excellent path for walkers and joggers.

The popular **Interurban Trail** is an 11-mile paved path that follows an old railroad route across Lynnwood and continues north all the way to Everett. Or get the locals to give you a tour—visit the shoe store **Running in Motion** (410 Main St., Ste. B, 425/774-0637, www .runninginmotion.com) at 8:30 A.M. Sunday to join its free weekly runs around town.

Mountain Biking

Spin your way through the miles of singletrack carved throughout the greenery within **Japanese Gulch** in Mukilteo. This forested slice of private land rests on a ravine and is accessible from Mukilteo Boulevard. Park in the lot at **Centennial Park** (1126 5th St.) and cross the street to ride. The park offers a nice square of grass to sit on during a leisurely postride picnic.

Golf

Harbour Pointe Golf Course (11817 Harbour Pointe Blvd., 425/355-6060 or 800/233-3128, http://harbourpointegolf.com, greens fees $22–67, carts $14), a challenging, water-dependent set of links so well-tended it seems as if the groundskeepers use grooming shears instead of lawnmowers.

If you just want a quick golf fix, **Ballinger Lake Golf Course** (23000 Lakeview Dr., Mountlake Terrace, 425/774-4940, www .ballingerlakegolf.com, $17) is a well-maintained nine-hole municipal course not far from Mukilteo and Edmonds. The pretty water of Ballinger Lake plays a part in two holes.

ACCOMMODATIONS
Under $100

There might not be much to see in nearby Lynnwood, but it is a good halfway point when you're looking for an affordable base of operations for exploration into Seattle and Snohomish County.

There are a number of chain hotels clustered

right near the I-5/I-405 junction and between Highway 99 and I-5 east of Edmonds, but for a consistently affordable option, consider **Hotel International** (5621 196th St. SW, 425/771-1777 or 800/626-5750, $65 s, $85 d), an independent hotel with tidy and spacious rooms, an indoor spa, and very gracious staffers.

Of course, if you're headed to Edmonds or Mukilteo for the charm of the neighborhood, then a friendly bed-and-breakfast is probably more your speed. Mukilteo offers two B&Bs that won't break the bank. Two miles north of downtown Edmonds, **Maple Tree B&B** (18313 Olympic View Dr., 425/774-8420, http://themapletreeb_b.home.comcast.net $100 d) rests atop a bluff facing the sound and the Olympics beyond. Soak up the view from the solarium, and once the sun goes down, check out the constellations from the telescope set up there. The single guest room has a private bath, and a light breakfast is served.

$100-150
If those two small establishments are booked, or if you're looking for a full-service hotel in Edmonds proper, then you'll want to stay at **Best Western Plus Edmonds Harbor Inn** (130 W. Dayton St., 425/771-5021 or 800/441-8033, www.nwcountryinns.com/harbor, $125–139 s or d). The decor is modern, a light breakfast is included, and guests pay just $5 extra for access to an excellent health club with lap pool, racquetball, and tennis courts right next door. Suites with jetted tubs, fireplaces, and kitchenettes are available for $189.

Mukilteo also offers a pair of bed-and-breakfasts at moderate rates. Most remarkable is **Hogland House** (917 Webster St., 425/742-7639, www.hoglandhouse.com, $125 d), a Craftsman bungalow home built in 1906. The home has been in the innkeeper's family for over 60 years; she'll treat you to local lore as well as a country breakfast.

The smaller **By the Bay B&B** (821 4th St., 425/347-4997, www.bythebay.net, $80–110 d) has a guest room in the main house and a private cottage for families on its property.

Breakfast is a simple continental spread, and guests are encouraged to enjoy the lovingly tended English garden on the property.

$150-200
Mukilteo's major hotel is the posh **(** **Silver Cloud Inn** (425/423-8600 or 800/311-1461, www.scinns.com, $159–189 d), the only Mukilteo hotel right on the water. Many of the rooms have stunning views of the water and passing ferries to Whidbey Island. Complimentary Wi-Fi is provided, as is a continental breakfast and a local shuttle. Luxurious rooms with private hot tubs and fireplaces are $219–289.

Camping
Road-trippin' RV owners looking for a place to park their rigs close to Seattle's sights might consider the clean and reasonably priced **Twin Cedars RV Park** (17826 Hwy. 99, Lynnwood, 425/742-5540 or 800/878-9304, $30 full hookup). Spaces are a little tight, and it's not the most private of parks, but it'll take big rigs and has pull-through sites.

FOOD
Mukilteo
Enjoy an espresso and pastry in the flower-filled courtyard at **Whidbey's Coffee Co.** (619 4th St., 425/348-4825, www.whidbeycoffee.com, 7 A.M.–5 P.M. daily, $5). Hidden away at the top of the hill overlooking the ferry, this is a great place to escape the traffic on a sunny morning.

Mukilteo has one of the Ivar's chain of seafood restaurants, but you're better off heading uphill to **(** **Arnie's** (714 2nd St., 425/355-2181, www.arniesrestaurant.com, 11 A.M.–9 P.M. Mon.–Fri., 11:30 A.M.–10 P.M. Fri.–Sat., $20) for water views from two levels. Enjoy very good lunches and dinners of salmon and other seafood, along with chicken, steaks, and a Sunday champagne brunch.

Legend has it that back in the 1920s, Al Capone used to distill whiskey and smuggle it out to his docks from a tunnel underneath the big brick mansion that now hosts **Charles at Smuggler's Cove** (8310 53rd Ave. W., 425/347-2700, www.charles atsmugglerscove.com, 11 A.M.–2 P.M. Tues.– Fri. and 5–10 P.M. Tues.–Sat., reservations recommended, $25). He'd probably find the restaurant sufficiently classy to impress his rich gangster buddies—this cozy and authentic French restaurant is a birthdays-and-anniversaries sort of place. You're likely to rub elbows with Boeing execs wining and dining clients as you look over the vistas of Possession Sound from the window and sup on superb continental fare.

Edmonds

For a heartier breakfast, **Pancake Haus** (530 5th Ave. S., 425/771-2545, 6 A.M.–3 P.M. Mon.–Fri., 6 A.M.–2 P.M. Sat.–Sun., $9) in Edmonds is a lock for the best breakfast in the area. This 30-year-old legend is the Wonka of pancakes, with every imaginable ingredient including fruits, chocolate, and even bacon.

Arnie's (300 Admiral Way, 425/771-6533, 11:30 A.M.–9 P.M. Sun.–Thurs., 11:30 A.M.– 10 P.M. Fri.–Sat., $20) has a twin location in Edmonds, just two blocks south of the ferry terminal. The bar here is a perfect perch to settle in and watch the sun set over the ferries.

Chanterelle (316 Main St., 425/774-0650, www.chanterellewa.com, 8 A.M.–3 P.M. and 4–9 P.M. Mon.–Sat., 8 A.M.–1 P.M. Sun., $16) is a popular downtown bistro and espresso bar, with offerings ranging from the quick and simple to rich and exotic.

INFORMATION AND SERVICES

The friendly folks at the log cabin **Edmonds Visitors Bureau** (120 5th Ave. N, 425/776-6711, www.edmondswa.com, 9 A.M.–4 P.M. Mon.–Fri., 11 A.M.–3 P.M. Sat. in summer, 9 A.M.–4 P.M. Mon.–Fri. in winter) will be happy to provide you with maps and current information.

The **South Snohomish County Chamber of Commerce** (3400 188th St. SW, 425/774-0507, www.s2c3.com, 8 A.M.–5 P.M. Mon.–Thurs., 8 A.M.–4 P.M. Fri. year-round) has local information.

Contact the city of **Lynnwood** (425/775-1971, www.ci.lynnwood.wa.us) for additional details on the area.

GETTING THERE AND AROUND
By Ferry

Both Edmonds and Mukilteo are known as gateways in the Washington State Ferry system. Edmonds is the departure point to Kingston on the Kitsap Peninsula, which connects to the Olympic Peninsula. Meanwhile, Mukilteo is the busiest ferry terminal in the state, with service to Whidbey Island.

The **Washington State Ferry** (206/464-6400 or 888/808-7977, 800/843-3779 for automated information, www.wsdot.wa.gov/ferries) crossing from Edmonds to Kingston takes 30 minutes and leaves about every 40 minutes during the day. Summertime fares are $15.20 one-way for car and driver, $7.10 for passengers or walk-ons.

WSF has service between Mukilteo and the town of Clinton on the south end of Whidbey Island every half hour 5 A.M.–2 A.M. The 20-minute crossing costs $4.20 round-trip for passengers or walk-ons, $1 extra for bikes, and $9.00 one-way for car and driver. You only pay on the westbound leg of the trip (leaving Mukilteo). Busiest times are during the weekday commute periods, Saturday morning (after 9 A.M. when going to Whidbey), and late in the afternoon on Sunday.

By Train

From **Edmonds Station** (210 Railroad Ave.), catch a connection on **Amtrak's Cascades** route from Oregon to Vancouver, British Columbia. Ride to Seattle to connect to the eastbound Empire Builder to Spokane and Chicago, and the southbound Coast Starlight with stops all the way down to San Diego. For information on Amtrak, visit www.amtrak.com or call 425/778-3213 or 800/872-7245.

Mukilteo Station (920 1st St., 888/889-6368, www.soundtransit.org), is a hub for the Sound Transit *Sounder* train, which will get you to Everett ($2.75) Edmonds ($3.25) or Seattle ($4), leaving four times daily in each direction between 6 A.M. and 7:30 P.M. The train will get you from Mukilteo to Seattle in just under an hour. Leaving from Edmonds shaves 30 minutes off of your rail-time.

By Bus

Community Transit (425/778-2185 or 800/562-1375; www.commtrans.org) covers nearly all of Snohomish County, with service south to Seattle and east as far as Snohomish and Darrington.

Whidbey Island

The longest island in the lower 48 states, Whidbey Island encompasses 208 square miles in its 45-mile length, but there's no spot on the island more than five miles from the water. The island is a favorite place for a Sunday-afternoon drive, with motorists typically starting the day by taking the Mukilteo–Clinton ferry to the south end of the island and winding their way north to stop and gawk at the impressive waterway and bridge at Deception Pass State Park. But to really see Whidbey, you'll need more than a hurried day trip. Take the time to explore the many natural areas and historic sites, camping out in one of the excellent state parks or staying in a B&B to enjoy the full benefits the area has to offer. If you choose the leisurely route, consider doing it by bike. Many miles of quiet back roads wind between quaint hamlets like Coupeville and Langley, and you'll have the chance to spin by serene shoreline and picturesque agricultural land throughout Ebey's Landing National Historical Reserve.

CLINTON AND LANGLEY

The southern gateway to Whidbey Island, Clinton rests on a bluff overlooking the ferries that chug across Possession Sound to unload at the docks here. You'll pass through it in a blink on your journey northward to Langley, a charming little town best enjoyed without a watch or a cell phone. Langley lies along the waters of Saratoga Passage, with views of Camano Island and the North Cascades on a clear day. It is a getaway dream-town, with boutiques, bed-and-breakfast inns, and galleries galore.

Sights

DOWNTOWN LANGLEY

The main attraction in Langley is simply the charismatic town itself, perched right above Puget Sound. A favorite downtown spot for photos is the life-size bronze *Boy and Dog* by local sculptor Georgia Gerber. The 160-foot fishing pier offers great views and a chance to test your fishing pole, and the beach here is a popular place for picnicking and swimming. **South Whidbey Historical Museum** (312 2nd St., 360/730-3367, www.southwhidbeyhistory .org, 1–4 P.M. Sat.–Sun.) has local memorabilia in a century-old building.

WHIDBEY ISLAND WINERY

Stop for a picnic overlooking the vineyard and apple orchard at Whidbey Island Winery (5237 S. Langley Rd., 360/221-2040, www.whidbey islandwinery.com, noon–5 P.M. Thurs.–Sun.), a family vintner. The tasting room here offers sips of creative rhubarb wines and vintages fermented from estate-grown Madeline Angevine grapes.

Entertainment and Events

The **Whidbey Island Center for the Arts** (565 Camano Ave., 360/221-8268 or 800/638-7631, www.wicaonline.com) features concerts

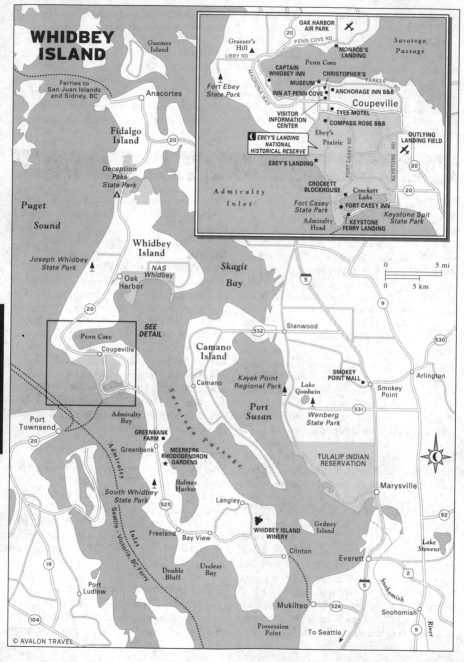

WHIDBEY ISLAND

Guemes
Island

Ferries to
San Juan Islands
and Sidney, BC

Anacortes

Fidalgo
Island

20

Puget
Sound

Deception
Pass
State Park

Joseph Whidbey
State Park

Whidbey
Island

NAS
Whidbey

Oak
Harbor

Skagit
Bay

20

Penn Cove

SEE
DETAIL

Coupeville

Port
Townsend

20

Admiralty
Bay

GREENBANK
FARM

Greenbank

MEERKERK
RHODODENDRON
GARDENS

Camano
Island

Camano

Kayak Point
Regional Park

Lake
Goodwin

Wenberg
State Park

Port
Susan

Stanwood

532

531

SMOKEY
POINT MALL

Smokey
Point

Arlington

530

5

9

TULALIP INDIAN
RESERVATION

Marysville

19

South Whidbey
State Park

525

Holmes
Harbor

Langley

Freeland   Bay View

WHIDBEY ISLAND
WINERY

Gedney
Island

Clinton

Everett

92

Lake
Stevens

Port
Ludlow

Double
Bluff

Useless
Bay

5

2

104

Possession
Point

To Seattle

Mukilteo

526

Snohomish

9

Snohomish River

© AVALON TRAVEL

DETAIL:

OAK HARBOR
AIR PARK

20

PENN COVE RD

Grasser's
Hill

LIBBY RD

Fort Ebey
State Park

MONROE'S
LANDING

Saratoga
Passage

Penn Cove

CAPTAIN
WHIDBEY INN

CHRISTOPHER'S

INN AT PENN COVE

ANCHORAGE INN B&B

Coupeville

PARKER RD

VISITOR
INFORMATION
CENTER

TYEE MOTEL

COMPASS ROSE B&B

EBEY'S LANDING
NATIONAL
HISTORICAL RESERVE

Ebey's
Prairie

MADRONA WAY

FORT CASEY RD

KEYSTONE RD

OUTLYING
LANDING FIELD

20

EBEY'S LANDING

CROCKETT
BLOCKHOUSE

Crockett
Lake

20

Fort Casey
State Park

FORT CASEY INN

KEYSTONE
FERRY LANDING

Keystone Spit
State Park

Admiralty
Head

Admiralty
Inlet

0   5 mi

0   5 km

NORTH PUGET SOUND

LANGLEY FOUNDED BY GANGLY TEEN

Langley is probably the only Washington town founded by a teenager. In 1880, an ambitious 15-year-old German immigrant, Jacob Anthes, settled here. Because he was too young to file for a homestead, Anthes spent $100 to buy 120 acres of land, adding to his holdings with a 160-acre homestead claim when he reached 21. He later built a store and post office and teamed up with Judge J. W. Langley to plot the new town.

and plays throughout the year. The historic **Clyde Theatre** (1st St., 360/221-5525, www.theclyde.net, $6) is the only place to watch first-run movies on the south end of Whidbey Island.

In late February, hundreds of wannabe detectives converge on Langley to search out the culprit in the annual **Langley Mystery Weekend** a participatory bit of theatre that takes over the whole town. Langley's popular **Choochokam Festival of the Arts** (360/221-7494, http://choochokamarts.org) is held the second weekend of July with a juried arts festival, food, crafts, music, and dancing. Langley puts its own twist on the ubiquitous summer fair with the **Island County Fair** (360/221-4677, www.islandweb.org/fair), a four-day event in late August that includes a logging show, carnival, parade, music, and 4-H exhibits.

Just a little past the time when tourists leave and things get back to normal, gypsy jazz comes to visit at **DjangoFest Northwest** (800/638-7631, www.djangofest.com/nw). The September show is named after Belgian-born Gypsy Django Reinhardt, who blended the music of his youth with the energetic and revolutionary jazz scene of the 1930s and beyond. Festival-goers are treated to an exotic musical art played by musicians from around the world. You can even pick up a few skills at one of the workshops that are generally led by big-name artists.

The Langley Woodworkers Guild takes some serious pride in its work and likes to show it off at the annual **Woodpalooza** (5603 S Bayview Rd., www.whidbeywoodworkers.com, free) lasting from September through October. The Woodworker's Guild rolls out its very best work from the last year and puts it out for appreciative eyes.

Langley's galleries are open for evening **Art Walks** on the first Saturday of each month.

Shopping

Tiny Langley is home to many art galleries, maybe best represented by **MUSEO** (215 1st St., 360/221-7737, www.museo.cc, 11 A.M.–5 P.M. daily). It holds monthly shows for new artists or collections and has some really fascinating Northwest-inspired sculpture, to say nothing of its knockout paintings, glass, and ceramics. **Lowry-James Rare Prints & Books** (101 Anthes Ave., 360/221-0477, www.lowryjames.com, 10 A.M.–5 P.M. Wed.–Sun) may well be the definitive rare prints and books store in the region. The store is like a history museum full of original charts, manuscripts, and prints that, for a price, you can take home with you. If you are a naturalist or just a lover of expert illustration, your heart will skip to see original work by John James Audubon available for purchase and suitable for framing.

South Whidbey Commons (124 Second St., 360/221-0127, http://southwhidbeycommons.org) seems like the Seattle same-old: a bookstore and a coffee shop. Making a good latte and a buck while you're at it is just the beginning for this nonprofit. Yes, they have a wide variety of used books, but their greater goal is to create a solid community, even for folks on vacation. It's a great place to browse some old classics while breaking away from that outsider feel that can make travel tough at times. Whidbey Island is a dream-home not just for people, but for alpacas, too! A handful of farms dot the island, but **Sonshine Farm** (5662 Crawford Rd., 360/321-5772, http://sonshinefarmofwhidbeyisland.com, call to visit any day) wins the prize for best alpaca goods. Its by-appointment shop will amaze you with its soft, sturdy, and warm alpaca-fur woven goods. If you're a do-it-yourselfer, stock up on alpaca yarn. You'll even meet the friendly fur-donors themselves.

Puppets are for all ages, a point no better proven than at **Act II Books and Puppets** (11 Anthes Ave., Unit B, 360/221-4442, www .kidsbooksandpuppets.com, 11 A.M.–5 P.M. Mon.–Sat., noon–4 P.M. Sun.). The little store is packed to the rafters with the Folkmanis line of stage and finger puppets. Amazingly realistic, these puppets are collectable, and the store sells discontinued puppets in the collection. Books, videos, and silly hats are all fun for kids both big and little.

Sports and Recreation

Driving or biking around Clinton's rural, wooded back roads provides fresh air and great views. Take windy Deer Lake Road to **Deer Lake Park** for swimming, boating, and fishing in a secluded, wooded area. From Highway 525, go left on Maxwelton Road, and stay on it all the way to Maxwelton Beach in **Dave Mackie County Park,** where you'll find the island's best Dungeness crabbing, along with shallow water for swimming.

Possession Beach County Park covers just two acres at the southern tip of Whidbey Island; it is a popular fishing site and a peaceful spot to enjoy the view, with occasional whale and eagle sightings adding to the pleasure.

Accommodations

Feeling spontaneous? Stop by the Langley Chamber of Commerce **visitors center** (208 Anthes Ave.) to see photos of local lodgings available for the night. Vacancies are posted in the front window each night after 5 P.M.

$100-150

The rambling **Ashingdon Manor B&B Inn** (5023 Langley Rd., 360/221-2334 or 800/442-4942, www.ashingdonmanor.com, $129–179 s or d) is one of the more distinctive local inns, with a 14-acre country location, six guest rooms

with private baths (three with fireplaces), a grand piano, and a lovely pond and patio. The rate includes a gourmet breakfast prepared by a professional chef, who also happens to be a co-owner.

Some of the most affordable south Whidbey digs are at **Langley Motel** (526-B Camano Ave., 360/221-6070, www.langleymotel.com, $105–125 d). This little inn features four contemporary casual rooms.

Located on pastureland overlooking Sunlight Beach, **The Farmhouse** (2740 E. Sunshine Ln., 360/321-6288 or 888/888-7022, www.farmhousebb.com, $129–179 d) has four suites, all with fireplaces, private baths (two with jetted tubs), outside entrances and decks, and kitchens. The refrigerators are stocked for a full breakfast, and guests have access to an outdoor hot tub.

Soak up the views across Saratoga Passage at **Eagles Nest Inn** (4680 E. Saratoga Rd., 360/221-5331, www.eaglesnestinn.com, $125–175 d), a pretty four-story octagonal home tucked into a wooded lot adjoining the Saratoga Woods Preserve trail system. After a hike, relax in the hot tub or enjoy the private decks and grand piano.

Families who may find a trip to a bed-and-breakfast too expensive or nerve-wracking have an option at **Sweetwater Cottage** (6111 S. Cultus Bay Rd., 360/341-1604, www.whidbey .com/sweetwater, $150 s or d), a secluded two-bedroom cottage with a kitchen, woodstove, and sauna on 22 forested acres. You can even bring along your furry family—horses and other pets are allowed here.

$150-200

The **Primrose Path Cottage** (3191 E. Harbor Rd., 360/730-3722 or 800/333-4724, www .primrosepath.net, $129–200 d, $20 per extra person up to six people) is another private family-friendly space. This charming 1928 two-bedroom cottage in the woods has a path to a private beach and a relaxing hot tub.

All of the rooms at **Country Cottage of Langley B&B** (215 6th St., 360/221-8709 or 800/713-3860, www.acountrycottage.com, $139–189) have water views and private decks;

two of them even have hot tubs. The breakfasts here are the stuff of legends—innkeepers use local produce to create gourmet fare.

For downtown lodging at its best, stay at **Garden Path Inn** (111 1st St., 360/221-5121, www.gardenpathsuites.com, $125–175), where the two attractive suites include a continental breakfast.

$200-250

Rest your weary head at the expansive and modern ◖ **Saratoga Inn** (201 Cascade Ave., 360/221-5801 or 866/749-5565, www.saratogainnwhidbeyisland.com, $155–255 s or d, $375 suite), right in town. This 15-room hideaway offers more privacy than a typical B&B, but still delivers the goods with a hot buffet breakfast. The spacious rooms are attractively appointed, and all include gas fireplaces.

Boating fans can find a comfortable port at **Boatyard Inn** (200 Wharf St., 360/221-5120, www.boatyardinn.com). You can hear the rigging pinging against the masts at the public marina right next door to this architecturally distinctive inn. The sloping corrugated roofs and colorful siding pay homage to the old salmon and shellfish canneries of the Puget Sound, now mostly lost to history. There are also 10 modern beachfront studios ($195 d) or loft units ($250 for up to four) with kitchens, fireplaces, and decks.

OVER $250

The luxurious **Inn at Langley** (400 1st St., 360/221-3033, www.innatlangley.com) has zen-inspired rooms ($275–295 d), suites ($395 d), a cottage ($495 d), and full apartments ($595), each with its own private patio overlooking Saratoga Passage, a whirlpool tub, fireplace, and a delicious quiche and granola breakfast. A two-night minimum applies on weekends. The Inn is also the home of Spa Essencia, offering massage, aromatherapy, body masks, and more.

Those looking for a homey spot convenient to the ferry terminal can cozy up in **Sunset Cottage** (360/579-4445, www.whidbeynet .net/beach, $125–275 d). The cottage features

a king-size bed, full kitchen, and patio. It sits along sandy Maxwelton Beach, a good place to spot the bald eagles that also call the island home.

Food

When a town is as full of community spirit as Langley, locals take pride in everything they do, including running restaurants. It's almost a challenge to get a bad meal in this town. **Café Langley** (113 1st St., 360/221-3090, www.cafelangley.com, 11:30 A.M.–2:30 P.M. and 5–9 P.M. daily, $17) has a huge local following who come for great Greek and Middle Eastern dishes.

It's less fancy, but it's still fun to visit the ◖ **Village Pizzeria** (106 1st St., 360/221-3363, 11:30 A.M.–9 P.M. daily, $15). It serves up delicious, thin-crust, New York–style pies that taste best when enjoyed at the outdoor tables with great views of the water.

Located atop a hill that's a 10-minute walk from downtown, **China City** (510 Cascade Ave., 360/331-8899, www.chinacityrestaurant.com, 11 A.M.–9 P.M. daily, $10) serves excellent Chinese meals in an upscale setting. Big windows and a small patio offer striking 180-degree views of Saratoga Passage and the Cascades, while tall evergreen trees accent the yard. Prices are reasonable and the atmosphere is relaxed.

Langley Village Bakery (221 2nd St., 360/221-3525, 8 A.M.–5 P.M. Wed.–Sun.) bakes out-of-this-world breads and sweets along with a Tres Leches cake that might well change your life. At the **South Whidbey Tilth Farmers Market** (Hwy. 525 at Thompson Rd., 360/579-1871, www.southwhidbeytilth .org, 11:30 A.M.–3:30 P.M. Sat. and 4–7 P.M. Wed. mid-May–Oct.) offers all-organic fruits and vegetables. For those who just can't get enough farmers market action, the **Bayview Farmers Market** (Bayview Rd. at Hwy. 525, 360/221-6903) is open every Saturday from 10 A.M.–2 P.M.

Information and Services

Clinton's chamber of commerce can be

contacted at 360/341-3929 or www.clinton chamberofcommerce.org, and **Langley South Whidbey Chamber of Commerce** (208 Anthes Ave., 360/221-6765, www.visitlangley.com) is open to answer questions in person every day 10 A.M.–5 P.M. all year.

The **Langley Library** (360/221-4383, www.sno-isle.org) is located at 104 2nd Street.

Getting There and Around

The **state ferry** (206/464-6400, 888/808-7977, or 800/843-3779 for automated information, www.wsdot.wa.gov/ferries) leaves for Clinton from Mukilteo every half hour 5 A.M.–2 A.M., and the 20-minute crossing costs $4.20 round-trip for passengers or walkons, $1 extra for bikes, and $9 one-way for car and driver. You only pay on the westbound leg of the trip, so if you drive down Whidbey via the Deception Pass Bridge, your ride is free. Busiest times are during the weekday commute periods, Saturday morning (after 9 A.M. when going to the island), and late afternoon on Sunday. Sunday evenings after 7 P.M. are quieter, so just enjoy the island and let folks in a hurry wait in the traffic jams while you sit on a beach or in a café.

Island Transit (360/321-6688 or 800/240-8747, www.islandtransit.org) offers free bus service Mon.–Sat. throughout Whidbey Island. From the ferry terminal in Clinton, you can catch Route 1 for service to Freeland, Greenbank, Coupeville, and Oak Harbor via Highway 20. Or catch Route 7 with service to Langley and Freeland.

FREELAND AND GREENBANK

Freeland was founded in 1900 by a utopian group of socialists. They formed a cooperative, the Free Land Association, and each contributed $10 toward five acres of land. The balance was to be paid off through cooperative labor. Their experiment didn't last long, but the name stuck. Today it is an unassuming little town with a few quiet parks ideal for picnics on the way to the ferry terminal or Oak Harbor.

Also worth a stop is the pinprick-small "town" of Greenbank. The turn-of-the-20th-century general store, restaurant, and post office are easy to miss—but you can't miss the big red barn marking Whidbey Island Greenbank Farm, an icon for the entire island.

Sights and Recreation

PARKS

Find a small, sunny picnic area and a boat launch at **Freeland Park** on Holmes Harbor, about two streets over from "downtown" Freeland—just look for the water. The beach is popular with clammers. **Double Bluff Beach Park,** three miles south of Freeland, is an interesting place to explore and a good place to find big chunks of soft coal that eroded from the cliff. Do not try to climb these unstable bluffs; a number of people have been injured trying to do so.

WHIDBEY ISLAND GREENBANK FARM

At one point the Whidbey Island Greenbank Farm (360/678-7700, www.greenbankfarm.com) was the largest loganberry farm in the world. After the owners closed it down in 1996, local citizens persuaded the county to purchase it in 1997.

Today, new loganberry vines have been planted, and the farm's gift shop (10 A.M.–5 P.M. daily in summer) sells loganberry wine (produced elsewhere), along with grape and fruit wines from small local wineries. **Sundays at the Farm** feature local foods, goods, and live music, 11 A.M.–3 P.M. Sunday May–mid-October. The third weekend of July brings the **Loganberry Festival,** featuring a pie-eating contest, arts and crafts, live music, and food stands.

SOUTH WHIDBEY STATE PARK

Easily the island's most underrated park, South Whidbey State Park (360/331-4559, www.parks.wa.gov) on Smuggler's Cove Road (halfway between Greenbank and Freeland) has outstanding hiking, campsites, striking Olympic views, and a narrow, sandy beach.

If you seek solace, wander through the park's 85 acres of old-growth Douglas fir and red cedar, which protect resident black-tailed deer, foxes, raccoons, rabbits, bald eagles, ospreys, and pileated woodpeckers. Be sure to hike **Wilbert Trail,** a 1.5-mile path that circles through these ancient forests; it starts directly across from the park entrance.

You can also camp at South Whidbey State Park ($22 for tents, or $31 for RVs with hookups, open late Feb.–Oct.). Make reservations ($7 extra) at 888/226-7688 or www.parks.wa.gov.

MEERKERK RHODODENDRON GARDENS
The delightful Meerkerk Rhododendron Gardens (360/678-1912, www.meerkerk gardens.org, 9 A.M.–dusk daily summer, 9 A.M.–4 P.M. Wed.–Sun. winter, adults $8, children under 16 free) boast more than 1,500 varieties of rhododendron species and hybrids on a 53-acre site just south of Greenbank off Resort Road. First planted by Max and Anne Meerkerk in the 1960s, the gardens are now maintained by the Seattle Rhododendron Society and are a major tourist attraction. Peak season for "rhodies" is in late April and early May. Leashed dogs are allowed.

Accommodations
UNDER $100
Families traveling with Fido and not a lot of dough will sleep soundly at the simple **Harbour Inn Motel** (1606 E. Main St., 360/331-6900, www.harbourinnmotel.com, $101–110 d). This pet-friendly motel with outdoor corridors has 20 rooms, some with kitchenettes, and serves a generous continental breakfast.

Situated on five secluded acres, **The Yoga Lodge** (3475 Christie Rd., 360/678-2120, www.yogalodge.com, $65–125) is a peaceful place to spend a night surrounded by gardens and trees. Those with allergies will breathe easier knowing that the Lodge caters to those with chemical sensitivities, cleaning only with natural products. There are three quiet guest rooms here with a shared bathroom, and rates include an organic vegetarian or vegan continental breakfast and use of the wood-fired sauna. Guests can join in midweek yoga lessons ($15 per person) or private lessons on weekends ($70 for two).

$100-150
Watch the goats and llamas graze the pastures at **Bay Breeze B&B Cottages** (5660 S. Double Bluff Rd., 360/321-4277 or 888/547-4179, www.baybreezecottages.com, $129–150 d), a delightful retreat that sits next door to a flower farm and less than 1.5 miles from the off-leash Double Bluff beach. Both cottages come with a private bath, indoor hot tub, fireplace, and kitchenette.

Another beachfront guesthouse possibility is **Bush Point Wharf** (229 E. Main St., 360/331-0405 or 800/460-7219, www.whidbey.com/bushpoint), which has two guest suites ($115 s or d) and a three-bedroom penthouse ($195 d), all with private baths, a deck, and hot tub.

$150-200
Set amid 25 wooded acres, **Guest House Log Cottages** (3366 S. Hwy. 525, 360/678-3115, www.whidbey.net/logcottages) is a quiet, kid-free retreat that mingles four-star amenities with the down-home style of cedar cabins. Accommodations include a modern log home ($325 d) with fireplace, indoor hot tub under a glass ceiling, and king bed, plus five cottages ($165–235 d) with fireplaces, kitchens, and jetted tubs. All have access to the outdoor pool, hot tub, and small exercise room, along with make-it-yourself breakfasts.

Those bringing wee ones may prefer **Smugglers Cove Haven B&B** (3258 Smugglers Cove Rd., 360/678-7100 or 800/772-7055, www.smugglerscove.com, $125–175 s or d), which has three private units, each with a woodstove, kitchen, and make-it-yourself breakfast.

OVER $250
For the ultimate in luxury, stay at **Cliff House B&B** (727 Windmill Dr., 360/331-1566, www.cliffhouse.net) where the stunning modern home ($495 d) sits atop a cliff over Admiralty Inlet and has a hot tub, king-size bed, stone fireplace, and gourmet kitchen. A light breakfast is in the fridge. Also on the 13 acres of wooded land is a cottage with equally grand vistas for $175 d. There is a two-night minimum stay either way you choose.

NORTH PUGET SOUND

Food

Upscale elegance is always on the menu at 【 **Gordon's on Blueberry Hill** (5438 Woodard Ave., Freeland, 360/331-7515, $19, 11:30 A.M.–2 P.M. and 5–10 P.M. Tues.–Fri., 4–10 P.M. Sat.–Sun.). The nouveau-Northwest cuisine it serves within a bustling ranch-style house in Freeland is good enough to make Gordon's the island's destination restaurant. The owner-chef here mixes local ingredients such as mussels and homegrown herbs with flavors of Asia and Europe. Try unique dishes such as tandoori-style game hens ($19) or butternut squash ravioli in Sambuca cream sauce ($19).

Freeland Café (1642 E. Main St., 360/331-9945, www.whidbey.com/freelandcafe, 6 A.M.–9 P.M. daily, $10) is an old-time diner with breakfast served anytime, the twist being its Hawaiian and Asian specialties. Still, it's always popular with locals when they've got a hankering for a burger.

For a slice of warm pie à la mode, nobody beats those baked up at 【 **Whidbey Pies Cafe** (765 Wonn Rd., 360/678-1288, whidbeypies. com 10 A.M.–5 P.M. Mon.–Sat., 10 A.M.–8 P.M. Sun. May–Sept., 11 A.M.–4 P.M. Mon.–Fri., 10 A.M.–5 P.M. Sat.–Sun. Oct.–Apr.) at Greenbank Farm, which features the farm's renowned loganberries.

Information and Services

The **Freeland Chamber of Commerce** (1640 Main St., 360/331-1980, www.islandweb.org/freeland) is open 11 A.M.–3 P.M. Tuesday–Saturday. The **Freeland Library** (360/331-7323, www.sno-isle.org) is located at 5495 Harbor Avenue.

Getting There

Ride **Island Transit** (360/321-6688 or 800/240-8747, www.islandtransit.org, free) to Freeland and Greenbank from Clinton on Route 1 and from Langley to Freeland on Route 5.

COUPEVILLE

The second oldest town in Washington, the "Port of Sea Captains" was founded and laid out in 1852 by Capt. Thomas Coupe, the first man to sail through Deception Pass. The protected harbor at Penn Cove was a perfect site for the village that became Coupeville, and timber from Whidbey was shipped from here to San Francisco to feed the building boom created by the Gold Rush.

Today, modern businesses operate from Victorian-era buildings amidst the nation's largest historical preservation district. Downtown has an immaculate cluster of false-fronted shops and restaurants right on the harbor and a long wharf that was once used to ship local produce and logs to the mainland. Coupeville has become a bit of a haven for artists of all stripes over the years, a fact that lends a certain whimsical and colorful feel to this little town.

Sights
【 EBEY'S LANDING NATIONAL HISTORICAL RESERVE

With its bucolic farmland, densely wooded ridges, and steep shoreline bluffs, Ebey's Landing (360/678-6084, www.nps.gov/ebla) has the most striking coastal view on Whidbey. No wonder parts of the 1999 movie *Snow Falling on Cedars* were filmed here.

Unfurling over 25 square miles of rich farmland, this was the first designated national historical reserve in America. The rolling hills and whispering winds of the sound are the main attraction here, easily enjoyed by car or bike over the quiet ribbons of scenic blacktop that run through the reserve.

Whidbey Island's original inhabitants, the Salish tribe, enjoyed the rich resources of both the sea and the land and used fire to keep the prairies open here. It was these prairies that attracted settlers in the 1850s, who then used the Homestead Act to carve out farms and homes for their families. Today much of the land in Ebey's Landing is still privately owned—in fact, the reserve's boundaries encircle the entire historic town of Coupeville—but there are a trio of scenic state parks perfect for throwing down a blanket or going for a nature walk.

Among them is the tiny **Ebey's Landing State Park,** the site where island pioneer

Isaac Ebey landed his boat to gain access to the nearby fertile land that he homesteaded in 1850. Because this is the thinnest point in the island, Ebey's Landing later became a popular beach for locals to land in order to cross overland to the eastern shores of Whidbey at Penn Cove. There is still an 1858 ferry house that serviced these travelers standing at the site.

In Coupeville you'll find one of the original Whidbey Island fortifications: the **Alexander Blockhouse,** built in 1855, stands outside the museum, along with a shelter housing two turn-of-the-20th-century Native American racing canoes. Historical Reserve headquarters are upstairs from the museum. Also out front are attractive gardens with herbs and drought-tolerant plants. Additional blockhouses can be found at the Sunnyside Cemetery, just south of town, and near Crockett Lake.

FORT CASEY STATE PARK

Once a part of the Iron Triangle that guarded the entrance to the Puget Sound and the Bremerton Naval Shipyard, Fort Casey has long since seen the retirement and meltdown of the 10-inch disappearing carriage guns that stood sentinel there during the turn of the 20th century.

Nowadays it is home to a state park (12901 Hwy. 20, 360/679-7391, www.parks.wa.gov) that not only gives a glimpse into Army life back in the day but also offers spectacular Olympic views along two miles of beach. The park is a prime spot for hiking, too.

Much of the fort is open for public viewing, including ammunition bunkers, observation towers, and dark, spooky underground storage facilities. Military buffs will get a kick out of the two carriage guns brought in during the 1960s as replacements for the long-decommissioned originals.

Be sure to visit the **Admiralty Head Lighthouse Interpretive Center** (360/240-5584, www.admiraltyhead.wsu.edu, 11 A.M.–5 P.M. daily June–Sept., with reduced hours the rest of the year) where you can learn more about coastal artillery and the 1890 defense post. The lighthouse itself has not been

used since 1927, but you can climb to the top for a wonderful view of Puget Sound and the Olympic Mountains.

FORT EBEY STATE PARK

Located southwest of Coupeville on Admiralty Inlet, Fort Ebey State Park (360/678-4636, www.parks.wa.gov) has campsites (standard $22, RV hookups $28), a large grassy area, three miles of beach, and two miles of hiking trails within its 644 acres. The fort was constructed during World War II, though its gun batteries were never needed for coastal defense.

The concrete platforms remain, along with cavernous bunkers, but the big guns have long since been removed. Due to its location in the Olympic rain shadow, the park is one of the few places in western Washington where cactus can be found. The park also hosts stands of second-growth forests and great views across the Strait of Juan de Fuca.

ISLAND COUNTY HISTORICAL MUSEUM

The Island County Historical Society Museum (Alexander and Front Sts., 360/678-3310, www.islandhistory.org, 10 A.M.–5 P.M. Wed.–Mon. May–Sept., 11 A.M.–5 P.M. Fri.–Mon. the rest of the year, $3 adults, $2.50 seniors, students, and military personnel, $6 families, free for kids under 6) has pioneer relics and oddities such as a shadow box with flowers made from human hair and newsreels from the 1930s on the Indian Water Festival. While at the museum, pick up a brochure describing the walking tour of the town's beautiful Victorian buildings. It lists dozens of Coupeville's historical buildings and tells family histories of many of the owners.

Festivals and Events

Lots of events take place in tiny Coupeville, starting with the **Penn Cove Mussel Festival** the first weekend of March, with scavenger hunts, arts and crafts, and mussel cooking competitions. The **Penn Cove Water Festival** in early May includes tribal canoe races, Native arts and crafts, and Native foods

PENN COVE MUSSELS

Right in the midst of the cozy bed-and-breakfasts, antique shops, and small-town splendor of Whidbey Island lies one of the oldest and largest mussel farms in the United States. The Stillaguamish and Skagit Rivers bring the area a nutrient-rich outflow, and the additional sunshine provided by the Olympic rain shadow makes sure the plankton on which these mussels feed is especially nourishing. The result is a fat, sweet mussel that tastes just as wonderful in a creamy white-wine sauce as it does with just a few drops of butter and a sprig of basil. Penn Cove Shellfish has won multiple awards for quality and taste and is one of the few seafood brands to which connoisseurs are strongly loyal.

curvy road's namesake, the Pacific madrona tree, whose distinctive red bark and leathery green leaves line the route. Quite a few summer cottages and cozy homes can be found here, along with the one-of-a-kind **Captain Whidbey Inn.** Offshore there are dozens of floating pens where mussels grow on lines hanging in Penn Cove. On the northwest corner of Penn Cove, Highway 20 passes scenic **Grasser's Hill,** where hedgerows alternate with open farmland. Development restrictions prevent this open country from becoming a mass of condos. Just north of here are the historic **San Juan de Fuca School House** and Whidbey Inn.

Another scenic route crawls along Hill Road, two miles south of Coupeville. Follow it through the second-growth stand of Douglas fir trees. It emerges on a high bluff overlooking Admiralty Inlet before dropping to the shoreline at tiny Ebey's Landing State Park.

WATER SPORTS

Anglers, divers, and pleasure boaters will find the area around Coupeville an ideal place to get their craft out into Puget Sound. There are two boat ramps at Fort Casey State Park and a boat launch, small marina, and fuel dock at the Coupeville Wharf along Penn Cove.

Visit with the whale skeletons hanging in the wharf building and then get on the water at **Harbor Gift & Kayak Rental** (26 Front Street in Coupeville, 360/678-3625, $25 per hour single, $35 per hour double). Despite the sound of the name, you can't rent gifts, which is good, because what would the recipient think, anyways?

Just offshore from Fort Casey State Park is the **Keystone Jetty underwater park,** a marine reserve that gives divers the opportunity to explore a forest of kelp and come face to face with lingcod, crab, and sculpin, among other critters. The park is particularly popular for its abundant population of waving plumose anemones.

The closest place for scuba divers to get their tanks filled, rent equipment, and schedule chartered dives is in Oak Harbor, at **Whidbey Island Dive Center** (1020 NE 7th Ave., #1, 360/675-1112, www.whidbeydive

and entertainment. The **Coupeville Arts and Crafts Festival** on the second weekend in August features a juried art show that attracts participants from across the Northwest, plus arts and crafts exhibits, food, music, and entertainment. Also, in recent years, the Pacific Northwest Art School (360/678-3396, www.pacificnorthwestartschool.org) has sponsored an August **Plein Air** art show where artists demonstrate that sometimes it's really nice to get out of the studio and into nature.

On Sundays in July and August, **Concerts on the Cove** (360/678-4684) are held in the Town Park pavilion, featuring a wide variety of music. The **Coupeville Farmers Market** (8th and Main Sts., 360/678-6757) is held 10 A.M.–2 P.M. Saturday April–mid-October.

On the first Saturday of December, the **Greening of Coupeville** is a popular craft bazaar and tree-lighting festival. A number of historical homes are open for this event.

Sports and Recreation

SCENIC DRIVES

Head northwest from Coupeville along Madrona Way to take a ride underneath the

.com, 10 A.M.–5 P.M. Mon.–Tues., 9 A.M.–6 P.M. Wed–Sat., 10 A.M.–4 P.M. Sun.).

One of the major draws within Fort Ebey State Park is **Lake Pondilla**. This glacial sinkhole is a delight both for bass fishermen and swimmers. Follow the signs from the north parking lot at the park for a two-block hike to the lake.

HIKING

From the small parking area at the water's edge at Ebey's Landing State Park, hike the 1.5-mile trail along the bluff above **Parego Lagoon** for a view of the coastline, Olympics, and the Strait of Juan de Fuca that shouldn't be missed. If you hit the seasons right, the lagoon may be teeming with migratory birds, so bring some binoculars. Return along the beach, or continue northward to Fort Ebey State Park (three miles from Ebey's Landing). Along the way, keep your eyes open for gem-quality stones such as agate, jasper, black and green jade, plus quartz and petrified wood.

Another trail leads 1.4 miles from Ebey's Landing to **Sunnyside Cemetery,** where you can look north to snowcapped Mt. Baker and south to Mt. Rainier on a clear day. The cemetery is also accessible from Cook Road. The **Davis Blockhouse,** used to defend against Tlingit and Haida attacks, stands at the edge of the cemetery; it was moved here in 1915.

From the north parking lot at Fort Ebey, follow trails that lead south along the bluffs down to the beach. After consulting a tide chart and taking a bit of care, adventurous folks can continue all the way to Fort Casey State Park, eight miles away.

Accommodations

Coupeville is blessed with many historic buildings, several of which have been turned into delightful B&Bs and inns. Unfortunately, they are priced accordingly and equally likely to be full on summer weekends. Be sure to make advance reservations.

UNDER $100

Tyee Motel (405 S. Main St., 360/678-6616,

www.tyeehotel.com, $64–80 s or d) has nine comfortable no-frills sorts of rooms and an attached restaurant and lounge.

Anchorage Inn B&B (807 N. Main St., 360/678-5581 or 877/230-1313, www.anchorage-inn.com, $95–149 s or d) offers seven guest rooms, each with their own Victorian-inspired theme and private baths.

$100-150

The **Compass Rose B&B** (508 S. Main St., 360/678-5318 or 800/237-3881, www.compassrosebandb.com, $115 s or d), is housed in a striking 19th-century Queen Anne home packed with antiques. The friendly owners provide two handsomely appointed rooms with a shared bath.

Coupeville Inn (200 NW Coveland St., 360/678-6668 or 800/247-6162, www.thecoupevilleinn.com, $105–145 s or d) has spacious pet-friendly motel rooms with waterside views of Penn Cove.

Garden Isle Guest Cottages B&B (207 NW Coveland St., 360/678-5641 or 877/881-1203, www.gardenislecottages.com, $120–140 d) features two cottages with kitchens and a continental breakfast is included. One cottage has a gas fireplace, and both share an outside hot tub.

The Victorian Italianate-style **Inn at Penn Cove B&B** (702 N. Main, 360/678-8000 or 800/688-2683, www.whidbey.net/penncove, $99–140 s d) provides four guest rooms with private baths and fireplaces. Kids are accepted with advance notice. The building is also home to the popular The Cove Thai Cuisine restaurant.

$150-200

 Captain Whidbey Inn (2072 W. Captain Whidbey Inn Rd., 360/678-4097 or 800/366-4097, www.captainwhidbey.com) has European-style rooms with shared baths ($99–199 d) and suites ($190 d) inside this classic two-story inn built in 1907 from madrona logs. Also here are modern cabins and cottages ($193–230 d). The gardenlike grounds face Penn Cove. Even if you aren't staying here, be sure to stop and take in the scenery or sip a drink in the bar. The lodge also operates a 52-foot wooden ketch, the *SV Cutty Sark*, with regularly scheduled sailing trips.

Right next to Fort Casey State Park, **Fort Casey Inn** (360/678-5050 or 866/661-6604, www.fortcaseyinn.com) consists of 10 restored Georgian revival homes that served as officers' quarters during World War I. These large two-story homes are divided into two duplex units each, with full kitchens and private baths. The basements were built to be used as bomb shelters in case of attack, and some still have the original steel-shuttered windows. These duplexes rent for $165–175 for up to four people. One motel-style unit is also available for $85 s or d.

CAMPING

A small and crowded campground (360/678-4519, www.parks.wa.gov, $22 for tents, $27 for RVs with hookups) at Fort Casey is open year-round and has showers. These exposed sites are right on the water next to the busy ferry terminal. No reservations are accepted, so get here early to be assured of a site on summer weekends.

You can also try **Rhododendron Campground** two miles east of Coupeville on Highway 20. It's easy to miss; look for the small blue camping sign on the highway. Here you'll find 10 in-the-woods campsites ($15/day) in a second-growth stand of Douglas fir trees and rhododendrons that bloom each April and May.

Food

The townies on Whidbey like to take their squeezes out on dates to (**Christopher's** (103 NW Coveland St., 360/678-5480, www.christophersonwhidbey.com, 11:30 A.M.–2 P.M. Mon.–Fri., noon–2:30 P.M. Sat. and 5–9 P.M. daily, $18). They don't come for the view—there isn't one—or trendy decor. The main attraction here is the food. The chef simmers art on the stove, with creations such as baked raspberry salmon ($20.95) and bacon-wrapped pork tenderloin with smoked cheddar gratin ($17.95).

Get dependably good pub grub—including

fish and chips, Reubens, and mussel chowder—at **Toby's Tavern** (8 NW Front St., 360/678-4222, 11 A.M.–10 P.M. daily, $10). The 1884 red building *is* a bar, so no kids allowed. Toby's even has its very own microbrew.

The Oystercatcher (901 Grace St., 360/678-0683, www.oystercatcherwhidbey.com, 5–8 P.M. Thurs.–Sun., closed Mon.–Tues., entrées $25) is a delightful little out-of-the-way restaurant behind the *Coupeville Examiner* newspaper office. The short but sophisticated menu changes frequently but always includes shellfish hors d'oeuvres.

You can also get a mussel appetizer and a drink and enjoy the quiet ambience in the dining room at **Captain Whidbey Inn** (2072 W. Captain Whidbey Inn Rd., 360/678-4097 or 800/366-4097, www.captainwhidbey.com, 5–9 P.M. daily), which offers unparalleled views of Penn Cove. Reservations required; dinner entrées run $18–25.

Information and Services

Coupeville lacks a visitors center, but the museum has local brochures, or you can get them from the **Central Whidbey Chamber of Commerce** (360/678-5434, www.centralwhidbeychamber.com). The **Coupeville Library** (360/678-2911, www.sno-isle.org) is located at 788 NW Alexander Street.

Getting There and Around

From the Olympic Peninsula, board the **ferry** in Port Townsend to arrive at the Keystone landing next to Fort Casey State Park approximately 30 minutes later. These ferries operate about every 45 minutes 7 A.M.–10 P.M. in the summer, and one-way fares are $2.75 for passengers ($0.35 extra one-way for bikes), and $11.70 for car and driver. Be ready for a two-hour wait during peak times on summer weekends.

Island Transit (360/678-7771, or 800/240-8747, www.islandtransit.org) has free bus service Monday–Saturday throughout Whidbey.

OAK HARBOR

Full of Irish, Dutch, and general sailing folk influence, the town of Oak Harbor takes its name from the many ancient Garry oak trees that once grew here—few are left, but those remaining are protected by law. Part of a strategic naval chokepoint, Oak Harbor saw a flood of men and materiel during World War II, briefly changing the sleepy little town into a hub of activity. Today the Whidbey Island Naval Air Station just outside Oak Harbor is the only naval aviation support base in the Pacific Northwest.

The city's historic downtown faces the water and retains some maritime character. While not as scenic as the wide-open, rolling meadows and cool, damp woods elsewhere, the convenience of town makes up for it somewhat. Oak Harbor is the cheapest place to pick up gas and groceries on the island, and there are a number of affordable motels here.

Sights

Windjammer Park (360/679-5551), at the end of Beeksma Drive, has a sandy beach, picnic tables, swimming and wading pools, tennis and baseball facilities, campsites along the lagoon, and a Dutch-style windmill. There's a nice view of the harbor from here, and a great playground. Look for ducks along the shore. **Dugualla Bay State Park** (E. Sleeper Rd., 360/279-4500) is a small undeveloped park with almost a mile of muddy shoreline. The park is a good spot to watch birds and other wildlife and peek across the channel at Goat Island.

See the sculpture and public art at **Fort Nugent Park** (2075 SW Ft. Nugent St., 360/279-4500). Oak Harbor established the first "1 Percent for Art" program in the region, which diverts 1 percent of money usually used to maintain infrastructure and services to fund public art projects instead. An $80,000 art blitzkrieg is planned for the next few years that would install statuary and sculpture in the most traveled points of town.

Entertainment and Events

Whidbey Playhouse (730 SE Midway Blvd., 360/679-2237 or 800/606-7529, www .whidbeyplayhouse.com) produces five shows

throughout the season, ranging from plays to musicals to variety shows and mysteries. Tickets are $16 for all seats.

For something a little different, **Blue Fox Drive-In Theatre** (1403 Monroe Landing Rd., 360/675-5667, www.bluefoxdrivein .com) is one of the last outdoor movie theaters in Washington. Not to mention, they have go-karts!

The last weekend in April, Oak Harbor's Dutch roots appear as it hosts **Holland Happening**—a downtown street festival, parade, international dance festival, Dutch dinner, and tulip show in Holland Gardens. The **4th of July** celebration includes a parade and fireworks, followed in mid-July by **Whidbey Island Race Week** (360/675-6399, whidbey islandraceweek.com), one of the top 20 yachting regattas in the world. In early December, the **Christmas Boat Parade** departs from Oak Harbor, proceeding around Penn Cove to the Coupeville Wharf and back.

Sports and Recreation

Smith Park at Midway Boulevard has an impressive grove of old Garry oak trees as well as a large erratic boulder left behind by the last ice age.

Joseph Whidbey State Park (www.parks .wa.gov) just south of the Naval Air Station on Swantown Road, is largely undeveloped, with picnic tables and a few trails. The real attraction here is a long and scenic beach, one of the most beautiful on the island.

The city is home to the 18-hole **Gallery Golf Course** (Crosby Rd., 360/257-2295, $16 civilian, $9 military), run by the U.S. Navy with most of its use by Naval personnel. The course is playable by the public, however, and rental clubs are available.

Accommodations

It might not be Whidbey's most idyllic town, but Oak Harbor can be just the right post on which budgeting families can hitch for the night. Lodging options are less expensive, and the town has an abundance of fast-food joints and grocery stores.

NORTH PUGET SOUND

Kitchenette units are more expensive at **Auld Holland Inn** (33575 Hwy. 20, 360/675-2288 or 800/228-0148, www.auld-holland-inn.com, $40–149 d) but worth the extra couple of bucks, as they are a bit more charming and clean. This Dutch-style motel has a whirling windmill outside and old-country furnishings with floral linens within. Amenities include an outdoor pool and hot tub, sauna, tennis court, exercise room, and lawn games.

Though slightly more expensive than the motel competition, **Coachman Inn** (35959 Hwy. 20, 360/675-0727 or 800/635-0043, www.thecoachmaninn.com, $98–209 d) should be on the summertime short list. The well-tended rooms range from the basic to suites and even an indoor hot-tub honeymoon room. There's an outdoor pool and exercise room, and continental breakfast is included.

Nicest of the bunch is **Best Western Harbor Plaza** (33175 Hwy. 20, 360/679-4567 or 800/927-5478, $90–140 d), which kids love for the deluxe breakfast's do-it-yourself waffle maker and the fresh popcorn and cookies served in the afternoon. Rack rates here are some of the priciest in Oak Harbor, but you're also more likely to get a deep discount online for this place than any other accommodations in Oak Harbor. The property has an outdoor pool, hot tub, and fitness center.

Food

Like any town that plays host to our men and women in uniform, Oak Harbor's restaurants fall into the traditional American food groups: burgers, pizza joints, and steakhouses.

The best among classic American eateries is the aviation-themed **Flyers** (32295 Hwy. 20, 360/675-5858, www.eatatflyers.com, 11 A.M.–9 P.M. daily, $15), This kid-friendly brewpub has a huge menu featuring salads, prime rib and steaks, seafood, and even lamb shanks. Sure to satisfy big parties with different tastes.

For Cantonese and Szechuan meals, stop by the friendly **China Harbor** (630 SE Pioneer Way, 360/679-1557, chinaharborbistro.com, 11 A.M.–11 P.M. Mon.–Sat., 2 P.M.–midnight Sun., $9). For quality Mediterranean food, try **Zorba's** (841 SE Pioneer Way, 360/279-8322, 11 A.M.–9 P.M. Mon.–Sat., $13). You'll find staples like gyros and moussaka along with some traditional Italian dishes. It can get busy and loud in the evenings.

If you intend on touring the island for the day, stop by **Bayleaf** (720 SE Pioneer Way, Ste. 1-B, 360/675-6600, www.bayleaf.us, 11 A.M.–6 P.M. Tues.–Fri., 10 A.M.–5 P.M. Sat., noon–4 P.M. Sun.) first for some picnic provisions. This little store is a foodie's delight, serving up artisan cheeses, cured meats, olives, fresh rustic breads, and a good selection of wine to pair with it all.

The **Oak Harbor Public Market** (360/675-0472) is held 3–7 P.M. on Thursdays June–September next to the visitors center.

Information

The **Oak Harbor Visitor Center** (32630 Hwy. 20, 360/675-3535, www.oakharborchamber.com) is open 9 A.M.–5 P.M. Monday–Friday all year, plus 10 A.M.–4 P.M. Saturday in the summer. The **Oak Harbor Library** (360/675-5115, www.sno-isle.org) is located at 1000 SE Regatta Drive.

Getting There and Around

Catch **Island Transit** (360/321-6688 or 800/240-8747, www.islandtransit.org, free) Route 1 in Oak Harbor bound for parts south and Clinton. Route 5 snakes north all the way off the island to Mount Vernon.

Ride on **Airporter Shuttle** (360/380-8800 or 800/235-5247, www.airporter.com) between Oak Harbor and Sea-Tac Airport.

DECEPTION PASS STATE PARK

Washington's most popular state park, Deception Pass is best known for the spectacular green bridge that spans the narrow waterway that flows between Fidalgo and Whidbey Islands. When Capt. George Vancouver first visited the waterway in 1792, he thought it was an inlet and called it Port Gardner. When he realized that he'd made a mistake and that

© ERICKA CHICKOWSKI

Washington's most scenic bridge, Deception Pass Bridge

it was actually a tidal passage, he renamed it Deception Pass, probably not without some embarrassment. The name has a second meaning, too. The swirling, tricky waters here have befuddled many a sailor since Vancouver.

Nine miles north of Oak Harbor on Highway 20, the 3,600-acre park covers ground on both ends of the bridge and offers facilities that rival those of some national parks: swimming and fishing at two lakes, four miles of shoreline, 28 miles of hiking trails, fresh and saltwater fishing, boating, rowboat rentals, boat launches, viewpoints, an environmental learning center, and several hundred campsites.

Sights

Completed in 1935, **Deception Pass Bridge,** a steel cantilever-truss beauty built by the Civilian Conservation Corps (CCC), which also built many other park structures. The bridge towers 182 feet above the water. It's estimated that each year more than three million people stop at the bridge to take a dizzying look over the edge or to enjoy the sunset vistas. The

best view of this architectural marvel, though, is from below. Check out the trusses from their underbelly at the south end of the bridge. The beach below is accessible by taking the road to the North Beach picnic area.

Bowman Bay is just north of the bridge on the west side of the highway and has campsites, a boat launch, and a fishing pier. The **CCC Interpretive Center** (Thurs.–Mon. summers only), can be found here as well, which chronicles the work and impact of the Civilian Conservation Corps of the 1930s.

Rosario Beach, just north of Bowman Bay, features a delightful picnic ground with CCC-built stone shelters. The **Maiden of Deception Pass** totem pole here commemorates the legend of a Samish girl who became the bride of the water spirit.

Sports and Recreation
WATER SPORTS

Only electric motors, canoes, or rowboats are allowed on the park's lakes. The most visible of the two is **Pass Lake,** around which Highway

© ERICKA CHICKOWSKI

The state park system's prize jewel, Deception Pass State Park offers two excellent freshwater fishing lakes, Pass Lake and Cranberry Lake.

20 curves. This is a fly-fisher's delight, and on any given weekend you're likely to see plenty of anglers looping their lines overhead as they bob in float-tubes. Fishing is catch-and-release only. You can observe beaver dams, muskrats, and mink in the marshes on the south side of shallow **Cranberry Lake,** which also hosts a seasonal concession stand. There's good fishing for trout here, and the warm water makes it a favorite swimming hole. The waters around the pass are also a magnet for anglers, with good saltwater fishing for lingcod, salmon, smelt, and bottom fish. One of the best holes for some leisurely shore fishing is **Hoypus Point,** at the end of Coronet Bay Road.

Anglers and pleasure boaters can get their craft in the water at the one-lane launch at Bowman Bay. But be aware that the tricky waters of the pass still require skill to navigate. At peak tide the current can reach up to eight knots.

This warning is especially important for kayakers—don't even think about crossing the pass by paddle unless you have years of experience.

Instead, stick to the calmer waters along the rest of the park's shorelines, which can provide hours of exploration and a chance to find seals, porpoises, and other marine life along the way. **Anacortes Kayak Tours** (800/992-1801, May–Oct., $35 adults, $25 children) caters to first-time paddlers and those without their own boats during its 1.5-hour guided trips within Bowman Bay.

If you are set on riding through the pass but you don't have the boat or the maritime skills, then hop aboard *The Island Whaler,* a most-unusual open-deck jet catamaran run by **Deception Pass Tours** (360/914-0096 or 888/909-8687, www.deceptionpasstours.com, $21 adults, $19 children), which runs hourly boat tours from April through October. Tickets are sold at a concession in the parking lot on the south end of the bridge.

If you get your kicks below water rather than over it, then bring your dive gear out to Rosario Beach. Just offshore is an underwater park that stretches all the way to Northwest Island.

HIKING

A scenic trail leads down from the southwest side of the bridge to a lovely rocky beach strewn with bleached driftwood.

A 15-minute hike to the highest point on the island, 400-foot **Goose Rock,** provides views of the San Juan Islands, Mt. Baker, Victoria, and Fidalgo Island, and possibly bald eagles soaring overhead. The trail starts at the south end of the bridge, heading east from either side of the highway; take the wide trail as it follows the pass, then take one of the unmarked spur trails uphill to the top. A half-mile hiking trail circles Rosario Head, the wooded point of land that juts into Rosario Bay. The shoreline is the perfect place to explore tide pools.

Other hiking trails lead throughout the park, ranging from short nature paths to unimproved trails for experienced hikers only.

Camping

With 178 campsites, **Deception Pass State Park** (41020 SR 20, 360/675-2417, www .parks.wa.gov) offers some of the best camping in this part of Washington, with tall Douglas fir trees and a gorgeous lakeside setting. Just be prepared for the crowds—it's no secret this one is a gem. The primary campground along Cranberry Lake has year-round sites, and a second campground (open summers only) is just north of the bridge at Bowman Bay. The cost for both is $12–25 for tents, $29–36 for RVs including hot showers and disposal stations. Make reservations ($6.50–8.50 extra) at 888/226-7688 or www.parks.wa.gov. Head to the park's outdoor amphitheater on weekend evenings in the summer for natural history lectures and slide shows.

If the public campground is full—and it does fill up frequently—RVers can try **Quinn's Deception Pass Campground** (5050 N. Hwy. 20, 360/675-9597). And there's always the local Wal-Mart (1250 SW Erie St.) lot, which becomes an unofficial RV park each summer.

THE MAIDEN OF DECEPTION PASS

The Samish Tribe have a legend that explains the plentiful shellfish on local beaches. The Maiden of Deception Pass, Ko-Kwal-Alwoot, was possessed of exceptional beauty, a fact not lost on the sea spirit. The spirit confessed his love to the maiden and often dropped by to pitch woo as she collected clams on the beach. As will happen, the sea spirit eventually decided that the time was right and he would go ask the maiden's father for her hand in marriage. Unsurprisingly, the father was less than enthused, asking how he might hope to provide for his daughter – a daughter who would immediately drown, probably before the wedding reception had even ended. The relentless sea spirit gently tried to convince the father by bringing down drought and famine on him and his family. Eventually, the offer was warmly accepted, the father agreeing that yes, mistakes were made. The father asked one thing, though. Still not convinced of his daughter's ability to not die while occupying her nuptial home, he asked that the maiden be sent home once a year so he could check up, after the fashion of many fathers-in-law through the present day. It was quickly agreed and they were off. For many years, Ko-Kwal-Alwoot returned faithfully, but each time, she was more covered with barnacles and more generally sealike in attitude. After watching this uncomfortable spectacle for four years, the people let her know that, really, the visit wasn't so necessary and she mustn't go through the trouble on their behalf, and gave her their best wishes and said goodbye. Instead of the visit, the once-beautiful maiden makes sure that the beach is strewn with shellfish and that the springs are clear and clean.

The unabridged legend is inscribed on a story pole on Fidalgo Island. To get there, follow Highway 20 to Fidalgo Island, go west at Pass Lake, following the signs for Bowman Bay and Rosario Beach, and hike the trail toward Rosario Head.

Everett

Flanked by craggy mountains to the east and sweeping vistas of Whidbey Island to the west, Everett is at heart a blue collar community. Sailors, lumbermen, and workers at the nearby Boeing plant rub elbows with the techies of Seattle who can't quite fork out the green for more urban digs. Highway 2 begins to wind eastward to Stevens Pass and Wenatchee here, and the Snohomish River curves north on the edge of town on its way to Puget Sound.

SIGHTS
◖ Future of Flight Center and Boeing Tour

Aviation buffs can get a close-up look at how Boeing puts together its giant 747, 767, 777, and 787 jets at its gargantuan Everett factory plant. Big aircraft need a big building—this structure is the largest building in the world, measured by volume. The facility is so huge that you'll sometimes see workers riding on one of the company-provided bicycles that help get them around in a hurry.

The tour begins at the slick Future of Flight Center (8415 Paine Field Blvd., 425/438-8100 or 800/464-1476, www.futureofflight.org, $18 adults, $12 children under 15), where kids and kids-at-heart flock to the 727 flight deck to imagine they're at the controls. Visitors will also encounter narrated videos on Boeing innovations, flight simulators, and a 200-yard runway with the nose of a 727 about to take off.

Then it is on to the assembly line tour, a 90-minute walk through the building and onto an observation deck that overlooks shiny airplanes under construction.

For security reasons, visitors are not allowed to bring cameras, cell phones, purses, or other personal items on the tour. Babies and toddlers are also banned from the tour and there is no daycare on premises, so plan accordingly. Tours begin on the hour starting at 9 A.M., with the

a view over the Everett waterfront

© ERICKA CHICKOWSKI

last tour departing at 3 P.M. Reservations are highly recommended.

Jetty Island

Families flock to Jetty Island (425/257-8300, www.everettwa.org) as regularly as the waterfowl and sea mammals. This two-mile stretch of sand is a happy byproduct of dredging done at the nearby mouth of the Snohomish River.

The island is an ideal spot to strike out with binoculars dangling from your neck and a picnic basket from your arms. Don't forget a bathing suit—the shallow water nearby warms up to 70°F by August. A free passenger ferry (425/257-8300, www.everettwa.org) departs Marina Park for Jetty Island every half hour from July–mid-September.

Downtown Everett

In its early years, Everett was home to some of the timber industry's most successful entrepreneurs. These lumber barons built elaborate mansions in the north end of town on Grand and Rucker Avenues, many of which still stand.

They surround a small but well-restored commercial district around the vicinity of Hewitt Avenue from Broadway west to Grand Avenue. If you tour down Grand Avenue, be sure to stop at the grassy strip that is **Grand Avenue Park.** With your back to the stately homes in this neighborhood, you will get a panoramic view of Port Gardner and **Everett Marina,** the Puget Sound's second largest. That will whet your appetite for another great viewpoint at American Legion Park less than two miles away—simply head north on Grand Avenue and veer right to **Alverson Boulevard** when the road forks. You can't miss the grassy banks of the park sitting on the bluff.

Museums and Art

Paine Field is home to the **Museum of Flight Restoration Center** (425/745-5150, www .museumofflight.org, 9 A.M.–5 P.M. Tues.–Sat., $2 donation), where aircraft are restored before going on display at the interesting Museum of Flight in Seattle. The center is located in Building C-72. Get here from the Boeing Tour Center by returning to Highway 526 eastbound and taking the first exit (Airport Road). Head south on Airport Road for a mile, and turn right onto 100th Street SW. Building C-72 is on the right side.

The **Schack Art Center** (2919 Hoyt Ave., 425/259-5050, www.artscouncilofsnoco.org, 10 A.M.–6 P.M. Mon.–Fri., 10 A.M.–5 P.M. Sat., noon–5 P.M. Sun.), hosts a juried art show, and exhibits works of regional artists.

The award-winning **Imagine Children's Museum** (1502 Wall St., 425/258-1006, www .imagineCM.org, 9 A.M.–5 P.M. Tues.–Wed., 10 A.M.–5 P.M. Thurs.–Sat., 11 A.M.–5 P.M. Sun., $7.75) is a creative tiny town for tykes where kids can sharpen their imagination in more than a dozen unique play environments.

ENTERTAINMENT AND EVENTS
Nightlife

The sprawling **Manhattan Center** (1611 Everett Ave., 425/259-3551, www.clubbroadway.com) has live music just about every night, catering to a top-40, country, rock, and dance audience. Pool tables, darts, karaoke further provide the perfect atmosphere for off-track betting and pull tabs.

Get your fill of twang and twirls at **McCabe's American Music Café** (3120 Hewitt Ave., 425/252-3082, www.mccabes everett.com), which plays country music and offers a full slate of dance lessons. They also have a calendar packed with live shows.

Performance Venues

The 8,300-seat **Comcast Arena** (425/322-2600, www.comcastarenaeverett.com) at Everett Events Center is the largest concert venue in the North Sound region. The arena regularly hosts top-billed stars such as Justin Beiber, Guns N' Roses, and Duran Duran, not to mention wrestling, roller-derby, and circus events. This is also a favorite stopover for big-name ice-skating shows like *Disney on Ice.*

The Arts

Theatrical performances are held throughout the year in the new showpiece **Performing Arts Center** (2710 Wetmore Ave., 425/257-8600). The theater features touring musicals, plays, concerts, and regional performing arts groups, and also houses the **Arts Council Gift Gallery.** The remodeled **Historic Everett Theatre** (2911 Colby Ave., 425/258-6766, www.everetttheatre.org) is home to movies, concerts, and live theater productions throughout the year.

The **Everett Symphony** (425/257-8382, www.everettsymphony.org) performs at the Everett Civic Auditorium October through June. The **Port Gardner Bay Chamber Music Society** (360/658-1129, www.everettchorale.org) performs at the historic Hartley Mansion (2300 Rucker Ave.) during the winter months. For something less formal, the **Music in the Parks** program (425/257-8300) brings live music to local parks on Sunday and Tuesday afternoons in July and August.

Festivals and Events

Held on the first weekend in June, **Salty Sea Days** (425/339-1113, www.saltyseadays.org) features a parade, Navy ship tours, hydroplane races, an arts show, live music, and outrigger canoe races. Return in August for two days of blues music at **Blues by the Bay** (425/339-1113, www.bluesbythebay.com).

A summer-long recreational event from July–September sponsored by the parks department, **Jetty Island Days** (425/257-8300) includes free ferry rides to the island from Marina Village, guided nature walks, sailing and rowing regattas, concerts, and campfire programs, as well as beachcombing and bird-watching on a saltwater beach.

In late September, Everett garners national attention among anglers for its **Everett Coho Salmon Derby** (Port of Everett, 1111 Craftsman Way, 800/729-7678, www.everettcohoderby.com). It costs $25 to enter and you'll need your own boat, rigs, and tackle and a Washington fishing permit. This is the largest derby of its type on the West Coast, which makes it the largest one just about anywhere. The prize is upwards of $3,000. The pee-wee league awards around $100.

SHOPPING

The area's largest shopping center is in South Everett at **Everett Mall** (1402 SE Everett Mall Way, 425/355-1771, www.shopeverettmall.com), with over 140 small shops, as well as giant department stores Macy's and Sears. Everett Mall Way and intersecting Evergreen Way are also a mecca for discount shoppers, with enough strip malls to keep granny shopping for days.

In North Everett along the bay at **Everett Marina Village** (1728 W Marine View Dr, 800/729-7678, www.portofeverett.com), you'll find an 1890s-style waterfront marketplace with restaurants, gift shops and clothing stores.

The **Everett Public Market** (2804 Grand Ave.) has more than 100 antique dealers, plus fresh fish and produce, and Sisters Restaurant.

SPORTS AND RECREATION

Spectator Sports

The Seattle Mariners' Class-A farm team, the **Everett Aquasox** (3802 Broadway, 425/258-3673, www.aquasox.com), plays at Everett Memorial Stadium (3900 Broadway) from mid-June–Labor Day. The games offer great family fun. The Comcast Arena (425/322-2600, www.comcastarenaeverett.com) is the home rink for the **Everett Silvertips** (www.everettsilvertips.com), a major junior hockey team playing in the Western Hockey League.

Water Sports

If you've ever watched the elegant yet extreme kiteboarders as their kites fill with air, launching them off of the waves, and thought, "I wish I could try that," Everett could be your ticket to adrenaline-ville. The **Motion Boardshop** (8319 Aurora Ave N in Seattle, 206/372-5268, http://motionboardshop.com) offers classes at all levels and lets you borrow their equipment. Lessons take place at Everett's Jetty Island and range from rank beginner ($99) to blasting through the ranks, learning through doing ($349). They also rent out standup paddleboards for $25 per hour. **Northwest Fishing Charters** (206/949-0221, http://nwfishingcharters.com), offers seven-hour fishing trips for $180 per person, as well as private charters aboard its 28-foot boats. Washington State fishing permits are necessary for all guests and can be purchased in just about any sporting goods shop or online at fishhunt.dfw.wa.gov.

Swim and sunbathe in the summertime at **Thornton A. Sullivan Park at Silver Lake** (11400 W Silver Lake Rd., 425/257-8300, www.ci.everett.wa.us). A lifeguard is on duty from 11 A.M.–6 P.M. between late June and Labor Day.

PORT OF EVERETT

At first glance, the Port of Everett seems to be just like any other along the coast. Cargo ships haul containers in and out, commercial fishermen ply their trade and the marina is chock full of motor yachts and sailboats. This natural deep-water port does stand out a bit, though. Surrounded by state parks and lined with shops and residences, the port and marina have just a tad more personality than many facilities like it. The marina itself is equipped with 2,300 slips with water and electricity hookups, along with shower, laundry, and restroom facilities. Reservations for moorage ($0.55 per foot per night in winter, $0.75 per foot per night in summer) are accepted during the summer between Memorial Day and Labor Day and on a first-come, first-served basis the rest of the year. There are also pump-out and dump facilities, a fuel dock, and several restaurants on premises. Guests can stay up to six hours at no charge.

Skippers looking to get their craft into the waters of the Puget Sound should go a couple blocks away to the **10th Street Boat Launch** (10th St. and Marine View Dr., 425/259-6001, 4 A.M.–11 P.M. daily Apr.–Sept., 6 A.M.–7 P.M. daily Oct.–Mar., $8 per launch).

Golf

Perched on a hill overlooking the Everett waterfront, **Legion Memorial Golf Course** (144 W. Marine View Dr., 425/259-4653, http://everettgolf.com/leg, $36 adult, $28 senior or military) offers up some primo views of Puget Sound. The grounds are decent for municipal links at this price. Everett's other muni, the **Walter E. Hall Golf Course** (1226 W. Casino Rd., 425/353-4653, http://everettgolf.com/hall, $36) is a gentle course that presents the opportunity for a round with the family in a lightly wooded setting.

Running and Cycling

The paved 11-mile-long **Interurban Trail** connects Lynnwood with Everett and is very popular with cyclists and in-line skaters. Also check out the 1.6-mile **Lowell Riverfront Trail** located just off Lenora Street. Get local park information at 425/388-6600 or www1.co.snohomish.wa.us/Departments/Parks.

ACCOMMODATIONS
Under $100

There are a bevy of discount hotels and motels in the northern and southern outskirts of town. Particularly beware of many of the cut-rate offerings on North Broadway Avenue. Some of these joints are a health inspector's worst nightmare and attract a live-in crowd of questionable character.

One reasonably comfortable and secure option is **Sunrise Motor Inn** (8421 Evergreen Way/Hwy. 99, 425/347 1100 or 888/222 2112, www.sunriseinneverett.com $67–69 s or d), on the south end of town, with laundry facilities, free high-speed Internet, and recently remodeled rooms. It lays out a continental breakfast in the morning.

$100-150

Sometimes, it's just worth it to jump up a price bracket.

At the scenic Everett Marina, **◖ The Inn at Port Gardner** (1700 W. Marine View Dr., 425/252-6779 or 888/252-6779, www.innatportgardner.com, $140–189 d, $235 d for a deluxe suite) has the best hotel view in town. The cannery-style lodge is a good-looking specimen, though the furniture is a bit cheap for the image the exterior and lobby present. But rooms are clean, the staff cheerful, and the dockside location makes up for it. Tell the clerk if you are traveling on business—there is a generous midweek discount to road warriors. Pet-friendly.

If you prefer the predictability of chain hotels, your top pick should be the **Holiday Inn Downtown Everett** (3105 Pine St., 877/863-4780, www.holidayinn.com, $127–190 d). Just a stone's throw from the Everett Transit Center and downtown, and conveniently located right off the freeway, this airy tower hotel has clean and updated rooms, along with a pool, spa, cocktail lounge, and fitness center. Rooms face away from the freeway for a quiet night's sleep, and morning brings a breakfast buffet smorgasbord that is the envy of other establishments' measly continental offerings.

Camping
There are no nearby public parks with campgrounds, but **Lakeside RV Park** (12321 Hwy. 99 S, or 800/468-7275, $38) is on a three-acre lake with all hookups and facilities.

FOOD
Cafés
Start the day at **The Sisters Restaurant** (2804 Grand Ave., 425/252-0480, 7 A.M.–4 P.M. Mon.–Fri., $8), a friendly place with great breakfast specials and espresso coffees. Lunches include great soups (especially the chilled tomato and avocado), salads, veggie burgers, and homemade ice cream.

If you're down on the marina, find lunchtime panini sandwiches and other tasty light meals at **Meyer's Café** (1700 W. Marine View Dr., 425/259-3875, 6:30 A.M.–3 P.M. daily, $7). Enjoy BBQ so smoky that it sells its unused firewood out back at **The Depot Café and Smokehouse** (3201 McDugall Ave., 425/257-3140, www.depotcafebbq.com, 11:30 A.M.–3 P.M. Tues.–Wed., 11:30 A.M.–7 P.M. Thurs.–Sat.). The restaurant was built in an actual 1900s train depot; apt since the owner travels the country competing head

to head with other master craftsman of BBQ sauce at public contests.

Steak and Seafood
Everett Marina Village has a couple of popular seafood restaurants with views to match the food. **Anthony's HomePort** (1726 W. Marine View Dr., 425/252-3333, www.anthonys.com, 11 A.M.–3 P.M. Mon.–Sat. and 4:30–9:30 P.M. Mon.–Thurs., 4:30–10:30 P.M. Fri.–Sat., 3–9:30 P.M. Sun., brunch 10 A.M.–2 P.M. Sun., $30) has fresh Northwest and imported seafood flown in fresh daily, plus tasty fish and chips for a simpler meal. **Anthony's Woodfire Grill** (1722 W. Marine View Dr., 425/258-4000, www.anthonys.com, 11:30 A.M.–3:30 P.M. Wed.–Sun., and 3:30–9:30 P.M. Mon.–Thurs., 3:30–10:30 P.M. Fri.–Sat., 3:30–9:00 P.M. Sun., $16) serves steak, prime rib, pasta, seafood, and the unique margarita-infused crab entrée.

Located, unsurprisingly, on Silver Lake, **Emory's on Silver Lake** (11830 19th Ave. SE, 425/337-7772, www.emorys.com, 11 A.M.–2 P.M. Mon.–Sat. and 4 P.M.–close nightly, 10–2 P.M. Sun., brunch $20) is a pleasant, upscale place for seafood and steak.

International
For waterfront views while you enjoy your pasta or pizza, head to ◖ **Lombardi's Cucina** (1620 W. Marine View Dr., 425/252-1886, www.lombardiscucina.com, 11:30 A.M.–9:30 P.M. Sun.–Thurs., 11:30 A.M.–10 P.M. Fri.–Sat., 11 A.M.–2 P.M. Sun. for brunch, $15), a favorite lunchtime hangout for the suit-and-tie crowd and a very pleasant spot to take a date for late afternoon drinks and appetizers.

Enjoy Neapolitan cuisine in a colorful yet tasteful setting at **Gianni's Ristorante Italiano** (5030 Evergreen Way, 425/252-2435, www.giannisitaliano.com, 11 A.M.–9 P.M. Tues.–Thurs., 11 A.M.–10 P.M. Fri. 11:30 A.M.–10 P.M. Sat., 3–9 P.M. Sun., $15), so reminiscent of the Rat Pack days, you can almost hear Dino sing "That's Amore."

Spice of Thai (607 Everett Mall Way SE, 425/290-7900, 11 A.M.–9 P.M. Sun.–Thurs.,

11 A.M.–10 P.M. Fri.–Sat., $9) is one of those unexpected gems. Located in a strip mall, this small restaurant cranks out great curries, Thai eggplant, and other specialties at inexpensive prices.

Pub Grub

Sporty's Beef & Brew (6503 Evergreen Way, 425/347-1733, www.sportysbeefandbrew. com, 11 A.M.–2 P.M. Mon.–Sat., 11 A.M.–midnight Sun., $8) serves burgers and beer and attracts sports fans with its pull tabs, shuffleboard, three pool tables, and of course, large-screen televisions. Or head to the main Colby strip downtown where the **Flying Pig Brewing Co.** (2929 Colby Ave., 425/339-1393, 11 A.M.–9 P.M. Mon.–Thurs., 11 A.M.–midnight Fri.–Sat., 11 A.M.–9 P.M. Sun., $12) prepares a better menu. By day, servers bring out pub classics like pulled pork and French dip sandwiches and big burgers. But at night, the chefs really roll up their sleeves to serve gourmet dishes such as seafood cioppino, crab cakes, and rib eye with green peppercorn butter.

For beer and atmosphere on the waterfront, **Scuttlebutt Brewing Co.** (1205 Craftsman Way, Ste. 101., 425/257-9316, www.scuttlebuttbrewing.com, 11 A.M.–9 P.M. Mon.–Thurs., 11 A.M.–11 P.M. Fri.–Sat., 11 A.M.– 9 P.M. Sun., $10) wins the prize. Situated at Everett Marina, Scuttlebutt offers delicious fish and chips, perfect for washing down with their consistent, award-winning ales that run from light blonds to deep porters. The good brews are a magnet for locals during after-work hours.

Bakeries and Markets

On a cold Northwest day, there's nothing more inviting than the warm smell of fresh-baked breads, European pastries, and hot soups that greet you upon entering the door at (**Pavé Specialty Bakery** (2613 Colby Ave., 425/252-0250, www.pavebakery.com, 7 A.M.–5 P.M. Mon.–Fri., 7 A.M.–3 P.M. Sat., closed Sun.).

The **Everett Farmers Market** (425/347-2790, www.everettfarmersmarket.com) takes place at Port Gardner Landing in the marina 11 A.M.–4 P.M. Sunday June–October and offers great times and fresh food. There is live music every week, styles ranging from that old-timey sound to adult contemporary.

INFORMATION AND SERVICES

For maps and brochures, stop by **Everett Tourism and Vistor Services** (2000 Hewitt Avenue, Suite 120, 425/263-9001, www .snohomish.org, 10 A.M.–4 P.M. Mon.–Fri.).

The **Everett Public Library** (2702 Hoyt Ave., 425/257-8005, www.epls.org) allows only cardholders access to its Internet-enabled desktop computers, but free Wi-Fi is available for those with laptops.

GETTING THERE AND AROUND

The impressive **Everett Station** is the biggest multimodal station serving Snohomish County. Settled at the junction of Pacific Avenue and Smith Avenue, this is a major hub for local buses, Amtrak trains, and Sounder commuter trains.

By Bus

Everett Transit (425/257-8803, www .everettwa.org/transit) buses provide transportation within the city and to the Mukilteo ferry dock. Route 7 connects downtown to South Everett via Colby Avenue and Evergreen Way, and Route 2 connects North Everett and downtown to Boeing facilities. Fares are $0.75.

To get out of town, use **Community Transit** (425/353-7433 or 800/562-1375, www.comm trans.org). From Everett station, this service goes south to Lynnwood Transit Station near Edmonds and north to Arlington and Smokey Point via Route 201 and 202. Also from downtown, Routes 270, 271, and 275 service cities east, including Snohomish, Monroe, and Gold Bar. Route 280 will take you north to Granite Falls and Lake Stevens. Commuter service is available on Routes 510 and 513 to Seattle and 532 and 535 to Bellevue. Fares are $1.75 within Snohomish County and $4.50 to King County destinations.

For long-haul service along the I-5 corridor, **Greyhound** (800/231-2222, www.greyhound.com) is the best bet, linking Everett to Bellingham; Olympia; Vancouver, Washington; and other points south.

Travelers from Spokane or Boise may want to consider the **Northwestern Trailways** (800/366-3830, www.northwesterntrailways.com) line running across the mountains over Stevens Pass on Highway 2. Roundtrip fares to Spokane are about $80.

If you're flying into Sea-Tac Airport, **Shuttle Express** (425/981-7000 or 800/487-7433, www.shuttleexpress.com) has door-to-door van service between Sea-Tac and Everett; reservations are required.

By Train

Each weekday Sound Transit's commuter train the **Sounder** (206/398-5000, www.soundtransit.org) runs three times in the morning from Everett to Seattle, with stops at Mukilteo Station and Edmonds Station along the way, and three routes back again in the evening. The ride takes about one hour and costs $4.50 each way.

Amtrak trains serve the area from **Everett Station** (3201 Smith Ave. 425/258-2458 or 800/872-7245, www.amtrak.com). The *Empire Builder* heads south to Seattle and east to Spokane and Chicago. The *Cascades* provides daily train connections between Portland, Oregon, and Vancouver, B.C., via Mount Vernon and Bellingham.

Northern Snohomish County

Driving north from Everett on I-5, visitors will encounter a mixture of suburbs, outlet malls, and slower-paced rural enclaves all pointing to the logging and agricultural roots of Snohomish County. While towns such as Marysville, Arlington, and Lake Stevens are hardly tourism magnets, Snohomish County does have a few attractions and plenty of pretty country roads ready for a leisurely drive.

Coastal Camano Island has a pair of stunning state parks and cabins galore for a relaxing getaway. Tulalip Casino on the outskirts of Marysville is one of the top gambling resorts in the state. And southwest of Everett off Highway 2, the charming antique village of Snohomish provides a prime opportunity for window shopping and daydreaming about the good old days.

SIGHTS
Historic Snohomish

Attractive downtown Snohomish has a classic small-town feel and a real sense of the past. Settled in 1859 along the banks of the Snohomish and Pilchuck Rivers, Snohomish is a collection of eclectic historic homes and brick commercial buildings hosting some of the best antique shops in the state. The Museum at the heart of it all is the **Blackman Historic Museum** (118 Ave. B, 360/568-5235, http://blackmanhouse.org, noon–3 P.M. Sat.–Sun., $2 adults, $1 seniors or children), an 1878 pioneer mansion filled with area artifacts and Victorian furniture. Docent-led tours are available on Sundays only.

Camano Island State Park

Located 14 miles southwest from Stanwood, this state park (www.parks.wa.gov, open year-round) provides over a mile of shoreline and rocky beach along Saratoga Passage. The picnic tables on the park's west side provide striking views of Whidbey Island and the Olympics. Hiking trails, including a half-mile interpretive loop, wind through 600-year-old Douglas firs and maybe spot bald eagles and deer. Fish from the Point Lowell boat launch, or, season and conditions permitting, try your hand at clamming. The park's two camping areas have tent sites ($12–36, no hookups) and coin-operated showers.

Other Parks

In addition to nature trails, a duck pond, and

the **Rotary Ranch Petting Zoo** (360/659-8581, 10 A.M.–6 P.M. daily mid-May–mid-August), the 50-acre **Jennings Nature Park** (6915 Armar Rd. in Marysville, 360/659-3005) is home to the **Gehl House Historical Museum.**

Mother Nature's Window (100th St. NE and 55th Ave. NE in Marysville) is a private second-growth forest with an outdoor amphitheater and various carved objects.

Twin Rivers Park (SR 530 in Arlington, 425/388-6600) is grassy and green, with river access to the North Fork of the Stillaguamish River, just east of Arlington. Bring your Frisbees. This is one of the foremost disc golf courses in the Pacific Northwest.

Lundeen Park (10020 Lundeen Parkway in Lake Stevens, 425/334-1012) covers eight acres of shoreline just west of town, with a roped-off swimming beach, playground, picnic tables, and grand views across the water to the Cascade Range.

The city of Lake Stevens jumped to buy up **Wyatt Park** (10508 Chapel Hill Rd. in Lake Stevens), this little stretch of private beach, when it became available years ago. Now the public can enjoy lying in the grass, swimming, or launching their boats. Enjoy swimming at the west shore of Lake Stevens, or join the group of early-morning anglers sure to be there with the sun.

ENTERTAINMENT AND EVENTS
Casinos

Operated by the Tulalip Tribes, **Tulalip Casino** (off I-5 at exit 199, 360/651-1111 or 888/272-1111, www.tulalipcasino.com) offers slots, bingo, blackjack, craps, roulette, baccarat, and poker. This massive casino is the closest it gets to Vegas in Washington and gamblers will enjoy the on-site spa, hotel, and free valet parking. The **Angel of the Winds Casino** (3438 Stoluckquamish Ln., Arlington, 877/394-2210), also in Arlington is a more intimate affair than the Tulalip. It offers lower-key entertainment, like karaoke and trivia nights. It has slots and table games, as well as a poker room with frequent tournaments.

Pilchuck Glass School

The Pilchuck Glass School (360/445-3111, www.pilchuck.com) east of Stanwood was founded by Dale Chihuly in 1971, one of the world masters in the creation of glass sculptures. The school occupies a 64-acre wooded campus where both students and faculty live during their intensive May–September sessions. Public tours are given only during an early August open house. The school also puts on an immensely popular annual auction, held in Seattle in October.

Festivals and Events

Arlington's airport (360/403-3470, www.arlingtonwa.gov) is the third largest general aviation facility in Puget Sound and calls itself the world's largest ultralight airport. On the second weekend of July, it is home to the **Northwest Experimental Aircraft Association Fly-In** (360/435-5857, www.arlingtonflyin.org, $15), one of America's biggest fly-ins. Displays might include anything from experimental aircraft to fighter planes, to tanks, or even naval ships.

Also in Arlington, the Stillaguamish Tribe hosts the **Festival of the River and Pow Wow** (360/659-3248, www.stillaguamish.nsn.us/festival.htm) every August. This free event features a storytelling tent, a logging show, Stillaguamish cultural exhibits, a giant roving salmon puppet, and of course, a 5K fun-run.

In Marysville, the third week in June brings the **Strawberry Festival** (360/659-766, www.marysvillestrawberryfestival.com), the town's tribute to the slowly disappearing strawberry fields that once ringed the city. This is the area's biggest summer event, with parades, a carnival, car show, art and food booths, and adult trike races.

Starting in late September, several local farms create amazingly intricate corn mazes and open their pumpkin patches for family fun and frolics in the fields. Get a brochure showing the locations from the **Marysville Chamber of Commerce** (8825 34th Ave. NE, Suite C, 360/659-7700, www.marysvilletulalip chamber.com). The best corn maze is usually created by **The Farm at Swan's Trail** (7301

Rivershore Rd., 425/334-4124, www.thefarm1
.com).

In Snohomish, the biggest and most whimsical event is **Kla Ha Ya Days** (425/493-7824,
www.klahayadays.com) on the third week of
July. Kla Ha Ya is Snohomish for "welcome";
activities include a carnival, bed races, frog
jump, arts and crafts, and entertainment.
The **Snohomish Classic Car and Hot Rod
Display** (360/568-2525, http://cityofsnohom-
ish.com) is the last Sunday of September. Over
700 cars and trucks line the streets of downtown Snohomish.

SHOPPING
Antiques
With more than 15 local dealers in vintage
goods, Snohomish is justified in calling itself the "Antique Capital of the Northwest."
Antique shops of all sorts line First Street. It
is paradise for lovers of vintage toys, Victorian
furnishings, classic models of sailing ships,
Persian rugs, and delightfully musty clocks.
The biggest of all is **Star Center Antique
Mall** (829 2nd St., www.myantiquemall.com/
starcenter, 360/568-2131, 10 A.M.–5 P.M. daily),
where 200 dealers have small booths covering
such specialties as marbles, Chinese scrolls, or
historic newspapers. Down the street a little
bit, **Faded Elegance** (1116 1st St., Snohomish,
360/568-5333, http://fadedelegancestyle
.blogspot.com, 10 A.M.–6 P.M. Mon.–Sat.
11 A.M.–5 P.M. Sun.) has risen above the competition by offering the usual antiques, plus
hands-on classes, lectures by nationally recognized experts and design services. Give a call for
current class schedules. Bibliophiles also must
stop by **Uppercase Books** (611 2nd St., Ste.
L., 360/568-5987, www.uppercasebooksand
collectables.com), which has a trove of thousands of used, out-of-print, and rare books. The
decidedly non-elegantly named **Past Gas** (1003
1st St., 360/568-8815, www.pastgas-pegasus
.com) stocks fun and kitschy 1950s and 1960s
Route 66-style nostalgia and memorabilia.

Outlet Stores
Cozied right up to the Tulalip Casino, **Seattle**

Premium Outlets (10600 Quil Ceda Blvd.,
360/654-3000, www.premiumoutlets.com,
10 A.M.–9 P.M. Mon.–Sat., 10 A.M.–7 P.M.
Sun.) is the nicest outlet center in Western
Washington, with over a hundred primo shops
such as Coach, Burberry, Calvin Klein, and
Ralph Lauren taking up residence in this outdoor shopping complex.

SPORTS AND RECREATION
Cycling
The popular **Centennial Trail** follows an old
railway route connecting Snohomish with
Lake Stevens eight miles north. This paved
trail is a great spot for biking, in-line skating,
or running.

Scenic Flights and Balloon Rides
To get a glimpse of the rich farmlands, verdant forests, and towering peaks of Snohomish
County from up above, hop aboard one of the
colorful balloons launched by **Airial Balloon
Company** (360/568-3025, www.airialbal
loon.com, $200 and up). Or charter a person-
alized ride aboard a plane or helicopter with
Snohomish Flying Service (360/568-1541,
www.snohomishflying.com).

Water Sports
Covering 650 acres, **Kayak Point Regional
County Park** (15610 Marine Dr. in Stanwood,
425/388-6600, www1.co.snohomish.wa.us),
approximately 15 miles west of Marysville on
Marine View Drive, is home to windsurfing, a
boat launch, and a picnic area.

Wenberg County Park (15430 E. Lake
Goodwin Rd. in Stanwood, 360/652-7417 or
888/226-7688, www1.co.snohomish.wa.us) on
Lake Goodwin has a very popular swimming
beach, fishing for trout, waterskiing, a concession stand for fishing supplies, and snacks.

Golf
Nearby is the 18-hole **Kayak Point Golf
Course** (360/652-9676 or 800/562-3094,
www.golfkayak.com, $42), considered one of
Washington's better public courses. Duffers
can be glad the land wasn't developed as its

original purpose—a huge spirits refinery. Or can they?

Scenic Drives

For a delightful country drive, head southeast from Stanwood on the road to the tiny burg called **Silvana**. Along the way, you'll wind through wooded Prestliens Bluff, overlooking big dairy farms, haystacks, and aging barns.

ACCOMMODATIONS
Under $100

There are a number of cheap motor inns between Marysville and Mount Vernon. I found the best one in Arlington, off exit 206. The **Smokey Point Motor Inn** (17329 Smokey Point Dr., 360/659-8561, $69 s or $79 d) doesn't look like much from the outside, and the rooms probably haven't been updated in decades, but they are the absolute cleanest budget units along this stretch.

The best deals in this area are away from the freeways at Camano Island's two state parks. **Camano Island State Park** (2269 S. Lowell Point Rd, 360/387-1550, $65 for up to 5) rents rustic cabins in the woods that sleep five. These truly are roughing-it set-ups, as there are no kitchens; bathrooms and pay-showers are shared with campers. Outside each cabin is a covered porch, pedestal grill, fire ring, and picnic table.

One of Washington's newest state parks, **⟨ Cama Beach State Park** was a fishing resort built in the 1930s. The views are spectacular from the waterfront cedar cabins and bungalows lined up on the beach here. Standard cabins sleep five and come with refrigerator, sink, microwave, and a coffee pot. Showers are shared. Waterfront cabins go for $60 per night, while second row cabins rent for $65. The deluxe bungalows also sleep five and have similar amenities, with the addition of small private baths and a separate bedroom. They rent for $143 nightly.

All of the cabins at the two Camano Island parks lack linen service, so you'll need to bring along sheets and blankets, as well as kitchen implements.

$100-150

The comfortable **Inn at Snohomish** (323 2nd St., 360/568-2208 or 800/548-9993, www.snohomishinn.com) has standard motel rooms for $122 s or d, and ones with whirlpool tubs for $142 d.

Countryman B&B (119 Cedar, Snohomish, 360/568-9622 or 800/700-9622, www.countrymanbandb.com, $115–135 d with continental breakfast has three rooms with private baths on the second floor of an 1896 Stick-Eastlake Victorian home. Kids are welcome.

Cadyville Carriage House (304 Avenue A, 360/568-5390, www.cadyvillecarriage.com, $105) marries the charm of a B&B with the comfort of a suite. Units sleep four and include a full kitchen stocked for a make-it-yourself breakfast, free wireless, and a hot tub in the garden.

The **Inn at Barnum Point B&B** (464 S. Barnum Rd., Camano Island, 360/387-2256 or 800/910-2256, www.innatbarnumpoint.com, $125–225 s or d, including full breakfast) has three spacious guest rooms with private baths in a modern Cape Cod–style home on a bluff overlooking the water. Perfect for a quiet and romantic getaway. Kids accepted.

Medallion Hotel (16710 Smokey Point Blvd., at I-5 exit 206, 360/657-0500, www.medallionhotel.net, $109–119 s or d) is the newest lodging in town, offering expensive style at a discount price. All rooms include microwaves and fridges, and access to the heated indoor pool, hot tub, fitness center, and hot breakfast buffet. Restaurant and lounge on premises.

$150-200

Nearly a century old, the heavily restored **Camano Island Inn B&B** (1054 SW Camano Dr., 360/387-0783 or 888/718-0783, www.camanoislandinn.com, $125–230 s or d) has six waterfront guest rooms with private baths, a wraparound deck, and full breakfasts. Guests can rent kayaks to paddle along Saratoga Passage, and kids are welcome.

The stylish digs at **⟨ Tulalip Resort Casino and Spa** (10200 Quil Ceda Blvd., 888/272-1111, www.tulalipresort.com, $190–550 d) celebrate Northwest Salish traditional art by weaving it subtly into their decor. Expect plush linens, walk-in showers, and huge HDTVs. The suites ($310 and up) are over the top, many with jetted tubs, fireplaces, and even pool tables. The entire hotel is set up for reliable free wireless Internet.

Camping

Twelve miles north of Marysville and just south of Arlington, Lake Goodwin offers several camping choices. One of the favorites is at **Wenberg County Park** (360/652-7417 or 888/226-7688, www1.co.snohomish.wa.us, $19–20 for tents), which offers wide-open lawns dotted by lightly grouped pines for a gentle camping experience. Or motor over to **Lake Goodwin Resort** (4726 176th St. NW, 800/242-8169) right on the lake. Tent sites are $26 and RV sites with water, septic, and sewer are $40.

Year-round camping is available at **River Meadows County Park** (20416 Jordan Rd, 360/435-3441, www.co.snohomish.wa.us/parks, $12 for tents, $17 for hookups) several miles east of town on the South Fork of the Stillaguamish River. River Meadows Park offers enjoyable hiking trails, picnic grounds, and a mile of river shoreline for fishing.

Gamblers may want to park their RVs at **Smokey Point RV Park** (17019 28th Dr. NE, 360/653-8804, www.smokeypointrv.com $30/day or $175/week), a clean, comfortable park just five minutes away from the Tulalip Casino.

FOOD
Snohomish

Cabbage Patch Restaurant (111 Ave. A, 360/568-9091, 10 A.M.–10 P.M. Mon.–Fri., 8 A.M.–10 P.M. Sat.–Sun., $12) sells sandwiches, salads, pasta, beef, seafood, and homemade desserts in a historic house full of antiques, old furnishings, and some would say ghosts, as well. Should you see one, offer it a toast with Sondy's Favorite Pimms Cup or one of their other signature cocktails.

Collector's Choice Restaurant (215

Cypress Ave., 360/568-1277, 7 A.M.–1:30 A.M. daily, $15) serves a diverse menu of pasta, meats, and seafood. Step on up to the false-fronted **Oxford Saloon & Eatery** (913 1st St., 360/568-3845, www.theoxfordsaloon.com, 10 A.M.–2 A.M. daily, $10), with pub grub and local musicians on stage seven nights a week. Built in 1889, it is supposedly haunted by a 19th-century policeman claimed to have been killed here while breaking up a knife fight.

Mardini's (1001 1st St., 360/568-8080, www.mardinis.com, 11 A.M.–10 P.M. Mon.–Sat., 8 A.M.–10 P.M. Sun., $16) serves well-prepared pasta, seafood, chicken, and steaks in a romantic setting. There's also a full bar and plenty of wines to choose from.

Fred's Rivertown Alehouse (1114 1st St., 360/568-5820, www.fredsrivertownalehouse.com, 11 A.M.–11:30 P.M. Sun.–Thurs., 11 A.M.–12:30 P.M. Fri.–Sat., entrées $8–17) is a friendly pub with more than 30 beers on draft and dozens of malt scotches. The menu includes such treats as Thai chicken wraps, Caesar salads, and halibut tacos.

Get fresh fruits and veggies, honey, and nursery stock, at the **Snohomish Farmers Market** (425/347-2790, www.snohomishmarkets.com), held downtown 3–7 P.M. on Thursdays mid-May–September.

Marysville and Arlington

In business for over 70 years, Marysville's **Village Restaurant** (220 Ash St., 360/659-2305, www.villagepie.net, 6 A.M.–9 P.M. Sun.–Thurs., 6 A.M.–10 P.M. Fri.–Sat., $10) is famous for its "mile-high" meringue pies and other home-cookin' classics.

The best breakfast in Marysville (and arguably anywhere) is **Fanny's Restaurant** (505 Cedar St., 360/653-8164, 7 A.M.–2 P.M. Mon–Sat., 8 A.M.–2 P.M. Sun., $10), where just the biscuits and gravy are enough to make you a lifelong fan.

Over in Arlington, **La Hacienda** (210 W. Division, Arlington, 360/435-9433, 11 A.M.–10 P.M. Sun.–Thurs., 11 A.M.–11 P.M. Fri.–Sat., $12) serves a bit heavy but satisfying Mexican food. On the weekends locals crowd the large bar for karaoke and a few bottles of south-of-the-border suds.

From mid-June to mid-July, you can be a farmer for a day at **Biringer Farm** (21412 59th Ave NE, 425/259-0255, www.biringerfarm .com) and pick your own strawberries, raspberries, or tayberries. Or if you're not here to work, buy them prepicked and have a picnic at the old Berry Barn.

Stanwood and Camano Island

Head on down to (**The Chatter Box** (9819 270th St. NW, 360/629-0600, www.the chatterboxrestaurant.com, 11 A.M.–9 P.M. Tues.– Sat., noon–8 P.M. Sun., closed Mon., $12) to find one of the most creative restaurants in the area. Housed in a cute little farmhouse, you'd think you'd be limited to down-home country cookin'—but you'd be wrong. The menu is Asian fusion, with cuisine elements from Thailand, India, and Malaysia. If you're saddled with a picky eater, there are burgers here, too.

For more conventional fare, eat at **Jimmy's Pizza and Pasta** (9819 Hwy. 532, 360/629-6565, jimmyspizzaandpasta.com, 11 A.M.–9 P.M. daily), which serves surprisingly good pies compared with most small-town pizzerias.

Get fresh produce at the **Schuh Farms** (9828 Hwy. 532, 360/424-6982, 9 A.M.–6 P.M. daily Apr.–Dec.), a 300-acre farm with a five-acre homestead.

INFORMATION AND SERVICES

The **Snohomish Chamber of Commerce** (127 Ave. A, 360/568-2526, www.cityof snohomish.com, 9 A.M.–5 P.M. Mon.– Fri.) is located in the Firehouse Center. Unfortunately, it's closed on weekends. Pick up a brochure for the self-guided tour of the elegant Victorian-era homes that comprise the Snohomish National Historic District.

The **Whidbey Camano Islands Visitor Center** (360/629-7136, www.whidbey camanoislands.com/, 9 A.M.–2 P.M. Mon.– Fri.) is visible as you come onto Camano Island and can be a helpful source of all the latest info.

GETTING THERE AND AROUND

Community Transit (360/778-2185 or 800/562-1375, www.commtrans.org) has daily bus service throughout Snohomish County and on to Seattle.

Airporter Shuttle (360/380-8800 or 800/235-5247, www.airporter.com) offers direct service between Sea-Tac Airport and Snohomish County's major towns.

Island Transit (360/387-7433 or 800/240-8747, www.islandtransit.org) is a free bus system that offers weekday service around Camano Island.

Skagit Valley and Mount Vernon

The rich bottomland of the Skagit (SKAJ-et) Valley near Mount Vernon produces peas, potatoes, cabbage, cauliflower, broccoli, cucumbers, strawberries, raspberries, spinach, corn, vegetable seeds, and the area's best-known crops: daffodils, tulips, and irises. More than half the world's cabbage and spinach seeds are grown in the valley.

The city of Mount Vernon is the largest in the county, and in spring is certainly among the prettiest; tulips and daffodils are *everywhere,* from fields to yards to gas stations. The attractive downtown features brick-fronted buildings, planters filled with flowers, and a prosperous mixture of stores.

SIGHTS
Farms

A handful of farms invite the public to stroll through their display gardens and order bulbs for fall delivery. **RoozenGaarde** (15867 Beaver March Rd., 360/424-8531 or 866/488-5477, www.tulips.com/bloommap. cfm) offers retail and mail-order bulb sales, fresh-cut flowers, and a gift shop; it's open daily March–May, and Mon.–Sat. the rest of the year. The Dutch-style windmill is a local landmark.

Skagit Valley Gardens (18923 Peter Johnson Rd., just off I-5, 360/424-6760 in Mt. Vernon, www.skagitvalleygardens.com, 9 A.M.–6 P.M. daily) has additional floral displays in both spring and fall.

La Conner Flats Display Garden (15920 Best Rd., 360/466-3190, www.laconnerflats .com, dawn–dusk daily, $3 suggested) has 11 acres of proper English gardens, livestock, and an assortment of beautiful roses that tend to bloom March–September. Next door, **Christianson's Nursery** (15806 Best Rd., 360/466-3821, www.christiansonsnursery. com, 9 A.M.–6 P.M. daily) features 600 varieties of roses, plus rhododendrons, azaleas, dogwoods, and other flowering plants.

Washington State University has established three **display gardens** (16650 S.R. 536 in Mt. Vernon, 360/848-6120, www .mtvernon.wsu.edu) planted by students and other volunteers. The Master Gardeners Discovery Garden is beautifully landscaped and meant to suggest hardy plants for different areas of a visitor's yard—almost like a pattern-book. The Washington Native Plant Garden shows off local plants likely to thrive in Washington's climate, and the Western Washington Fruit Research garden, which experiments with growing different types of fruit not normally associated with Western Washington. The gardens are free and open dawn–dusk daily.

Edgewater Park

Sitting on the banks of the Skagit River near the center of Mount Vernon, Edgewater Park is a perfect slice of greenery to bring your family and a picnic basket after touring the flower fields. Wide-open lawns invite the kids to enjoy a spontaneous game of tag, and a playground on the premises provides another good way to burn off pent-up energy after having behaved so well during the tulip tour.

ENTERTAINMENT AND EVENTS
Lincoln Theatre

The Lincoln Theatre (712 S. 1st St., 360/336-8955 www.lincolntheatre.org) hosts a busy calendar ranging from Shakespeare to *The Rocky Horror Picture Show.* The ultra-classy 1920s-era building still has its original Wurlitzer organ—and, yes, it still works.

◖ Skagit Valley Tulip Festival

With its rich loamy soil and mild weather, the Skagit Valley is Washington's primary bulb-growing region and home to Washington Bulb Co., the largest producer of bulbs in America. From late March through April, more than 2,000 acres of the valley are carpeted with flowering daffodils, tulips, irises, and lilies; more than 40 million bulbs are produced annually. Many of the most successful fields were started by newly emigrated Dutch tulip masters following World War II.

The countywide Tulip Festival (360/428-5959, www.tulipfestival.org) is held over the

Get your picture taken at Tulip Town.

whole month of April. Attractions include bus tours, Skagit River trips, bike rides, street fairs, foot races, llama exhibits, antique shows, a salmon bake, volleyball tournaments, and art shows. Daily shuttle buses help alleviate the crowding, but be warned that this is a well-attended event, especially midday on weekends. After mid-January, get maps of the floral fields from the Mount Vernon Chamber of Commerce Office (listed below). Or just head west from Mount Vernon toward La Conner. Most of the fields are in an area bounded on the north by Memorial Highway 536, on the west by La Conner-Whitney Road, on the south by Chilberg Road, and on the east by the Skagit River. Crops are rotated to preserve the soil and to keep insect pests down, so last season's field of yellow daffodils may be home to a crop of flowering broccoli this year—more nutritious, but not nearly as photogenic.

There is an official photo platform at **Tulip Town** (15002 Bradshaw Rd., 360/424-8152) along with music, art, pony rides, kite flying, espresso coffee, cut flowers, and refreshments.

In Mount Vernon itself, the Tulip Festival action centers on a downtown **street fair** that includes art and craft vendors, music, magic, and of course, food.

Other Events

Skagit Valley's **Festival of Family Farms** (360/428 8547, www.festivaloffamilyfarms .com) is a hugely popular free event held the first week of October each year. Dozens of small local farmers throw open their barn doors and let you get a behind-the-scenes look at growing crops and animals, as well as family corn-mazes and other fun events.

Berry Dairy Days (360/757-0994) on the third weekend of June celebrates Burlington's agricultural roots, with a big parade, carnival rides, a road run, arts and crafts, pony rides, music, and strawberry shortcake served by cheerleaders.

In early July, the Celtic Arts Foundation hosts the **Highland Games** (360/416-4934, www.celticarts.org), an event full of traditional dancing, athletic events such as the caber toss and Braemar stone, sheepdog trials, plus harp, fiddle, and some quite interesting variations on the good old bagpipe.

The second weekend of August brings the **Skagit County Fair** (360/336-9453, www .skagitcounty.net/fairgrounds) to the fairgrounds on the southwest side of Mount Vernon off Blackburn Road. Expect interactive programs for the kids, agricultural exhibits, music, multiple food eating contests, and often rare or unusual animals on display.

SHOPPING

First Street in downtown Mount Vernon offers a leisurely stroll past bakeries, gift and clothing stores, and cafés. You're unlikely to have seen anything quite like **The Conway Muse** (18444 Spruce, 360/445-3000, www .theconwaymuse.com). Housed in a barn-inspired building, the shop sells art, provides space for auctions, and puts on countless musical, dance and spoken-word performances throughout the year. Art shows and even an on-site restaurant make it impossible to guess what you'll find when walking through the doors. And if you're tired of dealing with snooty tasting rooms or the shelf at your local grocery and just know you can do better yourself, pop in to **My Own Vintage** (312 Pine St., 360/336-3555, www.myownvintage.net). The owners can get you set up with all the necessities to start your own boutique winery from grapes to bottle labels. And your masterpiece would, of course, not be complete without cheese and they can set you up with cheese making supplies, too. It you are just an aspiring brewmaster, you'll also find a staggering selection of hops and grains.

If you prefer to shop in a mall, Mount Vernon and Burlington have several to choose from, including **Cascade Mall** (201 Cascade Mall Dr., 360/757-2070, www.shopcascade mall.com), with Sears, JCPenney, Macy's, plus dozens of others, along with **Prime Outlets Burlington** (234 Fashion Way, 360/757-3549) with more than 50 outlet stores.

SPORTS AND RECREATION
Skagit Speedway
The speed-through-it town of Burlington is home to Skagit Speedway (360/568-2529, www.skagitspeedway.com), with a pulse-pounding, adrenaline-burning mix of Supercross, Sprints, Hornets, and Quads. Call to find out about their frequent Ladies' Night promotions.

Cycling
With its nice flat roads and breathtaking views of Mount Baker and the Cascades, the farm country of Skagit Valley is a great place to bicycle. When the flowers are blooming, the scenery gets even better, although heavy Tulip Festival traffic on weekends might make the ride a bit less bucolic.

If you've left your wheels at home, stop by **Skagit Cycles** (1704 S. Burlington Blvd., Burlington, 360/757-7910, skagitcyclecenter.com, 10 A.M.–6:30 P.M. Mon.–Sat., noon–5 P.M. Sun.) to pick up a rental. The shop offers a variety of bikes for $40–100 a day. This is also a good stop to pick up spare tubes and other accessories.

Hiking
Breazeale Interpretive Center (360/428-1558, www.padillabay.gov, 10 A.M.–5 P.M. Wed.–Sun., free) has natural history and marine displays, hands-on exhibits for kids, and a range of programs. There is a short self-guided nature hike through the woods and fields, where you might see bald eagles, herons, ducks, or geese. Find it just north of Bay View State Park on Bay View-Edison Road.

Catch peekaboo views of the Olympics, San Juan Islands, and Skagit Valley farmland along the trails at **Little Mountain Park.** The highlight of the 490-acre park is the summit observation area, which offers an unobstructed panorama view from the 927-feet above the valley floor. To get there, follow Blackburn Road to Little Mountain Road.

ACCOMMODATIONS
Local motels and B&Bs fill up fast for the Tulip Festival. Be sure to make reservations at least a month ahead if you plan to visit during that time. Also note that nearby La Conner is another good sleepover spot from which to tour Mount Vernon and the flower fields.

Snuggled in the midst of 250 wooded acres three miles south of Mount Vernon, **Whispering Firs B&B** (19357 Kanako Ln., 360/428-1990 or 800/428-1992, www.whisperingfirs.com, $85–125 d) is a large, modern home with shaded seclusion. Four guest rooms have private baths, country-style breakfast, and there is a hot tub on the deck. Kids are welcome.

There are several chain motels along the I-5 corridor, but for a cheaper stay with similar quality rooms, give **Tulip Inn** (2200 Freeway Dr. in Mount Vernon, 360/428-5969 or 800/599-5969, www.tulipinn.net, $75–109 d) a try. Rooms are clean, if a bit worn, and the rate includes free wireless Internet and a modest continental breakfast each morning.

If the Tulip is booked, there are a couple of other independent motels good for a short stay, including the **Hillside Motel** (2300 Bonnie View Rd. in Mount Vernon, 360/445-3252, $59 s or $63 d), which has rooms with kitchenettes, and **Cocusa Motel** (370 W. Rio Vista in Burlington, 360/757-6044 or 800/628-2257, $75 s or $135 d), which has an outdoor pool.

For a step up in quality and better amenities such as an indoor pool, spa, fitness center, and business center, go for the **Fairfield Inn and Suites by Marriott** (9384 Old Hwy. 99 N., Burlington, 360/757-2717, $134–171 d) in Burlington. The Fairfield offers newer digs and close proximity to the Burlington outlets and chain restaurants.

Camping
Eight miles west of Burlington on Padilla Bay, **Bay View State Park** (360/757-0227, www.parks.wa.gov) has year-round campsites for $12 ($31 for RVs) across Bay View-Edison Road from the waterfront. Make reservations ($6.50 extra) at 888/226-7688.

During the fair, the **Skagit County Fairgrounds** (315 S 3rd St., 360/336-9453), makes several sites available. Reservations should be made far in advance.

There are a few nice RV parks in the area. **Burlington KOA** (6397 N. Green Rd., 360/724-5511 or 800/562-9154, www.koa.com, $42 for a pull-thru spot) has all the amenities you expect from a KOA park. **Riverbend Park** (305 W. Stewart Rd., 360/428-4044, $25) is basic but quiet and **Mt. Vernon RV Park** (1229 Memorial Hwy., 360/428-8787 or 800/385-9895, $29) is a nice park near stores that is a bit close to the train tracks, but not close enough to keep most campers up at night.

FOOD
Cafés and Diners
You'll find the most creative meal in town at the oddball ◖ **Chuck Wagon Drive-In** (800 N. 4th St., 360/336-2732, 11 A.M.–9 P.M. Sun.–Thurs., 11 A.M.–9:30 P.M. Fri.–Sat.). This is a burger lover's mecca, with weird concoctions such as peanut-butter burgers and hash-brown burgers on its extensive menu. It isn't just a gimmick, either; even plain old cheeseburgers are scrumptious here.

Wear flannel if you want to fit in at the mostly-locals **Mr T's Family Café** (503 W. Fir St., 360/428-8808, 6 A.M.–2 P.M. Mon.–Sat., 8 A.M.–2 P.M. Sun.). This down-home diner is a favorite among the area farmers, loggers, and truck drivers who come for the rib-sticking biscuits and gravy, enough to please the stomach and the wallet.

The Gardens at La Conner Flats restaurant serves delicious lunches and high tea (reservations required) 11 A.M.–4 P.M.

And to satisfy the sweet tooth, stop by **Big Scoop Sundae Palace** (327 E. College Way, 360/424-3558, www.bigscoopsundaepalace .com, 11 A.M.–10 P.M. Sun.–Thurs., 11 A.M.–11 P.M. Fri.–Sat.). This fun, old-school ice cream parlor scoops up share-worthy sundaes, shakes, and root beer floats. If you insist on actually eating a meal before your dessert, it conveniently serves burgers, hot dogs, and other diner fare.

Steak and Seafood
Max Dale's Steak & Chop House (2030 Riverside Dr., 360/424-7171, www.maxdales

.com, 11:30 A.M.–9:30 P.M. Mon.–Thurs., 4–10:30 P.M. Sat., 4–9 P.M. Sun., $25) serves steak, seafood, and prime rib in their tasteful western-themed dining room and lounge.

You can also get all-American steak and seafood at **Gentlemen Gene's Pub** (1400 Parker Way, 360/424-4363, www.gentlemen genespub.com, 10:30 A.M.–9 P.M. Sun.–Fri., 9 A.M.–11 P.M. Sat., $13). The pub has a huge drink menu including a dozen or so custom cocktails.

International
Pacioni's Pizzeria (606 S. 1st St., 360/336-3314, 11 A.M.–9 P.M. Mon.–Sat., 3–8 P.M. Sun.) bakes outstanding thin-crust, crunchy pizzas with fresh toppings, as well as equally good calzones and paninis.

For top-notch tacos and more, visit **Mexico Café** (1320 Memorial Hwy., 360/424-1977, http://mexicocaferestaurant.com, 11 A.M.–10 P.M. Mon.–Thurs., 11 A.M.–11 P.M. Fri.–Sat., 10:30 A.M.–10 P.M. Sun.), which offers tasty south-of-the-border fare, including scrumptious *chile verde* dishes and great margaritas.

Pub Grub
Skagit River Brewing Co. (404 S. 3rd St., 360/336-2884, www.skagitbrew.com, 11 A.M.–10 P.M. Mon.–Thurs., 11 A.M.–11 P.M. Fri.–Sat., 11 A.M.–9 P.M. Sun., $15) has six year-round and usually two seasonal craft-brewed beers on tap and upscale wood-oven-grilled and rotisserie foods on the menu.

Markets
Skagit Valley Food Co-op (202 S. 1st. St., 360/336-3886, www.skagitfoodcoop.com, 8 A.M.–9 P.M. Mon.–Sat., 9 A.M.–8 P.M. Sun.) sells locally sourced produce as well as wine and beer. Nonmembers are free to shop and a membership will set you back a cool $100 per year. The attached deli sells sandwiches and salads and is always slammed at lunchtime.

The area puts on the **Mount Vernon-Skagit Valley Farmers Market** (360/292-2648, www.mountvernonfarmersmarket.org)

by the river in downtown Mount Vernon 9 A.M.–1 P.M. Saturday May–October. Also try the **Burlington Farmers Market** (Cherry and Victoria Sts., 360/755-9717, 3–7 P.M. Friday May–Sept.).

At other times, stop by Burlington's **Country Farms Produce Market** (101 Orange Ave., 360/755-0488) for fresh locally grown fruits and vegetables.

INFORMATION

For maps, brochures, and festival information, contact the **Mount Vernon Chamber of Commerce** (105 East Kincaid St., Ste. 101., 360/428-8547, www.mountvernonchamber .com, 8:30 A.M.–5 P.M. Mon.–Fri., 9 A.M.–4 P.M. Sat., 10 A.M.–4 P.M. Sun. in the summer, closed Sun. in winter).

GETTING THERE AND AROUND

Skagit Transit (360/757-4433, www.skagit transit.org, $0.75 per ride or $1.50 for day pass) offers daily bus service throughout Skagit Country, including Mt. Vernon and Burlington. Of particular note is Route 615, which runs from Skagit Station (105 E. Kincaid St.) through farmlands and to La Conner. The station is also the landing point for a weekday express connector from Everett Station ($2) and a Monday–Saturday express route from Bellingham ($0.75).

Amtrak (800/872-7245, www.amtrak.com) provides daily train connections from Mount Vernon north to Vancouver, B.C., and south to Seattle on the Cascades train.

Airporter Shuttle (360/380-8800 or 800/235-5247, www.airporter.com) offers connections to Sea-Tac Airport. **Greyhound** (360/336-5111 or 800/231-2222, www.grey hound.com) has long-haul bus service from the Mount Vernon terminal at 1101 South 2nd Street.

Festival Transportation

During the tulip festival, the *Victoria Clipper* (360/448-5000 or 800/888-2535, $46 for adults, $29 children under 11) offers a special voyage from Seattle to La Conner. The package includes the cruise, a guided bus tour of the tulip fields, plus stops at two bulb farms and free time in La Conner.

La Conner

The oldest town in Skagit County, La Conner saw the arrival of its first white settlers shortly after the Civil War. They built dikes to tame the annual floods on the Skagit River and planted crops in the fertile soil, which proved some of the most productive in the world. In 1876, John Conner purchased a trading post and named the site after his wife, Louisa A. Conner (L. A. Conner eventually became La Conner).

Today La Conner is home to fewer than 900 people but is one of Washington's most-loved destinations. The town is nothing if not cute, with more frills and lace than a Victoria's Secret catalog. More than 160 local buildings in La Conner are on the National Register of Historic Places. Its galleries, gift shops, restaurants, museums, and 19th-century homes make for enjoyable exploring, and the bright-orange **Rainbow Bridge** across Swinomish Channel is a good spot for photographers to get a shot of the La Conner waterfront with a Mount Baker backdrop.

SIGHTS

Housed in an award-winning building in the center of town, the **Museum of Northwest Art** (121 S. 1st St., 360/466-4446, www.museum ofnwart.org, 10 A.M.–5 P.M. Tues.–Sat., noon–5 P.M. Sun.–Mon., $5 adults, $4 seniors, students $2, free for kids under 13) features paintings and sculptures by regional artists, including a room on glassmaking.

Skagit County Historical Museum (501 4th St., 360/466-3365, 11 A.M.–5 P.M. Tues.–Sun., $2 adults, $1 seniors and kids ages 6–12, free for under 5, $5 for families) sits high on a hill, with a panoramic view from the observation deck across the fields and farms of Skagit Valley. It features a variety of pioneer and native artifacts. Hours are extended during the Tulip Festival.

The 1891 **Gaches Mansion** (703 2nd St., 360/466-4288, 11 A.M.–5 P.M., Mon. and Tues.) contains turn-of-the-20th-century furnishings, while the upstairs houses the **La Conner Quilt & Textile Museum** (360/466-4288, 11 A.M.–5 P.M. Wed.–Sun., $7 adults, $5 military and students, free for kids under 12), with changing exhibits and a small gift shop that sells locally made quilts. Nearby is the old 1886 brick city hall as well as historic **Maple Hall,** which is a super popular wedding venue come spring and summer.

The little **Volunteer Fireman's Museum** on 1st Street contains a horse-drawn hand-pumped fire truck that saw service in San Francisco following the 1906 earthquake. It was later used by the La Conner Fire Department.

Pioneer Park is a quiet riverside green beneath tall Douglas fir trees next to Rainbow Bridge. No camping is permitted but feel free to roll out a picnic lunch. The **Fir Island Farms Reserve,** a waterfowl refuge south of La Conner on Fir Island, is one of 16 units making up the Skagit Wildlife Area. There is a gravel parking lot with disabled access, making it easy to watch for wintering snow geese and trumpeter swans.

ENTERTAINMENT AND EVENTS

In August, the **La Conner Classic Yacht & Car Show** sails into town, replete with classic motorcycles, wooden yachts, and car show staples. Also in August, the whole city goes slumming at the **White Trash Food Festival** at the Rexville Grocery (19271 Best Rd., 360/466-5522) where you may witness and participate in Cheez Whiz tastings, Spam canapés, and plenty of beer in cans. The season winds down with the **Art's Alive!** celebration in early November, featuring showings of artists and techniques throughout La Conner's 30-plus galleries. An event uniquely La Conner, the Rotary Club's **Annual Smelt Derby** is

Don't forget your pocketbook – La Conner offers blocks and blocks of cute shops.

© ERICKA CHICKOWSKI

NORTH PUGET SOUND

held in February and starts with a pancake breakfast, which provides the energy for the 5K/10K Smelt Run/Walk race to follow. Of course, the highlight is the smelt fishing, with awards for longest, smallest, weirdest, and other categories.

SHOPPING

The way to shop in La Conner is to meander through downtown at your own pace, stopping for food or drink as needed, and keeping a mellow pace. Art galleries, shops specializing in everything from olives to old fishing tackle, antique dealers, espresso bars, and restaurants line 1st and Morris Streets.

The Stall (712 1st St., 360/466-3162, 10 A.M.–5:30 P.M. daily) sells unusual folk art imports from all over the globe. The **Wood Merchant** (709 S. 1st St., 360/466-4741, 10 A.M.–5 P.M. daily) has gorgeous wooden furniture, cases, games, and other delights. **The Next Chapter Books** (721 S. 1st St., 360/466-2665, 9 A.M.–5 P.M. Mon.–Fri., 10 A.M.–5 P.M. Sat.–Sun. daily) sells books and espresso from its little shop on the east end of 1st Street.

SPORTS AND RECREATION
Boating

The Swinomish Channel is a peaceful body of water for paddling or rowing, though no local places rent boats. Luckily, in nearby Anacortes you can visit **Sea Kayak Shop** (2515 Commercial Ave., 360/299-2300, www.sea kayakshop.com), which rents boats, paddles, and gear and runs guided excursions.

Those with their own boats can find guest moorage at the **La Conner Marina,** complete with covered and open slips, electricity, water, showers, and laundry. Their summer rate is $1 per foot per night. Call 360/466-3118 for details.

ACCOMMODATIONS

La Conner is blessed with a number of delightful inns and historic B&Bs of the sort that attract the thousands of aesthetically minded folks who come for the Tulip Festival each year. As you read this, most lodgings are already booked for next year's festival. But if you roll in during any of the other 11 months, you should be able to find just the right option for you and your party.

$100-150

The distinctive cedar-shingled exterior of **La Conner Country Inn** (107 S. 2nd St., 360/466-3101 or 888/466-4113, www.laconnerlodging.com, $159 d) contrasts a bit with the simply furnished rooms, but they are clean and comfortable and the property is large enough that you might find a spot here when all the B&Bs fill up.

Window shoppers can't beat the location at **Hotel Planter** (715 1st St., 360/466-4710 or 800/488-5409, www.hotelplanter.com, $99–169 d), which sits in a 1907 building right smack in the middle of bustling 1st Street. The rooms are quaintly decorated to pay homage to the building's history, and there's a hot tub and gazebo in the garden courtyard. This establishment offers a reprieve for many adults, as it doesn't allow young children.

Right on the edge of town adjacent to open farm country, **The Inn & Day Spa** (117 Maple Ave., 360/399-1074, www.theheron.com, $99–159 d) is a Victorian-style country inn with 11 guest rooms, a backyard hot tub, an on-site day spa, and a gourmet breakfast buffet. All the big, bright rooms come with private baths, Egyptian cotton linens, flat-screen TVs, and wireless Internet. There are also three suites ($199) with fireplaces and one with a whirlpool tub for those rainy days when you'd like to stay in.

$150-200

◖ **Wild Iris Inn** (121 Maple Ave., 800/477-1400, www.wildiris.com) has seven luxurious guest rooms ($119–199 d), plus 12 view suites ($199 d) with jetted tubs, gas fireplaces, and outside decks. All guests can use the outdoor hot tub and are served a buffet breakfast. No kids under 12.

Esteps' Residence in La Conner (1st St.,

360/466-2116, www.estep-properties.com, $150–175 d) offers four condo properties scattered about town. Whether you'd like to stay right on 1st Street, on the waterfront, or hidden behind an 1880s storefront, they've got an efficiency for you.

$200-250
La Conner Channel Lodge (205 N. 1st St., 360/466-1500 or 888/466-4113, www.la connerlodging.com, $159–359 d) shares its ownership with the La Conner Country Inn and is a modern waterfront hotel with gas fireplaces, balconies, hot tubs, and a continental breakfast. Dock space is available for rent if you're traveling by boat.

Skagit Bay Hideaway (17430 Goldenview, 360/466-2262 or 888/466-2262, www.skagit bay.com, $199 or $179 for multiple nights) is a well-appointed contemporary home across the Rainbow Bridge from downtown with a rooftop hot tub and a breakfast basket each morning.

Camping
Bay View State Park (360/757-0227, www .parks.wa.gov), eight miles north of La Conner, allows camping year-round near its 1,285 feet of salty beach right on the Padilla Bay National Estuarine Sanctuary. Campsites run $12 ($31 for RVs with hookups). Make reservations ($6.50 extra) at 888/226-7688.

Head north to Fir Island for **Blakes RV Park & Marina** (1171-A Rawlins Rd., 360/445-6533 $15–35) for an RV park with laundry, showers, propane concessions, and a boat-dock (additional fee applies).

FOOD
Cafés
Start your day at **Calico Cupboard Café and Bakery** (720 S. 1st St., 360/466-4451, www .calicocupboardcafe.com, 7:30 A.M.–5 P.M. daily) for great homemade country breakfasts, soups, salads, and sandwiches. Don't miss out on their extensive specialty hash selection!

Nestled in a former seed warehouse, **◖ Seeds Bistro and Bar** (623 Morris St., 360/466-3280, www.seedsbistro.com, 11 A.M.–9 P.M. daily) brims with Skagit Valley pride and serves dishes featuring fresh local veggies and meats, just-off-the-boat fish and shellfish, and scrumptious homemade breads.

Pub Grub
Based out of the La Conner Country Inn, **Nell Thorn Restaurant and Pub** (702 S. 1st St., 360/466-9932, www.nellthorn.com, 10:30 A.M.–9 P.M. Sun.–Thurs., 10:30 A.M.–10 P.M. Fri.–Sat., $18) sits perched on a hill overlooking the Swinomish in a whimsically weathered cedar-shingled building. The menu takes pub food upscale with goat burgers and an optional fried duck egg, along with pasta, salads, and the like.

La Conner Brewing Co. (117 S. 1st. St., 360/466-1415, www.laconnerbrew.com, 11:30 A.M.–9 P.M. daily, $13) is a lively and noisy place with five kinds of brewed-on-the-premises beer, plus tasty wood-fired pizzas, quesadillas (one with mangos), soups, and salads. The pub is entirely nonsmoking, and the outside patio is perfect for warm summer evenings.

Just down the street is **La Conner Seafood and Prime Rib House** (614 1st St., 360/466-4014, www.laconnerseafood.com, 11:30 A.M.–8 P.M. Sun.–Thurs., 11:30 A.M.–9 P.M. daily), with waterfront dining, and offers prime rib, pasta, and seafood among others.

Kerstin's (505 S. 1st, 360/466-9111, http:// kerstinsrestaurant.com, noon–9 P.M. Mon.–Sat.) is a delightful place for Northwest meals of pasta, lamb, chicken, steaks, or seafood. Lunches are your best bet if you're on a budget; dinner entrées cost $25–29.

Markets
In the summer, be sure to stop at the **Hedlin's Family Farm** (12275 Valley Rd., 360/466-3977, 10 A.M.–6 P.M. daily May–Oct.) on the east edge of town for fresh corn, tomatoes,

peas, honey, strawberries, and other produce from its nearby farm.

INFORMATION

For local information, visit the **La Conner Chamber of Commerce** (4th and Morris, 360/466-4778 or 888/642-9284, www.la connerchamber.com, 10 A.M.–4 P.M. Mon.– Fri., 11 A.M.–3 P.M. Sat.–Sun. Apr.–Sept.).

GETTING THERE AND AROUND

Skagit Transit (360/757-4433, www .skagittransit.org) offers daily bus service from Mount Vernon to La Conner on Route 615. **Airporter Shuttle** (360/380-8800 or 800/235-5247, www.airporter.com) provides service between Sea-Tac Airport and La Conner.

Burlington to Bellingham

◖ CHUCKANUT DRIVE

Heading north up the coast from the Skagit Valley, you enter one of the most scenic stretches of highway in the state—Chuckanut Drive. This 11-mile portion of Highway 11 was the first state-designated scenic drive in Washington. Built as part of the now-extinct Pacific Highway, it leaves I-5 just north of Burlington and heads as straight as a cue stick across the black, flat soil of the Skagit Valley. The tiny towns of **Bow** and **Edison** have begun attracting artists, and several studios are open for weekend visits.

A short distance north of Bow, the highway runs head-on into the mountains that hover over Puget Sound; it's here that the fun begins. The road doesn't have a straight stretch for seven miles as it swoops and swerves along the face of a cliff, with grand views across to Anacortes, Guemes Island, and, farther north, the San Juan and Lummi Islands. With no shoulder, a narrow strip of pavement, and tight corners, it's a bit dicey for bikes (especially on weekends when traffic is heaviest), but the views are stunning.

© ERICKA CHICKOWSKI

Chuckanut Drive is a cruiser's dream road.

For more information on Chuckanut Drive, see the **Chuckanut Merchants' Association** (www.chuckanutdrive.com).

ENTERTAINMENT

Skagit Valley Casino Resort (just off I-5 at Exit 236 near Bow, 360/724-7777 or 877/275-2448, www.theskagit.com) is the biggest thing going in the area. They've got slots, double-deck blackjack, craps, roulette, keno, and more ways to suck your wallet dry. The resort also has a luxury hotel ($99–119 s or d), three restaurants, frequent live music, and karaoke on Thursdays.

SPORTS AND RECREATION

Seven miles south of Bellingham on Chuckanut Drive, **Larrabee State Park** (360/676-2093) was the state's first, created in 1923 when Charles Xavier Larrabee's family donated 20 acres in his honor—since grown to 2,683 acres. The park's 85 campsites range from tent-only ($12) to full-hookup RV ($36) sites, plus coin-operated showers. It's open year-round. Make reservations ($6.50 extra) at 888/226-7688 or www.parks.wa.gov. The park borders Samish Bay, with a boat launch, a sandy beach for sunning, and tidepools for marine explorations.

Nine miles of hiking trails include the southern end of the **Interurban Trail,** connecting the park with Bellingham. Other trails lead to scenic Fragrance and Lost Lakes for trout fishing, and to dramatic vistas from the 1,941-foot summit of **Chuckanut Mountain** (also accessible via a gravel road).

Continue north from Larrabee State Park to **Teddy Bear Cove,** located at the foot of the cliff just before you enter the Fairhaven District. For many years it was an unofficial nude beach, but the county purchased the land and started fining the au naturel crowd $125 per infraction in 1997. That doesn't stop some people from going sans clothes anyway.

ACCOMMODATIONS

◖ Chuckanut Manor (360/766-6191, www.chuckanutmanor.com) has a two-room suite over the restaurant with a spa and private deck. Nearby is a cottage with a hot tub, antique furnishings, a private deck, and kitchen. Both of these are $160 d including continental breakfast.

Alice Bay B&B (982 Scott Rd. on Sammish Island just west of Edison, 360/766-6396 or 800/652-0223, www.alicebay.com, $155 s or d) has a two-story unit where you can soak in the hot tub on the deck overlooking Alice Bay, take the rowboat out, or walk the private beach; rates include a full breakfast. Kids are welcome.

Samish Point by the Bay (447 Samish Point Rd., 360/766-6610, www.samishpoint.com, $185 s or d for the entire place) has four guest rooms with private baths in a secluded Cape Cod cottage facing Samish Bay. Outside, you'll find a hot tub and extensive gardens. There is a two-night minimum. The kitchen is stocked for a make-your-own breakfast. Kids over 12 only.

FOOD

Rhododendron Café (5521 Chuckanut Dr., Bow, 360/766-6667, www.rhodycafe.com, 11:30 A.M.–9 P.M. Wed.–Fri., 9 A.M.–9 P.M. Sat.–Sun., closed from Thanksgiving until the last Friday in January), at the Bow-Edison intersection, serves good food and is populated on weekends by bicyclists and weekend-drive aficionados, particularly during the morning hours when brunch is served.

As you drive north from Bow on Chuckanut Drive, you'll pass several good places to eat. Overlooking Samish Bay and the San Juans, **Chuckanut Manor Restaurant and B&B** (302 Chuckanut Dr., 360/766-6191, www.chuckanutmanor.com, 11:30 A.M.–9 P.M. Tues.–Thurs., 11:30 A.M.–10 P.M. Fri., 10:30 A.M.–11:30 P.M. Sat., 10:30 A.M.–6 P.M. Sun., closed Mon.), at the southernmost end of the drive, specializes in fresh seafood and continental dishes, a Friday night prime rib and seafood buffet, and a Sunday champagne brunch. The bar has the best and usually quietest seats in the house. The Chuckanut Clam Chowder here is to die for.

The oyster-sized **Oyster Bar** (240 Chuckanut Dr., 360/766-6185, www.the oysterbar.net, 11:30 A.M.–10 P.M. daily) is a cozy and romantic place clinging to the side of the mountain. The entire west-facing wall is windowed, offering superb sunset views of the San Juan Islands. This is arguably one of the best places in the state to sup on fresh oysters on a half shell—the house-made jicama slaw served as a side brings these slippery treats to a new level.

If you'd prefer to cook up your own fresh seafood smorgasbord, stop by the shoreline shop at **Taylor Shellfish Farm** (2182 Chuckanut Dr., Bow, 360/766-6002, www .taylorshellfishfarms.com, 9 A.M.–6 P.M. daily Apr.–Sept., 9 A.M.–5 P.M. daily Oct.–Mar.) for locally raised fresh oysters, clams, scallops, mussels, and Dungeness crabs (cooked while you wait).

Bellingham

Throw a hiking boot down any one of Bellingham's commercial thoroughfares and you're just as likely to land it in front of an outdoor sporting goods shop as you are in front of some passerby who, just for a second, might think "Hey, that isn't mine, is it?"

Yep, this is a town that is bonkers for bikes, skis, kayaks, and any other means of conveyance that will get them out into the pristine water, trails, and slopes that surround their neighborhoods.

The town is a microcosm of all the best that Western Washington has to offer, with beautifully restored historic buildings, extraordinary museums, and quirky boutiques and creative cafés.

It is also the last major outpost for Canada-bound travelers looking to cross at Blaine or Sumas and hearty travelers planning to take the rugged Alaska Marine Highway ferry.

SIGHTS
◖ Fairhaven
Fairhaven once banked on the arrival of the railroad, which would make the city, in the words of some backers, the next Chicago. In the 1880s, they imported laborers from all over, quickly throwing up the elaborate Italianate brick buildings still there today. Maybe town backers greased the wrong palms or maybe it was just blindingly obvious that the terminus should be in the better known and more developed city of Seattle less than 100 miles south, but Fairhaven lost out big-time. Staggering depression followed, both economic and, doubtlessly, emotional among the residents of what could have been New Chicago, Washington. Those old buildings

FAIRHAVEN'S ROWDY DAYS

The story of Fairhaven, Washington, is one all too typical of Western towns in the late 1800s. Rumors that the Great Northern Railway was going to select the town as its terminus sent people into a speculative frenzy, building grand houses, bars, and hotels. An opera house and, well, less respectable houses provided whiskey-fueled recreation. At its height, men slept in tents on the beach once the hotels filled up. Fistfights and gunplay left Fairhaven with a wild reputation. Ultimately, the terminus ended up in Tacoma, bursting the bubble that had sustained the town for a short time. The disappointment over the railroad coupled with a national financial panic quieted the rowdy town almost to the point of death. In 1903, Whatcom, Sehome, and Fairhaven – all on Bellingham Bay – decided to combine into a new town called Bellingham. These days, it's a lot more peaceful, if a little less fun.

now make up the **Fairhaven Historic District,** quieter and a little less speculative than it used to be in those grand old days. You can see its old buildings and Victorian homes in a walking tour. Maps are available from the **visitors bureau** (904 Potter St., 360/671-3990, www .bellingham.org) and various Fairhaven shops and restaurants.

Western Washington University

This 189-acre campus has five colleges and two schools for 12,000 students. The campus is known for its 22 sculptures in the **Outdoor Sculpture Garden.** Contact the Administration office (360/650-3000, www .wwu.edu) for campus tours.

Overlooking Bellingham Bay and accessible via a footpath from the university, the **Sehome Hill Arboretum** (Bill McDonald Parkway at 25th St., 360/778-7000, 6 A.M.–10 P.M. daily) provides splendid views of the San Juans and Mount. Baker, plus 70 acres of tall Douglas firs, wildflowers, and bigleaf maples preserved in their natural state. There are several trails and an observation tower that are open to the public.

Museums

Located on a high bluff overlooking Bellingham Bay, the must-see **Whatcom Museum of History and Art** (121 Prospect St., 360/676-6981, www.whatcommuseum. org, noon–5 P.M. Thurs.–Sun., adults $10, students, military, seniors $8, children 5 and under $4.50) is housed in the 1892 old city hall, an ornate redbrick building capped by a four-corner cupola and a tall clock tower. Today, the museum has grown to include two gorgeous nearby structures as well.

The main building contains historical displays, changing exhibits, Victorian clothing, woodworking tools, toys, and contemporary art. Also here is a small gift shop with unusual items from around the globe.

Two nearby structures house separate collections that are also part of the Whatcom Museum "campus." The **Lightcatcher** (250 Flora St., noon–5 P.M. Tues.–Sun.) across the

The Whatcom Museum of History and Art stands impressively over downtown Bellingham.

© ERICKA CHICKOWSKI

NORTH PUGET SOUND

street houses changing fine art and historical exhibits. The Lightcatcher also plays host to the Family Interactive Gallery in which children can interact with art and create some of their own. The **Syre Education Center** (201 Prospect St., 360/733-8769, noon–5 P.M. Sun., Tues., 1–4:45 P.M. Wed.–Fri., $2.50) displays artifacts and photographs interpreting local history, wildlife, and industry.

Make it a point to visit **Mindport** (210 West Holly, 360/647-5614, www.mindport .org, noon–6 P.M. Wed.–Fri., 10–5 P.M. Sat., noon–4 P.M. Sun. $2), a creative center that will amuse, fascinate, and educate both kids and adults. The exhibits are a mixture of "notouch" fine art and interactive sculpture mostly made from reused old junk, with a touch of whimsy thrown in. It's great fun.

For something completely different, check out the **American Museum of Radio and Electricity** (1312 Bay St., 360/738-3886, www.amre.us, 11 A.M.–4 P.M. Wed.–Sat., $5 adults, $2 children 11 and under). The collection has rare and historical radios, plus an

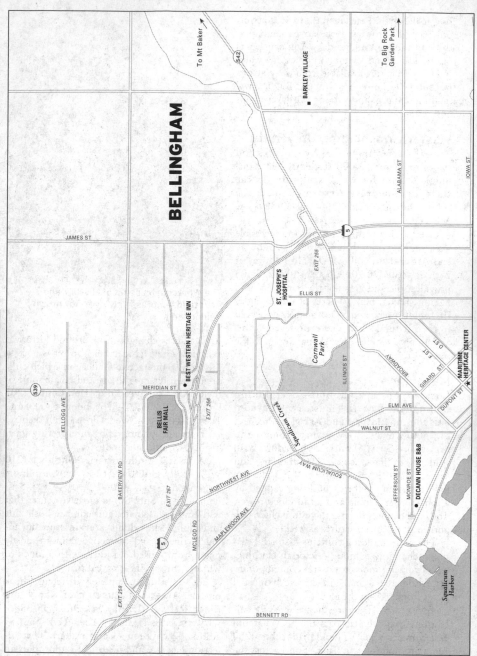

To Mt Baker

542

To Big Rock
Garden Park

BARKLEY VILLAGE

BELLINGHAM

ALABAMA ST

IOWA ST

JAMES ST

5

EXIT 255

ST. JOSEPH'S
HOSPITAL

ELLIS ST

Cornwall
Park

ILLINOIS ST

O ST

F ST

MARITIME
HERITAGE CENTER

BROADWAY

GIRARD ST

DUPONT ST

539

MERIDIAN ST

BEST WESTERN HERITAGE INN

KELLOGG AVE

BELLIS
FAIR MALL

EXIT 256

Squalicum Creek

ELM AVE

WALNUT ST

BAKERVIEW RD

EXIT 257

NORTHWEST AVE

SQUALICUM WAY

JEFFERSON ST

MONROE ST

DECANN HOUSE B&B

MCLEOD RD

MAPLEWOOD AVE

5

EXIT 258

Squalicum
Harbor

BENNETT RD

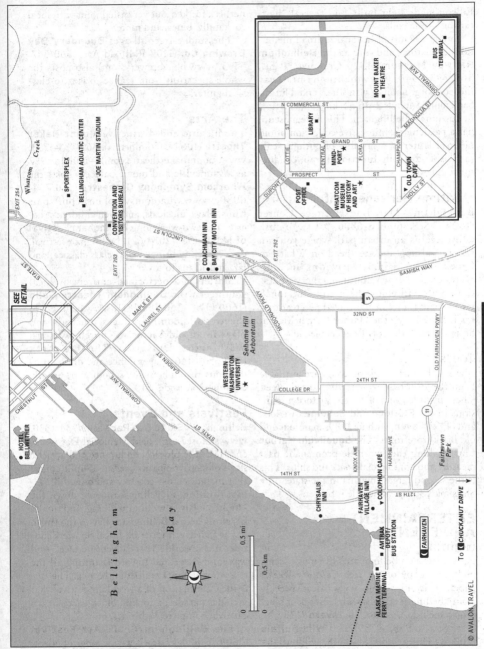

BUS TERMINAL

MOUNT BAKER THEATRE

CORNWALL AVE

N COMMERCIAL ST

LIBRARY

ST

CENTRAL AVE

GRAND ST

MAGNOLIA ST

CHAMPION ST

LOTTIE

MIND-PORT ★

FLORA ST

OLD TOWN CAFÉ

DUPONT ST

PROSPECT ST

POST OFFICE

WHATCOM MUSEUM OF HISTORY AND ART ★

HOLLY ST

SEE DETAIL

Whatcom Creek

EXIT 254

SPORTSPLEX

BELLINGHAM AQUATIC CENTER

JOE MARTIN STADIUM

CONVENTION AND VISITORS BUREAU

STATE ST

EXIT 253

LINCOLN ST

COACHMAN INN

BAY CITY MOTOR INN

SAMISH WAY

EXIT 252

SAMISH WAY

5

32ND ST

MAPLE ST

LAUREL ST

GARDEN ST

MCDONALD PKWY

Sehome Hill Arboretum

WESTERN WASHINGTON UNIVERSITY ★

COLLEGE DR

24TH ST

OLD FAIRHAVEN PKWY

CHESTNUT ST

CORNWALL AVE

STATE ST

HOTEL BELLWETHER

11

HARRIS AVE

KNOX AVE

14TH ST

COLOPHON CAFÉ

Fairhaven Park

Bellingham Bay

CHRYSALIS INN

FAIRHAVEN VILLAGE INN

12TH ST

AMTRAK DEPOT/ BUS STATION

FAIRHAVEN

To CHUCKANUT DRIVE

0.5 mi

0.5 km

0

0

ALASKA MARINE FERRY TERMINAL

NORTH PUGET SOUND

© AVALON TRAVEL

Edison-made light bulb, and several "hair-raising" Tesla coils.

Immerse yourself in local railroad memorabilia, history, and lore at the **Bellingham Railway Museum** (1320 Commercial St., 360/393-7540, www.bellinghamrailway museum.org, noon–5 P.M. Tues. and Thurs.– Sat., adults $4, kids 2–16 $2, kids under 2 free) in downtown Bellingham. This little museum has a particularly impressive collection of old railroad lanterns, a number of antique scale models, and a fully functional train conductor simulator.

Maritime Heritage Center

Bellingham's Maritime Heritage Center (1600 C St., 360/676-6806, 9 A.M. to dusk daily, free) is an urban park where you can fish for salmon and steelhead on Whatcom Creek, watch salmon spawning in mid-October, and learn about hatchery operation. Kids will enjoy the marine life touch tank where they can pet intertidal creatures. It's located inside the Harbor Center Mall at Squalicum Harbor off Roeder Avenue.

Tours

Maps of historic walking tours are available from the visitors bureau at 904 Potter Street. These include tours of stately Victorian mansions in the **Eldridge** and **Sehome** districts, and of **Fairhaven,** with its 1880s mansions and old brick storefronts. The **Squalicum Harbor** tour is along the two-mile promenade past pleasure and commercial boats and ships. This is the second-largest marina in the state; only Shilshole Marina in Seattle is bigger.

ENTERTAINMENT AND EVENTS
Nightlife

For the latest on Bellingham's live music scene, pick up a copy of the free *Cascadia Weekly* paper, or visit its website, www.cascadiaweekly .com/. Bellingham clubs with live rock or blues music include **Up and Up Tavern** (1234 N. State St., 360/733-9739), and **Wild Buffalo** (208 W. Holly, 360/752-0848, wildbuffalo.

net) is a funked-out yet casual joint with local rockabilly, blues, and more.

The smoke-free, all-ages **Boundary Bay Brewing Co.** (1107 Railroad Ave., 360/647-5593, www.bbaybrewery.com) also hosts the whole spectrum from reggae to jazz to classical guitar.

The Arts

The historic and distinctive **Mount Baker Theatre** (106 N. Commercial, 360/733-5793, www.mountbakertheatre.com)—built in 1927 as a vaudeville and movie palace—hosts the **Whatcom Symphony Orchestra** (360/734-6080, www.whatcomsymphony.com) plus films, plays, musicals, and even children's theatre. The two-week-long **Bellingham Festival of Music** (360/201-6621, bellinghamfestival. org) each July brings world-class classical and jazz musicians to town.

Staffed and performed entirely by local volunteers, the **Bellingham Theatre Guild** (1600 H St., 360/733-1811, www.bellingham theatreguild.com) produces musicals and plays in an old Victorian church. Western Washington University **Theatre Arts** (360/650-6146) stages dance and drama productions throughout the school year, usually coming in at under $10.

Festivals and Events

Bellingham's **Ski to Sea Race** (360/734-1330, www.skitosea.org), held Memorial Day weekend, tests the physical endurance and athletic skills of its participants over an 85-mile course that includes cross-country and downhill skiing, running, bicycling, canoeing down the Nooksack River, mountain biking, and finally kayaking across Bellingham Bay to the finish in the Fairhaven District. Local boosters consider it the world's first "adventure race," and was (and is) geared toward flaunting all the recreational opportunities in the area. The race is the culmination of a weeklong festival that includes parades, a rockin' block party, and a carnival complete with rides.

The **Bellingham Chalk Art Festival** (360/676-8548) attracts a wide range of talent, from kids to serious artists. Sidewalk "canvases" cost $25 each, and the event attracts some amazing talent.

SHOPPING
Fairhaven District
The Fairhaven District is Bellingham's most enjoyable place to stroll and shop. Several interesting shops and galleries can be found in the district. **Good Earth Pottery** (1000 Harris Ave., 360/671-3998, 11 A.M.–6 P.M. Mon.–Sat., noon–5 P.M. Sun.) has ceramics created by more than 50 artists; the cooperatively owned **Artwood** (1000 Harris Ave., 360/647-1628, www.artwoodgallery.com, 10 A.M.–6 P.M. Mon.–Sat., 10 A.M.–5 P.M. Sun.) sells handcrafted wooden furniture, jewelry, sculpture and more; and **Gallery West** (1300 12th St., 360/734-8414, www.artgallerywest.com, 10 A.M.–6 P.M. daily) sells art ranging from paintings, sculpture, pottery, Native art, and much more in their amply sized gallery.

    Brenthaven (200 W. Holly, 360/752-5537 or 888/212-5301, www.brenthaven.com, 11 A.M.–6 P.M. Mon.–Sat.) sews and sells high-quality day packs, shoulder bags, and soft luggage.

    A hugely popular community hub, **Village Books** (1210 11th St., 360/671-2626 or 800/392-2665, www.villagebooks.com, 10 A.M.–8:30 P.M. Mon.–Sat., 11 A.M.–7 P.M. Sun.) offers frequent promotions, book signings, and even a children's camp in the summer. If, like a true bibliophile, the musty smell of used books is practically an aphrodisiac for you, savor **Eclipse Bookstore** (915 Harris Ave., 360/647-8165), truly one of a dying breed.

Bellis Fair Mall
Massive **Bellis Fair Mall** (I-5 exit 256B, 360/671-5654, www.bellisfair.com), has over 150 shops (including Sears, JCPenney, Macy's, Kohl's, and Target), a food court, and a six-plex theater. Keep going out Meridian Street to enjoy the frenzy of shopping even more; here you'll find all the big discount chain stores, fast-food joints, motels, and hundreds of British Columbia license plates.

Antiques
Whatcom County has a good selection of antique shops and malls. In Bellingham proper, check out several along West Holly Street, particularly **Old Town Antique Mall** (427 W. Holly St., 360/671-3301, www.oldtown antiquemallbellingham.com, 10 A.M.–6 P.M. Mon.–Sat., noon–5 P.M. Sun.), which features a wide selection of collectibles from 40 dealers. Downstairs, at the same address, **Aladdin's Lamp Antique Mall** (427 W. Holly St., 360/647-0066, 10 A.M.–6 P.M. Mon.–Sat., noon–5 P.M. Sun.) sells jewelry, glassware, toys, and especially known for their selection of old vinyl records.

Art Galleries
Bellingham has a diverse arts community, with a number of pleasant galleries. **Allied Arts of Whatcom County** (1418 Cornwall Ave., 360/676-8548, www.alliedarts.org) has a large gallery that hosts a juried art show and a Re-Art show focusing on recycled materials. For two weekends in October, local artists open their studios to the public. Call 360/734-9472 or email info@studiotour.net for this year's slate of artists. In Barkley Village, **Hamann's Gallery & Gift** (2940 New Market, 360/733-8898) offers originals and prints, cards, candles, books and more for sale to the public. The **Blue Horse Gallery** (301 W. Holly St., 360/671-2305, www.blue horsegallery.com) features works from extremely talented regional artists. Enjoy their café and wine bar, as well as occasional live music. The **Pacific Marine Gallery** (700 W. Holly St., 360/738-8535, www.pacificmarine.com), is just a few blocks away. The unique gift shop, bookstore, and gallery has saltwater in its veins and is focused completely on maritime goods.

    Behind the visitors bureau office, you'll find **Jody Bergsma Gallery** (1344 King St., 800/237-4762, www.bergsma.com) showing the works of this prolific artist. See her brother's work at **Mark Bergsma Photographer Gallery** (1306 Commercial St., 360/671-6818), including multipanel landscape photographs.

SPORTS AND RECREATION
Parks

Whatcom County has one of the best collections of city- and county-owned parks in the state. In Bellingham alone there are more than 35 places that qualify as parks, including green belt areas, fitness areas, and trails. These parks range from less than half an acre to over a thousand acres. Details at 360/733-2900 or www.co.whatcom.wa.us/parks.

Beautiful **Samish Park** (I-5 exit 246 south of Bellingham, 360/733-2362) is a 39-acre county park along Lake Samish with swimming, fishing, boating, picnicking, hiking, and a children's play area. Rent canoes, kayaks, hydrobikes, paddleboats, or rowboats.

Whatcom Falls Park (1401 Electric Ave.) near Lake Whatcom has hiking trails, tennis courts, a playground, a picnic area, and a state fish hatchery on 241 acres.

With 12 acres on the lake itself, **Bloedel Donovan Park** (2214 Electric Ave.) has a swimming beach, boat launch, playground, and picnic area.

Lake Padden Park (4882 Samish Way) has over 1,000 acres of hiking and horse trails, a golf course, picnic areas, and a playground, plus swimming, fishing, and nonmotorized boating on the lake.

Thirty-eight acres of practically untouched canyon wilderness is yours for the hiking at **Arroyo Park** on Old Samish Road, with nature and horse trails and creek fishing.

Overlooking Lake Whatcom, **Big Rock Garden Park** (2900 Sylvan St.) includes a hundred varieties of rhododendron and azaleas, along with dozens of Japanese maples. Big Rock Garden is an oasis of tranquility, with forests and outdoor sculptures, as well as a pleasant venue for free summer concerts.

Hiking

Stop by the visitors bureau for descriptions of more than 20 hiking trails in and around Bellingham, including trails in **Whatcom Falls Park** and **Sehome Hill Arboretum.** Another 2.6 miles of paths circle Lake Padden Park.

The **Interurban Trail** is a six-mile path that follows a former railroad bed from Old Fairhaven Parkway south to Larrabee State Park. It is a great place for a jog or bike ride.

SKI TO SEA

No event highlights the joys of Bellingham's recreational opportunities more than the **Ski to Sea** (www.skitosea.com), the mother of all adventure races. This whopping seven-sport relay attracts teams of athletes from all over the world, who make their way speedily from Mount Baker cross-country skiing, downhill skiing, road cycling, canoeing, mountain biking, and finally, sea-kayaking. All told, the grueling race can take anywhere from 5.5 to over 8 hours to complete, all followed with a celebratory party in Fairhaven for those who can still stand and/or sit.

Climbing

Bellingham is home to the **American Alpine Institute** (1515 12th St., 360/671-1505, www.aai.cc), the nation's preeminent center for mountaineering education. The school's staff is made up of accomplished mountain climbers and educators who teach courses from the basics to advanced month-long programs. Classes are taught all over the world, with beginning mountaineering courses in the North Cascades. AAI also rents outdoor equipment.

Ice Skating

Strap on some skates and glide the rink at **Sportsplex** (1225 Civic Field Way, 360/733-9999, www.bellinghamsportsplex.com, $5.50 adults for adult skate (16 or over) or $2 community all-ages, skate rental $2.50), which offers year-round skating at its indoor facilities.

Golf

Tee off at the pastoral **Shuksan Golf Club** (1500 Axton Rd., 360/398-8888, www.shuksangolf.com, $45 weekends), a pretty and affordable course with ample elevation changes set by the gurgling Ten Mile Creek. You'll catch glimpses of the namesake Shuksan Mountain as you walk the course.

Gear Rentals

Rent bikes, skis, and snowboards, or practically anything else from **Fairhaven Bike & Mountain Sport** (1108 11th St., 360/733-4433, fairhavenbike.com, 9:30 A.M.–7 P.M. Mon.–Thurs., 9:30 A.M.–8 P.M. Fri., 10 A.M.–6 P.M. Sat., 11 A.M.–5 P.M. Sun.).

Water Sports and Tours

In the summer months you can swim at **Lake Padden Park** (4882 Samish Way, 360/676-6985), **Lake Samish** (673 N. Lake Samish Dr., 360/733-2362), and **Bloedel Donovan Park** (2214 Electric Ave., 360/676-6985).

Sail the San Juans (360/671-5852 or 800/729-3207, www.stsj.com) offers six-day fully crewed charters around the islands, departing from Bellingham. For those who'd rather fish from land, **Lake Padden** is the place to be.

Moondance Sea Kayaking Adventures (360/738-7664, www.moondancekayak.com) offers guided sea kayak tours from Bellingham.

You can rent sea kayaks, rowboats, and sailboats in summer from **Bellingham Bay Community Boating Center** (555 Harris Ave., 360/714-8891, www.boatingcenter.org), near the Bellingham Cruise Terminal. **Bellingham Boat Rentals** (3034 Silvern Lane, 360/676-1363) has canoes and pedal boats for rent on Lake Whatcom and is open May through August.

Several Bellingham companies offer breathtaking day-long Orca whale-watching trips for the ecotourist in you. For the best deal on the water, call **Island Mariner Cruises** (5 Harbor Esplanade, 360/734-8866 or 877/734-8866, www.orcawatch.com, $69 for adults, $59 for kids 11–18, or $39 for kids under 10). Their spotter high above in a seaplane is an almost-guaranteed whale sighting. Tours depart from the boat harbor in town. **San Juan Island Shuttle Express** (800/465-4604, www.orcawhales.com) operates the slickest ships for five-to six-hour naturalist-guided whale-watching cruises for $89 for adults, or $79 for seniors, active military, or students with ID. **Victoria-San Juan Cruises** (355 Harris Ave., 360/738-8099 or 800/443-4552,

© ERICKA CHICKOWSKI

Try fishing from the shores of one of Bellingham's lakes.

NORTH PUGET SOUND

www.whales.com) has all-day cruises from Bellingham to Victoria and back by way of the San Juan Islands. You'll sail aboard the *Victoria Star II,* a 100-passenger boat. The cost—including a seafood dinner—is $89 for adults, $84 for seniors, or $45 for kids. Tours are offered late May–mid-October.

ACCOMMODATIONS
Under $100

Surprisingly, for a town with so many college students, hippies, and vagabonding ski bums, there's no hostel in Bellingham proper. Travel 20 miles north to stay in pleasant Blaine at the quiet **Birch Bay Hostel** (7467 Gemeni St. in Blaine, 360/371-2180, www.birchbayhostel .org, $27.50 for a male or female dorm).

For cheap accommodations in town, North Samish Way near the university is the major motel thoroughfare. The quality is unpredictable and the neighborhood is a little sketchy, so be wary of that super cheap rate on the Internet at a motel you haven't vetted. One of the best values is at the **Coachman Inn** (120 N. Samish Way, 360/671-9000 or 800/962-6641, $60 s or d). The exterior here looks a bit worn, but inside the rooms are updated and clean. Plus it has an outdoor heated pool, hot tub, and sauna.

Another clean and safe establishment is **Bay City Motor Inn** (116 N. Samish Way, 360/676-0899 or 800/538-8204, $75 s or $85–95 d). As a plus, the rooms are accessible via indoor corridor, and there's a fitness center, billiard table, laundry facility, and free continental breakfast in the morning. Spend a little extra coin and rent one of three whirlpool-tub suites for $125 d.

Or just go for the bed-and-breakfast option. The eminently affordable ◖ **DeCann House B&B** (2610 Eldridge Ave., 360/734-9172, www.decannhouse.com, $99–115 d) has two guest rooms with private baths. This 1902 charmer was partially restored by hand by its owners, and is adorned with stained glass, heirlooms, and views of the San Juan Islands. Unwind with a cue stick or book in hand in the English-style library. This alluring room makes you wish for a smoking jacket and glass of brandy with its dark wood, floor-to-ceiling

bookshelves, and classic billiard table. Kids are accepted here by prior arrangement.

$100-150

Get out of town and stay at **Anderson Creek Lodge** (5602 Mission Rd., 360/966-0598, www.andersoncreek.com, $135–180). Llamas graze in the pasture on this 55-acre property 10 miles northeast of Bellingham. Rooms in the lodge have king-size beds, private baths, attractive wood paneling, and access to a hot tub.

$150-200

There are numerous big chain hotels near Bellis Fair Mall to choose from. I particularly enjoyed staying at the **Best Western Heritage Inn** (151 E. McLeod Rd., 360/647-1912 or 800/528-1234, www.bestwestern.com/heritageinn bellingham, $169 s or $199 d), a reasonably priced hotel complex with New England colonial-style buildings and interiors. The grounds are well tended, and there's an outdoor pool, hot tub, fitness center, airport shuttle service, and complimentary breakfast. The rooms sport super comfy mattresses, new linens, and big flat-screen TVs. The only downside is the traffic drone in some rooms—ask for a room facing away from the freeway.

The Victorian Italianate-style **Fairhaven Village Inn** (1200 10th St., 360/733-1311 or 877/733-1100, www.fairhavenvillage inn.com, $179–239 d) blends well with its historic Fairhaven neighbors. This distinctive boutique hotel is one of the best in Bellingham, with large rooms, luxe furnishings, bathrobes, free continental breakfast, and free Wi-Fi. The best rooms come equipped with gas fireplaces; the two-room suite ($289) comes with a large dining table and jetted tub. Some rooms are also pet friendly.

A large Craftsman home high on a hill overlooking Lake Whatcom, **South Bay B&B** (4095 S. Bay Dr. in Sedro-Woolley, 360/595-2086 or 877/595-2086, www.southbaybb .com, $149–245 d) is a quiet retreat featuring five guest rooms with whirlpool tubs, fireplaces, and private patios; rates include a big gourmet breakfast. This is a great romantic getaway.

$200-250

The ◖ **Hotel Bellwether** (1 Bellwether Way, 360/392-3100 or 877/411-1200, www .hotelbellwether.com, $202–264 d) offers Bellingham's most indulgent lodging, with a waterfront location, spacious rooms, balconies, Italian furnishings, gas fireplaces, and marble baths with jetted tubs. Regular suites with separate living areas run for $499. And honeymooners looking for a room to remember can book a spot in the eccentric three-level mini-lighthouse for $699—ask about the lighthouse package, which includes champagne and caviar, plus a three-course dinner served by your own private butler. No matter which room you choose, your puppy is welcome and for $35 extra will be spoiled with a pet bed, bowls, and a fresh-baked dog treat. A lavish breakfast buffet is available for an extra $11.95.

The swanky rooms at the waterfront **Chrysalis Inn and Spa at the Pier** (804 10th St., 360/756-1005 or 888/808-0005, www.the chrysalisinn.com, $209–325 s or d) are beautifully appointed, with such amenities as king-size beds, down comforters, fireplaces, fridges, high-speed Internet access, plus a substantial buffet breakfast. Suites ($299 d) also include whirlpool tubs, wet bars, and bay vistas. In-room spa treatments are available at additional cost. Fino Wine Bar and Restaurant is on the main floor and serves meals that match the elegance of the hotel.

Camping

The closest public campsites ($14 for tents, $20 for RVs) are seven miles south of Bellingham along Chuckanut Drive at **Larrabee State Park,** 14 miles north at **Birch Bay State Park,** and **Bellingham RV Park** (3939 Bennett Dr., 888/372-1224, www.bellinghamrvpark .info, $30 with full hookup and free Wi-Fi).

FOOD
Cafés and Delis

A particular favorite among health-conscious foodies is **Old Town Café** (316 W. Holly St., 360/671-4431, 7 A.M.–3 P.M. Mon.–Sat., 8 A.M.–2 P.M. Sun., $8), where the waitress is likely to have an armful of tattoos and the queue of customers is out the door on a weekend morning. They cook fresh, organically grown food without being self-righteous about it. The atmosphere is laid-back and noisy. Another

Bellingham's finest hotel: Hotel Bellwether

little breakfast gem is **The Daisy Cafe** (114 W. Magnolia St., 360/733-8996, www.thedaisy cafe.com, 7:30 A.M.–2:30 P.M. daily, $8) with a diverse breakfast and Sunday brunch menu. It's a favorite of the suit-and-tie crowd.

A slightly less casual dining experience can be found at **The Little Cheerful Café** (113 E. Holly St., 360/738-8824, www.little cheerful.com, 7 A.M.–2 P.M. daily, $8). The setting is casual with plenty of sidewalk seating, and the breakfasts are always great with ample portions. Cute and quirky, The Little Cheerful will cheerfully prepare your eggs benedict with salmon, crab cakes, or fresh veggies.

Swan Café (1059 N. State St., 360/734-8158, 8 A.M.–9 P.M. daily, $6), offers salads, fish, along with vegan and vegetarian pickings.

If you're in Fairhaven and want great sandwiches, bagels, quiche, or just a scoop of ice cream, drop by ⬛ **Colophon Café** inside Village Books (1210 11th St., 360/647-0092, www.colophoncafe.com, 9 A.M.–8 P.M. Mon.–Thurs., 9 A.M.–10 P.M. Fri.–Sat., 10 A.M.–8 P.M. Sun., $10). Be sure to give the unique African peanut soup a go—this rich, velvety concoction has a complex meaty flavor and a little bit of a spicy kick. Colophon is also great for Paul Bunyan–sized slices of carrot cake.

If you're searching for the great American burger, the car hop service at **Boomer's Drive In** (310 N. Samish Way, 360/647-2666, 11 A.M.–10 P.M. Sun.–Thurs., 11 A.M.–11 P.M. Fri.–Sat., $5) is sure to satisfy.

Steak and Seafood

Cliff House Restaurant (331 N. State St., 360/734-8660, www.bellinghamcliffhouse .com, 4:30–9:30 P.M. daily, $30) is famous for its whiskey crab soup, oyster bar, fresh seafood, and Angus beef. This is an old favorite with a big deck facing Bellingham Bay for alfresco dining.

The fair-weather favorite **Fairhaven Fish and Chips** (1020 Harris Ave., 360/733-5021, 11 A.M.–7 P.M. Mon.–Sat., noon–5 P.M. Sun.) is easy to find—just look for the red double-decker bus surrounded by patio umbrellas and tables. Step up to the bus window to order a basket of golden crispy deliciousness, plus clam chowder, Italian sodas, and ice cream.

Harborside Bistro (1 Bellwether Way, 360/392-3100 or 877/411-1200, www.hotel bellwether.com, 7 A.M.–9 P.M. Sun.–Thurs., 7 A.M.–9:30 P.M. Fri.–Sat., $25) is a charming place for fresh seafood or locally sourced bison tenderloin. It's right on the water at the

You can't miss the double-decker bus housing Fairhaven Fish and Chips.

© ERICKA CHICKOWSKI

luxurious Hotel Bellwether. A few steps away on the marina is **Anthony's at Squalicum Harbor** (25 Bellwether Way, 360/647-5588, www.anthonys.com, 11:30 A.M.–9:30 P.M. Sun.–Thurs., 11:30 A.M.–10:30 P.M. Fri.–Sat., $30), part of a Northwest chain of upscale seafood restaurants.

Dirty Dan Harris Steakhouse (1211 11th St., 360/676-1011, www.dirtydanharris.com, 5–9:30 P.M. Sun.–Thurs., 5–10 P.M. Fri.–Sat., $24) in the Fairhaven District serves corn-fed prime rib, steaks, and fresh seafood dinners in an 1800s-style saloon. It's named for Daniel Jefferson Harris, the feisty eccentric known for his iffy bathing habits who platted the town's streets, and sold lots to the thousands of folks who rolled into Fairhaven in 1883.

Italian and Pizza

D'Anna's Café Italiano (1317 N. State St., 360/714-0188, www.dannascafeitaliano.com, 11 A.M.–10 P.M. Mon.–Sat., 4–10 P.M. Sun., $13) is a charming little bistro specializing in homemade pasta, ravioli, and sausage. The chicken parmesan is the best around.

For pizza, **Rudy's Pizzeria** (1230 N. State St., 360/647-7547, www.rudysbham.com, 11 A.M.–11 P.M. Mon.–Thurs., 11 A.M.–midnight Fri., noon–midnight Sat., 4–10 P.M. Sun., $15) is popular with the college set and big families. Choose between a range of gourmet toppings, plus several types of crusts and sauces. An ever-changing slate of craft beers on tap and killer daily specials make a good thing better.

Other International

Fairhaven's **Dos Padres** (1111 Harris Ave., 360/733-9900, www.dospadres.net, 11:30 A.M.–9 P.M. Sun.–Thurs., 11:30 A.M.–9:30 P.M. Fri.–Sat., $10) serves up a combo of Tex-Mex dishes and Mexican classics. It's locally famous for margaritas and nachos. For a Mexican restaurant that offers delicious pork, beef and chicken dishes, as well as great vegetarian fare, check out **El Gitano** (1125 Sunset Dr., 360/714-1065, www.elgitano.com, 11 A.M.–10 P.M. daily $13). They grill up some of the area's best Southwestern-style meals at **Pepper Sisters**

(1055 N. State St., 360/671-3414, www.pepper sisters.com). Their cozy, funky location is a great complement to good food at a good price.

Café Akroterii (1219 Cornwall Ave., 360/676-5554, 11 A.M.–10 P.M. Mon.–Sat., 4–9 P.M. Sun., $14) invites you to enjoy a Greek salad with Old World leisureliness while watching the hustle and bustle of downtown Bellingham.

India Grill (1215 Cornwall Ave., 360/714-0314, www.indiagrill.us, 11 A.M.–3 P.M. and 4–9 P.M. daily, $11) is *the* place for Indian food, including tandoori and vegetarian specials.

For some good Thai food, two restaurants stand out. **Busara Siamese Cuisine** (324 36th St., Sehome Village Mall, 360/734-8088, 11:30 A.M.–9:30 P.M. daily, $11) cooks top-notch curries. Just about anything on the menu can be prepared with tofu rather than meat for those of the vegetarian persuasion. **Thai House Restaurant** (187 Telegraph Rd., 360/734-5111, www.bellinghamthaihouse .com, 11 A.M.–10 P.M. Mon.–Sat., noon–9 P.M. Sun. $10) has a traditional Thai menu with free delivery, even to hotels and guest houses. **Little Tokyo** (Barkley Village, 360/752-2222, www.littletokyowa.com, lunch 11 A.M.–9 P.M. Mon.–Fri., noon–9 P.M. Sat $15) is a casual sushi bar and Japanese restaurant considered by many to be the best in town. Different lunch and dinner specials every day mean there's always a super value for the choosing.

Pub Grub

Boundary Bay Brewery & Bistro (1107 Railroad Ave., 360/647-5593, www.bbay brewery.com, 11 A.M.–11 P.M. daily, $10) features several very flavorful house-brewed beers on tap and a menu focused around brats and burgers.

Markets and Bakeries

Bellingham's **Community Food Co-Op** (1220 N. Forest St. at Holly St., 360/734-8158, www .communityfood.coop, 7 A.M.–10 P.M. daily) is a natural and organic foods market that even stocks Mexican and Indian ingredients. **Haggen Foods** (2900 Woburn, 360/676-5300, 2814 Meridian St. 360/671-3300, 1401 12th St.

360/733-4370, www.haggen.com) runs three large gourmet markets around town. All three have pharmacies and comprehensive delis.

Downtown, **Avenue Bread Co.** (1313 Railroad Ave., 360/715-3354, 7 A.M.–4:30 P.M. Mon.–Sat., 9 A.M.–4 P.M. Sun.) strives to perfect the art of bread, from baguettes to biscotti. Add in some soup or a gourmet coffee drink to create the ideal antidote for the drizzles. For French pastries, say bonjour to **La Vie En Rose French Bakery** (111 W. Holly St., 360/715-1839, www.laviebakery.com, 8 A.M.–4 P.M. daily).

Now one of the largest in the state, the **Bellingham Farmers Market** (360/647-2060, www.bellinghamfarmers.org, 10 A.M.–3 P.M., Sat.–Sun., early Apr.–Oct.) is held in the parking lot at Chestnut Street and Railroad Avenue. Fairhaven stages a special at 11th and McKenzie, Wednesday **Fairhaven Farmers Market** (360/647-2060), noon–5 P.M. Wednesday June–September.

INFORMATION AND SERVICES

For maps, brochures, and general information, contact the **Bellingham and Whatcom County Convention and Visitors Bureau** (904 Potter St. at exit 253 off I-5, 360/671-3990 or 800/487-2032, www.bellingham.org, 9 A.M.–5 P.M. daily). An information booth at the Bellingham Cruise Terminal (where the Alaska ferry docks) is staffed Tuesday, Thursday, and Friday in the summer, and brochure racks are located inside the Bellis Fair Mall.

GETTING THERE AND AROUND
By Car

Downtown Bellingham makes up for its relatively small size with odd street intersections that send you off in the opposite direction you intended. It's as if someone laid out a grid and then took the downtown section and gave it a good twist. Make sure your GPS is ready for a good workout.

By Ferry

The **Bellingham Cruise Terminal,** located three blocks downhill from Fairhaven, is where you can catch ferries to the San Juans, Victoria, and Alaska. The terminal has reservation and ticketing booths for the **Alaska Marine Highway** (360/676-8445 or 800/642-0066, www.state.ak.us/ferry), which provides passenger and vehicle ferry service to Southeast Alaska destinations. Alaska ferries depart on Friday year-round, plus Tuesday in summer. The ticket office inside the terminal is open weekdays. Also here are a gift shop, storage lockers, and a little seafood café.

By Train

Amtrak (800/872-7245, www.amtrak.com) provides daily train connections on its modern Cascades train north to Vancouver, B.C., and south to Mount Vernon, Everett, Edmonds, and Seattle. It stops at the Fairhaven depot, just a short walk from the ferry terminal.

By Air

Alaska Airlines (800/252-7522, www.alaska air.com) operates flights out of Bellingham International Airport (www.portofbellingham .com) to Seattle. Many Canadians use this airport because they can get more convenient or cheaper flights to the U.S. **San Juan Airlines** (800/874-4434, www.sanjuanairlines.com) has scheduled service to the San Juan Islands, plus charters and scenic flights over Friday Harbor, Mount Constitution,Victoria, and many other destinations.

If you're flying into Sea-Tac Airport and can't make good connections, **Airporter Shuttle** (360/380-8800 or 866/235-5247, www.air porter.com) runs daily van service to Bellingham. Similarly, **Quick Shuttle** (604/940-4428 or 800/665-2122, www.quickcoach.com) runs service to Vancouver, British Columbia.

By Bus

Locally, **Whatcom Transit** (360/676-7433, www.ridewta.com) provides bus service Monday–Saturday to Bellingham, Ferndale, Lynden, and Blaine. **Greyhound** (360/733-5251 or 800/231-2222, www.greyhound .com) has nationwide bus connections from the Amtrak depot in Fairhaven.

North to Canada

Many road-weary travelers heading up to the Canadian border tend to let the scenery blur by along I-5 once they pass the outskirts of Bellingham, but there are a number of worthwhile stops along the way.

Just north of Bellingham, the little hamlet of Ferndale is home to one of the best collections of historic log buildings in the state and is a darned fine spot for a piece of pie and a cup of coffee.

Along the waterfront, Birch Bay's moon-shaped waters have drawn families from both sides of the border for generations to enjoy its warm waters come summertime. Similarly, Lummi Island and Semiahmoo Spit also offer a shoreside respite and a chance to walk quiet beaches, ply the waters for fish, and soak in the sunsets.

For a more terrestrial treat, little Lynden's shady streets and spinning windmills present travelers a taste of old-world Holland. Set amid the idyllic dairy fields and ruby red barns along Highway 539, this small town also offers visitors a chance to peek in at one of the best history museums they've never heard of.

All roads eventually lead to Blaine, the largest Canadian border crossings in the northwest. Before hopping in line, be sure to pull off at Peace Arch Park to walk the greens and take a gander at the white arch standing proudly as a testament to the long-lasting friendship between two countries.

SIGHTS
〔 Peace Arch

The 40-acre **Peace Arch State Park** at the Canadian border has beautifully landscaped grounds and gardens surrounding the Peace Arch, a symbol of friendship between the U.S. and Canada that stands with one "foot" in each country. The park was constructed in 1921 by American and Canadian volunteers and funded by Washington and British Columbia schoolchildren, who contributed from $0.01 to $0.10

Peace Arch

BORDERING ON FRIENDLINESS

East of Blaine is quite a physical statement of the relationship between the United States and Canada. As you drive east toward Sumas and Lynden, you can turn north off the main road and follow it until it makes a sharp right turn to the east again. Here you will notice a pair of two-lane blacktop highways running east and west, side by side, with only a swale separating them. That swale is part of the 3,000 mile international boundary between Canada and America, the longest unprotected boundary in the world.

each for the project. Pieces of the *Mayflower* and the Hudson's Bay Company steamer *Beaver* are included in the monument.

A path lined with rhododendrons, dahlias, and azaleas leads from the arch greens to a picnic area and playground. Get to the Peace Arch by heading north on 2nd Street into the parking lot; customs officers from both nations don't like folks stopping at the border crossing to enter the park.

Semiahmoo Spit

Head out the 1.5-mile-long Semiahmoo Spit to **Semiahmoo County Park** (360/371-5513), where you'll find restored salmon cannery buildings, and a museum (1–5 P.M. Sat., Sun. Memorial Day–Labor Day only) that depicts early fishing and cannery operations. The park itself is open daily year-round. The **Raven-Salmon Woman Totem Pole** stands outside as a testament to hundreds of years of Native American presence here. A paved bike path parallels the road along Semiahmoo Spit.

The **MV Plover** (360/332-5742, donations accepted), the oldest passenger foot ferry in Washington, runs a pleasant tour between Blain Harbor and Semiahmoo, noon–8 P.M. on summer weekends only, departing on the hour from Blaine and on the half hour from Semiahmoo.

Lummi Island

This little haven is home primarily to artists, weekenders, and a few thousand members of the Lummi Nation on the 13,000-acre Indian Reservation here. Many of the Lummi who live on the reserve still fish the waters in the style of their ancestors. Stroll the western shore along Legoe Bay to see them line up two by two in their small barks, spreading specialized reefnets between them.

Most of the island is private property with no public access, but you can ride the roads to a few public places around the island. Most notable among them is a checkerboard of land preserved by the Lummi Island Heritage Trust (360/758-7997). Largest among them is **The Otto Farm,** a 120-acre property that includes a 70-acre wildlife preserve located on Sunrise Road, between South Nugent Road and Seacrest Drive.

Readily accessible public beaches are scant on the island, with most only accessible by boat. The best bet for the boatless is a stretch of shoreline just north of the ferry terminal. Go north on Nugent Road until you reach a viewing platform and descend the adjacent stairs.

Historic Ferndale

Ferndale is a quiet little "Main Street" town on the northwest side of the Nooksack River whose major highlight is a pair of historic parks that have preserved a little slice of Whatcom County's past.

The mini-tour of Northwest heritage starts two blocks south of Main on 1st Avenue. **Pioneer Park** (360/384-6461) is home to eleven hand-hewn cedar log buildings dating back to the late 19th century, which were moved here one by one starting in the 1930s. Visitors can check out exhibits that range from aged photos to an old Linotype machine. Tours of the buildings are available 11:30 A.M.–4 P.M. Tues.–Sun. mid-May–mid-September, and cost $5 for adults, $3 for children 6–12, and free under 6.

Head south from town on Hovander Drive and Neilsen Road to **Hovander Homestead Park** (5299 Nielsen Ave., 360/384-3444, www.co.whatcom.wa.us/parks), where you'll find a century-old folk-style Victorian home and farm on the Nooksack River, a big red barn, milk house, and flower gardens (including 30 varieties of dahlias). There is a farmyard full of animals and even vending machines so that children can buy snacks for the goats, cows, rabbits, and more. Bring a blanket for some relaxing sprawling out by the river. Now a National Historic site, the park is open daily, but the homestead is open only in summer, Friday through Sunday. Admission is $3 per car. Tours are available in the summer noon–4:30 P.M. Thursday through Sunday.

Birch Bay State Park

Birch Bay's featured attraction is its beach, and one of the best places to enjoy it is the 193-acre Birch Bay State Park (360/371-2800, www.parks.wa.gov) at the west end of Helwig Road. This park follows two miles of shoreline along the bay, with campsites set back in the trees. The beach is a favorite place for swimming, kite flying, windsurfing, clamming, and volleyball. Other facilities include an underwater park, fishing, a public boat launch, a picnic area, and the Terrell Marsh nature trail through an estuary teeming with wildlife.

Lynden

Most of Lynden's early settlers were dairy farmers from the Netherlands, and the town now celebrates that heritage for the benefit of visitors from all over. The town has become a favorite stopping place for tourists from British Columbia, just three miles north, heading to Bellingham via Highway 539. Many downtown buildings have been outfitted with Dutch false fronts, you'll see provincial flags flapping in the breeze and more than one store sells its fair share of wooden shoes. Front Street, the main drag, is dominated by a four-story, 72-foot-tall windmill that is part of the Dutch Village Mall, which also has a 150-foot indoor "canal" with colorful koi fish, a theater, and shops along a simulated Dutch cobblestone street.

Be sure to stop by the **Lynden Pioneer Museum** (217 W. Front St., 360/354-3675, www.lyndenpioneermuseum.com, 10 A.M.–4 P.M. Mon.–Sat., $7 adults, $4 seniors and students free for kids under 5), which features a life-size turn-of-the-20th-century scene of

The Lynden Pioneer Museum features a life-size replica of historic Lynden.

downtown Lynden. Tromp downstairs for the real treat: a collection of dozens of antique cars and trucks, including a number of buggies, wagons, and sleighs.

FESTIVALS AND EVENTS
Ferndale
Ferndale has several of the county's best festivals. The **Scottish Highland Games** (360/647-8500, www.bellinghamhighland.org) take place at Hovander Homestead Park on the first Saturday in June, with bagpipe music, Highland dancing, dog trials, Celtic music, and the caber toss. Then comes the **Whatcom County Old Settlers Picnic** (360/384-1866) at Pioneer Park on the last weekend of July. More than an old-timers picnic, this century-old festival includes horse-drawn carriage rides, dancing, and a grand parade.

The Pacific Northwest was a little far afield during the War Between the States, but nevertheless, early August brings the **Civil War Re-enactment** of the historical Battle of Hovander Farm, featuring staged battles between the Blue and Gray armies. On the first weekend in December, volunteers dressed in turn-of-the-20th-century-style clothing take you through some yuletide history at the **Olde Fashioned Christmas at Pioneer Park** (360/384-3693).

Birch Bay and Blaine
Birch Bay Discovery Days (360/371-2070) is the main summer event, with a "clampetition" clamming contest, parade, golf tournament, and arts and crafts show. It's held in mid-July. The Birch Bay area also has monthly **sandcastle contests** all summer. For something different, come here on January 1 for the annual **Polar Bear Swim** (360/371-7800) with other hardy fools.

The annual **Hands Across the Border Peace Arch Celebration** (www.peacearch park.org/peacearchcelebration.htm) held the second Sunday in June, brings together veterans and Boy and Girl Scouts from the U.S. and Canada to celebrate friendly relations. After ceremonially transferring the flags, the gathering turns into a big merit-badge swap for the scouts.

Lummi Island
The **Lummi Stommish Water Festival** in mid-June is held on the Lummi Reservation and features competitive war-canoe races over a five-mile course, with up to 11 people in a canoe. Other activities include arts and crafts sales, dancing, and a salmon bake. For details, call the tribal office at 360/734-8180.

Lynden
Mid-August brings the largest event in all Whatcom County: more than 200,000 people come to the **Northwest Washington Fair** (360/354-4111 or 800/992-8499, www.nwwa fair.com), with farm animal exhibits, carnival rides, a tractor pull, auto racing, and musical entertainers.

Late August brings the testosterone-drenched **Lynden PRCA Rodeo** (1775 Front St., 360/354-4111) with traditional events like bull riding, saddle bronc riding, and the always-entertaining kids-only mutton bustin'. And if you happen to be in the area the first week of August, you'd be crazy to miss the **Annual Threshing Bee and Antique Tractor Show** (8837 Berthusen Rd. in Linden, 360/380-2317, www.psata.com), a celebration of all things old, useful, and motorized. The **Dutch Sinterklaas Celebration** in early December is a Christmas parade with lighted farm equipment, antique vehicles, horses, and floats, plus Sinterklaas (Santa Claus) atop a white horse.

SHOPPING
For a large variety of apples, cider, and gifts, drop by **BelleWood Acres** (231 Ten Mile Rd. in Lynden, 360/398-9187, 10 A.M.–6 P.M., www.bellewoodapples.com). It will also ship its delicious apples and related products around the world. Compulsive quilters really ought to see **Tangled Threads Quilt Shop** (202 6th St. in Lynden, 360/318-1567, www.tangledthreads quilts.com, 9 A.M.–5 P.M. Mon.–Sat.). The owners are quilters themselves and will put on coffee or tea if you call ahead. If you're the

type of traveler who would prefer the owners crack a cold one for you, visit **Dave's Sports Shop** (1738 Front St., Fairway Center in Lynden, 360/354-5591, 9 A.M.–8 P.M. Mon.–Fri., 9 A.M.–6 P.M. Sat., www.davessports.com). Dave's is the place to get the low-down on all hunting and fishing-related rules, regulations, tips and gear. It runs a series of hunter-education classes and can even help you export a firearm (legally) to Canada. There is also a Northwest-themed fine art gallery right there in the shop.

The **Peace Arch Factory Outlets** are just off I-5 at exit 270, six miles south of the border. Here you'll find 30 outlet stores open daily, including Levi's, Carters, Mikasa, Bass—all the usual suspects.

SPORTS AND RECREATION
Golf

One of the area's premier set of links, **Semiahmoo Golf and Country Club** (9565 Semiahmoo Pkwy., 360/371-7015 or 800/231-4425, www.semiahmoo.com, $90 weekends with special rates for resort guests) is the featured attraction at the sprawling Semiahmoo Resort, with two championship courses—one of which was designed by Arnold Palmer and both of which are regularly voted Washington's top courses. The Semiahmoo Course is a challenging 7,005 yards from tip to tip and is open to the public on odd days of the month. The companion course, The Loomis Trail Golf & Country Club, has the unique characteristic of having a water feature come in to play on all 18 holes. It is playable by the public on even days of the month.

In Lynden, **Homestead Golf & Country Club** (360/354-1196 or 800/354-1196, www.homesteadfarmsgolf.com, $50) maintains an elaborate 18-hole championship course laid-out where Dutch cows once grazed. One par–five hole features an island green. There's also a putting course, gourmet restaurant, and an impressive fitness center. All are open to the public.

Horseback Riding
Peace Arch Equestrian Center (360/371-

3109, www.peacearchequestrian.net) teaches private, semiprivate, and group lessons in horsemanship focused on respectful yet effective handling of the horse.

Hiking

Look for migratory birds and learn about the wetland environment at **Tennant Lake Interpretive Center** (at the end of Nielsen Rd. just south of the turnoff to Hovander Homestead, 360/384-3444). The grounds surrounding shallow and marshy Tennant Lake offer trails, an elevated boardwalk, and an observation tower. One of the park's highlights is the wheelchair-accessible **Fragrance Garden,**—with information in Braille and the opportunity to touch and smell more than 60 varieties of plants

The state-operated **Lake Terrell Wildlife Area** (four miles west of Ferndale, 360/384-4723, $11.50 day pass) picnic gives you a sporting chance of spotting loons, bald eagles, and other migratory birds. Launch your boat here to chase the lake's cutthroat and rainbow trout or just fish from the shore. Stop at the Department of Fish and Wildlife office or any sporting goods store to pick up your Discover Pass, good for Washington State Parks.

Amusement Parks

Kids of all ages love **Birch Bay Water Slides** (4874 Birch Bay-Lynden Rd., 360/371-7500, www.birchbaywaterslides.net, daily mid-May–Labor Day, $17.95 ages 6 and up, $11.95 ages 3–5 and seniors, free for tots). The park has slides ranging in adrenaline from the 60-foot "hydrocliff," to kiddie slides and sedate river-tubing, all with water heated to 80-plus degrees.

Miniature World Family Fun Center (4620 Birch Bay-Lynden Rd., 360/371-7700) is a celebration of fun on a smaller scale, including 18 holes of mini-golf, a mini-railroad ride through the woods, and the throaty growl of go-karts on an outdoor oval track. For those traveling with younger children, passenger go-karts are available so even the kids won't miss out on the fun.

ACCOMMODATIONS
Under $100

At the bottom of the price category in Birch Bay, but not in popularity or friendliness, is the 49-bed **Birch Bay AYH-Hostel** (467 Gemini St., Birch Bay, 360/371-2180, www.birchbay .net). Dorm beds are $14 per person for hostel members or $17 per person for others. Couples stay in one of four private rooms for the same rate, and families ($7 for kids ages 7–18, free for younger kids) stay in two adjacent rooms that share a bath. A full kitchen is on the premises. Reservations are advised if you're arriving in the summer. The hostel is closed 10 A.M.–5 P.M. daily, and October–April.

For a bit more privacy, **Driftwood Inn Motel** (7394 Birch Bay Dr., Blaine, 360/371-2620 or 800/833-2666, www.driftwoodinnmotel.com) offers studio units ($80 d), rustic cottages and suites with kitchenettes ($90 for up to four), and condo units ($180–190 for eight), all with access to the outdoor pool and canoe rentals.

Border-hoppers looking for a cheap night's stay will find a number of options in Blaine, including **Anchor Inn Motel** (250 Cedar St., Blaine, 360/332-5539, www.theanchorinn motel.com, $64 d, $67 d with kitchenette). Like other places in town, the rooms have older furnishings, but these are clean and well maintained. The owner is fluent in French, Farsi, Afghani, and, of course, English.

Lodging on Lummi Island is limited, but the all-amenity **Willows Inn B&B** (2579 West Shore Dr., Lummi Island, 360/758-2620, $205–650 d) is plenty of B&B for most visitors. The farm is a 21-acre spread with sweeping Georgia Strait views and private beach access. You'll stay in one of 14 guest rooms decked-out with super-relaxing whites and beiges. There's even a yurt that can be rented.

The town of Lynden is similarly quiet, with only a couple of options. Thankfully they're both interesting. Spend a night in a windmill at the **Dutch Village Inn** (655 Front St., Lynden, 360/354-4440, $79 s or $119 d), where six hotel rooms (three are in the windmill and two have hot tubs) feature Dutch furnishings and antiques.

Near the little town of Everson, southeast of Lynden, **Kale House B&B** (201 Kale St., 360/966-7027 or 800/225-2165, kalehouse.net, $95 d) is a peaceful house in the country with well-designed common areas for recharging those batteries, spiritually speaking. This early-20th-century home features a downstairs bedroom and upstairs suite and is a perfect centralized home base for the area. Both suites have private baths, one of which is a lovely claw-foot bathtub.

$100-150

Birch Bay is full of condo rentals for those who want a little more space to kick off their shoes.

Birch Bay Get Away (4973 Cottonwood Court, 877/627-2229 or 360/371-3730, www .birchbaygetaway.com, $119–199 d) has one-, two-, and three-bedroom cottages. Pay in Canadian currency for a 5 percent discount.

Located on the west side of Lummi Island, (**The Willows Inn B&B** (2579 W. Shore Dr., Lummi Island, 360/758-2620, www .willows-inn.com) is a standout option in the area. Willows has four rooms in the inn ($125 d), a honeymoon cottage ($155 d), and a guest house ($290 for up to six people). All include a three-course breakfast, private baths, a hot tub, and tranquility, as no kids are allowed here. The honeymoon cottage provides additional privacy and a magnificent view of the San Juans.

$150-200

Those looking to experience a bit of luxury in Lynden should look no farther than **Homestead Farms Golf Resort** (115 E. Homestead Blvd., 360/354-1196 or 800/354-1196, www.home steadfarmsgolf.com, $99–210 d), an ideal sanctuary for duffers and scratch golfers alike. The resort offers one- and two-bedroom vacation rentals as well as an indoor pool facility.

$200-250

Located at the end of a long sand spit guarding Blaine's Drayton Harbor, (**Semiahmoo Resort** (9565 Semiahmoo Pkwy., 800/770-7992, www.semiahmoo.com) is Washington's largest destination resort. The Inn at Semiahmoo is a part of a massive 800-acre development with facilities such as a 300-slip marina, athletic club, indoor/outdoor pool, hot tub, racquetball and tennis courts, full European spa, a movie theater, two championship golf courses), restaurants, lounges, and plenty of Puget Sound beachfront. Rates cover a wide range, from $189 d for a standard room up to $399 d for an executive suite with fireplace. Package rates are also available.

Camping

Public tent ($17) and RV ($23) sites are just a few miles northwest of Ferndale at **Birch Bay State Park** (5105 Helwig Rd.). Make reservations ($7 extra) at 888/226-7688 or www.parks.wa.gov. Fully hook up that four- or six-wheel behemoth at **Cedars RV Resort** (6335 Portal Way, 360/384-2622, $38 for full hookups, $28 for tents) which features a large heated outdoor pool, and a large area for tents. **Ball Bay View RV Park** (7387 Jackson Rd., 360/371-0334, www.ballbayview rvpark.com, $32) is an orderly park near the water. **Beachside RV Park at Birch Bay** (7630 Birch Bay Dr., 360/371-5962 or 800/596-9586, www.beachsidervpark.com, $33) is open year-round unlike many other nearby parks.

Tree-loving tent campers must try Lynden's **Berthusen Park** (8837 Berthusen Rd., 360/354-2424, $22 tents, $31 RVs), where 20 acres of virgin forest stands untouched.

FOOD
Ferndale

Locals love **Cedar's Restaurant and Lounge** (2019 Main St., 360/384-2847), especially for the breakfasts, but the attached cocktail lounge is a draw at any time of day, too. Another favorite is **Chihuahua Family Mexican Restaurant** (5694 3rd Ave., 360/384-5820) which attracts a fair number of Canadians south of their border.

Finally, those hoping to picnic at Pioneer Park can stop by **Haggen Foods** (1815 Main St., 360/380-6353, www.haggen.com) for deli items and express Chinese food takeout.

Birch Bay and Blaine

Locals often hop across the border to White Rock for good regional cooking, but there are options in Birch Bay and Blaine. In Birch Bay, summer-only **C Shop** (4825 Alderson Rd., 360/371-2070, www.thecshop.com, 11 A.M.–10 P.M. daily) is an old-fashioned candy shop that also happens to sell pizza and sandwiches.

For pastries, bagels, and conscience-comforting fair trade, organic, shade grown coffee, head to **Blackberry House** (321 H St., 360/332-5212, 6:30 A.M.–5 P.M. Mon.–Fri., 8 A.M.–3 P.M. Sat., $6).

Nicki's Restaurant (1700 Peace Portal Dr., 360/332-7779) serves the fattest, juiciest burgers in Blaine and the thickest milkshakes, too.

Out on the end of Semiahmoo Spit, the Semiahmoo Resort has a formal restaurant, **Stars** (360/371-2000 or 800/770-7992, www.semiahmoo.com) featuring expensive Northwest cuisine and a popular Sunday brunch, plus the less-fancy **Packers Lounge**, with delicious fish and chips.

La Bonne Maison (1830 Peace Portal Dr., 360/332-6178) is a nice French restaurant with surprisingly reasonable entrées. Reservations are required. Many more restaurants—including Thai and Greek eateries—can be found in the pretty town of White Rock, just across the border.

Lynden
Dutch Mothers Family Restaurant (405 Front St., 360/354-2174, 6 A.M.–4 P.M. Mon.–Thurs., 6 A.M.–8 P.M. Fri.–Sat.) will coddle you with hearty breakfasts, standard lunch, and country dinners. But if you don't try a slice of their "uber pie," you deserve a serious spanking.

The always-hopping **Lynden Dutch Bakery** (421 Front St., 360/354-3911, 7 A.M.–5 P.M. Mon.–Sat.) builds enormous sandwiches, but their pies and Dutch specialties like Olie Bollen may change your way of looking at the world.

Sink your teeth into a mesquite-grilled steak in nearby Everson at **Black Forest Steakhouse** (203 W. Main St., 360/966-2855, www.blackforesteverson) or have them fry up some schnitzel—they do German as well.

Located at the golf resort of the same name, **The Reserve Restaurant Lounge** (115 E. Homestead Blvd., 360/354-1196 or 800/354-1196, thereserverestaurantlounge.com) offers fine dining three meals a day, with vistas of Mt. Baker from the deck.

Watch as cheese makers work their craft at **Appel Farms Cheese** (6605 Northwest Rd., 360/384-4996, www.appel-farms.com), making a variety of traditional cheeses, including Dutch-style gouda, a European yogurtlike cheese called quark, and Indian paneer. It doesn't get fresher than their farm store, open Monday–Saturday 9 A.M.–6 P.M.

INFORMATION AND SERVICES

Find information about Blaine and surrounding towns at the **Blaine Visitor Information Center** (728 Peace Portal Dr., 360/332-4544 or 800/624-3555, 9 A.M.–5 P.M. daily April–Oct., 9 A.M.–4 P.M. Thurs.–Tues. the rest of the year).

GETTING THERE AND AROUND

Whatcom Transit (360/676-7433, www .ridewta.com) provides bus service Monday–Saturday to Bellingham, Lynden, Blaine, and the rest of Whatcom County.

Airporter Shuttle (360/380-8800 or 800/235-5247, www.airporter.com) runs direct bus service between Blaine and Sea-Tac Airport.

Lummi Island Access

From I-5, go west on Slater Road to Haxton Way on the Lummi Reservation and follow it to the ferry landing. The **county-owned ferry** (360/676-6692, $2 round-trip for cars, $1 passengers and drivers, free for kids, $0.50 bikes) makes eight-minute trips back and forth from Gooseberry Point on the mainland to Lummi Island every hour on the hour from 7 A.M. to midnight (more frequently during the commute period).

SOUTH PUGET SOUND

Snugged up between the heights of the Olympic Mountains to the east and the Cascade range to the west, the stunning terrain of the Puget Sound region defines the character of much of Western Washington. When the sun shines, the Puget Sound region is one of the most beautiful in the country—snowcapped peaks stand sentinel over glistening water and evergreen canopies.

Visitors will encounter a breathtaking diversity in ecology along the inlets and isles of the sound, from wetlands and marshes on the banks of the waters to verdant farmlands and wooded hills at the foothills of the nearby mountain ranges. The moderate climate and constant drizzle of the region cultivates a lush display of greenery. In spite of the explosion of growth that has hit the region in recent decades,

locals have respected the gift of such beautiful environs by maintaining an impressive network of county, state, and municipal parks that give residents and visitors the opportunity to explore by foot, paddle, pedal, saddle, sail, and ski.

The south sound is dominated by Olympia and Tacoma. The capital of Washington, Olympia draws travelers with tours of the capitol dome and its surrounding gardens and stately buildings. Tacoma, meanwhile, offers some of the best museums in the region, including the world famous International Museum of Glass, with creations blown by the city's favorite son, Dale Chihuly.

PLANNING YOUR TIME

Without a doubt, the best time to visit the South Puget Sound is mid-July–mid-August,

© ERICKA CHICKOWSKI

HIGHLIGHTS

◖ **Capitol Campus:** Grand halls, historic buildings, and lovely gardens all sit on the central grounds for the state's government (page 202).

◖ **Museum of Glass:** Built with the help of Tacoma resident and glassmaking superstar Dale Chihuly, this museum highlights the creative medium of glass (page 214).

◖ **Washington State History Museum:** Bar none, this is the best history museum in the state, highlighting the unique stories that make up Washington's heritage (page 216).

◖ **Point Defiance Park:** The sprawling waterfront grounds here are home to a well-regarded zoo, several historical museums, and innumerable spots to lay a blanket and picnic basket (page 217).

◖ **Tillicum Village:** Watch a traditional tribal dance, enjoy a salmon feast, and explore the re-created Native American village on Blake Island (page 246).

LOOK FOR ◖ TO FIND RECOMMENDED SIGHTS, ACTIVITIES, DINING, AND LODGING.

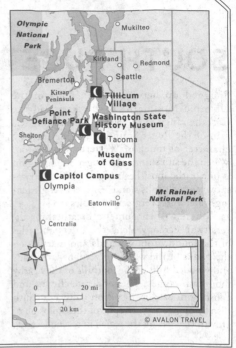

© AVALON TRAVEL

SOUTH PUGET SOUND

Tillicum Village totem pole

© JOY PRESCOTT/123RF.COM

when you are most likely to experience the bliss of blue skies and mountain views. Much of the rest of the year is dominated by seemingly ceaseless gray and drizzly weather, infrequently interrupted by a few days of glorious sunshine here and there.

If a little bit of cloud cover doesn't bother you, though, this is the mildest region of the state. The rain doesn't often pour, thunder and lightning are an anomaly, and it rarely snows. So live like the locals—throw on a raincoat

and don't let a little mist get in the way of your fun.

Just about all of the cities and towns in this chapter are easy day trips from Seattle if taken individually. For a more thorough tour of the region, including all of the museums and historic sights of Olympia and Tacoma and the recreational opportunities in the north sound, visitors should consider padding their schedule with a week or more on top of their Seattle itinerary.

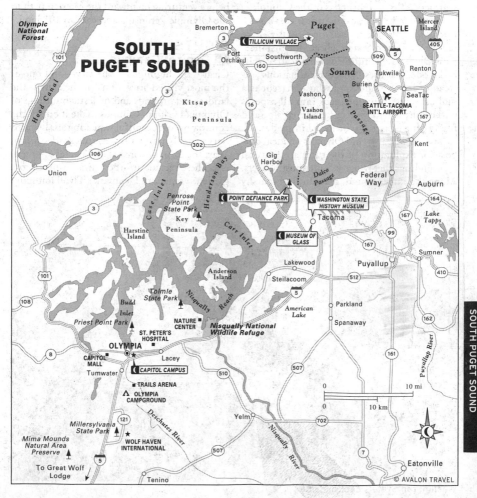

SOUTH PUGET SOUND

Olympia

The southernmost finger of the Puget Sound points to Olympia, almost a geographic exclamation point. Here sits the state capital, home to the Governor's Mansion and the Washington Capitol Campus. The sprawling lawns, sunken gardens, and stately buildings on campus sit along the reflective Capitol Lake and are an excellent place to have lunch after exploring the whispery halls and rotundas of the Capitol.

In spite of its political significance, this is a town that doesn't take itself too seriously. Take quirky Evergreen State College, for instance. This Olympia institution works on a free-spirited model that uses "narrative evaluations" instead of letter grades and whose mascot is a mollusk. The fun vibe seeps into all aspects of the culture here, where creative cuisine and funky art galleries can be found in spades.

Visitors will also find Olympia an ideal outpost for exploration of the rural and natural surroundings that fringe its outermost borders. Along the Puget Sound, one can find marshy wildlife reserves. To the south lie lonely country roads passing Christmas tree farms, cow pastures, and sleepy hamlets like Tenino, where folks still send the kids off to swim in the old sandstone quarry. Just south of the city, one can stumble upon the mysterious Mima Mounds in the prairies that unfold near Capitol Forest.

Olympia also marks the last exit along I-5 before venturing on toward the forested path to the Olympic Peninsula and the US 101 loop.

SIGHTS
◖ Capitol Campus

Clearly the highlight of the city—and one of the most-visited attractions in the state—the landscaped grounds and majestic buildings of Olympia's Capitol Campus make it one of the country's most beautiful state capitols. Located between 11th and 14th Avenues off Capitol Way, the campus consists of 55 acres of greenery. These include an arboretum, a sunken rose garden, a replica of Denmark's Tivoli fountain,

Washington State's capitol dome

© ERICKA CHICKOWSKI

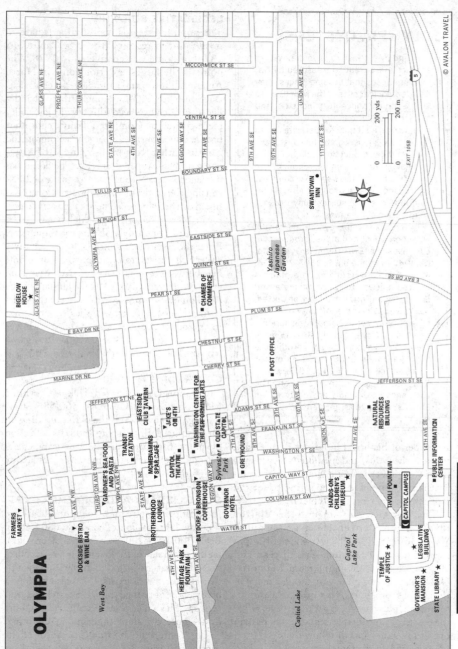

© AVALON TRAVEL

OLYMPIA OYSTERS

Tiny and sweet-tasting Olympia oysters are a culinary treat so treasured by Native Americans that in some places, they have left ancient piles of their shells up to 300 feet high! Midcentury industrial and municipal pollution, along with the accidental introductions of parasites alien to the area, almost completely destroyed the oyster bed production, but after years of rehabilitation it is on the rebound. The oysters range all the way down the West Coast, and several groups and government agencies are successfully working on restoring populations.

To see how Olympia oysters are raised, visit the largest and oldest producer (in business since 1876), **Olympia Oyster Co.** (SE 1042 Bloomfield Rd., 360/426-3354, www.olympiaoyster.com). The plant is located halfway between Olympia and Shelton along Totten Inlet. **Taylor United, Inc.** (www.taylorshellfishfarms.com) – the biggest producer of clams in the nation – grows and harvests shellfish from more than 3,000 acres of tidelands around the southern Puget Sound. Visit its oyster sheds and clam hatchery at SE 130 Lynch Rd., three miles south of Shelton. The shop sells fresh clams and oysters; call 360/432-3300 to arrange a tour.

a number of historical buildings dating back to the early 1900s, and memorials to veterans from World War I, World War II, Korea, and Vietnam. Come here in the spring to see the Japanese cherry trees in full bloom.

The best place to start is the **Visitor Information Center** (14th and Capital Way, 360/586-3460, www.visitolympia.com, 8 A.M.–5 P.M. Mon.–Fri. all year, and 10 A.M.–4 P.M. Sat.–Sun. from Memorial Day–Labor Day). Here you can get maps of the campus, brochures, postcards, and tour information, plus a metered parking space. All of the on-street parking is leased, so either park in one of the visitor lots or follow the signs from I-5 exit 105A to the free shuttle bus.

LEGISLATIVE BUILDING

The imposing Legislative Building is hard to miss. Built to resemble the U.S. Capitol, its 287-foot dome was completed in 1928. The dome is the largest exterior dome in North America. The central rotunda is the central attraction, with a 25-foot-long Tiffany chandelier suspended overhead (this was the last major piece created by Comfort Tiffany), enormous bronze doors, busts of George Washington and Martin Luther King Jr., Belgian marble steps, and gargoyle-capped draperies. The dome was damaged in the Nisqually Earthquake of 2001, causing the columns that support it to shift as much as three inches. The state has since performed heavy retrofitting, which has yet to be tested and hopefully won't be for some time. Enter the Senate and House of Representatives gallery chambers from the fourth floor. Come here between early January and early March on even-numbered years, or early January–mid-April on odd-numbered years, to see the legislature in session. Even when legislature is not in session, the capitol is open daily, with free 45-minute tours (360/586-3460, www.ga.wa.gov/capitol, tours hourly 10 A.M.–3 P.M.).

GOVERNOR'S MANSION

The Georgian-style redbrick Governor's Mansion (Capitol Grounds, 360/586-8687, www.ga.wa.gov.com) is the oldest building on the campus, dating back to 1908. Its collection of antique furniture from the American Federal period is available to tour most Wednesdays by reservation.

STATE LIBRARY AND SUPREME COURT

In addition to state and federal publications, the State Library (Point Plaza East, 680 Capitol Blvd., 360/704-5200, 8 A.M.–5 P.M. Mon.–Fri.), on the south side of the Capitol, houses a collection of murals, mosaics, paintings, and sculpture by Northwest artists. It has also become a bit of a hot spot for genealogy researchers in recent days. It's a nice place to sit inside on a rainy day—more common than not in Olympia.

The **Temple of Justice** (just north of the capitol building, 8 A.M.–5 P.M. Mon.–Fri.) is not a sequel to *Indiana Jones and the Temple of Doom,* though it may mean doom for certain individuals. Instead, this is where the State Supreme Court meets. It is open year-round for self-guided tours. The building also houses the Washington State Law Library.

Historic Sights

A few blocks away from the cluster of state governmental buildings, the **Washington State Capital Museum** (211 W. 21st Ave., 888/238-4373 or 360/753-2580, www.wshs .org, 10 A.M.–4 P.M. Sat., $2 adults, $1.75 seniors, $1 kids, free for under age six) houses permanent exhibits that include touchable baskets, other American Indian artifacts, and a re-created Salish Tribal Winter House. See lots more on the political and cultural history of Washington, including pioneer settlements and the early history of Northwest publishing, plus rotating exhibits, lectures, and programs. The building itself is quite an attraction, built in 1920 as a 32-room California mission–style mansion for banker C. J. Lord. After his death, it was deeded to the state as a museum.

Also just off the state government campus, at Legion Way and Franklin Street, the **Old State Capitol Building** (360/725-6025, 8 A.M.–5 P.M. Mon.–Fri.) was built in 1891 as the Thurston County Courthouse and served as the state capitol from 1903–1928. Today the flamboyant, turreted building—complete with gargoyles—houses the State Department of Public Instruction. The Old Capitol is open for self-guided tours and has historical exhibits in the hallways.

Pick up self-guided tour brochures describing Olympia's historic neighborhoods from the Thurston County Chamber (809 Legion Way., 360/357-3362, http://thurstonchamber. com). The small but ornate gingerbread-decorated Carpenter Gothic **Bigelow House** (918 Glass Ave. and East Bay Dr., 360/753-1215, www.bigelowhouse.org, 1–3 P.M. Sat.–Sun., free to examine, guided tours suggest a donation of $5 for adults, $3 students or seniors, $1 for age 12 and under) overlooks Budd Inlet. It is Washington's oldest surviving residential home and one of the oldest frame buildings in all of the Northwest. It was built in 1854 by Daniel and Ann Bigelow, early crusaders for civil rights and other causes.

Hands on Children's Museum

Olympia's Hands On Children's Museum (106 11th Ave SW, 360/956-0818, www.hocm.org, 10 A.M.–5 P.M. Mon.–Sat., noon–5 P.M. Sun., $6.95 seniors over 62, $7.95 ages 2–adult, $5.95 toddlers 12–23 mo., infants under 12 mo. free) has kid-sized exhibits teaching about health, ecology, and the maritime character of Western Washington from the natural to the industrial.

City Parks

With the Legislative Building so close to its shoreline, Capitol Lake acts as Olympia's unofficial reflecting pool. Enjoy the glassy waters from the lawns at Heritage Park, a grassy end stop on the lake just below the Capitol's hill. The park shows off with cherry blossoms in April, and swimming, sunbathing, sailing, hiking, biking, and picnicking the rest of the year. Each fall, the nearby Capitol Lake fish ladder is used by hundreds of king salmon returning home to spawn in the Deschutes River.

Across the street, jets of water shoot up, to the delight of bathing-suited kids at **Heritage Park Fountain** (6th Ave. and Water St.). The fountain runs 9 A.M. through 9 P.M. daily except for Wednesdays, when it is closed for maintenance.

Named for city founder Edmund Sylvester, downtown's **Sylvester Park** (7th Ave. and Capitol Way) hosts concerts in the gazebo in July and August on Friday at noon, and on Wednesday evenings. The park sits just behind the Old Capitol Building.

The **Yashiro Japanese Garden** (1010 Plum St., 360/753-8380, 10 A.M.–dusk daily, free) near Union Avenue was built in cooperation with Olympia's sister city of Yashiro, Japan. This small and peaceful park has a garden lantern of cut granite, a bamboo grove, and an 18-foot pagoda. A tranquil pond and waterfall are central features.

© ERICKA CHICKOWSKI

Don't forget to bring the kids' bathing suits when visiting Olympia. The Heritage Park Fountain is a favorite place to romp in the water.

Boat lovers can take a stroll at **Percival Landing Park** (222 Columbia St. NW), a waterside retreat with grassy lawns, lots of outdoor art, and a short boardwalk facing the Olympia harbor. Climb the **Percival Landing Tower** (open daylight hours only) at the north end of the Budd Inlet boardwalk for a panoramic view of the yacht-filled harbor with the Capitol behind, the Olympic Mountains, and freighters loading logs for Asian markets.

Priest Point Park (dawn–dusk daily) is a beautiful nature park that sits less than two miles away from downtown, but seems a world apart in terms of habitat. The wooded park hugs Ellis Cove along Budd Inlet with a mile of natural and quiet saltwater shoreline, including trails and picnic shelters. The park was the site of an 1848 Catholic mission that served as church and trading post for nearby Squaxin, Nisqually, Puyallup, and Snoqualmie tribes.

Nisqually National Wildlife Refuge
Birders will have a ball at Nisqually National Wildlife Refuge (360/753-9467, http://nisqually.fws.gov, dawn–dusk daily, $3), a massive nature preserve that protects one of the largest surviving estuaries in the state. Over 300 species of wildlife find sanctuary here, but the real stars of the show are the birds. Set up in one of the hidden photo blinds scattered on the trails here to spot some blue herons, bald eagles, red-tailed hawks, and more. Aim for a spring or fall visit to observe more than 20,000 geese and ducks as they fly their migratory pattern.

Snakes, salamanders, shrews, and bats are also common guests at the Refuge.

Tumwater Historic District
The 15-acre privately owned **Tumwater Falls Park** (110 Deschutes Way SW, Tumwater, 360/943-2550, www.olytumfoundation.org, free) is the site of the first American settlement in the Puget Sound region, started in 1845 by Leopold Smith, founder of the once-storied Olympia Brewing Company. The neatly landscaped grounds feature Schmidt's 1910 home, a boat launch into the Deschutes

River, hiking trails, and lots of hungry ducks. You may see king salmon heading up the fish ladders late August–October; they spawn in nearby tanks.

Nearby, the **Henderson House Museum** (602 Deschutes Way, 360/754-4217, 1 P.M.–4 P.M. Thurs.–Fri., suggested donation is $2) is a subdued, turreted late-Queen Anne that has photographic exhibits depicting life along the Deschutes River during the late 1800s and recent photos of Tumwater's people and events.

Nearby, find Tumwater's oldest home, **Crosby House** (703 Deschutes Way N, adjacent to Tumwater Falls Park, 360/943-9884, tours 1–4 P.M. Fri. & Sun., donation suggested). It was built in 1860 by the grandfather of singer and actor Bing Crosby, Capt. Nathaniel Crosby III, who came west in 1847 and inspired the whole Crosby clan to follow.

Wolf Haven International

This 80-acre wolf refuge (3111 Offutt Lake Rd. SE, 800/448-9653, www.wolfhaven.org, 10 A.M.–4 P.M. Mon., Wed–Sat., noon–4 P.M. Sun. Apr.–Sept., 10 A.M.–4 P.M. Sat., noon–4 P.M. Sun. Oct.–Jan. and Mar., closed Feb., $9 adults, $8 seniors, students, active duty military, $7 ages 3–12) north of Tenino, just off Old Highway 99, is a sanctuary for captive-born and displaced wolves. "Howl-ins" are summertime events featuring live music, mini-tours, and interactive eco-savvy children's activities.

Millersylvania State Park

Millersylvania State Park (12245 Tilley Rd. S., 360/753-1519) is an 842-acre wooded park with impressive stone picnic shelters and bathhouses as well as old-growth cedars and firs. Over half a mile of swimmable beaches stretch around Deep Lake. Enjoy fishing for rainbow trout and boating. Be sure to have a valid Washington fishing license, available at just about any sporting-goods store.

Mima Mounds

Thousands of unusual rolling hilly mounds dot the landscape of southwestern Washington. Explore them at the Mima Mounds Natural Area Preserve. The cleverly designed bumpshaped **Mima Mounds Interpretive Area** (Waddell Creek Rd. SW, 360/596-5144, dawn–dusk daily) provides some perspective on the National Natural Landmark. The building has interpretive displays and is the trailhead for several hikes, one of which is an Americans with Disabilities Act (ADA)–compliant halfmile loop. No one is quite sure how the regularly spaced mounds formed, but theories range from the effects of melting glaciers, vibrations from earthquakes, or even the persistent digging of thousands of little pocket gophers over the course of millennia.

ENTERTAINMENT AND EVENTS
Nightlife

Olympia has an active music scene, credited with launching alt-rock and indie bands like Sleater-Kinney and Bikini Kill, and providing temporary homes for members of Nirvana and Rancid. One of the most successful and wellknown indie labels, Kill Rock Stars, is based out of Olympia. Nightlife is lively, but don't expect New York or Los Angeles. Bars and clubs have a bit more of a mellow vibe down here. And odds are very good that they don't take credit or debit. If you want to hit the ground running, party like a local at **The Brotherhood Lounge** (119 Capitol Way N, 360/352-4153, http://thebrotherhoodlounge.com). The crowd is a young lewd, crude, and tattooed bunch. Reasonable drinks and a super-popular jukebox complete the scene. Every so often, local bands will play a set on its stage. **The Eastside Club Tavern** (410 4th Ave. E, 360/357-9985) could be said to be a bit of a step up on the food chain. The atmosphere is brighter and you have your choice of dozens of games from pinball to ping-pong to pool. But the draw is the extensive choice of microbrews on tap and maybe its coin-op Internet kiosk. If your tastes are even higher brow, try the **Dockside Bistro and Wine Bar** (501 Columbia St. NW, 360/956-1928, www.docksidebistro.com). It often has jazz and vocals performances. Its website's calendar can tell you who is playing when. The alternative-lifestyle heart of Olympia is **Jake's on 4th** (311 4th Ave. E, 360/956-3247) with a full bar, DJ, and coat-check for your finest finery. Occasional karaoke and drag shows bring in a weekday crowd that rivals the weekend dance scene.

Casinos

The **Lucky Eagle Casino** (360/273-2000 or 800/720-1788, www.luckyeagle.com, 9 A.M.–4 A.M. Sun.–Thurs., 9 A.M.–6 A.M. Fri.–Sat.) is on the **Chehalis Indian Reservation** between Rochester and Oakville, and has slots, table games, and a respectable poker room. They have a buffet and restaurants of varying size. Sometimes they host nationally known music and comedy.

Red Wind Casino (12819 Yelm Hwy., 360/456-3328, www.redwindcasino.com, 8 A.M.–5 A.M. daily) is operated by the Nisqually Indian Nation. They provide nearly 1,000 slot machines along with craps, keno, blackjack, roulette and a variety of table games. They offer periodic "comps" for their buffet, grill, and deli. Their cabaret focuses more on local acts.

Performing Arts

Olympia's **Washington Center for the Performing Arts** (512 Washington St. SE, 360/753-8586, www.washingtoncenter.org) is a state-of-the-art facility with plays, musicals, and concerts from the mainstream to the experimental. Both the **Olympia Symphony Orchestra** (360/753-0074, www.olympiasymphony.com) and the **Masterworks Choral Ensemble** (360/491-3305, www.mce.org) perform here.

Capitol Playhouse (360/943-2744, www.capitolplayhouse.com), located in the historic Capitol Theatre (612 E 4th Ave.), produces plays from September through May.

Olympia Little Theater (1925 Miller Ave. NE, 360/786-9484, www.olympialittletheater.org) is a small community theatre with a dedicated troupe of amateurs. They stage around seven plays per year, tending toward the light-hearted and fun.

Festivals and Events

Don't miss **Arts Walk Olympia** on the third weekend of April, with performances, literary, and art events, and tours of local galleries. Many downtown businesses—even furniture stores—open their windows for budding artists. The unique and whimsical **Procession of the Species** (360/753-8380 or www.procession.com) is the main event, with strange creatures and plants of every shape and form. A second Arts Walk (sans procession) takes place in April.

The **Wooden Boat Festival** (360/357-3370, www.olywoodenboat.org) held in mid-May at Percival Landing, includes a regatta, wooden boats open for public viewing, and a chance for kids to try their own hands at building a wooden ship.

The city's biggest summer festival is **Lakefair** (360/943-7344, www.lakefair.org), held the third weekend of July. Activities include a twilight parade, fireworks, a carnival, a 3K and 8K race, and the crowning of the Lakefair queen. From mid-July through August, Sylvester Park has **Music in the Park** (360/357-8948, musicintheparkolympia.com) concerts played mainly by Washington bands at noon on Wednesdays.

The fourth weekend in July brings all kinds of commotion to quiet Tenino with the **Oregon Trail Days,** including a parade, arts and crafts, entertainment, and a muzzle-loading camp.

The **Thurston County Fair** (360/786-5453, www.co.thurston.wa.us/fair) held the first full weekend in August at the County Fairgrounds in Lacey, is a relatively small affair with the pride of the local 4-H clubs, along with food and entertainers.

Harbor Days Festival (222 Columbia St. NW, 360/556-0498) at Percival Landing is highlighted by a regatta and vintage tugboat races on Labor Day weekend. December brings **Winterfest in Historic Tenino** featuring wagon rides, living history demonstrations, a gingerbread house competition, a quilt contest, and 1880s arts and crafts.

SHOPPING

Downtown Olympia has a number of art galleries and boutiques on 4th and 5th Avenues.

State of the Arts Gallery (500 Washington St. SE, 360/705-0317, www.thestateofthearts.com) is almost mind-blowingly diverse in style and media, and **Artists' Gallery** (113 Legion Way SW, 360/357-6920, www.theartistsgallery.com) lends their art all over town, and is staffed by the artists themselves.

Given that this is a government/college town, you'd expect to find good bookstores in Olympia. The biggest is **Orca Books** (509 4th Ave. E, 360/352-0123, www.orcabooks.com, 10 A.M.–9 P.M. Mon.–Sat., 11 A.M.–6 P.M. Sun.) is very much community oriented and rich in its offerings of local authors. They sell used and new books, staying open late most nights for browsers.

Capital Mall (625 Black Lake Blvd., 360/754-8017) is the area's largest indoor shopping mall with nearly 100 shops and restaurants anchored by REI and JCPenney. Just up Black Lake Boulevard is another shopping plaza, Capital Village, with grocery, drug, and hardware stores, plus a sprinkling of fast-food restaurants. **Shipwreck Beads** (2727 Westmoor Ct. SW, 800/950-4232, www.shipwreckbeads.com, 9 A.M.–6 P.M. daily) claims to have the world's largest selection of beads for sale, numbering in the billions.

SPORTS AND RECREATION
Capitol Forest
From Mima Mounds, continue north on Waddell Creek Road to Capitol Forest. The multiuse forest is divided into motorized use on the north end and nonmotorized use like hiking, horseback riding, and mountain biking or even mushroom picking on the south end. Camping is free but sites are only available May 1 through November 30. You will, however, need a "Discover Pass," a $10 permit available through most sporting goods stores. The fine is $99 for not having one, so it's best not to risk it.

Tolmie State Park
Tolmie State Park (five miles from exit 111, www.parks.wa.gov) has 1,800 feet of waterfront on Nisqually Reach with swimming, fishing, 3.5 miles of hiking trails, and an underwater park with an artificial reef. The park provides an outdoor shower for swimmers and divers near the lower restroom. Open for day use only.

Running, Hiking, and Cycling
Along Henderson Boulevard at **Olympia Watershed Park** (six miles north of Olympia on Boston Harbor Rd.), there is a two-mile hiking trail through woods, marsh, and streams.

Go to **Priest Point Park** to explore the three-mile loop that circles Ellis Cove through marsh and wooded land.

A six-mile paved cycling and walking trail leads from Martin Way in town north to Woodard Bay along an old railroad track. At Woodard Bay, the Dept. of Natural Resources has purchased 190 acres of land, managed as the **Woodard Bay Natural Resources Area.**

The **McLane Creek Nature Trail** (360/902-1234 or 800/527-3305 for directions) is a mile-long route that circles a beaver pond and meadow. To get a panoramic view of the area, follow the marked dirt road from Waddell Creek Road to 2,658-foot Capitol Peak, the highest point in the Black Hills.

Running parallel to Highway 507, the 7.5-mile **Yelm-Tenino Trail** is a rails-to-trails route that cuts through forest, pastures, wetlands, and creeks. This paved route is open to walkers, runners, and bikers. You can find a trailhead in Yelm behind the city hall (105 Yelm Ave. W), in Rainier between Centre and Minnesota Streets and in Tenino in the Tenino City Park on Washington Avenue.

Golf
The Golf Club at Hawks Prairie (8383 Vicwood Ln., 360/412-0495, www.hawksprairiegolf.com, $22–39 Mon.–Thurs. $35–51 Fri.–Sun. and holidays) offers two courses—the Northwest-inspired The Woodlands and the Scottish links-style The Links. Practice on their excellent driving range or rent clubs for $50 per set.

A well-kept municipal, the **Tumwater Valley Golf Course** (4611 Tumwater Valley Dr. SE,

SOUTH PUGET SOUND

360/943-9500, www.tumwatervalleygc.com) offers a comfortable round with awe-inspiring views of Mount Rainier.

Water Sports

Tenino lets the public swim in its old abandoned sandstone quarry, open mid-June–early September. Nonlocals pay $3.50 per person.

Just a few miles north of Olympia, you'll find little Boston Harbor and the **Boston Harbor Marina** (312 73rd Ave. NE, 360/357-5670), a year-round source of kayaks and sailboats for exploring the various inlets of the Puget Sound. The friendly staff will rent you a kayak for a full day at $45 in the summer or $30 in the winter. If you can show 'em you know what to do with it, you can rent a 25-foot Catalina sailboat for $110 for a full summer day or $80 per day in the winter. And if you long for the day before kayaks were king, rowboats and canoes are available for $25 per day summer or winter. Buy some live clams or smoked salmon on your way out.

Climbing

Practice your bouldering and belaying skills at **Warehouse Rock Gym** (315 Jefferson St. NE, 360/596-9255, www.warehouserockgym.com, $12 adult, $10 children 7–17, $5 children 4–6). Classes are held daily if you're just starting out.

Off-Road Driving

Motocross fans and four-wheelers may want to try out the 150-acre **Straddleline ORV Park** (16 mi. west of Olympia off Hwy. 8, 360/495-3243, www.promotopromotions.com, $5 adults, 12 and under, seniors, and military are always free)—$25 gets you a full hookup RV space with coin-op showers. Frequent races are held at the park.

ACCOMMODATIONS
Olympia

You can't beat the **Governor Hotel** (621 S. Capitol Way, 360/352-7700, www.olywagov.com, $99–170 d) location—it's cozied up next to the capitol campus closer than a lobbyist on voting days. It is right downtown with views of Sylvester Park and Capitol Lake. The building exterior is a bit drab, but the rooms inside are cheery enough and the list of amenities is pretty long for the rates you pay. There is an outdoor pool, a hot tub, a sauna, and an exercise room.

Also right in town, **Swantown Inn** (1431 11th Ave. SE, 360/753-9123 or 877/753-9123, www.swantowninn.com, $119–179 s or d) gets a few extra bonus points for style. This bed-and-breakfast is set in an 1887 Victorian mansion with four guest rooms and private baths. This little charmer is a secret weapon for tired adults in search of refuge—munchkins under 12 aren't allowed. Full three-course breakfasts are served each morning, and the inn has an on-site day spa up in the attic that offers two-hour treatments for $99.

In the dining room at **Inn at Mallard Cove** (5025 Meridian Rd. NE, 360/491-9795, www.theinnatmallardcove.com, $169–199 s or d, discounts for military, nurses, or certain airline employees), you have an unobstructed view of the Puget Sound and fresh breakfasts made from organic ingredients grown on-site. This waterfront English Tudor Home is nuzzled by forests and gardens. All three guest rooms come equipped with private baths, fireplaces, and terraces. Get a closer look at the Olympic Mountain views from a complimentary kayak, or if it rains, curl up with a tome next to the floor-to-ceiling bookshelves in the library here.

Vicinity of Olympia

Olympia and the bedroom communities of Tumwater and Lacey are chock full of chain motel options, particularly clustered around the I-5 corridor.

Those in town looking for a place to get comfy during an extended stay might do well to look into **Tumwater Inn & Suites** (5895 Capitol Blvd. SW, Tumwater, 360/943-8428, www.tumwaterinnsuites.com, $69–87 d). This extended-stay motel caters to government workers in town for the legislative session and has discounted weekly and monthly rates available.

Despite what you might think, it's possible to find quiet elegance and peace near Olympia. **The Inn at Mallard Cove** (5025 Meridian Rd. NE, 360/491-9795, www.theinnatmallard cove.com, $169–199), a big, beautiful English Tudor-style building, has three tasteful rooms full of antiques. Outdoors, you'll find three kayaks that you can borrow for free. Just a little paddle-power gets you to the nearby Nisqually Wildlife Refuge. Breakfasts are large but focused on healthy fare.

Olympia's most family-friendly hotel destination is **€ Great Wolf Lodge** (20500 Old Hwy. 99 SW, Grand Mound, 360/273-7718, www.greatwolf.com, $199–389 for four), a combination resort and water park that packs enough fun on its grounds to keep a family happy for a whole weekend. This enormous indoor facility has six slides, a six-story tube ride, three pools, a giant treehouse water fort, and more than 100 lifeguards to look after the kiddies. For mom and dad, there's a 12-room spa on premises. The spacious rooms are pricey, but all rooms are suites, and the rates are typically for four people and include two-day passes to the water park for each guest. Many rooms can accommodate up to eight, with an extra charge of $30 per person beyond four.

Camping

The closest public camping can be found alongside Deep Lake at **Millersylvania State Park** (12 mi. south of Olympia off I-5 at exit 95, 360/753-1519, www.parks.wa.gov). Tent ($22) and RV ($28) sites are available year-round. Make reservations ($6.50 extra) at 888/226-7688 or online.

Approximately 20 miles southwest of Olympia, **Capitol Forest** (www.wa.gov/dnr) has an abundance of primitive campsites ($10 Discovery Pass needed; no water). Contact the Department of Natural Resources at 360/902-1234 or 800/527-3305 for details and a map.

Olympia has an abundance of private tent and RV camping facilities, including several

just a few miles from the center of town. Best among them is **Olympia Campground** (1441 83rd Ave. SW, 360/352-2551, www.olympia campground.com, $19 tent sites, $28 full hookup RV sites), set on 10 acres of lightly wooded grounds. There is a ton of amenities, including a convenience store, a gas station, an ATM, a laundry room, a heated outdoor pool, and a game room with free Wi-Fi.

FOOD
Coffeehouses

Get your buzz on at any number of Olympia's coffeehouses, which often attract the younger Evergreen State College set.

The baristas at **Batdorf and Bronson Roaster** (513 Capitol Way S, 360/786-6717, www.batdorf.com) take their coffee very seriously. Often offering exotic African blends, Batdorf also takes great pride in being certified organic, fair trade, bird-friendly, shade grown, and do their best to operate with 100 percent renewable energy.

Cafés and Diners

€ McMenamins Spar Café & Bar (114 4th Ave. E, 360/357-6444, 7 A.M.–midnight Sun.–Thurs., 7 A.M.–1 A.M. Fri.–Sat.) is family-friendly, serving solid all-American breakfasts, lunches, and dinners. In business since the 1930s, the Spar has a decor to match: classic Northwest logging photos line the walls.

For an all-natural breakfast, lunch, or dinner, try the **Urban Onion** (116 Legion Way, 360/943-9242, www.theurbanonion.com, 11 A.M.–9 P.M. daily) in the old brick building at the corner of Legion and Washington. The varied and varying menu is casual enough for a come-as-you-are lunch but classy enough for a romantic dinner.

The cute little **Mason Jar** (408-C Cleveland Ave., 360/754-7776, themasonjar.net, 9 A.M.–4 P.M. Mon.–Fri. only) is a favorite Tumwater lunch spot with homemade soups, freshly baked breads, and sandwiches. The wall full of Mason jars will let you know you're in the right place.

Get some of the best pastries in southern Puget Sound at **Wagner's European Bakery & Café** (1013 Capitol Way S, 360/357-7268, 7 A.M.–6 P.M. Mon.–Fri., 7:30 A.M.–5 P.M. Sat., 8 A.M.–3 P.M. Sun.) where they also serve soups, salads, and sandwiches for lunch, as well as light breakfasts. A great spot for gluten-free brownies, if that's your thing. Be prepared for a line of state workers on weekdays at lunchtime.

Steak and Seafood

Waterfront and view restaurants aren't as common in Olympia as in other Puget Sound cities, but they do exist. At Percival Landing, **Dockside Bistro** (501 Columbia St. NW, 360/956-1928, http://docksidebistro.com, 11 A.M.–9:30 P.M. Tues.–Sat., 5–9:30 P.M. Sun.) offers a quiet little nook to enjoy the marina, a plate of Northwest flavors, and a glass of wine.

Budd Bay Café (525 Columbia St. NW, 360/357-6963, www.buddbaycafe.com, 6:30 A.M.–8:30 P.M. Mon.–Sat., 9:30 A.M.–8:30 P.M. Sun., entrées $20) at Percival Landing is open for all meals and has a popular $24 Sunday brunch buffet, with outdoor dining in summer featuring a marina view. If you're keen to sample famous Olympia oysters on the half shell, you won't regret doing it here.

Get Olympia oysters, geoduck clams, and other perfectly prepared seafood at **Gardner's Seafood and Pasta** (111 W. Thurston St., 360/786-8466, www.gardnersrestaurant.com, 5–9 P.M. Tues.–Sat., closed Sun.). This romantic epicurian's delight serves many local wines and has become one of Olympia's most popular restaurants. Reservations are definitely advised.

In front of the Olympia Brewery and overlooking Tumwater Falls, **(Falls Terrace Restaurant** (106 Deschutes Way, Tumwater, 360/943-7830, www.fallsterrace.com, 11 A.M.–8:30 P.M. Mon.–Thurs., 11 A.M.–9 P.M. Fri., 11:30 A.M.–9 P.M. Sat., 11:30 A.M.–8 P.M. Sun.) has moderately priced dinners featuring steak and seafood, as well as chicken, pork, and decadent salads. They also offer a Sunday brunch. The lounge features an outside deck, a favorite place to drop by for a drink. Reservations are highly recommended.

Asian

Saigon Rendez-Vous (117 5th Ave. W, 360/352-1989, 11 A.M.–8:30 P.M. Mon.–Fri., noon–8 P.M. Sat.–Sun.) is one of the best local Asian restaurants, with Vietnamese and Chinese menus and vegetarian or vegan specialties.

Get quick and reasonable meals at either location of **Happy Teriyaki:** downtown (530 Capitol Way S, 360/705-8000, 11 A.M.–9 P.M. Mon.–Sat., closed Sun.) and over in West Olympia (2915 Harrison Ave. NW, 360/786-8866, 11 A.M.–9 P.M. Mon.–Sat., closed Sun.). It's also known for great bubble-tea.

Italian

Casa Mia (716 Plum St., 360/352-0440, 11:30 A.M.–10 P.M. Mon.–Fri., 11:30 A.M.–11 P.M. Sat.–Sun.) is the Olympia location of a dependable Hoquiam-based Italian food franchise.

Meconi's Italian Subs (1018 Capitol Way S.

GOOEY DUCKS

Traveling through Western Washington, you're going to hear a certain term and find it quite the head-scratcher, asking yourself, what exactly is a gooey duck? It doesn't quack and you can't find it in the candy aisle. It's the way you pronounce **geoduck,** a gigantic clam weighing up to three pounds. Named after the Nisqually word for "dig deep," these enormous bivalves have been known to live up to 160 years and burrow between 2 and 360 feet beneath the subtidal mud. In many Asian countries, the geoduck is a delicacy, and an earnest search of Washington's Chinese, Japanese, and Korean restaurants is bound to turn up some geoduck on the menu. In addition to being the mascot of Evergreen State College, this slimy fellow is thought by some to be a powerful aphrodisiac.

Suite 101, 360/534-0240, 10 A.M.–8 P.M. Mon.–Fri., 10 A.M.–7 P.M. Sat., closed Sun.) makes the best East Coast–style subs in the Olympia area—very popular with state workers.

Pub Grub
The Fish Tale Brew Pub (515 Jefferson St. SE, 360/943-6480) offers a surprising contrast to Olympia's better-known brew. This small downtown brewpub produces four year-round beers and two seasonals, all with the unusual distinction of being brewed from organic ingredients. The café offers everything from steamer clams to schnitzel to bangers and mash. The pub is strictly 21 and over.

Dine in or take out at **Brewery City Pizza** (2705 Limited Ln. NW, West Olympia, 360/754-7800, 11 A.M.–10 P.M. Sun.–Thurs., 11 A.M.–11 P.M. Fri.–Sat.). Along with pizzas and calzones, they serve up weird appetizers like sweet potato fries and nachos italianos.

Markets and Bakeries
Located in a big building on the north end of Capitol Way, the popular multiday **Olympia Farmers Market** (700 Capitol Way N, 360/352-9096, www.olympiafarmersmarket.com, 10 A.M.–3 P.M. Thurs.–Sun. Apr.–Oct., Sat.–Sun. only Nov.–Dec.) is Washington's second largest after Pike Place Market. You'll find the expected fresh fruits and veggies, plus mushrooms, honey, nursery plants, and just about everything else. The market has entertainment throughout the summer.

Get fresh-squeezed apple cider, take-and-bake apple pies, eggs, honey, and more at **Lattin's Country Cider Mill** (9402 Rich Rd. SE, 360/491-7328, www.lattinscider.com, 9 A.M.–5:30 P.M. Mon.–Sat., 9 A.M.–4 P.M. Sun.). They are located just south of the Amtrak station in East Olympia. If you go in spring, ask to meet the new baby goats.

San Francisco Street Bakery (1320 San Francisco St. NE, 360/753-8553, 6:30 A.M.–7 P.M.

Mon.–Sat., 6:30 A.M.–6 P.M. Sun.) has a small café in a garden setting where you can try their organic breads and pastries.

INFORMATION AND SERVICES
For maps and general information, stop by the **Thurston County Chamber of Commerce** (809 Legion Way SE, 360/357-3362, thurstonchamber.com, 9 A.M.–5 P.M. Mon.–Fri. year-round). At the Capitol Campus, head to the **Public Information Center** (360/586-3460, 8 A.M.–5 P.M. daily). The headquarters office for **Olympic National Forest** (1835 Black Lake Blvd. SW, 360/956-2300, www.fs.fed.us/r6/olympic) is in Olympia.

GETTING THERE AND AROUND
Trains and Planes
Amtrak (800/872-7245, www.amtrak.com) serves Olympia along its north–south **Coast Starlight** route from Seattle to Los Angeles. The Amtrak station is in east Olympia at 6600 Yelm Highway.

There are no scheduled passenger flights to Olympia. Take a shuttle to Sea-Tac instead. **Capital Aeroporter** (360/754-7113 or 800/962-3579, www.capair.com) will get you there starting at $31 for a one-way trip.

By Bus
Intercity Transit (360/786-1881 or 800/287-6348, www.intercitytransit.com) has daily service to Olympia, Tumwater, and most of Thurston County. All buses have bike racks. The Olympia Transit Center is on State Street between Franklin and Washington Streets. You can even get a mobile app to help plan your route at onebusaway.org.

Greyhound (Capitol and 7th, 800/231-2222, www.greyhound.com) connects Olympia to Seattle, Tacoma, Portland, and other cities along the north–south I-5 corridor.

Tacoma

Washington's third-largest city is a community actively reinventing itself. Once a drab paper-mill town 30 miles south of Seattle, Tacoma is becoming a vibrant, charming metropolis with clean air, a University of Washington campus, and an eye on the future.

Most of the smelly mills have closed, and Tacoma's downtown is enjoying an urban renaissance that includes the presence of the Washington State History Museum, the International Museum of Glass, and the Tacoma Art Museum, all under the backdrop of majestic Mount Rainier.

Along with this fresh crop of visual wonders, old warehouses are becoming artists' lofts, a thriving theater district has been created, and a downtown plaza occupies the fountain-flowing, stroller-friendly heart of the city. Add to this a diverse 700-acre city park with a world-class zoo, a rambling public market, top-quality hotels and waterfront restaurants, and a spruced up shoreline.

SIGHTS
Museum Row
◖ MUSEUM OF GLASS

Tacoma's artistic gem, the 75,000-square-foot Museum of Glass (1801 Dock St., 253/572-931 or 866/468-7386, www.museumofglass.org, 10 A.M.–5 P.M. Mon.–Sat., noon–5 P.M. Sun. Memorial Day–Labor Day, closed Mon.–Tues. Labor Day–Memorial Day, $12 adult, $10 senior & military, $5 children) in downtown Tacoma, covers two acres along the waterfront, encompassing galleries and exhibition spaces, an enormous hot shop studio where you can watch artisans blow and cast glass, a theater for multimedia presentations, museum shop, and café. A highlight is the **Chihuly Bridge of Glass,** a 500-foot-long pedestrian bridge created by native son Dale Chihuly. The bridge takes you through a tunnel of brilliant light and color and crosses I-705, connecting the Glass Museum with the History Museum. Adjacent to the

Museum of Glass

© ERICKA CHICKOWSKI

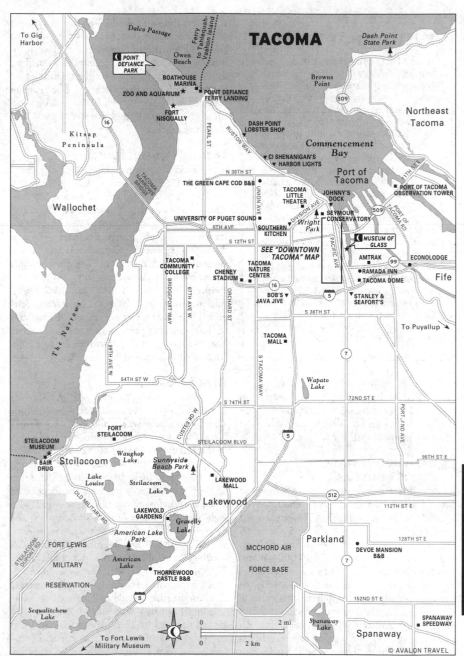

SOUTH PUGET SOUND

© AVALON TRAVEL

FULL OF HOT AIR

Tacoma is a town crazy about its glass art. You can thank Dale Chihuly for that. Born in Tacoma in 1941, this world-renowned glassmaker has made a name for himself through his wild and colorful pieces that often feature twisted tentacles and tendrils, uniquely patterned orbs, and a riot of colors. He helped found the Pilchuck Glass School in the 1970s, and brought a whole new level of notoriety to the American glass art scene, which has always played second fiddle to European centers like Murano, Italy.

Chihuly has been instrumental in the Tacoma downtown revitalization, helping to draw the International Glass Museum to town and donating thousands of unique pieces for his Bridge of Glass, which links the museum to Pacific Avenue. He's donated some of his best glass to the Tacoma Art Museum, and you can also find his work in businesses and restaurants around town. Legend has it that his trademark pieces over the bar at The Swiss were given in exchange for pints in his less glamorous days.

Glass Museum is another large glass sculpture called Water Forest that is the creation of artist Howard Ben Tré. Admission is free on the third Thursday of the month, when the museum is open until 8 P.M.

(WASHINGTON STATE HISTORY MUSEUM

Tacoma is home to the impressive Washington State History Museum (1911 Pacific Ave., 253/593-2830 or 888/238-4373, www.wshs .org/wshm, 10 A.M.–5 P.M. Wed.–Sun, $8 adults, $7 seniors, $6 ages 6–18 and military, free for kids under 6). This 100,000-square-foot building sits next to historic Union Station and repeats its rounded design in a series of three gracefully vaulted arches. Visitors walk through a maze of exhibits that include a Salish plank house and Native basket collection, dioramas of mining and logging towns, exhibits on the arrival of the railroad and the effect of the Depression and World War II, and a theater with an educational video about the Columbia River. Given the importance of high-tech industries in Washington, it comes as no surprise to find lots of interactive displays. Upstairs are galleries with temporary exhibits. The museum is joined to the restored Union Station by a scenic courtyard and amphitheater, a great spot for a lunch break.

TACOMA ART MUSEUM

The Tacoma Art Museum (1701 Pacific Ave., 253/272-4258, www.tacomaartmuseum.org, 10 A.M.–5 P.M. Wed.–Sun. 10 A.M.–8 P.M. Thurs., $10 adults, $8 students, seniors, and military, free under age 6) is best known for its paintings and other pieces from 19th- and 20th-century artists, plus its permanent exhibitions of Dale Chihuly glass. New exhibits come to the museum almost monthly, and there are frequent lectures and other activities, plus a museum shop with gifts, art books, and jewelry. There is no charge on the third Thursday of the month between 5 and 8 P.M., and active-duty military and their families are free from Memorial Day through Labor Day.

Other Museums

Over many years, the owner of Pierce County Refuse Co.—Harold E. LeMay—amassed the world's largest private collection of automobiles. Classic car fans should definitely stop at the **Harold E. LeMay Museum** (325 152nd St. E, 253/779-8490, www.lemaymuseum.org, 10 A.M.–5 P.M. Tues.–Sat., adults $15, children $5). This is officially the largest collection of antique and vintage vehicles in the world, with well over 1,900 cars, trucks, motorcycles, and even campers. In addition to the usual suspects, the collection features magnificent oddities like a 2004 Picklefork Ultra Boat-Car built on the TV show *Monster Garage.* The museum will be moving to a smaller but more central location in 2012, so be sure to call or click for directions.

The **Children's Museum of Tacoma** (936 Broadway, 253/627-6031, www.childrens museumoftacoma.org, 10 A.M.–5 P.M. Mon.–Sat., noon–5 P.M. Sun. $6 adults, $6 children, free for tots under 12 mos.) lets kids build, problem-solve, create art, and just plain have fun.

⟨ Point Defiance Park

Almost 702 acres of gardens, forests, footpaths, and shady picnic areas juts out into Puget Sound at Tacoma's Point Defiance Park. It reminds visitors of the best metropolitan parks in America, but once you've seen it, the cliff setting with its views and thick forest will make most other similar parks seem modest. This is an amazing place, with an array of attractions to please almost anyone. Originally set aside as a military reservation, the park was given to the city of Tacoma in 1888 for use as a public park.

POINT DEFIANCE ZOO AND AQUARIUM

The biggest attraction at the park is the Point Defiance Zoo and Aquarium (253/591-5335 or 253/591-5337, www.pdza.org, 8:30 A.M.–6 P.M. daily Memorial Day–Labor Day, 10 A.M.–4 P.M. daily the rest of the year, $16 adults, $15 seniors, $14 military, $12 ages 5–12, $8.25 tots 3–4, and free for kids under 3). The real draws here are the ocean exhibits. You'll discover a tropical reef filled with brilliantly colored fish, a huge cold-water aquarium with fish, jellyfish, eels, and other critters from the Puget Sound area, and the main event: a large tank where you can come face to face with more than 30 sharks, reaching up to 10 feet long. The Rocky Shores exhibit includes tufted puffins, harbor seals, Pacific walruses, beluga whales, and playful sea otters. Another favorite attraction is the polar bear area, which features them swimming in a deep pool. In August and September, the Friday evening **Zoosounds concerts** are fun for the whole family. In December, come in the evening to see the twinkling **Zoolights.**

JAPANESE AND BOTANIC GARDENS

Point Defiance Park is home to several beautifully maintained gardens. The Japanese garden features a pagoda built in 1914, plus pools, a waterfall, and immaculate landscaping. The park's botanic garden covers almost five acres. Whenever you come, you're likely to see the roses, iris, dahlias, rhododendrons, or native flowers in bloom.

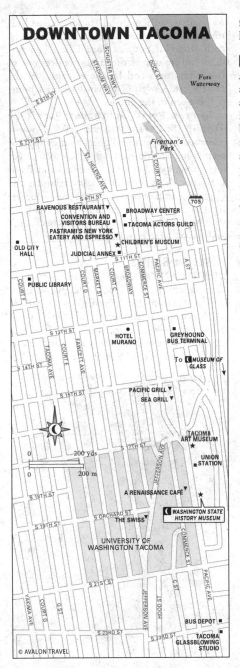

DOWNTOWN TACOMA

SCHUSTER PKWY
STADIUM WAY
DOCK ST
Foss
Waterway
S 4TH ST
S 5TH ST
Fireman's
Park
ST. HELENS AVE
S COURT AVE
S 9TH ST
705
RAVENOUS RESTAURANT ▾
CONVENTION AND
VISITORS BUREAU ▪ ▪ BROADWAY CENTER
PASTRAMI'S NEW YORK ▾ ▪ TACOMA ACTORS GUILD
EATERY AND ESPRESSO
OLD CITY ★ CHILDREN'S MUSEUM
HALL ▪
JUDICIAL ANNEX ▪
S 11TH ST
A ST
▪ PUBLIC LIBRARY
COURT C
MARKET ST
BROADWAY
COMMERCE ST
PACIFIC AVE
COURT D
COURT ▪
S 13TH ST
HOTEL ▪
MURANO
▪ GREYHOUND
BUS TERMINAL
TACOMA AVE
FAWCETT AVE
COURT E
S 14TH ST
To ⟨ MUSEUM OF
GLASS
S 15TH ST
PACIFIC GRILL ▾
SEA GRILL ▾
TACOMA
ART MUSEUM ★
S 17TH ST
JEFFERSON AVE
UNION
▪ STATION
0   200 yds
0   200 m
S 19TH ST
A RENAISSANCE CAFE ▾ ★
S ORCHARD ST
THE SWISS ▾
⟨ WASHINGTON STATE
HISTORY MUSEUM
S 19TH ST
COMMERCE ST
UNIVERSITY OF
WASHINGTON TACOMA
S 21ST ST
C ST
PACIFIC AVE
YAKIMA AVE
COURT G
G ST
JEFFERSON AVE
S 23RD ST
BUS DEPOT ▪
S 23RD ST
© AVALON TRAVEL
TACOMA
GLASSBLOWING
STUDIO

FORT NISQUALLY

Part of the Hudson's Bay trading post once located near present-day Fort Lewis, the buildings of Fort Nisqually Historic Site (5400 N. Pearl St. #11, 253/591-5339, www.fortnisqually.org, 11 A.M.–5 P.M. daily Memorial Day–Labor Day, with varying hours Wed.–Sun. the rest of the year, $6 adults, $5 active military and spouse, $4 ages 4–17, $5 seniors and students, free for kids under 3) were moved to Point Defiance and restored in the 1930s. The half dozen log buildings are still well cared for today, and volunteers in period garb frequently offer living history demonstrations.

Check out the storehouse built in 1851, considered the oldest standing building in Washington. Come here in May to celebrate Queen Victoria's birthday, in August for a mountain man encampment, or in October for a candlelight tour.

Other Parks

Lakewold Gardens (12317 Gravelly Lake Dr., 253/584-4106 or 888/858-4106, www.lakewold.org, 10 A.M.–4 P.M. Wed.–Sat., April–Sept., 10 A.M.–4 P.M. Fri.–Sat. Oct.–Mar, $7 adults, $5 seniors, military, and students, free kids under 12) is a 10-acre collection of rare plants, including blue poppies from Tibet. The gardens feature one of the largest collections of rhododendrons and Japanese maples in the Northwest. A lovely Georgian-style brick home is also open to the public.

Browns Point Lighthouse Park (201 Tulalip St. NE, 253/927-1042, www.metroparkstacoma.org) offers a sunny spot for picnicking or ship-watching. Here you've got a great view of downtown Tacoma and Point Defiance, Vashon and Maury Islands, the Olympics, and of course, the Sound. Tour the lighthouse and the keeper's cottage, complete with historical exhibits on Saturdays between 1 and 4 P.M., March through November.

Historic Sights

DOWNTOWN TACOMA

Completed in 1911, Tacoma's copper-domed **Union Station** (1717 Pacific Ave.,253/863-5173, www.unionstationrotunda.org, 8 A.M.–5 P.M. Mon.–Fri., closed weekends, free) was designed by the same firm that built New York's Grand Central Station and has a similar

Tacoma's most dramatic architecture can be found at Union Station.

© ERICKA CHICKOWSKI

GALLOPING GERTIE

One of the most famous few minutes of American film is the stunning collapse of the Tacoma Narrows Bridge in 1940. Open for a mere five months at the time of its fall, the bridge had been affectionately named "Galloping Gertie" for the undulating motion that motorists could feel as they drove over the 2,800-foot span. On November 7, 1940, the relatively moderate 40-mph winds had an unexpected effect on the bridge, causing the steel-and-concrete structure to twist and flap like a flag. The movement became more severe until the bridge finally collapsed, the dramatic moment caught on film by a local camera-shop owner. Thankfully, no humans were hurt, although an elderly cocker spaniel named Tubby, trapped in a car his owner had just ditched, fell to his death in the roiling waters below.

Today, two bridges carry traffic across Highway 16 between Tacoma and the Kitsap Peninsula, one built in 1950 and the other in 2007. The new bridges are sometimes referred to as "Sturdy Gertie" for their superior engineering.

sense of grandeur. The depot originally served as the terminus of the Northern Pacific's rail line. Today, the works of Tacoma-born glass artist Dale Chihuly fill its magnificent central space. A magnificent 18-foot cobalt-blue chandelier hangs from the high center. The station has become a much sought-after wedding and reception venue.

Old City Hall (S. 7th St. and Pacific Ave.) is a striking Italianate building downtown, patterned after a Florentine town hall. More than a century old, it is complete with a tall freestanding clock tower. In 2005, the building was purchased with the idea of converting it to condos, but the deal soured and the venerable old building and symbol of Tacoma has fallen into foreclosure.

STADIUM DISTRICT

The impressive Stadium District, located near **Stadium High School** on Tacoma Avenue, is a chateau-cum-Queen Anne wonderland built by timber and railroad barons of the late 19th century. The district is home to over 70 businesses, a handful of parks, and the Stadium Bowl, the West Coast's first stadium. Theodore Roosevelt, Warren Harding, and Franklin Delano Roosevelt stopped here, as did sports legends Babe Ruth and Jack Dempsey. Be sure to see the **William Ross Rust House** (1001 N. I St.), a curious neoclassical building with rococo and Victorian influences. It was built in 1905 as the home of president of the Tacoma

Smelter and Refining Company. It's privately owned and not open to the public, so do your touring from the sidewalk.

Wright Park (501 South I St.) is a shade-filled green with lawn-bowling greens, sculpture, fountains, and a delightful surprise: the **Seymour Conservatory** (253/591-5330, www.metroparkstacoma.org, 10 A.M.–4:30 P.M. Tues.–Sun., $5 donation). The glass-paned domed building hosts a bright array of tropical plants and cacti. This is a great indoor place to visit on a rainy winter day. The conservatory is one of the few places entrusted by the government to care for plants confiscated by Fish and Wildlife at the U.S./Canada border.

One of Tacoma's most unique museums is the **Karpeles Manuscript Library Museum** (407 S. G St., 253/383-2575, www.rain.org/~karpeles, 10 A.M.–4 P.M. Tues.–Sun., free). The museum displays rotating exhibits of one-of-a-kind original documents from all over the world, handwritten papers by Sigmund Freud, Albert Einstein, and Queen Elizabeth I's 1588 instructions for dealing with the Spanish Armada.

STEILACOOM

Located about 25 minutes southeast of Tacoma, the National Historic District of Steilacoom offers history buffs ample opportunity to take in some old-timey sights. Start at the **Steilacoom Town Hall and Museum** (1801

SOUTH PUGET SOUND

Rainier St., 253/584-4133, www.steilacoom .org/museum, 1–4 P.M. Tues.–Sun. Mar.–Oct., 1–4 P.M. Fri.–Sun. Nov.–Dec. and Feb., closed Jan., free), which will give you the scoop on the town's heritage as the first incorporated town in Washington Territory. Pick up the *Guide to Historic Steilacoom* here for a walking tour. It is located downstairs in the white New England–style Town Hall on Main and Lafayette.

Housed in a 100-year-old Congregational Church building, **Steilacoom Tribal Cultural Center and Museum** (1515 Lafayette St., 253/584-6308, 10 A.M.–4 P.M. Sat., $2 adults, $1 seniors and kids, children under 6 free, $6 families) documents the history of the Steilacoom tribe with exhibits that feature the prehistory of the Tacoma Basin, historical artifacts, and contemporary artistry.

East from the town of Steilacoom is **Fort Steilacoom** (253/584-2368), right next to the massive psychiatric hospital once named "Western Washington Hospital for the Insane." Meant to protect U.S. interests in then-Oregon Territory in the days following the Mexican-American War, the fort now features four small frame houses from when the fort was established in 1849. One of the buildings has an interpretive center and small museum open for summertime tours 1–4 P.M. on Saturday.

Military Museums

With two military bases surrounding the greater Tacoma region, there's a fairly decent chance you'll run across a few soldiers or airmen while wandering about town. Military buffs can bone up on their history at museums offered by each base.

Take exit 120 from I-5, 16 miles south of Tacoma, to the **Fort Lewis Military Museum** (www.lewis.army.mil/dptms/museum.htm, 253/967-7207, noon–4 P.M. Wed.–Sun., free) located in a 1918 Swiss-style building originally used as a Salvation Army center. The museum emphasizes Northwest military history, including displays of the dress uniforms from various eras, the history of the I Corps, and Gen. "Stormin'" Norman Schwartzkopf's Jeep (he was base commander here in the early 1980s).

Get a pass at the visitors office on the east side of the freeway near the main gate.

Indulge those jet-fueled fantasies at **McChord Air Museum** (253/982-2485, noon–4 P.M. Wed.–Fri., closed holidays, free), one mile east on exit 125. The museum owns several aircraft, including a C-47 Skytrain, an unmistakably 1960s-era T-33A Shooting Star, and the ugly but hard-hitting A-10A "Warthog." Weapon systems, uniforms, and other Air Force memorabilia are also on display.

ENTERTAINMENT AND EVENTS
Nightlife

One of the primary beneficiaries of Tacoma's rebirth as a haven of hip is the bar and club scene. For an exhaustive listing, pick up the free *Tacoma Weekly* (www.tacomaweekly.com) newspapers in racks around town.

The clubs are in an almost constant state of change but **The Swiss** (1904 Jefferson, 253/572-2821, www.theswisspub.com) has stood the test of time for a long time, hosting local rock, punk, and blues music along with a popular quiz night and weekly karaoke.

Jazzbones (2803 6th Ave., 253/396-9169, jazzbonestacoma.com) puts on jazz, comedy, local rock, and offers the chance to sing karaoke in front of a live band.

A neighborhood favorite is **Bob's Java Jive** (2102 S. Tacoma Way, 253/475-9843) a coffee-pot-shaped building on S. Tacoma Way with a neon-decorated handle and spout. The drinks of choice are beer and wine, not lattes and mochas.

The **Ale House Pub & Eatery** (2122 Mildred W., 253/565-9367, www.alehousepub .com, 11 A.M.–2 P.M. daily) has one of the largest selections of draft beer in the state, with an incredible 63 different beers on tap. The menu is reasonably priced and good—especially the ribs—and the big-screen TV is popular for sporting events.

Casinos

If games of chance are the thrill you're looking for, head to the 24-hour **Emerald Queen**

Casino (2102 Alexander Ave., 888/831-7655, www.emeraldqueen.com), a Mississippi River–style riverboat with blackjack, roulette, craps, and over 2,000 slots. Run by the Puyallup Tribe of Indians, the casino also hosts some major musical acts that you might remember from your late childhood.

Performance Venues

Tacoma rocks the Puget Sound with some of the biggest concerts of the region inside the **Tacoma Dome** (2727 E. D St., 253/272-3663, www.tacomadome.org), a distinctive blue bastion of the early 1980s that remains one of the largest wood-domed structures in the world. This is where you come to see U2 or Lady Gaga throw their megatours or watch monster trucks crush little subcompacts into lunch-pail sized cubes.

The Arts

Tacoma's **Broadway Center for the Performing Arts** (901 Broadway, 253/591-5890, www.broadwaycenter.org) is composed of a trio of theaters downtown near the intersection of 9th and Broadway Streets. Newest is the 302-seat state-of-the art **Theater on the Square,** sporting a yellow paintjob that's impossible to miss.

Housed in a large 1918 building modeled after a theater at Versailles, France, **Pantages Theater** is a former Vaudeville venue and neighbor to the eclectic Beaux Arts–style **Rialto Theater** (253/591-5894 for both), both of which share the privilege of staging comedy, dance, plays, films, and concerts.

For more than 75 years, the **Tacoma Little Theater** (210 N. I St., 253/272-2281, www.tacomalittletheatre.com) in the Stadium District has tackled all sorts of musicals, comedies, and dramas with their all-volunteer casts and crews. It's the oldest theater to stage continuous performances west of the Mississippi.

The **Tacoma Philharmonic** (253/272-0809, www.tacomaphilharmonic.org) presents classical music programs at the Pantages Theater five times a year. The decidedly more casual **Tacoma Symphony** (253/272-7264) shares the Pantages, but also performs at a variety of other venues throughout the season. Each season, the orchestra performs Kids Concerts in an old church, sometimes hosting visiting musicians. **Tacoma Musical Playhouse** (7116 6th Ave., 253/565-6867, www.tmp.org) is a community theater that is dedicated to performing musicals. The **Tacoma Opera** (1119 Pacific Ave., 253/627-7789, www.tacomaopera.com) performs classic and contemporary opera at the Pantages Theater. They sometimes offer non-English operas sung in translation and when not, often have a projector to show the English words.

Festivals and Events

Celebrate the New Year in a family-friendly booze-free sort of way at Tacoma's **First Night** (253/591-7205, www.firstnighttacoma.org) celebration, usually united by a theme. The party starts with free museum and gallery admission during the day and music, puppets, and setting lots and lots of things on fire in the evening.

Tacoma's big **Freedom Fair** (253/756-9808, www.freedomfair.com) on the 4th of July includes arts and cultural events, and live entertainment along the waterfront. A huge fireworks display blasts off at dusk, but the main attraction is the air show—one of the largest in the nation—featuring both civilian and military aircraft rocketing over Commencement Bay. The **Taste of Tacoma** (www.tasteoftacoma.com) takes in late June, with dozens of local restaurants providing food, two concert stages with live music and entertainment, and a beer garden.

Over two days in August, the Browns Point Improvement Club puts on a **Salmon Bake** (253/756-7336) at Browns Point.

The **Steilacoom 4th of July** includes a parade and street fair with food vendors, art booths, and live entertainment. Late July sees the Steilacoom **Dog-a-Thon** (253/383-2733), a benefit for homeless dogs at the Humane Society. Events include dogs riding scooters, sheepherding demonstrations, a dog show with a variety of prizes, and the inimitable doggie wet T-shirt contest. One of the region's few fall events, the **Steilacoom Apple Squeeze**

(253/584-4133) on the first Sunday of October lets you indulge that burning desire to make cider the old-fashioned way—with hand-cranked presses. Pony rides, crafts, magic, and homemade apple pies round out the day.

SHOPPING

In a great-big former railroad freight terminus, **Freighthouse Square** (25th and East D, a block north of Tacoma Dome, 253/305-0678) is Tacoma's indoor market-style shopping center with everything from pet supplies to clothes to good food. Not far away you can spend an afternoon hunting through used books at **Tacoma Book Center** (324 E. 26th St., 253/572-8248, www.tacomabookcenter.com). The quite-large independent bookstore buys and sells titles over just about every genre.

Broadway in downtown Tacoma makes for a lovely stroll on a lazy afternoon. More than 20 art galleries and more than a few antique shops dot **Antique Row** between 7th and 9th Streets in downtown Tacoma. There are clothing boutiques, tea shops, and even a supply shop for practitioners of Pagan witchcraft.

One of the most enjoyable window-shopping districts in Tacoma is the mostly upscale cluster of shops and boutiques called the **Proctor District** along the 2700 block of N. Proctor. Among them, **Pacific Northwest Shop** (2702 N. Proctor St., 253/752-2242, www.pacific northwestshop.com) stocks all kinds of things just so long as they were made in Washington, Oregon, Idaho, or British Columbia.

Many of the major national and regional stores can be found at the plus-sized **Tacoma Mall** (4502 S. Steele St., 253/475-4566, www .tacoma-mall.com) with 135 stores including Nordstrom, Macy's, and an Apple store.

SPORTS AND RECREATION
Spectator Sports

The Pacific Coast Baseball League is represented by the **Tacoma Rainiers,** a AAA farm club for the Seattle Mariners that plays at **Cheney Stadium** (2502 S. Tyler St., 253/752-7707, www.tacomarainiers.com), off Highway 16. With ticket prices starting at $5, taking in a minor-league game can certainly be some cheap summertime fun.

Point Defiance Park Natural Areas

Much of Port Defiance Park's wild nature remains from the early years, visible from a myriad of hiking paths (no bikes on unpaved trails) and a loop road that passes all the main sights. This loop road, **Five-Mile Drive,** winds through the park, offering a popular jogging, cycling, and driving route with viewpoints and picnic stops along the way. The outer loop is closed Saturday mornings (till 1 P.M.) to cars, giving joggers, cyclists, and in-line skaters free rein.

Owen Beach on Commencement Bay offers summer sun or a pleasant shoreline stroll any time of year. Rent a boat with a small motor at the Point Defiance **Boathouse Marina** (253/591-5325). The water off the point is popular with anglers, particularly during salmon season. Get fishing tackle at the shop here, or stop for a meal at the popular Boathouse Grill Restaurant next door. The state ferry to Vashon Island docks here as well. Point Defiance Park (253/305-1000, www.metroparkstacoma.org) is open every day from sunrise until 30 minutes past sunset.

Walking and Cycling

Lakewood Park (on Steilacoom Blvd.) has a trail that circles Waughop Lake. Drive down Dresdon Lane, then park by the barns to get to the trailhead.

A two-mile cycling and jogging path runs along Ruston Way, good for a breezy post-lunch or -dinner walk all the way down to Point Defiance, or just to the waterfront at **Commencement Park** or **Marine Park** along the way.

Tucked away where you'd least expect it is the **Tacoma Nature Center** (1919 S. Tyler St., 253/591-6439, www.metroparkstacoma.org). The 54 acres of marshland and evergreens are just a stone's throw from busy 19th Street, but this is a place to watch ducks and other birds. There are two miles of self-guiding nature trails. Trails are open 8 A.M.–dark daily; the interpretive center (8 A.M.–5 P.M. Mon.–Fri., 10 A.M.–4 P.M. Sat. year-round, donations) is filled with hands-on exhibits.

Water Sports

For a chilly-water swim, visit **Titlow Park** (just south of Narrows Bridge) and **Wapato Lake Park** (S. 72nd St. and Sheridan Ave.), where a lifeguard is present at its public swimming beaches in the summer. The five-acre **American Lake Park** (9222 Veterans Dr. SW., Lakewood) south of Tacoma near Fort Lewis has a swimming beach, too.

There are two parks with fishing piers on Commencement Bay. Also known as Sundial Park for the giant stone timepiece there, **Commencement Park** is the quieter of the two. **Marine Park** has more amenities, with a long narrow strip of shoreline with open grassy areas, picnic tables, a fishing pier, bait shop, and snack stand.

Golf

When the fairway is dry, golfers can expect to be rewarded with amazing views of Mount Rainer as they play some of Washington's best golf. **Allenmore Golf Course** (2125 S. Cedar St., 253/627-7211, www.allenmoregolfcourse .com, $28.50-$30), gives your driver a serious workout with its long, straight approaches. **Meadow Park Golf Course** (7108 Lakewood Dr. W, 253/473-3033, $31–36 18 holes, $15 executive) is an enjoyable municipal with an 18-hole championship course, a 9-hole executive, and a driving range. At **North Shore Golf & Country Club** (4101 North Shore Blvd. NE, 253/927-1375 or 800/447-1375, $26–35) rent clubs if you left yours at home. The club also runs a putt-putt obstacle course, horseshoes, and other kid-friendly events for the family traveler. **Classic Country Club** (4908 208th St. E in Spanaway, 253/847-4440, $20–49) offers tough contoured greens and fairways that demand precision. Classic is the home course of Professional Golfers Association player Ryan Moore.

Spas

Those looking to relax after a long day of walking museum row can take a break at **Savi Day Spa** (1320 Broadway, 253/627-2000, www.savi dayspa.com), a plush retreat based out of the Hotel Murano that offers full body massages ($30 for 25 min.), hot stone massages ($120 for 60 min.), and a number of foot and hand treatments on its menu of services.

Glassblowing

If you're digging all of the cool glass art around

© ERICKA CHICKOWSKI

An advanced glassblower crafts a piece at Tacoma Glassblowing Studio.

SOUTH PUGET SOUND

town and want to see if you have the chops to compete with Chihuly, take a walk to the end of Museum Row and enroll in a class at **Tacoma Glassblowing Studio** (114 S. 23rd St., 253/383-3499, $225 for two-day course). The teachers patiently explain the process of blowing glass, from heating the raw material to blowing to shaping and more. Your first time around might feel like helping Dad build a treehouse—there's a lot of hand-holding early on for safety reasons—but the teachers are really friendly and you get to see the advanced artists making some cool stuff.

ACCOMMODATIONS
Under $100
Many of the Tacoma area's motels are strung along Pacific Highway just off I-5, many in neighboring towns of Fife and Lakewood. **Rodeway Inn & Suites** (3100 Pacific Hwy. E, Fife, 253/922-9520 or 800/982-3781, $58 s or $64 d) has an outdoor pool for those toasty Tacoma summer days, plus a free continental breakfast. Pet owners can bring Fluffy with them for $10 more per night. In Lakewood, **Western Inn** (9920 South Tacoma Way, 253/588-5241, $80–100) is a clean and comfortable motel within easy range of Fort Lewis or downtown, whatever your need. It offers smoking and nonsmoking rooms and provides free wireless Internet. Furnishings are simple and the very epitome of the term "motel." The locale is maybe less than optimal, but rooms are clean and the staff is nice.

In Tacoma proper, **King Oscar Motel Tacoma** (8820 S Hosmer, 253/539-1153, http://koscar.net, $75–85) is a crisp, centrally located motel with an indoor pool, a laundry room, and a continental breakfast. After a long day on the road, you might be tempted to spring for the whirlpool tub suite for a pretty modest $145.

$100-150
For just a few extra greenbacks, get a big jump in quality over the average motel offerings around Tacoma at **Baymont Inn & Suites** (5805 Pacific Hwy. E, Fife, 253/922-2500 or 800/422-3051, www.guesthousefife.com, $109

s or $119 d). This completely renovated building has well-lit rooms with quality linens and mattresses. The facility offers a fitness center, pool table, complimentary hot breakfast, and free wireless Internet. There is also a spate of suite options, including a whirlpool tub suite ($165), an apartment with full kitchen ($189), and a spacious turret suite ($225) with huge windows, kitchen, and whirlpool tub.

The Green Cape Cod B&B (2711 N. Warner, 253/752-1977 or 866/752-1977, www.green capecod.com, $135–165 d) is a cozy 1929 Cape Cod antique-furnished home in north Tacoma where three guest rooms have private baths.

Built in 1911 and on the National Register of Historic Places, the elegant Colonial-style **DeVoe Mansion B&B** (208 E. 133rd St., 253/539-3991 or 888/539-3991, www.devoe mansion.com, $115–149 d) is situated on 1.5 acres. The mansion was the home of Emma DeVoe, a turn-of-the-20th-century suffragette whose efforts helped give Washington women the right to vote. The four guest rooms have antiques and private baths. Guests can soak in the garden hot tub.

$150-200
In the Stadium District, **Villa B&B** (705 N. 5th St., 253/572-1157, www.villabb.com, $150–250 d) is a grand Mediterranean-style mansion built in 1925. The Villa features four large guest rooms, verandas, and gardens. In addition to a big breakfast each morning, Villa also provides snacks, pop, and water at no extra cost.

An 1889 Queen Anne Victorian in the historic Stadium District, **Chinaberry Hill B&B** (302 Tacoma Ave. N, 253/272-1282, www .chinaberryhill.com, $149–245 d) is one of the most superb B&Bs in Tacoma. The home has a wraparound front porch, period furnishings, stained glass windows, and a separate carriage house for families or couples looking for privacy. Five guest rooms have private baths, and suites contain whirlpool tubs.

$200-250
Tacoma's landmark hotel is one of the nicest in all of Puget Sound—including downtown

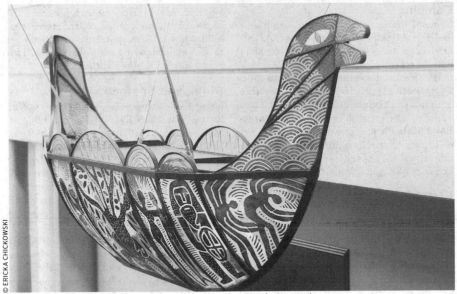

© ERICKA CHICKOWSKI

Tacoma's Hotel Murano features a museum's-worth of glass art.

Seattle. The one-of-a-kind ◖ **Hotel Murano** (1320 Broadway Plaza, 253/238-8000, www .hotelmuranotacoma.com, $199–229 d, $249–469 suites) pays homage to Tacoma's glassblowing scene in a big way. Named for the famous Italian glassmaking town, Murano will impress you right away with the enormous glass Viking boats crafted by Vibeke Skov, which are suspended from the lobby ceiling and reflect light differently throughout the day. From there it just gets better. There are pieces from all of the biggest glassmaking names around the world, including hometown hero Dale Chihuly, scattered through the lobby and posh lobby bar, the upstairs bistro, and the rest of the public nooks here. Most exciting are the individual pieces facing each elevator exit on every guest floor at this 21-floor tower. These glass pieces were specially commissioned for the hotel, and along each hallway there is an interpretive display honoring each artist's vision for the work and pictures showing the making of the piece. The rooms themselves are hardly a footnote to the story—they are stylishly decorated with modern furnishing, über-comfy

beds, and sumptuous linens. The service is top notch, without the pretension that would probably surround such a hotel if it were in Seattle.

Every second Tuesday of the month, the hotel opens for a tour led by docents from the Museum of Glass. Held at 2 P.M., the tour takes you through the public spaces, meeting rooms, and guest floors, which normally are not open to the public. The tour costs $5, with proceeds going to the Museum of Glass.

Over $250

There's nothing else in Washington like ◖ **Thornewood Castle B&B** (8601 N. Thorne Ln. SW, 253/584-4393, www.thornewood castle.com, $270–597 d, no kids allowed), a magnificent 1910 Tudor Gothic mansion on American Lake southwest of Tacoma, with a half-acre sunken English garden. Inside this 27,000-square-foot mansion you'll find 16th-century stained glass and other ornate furnishings. Five guest rooms have private baths. The Stephen King made-for-TV movie *Rose Red* was filmed here in 2000 for ABC.

SOUTH PUGET SOUND

Camping

Some of the nearest year-round camping is available at **Dash Point State Park** (5700 SW Dash Point Rd. in Federal Way, 360/902-8844) with beachfront sites for tents ($22) or RVs ($31). More campsites can be had at **Kopachuck State Park** (11101 56th St. in Gig Harbor, 360/902-8844) right on Puget Sound, about 12 miles northwest of Tacoma, and **Penrose Point State Park,** approximately 20 miles west of Tacoma on the Key Peninsula. Get information at 360/902-8844. Make reservations ($6.50 extra) at 888/226-7688, www.parks.wa.gov.

FOOD
Cafés and Grills

Bair Drug and Hardware (1617 Lafayette in Steilacoom, 253/588-9668, 9 A.M.–4 P.M. Tues.–Fri., 8 A.M.–4 P.M. Sat., 8 A.M.–2 P.M. Sun.) is an 1895 shop with a sampling of historic items on display and a 1906 soda fountain where you can still get a soda or sundae, along with something you wouldn't find in 1906—espresso coffees. Great baked goods and pies here as well.

Start out at **Knapps Restaurant** (2707 N. Proctor St., 253/759-9009, 6 A.M.–9 P.M. Sun.–Thurs., 6 A.M.–10 P.M. Fri.–Sat.) in the Proctor District, where you'll find the best breakfasts in Tacoma, from pancakes to eggs Benedict.

Located in north Tacoma near Point Defiance Park, the **Antique Sandwich Company** (5102 N. Pearl in Ruston, 253/752-4069, 7 A.M.–7 P.M. Wed.–Mon., 7 A.M.–10:30 P.M. Tues.) has a 1970s throwback vibe about it. It serves up warm, hearty soups like clam chowder, as well as salads, espresso, and sweets. Come back on Tuesday evening for live acoustic or folk music.

Primo Grill (601 S. Pine St., 253/383-7000, 11:30 A.M.–9:30 P.M. Mon.–Thurs., 11 A.M.–10:30 P.M. Fri., 5–10:30 P.M. Sat., 4:30–9 P.M. Sun.) has a wood-burning grill serving light Italian food in an architecturally tasty setting. If you're longing for some down-home cooking, **Southern Kitchen** (1716 6th Ave., 253/627-4282, www.southern kitchen-tacoma.com, 8 A.M.–8 P.M. Mon.–Thurs., 8 A.M.–9 P.M. Fri.–Sat., 8 A.M.–7 P.M. Sun.) where the menu of deep south meals includes catfish, pork chops, collard greens, barbecued ribs, and sweet potato pie. Don't forget to wash it down with a glass of sweet tea. This is a longtime Tacoma favorite.

Steak and Seafood

Located right on the water, **Harbor Lights** (2761 Ruston Way, 253/752-8600, 11 A.M.–9:30 P.M. Mon.–Thurs., 11–10:30 Fri.–Sat., noon–9 P.M. Sun.) is a Tacoma tradition, with giant steaks, four-pound buckets of clams, tasty fish and chips, and moderate prices. Or stop by just for the drinks and view of Commencement Bay.

Located on the Thea Foss Waterway with a view of the Museum of Glass, **《 Johnny's Dock** (1900 East D St., 253/383-4571, 10 A.M.–11 P.M. daily) has seen Tacoma through its downs and ups, serving classic seafood dishes to locals and visitors alike. It's a good place to pick up fish recipes, too—this is the home of the Johnny's Seasoning line of spices, which you can find at just about any grocery store around the nation.

If you want a sweeping Sound view, try the **Cliff House** (6300 Marine View Dr. at Browns Point, 253/927-0400 or 800/961-0401), upstairs 5–9:30 P.M. weekends, downstairs 11:30 A.M.–11 P.M. daily). The steak and seafood are very good, and the downstairs lounge offers the same view and a sandwich menu.

View the glittering lights of downtown Tacoma and the port from above I-5 at **《 Stanley and Seafort's** (115 E. 34th, 253/473-7300, stanleyandseaforts.com, 11–10 P.M. Mon.–Thurs., 4–11 P.M. Fri., 2–11 P.M. Sat., 2–10 P.M. Sun.). This is a true-blue Tacoma culinary institution, a no-brainer stop for locals on anniversaries, birthdays, and proms. It is one of those places where the meats, seafood, and desserts rarely if ever disappoint.

C. I. Shenanigan's (3017 Ruston Way, 253/752-8811, 11 A.M.–9 P.M. Mon.–Thurs., 11 A.M.–10 P.M. Fri.–Sat., 9:30 A.M.–9 P.M. Sun.) is a waterside restaurant stylistically inspired by old-timey canneries. Sit in a comfortable mahogany booth or take in the view from the deck seating. The crab and shrimp

Louie salad is but one of many house specials. Reservations certainly couldn't hurt.

The **Dash Point Lobster Shop** (6912 Soundview Dr. NE, 253/927-1513, www.lobstershop.com, 4:30–9 P.M. Sun.–Thurs., 4:30–10 P.M. Fri.–Sat.) sister to the **Lobster Shop South** (4015 Ruston Way, 206/759-2165, 11:30 A.M.–2:30 P.M. and 4:30–9:30 P.M. Mon.–Thurs., 11:30 A.M.–2:30 P.M. and 4:30–10:30 P.M. Fri., 4:30–10:30 P.M. Sat., 9:30 A.M.–1:30 P.M. and 4:30–9:30 P.M. Sun.) across the bay, is the original, simpler version, where you can't go wrong with the steaks, seafood, and even wine. There are great waterside views. Lobster Shop South is open for lunch and dinner, and also serves a substantial Sunday brunch. Definitely consider making reservations.

Asian

Throw a brick along 38th Avenue and chances are good it'll plunk down into a bowl of *pho* noodles. This is the epicenter of Tacoma's thriving Vietnamese community and is *the* place to go in the South Sound for fresh spring rolls, vermicelli noodle dishes, and, of course, *pho*. **Vien Dong Vietnamese** (3801 S. Yakima Ave., 253/472-6668, 9 A.M.–9 P.M. Mon.–Sat., 9 A.M.–8 P.M. Sun.) is all about delicious soups, hearty sandwiches, and great vegetables and tofu. Ambiance is a bit lacking, but don't let that scare you off.

Restaurants come and go, but for over a quarter century, **Fujiya Japanese Restaurant** (1125 Court C, 253/627-5319, 11 A.M.–2 P.M. Mon.–Fri. and 5–9 P.M. Mon.–Thurs., 5–9:30 P.M. Fri.–Sat., closed Sun.) has served up fresh sushi and creative rolls. The restaurant's founder gave up a career test-driving Honda sports cars in Japan to build up this Tacoma institution.

If you've just had a full day at Point Defiance and you've got to satisfy the little ones with Americanized Asian dishes, venture over to **Imperial Dragon** (6805 6th Ave., 253/565-5477, 11 A.M.–9:30 P.M. Sun.–Thurs., 11 A.M.–10:30 P.M. Fri.–Sat.), where you can find a compromise between traditional Chinese fare and kid-friendly sweet-and-sour dishes.

Italian

The Rock Wood Fired Pizza & Spirits (1920 Jefferson Ave., 253/272-1221, 11:30 A.M.–midnight Sun.–Thurs., 11:30 A.M.–1 A.M. Fri.–Sat.) is an individually owned Northwest pizza franchise serving up wood-fired pizzas and pasta and with attitude. Full of team spirit, the **Cloverleaf** (6430 6th Ave., 253/565-1111, 10 A.M.–midnight Sun.–Thurs., 10 A.M.–1 A.M. Fri.–Sat.) has tricked out an old warehouse to be a sort of miniature Safeco Field—the home of the Seattle Mariners. Order a pitcher of beer, a delicious steaming pie, and help cheer on the Mariners or Seahawks.

Ravenous Restaurant (785 Broadway, 253/572-6374, www.ravenoustacoma.com, 11:30 A.M.–2 P.M. Mon–Fri. and 5:30–9 P.M. Tues.–Sat.) is a little downtown bistro that makes flavorful Italian and Northwest cuisine. It's popular with the business-lunch crowd.

Mexican

The city's best Mexican entrées are served at **Moctezuma's** (4102 56th St., 253/474-5593, www.moctezumas.com, 11 A.M.–10 P.M. Sun.–Thurs., 11 A.M.–11 P.M. Fri.–Sat.). If the food is too spicy, cool down with their margaritas made with fresh-squeezed juice.

Pub Grub

The Swiss (1904 S. Jefferson, 253/572-2821, www.theswisspub.com, 11 A.M.–10 P.M. daily) is a friendly pub with 37 beers on tap, splendid Chihuly glass art, and surprisingly good sandwiches and pasta. The back room has pool and darts, plus live music on weekends.

Harmon Pub and Brewery (1938 Pacific Ave., 253/383-2739, harmonbrewingco.com, 11 A.M.–11 P.M. Mon.–Thurs., 11 A.M.–midnight Fri.–Sat., 11 A.M.–9 P.M. Sun.) is a big, bustling place with brewed-on-the-premises ales and porter, and a sound grasp of the classics like fish and chips, burgers, pizza, and pasta.

Located in a turn-of-the-20th-century firehouse, **Engine House No. 9** (611 N. Pine, 253/272-3435, www.ehouse9.com) pours nine fresh ales and features a pub menu of pizza, steaks, and salads.

Established in 1913, **Spar Tavern** (2121 N. 30th, 253/627-8215, 11 A.M.–midnight Mon.–Fri., 9 A.M.–midnight Sat.–Sun.) has great burgers, sandwiches, chili, and fishwiches. They'll even grill up a meatless garden burger for you. Don't show up with anyone under 21, though, or else it's no fishwich for you.

Katie Downs Tavern (3211 Ruston Way, 253/756-0771, www.katiedowns.com, 11 A.M.–2 A.M. daily) sits on a pier and attracts a good-sized jeans-and-sneakers crowd. Its modest selection of beer and wine is a good complement to deep-dish pizza and burgers. There's outdoor seating with a view during the summer. Its Washington Tavern License means 21 and older.

Markets and Bakeries

The **Tacoma Farmers Market** (253/272-7077, www.tacomafarmersmarket.com) now operates in three locations throughout Tacoma. The 6th Avenue Market has a sort of neighborhood feel with a handful of tented produce and goods vendors. It's held on Tuesdays from 3–7 P.M. May 3 through September 27. The Broadway Market is their first and still favorite market, full of performers, impromptu cooking classes, and the healthiest produce the region grows. It sets up shop on Thursdays 10:30 A.M. through 4 P.M., May 5 through October 27 at S. 9th Street and Broadway. For a lazy Sunday full of browsing fresh meats, veggies, and flowers, drop by S. 56th and Washington in south Tacoma 11 A.M.–3 P.M. Sundays June 5 to September 25.

INFORMATION AND SERVICES

For up-to-the-minute information on Tacoma and the surrounding area, head to **Tacoma-Pierce County Convention and Visitor Bureau** (1516 Pacific Ave. inside the Courtyard by Marriott, 253/284-3254 or 800/272-2662, www.traveltacoma.com, 8:30 A.M.–5 P.M. Mon.–Fri. year-round).

The main **Tacoma Public Library** (1102 Tacoma Ave. S, 253/591-5666, www.tpl.lib.wa.us) features an amazing stained-glass dome ceiling upstairs in the Northwest Room.

Wireless Internet access is provided free, even for noncardholders.

GETTING THERE AND AROUND
By Bus

Pierce Transit (253/581-8000 or 800/562-8109, www.piercetransit.org) has daily service to Puyallup, Gig Harbor, Lakewood, Steilacoom, Spanaway, Fife, Buckley, and every other town in Pierce country, along with commuter service to Seattle and Olympia. The bus station is located at 1319 Pacific Avenue. The **Tacoma Link** (www.soundtransit.org) is a light-rail service that connects downtown with the transit hub at the Tacoma Dome Station. The trains run every 10 minutes, Monday through Saturday, and every 10–20 minutes on Sunday. Even load your bike on if you choose. Some busses and trains offer free wireless while you ride.

Greyhound (253/383-4621 or 800/231-2222, www.greyhound.com) runs service along the I-5 corridor, connecting Tacoma with Portland, Seattle, and Vancouver. **Northwestern Trailways** (800/366-6975, www.northwesterntrailways.com) runs daily bus service between Tacoma, Seattle and Everett.

By Train

Amtrak (800/872-7245, www.amtrak.com) serves Tacoma from its passenger station at 1001 Puyallup Ave., between the tide flat area and I-5 in the eastern part of the city. The *Coast Starlight* train provides four-times-a-day service to the Puget Sound area from Portland, San Francisco, and Los Angeles.

By Ferry

The **Washington State Ferry** (425/355-7308, 888/808-7977, or 800/843-3779 for automated information, www.wsdot.wa.gov/ferries system) is an everyday method of transportation for hundreds of residents of the Puget Sound region. From Tacoma, however, it can only get you to Tahlequah on Vashon Island. Ferries depart from Point Defiance; summer fares are $4.55 round-trip for passengers and walk-ons, $19.45 round-trip for car and driver. Fares are collected only on the way to Vashon, not when you return.

Seattle-Tacoma International Airport

If you're flying into Tacoma, you'll arrive at the Seattle-Tacoma International Airport (better known as Sea-Tac). As the name suggests, it's about halfway between Seattle and Tacoma. **Capital Aeroporter** (800/962-3579, www .capair.com) offers door-to-airport service to Tacoma.

Kitsap Peninsula

The Kitsap Peninsula is an appendage to the Olympic Peninsula; in fact, visitors and locals alike sometimes confuse the two, thinking that anything west of Seattle must be the Olympic Peninsula. Not true: the Kitsap is separated from the Olympic Peninsula by Hood Canal.

The Kitsap is readily accessible by ferry from Seattle and Edmonds, and by the Tacoma Narrows Bridge from Tacoma. Its many back roads are favorite cycling destinations. Bainbridge Island is especially popular because of the easy access, diverse country, lack of traffic, and abundance of cafés and B&Bs. For a helpful map of recommended bike routes—plus all sorts of other local information—contact the **Kitsap Peninsula Visitor & Convention Bureau** (9481 Silverdale Way NW, 360/297-8200 or 800/337-0580 www.visitkitsap.com).

BREMERTON

The city of Bremerton—the largest settlement on Kitsap Peninsula—offers sweeping views of both the Cascades and the Olympics. It is dominated by a U.S. Navy base and the Puget Sound Naval Shipyard, both of which, of course, lend a sort of blue-collar (complete with shiny insignia) feel. The city is in the middle of various projects meant to revitalize the downtown area. There have been many setbacks including recession, fires, strikes, and conflicts with the Suquamish Indian tribe, but city leaders continue to work toward their goal of revitalization. The city has some interesting sights, including famous, tourable battleships and a naval museum, as well as good restaurants and inexpensive lodging.

Sights

The destroyer **USS Turner Joy,** hull number DD-951, was one of the chief players in the 1964 Gulf of Tonkin Incident that led to the escalation of the Vietnam War. The destroyer was decommissioned in 1982 and opened to the public in 1992 for self-guided tours. If you haven't been aboard a Navy ship before, a tour of the USS *Turner Joy* (300 Washington Beach Ave., 360/792-2457, www.ussturner joy.org, 10 A.M.–5 P.M. daily May 1–the third Sunday of Sept., 10 A.M.–4 P.M. Wed.–Sun. Oct.–mid-May, $12 adults, $10 seniors, $7 ages 5–12, free for active-duty military) will be an education, with its tight sleeping quarters and an impressive array of weaponry. They do a spooky "Haunted Ship" program at the end of October. Closed-toe shoes are a must and strollers are a no-go.

A number of other decommissioned (or "mothballed") Navy ships, including several

ANCHORS AWEIGH

When the U.S. Navy was looking to build the **Puget Sound Naval Shipyard** in 1891, Bremerton's deep harbor clinched the deal. Today the facility is where aging ships and submarines are overhauled or deactivated, with the large collection of floating relics of the "mothball fleet" visible from the waterfront. Over 9,000 civilians and 10,000 military personnel work here, making it one of the largest employers in the entire state.

SOUTH PUGET SOUND

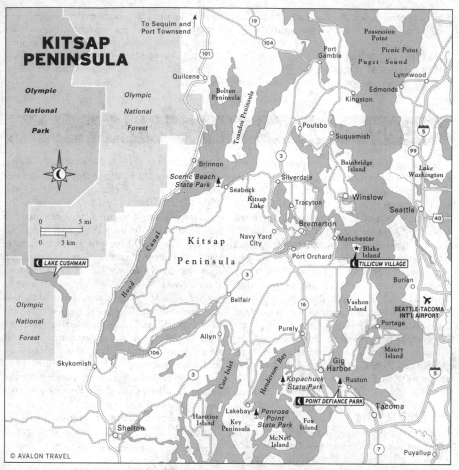

KITSAP
PENINSULA

To Sequim and
Port Townsend

Olympic

National

Park

Olympic

National

Forest

Quilcene

Bolton
Peninsula

Toandos Peninsula

Brinnon

Scenic Beach
State Park

Seabeck

Kitsap
Lake

Hood Canal

Kitsap

Peninsula

LAKE CUSHMAN

Olympic

National

Forest

Skykomish

Belfair

Allyn

Shelton

Harstine
Island

Lakebay

Key
Peninsula

Penrose
Point
State Park

McNeil
Island

Possession
Point

Port
Gamble

Picnic Point

Puget Sound

Lynnwood

Edmonds

Kingston

Poulsbo

Suquamish

Bainbridge
Island

Lake
Washington

Silverdale

Tracyton

Winslow

Seattle

Bremerton

Navy Yard
City

Manchester

Blake
Island

Port Orchard

TILLICUM VILLAGE

Burien

Vashon
Island

SEATTLE-TACOMA
INT'L AIRPORT

Purely

Portage

Maury
Island

Gig
Harbor

Ruston

Kopachuck
State Park

POINT DEFIANCE PARK

Tacoma

Fox
Island

Puyallup

0   5 mi

0   5 km

© AVALON TRAVEL

old carriers, frigates, and subs, sit at anchor awaiting sale or the scrapheap. They aren't open to the public, but **Kitsap Harbor Tours** (360/876-1260,) offers chartered boat tours for groups that will cruise around the ships.

Naval history buffs will also enjoy the excellent **Puget Sound Navy Museum** (251 1st St., 360/479-7447, 10 A.M.–4 P.M. Mon.–Sat., donations accepted), which allows visitors to tour the USS *John C. Stennis,* moored out back. Permanent exhibits teach about submarine warfare and ship building, while numerous touring exhibits help interpret local and global Naval operations.

Entertainment and Events

THE ARTS

The **Bremerton Symphony Orchestra** (360/373-1722, bremertonsymphony.wordpress.com) performs ambitious concerts throughout October–May in the Bremerton High School Performing Arts Center. **Bremerton Community Theatre** (599 Lebo Blvd., 360/373-5152, www.bremertoncommunitytheatre.org) produces comedy, drama, and musical theater performances for and by the local community. Free **Concerts on the Boardwalk** entertain listeners with rock 'n' roll classics, one of many talented Navy bands, folk, country, or bluegrass Friday evenings mid-July–mid-August.

Art has a home in Bremerton at **Collective Visions** (331 Pacific Ave., 360/377-8327, www.collectivevisions.com 10 A.M.–5 P.M. Tues.–Sat.), a bright and inviting gallery exhibiting practically all media including digital. The namesake of **Amy Burnett Gallery** (402 Pacific Ave., 360/373-3187, 10 A.M.–5 P.M. Wed.–Sat.www.amyburnettgallery.com) is a prolific artist, columnist, and radio host. She also curates the on-site Pyrex Museum.

FESTIVALS AND EVENTS

The third weekend of May brings an **Armed Forces Festival and Parade** (360/479-3579), featuring pancake breakfasts, golf tournaments, and a parade that usually draws some seriously top brass. In late August the **Kitsap County Fair and Stampede** (360/692-3655) comes to the Kitsap County Fairgrounds five miles north of Bremerton. Highlighted by a (Professional Rodeo Cowboys Association (PRCA) rodeo, the fair also includes a carnival, circus, and other entertainment. Join the Labor Day Weekend party at the **Blackberry Festival** (www.black berryfestival.org) on the boardwalk, with arts and crafts, food, music, a classic car show, and fun run. There's blackberry wine, scones, pie, soda, syrup, preserves, and shortcake. You're bound to walk away with seeds in your teeth.

Sports and Recreation

Three miles northeast of downtown Bremerton on Highway 306, **Illahee State Park** (3540 NE Bahia Vista Dr., 360/478-6460, www .parks.wa.gov) has campsites on 75 acres, with swimming beaches, a short but steep hiking trail, a boat launch, and a pier for fishing and lolling in the sun. Illahee State Park also has camping ($21 tents, $31 RV hookups) and showers year-round. Campers can also find showers at the Bremerton marina.

Hikers will enjoy the two-mile trek to the summit of 1,700-foot **Green Mountain** for spectacular views of Kitsap Peninsula, Puget Sound, and the Seattle skyline. From

downtown, take Seabeck Highway Northwest for two miles, turn left (west) on Holly Road, then take a left onto Tahuyeh Road for 1.25 miles to Gold Creek Road. Turn left onto Gold Creek and follow it for 1.5 miles to the trailhead on the left, before Gold Creek Bridge. Be sure to wear proper footwear since the trail is rocky and often wet.

Swim at **Wildcat Lake** (9205 Holly Rd. NW), where a seasonal lifeguard is on duty. Bathhouses, picnic areas, and a playground are provided for your enjoyment.

Accommodations

Bremerton has low-cost motels in spades, but do your homework ahead of time, as some of these places can be a little sketchy.

No need for worries at the **Flagship Inn** (4320 Kitsap Way, 360/479-6566 or 800/447-9396, www.flagship-inn.com, $69 s, $75–85 d), though. This place is a nice waterfront motel with gorgeous views and patios to enjoy them. Rooms are updated and clean and there's a heated outdoor pool on premises. As an added bonus, continental breakfast is served each morning.

You'll enjoy easy ferry access and modern rooms at **Hampton Inn and Suites** (150 Washington Ave., 360/405-0200, www.hamp toninn.com, $124–169 d), just about the nicest hotel in town. The marina-front hotel offers comfy beds and sparkling clean facilities that include a fitness center with an indoor lap pool, business center with free printing, wireless Internet, and valet parking.

Situated on a six-acre wooded site along Puget Sound, **Illahee Manor B&B** (6680 Illahee Rd. NE, 360/698-7555 or 800/693-6680, www.illaheemanorbandb.com, $130–220 d) offers the coziest stay in Bremerton. The six suites have private baths, most with fireplaces and whirlpool baths. The eclectically furnished and comfortable house was built in 1929. A full breakfast is served, and families can stay in the beach house.

Food

Get fresh seafood, steaks, pasta, salads, with a

great local wine list over the water at the **Boat Shed** (101 Shore Dr., 360/377-2600, www.the boatshedrestaurant.com, 11 A.M.–9 P.M. daily).

Enjoy gourmet french fries served up Belgian-style in little paper cones and with creative dipping sauces at **Fritz European Fry House** (94 Washington Ave., 360/479-1088, www.fritzfryhouse.com, 11 A.M.–10 P.M. Mon.–Thurs., 11 A.M.–11 P.M. Fri.–Sat., 10–8 P.M. Sun.), which also serves a nice selection of imported beers.

The best Italian food served this side of the Sound is masterfully plated at **La Fermata** (2204 E 11th St., 360/373-5927, 5–10 P.M. Tues.–Sat.), a romantic restaurant that specializes in Northern Italian dishes.

Enjoy a cup of joe and a breakfast burrito in the morning or a pop and a sandwich later in the day at the psychedelic **Hi-Lo's 15th St. Café** (2720 15th St., 360/373-7833, www .hilos15thstreetcafe.com, 7 A.M.–3 P.M. daily), a hippie-dippy place that has put together a consciousness-raising collection of hundreds of old Thermoses and lunch pails. It's sure to take several generations of diners back to their childhoods, if only for a moment.

Information and Services
The folks at the **Bremerton Area Chamber of Commerce** (286 4th St., 360/479-3579, 9 A.M.–5 P.M. Mon.–Fri. year-round, www .bremertonchamber.org) can answer most of your questions. They also have an information booth next to the ferry terminal.

Getting There and Around
From the Seattle waterfront you can take a 60-minute trip to Bremerton on the **Washington State Ferries** (360/842-2345, 888/808-7977, or 800/843-3779 for automated information, www.wsdot.wa.gov/ferries, one-way $7.10 extra passengers and walk-on, $6.25–15.20 car and driver, $6.65 motorcycle and driver, $1 extra bikes). Ferries depart about every 70 minutes for Bremerton. A passenger-only ferry (same rates) sails from Seattle five times a day and makes the run in 50 minutes. You'll probably end up paying $4–8 if you want to park

anywhere near downtown because so many folks from the Kitsap Peninsula park here and ride the ferry to Seattle.

Kitsap Transit Foot Ferry (360/373-2877, www.kitsaptransit.org, $1.50 one-way) also offers 10-minute ferry rides across the Sinclair Inlet between Bremerton and Port Orchard for foot traffic and bikes only. It's a seven-mile drive around the head of Sinclair Inlet to Port Orchard if you drive there instead. It also has daily bus service throughout the peninsula and meets all state ferries. All buses have bike racks.

Bremerton-Kitsap Airporter (360/876-1737 or 800/562-7948, www.kitsapairporter.com) offers shuttle buses to Sea-Tac Airport for just under $20.

PORT ORCHARD
Across the Sinclair Inlet from Bremerton, Port Orchard—the Kitsap County seat—has two distinctly different sides. The waterfront section is loaded with personality and faces the marina with covered walkways, colorful murals, antique shops, and cozy cafés. This contrasts sharply with the more generic, strictly functional section of chain stores and restaurants. Port Orchard still keeps a small fishing fleet, and boat sheds fill the harbor, but it is primarily a bedroom community for Seattle and Tacoma, and for Bremerton military workers.

Port Orchard was named after Orchard Bay, which the city overlooks. The town was founded in 1886 and became the county seat seven years later. It gradually shifted from being a sawmill town, to operating a major industrial pottery works, to supporting the naval shipyard, to its current status as a residential and tourist town.

Sights
From downtown, head two blocks uphill on Sidney Avenue to the **Sidney Art Gallery and Museum** (202 Sidney Ave., 360/876-3693, www.sidneymuseumandarts, 11 A.M.–4 P.M. Tues.–Sat., 1–4 P.M. Sun.), which combines regional fine art with displays and artifacts from Port Orchard's history.

Entertainment and Events

Port Orchard's most peculiar event is the **Seagull Calling Festival,** held on the Memorial Day weekend. Contestants in goofy costumes compete to see who can call in the most gulls. Participants are allowed to use breadcrumbs as their secret weapons. The weekend is jam-packed with pirate events, too. There is a murder-mystery weekend full of pirate flair, and a pirate dinghy race in which inventive scurvy dogs build wheeled "dinghies" out of recycled material and race them downhill. Food, demonstrations, and appalling sea-shanties round out the fun. The **Fathoms O' Fun Festival by the Sea** is Port Orchard's premier summer festival and one of the state's oldest, held from the last Saturday in June through the 4th of July. Highlights include a big parade, frog jump and snake races, and lots of food from local restaurants. **The Cruz,** on the first Sunday of August, invites more than 1,000 classic-car owners to show off their hot rods, museum pieces, or personality-rich jalopies. Don't try to fight the traffic—you definitely want to take a bus or ferry for this one.

Shopping

"Cute" is the operative term at Port Orchard's many antique, craft, and gift shops, which generally cater to an audience that appreciates lots of lace, chintz, and cinnamon-sweet smells. The first thing you'll notice about the **Victorian Rose Tea Room** (1130 Bethel Ave., 360/876-5695, 9 A.M.–5 P.M. Mon.–Fri., 8 A.M.–4 P.M. Sat.–Sun.) is that it's very pink. Very, very pink. Alongside the tearoom, you'll find a one-stop-shop for Alexander and Iacona dolls and Jim Shore collectables. Fans of kitschy old stuff should swing by the largest antique emporium in town, the **Olde Central Antique Mall** (801 Bay St., 360/895-1902, 10 A.M.–5:30 P.M. Mon.–Sat., 11 A.M.–5 P.M. Sun.); dozens of vendors are primed and ready to take you down memory lane.

Sports and Recreation

Follow Beach Drive from Port Orchard for a scenic approach to **Manchester State Park** (360/871-4065 or 888/226-7688, www.parks .wa.gov), six miles away at the entrance to Sinclair Inlet. The park's 111 acres include campsites ($21 tents, $31 RV hookups, $6.50 extra reservation fee), hiking, and interpretive trails, plus swimming, fishing, and scuba diving in Rich Passage. The main attractions here are various century-old military structures, built to protect the Bremerton Naval Shipyard from attack. These include a control center where underwater mines could be triggered remotely should enemy warships intrude on the inlet. The park is open from late April–early September.

The 200-acre **South Kitsap Community Park** (3200 SE Lund Ave.), two miles southwest of downtown, has hiking trails and a picnic area. A group of scale outdoor railroad buffs operate a 7.5-inch gauge train and offer free rides behind their functional mini–steam locomotives on a donation basis, 11 A.M.–4 P.M. daily June–mid-September). Swim or boat at **Long Lake County Park** (Lake Valley Rd. SE), approximately four miles south of Port Orchard.

If you're aiming to spend a day on the links while in the area, **Horseshoe Lake Golf Course** (15932 Sidney Rd. SW, 360/857-3326, hlgolf.com, $39–42) is a thinking-man's course with hardly a level patch of ground and cleverly designed doglegs. The BBQ restaurant at the 19th hole is so sticky, you might want to keep your glove on. For as much serenity as you can muster while struggling with that slice, play **McCormick Woods Golf Course** (5155 McCormick Woods Dr. SW, 360/895-0130, www.mccormickwoodsgolf.com, $45–59). One of the most beautiful courses in the Northwest, McCormick Woods was designed with constant input from the Audubon Society. No two holes border each other so it's easy enough to stay mellow among the firs and peaceful lakes, as long as you don't hit into them.

Accommodations

There are more hotel options in Bremerton, but Port Orchard does offer some decent hotel rooms at the **Comfort Inn** (1121 Bay St., 360/895-2666 or 800/465-4329, $89–119 d) that include microwaves and mini-fridges. The more expensive ones even come with whirlpool tubs. The property has an outdoor spa and an extensive continental breakfast that includes make-your-own waffles.

Another lovely option for the budget-minded traveler is **Reflections B&B** (3878 Reflection Ln. E, 360/871-5582, $65–110 d), a large two-story colonial-style home with four guest rooms, a hot tub, and gazebo. Rooms offer views of Port Orchard Passage, and a full breakfast is served. Couples will enjoy the silence—no kids are allowed at this place.

Families touring with older kids can check into **Little Clam Bay Bed and Breakfast** (7801 E Jessica Way, 360/871-0619, www.littleclambay.com, $160 d), a private little cottage only about a mile away from Manchester State Park. The second bedroom with twin beds is rented out for only $35 more per person and kids over 12 are welcome. The master bedroom has a large tub meant for two and there's a fireplace in the living room, plus a deck looking out over Little Clam Bay. On top of breakfast, the innkeepers serve late evening snacks each day.

Food

Right in front of the ferry dock, **Amy's on the Bay** (100 Harrison Ave., 360/876-1445, www.amysonthebay.com, 11 A.M.–10 P.M. daily) whips up great, super-fresh seafood. They also pour local wines and microbrews to wash down your meal.

For fresh tortillas and big plates of beans and rice, visit the popular **Puerto Vallarta** (1599 SE Lund Ave., Bethel Rd. and Lund Ave., 360/876-0788, 11 A.M.–10 P.M. Mon.–Thurs., 11 A.M.–11 P.M. Fri.–Sat., 10 A.M.–11 P.M. Sun.), serving up Mexican favorites.

Bay Street Ale House (807 Bay St., 360/876-8030, baystreetalehouse.com, 3–11 P.M. Tues.–Thurs., 3 P.M.–midnight Fri.–Sat., 3–10 P.M. Sun.) has a handful of microbrews on tap, distinctive pizzas, sandwiches, and other pub-type meals.

The **Port Orchard Farmers Market** (253/857-2657, pofarmersmarket.org) takes place behind Peninsula Feed Store on Bay Street 9 A.M.–3 P.M. Saturday May–October. This is one of the largest markets in the state

and features more than 100 vendors offering homegrown fruits and veggies, homemade crafts, and chainsaw art.

Information

Get information at **Kitsap Peninsula Visitor and Convention Bureau** (9841 Silverdale Way NW, 800/337-0580, visitkitsap.com, 10 A.M.–5 P.M. Mon.–Fri., 10 A.M.–2 P.M. Sat.).

Getting There and Around

Catch the **Washington State Ferry** (360/842-2345, 888/808-7977, or 800/843-3779 for automated information, www.wsdot.wa.gov/ferries, $19.45 one-way car and driver, $8.45 motorcycle and driver, $4.55 extra passengers and walk-ons, $1 extra bikes) from the Fauntleroy dock in West Seattle for the 35-minute ride to Southworth on the southeast side of the Kitsap Peninsula near Port Orchard. You can also catch a ferry from Southworth to Vashon Island every 90 minutes (one-way from Southworth $19.45 car and driver, $8.45 motorcycle and driver, $4.55 extra passengers and walk-ons, $1 extra bikes, one-way from Vashon free).

Kitsap Transit Foot Ferry (360/373-2877, $2 one-way) offers a 10-minute ferry ride across the Sinclair Inlet between Bremerton and Port Orchard for folks on foot or with a bicylcle. Should you choose to go by car instead, it's a seven-mile drive around the head of Sinclair Inlet to Bremerton.

Kitsap Transit (360/373-2877, www.kitsap transit.org, $2 one-way) provides daily bus service throughout the Kitsap Peninsula and Bainbridge Island and meets all Southworth ferries. **Bremerton-Kitsap Airporter** (360/876-1737, www.kitsapairporter.com) runs shuttle buses to Sea-Tac Airport every hour or so. Rates start at $16.

SEABECK

The small town of Seabeck occupies a point of land west of Silverdale on the east shore of Hood Canal, with dramatic panoramic views of the Olympic Mountains. It has a marina and a few restaurants and grocers, and it is a favorite of anglers. The oldest outdoor theater in the Northwest, **Kitsap Forest Theater** (206/542-7815, www.foresttheater.com) holds productions near Seabeck late May through June. The amphitheater's terraced log seats are beautifully backdropped by rhododendrons, Douglas firs, and hemlocks. In 1909, convenient parking wasn't the founder's highest priority, so be ready for the 0.3-mile hike from your car to the theater.

Scenic Beach State Park

Scenic Beach State Park has forested campsites (360/830-5079 or 888/226-7688, www.parks.wa.gov, $22 tent, $31 full-utility pull-through sites, $7 extra reservation fee), salmon fishing, oyster gathering in season, and Olympic Mountain views on Hood Canal. The 88-acre park becomes a waterfront wonderland when the spring rhododendrons are in bloom. The park is open for day use year-round, but the campground is only open from late April–late September. The restrooms and a handful of trails are Americans with Disabilities Act (ADA)–compliant.

Accommodations

Once the private residence of Col. Julian Willcox and built in 1936, the 10,000-square-foot waterfront **Willcox House Country Inn** (2390 Tekiu Rd. NW, 360/830-4492 or 800/725-9477, www.willcoxhouse.com, $199–259 d, no kids), on the Hood Canal south of Seabeck, was described as "the grand entertainment capital of the Canal region." Every room is angled to capture a water view, and the house is filled with marble and copper fireplaces and luxurious period furnishings. Outdoors, a 300-foot pier can accommodate guests' boats and float planes. Clark Gable once stayed in the room that now bears his name.

POULSBO

The quaint town of Poulsbo occupies the head of Liberty Bay and could pass for a tourist village on the coast of Maine. The main street is crowded with antique shops, cafés, galleries, high-quality craft boutiques, a chocolate shop, and a wonderful quilt shop. Sailboats bob in the busy marina just a few feet away, and old-fashioned lamps brighten the evening sky. Locals jokingly call the town "Viking Junction," and it doesn't take much to see that Poulsbo loves to play up its Norwegian heritage.

Many downtown buildings have Scandinavian decor and sell Norse Viking collectables and *tørrfisk*. The **Sons of Norway Hall** dominates Front Street downtown. People need to eat, however, and RV megadealers, real estate offices, and chain restaurants have moved in up the hill, sort of breaking the Norwegian spell but offering travelers some familiar conveniences.

Sights

Get friendly with sea cucumbers, starfish, sea anemones, and barnacles in the saltwater touchtank or watch a jellyfish flotilla at the fascinating **Marine Science Center** (18743 Front St. NE, 360/598-4460, www.poulsbomsc.org, 11 A.M.–4 P.M. daily, donations). View a huge gray whale skeleton and find out lots of information about Puget Sound sea creatures and the problems facing the ocean.

Stroll down the 600-foot shoreside boardwalk that connects **Liberty Bay Park** to the small arboretum at **American Legion Park.** Both parks have picnic areas, restrooms, and water access. Head uphill to the corner of 4th Avenue and Lincoln Road for the **Fordefjord Lutheran Church,** built in 1908.

Located about 15 minutes south of Poulsbo in Keyport, the home to the top-secret Naval Undersea Warfare Center, the **Naval Undersea Museum** (610 Dowell St., 360/396-4148, 10 A.M.–4 P.M. daily June–Sept., 10 A.M.–4 P.M. Wed.–Mon. Oct.–May, free) offers a less-secretive look at the world of undersea warfare. One of the most fascinating museums in Washington, it houses exhibits on the history of undersea warfare and exploration, from scale models of Navy subs to underwater archaeology to mines. A large globe details the mountainous floor beneath the oceans. Some of the most interesting items are the torpedoes—including such oddities as a 19th-century wind-up torpedo and a World War II Japanese version with space for a kamikaze human driver—plus a half-scale model of an undersea rescue vehicle that appeared in the movie *The Hunt for Red October*. Out front is the blimp-like Trieste II, which reached the bottom of the Marianas Trench—the deepest point on earth—in 1960.

Entertainment and Events

The Suquamish Tribe's **Clearwater Casino Resort** (1537 Suquamish Way NE in Suquamish, 360/598-8700) is a fun, cozy casino perfect for spending a little time inside. It stages frequent blackjack and poker tournaments for the supercompetitive and slots (some of which still take cash instead of tickets), craps, roulette and Pai Gow for challenging the house mano-a-mano. The Event Lawn is the site of occasional concerts and there is a dance club that opens its doors on Thursdays.

Poulsbo's calendar is packed with events celebrating the town's Scandinavian roots. The **Viking Fest** in mid-May celebrates Poulsbo's Norwegian heritage with a parade, arts and crafts show, and pancake breakfast. And, if you have a stomach of steel and a tongue tough as tarpaper, enter the lutefisk-eating contest. If lye-soaked whitefish isn't your thing, they've got burgers, too. On the third Saturday of October, the First Lutheran Church puts on a **Traditional Lutefisk Dinner,** with Norwegian meatballs and potatoes for those with less-hardy stomachs.

Sports and Recreation

SEA KAYAKING

Poulsbo's **Olympic Outdoor Center** (32379 Rainier Ave. in Port Gamble, 360/297-4659, www.olympicoutdoorcenter.com) is a great place to learn sea kayaking and white-water kayaking. Classes include the basics, special classes for kids, kayak rescue courses and roll clinics, and a comprehensive four-day sea kayak courses. The center also leads sea kayak trips and sells and rents kayaks if you want to head out on your own.

FISHING

Few areas of Washington offer such a diversity of fishing options. Take freshwater trout on the fly or battle salmon in the bay. Commercial fishing helped build the city and the thrill of the chase is still in the civic bloodstream. **Peninsula Outfitters** (19740 7th Ave., Suite E, 360/394-1599, www.peninsulaoutfitters.com) is passionate about fly fishing and will teach you as much as you are willing to learn. The full shop also offers regularly scheduled classes and once you have the confidence, they'll take you on a guided trip to pursue trout, lingcod, seabass, cutthroat trout, or just about anything with two fins and a tail. If you already know what you're doing, Owen Dam is a favorite place to take trout or sucker on a fly, spinning or baitcasting.

Accommodations

Be sure to make reservations well ahead for summer weekends. Like much of Western Washington, it is not unheard of for rooms in the area to be booked up a full year in advance.

The family-friendly property at **Poulsbo Inn** (18680 Hwy. 305, 360/779-3921 or 800/597-5151, www.poulsboinn.com, $99–125 d) includes an outdoor pool, hot tub, and playground. There's also a fitness center and free high-speed Internet. Not only does this property offer complimentary continental breakfast each day, it also serves soup in the winter Tuesday–Thursday. Rooms are tastefully decorated and up-to-date.

Farther away is **Foxbridge B&B** (30680 Hwy. 3 NE, 360/697-4875, www.foxbridge.com, $115 d, no kids), located a half mile from the Hood Canal floating bridge. This two-story home sits on five wooded acres with a panoramic view. Several rooms come with private baths, and a decadent three-course breakfast is served each morning. There is also a complimentary bike available for light use. At the time of this writing, it is closed for remodeling and plans on opening at the end of 2012.

Two miles away from downtown, the one-bedroom **Liberty Place Guest House** (360/779-4943, www.libertybayguesthouse.com, $125 d) overlooks Liberty Bay and affords guests quiet privacy, a sleeper-sofa in addition to the queen-sided bed, and a full kitchen and a deck to boot.

CAMPING

Enjoy the wide-open grassy lawns and quarter of a mile of shoreline at **Kitsap Memorial State Park** (360/779-3205, www.parks.wa.gov, $21 tents, $31 RV water/electric and dump privileges), about six miles north of downtown on Highway 3. There are ample picnic facilities, including rentable shelters with electricity and fire pits, as well as showers on-site.

A couple miles south of town, **Eagle Tree RV Park** (16280 Hwy. 305 NE, 360/598-5988, www.eagletreerv.com, $32 full hookups) offers RV owners another good option when the state park's sites fill up.

Food

Despite its small size, Poulsbo has one of the best collections of restaurants on the Kitsap Peninsula. **Poulsbohemian Coffeehouse** (19003 Front St., 360/779-9199, poulsbohemian.com, 7 A.M.–5 P.M. Mon.–Fri., 8 A.M.–5 P.M. Sat.–Sun.) is a friendly and funky gathering place, with giant chocolate chip cookies, cozy couches, local art, and frequent events like an ongoing fiction writer's workshop and movie discussion group.

Get delicious sandwiches and pastries at **Liberty Bay Bakery and Café** (18996 Front St. NE, 360/779-2828, 6 A.M.–3 P.M. Tues.–Sat., 8 A.M.–2 P.M. Sun., http://libertybay bakerycafe.bzlnk.com).

The first contemporary American multigrain "Ezekiel 4:9" style bread was baked up at **Sluys Poulsbo Bakery** (18924 Front St. NE, 360/697-2253, 4:30 A.M.–6:30 P.M. Mon.–Thurs. & Sun., 4:30 A.M.–7:30 P.M. Fri.–Sat.). Now known as Poulsbo bread, it is available worldwide under a variety of brands. The Sluys still has excellent pastries, Norwegian lefse, and coarse-grained European breads.

That's-a-Some Italian Ristorante (18881 Front St. NE, 360/779-2266, 11:30 A.M.–8:30 P.M. Mon.–Thurs., 11:30 A.M.–9:30 P.M. Fri.–Sat., 11:30 A.M.–8:30 P.M. Sun.) has the traditional red-checked tablecloths, but the Italian food and pizzas have West Coast influences, including an Anaheim chili penne.

Casa Luna (18830 Front St. NE, 360/779-7676, 11 A.M.–9 P.M. daily) is one of the more distinctive Mexican restaurants in the Puget Sound area. The ingredients are fresh and high-quality, packed with flavor and made to order in the open kitchen.

Arawan Thai Cuisine (225 Lindvig Way, 360/779-4888, Lunch 11:20 A.M.–2 P.M. Tues.–Fri., dinner 5–9:30 P.M. nightly) is just north of town in the basement of a small shopping mall, but the food is authentic and exceptional.

Molly Ward Gardens (27462 Big Valley Rd., 360/779-4471, www.mollywardgardens .com, 11 A.M.–2 P.M. and 6–9 P.M. Wed.–Sat., 10:30 A.M.–1:30 P.M. and 6–9 P.M. Sun., closed Mon.–Tues.) is Poulsbo's place to splurge on a great lunch or dinner. The menu emphasizes Northwest seafood, along with fresh salads and herbs from its beautiful gardens. This elegant restaurant serves only wild-caught fish, buys (or grows) organic ingredients, and even has their very own compost heap on site. The menu changes seasonally.

Information and Services

For information, visit the **Greater Poulsbo Chamber of Commerce** (19131 8th Ave. NE, 360/779-4848, www.kitsapedc.org, 9 A.M.–5 P.M. Mon.–Fri.). Drop by Poulsbohemian Coffeehouse to pick up a brochure detailing a walking tour of Poulsbo's historic buildings.

Getting There and Around

Kitsap Transit (360/377-2877 or 800/501-7433, www.kitsaptransit.org) provides daily bus service around the peninsula. **Bremerton-Kitsap Airporter** (360/876-1737 or 800/562-7948, www.kitsapairporter.com) offers shuttle buses to Sea-Tac Airport.

GIG HARBOR

Just across the Narrows Bridge from Tacoma, Gig Harbor is one of the most scenic little towns on Puget Sound. The picturesque village and its namesake harbor is postcard-perfect, with hundreds of sailing and fishing boats, tall pine trees, and a circle of seaside houses, all set against the backdrop of Mount Rainier.

SOUTH PUGET SOUND

If there ever was a town with the sea in its veins, it's Gig Harbor. The sheltered harbor provided the perfect locale for boatbuilding, an industry that over a century and a half turned out hundreds of purse seiners, gillnetters, tenders, and yachts. Today, those protected waters still provide safe harbor for hundreds of commercial fishing and pleasure craft.

But you won't need sea legs to enjoy the town. On land, there are plenty of upscale shops, galleries, good restaurants, and at least one tavern that will pour a pint for salty dogs and landlubbers alike.

Sights

HARBOR HISTORY MUSEUM

The Harbor History Museum (4121 Harborview Dr., 253/858-6722, www.harbor historymuseum.org, 10 A.M.–4 P.M. Tues.–Sat.) at the downtown waterfront offers exhibits that display and interpret antique ships and boats as well as a smattering of American Indian artifacts.

KOPACHUCK STATE PARK

You'd never expect so much solitude so close to a major city. Just 12 miles northwest of Tacoma off Highway 16 and seven miles northwest of Gig Harbor (follow the signs), Kopachuck (253/265-3606, www.parks.wa.gov, tents $17) has a campground (no RV hookups) and picnic areas. This 103-acre park is shaded by tall pines and has a beach for swimming, clamming, and fishing. It is one of Puget Sound's most beautiful parks, and even includes the small (5.5 acres) Cutts Island, a marine park only a short distance offshore with mooring buoys. Scuba divers come here to explore an underwater park with a sunken barge. Kopachuck's campground is open from late April–early October. Make reservations ($6.50 extra) at 888/226-7688 or www.parks.wa.gov.

Entertainment and Events

Gig Harbor's **Paradise Theater** (253/851-7529) stages musicals and plays throughout the year, often offering at least one night of dinner theater per show. In the summer, they often use an airy amphitheater as a special treat for the audience.

The **Tides Tavern** (2925 Harborview Dr., 253/858-3982) is a hoary old Gig Harbor institution that makes clam chowder and chili that will cut the chill of the most wicked winter rain. And if those don't work, a few pints of their house ale should do the trick. Spring and summer complement those classics with local music.

Gig Harbor's event of the year is June's **Maritime Gig Festival** (253/851-6865), a dock-side blowout. In one of the most cherished events, commercial fishing boats circle up while a priest from St. Nicholas Catholic Church passes in a motorboat, blessing the fleet. Stunning old wooden yachts and classic cars are everywhere, as are food booths, pirates, music stages, and fun activities for young scallywags. The **Gig Harbor Art Festival** (www .peninsulaartleague.com) on the third weekend in July gives local artists a chance to display their work among wandering magicians and drum circles. Plein air artists are invited to show their stuff as well. One of the most festive eco-events in Western Washington is October's **Donkey Creek Chum Festival** (253/853-7609) which, despite the improbable name, is a more improbable-seeming alliance between environmental groups and commercial fishermen. The festival is time for the Gig Harbor Commercial Fisherman's club to release the one million-plus salmon fry they've been incubating over the course of the year. Kayak races, a roaming costumed salmon mascot, and the unforgettable Chum Burgers make your trip to Donkey Creek Park well worth it.

Shopping

Downtown Gig Harbor is laid out along the water, with a variety of shops to lure browsers and restaurants to lure growling stomachs. A few galleries can be spotted near the mouth of the harbor, just down the road from the Tides Tavern. The **Ebb Tide Gallery of Gifts** (7809 Pioneer Way, 253/851-5293, www.ebbtide galleryofgifts.com, 10 A.M.–5 P.M. daily), is a handsome gallery run by 20 artists, the idea being to offer something for just about every taste and budget. The angler of the family can while away time waiting for the next fishing trip at the **Gig Harbor Fly Shop** (3115 Harborview Dr., 253/851-3474, www.gigharborflyshop .com).They'll even arrange that next trip for you and get you outfitted if you'd like. Walk north past the wharf to **Dog House Designs** (3308 B Harborview Dr.) for a unique canine experience. The owner is a 20-plus-year veteran of the dog-show circuit but gave it up to craft specialty dog toys, beds, and seasonal clothing.

Sports and Recreation

Rent powerboats, paddle boards, sea kayaks, and pedal boats from **Gig Harbor Rent-a-Boat** (8829 N. Harborview Dr., 253/858-7341, gigharborrentaboat.com).

Purdy Spit, located at the head of Henderson Bay (the upper end of Carr Inlet), is bisected by Highway 302 and is a favorite place to beachcomb, dig for clams, and windsurf. Before gunning for clams, check with the Washington Department of Fish and Wildlife at 360/902-2500 to learn about current restrictions and licensing.

In addition to Kopachuck State Park, camping is available at the private **Gig Harbor RV Resort** (9515 Burnham Dr., 253/858-8138 or 888/226-7688), which has RV sites for $37 and tent sites $20.

If you've decided you prefer water hazards to waterfront, you can play 18 at **Madrona Links Golf Course** (3604 22nd Ave NW, 253/851-5193, $27–30), the only public course in Gig Harbor. The 5,602-yard course won't knock you over, but if you need your fix, this is it. Kids are allowed, but probably won't win you any friends with the staff.

Accommodations

UNDER $100

The pleasant grounds at the pet-friendly **Westwynd Motel** (6703 144th St. NW, 253/857-4047 or 800/468-9963, www.west wyndmotel.com, $62–69 d, $75–105 suites) are a cut above most mom-and-pop motels. There's a pleasant lawn lined with flower beds,

a quiet picnic area, and a playground for the kiddies. Westwynd rents motel units, as well as apartments and suites with kitchens. Rooms are recently remodeled, styled with a homey flair, and are quite clean.

Twelve miles north of Gig Harbor on Glen Cove is the beautiful **Olde Glencove Hotel** (9418 Glencove Rd., 253/884-2835, www.glen covehotel.com, $75–95 s or d), built in 1897. This waterside retreat has been restored and transformed into a family-friendly bed-and-breakfast. The two guest rooms have private baths and a post-Victorian elegance.

Out in the rolling pastures of the tiny hamlet of Olalla, **Childs' House Bed and Breakfast** (8331 SE Willock Rd., 253/857-4252, www .childshouse.com, $85–100 d) has the distinct feeling of being a doll house big enough to sleep in. The five-acre grounds are surrounded by gardens and trees; also providing space for the occasional smoker—a rare thing among Washington B&Bs. The innkeeper strives to serve local seasonal ingredients in her daily breakfast spread.

$150-200

The best digs right in Gig Harbor are at **🄲 The Maritime Inn** ($129–198 d), a 15-room boutique hotel across the street from the marina and within walking distance of shops and restaurants in the village. Rooms are beautifully appointed, with plush linens, gas fireplaces, and a soothing neutral palette of beiges, browns, and seafoam green accents. Rooms are named after Gig Harbor boats of historical merit, and some have jetted tubs and water views. Complimentary wireless Internet and continental breakfast are included in the room rate.

If you'd like something a bit simpler, with a pool and a hot tub, **Best Western Wesley Inn** (6575 Kimball Dr., 253/858-9690 or 888/462-0002, www.wesleyinn.com, $109–185 d) is an attractive pick. It's not quite within walking distance of the waterfront, but awfully close by car. Rooms are stylishly decorated, there is a fitness center, and breakfast is complimentary. If being near the harbor isn't make or break,

SOUTH PUGET SOUND

The Inn at Gig Harbor (3211 56th St. NW, 253/858-1111 or 800/795-9980, www.innat gigharbor.com, $119 s or $149 d) is another good possibility. This large Craftsman-style hotel has a full spate of amenities, including a day spa, a well-regarded gourmet restaurant, a fitness center, an outdoor hot tub, and complimentary wireless Internet and continental breakfast. It offers a full spectrum of suites ($159–210 s or d) with amenities such as fireplaces, jetted tubs, wet bars, and kitchenettes.

$200-250
Westbay Guest Cottage (2515 48th Ave. NW, 253/265-3033 or 800/420-3033, www .westbaycottage.com, $145–250 d, sleeps four) is a beautiful waterfront home on Wollochet Bay with a deck, boat dock, and porch facing the water. This is not a B&B, but it does have a full kitchen and hot tub.

Food
Gig Harbor's most acclaimed venue for victuals and vino is the hip bistro ◖ **Brix 25** (7707 Pioneer Way, 253/858-6626, www .harborbrix.com, 4:30–9 P.M. Mon.–Thurs., 4:30–9:30 P.M. Fri.–Sat., 4:30–8:30 P.M. Sun.). Creative and sumptuous dishes such as piccata-style trout ($25) and duck in onion demi-glace ($29) are paired with an unparalleled wine list that features exclusively Washington and Oregon wines. Washington Wine Commission named Brix as the Wine Restaurant of the Year in 2008, and it is no wonder. There are over 25 wines that can be ordered by the glass or by a petite two-ounce serving to create your own wine flight.

Let your nose lead you to **Susanne's Bakery & Deli** (3411 Harborview Dr., 253/853-6220, www.susannesbakery.com, 7 A.M.–5 P.M. Tues.–Sun., closed Mon.). In the morning, pair up the freshly baked pastries and sweets with an espresso or latte. Come lunchtime, pick up a sandwich served on fresh-baked bread.

Arrive by car or by boat at the bustling **Tides Tavern** (2925 Harborview, 253/858-3982). This classic dive joint has a small harborside deck to enjoy the views while munching on a burger and a beer. Besides burgers, the Tides offers pizza, sandwiches, and the best local fish and chips, plus live music on weekends.

For something a little fancier served under the sun, **The Green Turtle** (2905 Harborview Dr., 253/851-3167, 11 A.M.–2 P.M. Tues.–Fri. and 4:30–9 P.M. Tues.–Sun., closed Mon.) also has a harbor-facing deck. The menu ventures eastward, with distinctively creative Thai- and Chinese-inspired meals. Lunch is pretty casual here, but reservations are recommended come dinnertime.

Or you can just do the takeout thing and picnic at Gig Harbor City Park. Pick up fiery hot Chinese food at **Harbor Monsoon Restaurant** (4628 Pt. Fosdick Dr. NW, 253/858-9838, www.harbormonsoon.com, 11:30 A.M.–10 P.M. Mon.–Thurs, 11:30 A.M.–11 P.M. Fri., noon–11 P.M. Sat., 2–9:30 P.M. Sun.) or very good, from-scratch pizzas, pasta, subs, and salads from **Spiro's Pizza & Pasta** (3108 Harborview Dr., 253/851-9200, spirosgh.com, 11 A.M.–10 P.M. Sun.–Thurs., 11 A.M.–11 P.M. Fri.–Sat.).

For the freshest local produce, baked goods, and crafts, head to the **Gig Harbor Farmers Market** (4701 Pt. Fosdick Drive, 253/884-2496, www.gigharborfarmersmarket.com) held 8:30 A.M.–2 P.M. Saturday Apr.–Sept.) or the second location downtown at Skansie Brothers Park on the water on Wednesday from noon–5 P.M.

Information and Services
The **Gig Harbor Chamber of Commerce** (3125 Judson St, 253/851-6865, www.gighar borchamber.com, 8 A.M.–5 P.M. Mon.–Fri.) can provide you with local brochures and information.

Getting There
Pierce Transit (253/581-8000 or 800/562-8109, www.piercetransit.org) has daily service from Gig Harbor to Tacoma and other parts of Pierce County. The **Bremerton-Kitsap Airporter** (800/562-7948, www.kitsap airporter.com) offers shuttle bus connections to Sea-Tac Airport.

Islands and Inlets

CARR AND CASE INLETS

The waters of Carr and Case Inlets are a kayaker's and leisure boater's dream sailing grounds. Still waters, relatively light boating traffic, and serene, wooded beaches add up to an ideal combination for boating bliss. With a number of public campgrounds scattered about the shores of these two waterways, it's easy to design a perfect multiday trip from campground to campground.

Anderson Island

Miles of roads and rural bike paths are the primary attractions to draw mainlanders to quiet Anderson Island. The restored Johnson Farm, founded by John Johnson in 1881, is the focus of the **Anderson Island Historical Museum** (9306 Otso Point Rd., 253/884-2135). The complex also is the proud home of the disembodied pilothouse off of the *Tahoma*, the island's ferry from 1939–1977. Local historical items are on display. Both the farm and the museum are open weekends during the summer and sporadically the rest of the year.

ACCOMMODATIONS

There are a handful of places to stay on the island. The kid-friendly modern log house at **The Inn at Burg's Landing B&B** (8808 Villa Beach Rd., 253/884-9185, www.burgslandingbb.com, $110–150 s or d) gives guests panoramic views of Mount Rainier and the Cascades. A covered deck with a hot tub overlooks the backyard fire pit and tree-dotted lawns leading to a private beach.

Watch herons glide over Little Vega Bay from the porch at **Anderson House on Oro Bay** (12024 Eckenstam-Johnson Rd., 253/884-4088 or 800/750-4088, www.andersonisland inn.com, $150 s or d, no kids). This beautifully restored 1920s Scandinavian farmhouse rests on a pasture surrounded by old-growth forests and an estuary. All four guest rooms have private baths, and a full breakfast is included.

GETTING THERE AND AROUND

Pierce County operates the small **Anderson Island-Steilacoom Ferry** (253/798-7250), which leaves Steilacoom Dock about every two hours. Round-trip summer fares are $19 for car and driver, $4.70 for passengers and pedestrians.

Key Peninsula

Penrose Point State Park (321 158th Ave. S., Lakebay, 253/884-2514 sprawls along two miles of shoreline just south of Home. This marine park is a favorite among pleasure craft and paddling enthusiasts, offering moorage and a boat dock. You can also explore by foot or bike on 2.5 miles of trails snaking through the park. Picnic tables and a large lawn and volleyball pit by the water make this an idyllic place for a picnic and a pickup game of soccer, Frisbee, or volleyball.

On the other side of Key Peninsula, facing Case Inlet, is **Joemma State Park** (20001 Bay Rd. KP S, Longbranch, 253/884-1944) at Whitman Cove. This is another boating hotspot, with a calm little beach and a big dock.

Harstine Island

Jarrell Cove State Park (www.parks.wa.gov, tents $17, no RV hookups), along a small cove on the north end of Harstine Island, has campsites and is open year-round. Get here on land by heading seven miles northeast of Shelton on Highway 3, crossing the bridge to Harstine Island, and then following the signs another five miles to the park. The 43-acre park is primarily used by boaters and is a fun place to explore in a kayak.

Jarrell's Cove Marina (E. 220 Wilson Rd., 360/426-8823) rents short-term RV spaces with hookups ($26) May–September. The marina and grocery store are open year-round, but gas is by appointment only during non-summer months.

VASHON ISLAND

Vashon Island is not the place to go if you're expecting a hot time on the ol' town. Cows and horses probably outnumber humans on this rock. The rural, slow-paced, homey environment is ideal for bike tours, not so much for barhopping. Vashon's residents are a mix of commuting yupsters, post-hippie artisans, retirees, and power-politics farmers.

Vashon Island was one of the many islands encountered in 1792 by Capt. George Vancouver, who, having named enough things after himself, decided to give this one to his Navy buddy, James Vashon.

Sights

FARMS AND MARKETS

Gourmet fruits and vegetables are a specialty of Vashon Island. The **Vashon Farmers Market** (206/567-5539, 10 A.M.–3 P.M. Sat. July–Sept.) in Vashon's Town Center is as much a social gathering as a place to buy island-grown food and island crafts.

Drive around and you'll see that Vashon Island is serious about agriculture. Vineyards, enormous cattle, cuddly alpacas, and gently swaying lavender give the feel of a farming fairyland when set against views of the Sound and the snowy mountains. The Farmer's Market is the best way to get to know the farmers and ranchers who put their backs into their work every day. Get a peek at the farms and ranches up close during fall's **Fall Farm Tour,** which punctuates harvest season in late September. The Chamber of Commerce (206/463-6217) will provide a tour booklet that will direct you to farms holding open houses.

Of very minor interest, there is a **"treed" bicycle** behind Sound Catering and Events—a tree that has gradually grown around a 50-plus-year-old bicycle, encasing it in a surrealistic natural display. There is a short trail leading to the curious sight.

PARKS

The shoreline of Vashon Island has a community park every couple of miles, circling the whole island. One of the most interesting is **Point Robinson Lighthouse** (3705 SW Point Robinson Rd., 206/463-1323) on the easternmost end of Maury Island, a manmade island adjacent to Vashon. The squat West Coast-style

© DAVID GAYLOR/123RF.COM

Point Robinson Lighthouse

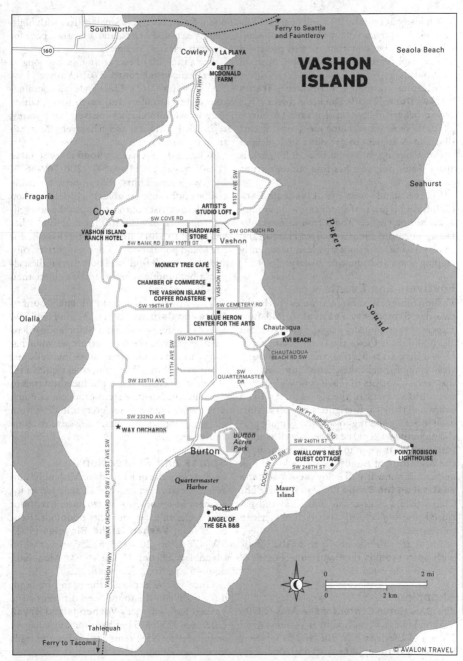

VASHON ISLAND

Southworth

Ferry to Seattle and Fauntleroy

160

Cowley ▼ LA PLAYA

● BETTY MCDONALD FARM

Seaola Beach

Seahurst

Fragaria

91ST AVE SW

Cove

ARTIST'S STUDIO LOFT ●

SW COVE RD

VASHON ISLAND RANCH HOTEL ●

THE HARDWARE STORE

SW GORSUCH RD

SW BANK RD ‖ SW 170TH ST ▼ Vashon

Puget

MONKEY TREE CAFÉ ●

CHAMBER OF COMMERCE ■

Olalla

THE VASHON ISLAND COFFEE ROASTERIE ▼

SW 196TH ST

VASHON HWY

SW CEMETERY RD

Sound

BLUE HERON CENTER FOR THE ARTS ■

Chautauqua

SW 204TH AVE

KVI BEACH ●

CHAUTAUQUA BEACH RD SW

111TH AVE SW

SW 220TH AVE

SW QUARTERMASTER DR

SW PT ROBISON RD

SW 232ND AVE

★ WAX ORCHARDS

SW 240TH ST

Burton

Burton Acres Park

POINT ROBISON LIGHTHOUSE ■

SWALLOW'S NEST GUEST COTTAGE

SW 248TH ST ●

DOCKTON RD SW

Quartermaster Harbor

Maury Island

VASHON HWY / 131ST AVE SW

WAX ORCHARD RD SW

● Dockton

ANGEL OF THE SEA B&B

0   2 mi

0   2 km

Tahlequah

Ferry to Tacoma

© AVALON TRAVEL

lighthouse was built in 1915 and continued its duty with an original Fresnel lens right up until 2008. The keeper's quarters are well-preserved and available as rentals. A gift shop is open on weekends.

A former armored embankment, **Tramp Harbor Dock** (21200 Dockton Rd. SW) is now a beautiful, peaceful place. The little park allows access to a long pier pointing east that allows anglers to get out a little deeper without having to have a boat. The park is also a prime point for heading out on a scuba adventure.

On the island's west side, **Lisabeula Park** (220th Rd.) is just perfect for throwing around a football or Frisbee. You'll find picnic tables facing out onto Quartermaster Harbor and Maury Island. Hiking trails lead past gently lapping water and a marine estuary.

Festivals and Events

Vashon's biggest summertime event is the two-day **Strawberry Festival** in mid-July. Expect parades, music, magic, and crafts, but the highlight is the festival's namesake fruit. If you love strawberries, there are enough strawberry funnel cakes, jams, sundaes, syrups, and smoothies to make yourself happy if not a little unwell in the stomach. And you can watch the local firefighters face off against each other competing to see who is most proficient in the tasks of the trade, as well as some fun games thrown in to up the excitement. In the beginning of August, aficionados of folk and country music will enjoy the **Americana Festival on the Sound** (206/463-5131). The island gives a stage to the best local and national unplugged and distinctly American musicians.

Local art galleries are open to the public with **open studios** the first two weekends of May and December.

Shopping

The **Blue Heron Center for the Arts** (19704 Vashon Hwy. SW, midisland at Vashon Island Hwy. and 196th St. SW, 206/463-5131, www.vashonalliedarts.org, 10 A.M.–5 P.M. Mon.–Fri., noon–5 P.M. Sat.) has a small gallery with high-quality arts and crafts, and a central space for concerts, classes, and plays.

For a little bit of everything, just so long as it's eclectic, visit **Kronos** (17610 Vashon Hwy. SW, 206/463-0061). Their style is a combination of bright colors and earth tones, which they weave into clothes, purses, housewares, refinished antiques, and whatever else it can fit in its store.

When a shop is named **Good Merchandise** (17601½ Vashon Hwy. SW, 206/769-8627, 11 A.M.–5 P.M. Thurs.–Mon.) need anything else be said? I suppose at least a little. The shop is the local artist's outpost, displaying and selling the work of over 100 local artists. That works out to a little under one-tenth of the entire island population. It's not just pottery, oils, and glass. You'll find local beeswax candles, alpaca fiber products, herbs, and way more than you'd expect.

The wooden false-front of **The Country Store and Gardens** (20211 Vashon Hwy. SW, 888/245-6136, www.countrystoreandgardens.com) gives you the (correct) impression that you've found an old-timey store that sells just about everything. The store stocks quite a bit of local farmer and ranch products and tries to specialize in Northwestern products as much as possible. They also sell everything else from oil lamp supplies to organic dog salve to china and silver.

Sports and Recreation

Cyclists love the quiet roads of Vashon Island. You can carry bikes aboard all state ferries for an extra $1 round-trip. Metro buses have front bike racks in case your legs poop out. Rent bikes from **Vashon Island Bicycles** (9925 SW 178th St. 206/463-6225, www.vashonislandbicycles.com, 11 A.M.–6 P.M. Mon–Sat., noon–4 P.M. Sun., $20 per day).

Once you've explored the island by land, dip a paddle in the sound for a different view. Vashon Park District's **Vashon Island Kayak** (206/463-9257, $15 per hour for single kayaks or full day for $55) rents sea kayaks and leads tours from Burton Acres Park.

Accommodations

UNDER $100

The least expensive place to stay on the island is unique 【 **Vashon Island Ranch Hostel** (12119 SW Cove Rd., 206/463-2592, www .vashonhostel.com, open May–Oct, $75 guest house, tent camping $13, tepees, covered wagons or dorm beds $15). This amusing Western-theme hostel is complete with tepees, covered wagons, a log bunkhouse, and barn. The lodge houses two dorms and has a full kitchen. Guests can also stay in the covered wagons and tepees, or pitch their own tent. An old fixed-gear bike is there for the borrowing and you can rent sleeping bags and lockers. Call in advance for pickup service at the Vashon Thriftway grocery store or the ferry terminal.

$100-150

Vashon Island has a number of delightfully romantic B&Bs and guest cottages, making this a great weekend getaway.

Families traveling with pets will feel comfortable in one of eight cottages by **Swallow's Nest Guest Cottages** (6030 SW 248th St., 206/463-2646 or 800/269-6378, www .vashonislandcottages.com, $105–230 d). The properties are located throughout the island, including one right on the Vashon Country Club, one right downtown, and one on a picturesque bluff overlooking the water.

Set on a lush five acres with flower gardens and ponds, **Artist's Studio Loft** (16529 91st SW, 206/463-2583, vashonbedandbreakfast. com, $119–215 d, two-night minimum on weekends) has two B&B rooms with full breakfast and separate entrances, a hot tub, woodstove, and a big continental breakfast. There are also four cottages that offer full kitchens in lieu of the prepared breakfast.

Once the home of the late Betty McDonald, author of children's books such as *The Egg and I,* the **Betty MacDonald Farm** (11835 99th Ave. SW, 206/567-4227 or 888/328-6753, www.bettymacdonaldfarm.com, $125–160 d) is now a tastefully romantic B&B just a few blocks from the ferry dock. The big old barn sits on six acres atop a bluff facing Mount Rainier and has a spacious upper loft with kitchen and woodstove. A separate cottage is popular with families. The fridges are well stocked for a make-your-own breakfast.

Food

There are only so many restaurants to choose from on Vashon, but there are still a few treasures to be found.

Operating out of a 120-plus-year-old former hardware store, the appropriately named restaurant **The Hardware Store** (17601 Vashon Hwy. SW, 206/463-1800, www.thsrestaurant .com, 11:30 A.M.–2:30 P.M. and 5–9:30 P.M. Mon.–Sun.) serves breakfast, lunch, and dinner daily. Their menu has quite a bit of breadth, offering vegetarian dishes, steak, seafood, and soups and salads. The real specialty of the house are the lahvosh "pizzas" made on Armenian cracker bread. The restaurant serves a special breakfast menu 8:30 A.M.– 2:30 P.M. Sunday.

If you're craving a taco or you just need to grab something before heading off the island, **La Playa** (1824 Vashon Hwy., 206/567-0020, www.laplayarestaurantvashon.com, 11 A.M.–10 P.M. daily) at the north end of the ferry terminal offers the best Mexican food on the island. Their walk-up espresso window opens at 5 A.M.

Information and Services

The **Vashon-Maury Island Chamber of Commerce** (17633 Vashon Hwy., 206/463-6217, www.vashonchamber.com) can be found in the main village of Vashon. Hours vary seasonally.

Getting There

Vashon is only 15 minutes by ferry from Tacoma and about the same from West Seattle. The **Washington State Ferries** (206/464-6400, 888/808-7977, or 800/843-3779 for automated information, www.wsdot.wa.gov/ ferries) float auto and passenger service to both the north and south ends of Vashon Island. The return trip is always free (round-trip fare

SOUTH PUGET SOUND

is charged on your way to the island), so you can arrive or depart from either end for the same price. There are four departure points for the island. To reach Heights Dock on the north end, you can take the half-hour passenger-only **King County Water Taxi** from downtown Seattle's Pier 50 for $4.50, cash only. This ferry operates daily, save holidays, and generally runs six trips both ways between 5:30 A.M. and 7 P.M. Bicycles and nonmotorized scooters are allowed for free. Two wheeled electrical vehicles are also allowed free.

By car or bus, you can take the frequent ferries from West Seattle's Fauntleroy terminal for $19.45 round-trip for car and driver. Passengers and walk-ons are $4.55 round-trip. Winter fares are lower. Ferries also connect Heights Dock with the Southworth ferry terminal on the Kitsap Peninsula, and the Tahlequah dock on the south end of Vashon Island with Tacoma's Point Defiance ferry terminal. Both of these ferry runs have the same rate schedule as from Fauntleroy.

Getting Around

The main town of Vashon is five miles from the ferry landing. **Metro Transit** (206/553-3000 or 800/542-7876, http://metro.kingcounty.gov, $2.50) operates route 118 Monday–Saturday, between both ferry terminals, through Vashon, and onto Maury Island. Route 119 offers direct service to and from downtown Seattle for $3 Monday–Friday.

Island Air (206/567-4697, www.san juan-islandair.com) sends off flightseeing trips over Puget Sound from Vashon Municipal Airport.

BLAKE ISLAND

Accessible only by boat, Blake Island has 476 acres of state park land with year-round camping ($21); sandy beaches for swimming, sunbathing, and clamming; fishing and scuba diving; a 0.75-mile loop nature trail; and 12 miles of other hiking trails. To reach the island from the Kitsap, **Blake Island Charters** (360/731-7776) sails from Port Orchard to Blake Island and any other South Sound

destination you'd like to add to your charter for $35 per hour.

◖ Tillicum Village

Blake Island's main attraction is Tillicum Village (206/933-8600, www.tillicumvillage .com). Argosy Cruises runs a four-hour trip from Seattle (daily May–Sept., $80 adults, $73 seniors, $30 kids, free for under age 4) and Bremerton (select summer dates) that provides visitors with an introduction to the culture of the Coast Salish people, residents of the Puget Sound area for thousands of years. The cedar longhouse salmon bake is maybe the main draw of the whole trip, but the show that explores Salish dance and traditions makes the trip more than just a salmon feast. Guests can also walk around the island, taking in views of the Sound.

BAINBRIDGE ISLAND

Just a 35-minute ferry ride from downtown Seattle, Bainbridge Island offers a comfortable escape from the hordes, a place where commuters retreat to rural waterside homes and retirees enjoy a peaceful escape from the workaday world. Over 20,000 folks call Bainbridge home today, and more move here every week.

Back in the 19th century, Bainbridge Island was home to the largest sawmill in the world. Today, though, the little island is mostly residential, owned by folks ranging from politicians to fishermen, 70 percent of whom commute by ferry to Seattle-area jobs. Although the entire island is officially incorporated as a city, activity is centered around the "town" of **Winslow**, located along Eagle Harbor where the ferry docks. Winslow is a genuine—albeit gentrified—hamlet with BMWs crawling the streets, yachts in the marina, and classical music in the cafés.

If you're arriving by ferry from Seattle, you'll find Winslow easy to sightsee by foot. Start on the shoreline footpath that heads west from the ferry to **Eagle Harbor Waterfront Park,** good for sunny-day picnics. If you're arriving by car, parking can be a real problem on weekends, and no on-street overnight parking is allowed.

Sights
BAINBRIDGE ISLAND HISTORICAL MUSEUM
The history of the island is interpreted in a 1908 schoolhouse, home to the Bainbridge Island Historical Museum (215 Ericksen Ave. NE, 206/842-2773, www.bainbridgehistory .org, 1–4 P.M. Wed.–Mon., 10 A.M.–4 P.M. Sat. in summer, $4 adults, $3 students and seniors, $6 family, kids under 5 free) in Strawberry Hill Park. The few exhibits cover Japanese internment in WWII, the plight of local American Indians, and a bit of local history.

PARKS AND GARDENS
Fay-Bainbridge State Park (206/842-3931, www.parks.wa.gov) covers a mere 17 acres but it offers some of the best over-the-water vistas of the Cascades and the twinkling lights of Seattle. Fay-Bainbridge also offers tent campsites ($21 for tents; $31 for RVs), plus hot showers and beach access with scuba diving and boating facilities at the island's northeast end. This is the closest public campground to Seattle—just a ferry ride and short drive or bus ride away—so it is very popular in the summer months. The park's open for day use year-round but only open to camping mid-April–mid-October.

Located six miles from the Winslow ferry terminal at the island's south end, **Fort Ward Park** is an island-owned public park with 137 acres for day-use picnicking, bird-watching, boating and scuba diving along the mile-long beach. There's no camping, but nature-lovers can walk the one-mile path that loops through the park. There are some interesting views of the WWII-era radio tower that was once operated by the U.S. Navy.

The 150-acre **Bloedel Reserve** (7571 NE Dolphin Dr., 206/842-7631, www.bloedel reserve.org, 10 A.M.–4 P.M. Wed.–Sun., $13 adults, $9 seniors and military, $5 kids 13–18, free for children under 13) is an unbelievable large and diverse public garden, full of native plants, a bog, pond, Japanese garden, and spacious lawns. In springtime, the rhododendrons bloom, making this bucolic parklike garden even more beautiful. The thousands of cyclamen plants compete to be a botany-oriented tourist's favorite.

WINERIES
One-quarter mile from the ferry terminal, **Bainbridge Island Vineyards and Winery** (682 Hwy. 305, Winslow, 206/842-9463) is the only place to buy this family-operated winery's limited-run wines, made from grapes grown on the island. The grounds are a refreshing spot for a lunch break, and the antique wine glass collection is worth a gander. Tours and tastings are held once a month, depending on availability of staff. Call ahead before dropping in.

Festivals and Events
In February, the popular **Chilly Hilly** bicycle marathon encourages upwards of 4,000 riders to pedal around Bainbridge in the sometimes-harsh wintertime. The **Fourth of July** brings a two-day street fair and parade to Winslow. You'll have to settle for watching Seattle's fireworks from 35 miles away. **Concerts in the Park** take place at Waterfront Park in Winslow on Wednesday evenings in July and August, and an **outdoor music festival** brings more performers to Waterfront Park in August.

Shopping
Downtown Winslow is jammed with gift and import shops, including several inside Winslow Green, a mini–shopping district of its own. In the center of town, **Eagle Harbor Books** (157 Winslow Way E., 206/842-5332, www.eagle harborbooks.com, 9 A.M.–7 P.M. Mon.–Wed. and Fri., 9 A.M.–9 P.M. Thurs., 9 A.M.–6 P.M. Sat., 10 A.M.–6 P.M. Sun.) has new and used titles as well as a coffee shop. To experience the cosmic vibe that is omnipresent in the Puget Sound, visit **Willows Naturally** (169 Winslow Way E., 206/842-2759). They stock aromatherapy supplies, countless dietary supplements, and food for your pampered yet vegetarian pet. If you're caught flat-footed by chilly, breezy drizzle, drop by **Lindsleys Classic Clothing for Bainbridge** (164 Bjune Dr., 206/780-5808, www.lindsleys.com). The

husband, wife, and black-and-white mutt team carry name-brand sportswear from the functional to the fabulous.

Sports and Recreation

Pick up a map of hiking trails on Bainbridge from the Chamber of Commerce office. The largest parcel of public land—280 acres—contains second-growth forests. Called **Grand Forest,** it's near the center of the island off Mandus Oldon Road and has three miles of paths. **Manzanita Park** is 120 acres of broadleaf woods with a two-mile hiking and equestrian trail through woods and wetlands. The park is near Miller Road and Day Road on the northwest side of the island.

Back of Beyond (181 Winslow Way, 206/842-9229, www.tothebackofbeyond .com, 10 A.M.–6 P.M. Mon.–Fri., 9 A.M.–dusk Sat.–Sun.) has sea kayak, canoe, sailboat, and rowboat rentals and tours from the Winslow waterfront.

For adventure under the water, try **Exotic Aquatics** (100 Madison Ave. N., 206/842-1980, exoticaquaticsscuba.com), which offers guided scuba dives in nearby waters. Come certified if you want to dive. It's a long and pricy course if you don't already have certificate in hand.

Take advantage of the island's many back roads, as well as those on Kitsap Peninsula, on the saddle of a rented bike from **Classic Cycle** (310 Winslow Way E., 206/842-9191, classic cycleus.com, 10 A.M.–6:30 P.M. Mon.–Fri., 10 A.M.–5 P.M. Sat., noon–4 P.M. Sun., $25 for two hours or $35 for the day).

Accommodations

There are dozens of little B&Bs tucked away in the residential areas of Bainbridge, but if you prefer a hotel, **Island Country Inn** (920 Hildebrand Ln. NE, 206/842-6861 or 800/842-8429, www.islandcountryinn.com, $113–133 s or d) has nicely updated deluxe guest rooms and suites. The property has an outdoor pool and hot tub, plus continental breakfast in the mornings. Several rooms can accommodate persons with disabilities.

One of the better B&B deals on the island, **The Captain's House** (234 Parfitt Way NE, 206/842-3557, $75–100 d) is a century-old home overlooking Eagle Harbor with rowboats, tennis courts, and an old-fashioned porch swing. The two guest rooms have private baths. There is no way to resist the charm of a guesthouse named the **Wacky Nut Farm** (10821 NE Wacky Nut Way, 206/780-1617, www.wacky nutfarm.com, $175–275). The farm is chiefly an equestrian center that boards horses, trains horses, gives lessons, and leads rides. Two guest rooms have queen beds and private baths. The guesthouse is a two-bedroom unit with a partial kitchen and an additional bunk-bed bedroom that can be added on at additional cost. Rooms are colorfully and creatively decorated while still conservative enough to please most eyes. In short, this property is a little girl's dream come true.

Our Country Haus B&B (18718 Ellingsen Rd. NE, 206/842-8425, www.ourcountryhaus .com, $150 d) is a private carriage house on two acres with gardens and pond, private bath, and kitchen. A continental breakfast is served.

Willow Brook Farm Cottage (12600 Miller Rd., 206/842-8034, www.willowbrookfarm. com, $165 s or d) is a private 1920s-era cottage on a 25-acre working organic farm. The cottage has a complete kitchen, separate living and sleeping rooms, and a hot tub on the deck.

One of the swankiest sleeping spots on the island, **Ashton Woods Retreat** (5515 Tolo Rd. NE, 206/780-0100, www.ashtonwoodsretreat .com, $275 d, $40 pet fee) sits on a secluded 10-acre wooded plot complete with quiet gardens and walking trails. Guests can borrow bikes from the property or just hoof it on two feet to the trails of Grand Forest. Enjoy the exercise with your pup—this is a very dog-friendly property. The rooms are extremely well appointed and private for a B&B-type property. Fresh-baked continental breakfast is brought to your door each morning rather than served at a communal table.

Food

Streamliner Diner (397 Winslow Way,

206/842-8595, www.streamlinerdiner.com, 7 A.M.–2:30 P.M. Mon.–Sat., 7:30 A.M.–2:30 P.M. Sun., and 5–9 P.M. Tues.–Thurs., 5–9:30 P.M. Fri.–Sat.) is famous for its hearty breakfasts that include wonderful hash browns and omelettes. It's popular with both locals and tourists, so be ready for a wait most mornings. For something lighter, get fresh-baked goods and espresso coffees at **Bainbridge Bakers** (140 Winslow Way W, 206/842-1822, www.bainbridgebakers.com, 6 A.M.–6 P.M. Mon.–Sat., 6 A.M.–5 P.M. Sun.). They offer hot lunches and fresh pastries, too. Or head to the historic brick building that houses **Pegasus Coffee House and Gallery** (131 Parfitt Way, 206/842-6725, www.pegasus coffeehouse.com, 7 A.M.–6 P.M. Sun.–Thurs., 7 A.M.–10 P.M. Fri.–Sat.). This is a fun place to enjoy a relaxing light lunch and espresso or, in the evening, a stiff cocktail, cold beer, or glass of wine.

Harbour Public House (231 Parfitt Way SW, 206/842-0969, harbourpub.com, 11 A.M.–midnight daily) has tasty on-the-water eats, including fish and chips and burgers, as well as plenty of beer on tap.

Order up some of the absolute best Southwestern food in the Northwest at the **San Carlos Restaurant** (279 Madison N, 206/842-1999 5–9 P.M. daily, plus Fri. lunch 11 A.M.–2 P.M.), two blocks from the Winslow ferry terminal. Their tapas menu is perfect for grazing.

Winslow's **Town & Country Thriftway** (343 Winslow Way, 206/842-3848) is a big gourmet grocery with an impressive wine selection. The deli has a menu of box lunches to buy, perfect for a quiet waterside lunch. The **Bainbridge**

Farmers Market (Madison Ave. and Winslow Way, 206/855-1500, 9 A.M.–1 P.M. Sat. mid-Apr.–Oct.) comes to the municipal parking lot with flowers, organic fruits and vegetables, handicrafts, international foods, and a variety of nonprofits offering information or asking for donations.

Information and Services

The **Bainbridge Island Chamber of Commerce Visitor Center** (590 Winslow Way E, 206/842-3700, www.bainbridgechamber .com, 9 A.M.–5 P.M. Mon.–Fri., 10 A.M.–3 P.M. Sat.) is at the top of the hill as you exit the ferry. You can also get info at the kiosk at the ferry terminal (10 A.M.–6 P.M. daily May–Oct., 10 A.M.–6 P.M. Sat.–Sun. Nov.–Apr.).

Getting There and Around

The **Washington State Ferry** ($15.20 one-way car and driver, $6.25 motorcycle and driver, $6.70 extra passengers and walk-on, $6.25 extra kayaks, $1 extra bikes) provides service between downtown Seattle and Winslow on Bainbridge Island every 50 minutes throughout the day. The crossing takes 35 minutes. Be ready for long delays—especially in the summer—if you're traveling on Friday and Sunday evenings.

Kitsap Transit (206/373-2877 or 800/501-7433, www.kitsaptransit.org) provides daily bus service around Bainbridge Island and the Kitsap Peninsula and meets all state ferries in Winslow. All buses have bike racks.

Tours of Bainbridge and surrounding areas are offered by **Taxis & Tours** (206/842-7660). It will also take you just about anywhere in the area, around the island or off.

SOUTH PUGET SOUND

Puyallup Valley to White River Valley

Puyallup (pyoo-AL-up) is fewer than a dozen miles southeast of Tacoma in the scenic, nearly level Puyallup Valley. The scenery is dramatic in Puyallup in the springtime, when Mount Rainier decides to peek out from under the clouds. This town's agricultural pace is an antidote to traffic jams and fast-paced living. It is home to September's Puyallup Fair, the most beloved fair in the Puget Sound. Puyallup also prides itself on its historic buildings and homes and the bucolic sights surrounding them.

SIGHTS

The 17-room Stick-Eastlake–style **Ezra Meeker Mansion** (312 Spring St., 253/848-1770, www.meekermansion.org, tours noon–4 P.M. Wed.–Sun. Mar.–mid-Dec., $4 adults, $3 students and seniors, $2 children under 12) was built by the city's founder and first mayor. Stained glass, inlaid fireplaces, and a grand staircase offer a glimpse into the lives of 19th-century kings of industry. Call ahead, as the house is periodically closed for restoration. Strollers are unkind to the floors and unfortunately not allowed.

Over in Sumner, the **Ryan House Museum** (1228 Main St., Sumner, 253/863-8936, 1–4 P.M. Sat., donations) showcases a Victorian farmhouse from 1875, with tall backyard trees and regional history displays. Named for the first mayor of Sumner, who lived here for many years, the home is open April–October and December only.

Auburn's **White River Valley Historical Museum** (918 H St. SE, 253/939-2783, www.wrvmuseum.org, 1:30–4:30 P.M. Thurs.–Sun. year-round, free) has artifacts from the early days in the valley, including old photos, a one-room schoolhouse, country store, and farm machinery.

VanLierop Bulb Farms

Two miles east of Puyallup, VanLierop Bulb Farms (13407 80th St. E, 253/848-7272 or 877/666-8377) was created by Simon VanLierop, a Dutch immigrant from a family with a long history of bulb growing. You can have them shipped or take them with you. The flower shop is open 9 A.M.–5 P.M. daily when the flowers are in bloom, mid-March–mid-April.

ENTERTAINMENT AND EVENTS
Entertainment

Play the ponies April through September at **Emerald Downs** (2300 Emerald Downs Dr., 253/288-7000 or 888/931-8400, www.emeralddowns.com, $7 preferred, free for general admission), the Seattle area's thoroughbred horse track. Stable tours are available on Saturday mornings by appointment.

The **Auburn Avenue Dinner Theater** (10 Auburn Ave., 253/833-5678) screens classic (and contemporary classic) films, and puts on tribute concerts, plays, and musicals. It's Washington's oldest and largest dinner theater.

Gamblers can try their luck at **Muckleshoot Indian Casino** (2402 Auburn Way S, 253/939-7484 or 800/804-4944, www.casino-fun.com), offering blackjack, craps, roulette, and slots. They also claim to have the largest poker room in the state. With several different restaurants in multiple different styles, chances are you'll find something you'll like.

For some four-wheel, fire-breathing fun, drop by **Pacific Raceways** (31001 144th Ave. SE, Kent, 253/631-1550, www.pacificraceways.com). There's drag racing once a month or so, and motorcycles and car and truck races and demonstrations just about every weekend.

Festivals and Events

Puyallup is home of the famous **Puyallup Fair** (Meridian St. and 9th Ave. SW, 253/841-5045, www.thefair.com). One of the nation's 10 largest, the fair runs for 17 days in September (starting the Friday after Labor Day) and attracts a crowd of more than 1.2 million

LAS VEGAS, WASHINGTON

Puyallup's marquee casino, the Emerald Queen Casino is one of the top draws for gamblers across Western Washington, with almost 2,000 colorful slots, tons of table-games, keno, and lots more. The house is run by the Puyallup tribe of American Indians. As in many other parts of the country, Indian gaming has gained a huge foothold, bringing casino-style gaming to communities that never would have allowed it otherwise. The casinos provide a source of income and employment for the various tribes and bands that often find themselves living in poverty otherwise. Some go so far as to call Indian gaming the "new buffalo" for its ability to single-handedly feed, clothe, and otherwise support American Indians. Across the state of Washington, 15 tribes operate over 20 casinos, ranging from the huge Tulalip tribe in Tulalip, Washington, to the much smaller Yakama-run Coulee Dam Casino.

fairgoers to its big-name concerts, livestock displays, a PRCA rodeo, carnival rides, and refreshments. Locals refer to it in shorthand simply as "the Puyallup." You can find gluten-free and vegetarian eats, but you're at the fair: punish your heart with a fried chicken sandwich with donuts as a bun, pizza on a stick, or deep-fried peaches and cream.

The **Spring Fair and Daffodil Festival** (253/627-6176, www.daffodilfestival.net) is a bit of a change of pace from the Puyallup Fair. This two-week series of events throughout Pierce County features Grand Floral Parades in Tacoma, Puyallup, Sumner, and Orting. Naturally, there is a coronation of a daffodil queen, the complete opposite of the huge Mutt Show, which awards dozens of categories of prizes to canines.

It is certainly offbeat, but quite a bit of fun when Puyallup puts on the annual **Alpacapalooza** (Meridian St. and 9th Ave. SW, 206/719-4978, www.alpacawa.org) the

last weekend of March. Billed as "2 days of Peace, Love and Livestock," it is a chance for fuzzy alpacas from over a hundred regional ranches to strut their stuff. As in a county fair, alpacas are judged and their breeders awarded prizes. Make friends with the fancy beasts and also get the chance to buy alpaca merchandise that defies the imagination.

SHOPPING

Shoppers head to the enormous **SuperMall of the Great Northwest** (1101 SuperMall Way, 800/729-8258 www.supermall.com, 10 A.M.–9 P.M. Mon.–Sat., 11 A.M.–6 P.M. Sun.), with over 140 outlet, "rack," and specialty stores located just off Highway 167 at 15th Street Southwest.

Also, **South Hill Mall** (3500 S. Meridian, 253/840-2828, www.southhillmall.com, 10 A.M.–9 P.M. Mon.–Sat., 10 A.M.–6 P.M. Sun.) has over 150 stores at the intersection of Highway 512 and South Meridian.

ACCOMMODATIONS
Puyallup

Those searching for a simple room to hang their hat after a night at the fairgrounds would do well to check into **Northwest Motor Inn** (1409 S. Meridian, 253/841-2600 or 800/845-9490, $54–100 d). This tidy little motel has an outdoor hot tub and is only a few minutes' walk to the fair.

Standing behind a white picket fence and two giant evergreens, **Hedman House** (502 9th St. SW, 253/848-2248, www.hedman house.com, $120 d) is also within walking distance of the fairgrounds. Relax on the porch swing or in front of the living room fire in the evening; come breakfast time you'll be treated to a sit-down breakfast in the country-themed dining room. The two rooms in the house share a bath, but for $25 extra you can reserve one room for a private stay. There's also a fenced-in backyard with a large deck and hot tub.

On the edge of town, **Tayberry Victorian Cottage B&B** (7406 80th St. E, 253/848-4594, $135) is a modern Victorian-style home with a wraparound porch and hot tub with a view of the valley. All three guest rooms are equipped with TVs and VCRs, and private baths featuring clawfoot tubs and bathrobes. Two-course full breakfasts are served each morning, and the inn caters to special dietary needs.

Best Western Park Plaza (620 S. Hill Pl., 253/848-1500 or 800/238-7234, www .bestwestern.com, $154–204 d) has the nicest hotel rooms in town, plus an outdoor pool and hot tub, in-room hot tubs, exercise facility, and continental breakfast.

Kent and Auburn

Up north between the I-5 and Highway 167 corridors, Kent and Auburn are teeming with every shape and size of chain hotel and motel. Their proximity to Sea-Tac makes them a convenient stopover when flying in or out of the region.

You can find a relatively cheap night's sleep at **Days Inn** (22420 84th Ave., Kent, 253/872-5525 or 800/443-7777, $64 s or $97 d). Amenities include a hot tub, continental breakfast, wireless Internet, and a desktop computer available for use 24 hours a day. You can choose a smoking or nonsmoking room.

For a few extra dollars, though, **Best Western Plaza by the Green** (24415 Russell Rd., 253/854-8767 or 800/835-3338, $99–209 s or d) is a better value. The hotel is situated on the 8th green of the Riverbed Golf Course, so be sure to ask for a room with a view. Guests are welcome to relax in the sauna, hot tub, and exercise room. Continental breakfast is complimentary, as is the airport shuttle.

For a homier stay, try **(Victorian Gardens Bed and Breakfast** (9621 S. 200th St., Kent, 888/850-1776, www.victoriangardensbandb .com, $135–155 d). This 1888 home is surrounded by an award-winning garden, lush green lawns, and a backyard pool. Sticking to the Victorian theme, three of the rooms are all floral and lace, but for those who prefer a more understated look, the Tuxedo Room is an elegantly masculine choice with rich purple-and-gray furnishings. All come equipped with private bath, refrigerator, TV, and wireless Internet.

Camping

Size doesn't matter at **Majestic Mobile Manor** (6906 52nd St. Court East in Puyallup, 253/845-3144 or 800/348-3144), which has well-landscaped grounds, a coin-laundry, and showers. The property can handle rigs up to 75 feet.

Park RVs or pitch a tent in Kent at **Seattle-Tacoma KOA Kampground** (5801 S. 212th St., 253/872-8652 or 800/562-1892, www .koa.com, $60 back-in full hookup sites, $34 tents). This is one of the few RV parks in the Seattle area.

FOOD
Puyallup

The deep, dark accent woods of the furnishings and decor at **(Hungry Goose Bistro** (1618 E. Main St., Puyallup, 253/845-5747, www.hgbistro.com, 11:30 A.M.–2:30 P.M. Mon.–Fri., 5–9:30 P.M. Sun.–Sat., 9 A.M.–2:30 P.M. Sat.–Sun. brunch) set the tone for a classy meal supping on Nuevo Bistro–style fare. Inventive entrées such as Dungeness crab macaroni and cheese ($17) light up the menu. On Saturday and Sunday, the Goose pulls out all the stops with a special brunch menu served 8 A.M.–3 P.M.

Another favorite Puyallup eatery is **Mama Stortini's** (3207 E. Main St., 253/845-7569, www.mamastortinis.com, 11 A.M.–9:30 P.M. Mon.–Thurs., 11:30 A.M.–10:30 P.M. Fri., noon–10:30 P.M. Sat., 11 A.M.–9 P.M. Sun.), a lively spot that focuses on Northwest cooking fused with French and Italian flavors.

For more traditional Italian fare—and the best local pizzas—try locally based chain **Casa Mia** (505 N. Meridian, 253/770-0400, 11 A.M.–10 P.M. Sun.–Thurs., 11 A.M.–11 P.M. Fri.–Sat.).

The popular **Puyallup Farmers Market** (330 S Meridian, 253/840-2631, 9 A.M.–2 P.M. Sat. April–Oct. and 9 A.M.–2 P.M. Sun. May–Sept.) features, among other things, fresh flowers, ripe cherries, and succulent apricots from local farms. The market is held downtown next to Pioneer Park. At other times, head out River Road to find the produce stands.

INFORMATION

The **Puyallup Area Chamber of Commerce** (41 7 E. Pioneer, 253/845-6755, www.east piercechamber.com, 9 A.M.–5 P.M. Mon.–Fri.) might be of some use for local information. They keep their office open year-round.

GETTING THERE

Pierce Transit (253/581-8000 or 800/562-8109, www.piercetransit.org) has daily bus service to Tacoma and other parts of Pierce County, along with Seattle and Olympia. **Capital Aeroporter** (253/754-7113 or 800/962-3579, www.capair.com) operates shuttle vans between Puyallup and Sea-Tac Airport.

Metro Transit (253/553-3000 or 800/542-7876, http://metro.kingcounty.gov) has bus service to Auburn, Kent, and the rest of King County.

Sea-Tac Airport Corridor

The southern end of King County encompasses several rapidly growing suburbs and industrial areas all centered around Sea-Tac Airport. This area was literally and figuratively built by logging and lumber. The massive logging company Weyerhaeuser is still headquartered here and is the top employer in Federal Way. Like the rest of Western Washington, the southern tip of the county is seeing a bit of gentrification, but as long as the timber giant remains, the area will always be significantly blue-collar.

SIGHTS
Renton

A simple monument marks the grave of **James M. "Jimi" Hendrix** in Greenwood Memorial Park, located east of town on NE 3rd at Monroe. Born in Seattle in 1942, Hendrix is remembered for his virtuosic electric-guitar stylings that changed American music forever. He died in London in 1970, but was flown to Washington to be buried in his hometown. Hundreds of people of all ages still make the pilgrimage to his grave each year, leaving behind tokens of all sorts, from flowers to pinwheels. Be sure to stop by the office near the cemetery entrance to sign the guestbook and read comments from visitors who arrive from around the globe. Seattle's Experience Music Project has much more on this rock legend.

SeaTac and Burien

Seahurst Park (SW 140th St., 206/988-3700), in the city of Burien, is bubbling with springs and the site of two streams and a patch of wetland. A sandy beach slopes down to Puget Sound.

Federal Way
WILD WAVES

Federal Way is best known 'round the Sound for its amusement and water park, Wild Waves (36201 Enchanted Pkwy. S., 253/661-8000, www.wildwaves.com, $35 adult, $30 child, hours vary, open May–Sept.). This enterprise is a nice summer destination to keep the whole family amused. The water park offers 400 feet of white-water rapids on its Raging River Ride, four giant water slides, a "beach" with artificial five-foot waves for bodysurfing, and all the water is heated, so don't worry about the weather. The dry side of the park has a 1906 carousel, bumper boats, a free-flight bird aviary, pony rides, children's museum, petting zoo, and scream-and-smile producing roller coasters.

PARKS AND GARDENS
The Rhododendron Species Foundation Garden (Weyerhaeuser Way, 253/661-9377, www.rhodygarden.org, 10 A.M.–4 P.M. Fri.–Wed. Mar.–May, 11 A.M.–4 P.M. Sat.–Wed. the rest of the year, $3.50 adults, $2.50 students and seniors, free for kids under 12) displays over 2,100 varieties of wild rhododendrons from around the world in a 24-acre garden. This is the world's

SOUTH PUGET SOUND

largest collection in one garden, and something is in bloom March–September. The garden is operated by the nonprofit Rhododendron Species Foundation, which also offers workshops, classes, and tours for members.

Just south of the Rhododendron Garden is **Pacific Rim Bonsai Collection** (33663 Weyerhaeuser Way S., 253/924-5206, www .weyerhaeuser.com/bonsai, 10 A.M.–4 P.M., free), operated by the Weyerhaeuser Corporation. The collection contains more than 90 bonsai trees, some more than 500 years old. The artistry of these tiny trees is truly impressive.

A couple miles north of Federal Way in Des Moines, **Saltwater State Park** (25205 8th Place S., 253/661-4956, www.parks.wa.gov) is a popular summer spot. The sandy beach is very popular for swimming, scuba diving, and sea kayaking, and a two-mile path loops through the forest. Tacoma and Seattle have sometimes competed ruthlessly against one another for dominance of the region. That's why representatives of Tacoma and Seattle met up in the 1920s to open this park by actually burying a literal hatchet in the soft sand here. The park is close to Sea-Tac Airport, and planes pass directly overhead while landing and taking off. It's a great place for plane-spotting.

Dash Point State Park (5700 SW Dash Point Rd.) is in Federal Way, five miles northeast of downtown Tacoma on Puget Sound, on Highway 509, aka Dash Point Road. On the Sound side of the park there's a beach, picnic tables, and trails that lead to the water. The water here is just about warm enough for swimming in the summertime.

ENTERTAINMENT AND EVENTS

In Federal Way, the **Red, White & Blues Festival** (Celebration Park, 253/835-7000) is a good place to celebrate freedom, listen to local blues musicians, get your sack on for a three-legged race, and maybe meet the mayor of Federal Way. In late August, the **Sand Sculpting Tournament of Champions** will leave you gaping open-mouthed at what these talented sand artists can do.

In June, SeaTac holds the **International Festival** (Angle Lake Park, 19408 International Blvd., 206/973-4680) with tons of world music, dancing, and food. It's a nice change of pace from parade and pancake breakfast festivals Sound-wide.

For over a decade, the blue building that towers over Renton, retailer IKEA, has sponsored **IKEA Renton River Days** (1055 S. Grady Way, 425/430-6528) in late July or early August. The city rolls out an Art Market in the park, showcasing local talent. In years past, there have been acrobatic circuses, rubber ducky races on the river, and of course, parades, food, and strolling musicians and magicians.

SHOPPING
Malls

Southcenter Mall (2800 Southcenter Mall, south of the intersection of I-5 with I-405 in Tukwila, 206/246-7400) has the major department stores Macy's, Nordstrom, JCPenney, and Sears, with 240 stores in total.

The **Commons at Federal Way** (1928 S. Commons., www.tcafw.com) has over 100 stores including Macy's and Sears and has a movie theater attached. Tukwila has its own **REI** (240 Andover Park W, 206/248-1938, www.rei.com), with camping and backpacking supplies galore.

Downtown Renton

For an exhaustive selection of Western garb, be sure to tie up at the state's largest cowboy shop, **Renton Western Wear** (724 S. 3rd, 425/255-3922 or 888/273-7039, www.rentonww.com). It's not all just hats and boots. Although there are a lot of hats and boots. Renton also has a considerable downtown antiques district along Wells Avenue South near 3rd.

SPORTS AND RECREATION

Just north of Federal Way on the Puget Sound, the Des Moines city marina is one of the largest in the area. Nearby is a 670-foot fishing pier that provides great views of the mountains for anglers and strollers. To the north of the pier is the **Des Moines Beach Park,** a 20-acre park with Des Moines Creek, to which salmon return each year.

Gene Coulon Memorial Beach Park (1201 Lake Washington Blvd. N. in Renton, 425/430-6700), has a nice swimming area that's clean and reasonably goose-free. It opens for season in mid-June and lifeguards are on duty from noon–8pm.

Renton's Maplewood **Golf Course and Driving Range** (4050 SE Maple Valley Hwy., 425/430-6800, $31 weekday, $37 weekend) is a fun municipal course with tight, tree-lined fairways and a driving range.

ACCOMMODATIONS

Renton

Situated right next to the greenery of Cedar River Park, **Quality Inn** (1850 Maple Valley Hwy., 425/226-7600 or 800/205-6936, $104–114) is a quiet and pleasant alternative to the SeaTac pack of motels. Several miles of trails await just outside the door, and the facilities include an exercise room and hot tub. Some rooms have kitchenettes. Rooms are tidy, and wireless Internet is included.

The nearby **Clarion of Renton** (3700 E. Valley Rd., 425/251-9591 or 800/578-7878, $99 s or $159 d) offers a free airport shuttle, has a hot tub, and serves continental breakfasts each morning.

SeaTac and Burien

The hotel alley along Highway 99 near the airport in the town of SeaTac was once a notoriously dirty and sketchy neighborhood, but over the last decade the area has really spiffed itself up. Older hotels have been remodeled and decrepit motels torn down in favor of newer establishments. As a result, there are fewer places that remain under $100 per night, but those that do are typically cleaner and safer than what used to be offered in this pool.

One of the best deals in the area is at **(** **Sea-Tac Crest Motor Inn** (18845 Pacific Hwy., 206/433-0999 or 800/554-0300, www .seataccrest.com, $45 s or $64 d), two blocks south of the airport. This is a friendly mom-and-pop operation that caters to no-nonsense

travelers. Rooms are accessible only by indoor corridor, with 24-hour front desk and security. Beds are reasonably comfortable and the units are spic and span—no need to wear socks in the room here. Coffee and muffins are served in the morning, there's free shuttle service to the airport (dial #20 from airport courtesy phones) and seven days of free parking are included with one night's stay.

For something a little slower-paced, but still convenient to the airport, **(** **Three Tree Point Bed & Breakfast** (17026 33rd Ave. SW, 206/669-7646 or 888/369-7696, www.3pointbnb.com) rests in the little town of Burien, about 10 minutes southwest of Sea-Tac. This waterfront inn is situated by a little point jutting out into the Puget Sound. There are two light and airy units here. First there's a deluxe suite ($200 d) with living room, dining room, separate bedroom, and laundry room. And then there's a cottage ($250) with bedroom and master bath, a beautiful kitchen with gas stove and oven, a living room with fireplace, and a laundry room. Both units come with a porch and some amazing water views. A gourmet breakfast is delivered to your kitchen each morning.

If you've got an early morning flight to catch, **Best Western Airport Executel** (20717 International Blvd., 206/878-3300, $100–130 s or d) is one of the best budget chain hotels on the International Boulevard strip. Rooms are very clean, furnishings are new, and access is only by indoor corridor. Get work done in the business center and then relax in the indoor pool, hot tub, and steam room. There's also a fitness center and a restaurant on-site. Wireless Internet is free, and a hot breakfast is served each morning starting in the wee hours at 5 A.M. The hotel runs a free shuttle to the airport.

Federal Way

Another clean and comfortable option is to motor south on Highway 99 down to the **Days Inn** (34827 Pacific Hwy. S, 253/838-3164, $82) in Federal Way. Beds are comfy and the building is very well kept. Though it is just off busy Highway 99, it is soundproofed well enough so that light sleepers should be able to rest peacefully. Rate includes free continental breakfast.

Camping

The wooded camping area on the east side of **Dash Point State Park** (5700 SW Dash Point Rd., 253/233-03221) has primitive sites ($12), tent sites ($21) and RV sites ($31). The park is open year-round. Make reservations ($6.50 extra) at 888/226-7688 or www.parks.wa.gov.

During the summer between late April and early September, **Saltwater State Park** (25205 8th Pl. S., Des Moines, 253/661-4956, www.parks.wa.gov) opens up their small campground to tent campers ($21).

FOOD
Renton

Rainier Avenue is Renton's major commercial byway, lined with big chain restaurants. But all hope is not lost. The best comestibles on this strip are found at **Royal Orchid Thai Cuisine** (104 Rainier Ave. S, 425/271-4219, royalorchidrenton.org, 11 A.M.–10 P.M. daily), which serves authentic Southeast Asian fare with a smile. The dining room is full of real orchids. Try one of the complex curry dishes.

Right across from the downtown train station, **Whistle Stop Ale House** (809 4th St. S, 425/277-3039, www.whistlestopalehouse.com, 11 A.M.–10 P.M. Mon.–Fri., 9 A.M.–10 P.M. Sat., 9 A.M.–3 P.M. Sun.) is a friendly locals bar and eatery with microbrews on tap and good sandwiches.

SeaTac and Burien

SeaTac is mostly dominated by fast-food chains, but there are a few charmingly quirky independent establishments along Highway 99.

For your first or last sample of Seattle's international flavor, try **Mango Thai Cuisine & Bar** (18613 International Blvd., 206/243-1888, www.mangoseattle.com, 11 A.M.–10 P.M. Mon.–Fri., noon–10 P.M. Sat.–Sun.). Its cold beer and hot curries please both local palates and airport travelers alike. And if you find yourself stranded at Sea-Tac in need of comfort food, drop by **Sharps Roaster & Alehouse** (18427 International Blvd., 206/241-5744, http://sharpsroasthouse.com, 11 A.M.–midnight daily). Two dozen draft beers and pulled pork sandwiches should keep anyone from getting homesick.

You can get the real deal in diner food at **Dave's Diner & Brews** (2825 S. 188th St., 206/277-7196, 6 A.M.–10 P.M. daily, lounge is open 10 P.M.–midnight weekends with a full menu), just about a block away from the airport. Get a big plate of chicken-fried steak swimming in flavorful gravy, with a side of real mashed potatoes, veggies, and a roll for under $10. Air travelers take note: Dave's also does box lunches to go for $8.59.

Federal Way

Redondo, just west of Federal Way on Puget Sound, has a fishing pier, boat launch, and one of the area's best restaurants: **(Salty's at Redondo** (28201 Redondo Beach Dr. S, 253/945-1363, www.saltys.com/seattle_south). Primarily a seafood restaurant, Salty's has one of the best sunset views around, and you can drink or dine outdoors on the pier in the summer months.

A good little dive for a light meal is **Lolli's Broiler & Pub** (32925 1st Ave. S. in Federal Way, 253/838-5929), a restaurant and tavern that serves huge burgers and good sandwiches, along with an extensive selection of beers on tap.

INFORMATION

For a handful of local brochures, drop by **Southwest King County Chamber of Commerce** (16400 Southcenter Pkwy., Ste. 210, 206/575-1633 800/638-8613, www.swkcc.org).

The **Renton Chamber of Commerce** (300 Rainier N, 425/226-4560, www.gorenton.com) is open 8:30 A.M.–5 P.M. Monday–Friday.

GETTING THERE AND AROUND

By Air

Seattle's airport is 12 miles south of town and midway between Seattle and Tacoma, hence the name, **Sea-Tac International Airport** (17801 International Blvd., 206/787-5388 or 800/544-1965, www.portseattle.org). All the major domestic, and many international, airlines fly into Sea-Tac. Foreign travelers can change money at the Thomas Cook booth in the main terminal.

Storage lockers are scattered around the airport, but you'll need to pass through security before you reach them. Another option is **Ken's Baggage and Frozen Food Storage** (206/433-5333, 5:30 A.M.–12:30 A.M. daily), located between carousels 12 and 13 in the baggage claim area. Yes, quite a few travelers are interested in storing frozen food, especially fish.

Also near the baggage claim is a volunteer-staffed **Visitor Information Booth** (9:30 A.M.–7:30 P.M. daily in the summer, brochures available at other times), along with car rental counters and kiosks with information on Metro buses, shuttle buses, and limo services. The airport website has updates on airport parking, weather and traffic conditions, ground transportation, and other services.

By Bus and Van

Metro Transit (253/447-4800 or 800/542-7876 http://metro.kingcounty.gov) provides bus service to Seattle and other parts of King County. **Pierce Transit** (253/581-8000 or 800/562-8109, www.piercetransit.org) operates service to Tacoma and other parts of Pierce County, along with Seattle and Olympia.

Renton Urban Shuttle (425/277-5555) has bus service around town for $2.50 per trip. Its route runs between the Tukwila Sounder train station and the Paccar truck factory. **Shuttle Express** (206/622-1424 or 800/942-7433, www.shuttleexpress.com) has van service to Sea-Tac Airport.

SAN JUAN ISLANDS

Scattered like emerald nuggets in the sapphire that is the Puget Sound, the San Juan Islands offer travelers a glimpse into the secret life they might have if they threw caution to the wind, quit their jobs, and gave up Starbucks and mall shopping for life.

Step aboard one of the state's trademark green-and-white ferries in Anacortes and glide over to one of the chain's four largest islands—Orcas, Lopez, Shaw, or San Juan—to find pastoral land grazed by livestock, winding country roads, and not a chain store or restaurant in sight. Peer over the shoreline to scan for orcas spyhopping and lobtailing in nearby waterways. Look overhead to spot bald eagles circling over lakes and glades hidden within island interiors.

While the thread of natural beauty unites these most popular San Juan Islands, each has its own unique personality and individual flair. Lopez Island attracts low-key people who care less than most about an extravagant lifestyle, people who are comfortable alone or in a small community. The island is quiet, rural, and a cyclist's paradise. San Juan Island contains the biggest town, Friday Harbor, with impressive dining, lodging, and recreation possibilities, including whale-watching and sea kayaking. San Juan is also rich in history, and home to San Juan Island National Historical Park, where a war nearly erupted over a pig. Orcas Island is the most rugged and beautiful of the San Juans, with the tallest mountains, best camping, and a relaxed atmosphere that attracts a lot of artists, writers, and free spirits. Shaw, the quietest island, is known for its residents' hands-off approach. Visitors are welcomed here but not

© ERICKA CHICKOWSKI

HIGHLIGHTS

◀ **San Juan Island National Historical Park:** Explore the American and British Camps of this two-site park that is preserved in remembrance of an international standoff started over a pig (page 269).

◀ **Roche Harbor:** Situated on the north side of San Juan Island, this is a classic little seaport resort community with historic roots (page 272).

◀ **Lime Kiln Point State Park:** Also known as Whale Watch Park, this is the best land-based spot on all of the islands to spot orcas (page 274).

◀ **Moran State Park:** The main attraction on Orcas Island, this massive park offers the best camping in the Puget Sound, pristine freshwater lakes, a tumbling waterfall, and the highest peak in all of the islands (page 285).

◀ **Obstruction Pass State Park:** Hidden away on Orcas Island, this remote little park offers a short hike down to a solitary beach filled with skipping stones and driftwood (page 287).

◀ **Lopez Island Country Sights:** Cycle the rural roads of Lopez and stop off to pick berries, watch cows munch the fields, and sip on organic wine (page 295).

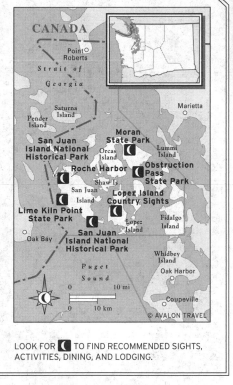

LOOK FOR ◀ TO FIND RECOMMENDED SIGHTS, ACTIVITIES, DINING, AND LODGING.

catered to, so the only lodging here is available under the great blue yonder at the island's small campgrounds. This is the place to get away from it all—including swarming tourists.

Wedged between the Washington mainland and Vancouver Island, the San Juan archipelago is more than just these four islands. The chain is made up of 786 islands at low tide and more than 172 named islands. Those with a boat can widen their base of explorations by paddle, sail, or motor to discover a kaleidoscope of tidepools, rocky shorelines, and hidden campgrounds enough to satisfy even the most pressing case of wanderlust.

To get to any of these islands by car, you'll pass through the mainland town of Anacortes,

a charming port city that definitely merits a stop for a night or two.

PLANNING YOUR TIME

No matter what the season, chances are you will catch more sunshine in the San Juans than anywhere else in the Puget Sound. Shielded by the Olympic and Vancouver Island mountains, the San Juans see less than 25 annual inches of rain, with the sun shining an average of 247 days a year.

The islands are immensely popular in the summer, particularly during the peak season of July and August when it is sunny and moderate— with temperatures rarely exceeding 85°F. If you plan a visit at these times, there may well be no

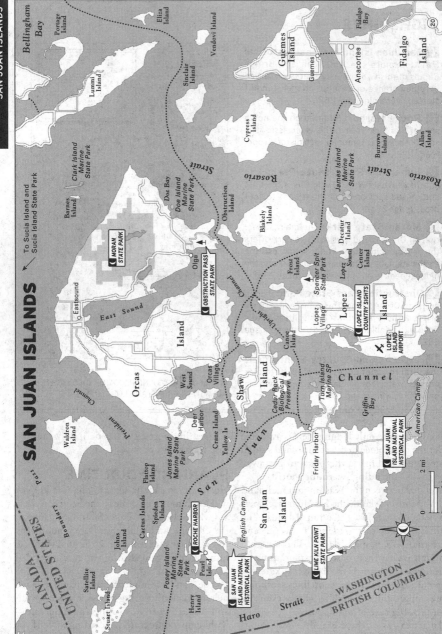

SAN JUAN ISLANDS

CANADA
UNITED STATES
Boundary

To Sucia Island and
Sucia Island State Park

MORAN STATE PARK

OBSTRUCTION PASS STATE PARK

Orcas Island

East Sound

Eastsound

Olga

Presidentᵖᵃˢˢ

Waldron Island

Flattop Island

Spieden Island

Johns Island

Satellite Island

Stuart Island

Cactus Islands

Posey Island Marine State Park

Henry Island

Pearl Island

ROCHE HARBOR

SAN JUAN ISLAND NATIONAL HISTORICAL PARK

English Camp

San Juan Island

LIME KILN POINT STATE PARK

Haro Strait

WASHINGTON
BRITISH COLUMBIA

Jones Island Marine State Park

Deer Harbor

Crane Island
Yellow Is

West Sound

Orcas Village

Shaw Island

Cedar Rock Biological Preserve

San Juan Channel

Friday Harbor

Griffin Bay

Turn Island Marine SP

SAN JUAN ISLAND NATIONAL HISTORICAL PARK

American Camp

Barnes Island

Clark Island Marine State Park

Due Bay

Doe Island Marine State Park

Olga

Obstruction Island

Blakely Island

Canoe Island

Lopez Village

Frost Island

Spencer Spit State Park

Lopez Island

LOPEZ ISLAND COUNTRY SIGHTS

LOPEZ ISLAND AIRPORT

Center Island

Decatur Island

James Island Marine State Park

Lopez Sound

Channel

Cypress Island

Rosario Strait

Burrows Island

Allan Island

Anacortes

Fidalgo Island

Fidalgo Bay

Guemes Island

Guemes

Sinclair Island

Vendovi Island

Eliza Island

Portage Island

Lummi Island

Bellingham Bay

Rosario Strait

2 mi

2 km

© AVALON TRAVEL

room in the inn, and not a lot of mangers available either. Save yourself a lot of headaches by making reservations far in advance, even if you plan on camping. At the older and more established B&Bs this means calling at least four months ahead of time for a midsummer weekend reservation. If you're looking for space on Memorial Day, the 4th of July, or Labor Day, make reservations up to a year in advance. Also plan on staying at least two nights, as most places on the islands require a minimum stay in the summer and sometimes year-round.

For the locals, September and October are the nicest months of the year: The tourists are gone, the weather is still warm and dry, with highs in the 60s and lows in the 40s or 50s, and the salmon are running. In the winter you'll find fewer fellow travelers and lower lodging rates (often 30 percent less), but the weather won't be quite as inviting and things won't be as green. December is the wettest month, with 4.5 inches of rain on the average and temperatures in the low 40s. It rarely snows in the San Juans, and when it does it lasts but a few days. Still, winter holidays (especially Christmas to New Year's) are likely to be booked well in advance.

For maps and other information before you arrive, contact the **San Juan Islands Visitor Information Service** (360/468-3663 or 888/468-3701, www.visitsanjuans.com) and request *Your Guide to the San Juan Islands,* packed with up-to-date information.

GETTING THERE
By Ferry

If you can take only one ride aboard a **Washington State Ferry** (206/464-6400, www.wsdot.wa.gov/ferries), the trip from Anacortes to the San Juans should be the one. When the ferry pulls away from the Anacortes dock, it is almost like departing on a cruise ship. The scenery is so beautiful that even amateur photographers can get spectacular sunset-over-the-islands shots. In the summer, ferries leave Anacortes at least a dozen times a day 4:30 A.M.–12:20 A.M., stopping at Lopez, Shaw, Orcas, and Friday Harbor, in that order; it takes roughly two hours from Anacortes to Friday Harbor.

Not every ferry stops on each island, but nearly all of them stop at Friday Harbor on San Juan Island. Ferries between Anacortes and Sidney, B.C., run twice a day in the summer and once a day the rest of the year. (Vehicle reservations are *required* for service between the San Juans and Sidney.) Some ferries serve food, espresso, beer, and wine and a duty-free shop can be found on ferries heading to British Columbia. For more information, call 360/293-8166 in Anacortes, 206/464-6400 in Seattle, 888/808-7977 statewide or 604/381-1551 in Victoria. Call 800/843-3779 for automated information.

During the peak summer season, it's wise to arrive at least two hours early on weekends, or an hour early on weekdays. On holiday weekends you may find yourself in line for up to five hours! Parking is available at the Anacortes ferry terminal if you're heading over on foot or by bike. Both San Juan and Orcas Islands have excellent bus services, so you really don't need a car there anyway. The terminal usually has information on current campsite availability at the San Juans parks (meaning they often say none are available) to help in planning where to stay that night. Avoid the crowds by traveling midweek, early morning, late evening (except Friday evenings), or better yet, by foot, kayak, or bike.

The ferry system operates on a first-come, first-served basis, with reservations available only for the routes from Anacortes to Sidney, B.C., and from Orcas Island or San Juan Island to Sidney. No reservations are accepted for travel to the San Juans—just get in line and wait like everyone else. In Anacortes, tune your radio to **AM 1340 "The Whale"** for broadcasts of current ferry status, including any backups or other problems.

Peak season fares to Friday Harbor, the last American stop, are $16.85 for passengers, $54 for car and driver. Bikes are $4 extra. Car-and-driver fares to the other islands from Anacortes are a few dollars less. Interisland ferries are free for passengers and bikes, and $23.50 for cars and drivers. Cash, credit cards, in-state checks, and travelers checks are accepted. Most of these rates are lower in the off-season.

Ferry travelers are only charged in the

westbound direction; eastbound travel within the San Juans or from the islands to Anacortes is free. (The only exception to this is for travelers leaving from Sidney, B.C.) If you're planning to visit all the islands, save money by heading straight to Friday Harbor, and then working your way back through the others at no additional charge.

If you're driving around the islands, be sure to fill your tank in Anacortes before getting on the ferry. Because of the cost of shipping fuel here (and because they can get away with it), gas stations on the islands charge at least 30 percent more for gas than on the mainland.

Once a day, a ferry continues on from Orcas and Friday Harbor to Sidney, B.C.; round-trip fares are $13.50 for passengers or $58.65 for car and driver.

The passenger-only *Victoria Clipper* (206/448-5000 or 800/888-2535, www.clipper vacations.com) has high-speed catamaran day trips between Seattle and San Juan Island ($75 for adults, $37.50 for kids round-trip).

Puget Sound Express (360/385-5288, www.pugetsoundexpress.com, $88.50 round-trip, bikes and kayaks $15 extra) provides passenger-only service between Port Townsend and Friday Harbor. The boat leaves Port Townsend daily April–October and stays in Friday Harbor long enough for a quick three-hour visit, or you can overnight there and return to Port Townsend later.

By Air
Kenmore Air (206/486-1257 or 800/543-9595,

www.kenmoreair.com) has scheduled floatplane flights from Lake Union in Seattle and Lake Washington in Kenmore to Friday Harbor and Roche Harbor on San Juan Island, to Lopez Islander and Fisherman Bay on Lopez Island, and to Rosario Resort and West Sound on Orcas Island. Peak fares are approximately $263 one-way. A 24-pound baggage weight limit is in effect for these flights, with excess baggage charged at $1/pound. Kenmore Air also offers charter service to other destinations in the San Juans and flightseeing trips.

San Juan Airlines (360/293-4691 or 800/874-4434, www.sanjuanairlines.com) has daily wheeled-plane flights from Anacortes and Bellingham to most of the San Juan Islands. Typically tickets cost $106–140 one-way. Charters are also available departing from Seattle's Boeing field starting at $130. San Juan Airlines (800/874-4434, www.sanjuanairlines.com) also offers flightseeing trips over the San Juans from Bellingham for about $190 for a half-hour flight on a five-seat aircraft.

Rose Air (503/675-7673, www.roseair.com) offers charter flights between Portland International Airport and the San Juan Islands. Charters start at $364 one-way for a three-seat flight.

Island Air (360/378-2376 or 888/378-2376, www.sanjuan-islandair.com) has custom charter flights and flightseeing trips from San Juan Island Airport. Fares vary, with a three-person flight from Seattle's Boeing Field to Friday Harbor starting at $275 one-way.

Anacortes

Many visitors know Anacortes (ah-nah-KOR-tez) only as the jumping-off point for the San Juan Islands, but this city of 15,000 is far more than a ferry dock on the tip of Fidalgo Island. It is one of the more pleasant cities of its size in the Puget Sound basin and has a casual, end-of-the-road atmosphere.

Although it's hard to believe, Anacortes is legally on Fidalgo Island; Swinomish Slough cuts

a sluggish, narrow swath from the La Conner area around the hills known as Fidalgo Head. The slough is kept open for boaters and is spanned by a beautiful arc of a bridge.

SIGHTS
Museums and Historic Buildings
The **Anacortes Museum** (1305 8th St., 360/293-1915, 10 A.M.–4 P.M. Mon.–Sat.,

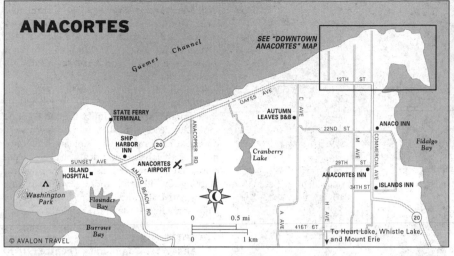

ANACORTES

SEE "DOWNTOWN ANACORTES" MAP

Guemes Channel

12TH ST

GAYES AVE

STATE FERRY
TERMINAL

AUTUMN
LEAVES B&B

C AVE

22ND ST

ANACO INN

SHIP
HARBOR
INN

ANACOPPER RD

20

*Cranberry
Lake*

M AVE

COMMERCIAL AVE

*Fidalgo
Bay*

SUNSET AVE

ANACORTES
AIRPORT

29TH ST

ISLAND
HOSPITAL

ANACO BEACH RD

ANACORTES INN

34TH ST

ISLANDS INN

*Washington
Park*

*Flounder
Bay*

H AVE

A AVE

0   0.5 mi

41ST ST

To Heart Lake, Whistle Lake,
and Mount Erie

20

*Burrows
Bay*

0   1 km

© AVALON TRAVEL

donation) houses local historical exhibits, photographs, and period furniture. Get another taste of the past in a walk around Anacortes to see the many small **historic murals** on local buildings. The visitors center has descriptions of each.

Other remnants of earlier days are scattered throughout town, including the historic sternwheeler **W. T. Preston** the pride and joy of the Snagboat Heritage Museum at 713 R Ave. next to the marina (360/293-1916, 11 A.M.–5 P.M. Sat.–Sun., $3 adults, $2 seniors, $1 kids, free for kids under 8). She was the last sternwheeler to operate on Puget Sound. Right next to the *Preston* is the 1911 Burlington Northern Railroad Depot (7th and R), plus the Anacortes Farmers Market on summer Saturdays.

Causland Park covers a city block at 8th Street and N Avenue; its colorful and playfully ornate mosaic walls and gazebo were built in 1920 with stones from area islands. The small amphitheater completes the old-timey feeling. Nearby are a number of 1890s homes and buildings, many restored to their original splendor. The home owned and built by Amos and Anna Curtis Bowman in 1891 stands at 1815 8th Street; at 807 4th Street, an architect's office is now housed in what was probably the finest bordello in the county in the 1890s.

Viewpoints

Five miles south of downtown Anacortes, 1,270-foot **Mount Erie** is the tallest "mountain" on Fidalgo Island. The steep and winding road leads 1.5 miles to a partially wooded summit, where four short trails lead to dizzying views of the Olympics, Mount Baker, Mount Rainier, and Puget Sound. Don't miss the two lower overlooks, located a quarter mile downhill from the summit. Get to Mount Erie by following Heart Lake Road south from town, past Heart Lake to the signed turnoff at Mount Erie Road. Trails lead from various points along Mount Erie Road into other parts of Anacortes Community Forest Lands.

For an impressive, low-elevation viewpoint of the Cascades and Skagit Valley, visit **Cap Sante Park** on the city's east side, following 4th Street to West Avenue. Scramble up the boulders for a better look at Mount Baker, the San Juans, and the Anacortes refineries that turn Alaskan oil into gasoline. Not far away, a short trail leads to **Rotary Park** next to Cap Sante Marina, where you'll find picnic tables overlooking the busy harbor.

Washington Park

Three miles west of downtown Anacortes, Washington Park is a strikingly beautiful picnic

© ERICKA CHICKOWSKI

downtown Anacortes

spot with 200 waterfront acres on Rosario Strait affording views of the San Juans and Olympics. Walk, bike, or drive the 2.3-mile paved scenic loop, and pull into one of many waterfront picnic areas. Other facilities include a popular boat launch, several miles of hiking trails offering views of the San Juans and the Olympics, a playground, and well-used campsites. The original park acreage was donated by one of Fidalgo Island's earliest pioneers, Tonjes Havekost, who said, "Make my cemetery a park for everybody." His grave stands on the southern edge of the park, overlooking Burrows Channel. Additional acreage was bought by the Anacortes Women's Club in 1922 with proceeds from the sale of lemon pies—they paid just $2,500 for 75 beachfront acres.

ENTERTAINMENT AND EVENTS
Nightlife
Get your live music fix on Friday and Saturday nights at three downtown bars, staging just about every kind of music. They are **Rockfish**

Grill & Anacortes Brewery (320 Commercial Ave., 360/588-1720, www.anacortesrock fish.com), **Brown Lantern Ale House** (412 Commercial Ave., 360/293-2544, www .brownlantern.com), and **Watertown Pub** (314 Commercial Ave., 360/293-3587).

Casinos
Swinomish Northern Lights Casino & Bingo (360/293-2691 or 800/877-7529, www.swin omishcasino.com) fires up slot machine tournaments all summer and deals blackjack, rolls craps, and spins roulette just across the Highway 20 bridge on Fidalgo Island. Use your winnings to buy native arts and crafts in the gift store, or enjoy some live music in the cabaret.

The Arts
The **Anacortes Community Theatre** (918 M Ave., 360/293-6829, acttheatre.com) makes locals into stars with its amateur productions of everything from well-known musicals to plays by emerging playwrights. The **Vela Luka Croatian Dance Ensemble** (www.velaluka .org) is a talented celebration of the Croation heritage of nearly a quarter of the residents of Anacortes.

Meet regional authors during book and poetry readings at the fiery independent **Watermark Book Co.** (612 Commercial Ave., 360/293-4277 or 800/291-4277, www.water markbooks.com, 8 A.M.–8 P.M. Mon.–Fri., 8 A.M.–5 P.M. Sat.–Sun.).

Festivals and Events
The **Anacortes Waterfront Festival** (www .anacortes.org/wff), held at Cap Sante Boat Haven in June, celebrates the city's maritime heritage with a docent-guided waterfront walking tour, boat show, radio-controlled sail boat regatta, and food, music, and magic. A bit livelier party for salty dogs happens in late August at the **Anacortes Workboat Races and Pirate Faire** (360/293-3522, www.ana cortesworkboatraces.com). Eye patches, parrots, and peg-legs abound during the festivities, which include a maritime swap meet, music, and thunderous tug-boat races.

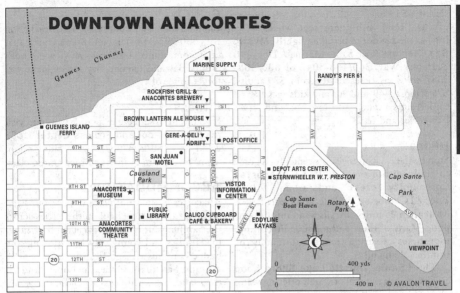

DOWNTOWN ANACORTES

The last weekend in July brings the oratory celebration of **An-O-Chords Annual Barbershop Concert and Salmon Barbecue** (360/293-1282, www.anochords.org) showcases some of the best a cappella harmony groups in the world, including the famous 50-man local An-O-Chords group. Tickets run from $16–25.

The **Anacortes Arts and Crafts Festival** (360/293-6211, www.anacortesartsfestival .com), held the first weekend of August, attracts more than 50,000 people and includes a juried fine-art show, high-quality arts and crafts booths, a children's fair, ethnic foods, antique cars, and plenty of live music and entertainment. The **Oyster Run** (360/757-1515) on the last weekend of September draws thousands of motorcyclists to Anacortes. You'll also find stunt bikers, a map of biker-friendly businesses, and oysters on the half shell. The event has gotten so big, some hotels book up a year in advance.

SPORTS AND RECREATION
Boating
Anacortes is home to the largest concentrations

of bareboat charters in North America; get a list from the visitors center (360/293-3832, www.anacortes.org). The sea kayak manufacturer Eddyline has a factory in nearby Burlington. Learn about kayaking through instruction or tours at the **Sea Kayak shop** (2515 Commercial Ave., 360/299-2300, seakayak-shop.com) along the Anacortes marina. You can also take boats out for a test paddle, rent a kayak, or try on some high-tech clothing.

Founded in 1913, **Marine Supply & Hardware Co.** (2nd St. and Commercial Ave., 360/293-3014, www.marinesupplyand hardware.com) is the oldest continuously operating marine supply store west of the Mississippi. The original oiled wood floors and oak cabinets make a great showplace for the nautical antiques, decorations, and even a few functional maritime objects. It's a fascinating place to visit. Be sure to pet the store cat!

Whale-Watching
Two local companies offer whale-watching trips from Anacortes. **Island Adventures** (360/293-2428 or 800/465-4604, www .island-adventures.com, $89 adults, $79

seniors, $49 ages 3–12, free for tots) boasts of a fast boat with guaranteed whale viewing—a pledge not to be taken lightly. **Mystic Sea Charters** (Cap Sante Marina A Doc, 710 Seafarers Way, 360/466-3042 or 800/308-9387, www.mysticseacharters.com, $89 adults, $79 seniors, $49 students and kids ages 17 and under) runs a stately 100-foot boat and serves free coffee and tea.

Hiking

Stop by the Anacortes visitors center for a guide to trails within the 2,200-acre **Anacortes Community Forest Lands** around Mount Erie and Cranberry, Whistle, and Heart Lakes. More than 25 miles of trails wind through the park. Many of these paths can be linked into loop hikes of various lengths to match the stamina of any hiker.

The 3.5-mile **Whistle Lake Shore Loop** circles this small body of water, offering water views, lots of birdlife, and old-growth stands of Douglas fir and cedar. An easy and almost-level path is the **Erie View Trail,** which departs from Heart Lake Road and follows a seasonal creek to a fine view of Mount Erie a mile out.

From the trailhead at the intersection of Mount Erie and Heart Lake Roads, hike the half-mile **Pine Ridge Loop Trail** for more views of Mount Erie and Sugarloaf. This moderately difficult hike takes from 1–2 hours. Another short hike is the 1.6-mile **Sugarloaf Trail,** starting on Ray Auld Drive six miles from its intersection with Heart Lake Road. Follow the trail from the marshy trailhead straight up, ignoring side trails, to be treated to views of Port Townsend, the San Juan Islands, and the Strait of Juan de Fuca to the west, and Bellingham to the north.

The Cranberry Lake area also has a number of hiking paths, including the mile-long **John M. Morrison Loop Trail,** which starts at the end of 29th Street. This easy loop hike provides bluff-top views of Cranberry Lake old-growth Douglas firs, some of which are seven feet wide.

Golf

Similk Beach Golf Course (12518 Christianson Rd., 360/293-3444) has an 18-hole course that takes some concentration—the views of both Similk Bay and Fidalgo Bay might make you forget to tee off.

Fitness

If you want to squeeze in a quick workout, visit the **Fidalgo Pool and Fitness Center** (1603 22nd St., 360/293-0673, www.fidalgopool.com) for a swim or instructor-led cardio class.

ACCOMMODATIONS

Anacortes is a natural place to rest your head before or after a long haul on the ferries across the San Juans. It is also an excellent base camp for families and young travelers sticking to a budget—rooms are significantly less expensive than on San Juan, Orcas, or Lopez, and all the islands are within easy reach for a day trip. Make reservations far ahead for the summer months; some places fill up by March for the peak season in July and August.

Under $100

Lake Campbell Motel (1377 Hwy. 20, 360/293-5314, $55–105 s or d) is four miles south of Anacortes along Lake Campbell. This is a good family place with microwaves and fridges in all the rooms; the more expensive ones contain full kitchens.

San Juan Motel (1103 6th St., 360/293-5105 or 800/533-8009, $72 s or $128 d, kitchenettes $85 s or $145 d) is a centrally located, clean place.

Anacortes Inn (3006 Commercial Ave., 360/293-3153 or 800/327-7976, www.anacortesinn.com, $72 s or d, suites $80–128) has rooms with fridges and microwaves, plus a seasonal outdoor pool.

Islands Inn (3401 Commercial Ave., 360/293-4644 or 866/331-3328, www.islandsinn.com, $89–149 d) has 36 comfortable motel rooms and two executive suites ($140 d) with fireplaces and jetted tubs. An outdoor pool and hot tub are there for the using, and the attached wine bar offers appetizers to go along with your glass of wine. The Islands also lays out a continental breakfast spread superior to most.

$100-150

Anaco Inn (905 20th St., 360/293-8833, www.anacoinn.com) is a well-kept inn where standard rooms are $79 s or d. Rooms with jetted tubs and kitchens cost $149 d, and apartment units run $149 d. A hot tub is available, and a continental breakfast is included.

With large rooms, an outdoor pool, hot tub, and continental breakfast, **Fidalgo Country Inn** (7645 S.R. 20, 360/293-3494 or 800/244-4179, www.fidalgocountryinn.com, $109–160 d) is located on the outskirts of town, convenient for those who would like to visit both Anacortes and La Conner. Larger suites with kitchenette, fireplace, and jetted tub are available for $159 d.

Anyone heading out to the San Juans by ferry should consider the homey **((Ship Harbor Inn** (5316 Ferry Terminal Rd., 360/293-5177 or 800/852-8568, www.shipharborinn.com), located near the ferry terminal. It is quiet and peaceful, with clean rooms ($109 d), cottages ($129 d) with kitchenettes and fireplaces, and several hot tub suites ($159–179 d).

$150-200

Autumn Leaves B&B (2301 21st St., 360/293-4920, www.autumn-leaves.com, $160–175 d) is a contemporary home with three romantic guest rooms furnished with French antiques. The private bathrooms all have jetted tubs and the fireplace has a remote control. Rates include a gourmet breakfast. Children over 14 are welcome. Smoking is not allowed anywhere on the B&B's grounds.

Camping

Three miles west of Anacortes, the city-run **Washington Park** (360/293-1918, $17 tents, $23 RVs with water and electrical hookups) has 73 campsites in the woods, with showers and boat launches. No reservations are accepted from nonresidents of Fidalgo and Guemes Islands.

Camp your camper or RVs at **Fidalgo Bay Resort** (4701 Fidalgo Bay Rd., 360/293-5353 or 800/727-5478, www.fidalgobay.com, $34.50–58), owned and operated by the Samish Indian Nation or **Pioneer Trails Campground** (7337 Miller Rd., 360/293-5355 or 888/777-5355, www.pioneertrails.com, $32–49 RV sites, $47–129 cabins). Pioneer Trails even has cozy cabins available for rent.

FOOD
Cafés and Delis

Start your day at **Calico Cupboard Café & Bakery** (901 Commercial Ave., 360/293-7315, 7:30 A.M.–4 P.M. daily) for great homemade country breakfasts and healthy lunches. Save room for dessert: the fudge pecan pie and apple dumplings are legendary.

For food with a side of sass, stop by **((Gere-a-Deli** (502 Commercial Ave., 360/293-7383, www.gere-a-deli.com, 7 A.M.–4 P.M. Mon.–Sat., closed Sun.). This funky little eatery offers cleverly named (and tasty) sandwiches, salads, soups, and homemade desserts. Munch away while enjoying the antique signs and advertisements lining the walls here.

Seafood

If your palate seeks something a bit more sophisticated and you have a bit more time to spare, try **Randy's Pier 61** (209 T Ave., 360/293-5108, www.pier61.com, 11:30 A.M.–9 P.M. daily, $22), on the waterfront, is a pleasant seafood restaurant with lobster, crab, and local oysters, to say nothing of the beautiful vistas of Guemes Channel. The Sunday brunch is a local favorite.

Contemporary

One might not expect it in the ho-hum hamlet of Anacortes, but there are actually two hip restaurants in town that could easily compete with most of the fashionable restaurants in Seattle.

Better of the two is **((Adrift** (510 Commercial Ave., 360/588-0653, www.adriftrestaurant.com, 8 A.M.–9 P.M. Mon.–Thurs.,

8 A.M.–10 P.M. Fri.–Sat., closed Sun.). Driftwood furniture and local art accent the interior here, fostering an inviting dining place with a cozy nautical theme that celebrates Anacortes's roots. The menu relies on fresh greens, seafood, poultry, and steaks, cooked up with a bit of international flair. On the seasonal dinner menu you're as likely to find Cuban pork sandwiches or Vietnamese chicken burgers as cioppino or steak. Adrift also serves hearty breakfasts and fresh lunches.

Pub Grub

You won't go wrong with a lunch or dinner at **Rockfish Grill & Anacortes Brewery** (320 Commercial Ave., 360/588-1720, www.anacortesrockfish.com, 11:30 A.M.–10 P.M. Sun.–Thurs., 11:30 A.M.–midnight Fri.–Sat., $15). Choices include seafood, pastas, wood-fired pizzas, and fresh ales from the on-the-premises brewery. Just down the street is **Brown Lantern Ale House** (412 Commercial Ave., 360/293-2544, www.brownlantern.com, 11 A.M.–11 P.M. Mon.–Wed., 11 A.M.–midnight Thurs., 11 A.M.–1 A.M. Fri.–Sat., $10), where the burgers and halibut fish and chips rock and the classic pool table sees plenty of action.

Markets

Get groceries at the big **Food Pavilion** store (1519 Commercial Ave., 360/588-8181). Get smoked salmon and fresh shellfish from **Seabear Smokehouse** (30th St. and T Ave., 800/645-3474, www.seabear.com). There are free tours daily in the summer.

The **Anacortes Farmers Market** (7th St. and R Ave., 360/293-9404, www.anacortesfarmersmarket.org) takes place 9 A.M.–2 P.M. Sunday from mid-May–mid-October.

INFORMATION AND SERVICES

For maps, brochures, and up-to-date information, drop by the **Anacortes Visitor Information Center** (819 Commercial Ave., 360/293-3832, www.anacortes.org, 9 A.M.–5 P.M. daily May–mid-Sept., 9 A.M.–5 P.M. Mon.–Fri., 10 A.M.–3 P.M. Sat., noon–3 P.M. Sun. the rest of the year). Across the street is a mural of Anna Curtis, for whom the town was named. The **Anacortes American** newspaper's website, www.goanacortes.com, is interesting to read and is full of local information and links.

Get clean with laundry facilities and coin-operated showers at the **Friday Harbor Marina** and **Roche Harbor Marina** (360/378-2688, www.portfridayharbor.org).

GETTING THERE AND AROUND

By Ferry

To reach the San Juan Islands or British Columbia via **Washington State Ferry** (206/464-6400, www.wsdot.wa.gov/ferries), you have no choice but to leave from Anacortes. Be prepared for a lengthy wait on summer weekends. Avoid the waits by leaving your car in the lot at the terminal ($25 for three days) and walking aboard; there's always space for walk-on passengers. A free park-and-ride lot is located at March Point eight miles east of here, and a shuttle bus transports you to the ferry terminal.

By Air

Departing from Anacortes Airport, **San Juan Airlines** (360/293-4691 or 800/874-4434, www.sanjuanairlines.com) offers commuter flights year-round to all three major islands.

By Bus

Skagit Transit (360/299-2424, www.skagit transit.org) has daily bus connections from Anacortes to Mount Vernon, La Conner, and other parts of Skagit County. **Airporter Shuttle** (360/380-8800 or 800/235-5247, www.airporter.com) offers daily shuttles between Anacortes and Sea-Tac Airport.

San Juan Island

The largest island in the archipelago, San Juan Island is about 20 miles long and 7 miles wide, covering 55 square miles. Picturesque Friday Harbor sits along the west side, its marina protected by Brown Island. Acting as the county seat, Friday Harbor is the only incorporated town in the islands and is the commercial center of the San Juans. It is a U.S. Customs port of entry, as is Roche Harbor on the other side of the island.

SIGHTS

◖ San Juan Island National Historical Park

In one of the stranger pieces of history, the killing of a pig by an American settler nearly set off a war between the United States and Britain. Fortunately, conflict was averted and the San Juan Islands were eventually declared American territory.

The sites where the American and British forces were based during the peaceful standoff are now part of the San Juan Island National

Historical Park (headquarters on Spring St. in Friday Harbor, 360/378-2240, www.nps.gov/sajh, 8:30 A.M.–5 P.M. daily Memorial Day–Labor Day, 8:30 A.M.–4:30 P.M. Mon.–Fri. the rest of the year). In the spring, the National Parks Service offers nature walks and bird-watching trips. Summertime brings guided historical walks and living history exhibitions on selected weekends. The office doubles as a small interpretive museum that manages to untangle the mess that was the Pig War. The park itself is in two sections on different ends of the island: American Camp and English Camp. Both sites have picnic areas and beach access for day use only. The grounds are open year-round.

AMERICAN CAMP

Located on the southeast corner of San Juan Island, American Camp sits on a windswept grassy peninsula six miles from Friday Harbor. This is a wonderful place on a sunny summer afternoon, with both the Cascades and

© ERICKA CHICKOWSKI

Get lost in the pastoral scenery on San Juan Island.

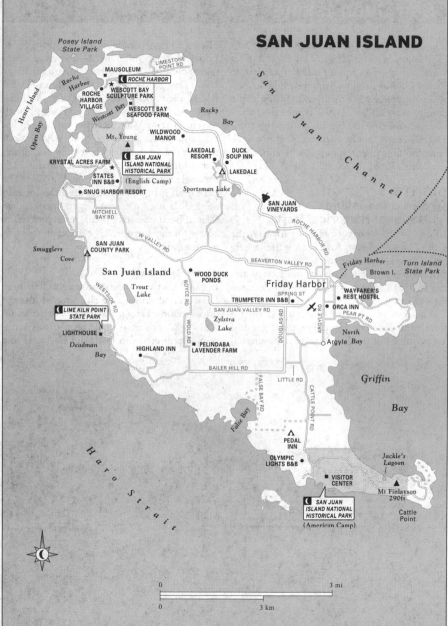

SAN JUAN ISLAND

Posey Island State Park
MAUSOLEUM
ROCHE HARBOR
Roche Harbor
LIMESTONE POINT RD
WESCOTT BAY SCULPTURE PARK
ROCHE HARBOR VILLAGE
Henry Island
Open Bay
Westcott Bay
WESCOTT BAY SEAFOOD FARM
Rocky Bay
Mt. Young
WILDWOOD MANOR
KRYSTAL ACRES FARM
SAN JUAN ISLAND NATIONAL HISTORICAL PARK (English Camp)
LAKEDALE RESORT
DUCK SOUP INN
STATES INN B&B
LAKEDALE
SNUG HARBOR RESORT
Sportsman Lake
SAN JUAN VINEYARDS
MITCHELL BAY RD
ROCHE HARBOR RD
Smugglers Cove
SAN JUAN COUNTY PARK
W VALLEY RD
San Juan Island
BEAVERTON VALLEY RD
Friday Harbor
Brown I.
Turn Island State Park
WESTSIDE RD
BOYCE RD
WOOD DUCK PONDS
Trout Lake
Friday Harbor
SPRING ST
WAYFARER'S REST HOSTEL
TRUMPETER INN B&B
ORCA INN
PEAR PT RD
LIME KILN POINT STATE PARK
WOLD RD
Zylstra Lake
DOUGLAS RD
ARGYLE RD
North Argyle Bay
LIGHTHOUSE
Deadman Bay
HIGHLAND INN
PELINDABA LAVENDER FARM
SAN JUAN VALLEY RD
BAILER HILL RD
LITTLE RD
Griffin Bay
FALSE BAY RD
CATTLE POINT RD
Haro Strait
PEDAL INN
OLYMPIC LIGHTS B&B
False Bay
VISITOR CENTER
Jackle's Lagoon
SAN JUAN ISLAND NATIONAL HISTORICAL PARK (American Camp)
Mt Finlayson 290ft
Cattle Point

0   3 mi

0   3 km

© AVALON TRAVEL

Olympics in view. It's also a satisfyingly lonely place to explore on a rainy winter day.

Two buildings remain at American Camp—an officers' quarters and a laundresses' quarters—along with a defensive fortification (redoubt) constructed by Henry M. Roberts of *Roberts' Rules of Order* fame. A long white picket fence circles the grounds, and a trail leads downhill past the old Hudson's Bay Company Farm site on Grandma's Cove. Other nature trails take off to Mount Finlayson (hardly a mountain at just 290 feet) and through the forests along **Jackle's Lagoon,** or you can explore driftwood-jammed **South Beach,** a wonderful place for a sunset walk on the sandy shores. This is the longest public beach on the island. The park is also home to thousands of rabbits whose ancestors were brought to the islands as a food source, but the inevitable happened and they keep multiplying. Birders come to American Camp to see the only nesting **Eurasian skylarks** in the United States; they were introduced to Vancouver Island early in the 1900s and a small number ended up here.

The **American Camp Visitor Center** is open 8 A.M.–5 P.M. daily in the summer, and 8:30 A.M.–4:30 P.M. Wed.–Sun. in winter. The

THE PIG WAR

San Juan Island on the northern edge of the Puget Sound is the site of one of the weirdest international incidents in American history. Two nations, confirmed adversaries, squared off for armed confrontation on this tiny island in 1859. Sloops of war sailed into harbor and positioned their guns. Camps were built and battle lines were drawn. Soldiers drilled in the rain and prepared for battle. Their cause? A British pig that couldn't be kept from eating American potatoes.

As Americans moved west along the Oregon Trail and settled in Washington, the British started to get cagey about the new residents in the area. The existing law of the land had called for joint occupation by Americans and British, a right that the Hudson's Bay Company had taken full advantage of, conducting trapping and trading operations throughout the Northwest. This arrangement had outlived its usefulness, however, and both sides met in 1849 to thresh out a more permanent solution. The resulting Oregon Treaty set a boundary formalizing U.S. and British land claims. Unfortunately, ambiguity in the wording of the treaty left it unclear who exactly owned San Juan Island. Both sides claimed sovereignty, and Hudson's Bay built a large sheep ranch here, while 25 or so Americans also settled in to farming the opposite side of the island.

This uneasy peace was soon to be disturbed by a pig in Her Majesty's service. The pig, which belonged to the Hudson's Bay Company, was fond of straying into American settler Lyman Cutlar's farm and sampling his crops. Numerous petitions to the company brought no solution, and in June of 1859, a frustrated Cutlar shot and killed the pig. This outrage led to both sides pleading for military intervention; in short order, both sides got their wish. An armed standoff ensued, although few probably imagined that this drizzly cold war would ultimately last 12 years. British Royal Marines established a base at English Camp on the northern shore of the island, while the Americans fortified the southern tip, known as American Camp. Each force's orders were the same: return fire if fired upon, but do not initiate attack.

Tensions waxed and waned as Americans were distracted by the Civil War and troubles elsewhere. During this time, it's said that both sides enjoyed fairly cordial relations, visiting each other's camps and playing against one another in sporting events. If any other livestock got out of line during this period, it went unrecorded. Finally in 1872, the dispute was submitted for arbitration to Germany's Kaiser Wilhelm I, who ruled in favor of the Americans. The British withdrew soon afterward, pigs and all, just barely having prevented what might have been one of the silliest wars in history.

museum provides interpretive displays and historical artifacts.

At the tip of the peninsula is **Cattle Point Interpretive Area,** where you'll find a picnic shelter in an old powerhouse and trails to a nearby lighthouse and beach.

ENGLISH CAMP

Ten miles from Friday Harbor on the northwest side of the island, English Camp (also known as British Camp) includes a restored hospital, a picturesque reconstructed blockhouse right on the water's edge, an impressive formal garden, and a small white barracks. The blockhouse and barracks are open 8:30 A.M.–4:30 P.M. daily in the summer, closed the rest of the year. The location is beautiful, with protected waters on both sides of Bell Point and spreading maple trees overhead, a sharp contrast to the barren American Camp. The mile-long **Mount Young Trail** leads from English Camp to the old British cemetery where six Royal Marines are buried, and then up through second-growth forests to 650-foot Mount Young with its gorgeous vistas of the archipelago. An almost-level nature path heads a mile out to the tip of **Bell Point.**

The Whale Museum

The Whale Museum (62 1st St. N. in Friday Harbor, 360/378-4710, www.whalemuseum .org, 9 A.M.–6 P.M. daily, $6 adults, $5 seniors, $3 ages 5–18 and students, free for kids under 5) has whale and porpoise displays, including the genealogy of Puget Sound orcas and full skeletons of an adult killer whale, a minke whale, and a baby gray whale. If you spot a whale anywhere around the San Juans, swimming or stranded, call the museum's 24-hour **Whale Hotline** at 800/562-8832.

San Juan Historical Museum

San Juan Historical Museum (405 Price St., Friday Harbor, 360/378-3949, www.sj museum.org, 10 A.M.–4 P.M. Wed.–Sat. and 1–4 P.M. Sun. May–Sept., 1–4 P.M. Sat. in October, March, and April, closed the rest of the year, $5 adults, $4 seniors, $3 ages 5–18, free for kids under 5). Housed in an 1890s farmhouse, the museum includes fascinating antiques, old photos, and historical artifacts. Outside, visitors can tour a collection of old farm equipment, the first county jail, a log cabin, and other historic buildings.

Krystal Acres Farm

If you're out for a cruise or a bike ride through the middle of the island, be sure to take a break at Krystal Acres Farm (152 Blazing Tree Rd., 360/378-6125, www.krystalacres.com), an alpaca ranch with lovely grounds and lightly bleating beauties grazing the pastures. Step inside to check out the woolen wares made from alpaca fur, which makes for some of the softest scarves and sweaters on the planet.

◖ Roche Harbor

Located on the north end of San Juan Island, Roche Harbor (360/378-2155 or

THE LIME WORKS OF SAN JUAN ISLAND

Mention a trip to the San Juan Islands and thoughts come to mind of whale-watching, shopping, leisurely bike rides, or just relaxing by the water. And while San Juan Island has always been a bit of a resort town, in the distant past, it was also a home of industry. Take a walk around the grounds of the historic Hotel De Haro in Roche Harbor and you absolutely cannot miss the lime works. These high-reaching ovens were once used to heat limestone until calcium oxide was formed, a process called calcining. The calcium oxide, or quicklime, was critical for whitewash, mortar, and plaster. By the 1930s, most of the pure limestone deposits had been depleted and the works closed. Today, you can still visit the lime works at the Hotel de Haro, or look out for orcas from another former hub of industry, Lime Kiln State Park.

© ERICKA CHICKOWSKI

Visit the alpacas at Krystal Acres Farm.

800/451-8910, www.rocheharbor.com) is a delicious step into the past. In 1886, John S. McMillin established the Roche Harbor Lime & Cement Co., mining lime deposits from 13 hillside quarries and processing the lime in brick-lined kilns along the shore. By the 1890s this was the largest lime works west of the Mississippi and required 4,000 acres of forest just to keep the kilns running. McMillin built a company town for his employees, had warehouses that extended hundreds of feet into the bay, and operated a general store on the wharf. His **Hotel de Haro** began as a log bunkhouse, but later grew into the distinctive three-story wood structure of today. McMillin's home is now a waterside restaurant, facing the protected harbor filled with sailboats.

Take some time to explore the area around the hotel (now on the National Register of Historic Places) and the little New England–style **Our Lady of Good Voyage Chapel,** built in 1892, and the only privately owned Catholic church in the nation. The bizarre family mausoleum (named "Afterglow Vista," no less) is approximately a mile from the hotel. Located north of the cottages and a quarter-mile hike up a dirt side road, the mausoleum's centerpiece is a stone temple packed with Masonic symbols and containing the family's ashes in chairs around a limestone table. There's even a broken column symbolizing the "unfinished state" of life, but the planned bronze dome was never added to this once-grandiose mausoleum. Pick up a brochure describing the mausoleum inside Hotel de Haro.

Wescott Bay Sculpture Park

As you approach Roche Harbor, it is pretty hard to miss the Wescott Bay Sculpture Park (across from the Roche Harbor Airstrip on Roche Harbor Road, dawn–dusk daily, free). This unique outdoor museum and promenade displays over 100 unique pieces of art on a 19-acre natural preserve. Art often changes with the seasons, featuring work in wood, ceramic, metal, glass, and stone. Nature lovers will also appreciate the interpretive displays scattered across the trails, which cross over freshwater and saltwater wetlands, forests, and meadows. The park is open rain or shine, with free umbrellas for use at the entrance gatehouse.

(Lime Kiln Point State Park

A good spot to watch for whales is from Lime Kiln Point State Park (www.parks.wa.gov) along Haro Strait on the island's west side; it's the only park in the country dedicated exclusively to whale-watching. Sit here long enough on a summer day (it may be quite a while) and you're likely to see killer whales (orcas), and possibly minke and pilot whales, Dall's porpoises, or harbor porpoises. Rangers are usually at the park in the summer and fall and can answer your questions. The small white lighthouse was built in 1914 and has a foghorn that announces its presence frequently. Researchers use the lighthouse to watch for whales and to determine if boats are affecting their behavior. If there aren't any whales to watch, you can just take in the vistas that stretch to Victoria. No camping is available at the park.

Bald eagles live on the island year-round; look for them between Eagle Cove and Cattle Point on the island's east side.

ENTERTAINMENT AND EVENTS

Nightlife

China Pearl (51 Spring St., 360/378-5254, noon–1 A.M. daily) hosts live music and opens up the dance floor on weekends.

For a friendly game of pool and some chit-chat with the locals, pop into **Herb's Tavern** (80 1st St., 360/378-7076). It's said that Sandra Bullock rented out the whole place a few years back.

Theater

The impressive **San Juan Community Theatre & Arts Center** (100 2nd St., 360/378-3211, www.sanjuanarts.org) is the center for local performing arts, with year-round musical programs and plays. Watch first-run films at **Royal Theatre** (209 Spring St., 360/378-4455).

Festivals and Events

In mid-May, the annual **Return of the Orcas Festival** (360/378-5240) brings kayak races, a whale calling contest, a clam chowder cook-off, and live music to Roche Harbor. A popular **Summer Arts Fair and Lavender Festival** on the third weekend of July includes art exhibits, food booths, and live music.

The **Fourth of July** brings a variety of fun events, including a parade, a 10K race, music, dancing, and evening fireworks. Don't miss the annual Pig War Picnic, featuring a Kiwanis-sponsored pulled-pork feast.

The four-day **San Juan County Fair** (360/378-4310, www.sanjuancountyfair.org) in mid-August features a sheep-to-shawl race, chicken and rabbit races, music, livestock judging, and, of course, carnival rides. The fairgrounds goes German every October during

---

KILLER ANTICS

When you go on whale-watching trips in the San Juans, or just hang around Lime Kiln State Park, see if you can spot some orcas fooling around. These spirited creatures come above the water level quite frequently. Here's a guide to some of their favorite moves:

- **Breach:** Anytime an orca breaks the surface of the water, that's called breaching. If you're ever lucky enough to see one jump completely out of the water, count your blessings. Called a full breach, this is a rarity.

- **Fin Slap:** Scientists don't quite know why they do it, but orcas frequently like to slap the water with their pectoral and dorsal fins.

- **Lobtail:** This is when the whale sticks its tail completely out of the water, waving it like a fan.

- **Spyhop:** That's when they peek out of the water with their head perpendicular to the waterline.

the local **Oktoberfest.** Come prepared to eat schnitzel, drink great-big beers, and do the chicken dance.

Wine-Tasting

San Juan Vineyards (3136 Roche Harbor Rd., 360/378-9463 or 888/983-9463, www.sanjuanvineyards.com) is housed in a century-old schoolhouse three miles out Roche Harbor Road. It produces a limited bottling of wines from the vineyard here, but most of its wine comes from eastern Washington grapes. Give them a call to set up a visit and wine-tasting.

There are no vineyards at **The Island Wine Company** (2 Cannery Landing next to the ferry dock in Friday Harbor, 360/378-3229 or 800/248-9463, www.sanjuancellars.com, 10 A.M.–6 P.M. daily), but the comprehensive wine store might let you sample wines made from eastern Washington grapes and bottled under its San Juan Cellars label.

SHOPPING
Bookstores

Friday Harbor has three good places to buy new books: **Griffin Bay Bookstore** (155 Spring St., 360/378-5511, www.griffinbaybook.com, 10 A.M.–6 P.M. daily), and the grandest bookseller in town, **Harbor Bookstore** (22 Cannery Landing, upstairs, 360/378-7222, 9:30 A.M.–5 P.M. daily). Because I'm partial to well-loved books, my favorite bookstore on the island is **Serendipity Books** (225 A St., at the top of the ferry lanes, 360/378-2665, 10 A.M.–5:30 P.M. daily), which offers used titles at good prices. The selection is fantastic, and titles are well organized.

Boutiques

You'll kick yourself if you visit Friday Harbor and don't go to see **Funk & Junk Antiques** (85 Nichols St, 360/378-2638, 11 A.M.–6 P.M. daily). It has a light-hearted name, but is the force behind most estate or business liquidations in town. This leaves it with a diverse, interesting, and valuable inventory that you're free to browse.

If you're on the lookout for unique beading supplies, try **The Garuda & I** (60 1st St, 866/448-5294, 11 A.M.–3 P.M. Sun.–Mon., 11 A.M.–4 P.M. Thurs.–Sat.). It has parties, classes, and displays of local artistry. You're doubtlessly wondering—a Garuda is a mythical Buddhist/Hindu bird.

The fun folks at **The Toy Box** (20 1st St, 360/378-8889), will do their best to put a smile on the face of you and your children at this whimsical store. It's the perfect place to find games or art supplies to help pass drizzly nights.

Galleries

Friday Harbor is home to several excellent art galleries, including **Waterworks Gallery** (315 Argyle, 360/378-3060, www.waterworksgallery.com, 11 A.M.–6 P.M. Mon.–Fri., 10 A.M.–5 P.M. Sat.–Sun.), a large, contemporary gallery with inventive paintings, prints, watercolors, and sculpture by island and international artists. **Sunshine Gallery** (85 Nichols St., 360/378-5819, 10:30 A.M.–5:30 P.M. Wed.–Mon., closed Tues.) focuses on watercolors, oils, gouache, and pastels. In March, they do a showing of top art by local preschool and elementary school artists-in-training. **The Garuda & I** (60 1st St., 360/378-3733 or 866/448-5294, www.thegarudaandi.com, 11 A.M.–3 P.M. Sun.–Mon., 11 A.M.–4 P.M. Thurs.–Sat.) is less a gallery than a celebration of all things beads and beading, with the best selection in the San Juans, guaranteed. If you didn't know that gourds could become fine art, enlighten yourself at **Island Studios** (270 Spring St., 360/378-6550, www.islandstudios.com), which features work from the many, many local artists, including paintings, stained glass, jewelry, pottery, and gourds.

SPORTS AND RECREATION
Bike and Moped Rentals

Although many folks bike around San Juan Island, it isn't as bike-friendly as slower-paced Lopez. Be ready for narrow roads and speeding cars.

Rent hybrid bikes ($9.50 per hour, $38 per day), road bikes ($12.50 per hour, $50 per day) or even tandems ($19 per hour, $76 per day) to cruise around San Juan Island from **Island Bicycles** (380 Argyle St., 360/378-4941, www.islandbicycles.com, 9 A.M.–6 P.M. daily).

Susie's Moped and Car Rentals (360/378-5244 or 800/532-0087, www.susiesmopeds.com, 9 A.M.–6 P.M. daily mid-Mar.–mid-Oct., $30–60 per hour or $65–130 per day) rents motor scooters in the summer from its two shops: one at the top of the ferry lanes in Friday Harbor (125 Nichols St.) and the other at the resort entrance in Roche Harbor Resort.

Sea Kayaking

One of the best ways to soak up the sights of San Juan Island is to haul out of Friday Harbor or Roche Harbor in a sea kayak and paddle along the shoreline. Doing so can give you a good vantage point to check out the lighthouses, madronas, and neat rocky outcroppings of the coast. It can also put you in prime position to look for whales, particularly along their favorite stretch of waterway, Haro Strait, which passes along the west edge of the island.

Those with little to no experience paddling should definitely consider a guided tour, as currents and tides can be tricky in these parts. **Crystal Seas Kayaking** (360/378-7899 or 877/732-7877, www.crystalseas.com) offers a three-hour round-trip out of Snug Harbor resort for $79. It also operates a unique two- to six-day kayak and bike tour, which overnights at area inns, stops at the nicer restaurants and enters remote areas and prime orca waters. Trip prices are all-inclusive and start at $780 per person. **Discovery Sea Kayak** (360/378-2559 www.discoveryseakayak.com) offers a neat nighttime bioluminescence tour ($99), the kayaks setting off galaxies of shimmering green light as you paddle.

Women kayakers can feel completely comfortable creating a sisterhood of the paddle at **Sea Quest Expeditions** (888/589-4253, www.sea-quest-kayak.com) where they organize two-, three-, and five-day kayaking, camping, and wildlife-spotting trips. Trips run between $349 and $800, and yes, they offer co-ed trips as well.

San Juan Kayak Expeditions (360/378-4436, www.sanjuankayak.com), is passionate about their gear and will rent you impeccably maintained fiberglass kayaks while offering advice for free. They rent double-kayaks only for single day ($100) and multiday ($99/day) trips. The cost includes free pickup from the ferry and all necessary equipment to have a fun and successful trip. They also offer expeditions led by experienced guides.

Whale-Watching

Summertime whale-watching has become a big business in the San Juans. The average price for a three-hour trip is $80.

The Puget Sound's resident pods of orca whales love the San Juans about as much as tourists do. Their prime salmon-hunting grounds are right around San Juan Island on Haro Strait, Trying to spot these black-and-white beauties is a must-see on any trip to the island. The best whale-watch tours and charters have a knowledgeable biologist or naturalist onboard and should operate eco-ethically by keeping at least 100 yards distance between the boat and the whales. As for actually spotting whales, most services claim a success rate of 95 percent or higher and offer refunds or free second-chance cruises if you get skunked. The colorful **Maya's Whale Watch Charters** (360/378-7996, www.mayaswhalewatch.biz) is run by the lovable Capt. Jim Maya, a funny and knowledgeable retired teacher whose clients rave about his tours.

If you've always wondered what whales sound like when they're talking to each other, climb aboard the *Odyssey,* an extensively refitted WWII Navy search and rescue boat outfitted with a special underwater hydrophone to pick up the whales' haunting cries. Run by the folks at **San Juan Excursions** (360/378-6636 or 800/809-4253, www.watchwhales.com, $79 adults, $53 children from 3–12), the three-and-a-half- to four-hour tours embark daily from Friday Harbor. They offer private charters and sea-kayaking as well. **San Juan Safaris** (360/378-1323 or 800/450-6858, www.sanjuansafaris.com) runs a very fast ship that brings 40 or fewer watchers aboard, ensuring a more personal experience. They offer a stunningly affordable combo package that will fly you from Seattle to the Island aboard a seaplane, take you on a 3.5-hour long whale-spotting cruise and then fly you back to Seattle when you'd like. It's a lot of fun for $325 per person.

Boat Charters, Sailing, and Fishing

As the forests of masts and rigging in Friday Harbor and Roche Harbor can attest, sailing and cruising is the preferred pastime on San Juan Island. If you don't have a boat of your own, there are a number of charter and cruise companies available to take you out on the water in style.

If you're looking to splurge, **Caramel Cruises** (360/378-9816 or 888/875-1774) offers three-hour afternoon sails aboard a 37-foot Hunter Legend sailboat for $384 per couple. Sunset sails, dinner cruises, and multiday sails are also available.

Fishing is another great way to see the islands. Whether your taste runs to hard-fighting salmon or deep bottom lingcod, you've struck gold in the San Juans. Before boarding any fishing boat in Washington, you'll need a saltwater fishing license, available at any sporting goods store. Bait and gear is almost always provided as part of the fare. The salmon season is variable—contact the Washington Department of Fish and Wildlife at 360/902-2500 or wdfw.wa.gov for the latest news. **A Trophy Charters** (360/378-2110, www.fishthesanjuans.com) runs a 29-foot fishing boat built for comfort and effectiveness, half-day trips starting at $95 per person, or **North Shore Charters** (360/376-4855) runs out of Oak Harbor, but offers pickup service on San Juan Island. They offer fishing charters virtually year-round.

POSEY ISLAND STATE PARK

This pinprick of an island covers just one acre and is located a quarter mile north of San Juan Island's Roche Harbor. Shallow waters and a

© ERICKA CHICKOWSKI

Friday Harbor marina

single primitive campsite ($10) make this a favorite spot for folks on kayaks and canoes in search of their own little island.

TURN ISLAND STATE PARK

Turn Island, just a quarter mile from San Juan's east shore and within easy kayaking distance of Friday Harbor, is a very popular place for picnickers and campers. It features 10 primitive campsites ($10), three mooring buoys, two beaches, and three miles of wooded hiking trails. There is a strict "no open flames" policy. No grills or fires except for liquid fuel and camp-stoves.

Diving

The San Juans offer the finest cold-water diving on earth and were a particular favorite of the legendary Jacques Cousteau. When the water is clear, one can glimpse a thriving ecosystem teeming with colorful fish, elegant anemones, coral, starfish, freaky octopi, and much more. You'll need your own gear to explore this marvel, but if you've packed in your tanks and are hungry for adventure and a continental breakfast, call **Diver's Dream Charters** (north end of Skyline Marina, 360/202-0076). It generally charters trips up to 12 divers, and one dive master from the shop will come along. Take a two- or three-tank dive and get a feel for this wholly unique undersea world.

Golf

The **San Juan Golf & Country Club** (2261 Golf Course Rd., 360/378-2254, www.san juangolfclub.com, $24 Mar.–May, $28 Jun.–Oct.) is a nine-hole public course. Golf fanatics who don't care about cold weather might want to give the course a go November–February, when they can play unlimited holes for $15 during the week and $20 on weekends. Tennis courts are also available here for public use.

Fitness

Fitness devotees might want to take advantage of one-day memberships at **San Juan Fitness and Athletic Club** (435 Argyle Ave., 360/378-4449, www.sanjuanislandfitness.com,

6 A.M.–8 P.M. Mon.–Fri., 9 A.M.–4 P.M. Sat., 11 A.M.–4 P.M. Sun.) For $17.77 you'll have access to the entire facility including court games, classes, and strength-training equipment, a sauna, and pool.

ACCOMMODATIONS

During the summer it's a good idea to make reservations several months ahead of time to be assured of a bed, particularly on weekends.

Call the **Bed & Breakfast Association of San Juan Island** hotline (360/378-3030 or 866/645-3030, www.san-juan-island.net) for availability at 25 or so of the finest local B&Bs; its website has links to B&B homepages.

Under $100

San Juan Island's lone hostel, **Wayfarers Rest** (35 Malcolm St., 360/378-6428, www.rock island.com/~wayfarersrest) is in a comfortable home with a full kitchen just a short walk from downtown Friday Harbor. The 10-bed hostel has dorm room beds for $30 per person and private double rooms for $70. Kids are welcome.

Another budget-conscious alternative in Friday Harbor is **Orca Inn** (700 Mullis St., 360/378-2724 or 877/541-6722, www.orca innwa.com, $84–99 d). Rooms are a little dated, more than adequate for the type of guests that will spend most of their time out on the water anyway.

Go inland for one of the best deals on the island. **States Inn B&B** (360/378-6240, www .statesinn.com, $100–180 d) is a country home on a working ranch with sheep, chickens, and alpacas seven miles northwest of Friday Harbor. This welcoming bed-and-breakfast serves up fresh cookies in the afternoon and distinguishes itself as one of the only B&Bs on the island to offer rooms for under $100 during peak summer months. All guest rooms have private baths. The inn caters to families and also offers a four-person cottage for $260 and a three-room suite for four for $260.

$100-150

Sitting right on the edge of Friday Harbor,

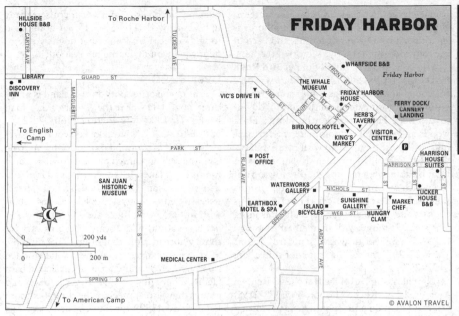

the rooms at **Discovery Inn** (1016 Guard St., 360/378-2000 or 888/754-0034, www.discovery-inn.com, $99–168) aren't much to sing about, but the grounds do have attractive gardens, a cedar sauna, hot tub, and sundecks.

Out in the open fields near American Camp, **Olympic Lights B&B** (360/378-3186 or 888/211-6195, www.olympiclights.com, $105–165 s or d) offers a slice of solitude and serenity to its guests. This 1895 Victorian farmhouse has four guest rooms with private baths and is surrounded by pleasant grounds that showcase amazing views of the Olympic Mountains in the distance.

$150-200

A spacious contemporary home with seven guest rooms and private baths, **Hillside House B&B** (365 Carter Ave., Friday Harbor, 360/378-4730 or 800/232-4730, www.hillsidehouse.com, $85–275 d) is notable for its atrium full of birds, flowers and trees, and great up-close harbor views. The home sits on an acre of wooded land just a half mile from town.

A mile west of Friday Harbor, **Trumpeter Inn B&B** (318 Trumpeter Way, Friday Harbor, 360/378-3884 or 800/826-7926, www.trumpeterinn.com, $130–199 s or d) is set on five pastoral acres, complete with a tranquil pond. The showcase of the property is the lovingly tended garden featuring several varieties of lavender and a well-placed hot tub from which to soak it all in. The five guest rooms in this contemporary home have private baths, and the rate includes a sumptuous breakfast.

For a real waterfront room, **Wharfside B&B** (360/378-5661, www.slowseason.com, $179–195 d) has two small staterooms aboard the gracious 60-foot sailing vessel *Jacquelyn,* docked at the Friday Harbor Marina. If you have the opportunity, splurge a little and spend the extra $75 for the optional four-hour cruise.

Those looking to stay closer to Roche Harbor and British Camp can consider **Wildwood Manor** (5335 Roche Harbor Rd., 360/378-3447 or 877/298-1144, www.wildwoodmanor.com, $280 d), a B&B in a large Queen Anne–style home atop a knoll above

Roche Harbor, with a view across the water to British Columbia. The lavish modern home is surrounded by 11 acres of forests, and each of the four rooms follows the Victorian theme.

The sleek, modern interior of (**Bird Rock Hotel** (35 1st St., 800/352-2632, www.bird rockhotel.com) comes as a pleasant surprise given the historic exterior of this, one of downtown Friday Harbor's oldest buildings. Dark woods and clean lines dominate the furnishings, which are highlighted with comfy pillowtop beds and big flat-screen TV monitors. A light breakfast can be brought directly to your room each morning or served in the downstairs salon; also the place to get the scrumptious cookies and lemonade served each afternoon. The smallest rooms with shared bathrooms go for $197–227 s or d, while "standard" rooms are $127–297 s or d. The "superior suites" are $127–297.

The charming **Hotel De Haro** (248 Reuben Memorial Dr., Roche Harbor, 360/378-2155) was built in 1886 and fronts a gracious formal garden and the harbor. The hotel's downstairs lobby is worth a look even if you aren't staying here, with historic photos and a big fireplace. Rates at the hotel start at $129 s or d for an old-fashioned room (bath down the hall and no TV) that faces the harbor, up to the presidential suite ($325 s or d) with its own fireplace and private bath. This one really is a presidential suite—Theodore Roosevelt slept here in 1906 when it was still room 2A.

$200-250

Snug Harbor Resort (1997 Mitchell Bay Rd., 360/378-4762, www.snugresort.com) is a cozy resort along Mitchell Bay on the west side of the island. Choose from a variety of waterfront cabins for $179–239 d, including the elevated Tree House suite with an especially good view. Boat and kayak rentals are available.

Earthbox Motel and Spa (410 Spring St., Friday Harbor, 360/378-4000, earthboxmotel. com, $197–247 d) looks like an old-school two-story motel, but don't be fooled. The rooms are newly furnished with hipster-in-paradise "retro-chic" decor. Enjoy the heated indoor pool, on-site day spa, and beach cruisers ready to be borrowed. There are 15 pet-designated rooms, so let them know that dog is your co-pilot when you make the reservation.

Over $250

One of my favorite spots on the island is set by three small lakes near the center of San Juan Island. (**Lakedale Resort** (360/378-2350 or 800/617-2267, www.lakedale.com) features a number of accommodation options, starting with the well-appointed but still down-to-earth rooms in its lakeside lodge, which go for $249 d in high season. The resort also has six attractive two-bedroom, two-bath lakeside log cabins with full kitchens. Rates are $399 d (plus $35 per extra adult). Cute "canvas cabins" are for those whose idea of "roughing it" is a bit more mild. These canvas tents have a solid wooden floor, a queen bed, and an adjacent shared bath facility They run at $289. Larger families and groups may also appreciate the three-bedroom Lake House ($599 for four), which features a greatroom with a fireplace, three bathrooms with whirlpool tubs, and a huge deck. Resort amenities include a hot tub, continental breakfast basket, rowboats, canoes, and paddleboats for rental at $10 per hour.

Right on the harborfront, **Friday Harbor House** (130 West St., 360/378-8455 or 866/722-7356, www.fridayharborhouse.com) overlooks the hundreds of boats moored in the harbor stylish rooms and suites for $250–325 s or d. Each of the inn's 23 rooms has a fireplace, a whirlpool tub, fridge, and harbor view. A continental breakfast is served each morning. A two-night minimum is in effect on summer weekends.

One of the nicest bed-and-breakfast options in Friday Harbor is offered by sister properties (**Harrison House Suites B&B** (275 C St., Friday Harbor, 360/378-2783 or 800/965-0123, www.harrisonhousesuites.com) and **Tucker House B&B** (260 B St., Friday Harbor, 360/378-2783 or 800/965-0123, www.tucker house.com). Set side by side and within easy walking distance of the ferry, these two establishments shine come morning, when the resident innkeepers serve up a dazzling multi-course meal sure to wow even the most experienced B&B veteran. Harrison House features five well-appointed suites (one is 1,600 square feet) for $185–375 and has hot tubs available for all guests. Tucker House offers a more traditional B&B experience in the rooms within its 1898 Victorian house ($125–225 s or d). It also has three cottages ($130–175 d) with private baths and woodstoves. Guests can use the hot tub, and kids are welcome in the cottages. Both Harrison House and Tucker House are pet-friendly.

Located on the west side of the island, **Highland Inn** (directions provided with reservation, 360/378-9450 or 888/400-9850, www.highlandinn.com) offers some of the finest lodging in the area, with two luxurious suites ($275 d), each with a king-size bed, steam showers, jetted tubs, and fireplace. A covered porch runs the length of the house, providing knock-your-socks-off views across Haro Strait; it's a great place to watch for orca whales, and a hot tub is on the grounds.

The classic 19th-century **Roche Harbor Village** (360/378-2155 or 800/451-8910, www.rocheharbor.com) at beautiful Roche Harbor offers a wide range of lodging options. Employees of the Roche Harbor Lime Company once occupied the rustic cottages, and all cottages have two bedrooms and full kitchens for $579–609 s or d. A number of condos are also available, starting at $235 for one-bedroom units up to $350 for three-bedroom condos. The modern condos, while functional, seem a little out of place in this historic and scenic setting.

Camping

Pitch a tent at the 12-acre **San Juan County Park** (along West Side Rd., 360/378-8420, www.co.san-juan.wa.us/parks, $30–42), a mile north of Lime Kiln State Park. The 1998 film *Practical Magic* was filmed here. Because this is the only public campground on the island, you'll need to make advance reservations for the summer. Call 360/378-1842 for reservations ($10 fee) between six days and three

months ahead of time. You may find space on a summer weekday, but weekends are usually fully reserved, especially in August. The park has a boat ramp and drinking water but no RV hookups.

Park that RV or pitch a tent at the spacious **Lakedale Resort at Three Lakes** (4313 Roche Harbor Rd., 360/378-2350 or 800/617-2267, www.lakedale.com), which offers a good compromise to families divided between the nature enthusiasts and lovers of creature comforts. The platform canvas cabins at Lakedale offer a camplike setting without the necessity of sleeping on the hard ground. Equipped with queen-size beds and sleeper sofas, these luxury campsites start at $149 for two adults and two kids. This rate includes a continental breakfast served up at the nearby canvas Longhouse each morning.

Lakedale also offers traditional tent sites ($20–42) and RV sites ($57) on the property, plus boat, fishing equipment, and bike rentals to better explore the 82-acre property and its surrounding lakes. It's located near the center of the island, 4.5 miles from Friday Harbor, and is open mid-March–mid-October.

RVs are also welcome at **Snug Harbor Marina Resort** (1997 Mitchell Bay Rd., 360/378-4762, www.snugresort.com, $30) where you'll also find tent sites, rentals of skiffs, fishing tackle, and crab pots. A small store has supplies and dive tank refills.

FOOD

San Juan Island has a wide range of restaurants and eateries, including some real gems. Unless otherwise noted, all the restaurants listed below are located in the town of Friday Harbor.

Cafés and Diners

Blue Water Bar and Grill (2 Front St., 360/378-2245, 9 A.M.–11 P.M. daily) is a good breakfast hangout, with a fun atmosphere, big omelettes, eggs Benedict, and a ferry-side location. The dependable lunches include fish and prawn baskets, Philly cheese steaks, and more.

For a simple breakfast or lunch near the ferry terminal, **Hungry Clam** (205 A St., 360/378-

THE SAN JUAN FOOD CHAIN

Folks who live in the San Juan Islands year-round are a special breed. Tough and self-reliant, locals take a great deal of rightly deserved pride in their unique home. Getting fresh food to the island is an expensive chore, however. These challenges led locals to turn to the islands' fertile farmland and agrarian roots, thus making locally sourced food a point of pride around here. Island farmers grow berries and produce, raise livestock, and pick their eggs fresh from the henhouse each day. And don't forget fresh Puget Sound seafood.

The local agricultural community has gone so far as to create the **Islands Certified Local** program to recognize those hospitality industry businesses in the community that support the "locavore" cause. Look for restaurants and bed-and-breakfasts with this seal of approval, and consider the fresh, delicious, and locally sourced food just one more of the many benefits of your ferry ride to the San Juans.

3474, 11 A.M.–7 P.M. daily), should satisfy. Find cheap and very good fish and chips served in a basket, plus clam chowder, burgers, and grilled chicken sandwiches.

No place in Friday Harbor serves healthier, heartier lunches than **(The Market Chef** (225 A St., 360/378-4546, 10 A.M.–4 P.M. Mon.–Fri.), a deli and bistro that offers up scrumptious sandwiches on house-made breads, inventive salads, and soothing soups, all made with organic and local ingredients.

San Juan Coffee Roasting Company (18 Cannery Landing, 360/378-4443 or 800/624-4119, www.rockisland.com/~sjcoffee, 9:30 A.M.–5 P.M. daily Apr.–Labor Day, 9:30 A.M.–5:30 P.M. daily) specializes in full and dark roasted coffees, sold by the hot, comforting cup or aromatic pound.

If you're in search of a great all-American burger, fries, and shake, head to **Vic's Drive-In**

(25 2nd St. N, 360/378-8427, 7 A.M.–7 P.M. Mon.–Fri., 8 A.M.–2 P.M. Sat., closed Sun.).

Lime Kiln Café (360/378-2155 or 800/451-8910, www.rocheharbor.com, 7 A.M.–4 P.M. in winter) offers quick meals at the Roche Harbor Resort. The fish, burgers, and fresh donuts might seem a little spendy for what you get, but they are a bargain compared with other resort offerings.

Steak and Seafood

Duck Soup Inn (50 Duck Soup Ln., five miles north of Friday Harbor on Roche Harbor Rd., 360/378-4878, http://ducksoupinn.com, 5–10 P.M. Tues.–Sun. summer, irregularly other times of year, $30), specializes in superb local seafood, along with a constantly changing, eclectic menu with an international flair. The country setting adds to the relaxed and romantic atmosphere. This is a favorite local spot for a special night out.

The Place Next to the Ferry Café (360/378-8707, 4:30–9 P.M. daily in summer, 5–8:30 P.M. daily the rest of the year) or just "The Place" gets the nod from locals who come here for the creative, seafood-rich menu and a semicasual atmosphere. The menu changes periodically, and as might be surmised from the name, this restaurant has a great location—on the marina adjacent to the ferry dock.

A mile east of Roche Harbor, **Westcott Bay Sea Farms** (904 Westcott Dr., 360/378-2489, www.westcottbay.com, 11 A.M.–5 P.M. daily, closed in winter) supplies local restaurants with gourmet oysters and clams; get them at the source for the freshest available. The farm also features several days each summer when you can pick your own oysters, timed around the lowest tides. Give them a call to find out when the time will be just right.

Friday Harbor House's **Harbor View Restaurant** (130 West St., 360/378-8455, www.fridayharborhouse.com, 11:30 A.M.–2 P.M., 5:30–9 P.M. daily, $28–34) is one of the top local dining establishments, with a menu that changes weekly, depending upon what's fresh.

Roche Harbor Resort's nicest fare can be

© ERICKA CHICKOWSKI

Serve yourself at Wescott Bay Sea Farms.

found at the second-story ◖ **McMillin's Dining Room** (248 Reuben Memorial Dr., 360/378-5757, 5–10 P.M. daily, $30). This swanky little pad is outfitted with a player piano and great views of the marina. It serves up fine steaks, mouthwatering pasta, and fresh seafood. Call for reservations at McMillin's, especially during the summer months.

International

Mi Casita (95 Nichols St., 360/378-6103, 4–8:30 P.M. Mon.–Sat.) is a good bet for family Mexican food. Pork lovers should definitely give the house specialty *carnitas* a try.

Finally, if you get a hankering for some sweet-and-sour chicken, **China Pearl** (51 Spring St., 360/378-5551) serves an Americanized Chinese menu. For great Thai food, swing by **Golden Triangle** (140 1st St., 360/378-1917), a casual eatery that serves curries, spring rolls, and other Thai staples.

Pub Grub

One of the most popular eating establishments

on San Juan Island is **Friday's Crabhouse** (65 Front St., 360/378-8801, www.fridayscrabhouse.com, 11:30 A.M.–7 P.M. daily) directly across from the ferry. Open summers only, this is the place for finger-lickin' fish and chips, shrimp cocktail, or grilled crab cakes, along with fajitas, burgers, and veggie burgers—most for under $10. Service is fast, making this a great last-minute stop while waiting for your ship to come in. In good weather, enjoy their open decks or eat inside. The decks also seat well-behaved, leashed dogs.

If you're looking for a leisurely lunch or a dinner cocktail in Roche Harbor, try **Madrona Bar & Grill** (360/378-2155 or 800/451-8910, www.rocheharbor.com, 11 A.M.–10 P.M.) for grilled and barbequed lunches on their waterside deck overlooking the harbor.

Markets

The **San Juan Farmers Market** (360/378-6301, www.sjifarmersmarket.com, 10 A.M.–1 P.M. on summer Saturdays) is held at the county courthouse parking lot, with lots of organic fruits, vegetables, berries, and flowers. Islanders are very particular about buying locally, so expect a good turnout and great produce.

The island's largest grocer is **King's Market** (160 Spring St., 360/378-4505), the San Juan Island's answer to the old-timey general store. They carry a full selection of fresh meats and fish and a deli, but also a full line of sportswear as well as just about everything you need for fishing, crabbing, or boating the area.

INFORMATION AND SERVICES
The **San Juan Island Chamber of Commerce Visitor Center** (1 Front St., 360/378-5240, www.sanjuanisland.org). Hours are 10 A.M.–4 P.M. daily.

Check your email for free at the **San Juan Island Library** (1010 Guard St., 360/378-2798, www.sjlib.org), or pay to do so at **The Menu Bar** (435 Argyle Ave., 360/378-1987, www.interisland.net/menubar) or **Madelyn's Bagel Bakery** (A St., 360/378-4545), above the ferry parking area.

Store luggage in the coin-operated **lockers** opposite the ferry terminal next to Friday's Crab House and clean your dirty laundry at **Sunshine Coin-Op Laundry** (80 Web St., 360/378-7223).

GETTING AROUND
Be warned, Friday Harbor has a big parking problem in the summer, and the city *strictly* enforces a two-hour downtown parking limit. Get back to your car three minutes late and you'll probably have a ticket pasted on the windshield.

The **Washington State Ferry** (206/464-6400, www.wsdot.wa.gov/ferries) stops right in Friday Harbor on San Juan Island. In the summer, ferries leave Anacortes at least a dozen times a day 4:30 A.M.–11 P.M.; nearly all of them stop at Friday Harbor.

By Bus
You don't necessarily need a car on San Juan Island, although things are spread out quite a bit. **San Juan Transit & Tours** (360/378-8887 or 800/887-8387, www.sanjuantransit.com) operates shuttle buses between Friday

a supply boat approaching Roche Harbor

© ERICKA CHICKOWSKI

Harbor and Roche Harbor, with stops at San Juan Vineyards, Lakedale Resort, Krystal Acres Alpaca Ranch, English Camp, Sculpture Park, and Roche Harbor. Buses operate May–September, and service is daily in summer and weekends only until mid-May. The cost is a reasonable $5 one-way, $10 round-trip, or $15 for an all-day pass, and buses can carry bikes and luggage. Be sure to carry exact change. The office is next to the Friday Harbor ferry in the Cannery Landing Building.

By Car and Taxi

Whether you're more of a compact-car person or a 4 x 4 or pickup person, **M&W Auto Rentals** (725 Spring St., 360/378-2794 or 800/323-6037, www.sanjuanauto.com/rental, $50–70 per day) has you covered.

Susie's Moped and Car Rentals (360/378-5244 or 800/532-0087, www.susiesmopeds .com) also rents convertible Chevy Trackers from its shop at the top of the ferry lanes in Friday Harbor. All reservations must be made by phone.

Call **Bob's Taxi & Tours** (360/378-6777 or 877/482-9426, www.bobs-taxi.com) for local rides year-round. Or just "hail" one of their signature dark green vans. Friday Harbor to Roche Harbor is around $22 for two people. Even if you've got nowhere in particular to go, but want to roam the island, they're happy to oblige.

Orcas Island

Known as "The Gem of the San Juans," Orcas Island is considered the chain's most beautiful island. It is definitely the hilliest—drive, hike, or bike to the top of 2,409-foot Mount Constitution for a panoramic view from Vancouver, B.C., to Mount Rainier. Orcas' most prominent mansion, Moran Mansion at Rosario Resort, regularly graces the pages of national travel magazines. The island—named by a Spanish explorer in 1792 for the viceroy of Mexico, not for the orca whales common in neighboring waters—is home to 3,500 people, half of whom seem to now operate real estate offices.

The ferry docks at the cluster of cafés and gift shops called **Orcas Village,** located on the south end of this horseshoe-shaped island. The tiny settlement of **West Sound** is eight miles northwest of the ferry landing and has a large marina, along with a couple of stores. Approximately four miles west of here is another little gathering place, **Deer Harbor,** with a handful of resorts and B&Bs, a couple of restaurants, charter sailboats, and kayak rentals. It's appropriately named for the many black-tailed deer in the area and throughout the San Juans. The town of **Eastsound** sits at the head of Orcas's horseshoe shape. This is the primary village on the island, and *the* place to go for groceries, gas, and a wide choice of gift shops, cafés, and galleries. It also probably has more lounging cats per shop than any other town in Washington!

SIGHTS
◖ Moran State Park

Near Eastsound, 5,252-acre Moran State Park (360/376-2326 or www.parks.wa.gov) is most popular for its steep, paved road to the 2,409-foot summit of **Mount Constitution,** where you'll discover a 52-foot stone observation tower constructed by the Civilian Conservation Corps in 1936. This is the highest point on the San Juans and offers a commanding view in all directions, from Mount Rainier to British Columbia. If you've ridden to the top by bike, it's an exciting ride back down. Another popular attraction is **Cascade Falls,** where Cascade Creek drops into a deep pool 100 feet below. A quarter-mile path leads to the falls, and you can continue uphill to two less-impressive waterfalls.

The park has more than 30 miles of other hiking trails, from easy nature loops to remote and rugged out-of-the-way hikes. Get a park map for details on all of these. A four-mile

ORCAS ISLAND

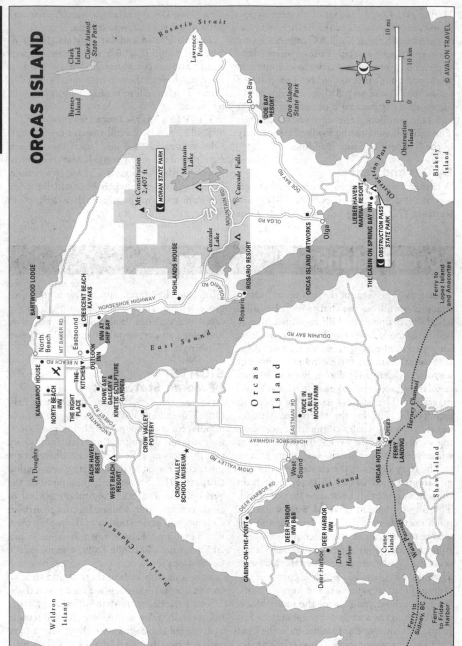

Rosario Strait

Clark Island State Park

Clark Island

Barnes Island

Lawrence Point

Doe Bay

Doe Bay Resort

Doe Island State Park

Obstruction Island

Blakely Island

Mt Constitution 2,407 ft

MORAN STATE PARK

Mountain Lake

Cascade Falls

DOE BAY RD

Obstruction Pass

MOUNTAIN RD

LIEBER HAVEN MARINA RESORT

OLGA RD

Cascade Lake

THE CABIN ON SPRING BAY INN

HIGHLANDS HOUSE

OBSTRUCTION PASS STATE PARK

ROSARIO RD

ROSARIO RESORT

ORCAS ISLAND ARTWORKS

Olga

BARTWOOD LODGE

Rosario

HORSESHOE HIGHWAY

CRESCENT BEACH KAYAKS

Eastsound

MT BAKER RD

North Beach

N BEACH RD

INN AT SHIP BAY

Ferry to Lopez Island and Anacortes

East Sound

KANGAROO HOUSE

OUTLOOK INN

DOLPHIN BAY RD

NORTH BEACH INN

THE KITCHEN

Orcas Island

THE RIGHT PLACE

HOWE ART GALLERY & KINETIC SCULPTURE GARDEN

Pt Doughty

ENCHANTED FOREST RD

ONCE IN A BLUE MOON FARM

EASTMAN RD

CROW VALLEY POTTERY

HORSESHOE HIGHWAY

BEACH HAVEN RESORT

Harney Channel

Orcas

WEST BEACH RESORT

CROW VALLEY SCHOOL MUSEUM

ORCAS HOTEL

FERRY LANDING

West Sound

CROW VALLEY RD

Shaw Island

West Sound

DEER HARBOR RD

President Channel

Waldron Island

CABINS-ON-THE-POINT

DEER HARBOR INN B&B

DEER HARBOR INN

Deer Harbor

Crane Island

Wasp Passage

Deer Harbor

Ferry to Sidney, BC

Ferry to Friday Harbor

10 mi

10 km

© AVALON TRAVEL

© ERICKA CHICKOWSKI

The views from atop Mount Constitution are the best on the islands.

loop trail circles Mountain Lake, offering a chance to see black-tailed deer, particularly in the morning and early evening. You can climb to the summit of Mount Constitution from Mountain Lake on a 3.7-mile path, or save your legs by catching a ride to the top and hiking downhill instead.

Moran State Park has several lakes that are popular for fishing, nonmotorized boating, and swimming in the cold water. Rent rowboats and paddleboats (summers only) at the largest of these, Mountain and Cascade Lakes, where you'll find good trout and kokanee fishing. Both also have boat ramps and fishing supplies. Cascade Lake has a roped-off swimming area in the summer, and the park is one of the most popular places to camp in the state.

◖ Obstruction Pass State Park

This postage-stamp state park is a perfect place to teach a young child how to skip stones. After hiking down the network of trails through madrona trees, you are greeted by a beach made up of a rainbow of buttery-soft pebbles washed smooth by the ocean tides. Take a seat on one of the innumerable bleached drift logs here, listen to the waves ripple through the stones, and see how many times you can get the flat ones to bounce off the water's surface. To get here from Eastsound, drive south along Olga Road, eventually passing through Moran State Park. Turn left onto Point Lawrence Road. Keep left as the road curves before making a slight right onto Obstruction Pass Road. Enjoy the twists and turns as the road becomes Trailhead Road and leads straight into the park.

Museums and Historical Sights

Located in a cluster of six pioneer log buildings, the **Orcas Island Historical Museum** (181 North Beach Rd., Eastsound, 360/376-4849, orcasmuseum.org, 11 A.M.–4 P.M. Wed.–Mon. late May–Sept., 11 A.M.–4 P.M. Sat. Oct.–mid-May, free) has a collection of artifacts and exhibits celebrating the island's Native and pioneer history.

See the little **Crow Valley School Museum** (2274A Orcas Rd., three miles southwest of Eastsound on Crow Valley Rd., 360/376-4849, 1–4 P.M. Thurs.–Sat. Memorial Day–Labor Day), where as many as 47 children of all ages crowded in for what was probably all the education they would ever get. Built in 1888, this classic one-room school has old desks, a great school photo collection, report cards, school clothes, toys, and other pieces from a bygone era.

The Funhouse (30 Pea Patch Lane 360/376-7177, www.thefunhouse.org, 11 A.M.–5 P.M. Mon.–Fri. in July and Aug., 3–5:30 P.M. Wed.–Sat. the rest of the year, $7 per person or $25 for a family) is a hands-on science center with more than 50 fun and educational exhibits. The Fun House also has special teens-only evening hours.

ENTERTAINMENT AND EVENTS
The Arts

The **Orcas Theatre & Community Center** (917 Mt. Baker Rd., 360/376-2281, www.orcascenter.org) hosts a variety of events nearly year-round in Eastsound, from concerts by nationally known musicians to theatrical performances and productions for kids.

Every Thursday at noon during July and August, head to the beautiful and historic Emmanuel Episcopal Church (242 Main St., 360/376-2352, in Eastsound for a free **Brown Bag Concert.**

Check out the latest movies at **Sea View Theatre** (360/376-5724) in Eastsound.

Festivals and Events

The first weekend of August brings a popular **Orcas Island Fly-In** (www.portoforcas .com) that features many antique planes. It's followed on the second Saturday of August by the **Library Fair** (360/376-4985, www.orcas library.org), a big community-oriented arts and crafts fair and book sale. In late August and early September, world-class musicians flock to Orcas Island for a two-week celebration of the small-orchestral group at the **Orcas Island Chamber Music Festival** (360/376-6636, www.oicmf.org). Multiple concerts are held across a number of generally intimate venues that always sell out quickly.

SHOPPING

Darvill's Bookstore (296 Main St., Eastsound, 360/376-2135, 9:30 A.M.–6 P.M. Mon.–Sat., 9:30 A.M.–5 P.M. Sun.) has a big selection of books on the San Juans and a cozy coffeeshop.

Whether you need to replace a broken string on your acoustic guitar, or you've always wondered what it would be like to play the ukulele, **Eastsound Instruments & Supplies** (221 A St, 360/376-3338, 10 A.M.–5 P.M. Mon.–Tues., 11 A.M.–6 P.M. Wed.–Thurs., 10 A.M.–4 P.M. Sat.) will help you strike the right note.

Orcas has a number of art galleries kept well supplied by the artists and craftspeople who live there. Come to buy or just browse at **The Orcas Island Artworks** (11 Point Lawrence Rd., 360/376-4408, www.orcasart works.com, 10 A.M.–6 P.M. daily) in Olga, owned by 40 or so local artists who work in just about every medium known to man. This is one of the oldest artist-owned cooperatives in the country.

Not far away, **Orcas Island Pottery** (338 Old Pottery Rd., Eastsound, 360/376-2813, www.orcasislandpottery.com, 10 A.M.–5 P.M. daily), the oldest pottery studio in the Northwest, is nestled among beautiful gardens and towering old-growth cedars and Douglas firs.

For a slightly unconventional take on sculpture, head west from Eastsound on Horseshoe Highway and look for the curious and playful welded metal mobiles hanging along the road. Follow the signs up Two Hills Road to reach **Howe Art Gallery & Kinetic Sculpture Garden** (236 Double Hill Rd., 360/376-2945, www.howeart.net, 10 A.M.–5 P.M. daily in summer, winter by appointment), where more of these large kinetic sculptures fill the grounds and a gallery. It's hard to beat for free artsy entertainment.

SPORTS AND RECREATION

Hiking and Cycling

Gnat's Nature Hikes (360/376-6629) will lead you on a custom guided hike through Moran State Park or to one of the outer island marine parks. Trips start at $25 per person for a 3.5-hour hike.

With its steep terrain and long roads, Orcas Island is definitely the toughest of the islands to get around on bike. However, it can be pretty fun if you're up for the challenge. In Eastsound you can pick up a rental steed from **Wildlife Cycles** (350 N Beach Rd., 360/376-4708, www.wildlifecycles.com, 10 A.M.–6 P.M. daily, winter hours vary so call ahead, $3–50 per day). If you prefer to rent a bike at the ferry and take the long haul into Eastsound or other remote parts of the island, **Dolphin Bay Bicycles** (360/376-4157, www.rockisland .com/~dolphin) is right at the ferry landing and rents bikes for $30 per day, which includes a helmet and lock.

Sea Kayaking

Orcas Island is as crazy for kayaks as the rest of the San Juans, and there are many spots along

© ERICKA CHICKOWSKI

The best sights in the San Juans are seen with paddle in hand.

the shoreline to launch a great adventure on the water. If you're planning on launching your own kayak, be forewarned that you may be subject to a launching fee ($5 at Deer Harbor) if you aren't on public lands.

Pick up last-minute supplies at **Shearwater Adventures** (360/376-4699, www.shearwater kayaks.com) in Eastsound, which sells kayak and camping gear, plus a slew of natural history books to learn about the areas you'll be paddling around. Shearwater is also one of the best-regarded tour companies, offering daily paddles from Rosario Resort, Deer Harbor Resort, and Doe Bay Resort starting at $69 for three hours.

For a unique paddling adventure, try your hand at the reins of the hand-built, traditional Aleutian–style kayaks used by **Osprey Tours** (360/376-3677 or 800/529-2567, www.osprey tours.com). The tours leave from Bartwood Lodge on the north end of the island and can range from one hour ($50) to a full six-hour day ($150). Box lunches can be purchased for longer tours.

Finally, you can just go it alone and rent single or double kayaks in Eastsound from **Crescent Beach Kayaks** (239 Crescent Beach Dr., Eastsound, 360/376-2464, www.crescent beachkayaks.com, 9 A.M.–6 P.M, daily, $50 per person half day or $18 per person per hour) or at Obstruction Pass from **Lieber Haven Marina Resort** (360/376-2472, www.lieber haven.com, 8 A.M.–8 P.M. daily, $10–35 per hour).

DOE ISLAND STATE PARK

Located just southeast of Orcas Island, Doe Island has five primitive campsites ($10) on a small, secluded island with a rocky shoreline. There are no mooring buoys, but it is just a short kayak paddle from the hot tubs at **Doe Bay Village Resort.**

Whale-Watching

Since San Juan Island is closer to Haro Strait, it's better suited for heading out on an orca adventure than Orcas Island is. However, if you won't be on San Juan, you can still find a couple of quality companies heading out from Orcas.

One of the most comfortable rides is aboard the 50-foot cruising yacht run by **Orcas Island Eclipse Charters** (360/376-6566, www.orcas islandwhales.com) in Orcas Landing. Eclipse guides Dan and Denise Wilks are contributors to the Center for Whale Research and they even played coastal marine patrol officers in the movie *Free Willy II.*

A less star-studded, but very experienced nonetheless, option is **Deer Harbor Charters** (360/376-5989 or 800/544-5758, www.deer harborcharters.com) in Deer Harbor, the longest-running whale-watching business on the island. The 30-plus year veteran of the waves offers a no-nonsense professional tour for $72.

Boat Charters and Rentals

Like San Juan Island, Orcas is a good departure point to motor or sail the outer islands in the San Juan archipelago. **Orcas Island Sailing** (360/376-2113, www.orcassailing.com) offers family- and couple-oriented sailing lessons out of Lieber Haven Resort. For $260, you get gentle instruction in handling one of two 19-foot boats. Extend the learning to an all-day session for $460. You can also feel the wind whip up the sails (and your hair) aboard the **Northwest Classic Daysails** (360/376-5581, www.classic daysails.com) sailing sloop, *Aura.* A three-hour sail for two is just $140.

If you prefer to motor out on your own, **Orcas Boat Rentals** (360/376-7616, www .orcasboats.com) rents runabout motorboats at Deer Harbor Marina, a two-hour run costing between $150–200 per day. It also provides water-taxi service, rents fishing tackle, and leads the occasional whale-watching tour.

Golf

The **Orcas Island Country Golf Club** (Orcas Rd. southwest of Eastsound, 360/376-4400, www.orcasisland.com/golf, $30) is a par-71 18-hole public course that prides itself on its environmentally sound fertilization and maintenance regimen. There's no driving-range, but

you can rent a full set of clubs if you left yours at home.

Fitness

Orcas Spa & Athletics (188 A St., Eastsound, 888/894-8881, www.orcasspaandathletics .com) is a full athletic club with racquetball court, swimming pool, saunas, hot tub, and more. Nonmembers can work out here for a $15 fee.

ACCOMMODATIONS

Anyone planning to stay on Orcas in the summer—particularly on weekends—should make reservations several months ahead of time to be assured of a space. Call the **Orcas Island Chamber of Commerce** (360/376-8888) or visit orcasislandchamber.com for the latest info on vacancies.

Under $100

During the summer it is nigh impossible to find a hotel or bed-and-breakfast willing to put you up for under $100 per night, and even in the winter it is no small feat. The cheapest lodging sans tent that you'll find on Orcas Island is at the hostel at **Doe Bay Resort and Retreat** (107 Doe Bay Rd. in Olga, 360/376-2291, www.doebay.com, dorm beds $35–50), a funky hippie enclave with a laid-back mix of characters eager to chat with solo adventurers and penny-pinching travelers. There are two private couples rooms in the hostel building for $75–100.

$100-150

One of the best lodging deals on the island can be had by those who prepare in advance. The **Camp Moran Vacation House** (360/902-8600, www.parks.wa.gov/vacationhouses/, $123) inside beautiful Moran State Park is one of a handful of vacation homes rented out by the state parks department. This spacious two-bedroom rental sleeps eight, and its large kitchen comes fully equipped. All you need to bring is bed linens and firewood for the fire ring in the private yard outside. The word is out about this super deal, though, so check with the parks department a year in advance to lock up your dates.

Couples seeking solitude on the beach need look no further than **Beach Haven Resort** (684 Beach Haven Rd., 360/376-2288, www .beach-haven.com), which has two-, three- and four-bedroom private little cabins right on the beach for $117–300 per night. For a special treat, try the Stargazer's Cottage with a skylight above the bed, a jetted tub, and a private beach. Beach Haven can also be family-friendly, offering two-, three- and four-bedroom cabins for $165–310 nightly. The property has a playground, horseshoe pit, and ping-pong table on-site.

Spread out across 33-acres along Otter Cove, **Doe Bay Resort and Retreat** (360/376-2291, www.doebay.com) is a legendary institution on the island dating back to the 1970s. The resort attracts a free-spirited and artistic-minded bunch, who come to relax in the property's soaking tubs and sauna, stretch their minds and bodies at the on-site yoga studio, and unwind with a cup of tea in the community lounge and library.

Though it continues to stay true to its down-to-earth roots, Doe Bay Resort has undergone a bit of a renaissance over the past several years, with many of its cabins getting a much-needed face-lift in the process. Woodstove cabins with community bathrooms and showers run $100–125 nightly. Between May and October, the resort rents out yurts for $110 per night. Full bathroom and kitchen cabins are also available, and range from $170–260 per night.

The resort has a small store with limited supplies, plus sea kayaking tours ($45 for three hours), a massage therapist on call, and a café featuring organic veggies grown on the property.

Deer Harbor Inn (68 Inn Ln. in Eastsound, 360/376-4110) is a two-story log-cabin-style lodge surrounded by an apple orchard near Deer Harbor, eight miles west of the ferry dock. The eight small guest rooms ($149 d) in the main lodge contain log furniture and private baths. Four private cottages ($239–385 d) have fireplaces and a two-night minimum in summer. All rates include a continental breakfast (in a picnic basket) and access to the hot tub. Kids and pets are welcome. Deer Harbor Inn is also home to a gourmet restaurant that interestingly features family-style service, housed in a farmhouse built in 1915.

On the north end of the island, **Coho Lodge** (178 Fossil Bay Dr., 360/376-2242, www.coho lodgeorcas.com, $105–145 d) is a charming old rustic lodge with 16 private rooms. Amenities include a tennis court, boat launch, and private moorage for guests. Kids are welcome.

North Beach Inn (360/376-2660, www .northbeachinn.com, $135 s or d, $17 extra person) in Eastsound has beachfront cottages on a beautiful private beach. The cabins all flaunt individual names and unique warm flair and come equipped with kitchens and fireplaces. Two bedroom and larger cabins are $240–280 for four people. Kids are welcome, as are pets for an additional charge. The inn is closed December–mid-February.

Outlook Inn (171 Main St., 360/376-2200 or 888/688-5665, www.outlookinn.com) is a beautifully restored 1888 hotel right in Eastsound with its own private beach. Classic economy rooms with shared baths and no TVs are available in the historic hotel for $84 s or d. Standard rooms in the hotel with private baths and TVs are $140 s or d, and a newer building contains deluxe suites with king-size beds, whirlpool tubs, and mini-bars for $259 s or d.

$150-200

Located on the southeast corner of Orcas Island near Olga, **Lieber Haven Marina Resort** (1945 Obstruction Pass Rd., 360/376-2472, www.lieberhavenresort.com) offers charming and affordable beachfront lodging in cottages, apartments, studios, and rooms, most of which contain full kitchens. Rates are $135–165 for up to four people. This is a great place for the family to relax and take in the harbor scene. Kayaks and motorboats are available for rent at the protected marina, and sailing trips, whale-watching, and fishing charters often depart from this port. The property also offers free Wi-Fi access.

For classic lodging, stay at beautiful

⟨ Orcas Hotel (360/376-4300 or 888/672-2792, www.orcashotel.com), a 12-room century-old Victorian inn overlooking the ferry landing in Orcas. Rates are $89–125 d for modest rooms with shared baths, or $89–218 d for those with private baths. The nicest of these is a suite with a private deck and hot tub. For ease of access, the location can't be beat; just get off the ferry and you're at your hotel. The hotel is a popular place for weddings and family gatherings, though it isn't exactly quiet, being so close to ferry traffic.

The accommodations at **The Inn at Ship Bay** (326 Olga Rd., just east of Eastsound, 877/276-7296, www.innatshipbay.com) are brand-new, but the centerpiece of the property is the 1869 farmhouse and surrounding plum, pear, and apple orchards. The inn features 10 staterooms ($100–195 s or d), one of which has been extensively retrofitted to fully accommodate travelers with disabilities. The staterooms have king-size beds, private balconies with water views, gas fireplaces, and fridges. There is one executive suite ($250 s or d) with a double bathroom and pull-out sleeper couch in the large living-room. Rates include a big continental breakfast. The house restaurant specializes in haute cuisine with a local touch.

The kangaroo is long gone, but the name remains at the **Kangaroo House** (just north of Eastsound Village, 360/376-2175 or 888/371-2175, www.kangaroohouse.com, $155–195 s or d), an attractive 1907 home outfitted with a big fireplace, period furnishings, decks, and a garden hot tub. Bought in the 1930s by a sea captain, Harold Ferris, the house picked up its name when he brought a young female kangaroo on one of his Australian voyages. Nowadays you'll only see the innkeepers bouncing around the house—during morning time, that is, when a truly memorable multicourse breakfast is served. Bird-watchers will appreciate the many species that come to the feeders in the surrounding yard. The five guest rooms have private or shared baths. Families are welcome, and the whole inn can be rented for $850.

$200-250

Rosario Resort & Spa (1400 Rosario Rd., 360/376-2222 or 800/562-8820, www.rosarioresort.com) is a famous and historic getaway five miles south of Eastsound, and the largest resort on the islands. It's well worth a look even if you can't afford to stay here. The perfect island setting and delightful amenities make it a very popular outdoor wedding location. The resort is housed in an early 1900s mansion that once belonged to shipbuilder and Seattle mayor Robert Moran. Moran wasn't blessed with musical talent, so he played the 1,972-pipe organ like a player piano and none of his guests were the wiser; organ concerts are still held frequently. The historic building—on the National Register of Historic Places—has been beautifully restored, offering fine dining, an indoor pool, hot tub, sauna, fitness facility, and massage (extra fee). Rooms cost $129–359 d, and suites are $179–459 d. These vary greatly in size, amenities, and the age of the furnishings, but just don't seem to quite match the beauty of the main building.

Once in a Blue Moon Farm (412 Eastman Rd., Eastsound, 360/376-7035, www.onceinabluemoonfarm.com) sits on a peaceful 35-acre farm estate with panoramic water and mountain views. The owners have their own menagerie of animals that includes goats, llamas, horses, ducks, and chickens, plus an old orchard with apple, plum, cherry, and pear trees. Five units are available for rent. The Alpaca Suite ($165) offers one queen bed, one twin, and a sleeping loft. The Barn Loft ($225) is a second-story queen, twin, and day sofa unit with full kitchen. The Secret Garden ($155) has one queen bed and one full bed in a sleeping loft as well as a mini-fridge and coffeemaker. The Lilac Suite ($225) has two queen-bed sleeping areas and a studio kitchenette, while the Rock Rose Suite ($155 d, up to $225 for nine) has two queen-bed sleeping areas plus a full kitchen and grazing sheep just outside the door.

Sitting right along the shoreline next door to Obstruction Pass State Park, **The Cabin on Spring Bay Inn** (360/376-5531, www

.springbayinn.com, $240) is a large airy cabin with a queen bed, old-style wood stove, and a fridge and dishwasher as part of its kitchenette. There is a second room with a twin bed and an HDTV. Guided kayak tours ($30) are led each morning by the owners, both retired park rangers. Short trails lead directly to the longer trails of neighboring Obstruction Pass State Park, and binoculars are available for borrowing. There is a maximum of three people, which may include children if desired. Leave the pets at home, however.

Over $250

Cabins-on-the-Point (2101 Deer Harbor Rd., Eastsound, 360/376-4114, www.islandcabins.com, $195–450 s or d) has six romantic cabins—popular with honeymooners—with woodstoves and full kitchens. Two of them include access to the hot tub, and all guests will enjoy the private beach. The most posh among them is **Highlands House,** a large two-bedroom house with a fireplace, open kitchen, hot tub on the deck, and impressive water vistas.

Camping

Some of Orcas Island's best camping is at **Moran State Park,** with more than 150 campsites in four different campgrounds along Cascade and Mountain Lakes, plus a separate bike-in area ($12). Tent sites are $22–25, with showers provided. Full utility sites run from $31–39. Due to the park's popularity, reservations are required in the summer months. All sites are preassigned, so check in at the pay station across from Cascade Lake when you arrive. Make reservations ($6.50 extra) at 888/226-7688 or www.parks.wa.gov. The campground is open year-round.

Obstruction Pass State Park is a little 80-acre park with a boat ramp, a beach, and 10 first-come, first-served walk-in campsites a half mile from the road. Sites are $14 per night and there is no potable water. The park is located at the end of Obstruction Pass Rd., 2.5 miles southeast of Olga.

Doe Bay Resort and Retreat (near Olga, 360/376-2291, www.doebay.com) has tent sites

(no RVs) for $25; the new-agey resort's accommodations include Hindu-themed cabins $80–600, yurts $85–120, campsites $45–55, and hostel beds $45–90. They also offer karma-cleansing kayak tours, yoga, massage, and an organic foods café.

Camp in comfort at the **West Beach Resort** (190 Waterfront Way, three miles west of Eastsound, 360/376-2240 or 877/937-8224, www.westbeachresort.com) in one of its canvas platform tents. The spacious tent cabins each have a queen-size bed, a futon, and a small writing desk. On the front patio, there is a private picnic table, barbecue grill, and fire pit. West Beach also offers tent campsites ($27–33) and RV hookups ($33–38) along the scenic beach. Or for those who insist on a permanent structure over their heads, they rent beachfront, ocean view, and garden cottages as well. The marina rents motor boats and kayaks and offers several tours during the summer.

FOOD

The "big city" on Orcas—Eastsound—has the best choice of food on the island, though you'll find a scattering of restaurants and cafés elsewhere.

Eastsound Area

Get quick Asian-influenced takeout fare—including Thai hot and sour soup, teriyaki chicken, and spring roll wraps—at **The Kitchen** (249 Prune Alley, 360/376-6958, www.thekitchenorcas.com, 11 A.M.–3 P.M. Mon.–Sat. closed Sun., $13). Calorie-counters beware at **The Lower Tavern** (46 Prune Alley, Langell St. at Orcas Rd., 360/376-4848, 11 A.M.–10 P.M. Mon.–Sat., 11 A.M.–9 P.M. Sun., $12), where you'll find the best fish and chips in town, great burgers and hearty soups. The televisions are always tuned to the big game, making this a good rainy day retreat.

In a uniquely San Juan Islands story, the founder of **Portofino Pizzeria** (A St., 360/376-2085, www.portofinopizzeria.com, 11:30 A.M.–8:30 P.M. daily, $18) founded and grew a lovely pizzeria and then sold it so he could go do some fishing. When the economic slump overwhelmed the new owners, they shut down. When Woody DeWoody, the original owner, heard the news, he couldn't help but buy back his baby and reopen—less because he expected profit and more because he thought the community should have at least one good pizzeria. It's plenty worth a visit for their deep-dish pizza and the view across Eastsound from the second-floor deck.

Inn at Ship Bay Restaurant (326 Olga Rd., 360/376-5886 or 877/276-7296, www.innatshipbay.com, 5:30–9:30 P.M., Tues.–Sat., $22), just east of Eastsound, is the best place to taste fresh oysters in the San Juans. This spacious old farmhouse overlooking Ship Bay attracts both visitors and islanders for a variety of fresh-from-the-sea daily specials. The menu changes almost constantly, but you can count on plenty of oceanic haute cuisine. The appetizer list always includes fresh oysters from Buck Bay, prepared in a multitude of ways.

Set inside the historic Outlook Inn **New Leaf Café** (171 Main St., 360/376-2200, www.newleafcafeorcas.com, $22) has a great view of East Sound and is conveniently located amid the hubbub of town. The New Leaf menu, like that of most local restaurants, focuses heavily on island-sourced seafood, goat cheese, and greens. The breakfast and dinner are fancy without being threatening and the classy but comfortable happy hour features cocktails both exotic and deliciously retro.

The West End

When you step off the ferry at Orcas, the grand old Orcas Hotel faces you. Inside is **Octavia's Bistro** (8 Orcas Hill Rd., 360/376-4300 or 888/672-2792, www.orcashotel.com, $14–24) with such offerings as filet of beef, peppercorn-crusted salmon, or chicken piccata.

Housed in a farmhouse built in 1915, **The Restaurant at Deer Harbor Inn** (360/376-4110 or 877/377-4110, www.deerharborinn.com, $20–38) is a spacious and comfortable eatery with outstanding meals. The wait staff serves up free bread and salads with every entrée to make the time pass a little faster until

the main course arrives. Large portions and family-style service make it worth the drive, even if you're staying near Eastsound.

The East End

Cafe Olga (11 Point Lawrence Rd., 360/376-5098), inside the Orcas Island Artworks building near Olga, has inexpensive café food, like sandwiches, greens, quiche, espresso, and its justly famous blackberry pie. A little out of the way, so expect some tasty solitude.

The Mansion Restaurant (1400 Rosario Rd., five miles south of Eastsound, 360/376-2152 ext. 400, www.rosarioresort.com, $18–24) at Rosario Resort & Spa, has spectacular views and romantic dining. Reservations are not strictly required, but you'll probably be sorry without them.

For a much more casual feel, eat at the **Cascade Bar & Grill**, also at Rosario Resort and Spa. It serves seafood and chips, burgers, hot dogs, and other summertime favorites. The grill is connected with a small market, open 7 A.M.–9 P.M. daily.

Markets

For groceries and other essentials, stop by the **Island Market** (360/376-6000) in downtown Eastsound. This is the largest grocery store in the islands, with tons of local and organic produce, an in-store bakery, and a deli.

The **Orcas Island Farmers Market** (Eastsound's Village Square, www.orcasislandfarmersmarket.org, 10 A.M.–3 P.M. Sat. Apr.–Oct.) sells the typical local produce, flowers, crafts. Also find mystical herbal products, wool felted toys, and nonprofit food and coffee.

Orcas Home Grown Market & Deli (8 N. Beach Rd., Eastsound, 360/376-2009, 8:30 A.M.–7:30 P.M. daily) has natural foods plus fresh crab and salmon in season. The deli always has daily specials and salads as well. The same folks also run the small **Orcas Market** (360/376-8860) at the ferry dock.

INFORMATION AND SERVICES

You can drop by the **Orcas Island Chamber of Commerce** (65 N. Beach Rd., 360/376-2273, orcasislandchamber.com) for a free map, visitor guide, and the latest news on local shops and inns. Check email for free at the attractive and modern **Orcas Island Library** (500 Rose St., Eastsound, 360/376-4985, www.orcaslibrary.org, 10 A.M.–7 P.M. Mon.–Thurs., 10 A.M.–5 P.M. Fri.–Sat., noon–3 P.M. Sun.).

The **Lopez Library** (2225 Fisherman Bay Rd., 360/468-2265, www.lopezlibrary.org) is housed in a bright red-and-white 19th-century schoolhouse just east of Lopez Village and **Ray's Pharmacy** (Templin Center, Eastsound, 360/376-2230) is a full pharmacy along with other drugstore-type staples like cosmetics, first aid supplies, and postcards.

GETTING AROUND

The **Washington State Ferry** (206/464-6400, www.wsdot.wa.gov/ferries) docks at Orcas Landing on the south end of the island. **Magic Air Tours** (360/376-2733 or 800/376-1929, www.magicair.com, $299 for two passengers) offers half-hour scenic biplane tours out of Eastsound Airport.

By Car and Taxi

Rent mopeds at the Orcas ferry landing from **Orcas Moped** (360/376-5266, www.orcas mopeds.com) for $25 per hour or $65 per day, or cars at $68–79 per day. **Orcas Island Shuttle** (360/376-7433, www.orcasislandshuttle.com) rents cars, convertibles, and vans delivered to your temporary home. And don't worry about drop-off—you're encouraged to leave the keys in it and walk away. They'll pick it up later. They even allow pets in the cars as long as they're in a carrier, also available for a fee.

Local taxis are operated by **Orcas Island Taxi** (360/376-8294). Typical fare for two between the ferry landing and Eastsound is $27.

By Bus

Bus service is available June through September from **Orcas Island Shuttle** (360/376-7433, www.orcasislandshuttle.com, $6 one-way, $12 all-day pass). The buses circle the island five times a day and are equipped to handle bikes ($1 extra). This shuttle service also offers group charters and tours of the island by reservation starting at $50 per hour.

Lopez Island

Because of its gently rolling hills and lack of traffic, Lopez is very popular with cyclists; views of the surrounding islands and mountains to the east and west poke out from every turn. Despite being one of the largest San Juan Islands, Lopez is probably the friendliest. Waving to passing cars and bicycles is a time-honored local custom, and failure to wave will label you a tourist as surely as a camera around your neck and rubber flip-flops.

The business center for the island is **Lopez Village,** where you'll find a scattering of cafés, shops, a museum, stores, and especially real estate offices—which should tell you something about the island's newfound popularity. A few more businesses can be found along pretty Fisherman Bay—filled with sailboats and other craft—but the rest of the island is essentially undeveloped. Note that many local businesses shut down for the winter.

SIGHTS
Lopez Historical Museum

Lopez Historical Museum (Weeks Rd., Lopez Village, 360/468-2049, http://lopezmuseum.org, noon–4 P.M. Wed.–Sun. during July and Aug., noon–4 P.M. Wed.–Sun. in May, June, and Sept., closed the rest of the year unless by appointment) contains assorted bits and pieces of local history like the first car driven on the island, old farm equipment, and historical photos. Outside, find a reef net boat and an aging tractor.

◀ Country Sights

Lopez's main attraction is its rural, pastoral countryside. The long stretches of hills, pastures,

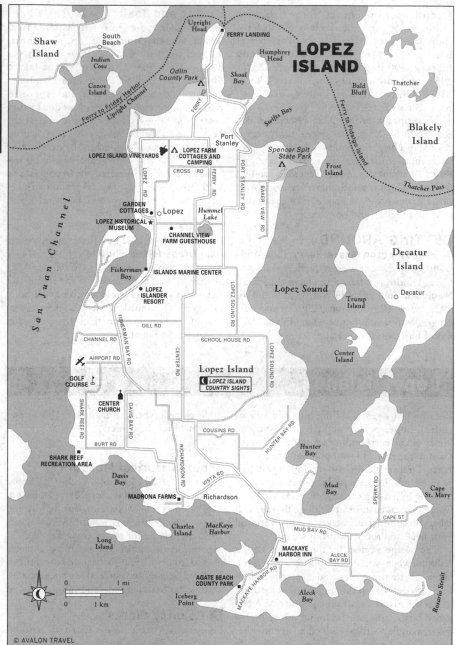

Shaw
Island

South
Beach

Indian
Cove

Canoe
Island

Upright
Head

FERRY LANDING

Humphrey
Head

**LOPEZ
ISLAND**

Odlin
County Park

Shoal
Bay

Bald
Bluff

Thatcher

Port
Stanley

Swifts Bay

LOPEZ ISLAND VINEYARDS

**LOPEZ FARM
COTTAGES AND
CAMPING**

Spencer Spit
State Park

Frost
Island

*Blakely
Island*

Thatcher Pass

CROSS   RD

S a n   J u a n   C h a n n e l

Ferry to Friday Harbor

Upright Channel

Ferry to Fidalgo Island

LOPEZ   RD

FERRY   RD

PORT STANLEY RD

BAKER   VIEW   RD

GARDEN
COTTAGES

Lopez

Hummel
Lake

LOPEZ HISTORICAL
MUSEUM

**CHANNEL VIEW
FARM GUESTHOUSE**

*Decatur
Island*

Decatur

Fisherman
Bay

ISLANDS MARINE CENTER

**LOPEZ
ISLANDER
RESORT**

Lopez Sound

Trump
Island

DILL RD

LOPEZ SOUND RD

SCHOOL HOUSE RD

CHANNEL RD

FISHERMAN BAY RD

CENTER   RD

LOPEZ SOUND RD

Center
Island

AIRPORT RD

**GOLF
COURSE**

Lopez Island

⟨ **LOPEZ ISLAND
COUNTRY SIGHTS**

**CENTER
CHURCH**

SHARK REEF RD

DAVIS BAY RD

RICHARDSON RD

COUSINS RD

HUNTER BAY RD

Hunter
Bay

BURT RD

**SHARK REEF
RECREATION AREA**

Davis
Bay

VISTA RD

MADRONA FARMS

Richardson

Mud
Bay

SPERRY RD

Cape
St. Mary

CAPE ST

Charles
Island

MacKaye
Harbor

MUD BAY RD

Long
Island

**MACKAYE
HARBOR INN**

ALECK
BAY RD

0   1 mi

0   1 km

**AGATE BEACH
COUNTY PARK**

MACKAYE HARBOR RD

Iceberg
Point

Aleck
Bay

Rosario Strait

© AVALON TRAVEL

© ERICKA CHICKOWSKI

outside the Lopez Historical Museum

orchards, and woods might just as well be New England. Cows and sheep are a common sight, including some exotic long-haired breeds at **Cape St. Mary Ranch** on the southeast end of the island. Also of interest are the bright fields of daffodils, tulips, lilies, gladiolus, and delphiniums at **Madrona Farms** (near the intersection of Richardson and Davis Bay Roads, 360/468-3441). For a complete list of nearly 50 Lopez farms, pick up the *Farm Products* brochure at the museum, or find details at www.lopezclt.org.

Lopez Island Vineyards (Fisherman Bay Rd., 360/468-3644, www.lopezislandvineyards.com, noon–6 P.M. Wed.–Sun.) is a small family winery that produces wines from their own organic grapes along with some imported from eastern Washington.

Bucolic Lopez Island is a delightful place to explore, but unfortunately, many of the beaches are privately owned and closed to the public—check for signage before traipsing to the shoreline.

Spencer Spit State Park

On the east side of the island, the 130-acre Spencer Spit State Park (360/468-2251, www.parks.wa.gov) has a mile-long beach for good year-round clamming, beachcombing, hiking, and picnicking. There are also seasonal campsites, mooring buoys, and an RV dump station, but no hookups. A brackish lagoon frequently has ducks and shorebirds, and black-tailed deer are a common sight in the evening.

Additional campsites and a boat launch are available at **Odlin County Park** (360/468-2496, www.co.san-juan.wa.us/parks) at the north end of the island, just a mile from the ferry landing. A two-mile-long sandy beach and numerous hiking trails add to the allure.

One of the few public beaches on Lopez Island is **Agate Beach,** located on the south end of the island at the end of MacKaye Harbor Road. This little park provides access to a beach filled with colorful wave-rounded stones. Another fine small park is **Shark Reef Recreation Area,** located at the south end of Shark Reef Road on the southwest side of the island. An easy half-mile path takes you through one of the few old-growth stands of trees left on Lopez to the rocky coastline. This is a good place to look for harbor seals, sea lions, and bald eagles.

FESTIVALS AND EVENTS

The big event in Lopez Village is the **Fourth of July,** with a parade, fun run, barbecue, and fireworks. In addition to being loads of fun, the event funds the public shower facilities in the heart of Lopez Village.

Also of note is the **Tour de Lopez** (360/468-4664, www.lopezisland.com/tourdelopez.htm), a noncompetitive bike tour of the island held each April. Riders choose from routes of 10–26 miles and are treated to lunch in the village once they've pushed their last pedal.

SHOPPING

Don't miss **Chimera Gallery** (360/468-3265, www.chimeragallery.com) in Lopez Village, a cooperatively run gallery with unusual blown-glass pieces, sweaters, pottery, and jewelry. Also of interest in the Village is **Gallery 10 Fine Art** (360/468-4910, www.gallery10 .com, noon–5 P.M. daily summer, noon–5 P.M. Thurs.–Mon. winter).

Get books from **Islehaven Books & Borzoi** (211 Lopez Rd., Lopez Village, 360/468-2132, www.islehavenbooks.com). The small bookstore prides itself on filtering out literary chaff and only offering quality volumes. The store is partially staffed by a little pack of Borzoi dogs. There is probably no other bookstore quite like it.

SPORTS AND RECREATION
Cycling

A favorite local activity is pedaling the 30-mile loop around Lopez Island. Once you get beyond the steep initial climb from the ferry dock, the rest of the island consists of gently rolling hills, perfect conditions for families.

Mountain bike rentals and tours are available from **Lopez Bicycle Works** (2847 Fisherman Bay Rd., 360/468-2847, www .lopezbicycleworks.com, 10 A.M.–6 P.M. daily Jun., July, and Aug., 10 A.M.–5 P.M. daily May and Sept.), along Fisherman Bay just south of Lopez Village will deliver rental bikes to you at the ferry terminal or your lodgings for a

small fee. Be sure to call ahead, as the owners are sometimes not in the shop during posted hours.

Water Sports

Lopez Island Sea Kayaks (360/468-2847, www.lopezkayaks.com, $25 per day single, $50 per day double plastic hulls, more for fiberglass) has sea-kayak rentals and tours from Fisherman Bay; inquire at Lopez Bicycle Works on Fisherman Bay Road. Staff can deliver the kayak to you anywhere on the island.

Harmony Charters (360/468-3310, www .cruisesanjuans.com) has a luxurious 65-foot classic motor yacht available for 1- to 10-day chartered cruises throughout the islands and even up to southeast Alaska. **Kismet Sailing Charters** (800/426-2313, www.abcyachts .com) has a fully custom 36-foot sailing yacht with two double staterooms and the option of having complete catered meals. They run three-day cruises that give you the choice of helping to crew the yacht or just taking it easy.

Golf

Lopez Island Golf Club (589 Airport Rd., 360/468-2679, lopezislandgolf.com, $25 weekday, $35 weekend for 18 holes) is a nine-hole course with separate tee-boxes so that it plays as 18 holes. Tuesdays and Thursdays are members-only days, but other days offer walk-on play with wait-times extremely rare. Not much water comes into play, but consider it a 2-stroke penalty to hit one of the local deer that sometimes come to nibble the fairway. The course does not rent clubs.

ACCOMMODATIONS

During the summer it's a good idea to make reservations a month or more ahead of time, particularly on weekends. Many of the resorts, inns, and cottages offer weekly rates.

$100-150

Located along Fisherman Bay, **Lopez Islander Resort** (2864 Fisherman Bay Rd., 800/736-3434, www.lopezfun.com) offers both motel-style units with one queen-sized bed ($119–139 s or d) and a three-bedroom house with full kitchens ($250–260 for up to five people). There's an outdoor pool, hot tub, and marina here, too.

Closer to town, **Channel View Farm Guest Cottage** (360/468-4415, www.channelviewfarm.com, $135 s or d with two-night minimum stay) is a quaint cottage with a full kitchen and bath with cottony robes. The loft makes a great place to read or nap, and it's within walking distance of Lopez Village. No children under 12. Please be aware! They take *only* cash or check.

For the perfect home away from home right in the village, check into the (**Garden Cottages** (360/468-4889, www.interisland.net/cc/, $150–200 for cottages or $125 for condo s or d). These two comfy little guesthouses and single condo unit each come equipped with a full kitchen, woodstove, queen-size bed, deck, and a washer and dryer for cleaning up after kayaking and biking the day away. On warm summer nights you can open the windows to take advantage of the Puget Sound breezes blowing through and wake up to the gurgling of the fountain in the lovingly maintained garden. Bring your pet to help enjoy the view.

Relax and enjoy the spectacular vistas of Jasper Bay from the gazebo at **Blue Fjord Cabins** (862 Elliot Rd., 360/468-2749 or 888/633-0401, www.bluefjord.com, $150 d). This quiet property has two Scandinavian-inspired chalet-style cabins with full kitchens in a secluded wooded setting. There is a minimum stay of two–three nights, depending on the time of year.

$150-200

Surrounded by floral gardens, **The Edenwild Inn B&B** (360/468-3238 or 800/606-0662, www.edenwildinn.com) is a contemporary Victorian-style inn right in Lopez Village. No children under 12 and no pets allowed here. The seven rooms all have private baths and range $170–195 d. The Grand Suite goes for $195 per night and has both a king and a queen bed. There is a $25 per person charge for more than two guests in the suite. They serve-up a lavish European breakfast every morning.

For delightful in-the-country lodging, stay at (**Lopez Farm Cottages and Tent Camping** (360/468-3555 or 800/440-3556, www.lopezfarmcottages.com, $180 d) on Fisherman Bay Road. The four immaculate and modern cottages come with kitchenettes, fireplaces, a continental breakfast, and an outdoor hot tub. The hosts bring a breakfast right to your door each evening, so treats await even the earliest of risers. Guests walk in the last 100 yards or so to preserve the quiet ambience. There is also a larger and more luxurious cottage with king-size bed and private hot tub for $215 d. You can drive up to this one, and it is wheelchair-accessible. The adjacent pasture has several friendly sheep.

If you're looking to stay on the secluded south end of Lopez, rest your head at the stately 1904 farmhouse at **MacKaye Harbor Inn** (888/314-6140, www.mackayeharborinn.com). The four rooms ($175–195 s or d) have shared or private baths, and the suite ($235 d) features a fireplace, private deck and antique furnishings. All are just a stone's throw from the water, where you can rent kayaks (guests only) to paddle around protected MacKaye Harbor. Children are accepted with advance reservations, and guests can borrow mountain bikes to explore the island. It is open year-round, unusual for these parts.

Camping

Camp at three comfortable parks on Lopez, none of which have RV hookups. If you're feeling grungy after a few nights in the wild, coin-operated showers are available at the public restrooms near Lopez Village Market and at the Islands Marine Center along Fisherman Bay.

Odlin County Park (360/468-2496, www.co.san-juan.wa.us/parks $5–15 for walk-in or bike-in sites, $20 or $22–25 for car-accessible sites), just a mile south of the ferry landing, has year-round waterfront campsites. The park has a boat ramp, a long sandy beach, and hiking trails. Call 360/378-1842 for summertime reservations ($5 fee, available up to three months ahead).

Spencer Spit State Park (360/468-2251, www.parks.wa.gov, open winter at reduced rates), five miles from the ferry landing on the east end of Baker View Road, has primitive ($12) and regular ($17–23) campsites, plus two Adirondack-style shelters ($25). A delightful sandy spit is a short walk from the campground. It fills early on summer weekends, so make reservations in advance ($7 extra) by calling 888/226-7688.

Lopez Farm Cottages and Tent Camping (Fisherman Bay Rd., 360/468-3555 or 800/440-3556, www.lopezfarmcottages.com, $45) has 10 nicely designed walk-in campsites in the woods with hammocks and Adirondack chairs, plus a central building for cooking and showers. Other amenities include barbecues, a fireplace, croquet, and badminton. These tent sites are perfect for couples; no children under 14 or RVs allowed. Open June–August only.

FOOD

One of Lopez Island's best qualities is its laid-back atmosphere. Unfortunately, this means that store and restaurant hours are pretty fluid, varying greatly depending on the seasons and the whims of the owners. Restaurants that close altogether during off season are noted;

call ahead to find out when the others will be open.

Love Dog Café (1 Village Center, Lopez Village, 360/468-2150, $15) serves fresh fish, steaks, and sandwiches year-round. The café is open for three meals a day and has a few tables on the patio.

☾ Holly B's Bakery (360/468-2133, http://hollybsbakery.com, open Apr.–late Nov., $4) in Lopez Village is *the* place to go for great breads, cookies, scones, and cinnamon rolls. Next door is **Caffe La Boheme** (1 Lopez Plaza, 360/468-3533, $4), where you can sip terrific espresso at tables out front. **Isabel's Espresso** (308 Lopez Rd., Lopez Village, 360/468-4114, $4) is a hip hangout with a large pooch-friendly outdoor deck that attracts locals. It sometimes has live music, too.

The locally beloved **Lopez Island Pharmacy** (352 Lopez Rd. Village Rd. in Lopez Village, 360/468-2616, www.lopezislandpharmacy.com, 9 A.M.–12:30 P.M., 1:15 P.M.–6 P.M. Mon.–Fri., $6) has an old-fashioned soda fountain and fills with locals at lunchtime.

The **☾ Bay Cafe** (9 Old Post Rd., Ste. C,

Bay Cafe on Lopez Island

Lopez Village, 360/468-3700, www.bay-cafe .com, $25) is maybe Lopez Island's overall best restaurant, serving dinners made up of proudly local seafood and grilled meats. Reservations are essential at this very popular place with a deck facing Fisherman Bay.

More on the grilled side, **Bucky's Lopez Island Grill** (211 Lopez Rd., Lopez Village, 360/468-2595, closed Oct.–Mar., $10) has the best burgers in town as well as great fish and chips, barbecued ribs, salads, and chicken.

The **Galley Restaurant and Lounge** (3365 Fisherman Bay Rd., 360/468-2713, www .galleylopez.com, $12) on Fisherman Bay is a friendly locals' joint best known for its enormous omelettes, steak, seafood, and even Mexican specialties. During fair weather, rooftop dining provides beautiful views.

Surprise yourself at the **Lopez Village Market** (162 Weeks Rd., 360/468-2266, www .lopezvillagemarket.com, 7:30 A.M.–8 P.M. daily) which has a wide selection of just about everything, including wine. They even carry camping supplies. The **Lopez Island Farmers Market** (www.lopezfarm-ersmarket.com) in Lopez Village runs from 10 A.M.–2 P.M. on Saturdays, mid-May–early September. Stop by for sustainably raised produce, pickles, chili sauce, and tons of art in multiple media.

INFORMATION AND SERVICES

Contact the **Lopez Island Chamber of Commerce** (360/468-4664, www.lopezisland .com) for local information, or pick up a free *Map and Guide of Lopez Island* from the museum or local real estate offices. Check your email at the **Lopez Library** (360/468-2265) near Lopez Village.

GETTING AROUND

The **Washington State Ferry** (206/464-6400, www.wsdot.wa.gov/ferries) docks at the north end of Lopez Island, approximately four miles from Lopez Village.

Other Islands

In addition to the three main islands, the San Juans consist of a myriad of smaller ones, including some islets that only appear at low tide. Shaw Island is served by the ferry system but is a mere seven square miles and has only one tiny public park among the otherwise private residential property. Of the remaining islands, only Blakely Island has a store and marina. It is accessible only by private boat or the small airstrip usable only by property owners. The other 170 or so are marine state parks, wildlife preserves, private property, or really, not much at all.

Getting There and Around

The state ferry does not stray beyond the four most popular islands (San Juan, Orcas, Lopez, and Shaw), and access to the others is generally by private boat or floatplane.

SHAW ISLAND

The least visited of the ferry-served islands, Shaw (pop. 200) is primarily residential and remains essentially undeveloped, with second-growth forests covering most of the land. "No Trespassing" signs limit access to all but a few beaches. The only business allowed by city decree is the unexciting **Little Portion Store** (360/468-2288) at the ferry landing. The tiny 60-acre Shaw Island County Park is the only place to stay here, with a boat launch, a few campsites, and some fire-rings.

ISLAND STATE PARKS

A number of the smaller islands in the San Juan archipelago are preserved as marine state parks and largely undeveloped. Access is by private boat or sea kayak. The parks have primitive campsites, no drinking water (bring plenty with

cyclists waiting for a ferry to dock

you), and no garbage collection. Sea kayaks are a popular island-hopping mode of transportation, but since some of the smaller islands are several miles out, be careful not to overestimate your ability. Sailboats and motorboats can tie up at mooring buoys in these marine parks for a fee, typically $0.50 per foot per day.

For information on the marine parks and the wildlife refuge, talk with folks at Lime Kiln State Park on San Juan Island (360/378-2044, www.parks.wa.gov).

Sucia Island State Park

Covering 564 acres, Sucia Island State Park is the largest and most popular marine state park, and with good reason. The U-shaped park sits a little under three miles north of Orcas Island and has numerous protected anchorages, 50 mooring buoys, 55 primitive campsites ($10),

and six miles of trails. The shoreline has delightful sandy beaches for sunbathing, clamming, and crabbing. In the past, they also proved delightful for rum-running and the smuggling of Chinese laborers from parts west. Offshore, you can scuba dive on sunken wrecks. Don't expect to be the only visitor on Sucia Island; on a summer weekend the waters around the island are jam-packed with U.S. and Canadian vessels of all description. The island is about 2.5 miles away from Orcas. Best to play it safe and hire a guide unless you're an experienced kayaker.

Outer Island Expeditions (360/376-3711, www.outerislandx.com) offers a once-daily ferry to Sucia from Orcas Island for $45 round-trip per person, plus $10 for a mountain bike or camping gear, $20 for a small kayak, or $35 for kayaks exceeding 12 feet.

OLYMPIC PENINSULA AND THE COAST

Washington's Olympic Peninsula juts up like a thumb hitchhiking a ride from Canada. This diverse 6,500-square-mile landmass ranges from remote rocky beaches to subalpine meadows, from majestic glacier-faced mountains to spooky rain forests. One of the most remarkable parts of the state, the peninsula has a rugged and wild beauty that embodies the spirit of the Evergreen State as much as any place in Washington. The beating heart of the peninsula is Olympic National Park, an unspoiled forest rich with old growth trees, wildlife, and awe-inspiring vistas. Beyond the park, the peninsula lives by the chainsaw, with lumber still providing paychecks for local residents. Tree farms abound, many with signs indicating when they were last cut and when the next round of logging will take place. The many large trucks hauling massive cut logs are a common sight.

HISTORY

American Indian tribes once sparsely inhabited the land now known as the Olympic Peninsula; evidence of their presence here dates back thousands of years. Coastal tribes lived off of the once-abundant salmon or hunted the Pacific gray whale, a tradition still practiced by treaty right by the Makah Tribe today. Starting in the 16th century, the region attracted the attention first of the Spanish, then the English, and finally, Americans. Due to the unforgiving landscape and the frequently hostile Makah, white settlement didn't take hold until 1851,

© ERICKA CHICKOWSKI

HIGHLIGHTS

◖ Fort Worden State Park: Explore underground bunkers, an airship balloon hangar, and even a marine science center in this park on the northeast corner of the Olympic Peninsula (page 320).

◖ Dungeness Spit: Walk the longest naturally occurring sand spit in the United States all the way to the end and reward yourself with a tour of the historic lighthouse (page 327).

◖ Hurricane Ridge: Peer over at Canada, Seattle, and even Mount Hood atop this amazing viewpoint. In the summer, the wildflowers abound here (page 334).

◖ Lake Crescent: Explore the vividly colored lake by boat, or just take a hike by the shore (page 340).

◖ Sol Duc Hot Springs: Nothing beats a posthike soak in Washington's most famous hot springs (page 341).

◖ Rialto Beach Area: The towering sea stacks dotted with evergreens, the enormous blanched driftwood logs, and the thundering surf all make for a dramatic visit to this stretch of shoreline (page 349).

◖ Hoh Rain Forest: Who says rainforests are only in South America? Bring a slicker and enjoy the magnificently mossy trees and shrouds of ferns covering this forest (page 350).

◖ Lake Quinault: Take a hike through the old-growth forest that surrounds this showcase of the Quinault Valley (page 353).

◖ Cape Disappointment State Park: Sitting at the mouth of the Columbia River, this is the most impressive of all the state parks, offering museums, beaches, wooded trails, lighthouses, and military history galore (page 374).

◖ Willapa Bay: Hunt for oysters, kayak the flats, and explore the islands at one of the nation's most pristine estuaries (page 376).

LOOK FOR ◖ TO FIND RECOMMENDED SIGHTS, ACTIVITIES, DINING, AND LODGING.

© ERICKA CHICKOWSKI

Road trippers will love the quiet roads of the Olympic Peninsula.

although the Spanish briefly held a fort here and trappers and explorers plied their trades in the area much earlier.

The peninsula has a long history of boom-and-bust cycles. Cities on the northern coast jockeyed over the right to collect customs charges from incoming shipping, while other towns rose up overnight in anticipation of the transcontinental railroad. Unfortunately for locals, in 1873 the railroad decided to end its route in Tacoma instead, dashing the region's hopes and sending it into decline. Still, the hardworking and genuine folks who live here have always found a way to survive, many of them depending on the timber and fishing trades to keep food on the table.

Farther south at the mouth of the Columbia River, Washington's coast holds an important historical position as the landing point of Meriwether Lewis and William Clark at the end of their transcontinental journey in 1805; they had finally "reached the great Pacific Ocean which we been so long anxious to See." Because game proved scarce and the Washington side of the Columbia lacked protection from winter storms, they crossed the river to build a winter camp called Fort Clatsop near present-day Astoria, Oregon.

CLIMATE

This area has an undeniable mystical quality, right down to the most unusual weather. Peninsular weather is dominated by the Olympic rain shadow. Simply put, the Olympic mountain range causes the moist sea air to dump its precipitation before crossing the high peaks. That's why cities directly east of the mountains see 10–17 inches of rain per year, but the western slope of the mountain might see upwards of 160 inches! Three-quarters of the national park's precipitation falls October–March, and even during the relatively dry months, it's best to be ready for rain. The geography helps keep temperatures mild, generally

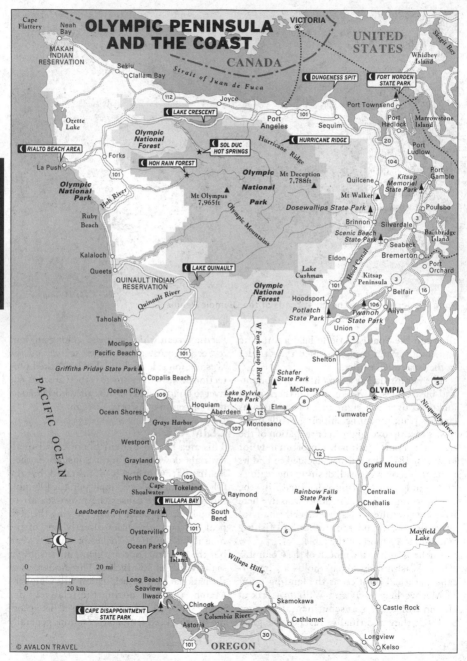

OLYMPIC PENINSULA AND THE COAST

VICTORIA
UNITED STATES
CANADA
Strait of Juan de Fuca
Cape Flattery
Neah Bay
MAKAH INDIAN RESERVATION
Sekiu
Clallam Bay
Ozette Lake
112
Joyce
Port Angeles
Sequim
DUNGENESS SPIT
FORT WORDEN STATE PARK
Whidbey Island
Port Townsend
Port Hadlock
Marrowstone Island
LAKE CRESCENT
101
Olympic National Forest
SOL DUC HOT SPRINGS
HURRICANE RIDGE
Hurricane Ridge
20
104
Port Ludlow
Kitsap Memorial State Park
Port Gamble
RIALTO BEACH AREA
Forks
HOH RAIN FOREST
La Push
101
Olympic National Park
Hoh River
Mt Olympus 7,965ft
Olympic Mountains
Olympic National Park
Mt Deception 7,788ft
Quilcene
Mt Walker
Dosewallips State Park
Brinnon
Poulsbo
3
Silverdale
Bainbridge Island
Ruby Beach
Scenic Beach State Park
Seabeck
Kalaloch
Eldon
Bremerton
Port Orchard
Queets
QUINAULT INDIAN RESERVATION
LAKE QUINAULT
Quinault River
Lake Cushman
Kitsap Peninsula
3
Belfair
16
Olympic National Forest
Hoodsport
Hood Canal
101
Taholah
Potlatch State Park
Union
106
Twanoh State Park
Allyn
3
Moclips
Pacific Beach
101
W Fork Satsop River
Shelton
Griffiths Priday State Park
Copalis Beach
Schafer State Park
McCleary
OLYMPIA
5
Ocean City
109
Lake Sylvia State Park
Hoquiam
Aberdeen
Elma
8
Nisqually River
Ocean Shores
Grays Harbor
107
Montesano
12
Tumwater
Westport
Grayland
12
Grand Mound
North Cove
Cape Shoalwater
105
Tokeland
Raymond
Rainbow Falls State Park
Centralia
Chehalis
WILLAPA BAY
Leadbetter Point State Park
South Bend
101
6
Oysterville
Ocean Park
Long Island
Willapa Hills
Mayfield Lake
0   20 mi
0   20 km
Long Beach
Seaview
Ilwaco
4
5
CAPE DISAPPOINTMENT STATE PARK
Chinook
Skamokawa
Castle Rock
Columbia River
Cathlamet
Astoria
30
Longview
Kelso
101
OREGON

PACIFIC OCEAN

ranging from the low 70s in summertime to the mid-40s in the winter.

PLANNING YOUR TIME

A ringed network of roads makes sightseeing easy here. Highway 101 follows three sides of the peninsula and joins Highways 8 and 12 to complete the loop. Visitors can continue their journey down Highway 101 past Willapa Bay all the way down to the Columbia River.

Trailheads within the Olympic National Forest require a **Northwest Forest Pass** (800/270-7504, www.discovernw.org, $30 annual, $5 daily).

Olympic National Park

Hard-core hikers and campers who think they've seen it all will never forget the wonder of the Olympic National Park, even after just one visit. The deep, damp rain forests, the frosted mountaintops, and the aquamarine rivers have a fantastical allure, seeming to leap from the pages of storybooks. Auto roads barely penetrate the park, but more than 600 miles of hiking trails meander through, crossing and connecting the park's virgin forest core, its matchless beaches, and its alpine peaks.

HISTORY

Few explorers dared enter the thick forests and steep slopes of the central Olympics until the end of the 19th century. In 1889—the heyday of sensationalistic reporting—the *Seattle Press* newspaper funded a small party of adventurers and tasked them with exploring the hinterland. The trip went about as well as can be expected from an excursion organized by the media. Plagued by poor planning, a brutal winter, and a string of mishaps, the group took six months to travel across the mountains before arriving on the Quinault Indian Reservation—starving, minus two mules and several dogs, and in desperate need of medical attention.

Seven years after the *Press* expedition, Congress created the Olympic Forest Reserve, which included much of the Olympic Peninsula. In 1909 President Theodore Roosevelt set aside much of the area for conservation by naming it Mount Olympus National Monument, and in 1938 President Franklin D. Roosevelt made the monument a national park, increasing the level of protection afforded to this wonder even more. The 62-mile coastal strip was added to the park in 1953. Today Olympic National Park sees over four million visitors a year.

ECOLOGY AND CLIMATE

The diversity of climate and geography in Olympic National Park's 908,720 acres of wilderness is one of many reasons it was among the 100 parks named a World Heritage Park by the United Nations in 1981. The park is home of the largest old-growth coniferous forest in the Lower 48 states, as well as 200 species of birds and 70 species of mammals, including Roosevelt elk, black bears, deer, bald eagles, and Olympic marmots.

Olympic National Park is probably most famous for the lush rain forests that carpet the western flanks of the mountains. Soaking up the ample rainfall, enormous spruce, cedar, fir, and hemlock trees covered with moss and lichen tower over the traveler, forcing a certain degree of perspective on life. The crystal-clear rivers and streams, the thick scent of fertility, and the tickle of mist on your eyelashes give this forest an unforgettable feeling of enchantment.

ORIENTATION

Olympic National Park is unique in that there are no roads running through its pristine center—the only way to visit the interior is to hike or ride horseback.

Interior Access

The biggest part of the park is smack dab in the middle of the peninsula, circled by the

OLYMPIC PENINSULA

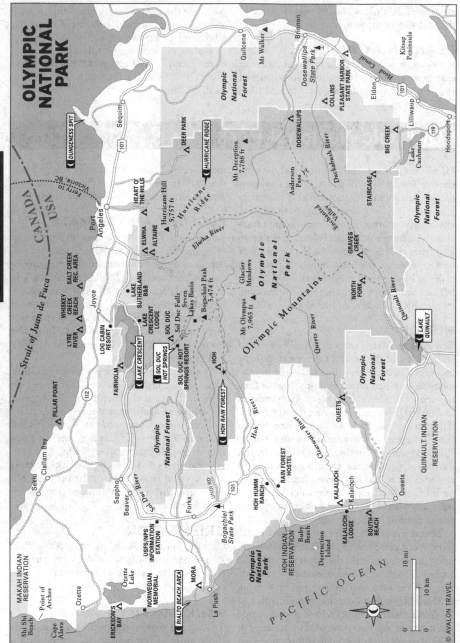

Highway 101 loop. That loop runs directly by the shores of Lake Crescent along its northern stretch and Lake Quinault along its southwest segment. Paved roads meander deeper into the park along the 101 loop at Hurricane Ridge near Port Angeles, Elwha west of Port Angeles, Sol Duc west of Lake Crescent, Hoh Rain Forest east of Forks, along the north and south shores of Lake Quinault, and at Staircase west of Hoodsport.

Coastal Access

Meanwhile, the coastal strips of the park stretch from the Makah Indian Reservation at Cape Flattery all the way down to the Quinault Indian Reservation at the Queets River, interrupted only by the Ozette, Hoh and Quileute Indian Reservations at the Ozette River, Hoh River and Quillayute River inlets, respectively. This skinny strip of gorgeous coastline is accessible with varying degrees of convenience.

To reach the remote northern park beaches it takes a good hour and fifteen-minute-drive from 101 along Routes 113, 112, and Hoko-Ozette Road to the trailhead at the northern tip of Ozette Lake. From there it is a three-mile hike to reach the actual shoreline. The 20-mile stretch from the northernmost tip of the park at Cape Alva all the way down to Rialto Beach is completely roadless, accessible only to hikers armed with tide maps, a car shuttle plan to get between Ozette and Rialto after the hike, and a sense of adventure.

Located in the center of the park's coastal strip, Rialto Beach is itself accessible by an easy 30-minute drive from 101 along Route 110 and Mora Road. Route 110 also takes you down to the Third Beach trailhead south of La Push. From here it is another roadless stretch for 17 more miles, once again only accessible to hardy overnight hikers.

The most accessible stretch of the Olympic National Park's coastline lies along its southern segment, from Ruby Beach down to South Beach, south of Kalaloch. The 101 loop runs along this entire portion of the park, with a number of access points along the way.

PARK INFORMATION

A $15 park entrance fee, good for seven days, is charged for vehicles, or $5 for those on foot or bikes. A variety of annual and lifetime National Park passes are also available from the park service. Entrance fees are collected at Elwha, Hurricane Ridge/Heart O' the Hills, Hoh, Sol Duc, and Staircase entrance stations. Backcountry users should be sure to request a copy of the *Olympic Wilderness Trip Planner* from the **Wilderness Information Center** (3002 Mount Angeles Rd., 360/565-3100, www.nps.gov/olym) in Port Angeles. **Wilderness use permits** ($5 for the permit, plus $2 pp/night) are required for backcountry camping; pick one up at the WIC or the ranger station nearest your point of departure. Because of overuse, summer quotas are in effect and reservations are required for overnight hikes in the Ozette, Flapjack Lakes, Hoh, Grand and Badger Valleys, Lake Constance, and Sol Duc areas.

Park Coverage

The various sights, recreation, and lodging opportunities offered by Olympic National Park are scattered about the peninsula. In-depth descriptions of park sites can be found in the sections covering the towns they're near.

HIKING THE COAST

The Olympic coastline, like any other wilderness area, has its share of dangers. Two dangerous situations are attempting to round headlands and getting stuck on the other side by incoming tides, and being struck by floating logs in the surf. Park Service offices have a helpful *Olympic Coastal Strip* handout with a map and dos and don'ts. Tidal action may also mean that local creeks and rivers will become difficult to cross at certain times. Always study a tide chart beforehand and be aware of your surroundings.

Hood Canal and Vicinity

Hood Canal is *not* a canal, but actually a long, glacially carved fjord. Like many other features in Washington, Hood Canal received its name from Capt. George Vancouver during his 1792 exploration of Puget Sound. He called it "Hood's Channel," after a British naval hero, Lord Hood, but a printer's error in Vancouver's report changed the word channel to canal. Separating Kitsap Peninsula from Olympic Peninsula with only about 1.5 miles of water, the 65-mile-long channel is hugged on the west side by Highway 101. It's a winding tidewater drive through second-growth forests with countless vistas of the waterway from every possible angle. Beyond the growing town of Shelton, much of the route is rural, dotted with resorts, summer homes, and restaurants serving up freshly shucked oysters.

In addition to the glorious vistas along the way, you'll discover camping and hiking at two state parks and on nearby Olympic National Forest and Olympic National Park lands, plus outstanding scuba diving and fishing.

SHELTON TO HOODSPORT

The peaceful blue-collar town of Shelton sits at the foot of Oakland Bay on the southwesternmost inlet of Puget Sound. Put on your plaid shirt and baseball cap to blend in with the locals and motor north from here to reach the southern "elbow" of Hood Canal. At the firework stands and bead outlets of the Skykomish Indian Reservation, you can either veer east along State Route 106 toward the scattered resort settlement of Union or keep on 101 toward the water sports–friendly town of Hoodsport. This is the place to get Forest Service and Park Service information and to stock up on food before heading north.

Sights

The **Mason County Historical Museum** (5th St. and Railroad Ave., 360/426-1020, noon–5 P.M. Tues.–Fri., noon–4 P.M. Sat., donations accepted), in Shelton's old library

building, emphasizes the importance of logging in Shelton's history with displays on railroad logging, historical photos, and artifacts.

"Tollie," the locomotive in downtown Shelton between 2nd and 3rd on Railroad Ave., is a 96-ton Shay logging engine that saw most of the country in its heyday. Behind it sits a red caboose housing the visitors center. Downtown Shelton has a number of antique shops scattered along Railroad Avenue.

Tour the Department of Wildlife's **Shelton Trout Hatchery** (7570 West Eells Hill Rd., approximately eight miles north of Shelton, 360/427-2188, 8 A.M.–5 P.M. daily). Continue up the road, turning right at the sign marking Denny Ahl Seed Orchard, and cross over the 440-foot-high **Steel Arch Bridge** that spans the Skokomish Gorge.

POTLATCH STATE PARK

Enjoy camping, diving, clamming, crabbing, and fishing in Hood Canal at Potlatch State Park (three mi. south of Hoodsport on Hwy. 101, 360/877-6947, www.parks.wa.gov). Have a picnic on the water, or explore the underwater park with scuba gear. The park is named for the feasts held by many Northwestern Indians, in which the exchanging of gifts was the primary focus. The campground ($22–25 for tents, $29–36 for RVs) is open year-round.

HOODSPORT WINERY

A small, family-run operation, Hoodsport Winery (23501 Hwy. 101, 360/877-9894 or 800/580-9894, www.hoodsport.com) produces wine from Puget Sound fruits and berries and is especially known for its rhubarb wine. It also has varietal grape wines, including a surprising cabernet sauvignon. The tasting room is open 10 A.M.–6 P.M. daily.

TWANOH STATE PARK

Twanoh State Park (seven mi. east of Union on Hwy. 106, 360/902-8608, www.parks .wa.gov, $10 day pass) is a very popular spot

© ERICKA CHICKOWSKI

Hood Canal

OLYMPIC PENINSULA

for picnicking beneath tall trees, and swimming and water-skiing on relatively warm Hood Canal. The park also features several miles of hiking trails along scenic Twanoh Creek, sturdy Civilian Conservation Corps–constructed structures from the 1930s, a tennis court, a concession stand with snacks and groceries, bathhouses, and camping in tent ($19) and RV ($26) sites with coin-operated showers.

Entertainment and Events

Little Creek Casino (91 W. Hwy. 108, 360/427-7711 or 800/667-7711, www.little-creek-casino.com, 8 A.M.–4 A.M. Sun.–Thurs., 8 A.M.–5 A.M. Fri.–Sat.) deals blackjack, craps, and roulette and hosts frequent no-limit Hold 'Em tournaments. If hunger strikes while your winning streak rolls on, try the inexpensive buffet dining or the surprisingly good café.

Early June's **Mason County Forest Festival** (www.masoncountyforestfestival.com) includes parades, a carnival, musical entertainment, arts and crafts, and logging competition in such

events as the Two-Man Double Buck, Speed Climb, Ax Throw, and the ever-popular Jack and Jill.

Mason County Fair & Rodeo (www.mason-countyfair.org) is held the last weekend in July at the fairgrounds. Highlights include live entertainment and traditional county fair favorites such as 4-H exhibits and cake and preserve competitions.

Come back in September for The West Coast Oyster Shucking Championship and Seafood Festival, aka **OysterFest** (www.oysterfest.org). The main event is high-speed oyster shucking, and those shells will fly. Surrounding the competition are two days of wine-tasting, an oyster cook-off, food booths, art and boating exhibits, dancers, bands, and magicians.

The holiday season brings Santa to Shelton during the annual **Christmas Parade and Bazaar** (www.sheltonchamber.org), held the first weekend in December with a parade by land and by sea.

The main summer event is **Celebrate Hoodsport Days,** with a street fair, food, kids' parade, and fireworks on the first full weekend of July.

August brings the annual **Hood Canal Salmon Derby** (360/790-6589, www.sschapterpsa.com/Derby_Page.htm), where $25 and some angling luck can win a $1,000 prize. Kids' events and a barbecue are all part of the fun.

Sports and Recreation

GOLF

Play a quick round of golf at **Lake Limerick Country Club** (790 E. Saint Andrews Dr., 360/426-6290, www.lakelimerick.com, $17) a fir tree–lined nine-hole course playable year-round.

MOUNTAIN BIKING

Mountain bikers can check out a relatively level nine miles of forested single-track just north of Shelton. The **Lower South Fork Skokomish Trail** can be reached by taking Highway 101 north of town, turning west on Skokomish Valley Road, taking Road 23 to the Brown Creek Campground and then following Forest Service Road 2394 for a bumpy quarter mile.

HUNTING

Shelton is a good departure point to enjoy some of Mason County's better hunting. Deer, elk, grouse, turkey, goose, and duck are all legal within season. Or, if you've got the guts, come out and take down a fearsome bear. Regulations are many and can be found at the **Washington Department of Fish and Wildlife** (360/902-2464, www.wdfw.wa.gov).

SCUBA DIVING

Scuba divers come to explore the amazingly diverse creatures in the deep, clear waters just offshore of Hoodsport. The lack of strong currents and minor tidal fluctuations help make this a good place for beginning divers. Visibility is best in the winter—to 50 feet—when fewer plankton are in the water.

Rent dive gear, get air refills, and take classes from **Hood Sport 'N Dive** (24080 N. Hwy. 101, a mile north of Hoodsport, 360/877-6818, www.hoodsportndive.com, 9 A.M.–5 P.M. Mon.,

Tues., Thurs., 9 A.M.–6 P.M. Fri., 8 A.M.–6 P.M. Sat., 8 A.M.–5 P.M. Sun.). This is also a good outfit to rent dive or sea kayaks from.

Accommodations

When it comes to chain motels in Shelton, **Super 8 Motel** (2943 N. View Cir., 360/426-1654 or 800/843-1991, www.super8.com, $68 s or $73 d) is about as good as it gets. The rooms aren't a disaster, but they aren't all that comfy either. Most guests—even nongamblers—would be better served heading into Hoodsport or splurging a little and checking in to the **(Little Creek Casino Resort** (91 W. Highway 108, 360/427-7711, www.littlecreek-casino.com, $145–275 d), which offers very nice rooms for reasonable rates. There's a spa on-site, plus an indoor pool and the ever-popular buffet restaurant.

The guest rooms at Union's elegant **(Alderbrook Resort and Spa** (7101 E. Hwy. 106, 360/898-2200 or 800/622-9370, www.alderbrookresort.com, $190–420 s or d) are simply but beautifully decorated, many augmented by views of the Olympic mountains. Its spa offers traditional services plus unique treatments such as ancient Hawaiian lomilomi massage. The downstairs Restaurant at Alderbrook showcases local seafood, and the bar serves beer, wine, and cocktails.

Robin Hood Village (6780 E. Hwy. 106, 360/898-2163, www.robinhoodvillage.com, $135–244 d) has seven cottages with hot tubs and kitchenettes. The smaller, older ones fit two people cozily, while the newer, larger ones are ideal for two couples.

Glen-Ayr Canal Resort (25381 N. U.S. Hwy. 101, 360/877-9522 or 866/877-9522, www.glenayr.com), 1.5 miles north of Hoodsport, is the most elaborate and diverse local resort, with motel rooms for $85–95 s or d. The one-bedroom suites start at $150. A hot tub, recreation room, and marina round out the amenities here. Or park at one of 38 RV sites with full hookups for $33–37 per day.

Sunrise Motel and Resort (24520 Hwy. 100 on the north side of Hoodsport, 360/877-5301, www.hctc.com/~sunrise) is a favorite of scuba divers and has rooms for $59–69 d. A package including a dorm bed for two nights and three days and including free air tank refills is $60 per person. RV sites are $30 per night, and pets cost an extra $10.

The **Waterfront Resort** (in Potlatch, 360/877-9422, motel $99 s or d, cabin $138–179 up to six) offers quite nice shore-view rooms, plus manufactured home–style cabins with kitchens. The resort also rents spaces to RV campers ($38–43 full hookups).

Food

A good place to start the day is **Pine Tree Restaurant** (102 S. 1st, 360/426-2604, 5 A.M.–8 P.M. daily) a family place with big breakfasts served all day, plus seafood and steak for dinner.

Owned by Taylor United and managed by Xinh Dwelley—a talented Vietnamese chef and former oyster-shucking champ—**⊂ Xinh's Clam & Oyster House** (221 W. Railroad Ave., 360/427-8709, 5–9 P.M. Tues.–Sat.) delivers such treats as hot and spicy seafood soup, oysters sautéed in black bean sauce, and grilled halibut.

If tasty affordable food beats out elegance as your chief concern, try **Suzan's Grill** (1927 Olympic Hwy. N., 360/432-8939, 8 A.M.–3 P.M. Sun.–Tues., 8 A.M.–7:30 P.M. Wed.–Sat.). This family-owned eatery trumpets "Nothing from Cans at Suzan's."

Also on-site is the **Robin Hood Pub** (6791 E, Hwy. 106, 360/898-4400, www.the robinhood.com, 5–9 P.M. Wed.–Sun.), which serves a full range of meals from a $12 burger and fries up to a $28 elk flank steak. Great desserts, too. **Union Country Store** (5130 E. Hwy. 106, 360/898-2641) has a small deli.

You can't visit the Hood Canal without feasting on some oysters. In Hoodsport, the place to do it is **⊂ The Tides** (27061 N. U.S. Hwy. 101, 360/877-8921), a family diner that serves up shellfish and smiles. Try the pan-fried oysters, its best dish.

Information and Services

For maps and festival information, contact the **Shelton-Mason County Chamber of Commerce** (in the caboose on Railroad Ave., 360/426-2021 or 800/576-2021, www.shelton chamber.org, 10 A.M.–4 P.M. Mon.–Fri., 10 A.M.–3 P.M. Sat.). Stop by the **Hood Canal Ranger Station** (360/877-5254, 8 A.M.–4:30 P.M. Mon.–Fri. year-round, plus 8 A.M.–4:30 P.M. Sat.–Sun. mid-May–mid-Sept.) in Hoodsport for Olympic National Forest and Olympic National Park information.

Mason General Hospital (901 Mountain View Dr., 360/426-3102) is the nearest emergency room to Shelton and Hoodsport. Hurt pets can be taken to **Shelton Veterinary Hospital** (104 E. J St., 360/426-2616).

Getting There and Around

Mason County Transit (360/427-5033 or 800/374-3747, www.masontransit.org) offers free bus service throughout the county and charges $1.50 one-way for trips to and from Olympia, Brinnon, and Bremerton. All buses are kitted-out with bike racks. **Olympic Air** (360/426-1477, www.olyair.com, $250 per hour) offers scenic flights over the area.

LAKE CUSHMAN AREA

Lake Cushman was a popular resort area at the turn of the 20th century, offering fishing, hiking, and hunting. By the 1920s, the two lakeside resorts had shut down and the city of Tacoma built a dam on the Skokomish River. When completed, the dam increased the lake's size tenfold to 4,000 acres. Though private summer homes are springing up around the lake, the area still has a decidedly remote feel, thanks in part to its protected neighbor, Olympic National Park, about 10 miles up the road.

Sights and Recreation

A once-upon-a-time state park, **Camp Cushman** (7211 N. Lake Cushman Rd., 360/877-6770, $5 day-use fee) is now managed by the Skykomish Tribe. This 500-acre plot of rugged forest, pristine shoreline, and shaded picnic areas draws in recreational enthusiasts of all stripes. Anglers love to vie for cutthroat, kokanee, and rainbow trout in the lake. Divers come to explore the sunken forest and an old resort that was here before the dam was built. Hikers enjoy the four miles of hiking trails, leading from lake's edge to deep woods. Others come to swim, water ski, and, in winter, cross-country ski.

Camp Cushman makes for a good base camp to explore the area. Follow Lake Cushman Rd. to a T intersection at road's end; go left and follow the lake's edge to 70-foot **Cushman Falls,** near the lake's northwest end, about 11 miles from Hoodsport. Or turn right at the T, then turn left in another 1.5 miles onto Big Creek Road 2419 for six miles to **Big Creek Viewpoint** for a sweeping view to the east.

The **Mount Ellinor Trail** leaves Road 2419 at the five-mile point; the trail heads up one mile for a view over Lake Cushman. Hiking trails lead into Olympic National Park from Staircase Trailhead at the head of Lake Cushman, providing a range of hiking options. The **Flapjacks Lake** area is accessed by hiking up the North Fork Skokomish Trail, and then turning up the four-mile side route to the lake. For longer hikes, you can continue up the North Fork Trail, which connects to others, providing a number of lengthy loop-trip options. A steep and challenging three-mile trail switchbacks from the campground to **Wagonwheel Lake,** gaining over 3,200 feet en route.

Golfers can enjoy the summer sunshine at the 9-hole, par 35 **Lake Cushman Golf Course** (210 West Fairway Dr., 360/877-5505, greens fees $31–33), four miles west of Hoodsport.

Accommodations

Cushman Lake Resort (4621 N. Lake Cushman Rd., 800/588-9630, www.lake cushman.com) has rustic cabins ($95–135 d) with kitchens and baths; canoe, personal watercraft, and boat rentals; a convenience store, plus tent ($20–27) and RV sites ($25–32) with power and water.

Camp in one of the two campgrounds at **Camp Cushman** (7211 N. Lake Cushman Rd., 360/877-6770, $20 tents, $26 RVs with hookups), with loads of nearby recreation

opportunities. The Forest Service's **Big Creek Campground** (877/444-6777, www.recreation .gov, $10, open May–Sept.) is nine miles up Highway 119.

For those looking to camp in Olympic National Park, check out **Staircase Campground** (www.nps.gov/olym, $12, no reservations), just west of Lake Cushman where Highway 119 ends, below the Staircase Rapids of the North Fork of the Skokomish River. This beautiful campsite has year-round camping surrounded by old growth forest. Chose a riverside site for the ultimate nighttime lullaby.

LILLIWAUP TO BRINNON

Heading north past Hoodsport, signs of settlement start to really peter out and the opportunities for recreation multiply. The Hamma Hamma and Dosewallips Rivers both enter Hood Canal along this stretch, producing some amazing estuarine environments that are ripe for exploration just off Highway 101. The small villages of Lilliwaup, Eldon, and Brinnon each offer a few limited services along the way, but it's best to come with the cooler packed so you can hit the trails early.

Whitney Gardens & Nursery

In Brinnon, seven acres of display gardens sprout up at Whitney Gardens & Nursery (306264 Hwy. 101, 360/796-4411, www .whitneygardens.com, 9 A.M.–dusk daily, $1 admission, $2 for a guided tour). Amble along a half mile of gravel paths that will take you past more than 3,000 rhododendrons, azaleas, and other flowering plants. It is especially stunning from mid-May–mid-June, but you'll find something in bloom all summer.

Scenic Drives

Turn off west two miles north of Eldon along the scenic **Hamma Hamma Road** (Forest Service Road 25) for sublime views of Mount Skokomish and the Brothers Wilderness areas. In the winter, bald eagles gather along the banks of the Hamma Hamma to feed on spawning salmon.

Look for elk along the scenic **Dosewallips Road** (Forest Service Road 2610), which heads west from Brinnon along the Dosewallips River toward the heart of the Olympics. Approximately three miles up the road, look for an unmarked turnoff by a bridge and small hydro plant to your right. From here, it is just a short walk to **Rocky Brook Falls,** an 80-foot waterfall worth the short jaunt. The road continues on for around another seven miles past this turnoff, at which point it abruptly ends at a washout that has left the last five miles into Olympic National Park severed. Environmental concerns and budget problems continue to delay the project, so expect the 10-mile stretch to suffice for several years to come.

Festivals and Events

The **Brinnon ShrimpFest** (360/796-4886) over Memorial Day weekend puts on an art fair, street dance, boat show, farmers market, and shrimp cooking contests. Bring along your decorated belt sander to participate in the zany Belt Sander Race.

Sports and Recreation

DUCKABUSH RECREATION AREA

Duckabush Road (Road 2519) heads west from Highway 101 four miles south of Brinnon, providing access to both the Brothers Wilderness and Olympic National Park. Two short trails—the **Interrorem Nature Trail** and **Ranger Hole Trail**—provide access to the densely forested country near the cabin. Continue a short distance up Duckabush Road to Forest Service Road 2530, and follow it 1.3 miles. From here, **Marhut Falls Trail** climbs 0.75 mile to this picturesque waterfall.

BROTHERS AND MOUNT SKOKOMISH WILDERNESSES

This 16,682-acre wilderness lies within Olympic National Forest and occupies a blip of land on the eastern flank of Olympic National Park. Wilderness permits are not required in the Brothers Wilderness. Only a few developed trails exist in the wilderness; the primary one is the **Duckabush River Trail,** which begins

a mile up from the Collins Campground in Duckabush Recreation Area. The trail climbs six miles to the park boundary, with a view from Big Hump rock. Once inside the park, you can connect to a maze of other routes through the high country. From Lena Lake Campground on Hamma Hamma Road, a hiking trail leads uphill to Lena Lake on the edge of the wilderness, and then on to **Upper Lena Lake** inside Olympic National Park. This is a perfect overnight backcountry trip.

Covering a little more than 13,000 acres, the Mount Skokomish Wilderness occupies steep terrain bordering the western edge of Olympic National Park. The **Putvin Trail** starts from Forest Service Road 25, approximately four miles beyond Lena Creek Campground on Hamma Hamma Road, and climbs steeply, rising more than 3,700 feet in less than four miles. The trail ends at rock-rimmed Lake of the Angels, just inside the ONP boundary.

BACKCOUNTRY HIKING

For those who want to dip their toes into backpacking, the Forest Service's **Elkhorn Campground** (free, open May–Sept.) features sites right along the river approximately three-quarters of a mile past the washout on Dosewallips Road. The gentle walk is a perfect one-night trip for those with young kids. You can extend the trip by walking further along the road-turned-trail about four miles to **Dosewallips Falls,** which cascades over enormous boulders just inside the Olympic National Park boundary. Stay nearby at **Dosewallips Campground** (www.nps.gov/olym, free, no reservations), a primitive site with no water and pit toilets that's about 5.5 miles away from the washout. A trailhead here provides access to the park backcountry via the West Fork and Main Fork Dosewallips trails. The site is not to be confused with the easier-access Dosewallips State Park.

BOATING AND FISHING

A half mile south of Brinnon on Highway 101, **Dosewallips State Park** covers 425 acres at the base of the Olympic Mountains, offering

OLYMPIC PENINSULA

both fresh- and saltwater activities where the Hood Canal comes together with the Dosewallips River. Clams are sometimes available here in season—check with the Washington Department of Fish and Wildlife (360/902-2700, www.wdwa.wa.gov).

Two miles south of Brinnon, **Pleasant Harbor State Park** has a protected dock adjacent to a private marina, but no boat launch or swimming facilities.

The secluded tidelands of **Point Whitney Beach** offer serene views of Hood Canal and prime clamming and oyster picking. Plus, you can learn how oysters, mussels, and clams are raised at the nearby **Point Whitney Shellfish Lab** (1000 Point Whitney Rd., 360/796-4601, 8 A.M.–4 P.M. daily Apr.–Sept. 4), run by the Washington Department of Fisheries.

Accommodations

C Mike's Beach Resort (38470 Hwy. 101, Lilliwaup, 360/877-5324 or 800/231-5324, www.mikesbeachresort.com, $70–130 d) is a fun and friendly place with a variety of accommodations, including dorm beds in a hostel with a full kitchen, cabins, and even Airstream RVs for rent. Tent spaces ($25) and RV hookups ($30) are also available, and pets are welcome throughout the resort. The main attraction here is the boat launch and dive facility; divers can fill tanks at the air station here, and for a fee even nonguests can launch boats or access the water from Mike's beach. There's great scuba diving at an artificial reef just offshore.

Houseboats for Two (360/796-3440 or 800/966-5942, www.houseboats4two.com, $225–245 d) rents private one-bed houseboats afloat on Pleasant Harbor near Brinnon. The accommodations are luxurious and include a hot tub, fireplace, and pool. This is a favorite honeymoon spot.

Elk Meadows B&B (3485 Dosewallips Rd., 360/796-4886, www.elkmeadowswa.com, $95 d, no kids under 14) is a big ranch-style home three miles up Dosewallips Road in the heart of elk country. Two guest suites have private baths, and a full breakfast is served each morning. Set right along Dosewallips River, Elk Meadows sprawling property also plays host to upscale, "Bring Your Own Bag" camping ($60). Unfurl the down inside a huge canvas tent set on a wooden platform and while the night away in front of a fire pit by the river.

CAMPING

Hamma Hamma Road begins two miles north of Eldon and continues to the edge of the Mount Skokomish Wilderness. Six miles up Hamma Hamma Road, **Hamma Hamma Campground** (877/444-6777, www.recreation.gov, $10, May–mid-Nov.) can accommodate tents and trailers up to 22 feet in length. Continue another two miles to **Lena Creek Campground** (877/444-6777, www.recreation.gov, $10, year-round), which provides access to miles of hiking. **Lena Lake Campground** is a free walk-in campground at this pretty lake, a three-mile trek from the Lena Creek Campground. Expect a compost toilet and no potable water at this fairly primitive site. Built by the Civilian Conservation Corps (CCC) in the 1930s, the historic **Hamma Hamma Cabin** (360/877-5254, $40) is available for groups up to six. This rustic abode has no running water.

Four miles south of Brinnon, head west on Duckabush Road (Forest Service Road 2519) to the rustic **Interrorem Ranger Cabin,** built in 1907 as headquarters for Olympic National Forest. Today the Forest Service rents this historic four-person cabin for $30; call 360/877-5254 for details. Keep going another mile up Duckabush Road to reach **Collins Campground** ($10, May–Sept.).

For prime views of the canal, the two best bets are at Dosewallips State Park and ($22–25 for tents, $29–36 for RVs) and **Seal Rock Campground** ($12, open May–Sept.). The former is one of the prettiest spots on the entire canal, but the Forest Service's Seal Rock is a great also-ran. Just north of Brinnon, it features saltwater-facing sites with great clam harvesting, as well as piped water and flush toilets. **Cove RV Park** (303075 U.S. Hwy. 101, 360/796-4723, $27 nightly, $170 weekly) has

RV hookups, plus bathrooms and showers. It is located three miles north of Brinnon.

Food

Brinnon's **Half Way House Restaurant** (41 Brinnon Ln. at Hwy. 101, 360/796-4715, 7 A.M.–8 P.M. Sun.–Thurs., 7 A.M.–9 P.M. Fri.–Sat.) has a gourmet chef and reasonable prices on seafood, steak, burgers, and lighter fare. This is also the place to go for a homemade breakfast. The **Geoduck Tavern** (307103 U.S. Hwy. 101, Brinnon, 360/796-4430, kitchen open 4–8 P.M. Tues.–Thurs., 11 A.M.–9 P.M. Fri.–Sat.) is a great place to soak up the local vibe. It serves up burgers and sometimes there's live music on weekends.

In Eldon, the **Seafood Store** (38546 N. U.S. Hwy. 101, 360/877-5811 or 888/877-5844, www.hamahamaoysters.com) sells fresh shucked, smoked, shell, and even pickled oysters! Tours of the facility are welcomed.

Getting There and Around

Jefferson Transit (360/345-4777 or 800/833-6388, www.jeffersontransit.com) bus service connects Brinnon with Port Townsend, Sequim, and Poulsbo. **Mason Transit** (360/427-5033 or 800/374-3747) runs free bus service south to Shelton and other parts of Mason County.

QUILCENE AREA

Tiny Quilcene has a rough-at-the-edges country feeling reminiscent of Northern California. The compact hamlet is made up of simple homes and trailers with piles of split wood in the yards and smoke curling from the chimneys. Chainsaw carving is considered high art and the surrounding cutover landscape looks like a bad haircut.

Sights and Recreation

BUCKHORN WILDERNESS

Covering 44,258 acres, the Buckhorn Wilderness occupies barren ridges and peaks topping 7,000 feet within Olympic National Forest and bordering on the extensive wilderness within Olympic National Park. The

Mount Townsend Trail begins from Forest Service Road 2760 off Road 27, northwest of Quilcene. This six-mile route climbs to the top of 6,280-foot Mount Townsend, providing incredible vistas in all directions. **Big Quilcene Trail** starts at the three-sided shelter 10 miles up Forest Service Road 2750 from Quilcene and follows the Big Quilcene River into the high country before switchbacking to the summit of Marmot Pass at 6,000 feet. From here, you can continue into Olympic National Park via the Constance Pass Trail. The Big Quilcene is famous for the multitudes of rhododendrons that bloom here in early summer. Contact the Hood Canal Ranger District (360/765-2200) for more information on the Buckhorn Wilderness.

MOUNT WALKER

The most popular viewpoint along Hood Canal is 2,804-foot Mount Walker, five miles south of Quilcene. A narrow gravel road leads to the summit, or you can hike up via a two-mile path through tall Douglas fir forests and a lush understory of huckleberry and rhododendron. The trail (or road) emerges onto a ridge with panoramic views of Seattle, Mount Rainier, and the Cascades to the east, and the Olympics to the northwest. Bring a lunch to enjoy at the summit picnic area.

Festivals and Events

Sit on hay bales and listen to chamber music while enjoying the mountain vistas and the antics of the event's iconic donkeys, which wander the pretty grounds at the **Olympic Music Festival** (360/732-4800, www.olympicmusicfestival.org). The Philadelphia String Quartet and guest artists perform these "Concerts in the Barn" 0.25 mile south of Highway 104 on Center Road.

Accommodations and Food

Hikers who prefer the comfort of crisp, clean sheets on a soft bed at the end of the trail will enjoy Quilcene's **Mount Walker Inn** (360/765-3410, www.mountwalkerinn.com, $65–108 s or d), a remote outpost of humble civilization on the edges of the peninsula's wilderness. Several rooms feature kitchenettes and all of them are kid- and pet-friendly, but none have telephones. These scenic woods are meant to be enjoyed without tethers anyway, right?

If you prefer to get a little closer to nature, the Forest Service's very popular **Falls View Campground** (877/444-6777, www.recreation .gov, $10; open May–Sept.) is 3.5 miles south of Quilcene and offers 14 RV sites without hook-ups and 16 tent sites. The half mile **Falls View Canyon Trail** drops down to the Big Quilcene River from the campground. Additional camp-sites can be found at **Lake Leland Park** (six mi. north of Quilcene, $12, open Apr.–Oct.), a small county facility that has a boat ramp

for small boats and a dock, plus a short na-ture trail.

Prime rib, roast beef, and seafood (includ-ing ultra-fresh local oysters) distinguish **The Olympic Timber House Restaurant** (295534 U.S. Hwy. 101, 360/765-3500, www.thetim berhouse.com, 11 A.M.–9 P.M. Mon.–Fri., 9 A.M.–9 P.M. Sat.–Sun.), a half mile south of Quilcene.

Information
The Olympic National Forest **Quilcene Office of the Hood Canal Ranger District** (295142 Hwy. 101, 360/765-2200) has maps and infor-mation on local camping and hiking options on both Forest Service and National Park lands.

Port Townsend and Quimper Peninsula

Standing on the northern tip of Quimper Peninsula—a point off the northeast corner of the Olympic Peninsula—Port Townsend is best known for its many excellent Victorian homes. Sandwiched between the perpetually snow-covered Olympic Mountains and the ship-filled Strait of Juan de Fuca, Port Townsend is a working town with much to see and explore. Many folks consider it one of the most interest-ing and beautiful towns in Washington.

The main port of entry to Puget Sound and the first town site on the Olympic Peninsula, the city's first building boom in the late 1800s is in evidence with the grand Victorian man-sions still standing today. Many of those old dames have been transformed into lavish B&Bs, and several galleries, shops, and gour-met restaurants have sprung up to serve visi-tors from near and far. Today the citizens of Port Townsend are a blend of blue-collar mill-workers, generally harmless tree-huggers, and wealthy newcomers and retirees who all enjoy the breathtaking views over Admiralty Inlet.

SIGHTS
Port Townsend's main attractions are its his-toric late 19th-century homes and businesses,

along with impressive Fort Worden State Park. Downtown's main boulevard, Water Street, consists of stout brick buildings filled with fine galleries, restaurants, and shops selling antiques, books, clothing, wines, and gifts.

One of the more distinctive town sights is the **Haller Fountain,** which features a bronze, scantily clad maiden emerging from a shell that is supported by water-spraying cherubs and fish. Theodore N. Haller donated the fountain to the city "in memory of early pioneers."

Port Townsend is still very much a seafar-ing town. Its Port Hudson Harbor is jammed with yachts, and quite a few boatbuilding businesses are based nearby. Of particular note is the **Northwest School of Wooden Boatbuilding** (42 N. Water St., 360/385-4948, www.nwboatschool.org, 8 A.M.–5 P.M. Mon.–Fri.), where several-day classes and six- and nine-month programs develop skills through intensive classes and hands-on projects. The facility is also open for self-guided tours by appointment.

Museums
Housed in the city's 1891 City Hall Complex, **Jefferson County Historical Society**

PORT TOWNSEND

NORTH BEACH PARK

FORT WORDEN STATE PARK

Point Wilson

POINT WILSON LIGHTHOUSE

DEFENSE WAY

MARINE SCIENCE CENTER
PUBLIC BOAT LAUNCH

CENTRUM OFFICE

49TH ST

ADMIRALTY AVE

ARTILLERY MUSEUM

EISENHOWER AVE

W ST

JEFFERSON COUNTY FAIRGROUNDS

COMMANDING OFFICER'S QUARTERS

KUHN ST

Admiralty Inlet

Inset:

HOLLY HILL HOUSE

ROTHSCHILD HOUSE

CITY HALL AND MUSEUM

HALLER FOUNTAIN

EARTHENWORKS

ROSE THEATRE

SILVERWATER CAFÉ

ANCESTRAL SPIRITS GALLERY

PALACE HOTEL

BELMONT HOTEL & RESTAURANT

PUBLIC HOUSE GRILL

PT CYCLERY

THE WATERSTREET HOTEL

CLAY ST · FRANKLIN ST · JEFFERSON · POLK ST · TYLER ST · JACOB ST · QUINCY · HARRISON ST · WASHINGTON ST · WATER ST

CHERRY ST · P ST · WALNUT ST · JACKSON ST

Chetzemoka Park

F ST

ADAMS ST · QUINCY ST

Park

HASTINGS AVE

ANN STARRETT MANSION

RAVENSCROFT INN

T'S RESTAURANT

Point Hudson

SWAN HOTEL

DISCOVERY RD · HAINES ST · SAN JUAN AVE · BLAINE ST · WALKER ST · KEARNEY ST · HARRISON ST · LAWRENCE ST · FRANKLIN · WATER ST · WASHINGTON ST

ST

WHIDBEY ISLAND FERRY

19TH ST

Kah Tai Lagoon Nature Park

Kah Tai Lagoon

JEFFERSON COUNTY COURTHOUSE

OLD CONSULATE INN

SEE DETAIL

SHERIDAN ST

CHAMBER OF COMMERCE

20

PORT TOWNSEND INN

BENEDICT ST

E SIMS WAY

HARBORSIDE INN

PORT OF PORT TOWNSEND

10TH ST

JEFFERSON GENERAL HOSPITAL

PORT TOWNSEND BREWING COMPANY

7TH ST

MANRESA CASTLE

← To Old Fort Townsend State Park

Port Townsend

0   0.25 mi

0   0.25 km

© AVALON TRAVEL

OLYMPIC PENINSULA

Museum (210 Madison St., 360/385-1003, www.jchsmuseum.org, 11 A.M.–4 P.M. daily, $4 adults, or $1 children 3–12), this excellent museum rambles over three floors of boat exhibits and models, intricate baskets, button and bottle collections, a Victorian bedroom, and even two buffalo-horn and bearskin chairs from an old photo studio. Downstairs is the old city jail, in use until the 1940s.

There's also a small museum inside the lobby of the **post office** (1322 Washington St.). During the 1880s, this imposing stone building served as the Customs House, the port of entry for all international traffic into Puget Sound.

Victorian Mansions

Stop by the visitor information center (440 12th St., 360/385-2722, www.enjoypt.com, 9 A.M.–5 P.M. Mon.–Fri., 10 A.M.–4 P.M. Sat., 11 A.M.–4 P.M. Sun.) to pick up a tour map of historic downtown and other parts of Port Townsend, including **Uptown,** which covers a block or so of Lawrence Street near Taylor Street. Created as a turn-of-the-20th-century shopping district for the genteel ladies living in the hilltop mansions, it was a yin to the yang of the formerly bawdy waterfront shopping district named "the most wicked city north of San Francisco" in the 1880s. Today, Uptown's mansions are elaborate B&Bs and offbeat stores. You'll discover great views across Admiralty Inlet from a tiny park at Monroe and Clay Streets.

The **Rothschild House** (Franklin and Taylor St., 11 A.M.–4 P.M. daily May–Sept., closed Oct.–Mar., $4 adults, $1 children 3–12) was built in 1868 by D. C. H. Rothschild, a Port Townsend merchant and a distant relative of Germany's famous Rothschild banking family. This restrained Victorian still has much of the original furniture, wallpaper, and carpeting, and it is surrounded by herb and flower gardens.

The **Manresa Castle** (651 Cleveland St., 360/385-5750 or 800/732-1281, www.manresacastle.com) is an 1892 mansion variously owned by a tycoon, the Jesuit Order, and a hotelier. A restaurant and lounge are on the premises, and an attractive rose and rhododendron garden provides a quiet place to enjoy the vista of Port Townsend and Admiralty Inlet.

Easily the most opulent Victorian structure in Port Townsend, the **Ann Starrett Mansion** (744 Clay St., 360/385-3205 or 800/321-0644, www.starrettmansion.com, noon–3 P.M. daily, $2 adults, kids under 12 free) is a National Historic Landmark and a favorite B&B. Take a tour or stay here to enjoy the luxury up close. The rooms are furnished with period antiques and offer outstanding views. Dormer windows in the dome admit light that illuminates a different red ruby stone for each season of the year.

Old Fort Townsend State Park

Old Fort Townsend State Park (4 mi. south of town off S.R. 20, turn east on Old Fort Townsend Rd., 360/385-3595, 8 A.M.–dusk daily, $10 day use parking) has campsites and seven miles of hiking trails through tall firs, sloping down to a 150-foot cliff along Port Townsend Bay. The 377-acre park is open mid-April–mid-September only. A fort was established here in 1856 to guard against possible American Indian attacks. The fort was used during World War II as an enemy munitions defusing station. In 1958 it was turned over to the State Parks Commission. A short self-guided historical walk starts at the display board near the park entrance.

◖ Fort Worden State Park

Capping Point Wilson, Fort Worden, along with Fort Flagler on Marrowstone Island and Fort Casey on Whidbey Island, served as the "Iron Triangle" of forts protecting the entrance to Puget Sound. Fort Worden's guns were never fired in battle, and advances in military technology made them obsolete almost as soon as they were in place. After the army left in 1953, Fort Worden served as a state detention center before becoming a state park in 1973. If the place seems familiar, it may be because much of the movie *An Officer and a Gentleman* was filmed here.

© NATALIA BRATSLAVSKY/123RF.COM

Point Wilson Lighthouse

Townsend Marine Science Center (360/385-5582, www.ptmsc.org, hours and days vary by exhibit, $5 adults, $3 kids 6–17, free for kids under 6, discounts Nov.–Mar.) offering intimate, hands-on relationships with local sea creatures, beach walks, and evening slide shows and lectures.

Oak Bay and Marrowstone Island

Those who choose to motor up to Port Townsend from the Kitsap Peninsula or the rest of the Hood Canal area would do well to take the slow route up along the gentle waters of Oak Bay on Oak Bay Road. The stretch from the Hood Canal Bridge all the way to Port Townsend will have you pass little villages such as Port Ludlow, Port Hadlock, and Irondale, as well as the pastoral Marrowstone Island. Each of these has a cluster of businesses and a number of fascinating historic homes, including **Hadlock Manor** on Curtiss Street in Hadlock, built in the 1890s by a Swedish sea captain.

Marrowstone Island's biggest attraction is **Fort Flagler State Park,** at the island's northern tip. Surrounded by water on three sides, the park is perfect for boating, picnicking, crabbing, and fishing. Wooded hiking trails and camping at beach sites are also available in this 783-acre park. Since it is in the Olympic rain shadow, the park gets lots of sun and only 17 inches of rain per year.

Fort Flagler joined with Fort Worden and Whidbey's Fort Casey to guard the narrow Admiralty Inlet against hostile incursions into Puget Sound. Built in the late 1890s, the fort served as a training center during the two World Wars. The massive gun emplacements were, thankfully, never needed for anything but gunnery practice. The fort was closed in 1955 and later became a state park. Today, nine gun batteries remain. From these, you can watch the ships, barges, sailboats, and fishing vessels cruise past; it's pretty easy to see why a fort was built on this strategic bottleneck.

Fort Flagler's spacious green parade grounds are bordered by barracks and gracious old officers' quarters. Several trails cut through wooded

Many of the fort's buildings remain, the highlight being the **Commanding Officer's House** (10 A.M.–5 P.M. daily June–Aug., noon–4 P.M. Sat.–Sun. Mar.–May and Sept.–Oct., one weekend per month Nov.–Feb., $2 adults, $1 kids 6–12, free for kids under 6) containing period Victorian furnishings. One of the old barracks buildings now houses the **Coast Artillery Museum** (360/385-0373, 10 A.M.–5 P.M. daily July–Aug., 11 A.M.–4 P.M. daily the rest of the year, $2 adults, $1 kids 6–12, free for kids under 6), where you'll learn how the enormous gun batteries out on the coastal bluffs worked.

Don't miss the photo op provided by the 1917 **Point Wilson Lighthouse.** No public tours of the building are offered, but the beach here makes for wonderful sunup or sundown strolls, with dramatic Mount Baker seeming to rise directly across the water.

Contemporary facilities include a campground, boat launch, tennis courts, underwater scuba-diving park, rhododendron garden, hiking trails, and a hostel. Also visit the **Port**

OLYMPIC PENINSULA

sections of the park. The **Marrowstone Point Lighthouse** (closed to the public) stands on the northeast edge of the fort, with massive Mount Baker creating an attractive photographic backdrop.

ENTERTAINMENT AND EVENTS

Bars

The Public House Grill & Ales (1038 Water St., 360/385-9708, www.thepublichouse.com, 11 A.M.–10 P.M. daily, $15) has live music on in-season weekends, and good pub food, especially for lunch. **Ajax Café** (21 N. Water St., Port Hadlock, 360/385-3450, www.ajaxcafe .com, 5–9 P.M. Tues.–Sun.) also has live music most weekend nights.

Theaters

A refurbished and reinvigorated old-time cinema house, **Rose Theatre** (385 Taylor St., 360/385-1089, www.rosetheatre.com) is a rare breed these days. A community theater that shows two titles a week, the Rose balances its love of the silver screen with a steady roster of concerts, plays, and music events that play in front of the red velvet curtains when the reels aren't running. The **Key City Public Theatre** puts on plays and musicals throughout the year at the Key City Playhouse (419 Washington St., 360/385-7396, www.keycitypublictheatre.org). The **Port Townsend Community Orchestra** (360/732-6898, www.porttownsendorchestra .org) performs at four free concerts each year between October and May.

Festivals and Events

Port Townsend's calendar is jam-packed with activities, many of which are sponsored by the nonprofit **Centrum Foundation** (360/385-3102 or 800/733-3608, www.centrum.org). These include events such as performances by jazz, bluegrass, blues, and classical musicians; folk dance festivals; plays; seminars; and readings by well-known authors. For a schedule of upcoming events, contact the Centrum Foundation.

Held the third week in May, the **Rhododendron Festival** (www.rhodyfestival .org) features a big Saturday parade, dances, antique and art shows, a carnival, rhododendron displays, and the pomp and circumstance of choosing rhododendron royalty.

The summertime music season kicks off with the **Festival of American Fiddle Tunes** (360/385-3102 x127, www.centrum.org) at the end of June, followed by mid-July's **Jazz Port Townsend,** which blends directly into the **Port Townsend Blues Festival** (360/385-3102 ext. 127, www.centrum.org).

The second weekend in August is reserved for the **Jefferson County Fair** (www.jeffco fairgrounds.com), the old-fashioned kind with livestock shows, 4-H displays, and a mud race. A particular highlight of the year's calendar is the **Wooden Boat Festival** (www.woodenboat .org) in early September, full of music, regattas, boat tours, and exhibitions.

Early October brings the fairly strange **Kinetic Sculpture Race** (www.ptkineticrace .org) to Port Townsend; costumed characters pilot human-powered mechanical sculptures over land and water in a race to the finish.

If you're in town on the first Saturday in December, you'll be able to join the fun as Santa arrives by ferry, and people gather to sing carols on Water Street and watch the **tree-lighting ceremony** (360/385-7911).

SHOPPING

Water Street houses numerous art galleries, antique shops, cafés, trendy gift shops, and an import toy store. **Ancestral Spirits Gallery** (921 Washington St., 360/385-0078, www .ancestralspirits.com, 10 A.M.–6 P.M. daily features an impressive blend of modern and traditional Native American art, masks, and jewelry. **Earthenworks Gallery** (1002 Water St., 360/385-0328, www.earthenworksgallery .com, 10 A.M.–5:30 P.M. daily) sells high quality, creative works—especially ceramics. **Gallery Walks** are held the first Saturday of each month, 5:30–8 P.M., during which galleries hang new works, serve refreshments, and often have artists on hand. Walks are self-guided, so just show up downtown and go for a walk!

FairWinds Winery (1984 Hastings Ave. W., 360/385-6899, www.fairwindswinery.com, noon–5 P.M. daily Memorial Day–Labor Day, noon–5 P.M. Fri.–Sat. Sept.–May) is a tiny family operation producing mainstream varietals as well as some unique offerings such as Aligote and its award-winning Fireweed Mead.

SPORTS AND RECREATION

Parks
Chetzemoka Park (900 Jackson St.) on Admiralty Inlet at Jackson and Roosevelt Streets is a small, shady park with eight flower gardens, picnicking, a bandstand, and beach access. Bird-watchers may be interested in **Kah Tai Lagoon Nature Park** (12th St. near Sims Way), which encompasses 85 acres of wetlands, grasslands, and woodlands, explorable through 2.5 miles of trails.

Water Sports
PT Outdoors (Flagship Landing on Water St., 360/379-3608, www.ptoutdoors.com) has kayak lessons, rentals, and tours. A kayak with paddles and life vest will run you $45 for a half-day's use. The 133-foot, 1913 schooner *Adventuress* (360/379-0438, www.soundexp .org) sails on voyages of all lengths throughout the summer and fall. Rates range from a $55 day cruise up to $450 for a three-night San Juans cruise. The ship allows no smoking nor alcohol, and all meals are vegetarian. **Brisa Charters** (360/376-3264, www.brisa charters.com, $75 per person) offers day and sunset sails aboard the 45-foot Lapworth sloop, the *Annie Too.*

South of Port Townsend, **Anderson Lake State Park** (Anderson Lake Rd. and Hwy. 20) is an isolated lake surrounded by trees. No camping or swimming, but it's a popular place to fish for cutthroat and rainbow trout, although toxic algae blooms in the lake have limited its use in the last few years.

The only real business on Marrowstone Island is **Nordland General Store,** which rents

sea kayaks. Tiny, boat-friendly **Mystery Bay State Park** (www.parks.wa.gov), just north of Nordland, has a picnic area, beach, pier, boat moorage, and protected waters for small boats, along with striking Olympic views.

Shine Tidelands State Park (www.parks .wa.gov) occupies a 13-acre spot at the north end of the Hood Canal Bridge and is popular with sea kayakers and windsurfers. No camping is allowed.

Bike and Gear Rentals
For mountain, touring, and tandem bike rentals, check **P.T. Cyclery** (252 Tyler St., 360/385-6470, www.ptcyclery.com). The store has created several maps of great mountain-bike rides in the area, for bikers looking for places to hit the trails. You can also rent bikes, sea kayaks, and camping gear from **Sport Townsend** (1044 Water St., 360/379-9711, www.sport townsend.com).

Fishing and Hunting
Peninsula Sportsman (360/379-0906, www .peninsulasportsman.com) outfits and guides a wide variety of family or individual expeditions, from salmon, trout, or halibut fishing to trophy hunting for sea ducks.

Golf
Local golf courses include the public 18-hole **Discovery Bay Golf Club** (7401 Cape George Rd., 360/385-0704, www.disco baygolf.com, $28 weekdays, $32 weekends). The **Port Townsend Golf Club** (1948 Blaine St., 360/385-4547, www.porttownsendgolf .com, $16/9 holes, $23/18 holes) is a municipal par-35, said to be the driest course on the Olympic Peninsula.

ACCOMMODATIONS
Port Townsend has some of the most exquisite lodging choices in the state, most notably the myriad old Victorian homes that have been turned into bed-and-breakfasts, along with a dozen or so motels and hotels, and an equal number of cabins and guesthouses.

OLYMPIC PENINSULA

The city is a popular destination, and reservations are advised, especially in the summer and on weekends. The chamber of commerce (360/385-2722, www.ptchamber.org) tracks local accommodations and can tell you where rooms are available.

Under $100

For a bit of a step up—and more privacy—try **Port Townsend Inn** (2020 E. Washington St., 360/385-2211 or 800/216-4985, www.porttownsendinn.com, $68 s or d). The normal rooms are pretty standard hotel fare with unremarkable furniture, but the grassy grounds are nice and there's an indoor pool and hot tub on the premises. Splurgers can upgrade to a whirlpool-bath suite ($168 d) with wet bar.

Built in 1885, the **Belmont Hotel and Restaurant** (925 Water St., 360/385-3007, www.thebelmontpt.com, $79–129 s or d), was once host to sailors, ship captains, and gamblers. The ornately decorated Italianate-style inn right in the heart of downtown offers guests a chance to savor the past.

The Waterstreet Hotel (635 Water St., 360/385-5467 or 800/735-9810, www.waterstreethotelporttownsend.com, $60–90 s or d, $140–160 suites) is on the second and third floors of the 1889 N. D. Hill Building, with Water Street Brewing and Ale House on the first level. Suites with private decks overlooking the bay are available.

Built in 1889, the **Palace Hotel** (1004 Water St., 360/385-0773 or 800/962-0741, www.palacehotelpt.com, $59–159 s or d), once the "Palace of Sweets" brothel, is a beautifully restored boutique hotel with antique furnishings, high ceilings, and old-world charm. Rooms come decorated with antique furnishings and high ceilings, some with shared and some with private baths. Continental breakfast is served daily.

$100–150

Harborside Inn (330 Benedict St., 360/385-7909 or 800/942-5960, www.harborside-inn.com, $119–179 s or d) is a 63-room waterfront motel with large rooms (each with a microwave, fridge, a private patio, and a striking view), an outdoor pool, hot tub, and continental breakfast.

A charming, three tier wedding cake Victorian house at the end of Water St. near Admiralty Inlet is home to **The Swan Hotel** (222 Monroe St., 360/385-1718 or 800/776-1718, www.theswanhotel.com). The property offers romantic little studio cottages ($160 d), suites ($99–145 d), and one penthouse unit ($275–400 d). The lodging is friendly to kids and dogs, even both at the same time.

Six miles west of Port Townsend on a bluff overlooking Discovery Bay is **Bay Cottages** (4346 S. Discovery Rd., 360/385-2035, www.baycottagegetaway.com, $150 s or d). The property's two cottages each include full kitchen, feather beds, and fresh flowers. Kids are welcome.

Holly Hill House (611 Polk St., 360/385-5619 or 800/435-1454, www.hollyhillhouse.com, $108–190 s or d), built in 1872, has been beautifully renovated to provide five guest rooms, each with a private bath. The parlor showcases the owner's collection of military aviation artwork and WWII memorabilia. The home is surrounded by tall holly and elm trees.

The best bet on Marrowstone is at **Fort Flagler State Park** (360/902-8600 or 888/226-7688, www.parks.wa.gov). Three of the fort's old buildings are rented out as vacation homes ($105–170) and the campground ($14 tents, $20 full hookups, $7 extra reservation fee, late Feb.–Oct.) accommodates tenters and RV campers. Coin-operated showers are available.

$150–200

One of Port Townsend's most remarkable bed-and-breakfast inns sits inside **❮ Manresa Castle** (651 Cleveland St., 360/385-5750 or 800/732-1281, www.manresacastle.com, $109–119 s or d, $169–229 suites), a unique 1892 castle-hotel with antique furnishings and bay views. Each room is unique, with one-of-a-kind antique furnishings and lavish linens. A spacious tower room set within the castle's turret is a favorite among honeymooners.

Ann Starrett Mansion (744 Clay St., 360/385-3205 or 800/321-0644, www.starrett mansion.com, $115–225) has nine rooms ($115–175 s or d) in the 1889 mansion and two in a separate cottage ($179–225 s or d). A gourmet breakfast is served.

Stay in a lovely turreted Queen Anne at ❰ **The Old Consulate Inn** (313 Walker St., 360/385-6753 or 800/300-6753, www.old consulateinn.com, $110–210 s or d), overlooking Port Townsend from atop a high bluff. Once the office of the German Consul, this 1889 beauty has fireplaces in two parlors, a large billiard and game room, and playable grand piano and antique organ. A gazebo encloses the hot tub. Eight guest rooms all have private baths. A gourmet breakfast is served.

Three short blocks from downtown, the elegant **Ravenscroft Inn** (533 Quincy St., 360/385-2784 or 800/782-2691, www.ravens croftinn.com, $150–210 s or d) features wide verandas with sound and mountain views in a custom-built B&B. The eight guest rooms have private baths, and two suites have fireplaces and tubs. Elegant gourmet breakfasts will get you out of bed, guaranteed.

The Inn at Port Ludlow (1 Heron Rd., 360/437-2222 or 800/732-1239, www.portlud lowresort.com, $169 d–$259) dominates Port Ludlow. Port Ludlow offers the utmost in luxury: large heated outdoor and indoor pools, hot tub, saunas, squash and tennis courts, paved bike paths, three nine-hole golf courses, and 300-slip marina on Port Ludlow Bay complete with rental sailboats. A wide variety of rooms are available, from standard rooms to four-bedroom suites that sleep eight.

$200-250

An interesting alternative lodging—especially for families and groups—is one of the former officers' homes in **Fort Worden State Park** (200 Battery Way, 360/344-4400, $183–508). The 32 houses have mostly been refitted with Victorian-style furnishings and modern conveniences. These cozy homes sleep 7–14 guests. Because of their popularity—especially during summer festivals—reservations for these houses should be made far in advance.

Camping

Stake your tents or pull your RVs up to the beachside campsites at **Fort Worden State Park** (360/385-4730, www.parks.wa.gov, $22–25 for tents, $29–36 for RVs), which hosts two fully developed campground sites with coin-op showers ready to accommodate the hordes during the summer rush and beyond. To get away from the crowds, try to snag one of five primitive tent sites hidden on the property.

Four miles south of town, **Old Fort Townsend State Park** (360/385-3595, www .parks.wa.gov, $22–25) has shady campsites under tall firs along Port Townsend Bay. It also has showers. The campground is open for camping mid-April–mid-September only.

RVers can park at the private **Point Hudson Resort** on the beach (360/385-2828 or 800/826-3854, $30–52 full hookups) or the campground adjacent to the **Jefferson County Fairgrounds** (4907 Landes St., 360/385-1013, www.jeff cofairgrounds.com/camping.html, $20).

FOOD
Cafés and Diners

Salal Café (634 Water St., 360/385-6532, 7 A.M.–2 P.M. daily) has a lovely sun deck and a wide variety of fresh breakfast and lunch options. Come here to enjoy the homemade jams and famous potatoes and salsa.

Lehani's (221 Taylor, 360/385-3961, 8 A.M.–6 P.M. daily) is another downtown spot for morning coffee and baked goods, delicious chocolate treats, and quick lunches.

Stop by **Sea J's Café** (2501 Washington St., 360/385-6312, 6 A.M.–8 P.M. Mon.–Sat., 7 A.M.–8 P.M. Sun.) for the best fish and chips in town.

As you drive through Quimper Peninsula, be sure to make time to stop off at the roadside **Chimacum Café** (9253 Rhody Dr., Chimacum, 360/732-4631, 6 A.M.–9 P.M. daily in summer,

6 A.M.–8 P.M. daily rest of year), a locals' favorite. The friendly staff serves big portions of the staple all-American foods: steaks, chicken, burgers, and chocolate malts.

Contemporary Northwest

Sandwiched between a launderette and a Radio Shack store, **(T's Restaurant** (2330 Washington St., 360/385-0700, www.ts-restaurant.com, 4–10 P.M. Wed.–Mon., closed Tues., entrées $20–31) is a big surprise. Step inside to find an elegant atmosphere and Italian-inspired Northwest seafood and meats.

Fountain Café (920 Washington St., 360/385-1364, 11:30 A.M.–3 P.M. and 5–9 P.M. daily) serves wide-ranging gourmet dishes full of local ingredients and fresh seafood in its small but charming backstreet location. It's a popular place, so be ready to wait for a table on summer weekends.

(Silverwater Café (Washington and Taylor Streets, 360/385-6448, 11:30–2:30 and 5–9 P.M. daily, entrées $10–15) is well known for fresh and reasonably priced pasta, meat, and seafood served in a bright and airy space.

International

Lanza's Ristorante/Pizzeria (1020 Lawrence St., 360/379-1900, 5–9 P.M. Tues.–Sat.) in Uptown has several kinds of excellent pizzas, plus outstanding home-cookin' in the form of antipasto and pastas. A simpler but nevertheless tasty choice is to get a slice of pie and a Coke at **Waterfront Pizza** (951 Water St., 360/385-6629, 11 A.M.–9 P.M. daily). It's the perfect place to try a sourdough-crust pizza if you've never had one before.

Ichikawa and Sushi Bar (1208 Water St., 360/379-4000, 11:30 A.M.–1:30 P.M. and 5–9 P.M. Tues.–Sat., closed Sun.–Mon.) serves up sushi, sashimi, and robata-yaki, as well as grilled and alder-smoked seafood, chicken, and steaks.

Pub Grub

Port Townsend Brewing Company (330 10th St., 360/385-9967, www.porttownsendbrewing.com, noon–8 P.M. Wed., noon–7 P.M. Thurs.

and Sat.–Tues., noon–9 P.M. Fri.) brews a variety of quality beers, including a pale ale, stout, IPA, and a bitter. You can check out the different flavors in the tasting room.

For the full sit-down brewpub experience, check out **Waterstreet** (126 Quincy St., 360/379-6438, noon–10 P.M. daily) with very tasty pub food like steamed mussels, oyster shooters, hearty burgers, and grilled sandwiches, plus several home-brewed beers to wash them down.

Markets

Located in Uptown, **Aldrich's Grocery** (940 Lawrence St., 360/385-0500, www.aldrichs.com, 7 A.M.–9 P.M. daily) has all the staples, but you'll also find gourmet specialties and a big wine selection. The deli here (Sally's) makes fantastic baked goods and the best soups around.

Find fresh fish and other seafood at **Key City Fish Co.** (307 10th St., 360/379-5516 or 800/617-3474, www.keycityfish.com, 10 A.M.–6 P.M. Mon.–Sat., closed Sun.), right next to the ferry terminal. They'll pack your fish in ice to take home aboard the ferry.

Get baked goods, organic produce, crafts, and flowers at the **Port Townsend Farmers Market** (360/379-5054) held downtown 8:30 A.M.–1 P.M. Saturday May–October and in Uptown 3:30–6 P.M. Wednesday May–August.

INFORMATION AND SERVICES

For local information and a ton of brochures, head to the **Port Townsend Chamber of Commerce Tourist Information Center** (440 12th St., 360/385-2722 or 888/365-6978, 9 A.M.–5 P.M. Mon.–Fri., 10 A.M.–4 P.M. Sat., and 11 A.M.–4 P.M. Sun.). For general tourist information about the town, look up www.ptguide.com on the Web.

Port Townsend Public Library (1220 Lawrence St., 360/385-3181) is one of the many Carnegie Libraries built early in this century.

The local emergency room is at **Jefferson Healthcare Emergency** (834 Sheridan St., 360/385-5600). Sick pets can find help at

Chimacum Valley Veterinary Hospital (820 Chimacum Rd., 360/385-4488) in nearby Port Haddock.

GETTING THERE AND AROUND
By Car and Bus
Parking can be a nightmare on summer weekends; avoid the hassles (and parking tickets) by parking at the **Park & Ride** (Haines Pl. and 12th St.); stop on the south side of town and hop aboard a **Jefferson Transit** bus (360/385-4777 or 800/773-7788, www.jeffersontransit.com), serving Port Townsend and Jefferson County, with connections to Port Angeles via Clallam Transit or the Kitsap Peninsula via Kitsap Transit.

By Ferry
Port Townsend is served directly by the **Washington State Ferry** (206/842-2345, 888/808-7977, or 800/843-3779 for automated information, www.wsdot.wa.gov/ferries/) from Keystone on the southwest side of Whidbey Island. The ferries depart about every 50 minutes, and in summer cost $3.05 one-way for passengers and walk-ons, $12.70 one-way for car and driver, $0.50 extra for bikes.

P.S. Express (360/385-5288, www.pugetsoundexpress.com, $85 round-trip, bikes and kayaks $15 extra) provides passenger-only service between Port Townsend and Friday Harbor on San Juan Island. The boat leaves Port Townsend daily April–October and takes you through Admiralty Inlet and the Strait of Juan de Fuca, where you're likely to see seals, sea otters, and orcas. The boat stays in Friday Harbor long enough for a quick three-hour visit, or you can overnight there and return to Port Townsend later.

OLYMPIC PENINSULA

Sequim

As storms pass over the Olympic Peninsula, they split in two; one part clings to the Olympics and the other is blown along by the strait's air currents, bypassing Sequim (pronounced skwim) like an island in the stream. The result is Sequim's famous "blue hole"—a miraculous gap in the sky of cerulean cloudlessness. It's sunny 299 days of the year and it rains less in Sequim than in Los Angeles.

SIGHTS
Museum and Arts Center
One block north of Highway 101 lies the Museum and Arts Center (175 W. Cedar St., 360/683-8110, www.sequimmuseum.org, 10 A.M.–4 P.M. Tues.–Sun., closed last Sun. of the month, $2 donation requested). Built to store the 12,000-year-old tusks, bones, and artifacts unearthed at Sequim's famous Manis Mastodon Site, the museum has branched out to include several antique cedar bark baskets, pioneer farming displays, and timber exhibits.

◖ Dungeness Spit
The word *Dungeness* (meaning sandy cape) is a fitting description for this 5.5-mile-long stretch of sand that creates Dungeness Bay. The **Dungeness National Wildlife Refuge** (Voice of America Rd., 360/457-8451, www.fws.gov/washingtonmaritime/dungeness, $3 per group) provides habitat for 250 species of birds on the nation's longest natural sand spit. As many as 30,000 birds rest at this saltwater lagoon during their migratory journeys.

Built in 1857, the **New Dungeness Lighthouse** at the tip of the spit is managed by volunteers and offers tours, but you'll have to hike a total of 10 miles round-trip to see it. It's a good idea to check the tide charts before starting out. For an overview of the area, hike the half-mile trail from the parking lot to a bluff overlooking Dungeness Bay. Clamming, fishing, and canoeing are permitted in this protected wildlife refuge, but no camping, dogs, firearms, or fires. The spit is closed to horses on weekends and holidays April 15–October 15.

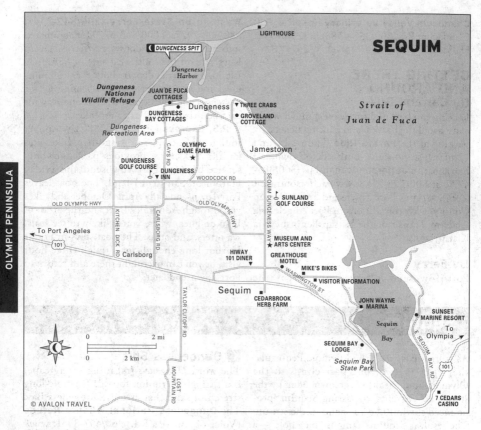

SEQUIM

Olympic Game Farm

The Olympic Game Farm (1423 Ward Rd., 360/683-4295 or 800/778-4295, www.oly gamefarm.com, 9 A.M.–5 P.M. daily May–mid-Oct., 9 A.M.–4 P.M. Feb.–May and mid-Oct.–Nov., $14 adults, $13 seniors and ages 6–12, free for kids under 6), a vacation and retirement home for Hollywood's animal stars, is a 90-acre preserve where Gentle Ben and over 200 other animals of TV and movie fame can be visited. Many of the Walt Disney nature specials were filmed here, along with parts of many feature movies. Hour-long guided walking tours are available daily mid-May–early September. The park is open all year for driving tours for the same prices. Follow the signs from Sequim five miles northwest to Ward Road.

Farm Tours

Dungeness Valley's mild climate is perfect for growing herbs, and it is now one of only two places in the world where lavender oil is produced (the other is France). Many farms grow lavender locally; visit www.lavendergrowers .org for more information. Gourmet cooks will enjoy a visit to Washington's first herb farm, **Cedarbrook Lavender and Herb Farm** (986 Sequim Ave. S, 360/683-7733, www.cedar brooklavender.com, 10 A.M.–5 P.M. Mon.–Sat.), where 200 varieties of herbs, teas, and flowers are organically grown.

© ERICKA CHICKOWSKI

Lavender farms scatter the country roads in Sequim.

Troll Haven

If you appreciate the unusual, drop by Troll Haven (360/797-7168, www.trollhaven. org) in Gardiner. This private residence is chock-full of sculptures and artwork depicting Scandinavian fairy-tale creatures. There are even live bison! Get here by heading east from Sequim on Highway 101 to Gardiner, and turning onto Gardiner Beach Road. Please respect the privacy of the landowners while viewing the art from a distance, or call in advance to request a tour.

John Wayne Marina

John Wayne loved the Northwest because he could visit the area and not be hounded by autograph seekers, and he especially loved the Strait of Juan de Fuca. The Duke liked it so much he bought land on Sequim Bay and donated it for a marina. The John Wayne Marina has 422 slips, a landscaped park and picnic area, and a bronze statue of the Duke as he appeared in the 1949 flick *She Wore A Yellow Ribbon*. Rent

boats here at **The Bosun's Locker** (360/683-6521, www.portofpa.com/marinas/john-wayne-marina.html, 9 A.M.–6 P.M. daily). Bosun's also sells John Wayne souvenirs.

ENTERTAINMENT AND EVENTS

Casinos

The enormous **7 Cedars Casino** (270756 Hwy. 101, 360/683-7777 or 800/458-2597, www.7cedarscasino.com), near Blyn at the head of Sequim Bay, has bingo, blackjack, craps, keno, poker, and roulette; it is run by the Jamestown S'Klallam Tribe. Inside, several restaurants serve a variety of cuisines from regional favorites to hot dogs and fries.

Festivals and Events

Maybe a festival celebrating ditch-digging doesn't excite you. But the **Sequim Irrigation Festival** (www.irrigationfestival.com) is the longest-running festival in Washington State, so it must have something going for it! Parades, art and flower shows, a carnival, fireworks, logging show, and a one-of-a-kind chainsaw carving contest (second largest in America!) commemorate the annual event, held on the first full week of May each year.

In July, the **Celebrate Lavender Festival** (877/681-3035, www.lavenderfestival.com) features tours of local lavender farms, speakers, and an open-air market offering food, music, and demonstrations.

SPORTS AND RECREATION

Recreation in the Sequim area focuses on the protected waters inside the inner harbor of Dungeness Bay, a favorite place for windsurfers and sea kayakers. The six-mile path to the lighthouse on Dungeness Spit is a very popular place for a seaside walk or horseback ride. **Dungeness Kayaking** (360/681-4190, www.dungenesskayaking.com, $100–150 per person, minimum of two) leads beginners on sea kayak trips around the bay.

Mountain bike rentals and tours of the nearby foothills are available from **Mike's Bikes** (551 W. Washington St., 360/681-3868, www.mikes-bikes.net, 10 A.M.–6 P.M. Mon.– Fri., 10 A.M.–5 P.M. Sat., closed Sun.). One superb full-day ride near Sequim is up **Forest Service Road 2860**, which winds up the side of the Dungeness River Valley (with spectacular views) to a junction with the end of the Lower Dungeness Trail. The 11-mile single-track descent to Gold Creek is one of the best on the Olympic Peninsula, if not the entire state. Get there by car via Palo Alto Road, which leaves Highway 101 three miles east of Sequim, following signs to Forest Service Road 28. The lazy can arrange for a lift up the dirt road, but the downhill ride just isn't quite as satisfying that way.

Northwest golfers will be in heaven in Sequim, where it is possible to play a round just about any month of the year. There are several championship courses within city limits, but the best is unquestionably the par-72 **Dungeness Golf Course** (north of Carlsborg on Woodcock Rd., 360/683-6344, www.dungenessgolf.com, $35–44 for 18 holes in summer), which keeps greens pristine and poses some good challenges with its well-positioned bunkers. It's also got a pretty decent 19th hole: the Dungeness Inn Restaurant.

ACCOMMODATIONS
Under $100
Greathouse Motel (740 E. Washington St./ Hwy. 101 E, 360/683-7272 or 800/475-7272, $75–85 s or d) includes a continental breakfast in the nightly rates. **Sequim West Inn** (740 W. Washington St., 360/683-4144 or 800/528-4527, www.sequimwestinn.com, $119–139 s or d) has rooms with microwaves and fridges.

$100–150
Sequim Bay Lodge (1788 Hwy. 101 E, 360/683-0691 or 800/622-0691, www.sequimbaylodge.com, $75–90 s or d), three miles east of town, has an outdoor pool and hot tub.

Dungeness Bay Cottages (140 Marine Dr., 360/683-3013 or 888/683-3013, www.dungenessbay.com, $130–180 d) is five miles north of town along the bay and has five cottages with full kitchens on a private beach.

East of Sequim, find **Sunset Marine Resort** (40 Buzzard Ridge Rd., Blyn, 360/681-4166, www.sunsetmarineresort.com, $135–260 d), where generally pet-friendly six-person cabins with kitchens are spread over cliffs and grassy shorelines.

Groveland Cottage (4861 Sequim-Dungeness Way, 360/683-3565 or 800/879-8859, www.grovelandcottage.com, $125–140 s or d) is a century-old house with a large lawn and pond five miles north of Sequim. Inside are five whimsical guest rooms with private or shared baths.

$150–200
Located across from the marina, **Sequim Bay Resort** (2634 West Sequim Bay Rd., 360/681-3853, www.sequimbayresort.com, $130–200 s or d) offers waterfront views from its lightly wooded property. The grounds are scattered with seaside cabins—some with kitchenettes—and campsites.

Just north of the main town are the **Juan de Fuca Cottages** (182 Marine Dr., 360/683-

4433 or 866/683-4433, www.juandefuca.com, $175–260 s or d), six fully equipped housekeeping cottages perched on a 50-foot cliff overlooking Dungeness Spit. A hot tub is available. There is a two-night minimum on weekends.

Flower fans won't want to miss the gardens at ◖ **BJ's Garden Café B&B** (397 Monterra Dr., Port Angeles, six miles north of Sequim, 360/452-2322 or 800/880-1332, www.bjgarden.com, $165–245), a Victorian-style B&B with award-winning greenery that's been featured in national magazines such as *Country Garden*. Each of the five guest rooms comes with fireplaces; some have jetted tubs.

$200-250

Colette's B&B (339 Finn Hall Rd., 360/457-9197, www.colettes.com, $195–395 s or d) is a luxurious 10-acre seaside estate with flower gardens, whirlpool baths, king-size beds, fireplaces, and gourmet breakfasts.

Camping

Dungeness Recreation Area (554 Voice of America West, 360/683-5847), a 216-acre Clallam County park at the base of the refuge, has camping February–October ($18) with showers, beach access, and a picnic area. **Sequim Bay State Park** (just east of Sequim on Hwy. 101, 888/226-7688, www.parks.wa.gov, $19 tent, $24 full hookups, $7 extra reservation fee) offers wooded tent sites, RV hookup sites, a boat launch, scuba diving, hiking, tennis courts, and superb views of Sequim Bay.

The Forest Service offers campgrounds in the mountains 11 miles south of Sequim via Forest Service Roads 2909 and 2958 at **Dungeness Forks Campground** ($10, open late May–early Sept.). This well-water and vault-toilet hideaway has 10 sites close to hiking and fishing. Trailers and motor homes might have a tough time on the road. Contact the Quilcene Ranger Station (360/765-3368) for details.

Sequim's best RV park is **Rainbow's End RV Park** (261831 Hwy. 101, 360/683-3863, $34 daily, $193 weekly), where you can catch rainbow and golden trout in the property's stocked fishing pond. This pet-friendly park offers a fenced off-leash area, laundry and shower facilities, and free wireless Internet. There's a creek bordering the property and plenty of views of the mountains.

FOOD

Start out the day at **Oak Table Café** (292 W. Bell, 360/683-2179, 7 A.M.–3 P.M. daily) where the breakfasts are filling and delicious (try the wonderful soufflé-style baked apple pancakes).

◖ **The Three Crabs** (Three Crabs Rd., 360/683-4264, noon–7 P.M. Sun.–Thurs., noon–8 P.M. Fri.–Sat.) has served Dungeness crab and other local seafood specialties for nearly 30 years at its waterfront location. It also has a retail seafood market. The crabs are well prepared, but the rest of the rather pricey menu isn't noteworthy.

Another place for fast and well-prepared lunches is **Hiway 101 Diner** (392 W. Washington St., 360/683-3388, 6 A.M.–8 P.M. Mon.–Thurs., 6 A.M.–9 P.M. Fri.–Sat., 7 A.M.–8 P.M. Sun.) a "fabulous '50s" family diner with the biggest local burgers. It's also popular for breakfast.

The **Double Eagle** (1965 Woodcock Rd., 360/683-3331, 4–9 P.M. Mon.–Fri., 9 A.M.–9 P.M. Sat.–Sun.) overlooking the Dungeness Golf Course, specializes in prime rib, steak, and seafood. **Tarcisio's** (609 W. Washington St., 360/683-5809, 7 A.M.–8 P.M. Sun.–Thurs., 7 A.M.–9 P.M. Fri.–Sat.) is the place to go for from-scratch pizzas.

Fans of Mexican food will enjoy **El Cazador** (531 W. Washington, 360/683-4788, 11 A.M.–9 P.M. Sun.–Thurs., 11 A.M.–10 P.M. Fri.–Sat.), which serves up the typical combination platter fare, but also has a very pleasant outside deck.

The **Sequim Open Aire Market** (2nd and Cedar, 360/683-9523) takes place 9 A.M.–3 P.M. Saturday late May–mid-October.

INFORMATION

For maps, brochures, and lots of local information drop by the helpful **Sequim-Dungeness Valley Chamber of Commerce Visitor**

Information Center (1192 E. Washington St., 360/683-6690 or 800/737-8462, www.visit sun.com, 9 A.M.–5 P.M. daily).

GETTING THERE

Clallam Transit (360/452-4511 or 800/858-3747, www.clallamtransit.com) connects Sequim with Port Angeles, Forks, and Neah Bay. **Jefferson Transit** (360/385-4777, www .jeffersontransit.com) has transportation east to Port Townsend and Poulsbo.

Olympic Bus Lines (360/417-0700 or 800/457-4492, www.olympicbuslines.com, $49 one-way) has a daily shuttle to Sea-Tac Airport.

Port Angeles

Port Angeles is the largest city on the northern Olympic Peninsula and the gateway to many of its pleasures. Its busy harbor, protected by the strong sandy arm of Ediz Hook, is visited daily by logging ships, fishing boats, and the Victoria ferry MV *Coho*. The view from the Port Angeles city pier is breathtaking: rocky Hurricane Ridge, made more ominous by a wispy cloud cover, seems to rise straight out of the turbulent waters of the Strait of Juan de Fuca. Because of its location as an entry point to both Vancouver Island (via the ferry) and to nearby Olympic National Park, Port Angeles bustles during the summer.

SIGHTS
Municipal Pier and Marine Laboratory

The best part of Port Angeles—outside of its proximity to Olympic National Park—is clearly the city pier. An observation tower at pier's end provides 360-degree views of the city, harbor, and majestic Olympic Mountains, while a sandy beach with picnic area is available for day use. Also located on the pier near the *Coho* ferry dock, the Arthur D. Feiro Marine Laboratory (360/417-6254, www .olypen.com/feirolab, noon–4 P.M. Sat.–Sun. year-round, 10 A.M.–8 P.M. daily in summer, $3 adults, $2 seniors, $1 for kids ages 3–17, and free for under age 2) features hands-on displays and exhibits of the area's sea life. More than 80 species are here, including sea slugs, eels, octopuses, starfish, and sea urchins.

Waterfront Trail

Stop by the downtown visitors center for a walking-tour brochure that leads you through the historical sights of Port Angeles. The city's Waterfront Trail is a delightful six-mile paved path that follows the downtown shoreline and continues out to the Coast Guard base on **Ediz Hook**—a 3.5-mile-long natural sand spit protecting the Northwest's deepest harbor. Along the way you're treated to views across to Vancouver Island and back toward town with the snowcapped Olympics in the background. Watch as freighters are guided in, or take out your own boat for fishing or sightseeing. Picnicking and beachcombing are also popular activities. Another place offering fine vistas across to Vancouver Island is from the top of the Laurel Street stairs, two blocks uphill from the *Coho* ferry dock.

Port Angeles Fine Arts Center

The Port Angeles Fine Arts Center (1203 E. Lauridsen Blvd., 360/417-4590, www.pafac .org, 11 A.M.–5 P.M. Wed.–Sun. Mar.–Nov., 10 A.M.–4 P.M. Wed.–Sun. Feb., free) is a bit out of the way, but well worth the side trip. Located on a hill, the building's enormous picture windows face north to Vancouver Island, offering panoramic vistas that pull your eyes away from the art on the walls. Walk outside to discover a small forest with gardens and a path leading to additional viewpoints. The Fine Arts Center features changing exhibits by prominent Northwest artists.

Olympic National Park Visitor Center

Located a mile out of town, the Olympic

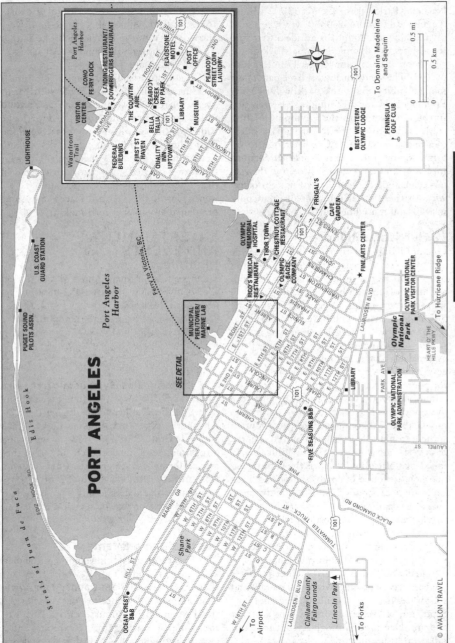

OLYMPIC PENINSULA

PORT ANGELES

Strait of Juan de Fuca

Ediz Hook

EDIZ HOOK RD

Port Angeles Harbor

LIGHTHOUSE

U.S. COAST GUARD STATION

PUGET SOUND PILOTS ASSN.

Ferry to Victoria BC

SEE DETAIL

MUNICIPAL PIER/TOWER/ MARINE LAB

OLYMPIC MEMORIAL HOSPITAL

RICO'S MEXICAN RESTAURANT

THOR TOWN

CHESTNUT COTTAGE RESTAURANT

OLYMPIC BAGEL COMPANY

FRUGAL'S

CAFE GARDEN

FINE ARTS CENTER

BEST WESTERN OLYMPIC LODGE

PENINSULA GOLF CLUB

To Domaine Madeleine and Sequim

OLYMPIC NATIONAL PARK VISITOR CENTER

To Hurricane Ridge

Olympic National Park

HEART OF THE HILLS PKWY

OLYMPIC NATIONAL PARK ADMINISTRATION

LIBRARY

PARK AVE

FIVE SEASONS B&B

CHERRY ST

PINE ST

MARINE DR

HILL ST

Shane Park

OCEAN CREST B&B

W 18TH ST

Clallam County Fairgrounds

Lincoln Park

LAURIDSEN BLVD

TUMWATER TRUCK RT

BLACK DIAMOND RD

To Airport

To Forks

LAUREL ST

© AVALON TRAVEL

DETAIL

Port Angeles Harbor

Waterfront Trail

VISITOR CENTER

COHO FERRY DOCK

LANDING RESTAURANT/ DOWNRIGGERS RESTAURANT

THE COUNTRY AIRE

PEABODY CREEK RV PARK

FLAGSTONE MOTEL

POST OFFICE

PEABODY STREET COIN LAUNDRY

BELLA ITALIA

LIBRARY

MUSEUM

FEDERAL BUILDING

FIRST ST HAVEN

QUALITY INN UPTOWN

RAILROAD AVE

FRONT ST

FIRST ST

SECOND ST

THIRD ST

FOURTH ST

CHASE ST

LINCOLN ST

LAUREL ST

OAK ST

VINE ST

0 0.5 mi

0 0.5 km

National Park Visitor Center (3002 Mount Angeles Rd., 360/452-0330, www.nps.gov/olym, daily year-round) is an ideal first stop for visitors to Olympic National Park or the very popular Hurricane Ridge, 17 miles south of town. The center includes a large panoramic map, exhibits about the park, a Discovery Room for kids, and a 12-minute slide show that introduces visitors to the Olympics. Nature trails lead through the forest to park headquarters, a block away. Get backcountry information from the summer-only **Wilderness Information Center** (directly behind the visitors center, 360/565-3100, www.nps.gov/olym/wic). Also here is the Beaumont log cabin, built in 1887 and moved here in 1962.

(Hurricane Ridge

One of Olympic National Park's most scenic and most visited areas, Hurricane Ridge rises over 5,200 feet seemingly straight up from the Strait of Juan de Fuca, providing an awesome contrast from sea level and breathtaking 360-degree views. The paved road starts at Race Street in Port Angeles, becoming Mount Angeles Road and then Hurricane Ridge Road as it snakes up mountainsides for 17 miles at an easy 7 percent grade; frequent turnouts allow for photo breaks. At the top, the **Hurricane Ridge Visitor Center** provides a must-stop location to peer across a meadow-and-mountain landscape that might have been imported straight from the Swiss Alps. This is one of the park's best areas for spotting wildlife; black-tailed deer often bound across the parking lot, marmots are found in nearby slopes, and black bears are occasionally visible from a distance. The ridge's name isn't without basis in fact: the first lodge at the summit lost its roof in a strong winter blast. The weather can change quickly up here; tune in to AM 530 in Port Angeles for weather and other park information.

Hurricane Ridge Visitor Center provides food service, a gift shop, winter ski rentals, and ski-tow service. It is usually open daily May–Sept., and on weekends only during October and mid-December through April. Park naturalists offer summertime walks and talks plus wintertime snowshoe treks. **Royal Victoria Tours,** 360/417-8006, offers three-hour (very hurried) bus tours up Hurricane Ridge daily at 1 P.M. from the ferry dock in Port Angeles; $21 adult, $12 kids age 5–16.

If the drop-offs and absence of guardrails on Hurricane Ridge Road made your palms sweat, you're in for a real treat on **Obstruction Point Road.** Starting from the Hurricane Ridge parking lot, this narrow gravel road (no RVs) follows the ridge for eight miles without a rail or fence, providing spectacular views for the strong-hearted. The road, constructed in the 1930s by the Civilian Conservation Corps, went as far as it could until a steep talus slope prohibited any further road-making.

ENTERTAINMENT AND EVENTS
Nightlife

Six miles west of town, **Annie M's Junction** (242701 W. Hwy. 101, 360/452-9880) offers occasional live music.

Check out the big screen at **Lincoln Theater** (132 E. 1st St., 360/457-7997) for the latest flicks.

The Arts

The **Port Angeles Symphony Orchestra** (360/457-5579, www.portangelessymphony.com) performs six concerts during the winter months. The **Port Angeles Light Opera Association** (360/457-5630, www.paloa.org) produces a musical each July. Live theater performances are given by **Port Angeles Community Players** (360/452-665, www.pacommunityplayers.com) year-round at the playhouse on Lauridsen Boulevard and Liberty Street.

Festivals and Events

The **Fourth of July** brings music at the pier, kids' events, and a big fireworks show off the beach. The **Clallam County Fair** (www.clallam.net/fair) comes to Port Angeles the third weekend of August, with a carnival, rodeo, horse shows, farming exhibits, and a crowd-pleasing smash-'em-up demolition derby.

Each Memorial Day weekend, the **Juan de Fuca Festival of the Arts** (360/457-5411, http://jffa.org) features a wide range of music, dance, comedy, kids' activities, arts and crafts, food, and more. For something a bit less formal, free **Concerts on the Pier** (360/452-2363) take place every Thursday evening mid-June–mid-September.

Another popular event is the **Forest Storytelling Festival** (360/417-5031, www.dancingleaves.com/storypeople), which attracts tale-tellers from the U.S. and Canada in late September or early October. End the year in style with a visit to the **Holiday Arts and Crafts Show** in mid-November, where local artisans display their works.

SHOPPING
Arts and Crafts

Port Angeles's downtown shopping district is centered on 1st Street, where you'll find shops, restaurants, galleries, and movie theaters. Several galleries carry artwork by local artists with Northwestern themes, including

Port Angeles offers a full day's worth of window shopping.

Waterfront Gallery (Landing Mall, 360/452-8165, 10 A.M.–5 P.M. daily) and **Olympic Stained Glass** (112 N. Laurel, 360/457-1090, 10 A.M.–5:30 P.M. Mon.–Fri., 10 A.M.–5 P.M. Sat., closed Sun.). For something completely different, head to **Pacific Rim Hobby** (124 A W. 1st St., 360/457-0794 or 800/994-6229, 10 A.M.–6 P.M. Mon.–Sat., noon–5 P.M. Sun.) for a voyage to model railroad heaven. The big HO-scale railroad village makes for fun gawking; look for such details as the giant insect attacking villagers.

Bookstores

Port Angeles has three good bookstores: **Odyssey Bookshop** (114 W. Front St., 360/457-1045, 9 A.M.–7 P.M. Mon.–Sat., 10 A.M.–5 P.M. Sun.), **Port Book and News** (104 E. 1st, 360/452-6367, 8 A.M.–8 P.M. Mon.–Sat., 8 A.M.–5 P.M. Sun.) and **Olympic Stationers** (122 E. Front St., 360/457-6111, 8:30 A.M.–5:30 P.M. Mon.–Fri., 10 A.M.–3 P.M. Sat., closed Sun.).

Outdoor Gear

Port Angeles is an ideal spot to gear up before venturing afield within the national park and the rest of the Olympic National Forest. Find a good selection of outdoor gear for sale at **Browns Outdoor** (112 W. Front St., 360/457-4150, www.brownsoutdoor.com, 9:30 A.M.–6 P.M. Mon.–Sat., noon–4 P.M. Sun.), including often forgotten essentials such as stove fuel, dehydrated goodies, and the like.

SPORTS AND RECREATION
Winter Sports

Between late December and late March, Hurricane Ridge is a popular winter destination for cross-country and downhill skiers, snowboarders, and tubers. A small **ski area** (360/452-0330, www.hurricaneridge.com) has two rope tows and a Poma lift. It's open on weekends and during the Christmas–New Year's holiday. Ski rentals, including cross-country and Telemark packages, are also available, along with ski lessons. Backcountry skiers will discover a wealth of open country at Hurricane Ridge—check avalanche conditions before heading out.

Park Service naturalists (360/452-0330) offer guided snowshoe walks on weekends and other times in the winter. Snowshoes are provided ($2 donation suggested). The visitors center—where you can warm up—and cafeteria are open winter weekends. The road to the top is open 9 A.M.–dusk Sat.–Mon. and is closed overnight or during storms. Entrance fees are charged on weekends. Call ahead (360/452-0329) for current road and weather conditions, and always come prepared for the worst. No overnight parking at the summit.

Bike and Kayak Rentals

Rent mountain and road bikes along with kayaks from **Sound Bikes and Kayaks** (120 E. Front St., 360/457-1240, www.soundbikeskayaks.com, 10 A.M.–6 P.M. Mon.–Sat., closed Sun.). Bikes are $10 per hour or $45 for the day and kayaks rent for $15 per hour or $50 per day.

Hiking

A number of trails begin at Hurricane Ridge, including 1.5-mile **Hurricane Hill Trail**, a paved walk to the top of 5,757-foot Hurricane Hill that passes picnic areas, marmot colonies, and spectacular vistas. A longer hike, the **Klahanee Ridge Trail,** follows the ridge's summit for four miles after leaving the paved trail near the marmot colonies. It continues downhill to Heart O' the Hills Campground, or you can return back to Hurricane Ridge.

In addition to these, visitors to Hurricane Ridge will find three other short paved trails through the flower-filled meadows with views of the Olympics. Longer paths lead downhill to the Elwha Valley and along the Little River. From Obstruction Peak, additional trails provide access into the heart of the Olympics.

ACCOMMODATIONS

Because of the popularity of Port Angeles in the summer months, it's a good idea to make reservations ahead of your visit. Stop by the visitors center to check the board for availability at local motels, B&Bs, and RV parks, or to use its phone to make reservations. The chamber of commerce website (www.cityofpa.com) has links to most local lodging places. Many of these offer free transport from the airport or ferry terminal upon request.

Under $100

The best deal in Port Angeles can be found at **Thor Town** (316 N. Race St., 360/452-0931, www.thortown.com, $14 dorm bed, $30 d private room), a free-spirited hostel set in a red barn-style farmhouse. Guests can make use of laundry facilities and the full kitchen, with the choice of buying food here or hopping on one of the hostel's rental bikes and picking up grub at the grocery store. This hostel has no lockout hours during the day.

Flagstone Motel (415 E. 1st St., 360/457-9494 or 888/304-3465, www.flagstonemotel.net, $49 s or $69 d) is a centrally located motel with an indoor pool and sauna; continental breakfast is included.

$100-150

Also with impressive views of the mountains and water is **Best Western Olympic Lodge** (140 Del Guzzi Dr., 360/452-2993 or 800/600-2993, www.portangeleshotelmotel.com, $130–219), with spacious rooms and continental breakfast. The hotel has an outdoor pool, hot tub, exercise room, and free airport and ferry shuttles.

The Five SeaSuns B&B (1006 S. Lincoln, 360/452-8248, www.seasuns.com, $129–175 s or d) is a grand 1926 Dutch Colonial home on spacious grounds. Inside are five guest rooms, shared or private baths, and period furnishings.

Perched on a hilltop, rooms at the **Quality Inn Uptown** (101 E. 2nd St., 360/457-9434 or 800/858-3812, $145–155) all have lots of light streaming through the floor-to-ceiling windows, with peekaboo views of the harbor and mountains. Rooms are pretty worn, but the hot breakfast, friendly staff, and reasonable rates balance this out a bit. Plus, the property is dog-friendly.

$150-200

Inn at Rooster Hill B&B (112 Reservoir Rd., 360/452-4933, www.innatroosterhill.com, $149–179 s or d) is a five-bedroom country house in the foothills of mountains outside of town. Breakfasts are hot and hearty and the inn accepts kids over 10 years old.

$200-250

Located halfway between Port Angeles and Sequim, **(Domaine Madeleine** (146 Wildflower Ln., 360/457-4174, www.domaine madeleine.com, $195–310 s or d) is an elegant waterfront estate overlooking the Strait of Juan de Fuca. The four guest rooms and a separate cottage (perfect for honeymooners) are luxuriously appointed, and a multicourse epicurean breakfast starts your day. The innkeepers speak French in addition to English.

Camping

No camping or overnight lodging is available at Hurricane Ridge, but several options are nearby. **Heart O' the Hills Campground** (five mi. south of Port Angeles on Hurricane Ridge Rd., $12) has year-round camping, with campfire programs offered July through Labor Day. Located at an elevation of 5,400 feet, **Deer Park Campground** ($10, mid-June–late September) sits at the end of a narrow 18-mile gravel road on the eastern edge of the park. No RVs are permitted, and it is not accessible from the Hurricane Ridge area.

RV owners hoping to catch a ferry to Victoria may find **Peabody Creek RV Park** (127 S. Lincoln, 360/457-7092 or 800/392-2361, $27 with full hookups) convenient. This very basic park isn't much more than a parking lot with utilities, but it is right next to the docks.

For a few more amenities, try **Conestoga Quarters RV Park** (40 Sieberts Creek Rd., 360/452-4637 or 800/808-4637, $25 with full hookups), which—in spite of cramped spaces—offers an off-leash area for dogs, showers, laundry facilities, free Wi-Fi, and a clubhouse. Also in town, **Crescent Beach RV** (2860 Crescent Beach Rd., 360/928-3344 or 866/690-3344, $40 with full hookups) is another pet-friendly private campground that offers access to a long, sandy beach, along with coin-op showers and laundry, plus a convenience store.

FOOD

Because of its location as a jumping-off point for Olympic National Park and Vancouver Island, Port Angeles is packed with high-quality eateries of all persuasions.

Cafés and Diners

The acclaimed **First Street Haven** (1st and Laurel, 360/457-0352, 7 A.M.–4 P.M. daily, 8 A.M.–2 P.M. Sun.) serves hearty breakfasts, along with reasonable sandwiches, quiche, pastas, and salads for lunch. The location is tiny, but the food is hard to beat and on Sundays you can gorge on breakfast all day long. The same owners run the equally popular **Chestnut Cottage Restaurant** (929 E Front St., 360/452-8344, http://chestnutcottage restaurant.com, 7 A.M.–3 P.M. daily) featuring creative egg dishes for breakfast, plus salads, pastas, fajitas, and burgers for lunch. The setting is cozy and friendly.

Another fine breakfast and lunch spot is **(Café Garden** (1506 E. 1st St., 360/457-4611, www.cafegardenpa.com, 6:30 A.M.–9 P.M. daily) where the menu covers the spectrum from Belgian waffles for breakfast to Asian stir fries and deli sandwiches for lunch. Dinner is well-presented and tasty, offering casual fare such as salads, pastas, and classics like meatloaf and pot pie.

Good breakfasts, along with the best local fish and chips, can be found at **Smuggler's Landing Restaurant** (115 E. Railroad Ave., 360/457-6768, www.smugglerslanding.com, 7 A.M.–9 P.M. daily).

Get the best burgers and fries anywhere around at **Frugals** (1520 E. Front St., 360/452-4320, 10:30 A.M.–10 P.M. Sun.–Thurs., 10:30 A.M.–11 P.M. Fri.–Sat.), a classic burger stand that can sate the meanest post-hike hunger. There's no seating—just drive up or walk up to order.

Steak and Seafood

Nestled into the basement of one of downtown

OLYMPIC PENINSULA

Port Angeles' historic buildings **Michael's** (117 B East 1st St., 360/417-6929, www.michaels dining.com, 4–10 P.M. daily) serves upscale specialties like prime rib and salmon as well as pizzas, pasta, and oysters. **The Bushwacker Restaurant** (1527 E. 1st, 360/457-4113, 4:30–9 P.M. daily) specializes in fresh seafood and prime rib and also has a good salad bar. Open for dinner only.

International

For tasty, reasonably priced, and authentic south-of-the-border meals, visit **Rico's Mexican Restaurant** (636 E. Front St., 360/452-3928, 11 A.M.–9:30 P.M. daily), with an extensive menu and daily specials.

Four miles east of Port Angeles, **C'est Si Bon** (23 Cedar Park Dr., 360/452-8888, 5–10 P.M. Tues.–Sun., closed Mon., entrées $20–25) prepares delicious local seafood with a French accent. The Olympics and rose garden views add to the luxurious ambiance.

Located downstairs from an organic grocery, **Bella Italia** (117B E. 1st St., 360/457-5442, 4–10 P.M. Mon.–Sat., 4–8:45 P.M. Sun.) blends traditional Italian cooking with a natural foods sensibility. The result is easily Port Angeles's finest Italian restaurant, with great desserts, too.

Bakeries

Pick up the freshest bagel on the peninsula with loads of cream cheese or filled up sandwich style at **Olympic Bagel Company** (802 E. 1st St., 360/452-9100, www.olympicbagel.com, 6 A.M.–3 P.M. Mon.–Sat., 7 A.M.–3 P.M. Sun., winter hours may vary), which serves lots of breakfast and lunch items, plus Tully's coffee.

Markets

Get the freshest local fare at **Port Angeles Farmers Market** (360/683-4642, 9 A.M.–3:30 P.M. Sat.) held year-round near the corner of 8th and Chase Streets. **Sunny Farms Country Store** (360/683-8003) has a large produce stand located halfway between Port Angeles and Sequim. Also sold here: everything from hanging plants to homemade pizzas. **The Country Aire** (117 E. 1st St., 360/452-

7175, 9 A.M.–7 P.M. Mon.–Sat., 11 A.M.–4 P.M. Sun.) has a big selection of natural and organic foods. For the freshest local seafood—along with canned and smoked specialties—stop by **Hegg & Hegg** (801 Marine Dr., 360/457-3344, 9 A.M.–6 P.M. Mon.–Sat., 10 A.M.–5 P.M. Sun.).

INFORMATION AND SERVICES

For maps, brochures, and more local information, contact the **Port Angeles Chamber of Commerce Visitor Center** (121 E. Railroad Ave., 360/452-2363, www.portangeles.org, 8 A.M.–9 P.M. daily Memorial Day–mid-Sept., 10 A.M.–4 P.M. daily the rest of the year).

Just a few steps away is the **Port Angeles-Victoria Tourist Bureau** (208 N. Laurel St., 360/452-1223, 7 A.M.–5 P.M. daily). Here the focus is on travel, motel, and B&B reservations for southwest British Columbia—particularly nearby Vancouver Island—but they can also make motel reservations for Port Angeles. Tons of British Columbia maps and brochures are free for the taking. Both the chamber of commerce and the tourist bureau are exceptionally helpful.

The **Olympic National Park Visitor Center** (3002 Mount Angeles Rd., 360/452-0330) can give you sightseeing, hiking, camping, and other park information.

Campers and backpackers will appreciate **Peabody Street Coin Laundry** (212 S. Peabody, 24 hours daily) after getting back to nature in Olympic National Park. **The Spa** (511 E. 1st St., 360/452-3257 or 800/869-7177) has been around since 1928, with Finnish-style steam rooms, massage, herbal body wraps, and a juice bar and tearoom. (The hostel is also here.)

GETTING THERE AND AROUND
By Ferry

Port Angeles is a major transit point for travelers heading to or from Victoria, B.C., just 18 miles away across the Strait of Juan de Fuca. The **MV Coho** (360/457-4491, www.cohoferry .com, $60.50 one-way for car and driver, $16.50 for passengers, $8.25 for kids 5–11, free under age 5, and $23 for bicycle and rider) sails on a 90-minute run between Port Angeles and Victoria four times daily in summer (mid-May through October), and twice daily the rest of the year. For specific departure times, contact the Black Ball ferry terminal at the foot of Laurel Street in Port Angeles. Vehicle space is at a premium on summer weekends and no reservations are accepted; get there very early to be assured of passage.

By Air
Alaska Airlines (800/252-7522, www.alaska air.com) provides daily commuter service from Victoria, B.C., and Sea-Tac Airport from Fairchild International Airport on the city's west side. **Kenmore Air** (www.kenmoreair.com) also flies from Seattle's Boeing Field three times a day.

Rite Bros. Aviation (360/452-6226, www .ritebros.com) offers flightseeing and charter flights over the Olympics from Port Angeles.

By Bus
Public bus service now extends throughout the Olympic Peninsula, making it possible to reach all the towns for a minimal fare on any of the four different public transit systems. **Clallam Transit** (360/452-4511 or 800/858-3747, www.clallamtransit.com) provides Monday–Saturday service around the Olympic Peninsula to Forks, Neah Bay, La Push, and Olympic National Park's Sol Duc Hot Springs and Lake Crescent. The buses have bike racks. They also connect with **Jefferson Transit** (360/385-4777 or 800/773-7788, www .jeffersontransit.com) in Sequim for Port Townsend and other Jefferson County points, and with **Grays Harbor Transit** in Queets for points to the south.

Olympic Bus Lines (360/417-0700 or 800/457-4492, www.olympicbuslines.com) offers van service connecting Port Angeles with Seattle and Sea-Tac Airport.

Port Angeles to Sol Duc

ELWHA RIVER VALLEY
Take Olympic Hot Springs Road south from Highway 101 just west of Port Angeles into the Elwha River watershed, best known for a bulwark project currently underway to demolish two dams and restore the river to its former pristine state. This river valley, a part of Olympic National Park, offers some of the closest remote hiking, camping, and rafting to Port Angeles.

Sports and Recreation
RIVER RAFTING
With Class II white-water conditions, the Elwha River is a popular destination for river-runners of all experience levels. Check with the Park Service for current flow conditions and precautions if you decide to run it yourself. **Olympic Raft and Guide Service** (360/452-1443, www.raftandkayak.com) leads scenic two-hour trips down the Elwha River ($54 adults, $44 kids), plus sea kayaking in Lake Crescent, Lake Aldwell, and Freshwater Bay.

HIKING
Nearly everyone in Washington knows of Sol Duc Hot Springs, but less well known are **Olympic Hot Springs,** located at the end of Boulder Creek Road, off Elwha River Road. The springs were once the site of a large resort, but today they are essentially undeveloped. A 2.5-mile trail leads to shallow rock-lined pools, where the water varies from lukewarm to 138°F. The Park Service discourages bathing and prohibits nudity (but that doesn't stop many folks from bathing au naturel).

Take the Elwha River Trail for two miles to **Humes Ranch,** built in 1889 by Grant Humes, who made his living leading wilderness expeditions and by hunting and trapping game. Today his cabin is on the National Register of Historic Places.

When a day hike is not enough, a number of hiking trails head into the backcountry from the Elwha area, and a variety of short and long hikes are available, including an across-the-park route that follows the Elwha Trail to Low Divide and then drops down to Quinault Lake on the North Quinault Trail, a distance of 44 miles.

For a north–south 44-mile trek, start at Lake Mills near Elwha on the **Elwha River Trail.** The trail runs 27.5 miles until it links up at Low Divide with the **North Fork Trail,** which follows the North Fork Quinault River until you reach the North Fork Ranger Station near Lake Quinault. You'll be hiking the route of James Halbold Christie, leader of the *Seattle Press* expedition across the then-unexplored Olympic Peninsula. It took Christie and his party six months and one black bear to complete the route in 1890; it should take you only four days and a packful of gorp.

Accommodations

Situated in a country home overlooking the Elwha River valley, **Elwha Ranch B&B** (360/457-6540, www.elwharanch.com, $140–165 d) has two guest rooms with private baths, a deck, and full breakfasts. The property features a private log cabin ($165) for those seeking a bit more seclusion.

Campers can pitch a tent at the **Elwha and Altaire Campgrounds** ($12) along the road north of Lake Mills.

◖ LAKE CRESCENT

Olympic National Park's Lake Crescent is an azure jewel set amid the emerald forests, and its origin myth is as interesting as the lake is beautiful: according to Native American legend, Mount Storm King once became so fed up with the fighting between the Clallams and Quileutes that he broke a rock off his head and threw it down at the warring tribes. The scientific view of Lake Crescent's origin isn't much different; it's attributed to ancient landslides that divided a glacial lake into two large sections (Lake Crescent and Lake Sutherland), sending water from Lake Crescent out the Lyre River.

Sights

Today, freshwater Lake Crescent, 624 feet deep and 8.5 miles long, is famous for its Beardslee trout, a subspecies that is large (some are in the 12- to 14-pound range) and a hard fighter when hooked. Swimming, boating, camping, picnicking, and, of course, fishing are popular lake activities. The lake has an impressive mountain-rimmed setting. The Park Service's **Storm King Ranger Station** (360/928-3380) is staffed during the summer months.

The nonprofit **Olympic Park Institute** (360/928-3720 or 800/775-3720, www.yni .org/opi) offers excellent hands-on field seminars covering such diverse topics as Makah basketry, ecology of the forest canopy, and wolf biology. Seminars last 2–5 days and some may be taken for college credit. They also have an Elderhostel. Headquarters for the institute is the historic Rosemary Inn, near Lake Crescent Lodge. Students stay in nearby cabins, and meals are served family style at the inn.

HIKING

From the ranger station, follow the **Marymere Falls Trail** 0.75 mile for a spectacular view of this 90-foot falls. Not a lot of water, but it's quite impressive nevertheless. Return via the Crescent Lake Lodge Trail for a two-mile loop hike.

The **Mount Storm King Trail** splits off from the Marymere Trail and climbs more than 3,000 feet in a bit over a mile, with fine views across the lake. The path ends before the summit, and the Park Service recommends against continuing to the top due to hazardous conditions.

A four-mile hike starting at Lyre River Road or North Shore Road at opposite ends of Lake Crescent, the **Spruce Railroad Trail** follows the tracks of the 1918 Spruce Railroad, built to supply spruce for World War I aircraft. The war was over before the railroad was completed, however, and the spruce was no longer needed. Two tunnels (closed) and depressions from the railroad ties remain. Besides a taste of local history, the almost-level hike provides a view of Lake Crescent.

CAMPING

Fairholm Campground ($12; open year-round), on the west end of Lake Crescent, has summertime naturalist programs on some evenings. The Forest Service's **Klahowya Campground** (nine mi. west of Lake Crescent on Hwy. 101, $12) opens sites May–mid-October.

Park RVs along Lake Sutherland at **Shadow Mountain RV Park** (360/928-3043).

Fairholm General Store (360/928-3020) on the west end of Lake Crescent, is open April–September, and has tent sites and RV hookups, plus motorboats, rowboats, and canoes for rent. It also serves meals in the café; eat alfresco on a deck overlooking the lake.

Accommodations

The lake has two concession-operated lodges around its perimeter. Built in 1916, **Lake Crescent Lodge** (360/928-3211, www.olympic nationalparks.com/accommodations, $99–158 d lodge, $180–231 cottages, Apr.–Oct. only) is a cozy place with a comfortable feeling from decades of guests, including President Franklin D. Roosevelt, who stayed here in 1937. Sit on the porch for incredible views of the mountains and Lake Crescent, or lounge in front of the big fireplace on a cool evening. The lodge has all sorts of accommodations, including lodge rooms (bath down the hall), cottages (some with fireplaces), and modern motel units. The lodge has a restaurant and gift shop, and rents rowboats.

Rent out motel rooms, rustic cabins, or waterfront A-frame chalets at **Log Cabin Resort** (three mi. from Hwy. 101 on E. Beach Rd., 360/928-3325, www.logcabinresort.net, $94–161 d, Apr.–Oct. only) at the northeast end of the lake. There are also camping cabins ($66) available for those with simple tastes. Many of the buildings have stood here since the 1920s. In addition to accommodations, the resort also has meals, a gift shop, grocery store, RV and tent sites, and rowboat, paddleboat, canoe, and kayak rentals.

East of Lake Crescent is the smaller Lake Sutherland, a popular place to swim. **Lake Sutherland Lodge B&B** (360/928-2111 or 888/231-1444, $65–90 s or d) is a modern log home with a covered deck facing the lake. The four guest rooms have private or shared baths, and a full breakfast is served.

SOL DUC

The wild and free Sol Duc River Valley offers hikers a chance to go deep into the mystical Olympic forests, experience soothing hot springs, and take a gander at one of the prettiest waterfalls on the peninsula.

Recreation

⟨ SOL DUC HOT SPRINGS

About 30 miles west of Port Angeles and 12 miles south of Highway 101, in Olympic National Park, is Sol Duc (SOLE duck) Hot Springs (9 A.M.–9 P.M. daily mid-May through Aug., till 8 P.M. in Sept., 9 A.M.–8 P.M. Sat.–Sun. Apr.–mid-May, and Oct., $10 adults, $6.50 two hours or less before closing, $7.50 seniors). Bask in the 99–105°F mineral water piped into three large outdoor pools. A fourth freshwater pool is also on the site. Massage is also available.

FISHING

Sol Duc is legendary for its steelhead fishing in winter, plus year-round chinook and king salmon fisheries. Avoid the hassle of schlepping your own gear and schedule a trip with **Piscatorial Pursuits** (800/347-4232, www .piscatorialpursuits.com, $300 per person per day), which provides guidance based on years of reading the river, a boat, and all the tackle necessary to land one for the record books. The guide even cleans the fish for you.

HIKING

Several trails head up the Sol Duc Valley. A favorite is the one-mile **Sol Duc River Trail,** which passes through enormous western hemlocks and Douglas firs to Sol Duc Falls, one of the state's best-known waterfalls. A footbridge crosses the deep gorge cut by the river. From here, you can climb another three miles (one-way) to **Deer Lake,** bordered by trees. For variety, return to the campground from Sol Duc Falls on the **Lovers Lane Trail,** a three-mile path along the south side of the river.

A fine loop trip for backpackers (wilderness permit required) is to head up the Sol Duc River Trail to Seven Lakes Basin, then uphill to the summit of Bogachiel Peak and back out for a round-trip of 22 miles.

Accommodations and Food

The springs were long known to the native peoples who first lived here, and white settlers were attracted to the area as a place of healing. By 1912, the area had an elegant hotel, theater, bowling alley, a 100-bed sanitorium, plus immaculately landscaped grounds with a golf course, tennis courts, and croquet grounds. A fire, begun by a defective flue, brought this to a crashing halt four years later. As the hotel burned to the ground, a short circuit caused the player organ to begin playing Beethoven's "Funeral March."

Today's **Sol Duc Hot Springs Resort** (360/327-3583, www.northolympic.com/solduc, $141–172 d, mid-May–Sept. only) isn't quite so lavish, but it does have a restaurant, grocery store, and gift shop, plus cabins (some with kitchenettes). A two-night minimum applies on holidays.

Outdoor lovers may prefer to pitch a tent at the Park Service's **Sol Duc Campground** ($12), open all year, but sometimes closed in the winter months due to flooding. Between July and Labor Day, park naturalists offer evening programs in the amphitheater some evenings.

Partway between Sol Duc and Forks, **Bear Creek Motel** (15 mi. northeast of Forks in the town of Beaver, 360/327-3660, www.hungry bearcafemotel.com, $55–95 d, $20 RV, $7 tent) makes a good stop for Olympic loop adventurers who just can't bear to drive past another mile marker. The **Hungry Bear Café** (5 A.M.–8 P.M. daily) here also makes a handy mealtime pit stop.

STRAIT OF JUAN DE FUCA

Highway 112 offers one of the most dramatic shoreline drives in Washington; the narrow road winds along cliff faces and past extraordinary views. The area is windswept and remote—the only radio stations to be found are from Canada—and the ocean is up close and personal much of the drive. At the end of the road,

72 miles from Port Angeles, Neah Bay sits on the 44-square-mile **Makah Indian Reservation** in virtual isolation, at the northwesternmost point of the contiguous United States. Anyone who has spent time in a remote Alaskan village will feel right at home in Neah Bay.

Sights
SALT CREEK COUNTY PARK

The scenic and diverse grounds at Salt Creek County Park (three mi. east of Joyce off Hwy. 112, 360/928-3441) is an open secret among Washingtonians. This is, hands down, the nicest municipal park on the peninsula. Situated three miles east of the village of Joyce, this was the site of Fort Hayden during World War II, and the concrete gun emplacements are still explorable, though the 45-foot-long guns are long gone. The fort sits on a bluffside, with grassy lawns and picnic areas adjoining campsites. A path down to the rocky beach offers lots of tidepools during low tide. Farther up the bluff are several miles worth of trails.

OTHER PARKS

The beaches beyond Slip Point Lighthouse, on the east end of Clallam Bay, are great for beachcombing and exploring the tidepools, and the area east of here is famous for its marine fossils. County parks in the Clallam Bay area are **Clallam Bay Spit,** a 33-acre waterfront park for day use only, and **Pillar Point County Park** (360/963-2301), just east of Clallam Bay. Pillar Point is a four-acre park with a boat launch.

MAKAH CULTURAL AND RESEARCH CENTER

In 1970, tidal erosion unearthed old Ozette homes that had been destroyed by a mud slide some 500 years earlier. The slide entombed and preserved the material, and 11 years of excavations by archaeologists from Washington State University unearthed one of the richest finds in North America. Find thousands of these artifacts at the Makah Cultural and Research Center (Hwy. 112 & Bay View Ave., 360/645-2711, www.makah.com, 10 A.M.–5 P.M. daily,

driftwood along the Strait of Juan de Fuca

$5 adults, $4 seniors and students) at Neah Bay. This is the finest collection of Northwest Coast Native American artifacts from precontact times, with treasures such as beautifully carved seal clubs and intricately woven baskets. A re-created 15th-century longhouse is the museum's centerpiece, which stands in contrast to a modern longhouse outside that's used for basketry and carving demonstrations.

Festivals and Events

Makah Days is the town's big annual festival, celebrating the day the reservation first raised the American flag in 1913. Held on the weekend closest to August 26, the three-day festival is highlighted by dances, a parade, fireworks show, salmon bake, canoe races, and bone games (Native American gambling). Also popular is the **Chito Beach Bluegrass Jamboree** in mid-June.

Sports and Recreation
CAPE FLATTERY
The **Cape Loop Road** provides an interesting drive or mountain-bike ride to the tip of Cape Flattery. The narrow dirt road is not for RVs. Pick up a route map at the museum, or head west from town to the Makah Tribal Center, and then turn right to the cape (left will take you to Hobuck Beach and a fish hatchery). About eight miles from town, you'll come to one of the few unlogged areas remaining on the cape, and the new **Cape Flattery Trail.** This boardwalk path leads downhill 0.75 mile to the rocky shoreline, with views of Tatoosh Island and **Cape Flattery Lighthouse,** built in 1858. Most folks return to Neah Bay the same way they came out, but mountain bikers and four-wheelers will enjoy the very rough road that leads back eastward around the cape to Neah Bay, passing a small waterfall with sculpted pools large enough to sit in on a warm summer day, and several miles later a dump that has to be one of the worst in the state of Washington (but a good place to look for ravens and eagles). The total length of this loop is approximately 16 miles.

POINT OF ARCHES AND SHI SHI BEACH
Near the north boundary of Olympic National

Park, Point of Arches is a testimony to the relentless power of the Pacific where, with a force of two tons per square inch, the ocean carved giant arches out of ancient rock. The Arches, legendary children of Destruction Island and Tatoosh Island, were pushed from Mother Tatoosh's canoe when she deserted her husband because, she said, "You'd probably grow up just like your father!" The bluffs above neighboring Shi Shi (shy-shy) Beach provide a vantage point for watching the spring and fall gray whale migrations; the best viewing season is March–May. This stretch of coastline features some of the finest beaches and tidepools anywhere on the Washington coast; you might even find remains of a shipwreck still visible.

LAKE OZETTE AREA

Located in the northwest corner of the coastal strip of Olympic National Park, eight-mile-long Lake Ozette is the third-largest natural lake in Washington. A 21-mile paved road heads southwest from Sekiu, ending at the **Ozette Ranger Station** (360/963-2725, open daily in summer, no set hours in winter) on the north end of the lake. This area has one of the most popular overnight hikes along the Olympic coast, and summer weekends attract outdoor enthusiasts. Parking costs $2 per day.

Two trails head to the coast from the ranger station. One leads southwest to **Sand Point**, three miles away; the other goes three miles northwest to **Cape Alva**—the westernmost point in the Lower 48. By hiking the beach connecting the two, you can create a triangular loop trip of 9.3 miles. You can also continue south on the beach for 2.3 miles to the **Norwegian Memorial,** a tribute to the victims of a 1903 shipwreck. There is much to explore in the Cape Alva area: fascinating tidepools, cannonball-shaped rocks, an anchor from one of the ships that ran aground here, and even an occasional Japanese glass ball. This is probably the best place to see wildlife in Olympic National Park, with bald eagles in the air, deer along the beach, sea lions and seals in the water, and migrating gray whales in fall and spring. This area contains the

largest population of sea otters in the Lower 48; look for them in the kelp beds off Sand Point. The **Wedding Rocks** area between Cape Alva and Sand Point is well known for its petroglyphs, carved by the original inhabitants of this land at an unknown time. Pick up a handout describing the petroglyphs from the ranger station.

Accommodations and Food
ALONG HIGHWAY 112

Right on the river and only a few steps from the Strait of Juan de Fuca, **Lyre River Recreation Area** offers free primitive campsites year-round. The best camping choice on the entire Strait, though, is at **Salt Creek County Park** (three mi. east of Joyce off Hwy. 112, 360/928-3441, $25 full hookups, $20 tent), a gorgeous park that accommodates tent campers and RVers alike and is surrounded by trails, an old fort, and loads of tidepools to explore.

Farther along the route in Sekiu, **Curley's Resort** (360/963-2281 or 800/542-9680, www.curleysresort.com, $50–105 s or d) has nice motel units and cabins with kitchenettes, as well as RV hookups, boat and kayak rentals, a dive shop, and even whale-watching trips through its Puffin Charters service.

Also of note is **Winter Summer Inn B&B** (360/963-2264, www.northolympic.com/ winters, $85–140 d), with decks overlooking the Clallam River and full breakfasts. The B&B has two rooms with private baths, as well as a separate studio apartment that doesn't include the breakfast.

NEAH BAY

Neah Bay lodging can leave much to be desired. The "resorts" are mostly shoestring operations dependent upon fishermen and hunters who don't mind ancient furnishings and marginally clean rooms. The nicest in-town motel is **The Cape Motel** (360/645-2250, $55–85 d) with rooms including kitchenettes. RV ($24) and tent spaces ($15) are available during summer only.

Washburn's General Store (360/645-2211, 9 A.M.–7 P.M. Mon.–Sat., 9 A.M.–6 P.M. Sun.)

sells groceries and has a deli with fresh sandwiches and espresso (this is Washington, after all), plus a small gift shop selling jewelry, baskets, carvings, and knitted items. **Raven's Corner Gifts & Indian Arts** sells local crafts and T-shirts with Makah designs.

Get seafood and burgers at **Warm House Restaurant** (1471 Bay View Ave., 360/645-2924, breakfast and dinner only).

LAKE OZETTE
The Lost Resort (360/963-2899 or 800/950-2899, www.lostresort.net, $65 cabin, $15 campsite) has a general store, deli, camping supplies, showers, and private campsites next to the lake. From February until May, the resort often runs a fun special—the price of a cabin is the temperature when you show up.

Because of overcrowding and resource damage, the Park Service has instituted a quota system for overnight hiking in the Ozette area between May 1 and September 30. (There are no restrictions on day use, however.) Make reservations at the Wilderness Information Center in Port Angeles (360/565-3100, www.nps.gov/olym/wic). If you don't have a permit, you might try arriving early to grab one of the 18 campsites accessible by car, but if those are gone, you'll have to drive all the way back to a private campground in Sekiu. The busiest times are weekends in July and August.

The small **Ozette Campground** has camping ($12) year-round, but get here early to be sure of a space (no reservations). The lake is a popular place for boats, canoes, and kayaks, but winds can create treacherous wave action at times. The free **Erickson's Bay** boat-in campground is halfway down the lake on the west side. There is good fishing for largemouth bass, cutthroat trout, kokanee, and other fish here.

Getting There
Clallam Transit (360/452-4511 or 800/858-3747, www.clallamtransit.com) provides daily bus service to Neah Bay and throughout the northern Olympic Peninsula.

Olympic Coast and Hoh Rain Forest

When the highway emerges on the coastline south of Forks, you will quickly become aware that the northern half of Washington's coastline is a picture of how the Pacific coast looks in brochures and calendar photos: pristine beaches, pounding waves, trees sculpted by relentless sea breezes.

Washington's rocky and essentially undeveloped Olympic coast is truly a national gem, and in 1994 it was declared the **Olympic Coast National Marine Sanctuary,** a designation that helps protect the shore and ocean from development. The coast contains rich fishing grounds; more species of whales, dolphins, and porpoises than anywhere on earth; some of the largest seabird colonies in the Lower 48; and an unparalleled beauty that attracts painters, photographers, and anyone with a sense of wonder. The shore is dotted with cliff-rimmed beaches and forested hills.

Farther inland, you'll encounter a different kind of spectacle—one of mossy trees, gurgling streams, and misty forests. These are the most famous woods in America, the Hoh Rain Forest. Bring your raincoat and a sense of adventure, and prepare to meander.

FORKS
The westernmost incorporated city in the Lower 48, Forks is the economic center and logging capital of the western Olympic Peninsula—a big handle for this town of 3,400 with one main drag. For travelers, the town's big selling point is its proximity to the west side of Olympic National Park and Pacific coast beaches. Also nearby is a modern University of Washington natural resources research facility.

Forks Timber Museum
The Forks Timber Museum (360/374-9663, 10 A.M.–4 P.M. daily mid-Apr.–Oct., free) has

LEISURELY LOGGING

If a 19th-century logger could have had a vision of what sort of tools future colleagues would get to use, he'd drop his ax and find the closest whiskey bar. Most people today have at least a basic idea of how modern logging is done. It involves diesel cranes, high-tensile steel cables, flatbed trucks, and long chainsaws. If the need is strong enough, the crew can call in a helicopter to help haul the harvest. And while this logging goes on even now, much of the cut stumps you're able to hike past were probably cut over a century ago.

In those days of almost impenetrable old-growth stands, when crews might cut a "one-log load" – an ancient tree that took up an entire railroad car by itself – loggers usually lived onsite for months if necessary. Using only an ax, men known as "fellers" would hack notches in the trees between four and 10 feet off of the ground. The notches would be big enough to hold a long wooden plank called the "springboard," which would let the fellers cut the tree where the trunk was more narrow. At that point, the loggers would hop up on the springboard and start whacking away at the tree until they took it down with the cry, "Timber!" If a tree was small enough, a crew would instead cut it down with a two-man handsaw.

The "bucker" then cut the tree into more manageable logs, which were slid down the often-hilly terrain along greased wooden skids and then hauled by horse to the nearest river or railway. Later in the game, loggers took advantage of new technology like the "steam donkey," a steam-powered winch, as well as gas-powered vehicles.

So how can you tell when a tree was harvested? Look at the stump on harder-wood trees. If you see matching notches toward the top and on either side of the stump, you know that tree was springboarded and probably cut in the decades before World War I.

historical exhibits that include a steam donkey, a logging camp bunkhouse, old logging equipment, and various pioneer implements. The real surprise is a large 150-year-old canoe that was discovered by loggers in 1990. Out front is a memorial to loggers killed in the woods and a replica of a fire lookout tower.

Bogachiel State Park

Six miles south of Forks on Highway 101, Bogachiel State Park (185983 Highway 101, www.parks.wa.gov, 8 A.M.–dusk year-round) encompasses 123 acres on the usually clear Bogachiel River (although Bogachiel comes from the Quileute for "muddy waters," funnily enough). Enjoy the short nature trail through a rain forest, or swim, paddle, or fish in the river—famous for its summer and winter steelhead, salmon, and trout.

Festivals and Events

Forks' **Fourth of July** is actually a three-day festival of fun that includes an art show, pancake breakfast, parades, a loggers show, frog jump, demolition derby, dancing, and fireworks.

Sports and Recreation

Right on the opposite side of the highway from the park entrance is Undi Road, which leads east five miles (the last two are gravel) to the **Bogachiel River Trailhead.** The trail follows the lush, infrequently visited rain forest valley of the Bogachiel River east for two miles through national forest land until reaching the edge of Olympic National Park, where the trail continues all the way up to Seven Lakes Basin (27 miles) or Sol Duc Hot Springs (27 miles). The lower section of trail in the rain forest is a lovely place for a day hike. Mountain bikers are allowed on the trail as far as the edge of the national park, but it's a pretty soggy ride.

Accommodations

Forks has the most lodging options on the west side of the 101 loop, though some of the motels can leave a little to be desired. The best bet for multiday stays is to opt for a B&B.

Families will enjoy the space that **Olympic Suites** (800 Olympic Dr., 1.5 miles north of Forks, 360/374-5400 or 800/262-3433, www.olympicgetaways.com/olympicsuites, $79–119 d) affords them. Here you'll find updated one- and two-bedroom suites with kitchens and free wireless Internet on a nicely wooded property. Pet owners will also find rooms here that accept Rover.

Another very clean motel choice is the **Pacific Inn Motel** (352 S. Forks Ave., 360/374-9400, www.pacificinnmotel.com, $58–89 and up), a basic but newish property that remains well-tended and cares for you with a friendly staff. There aren't a ton of amenities, but you will find coin-op laundry facilities and free coffee and tea in the lobby. Plus, *Twilight* fanatics will appreciate the special Twilight rooms decked out in dark, moody colors and posters from the teen vampire movie franchise.

The best choices in town are the bed-and-breakfasts. There are a number of off-the-beaten-path properties ideal for those looking to feel close to the natural surroundings around the town. For example, the **Fisherman's Widow B&B** (31 Huckleberry Ln., 360/374-5693, http://fishermans-widow.com, $125–135 d) is a comfy lodgelike home sitting right on the banks of the Sol Duc river, a favorite among anglers and kayakers who can head right out the back door for their daily adventures. The rooms are spacious and can accommodate up to five people, so adventuring groups can save some cash by sharing.

Also a favorite among anglers, especially fly-fishing fans, is **Brightwater House B&B** (360/374-5453 www.brightwaterhouse.com, $120–130 d), also on the Sol Duc and which boasts a liberal cancellation policy that allows anglers to change their plans when the river conditions change. The common River Room offers great views through its floor-to-ceiling windows. Pet-friendly, too.

Historic architecture buffs will best enjoy ◖ **Miller Tree Inn** (654 E. Division, 360/374-6806, www.millertreeinn.com, $130–230 d), a family- and pet-friendly inn that rests inside a well-cared-for 1914 homestead. The downstairs common rooms are especially homey, with rich wood paneling and a living room fireplace. Outside there's a back deck with a large hot tub overlooking the attractive grounds. You can also expect a full farmhouse breakfast.

CAMPING

Camp at **Bogachiel State Park,** four miles south on Highway 101 (360/374-6356, www.parks.wa.gov, $12 primitive tent site, $22 for tents, $31 for RV hookups), or at the Park Service's **Mora Campground** (open year-round, $10), 14 miles west of Forks, which offers summertime naturalist programs and nature walks.

FORKS FOR *TWILIGHT* FANS

"City of Forks," a notice in Forks reads, "Population: 3175 Vampires: 8.5." It might seem out of place in this out-of-the-way logging community on the remote Olympic Peninsula. But for those in the know, this is just one more sign that this obscure little town has been bitten by *Twilight* fever.

Seemingly overnight, Forks has been overrun with fans of the teenage vampire book series penned by Stephanie Meyer and adapted into multiple major motion pictures. Even though Meyer never visited the town before using it as the setting for her books, the good-natured folks of Fork have had fun with the fame. All around town you'll find *Twilight* T-shirts for sale, signs welcoming fans, menu specials, and even custom-decorated motel rooms. Sightseers will find a red pickup similar to the one driven by the heroine, Bella, parked out front of the visitors center, and the folks there have teamed up with the local chamber of commerce to offer a special *Twilight* tour of Forks. Included on the tour is a stop in front of Forks High School, where camera crews shot scenes for the movie. For more information, visit www.forkswa.com/HomeofTwilighttheBook.

Dispersed camping (pullouts off the road) is allowed on Forest Service lands throughout Olympic National Forest.

Park RVs at **Forks 101 RV Park** (901 S. Forks Ave., 360/374-5073 or 800/962-9964). Camp for free at Rayonier's **Tumbling Rapids Park** (11 mi. northeast of Forks along Hwy. 101, 360/374-6565).

Food

Meet the loggers over coffee and donuts at **The Coffee Shop** (314 Forks Ave. S, 360/374-6769, 5 A.M.–8 P.M. daily), with friendly waitresses and dependably good food three meals a day.

The **In Place** (320 S. Forks Ave., 360/374-4004, 6 A.M.–9 P.M. daily) is a good lunch spot, with deli sandwiches and great mushroom bacon burgers. They also serve pasta, steak, and seafood dinners.

A mile north of Forks at the La Push road junction on Highway 101, the **Smoke House Restaurant** (360/374-6258, 11 A.M.–9 P.M. Mon.–Fri., noon–9 P.M. Sat.–Sun.) is open daily for lunch and dinner with wonderful prime rib and a full menu of other all-American faves.

Pacific Pizza (870 Forks Ave. S, 360/374-2626, 11 A.M.–9 P.M. Sun.–Thurs., 11 A.M.–10 P.M. Fri.–Sat.) has the best local pizzas and pasta.

The **Forks Farmers Market** (360/374-6623, 10 A.M.–2 P.M. Fri.–Sat. May–mid-Oct.) takes place next to Sully's Drive-In at the north end of town.

Information and Services

Get local information on the south end of town at the helpful **Forks Chamber of Commerce Visitor Center** (1411 S. Forks Ave., 360/374-2531 or 800/443-6757, www.forkswa.com, 9 A.M.–5 P.M. daily in summer, 10 A.M.–4 P.M. daily rest of the year).

The **Olympic National Forest and Park Recreation Information Office** (551 Forks Ave. N, 360/374-7566, 8:30 A.M.–12:30 P.M. and 1:30–5:30 P.M. daily in summer, 8:30 A.M.–12:30 P.M. and 1:30–5:30 P.M. Mon.–Fri. the rest of the year) is housed in the transportation

building. Stop here for recreation information, maps, and handouts, and to take a look at the big 3-D model of the Olympic Peninsula.

Getting There and Around

Local buses all stop at the transportation building (521 N. Forks Ave.) in Forks. **Clallam Transit** (360/452-4511 or 800/858-3747, www.clallamtransit.com) provides daily service north to Port Angeles and Neah Bay, and west to La Push. Catch the free **West Jefferson Transit** (800/436-3950, www.jeffersontransit.com) bus, south from Forks to Kalaloch, Queets, and Lake Quinault. At Lake Quinault, join the Grays Harbor Transit system for points south and east.

LA PUSH AREA

A 14-mile road heads west from Forks through the Bogachiel/Quillayute River Valley. The road ends at La Push, a small village bordering the Pacific Ocean on the south side of the Quillayute River, and the center of the **Quileute Indian Reservation.** The name La Push was derived from the French (*la bouche,* meaning mouth), a reference to the river mouth here. It is an attractive little town with a fantastic beach for surfing and kayaking in the summer or watching storm waves in the winter.

Sights and Recreation

The main attraction at La Push is simply the setting: James Island and other rocky points sit just offshore, and waves break against First Beach. The small **Quileute Tribe Museum** (8 A.M.–3 P.M. Mon.–Thurs., 2–4 P.M. Fri.) housed in the Tribal Center office, has a few artifacts. Ask here for local folks who sell beadwork and other handicrafts, and about ocean and river tours in traditional cedar canoes.

Mora Road branches off from La Push Road three miles east of La Push and provides access to **Rialto Beach** within Olympic National Park. It's pretty easy to tell you've entered public land; instead of clear-cuts, you'll find tall old-growth trees. Mora Campground is here, and the beach is a favorite picnicking area and starting point for hikers heading north along the wild Olympic coast. The town of La Push is just across the wide river mouth to the south.

RIALTO BEACH AREA

This is one of the most popular entry points for the coastal strip of Olympic National Park. Rialto Beach is on the north side of the Quillayute River, just west of the Mora campground and ranger station. The 1.5-mile beach is popular with folks out for a stroll or day hike, but continue northward and the crowds thin out as the country becomes a jumble of sea stacks—remnants of the ancient coast. Hole in the Wall is one of the most interesting of these. This treacherous stretch of shore has claimed many lives, as memorials to Chilean and Norwegian sailors attest. The 21 long and remote miles between Rialto Beach and the Ozette Ranger Station feature abundant wildlife—including bald eagles, harbor seals, shorebirds, and migrating whales at different times of the year. The resident raccoons are here year-round, so hang your food in a hard-sided container!

A popular day hike from the La Push area is **Second Beach,** an easy 0.75-mile trail that starts just south of La Push, followed by 1.5 miles of beach, tidepools, and sea stacks, including a pointed one called the Quillayute Needle. You can camp at a couple of points under the trees, making this some of the most accessible beach camping in the state.

Park at Third Beach, just south of the Second Beach trailhead, for a challenging hike all the way down to **Oil City,** 17 miles away on the north side of the Hoh River. Be sure to carry a tide chart. Oil City neither has oil nor is it a city. Three different exploration parties came here in search of oil—attracted by crude seeping from the ground just north of here. During the 1930s, 11 exploratory wells were drilled and a town was platted, but there simply wasn't enough oil to justify development. A part-paved, part-gravel road leads 11 miles from Highway 101 to the Oil City trailhead.

Clallam Transit (360/452-4511 or 800/858-3747) provides daily bus service to La Push from Port Angeles and Forks. Hikers can catch the bus as far as the turnoff to Rialto Beach and walk or hitch the final three miles.

OLYMPIC PENINSULA

© NATALIA BRATSLAVSKY/123RF.COM

Second Beach

Festivals and Events

The unannounced **Surf Frolic Festival** in January attracts surfers and kayakers, but the big event is **Quileute Days** in mid-July, with a tug-of-war, bone games, a fish bake, canoe races, and fireworks.

Accommodations

The obvious pick in La Push for lodging, **Quileute Oceanside Resort** (320 Ocean Dr., 360/374-5267, www.quileuteoceanside.com/, $45–240 s or d) offers a range of options, everything from bare-bones camper cabins and simple motel rooms on up to duplex units and brand new cabins facing the breathtaking seastacks.

It is activities central at **Three Rivers Resort** (360/374-5300, www.forks-web.com/threerivers, $89–99 up to 4), which offers guided fishing trips, horseback rides, and float trips at the intersection of La Push and Mora Roads (halfway between Forks and La Push). This pet-friendly establishment is also a good spot to bring Spot.

Manitou Lodge (360/374-6295, www.manitoulodge.com, $139–179 d) is a modern country lodge on 10 acres of forested land off Mora Road. Seven luxurious guest rooms with private baths are $139–179 s or d, including a full breakfast. Also on the property are two cedar-shingle camping cabins ($69–99 d) available spring through fall only. Book up to six months ahead for summer weekends. A gift shop here sells quality baskets, woodcarvings, and beadwork.

CAMPING

Olympic National Park's **Mora Campground** (open year-round, $10) is a pretty in-the-trees place to pitch a tent. Check with the ranger station here for summertime naturalist programs and nature walks.

RV owners can pull their rigs into **Lonesome Creek RV Park** (360/374-4338, $30–35 full hookups), which offers many sites with ocean views. RVers can also park at nearby **Three Rivers Resort** (360/374-5300, www.forks-web.com/threerivers, $18 with full hookups).

Food

There are no restaurants in La Push, but you can get locally famous burgers plus soups and sandwiches east of town at **Three Rivers Resort** (360/374-5300, 11 A.M.–9 P.M.).

Information and Services

The Olympic National Park's **Mora Ranger Station** (360/374-5460) next to the Mora Campground is usually staffed daily June–August, but the rest of the year it's catch-as-catch-can. Stop by for a tide chart and information on hiking along the coast. Rangers offer daily beach walks and short guided hikes, and summer campfire programs on Friday–Sunday nights at the amphitheater.

Getting There

Clallam Transit (360/452-4511 or 800/858-3747, www.clallamtransit.com) provides daily bus service to La Push and other parts of the Olympic Peninsula, transporting you south as far as Lake Quinault, and north to Port Angeles and Neah Bay.

HOH RIVER VALLEY

Heading south from Forks on Highway 101, you pass through the heart of the Olympics and get a taste of the economic importance of logging and how it has changed the landscape. Despite reductions in the amount of timber cut in recent years on Forest Service lands, you're bound to meet a constant parade of trucks laden with logs from private land and reservations.

(Hoh Rain Forest

One of Olympic National Park's most famous sights is also one of its most remote. Fourteen miles south of Forks is the turnoff to the world-famous Hoh Rain Forest, located at the end of the paved 19-mile Upper Hoh Road. The road follows the Hoh River through a beautiful valley with a mix of second-growth stands and Department of Natural Resources clear-cuts. Once you enter the park, old-growth stands dominate. The **Hoh Rain Forest Visitor Center** (360/374-6925, 9 A.M.–7 P.M. daily July–Aug., 9 A.M.–4 P.M. daily the rest of the

© ERICKA CHICKOWSKI

Moss grows everywhere in the Hoh Rain Forest.

year) offers interpretive exhibits and summertime guided walks and campfire programs. Stop by for brochures, information, books, and educational exhibits on the life of the forest and the climate. It rains a *lot* here; 140 inches of rain per year keep this forest perpetually green and damp under towering conifers over 200 feet tall and up to 10 feet wide. The driest months are July and August.

Two short interpretive trails lead through the lush spikemoss-draped forests behind the visitors center. Lacy ferns carpet the forest floor, and some even survive in the tops of the bigleaf and vine maples. A paved wheelchair-accessible mini-trail is directly behind the center, and the **Hall of Mosses Trail** offers an easy 0.75-mile loop.

Shopping
Five miles up the Hoh Rain Forest Service Road is **Peak 6 Adventure Store** (360/374-5254, 9:30 A.M.–5:30 P.M. daily) selling all sorts of camping and climbing gear and clothes. The owners are friendly and knowledgeable about local trails, and prices are reasonable.

Sports and Recreation
HIKING
Spruce Nature Trail covers a 1.25-mile loop that crosses a crystalline spring-fed creek and then touches on the muddy, glacially fed Hoh River. More adventurous folks can head out the **Hoh River Trail**, an 18-mile path that ends at Blue Glacier and is used to climb Mount Olympus. Hikers heading into the wilderness need to pick up permits at the visitors center or the Wilderness Information Center in Port Angeles.

CLIMBING
Climbing the glacier-clad 7,965-foot **Mount Olympus** is a 44-mile round-trip trek. From the Hoh Ranger Station—the closest and most popular departure point—hike 12 flat miles along the Hoh River Trail, then another five steep ones to the Olympus base camp, Glacier Meadows. Crossing Blue Glacier and the Snow Dome requires rope, an ice ax, crampons, and mountaineering skills; a hard hat is advised because of rock falls near the summit. The eight-mile climb from Glacier Meadows to the summit takes about 10 hours. The best months for climbing are late June through early September, the driest months in the park; prior to that time mud and washouts may slow you down.

Inexperienced climbers and those unfamiliar with the area would be wise to hire a guide to accompany them up to the top. National park guide service contracts change year by year, but one company is a perennial fave: **Mountain Madness** (3018 SW Charlestown St., Seattle, 206/937-8389, www.mountain madness.com, $950) runs five-day treks to the top of Olympus meant for beginners on up.

Accommodations
Budget travelers will want to check out the quirky **Rain Forest Hostel** (23 mi. south of Forks on Hwy. 101, 360/374-2270, $10 pp, $5 kids). The hostel is out in the sticks and has two dorm rooms with bunk beds, a family room, and a trailer outside for couples. It's closed 10 A.M.–5 P.M., lights out at 11 P.M., and no booze is allowed. Guests are asked to do 15 minutes of chores in the evening or morning

before departure. Those without vehicles can catch the West Jefferson Transit bus.

Bring your own bedding to the rustic roadside cabins at **Hoh River Resort** (15 mi. south of Forks on Hwy. 101, 360/374-5566, www.hohriverresort.com, $65 s or d), a quiet property perfect for families and others who may not feel like camping in rain forest country. Tent ($17) and RV ($25) spaces are also here.

Animal lovers will fall head over hoofs for the ❰ **Hoh Humm Ranch** (20 mi. south of Forks on Hwy. 101, 360/374-5337, www.olypen.com/hohhumm, $35 s or d), where innkeepers raise a zoo's worth of critters: llamas, strange breeds of cattle, goats, sheep, ducks, geese, rhea birds, and Asian Sika deer. Stay in one of five guest rooms with shared bathrooms at a steal of a rate.

CAMPING

The Park Service's ❰ **Hoh Rain Forest Campground,** 19 miles east from Highway 101 at the end of the road, is open year-round with in-the-trees camping for $10. The visitors center has evening naturalist programs in the summer.

The Department of Natural Resources has five small, free, year-round campgrounds near the Hoh River: **Hoh Oxbow Campground** (near milepost 176), **Cottonwood Campground** (two miles west on Oil City Rd.), **Willoughby Creek Campground** (3.5 miles east on Hoh Rain Forest Rd.), **Minnie Peterson Campground** (4.5 miles east on Hoh Rain Forest Rd.), and **South Fork Hoh Campground** (6.5 miles east on Hoh Mainline Rd.). Willoughby Creek is right on the river but has just three sites.

Food

Be sure to bring food if you plan to spend the whole day at the Hoh, as dining options are very limited. Your only option is at the park entrance, where you'll find **Hard Rain Cafe** (5763 Upper Hoh Rd., 360/374-9288, www.hardraincafe.com, 9 A.M.–7 P.M. daily), a quiet little mercantile and burger stand that's good for lunches and quick bites on the way in or out of the park.

RUBY BEACH TO KALALOCH

The southern end of Olympic National Park's coastal strip is the most accessible, with Highway 101 running right along the bluff for more than a dozen miles. Short trails lead down to the water at half a dozen points, and at the southern end one finds the town (of sorts) called Kalaloch, with a comfortable lodge, two Park Service campgrounds, and other facilities. Beach camping is not allowed along this stretch of the coast.

Ruby Beach Area

Highway 101 rejoins the coast at Ruby Beach, part of Olympic National Park, just south of the mouth of the Hoh River. A very popular trail leads down to beautiful sandy shoreline dotted with red pebbles (garnets, not rubies), with piles of driftwood and the flat top of **Destruction Island** several miles offshore. The island is capped by a 94-foot lighthouse.

South of Ruby Beach, the highway cruises along the bluff, with five more trails dropping to shoreline beaches, creatively named Beach 1, Beach 2, Beach 3, and so on. A massive western red cedar tree stands just off the highway near Beach 6.

Kalaloch

The bluff and beach called Kalaloch, in Olympic National Park, has a campground, gas station/country store, and the ❰ **Kalaloch Lodge** (360/962-2271 or 866/525-2562), operated as a park concessionaire. The lodge consists of three different types of facilities: the 1950s-era main lodge ($180 d), cabins of various types ($220–335), and the Seacrest House Motel ($202–220). There are no TVs in the rooms, but the sitting room has one for those who can't miss their shows. Some of the cabins have kitchens and offer waterside views. Make reservations far ahead for the nicest rooms or the bluff cabins; some are reserved 11 months ahead of time for July and August. The lodge also runs a café, gift shop, and lounge.

Across from the lodge is the Park Service's **Kalaloch Visitor Information Center** (360/962-2283, daily June–Sept., with variable hours the rest of the year) where you'll find natural history books, maps, pamphlets, and tide charts for beach walking.

The National Park Service's **Kalaloch Campground** ($12; open year-round) sits on a bluff overlooking the beach. During the summer, attend campfire programs or join a tidepool walk at Beach 4. The primitive **South Beach Campground** ($8, open summers only) is on the southern edge of the park three miles south of Kalaloch. These are the only two campgrounds on the dozen miles of Pacific shoreline between Queets and the Hoh Reservation.

Queets and Quinault

QUEETS RIVER AREA

South of Kalaloch, Highway 101 crosses the **Quinault Indian Reservation,** where you get to see what clear-cuts really look like. A narrow corridor of Olympic National Park extends along the Queets River, protecting a strip of old-growth timber bordered by cut-over DNR and private lands. The gravel Queets River Road (well marked) follows the river eastward from Highway 101, ending 14 miles later at **Queets Campground.** This free, primitive campground has no running water, but it is open year-round. A seasonal ranger station is also here. The **Queets Loop Trail** departs the campground for an easy three-mile walk through second-growth forests and fields where elk are often seen. Another route, the **Queets Trail,** is more challenging. It requires the fording of Queets River near the campground—wait till late summer or fall for this hike, and use caution—and then continues along the river for 15 miles, passing through magnificent old-growth stands of Sitka spruce. Not for beginners, but an impressive hike.

Olympic Raft & Kayak (360/452-1443 or 888/452-1443, www.raftandkayak.com) leads relaxing float trips down the Queets River each spring.

The Quinault Reservation beaches, from just south of Queets almost to Moclips, have been closed to the public since 1969. However, you can arrange for an escorted tour of Point Grenville or Cape Elizabeth, two good bird-watching spots, by calling 360/276-8211.

The Department of Natural Resources has additional free campsites approximately 14 miles up Hoh-Clearwater Mainline Road. The turnoff is at milepost 147 on Highway 101 (three mi. west of the Queets River Rd. turnoff).

☾ LAKE QUINAULT

Surrounded by steep mountains and dense rain forest, Lake Quinault is bordered on the northwest by Olympic National Park and on the southeast by Olympic National Forest; the lake itself and land to the southeast are part of the Quinault Reservation and subject to Quinault regulations. Located at the southwestern edge of Olympic National Park, Lake Quinault is a hub of outdoor activity during the summer months. This very scenic tree-rimmed lake is surrounded by cozy lodges, and level hiking trails provide a chance for even total couch potatoes to get a taste of the rain forest that once covered vast stretches of the Olympic Peninsula.

The Quinault Rain Forest is one of three major rain forests that survive on the Peninsula; here the annual average rainfall is 167 inches, resulting in enormous trees, lush vegetation, and moss-carpeted buildings. If you arrive in the rainy winter months, bring your heavy rain gear and rubber boots, not just a nylon poncho and running shoes. If you're prepared, a hike in the rain provides a great chance to see this soggy and verdant place at its truest. July and August are the driest months, but even then it rains an average of three inches. Typical Decembers see 22 inches of precipitation.

OLYMPIC PENINSULA

© ERICKA CHICKOWSKI

Lake Quinault

Sports and Recreation

DAY HIKING

The Quinault area is a hiker's paradise, with trails for all abilities snaking through a diversity of terrain. The 10-mile **Quinault National Recreation Trail System,** accessible from Willaby and Falls Creek Campgrounds and Lake Quinault Lodge, provides several loop trail hiking opportunities along the lakeshore and into the rain forest. Easier still is the half-mile **Quinault Rain Forest Nature Trail,** where informative signs explain the natural features. A good hike for those traveling with small children begins at North Fork Campground, following the Three Lakes Trail for the first mile to **Irely Lake.** The half-mile **Maple Glade Rain Forest Trail** begins at the Park Service's Quinault Visitor Center on North Fork Road.

Another easy jaunt is the **Graves Creek Nature Trail,** a one-mile loop that begins at the Graves Creek Campground on the South Shore Road. From the same starting point, the **Enchanted Valley Trail** takes you through a wonderful rain forest along the South Fork of the Quinault River. Day hikers often go as far as Pony Bridge, 2.5 miles each way, but more ambitious folks can continue to Dosewallips, a one-way distance of 28 miles.

BACKCOUNTRY HIKING

You'll find two across-the-park hikes that begin or end in the Quinault area, one heading northeast over to Dosewallips, and the other heading north over Low Divide to the Lake Elwha area.

The 11,961-acre **Colonel Bob Wilderness** borders the South Shore Road just east of Quinault Lake and has a couple of popular backcountry paths. For an overnight hike, the seven-mile (each way) **Colonel Bob Trail** provides views of Mount Olympus, Quinault Valley, and the Pacific Ocean from its 4,492-foot summit and passes through impressive rain forests. Drive past Lake Quinault on South Shore Road until you see the trailhead on the right. The two-mile **Fletcher Canyon Trail** doesn't get a lot of use, but it's a fine chance to see virgin timber and a pretty waterfall. The trail starts from South Shore Road just before it enters the park. Access to the wilderness from the south side is via Forest Service Road 2204, northeast from the town of Humptulips. If you enter from this remote area, be sure to visit the beautiful Campbell Tree Campground (free) and to check out the **West Fork Humptulips River Trail** that departs from the campground.

A 21-mile loop begins near the North Fork Campground, heads up the **Three Lakes Trail** for seven miles to three shallow alpine lakes, and then turns down the **Elip Creek Trail** for four miles before catching the **North Fork Trail** back through dense rain forests to your starting point. An added advantage of this loop is the chance to see the world's largest Alaska cedar, located just off the trail approximately a mile east of Three Lakes.

Accommodations

The rambling **Lake Quinault Lodge** (345 S. Shore Rd., 360/288-2900 or 800/562-6672, www.visitlakequinalt.com, $143–300 d) sits

in a magnificent throne of grassy lawns and lakeside shores near the shroud of Quinault's old-growth forests. This is how a lodge should look, with a darkly regal lobby interior and a big central fireplace surrounded by comfortable couches and tables. There are activities galore, with an indoor pool and sauna, lodge-led tours of the Quinault area, and seasonal boat rentals on the property. Inside the rooms, though, the lodge shows its wear as a "classic" lodge with tight quarters and less than luxury furniture that may make some guests feel taken aback by the premium prices. Visitors who go into a stay with the understanding that the premium is for the location and the history will likely come away much more satisfied than those expecting a four-star resort experience.

Those looking to get a bit more bang for their buck will feel more comfortable in the fireplace cabins offered at **Rain Forest Resort Village** (360/288-2535 or 800/255-6936, www.rainforestresort.com, $149–199 d), just a short way up South Shore Road. This nice little property also sits on the waterfront with its own banked lawns. Cabins are a bit rustic, but updated and

© ERICKA CHICKOWSKI

Lake Quinault Lodge

roomier than lodge rooms. The resort also has some run-down motel rooms ($95–105 d) that will do in a pinch for those who won't spend much time there. There's also a good restaurant and lounge, a general store, laundry, RV hookups, and canoe rentals on-site. Whether you stay there or not, be sure to wander on the grounds and spot the world's largest Sitka spruce. This thousand-year-old behemoth is more than 19 feet in diameter and 191 feet tall.

For the absolute nicest place in Quinault, you'll have to travel to the other side of the lake. This is the quieter, less-developed side and home to **((Lake Quinault Resort** (314 N. Shore Rd., 360/288-2362 or 800/650-2362, www.lakequinalt.com, $169–199 d), which rents out sparkling clean and very updated townhouse and kitchenette units facing the lake. Units all line up along a picturesque deck overlooking the property's lawn and the lake. This is a primo spot to watch the winds whip up the water in winter or sailboats lazily float by in summer. Across the road, a trail leads to the world's largest western red cedar—63 feet in circumference and 159 feet tall.

Between north and south sides of the road in the little town of Amanda Park, **Quinault River Inn** (8 River Dr., 360/288-2714, $105 d) offers clean and comfortable rooms convenient to the highway and to all of Lake Quinault's destinations. This is a favorite spot of anglers, who enjoy access to launch boats on the Quinault River, which flows behind the property. But new owners have given this place quite a face-lift, so it is nicer than many peninsula motels catering to the fishing and hunting crowd.

CAMPING

Choose from seven different public campgrounds in the Lake Quinault area. The Forest Service maintains three campgrounds on the south shore of Lake Quinault: **Falls Creek** (open late May–mid-Sept., $14); **Gatton Creek** (no water, open late May–mid-Sept., $11); and **Willaby** (open mid-April–mid-Nov., $14). Willaby is the nicest of these and has a boat ramp. Olympic National Park campgrounds

are more scattered, and all three are open year-round. **July Creek** ($10) is a walk-in campground on the north shore of the lake. **Graves Creek** ($10) is near the end of the South Shore Road, 15 miles from the Highway 101 turn-off. The free **North Fork Campground** is at the end of the North Shore Road. It does not have running water and is not recommended for RVs.

Check out **Rain Forest Village Resort** (516 S. Shore Rd., 360/288-2535 or 800/255-6936, $25 with water and electric hookups) for serene lakefront RV sites. The property is the only campground by the lake with showers on premises, and it also sports a restaurant and general store. Another RV option is **Quinault River Inn** (360/288-2237, $21–25), which is convenient to the gas station and restaurants of Amanda Park.

Food

Get groceries at the **Mercantile** (352 S. Shore Rd., 360/288-2620, hours vary—call ahead) across the road from Quinault Lodge. The snack bar sells pizzas, burgers, milk shakes, espresso, and sandwiches. Quite good meals are available at **Quinault Lodge** (360/288-2571, entrées $14–20) and just up the road at **Rain Forest Resort** (360/288-2535). The tiny village of Amanda Park on the west end of the lake along Highway 101 has a fine old country store with narrow aisles and sloping wooden floors.

Information and Services

The Forest Service's **Quinault Ranger District Office** (360/288-2525, 8 a.m.–4:30 p.m. daily in summer, Mon.–Fri. the rest of the year), next door to Quinault Lodge on the south side of the lake, gives out informative handouts and offers guided nature walks and talks at the lodge in the summer.

Or stop by the Olympic National Park **Quinault River Ranger Station** (5.5 mi. up North Fork Rd., 9 a.m.–5 p.m. daily June–Labor Day, intermittently the rest of the year) for brochures, maps, and information on the park. The area around the station is a good place to see Roosevelt elk, especially in early summer and after September.

In **Amanda Park** along Highway 101 you'll find the essentials: a motel, library, church, school, general store, gas station, post office, café, and liquor store.

Getting There and Around

A road circles Lake Quinault, with side routes up both the East and North Fork of the Quinault River for a total of 31 scenic miles. While most of the road is paved, the upper few miles are gravel. This makes a great bike ride. One of the nicest sections is up South Shore Road, which passes scenic **Merriman Falls** and continues through towering old-growth forests to Graves Creek Campground.

West Jefferson Transit (800/436-3950, www.jeffersontransit.com) provides free daily bus service between Forks and Amanda Park. Continue southward from Lake Quinault on **Grays Harbor Transit** (360/532-2770 or 800/562-9730, www.ghtransit.com) to Moclips, Ocean Shores, and Aberdeen.

North Beach

Grays Harbor—one of just three deepwater ports on the West Coast—forms the southern border to the Olympic Peninsula. The northwestern part of the bay and the Pacific Coast north to the Quinault Reservation is commonly called North Beach. Towns included in this 22-mile long stretch of beachfront are Moclips, Pacific Beach, Copalis Beach, Ocean City, and Ocean Shores.

Some commercial development has occurred along this stretch, but the only significant development is Ocean Shores. This resort/residential complex was developed as a summer resort area in the 1960s and '70s and has never become as popular as its developers expected, in part because of the overcast, damp, windy weather, and in part because it lacks the offshore rugged beauty of, say, Cannon Beach, Oregon. Still, it is one of the most popular resort areas on the Washington coast.

MOCLIPS TO OCEAN CITY

Two small settlements—Moclips and Pacific Beach—occupy the northern end of the North Beach region, with a handful of stores, lodging places, and cafés. The drive from Moclips south to Ocean Shores marks the transition from the timber-dominated lands of the Olympic Peninsula to beachside resorts. Between Moclips and Copalis Beach, Highway 109 winds along the crest of a steep bluff, with dramatic views of the coastline. From Copalis Beach southward to Ocean Shores, the country is far less interesting and the highway straightens out on the nearly level land. The broad sandy beaches are backed by grassy dunes and fronted by summer and retirement homes. The entire 22 miles of beach between Moclips and Ocean Shores is open to the public, with various vehicle entry points along the way.

The pocket-sized town of Copalis Beach has a cluster of older buildings on the Copalis River, along with RV parks, motels, and gift shops. Ocean City, three miles farther south, is a bit larger, consisting mostly of simple homes set in the trees.

Sights and Recreation

Crane your neck upward to get a load of the kites afluttering at one of the most popular shoreline parks on the North Shore stretch, **Pacific Beach State Park** (49 2nd St.). Plunked down right in the middle of Pacific Beach's cute village atmosphere, the park offers beach lovers a meandering sandy reach adorned with sea-oat covered dunes. The camping facilities draw in lots of RVing families, making this a great spot for folks looking to get the little ones to socialize.

Just west of Copalis Beach, **Griffiths-Priday State Park** (www.parks.wa.gov) is a quieter day-use facility at the mouth of the Copalis

River. This is a birder's delight, as the Copalis Spit here is one of three snowy plover breeding grounds on the Washington coast. Visitors must be mindful, because this endangered species is very sensitive to human intrusion. To protect the plovers, large areas of the beach north of the park entrance are closed to the public—from the high-tide mark to the dunes—between mid-March and late August. The restricted areas are marked on the map at the park entrance. A boardwalk leads to the beach, where you can dig for razor clams below the tide line.

The **Anderson Cabin** (360/289-3842) on the east side of the highway is open in the summer. Built of beach logs in the 1920s, the cabin contains period furnishings and a display on local author Norah Berg.

Copalis Beach and Ocean City are "Home of the Razor Clam." The State Department of Fisheries sponsors **clam-digging clinics** (360/249-4628, www.parks.wa.gov) and **beach walks** throughout the summer at Ocean City State Park to prepare you for the short, intense razor clam season.

Festivals and Events

The **Chief Taholah Day Celebration** in early July includes arts and crafts, a powwow, salmon bake, canoe races, a parade, and games on the reservation. The **Kelper's Parade & Shake Rat Olympics** is Pacific Beach's festival, featuring two parades on Labor Day weekend. It's followed in mid-September by a **Sandcastle Sculpture Contest** open to everyone.

Ocean City sponsors the area's big 4th of July **Fire O'er the Water** fireworks and picnic, with live music and arts and crafts. In early August, Copalis Beach comes alive with **Copalis Days,** featuring a car parade, street dancing, and food booths. Head to Copalis Beach in mid-September for a popular **Sandsculpture Contest** with contestants of all levels of ability.

Accommodations

You'll find the most dining, lodging, and convenience options in the Moclips and Pacific Beach area. The most RV camping choices fall in Copalis Beach.

Watch the sunset from the veranda at **Moonstone Beach Motel** (4849 Pacific Ave., Moclips, 360/276-4346, www.moonstone moclips.com, $99–139 for four), a simple beachfront property with large kitchenette units that can capably handle families.

The nicest resort in the area is unquestionably ❲ **Ocean Crest Resort** (Moclips, 360/276-4465 or 800/684-8439, http://ocean-crestresort.com, $69–189), set on a wooded bluff over Moclips Beach. There's an indoor pool, sauna, hot tub, and exercise rooms, plus the best restaurant in town. The rooms are not luxurious, but they are the best-maintained units north of Ocean Shores. You'll get fireplaces and full kitchens with the pricier rooms. Be sure to reserve far in advance; this place is not a secret.

Beachwood Resort (3009 Hwy. 109, Copalis Beach, 360/289-2177, www.ilove beachwood.com, $110–120) is a summertime pick among families who like the outdoor pool, hot tub, and sauna facilities. Also on premises is a game room and playground for the kiddies, plus a tower overlooking the beach to set up the perfect sunset photo.

CAMPING

The 10-acre **Pacific Beach State Park** (49 2nd St., 360/276-4297 or 888/226-7688, www.parks.wa.gov, $22–25 for tents, $31 for RVs with hookups, $7 extra reservation fee) in Pacific Beach offers beachfront campsites that put visitors in prime position for early morning beachcombing or afternoon kite flying. The park is open for camping late February–October, and on weekends and holidays the rest of the year.

Copalis has the best selection of RV parks among all for North Shore cities. Active families will dig the recreation room at **Riverside RV Park** (6 Condra Rd., Copalis Beach, 360/289-2111, www.riversidervresort.net, $21 full hookup, $16 tent), which includes darts, billiards, and other games. Plus, outside you'll find horseshoe pits, shuffleboard, a playground, and a hot tub. This park is also right next to the Copalis River, so you don't have to wander far in the morning to start fishing; once done, clean up your catch at the clam- and fish-cleaning station. There are showers on-site, plus a convenience store.

Food

There aren't a whole lot of dining options in Copalis Beach or Ocean City—drive north to Moclips or, better yet, south into Ocean Shores for grub. For ocean-view dining, try the excellent **Ocean Crest Restaurant** (360/276-4465, 8:30 A.M.–2:30 P.M. and 5–9 P.M. daily) at the Ocean Crest Resort in Moclips. The varied dinner menu features Northwest specialties, steak, and seafood, with weekend entertainment in the lounge. They've got good breakfasts, too. Be sure to ask for a window seat—the views are amazing.

If you rent a unit with a kitchen, pick up supplies at **D and K Grocery** (58 Main St., Pacific Beach, 360/276-4400).

Information

Gather information at the **Washington Coast Chamber of Commerce** (2616 Hwy. 109, Ocean City, 360/289-4552 or 800/286-4552, www.washingtoncoastchamber.org, 11 A.M.–5 P.M. Thurs.–Mon. in summer, 11 A.M.–5 P.M. Mon. and Thurs.–Sat., 10 A.M.–2 P.M. Sun. the rest of the year).

Getting There and Around

Grays Harbor Transit (360/532-2770 or 800/562-9730, www.ghtransit.com) has daily service throughout the county, including Moclips to Ocean Shores.

It may not be on your map, but Moclips is connected to Highway 101 by the 20-mile-long Moclips-Quinault Road. Once a rutted and bumpy gravel road, this stretch is now paved and makes a great shortcut between Quinault and the beaches.

OCEAN SHORES

Occupying the six-mile dune-covered peninsula at the north side of the entrance to Grays Harbor, Ocean Shores brings in millions of visitors every year who come to make sand-castles, fly kites, play miniature golf, and ride bumper cars. Bikes, mopeds, and go-karts are

OLYMPIC PENINSULA

Ocean Shores is a favorite among sandcastle "contractors."

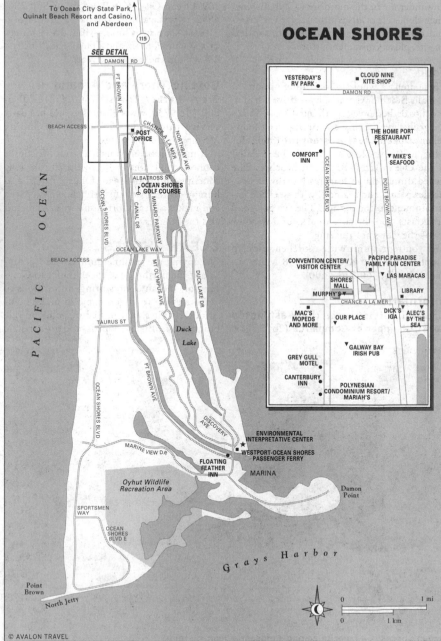

OCEAN SHORES

To Ocean City State Park,
Quinalt Beach Resort and Casino,
and Aberdeen

115

SEE DETAIL

DAMON RD

PT BROWN AVE

BEACH ACCESS

POST OFFICE

CHANCE A LA MER

NORTHBAY AVE

ALBATROSS ST

OCEAN SHORES GOLF COURSE

OCEAN SHORES BLVD

CANAL DR

MINARD PARKWAY

OCEAN LAKE WAY

BEACH ACCESS

MT OLYMPUS AVE

DUCK LAKE DR

TAURUS ST

Duck Lake

PACIFIC OCEAN

FT BROWN AVE

OCEAN SHORES BLVD

DISCOVERY AVE

MARINE VIEW DR

ENVIRONMENTAL INTERPRETATIVE CENTER

WESTPORT-OCEAN SHORES PASSENGER FERRY

FLOATING FEATHER INN

MARINA

Oyhut Wildlife Recreation Area

SPORTSMEN WAY

OCEAN SHORES BLVD E

Damon Point

Point Brown

North Jetty

Grays Harbor

© AVALON TRAVEL

Detail inset

YESTERDAY'S RV PARK

CLOUD NINE KITE SHOP

DAMON RD

THE HOME PORT RESTAURANT

COMFORT INN

MIKE'S SEAFOOD

OCEAN SHORES BLVD

POINT BROWN AVE

CONVENTION CENTER/ VISITOR CENTER

PACIFIC PARADISE FAMILY FUN CENTER

LAS MARACAS

SHORES MALL

LIBRARY

MURPHY'S

CHANCE A LA MER

DICK'S IGA

ALEC'S BY THE SEA

MAC'S MOPEDS AND MORE

OUR PLACE

GALWAY BAY IRISH PUB

GREY GULL MOTEL

CANTERBURY INN

POLYNESIAN CONDOMINIUM RESORT/ MARIAH'S

0   1 mi

0   1 km

the mode of transportation of choice to explore the beachfront lanes in town.

Sights and Recreation
WILDLIFE-WATCHING

The **Ocean Shores Environmental Interpretative Center** (five mi. south of town center at the marina, 360/289-4617, www.ocean shoresinterpretivecenter.com, 11 A.M.–4 P.M. Sat.–Sun.) displays exhibits on local floral and fauna, as well as the natural history of the area.

A pair of wildlife reserves on the southern end of the peninsula offer outstanding bird-watching. **Damon Point** (a.k.a. Protection Island) is an important breeding area for the rare snowy plover and semipalmated plover. This is the only place in the world where both species breed in the same habitat. Parts of Damon Point are closed March–September to protect the plovers, but the wet sands in the tidal zone are open to fishing and walking.

Nearby, **Oyhut Wildlife Recreation Area** at the south end of the peninsula is another good place for bird-watching, with trails through the marshy landscape. Also on the south end of the peninsula, **North Jetty** reaches a mile out into the Pacific and is a great place to fish, watch storm waves, or enjoy the sunset.

BEACHES

The beach at Ocean Shores allows vehicles to drive along the hard-packed sand. There are six access points in town—just head south along Ocean Shores Boulevard and look for the turn-offs. Signs are posted with beach driving regulations and safety warnings. Pedestrians have the right-of-way; cars must yield. Drive only on the higher hard sand, not in the water, on the clam beds, or in the dunes, and observe a 25-mph speed limit.

Beachcombing is a favorite activity on the six miles of sandy beach along Ocean Shores, as is digging for razor clams in season (generally in March and October). Check with the chamber of commerce for the regulations and where to buy a license.

CYCLING AND HORSEBACK RIDING

Rent mopeds and bicycles at **Apollo Activities** (Shores Mall on Chance A la Mer, 360/289-3830)

Sasquatch loves to surf the cold waters here.

or **This & That** (748 Ocean Shores Blvd., 360/289-0919).

Ride horseback along the shore on steeds provided by **Chenois Creek Horse Rentals** (360/533-5591). Or, for a unique equine experience, try out the "horse camp" run by **Nan-Sea Stables** (360/289-0194, $60). Adults and kids are all welcome at Nan-Sea's ranch, where you'll learn to care for horses, to properly muck a stall, and take a trail ride during this four-hour long camp.

KITE FLYING

Ocean Shores is a great place for kite flying, with strong offshore winds much of the year. If you didn't bring your own, head to one of several local kite shops, including **Ocean Shores Kites** (172 W. Chance A La Mer, 360/289-4103, www.oceanshoreskites.com. com, 10 A.M.–6 P.M. Mon.–Fri., 9 A.M.–6 P.M. Sat., 9 A.M.–5 P.M. Sun.) and **Cloud Nine Kite Shop** (380 Hwy. 115, 360/289-4424, 10 A.M.–6 P.M. Mon.–Fri., 9 A.M.–8 P.M. Sat., 9 A.M.–7 P.M. Sun.).

BOATING

With all that ocean out there, it's easy to overlook Ocean Shores' six-mile-long **Duck Lake,** but it's a haven for small boats, canoes, anglers (trout, bass, and crappie are all here), swimmers, and water-skiers. You can launch your boat from City Park, at Albatross and Chance A La Mer, or Chinook Park Boat Launch on Duck Lake Drive. At the south end, the lake connects with a maze of canals that lead past housing developments. Pick up a map before heading out, since these channels can be confusing.

Rent boats and canoes from **Summer Sails** (360/289-2884) located on the canal at the south end of Point Brown Avenue.

GOLF

At Canal and Albatross in Ocean Shores, **Ocean Shores Golf Course** (360/289-3357) is an 18-hole championship course open to the public.

PLAY CENTERS

Pacific Paradise Family Fun Center (767 Minard Ave., 360/289-9537, 11 A.M.–6 P.M. Mon.–Tues. and Thurs.–Fri., 10 A.M.–6 P.M. Sat.–Sun., closed Wed., closed Dec. 1–Dec. 26) has miniature golf, an entertainment center, bumper boats, and even more fun options for kids.

Festivals and Events

Ocean Shores hosts an annual **Beachcombers Fun Fair** at the convention center in early March. See displays of glass floats and driftwood art, and sample the fresh seafood. Ocean Shores' annual **Festival of Colors,** held each May, is family fun with a sandcastle contest, arts and crafts bazaar, and kite festival. The **International Kite Challenge** competition is held out on the beach in the first week of June. In late July, the leather-jacket crowd rolls into Ocean Shores for the **Harley Owners Group Sun & Surf Run,** an event that attracts 2,000 bikes and riders. The **Dixieland Jazz Festival** in early November features acts from all over the Northwest at the convention center and around town.

Shopping

Ocean Shores' **Shores Mall** has bike and moped rentals, a kite shop, bank, clothing store, and state liquor store on Chance A la Mer, just before the beach. In Homeport Plaza on Point Brown Avenue, Ocean Shores' **Gallery Marjuli** (360/289-2858) is open daily with art and gifts created by Northwest artists. **Tide Creations Gift Shop** (Point Brown Ave., 360/289-2550) near the marina has thousands of items, from kites and windsocks to fudge.

Accommodations

Ocean Shores has more than two dozen motels, along with dozens more private home rentals. Note that many places have a two-night minimum on weekends and July–August, and a three-night minimum on holidays. On holidays, the **chamber of commerce** (360/289-0226 or 800/762-3224, www.oceanshores.org) keeps track of room availability.

UNDER $100
Floating Feather Inn (982 Point Brown Ave. SE, 360/289-2490 or 888/257-0894, $85–130 s or d) has two decks facing the Grand Canal. Four guest rooms and a separate family-friendly cabin all have private baths and a breakfast buffet.

$100-150
Canterbury Inn (643 Ocean Shores Blvd. NW, 360/289-3317 or 800/562-6678, www.canterburyinn.com, $130–190 d) has studios with kitchenettes, along with one- and two-bedroom suites with full kitchens and fireplaces ($204–260 d). The beachfront complex, which has many privately owned units, has a large indoor pool and hot tub. There is a two-night minimum.

$150-200
With its gray-shingled roof in the shape of a stylized gull with its wings spread, the **Grey Gull Motel** (651 Ocean Shores Blvd. SW, 360/289-3381 or 800/562-9712, www.thegreygull.com, $160–260 d) appears (from the appropriate angle) in imminent danger of flying away. The hotel has modern, spacious efficiencies, one- and two-bedroom suites, as well as penthouses ($350 d). There is a two-night minimum on summer weekends. Amenities include a sauna and outdoor pool.

Situated north of Ocean Shores on land purchased by the Quinault tribe, **Quinault Beach Resort and Casino** (78 Hwy. 115, 360/289-9466 or 888/461-2214, www.quinaultbeachresort.com, $179 d, $349–549 suites) offers the area's most spacious and comfortable rooms, most with ocean-facing views. Service is very good, and the hotel has a full-service spa with sauna and massage service, walkways out over the dunes to the beach, a nice restaurant, and a café. Plus, of course, there's a full casino.

Polynesian Condominium Resort (615 Ocean Shores Blvd. NW, 360/289-3361 or 800/562-4836, www.thepolynesian.com, $149–229 d) caters to families with its indoor pool, game room, sauna, and hot tub. Choose among hotel rooms, kitchenette efficiencies, or full suites with kitchens and fireplaces. There's a two-night minimum in the summer.

CAMPING
One of the only sites in town is **Yesterday's RV Park** (512 Damon Rd., 360/289-9227, $16 tent, $25 full hookup), which offers sites for RVs and tents right on the beach. All sites have fire rings, and there are showers on premises.

Less than two miles north of Ocean Shores on Highway 115, **Ocean City State Park** (360/289-3553, www.parks.wa.gov) affords a little breathing room out of the town's bustle, with campsites in the trees, picnicking, two little ponds for bird-watching, and a path leading through the dunes to the beach.

Food
Our Place (676 Ocean Shores Blvd. NW, 360/289-8763, 6 A.M.–2 P.M. daily) is a tiny eatery with inexpensive but filling breakfasts and all-American lunches.

The Home Port Restaurant (857 Point Brown Ave., 360/289-2600, 8 A.M.–9 P.M. Sun.–Thurs., 8 A.M.–10 P.M. Fri.–Sat.) serves three meals, including good breakfasts and specialties such as salmon, Dungeness crab, and steak and lobster dinners.

Find very good south-of-the-border meals at **Las Maracas Mexican Restaurant** (729 Point Brown Ave. NW, 360/289-2054, 11:30 A.M.–9 P.M. daily).

Mariah's (615 Ocean Shores Blvd. NW, 360/289-3315, 4–9 P.M. daily) at the Polynesian Resort is the most upscale local restaurant, with seafood, steak, and pasta, along with a weekend breakfast buffet. The lounge has live music Friday and Saturday evenings.

Alec's by the Sea (131 E Chance A La Mer NE, 360/289-4026, 10 A.M.–8 P.M. Sun.–Thurs., 10 A.M.–9 P.M. Fri.–Sat.) next to Dick's IGA, has low prices and a big menu that includes burgers, fresh clams, salads, steaks, pasta, seafood, and chicken.

Galway Bay Irish Pub (676 Ocean Shores Blvd., 360/289-2300, http://galwaybayirishpub.com, 11 A.M.–10 P.M. daily) makes great clam chowder.

OLYMPIC PENINSULA

Be sure to follow the rules while visiting the beaches.

Mike's Seafood (830 Point Brown Ave. NE, 360/289-0532, www.oceanshoresseafood.com, 10 A.M.–8 P.M. Mon.–Sat., 11 A.M.–7 P.M. Sun.) sells fresh-cooked crab from a roadside stand.

Get homemade ice cream, fudge, and chocolates from **Murphy's Candy and Ice Cream** (in the Shores Mall, 360/289-0927, 9 A.M.–9 P.M. daily in summer, noon–8 P.M. Mon.–Tues. and Thurs.–Fri., 10 A.M.–8 P.M. Sat., 10 A.M.–6 P.M. Sun.).

Information
Get information from the helpful folks at **Ocean Shores Chamber of Commerce Visitor Information Center** (120B W. Chance A La Mer, 360/289-2451 or 800/762-3224, www.oceanshores.org, 9 A.M.–5 P.M. Mon.–Fri., 10 A.M.–4 P.M. Sat.–Sun.).

Getting There and Around
Grays Harbor Transit (360/532-2770 or 800/562-9730, www.ghtransit.com) has daily bus service throughout the county, connecting Ocean Shores with Aberdeen, Lake Quinault, and Olympia. Ocean Shores has an airport, but no commercial service.

The **Westport-Ocean Shores Passenger Ferry *El Matador*** (360/289-0414, $10 round-trip, free for kids under 4) is a 74-foot passenger boat with service to Westport. Gray whales are often seen along the way. The ferry leaves six times a day and takes 20–40 minutes, with daily service mid-June–Labor Day, and weekends-only service mid-April through mid-June and in September. There is no service the rest of the year. The boat leaves from the marina; get tickets at the Marina Store.

Grays Harbor and Vicinity

Discovered in 1792 by Capt. Robert Gray, an American en route to China to trade sea otter pelts for tea, Grays Harbor is presided over by Aberdeen and Hoquiam (HO-qwee-um). Grays Harbor has long been a major center for the timber industry, and the surrounding country bears witness to this. Heading toward Aberdeen and Hoquiam from any direction leads you through mile after mile of tree farms, with second- or third-growth forests interspersed with newly logged hillsides.

ABERDEEN AND HOQUIAM
Zipping up Highway 12 and then Highway 8 on the way to Olympia, the southern link in the Olympic loop is dotted by a few little burgs until you reach the easterly tip of Grays Harbor. Here the twin cities of Aberdeen and Hoquiam are separated only by the Hoquiam River. Primarily working-class mill towns, they offer weary peninsula and coast travelers a good opportunity to gas up, fill up, and catch some zzz's before hitting the road again. If you stop,

be sure to check out the historical sights around town, particularly the Grays Harbor Seaport.

Sights

GRAYS HARBOR HISTORICAL SEAPORT

Capt. Gray's discovery of the harbor in the 18th century was only the beginning of what was to become the area's love affair with the sea. The calm waters of the harbor and the ready supply of timber made Aberdeen an ideal shipbuilding headquarters from its early beginnings in the 19th century. Between 1887 and 1920 her port saw off some 130 new ships.

Today the Grays Harbor Historical Seaport (813 West Heron St., Aberdeen, 360/532-8611, www.historicalseaport.org) highlights the rich maritime heritage of the region, acting as host to two magnificent tall ships. The first, *Lady Washington,* is a full-scale replica of one of the ships in Gray's discovery fleet. This fluttering spectacle of spindly masts and oiled decks carries the honor of sailing as Washington State's Official Ship and is typically in the historical seaport at least two months out of the year, along with her companion ship, the *Hawaiian Chieftain,* a steel-hulled, topsail ketch. (The rest of the year they are featured in maritime and tall-ship festivals up and down the West Coast). While in port, *Lady* is open for tours (10 A.M.–1 P.M. daily, $3 adults, $2 seniors and students, $1 children) and offers outstanding three-hour sailing trips most afternoons and weekend evenings ($55 adults, $45 children). The crew is entirely in costume. Schedules change year by year, so be sure to check the Seaport website for up-to-date information.

You might also ask about volunteering aboard the *Lady.* This is not for everyone—simple food, cramped quarters, limited water, and lots of hard work—but at least you aren't subjected to floggings or surgery without anesthesia. No grog either. This is an incredible chance to learn about sailing the old-fashioned way.

MANSIONS AND MUSEUMS

In 1897, lumber baron Robert Lytle built **Hoquiam's Castle** (515 Chenault Ave.,

Hoquiam, 360/533-2005, 10 A.M.–5 P.M. daily in the summer, 11 A.M.–5 P.M. Sat.–Sun. the rest of the year, closed in Dec., $4 adults, $1 kids), a stunning maroon-and-white, three-story spectacle that's been restored to its original luster, with the original oak woodwork. It's completely furnished in turn-of-the-20th-century antiques, Tiffany-style lamps, and cut-crystal chandeliers. Half-hour tours are offered throughout the day. The hillside mansion overlooks town and has a distinctive monkey-puzzle tree outside.

Another wealthy lumber magnate, Alex Polson, once owned the largest logging operation in the world, Polson Logging Company (now a part of Rayonier). In 1923 he funded the building of a home for his son and daughter-in-law on property adjoining his own house. This 26-room **Polson Museum** (1611 Riverside Ave., 360/533-5862, www.polsonmuseum.org, 11 A.M.–4 P.M. Wed.–Sat., noon–4 P.M. Sun. Apr. 1–Dec. 23, noon–4 P.M. Sat.–Sun. Dec. 27–Mar. 31, $10 families, $4 adults, $2 students) is now named in his honor. Alex Polson's own home was razed after his death in 1939; his widow didn't want anyone else to live in it. The site of their home is now a small park with a rose garden, historic logging equipment, and a blacksmith shop. The museum houses all sorts of memorabilia: a magnificent old grandfather clock, a fun model railroad, a model of an old logging camp, a two-man chainsaw, and even an old punching bag.

The **Aberdeen Museum of History** (117 E. 3rd St., 360/533-1976, 10 A.M.–5 P.M. Tues.–Sun., free) displays exhibits of local history, including a century-old kitchen and bedroom, pioneer church, blacksmith shop, four antique fire trucks, a dugout canoe, thousands of pro-union buttons, and a short video about the great fire of 1903 that destroyed 140 buildings. There's lots of offbeat what-was-that-used-for stuff here.

GRAYS HARBOR NATIONAL WILDLIFE REFUGE

Due west of Hoquiam off Highway 109, Grays

Harbor National Wildlife Refuge (360/753-9467, http://graysharbor.fws.gov) is a 500-acre wetland in the northeast corner of Grays Harbor Estuary. This is one of the most important staging areas for shorebirds in North America, attracting up to a million birds each spring. The two dozen shorebird species that visit the basin include the western sandpiper, dunlin, short- and long-billed dowitcher, and red knot; other birds seen here are the peregrine falcon, northern harrier, and red-tailed hawk. A one-mile path leads to the viewing areas, but bring your boots since it's often muddy. The best viewing time is one hour before and one hour after high tide.

Entertainment and Events

The **Driftwood Players** (120 E. 3rd in Aberdeen, 360/538-1213), a community theatrical company, puts on several plays a year at Driftwood Playhouse.

Kick the year off with a fun time at Aberdeen's **Dixieland Jazz Festival,** held on Presidents Day weekend in mid-February. The **Grays Harbor Shorebird Festival** in late April—the peak of the migration—includes bird-watching field trips and workshops. In early May, the city's **Grays Harbor Discovery Days Celebration** attracts longboats from throughout the Northwest for rowing and sailing races.

Hoquiam's **Loggers Playday,** held the second weekend in September, is an opportunity for sedentary executives to see what real work is all about. After kicking off the event with a parade and salmon barbecue, loggers compete in ax-throwing, log-chopping, and tree-climbing events. Evening brings a big fireworks show.

Elma is home to the county fairgrounds, where you can take in an indoor pro rodeo in late March, horse racing in late July, the old-fashioned **Grays Harbor County Fair** in mid-August, and Saturday night auto racing.

Sports and Recreation

At E. 9th and N. I Streets, Aberdeen's **Samuel Benn Park** has rose and rhododendron gardens, tennis courts, a playground, and picnic facilities. **Lake Aberdeen** at the east entrance to town has swimming and nonmotorized boating and play equipment. For an indoor pool, head to the **Hoquiam Aquatic Center** (717 K St., 360/533-3474).

About a mile north of Montesano off Highway 12, **Lake Sylvia State Park** (360/249-3621, www.parks.wa.gov, open late March–Sept.) encompasses 233 acres around this narrow but scenic reservoir. The lake was created by a dam built in 1909 to supply water and power and is a popular place to swim, canoe, or fish. Two miles of trails circle the lake and connect with two more miles of trail in adjacent **Chapin Collins Memorial Forest.** Be sure to check out the four-foot wooden ball, carved by loggers from a spruce log and used for log rolling until it became waterlogged and sank. The ball was rediscovered in 1974 when the lake level was lowered and is now on display.

Lake Wynoochee, approximately 35 miles north of Montesano, is a popular summertime fishing, hiking, and swimming area within Olympic National Forest.

Accommodations

The twin cities of Aberdeen and Hoquiam are less vacation destinations and more convenient stopovers on the way to other points on the peninsula and coast such as Ocean Shores, Lake Quinault, and Kalaloch. Many of the hotels and motels are on the shabbier side of rundown, but there are a few exceptions.

One acceptable choice is the **Guest House Inn and Suites** (701 East Heron St., Aberdeen, 360/537-7460, www.guesthouseintl.com), a clean place that has the only motel pool in town. Guests are invited to munch on a simple continental breakfast each morning.

There are also a couple of very nice bed-and-breakfasts in town. Most impressive among them is the gorgeous **Hoquiam's Castle B&B** (515 Chenault, 360/533-2005 or 877/542-2785, www.hoquiamscastle.com, $145–195 s or d), which features rooms with four-poster beds, claw-footed tubs, and more dainty linens than you can shake a stick at. Breakfast in the morning is an elaborate affair that should sate even the hungriest hikers before heading out into the woods.

Check out some amazing panoramas of the harbor at the colonial revival-style **A Harbor View B&B** (113 W. 11th St., 360/533-7996, www.aharborview.com, $149–225 s or d, no kids under 12). Sitting high on a hill, this bed-and-breakfast offers five bedrooms furnished in Victorian period pieces and colorful quilts. All rooms include private baths, TVs, and wireless Internet.

The **Grays Harbor Hostel** (6 Ginny Ln., Elma, 360/482-3119, www.ghostel.com, $18 s shared bath, $35 s or d private bath) is a sprawling ranch house situated on eight acres of land. The spotless facilities include an outdoor hot tub, two common rooms, a kitchen, and storage rooms. Blankets and pillows are available, and there's even an 18-hole disc golf course. Open all year, but don't expect to lounge about—the doors lock between 9 A.M.–5 P.M. daily, when the hostel is not open to guests. Tent space is available for cyclists.

CAMPING

Campsites are available at **Lake Sylvia State Park** (360/249-3621, www.parks.wa.gov, open late Mar.–Sept., $9–14 for tents, no hookups) near Montesano, approximately 12 miles east of Aberdeen.

Situated near 20 acres of heavily wooded wilderness, near a creek with catchable crawdads, **Arctic Park** (893 Hwy. 101, Aberdeen, 360/533-4470, http://users.techline.com/articrv/, $22 with full hookups, $10 tents) offers an unusual amount of privacy over the typical corral-type RV park, with vegetation separating many sites. The owners grow a garden with veggies and berries that guests are welcome to pick, and the property includes showers, a volleyball court, and a convenience store. Nearby there's 1.5 miles of trails that run through the forest.

Follow the signs for 12 miles north of Elma to **Schafer State Park** (www.parks.wa.gov, open Apr.–Sept. only, $13 for tents, $19 for RVs) on the Satsop River. Originally a park for Schafer Logging Company employees, today it

has public campsites, riverside picnic areas, and a fine collection of mossy trees. There is good fishing for steelhead (late winter) and sea-run cutthroat (summers) in the East Fork of the Satsop River.

Food

In business since 1945, **Duffy's** is the local family restaurant, featuring a varied, inexpensive-to-moderate seafood and steak menu and great blackberry pies. Try this local favorite at two locations, one in Aberdeen (1605 Simpson Ave., 360/532-3842, 6 A.M.–10 P.M. Sun.–Thurs., 6 A.M.–11 P.M. Fri.–Sat.) and one in Hoquiam (825 Simpson Ave., 360/532-1519, 11 A.M.–10 P.M. Tues.–Sat., 11 A.M.–9 P.M. Sun.–Mon.).

Aberdeen's **Breakwater Seafood** (306 S. F St., 360/532-5693, 9:30 A.M.–7 P.M. Mon.–Sat., 11 A.M.–6 P.M. Sun.) is a seafood market/restaurant with good chowder and fresh fish and chips to eat in or take out.

Reservations are recommended for dinner at **Mallard's** (118 E. Wishkah, 360/532-0731, 5–7:30 P.M. Tues.–Sat.), a small place with good quality European-style cuisine prepared by a Danish chef, with daily specialties.

The atmosphere is elegant but not stuffy at **Bridge's** (112 N. G St., Aberdeen, 360/532-6563, 11 A.M.–9 P.M. Mon.–Sat., 4–9 P.M. Sun.), which serves prime rib, steak, and seafood dinners, including razor clams. It is open for lunch and dinner daily plus Sunday brunch.

Billy's Bar & Grill (322 E. Heron, Aberdeen, 360/533-7144, 8 A.M.–10 P.M. Mon.–Sat.) is a restored saloon that serves delicious and reasonably priced steaks, seafood, and burgers.

Decent Italian food and the best local pizzas are at **Casa Mia Pizza** (2936 Simpson Ave., Hoquiam, 360/533-2010, 11 A.M.–midnight Mon.–Thurs., 11 A.M.–1 A.M. Fri.–Sat., 11 A.M.–10 P.M. Sun.).

The **Hoquiam-Grays Harbor Farmers Market** (360/538-9747, 9 A.M.–6 P.M. Tues. and Thurs.–Sat. year-round) takes place at Hoquiam's Levee Park, on the river on Highway 101 North.

OLYMPIC PENINSULA

Information

The **Grays Harbor Chamber of Commerce and Visitor Center** (506 Duffy St., Aberdeen, 360/532-1924 or 800/321-1924, 9 A.M.–5 P.M. daily) is a good place to find out about the twin cities of Aberdeen and Hoquiam, along with other county towns.

Getting There and Around

Aberdeen and Hoquiam are well served by **Grays Harbor Transit** (360/532-2770 or 800/562-9730, www.ghtransit.com). Buses take you throughout the county seven days a week, including Lake Quinault, Westport, Ocean Shores, and even east to Olympia. **Pacific Transit System** (360/875-9418 or 800/875-9418) provides bus service southward to Raymond, Long Beach, and Astoria, Oregon.

WESTPORT

Ragged-at-the-edges Westport is quite unlike its more polished cross-bay twin, Ocean Shores. Westport once called itself "The Salmon Capital of the World." Commercial fishing and crabbing boats still line the waterfront and you're sure to see fishermen driving beat-up old pickups through town. But it's also a hub for charter fishing services and is home to plenty of waterfront shops offering kitschy gifts, saltwater taffy, and kites.

Sights

WESTPORT MARITIME MUSEUM

Housed in a magnificent 1939 Coast Guard station, **Westport Maritime Museum** (2201 Westhaven Dr., 360/268-0078, http://westportwa.com/museum, 10 A.M.–4 P.M. daily June–Sept., noon–4 P.M. Wed.–Sun. Oct.–May, $3 adults, $1 kids) is capped by six gables and a watchtower with a widow's walk. Walk inside to see Coast Guard memorabilia and cranberry and logging industry exhibits. On your way off the property, be sure to check out the massive lens from the now destroyed 1888 Destruction Island Lighthouse, and the glass cases displaying skeletons of gray whales, minke whales, sea lion, and porpoises.

a fishing boat in Westport

PARKS AND BEACHES

Head to the 0.75-mile **South Jetty** at the end of State Park Access Road for a chance to fish, look for birds and marine mammals, or watch the winter storms roll in. Use care on the slippery rocks. The road passes Half Moon Bay, popular with scuba divers. A tall **observation tower** on the east end of Nettie Rose Drive in town provides a fine vantage point to view freighter activity, scenery, sunsets, or an occasional whale, and a lower **ramp tower** on the east end of Nettie Rose looks into the marina. In front of this is a small memorial to fishermen lost at sea.

Entertainment and Events

Westport's **World Class Crab Races & Feed** in mid-April is not a good time to be a crab; the races are followed by a big crab feed. Live music is also featured. The **Blessing of the Fleet,** held annually in May, includes a memorial service for people lost at sea and demonstrations of Coast Guard sea-air rescues. Held in early July, the two-day **Kite Festival** has contests for the youngest and oldest kite flyers, best crash event, longest train of kites, and more. Mid-July has the **Longboard Classic Surf Festival,** attracting top longboard surfers from throughout the Northwest. In August, an **International Nautical Chainsaw Carving Contest** (no, it is not done underwater), and the **Brady's Oyster Feed** both come early in the month.

A very popular event—it's been going on for more than 50 years—is the **Westport Seafood Festival** on Labor Day weekend. Taste salmon, oysters, crab, and all sorts of other fresh-from-the-sea foods, with musical accompaniment.

Sports and Recreation

WESTHAVEN STATE PARK

Open for day use only, Westhaven State Park (Hwy. 105 just north of Westport, www.parks .wa.gov) is popular with rockhounds, beachcombers, and divers. Surfers and sea kayakers find some of the most consistent waves in Washington. The jetty was built here to increase the velocity of the seagoing water,

collected from six rivers flowing into Grays Harbor. Prior to the construction of the jetty, deposits of sediment mandated annual channel dredging. The jetty worked—the channel hasn't required dredging since 1942.

WESTPORT LIGHT STATE PARK

Westport Light State Park (www.parks.wa.gov), about a mile south of Westhaven off Highway 105 (continue straight when 105 goes left), is another day-use park good for kite flying, rockhounding, and fishing for ocean perch, but no camping. A paved, mile-long **Dune Interpretive Trail** wanders through the dunes, providing several observation platforms that overlook the water. There's vehicular beach access here, but the sand is considerably softer than at other drivable beaches; be careful if you don't have four-wheel drive. Check with the park for regulations on beach driving, since some sections are closed part or all of the year. The classic **lighthouse** inside the park—the tallest on the West Coast—was built in 1898 and is visible from an observation platform on Ocean Avenue. The building is closed to the public, but tours may be offered by the museum. The lighthouse originally stood much closer to the water, but the accretion of sand has pushed the beachfront seaward.

TWIN HARBORS STATE PARK

On Highway 105, two miles south of Westport, **Twin Harbors State Park** (www.parks.wa.gov) has campsites, a 0.75-mile sand dune nature trail, picnic areas, and a playground. This is one of the most popular oceanside campgrounds, especially when razor clam harvesting is allowed (usually March and October). Twin Harbors is open for day use all year.

FISHING AND CLAMMING

Even the casual visitor to Westport will see that this is a major sport and commercial fishing port. The harbor is packed with vessels of all dimensions, and charter operators line the marina. You don't have to charter a boat to go fishing; the whole stretch from Westport to North Cove is popular for surf fishing.

OLYMPIC PENINSULA

The rock jetty near Westhaven State Park is a good spot for catching salmon, rockfish, lingcod, surf perch, and crabs. In September and October, a coho salmon run returns to the marina area (the young are raised in pens here, so this is "home"). Clamming is seasonal and requires a license; see the chamber of commerce for a copy of the regulations. The 1,000-foot-long **Westport Fishing Pier,** off the end of Float 20 at the Westport Marina, is another landlubber fishing option.

Offshore rocks and reefs are feeding grounds for salmon, bottom fish, halibut, and even albacore tuna; take a charter boat to find the best spots, not to mention having your fish cleaned and ready to cook by the time you get back to shore. The charter services all charge about the same amount, so when you call for reservations be sure to check whether the price includes bait and tackle, cleaning, and sales tax, to see if your "bargain" is really a good deal. Note, however, that most departures are at the frightfully early hour of 6 A.M., with a return around 3:30 P.M. Be sure to take along your seasickness pills. Some companies also offer overnight trips that head far offshore in search of tuna. Wander along Westhaven Drive to check out the various charter companies, or get a listing of boats from the visitors center. Expect to pay around $125 per person for halibut charters, $375 for tuna, or $60–75 pp for coho salmon or bottom fishing.

WHALE-WATCHING

Many of the local fishing charter operators provide whale-watching trips March–May, when the gray whales are heading north from their winter quarters off Baja California. Get a list of operators from the visitors center. Expect to pay $20–30 for a three-hour trip. You may also spot whales from the jetty or from the Westport viewing towers. The passenger ferry to Ocean Shores is an inexpensive way to watch for the whales that periodically wander into Grays Harbor. The Maritime Museum offers weekend whale-watching seminars, films, and workshops in season.

SURFING

Surfers can check out the waves at Westhaven State Park, one of the most popular surfing beaches in the state. The manmade jetty here has developed the most consistent point break in Washington, making it well worth braving the icy waters when it is firing. Rent surfboards and wetsuits from the **Surf Shop** (207 Montesano St., 360/268-0992).

Accommodations

Most Westport accommodations are straightforward, down-to-earth affairs. Many have kitchenettes, but only a few offer hot tubs or pools. As one owner told me in her broken English, "No pool—big giant ocean out there!" Contact the **chamber of commerce** (360/268-9422 or 800/345-6223 www.westportgrayland-chamber.org) for a list of rental homes in the Westport area.

Most of the rooms at **Alaskan Motel** (708 N. 1st St., 360/268-9133 or 866/591-4154, www.westportwa.com/alaskan, $60–82 s or d) are simple kitchenette units, though there are some newer guest cottages with enclosed decks ($140–165 d).

A three-story building in the boat basin, **Coho Motel** (2501 N. Nyhus, 360/268-0111 or 800/572-0177) has rooms for $49–54 s or d, and third-floor suites for $68 d. The owners also manage a popular charter fishing operation.

An unpretentious, one-story motel with a gazebo for fresh fish barbecues, **Mariners Cove Inn** (303 Ocean Ave., 360/268-0531 or 877/332-0090, www.marinerscoveinn.com, $59–74 s or d) has clean, modern hotel rooms.

It might fool you at first glance, but **Chateau Westport Motel** (710 Hancock, 360/268-9101 or 800/255-9101, www.chateauwestport.com, $111–124 d, suites $217–383) is actually pretty nice inside. The rooms are comfortable and well equipped, many with balconies and ocean views. The hotel has an indoor heated pool and hot tub. Facilities also include a horseshoe pit and playground, plus free Wi-Fi. As an added bonus, the free continental breakfast starts at the dark hour of 4:30 A.M. for those headed out on fishing trips.

There might not be a pool, but fun-lovin' families will appreciate the go-kart track right on the property at **Breakers Motel** (971 Montesano St., 360/268-0848, www.westportwa.com/breakers, $94–140 d). The motel offers standard rooms and kitchenette units, as well as newer hot-tub suites ($210–230).

Built in 1898 and surrounded by tall evergreens, **Glenacres Inn B&B** (222 N. Montesano St., 360/268-9391 or 800/996-3048, $80–135 d) is the most interesting place to stay in Westport. The B&B has eight guest rooms with private baths, and guests are treated to a full breakfast. A gazebo encloses the hot tub.

CAMPING

Camp at the very popular **Twin Harbors State Park** (two mi. south of town, 888/226-7688, www.parks.wa.gov, $17 tent, $21 full hookups, $7 extra reservation fee). Some campsites are just steps away from the beach, and showers are available. The campground is open late February–October.

Westport is jam-packed with RV parks catering to the fishing crowd. Perhaps the most laden with amenities, **American Sunset Resort** (360/268-0207 or 800/569-2267, www.americansunsetrv.com, $29 full hookups, $19 tent) offers a heated outdoor pool, horseshoe pits and playgrounds, showers, and laundry facilities, plus free Wi-Fi. The property is pet friendly, offers plenty of space for larger rigs, and sports a convenience store and a special area for tent campers. It even rents out two permanent trailers parked at the property.

Food

Because of the early morning departure of fishing charters, several local cafés are already open when the clock strikes five in the morning. Another recommended lunch place with a salad bar and good seafood is **Barbara's by the Sea** (2323 Westhaven Dr., 360/268-1329, 8 A.M.–6 P.M. Mon.–Thurs., 8 A.M.–8 P.M. Fri.–Sat.) across from the marina. **Las Maracas Mexican Restaurant** (202 W. Ocean Ave.,

360/268-6272, 11 A.M.–8 P.M. daily) makes good enchiladas, tostadas, and chimichangas.

You'll find a "surf and turf" menu that includes oysters, halibut, and prawns, along with steaks and pasta, at **King's LeDomaine** (105 Wilson St., 360/268-2556, 7 A.M.–9 P.M. daily).

Buy freshly shucked oysters to go from **Brady's Oysters** (3714 Oyster Place E, 360/268-0077, 9 A.M.–6 P.M. daily). This company was the first to grow oysters on suspended lines, a method that many claim produces a more delicately flavored oyster. You can often buy ultra-fresh fish from commercial fishermen at the marina, and fresh-cooked crab at **Merino's Seafood** (301 E. Harbor St., 360/268-5324, 10 A.M.–6 P.M. daily in summer, 10 A.M.–4 P.M. Sat.–Sun. in winter).

Information

Find maps, brochures, and festival and tour information at the **Westport-Grayland Chamber of Commerce Visitors Center** (2985 N. Montesano St., 360/268-9422 or 800/345-6223, www.westportgrayland-chamber.org, 9 A.M.–5 P.M. Mon.–Fri. year-round, plus 10 A.M.–3 P.M. Sat.–Sun. May–Sept.).

Getting There and Around

Grays Harbor Transit (360/532-2770 or 800/562-9730, www.ghtransit.com) provides daily bus service throughout the county, including Grayland, Aberdeen, Lake Quinault, Ocean Shores, and even to Olympia.

The **Westport-Ocean Shores Passenger Ferry El Matador** (360/268-0047) is a passenger ferry that runs between Ocean Shores and Westport for $8 round-trip (free for kids under 5). The ferry leaves six times a day, with daily service mid-June–Labor Day, and weekend-only service early May–mid-June and in September. There's no service the rest of the year. The ferry departs from Float 10 at the Westport marina.

CRANBERRY COAST AND NORTH WILLAPA BAY

The section of coastline between Westport and North Cove is known as both South Beach and

CRANBERRIES

Grown by local American Indians for centuries, the cranberry was introduced to Finnish settlers on the coast in the early 1900s. Cranberries grow on vines in acidic and wet peat bogs. Nearly all of the 130 cranberry farms in the state are family-run operations averaging just 11 acres each. They typically sell the crop to Ocean Spray Cranberries, a farmers' cooperative best known for its juice cocktails. The company runs two plants in southeast Washington: at Grayland and in Long Beach.

The Cranberry Coast of Washington runs between Grays Harbor south to Tokeland. The most interesting times to visit the cranberry bogs are in mid-June, the peak blooming season, or mid-October, to see the harvest. If you choose to go in October, it's more informative and interesting to join the bus tour and Grayland's Cranberry Harvest Festival.

the Cranberry Coast—the former because it is the southern entrance to Grays Harbor, the latter because of the bogs east near Grayland that produce much of the state's cranberry crop. The area is especially popular for sportfishing, but also offers long beaches, good surfing, and reasonably priced lodging. The beaches are favorites of poststorm beachcombers who still turn up an occasional glass ball from old Japanese fishing floats.

Continuing south, Washington's coastline wraps around Willapa Bay, the 25-mile-long inlet protected by the Long Beach Peninsula. It is believed to be the cleanest and least developed estuary on the West Coast of the Lower 48 states. Locals posit that these waters produce the best-tasting oysters in the nation (a claim disputed by folks in Grays Harbor and Shelton). Highways 105 and 101 skirt Willapa's scenic marshy shoreline, and tree farms carpet the surrounding hills. This is timber country. A handful of small settlements—notably Raymond and South Bend—offer accommodations and meals.

Sights and Recreation

The crimson crush of cranberry bogs is this quiet region's biggest claim to fame. Visitors can get a roadside tour of the local crop along the aptly named Cranberry Road, as well as Larkin and Turkey Roads. If the tour sparks your interest and you plan on driving farther south, be sure to check out the **Cranberry Museum** on the Long Beach Peninsula.

A mile south of Grayland on Highway 105, **Grayland Beach State Park** (off Midway Beach Rd., 888/226-7688, www.parks .wa.gov) has 7,450 feet of ocean frontage, 200 acres for picnicking and camping, and a self-guided nature trail through huckleberry, Sitka spruce, and lodgepole pine. This is a popular place to dig for clams.

Hikers and cyclists will enjoy the 3.5-mile **Rails to Trails** paved path that follows the river from Raymond to South Bend. Along the way, look for the historic *Krestine*, a majestic, 100-foot sailing ship that plied the North Sea waters for many years. Follow the signs up the hill to the **Pacific County Courthouse,** built in 1910 and covered by an immense, multicolored stained-glass dome over mosaic-tile flooring. This "gilded palace of reckless extravagance" as it was called, was built at the then-extravagant cost of $132,000, but not everything is as it appears: the marble columns are actually concrete painted to look like marble.

Entertainment and Events

The third weekend of March, Grayland-area artists display their driftwood and shell creations at the town's **Beachcombers Driftwood Show.** The **Fourth of July** means a big fireworks display over Booming Bay, and a fun run, arts and crafts, and food booths in Grayland. Early October brings the **Cranberry Harvest Festival** with bog tours, a cranberry cook-off, parade, and dancing.

For some day-to-day excitement, try your luck at **Shoalwater Bay Bingo and Casino** (at the Hwy. 105 turnoff to Tokeland, 360/267-2048 or 888/332-2048, www.shoalwaterbay casino.com).

Accommodations

Check into **Grayland Motel & Cottages** (2013 Hwy. 105, 360/267-2395 or 800/292-0845, http://westportwa.com/graylandmotel, $55–93 s or d) and you'll be able to walk out your door to the beach. This family- and pet-friendly facility has a play area for kids and dogs. It also offers complimentary clam guns and shovels to its guests, plus a sink outside to clean them once you catch them.

Or try **Grayland B&B** (1678 Hwy. 105, 360/267-6026, $110 s or d) for a homier atmosphere. The proprietors let out two bedrooms with a shared bath in a two-story home built in the 1930s.

A focal point in Tokeland is the wonderfully old-fashioned **Tokeland Hotel** (Kindred Rd. and Hotel Rd., 360/267-7006, www.tokelandhotel.com, $55 s, $65 d). Built as a home in 1885, it became an inn in 1899 and is now on the National Register. The hotel and town are named for Chief Toke, whose daughter married a worker at the lifesaving station here. Together they built a home that was later turned into the Tokeland Hotel. Now on the National Register of Historic Places, it's said to be the oldest resort hotel in Washington, and the spacious front lawn, brick fireplace, and jigsaw puzzles provide an air of relaxation. The restored hotel has upstairs rooms with bath down the hall; reserve several weeks ahead for summer weekend stays. The restaurant, in an open dining room overlooking Willapa Bay, serves three meals a day, specializing in reasonably priced seafood ($10–15 entrées).

The Russell House B&B (902 E. Water St., 360/875-5608 or 888/484-6907, www.russellhousebb.com, $75–145 s or d) is a beautiful antique-filled Victorian mansion with views of Willapa Bay. The four guest rooms have private or shared baths, a full breakfast is served, and kids are accepted.

CAMPING

Grayland Beach also has 60 campsites, all with shower access and hookups for $20 ($7 extra for reservations), and is open year-round.

Park RVs at the well-maintained **Kenanna RV Park** (2959 S. Hwy. 105, 360/267-3515 or 800/867-3515, www.kenannarv.com, $25 full hookups, $15 tent).

Camp along the bay at **Bruceport County Park** (five mi. northeast of South Bend on Hwy. 101, 360/875-6611, $10–13 tent, $21 full hookups). Camping and great views across the bay are available nearby at **Bush Pioneer County Park** (2nd and Park, Bay Center, open summers only).

Food

Both Grayland and Tokeland are pretty quiet settlements. It makes for nice little getaways, but the drawback is there aren't a whole lot of restaurant options. Most days of the week you can nosh on the comestibles served up at **Mutineer Restaurant** (2120 Hwy. 105, Grayland, 360/267-2077, 8 A.M.–8 P.M. Thurs.–Mon.), which serves all three meals. If you stop by for lunch or dinner, be sure to try some clam chowder.

For those serious about their seafood, head to **Nelson Crab, Inc.** (3088 Kindred Ave., Tokeland, 360/267-2911, 9 A.M.–5 P.M. daily) for fresh-cooked crab and other seafood for picnics and cookouts.

The Boondocks Restaurant (1015 W. Robert Bush Dr., 360/875-5155 or 800/875-5158) is *the* place to eat in South Bend. The specialty, not surprisingly, is oysters, and for breakfast (served anytime) you'll get "hangtown fry," fresh pan-fried Willapa oysters. Also featured are seafood quiche, pastas, veal, and fresh fish.

Information

The small **Cranberry Coast Chamber of Commerce** (2190 Hwy. 105, 360/267-2003 or 800/473-6018, www.cranberrycoast.com) is next to Grandma's Treasure Chest store.

Get information about Raymond and South Bend at the **Raymond Chamber of Commerce** (415 Commercial St., 360/942-5419, http://visit.willapabay.org, 11 A.M.–9 P.M. daily).

Getting There

Grays Harbor Transit (360/532-2770 or 800/562-9730, www.ghtransit.com) provides daily bus service throughout the county, including Westport, Aberdeen, Lake Quinault, and Ocean Shores.

Long Beach Peninsula

The Long Beach Peninsula is a 28-mile-long strip of sand and fun off the southwestern corner of Washington. Locals call it the "World's Longest Beach," though you're bound to hear disagreement from folks in Australia and New Zealand. Be that as it may, this is one *very* long stretch of sand, and a favorite getaway for folks from Seattle and Portland.

The peninsula is the kind of place where you'll find driftwood decorating the shelves and rubber boots on the porch of every weather-washed cottage. It rains over 70 inches a year here, so be ready to get wet even in the summer.

The central tourist and commercial town on the island, the town of Long Beach sports the most walkable downtown village on the coast, with little shops and restaurants. As you venture to the north end of the peninsula you'll find beautifully restored century-old homes in Oysterville, and an isolated natural area at Leadbetter Point.

SIGHTS
◖ Cape Disappointment State Park

Ignore the name—Cape Disappointment State Park (360/642-3078, www.parks.wa.gov) is anything but a letdown. Arguably the most scenic state park in Washington, this 1,882-acre recreational retreat offers dramatic vistas across the mouth of the Columbia River, old-growth forests, incredible fishing, century-old military fortifications, historic lighthouses, and an impressive museum dedicated to Lewis and Clark.

This is the spot where Meriwether Lewis and William Clark stood in November of 1805, finally having "reached the great Pacific Ocean which we been so long anxious to See." Because game proved scarce and this side of the Columbia lacked protection from winter storms, they crossed the river to build a winter camp called Fort Clatsop near present-day Astoria, Oregon. The fascinating museum

© ANATOLIY LUKICH/123RF.COM

Cape Disappointment Lighthouse

WHAT A LETDOWN

Located at Washington's southernmost point, **Cape Disappointment** earned its name in 1788 from British fur trader John Meares, who was searching for the fabled Northwest Passage. He had heard tales of an enormous river near here from a Spanish description written in 1775. Meares never found the river, and certainly didn't find the Passage. The mighty river is surprisingly easy to miss from the sea and even Captain George Vancouver sailed right past it. The river wasn't officially "discovered" until 1792, when American Capt. Robert Gray sailed his *Columbia Rediviva* into the colossal disappointment of a river mouth.

at **Lewis and Clark Interpretive Center** (360/642-3029, 10 A.M.–5 P.M. daily) honors the famous duo and is one of the must-see places on Long Beach Peninsula. The interpretive center has enormous windows with expansive views of Cape Disappointment Lighthouse, the Columbia River, and the mighty Pacific.

You can see the mouth of the Columbia by turning right at the concession area and driving to the road's end; park here and walk through the sand to the lookout atop North Jetty. **Cape Disappointment Lighthouse** is the Northwest's oldest, built in 1856; follow the quarter-mile trail from the interpretive center or a steep quarter-mile path from the Coast Guard Station.

The commanding presence and strategic location of Cape Disappointment made it a vital fort location for the new Oregon Territory. The initial cannons arrived in 1862, and **Fort Canby** went on to protect the mouth of the Columbia for 95 years. Many of the old bunkers and gun emplacements remain, making for interesting explorations.

Ilwaco

Historic Ilwaco (ill-WOK-o) is a charter, sports,

and commercial fishing town on the south end of the Long Beach Peninsula, with docks on protected Baker Bay. The town was named for a Chinook leader, Chief Elowahka Jim. Walk around town to find five murals on the sides of local businesses, and some wonderful old buildings. Ilwaco's old Fire Station No. 1 on Lake Street contains the "Mankiller," an 1846 hand-pumper that was the first fire-fighting apparatus of its kind in Washington Territory. You can view the Mankiller through a window when the building isn't open. Just north of Ilwaco is a pullout along scenic Black Lake; paddleboats are available for rent here in the summer (360/642-3003).

Visit the excellent **Ilwaco Heritage Museum** (115 SE Lake St., 360/642-3446, 9 A.M.–5 P.M. Mon.–Sat., noon–4 P.M. Sun. in summer, 9 A.M.–4 P.M. Mon.–Sat. fall–spring) for a look into Pacific Coast history via models, Native American exhibits, and photographs of early settlers' fishing, oystering, and logging methods, along with Cape Disappointment shipwrecks and rescues. Of particular interest is a detailed scale model of the Columbia River estuary, and a display on the *Sector* ($3 adults, $2.50 seniors, $1 children under 12), a 26-foot boat that Gérard D'Aboville rowed from Japan to Ilwaco in 1991.

Washington State Parks conducts tours of historic **Colbert House** (360/642-3078, $1) at the corner of Spruce and Quaker Streets daily in the summer.

Long Beach

Long Beach makes up the commercial core of the peninsula, with all the typical beachfront services, including kitschy gift shops, fish-and-chips takeouts, real estate offices, kite stores, saltwater taffy shops, strip malls, RV parks, motels, and bumper boat, go-kart, and miniature golf amusement parks. Not everything is tacky, but don't come here expecting a classy, romantic experience; this is a family fun-for-all place. In the summer Long Beach hums with traffic and the ringing of cash registers; in winter it slows to a quieter pace but is still popular as a weekend getaway.

Several fine murals grace the sides of buildings in Long Beach. One of the peninsula's most photographed local spots is the **"World's Longest Beach" arch** that rises over Bolsted Street as you head toward the ocean. An elevated and wheelchair-accessible **boardwalk** takes off from here and continues a half mile south to 10th Street; it's a great place for romantic sunset strolls. The gravel **Dune Trail** extends for two miles across the dunes, from 17th Street S to 16th Street N, and is popular with cyclists and hikers.

A cautionary note: Contrary to expectations, the 28 miles of sandy beach on Long Beach Peninsula are not safe for swimming. Not only are there dangerous undertows and riptides, but rogue waves can occur, and there are no lifeguards. Every year waders or swimmers get trapped in these bitterly cold waters. Locals looking for a swim generally head to Waikiki Beach.

WORLD KITE MUSEUM

Befitting its beachside location, Long Beach is home to the World Kite Museum and Hall of Fame (3rd St. NW and Pacific Hwy., 360/642-4020, www.worldkitemuseum.com, 11 A.M.–5 P.M. daily May.–Sept., 11 A.M.–5 P.M. Fri.–Mon. Oct.–Apr., $5 adults, $4 seniors, $3 children). Inside, you'll learn the history of kites and how they were used during wartime and in developing airplanes. Also here are kites from around the globe, a re-created Japanese kite artist workshop, and a gift shop. The museum offers kite-making workshops the first Saturday of the month May–August.

CRANBERRY ATTRACTIONS

Around 600 acres of cranberries are grown in the Long Beach Peninsula area, and you're bound to see them growing along Highway 101 as you approach the peninsula. Cranberries were originally called "crane berries" by early settlers who thought the blossoms resembled cranes' heads. Ocean Spray Cranberries, Inc. has a processing plant on Sandridge Road in Long Beach, and a second one in Westport. **Anna Lena's Pantry** (111 Balstad Ave., Long Beach, 360/642-8948 or 800/272-6237, 10 A.M.–5 P.M. Mon.–Thurs., 10 A.M.–5:30 P.M. Fri.–Sat., 10 A.M.–4 P.M. Sun.) sells locally made cranberry products.

About a mile northeast of Long Beach is the **Cranberry Museum & Gift Shop** (Pioneer Rd., 360/642-5553, 10 A.M.–5 P.M. Fri.–Sun. May–mid-Dec., free). Operated jointly by the University of Washington and the Pacific Coast Cranberry Research Foundation, the museum shows old and new ways of growing and harvesting cranberries. Visitors can walk the adjacent 10-acre demonstration cranberry bog at any time to learn about this unique crop. Try to time your visit for June, the peak bloom season, or October, to see the harvest.

Ocean Park

Once the Pacific Highway (aka Highway 103) exits the north end of hectic Long Beach, you are suddenly in an almost flat landscape of lodgepole pine trees and scattered summer and retirement homes. You can't see the ocean or Willapa Bay from here, but there are access points all along the way, including at Klipsan Beach. After 11 miles of this, the highway widens into the sedate town of Ocean Park. Stop on the south side of 256th just west of Highway 103 to see the **Wreckage,** a unique house constructed in 1912 from logs salvaged after a storm broke apart a raft of logs being towed off the coast.

Loomis Lake State Park (south of Klipsan Beach) has picnic tables on the ocean, not the lake; the real Loomis Lake is about a quarter mile north.

◖ Willapa Bay

No matter which way you shuck it, the truth is that the Willapa Bay towns of Nahcotta and Oysterville are quite literally defined by the slurpy sweet meat of the mollusk of love. The latter's name says it all, while the former's namesake is Chief Nahcati, the Chinook leader who first clued the white man into the oystery bounty of the bay.

The oyster beds are closed to the public, but interpretive signs next to Nahcotta's Willapa Bay

Field Station explain local ecology and the lives of shellfish. **Willapa Bay Interpretive Center** (south side of the Port of Peninsula breakwater, Nahcotta, 360/665-4547, www.opwa.com/interp, 10 A.M.–3 P.M. Fri.–Sun. late May–mid-Oct.) displays exhibits on the oyster industry and the natural history of Willapa Bay.

You can purchase fresh oysters and other seafood in Nahcotta at **Wiegart Brothers Oyster Co., Bendiksen's East Point Seafood Co.,** or the smaller **Hilton's Coast Oyster Company.** Or stop at **Oysterville Sea Farms** (360/665-6585, www.oysterville.net) for fresh or smoked oysters and clams.

A number of homes constructed during the town of Oysterville's heyday have been restored and are now part of the **Oysterville National Historic District.** For a self-guided walking tour map, visit the beautiful white-and-red **Oysterville Baptist Church,** built in 1892. On Sunday afternoons in summer the church comes alive with vespers programs featuring an ecumenical mix of secular and religious music.

Further south, the historic homes make way for natural beauty, with much of the southeastern shore preserved within the **Willapa National Wildlife Refuge.** Refuge headquarters are about 10 miles north of Seaview along 101, near mile marker 24. Here you can meander along an interpretive art trail and keep on the lookout for deer, elk, and spawning salmon in pristine streams.

ENTERTAINMENT AND EVENTS
Nightlife
Every Saturday all summer long, you'll find free concerts in Long Beach's downtown gazebo. Seaview's **Sou'wester Lodge** (360/642-2542) often has concerts, lectures, or poetry on Saturday nights. During the summer and fall, **Nick's West** (1700 Pacific Ave. S, 360/642-5100) has country or rock bands on the weekends.

Festivals and Events
In April, come to Long Beach for the **Ragtime**

Rhodie Dixieland Jazz Festival. Then comes Ocean Park's **Garlic Festival,** held the third weekend of June, which features garlic shucking and garlic eating contests, plus all sorts of garlicky meals. Bring a couple of bottles of Listerine along. Long Beach hosts the annual 4th of July **Fireworks on the Beach,** and Ocean Park has a popular **Street Fair** the same weekend. Then comes **Sandsations Sand Sculptures** at the end of the month.

The year's biggest event, the **Washington State International Kite Festival** (www.kitefestival.com) lasts the entire third week of August and draws well over 200,000 spectators and participants. This is the largest kite festival in the western hemisphere, and every day brings a different contest, ending with Sunday's grand finale in which the sky teems with upwards of 4,000 kites of all sorts. The world record for keeping a kite aloft (over 180 hours) was set here in 1982.

Ocean Park hosts an enormously popular classic car show, the **Rod Run to the End of the World,** on the second weekend of September that ends with a 15-mile-long parade. The annual **Cranberrian Fair,** held in Ilwaco in mid-October, celebrates more than a century of coastal cranberry farming. Bog tours give you the chance to see the flooded fields with thousands of floating berries awaiting harvest. It's followed the third weekend of October by **Water Music Festival,** with chamber music concerts all over the peninsula.

SHOPPING
It may be campy, but you definitely don't want to miss **Marsh's Free Museum** (409 S. Pacific Ave., 360/642-2188, www.marsh freemuseum.com), a huge souvenir shop in downtown Long Beach. Inside is a delightful collection of the tasteless and bizarre, much of it from old amusement parks, traveling shows, and attics. You'll find an impressive collection of glass fishing balls, the world's largest frying pan, a vampire bat skeleton, an old bottle with a human tapeworm, a gruesome photo of a 1920 triple hanging, and a two-headed calf. Drop a nickel for a flapper-era peep show, pay a

dime to test your passion factor on the "throne of love," or search the jam-packed shelves for a stupid postcard, goofy T-shirt, cheap trinket, or bright seashell. Oh, and you won't want to miss "Jake the Alligator Man," stuck in a back corner inside a glass aquarium; he once starred in that arbiter of tabloid discernment, the *Weekly World News.* If you like kitsch, you'll rate this as Washington's finest gift shop! Out front of Marsh's is a small climbing wall ($5 per climb).

The Long Beach Peninsula is one of the best places in Washington for kite flying. Pick up kites, string, supplies, and advice at **Above It All Kites** (312 Pacific Blvd. S, Long Beach, 360/642-3541, www.aboveitallkites.com, daily 9 A.M.–5 P.M.).

Wiegardt Studio Gallery (2607 Bay Ave., 360/665-5976, www.ericwiegardt.com, 11 A.M.–4 P.M. Mon.–Fri., 11 A.M.–5 P.M. Sat. July–Aug., 11 A.M.–4 P.M. Fri., 11 A.M.–5 P.M. Sat. Sept.–June) contains the watercolor works of Eric Wiegardt, one of several respected local artists. Wiegardt runs numerous art workshops throughout the year, so be sure to check the website for the schedule during your trip.

Shoalwater Cove Gallery (1401 Bay Ave., 360/665-4382, www.shoalwatercove.com, 11 A.M.–5 P.M. daily spring–fall, winter hours vary) has beautifully detailed pastels by Marie Powell.

SPORTS AND RECREATION
Cape Disappointment State Park
North Head Lighthouse was built in 1898 and stands above Dead Man's Hollow, named for the sailors of the ill-fated *Vandelia,* which sank here in 1853. The lighthouse is no longer used; today marine lanterns shine out instead from North Head. The lighthouse is a short walk through the trees from the upper parking lot, or a two-mile hike from McKenzie Head (just west of the campground). **Lighthouse tours** (360/642-3078, $1) are given daily during the summer. To the south are the dunes and driftwood piles of **Benson Beach** (no vehicles allowed), with Long Beach pointing its finger northward. **West Wind Trail** leads a mile north

from the lighthouse through the old-growth forests to Beards Hollow. From there you can continue along the beach all the way to the town of Long Beach, four miles away.

North Head is a favorite place to watch for migrating gray whales heading north March–May or south late December–early February. It's also an awe-inspiring place during winter storms when waves pound hard against the rocks below.

Tiny **Waikiki Beach** is a favorite local spot for picnics and swimming in the summer (no lifeguard is present). The beach received its name when a Hawaiian sailor's body washed ashore here after his ship was wrecked in a failed attempt to cross the Columbia River bar in 1811. You can follow a trail uphill from Waikiki to the Lewis and Clark Interpretive Center, and then on to Cape Disappointment Lighthouse.

For a taste of old-growth forests, take the 1.5-mile **Coastal Forest Trail** that begins at the boat ramp along Baker Bay. This is a very enjoyable loop hike.

Leadbetter Point State Park
The northern tip of Long Beach Peninsula is capped by two publicly owned natural areas, Leadbetter Point State Park, and a portion of the Willapa National Wildlife Refuge. Leadbetter has a 1.5-mile trail through the evergreen forest, connecting both parking lots. From the north lot, you can enter Willapa and walk through stunted lodgepole pine forests to beachgrass-covered sand dunes along the Pacific Ocean, or head down to the shore of Willapa Bay for a beach walk. The northern end of Willapa National Wildlife Refuge is closed to all entry April–August to protect the threatened snowy plover that nests on the dunes here. This area is also a very important sanctuary for waterfowl, particularly during spring and fall migrations. Bird-watchers will see thousands (and sometimes hundreds of thousands) of black brant, Canada geese, dunlin, plovers, sandpipers, and other birds in the marshes and beaches during these times. No fires or camping are allowed.

Kite Flying

Long Beach is best known for its delightful beach, a favorite of kite enthusiasts. If you don't own a kite, several local shops sell them for all levels of flying ability.

Fishing and Boating

Ilwaco is home to the peninsula's fishing fleet. Some of the more popular excursion companies include **Sea Breeze Charters** (185 Howerton Way SE, 360/642-2300, www.seabreeze charters.net) and **Pacific Salmon Charters** (191 Howerton Way, 360/642-3466, www .pacificsalmoncharters.com), both of which lead deep-sea fishing trips off the coast for rockfish, flounder, sole, lingcod, salmon, and sometimes albacore tuna. They also lead river trips for those in hope of hooking salmon and the Columbia River's mighty sturgeon.

Or stay on shore to fish: more than 230 ships were wrecked or sunk on the Columbia bar before jetties were constructed to control the sand. The longest of these is **North Jetty** at Cape Disappointment State Park, which reaches a half mile out from the end of the cape and is a popular place to fish for salmon, rock cod, perch, and sea bass.

Clamming is a popular pastime on the sandy stretches of Long Beach. All it takes is a bucket and a shovel, but clam guns can help the success rate. Most people have the best luck about an hour before low tide. Check the Washington State Department of Fish and Wildlife's website (www.wdfw.wa.gov) for information on clamming and fishing seasons and to buy licenses. You can also pick up licenses, fishing tackle, and clamming gear at **Ed's Bait and Tackle** (207 2nd Ave. SW, Ilwaco, 360/642-2248).

Use the boat ramp at the Willapa National Wildlife Refuge to push off toward **Long Island,** a protected, old-forest-covered island accessible only by boat. The muddy tide flats and rich salt grass marshes ringing the island are important resting and feeding areas for migratory waterfowl, and Roosevelt elk frequently swim their way over to graze here. A 0.75-mile trail meanders through an ancient grove of enormous cedars that's carpeted with lush mosses, and the island has five primitive campgrounds that often fill up on summer weekends (bring your own water, no reservations). The paddle to the southern tip of the island is only about a quarter of a mile, but navigation can be tough due to tidal fluctuations—during low tide, you can practically walk out to it.

Bike and Moped Rentals

Rent mopeds, bikes, and surreys from **Long Beach Moped** (Sid Snyder Dr., just west of the stoplight at Pacific Hwy. 103, 360/289-3830, 9 A.M.–dark daily Memorial Day–mid-Sept., 9 A.M.–dark Fri.–Sun. the rest of the year).

Horseback Riding

Horse enthusiasts can participate in guided beach rides offered by **Skipper's Equestrian Center** (S Blvd. and 10th St., 360/642-3676, $25 per hour) or **Back Country Wilderness Outfitters** (10th St. S, Long Beach, 360/642-2576, www.backcountryoutfit.com, $20 per hour).

Golf

Two local golf courses are open to the public: **Peninsula Golf Course** (Long Beach, 360/642-2828) and **Surfside Golf Course** (north of Ocean Park, 360/665-4148).

ACCOMMODATIONS

Lodging can be hard to come by on summer weekends, especially during the big festivals. Many rooms are booked a year ahead for Memorial Day weekend, the International Kite Festival in August, and Labor Day weekend. It's a good idea to reserve 2–4 weeks ahead for other summer weekends.

Ilwaco

In Ilwaco, **Heidi's Inn** (126 Spruce St., 360/642-2387 or 800/576-1032, $79–99 s or d) is a tidy, simple little motel that accepts pets.

Owned by the same folks who run the Shelburne Inn in Seaview, **China Beach Retreat** (222 Capt. Robert Grey Dr., Ilwaco,

360/642-5660 or 360/642-2442, www.china beachretreat.com, $215–245) is a lovely 1907 house set amidst an orchard near the mouth of Columbia River. The house is beautifully decorated.

History buffs can stay in one of three historic three-bedroom **Lighthouse Keeper's Residences** (360/642-3078) at Cape Disappointment State Park). The head lighthouse keeper's residence ($377) offers the best views of the lighthouse and the mouth of the Columbia, and assistant lighthouse keepers' residences ($267) are nearby. All homes sleep six and feature fully equipped kitchens and living rooms with TVs and DVD players.

Long Beach

Equipped with a hot tub, sauna, and a small fitness center, **Our Place at the Beach** (1309 S. Ocean Beach Blvd., Long Beach, 360/642-3793 or 800/538-5107, www.willapabay .org/~opatb, $52–67 d) has 23 rooms, many with ocean views, each with a fridge. Two larger cabins are also available.

About a mile north of downtown, **The Breakers** (Hwy. 103 and 26th St., 360/642-4414 or 800/219-9833, www.breakerslong beach.com, $119–139 s or d) offers pretty standard motel rooms, plus spacious one- or two-bedroom suites with kitchens ($179–278) for up to four. Amenities include an indoor pool, sauna, and hot tub.

Anchorage Cottages (2209 N. Boulevard St., Long Beach, 360/642-2351 or 800/642-2351, www.theanchoragecottages.com, $80–128) provides beachside units with either one or two bedrooms, most with fireplaces, as well as more spacious two-bedroom cottages with fireplaces. All units have fully equipped kitchens.

There are also several B&Bs right in town. Set within a contemporary home, **A Rendezvous Place Bed and Breakfast** (1610 California Ave. S, Long Beach, 360/642-8877 or 866/642-8877, www.rendezvousplace.com, $129–169 d, suite $219) is one of the rare bed-and-breakfasts that doesn't have so many antiques that you feel like you're in a mausoleum or fear you're going to break something expensive. Rooms are comfy and nicely decorated, and outside there is a hot tub and deck overlooking the private backyard.

Another option is **Boreas B&B** (607 N. Boulevard St., 360/642-8069 or 888/642-8069, www.boreasinn.com, $160–179 s or d), a quiet and cozy 1920s beachfront home with airy and light-colored interiors and an enclosed sundeck with a hot tub. The four guest rooms have shared or private baths. The proprietors also rent out a family- and pet-friendly cottage next door.

Seaview

The oldest continuously used lodging in Washington, Seaview's acclaimed **C Shelburne Inn** (4415 Pacific Way, 360/642-2442 or 800/466-1896, www.shelburneinn .com, $139–199 d) sits within an elegant 1896 Victorian building. The inn is packed with tasteful antiques, stained-glass windows (from an old English church), and original artwork. TVs would be jarring in such a quaint little place, so don't expect to tune in during your stay. A full country breakfast is included; for many, it's the highlight of their stay. The inn is, however, located just a few feet from busy Pacific Highway, and roadside rooms can be quite noisy. Also beware of the ghost who is rumored to wander the third floor some nights.

But if you want a friendly place with a funky sense of nostalgia, character, and charm, look no farther than Seaview's **C Sou'wester Lodge** (38th Pl., 360/642-2542, www.sou westerlodge.com). Here, literary owners Leonard and Miriam Atkins have created a rustic and offbeat haven for those who appreciate simple comforts. The accommodations include "Bed and Make Your Own Damn Breakfast" rooms in the stately three-story lodge ($119–199 d) built in 1892 as a summer estate by Henry Winslow Corbett, a wealthy timber baron, banker, and U.S. senator from Oregon. Outside are weathered beach cottages ($129–139 d) furnished in "early Salvation Army" decor, and even a hodgepodge of 1950s-era trailers ($69–179 d). Tent and RV space are also available. Artists and writers often "book in" for months at a time, relaxing in this cozy and informal lodge. On many Saturday nights, the sitting room comes to life with lectures, concerts, or poetry. You're likely to find everything from chamber music to discussions on Sufism.

Ocean Park

Next to a small pond frequented by ducks and the occasional blue heron is **Shakti Cove Cottages** (1204 253rd Pl., Ocean Park, 360/665-4000, www.shakticove.com, $80–90 d) with 10 cabins nestled in a grove of trees.

Covered in sea-salt-weathered clapboard, **Klipsan Beach Cottages** (22617 Pacific Hwy., Ocean Park, 360/665-4888, www .klipsanbeachcottages.com, $130 d, $155 for four, $215 for six) are comfortable older cottages with kitchens and ocean views. This is a quaint place with a lovely meadow on one side and a row of tall pine trees on the other, 200 yards from the beach.

The modern Victorian-style **Caswell's on the Bay B&B** (25204 Sandridge Rd., Ocean Park, 360/665-6535, www.caswellsinn.com, $160–210) offers friendly and comfortable accommodations facing Willapa Bay. This is a quiet and relaxing place on a three-acre spread. Five guest rooms are furnished with antiques and private baths.

Camping

Cape Disappointment (888/226-7688, www .parks.wa.gov) is one of the most popular places to camp in Washington, welcoming tent ($22) and RV ($31 with full hookups) campers, plus groups of four or less seeking shelter in its permanent yurts ($50 up to six). If you need to clean up, there are coin-operated showers on premises. The campground—within a few yards of beautiful Benson Beach—is open all year.

Great camping for tents or RVs can be had at Cape Disappointment, and RVers will find more than 20 different parking lot/campgrounds along the Long Beach Peninsula. Get a complete listing at the visitors center,

or just drive along Pacific Highway until one looks acceptable. For unbeatable oceanfront access, **Andersen's RV Park** (1400 138th St., Long Beach, 360/642-2231 or 800/645-6795, www.andersensrv.com, $45 oceanfront with full hookups, $35 regular full hookups) is the way to go. This dog-friendly park is just a few yards from the sand and surf—grab a fishing pole and tromp through the dune trail to spend the day fishing. There's even a fish- and clam-cleaning station on the property. Facilities also include hot showers and wireless Internet. There are no open fire pits, to preserve the dune grasses, but guests can rent enclosed fire containers ($6/day). Another well-maintained and friendly option, **Driftwood RV Park** (1512 N. Pacific Hwy., 360/642-2711 or 888/567-1902, www.driftwood-rvpark.com, $36 with full hookups) offers grassy sites with lots of space to unwind. Rent a clam gun here to take out to the beach and then use the clam- and fish-cleaning station on premises.

FOOD

Long Beach

In downtown Long Beach, **◖ Cottage Bakery** (118 S. Pacific Ave., 360/642-4441, 4 A.M.–6 P.M. daily) has cabinets filled with sticky-sweet old-fashioned pastries. It's a favorite place for a coffee and dessert while watching the people stroll by.

Dooger's Seafood & Grill (900 Pacific Ave. S, Long Beach, 360/642-4224, daily 11 A.M.–9 P.M.) is a bit formulaic, but it is one of the best seafood restaurants in town, with brags about its sourdough bowls full of homemade clam chowder, fish and chips, pan fried oysters, and salads with fresh bay shrimp.

The kiddies will appreciate the pirate-themed **Castaways Seafood Grill** (208 Pacific Ave. S, 360/642-4745, www.castawaysseafoodgrille .com), a lively seafood eatery with loads of golden-fried fishies, plus burgers, sandwiches, and salads.

Corral Drive-In (2506 Pacific Ave. N, 360/642-2774, 11 A.M.–7 P.M. Mon.–Fri., 11 A.M.–8 P.M. Sat.–Sun.) is another very family-friendly joint. This place is known 'round

Washington as the home of the pie-tin sized Tsunami burger—a beast of a sandwich that can literally feed six people. Get the napkins ready, because it sure is messy!

For beef Philly-style, saunter over to **Surfer Sands** (1113 Pacific Ave. S, Long Beach, 360/642-7873, 10 A.M.–5 P.M. Sat.–Thurs., 10 A.M.–7 P.M. Fri.), a roadside stand that specializes in ooey-gooey cheese steaks. Summer brings variable extended hours—call ahead.

Seaview

Two Seaview restaurants vie for the breakfast crowds. **Laurie's Homestead Breakfast House** (4214 Pacific Hwy., 360/642-7171, 6:30 A.M.–1 P.M. daily) has a seven-page breakfast menu and very good food. Across the street is **Cheri Walker's 42nd St. Café** (360/642-2323, 8 A.M.–2 P.M. Thurs.–Mon., 9 A.M.–2 P.M. Tues. and 4:30–8:30 P.M. Sun.–Thurs., 4:30–9 P.M. Fri.–Sat.) with traditional American breakfasts, lunches, and dinners. The restaurant features iron-skillet fried chicken, pot roast, steaks, and seafood, with homemade bread and jam, all served in heaping helpings.

Chico's Pizza (Hwy. 103, right near Sid's Market, Seaview, 360/642-3207) makes tasty pizzas and pastas.

Seaview is also home to one of the peninsula's finest dining options, **The Depot** (38th & L, Seaview, 360/642-7880). Cozied up inside of a restored train station, this creative café plates inventive dishes like grilled wild boar on mashed fava beans and house-made cannelloni stuffed with fresh crab and saffron béchamel sauce.

Ocean Park

The Dunes Restaurant (1507 Bay Ave., Ocean Park, 360/665-6677, 7 A.M.–8 P.M. Sun.–Thurs., 7 A.M.–9 P.M. Fri.–Sat.) serves fresh fish, clam chowder, and Saturday night prime rib. Another good spot to nibble on seafood is **Pilot House Restaurant and Lounge** (1201 West Bay Ave., 360/665-3800, 6:30 A.M.–8 P.M. Sun.–Thurs., 6:30 A.M.–9 P.M. Fri.–Sat.), which serves steaks and pastas along with an ocean view. This is also a convenient

spot for country-style breakfasts. In the same building above Pilot House, **Luigi's** (1201 Bay Ave., 360/665-3174, 5–8 P.M. Sun.–Thurs., 4–8 P.M. Fri.–Sat.) bakes up pizza and other Italian classics in a casual setting.

INFORMATION AND SERVICES

Get information at the **Long Beach Peninsula Visitors Bureau** (at the junction of Hwys. 101 and 103, 360/642-2400 or 800/451-2542, www.funbeach.com, 9 A.M.–5 P.M. Mon.–Sat. and 9 A.M.–4 P.M. Sun. in summer, 9 A.M.–4 P.M. Mon.–Sat. fall–spring). Call **Long Beach Info-Line** (800/835-8846) for a recording of current activities, festivals, fun things to do, B&Bs, and more.

The two local **public libraries** are in Ilwaco (158 1st Ave. N, 360/642-3908) and in Ocean Park (1308 256th Pl., 360/665-4184).

GETTING THERE AND AROUND

The Long Beach Peninsula is divided by two parallel main roads: Highway 103, going through the commercial centers on the ocean side, and Sandridge Road, passing the largely residential sections on the bay side. The roads intersect at Oysterville, where only one road continues to Leadbetter Point.

Pacific Transit System (360/642-9418 or 800/642-9418, Mon.–Sat.) has countywide bus service, and dial-a-ride service in certain areas. The system connects with Grays Harbor Transit buses in Aberdeen, and also crosses the bridge to Astoria, Oregon. There is no Greyhound service to the area, and the nearest airport with commercial service is in Astoria. For taxi service, call **Limo Cab** (360/642-4047).

Approximately 15 miles of Long Beach are open to driving during the summer, but stay on the hard-packed sand, away from the car-eating soft sand and rich clam beds along the water's edge. The sand dunes are off-limits to all vehicles. The maximum speed is 25 mph, and it *is* enforced. Check at the visitors center for a current description of areas open to beach driving.

Lower Columbia River

The twin blue-collar cities of Longview and Kelso are at the nexus of I-5 and the Lower Columbia River. This freeway stopover has a long history in fishing and timber, and is a portal to the Columbia River mouth and the Long Beach Peninsula, 70 miles to the east. Sitting approximately 40 miles north of Portland and just 11 miles south of the Spirit Lake Highway turnoff, it is also a gateway to the City of Roses and Mount St. Helens.

Most tourists heading from I-5 in Longview and Kelso choose to rumble along the lower Columbia River from the southern Oregon side in order to reach the Long Beach Peninsula. The route along Highway 30 is faster, and it allows visitors to stop off in the unique outpost of **Astoria, Oregon,** before heading over the 4.4-mile Astoria-Megler Bridge, the longest continuous-truss span bridge on the continent.

On the Washington side of the Columbia River, Highway 4 hugs the riverbank for long stretches. This is the road less traveled. Tall cottonwood trees line the riverbanks; high rocky cliffs and Douglas fir trees line the slopes above the highway.

LONGVIEW AND KELSO
Sights

The beautiful **Lake Sacajawea Park** bisects Longview along Nichols Boulevard with a string of serene lakes surrounded by grassy hillsides, shady trees, and a gravel jogging/cycling path.

R. A. Long Park (aka Civic Center) is a grassy green in the city's core, at the intersection of Olympia and Washington Ways. Surrounding the green are many of the city's oldest buildings, including the wonderful red-brick **public library** donated by the town's founder and finished in 1926.

Just up Olympia Way from the Civic Center, the **Nutty Narrows** (600 Louisiana St.) is the

© GINO RIGUCCI/123RF.COM

A cargo ship glides under the Astoria-Megler Bridge on the Columbia River.

OLYMPIC PENINSULA

world's only sky bridge for squirrels. Builder and developer Amos J. Peters built it in 1963 to save the critters as they attempted to cross the busy street. Peters is honored for his effort with a many-times-greater-than-life-size squirrel sculpture between the library and sky bridge.

Visit the **Cowlitz County Historical Museum** (405 Allen St., Kelso, 360/577-3119, www.co.cowlitz.wa.us/museum, 9 A.M.–5 P.M. Tues.–Sat., 1–5 P.M. Sun.) to see well-presented Chinook and Cowlitz artifacts, a cabin from 1884, historic photos from the heyday of logging, and changing exhibits.

Entertainment and Events

The **Columbia Theatre** (1231 Vandercook Way, 360/423-1011), a legacy from the prosperous 1920s, hosts local theater and dance groups as well as national acts. The **Southwest Washington Symphony** (360/425-5346) gives performances there November–April. During July and August, music lovers head to Lake Sacajawea for free Sunday **concerts in the park** featuring everything from tuba fests to country-western bands.

In late June, the **Cowlitz River Canoe Race** is a fast 14-mile river run that starts in Castle Rock and pulls out at Kelso. The Independence Day **Go 4th Celebration** is said to be one of the largest in the country, with a parade, logging show, rubber-duck race, concession stands, and a big fireworks show. In mid-July, the **Summer Arts Festival** attracts artisans from throughout the Lower Columbia. Held at the fairgrounds in late July or early August, the **Cowlitz County Fair** (360/577-3121) has exhibits and entertainment, including the Professional Rodeo Cowboys Association (PRCA) Thunder Mountain Rodeo. In late August, the **Unique Tin Weekend** features old cars, street cruising, and dancing at the fairgrounds.

On the last Sunday of August, the **Three Rivers Air Show** attracts stunt pilots, hang gliders, hot-air balloons, military aircraft, and private planes of all types. The **Kelso Highlander Festival,** held the second weekend of September each year, features a parade, wine festival, art show, rubber-duck race, Scottish bagpipe music, dancing, and food at Tam O'Shanter Park.

Shopping

Pick up clothes and other essentials at the sprawling **Three Rivers Mall** (just off I-5 at Longview/Kelso exit 39, 351 Three Rivers Dr. #116, 360/577-5218, www.threeriversmall .com, 10 A.M.–9 P.M. Mon.–Sat., 11 A.M.–6 P.M. Sun.), home of big retailers such as Macy's, JCPenney, Sears, and scores of smaller specialty shops.

Stop by **Broadway Gallery** (1418 Commerce Ave., 360/577-0544, 10 A.M.–5:30 P.M. Mon.–Sat.) to see an outstanding collection of southwestern Washington art produced by more than 30 area artists, including jewelry, pottery, watercolors, weaving, baskets, sculpture, and more.

Sports and Recreation

Play a round of golf at **Mint Valley** (4002 Pennsylvania, Longview, 360/577-3395, www .mint-valley.com).

If you have a canoe, the Cowlitz River from Castle Rock to Longview is a scenic 16-mile float. The current can be strong and sandbars are visible at low water, but there are no major obstructions along the way.

Windsurfers flock to the Columbia River west and south of Longview, where wind conditions are often perfect for intermediate-level boarders.

Accommodations

Built in 1923, **Monticello Hotel** (1405 17th Ave., Longview, 360/425-9900, $60 d) is a redbrick Italianate beauty that still stands as Longview's most elegant structure. The well-appointed luxury suites ($200–250 d) are some of the nicest in the area, and the modest regular rooms in the hotel's adjoining annex are comfortable and reasonable choices for budget travelers. The location can't be beat, as the building faces R. A. Long Park from 17th Avenue.

Sitting on 26 acres outside of town, **Rutherglen Mansion B&B** (420 Rutherglen Rd., 360/425-5816, www.rutherglenmansion.com, $95–125 d) offers three daintily decorated rooms under its English Colonial eaves. Each comes with private bath and fireplace. The hostess serves a full breakfast each morning and spreads a gluttonous Sunday brunch. The restaurant downstairs also serves dinners nightly except Sunday.

Super 8 Motel (250 Kelso Dr., 360/423-8880 or 800/800-8000, www.super8.com, $69 s, $79 d) offers some of the best budget rooms in the area, along with an indoor pool. **Comfort Inn** (440 Three Rivers Dr., 360/425-4600 or 800/228-5150, $79–109 s or d) is another good chain hotel. The property has an outdoor pool and continental breakfast, plus free Wi-Fi.

For a more personal touch at budget prices, check one of two friendly mom-and-pop motels in town. The **Town House Motel** (744 Washington Way, 360/423-7200, www.townhousemo.com, $50 s, $65 d) offers tidy rooms that include microwaves, fridges, and free high-speed Internet. The property has an outdoor heated pool, and continental breakfast is served each morning.

There's no pool at **Hudson Manor Inn** (1616 Hudson, Longview, 360/425-1100, www.hudsonmanorinn.com, $60 s, $80 d), but the rooms are a little more nicely decorated and also include fridges and microwaves. Hudson has free wireless Internet, plus a free business center and complimentary continental breakfast. The owners here are especially kind.

Campers will enjoy the lush green lawns and breezy deciduous trees scattered around the pleasant **Brookhollow RV Park** (2506 Allen St., 360/577-6474 or 800/867-0453, www.brookhollow.com, $30 d full hookup, $1 extra for kids and pets), which offers campsites and RV hookups in the heart of Kelso. The closest public camping spaces are at Lewis and Clark State Park, near Winlock.

Food

Big breakfast lovers should make haste to give some meaning to the name at **Stuffy's Restaurant** (418 Long Ave., 360/423-6356, 6 A.M.–9 P.M. Mon.–Fri., 7 A.M.–9 P.M. Sat.–Sun.), which features an extensive menu, friendly family service, and enormous servings.

Or nosh on hearty sandwiches and soups, as well as cold smoothies at **Old Creekside Deli** (1323 Commerce Ave., 360/423-7225, 10 A.M.–4 P.M. Mon.–Fri., 11 A.M.–4 P.M. Sat., closed Sun.). Pick up a book at the **Benevolent Bookworm** across the street and plunk yourself down at a courtyard table to read.

Henri's Restaurant (4545 Ocean Beach Hwy., 360/425-7970, 11 A.M.–10 P.M. Sun.–Thurs., 7 A.M.–10 P.M. Fri.–Sat.) is a popular spot for the "power-lunch" business crowd. Specializing in moderately priced salmon or steak dinners and an impressive wine collection, it's open weekdays for lunch, Mon.–Sat. for dinner.

Located in—of all places—the bowling alley, ◖ **Hilander Restaurant** (1509 Allen St., 360/423-1500, 6 A.M.–midnight daily) is a real surprise. This locals' favorite serves great strawberry waffles and big omelettes for breakfast, a salad bar, homemade soups, and tasty halibut fish and chips.

Yan's Chinese Restaurant (300 Long Ave. W, 360/425-3815, 11 A.M.–10 P.M. daily) has reasonable prices and serves up ample portions.

The **Cowlitz Community Farmers Market** (7th and Washington, 360/425-1297, 8 A.M.–1 P.M. Tues. and Sat. April–Oct.) has fruit, flowers, fresh vegetables, honey, bedding plants, berries, and more.

Information

The **Kelso Visitors Center** (just east of the I-5 entrance ramp at 105 Minor Rd., 360/577-8058, 9 A.M.–5 P.M. daily May–Oct., Wed.–Sun. only Nov.–Apr.) provides local information and a small exhibit for those who may have missed the *real* Mount St. Helens visitors centers closer to the mountain. This one has a 15-foot model of the volcano and Toutle River valley, plus photos and exhibits of the 1980 eruption.

Getting There and Around

Community Urban Bus Service (254 Oregon Way, 360/577-3399) provides local service in the Kelso-Longview area Monday–Saturday.

Getaway Express (360/636-5656, $70 one-way) operates shuttle van service between Longview/Kelso and Portland International Airport.

Amtrak (501 S. 1st Ave., Kelso, 800/872-7245, www.amtrak.com) trains head north from Kelso to Centralia, Olympia, Tacoma, Seattle, and points beyond, and south to Vancouver, Portland, and California. Service is four times a day. Catch a **Greyhound** (360/423-7380 or 800/231-2222, www.greyhound.com) at the train station (501 S. 1st Ave.) in Kelso.

HIGHWAY 4

As you drive west, the lower Columbia is marked by a series of islands, many little more than sandbars with a fringe of willows and grass. The road banks away from the river at Skamokawa, where it heads toward the sinuous Grays River, which cuts a wide swath, with bucolic farms and fields on both sides and timber country climbing the hillsides.

Sights

The first town you'll encounter after Longview is the little burg of Cathlamet. Stop to visit the small **Wahkiakum Museum** (360/795-3954, 11 A.M.–4 P.M. Tues.–Sun. June–Sept., 1–4 P.M. Thurs.–Sun. Oct.–May, $5 adults, $1 kids), which contains photos and exhibits on early logging practices. Next door is Strong Park and Waterfront Trail. In the park is an unusual geared steam locomotive that hauled logs up steep grades from 1923–1958.

Just south of town lies the only populated island in the lower Columbia. Settled by dairy farmers from Switzerland and Scandinavian fishermen, Puget Island offers 27 miles of quiet country roads on rolling hills ideal for a Sunday afternoon drive or bike ride. It is connected by a bridge across a narrow channel.

Just west of Cathlamet is the 4,400-acre **Julia Butler Hansen National Wildlife Refuge** (360/795-3915, www.r1.fws.gov),

established in 1972 to protect the few remaining Columbian white-tailed deer around the lower reaches of the river. Brooks Slough Road and Steamboat Slough Road circle the refuge, offering a chance to see the small deer sharing grazing rights with dairy cattle and numerous birds, including bald eagles. To protect the deer from disturbance, hiking is prohibited, but you may see them from a blind located at a highway pullout.

Set up in an 1894 schoolhouse in Skamokawa, **River Life Interpretive Center** (1394 W. Hwy. 4, 360/795-3007, noon–4 P.M. Wed.–Sat., 1–4 P.M. Sun.) features historical photos, artifacts, and regional displays. Be sure to stop here and climb the belfry for extraordinary views over the Columbia River estuary.

Follow the signs from Rosburg to the only covered bridge in Washington still in use. The 158-foot-long **Grays River Covered Bridge** was built in 1905 and covered five years later. The bridge was carefully restored in 1989 and is now a National Historic Landmark. A **Grays River Covered Bridge Festival** is held at the local Grange each August, and includes a parade, crafts booths, music, and a logging contest.

Just a couple of miles west of the Astoria-Megler Bridge on Highway 101, **Fort Columbia State Park** (360/642-3028, www.parks.wa.gov, 10 A.M.–5 P.M. daily Apr.–Sept.) came to be in the late 1890s when it and Forts Canby and Stephens, formed a triad of military bases guarding the mouth of the Columbia. The park's grounds hold dozens of original buildings, along with various concrete batteries and two rapid-firing six-inch guns that face out over the mouth of the Columbia. A couple of delightful trails wind through the steep country along the river and an interpretive center in the enlisted men's barracks features two floors' worth of history. History buffs should also make time for the old **Commander's House,** furnished with period pieces.

Sports and Recreation

The best spot to enjoy the recreational opportunities offered by the lower Columbia is in

Skamokawa with its quiet estuaries, sloughs, and inlets. Launch motorized craft from **Skamokawa Vista Park** (360/795-8605) or wade in at the park's sandy swimming beach (no lifeguard). This is also a good place to watch ships crossing the treacherous Columbia River Bar; the busiest time is an hour before or an hour after low tide. When conditions are rough, you'll see enormous swells and waves breaking over these sandbars.

Things are much calmer and more serene along the protected waters of Steamboat Slough, a favorite paddling spot of the guides who lead kayak tours run by **Skamokawa Center** (www .skamokawapaddle.com, $70 one-day tour). The center also offers independent paddlers the chance to rent their own canoes ($40 for two hrs.) or kayaks ($20 two hrs.). Cyclists can also pick up cheap bike rentals ($12 per day) to tour the quiet country roads of Skamokawa, Cathlamet, and Puget Island.

Accommodations

Head into Cathlamet for a solid roof over your head. **Bradley House Inn** (61 Main St., Cathlamet, 360/795-3030, $79–99 d) is set literally on Main Street, offering a small-town America brand of hospitality in a 1907 Eastlake-style home. This former lumber baron mansion offers views of the town, the river, and Puget Island.

Pitch a tent or pull up small campers halfway between Longview and Cathlamet at **County Line Park** (2076 E. Hwy. 4, Cathlamet, 360/577-3030, $10 with electric hookups), set right on the river. There are grassy banks for picnicking and plenty of spots to settle down and plunk a line into the water.

You can extend your stay on Puget Island by checking into **Redfern Farm B&B** (277 Cross Dike Rd., 360/849-4108, $55–65 s or d) where the two guest rooms have a private bath and hot tub. A full breakfast is served, and children are not permitted.

Farther along the route, restored **Skamokawa Inn** (1391 W. Hwy. 4, Skamokawa, 360/795-8300 or 888/920-2777) is the unofficial town square. You'll find a general store, post office, and café at the inn, along with a recreation center that rents kayaks and runs water trail tours. Lodging in the inn ($80 s or $90–95 d) includes a full breakfast. Bring big groups this way—also on the property are apartment and suite rentals sleeping 4–20 ($145–400).

Paddlers, RV enthusiasts, tenters, and even those who don't like roughing it too much can find a comfy camping option at the waterfront **Skamokawa Vista Park** (13 Vista Park Rd., 360/795-8605). The park offers simple tent sites ($16), RV hookups ($23), and even yurts ($36–46). Be sure to make a reservation for RV spots and yurts, as this is a popular spot.

Travelers can rent one of two historic guesthouses at Fort Columbia State Park (two mi. west of Astoria-Megler Bridge, 360/642-3078, www.parks.wa.gov/fortcolumbia). The first is **Scarborough House** ($268), a restored fort building with accommodations to sleep up to 12 people in four bedrooms, with a full kitchen. The house is named for Captain James Scarborough, who first built a cabin on the land where the fort now stands. Also available is **Steward's House** ($165), a quaint and historic two-bedroom home that sleeps four and has an excellent view of the Columbia River.

COLUMBIA RIVER GORGE AND WINE COUNTRY

Follow the course of the mighty Columbia River from Vancouver eastward and you'll experience a parade of photogenic panoramas. From the sheer basalt cliffs diving into the river's depths along the Columbia Gorge to the windswept wheat hillocks of Walla Walla to the shady apple orchards of Yakima, the region is the stuff of postcards.

It's not just a feast for the eyes, either: This is Washington wine country. Resting at the same latitude as the famed French wine chateaus of Bordeaux and Burgundy, central Washington's distinct landscapes are bound together in the pursuit of perfecting reds and whites. Over the last decade, the state has seen an explosion in wineries—from slightly over 100 in 1997 to more than 500 now. Most of those new growers and winemakers have set up shop in central Washington, home of seven of the eight official wine appellations in Washington.

A day's drive can put you in position to walk the rows at scenic vineyards and chat up winemakers in their cozy tasting rooms. Wine country wanderers will also find artisan cheeses, freshly picked fruits, and other culinary delights dished up in the hidden countryside cafés and bistros that have sprung up from the region's viticultural boom. And you needn't worry about the scale after your gastronomic excess: The region offers plenty of outdoor activities that will make a four-course meal and a bottle of wine seem well justified by day's end.

Cyclists can spin on serpentine bands of blacktop winding through the country past historic train depots and scenically dilapidated barns.

© ERICKA CHICKOWSKI

HIGHLIGHTS

(Vancouver National Historic Reserve: History buffs will be in heaven here, exploring a reconstructed Hudson's Bay Company fort, turn-of-the-20th-century barracks, and a historic airfield (page 394).

(Beacon Rock State Park: Lewis and Clark spotted this gigantic volcanic rock on their journey west. Climb to the top of the rock for the best view of the Gorge (page 403).

(Columbia Hills State Park: With pretty views, rock climbing, and fishing galore, this

park is best known for its amazing collection of petroglyphs and pictographs (page 413).

(Maryhill Museum of Art: Dubbed "Castle Nowhere," this remote museum is remarkable for its collections of Rodin sculptures and chess sets (page 415).

(Gorge Waterfalls: Set on the south side of the Gorge, the plunging waterfalls along the Historic Columbia River Highway are some of the most beautiful in the United States (page 423).

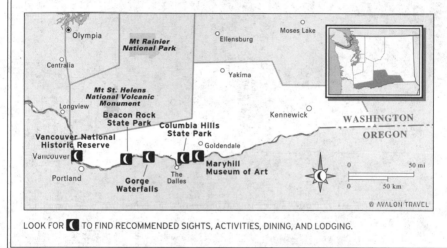

LOOK FOR (TO FIND RECOMMENDED SIGHTS, ACTIVITIES, DINING, AND LODGING.

COLUMBIA RIVER GORGE

Hikers and equestrians can scramble through rugged multiuse trails in ponderosa stands, desert wildflowers, and sylvan canyons. And watersports lovers will be in heaven—temperatures soar on the dry eastern side of the Cascades, making the prospect of a good drenching more than appealing. Experience the wind-whipped excitement of kiteboarding or windsurfing the Columbia River. Or enjoy a lazy afternoon tubing or fly-fishing its tributaries.

So slip on your driving gloves and prepare to hit the road. Even the most remote

outposts along the Gorge and the rest of central Washington's country roads are well worth the trip.

In 1986, President Ronald Reagan signed into law a measure that established the **Columbia River Gorge National Scenic Area,** encompassing 292,000 acres on both sides of the river from Washougal to Maryhill. The national scenic area is managed jointly by the U.S. Forest Service, the states of Washington and Oregon, and six local counties across both states. Headquarters for the scenic area are in

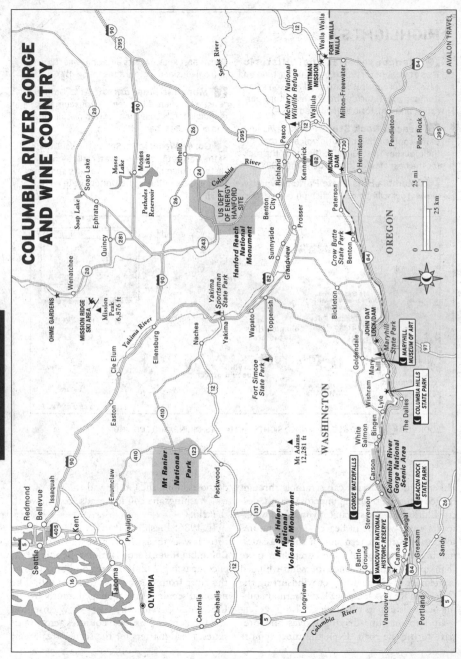

COLUMBIA RIVER GORGE

COLUMBIA RIVER GORGE AND WINE COUNTRY

© AVALON TRAVEL

Hood River, Oregon; call 541/386-2333 for details.

A $5 National Forest Recreation Day Pass is required for parking at all Forest Service trailheads in the scenic area. Or pick up an annual Northwest Forest Pass ($30) that is valid for most national forest trailheads in Washington and Oregon. Get one from most local sporting-goods stores, any Forest Service office (800/270-7504), or at www.fs.fed.us/passespermits.

HISTORY

In 1792, American trading captain Robert Gray discovered the great Columbia River on his journey to become the first American to sail around the world. Gray claimed the river and its huge drainage area for the United States, naming the river after his ship, the *Columbia Rediviva* (Columbus Lives Again). After Gray's discovery, Vancouver sent William Broughton out to explore the upriver territory for England; Broughton asserted that Gray hadn't found the true channel and claimed the river for His Royal Majesty, the King. After Broughton's claim, the United States and Great Britain were unable to come to terms on the ownership of Oregon Country, a fur- and lumber-rich land that included the Northwest Coast of North America. In 1818, the two powers agreed to share the land until a long-term arrangement could be reached, but seven years later the British-owned Hudson's Bay Company moved its headquarters from Fort George, at the mouth of the Columbia, to Fort Vancouver, 100 miles inland, in hopes of solidifying the British claim to the region.

Fort Vancouver became the Pacific Northwest's commercial and cultural center for fur trading from Utah to Hawaii; shops, fields, pastures, and mills made the fort a self-sufficient, bustling pioneer community. The most famous Columbia River explorers were Meriwether Lewis and William Clark. Northwesterners won't be surprised to hear that Lewis and Clark recorded 31 consecutive days of rain during their visit to the region!

The region's historic brush with the Corps of Discovery piqued American interest in what was then called "Oregon Country." The floodgates opened in 1843, when the Applegate Wagon Train, the largest wagon train ever assembled anywhere, left Independence, Missouri. Under the leadership of Dr. Marcus Whitman and guided by mountain man Bill Sublette, the pioneers made it all the way to the Columbia and Willamette Rivers by September of that year. It had taken six long months to travel the 2,000 miles, but they had shown that the "Oregon Trail" route was feasible. Thousands of Americans seeking open vistas and economic opportunity would follow in the next two decades. The march west along the Oregon Trail is regarded as the greatest peacetime migration in America's history.

The Columbia River Gorge lay near the end of the journey for emigrants heading west and posed the last major obstacle along the way. The narrow confines of the gorge forced them to dismantle their wagons and load them onto log rafts to float down the river as far as the Cascades, which they portaged before continuing by raft to the area of present-day Portland. Treacherous rapids, strong currents, and high winds caused the deaths of many people almost within sight of the promised land. Completion of the Barlow Road in 1846—a toll route that avoided the gorge by heading south around the south shoulder of Mount Hood—provided a safer alternative to the Willamette Valley. It cost pioneers an exorbitant $5 a wagon and $0.10 a head for livestock to use the road.

These droves of pioneering Americans would happily pay the fee, though, as they were drawn to Oregon's fertile Willamette Valley farmland, a migration that eventually led to the division of the territory along the 49th parallel in 1846—a boundary that put Britain's Fort Vancouver squarely on American soil. By 1860 all of Fort Vancouver was in the hands of the U.S. Army. Decay and fire had destroyed all of the remaining structures by 1866. The Army constructed new buildings on the slope behind the fort at **Vancouver Barracks,** including officers' quarters, barracks and other facilities.

COLUMBIA RIVER GORGE

CLIMATE

The scenery along the route blends the green forested hills of the western section into the dry basaltic and barren hills of the eastern half. In a distance of just 40 miles—from Cascade Locks to The Dalles—average annual rainfall changes by 40 inches! The gorge has its own climate, and temperature extremes on the east side range from zero or less in winter to 110°F of dry heat in summer. It isn't unusual to descend into the Gorge and into a gale because this narrow gap is the only place weather systems can push through the towering mountains. Sometimes in the winter a sudden arctic blast comes down the Gorge to create an ice storm, which, around these parts, they call a "silver thaw."

PLANNING YOUR TIME

This stretch of the Columbia River is treasured by residents of both Washington and Oregon. No matter the season, no matter the weather conditions, the Gorge is always beautiful. You can choose your pace: I-84 roars along the Oregon side of the Gorge at river level, blasting through the rocky hills through a number of tunnels. On the Washington side, things are a little more relaxed. A cross between country road and highway gently follows the contours of the land and the bends of the river. On the western stretch, the Lewis and Clark Highway (State Route 14) winds through maple and Douglas fir forests punctuated by stunning vistas into the river valley far below.

The gorge between I-5 and Highway 97 is heavily traveled on both sides of the river, but the area from Highway 97 at Maryhill Museum east to Paterson is the less so, so expect fewer services. The descriptions in this chapter follow the Washington side of the river from Vancouver to McNary Dam, where the highway heads away from the river and north to the Tri-Cities area, and on the Oregon side from Troutdale to The Dalles.

Crossing the Columbia

Obviously, in a region centered around a dramatic river gorge, the placement of bridge

COLUMBIA RIVER GORGE

© ERICKA CHICKOWSKI

The Columbia River Gorge is a bi-state region enjoyed best from both Washington and Oregon.

THE BRIDGE OF THE GODS

The Klickitat, Yakima, and Warm Springs people of the Pacific Northwest all share a legend describing the creation and destruction of a massive stone bridge spanning the Columbia River between Skamania County and Cascade Locks, Oregon. According to the Klickitat version, two great chiefs, Klickitat and Wy'East, were given rich new lands by the Great Spirit, their respective lands separated by the Columbia. As a symbol of peace, the Great Spirit built an enormous bridge across the river, connecting the two territories. Unfortunately, the two groups took to fighting, and in the ensuing chaos, the enormous bridge was destroyed.

It's believed that the legend refers to a historical event – roughly 500 years ago, a powerful landslide was said to have blocked the Columbia River until the water flow eroded all but a slender bridge that crossed the river. Eventually, that bridge collapsed, but the rocks from the bridge have come to form the Columbia Rapids. Today, the modern steel-and-concrete Bridge of the Gods spans the river close to where the legendary bridge was thought to have been. In order to cross, you no longer have to contend with Loo-Wit, the appointed guardian of the bridge, but you will have to pay a buck in tolls.

crossings will play an important part in your trip planning. From the greater Portland/Vancouver region to the eastern edge of the National Scenic Area at Maryhill, you'll find six Columbia River bridges crisscrossing the Washington and Oregon state line. Two of the biggest run from Vancouver into Portland via I-5 and I-205, with the former rolling into downtown Portland and the latter further east near the Portland International Airport.

The next crossing isn't for another 35 miles further east. There, between Cascade Locks, Oregon, and the outskirts of Stevenson, Washington, the Bridge of the Gods runs over a narrow Columbia River passage, so named for an ancient land bridge that once formed here from a massive rock slide. The bridge costs $1 to pass each way. It is also, interestingly, the route Pacific Crest Trail hikers take to hike their way up the Washington section of the trail. Just east of the Bonneville Dam and west of Stevenson's nicer lodging, plus several miles east of Oregon's most accessible Gorge waterfalls, this link provides a nice means to connect shorter loops on the "wet"western portion of the Gorge byways.

A little over 20 miles past that, the Hood River Bridge connects Hood River, Ore. with White Salmon, Washington. This river crossing gives Gorge travelers the ability to stay in the nicer accommodations in Hood River while still being able to pop over to enjoy the rafting and fishing on the White Salmon River and enjoy the wildflower-studded trails of Washington in this section of the Gorge. Over 20 miles east of that The Dalles Bridge provides a vital link between the largest city within the National Scenic Area and the windswept Columbia Hills area of Washington. Many campers who stay at Washington's Columbia Hills State Park cap off their trip with a meal in The Dalles.

The last bridge within the Gorge's designated scenic area is an additional 20 miles east. The Sam Hill Memorial Bridge crosses the Columbia to connect Maryhill, Washington, to Biggs Junction, Oregon, and offers the opportunity to take the grand loop of all of the Gorge from either side of the river. If you were to start in Vancouver, drive east through Maryhill and Biggs Junction and then back west through Portland and Vancouver, the total drive time would equal about 4.5 hours straight through.

Vancouver

Situated in the crook of the elbow bend in the Lower Columbia River, Vancouver serves as a gateway to the Columbia Gorge, Mount St. Helens, and Portland just across the river. The unique riverside geography allows Vancouver to hang on to its slow-paced charm in spite of its inclusion in the metropolitan Portland scene, giving visitors a healthy blend between big city convenience and small-town relaxation. Much of the city's appeal is drawn from its colorful history, which is vividly illustrated at the town's premier attraction, the Vancouver National Historic Reserve.

SIGHTS
◖ Vancouver National Historic Reserve

No trip to Vancouver would be complete without an excursion to the Vancouver National Historic Reserve (from I-5 take E. Mill Plain Blvd. and turn left at Fort Vancouver Way), a trove of history and scenery that unfolds over hundreds of acres. Curious travelers will stumble

Fort Vancouver's recreated stockade

© ERICKA CHICKOWSKI

upon a reconstructed Hudson's Bay trading post, the only complete row of restored 19th-century officers' homes in the nation, and one of the oldest operating airfields in the country.

FORT VANCOUVER NATIONAL HISTORIC SITE

In this scenic park, the visitor will find accurate reconstructions of 6 of the 27 buildings the Hudson's Bay Company built here in 1845 to protect its fur-trapping interests. Surrounded by a tall wooden stockade and guarded by a three-story tower once armed with eight three-pound cannons, it's easy to get wrapped up in the history of the area.

Other reconstructed buildings include a blacksmith's shop, bakery, Native American trade shop, storage house, and the elegant residence of Dr. John McLoughlin, the chief factor. Although McLoughlin had been charged with keeping the American traders out of the market, he realized that their participation was far more practical. He later became an American citizen, moved to Oregon City, and is now hailed as the "Father of Oregon."

Historic Fort Vancouver (360/816-6230, 360/816-6200 for recorded info, www.nps .gov/fova, 9 A.M.–5 P.M. Mon.–Sat., $3 adults, kids under 15 free) offers a tour with a visit to the fully restored home of John McLoughlin, along with a visit to the working blacksmith shop where you will learn how the Hudson's Bay Company produced beaver traps and other goods. Today the shop is used to train apprentices to create iron pieces for National Park Service historic facilities across the nation. Also of interest during the tour are the living history activities that take place all summer. The fort's period gardens are interesting to view, and gardeners will be happy to tell you of the crops that were—and are—grown here.

A block north of the fort is the **visitors center** (1511 East Evergreen Blvd., same hours as the fort), where you can watch a 15-minute orientation video and view displays on

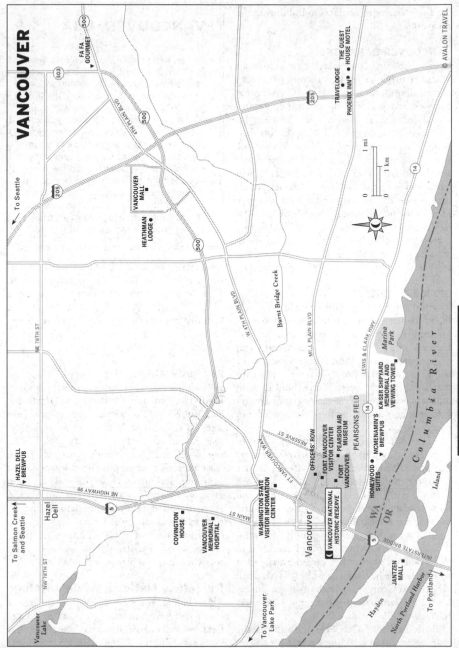

VANCOUVER

To Seattle

To Salmon Creek and Seattle

To Vancouver Lake Park

To Portland

COLUMBIA RIVER GORGE

© AVALON TRAVEL

FA FA GOURMET

TRAVELODGE
PHOENIX INN ●
THE GUEST HOUSE MOTEL

VANCOUVER MALL ●

HEATHMAN LODGE ●

Burnt Bridge Creek

W. 4TH PLAIN BLVD

M.L. PLAIN BLVD

LEWIS & CLARK HWY

Marine Park

KAISER SHIPYARD MEMORIAL AND VIEWING TOWER

McMENAMIN'S BREWPUB

HOMEWOOD SUITES

PEARSONS FIELD

OFFICERS' ROW
FORT VANCOUVER VISITOR CENTER
PEARSON AIR MUSEUM
FORT VANCOUVER
● VANCOUVER NATIONAL HISTORIC RESERVE

RESERVE ST.

FT. VANCOUVER WY.

WASHINGTON STATE VISITOR INFORMATION CENTER

COVINGTON HOUSE ■
VANCOUVER MEMORIAL HOSPITAL ■

MAIN ST.

NE HIGHWAY 99

HAZEL DELL BREWPUB

Hazel Dell

NE 78TH ST

NW 78TH ST

Vancouver Lake

Vancouver

Columbia River

Hayden Island

North Portland Harbor

INTERSTATE BRIDGE

JANTZEN MALL

WA
OR

0   1 mi
0   1 km

the fort along with artifacts found during the excavations.

VANCOUVER BARRACKS

Established in 1849 after the Whitman Massacre in Walla Walla, Vancouver Barracks played an important role in the U.S. Army for over a century. It was the central command post during the Northwest Indian Wars, and it was a mobilization center during the Spanish-American War and both World Wars. The site was continuously occupied by the Army and National Guard until 2011, when it was turned over to the National Park Service. It is now available to tour under its new name, Fort Vancouver National Historic Site. Take a stroll down the sun-speckled, tree-lined Barnes Street and McClellan and Hatheway Roads to get a close look at the picturesque brick structures built around the turn of the 20th century.

OFFICERS' ROW

The only complete row of restored Army officers' homes in the nation is at Vancouver's Officers' Row National Historic District. The homes occupy one side of a tree-shaded street and are now used by local businesses; opposite is spacious **Central Park**—a favorite place for locals to relax on a sunny day. Find here an old Army cemetery with the graves of around 1,400 soldiers, including four Medal of Honor recipients.

The two most famous buildings on Officers' Row are houses named for General George C. Marshall and President Ulysses S. Grant. The **Marshall House** (1313 Officers' Row, 360/693-3103, 9 A.M.–5 P.M. Mon.–Fri., and on select Saturdays) is open for free tours and has videotapes describing the fort and Officers' Row. The building is very popular for weddings and other events, so it is often closed to the public on weekends. Named for the man who authored the famous post-WWII Marshall Plan, it was George C. Marshall's home during his time as commanding officer at Vancouver Barracks, 1936–1938.

Built in 1849, **The Grant House** is the oldest remaining building on Officer's Row.

VANCOUVER, USA

The name, honoring Capt. George Vancouver, who explored the Columbia River in 1792, came from the Hudson's Bay post named Fort Vancouver. While the city was still part of the Oregon Territory, the Oregon Territorial Legislature named it Columbia City. However, in 1855, the legislature changed it back to its original name, creating a situation that will always cause confusion. Locals point out that Vancouver, British Columbia, is a Johnny-come-lately city and if any name should be changed, it should be the Canadian one. That prospect is doubtful. To help avoid confusion, the city is often referred to as Vancouver, USA, or specifically as Vancouver, Washington.

This stately home was built as the commanding officer's residence and is now home to **The Restaurant at Historic Reserve** (360/906-1101). While President Grant never actually lived in the house, he was a frequent visitor during his time as the post's quartermaster in the 1850s.

PEARSON AIRFIELD

Ever wanted to strap into a genuine flight simulator? The **Pearson Air Museum** (1115 E. 5th St., 360/694-7026, www.pearsonairmuseum .org, 10 A.M.–5 P.M. Wed.–Sat., $7 adults, $5 seniors and active duty military with ID, $3 ages 6–12, free for kids under age 6) offers you the chance. The museum also displays dozens of aircraft and memorabilia from all periods in aviation history. The adjacent Pearson Airfield is one of the oldest operating fields in the nation; its first landing was a dirigible that floated over from Portland in 1905, and the first plane arrived seven years later. This was also where the Russian transpolar flight ended in 1937.

Ridgefield National Wildlife Refuge

About half an hour north of Vancouver, nature lovers will have ample opportunity to explore fields, woodlands, and wetlands at Ridgefield National Wildlife Refuge (1071 S. Hillhurst

COLUMBIA RIVER GORGE

Rd., 360/887-4106, www.fws.gov/ridgefield refuges), which fans over 5,150 acres around the marshy lower Columbia River. Bring your binoculars in winter, when up to 10,000 geese and 40,000 ducks land here. Hiking and fishing are permitted—the two-mile **Oaks to Wetlands Wildlife Trail** is popular with all ages. Parts of the refuge are closed October–mid-April.

Clark County Historical Museum

The Clark County Historical Museum (1511 Main St., 360/993-5679, http://cchmuseum.org, 11 A.M.–4 P.M. Tues.–Sat., $4 adults, $3 students and seniors, $2 children 6–18, $10 for a family of four, free for historical society members and children under 5) hosts a changing lineup of exhibits related to Clark County History.

St. James Church

Be sure to drive by the St. James Church (12th and Washington Sts.). Built in 1885, this was the first Gothic Revival-style church in Washington and is home to the state's longest-standing Catholic congregation.

Parks

Marine Park occupies the site of the Kaiser Shipyards, where "Rosie the Riveter" hurriedly constructed more than 140 ships during World War II before the facilities were decommissioned and dismantled. Today you can climb a three-story riverside tower next to Kaiser Center for dramatic views of Vancouver and Portland. Also in the park is the new **Water Resources Education Center** (4600 SE Columbia Way, 360/696-8478, 9 A.M.–5 P.M. Mon.–Sat., free). The center houses hands-on exhibits, a video theater, and a 350-gallon aquarium filled with Columbia River creatures. Not far away is the **Chkalov Monument,** commemorating the Soviet transpolar flight of 1937, when three Russian aviators were the first to cross over the north pole and into America.

Old Apple Tree Park, along the river just east of I-5, honors what is believed to be the oldest apple tree in the Northwest. The tree was planted in 1826 and still bears small green apples each summer.

Shady **Esther Short Park** (W. 6th and Esther) contains the historic Slocum House Theater, along with a Victorian rose garden, playground, and a monument to pioneer women. The site is a popular one for festivals and concerts throughout the summer.

ENTERTAINMENT AND EVENTS
Nightlife

Enjoy the Columbia River view from **Beaches Restaurant & Bar** (1919 SE Columbia River Dr., 360/699-1592, www.beachesrestaurantandbar.com, 11 A.M.–9 P.M. Sun.–Mon., 11 A.M.–10 P.M. Tues.–Sat., bar open until 2 A.M.), a fun place with tasty appetizers, a diverse menu, and a hopping bar. Also facing the river is **Who-Song and Larry's Cantina** (111 E. Columbia Way, 360/695-1198, 11 A.M.–10 P.M. Sun.–Thurs., 11 A.M.–11 P.M. Fri.–Sat., bar open until 2 A.M.), where singing waiters are a local phenomenon.

The Arts

Tired of living in Portland's shadow, proud Vancouverites have worked hard to establish a lively arts and entertainment scene of their own. Skip the bridge, and check out some of these local venues.

Listed on the National Register of Historic Homes, the 60-seat **Slocum House Theater** (360/696-2497, www.slocumhouse.com) was built in 1867. The theater stages productions year-round.

Music lovers need not venture south to enjoy a quality performance. The unique **Vancouver Symphony Orchestra** (360/735-7278, www.vancouversymphony.org) attracts talented local musicians and a roster of traveling professionals to its full season of classical performances. Its venue, Skyview Concert Hall (1300 NW 139th St.), is wonderfully intimate and acoustically striking. The season runs September–May annually.

The city's well-attended **Six to Sunset** (360/619-1111, www.cityofvancouver.us, free) concert series in central Esther Short Park sets out to offer something for everyone. These weekly summertime concerts range from orchestral music to Beatles cover bands to contemporary rock. Food vendors and blanket seating complete the town carnival atmosphere.

Festivals and Events

Don't miss the annual **Vancouver Rodeo** (360/896-6654, www.vancouverrodeo.com), a four-day benefit show taking place around the 4th of July. Look for bull-riding, dances, and even pony rides for the little 'uns. Also in summer, the annual **Fort Vancouver Brigade Encampment** fills the fort with trappers and traders dressed in 1840 period costumes. There are tepees, baking and cooking demonstrations, tomahawk throwing, and other demonstrations.

On the first Saturday in October, the locals get together to venerate their nearly two-century-old apple tree at the sensibly named **Old Apple Tree Festival** (360/619-1108, free). The festival focuses on environmental and historical preservation, and the Urban Forestry Commission is on hand to give away free cuttings from the legendary tree itself. In early October, don't miss the very popular **Fort Vancouver Candlelight Tours** with interpreters dressed in 1840s period clothing.

The **Christmas Ship Parade** (www.christmasships.org) is another favorite event, with decorated vessels plying the Columbia and Willamette Rivers on the second and third weeks of December. You'll also find Officers' Row decorated with traditional evergreens for the holidays, plus concerts and carriage rides to get you in the spirit of the holidays.

SHOPPING

The two-level **Vancouver Mall** (8700 NE Vancouver Mall Dr., 360/892-6255, www.westfield.com/vancouver) has over 115 shops, restaurants, and services, including JCPenney, Macy's, Nordstrom, Sears, and Old Navy. It is hard to miss at the junction of I-205 and Highway 500.

SPORTS AND RECREATION

The 14-foot-wide, paved **Columbia River Waterfront Trail** follows the shore eastward for 3.5 miles from downtown to Tidewater Cove. It's a wonderful place for a sunset stroll or bike ride. Find trailheads at Wintler Community Park, Marine Park, Waterfront Park or downtown Vancouver.

Vancouver Lake Park (6801 NW Lower River Rd., 360/487-7100, daily 7 A.M.–dusk, $3 cars, free for pedestrians and bikes), three miles west of downtown, is a local hot spot for both sailboarders and anglers. The nearly 300-acre strip of land offers picnicking, swimming, and fishing, plus grassy and shady areas. It is also home to one of the largest great blue heron rookeries in the region, and bald eagles can be found roosting in the trees during the winter months.

A 2.5-mile hiking trail connects Vancouver Lake park with **Frenchman's Bar Park** (9612 NW Lower River Rd., 360/619-1123, 7 A.M.–dusk daily, $3 cars, free for pedestrians and bikes) along the Columbia River, where there is a public beach for swimming, fishing access, and a very popular sand pit with eight volleyball courts set up in the summer.

There are no lifeguards at either park, which is why most families prefer **Salmon Creek Park** (off NW 117th St., 360/696-8171), a small lake with trained professionals on the lookout during the summer months.

ACCOMMODATIONS

While comfy lodging is plentiful on the Washington side of the river, dozens of motels and a hostel are also available in Portland, Oregon.

Under $100

Right in downtown Vancouver, near I-5, there is an **Econolodge** (601 Broadway, 360/693-3668, $70 s or $80 d) with standard motel rooms with fridges and microwaves. Whirlpool-bath rooms are also available.

For the touch of home that only a B&B can offer, try the **Briar Rose Inn** (314 W. 11th St., 360/694-5710, $75 d), a lovely 1908 Craftsman in the center of downtown. The four rooms, two of which have private baths, have wireless Internet, and the unbeatable "Grandma's house" feel of antique sumptuousness.

There are two Shilo Inn locations in the metropolitan Vancouver area. Pass up the one downtown on East 13th; it is ho-hum at best. Instead, visit **Shilo Inn & Suites Salmon Creek** (13206 NE Hwy. 99, 360/573-0511, www.shiloinns.com, $79–89 s or d) in Hazel Dell. It may not look special from the outside, but walk through the door and you'll see it is a class above most chains. The interiors are brand new and immaculate at this well-tended hotel. The property has a pool, spa, and sauna. Beds are comfortable and rooms have fridges and microwaves. There's also free Wi-Fi, continental breakfasts, and cookies during the day.

$100-150

Convenient to downtown and the fort district, **Red Lion Vancouver at the Quay** (100 Columbia St., 360/694-8341 or 800/733-5466, www.redlion.com, $100 s or $110 d) sits right at the base of the I-5 Interstate Bridge next to a 1.8-mile riverfront trail. Ask for a room with a view of the river to watch the lights of Portland twinkle over the Columbia. The furnishings and bathroom fixtures are a bit tired, but the rooms are clean and the linens are new. There's an outdoor pool, fitness center, business center, and a restaurant and lounge on premises. The hotel also offers free wireless Internet and a free Portland airport shuttle to its guests. Plus, it is pet-friendly.

East of downtown, just off of I-205, is **Phoenix Inn** (12712 SE 2nd Circle, 360/891 9777 or 888/988-8100, www.phoenixinnsuites .com, $129 s or $134 d) with 98 mini-suites. A free continental breakfast buffet is included, along with an indoor pool and hot tub.

$150-200

Residence Inn by Marriott (8005 NE Parkway Dr., Orchards, 360/253-4800 or 800/331-3131, www.residenceinn.com, $159 s or $189 d) has apartment-style rooms with kitchens and fireplaces, plus an outdoor pool, hot tub, and airport shuttle.

The **Heathman Lodge** (7801 NE Greenwood Dr., 360/254-3100 or 888/475-3100, www .heathmanlodge.com, $119–159 s or d) is not affiliated with the uber-luxurious Heathman Hotel across the Columbia in Portland, but it is one of the nicest hotels in Vancouver. It features spacious rooms and rustic lodge-style touches like wood beams, leather lampshades, and hand-crafted furniture, as well as modern comforts like an indoor pool and complete exercise facility.

Homewood Suites by Hilton Hotel (701 SE Columbia Shores Blvd., 360/750-1100 or 800/225-5466, www.homewood-suites.com, $169 s or d) is a luxurious business hotel right on the Columbia River with kitchen suites.

$200-250

The Frank Lloyd Wright-esque **Bridge View Bed and Breakfast** (11734 SE Evergreen Hwy., 360/609-1381, www.bridgeviewbandb .com) was custom designed to pleasingly complement the aesthetics of the Glen Jackson Bridge under which it stands. The giant greatroom features a curving bank of floor-to-ceiling windows that presents views of this larger-than-life bridge and the Columbia River. The interior is also a compilation of luxe modern furnishings with shared amenities like a full kitchen, dining room, and living room with large-screen HDTV and surround sound. About 10 minutes east of downtown, the house has an upstairs master suite ($210) with a whirlpool tub, walk-in shower, and double-sink bathroom, plus a separate office with built-in cabinet desk. Downstairs are two standard rooms ($80) with double bed in each.

Camping

The closest public campgrounds are **Paradise Point State Park** (360/263-2350), 16 miles north on I-5 near Woodland, and **Battle Ground Lake State Park** (360/687-4621), 20 miles northeast of town in Battle Ground. Campsites are reservable May through September by calling 888/226-7688 or visiting www.parks.wa.gov.

Private parks in the area include **Vancouver RV Park** (7603 NE 13th Ave., 360/695-1158, $22–38) and **99 RV Park** (1913 NE Leichner Rd., 360/573-0351, $20–29) in Salmon Creek.

FOOD

It's a fact that many Vancouver locals cross the bridge into Portland for the bonanza of restaurants the big city offers. But for the smaller-town feel and the personal attention that comes with it, save the travel time and explore the local treats Vancouver has available.

Cafés

One place wins hands-down on the Vancouver breakfast front: **Dulin's Village Café** (1905 Main St., 360/737-9907, 7 A.M.–3 P.M. daily), with great home fries, omelettes, and wholewheat pancakes. It's also popular at lunch with the downtown crowd.

Travelers can relax with an espresso and croissant at **Java House** (210 W. Evergreen Blvd., 6 A.M.–5 P.M. Mon.–Fri., 8 A.M.–2 P.M. Sat., closed Sun., 360/737-2925) or **Paradise Café** (1304 Main St., 360/696-1612, 7 A.M.–5 P.M. Mon.–Fri., 8 A.M.–4 P.M. Sat., closed Sun.). Paradise also has a deli with fresh sandwiches.

Tommy O's Aloha Café (210 W. Evergreen Blvd., 360/694-5107, 6 A.M.–9 P.M. Sun.–Thurs., 8 A.M.–9:30 P.M. Fri.–Sat.), at the Vancouver Market Place, has interesting and healthy lunches like stir-fry with tofu, teriyaki burgers, and spicy chicken or beef bento, as well as soups and sandwiches.

If you can handle the suited throngs that line up at **Rosemary Café** (1003 Main St., Vancouver, 360/737-7611) during workday lunch hour, your patience will be rewarded. This homey café in downtown Vancouver slaps together some of the best sandwiches the city has to offer. My fave is the super grilled cheese sandwich with multiple types of cheeses on parmesan artisan bread. Rosemary also mixes remarkably fresh salads and homemade soups—I haven't tried it, but I heard the lady next to me raving about the beer cheese soup.

Contemporary Northwest

Enjoy stylish lunches and dinners in an elegant, historic setting at **The Grant House** (1101 Officers' Row, 360/906-1101, www.restauranthr.com, entrées $22), which is right inside a historic officer's house in Vancouver's Historic Reserve. Pick from a menu of glazed, grilled, and baked seafood, chops, and chickens. The restaurant also throws open the doors on Sunday mornings to serve a special brunch menu.

Seafood

On the banks of the Columbia, **Joe's Crab Shack** (101 E. Columbia Way, 360/693-9211, 10 A.M.–10 P.M. Sun.–Thurs., 10 A.M.–11 P.M. Fri.–Sat.) makes up a mess of large and delectable portions of seafood.

Italian and Pizza

Try **Bortolami's Pizzeria** (9901 NE 7th Ave., 360/574-2598, www.bortolami.com, 11:30 A.M.–8 P.M. Mon.–Tues., 11:30 A.M.–9 P.M. Wed.–Thurs., 11:30 A.M.–10 P.M. Fri., noon–9 P.M. Sat., 1–8 P.M. Sun.) for gourmet pies and a good selections of microbrews on tap. Or mosey over to **Little Italy's Trattoria** (901 Washington St., 360/737-2363, http://littleitalystrattoria.com, 11 A.M.–9 P.M. Mon.–Thurs., 11 A.M.–10 P.M. Fri.–Sat., 1–9 P.M. Sun.), which not only has good pizzas, but also a satisfying selection of Italian pasta and lasagna.

There's nothing like a perfectly crafted plate of from-scratch pasta to bring out the flavors of a locally made merlot. **Café Al Dente Italian Restaurant and Wine Bar** (907 Main St., 360/696-3463, www.cafealdente.net, 11 A.M.–9 P.M. Tues.–Sat.) offers the ideal combination of delectable homemade pastas and sauces with winning wine pairings for a blissful culinary experience.

Thai

For an authentic taste of Asia, try **Thai Orchid Restaurant** (1004 Washington St., 360/695-7786, www.thaiorchidrestaurant.com, 11:30 A.M.–9:30 P.M. Mon.–Fri., noon–9:30 P.M. Sat.–Sun.), serving Thai curries, noodles, and desserts.

Greek

Hidden House is named for its builder, Lowell M. Hidden, and not for any difficulty you'll have finding it. **The Touch of Athens at Hidden House** (100 W. 13th St., 360/695-

6198, 11 A.M.–2 P.M. and 5–9 P.M. Mon.–Fri., 5–10 P.M. Sat.) offers traditional Greek foods and atmosphere, complete with belly dancing and accordion music on weekend evenings.

Pub Grub and Burgers

Hazel Dell Brew Pub (8513 NE Hwy. 99, 360/576-0996, www.hazeldellbrewpub.com, 11:30 A.M.–9 P.M. Mon., 11 A.M.–10 P.M. Tues.–Fri., noon–10 P.M. Sat., 4–9 P.M. Sun.) serves pub meals, including fish and chips, burgers, and pasta in a lively, noisy setting to accompany its 14 different brewed-on-the-premises beers. And the setting of **McMenamins of the Columbia Brew Pub** (1801 SE Columbia River Dr., 360/254-3950, www.mcmenamins.com, 11 A.M.–11 P.M. Sun.–Thurs., 11 A.M.–1 A.M. Fri.–Sat.) is sublime, sidled up to the river on Hidden Way just east of Marine Park.

The sporting set is always at home at **Out-A-Bounds** (14415 SE Mill Plain Blvd., 360/253-4789, 11 A.M.–1:30 A.M. daily), chowing down on traditional sports-bar fare like wings, burgers, and beer.

You'll find pretty much the best fast-food burgers in the state, if not all of the Pacific Northwest at **Burgerville USA** (www.burgerville.com)—yes, Seattleites, even better than Dick's. The flagship store (360/694-4071, 7 A.M.–10 P.M. daily) is at 7401 East Mill Plain Boulevard, where the first Burgerville opened in 1961 and let loose the goodness. But I find the coolest location is (**Burgerville's second shop** (307 E. Mill Plain Blvd., 360/693-8801, 7 A.M.–10 P.M. Mon.–Sat., 8 A.M.–10 P.M. Sun.) ever opened; it's the only one that has been left as a walk-up stand, as it originally was built in the early 1960s. All of the food at any Burgerville is cooked with fresh ingredients, with a special focus on seasonal, local ingredients like thick-cut sweet Walla Walla onions for the fried rings and tart Northwest blackberries in the shakes and lemonade. The chain has a commitment to environmental sustainability and a policy of paying fair wages, so you're likely to be greeted with a smiling face when you step up to the counter.

Vancouver's best burgers are at Burgerville USA.

Markets

The **Vancouver Farmers Market** (5th and Ester Sts., 360/737-8298, http://vancouverfarmersmarket.com, 9 A.M.–3 P.M. Sat., 10 A.M.–3 P.M. Sun., Mar.–Oct.) takes place downtown. It's a great place to look for local produce, herbs, arts and crafts, baked goods, and entertainment.

INFORMATION AND SERVICES

For maps or other information, visit the **Washington State Visitor Information Center** (750 Anderson St., 360/750-1553, 8 A.M.–5 P.M. Mon.–Fri., 8:30 A.M.–5 P.M. Sat.–Sun.) located in the O. O. Howard House of Vancouver Historic Reserve. Also helpful is the **Greater Vancouver Chamber of Commerce** (404 E. 15th St., 360/694-2588 or 800/377-7084, www.vancouverusa.com), reachable by taking a left off the I-5 Mill Plain exit 1D.

The **Gifford Pinchot National Forest Supervisor's Office** (10600 NE 51st Circle, Orchards, 360/891-5000, 360/891-5009 for recorded recreation information, 8 A.M.–5 P.M. Mon.–Fri.) is in Vancouver. Stop by for details on Mount St. Helens and other nearby outdoor attractions.

Emergency medical services are provided by **Legacy Salmon Creek Hospital** at (2211 NE 139th St., 360/487-1000). Pet medical care is available at **VCA East Mill Plain Animal Hospital** (9705 East Mill Plain Blvd., 360/892-0032).

GETTING THERE AND AROUND

The local transit system is **C-TRAN** (360/695-0123, www.c-tran.com, $1.60–2.45 per ride, $3.85 all-day pass, $3.35 express ride to Portland), which provides daily service throughout Clark County, as well as to downtown Portland.

For cross-country trips, contact **Greyhound** (613 Main St., 360/696-0186 or 800/231-2222, www.greyhound.com).

Amtrak (360/694-7307 or 800/872-7245, www.amtrak.com) trains stop at a classic early-1900s depot at the foot of West 11th Street, with daily connections north and south on the Coast Starlight, and eastward up the Columbia River aboard the *Empire Builder.*

For air service, head south across the Columbia River to **Portland International Airport** (7000 NE Airport Way, Portland, OR, 877/739-4636, www.flypdx.com), second only in the Pacific Northwest to Sea-Tac International Airport. The airport is serviced by all the major domestic and international airline carriers and is a major hub for Alaska Airlines, which offer dozens of flights to Seattle, Spokane, and other nearby Northwest destinations.

The main parking lot is $24 per day or $3 per hour here, with long-term economy parking for $10 per day. Dozens of shuttle and van carriers service Vancouver from here, including **Blue Start Transportation Group** (800/247-2272, www.bluestarbus.com, $24–32), which offers door-to-door shuttle service.

Pearson Air Field (VUO, within Vancouver National Historic Reserve) provides services to private pilots.

COLUMBIA RIVER GORGE

Lewis and Clark Highway

While the trip along Highway 14, known also as Lewis and Clark Highway, does offer some beautiful Gorge scenery, by the time you arrive at Maryhill Museum you may feel that Columbia River trek is a bit longer than it looks on the map. This is truly a remote part of the state, so stock up on soft drinks, chips, and other necessities first.

Also keep your eyes peeled for speed limit signs. The now-you-see-'em, now-you-don't towns that you'll whiz by require slower speeds within their sometimes hard-to-gauge boundaries, creating speed traps that are zealously checked by local cops.

CAMAS AND WASHOUGAL AREA

While the sight and scent of the enormous Georgia-Pacific paper mill seem to dominate Camas, Camas and neighboring Washougal are attractive small towns right along the Columbia, with big trees lining the main route.

Sights and Recreation

The **Two Rivers Heritage Museum** (Front and 16th Streets, 360/835-8742, 11 A.M.–3 P.M. Tues.–Sat., $3 adults, $2 seniors, $1 ages 6–18) in Washougal has local historical artifacts and photos. A lovely walking path along the Columbia River levee leaves from Steamboat Landing Park in Washougal.

The **Rocket City Neon Museum** (1554 NE 3rd Ave., Camas, 360/571-5885) is one of the more unusual museums in Washington, with hundreds of neon signs, some more than 50 years old.

On Highway 14 between Washougal and North Bonneville, the **Cape Horn Viewpoint** (milepost 25) provides a good spot for photographing the dramatic west entrance to the Gorge and for viewing massive Beacon Rock.

For a short and scenic side trip, take Cape Horn Drive downhill to the river, through overhanging maples and Douglas fir trees.

Washougal's claim to fame is the **Pendleton Woolen Mill** (17th and A Sts., 503/226-4801 or 800/568-2480, www.pendleton-usa.com), in operation since 1912 and still producing its acclaimed woolen products. The mill gives guided tours by appointment. An outlet store here sells seconds and overstocked items.

Camas has a summer-only outdoor **swimming pool** (120 NE 17th, 360/834-2382).

Festivals and Events

Camas Days (360/834-2472), held annually on the fourth weekend of July, includes a parade, wine and microbrew street, live entertainment, craft and food booths, and of course, the bathtub races, which are not to be missed.

Accommodations and Food

For the most basic of accommodations, consider staying at the **Rama Inn** (544 6th St., Washougal, 360/835-8591, $55 s or $65 d), which has an outdoor pool on premises.

The stately colonial Greek-revival **Fairgate Inn** (2213 NW 23rd Ave, Camas, 360/834-0861, $125–175 d) makes an attractive alternative to more humble lodgings. All eight of the elegant rooms come complete with private bath, fireplace, high-speed Internet, and a full breakfast served in the dining room.

Information

Get answers to your questions at the **Camas-Washougal Chamber of Commerce** (422 NE 4th Ave., Camas, 360/834-2472, www.cwchamber.com, 9 A.M.–5 P.M. Mon.–Fri.).

◖ BEACON ROCK STATE PARK

Beacon Rock State Park (509/427-8265, www.parks.wa.gov) is 35 miles east of Vancouver on Highway 14, and just west of the little town of North Bonneville. You can't miss it; the centerpiece of the park is an 848-foot-high ancient volcano core believed to be the largest such

© ERICKA CHICKOWSKI

Climb to the top of Beacon Rock for amazing views of the Columbia River.

monolith in North America. Lewis and Clark named it when they traversed the Gorge in 1805.

Hike the steep one-mile trail to the pinnacle for spectacular views of the Gorge; the trail boasts a 15 percent grade, but handrails make the hiking both easier and safer. This and other trails provide 14 miles of hiking in the park. Advanced climbers only may attempt to climb on the south side of the rock, but it is closed part of the year to protect nesting hawks; register at the trailhead. The main part of the park is north of the highway, and old roads are perfect for mountain biking and horseback riding. A four-mile trail switchbacks to the 1,200-foot summit of **Hamilton Mountain,** passing the very scenic Rodney Falls. Anglers can launch their boats from the boat ramp to catch Columbia River white sturgeon, and campers can stay in the densely forested sites (no RV hookups) for $19, $10 for an extra vehicle. The campground is open April–October. A smaller state park campground below the noisy railroad tracks along the river is open all year, but there are no showers. Campers can take

COLUMBIA RIVER GORGE

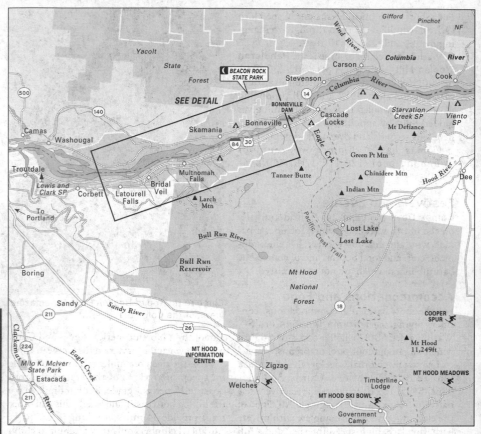

showers at the nearby private Beacon Rock RV Park (360/427-8473).

BONNEVILLE DAM AREA

Bonneville Dam snakes across the Columbia in three sections, connecting the shorelines and Bradford and Cascades Islands. This was the site of the famous Columbia River Cascades that made travel down the river so treacherous for Oregon Trail emigrants. An Army base, **Fort Cascades,** was constructed on the Washington side of the Cascades in the early 1850s and remained in use until 1861. Today, Fort Cascades Historic Site has an interesting 1.5-mile loop path with interpretive signs describing the area's rich history.

Bonneville Dam

The original Bonneville Dam and power plant were built here between 1933 and 1937; a second plant was added on the Washington shore in 1981. Together they produce over a million kilowatts of power that feed into the grid for the Northwest and California.

Visit the **Bonneville Second Powerhouse** visitors center (509/427-4281, 9 A.M.–5 P.M. daily, closed major holidays), on the Washington side of the Bonneville Dam, to see the inner workings of the powerhouse (including a peek inside a spinning turbine) and informative displays. You'll feel dwarfed by the enormity of the river, dam, and surrounding hills. Windows offer a chance to watch coho,

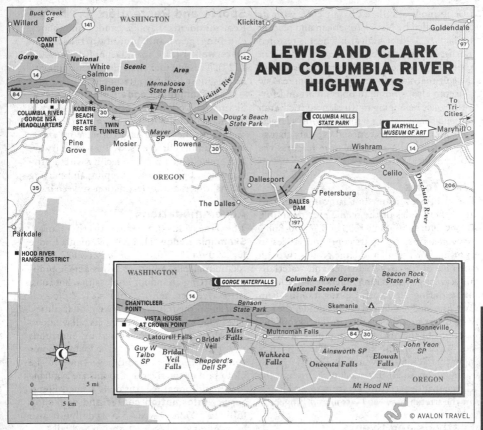

LEWIS AND CLARK AND COLUMBIA RIVER HIGHWAYS

© AVALON TRAVEL

sockeye, and king salmon, along with steelhead, shad, lamprey, and other fish as they head upstream each summer and fall.

Cross **The Bridge of the Gods** ($1 toll for autos) into Oregon and visit the original **Bonneville Lock and Dam** (541/374-8820), a popular tourist spot with continuous presentations, exhibits, and fish viewing.

STEVENSON

The small town of Stevenson has been the governmental seat for Skamania County since 1893, but it is only now starting to come into its own. An enjoyable museum, one of the fanciest lodges in Washington, and hordes of summertime windsurfers and kiteboarders give life to the awesome natural surroundings. **Rock Creek Park** (Rock Creek Dr. and Rock Creek Park Rd.) on the west side of town provides an excellent place for beginner sailboarders and kitesurfers to practice their art.

Columbia Gorge Interpretive Center

Located a mile west of Stevenson, this award-winning museum (990 SW Rock Creek Dr., 800/991-2338, www.columbiagorge.org, 10 A.M.–5 P.M. daily, closed Thanksgiving, Christmas, and New Year's Day, $7 adults, $6 seniors and students, $5 ages 6–12, free for kids under 6) looks across Rock Creek Cove to the mighty Columbia River. Highlights include an enormous simulated basalt cliff, with its crevices filled by Native American and pioneer artifacts, a 37-foot-high fish wheel, a restored Corliss steam engine, and Native American artifacts. Another section introduces you to the spiritual side of the Columbia Gorge. The museum also is home to objets d'art and furniture once belonging to Russian mystic Baron Eugene Fersen, along with the world's largest collection of rosaries. Special exhibits change frequently, and a museum store features the works of local artisans.

Wine Tours

Based in Stevenson, but running tours all along both sides of the scenic area, **Martin's Gorge Tours** (503/349-1323 or 877/290-8687, www.martinsgorgetours.com) specializes in running both small and large groups through the best of the area's wineries and waterfalls all year long, plus taking hikers on wildflower hunts during the colorful spring months. Run by a knowledgeable and affable guide, the service offers a laid-back way to check out big portions of the area while sipping vino without worry of driving impaired. The company's signature Wine and Waterfall Tour ($99) will take you on an all-day adventure through the Gorge that departs directly from several hotels on the stretch between Carson and Bingen.

Festivals and Events

The **Fourth of July** brings the usual fireworks, picnics, and concessions to Skamania County; the best way to see the fireworks is aboard the sternwheeler *Columbia Gorge* (503/224-3900, www.portlandspirit.com), which offers a special tour. In late July, the **Columbia Gorge Bluegrass Festival** (800/989-9178, www.columbiagorgebluegrass.net) brings foot-stompin' music, contests, dances, and plenty of food all day long at the Rock Creek Fairgrounds in Stevenson. The annual **Skamania County Fair and Timber Carnival** (509/427-3979), held in August, offers entertainment, a parade, timber contests, exhibits, and food. The fair prides itself on being one of the last original free fairs.

Sports and Recreation

Rent sailboards, kayaks, canoes, snowshoes, climbing gear, and mountain bikes from **Waterwalker** (21 Carson Depot Rd., 509/427-2727). This popular store also offers sailboard lessons most summer afternoons.

The **Skamania Lodge Golf Course** (SW Skamania Lodge Dr., 509/527-2541, www.skamania.com, $40–65) reigns as the nicest set of links the Gorge has to offer. With amazing Columbia cliff views, well-tended fairways and greens and a practice facility with a driving range, bunker, and chipping and putting greens, this is a true destination-style course.

Accommodations

The finest luxury resort in the Gorge, **Skamania Lodge** (1131 SW Skamania Lodge Dr., 509/427-7700 or 800/221-7117, www.skamania.com, $209–289 d) is a huge property sporting an indoor pool, sauna, hot tubs, fitness center, tennis courts, 18-hole golf course, hiking trails, and convention facilities. The lodge has a classic feeling. Its tall windows face the Columbia River and an enormous river rock fireplace heats up the lobby. Rooms come in various sizes and have views of the mountain or the river. Pet rooms are available for an additional fee. Inside is a small Forest Service **information center and bookshop** (509/427-2528, 9 A.M.–5 P.M. daily). It also hosts guest speakers each spring and fall.

If those rates are a little rich for your blood, **Columbia Gorge Riverside** (509/427-5650, www.cgriversidelodge.com, $79–199 d) offers a cozy atmosphere in its modern, well-appointed log cabins along the Columbia River near Stevenson. It has no phones or TVs, but each has a kitchen, back deck, and access to the hot tub.

Park RVs at **Lewis & Clark RV Park** (509/427-5982, $20 nightly) in North Bonneville, which offers well-spaced campsites on its grassy and tree-shaded property.

Food

Joe's El Rio (193 Hwy. 14, 509/427-4479, 4–9 P.M. daily) has authentic Mexican cuisine to eat in or carry out.

© ERICKA CHICKOWSKI

Skamania Lodge

Skamania Lodge serves gourmet Northwest cuisine three meals a day in an elaborate and busy setting. Be ready to drop $40 or more per person for dinner and be sure to get reservations, especially on summer weekends. The Sunday brunch is especially popular.

Information

The **Stevenson Chamber of Commerce and Visitor Information Center** (167 NW 2nd, 800/989-9178, www.skamania.org, 8 A.M.–5 P.M. daily in summer, Mon.–Fri. only in winter) is the place to go for the scoop on Stevenson.

Getting There

Bus service to these parts is close to non-existent. Vancouver's **C-TRAN** (360/695-0123, www.c-tran.com) will get you as far east as Camas and Washougal. Cross over to the Oregon side for Greyhound bus service along I-84.

CARSON AREA

Just a few miles east of Stevenson is the little town of Carson, known for its hot springs and

as an entry point into Gifford Pinchot National Forest. The drive north from Carson to the east side of Mount St. Helens offers photographic and recreational opportunities aplenty.

Sights

Historic **Carson Hot Springs Resort** (509/427-8292 or 800/607-3678, www.carson hotspringresort.com) has been drawing visitors to its 126°F natural mineral baths since 1876. The St. Martin Hotel was built in 1897 and cabins were added in the 1920s. Hot mineral baths and wraps ($20), and one-hour massages ($60) are available and still the chief draw.

The **Big Lava Bed Geologic Area** encompasses 12,500 acres of lava beds, the eerie remains of an ancient volcano. The steep walls of the tree-covered crater rise 800 feet on the north end of the area, sheltering a meadow deep inside. When exploring the lava beds, be sure to bring plenty of water and keep track of your wanderings, since there are no marked trails to follow. It's even rumored to be haunted. Get here by heading north up Cook-Underwood Road from the town of Cook, eight miles east of Carson on Highway 14. It turns into South

Prairie Road (Forest Service Road 66) after several miles and continues to the lava beds, approximately 14 miles up. The road follows the east side of the lava for the next 10 miles or so.

Festivals and Events

For a walk far on the wild side, plan your trip to catch Carson's **Bigfoot Daze** festival, held on the last weekend of August every year. The wacky festival features talks and panels on the legendary beast plus a costume contest, Sasquatch yell contest, and a chili cook-off.

Sports and Recreation

Several day hikes await the adventurous, including the **Bob Kuse Memorial Trail,** leading to the 1,000-foot summit of **Wind Mountain,** a three-mile hike that provides dramatic views over the Columbia Gorge and a peek at historical Indian vision-quest sites. The trailhead is a mile up Wind Mountain Road on the east side. Be on the lookout for rattlesnakes during the summer months!

For a good view of the area's peaks, take a short hike to the top of **Little Huckleberry Mountain,** best hiked mid-July–October. Take Forest Service Road 66 (along the east edge of the lava bed) to the 49 trailhead; climb the steep grade for 2.5 miles to the summit and a refreshing berry break. The trail is open to hikers, equestrians, and mountain bikers.

A $5 National Forest Recreation Day Pass is required for parking at all Forest Service trailheads in the scenic area. Or pick up an annual **Northwest Forest Pass** ($30) that is valid for most national forest trailheads in Washington and Oregon. Get one from most local sporting-goods stores, any Forest Service office (800/270-7504), or at www.fs.fed.us/passespermits.

Accommodations and Food

Service is known to be a bit iffy, and even the recently renovated rooms are a bit creaky at **Carson Hot Springs Resort** (509/427-8292 or 800/607-3678, www.carsonhotspringresort .com). But the hotel rooms ($80 d) and basic cabins ($60 d) at this historic hot springs are a convenient stopover for those seeking a soak in the soothing spring water. Reserve early if you plan to stay on a weekend. The restaurant serves three meals a day, none of which is likely to wow you.

For something a little nicer, 【 **Carson Ridge Cabins** (509/427-7777, $220–415) redefines "roughing it." The luxury cabins look out

Carson Ridge Cabins

© ERICKA CHICKOWSKI

to verdant Gorge and Cascade hillsides that can be enjoyed from each unit's private porch and charming log-swing. Rooms are decked out with all of the little amenities that add up to an epic vacation: whirlpool tubs controlled with wireless remotes, gas fireplaces,, plush robes, and big flat-panel televisions. Many of the wood furnishings are one-of-a-kind, custom-built pieces. Choose between enjoying the deliciously gourmet breakfast from a cozy dining area or have it directly delivered to your door for maximum privacy. If you can time it right, the property's monthly community dinner is a real treat.

Several Forest Service campgrounds are north of Carson off Wind River Road. Closest is **Panther Creek Campground** (open mid-May–mid-Nov.) nine miles up Wind River Road, and 1.5 miles up Forest Service Road 6517. This tranquil campground is on a stream and has water spigots and toilet facilities. **Beaver Campground** (mid-Apr.–Oct.) is 12 miles up Wind River Road and offers easy RV parking, fishing, and hiking. A shaded, lightly used respite, **Paradise Creek Campground** (mid-May–mid-Nov.) is 21 miles up Wind River Road, and another 6 miles on Forest Service Road 30. All three of these campgrounds range $17–34; make reservations ($9 extra) at 518/885-3639 or 877/444-6777.

Big Cedars County Park (north of Willard on Oklahoma Rd.) has 28 primitive campsites available; there are 23 more at **Home Valley County Park** (509/427-9478), along with a coin-operated shower. RVers can park at **Carson Hot Springs Resort** (509/427-8292).

WHITE SALMON AND BINGEN

Continuing eastward from Carson and Home Valley, the highway passes the trailhead (Forest Pass required for parking) for **Dog Mountain Trail,** a rugged, switchback-filled, 3.5-mile climb to the summit of this 2,900-foot peak.

This is a good chance to stretch your legs and enjoy wildflower-filled meadows in spring. Beyond the trailhead, the Lewis and Clark Highway cuts through five short tunnels and the landscape begins to open up, with fewer

trees and broader vistas. At Cook-Underwood Road, you'll encounter **Little White Salmon/Willard National Fish Hatchery** (13 miles east of Stevenson) and the **Spring Creek National Fish Hatchery** (2 miles west of the Hood River Bridge). Both are free to visit and open 7:30 A.M.–4 P.M. daily. Their goal is the re-establishment of a self-sustaining coho salmon fishery in the Wenatchee River Basin.

The German-themed speed-trap known as Bingen straddles Highway 14; its bigger twin, White Salmon, is just 1.5 miles up the hill. White Salmon has several Bavarian-style buildings and a 14-bell **glockenspiel** mounted above its city hall. The only one of its kind on the West Coast, it chimes hourly 8 A.M.–8 P.M. and plays music on holidays. East of these two towns, the road continues along the river's edge and through the tiny village of **Lyle.**

Gorge Heritage Museum

A well-preserved 1911 church provides the home of the **Gorge Heritage Museum** (202 E. Humbolt, Bingen, 509/493-3228, 11:30 A.M.–4:30 P.M. Thurs.–Sun. late May–Sept.). The collection includes local pioneer relics, Native American artifacts, and historic photos.

Wineries

Wineries around this stretch of Highway 14 fall within the Columbia River Gorge (www.columbiagorgewine.com) bi-state viticultural appellation. Standing as they are on the wetter side of the mountains, the vineyards here tend to produce more delicate wines than the rest of Central Washington. The region also makes for a change of scenery compared to the rest of Washington wine country, with vineyards surrounded by more trees and vegetation than wheat fields and sagebrush.

Set on a hill overlooking Mount Hood and the Gorge, **Wind River Cellars** (196 Spring Creek Rd., Husum, 509/493-2324, www.windrivercellars.com, 10 A.M.–6 P.M. daily, closed Dec. 15–Jan. 1, $5 tasting fee is waived if you purchase a bottle) is located off Highway 141 in Husum. Try the estate-grown white riesling in the tasting room, which is set within the

COLUMBIA RIVER GORGE

winery's lovely cottage with sloping eaves and cedar deck.

Check out the all-natural winemaking process at **Klickitat Canyon Winery** (6 Lyle-Snowden Rd., Lyle, 509/365-2900, www.columbiagorgewinery.com), which prides itself on its from-the-earth methods. The wines here are fermented using only the yeast on the grapes—winemakers don't add any bi-sulfites and 100 percent of its grapes come from the Columbia Gorge, making its vintages a true reflection of the region's terroir. Klickitat offers tours and barrel room tastings noon–6 P.M. Saturday–Sunday.

Plan ahead and call **Gorge Crest Winery** (509/493-2026, www.gorgecrest.com) to schedule a tasting appointment in its modern but comfortable big red barn winery center. The grounds are gorgeous—a favorite for weddings.

Sports and Recreation
RIVER RAFTING
Between Klickitat Gorge and the White Salmon River, the area has enough thrills and spills for the hardest-core river rat. Here, you can find runs in the intermediate skill level class III up through the experts-only class V rapids, along with plenty of experienced pros to guide you through. The best rafting tends to run from May–June. Expect one-day trips to cost around $100, depending on your choice of runs.

Attracting some of the biggest names in the whitewater kayaking world, **Wet Planet** (860 Hwy. 141 in Husum, 877/390-9445, www.wetplanetwhitewater.com) offers a half-day trip through the Wild and Scenic White Salmon River that ends in a rollercoaster ride down the 13-foot Husum Falls. This outfitter takes you through some of the prettiest and most exciting portions of the upper White Salmon from a private put-in that's 2.1 miles upstream from where most local outfitters launch. If you're feeling particularly adventurous, try leaping off a basalt ledge into the river on the trip's optional cliff jump.

All Rivers Adventures (800/743-5628, www.alladventuresrafting.com) provides full-service river guidance and even owns a private ranch available for barbecues and volleyball

canoeing the White Salmon River

© ERICKA CHICKOWSKI

COLUMBIA RIVER GORGE

after your run. **Blue Sky Outfitters** (800/228-7238, www.blueskyoutfitters.com) guides one-day and overnight trips. **Wildwater River Tours** (800/522-9453, www.wildwater-river.com) takes a wide variety of trips and even offers guide training, if white water truly gets in your blood.

HORSEBACK RIDING

North Western Lake Riding Stables (509/493-4965, www.nwstables.com) has horseback rides near White Salmon ranging $40–160 per person. Rides can be had between 8 A.M. and sunset, weather permitting.

BIKE RENTALS

Cross the river to Oregon to pick up a rental bike at **Discovery Bikes** (116 Oak St., Hood River, Oregon, 541/386-4820, $20–55 per day), which keeps a huge corral of mountain bikes, road bikes, and kiddie bikes with training wheels on hand for visitors.

Festivals and Events

White Salmon's **Spring Festival** (509/365-4565, www.whitesalmonspringfestival.com) on the third weekend of May in Rheingarten Park includes a parade, food, entertainment, and a chili cook-off. Or, for some autumnal fun, pay a visit to Bingen's **Huckleberry Fest** (509/637-0411, www.huckleberryfest.com) on the second weekend of September. The parade and talent show play second fiddle to the main attraction: the huckleberry products. If it can be made with huckleberries, you can try it here.

Accommodations

A cozy inn with a long history is **Inn of the White Salmon** (172 W Jewett Blvd., 509/493-2335 or 800/972-5226, www.innofthewhitesalmon.com, $90 s or $106–135 d) in White Salmon. This homey hideaway features charming decor, wireless Internet, a fireplace, hot tub, and delicious gourmet breakfasts. Most rooms have private baths, but if you're looking for a bargain, ask about the eight-bed hostel room ($25 per person).

For a break from the norm, the **Columbia**

River Gorge Hostel (Humboldt and Cedar Streets, 509/493-3363, www.bingenschool.com) might be just your style. This restored 1938 schoolhouse offers 48 hostel beds ($19 pp) and six private rooms ($49 d). This place is a big hit with visiting windsurfers and rock climbers—so much so that windsurfing rentals and lessons are offered on-site and one of the Inn's amenities is a private climbing wall. A weight room, indoor basketball court, and kitchen area are among the hostel amenities. The Inn is home to memorabilia from the old school days. Reservations are recommended in midsummer.

Right on the northern side of the Hood River Bridge, **Bridge RV Park and Campground** ($39) runs a well-manicured park with riverfront access and pretty views of the Gorge. Its location puts it within easy striking distance of Hood River and all of the Washington-side recreation activities. With full hookups for RV campers and shady tent spots, plus a spic-and-span shower and laundry facilities, this is a comfortable camping spot to serve as base camp for multiday Gorge explorations.

Food

Those craving a hearty breakfast can count on satisfaction at **Big River Diner** (740 E. Steuben St., Bingen, 509/493-1414, 8 A.M.–8 P.M. daily), which serves ample portions of old favorites like biscuits and gravy, pancakes, and eggs.

For something homier, **Inn of the White Salmon** (509/493-2335) pulls out its dining chairs to nonguests who'd like to partake in its locally famous country breakfasts ($10). Phone ahead for reservations.

The wine and brewery scene has definitely benefited White Salmon from a culinary perspective, as the area is slowly attracting chefs interested in the region's legacy in vino and fresh produce. **Henni's Kitchen and Bar** (120 E Jewett, 509/493-1555, 5–9 P.M. daily) is a testament to that. A gastropub-style establishment with exposed brick walls and moody lighting, the wine and beer selection is extensive and daring and the bartenders also know how to make a mean cocktail to go along with the selection of small plates and gourmet entrées like pork loin stuffed with apricot sausage over polenta and green beans or house-made gnocci with chanterelle mushrooms and spinach in leek cream.

Road-trippin' families toting little ones should consider unloading the minivan at **Solstice Wood Fire Café** (415 W. Steuben St., Bingen, 509/493-4006, www.solsticewood firecafe.com, 11:30 A.M.–2 P.M. and 5–8 P.M. Mon.–Thurs., 11:30 A.M.–2 P.M. and 5–9 P.M. Fri., 11:30 A.M.–9 P.M. Sat., 11:30 A.M.–8 P.M. Sun.). This kid-friendly restaurant has a special play area and a chalkboard for the kids to unload a little of that pent-up road trip energy. The food's delish, too, with a menu full of wood-fired pizzas, sandwiches, and salads. The pizzas range from plain for picky eaters to inventive, such as the combo with chicken, potatoes, and sweet peppers.

Information and Services

Get regional information from the **Mount Adams Chamber of Commerce** (509/493-3630, business.gorge.net/mtadamschamber, 8 A.M.–5 P.M. daily June–Sept., Mon.–Fri. only the rest of the year) next to the toll bridge just west of Bingen.

Emergency medical services are provided by **Skyline Hospital** (211 Skyline Dr., 509/493-1101) in White Salmon. Pets can go to **Alpine Veterinary Hospital** (208 Lincoln Dr., 509/493-3908) in Bingen.

Getting There

The Bingen **Amtrak** (509/248-1146 or 800/872-7245, www.amtrak.com) station is located at 800 Northwest 6th Street. Service is daily, heading west to Vancouver and Portland, and east to Wishram, Pasco, Spokane, and all the way to Chicago.

LYLE TO WISHRAM

A transformation begins east of the Lyle area as the country opens up into rolling dry hills of grass and rock. In this desolate place the rumble of long freight trains and the sounds of tugs pushing barges upriver mingle with those of nature to create a hauntingly resounding symphony.

Wineries

There are no gimmicky attractions or kitschy gift shops at **Syncline Wine Cellars** (111 Balch Rd., 509/365-4361, www.syncline wine.com). Nope, it's all about the wine here at this family-run vintner that's tucked away on a piece of country property up in the hills above Lyle. The tasting room is simply a marble-topped bar placed in the corner of the property's barrel room, giving the vino center stage. Known best for its work with rhone and burgundy varietals, this winery's prized vintage is its cuvee elena, a blend of grenache, mourvedre, syrah and carignan.

A super-fun winery located on a remote stretch of road near Columbia Hills State Park, **Marshal's Winery** (158 Oak Creek Dr., 509/767-4633) never takes itself too seriously. The tasting room is done up similar to your grandad's rumpus room, with picnic tables adorned with simple tablecloths and serving M&Ms and Cheetos as palate cleansers. Marshall's bold barbera is the highlight here.

Marshal's Winery

© ERICKA CHICKOWSKI

petroglyphs at Columbia Hills State Park

◖ Columbia Hills State Park

With dramatic views of the river, an amazing collection of some of the oldest petroglyphs and pictographs in the Northwest and plenty of opportunity for recreation, Columbia Hills State Park stands out as one of the jewels of the Gorge's hot and grassy dry side. Located two miles east of Highway 197 on Highway 14, the park has good trout and bass fishing at Horsethief Lake, accessible from your boat or one of the park's rentals, with two boat launches—one on the lake, one on the river. Nearby is 500-foot-high **Horsethief Butte,** a favorite of rock climbers. And finally, the park's most draw-worthy asset is its collection of petroglyphs and pictographs, which were transplanted here after being carved off the nearby cliffsides to make way for The Dalles Dam. The campground at the park (509/767-1159, open Apr.–Oct.) has four standard sites ($17), eight partial utility sites ($23), six primitive sites ($12), a dump station, and a restroom.

Doug's Beach State Park

This tiny park is a staging area for the throngs of windsurfers who come here all summer long to play on the Columbia River. This is not a place for beginners since the swells can reach six–eight feet at times. There's no water or camping, but it does have outhouses. The park is located 2.5 miles east of the town of Lyle along Highway 14, and 7 miles west of Columbia Hills State Park. Park hours are 6:30 A.M.–dusk in summer and 8 A.M.–dusk in winter.

Getting There

Amtrak (800/872-7245, www.amtrak.com) trains stop at the little settlement of Wishram, nine miles east of The Dalles dam. Service is daily, heading west to Bingen, Vancouver, and Portland, and east to Pasco, Spokane, and continuing all the way to Chicago.

GOLDENDALE AREA

Highway 97 heads north from the Columbia to the little town of Goldendale, 10 miles away, passing scores of cows, happily munching away or taking it easy along the route. The horizon is dominated by the snowcapped summits of Mount Hood to the south and Mount Adams, Mount St. Helens, and Mount Rainier to the west. North of Goldendale, Highway 97 climbs through ponderosa pine forests as it reaches 3,107-foot **Satus Pass,** before descending into the scenic and lonely Yakama Reservation, and finally the town of Toppenish in Yakima Valley, 50 miles away. Goldendale began when the first farmers and loggers settled here in 1879 and has grown slowly over the decades since.

Sights and Recreation

Goldendale's 20-room **Presby Mansion** (127 W. Broadway, 509/773-4303, 10 A.M.–4 P.M. Mon.–Thurs., 9 A.M.–5 P.M. Fri.–Sun. mid-Apr.–mid-Oct., $4.50 adults, $1 ages 6–12, free for children under age 6) is the home of **Klickitat County Historical Museum.** Built in 1902, this magnificent white-clapboard mansion is filled with pioneer furnishings,

© ERICKA CHICKOWSKI

Goldendale Observatory

historic photos, farm equipment, and other artifacts. Be sure to check out the annual Christmas lighting party on the first Sunday of December.

Head a mile north of town and uphill through open ponderosa pine forests to **Goldendale Observatory State Park** (509/773-3141, www.parks.wa.gov), where you'll find one of the nation's largest telescopes open to public viewing as well as several smaller portable telescopes. Take a tour and enjoy free audiovisual programs, displays, and demonstrations 2–5 P.M. and 8–midnight Wednesday–Sunday April–September, 2–5 P.M. and 7–10 P.M. Friday–Sunday in winter.

Festivals and Events

G'day Goldendale Community Days (509/773-3677) in early July features arts and crafts, ethnic food, a flea market, antique auction, beer garden, and parade. If the antique auction doesn't get your adrenaline pumping quite enough, check out Goldendale's

annual **4th of July Demolition Derby and Motocross Race** (509/250-0206) at the Klickitat County Fairgrounds. The **Klickitat County Fair and Rodeo** (509/773-3900) is another thrill-ride held over Labor Day weekend, including a carnival, parade, and chute after chute of angry bulls! This is one little town that knows how to do "extreme."

Accommodations

Lodging options are few and far between in this area. The best choice in town is **Quality Inn** (808 E. Simcoe Dr., 509/773-5881 or 800/358-5881, $8, or $99 d), which sports a seasonal outdoor pool, continental breakfast, and clean motel units. The price is a little over the top, mostly because they know they've gotcha.

A cheaper alternative is the **Ponderosa Motel** (775 E. Broadway St., 509/773-5842, $60 s or $70 d), which is not quite as nice as the Quality Inn, but makes up for it with friendly and attentive service.

Out in the pine country north of Goldendale, **Pine Springs Resort** (2471 Hwy.

97, 509/773-4434, www.pinespringsresort
.net) is a neighborly retreat offering small cabins ($89), RV hookups ($22) and tent camping
($13). The social center of the place is a cozy
snack bar with a rustic pine counter and stools
and a big-screen TV. Also on premises are a
game room, laundry room, grocery store, and
gift shop. Dogs are welcome, and rates include
free wireless Internet access.

Camp at **Brooks Memorial State Park**
(509/773-4611, www.parks.wa.gov), 15 miles
north of Goldendale on Highway 97. Tent ($19)
and full-utility RV ($27) sites on 700 forested
acres are available year-round. Enjoy the nine
miles of hiking trails through cool coniferous
forests and good trout fishing in the Klickitat
River. The park has great cross-country skiing
in winter, too.

Food

Tucked away into a restored Folk Victorian
cottage on a quiet downtown Goldendale
street, **The Glass Onion** (604 S. Columbus
Ave., 509/773-4928, www.theglassonionrestau
rant.com, 11 A.M.–4 P.M. Wed., 11 A.M.–9 P.M.
Thurs.–Sat.) is a secret little treasure that foodies will want to take a detour to visit while
rambling the vineyards of the Gorge. The seasonal menu is short, but every dish is an artfully plated symphony of flavors, such as the
from-scratch pea soup and the grilled pork
tenderloin served with ratatouille. Don't skip
a salad with that entrée—they are as fresh as it
gets. Check out the fine-art photos displayed
on the walls while waiting for your dishes—
they're taken by the chef's wife, a professional
photographer.

For more day-to-day fare, **Gee's Family
Restaurant** (118 E Main St., Goldendale,
509/773-6999, 10:30 A.M.–9:30 P.M. Mon.–
Sat., 11:30 A.M.–8:30 P.M. Sun.) has decent
Americanized Chinese dishes. Interestingly
enough, it also grills up Goldendale's best
burgers. These suckers are big enough for a
couple of lumberjacks to split.

Sodbuster's Restaurant (1040 E.
Broadway, Goldendale, 509/773-6160,
6 A.M.–9 P.M. Mon.–Sat., 6 A.M.–8 P.M. Sun.)
is also a reliable choice with its versatile diner
menu. It's got the best breakfast fare in town.

Information and Services

For local information, stop by **Goldendale
Chamber of Commerce** (903 E. Broadway,
509/773-3400, www.goldendalechamber.org,
9 A.M.–3 P.M. daily June–Sept., Mon.–Fri. only
the rest of the year).

Emergency medical services are provided by
Klickitat Valley Hospital (310 S. Roosevelt,
509/773-4022), while ailing pets can find succor at **Mid-Columbia Veterinary Clinic** (417
E. Broadway, 509/773-4363).

MARYHILL

Named after the daughter of businessman
Sam Hill, the little settlement of Maryhill
now boasts just 38 permanent residents. Hill
dreamed that his town would one day become
a thriving Quaker settlement, a wish that never
materialized. The railroad man and campaigner
for good roads left his mark nevertheless.

Although many of his original town buildings burned, Hill's mansion and the scale replica he built of Stonehenge as a war memorial
still stand as a symbol of his hopes. The dusty
intersection of Highways 14 and 97 may be remote, but it offers the wandering traveler some
unique sights and some wonderful wines to add
to the mystique of this place.

Sights
◖ MARYHILL MUSEUM OF ART

You'd be hard-pressed to find a collection more
wonderfully eclectic than that of the Maryhill
Museum of Art (35 Maryhill Museum Dr.,
509/773-3733, www.maryhillmuseum.org,
9 A.M.–5 P.M. daily Mar. 15–Nov. 15, closed
the rest of the year, $7 adults, $6 seniors, $2
ages 6–16, free for kids under 6). The beautiful 1914 concrete-and-steel home was originally built as a mansion for Sam Hill but
now houses exhibits ranging from an extensive selection of Auguste Rodin sculpture to
hundreds of international chess sets to a full
gallery of memorabilia related to Queen Marie
of Romania, a close friend of Sam Hill's. Along

CASTLE NOWHERE

The Northwest has no Hearst Castles or Winchester Mystery Houses, no Death Valley Scotties. In that favorite tourist category of eccentric mansions, the Northwest offers only the **Maryhill Museum of Art,** a place whose evolution from barren hillside to empty palatial home to museum took 26 years.

The museum – jokingly called "Castle Nowhere" – stands in isolated splendor on a bleak, sagebrush-strewn section of desert along the Columbia River, 100 miles east of Portland and Vancouver and 60 miles south of Yakima. This was just the setting that Seattle attorney and entrepreneur Sam Hill wanted when he was searching for a home site early in the 20th century.

Hill's most extravagant venture was an attempt to establish a utopian Quaker town "where the rain of the west and the sunshine of the east meet." He purchased 7,000 acres on the north side of the Columbia River south of Goldendale, and in 1914 began building his concrete palace, which was to be the farm's centerpiece. He named the spread Maryhill, after his wife, daughter, and mother-in-law, all three named Mary Hill. Hill attempted to interest Quakers in investing in his community. He built them a meeting hall and a few other facilities as enticement, but the Quakers declined. His wife, too, refused to live in this godforsaken place, taking the children and returning to Minnesota. All of the buildings constructed for the utopian town were destroyed in a fire in 1958.

About three miles upriver from the museum, just east of Highway 97, Hill built a concrete replica of **England's Stonehenge,** as it might have looked when intact, and dedicated it to the Klickitat County soldiers who died in World War I. Hill also built the **Peace Arch** that marks the U.S./Canadian border at Blaine, Washington.

The World War I years saw the mansion incomplete and bereft of inhabitants. After the war, President Herbert Hoover appointed Hill to a commission to help with Europe's reconstruction. There he met the three women who were responsible for Maryhill becoming a museum: Loie Fuller, a modern-dance pioneer at the Folies Bergère; Alma Spreckels, of a prominent California sugar family; and Queen Marie of Romania, whose country Hill aided during the post-war recovery period.

Fuller was particularly enthusiastic about the project and introduced Hill to members of the Parisian artistic community. Hill soon bought a large Auguste Rodin collection of sculptures and drawings.

When the 1926 dedication of the still-unfinished museum neared, Queen Marie agreed to come to New York and cross America by train to attend the ceremonies. She brought along a large collection of furniture, jewelry, clothing, and religious objects to be donated to the museum. Today her collection is one of the museum's largest.

Hill died in 1931 and was interred just below

with the surprisingly large permanent collection, Maryhill attracts top-notch traveling exhibits as well. Be sure to enjoy a moment on the patio watching the peacocks roam the grounds while enjoying the Columbia River vistas that brought Sam Hill here.

WINERIES

Overlooking the depths of the Gorge, **Cascade Cliffs Winery** (8866 Hwy. 14, 509/767-1100, www.cascadecliffs.com, 10 A.M.–6 P.M. daily) produces some deliciously obscure red wines.

The winery has the distinction of bringing the first Washington-grown barbera wine to market and is one of the few Washington wineries to produce nebbiolo. The exposed-beam warehouse tasting room (11 A.M.–5 P.M. Fri.–Sun. Apr.–Nov.) gives visitors the opportunity to sample wines.

The real centerpiece of the Gorge's winery scene, **Maryhill Winery** (9774 Highway 14, Goldendale, 877/627-9445, www.maryhill winery.com, 10 A.M.–6 P.M. daily) sits next door to the museum on a terraced cliff over the Stonehenge monument, overlooking the river. At the time of Hill's death, the museum still wasn't quite complete. Alma Spreckels took over the project, donating many pieces from her extensive art collection and seeing to it that the museum was finished and opened in 1940. On that occasion *Time* magazine called it "the loneliest museum in the world."

Sam Hill's original 7,000-acre spread remains intact, and the museum of sculpture, art, and trappings of Romanian and Russian nobility is worth the drive into the hinterlands. Standing on the veranda might feel a bit lonely, but the view is breathtaking and helps answer the question, "What in Sam Hill was he thinking?"

© ERICKA CHICKOWSKI

Stonehenge replica at Maryhill

Maryhill State Park's lush vegetation. Its comfortable tasting room and patio afford the most breathtaking scenery at any winery in the state. Much of the vineyard sits on a level below the tasting room terrace, its rows seemingly extending to the very lip of the Gorge. The panoramic view of the vineyard, the Gorge, and Mount Hood in the background make for unbelievable sunsets. The patio is pleasant when the wind doesn't whip up too much, and the tasting room itself is an elegant affair with a river-rock fireplace and an enormous 12-foot-

high oak and inlaid mirror bar built during the turn of the 20th century. Also on the premises right next to the winery arbor and tasting room is the brand new 4,000-seat Maryhill Winery Amphitheater, which draws summertime shows such as B. B. King and Crosby, Stills and Nash.

STONEHENGE REPLICA

Three miles east of Maryhill is another unexpected attraction. On a hilltop surrounded by open grass and sage sits a poured-concrete **replica of England's Stonehenge** (7 A.M.–10 P.M. daily) but with all the monoliths neatly aligned. Built by Sam Hill, an ardent Quaker and pacifist, the array is a monument to Klickitat county's 13 men who lost their lives in World War I. It is meant to illustrate the needless human sacrifice of war and is believed to be the nation's first World War I memorial. The ashes of Sam Hill himself are in an urn just down the slope from Stonehenge.

ORCHARDS AND FRUIT STANDS
Just down the hill from the Stonehenge replica are fruit orchards surrounding the small settlement of Maryhill, with its New England–style white church and old steam engine. The **Maryhill Fruit Stand** and **Gunkel Orchards** sell some of the finest peaches, apricots, cherries, and other fresh fruits that you'll ever taste.

Sports and Recreation
Maryhill State Park (509/773-5007) is five miles east of the Maryhill Museum and right along the Columbia River near the intersection of Highways 14 and 97. Maryhill State Park offers Columbia River waterfront access for boating, windsurfing, and fishing. A $7 fee grants you all-day access to one of two boat launches and a nearby dock. Once you dry off, you can also unwind taking a stroll and looking for waterfowl along 1.1 miles of trails here. The park is open for day use 6:30 A.M.–dusk in summer and 8 A.M.–dusk the rest of the year. You can also camp here year-round, in 50 full-utility RV campsites ($24), 20 standard tent sites ($17), and showers. Make reservations ($7 extra) at 888/226-7688 or www.parks.wa.gov. A **Travel Information Center** here has Columbia Gorge and Washington State information seasonally.

You can also camp or park RVs along the river at **Peach Beach Campark** (509/773-4698).

EAST TO TRI-CITIES
The stretch of Highway 14 between Maryhill and McNary Dam is some of the most sparsely populated country in Washington. Dry grassy hills provide grazing land for cattle, and a few scattered old farmsteads are slowly returning to the land. The land is bisected by tall power lines marching like misshapen insects over the landscape. There's not much traffic here, so tune in to the Spanish-language radio station, KDNA (FM 91.9) for music. Two bucolic settlements—**Roosevelt** and **Paterson**—are the only signs of human life on this side of the Columbia.

John Day Lock and Dam
The John Day Lock and Dam, 24 miles upriver from The Dalles and 6 miles east of Stonehenge, gave birth to Lake Umatilla and produces enough electricity for two cities the size of Seattle. Here you'll find one of the largest single-lift locks in the world, hefting vessels 113 feet. At the dam on Oregon's I-84, enjoy the fish-viewing room, visitors' gallery, and Giles French Park, which has a boat launch, a picnic area, and fishing.

A good portion of the power generated is used in the enormous Columbia Aluminum Corporation plant that stretches for two-thirds of a mile next to the dam. Camp for free at undeveloped **Cliffs Park,** approximately three miles off the highway on John Day Road.

Bickleton
For a pleasant side trip, drive north from Roosevelt to the farming town of Bickleton, with a friendly café on one side of the street and a tavern on the other. Bickleton has the unique distinction of being the bluebird capital of the world; houses for the little guys are everywhere. The bluebird housing project started in the 1960s when Jess and Elva Brinkerhoff built one, then another and another, and soon it was a community project. When the birds leave for the winter, the 700 houses are taken down, cleaned, and painted if they need it. Spring is the best time to view the bluebirds, but you're likely to see them all summer long.

In Cleveland Pioneer Park, four miles west of town, is a delightful old **carousel** with 24 wooden horses and a musical calliope. Built at the turn of the 20th century, the carousel has been here since 1928 and is a rare type that moves around a track. The horses are locked away in a secret location with the exception of a two-day period each summer: during the **Alder Creek Pioneer Picnic and Rodeo** in mid-June. This is the oldest rodeo in the state of Washington and also a cheap thrill at only $7.

For another piece of history, visit **Bluebird Inn** (121 E. Market St., 509/896-2273), said to be Washington's oldest tavern. Built in 1892, it has a classic century-old Brunswick pool table with leather pockets (still in use), along with other local artifacts.

The **Whoop-N-Holler Ranch Museum** (East Rd. between Bickleton and Roosevelt, 509/896-2344, 10 A.M.–4 P.M. Apr.–Sept., $3) contains a lifetime of collecting by Lawrence and Ada Whitmore. Two large buildings are filled with antique cars, as well as local historical items and family heirlooms that tell the interesting story of the Whitmore family. This is one of the largest collections of antique and classic cars in the state.

Wineries

Get lost in the sweet desolation of the Horse Heaven Hills viticultural region. Call ahead and make an appointment with **Destiny Ridge Vineyard** (509/786-3497), estate vineyard of Prosser-based Alexandria Nicole Cellars and a major grower for dozens of other wineries. Take in the sweeping views of the Columbia River as winemakers take you on a 2.5-hour tour ($35) of the vineyards followed by a barrel room tasting with light hors d'oeuvres. The vineyard also recently began a "glam-camp" program. Cozy up in a 14- by 17-foot platform tent equipped with electricity and water. Campers will be serviced with food to fire up a barbecue dinner and a breakfast in the vineyards for a one-of-a-kind getaway. Call for pricing.

Also here in the hills of the state's most remote region, **Columbia Crest Winery** (Hwy. 221, Columbia Crest Dr., Paterson, 509/875-2061, www.columbia-crest.com, 10 A.M.–4:30 P.M. daily) is perched just north of Paterson with its own commanding view across the Columbia River and adjacent vineyards. Founded in 1962, and now one of Washington's largest wine producers, Columbia Crest operates much of the winery below ground, making it easier to maintain cool temperatures throughout the year.

Crow Butte State Park

Located at the site of one of many camps used by the Lewis and Clark Expedition, this 1,312-acre park sits along a lonesome stretch of highway halfway between the little towns of Roosevelt and Paterson. It offers boating, swimming, fishing, and waterskiing, with tent ($19) and RV sites ($24) and coin-operated showers. The campground is open daily late March–late October, plus winter weekends. Make reservations ($7 extra) at 888/226-7688 or www.parks .wa.gov. Crow Butte State Park covers half of an island created when the John Day Dam backed up the river to form Lake Umatilla; the other half is within **Umatilla National Wildlife Refuge** (509/546-8300, http://midcolumbiariver.fws.gov/Umatillapage.htm), which straddles both sides of the Columbia. A 0.75-mile trail leads to the top of Crow Butte (671 feet), with views across the Columbia to Mount Hood when the weather permits; keep your eyes open for rattlesnakes. The Umatilla National Wildlife Refuge has an overlook a few miles east of Crow Butte where you can peer across the river below while browsing a brochure describing the refuge and its abundant waterfowl.

McNary Dam

By the time you reach the McNary Dam area, the land has opened into an brushy desert of sage and grass broken only by center-pivot irrigation systems. The Columbia River's McNary Lock and Dam, 30 miles south of Pasco in Umatilla, Oregon, creates 61-mile-long Lake Wallula, which reaches up past the Tri-Cities to Ice Harbor Dam.

The **McNary National Wildlife Refuge,** next to McNary Dam, has a mile-long hiking trail popular with bird-watchers. Area species include hawks, golden and bald eagles, and prairie falcons.

Information and Services

This is remote country; the combined population of Roosevelt and Paterson is a minuscule 301. As a result, services are extremely limited. If you're coming from the west and your gas tank isn't full, be sure to take the 30-minute side trip up to Goldendale to fill up. From the west or north, gas up in the Tri-Cities or Prosser. Failing to do so could wreck a trip, leaving you stranded for hours in the hot sun.

If you're starving, Roosevelt has a very basic roadhouse establishment, **M&T Bar & Grill** (215 Roosevelt Ave., Roosevelt, 509/384-9440). Paterson has no restaurant, but it does have the small **Paterson Store** (48201 Paterson Ave., 509/875-2741) with basic provisions.

Columbia River Highway

The Oregon side of the Columbia River offers the fastest routes east to the warmer part of the region via I-84, which runs the length of the Gorge and then some. But there are also plenty of opportunities along this route to take it slow along impressive historic back roads and enjoy the sprays and cascades of one of the prettiest collections of waterfalls in the lower 48.

TROUTDALE

Known as the Gateway to the Gorge, Troutdale is the first town you'll encounter when getting off I-84 to take the slower, more scenic Historic Columbia River Highway through some of the best parts of the southern Gorge. It makes for a good stop to gather last-minute details about scenic points along the way and fill up gas tanks and bellies on the way in or out.

Sights

If you can get the timing down just right, the Troutdale Historical Society (503/661-2164, www.troutdalehistory.org) runs an inviting trio of museums that it opens up on the third Saturday of each month between 10 A.M. and 2 P.M. or by appointment. Built in 1900 by the son of Troutdale's founder, the **Harlow House Museum** (726 E. Historic Columbia River Hwy.) features period furnishings and several collections from local families that include vintage hats and ruby glass. The **Barn Museum** (726 E. Historic Columbia River Hwy.) features a growing collection of old farm equipment and other rotating exhibits. And the **Rail Depot Museum** (473 E. Historic Columbia River Hwy.) displays over 100 years' worth of train memorabilia, along with a Union Pacific caboose outside. In addition to the Saturday hours, this museum is also open 10 A.M.–4 P.M. Tuesday through Friday. It's located right at Depot Park, a pretty little municipal green space with access to the Sandy River and Beaver Creek.

Entertainment and Events

No need to dust off the ol' tuxedo to order a cocktail at **Shaken Martini Lounge** (101 W Historic Columbia River Hwy., 503/512-7485), but be ready to drink it up Bond-style at this 007-inspired lounge. The drinks are named after various Bond girls, decor is done up in sleek reds and blacks, and on Thursday nights the owner even shows Bond movies. If that sounds a might fancy for your tastes, head down the street to **Brass Rail Tavern** (108 E Historic Columbia River Hwy., 503/666-8756), a good old fashioned hole-in-the-wall that'll do right by you with a pool table, plenty of pitchers to pour and a game on the TV.

The many pubs of **McMenamins Edgefield Resort** (2126 SW Halsey St., 503/669-8610, www.mcmenamins.com) are like an amusement park for drinkers. Click together the billiard balls at Lucky Staehly's Pool Hall, pay homage to the Grateful dead at the tiny Jerry's Ice House, and check out the pipe sculptures and woodstove at the Distillery Bar, all of which are just a few of the drinking establishments set on the unique property.

Shopping

Troutdale is also the gateway to shopping deals as the home to the **Columbia Gorge Premium Outlets** (450 NW 257 Way, 503/669-8060, wwww.premiumoutlets.com/columbiagorge, 10 A.M.–8 P.M. Mon.–Sat., 10 A.M.–6 P.M. Sun.), a huge high-roller outlet mall with stores such as Calvin Klein, Gap Outlet, Eddie Bauer Outlet, and Adidas to choose among. All told, the complex hosts 45 stores.

Sports and Recreation

The trout in Troutdale is actually the king of trouts, the steelhead. The adjacent Sandy River, which dumps into the Columbia on the outskirts of town, is known as one of the most bountiful steelhead fisheries in the entire state. If you're prepared to brave the icy waters during steelheading's wintery season, try your hand at **Sandy River Delta Park** or **Dabney State Recreation Area.** Pick up tackle, gear and some tips at **Jack's Snack N Tackle** (1208 E. Historic Columbia River Hwy., 503/665-2257, www.jackssnackandtackle.com, 8:30 A.M.–5 P.M. Mon.–Sat.). Or let a guide handle the details so you can concentrate on reeling in the hard-fighting fish. The **Hook Up Guide Service** offers a full- ($175 pp) and half-day ($100) service that includes all equipment and licenses. All you need to do is show up.

Accommodations

Built over a century ago as the county poor farm and old folks' home, the estate at [C] **McMenamins Edgefield** (2126 SW Halsey St., 503/669-8610, www.mcmenamins.com) charms guests with its whimsical play on the 74-acre property's history. Some of the farm land continues to produce veggies and herbs to supply the Edgefield's signature restaurant, the main dormitory has been restored and kitted out as a comfortable lodging house offering a range of European-style rooms, and many other original buildings have been transformed into unique watering holes that serve McMenamins' signature ales. A bit of a theme park for big kids, Edgefield also features two par-three golf courses, a spa, and tons of unique art to spice up a stroll around the grounds. The accommodations themselves are a lot more comfortable than the property's down-on-its-luck history would lead you to believe, with soft beds and funky furnishings galore. Guests who want a bit more privacy can even choose between a few suites with private baths. Solo travelers will also dig the option of laying up in one of the Edgefield's first-come, first-served hostel beds or reservable twin bed private rooms. Designed to be a bit of an oasis from everyday life, none of the rooms are equipped with TVs or telephones. But then again, given the choices for imbibing around here, the proprietors may well be saving you an embarrassing case of drunk dialing. If you absolutely need it, there's free Wi-Fi in a number of the public areas.

Food

Set up just beyond the century-old Sandy River Bridge along the east bank of the river on the edge of town, **Tad's Chicken 'n' Dumplins** (1325 E. Historic Columbia River Hwy., 503/666-5337, http://tadschicdump.com, 5–10 P.M. Mon.–Fri., 4–10 P.M. Sat.–Sun.) serves stick-to-yer-ribs dinners that make a perfect end-cap to a day exploring the Gorge. With views of the Sandy River through windows draped in red-checkered curtains, Tad's seats you in comfy red vinyl and wood booths. Upriver from that, a bit further outside of town, **Shirley's Tippy Canoe** (28242 E. Historic Columbia River Hwy., 503/492-2220, www .shirleysfood.com, 8 A.M.–8 P.M. daily) sports a huge patio overlooking the Sandy's waters and a long menu of home cookin' served throughout the day.

The nicest restaurant at McMenamins Edgefield, **Black Rabbit Restaurant** (2126 SW Halsey St., 503/492-3086, www.mc menamins.com) serves beautifully presented dishes made with seasonal produce grown on the organic plots scattered across the property's 74 acres.

Information and Services

The **Troutdale Visitor Center** (226 W. Historic Columbia River Hwy., 503/669-7473,

8:30 A.M.–4:30 P.M.) is staffed with friendly and helpful locals who can direct you to the best that the Oregon side of the gorge has to offer with a bundle of maps, brochures, and personal stories.

HISTORIC COLUMBIA RIVER HIGHWAY

The sun-dappled blacktop curves that snake their way east from Troutdale are what the Gorge is best known for. This take-it-slow alternative to I-84 runs parallel to the freeway but higher up on the Gorge's bluffs for unparalleled views. Vista points interrupt the lush canopy here at numerous points along the way, as do a number of impressive waterfalls, including the second-highest year-round waterfall in the States.

Sights
VIEWPOINTS
The **Portland Women's Forum State Scenic Viewpoint** (9 mi. east of Troutdale on Historic Columbia River Highway) presents the first breathtaking view of the Gorge from the vantage of the Historic Columbia River Highway. In the foreground you can see Crown Point with the distinctive Vista House at its tip, while in the distance the ribbon of river snakes its way through basalt walls. The air is redolent with blackberry fragrance in the summer from the vines growing up the hillside here, and if you come in August, you might be able to pick a few to munch while taking in the sights.

If the day is clear and you've got the time, about a half mile east of the Women's Forum overlook, the turnout to Larch Mountain Road will take you 14 miles up to the jaw-dropping panoramic of **Sherrard Viewpoint.** At an elevation of 4,055 feet and with tons of unobstructed views of the Cascades at the picnic area here, on a day with good visibility you can see Mounts St. Helens, Rainier, Adams, Hood, and Jefferson.

VISTA HOUSE AT CROWN POINT
Standing as a beacon of the historic highway on the promontory at Crown Point, Vista House (40700 Historic Columbia River Hwy., 503/695-2230, http://vistahouse.com,

the view from Vista House at Crown Point

COLUMBIA RIVER GORGE

© ERICKA CHICKOWSKI

9 A.M.–6 P.M. daily) was conceived when the road was built as "an observatory from which the view both up and down the Columbia could be viewed in silent communion with the infinite." The vistas are definitely worth the stop, but the building itself isn't too shabby, either. Constructed in 1918, this hexagonal Art Nouveau beauty features a beautiful marble rotunda and exterior rock work done by the same Italian masons who crafted the picturesque retaining walls and bridges across the highway. The ruggedly elegant masonry is accented by windows inlaid with green opalized glass and a green tiled roof that complements the palette of the river and surrounding vegetation. The building is a great place to order a latte, make a restroom stop and check out the views from the second-story wraparound veranda before taking on the highway's waterfalls.

◖ GORGE WATERFALLS

Without a doubt, the waterfalls that thunder, cascade, and splash their way down the cliffs beside the Historic Columbia River Highway are the highlight of the drive. The high concentration of falls in the area only makes sense given the geography of the area. With an amazingly active watershed springing up from nearby Mount Hood's glaciers and springs, and a steep embankment of volcanic rock standing between these tributaries and the mighty Columbia, there's only one way for the water to reach its final destination, and that is down, down, down. Lucky for us that it happens in such a dramatic fashion.

The following falls are the most easily accessible along the route, viewable from pull-out areas or short jaunts of under a mile roundtrip. These offer the best sights for the least amount of effort—it's the type of tour you'd feel comfortable taking granny along for. The first stop you'll come across will be a few miles past Corbett, for the faucetlike **Latourell Falls,** which plunges directly down over a columnar basaltic cliff. You can snap plenty of pictures directly from the parking lot or take a 15-minute stroll along a trail from there to get right up to the splash pool.

A bit further down the highway, **Bridal Veil Falls** is a little harder to reach, but worth the 0.6-mile round-trip trek. The only falls that tumble down below the highway, this 118-foot set of tiered horsetail falls is surrounded by mossy cliffs and its own veil of green leaves that make for a pretty snapshot from the viewing platform built across from the bottom tier's splash pool. Parking is ample here and the trail down to the falls is well maintained, but it is not accessible to those with wheelchairs.

But that's OK, because the next few falls offer plenty of ooos and ahhs directly from pavement. Just east of the Bridal Veil parking lot, the lot for **Wahkeena Falls** offers a great look at the cascading gush that gets its name for the Yakama tribe's word for "most beautiful." A short 0.4-mile roundtrip walk to a bridge near the falls will get you close enough to feel the mist coming off of this gushing wonder. And immediately after that on the highway comes the crown jewel of the Gorge's waterfalls, **Multnomah Falls.** Towering almost three times the average height of most of the notable falls in the Gorge area, Multnomah is the second-highest year-round falls in the entire country. With a huge parking lot, a nice restaurant and gift shop on site, and plenty of benches scattered around the paved paths that lead to viewpoints, Multnomah makes for a wonderful afternoon stopover.

The historic highway continues on for another four miles or so east until it joins back up with I-84. Don't be tempted to consider yourself all waterfalled out before heading off the highway—about halfway between Multnomah and the freeway junction, pretty **Horsetail Falls** fans itself over the cliffs just off the highway. Do yourself a favor and at least stop off for a quick peak and a few pics.

Sports and Recreation
WATERFALL HIKES
If you're willing to get out of the car for a while and strap on some sturdy shoes, there are lots of additional waterfall views to be earned by hiking the Forest Service trail system that can be accessed at numerous points along the

© ERICKA CHICKOWSKI

Latourell Falls

highway. Many of these trails can be linked together into gratifying loop hikes. For example, on the west end of the waterfall district, the **Latourell Falls** loop hike is a 2.15-mile loop from the falls parking lot that will take you to an overlook above the main lower falls and past a set of upper falls higher up the creek. The 480-feet of elevation gained by the trail may not seem much on paper but it all comes at once through a steep initial climb on either direction of the route.

Starting from the **Wahkeena Falls** trailhead, a two-mile out-and-back route will take you past numerous upper falls along Wahkeena Creek to the final destination of **Fairy Falls,** a fan-shaped waterfall that can be enjoyed from a hewn log bench at its foot. Along the route, don't miss the very short spur trail to **Lemmon's Viewpoint,** which even surpasses many of those roadside overlooks you thought unbeatable. If you've got the endurance, you can continue past Fairy Falls for a 5.5 mile loop that'll hook east at the Trail 420 junction and back north at the Trail 441 junction past

a pair of out-of-the-way waterfalls, **Ecola Falls** and **Weisendanger Falls,** before taking you down past **Multnomah Falls** and the nearby lodge. A 0.2-mile spur to a great overlook on Multnomah makes for a worthy add-on before continuing down.

From the **Horsetail Falls** parking lot you can set out on a 2.5-mile loop up past its horsetail cousins, **Ponytail Falls** and **Middle Oneonta Falls.** The hike ends with about a half-mile walk along the highway shoulder.

Accommodations

Owned by the original family that built it in 1926, the **Bridal Veil Bed and Breakfast** (across the street from Bridal Veil Falls, 503/695-2333, www.bridalveillodge.com, $139–149) stands as the only lodging establishment right in the Multnomah waterfall district. Right across the parking lot from Bridal Veil Falls, this antique-laden inn serves full breakfasts that include dishes such as Dutch babies or quiche. Many of the period furnishings have been passed down the generations by the family and there's even a photo album featuring post cards to and from the home's first occupants to peruse over coffee.

A midcentury home built using largely recycled materials and to emulate Frank Lloyd Wright's architectural style, **Brickhaven Bed and Breakfast** (38717 E. Historic Columbia River Hwy., 503/695-6326, http://brickhaven.com, $100–125) lies perched upon a hillside overlooking the Gorge, just east of Corbett. All the rooms have views of the river and a public-area sitting room features a heart-stopping panorama from an oversized floor-to-ceiling window.

CAMPING
Set on the easternmost end of the Historic Columbia River Highway, **Ainsworth State Park** (17 mi. east of Troutdale at Exit 35 off of I-84, 503/695-2301, www.orgegonstateparks.org, mid-Mar.–Oct.) offers a range of camping opportunities within day hiking distance to the Multnomah waterfall district. RVers will enjoy the dozens of full hookup sites($20), half of which are pull-through sites to accommodate bigger rigs. There's even a site for campers with disabilities and a handful of walk-in tent sites ($17) for those who'd like to sacrifice amenities for solitude. The campground offers bathrooms with flush toilets and hot showers, and there's an amphitheater that hosts interpretive programs. So what's the catch? Well, all sites are first-come, first-served, so summer planning can be tricky when the throngs arrive.

Food
With big skylights looking up toward Multnomah Falls, the **Multnomah Falls Lodge** (50000 E Historic Columbia River Hwy., 503/695-2676, www.multnomahfallslodge.com, 8 A.M.–9 P.M. daily) dining room feels a bit like an oversized, homey greenhouse. Servers are extra friendly here, always willing to take a snapshot and quick with the orders. Food is fresh and above par compared to other similar destination restaurants, if a bit overpriced. But you're paying for the view, so put a smile on and enjoy it for what it's worth. In the

summer the reservations can get tight, particularly for dinner, so plan ahead. Also, don't be fooled by the name. Though the historic building was originally built for accommodations, this "lodge" only operates as a restaurant.

With so few dining options around these parts, **Corbett Country Market** (36801 E. Historic Columbia River Hwy., 503/695-2234) is a welcome sight for hikers or travelers dying for something to eat or a nice sip of something warm. For the better part of a century, the little country story has been pumping gas and offering up comestibles to road-weary travelers. In addition to coffee, muffins, packaged snacks, and the like, this store sells some delicious homemade beef jerky and local produce.

Information and Services
The U.S. Forest Service runs a **visitors center** at Multnomah Lodge, where you can pick up trail maps, books, and other information about the area.

If you don't plan on taking the scenic route the whole way through from Troutdale, there are a number of access points from I-84 to shortcut your way through to the points that interest you. Exit 22 will bypass the Troutdale and Sandy River areas and deliver you directly to Corbett near the Women's Forum Overlook and the Vista House. Exit 28 will deliver you to the Bridal Veil area and Exit 31 will drop you directly to Multnomah Falls. If you'd like to take the whole route east to west, get off at Exit 35.

Beyond Troutdale, public transit from Portland drops off. If you'd rather enjoy the drive as a passenger, **EcoTours of Oregon** (www.ecotours-of-oregon.com) offers an all-day Columbia River Gorge Waterfalls and Mount Hood Loop Tour for $69.50 per person.

CASCADE LOCKS AND VICINITY
Before the Columbia was tamed through a series of dams, the area around Cascade Locks was a roiling tumble of whitewater that was enough to put gray in the youngest of sailors'

beards. The Cascade Rapids descended about 40 feet through a narrow two-mile chute that had to be bypassed by sternwheelers using a locks and canal system that gave the town its name when it was built in 1896. Just over 40 years later, the Bonneville Dam flooded out the rapids and most of the locks, but the town kept its name and still celebrates its early role in river navigation. You can still see a portion of the locks at the town's biggest riverside park, from which a sternwheeler fittingly sets sail each day for a scenic river tour of the Gorge.

Sights
BONNEVILLE DAM
Located four miles west of Cascade Locks, the Oregon side of the Bonneville Dam will give you a look at the dam's first powerhouse and spillway, as well as the dam's navigation locks and the Bonneville Fish Hatchery, which has a big viewing area for steelhead and salmon spawning in the fall, plus a tank that's home to Herman the Sturgeon, an enormous 10-foot, 450-pound white sturgeon who has called the Columbia his home for 70 years. Start your tour at **Bradford Island Visitors Center** (541/374-8820, 9 A.M.–5 P.M. daily, free).

STURGEON

The Columbia River Basin is home to an ancient monster – several thousand, in fact. The white sturgeon is the country's largest freshwater game fish, and it just happens to love the depths below any of the Columbia's dams. Measuring up to 18 feet in length and weighing up to 1,500 pounds, these prehistoric behemoths are often chased by both commercial and recreational fishermen. Check current regulations before wetting a line, and before preheating the oven, bear in mind that these bottom-feeders have plenty of time to soak up toxins over their 100-plus-year lifespan.

HISTORIC LOCKS AND MARINE PARK
Tucked into the manmade watery alcove that made the town what it is today, the **Cascade Locks Marine Park** overlooks remnants of the historic locks that once bypassed Cascade Rapids on the Columbia today. While much of the locks structure was submerged once the Bonneville Dam was built, park visitors can still see evidence of the locks, and just over a pedestrian bridge, serene little **Thunder Island** remains as a byproduct of the canal that was built as part of the 1896 boat-moving project. Today, Thunder Island and the rest of the grounds on the main shore are a great place to take a stroll and enjoy the scenery of passing sailboats and pleasure craft cruising by.

While you're at the park, take a minute to pop in to the **Cascade Locks Historical Museum** (noon–5 P.M. daily May–Sept., free), set inside one of three century-old locks tender's house that stand at the park today. Featuring an old Oregon Pony steam locomotive, memorabilia, artifacts, and photos, the museum provides perspective on the history of the Gorge and the role of sternwheelers and steamboats on the river in the town's bygone era.

If you want to get a little more hands-on with your appreciation of paddleboats, hop aboard the triple-decked sternwheeler *Columbia Gorge* (503/224-3900, www.portlandspirit .com, May–Oct., $28 adult, $18 kids), which boards several times a day from the park. The cruise aboard this craft will present views of the steep basalt cliffs up and down the river during a two-hour narrated tour.

SODERBERG BRONZE
The first bronze foundry opened in the U.S. by a woman, **Soderberg Bronze** (101 Wanapa St., 503/803-9414, www.heathersoderberg .com, 10 A.M.–6 P.M. Thurs.–Mon.) is a studio and foundry run by Heather Soderberg, a one-time child sculpting prodigy and now well-respected artist who sculpted the town's *Sacagawea, Pomp and Seaman* centerpiece over in Marine Park. The foundry offers daily tours. Call ahead for the schedule.

Entertainment and Events

NIGHTLIFE

Throw back a pint, share trail stories with PCT through-hikers, and play a little video poker at the dark and cozy **Pacific Crest Pub** (500 WaNaPa St., 541/374-9310, www.pacificcrestpub.com). Housed in a century-old building, the tavern caters to hikers, offering brochures, maps and other information, and keeping a lively PCT register to chronicle all of the intrepid trekkers who pass by making the Mexico-to-Canada journey.

FESTIVALS AND EVENTS

Held each June, the long-running **Sternwheeler Days** (www.cascadelocks.net/sternwheelerdays) festival at Marine Park celebrates Cascade Locks' riverside history with a sailing regatta and demonstrations from mountain men.

From opening day of boating season in June through its close in September, the locally based **Columbia Gorge Racing Association** (http://cgra.org) hosts a range of sailing regattas and clinics in Cascade Locks.

In early September, the Pacific Crest Trail Association holds **Pacific Crest Trail Days** (www.pcta.org) at Marine Park, where through-hikers gather to camp at Thunder Island, meet old friends they made on the trail, hear about new outdoor products and do a little maintenance on nearby segment of the PCT. Later in September, the **Festival of Nations** (541/553-4883) is a celebration of local Native American heritage that coincides with the spawning of the salmon. Also held at Marine Park, the event hosts children's crafts, tribal performances and a mini-Pow Wow.

Shopping

Featuring a little of this and that right next door to the Pacific Crest Pub, **The Cottage Gifts & Antiques** (502 WaNaPa St., 541/374-5414) sells from a varied collection of art, antiques, and even gemstones. Similarly eclectic, **Lorang Fine Art & Gorge-ous Gifts** (96 WaNaPa St., 541/374-8007, www.lorangfineart.com) displays and sells oil, acrylic, pastel, and watercolor work from 40 different artists, plus wood and basket pieces, Native American masks, glass art, and jewelry. The real highlight of the shop is the owner's steel and bronze sculptures.

Sports and Recreation

HIKING

Across the entire 2,000-plus miles of the **Pacific Crest Trail,** Cascade Locks is the only incorporated town through which the trail runs directly. It's no surprise, then, how many through-hikers take a day or two here to chomp down some burgers, sleep in a fresh bed and pick up a care package before heading over the Bridge of the Gods to tackle the Cascades in Washington. If you're looking to day hike the PCT, the rest stop just south of the bridge makes a great trailhead for a 4.4-mile out-and-back trip along the trail to **Dry Creek Falls.** After about two miles headed southeast from the trailhead, veer right onto Dry Creek Trail to reach the falls. Along the way, you'll come across an old **shoe tree,** which for years has gathered its "fruit" as hikers have tossed their old kicks up in the branches here.

One of the premier hiking trails on either side of the Columbia River Gorge, **Eagle Creek Trail** runs through Northwest rain forests, across impressive footbridges spanning basalt cliffs, and through narrow openings blasted directly into the cliffsides almost a century ago when the historic highway was built nearby. The real draw, though, are the waterfalls. Passing six major waterfalls in six miles, and many more little tumblers and babbling brooks along the way, the stretch is Xanadu for falls fans. For a moderate day hike, try the 4.4-mile round-trip to **Punchbowl Falls.** With only about 400 feet of elevation gain, this satisfying route ends at the 30-foot gusher and passes a viewpoint that overlooks the 100-foot Metlako Falls.

Day hikers with more stamina may want to set their sights on the 12-mile, 1,200-foot gain round-trip to **Tunnel Falls,** a 175-foot plunging falls that uniquely features a trail that was tunneled by dynamite behind the waterfall wall

THE PACIFIC CREST TRAIL

The Pacific Crest Trail, or PCT for those in the know, is really hundreds of trails that link together and run from Mexico all the way up the map to Canada, passing through forests and wilderness far away from civilization. The most dramatic and beautiful part of the trail is the part running through the mountains, rivers, and primordial woods in the state of Washington.

On horseback or on foot, you'd be hard-pressed to find a path that shows off more of Washington than the PCT. Crossing from Oregon, the traveler first comes across The Bridge of the Gods, an awe-inspiring passage across the Columbia River, before beginning a long climb out of the river valley. Then, a long trek through dry lands and ancient lakes leads past the mammoth round top of Mount Adams and across the severe and jagged Goat Rocks Wilderness. Your reward is the unique chance to hike over the Packwood Glacier; small, but a glacier nonetheless.

The trail misses few of the state's highlights, so of course a section skirting Mount Rainier is mandatory. A long stretch through the mysterious North Cascades full of old-growth trees and deep, clear lakes follows, leading the hiker deeper and deeper until he or she arrives at remote Lake Chelan. From there, things only get wilder approaching the border. The hiker or equestrian passes through the rugged, mountainous Pasayten Wilderness toward the ultimate payoff: views of hundreds of glaciers and year-round snowfields. A little farther leads to Monument 78, the Canadian border, and a deep sense of peace and a well-deserved sense of accomplishment. And hopefully a good rest before taking the long way back home.

and then on a blasted ledge halfway up the cliff where the water shoots over. This trail can also be backpacked, though the competition for the limited sites along the way is fierce in summer months. Hikers who choose to turn it in to a multiday loop will find that the trail syncs up with the PCT after 13.3 miles at Wahtum Lake and back down Benson Plateau to the trailhead on **Ruckel Creek Trail** for a total of almost 27 miles. To reach the Eagle Creek trailhead, take exit 41 off of I-84 eastbound and follow the road east until it ends a mile later. The exit only comes off the eastbound lanes, so if you are coming from Hood River, you'll need to take exit 40 and backtrack east a mile to the next exit. Parking at the trailhead requires a $5 Northwest Forest Pass.

HISTORIC COLUMBIA RIVER HIGHWAY STATE TRAIL
Extend your appreciation for the winding, scenic curves of the historic highway that much of I-84 replaced by walking or cycling the Historic Columbia River Trail. Oregon State Parks administers a couple of disconnected sections of pavement restored from some of the abandoned parts of the highway, one of which runs west from the parking lot at the Bridge of the Gods five miles over to Moffett Creek. With moss and shaded wildflowers decorating the path and views of the river and Bonneville Dam, this is a class act spot for a spin.

BOATING AND FISHING
The exposed concrete left over from the canal and locks over at **Marine Park** make for a popular fishing pier these days. The water flowing through this manmade feature seems to attract an ample supply of fish and the park features a fish cleaning station near the restrooms. The park also sports two boat launches for those who want to venture further out in the river. The adjacent marina features free moorage and dump station facilities for up to 72 hours. If you need to pick up tackle, bait, or even a fancy new rod, check out **Columbia Action Custom Rods** (502 WaNaPa St., 541/374-5414).

Accommodations and Camping
Perched along the river just east of the Bridge of

the Gods, **Best Western Plus Columbia River Inn** (735 WaNaPa St., 541/374-8777, $130 d) hosts the best digs in town. Meticulously clean with fresh furnishings and a whirlpool tub and pool facility, it'll satisfy most road-trippers. Ask for a riverside room with a balcony to soak up the view. Just be aware that the scenery comes with a caveat: the hotel overlooks the river *and* the railroad tracks that run above it. Light sleepers may not be fans, but kids will love the choo-choos and the housekeepers at least provide earplugs alongside the conditioner and shampoo bottles each day.

For a slightly cheaper alternative, **Bridge of the Gods Motel and RV Park** maintains a collection of motel rooms ($69–119) and self-contained cabins ($119–149) in its log-cabin-style buildings. Both options come equipped with kitchenettes, jetted tubs, and free Wi-Fi, and the property also has laundry facilities on site to clean up those rain and waterfall-soaked hiking clothes. The grounds also host RV overnight spots, but there are nicer camping options in town. The best bet is at **Marine Park Campground** ($25 hookups, $15 tent), right in the city's pride and joy park. The small campground offers a handful of sites with water and electric hookups, showers, and a dump station. There's a playground on the property, free Wi-Fi and even a book exchange. Best yet, the waterfront location can't be beat. For a bit more serenity, tent campers and RVers with small rigs who can do without hookups may prefer **Herman Creek Campground** (Frontage Rd. and Herman Creek Rd., $10) on the eastern outskirts of town. This Forest Service site offers a quiet stay under a piney canopy, with water spigots and vault toilets. The site is a trailhead for several routes, including the Pacific Crest Trail. The site doubles as a horse camp, so PCT riders can bring their horse trailers and steeds here.

Food

For the best hunk o' ground beef this side of Hood River and a fantastic view of the river and the Bridge of the Gods, **Charburger** (745 NW WaNaPa St., 541/374-8477) is the place

to go. To fill the limited dining options of the area, this burger stand also runs a bakery, cooks up a number of breakfast items, lays out a salad bar during lunch and dinner, and even serves lighter fare such as salmon burgers to sate calorie counters.

East Wind Drive-In (395 NW WaNaPa St., 541/374-8380) also does burgers, but the big neon sign of a penguin hefting an oversized cone should be your cue to where the real priorities are here. When the sun's shining, nothing beats a sweet treat from East Wind.

Information and Services

Get information about Marine Park and the rest of the town's amenities at **Port of Cascade Locks.** The steady stream of boot-clad backpackers streaming through the doors at the **Cascade Locks Post Office** are PCT through-hikers who like to mail food ahead here to help them finish the rest of their journey up in Washington. Check out the PCT register at the post office to sign in or look at who's been hiking by here. Hikers can also find pay showers at the **Marine Park Campground.**

HOOD RIVER

The central hub of recreation and repast in the Columbia Gorge, Hood River is at once sophisticated and homespun. "The Hood" is home to way more than its fair share of amazing restaurants for a town of its size, attracting culinary talent with its backdoor proximity to quality farms, orchards, and vineyards and its strong concentration of local microbreweries and wineries. At the same time, locals never take themselves too seriously and you'll never get an uptight vibe in town.

You can probably credit that to the fun mix of growers and outdoor enthusiasts who live here and share a love for the natural beauty of the Gorge and Mount Hood around them. Many farmers and orchardists have lived off of bountiful Hood River Valley harvests for generations. At the same time, recreation junkies have for decades been drawn to the Hood for the area's perfect combination of weather and geography. At the nexus of the Columbia River

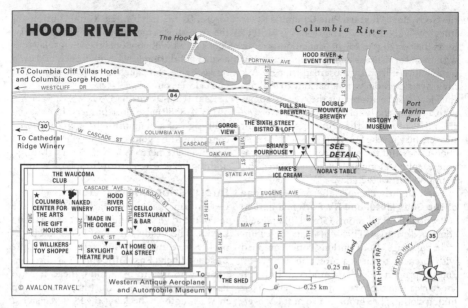

COLUMBIA RIVER GORGE

and Hood River, and just an hour north of Mt. Hood, the town is a perfect jumping off point for natural exploration by bike, boat, board, or boot. The sizzling summers invite the active set to get wet, and the blustery wind tunnel created by the Gorge here has contributed to make this the windsurfing and kiteboarding capital of the world. Meanwhile, in winter the consistent layer of powder on Mount Hood and its foothills prompts skiers to break out the bindings and wax for downhill and cross-country action.

Sights
WESTERN ANTIQUE AEROPLANE AND AUTOMOBILE MUSEUM

Known around town simply as WAAAM (1600 Air Museum Road, 541/308-1600, www.waaamuseum.com, 9 A.M.–5 P.M. daily, $12 adults, $10 seniors and veterans, $6 students, free children 4 and under and active military), this repository of antique machines that go "vroom" is sure to rev any gearhead's engine. With a collection of 75 aircraft, including a 1917 Curtiss JN4D Jenny, WAAAM's flying history primarily spans the early two decades of flight. In addition, you can find over 100 autos and

military jeeps, including a 1914 Ford Model T Depot Hack, several Model As and early Dodge, Mercury, and Studebaker cars.

THE HISTORY MUSEUM AT HOOD RIVER

The town's historical museum (300 E. Port Marina Dr., 541/386-6772, 10 A.M.–4 P.M. Mon.–Sat., noon–4 P.M. Sun. Apr.–Aug., noon–4 P.M. daily Sept.–Oct., $3 adults, free kids 10 and under and military) displays a range of permanent exhibits that includes dolls from pioneers in the valley, Native American beadwork and basketry, and artifacts that offer a look into over a century of history in Hood River Valley.

FRUIT LOOP

The bountiful orchard rows, rustic barns, putt-putting tractors, and farm dogs of the Hood River Valley lie in the shadow of Mount Hood, making the valley's back roads some of the most scenic in all of the Northwest. The locals affectionately refer to the 35-mile loop of Highway 35 running south and connecting down in Parkdale with Dee Highway 281 as the Fruit Loop. All along the route, participating farms, orchards, fruit stands, and more invite visitors to their grounds to take pictures, sample products, and pet animals. A fold-out brochure featuring information on more than 30 stops on the loop is abundantly available in town. The following are a few of the best things to see and do along the route.

Come watch furry alpacas scamper and lounge in their paddocks at **Cascade Alpacas** (4207 Sylvester Dr., 541/354-3542, www .foothillsyarn.com, 11 A.M.–4 P.M. Sat.–Sun. Mar., 11 A.M.–4 P.M. Fri.–Sun. Apr.–May and Nov.–Dec. 18, 11 A.M.–5 P.M. daily June–Oct.). These long-necked cuties are prized for their extremely soft wool and their friendly dispositions compared to their South American cousin, the llama. On the property you can get your hands on skeins of that wool, plus scarves, hats, socks, and sweaters made from the stuff.

Just a few minutes from downtown, **Wilinda Blueberry Patch** (730 Frankton Rd., 801/556-7964, 9 A.M.–6 P.M. daily July–Labor Day) opens its blueberry field to u-pickers between July and Labor Day. The patch grows a number of blueberry varieties that ripen at different times throughout that two-month window.

Visit **Lavender Valley Lavender Farm** (3925 Portland Dr., 541/386-1906, www .lavendervalley.com, 10 A.M.–6 P.M. daily June–Labor Day, 10 A.M.–5 P.M. Thurs.–Sun. Sept., 11 A.M.–4 P.M. Sat.–Sun. Oct.) in July to catch the lavender bloom at its peak for incredible pictures of purple fields backdropped by the imposing glaciers of Mount Hood. Open April through October, the farm runs a u-cut operation when in bloom, allowing visitors to pick from 70 varieties of lavender straight from the field. The rest of the months, enjoy the art gallery featuring hand-painted glass and get a whiff of the lavender oil that's distilled on the property in the late summer and fall.

More than just a fruit stand, **Mountain View Orchards** (6670 Trout Creek Ridge Rd., 541/352-6554, www.mtvieworchards.com, 9 A.M.–5 P.M. daily mid-July–Oct.) usually has enough activities on the property to keep the typical family busy for a good couple of hours. The owners have built three hiking trails on

© ERICKA CHICKOWSKI

Mount Hood rises above Hood River.

© ERICKA CHICKOWSKI

The petting zoo at Draper Girls Country Farm is a hit with the younger set.

the property for folks to explore, frequently run tours, host hayrides on the weekends, and put together a full slate of events during the month of October. The bakery on the property serves pie à la mode and runs a cider mill for fresh-pressed cider. And, unsurprisingly, the orchard offers u-pick apples, pears, peaches, cherries, pumpkins, and corn, depending on the season.

U-pick enthusiasts with a soft spot for farm animals may also want to consider stopping by **Draper Girls Country Farm** (6200 Hwy. 35, 541/352-6625, www.drapergirlscountry farm.com). In addition to u-pick of fruit by the bushel, and a store with some amazing jams and fruit butters, Draper Girls has a petting zoo featuring sheep, goats, pigs, and more.

Set up on a side road right along the Fruit Loop route, **Glassometry Studios** (3015 Lower Mill Dr., 541/354-3015, www.glass ometry.com) gives intrepid visitors the opportunity to feel the heat of the kiln with a special four-hour hands-on workshop ($200 pp for two, $180 pp for four). Even if you don't plan to work in the studio, the shop's artists display a pretty glass garden outside and sell their wares from a store that features windows looking into the work area.

MOUNT HOOD SCENIC RAILROAD
If you've already been cooped up in the car long enough, skip the Fruit Loop drive and see the Hood River Valley by train instead. Take the excursion train from the town of Hood River 22 miles all the way down to its terminus in Parkdale for a four-hour round-trip tour. Or do a two-hour trip to Odell. On some weekends the railroad spices rides up with a Western Train Robbery–themed train great for kids who want to help be on the lookout for train robbers who'll try to stop the train to carry out their old-timey larceny. Mount Hood Scenic Railroad also offers a number of brunch and dinner excursions within its equipped dining cars, including a very fun Murder Mystery Dinner Train.

VIEWPOINTS
There are a number of tripod-friendly places in and around Hood River to take in panoramic views of the Gorge and Mount Hood. At the little Ruthton Park, **Ruthton Point Overlook** (0.4 mile west of Columbia Gorge Hotel on Westcliff Dr.) presents a view of Ruthton Point and Washington cliffs in the distance, as well as passing trains as they snake their way just below at river level. And at **Panorama Point County Park,** clear days will give you vistas of Mount Hood towering over the orchards and vineyards of the fertile Hood River Valley. The park is only about three miles out of the central downtown district. Just take State Route 35 south to Eastside Road, take a left, and follow the signs to the park.

FULL SAIL BREWERY TOUR
The driving force behind Hood River's heritage as the microbrewery Mecca in the Gorge region, Full Sail Brewery has been concocting its suds by the Columbia since 1989. A beloved institution among the boardheads, farmers, and even vintners in the Hood, Full Sail throws open its brewery doors for an informative half-hour tour four times a day. The guides will

COLUMBIA RIVER GORGE

show you the equipment and the fresh ingredients that go into the beer that goes out the door and will tell you about how the upstart brewery started here out of a defunct fruit cannery. The tour ends in the Full Sail Tasting Room, where you can give most of its stock a sip for $1.

WINERIES

Set up right next to the Mount Hood Scenic Railroad depot, **Springhouse Cellar's** casual tasting bar is driven by a unique innovation: wine on tap. Committed to sustainable winemaking, Spinghouse serves up a red and a white wine stored within its old cannery building cellar upstairs via a unique tap system that gives the winery the ability to offer wine refills to anyone who comes with a cleaned out, empty wine bottle in hand. The winery isn't just about schtick, though, serving some delicious wines from bottles as well. Try the surprisingly complex Cherry Ort or the house specialty Ruins Red, a sangiovese/merlot/cab blend named after the old remnants of a distillery on the property.

Just a few minutes from downtown, the tasting room at **Cathedral Ridge Winery** is run out of a little cottage flanked by vineyard rows and a grassy picnic area bedecked with old barrels full of flowers and an incredible view of Mount Adams to the north. Inside, the wines take center stage, serving with some of the best reds south of the Columbia. The reserve syrah and the reserve cabernet are worth the trip all by themselves.

Focused primarily on Italian varietals, **Marchesi Vineyards** goes all out to embrace its owner's Italian winemaking heritage in the tasting room. Expect a warm reception, red checkered cloths, a mural imported from Italy's Piedmonte growing district and some Italian olive trees outside on the patio to complete the effect. The winery's sangiovesi and experimental dolcetto are both the highlights of this tasting stop along the Fruit Loop.

With a bar featuring ornately carved accents and giant mirrors, a dramatically high ceiling and huge windows with sweeping views of its vineyards and Mount Hood in the skyline, **Mt. Hood Winery** runs one of the classiest tasting rooms in the entire Hood River Valley. With vines growing on a 100-year-old farm along the

the tasting room at Mt. Hood Winery

Fruit Loop that still tends an impressive pear orchard, the wine here often features fruity flavors that are imparted through soil long used to apples, cherries, and pears. Try the pinot noir, or for something unique, the pear wine stands as a sweet but extremely crisp summer wine.

For a whirlwind tour of the best wines the Gorge has to offer, stop at **The Gorge White House** on your way back from the Fruit Loop. The said house is a century-old Dutch Colonial home on a farm with an equally long heritage. It's been converted inside to a tasting room that serves more than 30 wines from a smattering of local vintners, plus tastes of local microbrews. While you're there, you can venture out into the farm's u-cut flower fields to pick out a bouquet for that special someone.

Entertainment and Events
NIGHTLIFE
Enjoy live music most weekends from the stage at **Wacouma Club** (207 Cascade Ave., 541/387-2583, www.waucomaclub.com, 4 P.M.–2 A.M. Mon.–Fri., 9 A.M.–2 A.M. Sat.–Sun.), an established stop for local bands in the area, who come to play the small stage at this cozy joint. You can also take a seat at its long wooden bar on Tuesday nights to enjoy the rhythms played soulfully at its weekly blues jam session.

A serious winery with a cheeky name, **Naked Winery & Orgasmic Wine Company** frequently hosts bands on the weekends and competes with Wacouma through its own Tuesday evening jazz nights.

A movie house at a pizzeria? Yes indeedy. **Skylight Theatre Pub** screens first-run movies from its digs inside Andrew's Pizza, letting audiences enjoy a pie and some local beers while being thrilled and chilled. That's a might better than popcorn and Jujubees, don't you think?

If you're looking to rub elbows with the hard-charging boardheads, mountain bikers, and other long-time locals, motor south of downtown to the out of the way establishment **The Shed.** A no-nonsense spot equipped with booths and video poker machines, The Shed serves a mean cocktail and offers a pool table to while the night away.

THE COLUMBIA CENTER FOR THE ARTS
An institution in the Hood for over three decades, Columbia Arts Stage Troup, or **CAST**, presents plays, musicals, dance performances, and concerts out of the Columbia Center for the Arts (215 Cascade St., 541/387-8877, www.columbiaarts.org). In addition, the venue hosts lectures and films and runs an art gallery (11 A.M.–5 P.M. Wed.–Sun.) heavy on local talent.

FESTIVALS AND EVENTS
From May through October, many businesses in downtown Hood River band together to host a fun **First Friday** event. On the first Friday of each month, stores stay open late, run specials, host music and activities, and feature art and gifts tailored for the strong out-of-towner contingent visiting during the warmer months.

Strong swimmers can put themselves to the ultimate test on Labor Day, when Hood River plays host to the **Roy Webster Cross-Channel Swim.** The event ferries out a group of cap-and-goggled freestylers to the other side of the Columbia River and deposits them in the water to swim 1.1 miles across and back to Hood River. It's a challenging, chaotic field, often with 500 or more sets of swim caps, arms, and legs churning the water to reach the shore.

For close to 60 years, Hood River Valley has celebrated the annual bloom on its fruit trees during April's **Blossom Fest** (541/386-2000, http://hoodriver.org/blossom-fest). The events tied to the fest range from a Craft Show to a fire department all-you-can-eat-breakfast, with little mini-shindigs across the valley. This is the prime time to drive the Fruit Loop, with many of the stops on the route participating with activities on their properties.

Held each year on the first Saturday of October, **Hops Fest** honors its prime beer-making crop with an event centered around the ales, ambers, porters, and more that have brought the Gorge so much fame as a craft brewing capital in the States. Expect to have the hop-portunity to try dozens of different beers, many of them specially brewed to feature the distinctive taste of freshly harvested hops.

In mid-October, **Harvest Fest** marks the end of growing season for the Hood River Valley. Shop for fresh fruits and veggies at Produce Row, which offers up delights like Anjou pears, heirloom apples, pumpkins, and roasted nuts. Participate in an annual pie-eating contest, take a horse-drawn carriage ride, enjoy live music, or just get your fill tasting delicacies like artisan jams, chocolate-covered nuts, and smoked salmon for sale.

In December Hood River is frequently blanketed with a light layer of snow, making perfect scenery for the month-long slate of events during **Hood River Holidays.** Things are typically kicked off the first weekend of the month with a holiday parade down Oak Street and the lighting of downtown twinklers. Throughout the month wineries usually offer special tastings, Santa can be found frequently at downtown Santaland, and Mount Hood Railroad runs a special Polar Express train through the valley.

Shopping

With its cute collection of mom-and-pop boutiques and gift shops tucked into historic buildings, downtown Hood River's Oak Street is a vacation shopper's ideal walkway, filled with window shopping and souvenirs.

Featuring furnishing and unique decor items, **At Home on Oak Street** sells a unique smattering of accents surely not to be replicated by neighbors back home. Nearby, **Made in the Gorge** (108 Oak St., 541/386-2830, www.madeinthegorge.com, 10 A.M.–5 P.M. daily) displays a well-rounded mix of jewelry, painting, pottery, and sculpture created by local artists from in and around Hood River.

For more conventional tourist T-shirts, novelty gift snacks, and other souvenir baubles, **The Gift House** (204 Oak St., 541/386-9234, www.hoodrivergifthouse.com) has your bases covered. Pick up smoked salmon, chocolate-covered huckleberries, or fresh jam without having to take a drive out on the Fruit Loop. And kids and the young at heart will find a stop at **G Willikers Toy Shoppe** (202 Oak St., 541/387-2229, 10 A.M.–6 P.M. Mon.–Sat.,

10 A.M.–5 P.M. Sun.) to be mandatory. This toy store sells a wide range of games, stuffed animals, books, educational items, and other quality playthings that only the best elves on Santa's production line are put in charge of.

Sports and Recreation
WINDSURFING AND KITEBOARDING
The undisputed hub of wind-borne watersports in the Gorge, Hood River draws self-proclaimed boardheads from around the world, who flock here to ply the windy and scenic waters of the Columbia. Also known as sailboarding, windsurfing is powered by a mount that looks like a cross between a surfboard and a sailboat. An extreme sport around these parts for decades, sailboarding will always remain in vogue to some degree, but of late it has been supplanted in the hearts of many of the Gorge's adrenaline junkies by kiteboarding. Also referred to as kitesurfing, this high-octane sport sends enthusiasts careening over the water on a wakeboardlike mount powered by a line attached to a large C-shaped sail.

Both are technical sports that'll take some degree of education and training to get started. Fortunately Hood River has the highest concentration of schools for both in the entire country. If you take a lesson in town, more likely than not you'll be meeting at either the **Hood River Sailpark** (300 E. Port Marina Dr.) or the **Hood River Event Site** (north end of 2nd St. off of I-84 exit 63) each on either side of the Hood River outlet into the Columbia and both popular launch sites for boardheads of all experience levels. Try Hood River WaterPlay for a range of windsurfing lessons that run the gamut from a Quick Start two-hour ($69) lesson to a full two-day, six-hour U.S. Sailing sanctioned windsurf class ($199) that affords you free time on the company's equipment at its beginner beach throughout the sailing season after graduation. Meanwhile, for kiteboarding, the Port of Hood River has sanctioned six different outfits to teach classes from local launch spots. Located at a stand over at the Event Site, **New Wind Kite School** (541/387-2440) runs an individualized full-day

COLUMBIA RIVER GORGE

SURFING THE WIND

Because the Columbia is the only major break in the Cascade Range, it acts as an 80-mile-long wind tunnel. The wind blowing through the Columbia Gorge provides some of the best windsurfing and kiteboarding conditions in the nation. In 1991, a windsurfer set the national speed record, 47.4 miles per hour, here. This place isn't for beginners: gusty winds, large waves, a strong current, and frigid water make the Gorge challenging for even experienced sailors, and the constant parade of tugs and barges adds more hazards. Winds average 16 mph between March and mid-October, but most surfers and boarders prefer to come in July and August when the water is warmer and the current is slower.

The most protected waters in the Gorge are at Vancouver Lake near Vancouver, and at Horsethief Lake near the Dalles bridge, but here strong winds may make it difficult for the beginner to return to the upwind launch area. A good place to learn is The Dalles Riverfront Park, just across the river in Oregon, where you can take lessons and rent equipment in a relatively protected location. Board rentals are also available in Stevenson and Bingen, Washington, and Hood River, Oregon. If you just want to watch, the best place is near the Spring Creek Fish Hatchery three miles west of Bingen, where you may see upwards of 300 boarders on a windy August day.

Several good places for intermediate-level boarders are near Stevenson, Home Valley, Bingen, and Avery Park (east of Horsethief Lake). Avery Park is especially good because it has a long, straight stretch of river that gets nicely formed waves.

Expert-level conditions can be found at Swell City, four miles west of the Bingen Marina; the Fish Hatchery, 3.5 miles west of White Salmon; Doug's Beach, 2.5 miles east of Lyle; Maryhill State Park, where the river is less than a half mile wide; and the east end of the river near Roosevelt Park. Experts head to The Wall, 1.5 miles east of Maryhill State Park.

For general information on the sport, contact the Columbia Gorge Windsurfing Association (541/386-9225, www.cgwa.net) in Hood River, Oregon.

More than 50 sites provide access on both sides of the Columbia River; check with local shops for details. For up-to-date wind conditions, listen to radio stations 104.5 FM and 105.5 FM, or check with windsurfing shops in Hood River, Oregon – the center of the windsurfing universe. On the Web, head to www.windance.com for live Gorge "windcams" and weather updates. Showers are available at the Lyle Merc store or the Bingen School Inn.

Introduction to Kiteboarding for 1–2 people ($254–320 pp), as well as a two-day Fast Track Camp ($414 pp) for two that will really get you jump-started by getting you out on the water quickly through Jet Ski–assisted lessons.

VIENTO STATE PARK

One of the premier plots of state park land along the Gorge lies about eight miles west of Hood River. The aptly named Viento—in Spanish it means "wind"—brings together some beautiful riverfront property that sprawls south past the freeway into the waterfall-laden scenery the Oregon side of the Gorge is known for. On the river, windsurfers and kiteboarders take advantage of convenient access to launch their rigs. And for tumbling water, take the one-mile, fully accessible paved trail to the Starvation Creek waterfall along a now-defunct section of the Historic Columbia River Highway.

KOBERG BEACH
STATE RECREATION SITE

Just a couple miles east of Hood River, Koberg Beach was the town's go-to riverfront site when it was a tony little resort for most of the first half of the 20th century. The resort is gone but the beach along the Columbia remains a favorite place to recreate, with wind-sport enthusiasts and anglers taking full advantage of easy river access. The beach is conveniently right off of I-84, but the towering basaltic **Stanley Rock** keeps freeway noise down to a minimum.

MOUNTAIN BIKING
Mountain bikers will find a little something for every riding style and ability among the spaghettilike collection of trails curving through **Post Canyon** just south of town. Twisting and turning through land owned by the Hood River County Forestry Department, these shared use trails extend out to 89 miles of exploration from multiple staging areas, but Post Canyon is the most popular with the mountain biker set. To get there, take Country Club road for 1.4 miles from Oak Street and turn right onto Post Canyon Road for about half a mile until it turns to gravel. You can park there and ride another 1.2 miles up the road to the first trailhead, or chance it with your car along the bumpy road to see if the limited parking at the end of the road isn't full.

The quintessential ride in the Hood River region lies on the 11.7-mile **Surveyor's Ridge** trail, a demanding and serpentine line of singletrack that's most frequently ridden as a shuttle-ride. With more than 2,000-feet in elevation gain, much of it in very steep sections leading up and along the ridgeline that offers incredible views of Mount Hood and the Hood River Valley. To reach the trailhead from the south end, take State Route 35 26 miles from Hood River to Forest Service Road 44. Take a left and follow that for 3.5 miles to Road 620. The trail crosses it just a few yards away. From the north end, take Highway 35 south for 14 miles and turn left on Pine Mont Drive. Follow it five miles to Road 630, where you'll take a right and follow it to the parking area.

To get info on these and other local trails, pick up spare tubes and parts or rent a bike, check out **Discover Bicycle** (210 State St., 541/386-4820, http://discoverbicycles.com, 10 A.M.–6 P.M. Mon.–Sat., 10 A.M.–5 P.M. Sun.).

WHITEWATER RAFTING
Take a tumbling and scenic ride on the town's namesake waterway with **Northwest Rafting Company** (116 Oak St., Ste. 4, 541/450-9855, www.nwrafting.com, $135) on its full-day Hood River whitewater rafting tour. Starting in the exciting Class II and Class IV rapids of the river's West Fork, the ride calms down through the bucolic Hood River Valley for some beautiful views. Lunch is held near Punchbowl Falls and the ride floats its way all the way back right into town.

Accommodations
You can't beat the convenient location of **Hood River Hotel** (102 Oak St., 541/386-1900 or 800/386-1859, www.hoodriverhotel.com, $89 and up), an old brick hotel set downtown right in the mix of Oak Street's shops and restaurants. Rooms are a bit cramped, but the property features cheap parking ($5), a fitness center with sauna and whirlpool tub, free wireless and accepts pets in some rooms. Snag a suite for more space to spread out and a fully equipped kitchen or kitchenette.

Fans of historic hotels will probably enjoy **Columbia Gorge Hotel** (4000 Westcliff Dr., 541/386-5566 or 800/345-1921, www.columbiagorgehotel.com, $159 and up) better. First gaining prominence in the era of the Historic Columbia River Highway's heyday, this stately lodge overlooks an impressive rocky Gorge vista from its bluffside position. Furnishings, wallpaper, and art all hearken back to a rose-colored time when the establishment played host to bigwigs like Presidents Roosevelt and Coolidge, Rudolph Valentino, and Jane Powell. In the lobby an elevator operator runs a turn of the century lift and you'll spot floral patterns and intricate moldings galore. Of course, like many historic accommodations, this one comes with the floorboard creaks and temperamental plumbing as part of the package. But the views and ambiance contribute to a fun experience. The hotel exterior and grounds are accented by a barrel-tiled roof and mason work done by the same Italian craftsmen who worked on the highway bridges and the Vista House on Crown Point. These features are complemented by carefully tended and colorful gardens and there are ample viewpoints on the grounds to watch the river take its course. There's even a gushing 200-foot waterfall on the property. It's worth a visit even if you don't intend to stay there.

If you like the waterfall and grounds but prefer a newer establishment, the adjacent **Columbia Cliff Villas** (3880 Westcliff Dr., 541/436-2660 or 866/912-8366, $169 and up) should be a good fit. Featuring the same dramatic Gorge views and sharing the grounds and spa amenities with the Columbia Gorge Hotel, the sparkling new condo buildings of the Villas all come with flat screen TVs, coffee makers, and plush beds. Many rooms have gas fireplaces and spacious river-view patios. There are also many multibedroom suite options with full kitchens, making this a pleasing place to set up larger families. Decor is casual elegance, with granite and marble accents in the kitchens and bathrooms, and fine linens and furnishing throughout. The property offers free Wi-Fi, nanny services, room service, and in-room spa treatments to round out the amenities.

The meals are deliciously filling and the conversation convivial around the breakfast table at **Seven Oaks Bed and Breakfast** (1373 Barker Rd., 541/386-7622, www.sevenoaks bb.com, $160 d). Owned by an energetic couple who raised their kids in Hood River and have an intimate familiarity with the area, the inn is run out of a pretty Craftsman home with a porch and swing facing a lush lawn and nicely tended garden. A few minutes away from Hood River's central district, Seven Oaks strikes a delicate balance of convenience and country ambiance. The grounds here sport a great big barn with a chicken coop, awesome views of Mounts Hood and Adams and a sun deck with a whirlpool tub. Not a stitch of lace or froufrou floral patterns will clutter up your rooms here. Just crisp, white linens, an incredibly soft mattress, and early American furnishings to add a little flavor to the tasteful decor.

Just one block off of downtown's Oak Street and within walking distance to some of the area's best pubs, the porch wrapping around the Victorian-style house at **Gorge View** (1009 Columbia St., 541/386-5770, http://gorgeview .com, $85–95) bed-and-breakfast overlooks the mighty Columbia and Mount Adams. Catering

Catch a quiet night's rest at Seven Oaks Bed and Breakfast.

to the outdoor enthusiast crowd, Gorge View offers plenty of storage space to hold your sporting gear and serves a hearty morning breakfast in its country-style dining room.

Resting in a vibrant Hood River Valley farm and orchard with a breathtaking view of Mount Hood, **Sakura Ridge** (5601 York Hill Dr., 877/472-5872, http://sakuraridge.com) is tucked between rows of fruit trees and gentle pastures dotted with sheep and lamb. Bedecked in natural wood siding, the Sakura lodge hosts large rooms with private baths, most featuring private decks that face the mountain. Breakfast highlights the fruit of the farm's harvest, featuring fresh herbs and produce and eggs straight from the property's chicken coop.

CAMPING

Open mid-March through October, **Viento State Park** runs a first-come, first-serve campsight featuring 56 RV sites with electric and water hookups and an additional 18 sites just for tenters. The RV loop offers great access to the river, but its proximity to the busy railroad tracks that run through the park may disturb light sleepers, especially from sites A1 through A31.

Tenters looking for a quieter spot closer to town may prefer **Tucker Park** (five mi. south of Hood River on Hwy. 281, 541/386-4477), situated right along the waters of Hood River. You'll find 94 tent sites ($18 normal, $22 riverside) and a handful of RV sites with water hookups ($19). Again, this spot doesn't accept reservations.

RV campers who want to lock in a spot at a park with amenities may want to head across the Hood River Bridge, where on the Washington side there lies a very convenient spot named the **Bridge RV Park and Campground** (652714 SR 14, 509/493-1111, www.bridgerv.com).

Food

CAFÉS AND BAKERIES

A reimagining of the classic diner, coffee-shop-style, **Ground Espresso Bar and Cafe** (12 Oak St., 541/386-4442, http://groundhoodriver.com, 6 A.M.–4 P.M. daily) is bedecked in decor featuring midcentury touches like plastic bucket seats, hula girl wall hangings, and an orange and brown motif. In addition to the lattes and cappuccinos, you can get yourself a beer or wine and the food presents a tasty mix of fresh pastries and breakfast sandwiches, paninis, salads, and smoothies.

PUB GRUB

It's a raucous scene inside **Brian's Pourhouse's** (606 Oak St., 541/387-4344, www.brianspourhouse.com, 5 A.M.–11 P.M. daily, main courses $15–22) little white clapboard house, fitting for one of Hood River's few late-night dining establishments. Its seasonal menu is built around bold flavors, with a handful of salads and small plates complementing stick-to-your-rib entrées like hanger steak and grilled lamb sirloin. Brian's also offers several pub favorites like burgers, pizza, and its house-specialty fish tacos.

With a similarly effervescent atmosphere, **Double Mountain Brewery Taproom** (8 4th St., 541/387-0042, 4–11 P.M. Tues.–Thurs., 11:30 A.M.–11 P.M. Fri.–Mon.) lays out a varied menu but the real attraction is its brick-oven pizza. Baked up fast in a super-hot oven, this is East Coast–style pizza with nice bits of char on the crust and plenty of gooey cheese. Pizza snobs, I dare you to turn your nose up at this pick—it's good enough to compete with arguably the best microbrew selection created in the Hood.

Hands-down, though, **Full Sail Tasting Room and Pub** (506 Columbia St., 541/386-2247, 11:30 A.M.–10 P.M. daily) offers the best overall menu and the nicest atmosphere for families—particularly during the lunch hours. Try the special Full Sail Burger with smoked gouda and caramelized onions or go with a healthier but quite delicious turkey and brie. And don't forget dessert—several unique sweets feature Full Sail beer as ingredients, including the unique Session Black Float with ice cream dolloped into a glass of black lager.

CONTEMPORARY NORTHWEST

A high-class restaurant that could easily compete with the best Seattle or Portland has to

COLUMBIA RIVER GORGE

offer, **Celilo Restaurant and Bar** (16 Oak St., 541/386-5710, www.celilorestaurant.com, 11:30 A.M.–3 P.M. and 5–9 P.M. Mon.–Sat., 9 A.M.–3 P.M. and 5–9 P.M. Sun., $14–24) creates a warm and classy atmosphere with a dining room done up in honey-colored maplewood and earth-tone fabrics, low lighting, and an attentive staff at your call to serve amid it all. The food is the real show-stopper. A daring mix of seasonal fare creatively presented, Celilo's rotating menu fixates on the fruit and veggies grown in Hood Valley, paired with the chef's delicate sauces and seasonings. Menu picks featuring the hanger steak are a dependable choice here.

Nibblers will delight at the small plate selection at **C Nora's Table** (110 5th St., 541/387-4000, www.norastable.com, 5–9 P.M. Tues.–Thurs, 5–10 P.M. Fri.–Sat.), a laid-back but gourmand café that speaks the language of local—ingredients are freshly plucked from the proverbial back door. Just about everything is house-made, even the pickles, the ketchup, and the beer crackers. If the scallops are on the menu, drop all competing plans and order them. Plump and crispy on the outside with the melt-in-your-mouth middles, these are the shellfish of your daydreams.

You'll have quite a decision to make at **The Sixth Street Bistro and Loft** (6th St. and Cascade Ave., 541/386-5737, 11:30 A.M.–9:30 P.M. Sun.–Thurs., 11:30 A.M.–10 P.M. Fri.–Sat., $8–16), which plates up plenty of epicurean choices but also grills up the best burger in town. Whether you choose the Damn Good Cheeseburger or a colorful salad, you'll be able to enjoy it on the nicest patio on town, which sits on a quiet downtown side street and is strung with pretty white lights that twinkle in the evening hours.

DESSERT
Pinched into an adorable postage-stamp-sized green cottage, **C Mike's Ice Cream** (504 Oak St., 541/386-6260) scoops out luscious house-made cones and cups. In-season huckleberry shakes are enough to make you moan and the chocolate-chunked Galaxy really is out of this world. Enjoy it in the yard next to the cottage or scurry across the street to the hillside library lawn to watch downtown passersby and get some peek-a-boo glimpses of the Gorge.

MARKETS
If you're planning on picking up treats along the Fruit Loop drive, wait to completely stock up before you've had a chance to try some samples at **Packer Orchards and Bakery** (3900 SR 35, 541/234-4481, http://packerorchardsandbakery.com, 10 A.M.–6 P.M. daily). There are no gimmicky sights here, just the best darned jams, fruit butters, and pastries in the entire valley. Outside the shop you'll also be able to pick from bins overflowing with a wide selection of fresh fruits and veggies.

Don't just stop at the **Gorge White House** for the wine—a little out-building beside the house also delights with a unique smattering of fruits and prettily bottled house-made sauces. The coffee-merlot chocolate sauce tastes great with those apples you picked up on the Fruit Loop and the pear walnut sauce tosses well in any fruit or spinach salad.

You don't have to drive the Fruit Loop to tap into the fresh produce of the Hood River Valley. Pick up a bushelful of organic veggies or fruit at **Mother's Market Place** right in town. This small but bountiful market also runs a deli jammed with healthy and tasty options, many of which are vegan or gluten-free.

Information and Services
Hood River's go-to source of travel and tour information can be found at the city's main **visitor center** (20 E Port Marina Dr., 541/386-2000 or 800/366-3530, www.hood river.org, 9 A.M.–5 P.M. Mon–Fri. year-round, also 10 A.M.–5 P.M. Sat. May–Oct.) near the marina.

Transportation Network of The Dalles and **Columbia Area Transit** (http://community.gorge.net/hrctd) offer a fixed-route bus service between Hood River and Portland that runs every Thursday ($8 one-way), heading westbound in the morning and eastbound in the afternoon. The same service provider also runs a fixed-route service Monday through Friday between The Dalles and Hood River ($3 one-way). Buses arrive at and leave from the CAT station (224 Wasco Loop). Greyhound (www .greyhound.com) also offers bus service from this location, but you can't buy tickets at the station here.

THE DALLES AND VICINITY

East of Hood River, the Gorge takes a turn toward decidedly drier weather, with pine trees transitioning into grassy, sunny hillsides. Fortunately, this section of the south Gorge is home to some of the best riverside state parks and oxbow lakes in which adventuresome boaters, swimmers, and boarders can cool off in the water. At the eastern end of this stretch of I-84, The Dalles is a working class town that sports the largest population in the Gorge. Home to the fantastic Columbia Gorge Discovery Center and linked to Washington by The Dalles Dam and a peach-colored trussed bridge, the city presents a convenient spot to rest or take in a no-frills bite before making a U-turn north or south on a bi-state Gorge loop

drive. In between "the Hood" and The Dalles, the tiny town of Mosier is worth a mosey if you've got the time for delicious ice cream and a bike-ride through some 90-year-old tunnels blasted for the first Gorge highway.

Sights and Recreation
MOSIER TWIN TUNNELS
Explore one of the most popular abandoned stretches of the Historic Columbia River Highway from Mosier. Rehabilitated for walking and cycling, the paved **Twin Tunnels** trail runs five miles and passes through two tunnels that dig straight through the craggy basalt so familiar in this region. Stop in the tunnel to look through the cutaways to views of the Gorge, and check out the inside of the rock walls to see if you can spot the places where some travelers in 1921 carved their names while trapped there during a snowstorm.

MEMALOOSE STATE PARK
Situated directly in the hottest part of the Gorge, Memaloose State Park's 100-degree summer days can easily be relieved under the

COLUMBIA RIVER GORGE

© ERICKA CHICKOWSKI

A classic car crosses into The Dalles in style.

pretty maples and willows that shade and decorate this riverfront park. Windsurfers and kiteboarders can further cool off in the river from the popular launch point here, which provides views out to the island that gives the park its name. This was a sacred island to the Chinook Indian tribes of the Gorge, who used to lay their dead on open pyres there.

MAYER STATE PARK
Another favorite sunny-side destination in the Gorge, Mayer State Park holds within it some stunning views and a popular lake for fishing and swimming. First the view: the park covers a dramatic hillside overlooking the Gorge called Rowena Crest, which is summited by the twisting, turning segment of the Historic Columbia River Highway that runs through the park. It can also be hiked by trail. On the river itself, Mayer presents a place to launch windsurfing and kiteboarding equipment, plus a boat ramp.

COLUMBIA GORGE DISCOVERY CENTER
The pre-eminent museum in all of the Gorge makes its home in the unassuming town of The Dalles. The Columbia Gorge Discovery Center lays out a fascinating mix of exhibits detailing the geography, flora, fauna, history, and culture of the region. With presentations on the Lewis and Clark expedition, the building of the historic highway, and even an up-close-and-personal birds of prey demonstration, this museum makes the drive to The Dalles well worth it even if that's the only thing you do on the eastern section of the Gorge.

THE DALLES DAM
"The Dalles" is from the French (*La Grand Dalle de la Columbia,* meaning flagstone), a reference to the basaltic rocks lining the narrows. In the pre-dam days, this was the most dangerous point in the river for early navigators who approached a virtual staircase of rapids called Celilo Falls. Most Oregon Trail travelers opted to portage around the rapids at The Dalles. For centuries the falls were a major fishing spot for Native Americans who caught salmon as they

headed upstream to spawn. When Lewis and Clark visited this area in 1805, they reported a village of 21 large wooden houses and called the place a "great emporium . . .where all the neighboring nations assemble."

The Dalles Dam (exit 87 off of I-84, 541/506-7819) was completed in 1957 and the half-mile-long powerhouse now produces some 1.8 million kilowatts of power. Some salmon still make it up this far, and Native American fishing platforms can occasionally be found on both sides of the river. Check out the dam with a free tour through the power generation and fish passage areas. Tours leave the dam's visitor center at 11 A.M. and 2 P.M. on weekends between Memorial Day and Labor Day. Visitors have to be U.S. citizens, over 16 years old and must come with photo ID.

FORT DALLES
The Dalles initially sprang up as a pioneer and military outpost in the 19th century. Learn about the area's history, check out pioneer and military artifacts, and an interesting collection of antique wagons at **Fort Dalles Museum and Anderson Homestead** (500 W. 15th St, 541/296-4547, 10 A.M.–4 P.M. daily, $5). The museum is inside the old Surgeon's Quarters, the only remaining building left of the fort. Nearby, the Anderson Homestead is a quaint little cottage built of hand-hewn logs in 1895 and now furnished with antiques representative of the era.

DESCHUTES RIVER RAFTING
Splash your way up and over the Deschutes River east of The Dalles on a half-day, full-day, or overnight expedition led by **All Adventures Rafting** (509/493-3926, www.alladventuresrafting.com, $79 for full-day trip). This longtime river-running outfit has been guiding these waters for over 40 years and can arrange exciting class III through class IV trips or set something up calmer for a raft and fish combination trip. Unlike many of the Columbia tributary whitewater trips that take you through frigid waters that require many layers of neoprene, this hot-weather trip is a tank-top and

sandals type run the way that most people envision rafting should be.

Entertainment and Events

Check out the gorgeous 1900s-era backbar at the historic **Baldwin Saloon** (205 Court St., 541/296-5666). Serving some of the finest wines the Gorge has to offer, the saloon is a might bit less rough and tumble than back when it was built in 1876 right near the town's train tracks. A squat brick building that's been restored with care, it is now highlighted by an 18-foot mahogany backbar with big scrolled columns and an original mirror trimmed with stained glass paneling.

Held the second weekend in July, the **Fort Dalles Days and Rodeo** (http://fortdalles days.com) is the big shindig in town each year. Expect to see the buckin' broncs of a pro rodeo, plus a street fair and 5K fun run.

Accommodations

Hidden away on a Gorge-view property featuring a colorful garden, a creek, and a little pond, **The Mosier House** (704 Third Ave., 541/478-3640 or 877/328-0351, www.mosierhouse .com, $85–145) lies in a beautiful Queen Anne Victorian built by the little town's founder in 1904. Each of the five rooms has its own unique benefits—one with pretty stained glass windows, another with a beautiful Gorge vista, another with a garden view, and so on.

The only hotel settled directly in the middle of The Dalles' historic district, **The Dalles Inn** (112 W. 2nd St., 888/935-2378) presents an affordably posh alternative. With sleek linens, pillow-top beds, flat screen televisions, and free Wi-Fi, rooms come with all the goodies. Also included are in-room coffee makers, fridges, and microwaves. The property sports a heated pool and fitness center and is extremely pet-friendly.

Even though the building's designed to look like a quaint farm building, **Cousins Country Inn** (2114 W. 6th St., 541/298-5161) won't make you feel like you're staying in a barn. The neutral palette and clean lines of the guest rooms feel more like a trendy urban inn.

Flat screen TVs, free Wi-Fi, and leather seats are the norm and some rooms come with fireplaces. The pool here is small, but there's a nice indoor whirlpool and you'll be able to work out for free at an offsite fitness center.

A boutiquey twist on the typical roadside stopover, **Celilo Inn** (3550 E. 2nd St., 541/769-0001) has sweeping views of the Gorge. Accented with chocolate-colored backboards and wine-colored chairs and throw pillows, the classy rooms appeal to the wine-taster crowd who come here after a day tasting at Maryhill across the river. Enjoy a glass of wine on the patio or take a dip in the pool, both of which face the Columbia.

Food

Sharing a spic-and-span showroom garage with mint-condition vintage Porches in the tiny village of Mosier, **Route 30 Classics & Roadside Refreshments** serves delicious ice cream—huckleberry cheesecake is my favorite—and cold drinks. It makes a perfect stop after taking a ride through the nearby Twin Tunnels.

Overlooking the Gorge with a view of The Dalles Bridge, **The Bistro at Waters Edge** (541/506-5777, 6 a.m.–9 p.m. Mon.–Fri., 7 a.m.–8 p.m. Sat., 11 a.m.–6 p.m. Sun.) is run out of an airy space with plenty of windows. Serving a unique selection of sweet and savory crepes, plus flatbread pizza and typical café sandwich and salad fare, the Bistro presents a healthful alternative to many of the diner and drive-through options just off The Dalles's I-84 off-ramps. The patio's view is nice, but hold onto the napkins because its prime vantage point also lies right in the Gorge's blustery wind currents.

If it is a big, juicy burger that you crave, though, keep driving to **Big Jim's Drive-In** (2938 E. 2nd St., 541/298-5051, 10 a.m.–10 p.m. daily), a Gorge institution that's been running its fryers for over 40 years. If you're in a non-traditional fried spuds mood, give the joint's yummy Tater Tots a go and don't forget to pair your meal with a thick shake.

Serving up south-of-the-border specials, **La Fogata** (1204 Yakima Valley Hwy.,

509/839-9019, 11 A.M.–9 P.M. daily) is a simple taqueria that whips up a mean street taco. Pick from everything from standard carne asada to succulent beef cheek to fish, and slather on the freshly made salsa to complete the fiesta in your mouth. With only a couple of tables inside and a few picnic tables set up outside, this popular place can get crowded at times, but the wait is worth it.

Gussied up in a barn-red building with a shiny green tractor plopped down right in the middle of the dining room, **Cousins Restaurant and Lounge** plays up its country theme to the last, serving big portions of farm-style dishes like pot roast and meatloaf, accompanied by drinks served in Mason jars.

On the other end of the sophistication spectrum, **La Petite Provence** (408 E. 2nd St.), is a boulangerie and patisserie with deliciously fragrant French onion soup, crusty baguettes, and delectable sandwiches. A meal here is left unfinished without a sweet ending—the tortes, cookies, and sweet pastries can't be missed.

For a change of pace, you can switch your French accent to an Italian one and swing by **Romul's** (312 Court St., 541/296-9771, www .romuls.com) right down the street. A casual café with all the standard faves—calamari, lasagna, ossobuco—it does also surprise with a few dishes. Some delicious departures include stuffed grape leaves, pork schnitzel, and roasted duck cappelini.

Information and Services

You can gather information on local lodging, recreation and events at **The Dalles Chamber of Commerce** (404 W. 2nd St., 541/296-2231, www.thedalleschamber.com, 10 A.M.–5 P.M. Mon.–Fri.). **The Transportation Network of The Dalles** and **Columbia Area Transit** (http://community.gorge.net/hrctd) offer a fixed-route bus service between The Dalles and Portland that runs every Thursday ($8 one-way), heading westbound in the morning and eastbound in the afternoon. The same service provider also runs a fixed-route service Monday through Friday between The Dalles and Hood River ($3 one-way). Buses arrive at and leave from **The Dalles Transportation Center** (201 Federal St.). Greyhound (www .greyhound.com) also offers bus service from this location.

Yakima Valley

Yakima (YAK-a-ma) has become one of the largest cities in Central Washington and the commercial hub for the Yakima Valley. Eastern settlement was strongly resisted by the confederated tribes and bands of the Yakama Nation in the early 1800s. With the end of the 1855 Indian War and the settling of the Yakama People on a reservation, ranchers and farmers took their place, raising apples, pears, hops, and mint in large amounts. The volcanic soil practically farms itself. Today, Yakima relies on those crops still, as well as huge fields of hops for beer brewing. Yakima is also the source for the vast majority of grapes shipped all over the state to fuel the passion of boutique vintners. The extensive manpower needs of agriculture have brought a small army of men and women of Mexican extraction to the area. Thus, the valley has developed a rich culture of top-notch Mexican restaurants and upbeat music, far away from the border. Here, I-82 cuts across the north side of the valley, with the older Highway 22 following a parallel route on the south side. Several small towns dot the route between Yakima and the Tri-Cities; the largest are Zillah, Granger, Sunnyside, Grandview, and Prosser.

SIGHTS
Historic Yakima

The North Front Street Historical District boasts some of Yakima's oldest buildings, including the 1898 Lund Building and the Northern Pacific Railroad depot.

Three miles northwest of Yakima on

© ERICKA CHICKOWSKI

Wander the streets of Toppenish to see the city's murals.

Highway 12 you'll find the mysterious **Indian Painted Rocks,** a state historical site. Although the pictographs were partially destroyed by an early irrigation flume, some remain at Naches Highway and Powerhouse Road. The cliffs nearby are popular with local rock climbers.

The **Ahtanum Mission** (17740 Ahtanum Rd., 509/966-0865), east of Yakima along Ahtanum Creek, was built in 1852 by Catholic priests. During the Yakama Wars of the 1850s, the relationship between the priests and Yakamas led U.S. Army soldiers to the unlikely conclusion that the missionaries were providing the Yakama warriors with arms and munitions. A group of soldiers thus torched the mission in the middle of the night. The church was rebuilt in 1869 and is still used today. You can visit the mission and surrounding park for a small fee.

Toppenish Murals

Toppenish boasts that its chief recreation is watching paint dry. The city of murals and false-front Western buildings is a draw for lovers of outdoor art. Topics are generally of the sagebrush, saddles, and steam train variety.

Visit the chamber of commerce (11 S. Toppenish Ave., 509/865-3262, www.toppenish.net, 10 A.M.–4 P.M. Mon.–Sat. Apr.–Oct.) to pick up a map of the 80-plus wall-art pieces, or hop aboard one of the wagon rides offered by **Toppenish Mural Tours** (509/697-8995, $12 adults, $5 kids, 10 A.M.–1 P.M. Mon.–Sat.) that leave from the depot area on one-hour tours May–September.

Museums

Start your visit to Yakima at the large **Yakima Valley Museum** (2105 Tieton Dr., Yakima, 509/248-0747, www.yakimavalleymuseum.org, 10 A.M.–5 P.M. Mon.–Sat. and 11 A.M.–5 P.M. Sun., $5 adults, $3 students and seniors, $12 families, free for under age 5). It boasts an extraordinary collection of Yakama Native American artifacts, Oregon Trail, and local fruit tree industry exhibits. Boxcars, shops, and tool sheds are arrayed around the property and available for self-guided touring.

COLUMBIA RIVER GORGE

YAKAMA RESERVATION

Toppenish is the capital of the Yakama Indian Nation and the commercial center for the 1.37-million-acre Yakama Reservation (509/865-5121). The tribal council decided in 1994 that the correct spelling for their tribe is Yakama, rather than Yakima, although it is formally known as the Confederated Tribes and Bands of the Yakama Nation. The reservation is home to approximately 5,000 Native people from 14 different tribes and bands, along with another 20,000 non-Indians. The Yakamas run several businesses including a furniture factory, a juice bottler, orchards, ranches, a casino, and a sawmill. The westernmost edge of the reservation includes land within the Mount Adams Wilderness, and a permit is required for camping, fishing, or hunting.

The **American Hop Museum** (22 S. B St., Toppenish, 509/865-4677, www.american hopmuseum.org, 10 A.M.–4 P.M. Wed.–Sat., 11 A.M.–4 P.M. Sun. May–Sept., closed Mon.–Tues., $3 adults, $2 students, free for children under 5) is the only one of its kind, shining a bright spotlight on the underappreciated hops, a vital bittering ingredient in the production of beer and ale and a huge local cash-crop.

The once-bustling 1911 railroad depot near Toppenish town square is home to a shrine to a force that made most of the northern half of Washington possible. No, not glaciers. The **Northern Pacific Railway Museum** (10 S. Asotin Ave., 509/865-1911, 10 A.M.–4 P.M. Tues.–Sat. and noon–4 P.M. Sun. May–Oct., $5). Explore rail and steam artifacts and a restored telegraph office.

The impressive **Yakama Cultural Heritage Center** (100 Spiel-yi Loop, 509/865-2800, www.yakamamuseum.com, 8 A.M.–5 P.M. daily, $5 adults, $3 seniors and children 11–18, $1 children under 10, $12 family of four, free for enrolled Yakama members) on the Yakama Reservation features a museum that tells the story of the Yakama Nation from its beginnings to the present, a library specializing in Native American books, a theater that presents first-run movies and stage productions, a restaurant, and an RV park.

Fort Simcoe State Park

Head 27 miles west from Toppenish through the heart of the Yakama Reservation to peaceful Fort Simcoe State Park (509/874-2372, www .parks.wa.gov, 6:30 A.M.–dusk daily April–Oct., free). The drive takes you through fields of grapes and hops, past fast-growing Heritage College, past Native American burial grounds with decorated gravesites, to the reconstructed remains of a U.S. Army fort built to guard the frontier in 1856.

Other Parks

More than 250 species of birds live in the marshy **Toppenish National Wildlife Refuge** (five mi. south on Hwy. 97, then south a half mile on Pump House Road, 509/865-2405). The interpretive center and nature trail will get you started.

The **Yakima Area Arboretum** (1401 Arboretum Drive, 509/248-7337, www .ahtrees.org, dawn–dusk daily) is a peaceful 46-acre park with a Japanese garden and bird sanctuary, plus over 2,000 specimens of native and exotic woody plants near I-90 and Nob Hill Boulevard.

Across the Yakima River from Union Gap, bird-watchers will want to visit the **Hazel Wolf Bird Sanctuary** at the Wenas Creek Campground in the Wenas Valley, five miles west of Selah on Wean Road. Over 100 species of birds have been sighted in the 40-acre sanctuary.

Wineries

Yakima Valley is one of the premier wine-growing regions in the entire state, covering two distinct viticultural appellations, Yakima Valley and Rattlesnake Hills. Stop at local visitors centers for a map of more than two dozen local wineries, or request a copy from the **Yakima**

Valley Wine Growers Association (800/258-7270, www.yakimavalleywine.com).

UPPER YAKIMA VALLEY

No need to truck deep into the valley for a charming vineyard experience. Keep close to the city and visit **The Tasting Room Yakima** (250 Ehler Rd., 509/966-0686) out near Cowiche Canyon. Here you'll encounter a small turn-of-the-20th-century farmhouse that acts as a cooperative tasting room to three boutique wineries. Outside, there is a verdant lawn and a patio, a well-tended garden, and a small chicken coop. All of this is adjacent to a small nine-acre biodynamic vineyard and over 80 more acres of sage land open to hiking.

RATTLESNAKE HILLS

The pleasantly fragrant vineyard grounds at **Bonair Winery** (500 S. Bonair Rd., Zillah, 509/829-6027, www.bonairwine.com,

10 A.M.–5 P.M. daily) also present great views of the mountain and of nearby orchards. Stop by the shady pond to give Bonair's resident Aussie shepherd dog a scritch behind the ears before heading into the new pale-yellow French chateau tasting room. You'll be greeted with a smile by the friendly owners, who have the gift of gab. Call ahead to arrange a guided vineyard or winery tour ($10).

Sit on a bench near a giant wine barrel to sip a glass and survey the surroundings at the **Hyatt Vineyards Winery** (2020 Gilbert Rd., Zillah, 509/829-6333, www.hyattvineyards.com, 11 A.M.–5 P.M. daily April–Oct., 11 A.M.–4:30 P.M. daily Nov.–Dec. and Feb.–Mar., closed Jan.). An immaculate lawn, colorful rose garden, and a giant windmill sit directly outside the tasting room patio. Surrounding them are acres of orderly vineyard rows.

The McDonald Mercantile building houses **Piety Flats Winery** (2560 Donald-Wapato

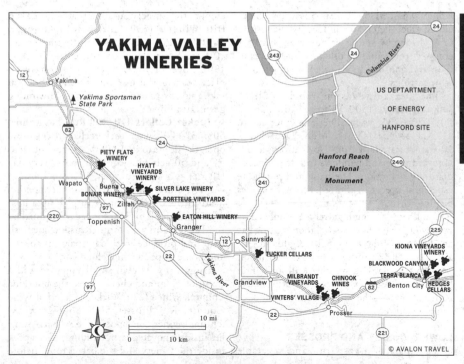

© ERICKA CHICKOWSKI

Walk the vineyards in the Yakima Valley for a closer look at the growing grapes.

Rd., 509/877-3115, 11 A.M.–5 P.M. Fri.–Sun., closed Dec.–Feb.). Surrounded by a lawn and table shaded by young walnut trees, this 1911 country store building offers bric-a-brac, candies, and gourmet foods to go along with the wine tastings.

The mezzanine tasting room at **Silver Lake Winery** (1500 Vintage Rd., Zillah, 509/829-6235, www.silverlakewinery.com, 11 A.M.–4 P.M. Thurs.–Mon. Dec.–Mar., 10 A.M.–5 P.M. daily Apr.–Nov.) affords a nice vineyard view and windows into the winery's distilling operation. The patio and porch are especially pretty in the fall when the leaves begin to turn.

You'll wind through gravel roads hugged by grapevines to get to the barrel room tasting bar at **Portteus Vineyards** (5201 Highland Dr., Zillah, 509/829-6970, www.portteus.com, noon–5 P.M. daily in summer, call for winter hours). Don't let the warehouselike atmosphere scare you away—the winemakers here produce some prized reds.

LOWER VALLEY AND PROSSER

Once a part of a vast fruit and vegetable empire, the cannery building that holds **Eaton Hill Winery** (530 Gurley Rd., Granger, 509/854-2220, www.eatonhillwinery.com, 10 A.M.–5 P.M. daily) dates back to the early 1900s. See for yourself how barrels have replaced cans in this historic structure while you take a sip or two of the winery's award-winning gewürztraminer.

Tucker Cellars (70 Ray Rd., Sunnyside, 509/837-8701, www.tuckercellars.net) throws open the doors to its 10,000-square-foot facility and 50-acre vineyards for tours every day (10 A.M.–5 P.M. in summer, 10 A.M.–4 P.M. in winter). Once you've worked up an appetite, head to the on-site market to pick up a host of gourmet food grown, cooked, or canned by the Tucker family. Favorite treats include fresh fruit and produce, pickled asparagus spears, and home-popped white cloud corn.

Hugged by its own small vineyard and a stand of plum and cherry trees, the boutique **Chinook Wines** (220 Wittkopf Ln. off of Wine Country Rd., Prosser, 509/786-2725, www .chinookwines.com, noon–5 P.M. Sat.–Sun.) lies inside renovated farm buildings. Get a peek inside the winery and the barrel room before

ICE WINE

While a disaster for many, for some Washington vintners, crystalline frost over ripe grape clusters is a beautiful sight. In these parts, such a picture portends the prospect of ice wine, an intensely flavorful and sweet concoction that can only be produced when the stars align just so to give wineries the chance to create it.

Ice wine is pressed from grapes that have frozen while still on the vine. In order to make this happen, vineyards must take a gamble. They'll reserve a selection of grapes past harvest time, protecting them with nets from hungry birds and other critters, and hope that the frost falls before the grapes go bad. If the weather doesn't cooperate, the vine's precious cargo is lost.

If it does, the grapes must be picked immediately so they can be squeezed while still frozen. When a grape freezes on the vine, it's only the water in the fruit that seizes up. The sugars and solids in the grape remain unfrozen. So when it is pressed, that fruit yields only a fraction of the liquid a normal grape would, but it is a highly concentrated juice.

Ice wine is prized not only for its smoothness and flavor, but also for its rarity. Because it is produced so infrequently and because the grapes yield much less ice wine than normal wine, expect to pay a premium. But if you have the means, do give it a try. It is the smoothest dessert wine you'll ever sip.

Vintner's Village complex, a hub of 12 distinct wineries, and **The Winemaker's Loft** (357 Port St., 509/786-2705, 11 A.M.–6 P.M. daily), a new winery "incubator" that helps upstart winemakers experiment and launch their own brands. Some of the highlights among the Vintner's Village dozen include **Milbrandt Vineyards** (508 Cabernet Ct., 509/788-0030), which serves a varied tapas and salad menu to go with its vintages, and **Thurston Wolfe Winery** (588 Cabernet Ct., 509/945-4292, 11 A.M.–5 P.M. Thurs.–Sun.), known best for its full-bodied zinfandel, syrah, and sangiovese.

Also at the village is the funky **Airfield Estates** (560 Merlot Dr., 509/786-7401, www.airfieldwines.com, 11 A.M.–5 P.M. Sun.–Thurs., 10 A.M.–5 P.M. Fri.–Sat.), a lively winery whose decor plays off of its vineyard history—the vines were all planted around an old World War II airbase. The winery was built to resemble an old military hangar, including a 40-foot water tower that acts as a VIP tasting room and wine library for the facilities. Big band music pipes inside when you step into the gorgeous building and get a look through the giant picture windows that frame the barrel room. Airfield is open one hour later on summer Saturdays.

While you're in town, be sure to also drop in on **Desert Wind Winery** (2258 Wine Country Rd., Prosser, 509/786-7277), a handsome new winery that eschews the typical chateau motif. The buildings are made up like an old New Mexico adobe hut, with eclectic Southwest decor to match within the luxury tasting room. The property is also home to a four-room bed-and-breakfast and a sumptuous fine-dining establishment.

Benton City

The quiet small town of Benton City provides a sharp contrast to the bustling Tri-Cities, just a few miles to the east. Stop here to enjoy the lush valley with vineyards and fruit trees.

Melt into the comfy leather chairs inside the tasting room at **Kiona Vineyards Winery** (44612 N. Sunset NE, Benton City,

heading into the farmhouse tasting room. The personable owners happily welcome people to wander the grounds and spread out blankets and baskets in the shady garden picnic area. Be sure to bring some food that will pair well with the specialty sauvignon blanc.

The town of Prosser is a good place to survey the Yakima Valley wine scene without having to drive all over the countryside. In addition to the tasting rooms and wine bars scattered over town, Prosser is also home to the unique

509/588-6716, noon–5 P.M. daily). Step outside on the patio and lawn for a nice view of Red Mountain.

The facilities at **Blackwood Canyon** (53258 N. Sunset Rd., 509/588-7124, www.black woodwine.com, 10 A.M.–6 P.M. daily, $10 standard, $25 reserve) are nothing to get excited about, but that would detract from the wine anyway. The winery sits at the end of a rough gravel road in the middle of the vineyards, and the tasting room is just a counter in the warehouse. The real star of the show is the eccentric winemaker, a believer in old-method, small-batch fermentation processes that produce, hands down, the best wines in Yakima valley. If you have the time, he'll take you through several hours of tasting, even bringing out bits of food he's prepared to pair with his masterpieces. The chardonnays, cabernets, and late-harvest wines are quite distinctive.

Tour through the cool, dark wine-storage caves at **Terra Blanca** (34715 N. DeMoss Rd., Benton City, 509/588-6082, www.terrablanca .com, 11 A.M.–6 P.M. daily) on Red Mountain. The $15 tour (noon and 3 P.M. Sat.–Sun.) allows you to walk the caves, the fermentation bays, the barrel room, and the vineyard, followed up with a chance to taste the fruit of all the labor.

ENTERTAINMENT AND EVENTS
Performing Arts
The **Yakima Valley Community Band** (www .yakimacommunityband.org) has free concerts on Wednesdays and Thursdays throughout the summer, as well as a spring program. Summer concerts are held in one of several parks and create perfect opportunities for relaxing. The **Yakima Symphony Orchestra** (32 N. 3rd St., 509/248-1414, www.yakimasymphony .org) performs a diverse season of music at the Capitol Theater October–April.

A new hub of Yakima's performance community, **The Seasons Performance Hall** (101 N Naches Ave., 509/453-1888, www.theseasons yakima.com) has some of the best acoustics east of the Cascades. This grand old building was converted from an old Seventh-day Adventist church and now draws quality jazz, classical, Latin, and world-beat musicians.

The historic **Capitol Theater** (19 S. 3rd St., 509/853-2787, www.capitoltheatre.org) is a beautifully restored 1920 theater, now hosting a full schedule of musical, theatrical, and Broadway productions.

Festivals and Events
The most popular local event is the **Central Washington State Fair** (1301 S. Fair Ave., 509/248-7160, www.fairfun.com) held in late September, which features a PRCA championship rodeo, hypnotists, carnival, nationally recognized musical talent, nitro-fueled demolition derby, and agricultural displays The **The Central Washington Antique Farm Expo** (509/457-8735) on the third weekend of August features an old-time threshing bee and working displays of farm equipment at the Central Washington Agricultural Museum.

The biggest annual wine event is the **Yakima Valley Spring Barrel Tasting** (800/251-0751) in late April, when the wineries pour samples of their new releases straight from the barrel and offer tours, hors d'oeuvres, and educational exhibits. All 25 wineries are open 10 A.M.–5 P.M. during this three-day event.

Dog lovers will enjoy Prosser's **National Championship Chukar Field Trials** on the last weekend in March. It attracts English pointers and shorthairs from all over the country.

Treaty Days and the All-Indian Rodeo and Pow Wow in nearby White Swan is held in early June to celebrate the signing of the Treaty of 1855. The rodeo features the Yakama Nation in a powwow and parade.

Fort Simcoe (509/874-2372) puts on a great show in June also, complete with living history presentations, traditional tribal dance, a flag-raising ceremony, military re-enactors, antique car shows, and best of all, free cake!

The 4th of July weekend brings a frenzy of activity to Toppenish: the **Pow Wow & Rodeo** (509/865-5566) is an event with something for everyone—a carnival, nightly rodeos, dancing, fireworks, a Wild West parade featuring cowboys, cowgirls, and Yakama people in full regalia, an antique power show, and arts and crafts booths.

The **Prosser Wine & Food Fair** (800/408-1517) on the second Saturday of August is the largest outdoor wine and food show in the state, attracting thousands of people for a chance to sample wine, beer, and food. The event usually sells out, so order advance tickets. It's only open to people over age 21.

In September, the Yakima Valley girds up to go ga-ga for the great **Grandview Grape Stomp** (114 Grandridge, 509/882-2100). In the town's grandest gala of the year, groups of three grapple to gouge grapes as in times gone by and gain some Grandview glory. And also a trophy. A fee of $30 gains you general admission and covers family activities galore.

The **Prosser Balloon Rally and Harvest Festival** (1230 Bennett Ave., www.prosser balloonrally.org) on the third weekend of September attracts balloon enthusiasts for morning launches and nighttime lighted balloons.

Late into the season, November brings **Tribal Jam** (509/865-5363, $25), a showplace for some of the country's best American Indian musicians and singers. The show is held at the Heritage Theater at the Cultural Heritage Center.

The season starts to winds down with **Thanksgiving in Yakima Valley Wine Country** (509/965-5201), which features food and wine-tasting at most local wineries. This is one way to taste a variety of gourmet foods and to get recipe ideas.

In early December, the **Country Christmas Lighted Farm Implement Parade** features bulb-bedecked tractors, farm machinery, and horse-drawn carriages and wagons in one of the premier lighted parades in the northwest. Call the Sunnyside Chamber of Commerce (509/837-5939) for details.

SHOPPING

At Yakima Avenue and North 1st, a trainful of 22 old railroad cars and pseudo-Victorian buildings house the **Track 29 Shopping Mall**

with gift shops and eateries. Several antique shops are inside the adjacent **Yesterday's Village.**

Several downtown art galleries offer high-quality works, including **Simon Edwards Gallery** (811 W. Yakima Ave., 509/453-7723).

Toppenish is rife with antique stores, craft shops, and gift shops. **The Amish Connection** (509/865-5300) has handcrafted Amish furniture, dolls, quilts, and other items. A few doors away is **Kraff's** (509/865-3000), the largest retailer of Pendleton blankets in the United States. **Roses Native Designs** (202 S. Toppenish Ave., 509/865-9325) offers local Native American art and crafts. For authentic Native American arts and crafts, visit the gift shop at **Yakama Nation Cultural Heritage Center.**

SPORTS AND RECREATION
Racing
The **Yakima Speedway** (1600 Pacific Ave., 509/248-0647, www.yakimaspeedway.us) hosts auto racing every Saturday night April–early October, ranging from Super Stocks to Youth Hornets. If that doesn't completely get your motor running, take part in the annual **Vintiques Northwest Nationals** (www.vintiques.com) car show and Rod Run held in late July and early August. You're bound to see some of the Northwest's finest mechanical muscle right here, plus a parts-oriented swap-meet, drag racing events, food, camping, and a carnival atmosphere.

Spectator Sports
Yakima County Stadium (1220 Pacific Ave., 509/452-1450) is home to the **Yakima Bears** (509/457-5151, www.yakimabears.com), a short-season class-A affiliate of the Arizona Diamondbacks. Games are affordable and the team offers several promotions throughout the June–September schedule.

Scenic Drives
Driving on I-82 between Ellensburg and Yakima, you'll realize that Central Washington

isn't the flat, boring terrain you might have heard about. As the road snakes up treeless ridges over 2,000 feet high, the far-off brown hills look as if they're covered with soft velvet; up close, it resolves into sagebrush, scrub, and grass. Pull into the rest stop at the south end of the Fred Rodmon Memorial bridge for a stunner of a view of the icy summits of Mount Adams and Mount Rainier in the distance.

The **Jacob Durr Wagon Road** (aka Wenas Road) is not recommended for vehicles without four-wheel drive. It was once the only route linking Yakima and Ellensburg; today, it's surely the most scenic, climbing over Umtanum Ridge for a 360-degree view of the Cascades and Yakima Valley. Drive north from Selah on N. Wenas Avenue, which becomes Wenas Road, the old Durr Wagon Road. The more standard route northward (I-90) also offers excellent vistas from the **Manatash Ridge Viewpoint** into the lush Kittitas Valley, with the Wenatchee Mountains rising behind the town of Ellensburg.

Water Sports

Yakima's **Franklin Park** (21st Avenue and Tieton Drive), has a big pool with a slippery spiral water slide. The grassy hills at this park are also a local hot spot for sledding in the winter.

At **Eschbach Park** (4811 South Naches Rd., 509/574-2435, www.co.yakimacounty.us), five miles past the fish hatchery on the Old Naches Highway, rent a tube or kayak and take a lazy float down the Naches River. The day-use, 168-acre county park offers boating, swimming, picnicking, and play areas.

Many locals also float, water ski, or fish (trophy-sized rainbows for catch-and-release fishing only) in the beautiful 27-mile **Yakima River Canyon** (509/665-2100) between Ellensburg and Yakima owned by the private Nature Conservancy. The river is paralleled by State Highway 821, with several boat ramps and picnic sites along the route and is home to the greatest concentration of nesting raptors in the state.

Before you head out to swish your rod around, pick up a few flies and nymphs from **Fairbanks Out Centers** (423 West Yakima Ave., Yakima, 509/457-3474), whose helpful staff can point you in the right direction if you know what you're doing or sign you up for one of their guided excursions if you don't.

Cycling

The Yakima Valley farming country makes for great back-roads cycling, with a multitude of possible loop trips. Get a map of local cycling routes from the visitors center. Unfortunately, there are absolutely no bicycle rental shops in the Yakima Valley, Tri-Cities, or Walla Walla Valley areas. Pick up a rental on the way. If you are headed over via I-90, stop off at **Cle Elum Bike and Board** (316 W. 1st St., 509/674-4567). Or try one of the numerous rental shops in the Gorge if you are coming in from parts south.

If you need some supplies or want to buy a new ride in Yakima, **Jake's Bike Shop** (507 W. Nob Hill Blvd., 509/469-9602) is a friendly local bike store that does right by its customers.

Golf

Yakima has quite a few public courses. The **Apple Tree Resort** (8804 Occidental, 509/966-5877, www.appletreeresort.com, $50 nonresidents) features a signature par 3 17th hole—a tricky forced carry on to an apple-shaped island. **Suntides** (231 Pence Rd., 509/966-9065, $25) offers a par-70 course. The city-owned, executive-length **Fisher Park Golf Course** (823 S. 40th Ave., 509/575-6075) can be a nice, quick indulgence at $9.25 for nine holes. You can even rent clubs here. The **Westwood West Golf Course** (6408 Tieton Dr., 509/966-0890) is another executive course with a driving range. Nine holes will run you $28.

Hiking

The **Yakima River Greenway** encompasses 3,600 acres east of the city, connecting Selah, Yakima, and Union Gap along a 10-mile paved biking and walking path.

Cowiche Canyon is a scenic and remote

rocky canyon just a few minutes west of Naches. The abandoned railroad line ribbons along and across Cowiche Creek, passing distinctive rock formations, with some that resemble the Easter Island faces. The canyon is managed by Cowiche Canyon Conservancy (509/966-8608, www.cowichecanyon.org), which produces a brochure on the three-mile trail. To continue your journey, follow the out-and-back Uplands Trail spur off of the main trail. You can follow that about 1.5 miles to a shady grove of birch trees before returning.

ACCOMMODATIONS

Most of Yakima's in-town motels can be found along the Highway 97 corridor through town (1st Street).

Under $100

Cruise into town on Highway 82, cross the Yakima River, and take 1st to find the **Days Inn** (1504 N. 1st St., 509/248-3393 or 800/248-3360, $70 s or $75 d). Also affordable (and pet-friendly) is **Howard Johnson Plaza** (9 N. 9th St., 509/452-6511, $75 s or $95 d).

For valley accommodations, **Best Western Lincoln Inn** (515 S. Elm St., Toppenish, 509/865-7444 or 800/222-3161, www.bestwestern.com, $80s or $90 d) is the best choice in Toppenish, with its indoor pool, hot tub, exercise room, fridges, microwaves, and continental breakfast.

Farther east, **Sunnyside Inn B&B** (804 E. Edison, Sunnyside, 509/221-4195 or 800/221-4195, www.sunnysideinn.com, $89–99 d) is situated in the 1919 Fordyce house and has thirteen spacious rooms with private baths, eight of which feature whirlpool tubs. A hearty country breakfast is served, and kids are accepted.

Also in Sunnyside, **Country Inn and Suites** (408 Yakima Valley Hwy., Sunnyside, 509/837-7878 or 800/578-7878, $55 s or $66 d) has a heated outdoor pool, hot tub, and continental breakfast.

When you drive into Prosser, you can't miss **The Barn Motor Inn** (490 Wine Country Rd., 509/786-2121, $50 s or $55 d). Just like the name tells you, this motel is fashioned like a

big red country barn. Rates are pretty good for the level of cleanliness and comfort offered by the rooms here. There's a pool and a restaurant on-site. You can also park RVs in the trailer facility around back ($17.50).

$100-150

Quality Inn Comfort Suites (I-82 and Valley Mall Blvd., 509/249-1900 or 800/228-5150, www.choicehotels.com, $129 s or $140 d) looks out over islands in the Yakima River. This all-suites motel has an indoor pool, hot tub, exercise room, continental breakfast, and free wireless Internet.

Holiday Inn Express (1001 E. A St., 509/249-1000 or 800/315-2621, www.hiexpress.com, $140 s or d) features an indoor pool, hot tub, fitness room, and continental breakfast. An extra $20 will warm the staff toward the idea of your pet staying the night with you.

A classic Queen Anne Victorian built in 1889, **A Touch of Europe B&B** (220 N. 16th Ave., 509/454-9775 or 888/438-7073, www.winesnw.com/toucheuropeb&b, $123–136 s or d) serves candlelit European breakfasts (included in rate), high tea ($30), and lavish five- to seven-course dinners ($50) in its elegant dining room. The German- and English-speaking owners provide an acre of shady grounds and three well-appointed guest rooms in a relaxing adults-only environment.

At the **Birchfield Manor B&B** (2018 Birchfield Rd., 509/452-1960 or 800/375-3420, www.birchfieldmanor.com, $119–220 d), guests may sample from a wine cellar amply stocked with local vintages. The biggest local B&B, Birchfield plumps the pillows for guests in four luxurious rooms in the 1910 main house and four adjacent, newer cottages. All rooms have private baths with whirlpool tubs, and some are equipped with gas fireplaces and private decks. The parklike grounds contain a swimming pool. Breakfasts are memorable, and dinners in the restaurant here are some of the finest around (Thurs.–Sat., $27–38 for full dinners). Ask about the golf packages in partnership with the Apple Tree Resort.

COLUMBIA RIVER GORGE

Orchard Inn B&B (1207 Pecks Canyon Dr., 509/966-1283, www.orchardinnbb.com, $109–129 d) is a lovely contemporary home tucked away in an orchard of cherry trees. The three guest rooms have private baths, private entrances, and the use of outdoor gazebos. A full, slow-food breakfast is served. The friendly bilingual (German and English) owners welcome kids and well-behaved dogs on approval.

$150-200

Feed a horse an apple grown right outside your door at **Cherry Wood Bed and Breakfast** (3271 Roza Dr., Zillah, 509/829-3500, www.cherrywoodbandb.com, $145–165 d), a fun little gem hidden away on a working farm in Zillah. This quirky inn offers a few different lodging options. First there are very comfortable and well-appointed rooms within the farmhouse, available year-round. Then there are the luxury teepee and themed retro trailers that open up in the warm summer months. Many guests stick around after breakfast for the host's guided horseback winery tours ($150), offered by appointment.

Over in Grandview, you'll be pampered from the get-go when you set your suitcases down at **Cozy Rose Inn B&B** (1220 Forsell Rd., 509/882-4669, www.cozyroseinn.com, $189 d). Lush tapestries, soft bedding, and smartly painted designer rooms await you here. All suites come with whirlpool tub and big-screen TV, and each has individual amenities including fireplaces, fridges, and private entrances. For maximum romance, breakfast can be delivered to your door and a special dinner can be arranged with the innkeeper.

Over $250

Dust off your fancy cowboy hat and tuck yourself in the luxurious rooms at the Southwest-style **Desert Wind Winery Inn** (2258 Wine Country Rd., Prosser, 509/786-7277, www.desertwindwinery.com, $250–300 d). The concert-hall-sized suites all come equipped with gas kiva fireplaces, large-screen TVs with Bose sound and DVD players, and balconies overlooking the winery courtyard and the Yakima River.

Camping

About a mile east of town off I-82, an oasis of green awaits at **Yakima Sportsman State Park.** Year-round, kids can fish the pond, stocked with bluegill, trout, catfish, and carp. Adults can try their luck on the nearby Yakima River. Tent sites run $21 and RV sites are $31. Americans with Disabilities Act (ADA)–compliant sites are available, as are coin-operated showers. Be sure to tackle the miles of hiking trails while you're here. Make reservations ($7 extra) at 888/226-7688, www.parks.wa.gov.

Wenas Creek Campground is home to the Hazel Wolf Bird Sanctuary in the Wenas Valley. Camping here is primitive—we mean it! There is no fresh water available and you can expect to dig your own trenches.

Trailer Inns (1610 N. 1st St., 509/452-9561 or 800/659-4784, www.trailerinnsrv.com, $22–40 depending on electricity needed) has a heated pool and a propane concession.

The **Yakama Nation Resort RV Park** (280 Buster Rd., 509/865-2000 or 800/874-3087, www.winesnw.com/YakNtnRVListing.htm), next to the Cultural Heritage Center has 125 parking spaces for RVs ($32), plus 14 very popular tepees ($30–50), a tent-camping area ($20), outdoor pool, hot tub, two saunas, exercise room, and other facilities.

FOOD
Yakima

One of the top 10 most-visited drive-ins in the country, **Miner's Drive-In** (2415 S. 1st St., 509/457-8194, 8:30 A.M.–4 A.M. daily) is a Yakima institution. The loyal customers line up for the flying-saucer-sized burgers and golden onion rings. Miner's also serves a book-length list of milk shake flavors. Freshness is the key here—you'll see the phrase "Nothing is cooked until you order it!" on signs in the store.

Looking for just the cure for a wine-induced hangover? Head to the local greasy spoon, **Mel's Diner** (314 N. 1st St., 509/248-5382, open 24 hours) and get yourself a big ol' breakfast with a fresh cup or three of coffee served up by waitresses who'll call you "hon."

Jack's Sports Bar (432 S. 48th Ave.,

Nosh on the best burgers in Yakima at Miner's Drive-In.

509/966-4340) is a fun place with burgers, sandwiches, and a big-screen TV, open till 1:45 A.M. on the weekends.

One of Yakima's finest supper spots, **Birchfield Manor** (2018 Birchfield Rd., two mi. east of the city on Birchfield Rd., 509/452-1960 or 800/375-3420, www.geopics.net/birchfield, dinner Thurs.–Sat.) seats diners in a restored 1910 farmhouse. Formal dinners are complemented by a vast selection of Yakima Valley wines. The innovative cuisine changes seasonally, but there is always a perfect filet mignon. Reservations are essential.

In the historic district, **The Greystone Restaurant** (5 N. Front St., 509/248-9801, entrées $30) aspires to be a fine dining establishment on par with big city cousins over in Seattle, and it certainly does have some strong points. The towering ceilings with antique molding and the ruggedly elegant exposed stonework certainly make for a dramatic dining room, and the food is delicious, even if the service is lacking. Your best bet is to bring some lively companions to pass the time, sit in the

lounge, and order a bottle of wine with some scrumptious light appetizers.

Then head across the street to **The Depot Restaurant and Lounge** (32 N. Front St., 509/949-4233, 11:30 A.M.–10 P.M. daily, entrées $20), in Yakima's old 1910 Pacific Northern Railroad station, which has an equally exciting dining room and none of the pretense. The depot is beautifully restored, and you'll likely spend parts of dinner looking upward, mouth agape, at the molding and scrollwork in the domed ceiling. The chef dishes out mouthwatering plates of seafood, chops, and fresh salads at extremely reasonable prices.

Yakima far and away has the area's best Mexican restaurants, a gift from the many workers of Mexican descent that come here and make the region's agriculture such a success.

One of the best spots in town is at **Los Hernandez** (3706 Main St., Union Gap, 509/457-6003, 11 A.M.–6 P.M. Tues.–Fri., 10 A.M.–7 P.M. Sat., 11 A.M.–6 P.M. Sun., closed Mon.), which serves homemade tamales better than you'll get even in Southern California. You'll regularly see folks load up coolers full of them to take home. If you go in springtime, be on the lookout for the inventive asparagus tamales. They may sound strange, but they sure are delicious.

Santiago's Gourmet Restaurant (111 E. Yakima Ave., 509/453-1644, www.santiagos.org, 11:30 A.M.–2 P.M. and 5–9 P.M. Mon.–Fri., 5–10 P.M. Sat., closed Sun.) is a lively and popular Mexican restaurant with all the standards and excellent daily specials.

El Pastor (315 W. Walnut, 509/453-5159, 11 A.M.–8 P.M. Mon.–Fri., noon–8 P.M. Sat.) is a small place with inexpensive and delicious Mexican dishes. Find lots more *tortillerias* and *panaderías* on South 1st Street heading toward Union Gap.

For gourmet Italian food and Northwest specialties, visit **Gasparetti's** (1013 N. 1st St., 509/248-0628, http://gasperettisrestaurant.com, 11 A.M.–midnight daily). The pastas are all freshly made, and desserts are a real treat. Interestingly enough, it is also well known for its onion rings. You really can't do wrong giving them a try.

© ERICKA CHICKOWSKI

COLUMBIA RIVER GORGE

Let the chef win you over at **Keoki's Oriental Restaurant** (2107 W. Lincoln Ave., 509/453-2401, 11 A.M.–2 P.M. and 4–10 P.M. daily), where the cooking takes place at your table teppanyaki-style. The teriyaki steak is always a pleaser.

Finding food out in the winery back roads can be a hit-or-miss affair. Load up on picnic supplies in town before you head out to ensure a happy and fulfilling wine excursion. **Deep Sea Deli** (20 N. 9th Ave, 509/248-1484, 9 A.M.–6 P.M. Mon.–Sat., closed Sun.) stocks specialty cheese, meats, and crackers. It also smokes its own salmon right on the property. Or leave the lunch packing up to **Buhrmaster Baking Co. and Restaurant** (117 E 3rd Ave in Selah, 509/469-9973, www.buhrmaster bakingco.com, 8 A.M.–8 P.M. Mon.–Fri., 11 A.M.–8 P.M. Sat., closed Sun.), which prepares box lunches to go for wine tourists.

Fresh fruit, vegetable stands, and U-pick places can be found throughout the Yakima Valley. From Yakima, the easiest way to find them is to take Highway 97 and exit off Lateral A Road. Head down south and let the signs guide you. The farm roads are ruler-straight, so it is pretty much impossible to get lost.

One sure winner is **Barrett Orchards** (1209 Pecks Canyon Rd., 509/966-1275, www .treeripened.com), where you can pick cherries, pears, apples, peaches, or whatever is in season. Or let them do the work and buy from its farm store. It's also fun to just head down Highways 97 and 22 until something looks interesting— hand-painted signs are as numerous as the fruit they advertise.

Valley Eats

Toppenish's strong Mexican culture is evidenced in the town's restaurants, clothing stores, and songs on the radio. **Taqueria Mexicana** (105½ S. Alder St., 509/865-7116) has the best south-of-the-border meals in town.

Also near Toppenish, the **Yakama Nation Cultural Center** (100 Spiel-yi Loop, 509/865-2800) has a popular restaurant with a large salad bar, salmon, buffalo, and fry bread. The Sunday brunch is very popular.

You'll discover the best burgers around, along with floats, shakes, and cold drinks, at the old-fashioned soda fountain in **Gibbons Pharmacy** (117 S. Toppenish Ave., 509/865-2722).

Sunnyside's big Darigold cheese factory is one of the largest cheese plants in the nation. **Darigold Dairy Fair** (400 Alexander Rd., 509/837-4321, www.darigold.com) has self-guided tours, fun exhibits (including flying cows), and videos, plus fresh ice cream, cheeses, sandwiches, and gifts.

Snipes Mountain Brewing Inc. (905 Yakima Valley Hwy., Sunnyside, 509/837-2739, www.snipesmountain.com, 10 A.M.–10 P.M. Sun.–Fri., 11 A.M.–11 P.M. Sat.) is hard to miss. It's the huge log-and-lodgepole building near the center of town, with a brewery behind glass and a diverse menu that includes everything from wood-fired pizzas to seafood satay. It's very popular, with a lively atmosphere and tasty grub.

The Barn Inn and Restaurant (490 Wine Country Rd., 509/786-1131, www.thebarn motorinn.com) on the west end of Prosser is one of the best local restaurants for all-American steak and seafood platters; munch the great appetizers while watching sports on the big-screen TV. Another local favorite is **Picazo 717** (717 6th St., 509/987-1607, www.picazo717.com), an arty, modern tapas and wine bar that serves food that will make you want to sing. Try the daring shellfish cakes ($10) with shrimp, crab, and scallops drizzled with a poblano remoulade. Or bring a friend and order the paella for two ($34). The well-educated staff is ready to offer the perfect wine pairing from the jam-packed cellar.

The **Prosser Farmers Market** (509/786-9174, 8 A.M.–12:30 P.M. Sat. June–Sept.) takes place in the city park.

INFORMATION AND SERVICES

For maps, brochures, and current festival information, contact the **Yakima Valley Visitors and Convention Bureau** (10 N. 8th St., 509/575-3010 or 800/221-0751, www.visit yakima.com, 8 A.M.–5 P.M. Mon.–Fri. all year, plus 9 A.M.–5 P.M. Sat. and 10 A.M.–4 P.M. Sun. May–Oct.).

Emergency medical service is provided by **Yakima Valley Memorial Hospital** (2811 Tieton Dr., 509/575-8000) in the city. Emergency medical care is also available at the 63-bed **Toppenish Community Hospital** (502 West 4th Ave., 509/865-3105) which, along with high-tech care, also provides a Native American Spiritual Care Center featuring facilities for performing healing rituals and ceremonies. **Sunnyside Community Hospital** (10th & Tacoma, 509/837-1500) runs a 24-hour ER.

Sick pets are welcomed at **Pet Emergency Service** (510 W Chestnut Ave., 509/452-4138) in Yakima or at the **Wapato Toppenish Veterinary Clinic** (Hwy. 97 and Branch Rd., 509/865-3435).

GETTING THERE AND AROUND
By Air
The **Yakima Air Terminal-McAllister Field** (2300 West Washington Ave., 509/575-6149) is the largest airport in the area. **Alaska Airlines** (800/252-7522, www.alaskaair.com) provides daily passenger service to and from Sea-Tac Airport.

Several rental car agencies have desks here as well.

By Bus
Yakima Transit (509/575-6175, www.ci.yakima.wa.us/services/transit/) serves the Yakima area, including the municipal airport, with Monday–Saturday service.

For local tours, contact **Accent! Tours** (509/575-3949 or 800/735-0428, www.accenttours.com).

To get out of town or across the country, hop aboard **Greyhound** (509/457-5131 or 800/231-2222, www.greyhound.com) from its Yakima station (602 East Yakima Ave.). Greyhound also stops in Toppenish (at the Branding Iron, 509/865-3773) and Sunnyside (13th St. and Hwy. 12, 509/837-5344).

Tri-Cities

The sun-scorched confluence of the Snake and Columbia Rivers marks the end of a straight-shot journey along Highway 14 and the Columbia Gorge. Here you'll find an industrious trio of cities—Kennewick, Pasco, and Richland—at the rivers' junction. The Tri-Cities are book-ended by the Yakima and Walla Walla Valleys, surrounded by bountiful fields of potatoes, grains, fruits, and veggies, much of which is exported to Pacific Rim countries.

So how does a collection of agricultural towns grow into a metropolitan area with more than 120,000 people? The answer lies north of Richland at Hanford Site, birthplace of the Manhattan Project and home to the decommissioned nuclear munitions plant whose cleanup has funneled more than $12 billion into the local economy. Lucky visitors can get an up-close look at selected portions of Hanford site during limited tours offered by the Department of Energy.

SIGHTS
Hanford Site
In a cloak of secrecy that not even the workers who built it could see through, Hanford's Plant B reactor was the birthplace of the atomic age. This was the first large-scale plutonium production reactor ever to be built, creating a supply chain of radioactive materials that made it possible to create the first atomic bomb and Fat Man, the bomb that was dropped over Nagasaki, Japan, contributing to the end of World War II.

Since being decommissioned in 1968, Plant B has been meticulously scrubbed as a part of a decades-long, $1 billion-per-year cleanup of the entire Hanford Site nuclear complex. Though this historic reactor is still contaminated with radiation, visitors can't be harmed simply by coming into contact with objects there.

For several years now the Department of Energy has offered selected road tours around

COLUMBIA RIVER GORGE

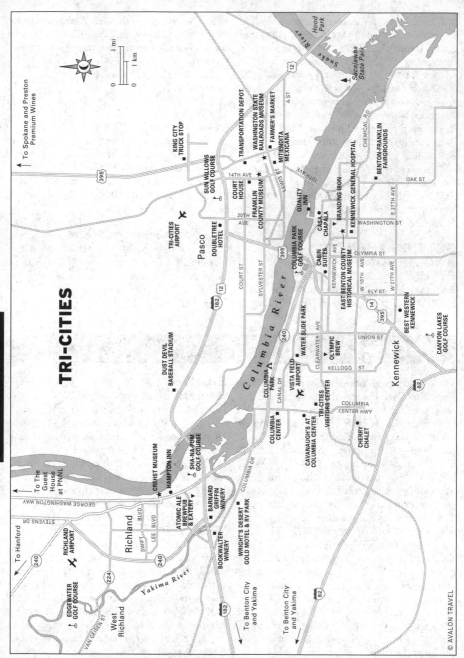

TRI-CITIES

limited areas of Hanford that include a walking tour of Plant B (www.hanford.gov/public tours). In order to book a slot, you must be an adult U.S. citizen who can plan well in advance. Online bookings fill up extremely quickly once the DoE announces the tour schedule. The only way to snag a free ticket is to regularly check the website. Plant B's availability may soon be opening up, though. In 2008 the building was placed on the National Registry of Historic Places, and DoE officials are currently working on plans to open the reactor to more public visits.

In spite of Hanford's toxic legacy, in a remarkable twist of fate it was also single-handedly responsible for preserving the last free-flowing, nontidal stretch of the "River of the West." The 51-square-mile buffer needed to protect outsiders from Hanford and vice versa during World War II and the Cold War is now protected as **Hanford Reach National Monument,** an amazing preserve that helps sustain healthy runs of chinook salmon and offers safe haven for deer, coyotes, bobcats, white pelicans, and other flora and fauna. For more information,

A NUCLEAR LEGACY

Cruise around the Tri-Cities and you'll find Atomic Ale Brewpub & Eatery, Atomic Body Shop, Atomic Laundry, Atomic Foods, and Atomic Health Center. The local high school team's name is the Bombers, with an atomic mushroom cloud as its emblem. There's a reason for this – the 560-square-mile Hanford Site just north of Richland, the source of much of the plutonium in America's nuclear arsenal.

During World War II, the United States began a frenzied race to develop an atomic bomb. The first controlled nuclear chain reaction experiments were conducted in late 1942, and within a few months the government had selected the Hanford site for its plutonium production plant. The location seemed perfect: remote enough for secrecy and safety, but still near railroads, an abundant source of water for cooling, and hydroelectric power for energy. The entire Manhattan Project was conducted with such secrecy that few of the construction workers knew what they were building. Three plutonium production reactors came online in time to provide the concentrated nuclear material for the bomb dropped on Nagasaki, Japan.

During the Cold War, the need for plutonium began to taper off, and the facility closed its doors, although the Hanford Site is still home to a Washington Public Power Supply System (WPPSS) nuclear plant.

After the closing of the last plutonium

reactor, the environmental problems that had been shrouded in secrecy for more than 45 years began to surface. Left behind were 54 million gallons of radioactive waste and powdery radioactive iodine spread around the local flora. Quite a bit of waste was stored in leaky containers that had gradually drained into the groundwater.

In 1994, the U.S. Department of Energy, the Washington State Department of Ecology, and the U.S. Environmental Protection Agency began the full-scale cleanup. The easiest problems at Hanford have been resolved in the last few years, but real problems remain, particularly the toxic stew of radioactive waste that sits in underground tanks or has escaped into the ground.

One surprising effect of the shutdown of Hanford and subsequent cleanup has been that it has spawned economic growth in the Tri-Cities. Billions of dollars in federal funds have flowed into the region, providing employment for thousands of engineers, spill experts, construction workers, and others. With an eventual price tag of somewhere between $30 billion and $100 billion, the environmental cleanup has proven to be a far bigger project than the reactors ever were. Due to the need for professionals to perform local research, the little town of Kennewick has managed to attract a higher concentration of PhDs per capita than in any other town in the western United States.

COLUMBIA RIVER GORGE

contact the U.S. Fish and Wildlife Service Monument/Refuge headquarters at 509/371-1801 or www.hanford.gov/doe/culres.

Museums

The **Columbia River Exhibition of History, Science, and Technology** (95 Lee Blvd., Richland, 509/943-9000, www.crehst.org, 10 A.M.–5 P.M. Mon.–Sat., noon–5 P.M. Sun., $4 adults, $3 seniors, $2.50 children) best illustrates the Tri-Cities' split personality with agricultural and natural displays on one side, and nuclear exhibits on the other. Try out a "hot cell" manipulator arm or learn to name all the local Columbia fish species on sight.

The **Washington State Railroads Historical Society Museum** (122 N. Tacoma Ave., 509/543-4159, www.wsrhs .org, noon–4 P.M. Thurs.–Fri., 9 A.M.–3 P.M. Sat., $2 adults, $1 senior and teen, free 12 and under) has railroad memorabilia inside and display of antique locomotives and railcars outside.

City Parks

Columbia Park (509/783-3711, www.ci .kennewick.wa.us, open year-round) forms a 609-acre border along the south shore of the Columbia River (Lake Wallula) in Kennewick, with four boat ramps for fishing and waterskiing, an 18-hole golf course, tennis courts, a picnic area, nature trails, and campsites ($7) and RV spaces ($11). One of the main attractions is a six-mile paved path that's a favorite of cyclists, in-line skaters, joggers, and lovers out for a riverside stroll. Two other popular spots are the **Columbia Park Family Fishing Pond** and **Playground of Dreams.** The pond was built by a consortium of community groups, and the playground was constructed in five days with help from over 5,000 volunteers.

Lake Sacajawea

Nine miles east of Pasco on the Snake River, **Ice Harbor Lock and Dam** is the first of four dams on the Lower Snake, with one of the highest single-lift locks in the world, rising 103

feet. Take a self-guided tour, watch the eager fish climb the ladders, or stop by the visitors center (9 A.M.–5 P.M. daily Apr.–Oct.).

The dam creates Lake Sacajawea, accessible for fishing, waterskiing, or swimming at **Levey Park** on the Pasco-Kahlotus Road on the lake's west side, and Charbonneau and Fishhook Parks on the east side. **Charbonneau Park** (14 mi. northeast of Pasco, 509/547-7783, Apr.–Oct., $18–22) and **Fishhook Park** (off Highway 124, May–mid-Sept., $14–22) have campsites with water, fire rings, and showers. Make reservations for both these Army Corps of Engineers campgrounds at 518/885-3639, 877/444-6777, or www.reserveusa.com.

Lake Wallula

Five miles east of Kennewick off Finley Road, **Two Rivers County Park** is open daily for boating, swimming, and picnicking along the Columbia River/Lake Wallula.

The U.S. Army Corps of Engineers operates **Hood Park** (four mi. southeast of Pasco, 877/444-6777, May–mid-Sept., $18–20), just east of Pasco for boating, swimming, and picnicking. You can also camp here, on the Snake River near its confluence with the Columbia. Make reservations at 518/885-3639, 877/444-6777, or www.reserveusa.com.

Sacajawea State Park

Two miles east of Pasco off Highway 12, Sacajawea State Park (509/545-2361, www .parks.wa.gov, 6:30 A.M.–dusk Wed.–Sun. Apr.–Sept.) sits at the confluence of the Snake and Columbia Rivers at the site where Lewis and Clark camped in 1805 on their way to the Pacific Ocean. You can fish, water-ski, or picnic here. An **interpretive center** (1–5 P.M. Fri.–Tues.) contains exhibits on Sacajawea—the Shoshone woman who acted as interpreter for the Lewis and Clark party—plus information about the expedition, videos, and Native American artifacts.

Juniper Dunes Wilderness

This 7,140-acre parcel of Bureau of Land

Management (BLM) wilderness (509/536-1200) is 16 miles northeast of Pasco on Pasco-Kahlotus Road. It contains the six largest remaining western juniper groves in Washington, along with sand dunes that top 120 feet high and are up to 1,200 feet long. Access is only through private land, so you'll need to get the permission of local ranchers to reach the dunes, and you may need a 4WD vehicle for the last several miles of road. There are no trails or drinking water, and summer temperatures often exceed 100°F, so come prepared. The best time to visit is in the spring and fall, when temperatures are more moderate.

Wineries

Most of the best wine-tasting around the Tri-Cities can be found to the east in the Yakima Valley and to the west in Walla Walla valley. However, travelers on a tight schedule can still find enough wineries close by to fill up a pleasant afternoon.

The parklike grounds at **Preston Premium Wines** (509/545-1990, www.prestonwines .com, 10 A.M.–5:30 P.M. daily) are perfect for a grassy reverie. The second-story deck off the tasting room overlooks the vineyards and a grassy area lined with birch trees and flower beds. Take a stroll and enjoy the antique tractors and shady gazebo. The tasting room sells a selection of gourmet goodies to get that picnic started on the right foot.

Ask the expert staff at **Bookwalter Winery** (894 Tulip Ln., Richland, 509/627-5000, www.bookwalterwines.com, 10 A.M.–8 P.M. Mon.–Tues., 10 A.M.–11 P.M. Wed.–Sat., 10 A.M.–6 P.M. Sun.) for help pairing tasting wines with the artisan cheeses and meats offered in its first-rate tasting room. Slide into a stool at the tasting bar or set up shop in the garden patio. In the evening hours you'll be serenaded by the live music acts that play here. If you go to Bookwalter, be sure to make time to also stop in at neighboring **Barnard Griffin Winery** (878 Tulip Lane, Richland, 509/627-0266, www.barnardgriffin.com, 10 A.M.–5 P.M. daily).

ENTERTAINMENT AND EVENTS
Nightlife

The **Louie's Lounge** (1101 N. Columbia Center Blvd., Kennewick, 509/783-0611) at Red Lion Columbia Center hosts lively karaoke nights on Friday, Saturday, and Sunday. **Branding Iron** (109 W. Kennewick Ave., 509/586-9292, www.brandingironnightclub .com, 4 P.M.–1:30 A.M. Wed.–Sat.) plays live country and other types of music and opens up its big dance floor Thursday–Saturday and hosts karaoke on Wednesday.

The Arts

For those of classical taste, enjoy events staged by the **Mid-Columbia Symphony** (1177 Jadwin Ave., Richland, 509/943-6602, www.mid columbiasymphony.org), which has been around for more than 50 years. The **Mid-Columbia Regional Ballet** (1405 Goethals, Richland, 509/946-1531, www.midcolumbiaballet.org) stages a spring program as well as the wintertime favorite, *The Nutcracker.* **Columbia Basin College Performing Arts** (509/547-0511) at Columbia Basin College offers live concerts, theater, gallery showings, and literary events.

Festivals and Events

The festival season kicks into high gear with the **Cinco de Mayo** parade and festivities in Pasco. The **Columbia Valley Wineries Barrel Tasting** in early June is a favorite introduction to local wineries.

Richland's **Sunfest** (509/736-0510) is a summer-long series of weekend activities that feature international food, music, and dancing. Sunfest events include the **Tri-Cities Children's Festival** in mid-June, **Ye Merrie Greenwood Renaissance Faire** in late June, and the **Sidewalk Art Show** in late July—southeast Washington's largest arts and crafts show.

The Tri-Cities' biggest event is the annual **Unlimited Hydroplane races** on the Columbia River, the highlight of the late-July **Columbia Cup** (509/547-2203, www.waterfollies.com). The action centers on Columbia Park in Kennewick, but you can also watch from the Pasco side if

COLUMBIA RIVER GORGE

you don't mind the sun in your face. Get to the park early on Friday or Saturday to take a pit tour before the races. A talent show, parade, and military aerial demonstrations round out the **Tri-Cities Water Follies** week.

Kennewick hosts the **Benton Franklin Fair and Rodeo** (1500 S. Oak St., 509/586-9211, http://bentonfranklinfair.com) every August, with top entertainers performing at the fairgrounds, including the Atomic City Rollergirls—if you're lucky. November brings the **Tri-Cities Wine Festival** (509/736-0510, www.tricitieswinefestival.com) to Kennewick, featuring 60 different wineries.

SHOPPING

Columbia Center (1321 N. Columbia Center Blvd., 509/783-2108, 10 A.M.–9 P.M. Mon.–Sat., 11 A.M.–7 P.M. Sun.) in Kennewick is the Tri-Cities' largest shopping mall, with 100 stores including Macy's, Sears, and JCPenney.

SPORTS AND RECREATION
Cycling
The Sacajawea Heritage Trail is a 22-mile contiguous path linking Tri-Cities' parks. Kennewick's **Columbia Park** has a popular six-mile paved, nearly level path, and Richland's Riverfront Trail offers a shady seven-mile option for biking or in-line skating.

Boating
Rent pontoon boats at **Columbia Park Marina** (1776 Columbia Dr. SE, Richland, 509/783-3802).

Racing
At Kennewick's Benton-Franklin Fairgrounds, **Sundowns Horseracing Track** (E. 10th Ave., 509/582-5434) hosts quarterhorse racing in the spring and fall.

Golf
Golfers have plenty of courses to choose from in the Tri-Cities area. **Columbia Point Golf Course** (225 Columbia Pt. Dr., Richland, 509/946-0710, http://playcolumbiapoint.com, $35–45) is a municipal that doesn't look like

a municipal. The rolling, mounded fairways and water features make for a fun 18. **Canyon Lakes Golf Course** (3700 Canyon Lakes Dr. in Kennewick, 509/582-3736, www.canyonlakes golfcourse.com, $51–54) is a slope 129 from the black tees. Hole 12 has a massive, undulating 12,000-square-foot green. And **West Richland Municipal Golf Course** (4000 Fallon Dr., 509/967-2165) is a straight links-style course following the banks of the Yakima River.

Spectator Sports
The Tri-Cities is home to two professional teams. The **Tri-City Dust Devils** (509/374-2757, www.dustdevilsbaseball.com), a Colorado Rockies "A" team, play at Pasco Stadium (6200 Burden), while the **Tri-City Americans** (509/783-9999, www.amshockey.com) smack the puck in the Western Hockey League.

ACCOMMODATIONS
It's a good idea to book your lodging well ahead, especially during July when the hydroplane races attract throngs of visitors from across the Northwest.

Under $100
Travelers on a shoestring budget will surely appreciate the facilities of **The Guest House at PNNL** (620 Battelle Boulevard, Richland, 509/943-0400, www.pnl.gov/guesthouse), a somewhat under-the-radar establishment run by the Pacific Northwest National Research Laboratory to provide lodging for visiting scientists and government workers. The unique 81-room inn offers utilitarian units reminiscent of college dorms. All guests can take advantage of the grounds' courtyard, exercise room, and coin-operated laundry machines. There are several room types to choose among. A standard dorm ($35 s) comes with a single twin bed and private bath. These are clustered in groups of 6–8 rooms with shared living room, dining room, and fully equipped kitchen. Queen studios ($75 s or $85 d) are larger private set-ups with microwave, fridge, and coffeemaker—bring your own utensils. The one-bedroom apartments ($80 s or $90 d) have a separate

bedroom with desk, a living room with hide-a-bed, and a fully equipped kitchen.

If government-style quarters aren't your thing, then try **Wright's Desert Gold Motel & RV Park** (611 Columbia Park Trail in Richland, 509/627-1000 or 800/788-4653, http://wrightsdesertgold.com, $47 d). This tight and tidy motel park has an outdoor pool, hot tub, and game room.

Quality Inn (7901 W. Quinault Ave., Kennewick, 509/735-6100 or 800/205-6938, www.scinns.com, $84–94 s or d) has nice rooms, a full breakfast, a hot tub, and a sundeck.

Settled back in a residential neighborhood, **Cabin Suites** (115 N. Yelm St., Kennewick, www.cabinsuites.com, 509/374-3966, $75–95 s or d) isn't a real cabin per se, but all three rooms are alluringly decorated with rough-hewn log bed frames and plaid flannel linens. This is a private B&B, as the innkeepers don't live on-site, only coming in the morning to serve breakfast. For maximum seclusion, the whole house can be rented for $195.

$100-150

All three of the Tri-Cities are full of reasonably priced chains. One of the best values is **Hampton Inn** (486 Bradley Blvd., 509/943-4400, www.hampton-inn.com, $117 d) in Richland. This snappily decorated establishment faces the Columbia River, offering dock facilities for boaters and a pretty view for the rest of us. Do yourself a favor and plunk down an extra $20 for a room with a view. The property has a fitness center and a hot tub and offers a continental breakfast and a complimentary airport shuttle.

Another good bet is **Best Western Kennewick** (4001 W. 27th Ave., Kennewick, 509/586-1332, www.bestwestern.com/kennewick, $85–130 d), a clean and friendly property with a raft of amenities. There's an indoor pool, hot tub, sauna, and fitness center, plus a business center. Pets are welcome, and there's room outside to walk them. The hotel serves a hot breakfast buffet with French toast, biscuits and gravy, sausage, bacon, and more. Come evening time, staff sets out warm cookies. Suites

with whirlpool bath and fireplace are available for $170.

Relax to the sound of a gurgling fountain waterfall on the shady and secluded patio at **Cherry Chalet** (8101 W. 10th, Kennewick, 509/783-6406, $160 d). This modest suburban-style home is cloistered on a 20-acre cherry orchard that's close enough to Kennewick to offer easy access to restaurants and activities.

Camping

Private RV parks in the Tri-Cities area include **Columbia Mobile Village** (4815 W. Clearwater Ave., Kennewick, 509/783-3314), **Desert Gold RV Park** (611 Columbia Dr. SE, Richland, 509/627-1000, http://wrightsdesertgold.com), **Green Tree RV Park** (2200 N. 4th, Pasco, 509/547-6220) and **Trailer City Park** (7120 W. Bonnie Ave., Kennewick, 509/783-2513, wwww.tri-citiesrvpark.com, $25).

FOOD
International

Casa Chapala #1 (107 E. Columbia Dr., Kennewick, 509/582-7848) has fresh Mexican food and ultra-fresh tortillas. They also have restaurants in Pasco and Richland.

Emerald of Siam (1314 Jadwin Ave., Richland, 509/946-9328, 11:30 A.M.–2 P.M. Mon.–Fri. and 5–9 P.M. daily) creates authentic and delicious Thai food and has an inexpensive lunch buffet weekdays ($8) and a popular dinner buffet on Friday and Saturday ($14).

Mandarin House (1035 Lee Blvd., Richland, 509/943-6843, 11 A.M.–2 P.M. and 4–9 P.M. Mon.–Fri., 4–9:30 P.M. Sat., closed Sun.) has the best local Chinese food.

Located in a cozy old railroad dining car, **Monterosso's Italian Restaurant** (1026 Lee Blvd., Richland, 509/946-4525, 5–10 P.M. Mon.–Thurs., 5–10 P.M. Fri.–Sat.) simmers and stews classic Italian cuisine and nightly seafood specials. Reservations are recommended.

Steaks and Burgers

For seafood, steak, prime rib, and pasta with outside riverside seating, head to **Cedars Restaurant and Lounge** (7 Clover Island, next to the Quality Inn, 509/582-2143, 5–9 P.M. Sun.–Thurs., 5–10 P.M. Fri.–Sat.).

Probably because Yakima Valley and Columbia Basin lead the nation in hops production, the Tri-Cities have become a center of microbrewed beer. **Atomic Ale Brewpub & Eatery** (1015 Lee Blvd., Richland, 509/946-5465, www.atomicale brewpub.com, 11 A.M.–10 P.M. Mon.–Thurs., 11:30 A.M.–11 P.M. Fri.–Sat., 11 A.M.–8 P.M. Sun.) is the oldest among dozens of local microbrewers. Its beers include the appropriately named Plutonium Porter, Atomic Amber, and Half-Life Hefeweizen. The menu centers on wood-fired pizzas, though they also have steaks, seafood, and bratwurst. There's live music every Monday evening.

Kimos at Rattlesnake Mountain Brewing Company (1250 Columbia Center Blvd., Richland, 509/783-5747, www.rattlesnake mountainbrewing.com, 3–11 P.M. Mon.–Thurs., 11 A.M.–1 A.M. Fri., 9 A.M.–1 A.M. Sat., 9 A.M.–10 P.M. Sun.) is one of the nicer local places and also features outside dining along the Columbia River. Oriental wasabi chicken salad and Rattlesnake Buffalo wings attract attention on its reasonably priced menu.

Markets

Visit the **Pasco Farmers Market** (4th Ave. and Columbia St., 509/545-0738, 8 A.M.–noon Wed. and Sat. May–Nov. for local produce, sausages, fresh breads, and arts and crafts. The **Kennewick's Southridge Farmers Market** (corner of Kennewick Ave. and Benton St., 509/528-4592, http://southridgefarmersmarket. com, 4–8 P.M. Thurs., Southridge Village) is small but has a particular hometown feeling.

Adam's Place Country Gourmet (910 E. Game Farm Rd., Pasco, 509/582-8564, www.adamsplacecountrygourmet.com, 10 A.M.–6 P.M. Mon.–Fri., 10 A.M.–2 P.M. Sat., closed Sun.) is located in an apple orchard and makes all sorts of sweet confections, even chocolate-covered pizzas.

Country Mercantile (232 Crestloch Rd., 10 mi. north of Pasco, 509/545-2192, www.country mercantile.com, 7 A.M.–8 P.M. daily) has a produce market and ice-cream parlor, and provides "agricultural entertainment" in October that includes a seasonal corn-field maze, petting zoo, and pumpkin patch. It's great fun for families.

INFORMATION

Pick up all the current maps and information you need from the **Tri-Cities Visitor and Convention Bureau** (7130 W. Grandridge Blvd. in Kennewick, 509/735-8486 or 800/254-5824, www.tcrchamber.com, 8 A.M.–5 P.M. Mon.–Fri.).

GETTING THERE AND AROUND
By Bus and Train

Public transportation comes together at the **Transportation Depot** (535 N. 1st Ave.) in Pasco. Here you can catch a local bus from **Ben Franklin Transit** (509/735-5100, www .bft.org, $1, $2.75 all-day pass) for service to the three cities and the airport Monday–Saturday. **Greyhound** (509/547-3151 or 800/231-2222, www.greyhound.com) also stops here, as does **Amtrak** (509/545-1554 or 800/872-7245, www .amtrak.com), whose *Empire Builder* train provides daily service east to Spokane, Minneapolis, and Chicago, and west to Portland.

By Air

Departing from the Tri-Cities Regional Airport in Pasco are **Alaska Airlines** (800/252-7522, www.alaskaairlines.com), **Delta Air Lines** (800/221-1212, www.delta.com), and **United Express** (800/241-6522, www.ual.com).

Bergstrom Aircraft (509/547-6271) offers flightseeing trips out of the Richland airport over the Tri-Cities area for $99 for up to three people on a Cesna 172.

Tours

Columbia River Journeys (509/734-9941 or 888/486-9119, www.columbiariverjourneys .com) runs jetboat trips to Hanford Reach. As you cruise up the river, you'll see heron rookeries, curious coyotes, huge salmon beds, and the surreal Hanford reactors along the horizon.

Walla Walla

As you drive toward Walla Walla from the east, Highway 12 takes you past mile after mile of gently rolling wheat growing out of the rich chocolate-brown soil. It's enough to make Midwest farmers drool. The strip-cropped patterns of plowed and fallow land look like cresting waves, with the Blue Mountains bordering the southeast horizon. The valley enjoys a long growing season, with wheat, potatoes, asparagus, peas, alfalfa, grapes, and the famous Walla Walla sweet onions as the big money crops. Livestock and dairy products are also significant parts of the economy.

If you arrive in the pretty town of Walla Walla on a hot summer day, you'll probably wonder, at least momentarily, if you took a wrong turn somewhere and drove to New England. Walla Walla is an oasis in arid eastern Washington. Here, trees have been cultivated for decades and offer much-needed shade and visual relief from the sameness of the eastern Washington landscape.

The Lewis and Clark party passed through the Native American hunting grounds here in 1805, but the first permanent white settlement wasn't until some time later. Dr. Marcus Whitman, a doctor and Presbyterian missionary, arrived in 1836 and established a settlement he called Waiilatpu. The Cayuse, suffering from measles that Whitman could not cure and resentful of Whitman and his party's aggressive conversion techniques, massacred 15 of the settlers in 1847, including Whitman and his wife. This put a bit of a damper on local white settlement until the Treaty of 1855 reopened the region to American migration.

In 1856, Col. Edward Steptoe built **Fort Walla Walla** at Mill Creek to keep the peace. The surrounding town was later named Walla Walla, meaning "Many Waters" in the Cayuse tongue. In 1859, the city was named the county seat and has since witnessed many booms and busts, from a minor gold rush in neighboring Idaho to disastrous fires that razed the entire

© ERICKA CHICKOWSKI

log cabin at Fort Walla Walla

COLUMBIA RIVER GORGE

town to the renaissance in the local wine industry that has made the town well known today.

SIGHTS
Museums

Step back in time with a visit to the **Fort Walla Walla Museum Complex** (Dalles Military & Myra Road, 509/525-7703, www.fortwalla wallamuseum.org, 10 A.M.–5 P.M. Tues.–Sun. Apr.–Oct., $7 adults, $6 seniors and students, $3 ages 6–12, free for younger kids). This excellent museum features 15 original and re-created pioneer buildings. A 19th-century cemetery containing the bodies of both Native Americans and cavalry soldiers borders the property. A short nature trail and campground is nearby.

Visit the **Kirkman House** (214 N. Colville, 509/529-4373, www.kirkmanhousemuseum .org, 10 A.M.–4 P.M. Wed.–Sat., 1–4 P.M. Sun., $5 adults, $2 students and seniors), a redbrick mansion built in 1880 by entrepreneur William Kirkman. The ornate Italianate-style structure features a widow's walk and figurehead keystones and is on the National Register of Historic Places.

Kids will be nearly overcome with wonder and delight at the **Children's Museum of Walla Walla** (77 Wainwright Place, 509/526-

ONION POWER

Although wheat is the most important crop in the Walla Walla area, onions are the town's claim to fame. The famous Walla Walla sweet onions were developed from Spanish and Italian varieties first brought here in the late 19th century. These mild-flavored, juicy, large onions actually have almost no sugar, but they have only half the sulfur of other onions. And it's the sulfur that gives onions their strong bite and causes tears.

© ERICKA CHICKOWSKI

Pick up a bag of Walla Walla sweets while you're in town.

7529, www.cmwallawalla.org, 10 A.M.–5 P.M. Thurs.–Sun., $4). The tykes can jump around on stage in costume along with life-size puppets at the Enchanted Theater. The Bug Patch Party Room is full of flowers and various kinds of insects. Kids can pretend to shop at the Wee Walla Walla Harvest Market, and visit a make-believe doctor's office, Mexican restaurant, or Construction Junction. Check the website for special events planned throughout the year.

Walking Tour

Pick up a brochure from the chamber of commerce for a walking tour of the historic downtown area. Some of the sights you'll pass are the 1917 **Liberty Theatre,** built on the site of the original army fort at W. Main and Colville, and the **Dacres Hotel,** built in 1899 at W. Main and 4th. The **Reynolds-Day Building,** on Main between 1st and 2nd, was constructed in 1874. Washington's first State Constitutional Convention was held here in 1878. It's hard to miss the 10-story **Marcus Whitman Hotel,** built in 1928 at 2nd and W. Rose, the brick centerpiece of downtown. The **Baker Boyer Bank** is the oldest bank in Washington and one of the few independent banks left in the state. Its seven-story home office at the corner of Main and 2nd Streets was built in 1910 and was the town's first "skyscraper."

If you've got a kitchen and a barbecue in your hotel unit, grab a bag of sweets while in Walla Walla and wow your travel companions with the following recipe.

GRILLED AND ROASTED WALLA WALLA SWEETS WITH PINE NUT BUTTER

4 medium Walla Walla sweet onions, peeled and cut in half from top to bottom

1 tablespoon olive oil

½ cup pine nuts, toasted

3 ounces unsalted butter, softened

½ teaspoon lemon zest

½ teaspoon chopped fresh rosemary

¼ teaspoon freshly ground black pepper

¼ teaspoon salt, or to taste

⅓ cup freshly grated parmesan cheese

2 tablespoons toasted pine nuts, lemon wedges, and rosemary sprigs for garnish

1. Toast the pine nuts in a 350°F oven for 6-7 minutes, or until golden brown. Cool. Caution: pine nuts burn easily.

2. Preheat the oven to 375°F and prep an outdoor grill. Brush onions with oil and place cut side down on the preheated grill. Once grill marks form, put onions on a cookie sheet and cook in oven for another 25 minutes, or until tender. Barbecue step can be replaced by broiling – just be sure to let the oven cool once you are ready to finish cooking.

3. While onions are cooking, take roasted pine nuts and pulse them in a food processor until finely ground. Then put butter, lemon zest, rosemary, black pepper, and salt in the bowl and process until smooth. If you're traveling, you'll need to improvise: place pine nuts in a zip-top bag and crush finely with a frying pan. Place in a bowl and mix with the rest of the ingredients.

4. Spread pine nut butter over the cooked onions and put back in oven until butter is melted.

5. Serve warm, with grated parmesan and a few extra pine nuts sprinkled over them.

Recipe courtesy of the Walla Walla Sweet Onion Marketing Committee and Chef Tom Douglas, who serves this dish at Dahlia Lounge in Seattle.

COLUMBIA RIVER GORGE

Founded in 1859, **Whitman University** (www.whitman.edu) was the first higher education center in the West and is home to 1,300 students. The campus is just west of downtown Walla Walla. The tall clock tower, built in 1900, is on the National Register of Historic Places.

Big Trees and Parks

Walla Walla is famous for its tall, stately trees, a heritage from pioneer settlers who wanted a reminder of their eastern homes. A booklet, available at the chamber of commerce, describes some of the largest of these, including the 25 different individual trees among the biggest in Washington. One of the trees, a 21-foot-in-circumference catalpa on the Whitman College campus, is the largest in America. The 47-acre **Pioneer Park** (Alder St. and Division St.) contains many more state-record trees. This well-kept city park was originally a cow pasture but now includes—in addition to marvelous forested areas—an aviary, rose garden, duck pond, swimming pool, gazebo, brass cannon, and picnic tables. The design for Pioneer Park came from John C. Olmstead, creator of New York's Central Park. **Fort Walla Walla Park** is home to more tall trees, along with the Fort Walla Walla Museum. **Mountain View Cemetery** (on S. 2nd Ave. near Abbott Rd.) dates back to 1853 and is considered one of the most attractive in the state.

Farm Tours

West from Walla Walla lies farming country with a Midwestern look; this could just as well be Nebraska. Far to the southeast lie rolling tree-covered hills that rise into the Blue Mountains. A blanket of snow covers the summits till late summer.

Take a dip in a sea of purple at the **Blue Mountain Lavender Farm** (345 Short Rd., 509/529-3276, www.bluemountainlavender .com) in nearby Lowden. Owned by a French-American family, the farm was inspired by nostalgia for the extensive lavender fields in the south of France. An on-site gift shop sells dozens of luxurious items made from the local crop. Call ahead for tours.

Whitman Mission

You can get the whole story of Marcus and Narcissa Whitman's pioneer mission on the Oregon Trail at the Whitman Mission National Historic Site (28 Whitman Mission Rd., 509/529-2761, www.nps.gov/whmi), seven miles west of Walla Walla on Highway 12. None of the original buildings remain, but you can walk self-guided trails to the mission site, grave, monument, and locations of the first house, blacksmith shop, and gristmill. Cultural demonstrations—including adobe brick making, beadwork, moccasin making, and butter churning—take place on summer weekends.

Maintained by the National Park Service, the visitors center here (8 A.M.–6 P.M. daily mid-June–Labor Day, 8 A.M.–4:30 P.M. daily the rest of the year, closed Thanksgiving, Christmas, and New Year's, $3 adults, free for kids under 16) contains a diorama of the Whitman mission, plus artifacts found here and an informative exhibit about the Cayuse tribe and the sad end to the Whitmans' work.

The grounds are open till dusk year-round. Be sure to walk up the hill to the **Whitman Memorial,** a 27-foot-tall obelisk overlooking this lonely place. Come here on a late fall day with the clouds overhead, the brown grass at your feet, great blue herons on the shore of the pond, and a chilly west wind to really appreciate the peaceful wildness that both the Cayuse and the Whitmans loved.

Wallula

The tiny settlement of Wallula stands along the east shore of Lake Wallula, the Columbia River reservoir created by McNary Dam. Look for **Two Sisters,** twin basalt pillars that the Cayuse legends said were two sisters who had been turned to stone by that trickster, Coyote. A plaque in Wallula commemorates one of the earliest garrisons in the Northwest. In 1818, the Northwest Fur Company established **Fort Nez Percé** at the junction of the Walla Walla and Columbia Rivers. The fort soon became a center for fur trade in the region. Fearing Native American attacks, the company built two strong outer walls and armed the men heavily; it was soon being called the "Gibraltar of the Columbia." In 1821, the British-owned Hudson's Bay Company took over the business, later renaming it Fort Walla Walla. The fear of attacks intensified, and in 1856 the company abandoned the fort rather than risking capture. The fort's commander ordered his men to dump the black powder and shot balls into the Columbia River to keep them out of Cayuse hands. Shortly after his men abandoned the fort, American Indian warriors burned it to the ground.

Two years later a new Fort Walla Walla rose, this time as a U.S. Army military garrison farther up the river. This fort would eventually become the center around which the city of Walla Walla grew. The original fort site later grew into the town of Wallula, but in the late 1940s, construction began on the McNary Dam downstream along the Columbia River. After its completion, the old town and fort site were inundated, and the town's residents moved to higher ground.

Wineries

Walla Walla Valley is one of Washington state's eight official viticultural appellations and is best known for cabernet sauvignon, merlot, riesling, and chardonnay grapes. There are dozens of wineries in and around town. As you head close to city limits from the west, you'll encounter the very attractive **Three Rivers Winery** (5641 West Hwy. 12, 509/526-9463, www.threeriverswinery.com, 10 A.M.–5 P.M. daily). The tasting room and winery building sit on a bank overlooking the vineyard and a large grassy area with a small three-hole pitch-and-putt course. The building itself is an impressive combination of river rock, pitched roofs, and warm-red exposed wooden beams. Inside there's a river rock bar and fireplace to keep you cozy while tasting. Try the estate-grown gewürztraminer; it is superb.

Visit **Woodward Canyon Winery** (11920 W. Hwy. 12, 509/525-4129, www.woodward canyon.com, 10 A.M.–5 P.M. daily), about 10 miles west of town in Lowden, for a taste of top-quality chardonnay and cabernet sauvignon. The $5 tasting fee is refundable with any

purchase. **L'Ecole No. 41 Winery** (509/525-0940, www.lecole.com, 10 A.M.–5 P.M. daily), also in Lowden, specializes in semillon and merlot wines. The tasting room is an old schoolhouse—relax by doodling on the chalkboard as you sip. Tasting fees are a refundable $5.

Other notable Walla Walla wineries include the largest local winery, **Waterbrook Winery** (31 E. Main St., 509/522-1262, www.water brook.com, 10 A.M.–6 P.M. Sun.–Thurs, 10 A.M.–8 P.M. Fri.–Sat.).

ENTERTAINMENT AND EVENTS
The Arts
The **Walla Walla Symphony Orchestra** (26 E. Main, 509/529-8020, www.wwsymphony .com) has been performing since 1907 and is the oldest continuously performing symphony in the West. Its season runs October–May, with the special Mares 'n' Music performance falling in June.

Founded in 1944, the **Walla Walla Little Theatre** (1130 E. Sumach, 509/529-3683, www .ltww.org) is a community theater that produces four plays each season. **Harper Joy Theatre** at Whitman University (345 Boyer, 509/527-5180) also stages several student productions each year, and the local community college puts on **Outdoor Summer Musical** productions at Fort Walla Walla amphitheater each July.

Art buffs will want to visit the **Clyde and Mary Harris Gallery** (509/527-2600) at Walla Walla College, focusing on faculty, student, and regional shows. Other galleries include the **Sheehan Gallery** (509/527-5249, www .whitman.edu/sheehan) at Whitman College, home of the Davis Collection of Asian Art. The **Carnegie Art Center** (109 S. Palouse, 509/525-4270, www.carnegieart.com, 11 A.M.–4:30 P.M. Tues.–Sat., free) sits on the site of the historic 1855 Great Indian Council. Once a public library, the 1904 building is home to a pottery studio and a changing gallery of largely regional artwork.

Festivals and Events
A popular event with photographers is the

Walla Walla Balloon Stampede held in mid-May. The Northwest's signature hot-air balloon rally stages concerts, arts and crafts displays, and plenty of food to go along with the racing fun. A big **Fourth of July** at Pioneer Park is followed by the **Walla Walla Sweet Onion Harvest Festival** a week later. Labor Day weekend's **Walla Walla Frontier Days Fair & Rodeo** (509/527-3247) brings ropin', wrasslin', racin', and ridin' to the Walla Walla County Fairgrounds. In mid-September, the **Fall Harvest and Community Festival** at Fort Walla Walla Museum provides a chance to learn about pioneer life.

SPORTS AND RECREATION
Cycling
Enjoy the bike path from Cambridge Drive to Rooks Park, or from 9th and Dalles Military Road to Myra Road. For a more adventurous ride, head out scenic Old Milton Highway south of town. It's especially pretty in the fall.

Fishing
Walla Walla is a fly fisher's paradise, giving you the drop on unsuspecting trout, smallmouth bass, and the mighty steelhead. **Stone Creek Fly Fishers** (509/520-7039, http://stonecreek-flyfishers.com) teaches introductory classes for beginners, including special classes for women and children. Guide service is also available.

Swimming
Outdoor summer-only swimming pools (509/527-1099) include one in Jefferson Park (9th Ave. and Malcolm St.) and a 50-meter pool on Rees Avenue at Sumach Street.

Golf
Veteran's Memorial Golf Course (201 E. Rees Ave., 509/527-4507, http://vetsgolf.com), off Highway 12, is an 18-hole course open to the public. Greens fees are $29 for 18 holes or $16.75 for just the front nine.

ACCOMMODATIONS
Under $100
Colonial Motel (2279 E. Isaacs, 509/529-1220,

www.colonial-motel.com, $59 s or $79 d) is a rare local-family-owned motel with a nice view and a running waterfall on-site.

$100–150
For splendid semi-private downtown digs, check in at **The Wine Country Inn** (915 Alvarado Terrace, 509/386-3592, www.wallawallawine country.net, $150 d). The simply and tastefully appointed rooms offer wireless Internet access, 1930s flair, and private baths. Be sure to take advantage of the knowledge of the innkeepers, both of whom are long-time residents of the area.

$150–200
Prepare to relax hard-core when you check in to one of the three rooms at the **Inn At Blackberry Creek** (1126 Pleasant St., 509/522-5233, www.innatblackberrycreek.com, $144–239 d) Cozy rooms pay homage to artists Cézanne, Monet, and Renoir. The Inn is well located for visiting shops and historic sites.

The elegant **Marcus Whitman Hotel and Conference Center** (6 W. Rose St., 509/525-2200 or 866/826-9422, www.marcuswhitman

the lobby at Marcus Whitman Hotel

© ERICKA CHICKOWSKI

hotel.com, $169–194 s or d) first opened in 1927. After a major renovation, the 127-room hotel is once again Walla Walla's premier lodging choice, with 22 suites also available.

The **Fat Duck Inn** (527 Catherine, 509/526-3825 or 888/526-871, http://fatduckinn.com, $178–205 d) is a smartly decorated Craftsman cottage offering four suites and a gourmet breakfast. Amenities include a complimentary wine hour, with tastings of local vintages and the option of enjoying a delicious dinner right in its dining room for an additional charge. Well-behaved dogs are welcomed with prior arrangements.

$200-250

Take your pick when you stay at the **Walla Walla Inns** (123 East Main St., 509/301-1181 or 877/301-1181, www.wallawallainns.com, $115–325 s or d): stay in one of the six rooms at its historic downtown property or at the more tranquil hilltop Vineyard property. Children of all ages are welcomed here. The Inn pulls out all the stops for canine companions, too. A $100 nonrefundable pet fee gets you toys, treats, furniture, and even a crate, so your tail-wagger can pack light.

A unique lodging experience (unless you could be considered "livestock") is provided by the **Inn at Abeja** (2014 Mill Creek Rd., 509/522-1234, www.abeja.net, $245–295 d). The original outbuildings of this 100-year-old farm have been converted into tony, light-filled guest cottages and suites. The 35-acre vineyard property is the picture of country comfort. You can be proud to tell your friends you slept in a chicken coop. Reservations for popular local and winery events are filled by lottery.

Complimentary telescopes supplement the stellar accommodations at Touchet's **Cameo Heights Mansion** (1072 Oasis Rd., 509/394-0211, http//cameoheightsmansion.com, $199–249 d). The suites, a few of which have private entrances, are decorated after a variety of European, Mediterranean, and Asian styles. The rich breakfast might just convince you to stick around for the gourmet nighttime offerings, including an optional private four-course fondue feast.

Camping

For information on hiking and camping in the Blue Mountains of Umatilla National Forest, visit the **Walla Walla Ranger Station** (1415 W. Rose St., 509/522-6290, www.fs.fed.us/r6/uma).

RVs can park and dump at **Four Seasons RV Resort** (1440 Dalles Military Rd., 509/529-6072, $28 per night or $168 for seven days), a privately run campground.

Tent campers can pitch at **Lewis and Clark Trail State Park** (509/337-6457), 26 miles northeast of Walla Walla. Standard tent sites large enough to fit RVs are available April 1–September 15. Primitive sites are open year-round. No reservations are accepted at this park.

FOOD
Cafés and Diners

Start your day at **Clarette's Restaurant** (15 S. Touchet, 509/529-3430, 6 A.M.–8 P.M. daily) for the best home-style breakfasts in Walla Walla. Also of note for lunch is **Cookie Tree Bakery & Café** (23 S. Spokane, 509/522-4826, www.cookietreebakeryandcafe.com, 7:30 A.M.–2:30 P.M. Mon.–Sat.), with homemade breads and pastries. **Blue Mountain Tavern and Casino** (2025 E. Isaacs Ave., 509/525-9941) serves excellent sandwiches for lunch and shows big-screen TV sports at night. No kids are allowed here.

Although Walla Walla has all the standard fast-food eateries (out on Wilbur and Isaacs), you'd do far better visiting **The Ice Burg** (616 W. Birch, 509/529-1793, 11:30–10 P.M. Sun.–Thurs., 11:30 A.M.–11 P.M. Fri.–Sat.). This popular drive-in makes great hamburgers and wonderful banana shakes.

International

The Walla Walla area has a rich Italian heritage, best illustrated by the sweet Walla Walla onion—developed by an Italian transplant to the area—and the tasty pasta houses in town. A good example is **T. Maccarone's** (4 S. Colville St., 509/522-4776, www.tmaccarones .com, 11 A.M.–2 P.M. and 4–9 P.M. Mon.–Fri., 9 A.M.–2 P.M. and 4–9 P.M. Sat.–Sun.), a trendy place downtown that puts its own twist on traditional Italian fare. This is the best place in town to pair a Walla Walla red wine with antipasto.

The food isn't as good at **Lorenzo's** (1415 Plaza Way, 509/529-6333, 11 A.M.–9 P.M. daily), but it has a fun atmosphere and works well for starving students and money-minding families. It offers an all-you-can-eat buffet 11 A.M.–2:30 P.M. ($7.49) and 5–8 P.M. daily ($9.49). Kids 12 and under eat for $0.59 per year of age.

Looking for Mexican meals and great margaritas? Head to **El Sombrero's** (428 Ash St, 509/525-2598) for big portions and a bunch of big hats. **La Casita** (315 S. 9th Ave., 509/522-4941) has noteworthy pico de gallo and can accommodate large groups.

Pub Grub

Mill Creek Brewpub (11 S. Palouse St., 509/522-2440, http://millcreek-brewpub.com, 11 A.M.–11 P.M. Mon.–Sat., noon–9 P.M. Sun.) is a fun place with fresh-brewed beer on tap and pub grub from the kitchen.

Bakeries and Markets

Although Walla Walla has the big chain markets, one grocer is noteworthy: **Andy's Market** (1117 S. College Ave., 509/529-1003, closed Sat.) out in College Place. Because of the Seventh-day Adventist college nearby, this large market is almost entirely vegetarian. You'll find a few frozen meat items (but no pork), lots of frozen and canned "vegemeat" products, bulk foods, and plenty of gluten-free foods.

Not far away is **Rodger's Bakery** (166 N. College Ave., 509/522-2738) with breads, bagels, breadsticks, and hot soups. **John's Wheatland Bakery** (1828 E. Isaacs, 509/522-2253) is another excellent bake shop that uses fresh local ingredients.

INFORMATION

For local information, contact the **Walla Walla Chamber of Commerce** (29 E. Sumach, 509/525-0850 or 877/998-4748, www.wwv chamber.com, 8:30 A.M.–5 P.M. Mon.–Fri. all year, plus 9 A.M.–4 P.M. Sat.–Sun. in the summer).

GETTING THERE AND AROUND

Valley Transit (509/525-9140, www.valley transit.com) serves the Walla Walla and College Place area Monday–Saturday. The **Greyhound depot** (509/525-9313 or 800/231-2222, www.greyhound.com) is at 315 N. 2nd Street.

Walla Walla Regional Airport is at 310 A Street and provides passenger terminals for **Alaska Airlines** (800/252-7522, www.alaska air.com) service to Seattle and Portland. **Blue Ridge Aircraft** is the local fixed-based operator (FBO). Information is available at 509/529-4243.

COLUMBIA RIVER GORGE

NORTH CASCADES

The Cascade Range is Washington's great divide. In addition to creating almost opposite climates on either side of the state, the mountains also serve as a political and psychological barrier between east and west, resulting in what seems like two states within one.

Crossing the Cascade passes in winter—an adventure many Washingtonians prefer to forgo—is an experience that thousands of avid skiers tolerate to reach the slopes. They simply learn to live with the snow tire and chain requirements, snow-packed and icy roads, and occasional pass closures.

In summer, the Cascades take on a more benign image and become a popular destination for all manner of travelers, who have a wide variety of places and experiences from which to choose. Millions of acres have been set aside for recreation. The North Cascades and the areas around Mount Baker and Mount Adams, along with numerous wilderness areas and wildlife refuges—all constitute the backbone of Washington's outdoor recreation.

PLANNING YOUR TIME

The northern part of the Cascade mountain range is what some meteorologists like to call a "convergence zone." Basically, because the Olympic Mountains block rain and foul weather from passing over its peaks, the unstable air that creates it must go somewhere. It flows around the Olympics to the north and to the south, eventually converging at the North Cascades. What this means to you, intrepid visitor, is that this area tends to get dumped on, particularly in the winter.

© ERICKA CHICKOWSKI

HIGHLIGHTS

◖ Heather Meadows Area: One of the North Cascades' best year-round recreational destinations, this serene spot at the base of Mount Baker is equally beautiful blanketed with snow or flowers (page 477).

◖ Ross Lake: Get a bird's-eye view of this massive reservoir from the trails that summit nearby peaks, or see it from water level on a motorboat or canoe (page 498).

◖ Lake Chelan: This is the state's longest lake and a favorite summertime destination for travelers looking to splash around and then dry out under central Washington's hot summer sun (page 513).

◖ Stehekin: Reachable only by boat, this little mountain hamlet is a hub for hikers exploring deep into the Cascades National Park, Lake Chelan-Sawtooth Wilderness, or Glacier Peak Wilderness (page 521).

◖ The Bavarian Village: Cozied up under mountainsides that look strikingly similar to the Alps, Leavenworth dresses up as a delightfully campy Bavarian town (page 526).

◖ Alpine Lakes Wilderness Area: Crystalline lakes, craggy mountaintops, and emerald meadows await the hardy adventurer willing to trek into this pristine wilderness (page 536).

◖ Wallace Falls State Park: You can see this white gush of water from Highway 2, but don't just zoom by. The trails that take you up close are well worth the effort (page 539).

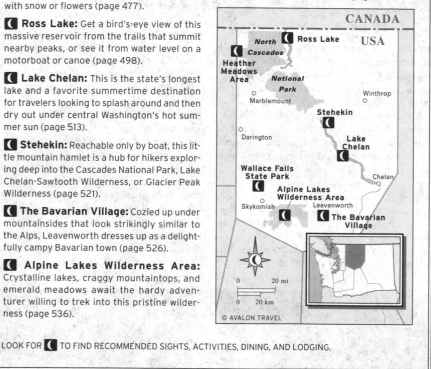

LOOK FOR ◖ TO FIND RECOMMENDED SIGHTS, ACTIVITIES, DINING, AND LODGING.

This is great news for skiers and snow-sports enthusiasts, but it can be a travel inconvenience. By November or so the Highway 20 pass is closed until springtime snowmelt, leaving Highway 2 as the only viable pass north of I-90. Even then, things can be tricky over Stevens Pass, so it is imperative that travelers check out snow reports and carry chains at all times. Also, be sure to plan loads of extra time to get to the Methow Valley, which can take up to six hours of travel depending on pass conditions. And you can forget about traveling the

rugged Mountain Loop Highway during these months, as its interior stretches are impassable once the snow falls.

In the summer, things open up considerably, and the favored route east is definitely the scenic Highway 20. It twists and turns directly through North Cascades National Park, by wild rivers, glacier lakes, and breathtaking passes. However, these mountains are unpredictable, so be sure to bring lots of layers of clothing—particularly if you plan on hiking or camping. It is not unusual to see summertime

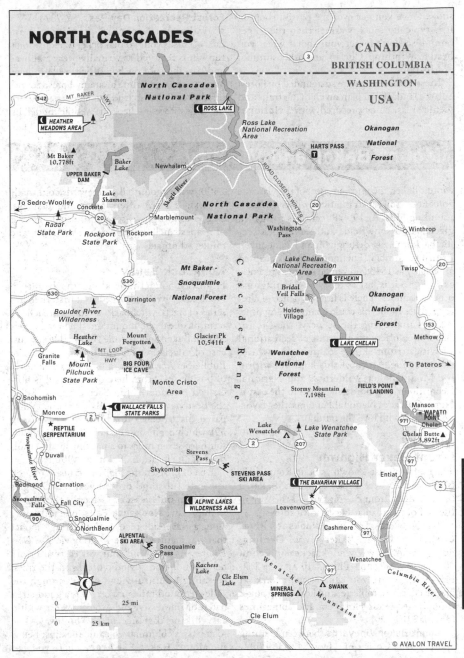

NORTH CASCADES

CANADA
BRITISH COLUMBIA

WASHINGTON
USA

3

North Cascades
National Park

ROSS LAKE

Ross Lake
National Recreation
Area

Okanogan

HARTS PASS

National

HEATHER
MEADOWS AREA

Mt Baker
10,778ft

Baker
Lake

Newhalem

Forest

UPPER BAKER
DAM

Lake
Shannon

To Sedro-Woolley

Concrete

Radar
State Park

Rockport
State Park

Rockport

Marblemount

20

North Cascades
National Park

ROAD CLOSED IN WINTER

20

Washington
Pass

Winthrop

530

Mt Baker -

Snoqualmie

National Forest

Darrington

Lake Chelan
National Recreation
Area

STEHEKIN

Bridal
Veil Falls

Twisp

20

Okanogan

530

Boulder River
Wilderness

Heather
Lake

Mount
Forgotten

MT LOOP
HWY

BIG FOUR
ICE CAVE

Glacier Pk
10,541ft

Holden
Village

National

Forest

153

Methow

LAKE CHELAN

To Pateros

Granite
Falls

Mount
Pilchuck
State Park

Monte Cristo
Area

Wenatchee

National

Forest

Stormy Mountain
7,198ft

FIELD'S POINT
LANDING

Snohomish

Monroe

WALLACE FALLS
STATE PARKS

Manson

WAPATO
POINT

Chelan

REPTILE
SERPENTARIUM

2

Lake
Wenatchee

Lake Wenatchee
State Park

971

Chelan Butte
3,892ft

Duvall

207

Redmond

Carnation

Stevens
Pass

Skykomish

STEVENS PASS
SKI AREA

2

THE BAVARIAN VILLAGE

97

Entiat

2

Snoqualmie
Falls

Fall City

ALPINE LAKES
WILDERNESS AREA

Leavenworth

90

Snoqualmie

NorthBend

ALPENTAL
SKI AREA

Snoqualmie
Pass

Cashmere

97

Wenatchee

Kachess
Lake

Cle Elum
Lake

MINERAL
SPRINGS

SWANK

Columbia River

0   25 mi

0   25 km

Cle Elum

© AVALON TRAVEL

snow. Once you get over the passes, though, it is typically much warmer than the Puget Sound, so don't forget your shorts when you head to Winthrop, Chelan, and other summer destinations.

Most of these areas are surrounded by Forest Service land. If you plan on enjoying trails and scenic areas, come prepared with a **National** **Forest Recreation Day Pass** (877/874-6775, www.discovernw.org, $5 per day, $30 annual). This is your golden ticket to recreational fun—it is required at virtually every trailhead and parking spot on Forest Service land here. You can get one online or at any Forest Service office. You can also find them at certain sporting goods stores—check the website for details.

Mount Baker and Vicinity

Mount Baker, the northernmost of the Cascade volcanoes, towers dramatically over the surrounding hills. At 10,778 feet, it is bathed in glaciers and snowfields and serves as a scenic backdrop for Bellingham and Vancouver, British Columbia. The mountain has erupted as recently as 1843 and vented steam as recently as 1975, so it is just as feisty as Washington's other volcanoes. There is little evidence of a return to life—but this could change at any time. Besides improving the scenery, the Mount Baker area offers up a wealth of recreational activities, from skiing to hiking to whitewater rafting. Much of this land lies within the Mount Baker Wilderness and National Recreation Area. Bordering them to the east is North Cascades National Park, another favorite of those who love the outdoors.

SIGHTS
Mount Baker Highway
The highway, also known as State Route 542, is the primary access road to Mount Baker, a 62-mile drive from Bellingham all the way to the end of the road at Heather Meadows.

The Nooksack Tribe runs **Nooksack River Casino** (5048 Mt. Baker Hwy., Deming, 360/592-5472, www.nooksackcasino.com, 10 A.M.–1 A.M. Sun.–Thurs., 10 A.M.–3 A.M. Fri.–Sat.), where you can try your hand at blackjack, craps, roulette, and keno. The poker room deals Texas Hold 'em and sometimes Omaha Hi/Low.

Mount Baker Vineyards (between Deming and Nugents Corner on Hwy. 542, 360/592-2300, www.mountbakervineyards.com, daily 11 A.M.–5 P.M.) offers tours and tastings. The vineyard grows several unusual varieties of grapes, including madeline angevine and müller–thurgau.

Nooksack Valley
Highway 542 climbs along the beautiful Nooksack River Valley, gently at first, then in a series of steep switchbacks as you approach the terminus near the mountain. The road enters Mount Baker-Snoqualmie National Forest just east of Glacier, where you'll find the Glacier Public Service Center, along with a handful of businesses. From here on, the road is officially a National Forest Scenic Byway. Enjoy the best views of Mount Baker at the end of paved Glacier Creek Road (Forest Service Road 39), which begins just east of Glacier and heads south for seven miles to a parking lot and trailhead at an elevation of almost 2,900 feet.

East of Glacier, the highway cruises through a wonderful stand of 700-year-old Douglas firs. Seven miles east of Glacier is the turnoff to impressive **Nooksack Falls** (one mile away along a gravel side road), a thundering cataract that was featured in the 1978 movie *The Deer Hunter*. As you wend your way eastward from here, you'll find periodic breaks in the trees, revealing beautiful views down through the valley. Around mile marker 44 is a good-sized patch of impressive old-growth forest within easy hiking distance of the highway. The road passes columnar volcanic rock just below the **Mount Baker Ski Area,** where you can

BACK IN THE DAY . . . .

Mount Baker has been a source for year-round recreation since 1868, when librarian-turned-mountaineer Edmund Coleman and his party climbed to the summit after two failed attempts. Either poor planners or extremely conscious of pack weight, the entire climbing party shared one plate and spoon and ate only bacon, bread, and tea during the 10-day ascent. By 1911, the mountain had become an integral part of the Mount Baker marathon, a 118-mile round-trip between Bellingham and the summit using any mode of transportation in addition to at least 24 miles on foot. The marathons were discontinued two years later, after one competitor fell into a crevasse, though he lived to tell about it. More recently the race has been revived as the 85-mile **Ski to Sea Marathon,** where teams begin by skiing down Mount Baker, and relays of bike riders, paddlers in canoes, and runners complete the course to Puget Sound.

purchase snacks on summer weekends or full meals in the winter, and then circles **Picture Lake,** a small lake that is ringed by wildflowers in early summer and reflects jagged Mount Shuksan year round. Save some space on your memory card—this one really is a stunner.

◖ Heather Meadows Area

The highway ends at 5,200-foot **Artist Point.** Known as Heather Meadows, this is the only alpine area in the North Cascades accessible by car. The scenery is amazing and there are hundreds of miles of hiking trails to explore in late summer. The stone-walled **Heather Meadows Visitor Center** (milepost 56 on S.R. 542, 10 A.M.–4 P.M. daily July–September) offers local information and a pretty view of Bagley Lakes.

Heather Meadows, stuck between Mount Baker and Mount Shuksan, has been drawing

tourists since the first lodge was built here in 1927. The lakes, meadows, and rock formations surrounded by snowcapped peaks were the setting for parts of Clark Gable's *Call of the Wild.*

The road to Picture Lake is kept plowed all winter, but the last five miles from here to Artist Point close with the first snows—generally mid- to late October—and usually don't open till late July. Because of the short season, August and September weekends are usually busy. If possible, a midweek trip might offer a bit more wilderness solace.

SHOPPING

Everybody stops at the quaint **Everybody's Store** (5465 Potter Rd., Deming, 360/592-2297, 7:30 A.M.–7 P.M. Sun.–Thurs., 8 A.M.–8 P.M. Fri.–Sat.), just south of Mount Baker Highway on the route that links it to the North Cascades Highway, State Route 9. The self-described "exotic grocery" makes up delicious sandwiches, sells cheese and local wine, clothing—everything to Native American and African musical instruments. You'll be amazed how much browsing you can do in such a little store.

SPORTS AND RECREATION

River Rafting

The Nooksack River emerges from Nooksack Glacier, high up Mount Shuksan, and drops over Nooksack Falls before entering a wild gorge. After four miles of class II–III white water, the silt-laden waters emerge into the lower river delta, providing fine views of Mount Baker and the chance to observe bald eagles and other wildlife. Several rafting companies offer eight-mile white-water trips down the Nooksack from Glacier to Deming June–August, including **River Recreation** (800/464-5899, www.riverrecreation.com, $78–88), which gives participants the option to ride in a raft with the rest of the group or in an individual inflatable kayak. Whichever you pick, you'll be treated to a buffet lunch at the end of the trip.

A more leisurely summertime float that's

NORTH CASCADES

extremely popular with inner tubers and families is the South Fork of the Nooksack River from Acme to Van Zandt.

Hiking

More than 200 miles of hiking trails meander through the Mount Baker district, and, fortunately for hikers, all of them are closed to motorized vehicles. The variety of trails is great: both backpackers and one-milers alike can find striking scenery within their reach. Wilderness permits are not needed for hiking within the Mount Baker Wilderness, but be sure to get one at the Glacier Public Service Center if you will be entering North Cascades National Park from the Mount Baker area.

One of the most popular local day hikes is the 3.5-mile round-trip **Heliotrope Ridge Trail** to the edge of **Coleman Glacier,** the starting point for Mount Baker summit climbs.

An easy four-mile round-trip hike leaves from the end of Twin Lakes Road off Mount Baker Highway to a lookout atop **Winchester Mountain,** with excellent views of Mount Baker, Mount Shuksan, and the North Cascades.

Popular with equestrians and hikers alike is the six-mile round-trip **Skyline Divide** trail, beginning 13 miles up Road 37 and providing ample Baker views and wildflower meadows.

LOOP TRIPS

Only a few loop trails are suitable for overnight trips; most Mount Baker trails are walk-in, walk-out propositions. Still, the scenery here is good enough to see twice. **Excelsior Pass** makes for a fairly short but respectable loop, gaining a torturous 3,800 feet. It then follows the **High Divide Trail** for four miles, with spectacular views of Baker and Shuksan, and returns to Road 3060 via **Welcome Pass** for 1.8 miles. The descent is via 67 demented switchbacks. Sections of this loop make popular, albeit difficult, day hikes. To stretch it out, travel north for three miles past the Excelsior Pass/High Divide junction to **Damfino Lakes** and Forest Service Road 31.

The **Copper Ridge-Chilliwack Loop Trail** is an extremely popular 35-mile trek into Mount Baker Wilderness and North Cascades National Park that begins from the Hannegan Campground at the east end of Forest Service Road 32. The first four miles are gentle, but after that the trail climbs abruptly to **Hannegan Pass,** then back down to a fork at the entrance to North Cascades National Park. The right fork continues east over Whatcom Pass and eventually to Ross Lake. Take the left fork instead, and climb along the spine of **Copper Ridge,** with vistas across the top of the Cascades. From here, the trail drops into Indian Creek, where you join the Chilliwack Trail for the return trip along Chilliwack River. A cable car provides a crossing over the river. This trail is best hiked from late July through September and even that late, an ice-ax might be necessary to cross steep snow sections. Wilderness permits are required for this hike, and are available at the Glacier Public Service Center.

HEATHER MEADOWS HIKES

The Heather Meadows area is an immensely

© ERICKA CHICKOWSKI

The banks of the Nooksack River are an ideal hiking destination.

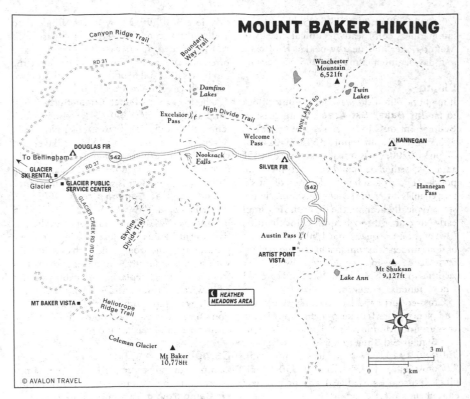

MOUNT BAKER HIKING

Canyon Ridge Trail

Boundary Way Trail

RD 31

Winchester Mountain 6,521ft

Damfino Lakes

Twin Lakes

TWIN LAKES RD

Excelsior Pass

High Divide Trail

Welcome Pass

HANNEGAN

DOUGLAS FIR

To Bellingham

542

Nooksack Falls

SILVER FIR

GLACIER SKI RENTAL

RD 37

Glacier

GLACIER PUBLIC SERVICE CENTER

542

Hannegan Pass

GLACIER CREEK RD (RD 39)

Skyline Divide Trail

Austin Pass

ARTIST POINT VISTA

Mt Shuksan 9,127ft

Lake Ann

HEATHER MEADOWS AREA

MT BAKER VISTA

Heliotrope Ridge Trail

Coleman Glacier

Mt Baker 10,778ft

0   3 mi

0   3 km

© AVALON TRAVEL

popular late-summer hiking area. Access is easy, since the Mount Baker Highway (Highway 542) ends at 4,700-foot Austin Pass, with trails branching out in all directions for all levels of ability. Easiest is the **Artist Ridge Trail,** a mile-long loop with interpretive signs and views all the way to Mount Rainier on clear days. The first 200 feet are wheelchair-accessible. Another easy path, **Fire and Ice Trail,** is paved to an overlook above Bagley Lakes.

Starting at Austin Pass near the end of Mount Baker Highway, the four-mile one-way hike to **Lake Ann,** one of the Cascades' most beautiful high-country lakes, is a popular route with day hikers and the major approach trail to 9,127-foot Mount Shuksan. Lake Ann Trail is often covered by snow till late summer.

From the end of Highway 542 at Artist Point, follow the steep 2.5-mile trail up lava cliffs to the appropriately named, flat-topped **Table Mountain.** Enjoy incredible views of Mount Baker and Mount Shuksan from here.

The 5.5-mile **Chain Lakes Trail** begins at the end of the road, traverses Table Mountain, and passes a series of alpine lakes. Beyond this, the trail climbs over Herrmann Saddle, enters the Bagley Lakes basin, and ends near the Mount Baker Ski Area. For a return loop, take the **Wild Goose Trail** back to Artist Point.

Climbing

Mount Baker offers one of the most challenging and rewarding climbs in the cascades. This one is not for beginners, so don't attempt to climb Mount Baker without previous alpine climbing experience. The trail begins from Road 39 off Mount Baker Highway and gains 1,500 feet along the way. **Mountain Madness**

NORTH CASCADES

(206/937-8389 or 800/328-5925, www.moun tainmadness.com) leads technical climbs of Mount Baker and nearby peaks. It offers a four-day beginner climb for $995 per person.

Skiing

It might be out of the way, but ski-bums flock to **Mount Baker Ski Area** (56 mi. east of Bellingham on Mount Baker Hwy., tickets 360/734-6771, ski report 360/671-0211 or 206/634-0200, www.mtbakerskiarea.com, $51 adult, $45 senior, $37 children) for its premium powder. The geography and elevation of the ski area enables it to run the longest seasons in the state, typically keeping the lifts running from early November through April. Eight chairlifts (two of these are quads) put 1,500 vertical feet of slope under-ski, from machine-groomed intermediate runs to open powder bowls. Other facilities include a big day lodge, child care, ski school, rentals, restaurant, and bar.

Cross-country and backcountry skiers will find plenty of trails to keep them happy in the area around Mount Baker. For rentals, contact **Glacier Ski Shop** (9966 Mt. Baker Hwy., 360/599-1943, www.glacierskishop.com, $25 cross country, $35 telemark, $30–40 alpine). It also sells used gear and demos new equipment.

ACCOMMODATIONS

Accommodations near Mount Baker mostly take the form of cabins, B&Bs, and condos. The closest lodgings are in the town of Glacier, 15 miles below Mount Baker Ski Area. Note that many places require a two-night minimum on weekends and have higher rates around Christmas and New Year's Day. Call well ahead for weekend reservations during the ski season.

One of the best sources of options is the well-rounded reservation service offered by **Mt. Baker Lodging** (360/599-2453 or 800/709-7669, www.mtbakerlodging.com), lets you check availability of several vacation rentals and book online or over the phone.

Three chalet-style cabins make up the **C Mt. Baker B&B** (9447 Mt. Baker Hwy.,

Glacier, 360/599-2299, www.mtbakerbed andbreakfast.com, $80–110), the closest B&B to the ski area. It serves a full breakfast and offers a steaming hot tub perfect to soothe the old bones after a day of hiking or skiing. Two of the three cabins share a bath.

The log cabin **Glacier Guest Suite** (8040 Mt. Baker Hwy., 360/300-7341, www.mt-baker .com, $79–145 s or d) overlooks Nooksack River Valley with views of Mount Baker and the 100-acre farmstead it sits on. The cabin comes with a kitchenette and fireplace, and a continental breakfast is served each morning.

The Logs at Canyon Creek (9002 Mt. Baker Hwy., 360/599-2711, $125 s or d, $125 log cabins, $270–300 vacation rentals) has five private cabins for those looking for a true getaway into the woods and a chance to relax with friends or family with nothing to distract from a roaring fireplace. The cabins do not have wireless Internet. Or TVs. Or phones. And they're darn proud of it. The larger vacation homes have 2–3 bedrooms, TV & DVD, dishwasher, and washer and dryer.

Camping

Camp at one of three Forest Service campgrounds in the Mount Baker area. **Douglas Fir Campground** (two mi. east of Glacier on Mount Baker Hwy., 518/885-3639 or 877/444-6777, www.recreation.gov, mid-May–mid-Sept., $16–18, $9 extra reservation fee), is situated in a beautiful old-growth forest along the Nooksack River and is open all winter. **Silver Fir Campground** (13 mi. east of Glacier, 518/885-3639 or 877/444-6777, www.recreation.gov, mid-May–mid-Sept., $16–18, $9 extra reservation fee) has campsites along a wide gravelly river bank, most with great mountain views especially beautiful just after sunrise on a fair day. **Hannegan Campground** (17 mi. east of Glacier and right next to the Mount Baker Wilderness on Forest Service Road 32, mid-May–mid-Sept.) is a primitive campground with no running water and no fees.

The 411-acre **Silver Lake County Park** (three mi. north of Maple Falls, 360/599-2776, $22 electric and water, $17 no hookups) has a beautiful day lodge/information center, year-round camping and partial RV hookups, showers, swimming, plus boat rentals. Dispersed camping is free on Forest Service land below milepost 52. Avoid alpine meadows, don't blaze new trails, and be sure to pack out all of your trash. Otherwise, any flat spot off the road is OK.

FOOD

◖ North Fork Beer Shrine (6186 Mount Baker Hwy., Deming, 360/599-2337, www .northforkbrewery.com, 2–9 P.M. Mon.–Fri., noon–9 P.M. Sat.–Sun.) runs a pizzeria that is really an excuse to get you to try its IPAs, hefeweizen, and barley wine. It will set you up with a traditional red-sauce pizza or a white garlic sauce that you can top with smoked salmon if you're feeling particularly Northwest-y. Be careful with your beer intake—the Shrine has an ordained minister on duty and a stained glass window. Yours would be far from the first wedding to take place here. If you love fresh homemade pasta, don't miss **Milano's** (9990

Mount Baker Hwy., Glacier, 360/599-2863, 9 A.M.–8:30 P.M. Mon.–Fri. 9 A.M.–9 P.M., Sat.–Sun. 10 A.M.–9 P.M.). The atmosphere is decidedly casual and the specials are inventive and tasty. Milano's also has a deli for lunchtime sandwiches, and Tuesday night pizzas.

INFORMATION AND SERVICES

Glacier Public Service Center (34 mi. east of Bellingham on Mount Baker Hwy., 360/599-2714, mid-Jun.–mid-Sept. 8 A.M.–4:30 P.M. daily, weekends only Oct.–May) is the place to go for information on Mount Baker and surrounding areas. Rangers here also issue backcountry permits.

Heather Meadows Visitor Center (at the end of Mt. Baker Hwy., July–Sept. daily 10 A.M.–5 P.M.) offers a variety of interpretive activities on late summer weekends. You can also pick up maps and information at the **Mount Baker Ranger District** (810 Hwy. 20, Sedro-Woolley, 360/856-5700, www.fs.fed.us/r6/mbs) offices.

The Mountain Loop: Granite Falls to Darrington

The scenic Mountain Loop Highway, one of the state's most popular weekend drives, connects Granite Falls to Darrington via a 55-mile-long road. From Granite Falls, the road is paved for the first 22 miles as it follows the South Fork of the Stillaguamish River to its headwaters at Barlow Pass, entering the Mount Baker-Snoqualmie National Forest near Verlot. Numerous campgrounds and hiking trails offer diversions along the way, and access to three fabulous swaths of wild mountain country: Boulder River Wilderness, Henry M. Jackson Wilderness, and Glacier Peak Wilderness. North of Barlow Pass, the road turns to gravel and becomes narrow and winding as it drops along the Sauk River. It remains gravel for 14 miles before returning to pavement for the last seven miles to Darrington. West of Darrington, the Mountain Loop Road passes through a wide valley bisected by the North Fork of the

Stillaguamish River and filled with hay piles, beehives, horses, sheep, chickens, hogs, big red barns, cut-your-own Christmas tree farms, lumber mills, clear-cuts, and regenerating stands of trees. Openings provide glimpses of the snowy peaks that cap the Cascade Range.

History

Parts of today's Mountain Loop Highway overlay trails that were used for centuries by the Native Americans who first inhabited these lands. The 1889 discovery of gold and silver in the Monte Cristo area led to a mad rush of miners and others attempting to get rich quick. To transport the (assumed) mineral wealth, a railroad was constructed from Monte Cristo over Barlow Pass, down the canyon created by the South Fork of the Stillaguamish River, through the new town of Granite Falls, and on to Everett, where the ore would be refined.

NORTH CASCADES

With cessation of mining, the Monte Cristo area began attracting tourists, and the trains turned to offering weekend excursions into the mountains. Business flourished in the 1920s, and hotels were added in Silverton and near Big Four Mountain. All this came to a screeching halt following the stock market crash of 1929. The railroad shut down in 1936, and the old railroad grade became an automobile road. Two years later, the Civilian Conservation Corps (CCC) began construction of a narrow mountain route north from Barlow Pass to Darrington, completing the final link in today's Mountain Loop Highway.

Weather

The Darrington area is an anomaly in the Cascades. Whereas the Seattle area receives 30–40 inches of rain per year, Darrington gets an average of 80 inches, while Monte Cristo gets over 140 inches, creating a dense rain forest much like those found in the Olympic Mountains. The low elevation here means questionable snowfall, though cross-country skiing and snowmobiling are popular area activities.

It is imperative to carry adequate clothing while hiking in this part of the Cascades, even if you're out on a short hike. The weather is unpredictable and can deal you a fatal surprise any time of year. Logging roads are popular snowmobile routes in winter, but that portion of the road over 2,361-foot Barlow Pass is blocked by snow beyond Elliott Creek on the north side and Deer Creek on the south side from mid-November–mid-April.

HIKING

More than 300 miles of trails lie within the Darrington Ranger District. Many of these are maintained by volunteers, so do your part to keep them clean. Parking-area theft is a major problem in this isolated area, so don't assume your valuables are safe in the trunk. Leave them at home or carry them with you. Report all thefts to a ranger station or the county sheriff. The following hiking trails are listed in a roughly northeastward progression from

Check the weather reports – these parts can stay snowy as late as June.

© ERICKA CHICKOWSKI

Verlot to Darrington along the Mountain Loop Highway.

Mount Pilchuck State Park

The 5,324-foot Mount Pilchuck (6.9 mi. up Forest Service Rd. 42, www.parks.wa.gov) offers a challenging day hike, with dramatic 360-degree views of the Cascades and Puget Sound from the summit. Get to the trailhead by heading a mile east of Verlot Public Service Center and turning onto Forest Service Road 42. Follow it seven miles uphill to the park entrance at an abandoned ski area. Allow five hours for the six-mile round-trip hike, and be prepared for a 2,300-foot gain in elevation and some boulder hopping at the end. The hike is best in late summer. Drinking water is scarce along the trail, so take plenty with you. Mountain climbers practice their techniques on the rugged northeast side of Mount Pilchuck. Be sure to sign the climbers' register at the Verlot Public Service Center (33515 Mountain Loop Hwy., 360/691-7791) before doing so.

Heather Lake

The subalpine forests and meadows are as much the attractions as the clear mountain lake on the four-mile round-trip hike to Heather Lake. To reach the trailhead, take Forest Service Road 42 for 1.5 miles, then hike up an old logging road before reaching the forest and then open meadows. Allow three hours; elevation gain is 1,100 feet. Because of its easy access, Heather Lake is a very popular day-hiking spot on summer weekends.

Lake 22

Late spring is a good time to hike the 2.7 mile trail to Lake 22 (No. 702), a scenic alpine lake whose ho-hum name doesn't do it justice. When you get to the lake you're likely to be greeted by waterfalls and mini avalanches crashing off the cliff walls butting up to the lake (but safely away from the trail). The trail starts two miles east of the Verlot Ranger Station, passing through an old-growth western red cedar forest on the way to the mountain lake. Allow four hours for the 1,400-foot elevation gain. No camping is allowed in the area.

Boulder River Wilderness

Established in 1984, the 49,000-acre Boulder River Wilderness occupies the low range of mountains between Verlot and Darrington. A handful of trails provide access to the wilderness from various sides, but travel off these paths can be a challenge in this rugged and oft-brushy terrain. The main attraction is Three Fingers, a 6,850-foot peak offering outstanding alpine vistas.

The 6.7-mile one-way trail to **Tin Pan Gap** and **Three Fingers Mountain** is a popular overnight hike. From Verlot, go west on Mountain Loop Highway for four miles, then head north on Forest Service Road 41, following it 18 miles to the trailhead at Tupso Pass. The trail climbs through dense forest for 2.5 miles to four-acre Saddle Lake; continue for another 2.3 miles through meadows to Goat Flat, an oft-crowded camping spot. Use only a campstove; fire rings leave near-permanent scars in these fragile meadows. The trail reaches Tin Pan Gap after about six miles; from here, the hike becomes a technical climb (not for the inexperienced) over Three Fingers Glacier and a scramble to the top of Three Fingers Mountain and the old fire lookout.

Ice Cave

The **Big Four Ice Cave trail** (No. 723) is a favorite two-mile round-trip hike, starting 26 miles from Granite Falls at the Big Four Picnic Area. The hike begins on boardwalks over a beaver-created marsh, then heads through a dense forest and across the South Fork of the Stillaguamish River to the ice caves and a view of 6,135-foot Big Four Mountain. The caves are created when water and wind form a channel under heavy snow piles left by avalanches. They are generally exposed in late July and are visible through October. Admire them from afar, since the caves are very unstable and falling ice can cause injury or death. In winter and spring the snowfield is especially susceptible to avalanches.

Mount Forgotten Meadows

A full-day hike to an alpine meadow starts 26 miles from Granite Falls and heads up 6,005-foot **Mount Forgotten** for an eight-mile round-trip hike. Take the Mountain Loop Highway 15 miles east from the Verlot Public Service Center, then go north on Perry Creek Road (No. 4063) for a mile to the Perry Creek trailhead. The trail climbs past **Perry Creek Falls** at about two miles, heading through an old-growth forest for another 1.7 miles to the first meadow. Allow seven hours to reach the meadows at 5,200 feet, an elevation gain of 3,100 feet. The trail continues through meadows to Mount Forgotten's climbing route (for experienced alpine climbers only).

Monte Cristo Area

The magnificent alpine-topped 103,591-acre **Henry M. Jackson Wilderness Area** is accessible from several trailheads on the eastern end of the Mountain Loop. The most popular hiking paths lead to and through the old mining town of Monte Cristo. In the 1890s, over a thousand people flocked to the mountains hoping to cash in on local gold and silver strikes. The metal was hard to get to and expensive to get out, but the mines languished on until a collapsing national economy shut them down in 1907. Since then, the town site has been gradually reclaimed by the forest. No original buildings remain, but the fireplace and foundation of the once-luxurious Big Four Inn stands as a mute reminder of the town's earlier glory. By the 1920s, there wasn't much call for the railroad that ran to Monte Cristo anymore, and so it was converted to today's Mountain Loop Highway.

Get here by driving 20 miles east from Verlot to Barlow Pass, where the four-mile side road to Monte Cristo begins. Floods in 1980 and 1990 left it impassable to cars, but it remains a popular place for mountain bikers and hikers in the summer, and cross-country skiers and snowmobilers in the winter. Check at the Forest Service offices in Darrington or Verlot for current road and bridge conditions. The Forest Service's free **Monte Cristo Campground** is a tricky four-mile walk-in that involves fording a

river without the help of a bridge. Once there, your only service is an outhouse, but it does offer a pleasant overnight stay very near the ghost town.

Glacier Basin Trail (No. 719) is a popular two-mile hiking route from Monte Cristo into nearby high country. The trail follows an old railroad grade for the first half mile, then climbs steeply past Glacier Falls, around Mystery Hill, and into gorgeous Glacier Basin, gaining 1,300 feet in elevation. The route passes all sorts of rusting mining equipment, pieces of the cable tramway, and old mine shafts on the way. Bring your stove, since no campfires are allowed in the high country, and avoid camping on the fragile meadow areas. Good campsites can be found at Ray's Knoll and Mystery Ridge.

Another very steep trail (No. 708, 4.4 miles one-way) climbs over **Poodle Dog Pass,** crossed by many a would-be miner on their way to town from the east. This trail leaves from the Monte Cristo town site, ascends to Silver Lake, and then on to an open ridge offering panoramic views of the surrounding mountains.

Glacier Peak Wilderness

Covering 576,865 acres—35 miles long by 20 miles wide—massive Glacier Peak Wilderness is one of Washington's largest stretches of wilderness landscape. Its dominant geologic feature, Glacier Peak, is a dormant volcano, last erupting some 12,000 years ago. Today, true to name, its 10,541-foot summit is almost completely encircled by glaciers. In the Glacier Peak Wilderness, you're likely to see deer, blue grouse, and marmots, plus an occasional lynx, mountain goat, or cougar. Deep snow buries much of the wilderness high country till late June, and some trails are not free of snow until mid-July.

More than 450 miles of backcountry trails provide diverse hiking opportunities in the wilderness, with access from all sides, including the Marblemount, plus the Lake Chelan, Stehekin, and Entiat River areas. The western side of the wilderness reaches almost to the

Mountain Loop Highway, with access via several Forest Service spur roads. The ultimate hiking experience, the **Pacific Crest Trail,** cuts right through the heart of Glacier Peak Wilderness, following the ridges for 60 miles of ascending and descending paths.

One of the most popular paths in the Glacier Peak Wilderness, **White Chuck Trail** (No. 643) was badly damaged when the river rerouted itself during a 2003 storm that ravaged many parts of the North Cascades. The storm completely consumed the popular Kennedy Hot Springs along the trail. The bridge has since been repaired and the trail is open to the public, again providing six miles one-way cutting through old growth forest and offering beautiful mountain views. Call Verlot Public Service center (360/691-7791) for the most up-to-date info on this trail, which acts as a major junction with the Pacific Crest Trail and other side trails in the Wilderness.

The Pacific Crest Trail is accessible from the west side at various points off the Mountain Loop Highway. One of the best of these is the **North Fork Sauk Trail** (No. 649), an 8.4-mile path offering a gentle riverside route through a magnificent old-growth cedar forest, before relentlessly switchbacking upward to the Pacific Crest Trail, gaining 3,900 feet en route. An excellent loop hike (26 miles round-trip) is to continue south on the PCT to its junction with the **Pilot Ridge Trail** (No. 652), and then follow that trail back downhill past alpine lakes to its junction with the North Fork Sauk Trail. The Pilot Ridge Trail offers hikers vistas of Glacier Peak and Mount Rainier, but be sure to carry plenty of water, since portions of this loop hike lack water sources. Get to the North Fork Sauk trailhead by driving east from the Verlot Public Service Center for 27 miles (or south from Darrington for 20 miles) and turning east onto Sloan Creek Road 49 near the Bedal Campground. The trailhead is located 6.6 miles up, where the road crosses Sloan Creek.

Darrington Area Trails

Several short paths provide fun day hikes in the Darrington area. **Old Sauk Trail** (No. 728) is an easy three-mile stroll that departs from Clear Creek Campground, four miles south of Darrington. The trail parallels the Sauk River, passing riverside alder stands and moss-covered cedar stumps. Salmon and steelhead spawn in Murphy Creek at the southern end of the Old Sauk Trail.

A three-mile path, **Beaver Lake Trail** (No. 629), starts across from White Chuck Campground, 10 miles south of Darrington. The trail sits atop an old railroad grade and crosses beaver ponds, continuing through a beautiful stand of old-growth cedar trees, and finally looping back to the Mountain Loop Highway. These are good mountain bike trails, too.

Another hike through virgin timber is the **Boulder River Trail** (No. 734). Get here by heading 8.2 miles west from Darrington, turn south onto French Creek Road 2010, branch right after a mile, and then follow it another 2.8 miles to the trailhead. In addition to thick old-growth forests, this four-mile trail passes a delightful series of Boulder River waterfalls and cascades.

RIVER RAFTING AND KAYAKING

The **Sauk River,** a National Wild and Scenic River that rises in the Henry M. Jackson Wilderness and joins the Skagit River near Rockport, offers a combination of fast and complex rapids, fantastic mountain scenery, and plenty of wildlife. **Orion Expeditions** (509/548-1401, http://orionexp.com, $75–90) runs trips that start 10 miles upriver and end in Darrington, with lots of class III–IV white water along the way. The primary season is May–mid-August. Orion provides lunch after the trip.

The **Suiattle River** (soo-AT-ul) starts in the Glacier Peak Wilderness and meets the Sauk River north of Darrington. This is a good white-water river for families and beginners, with great mountain scenery and lots of small rapids along the 13 miles of river. Because of its glacial origins, the

NORTH CASCADES

Suiattle has a milky, silt-laden appearance and braided channels. The main season for river-running is June–early September. Both **Blue Sky Outfitters** (800/228-7238, www.blueskyoutfitters.com) and **North Cascades River Expeditions** (800/634-8433, www.riverexpeditions.com) send rafts down the Suiattle, with lunch served after.

Experienced, do-it-yourself river runners can also enjoy the challenges of the Sauk and Suiattle Rivers on their own. The Suiattle is the tamer of the two, rated class II–III from Boundary Bridge to the Sauk River; it's not navigable within the national forest due to logjams, hidden stumps, and debris. Put in at Boundary Bridge. The Sauk River ranges from class I–V; from the White Chuck launch area to Clear Creek it's a IV or V, with difficult rapids through narrow passages. From Bedal to White Chuck, the river is classified as a class III–IV, and below Clear Creek it ranges from class I–III. North of Darrington, the river is considerably calmer and is popular for canoeing.

CANOEING AND FISHING

The Darrington District boasts a large number of small lakes, some of which provide excellent fishing. Getting out on the water is a great way to take in the mountain scenery and spot some local wildlife.

Paddlers and rafters will enjoy exploring six-acre **Coal Lake,** a subalpine lake at 3,600 feet elevation. Go east on the Mountain Loop Highway for 15 miles from the Verlot Public Service Center, then go north on Coal Lake Road 4060 for 4.5 miles to the trailhead. Carry your boat about 50 feet to the lake, where you'll find a limited number of campsites that fill up quickly. You can fish for cutthroat and brook trout on a fly or reel.

Another lake with easy canoe and raft access is five-acre **Canyon Lake.** From the Verlot Public Service Center, drive four miles on the Mountain Loop Highway to Road 41; turn right, continuing for two miles to Green Mountain Road 4110. Turn right again (heading east now), driving almost 1.4 miles to Road

4111; follow this road for 10.75 miles to the trailhead on the left side of the road. Carry your boat along the 50-foot trail to Canyon Lake, surrounded by trees and a few campsites. Brook trout and cuttys will sometimes take a fly or lure.

CROSS-COUNTRY SKIING

Skiers and snowshoers can count on solitude when exploring the Darrington District as most roads aren't plowed and snowfall is unpredictable at this low elevation. Any existing snow here is often wet and difficult to ski through. Still determined? Take these routes as suggestions; if the roads themselves aren't snow-covered, keep driving along the route until you come to some that are.

From Highway 530 on the way to Darrington, go south on **French Creek Road 2010** to the snow line, and then ski uphill from there. The road takes you through dense forest and switchbacks for great views and a fast downhill trip back. Or, from the Darrington Ranger Station, drive north on Highway 530 for 6.5 miles to **Suiattle River Road 26;** follow it till you hit snow, and then ski up the road and along the river. Enjoy views of Glacier Peak along the way.

On the Granite Falls side, the **Big Four** area is very popular with skiers, snowshoers, snowmobilers, and winter hikers; take the Mountain Loop Highway 23 miles from Granite Falls to the end of the maintained road at Deer Creek Road 4052. Ski two miles from the parking area to Big Four Picnic Area, following the South Fork of the Stillaguamish River; continue another mile to the snowfield near the Big Four Ice Cave. The avalanche danger here is severe; don't travel beyond the edge of the clearing—it's the force of avalanches that created and maintains that clearing! Allow 3–5 hours round-trip; this route is suitable for beginning skiers.

A more challenging route is the **Deer Creek/ Kelcema Lake Ski Route,** which follows Deer Creek Road uphill to Kelcema Lake, a distance of 4.6 miles, with an elevation gain of 1,600 feet. Allow 5–7 hours for the round-trip, and avoid it during periods of high avalanche danger. Get here by heading 12 miles east from the Verlot Public Service Center to the end of snow plowing and the start of the ski route. No snowmobiles are allowed here.

Another popular cross-country ski route (for advanced skiers only) begins at the Deer Creek parking area and continues 11 miles to the old mining town of Monte Cristo, gaining 1,275 feet in elevation en route. This is best done as an overnight trip due to its length; be sure to check on avalanche conditions before heading out.

INFORMATION

Get detailed camping, hiking, and historical information at the Mount Baker-Snoqualmie National Forest's **Verlot Public Service Center** (11 miles east of Granite Falls, 360/691-7791, 8 A.M.–4:30 P.M. daily June–Labor Day, 8 A.M.–4:30 P.M. Thurs.–Mon. spring and fall, closed in winter). The **Darrington Ranger District** (1405 Emmens St., Darrington, 360/436-1155, www.fs.fed.us/r6/mbs, Mon.–Fri. 8 A.M.–4:30 P.M.) is another good source of local info.

GRANITE FALLS

Granite Falls sits at the southwest end of the Mountain Loop Highway with Pilchuck Mountain offering a dramatic backdrop. The town was founded in 1889 to serve as construction headquarters for the mines at Monte Cristo. Later, it grew into a way station and center for logging and farming in the area. Because of its location at the base of the Cascades, the town provides a jumping-off point for hikers, campers, cross-country skiers, and snowmobilers exploring the Mount Baker-Snoqualmie National Forest.

Sights

The **Granite Falls Museum** (109 E. Union St., 360/691-2603, www.gfhistory.org, 1–4 P.M. Sun. in summer, closed in winter) houses local memorabilia; check out the cross section from an enormous 1,200-year-old Douglas fir tree in the front.

Just east of town is the **Granite Falls Fish Ladder,** the world's longest vertical-baffle fish ladder when it was built in 1954. Stop here to marvel at the raging South Fork of the Stillaguamish River as it roils over the falls (actually more of a giant rapids) for which the town was named. Salmon swim up a 240-foot tunnel dug through the granite.

Accommodations and Food

Step out onto the deck at **❰ The Country Cedar Inn** (5732 Robe Menzel Rd., 360/691-3830, www.countrycedarinn.com, $99–149 d) and get a close-up view of Mount Pilchuck and Three Fingers. Nestled in the foothills of the Snohomish Cascades, this quiet bed-and-breakfast is set within a beautiful cedar-sided home built with lumber milled from trees cut right on the forested five-acre property. All rooms come with private bathrooms; in addition to a home-style breakfast each morning, guests are treated to homemade cookies in the afternoon and sometimes dessert in the evening. There is also an option to order a four-course dinner in the evening.

Walk down the main drag to find several places with standard fare, including **Ike's Diner** (101 W Stanley St., 360/691-6636, Mon.–Fri. 8 A.M.–8 P.M., Sat.–Sun. 8 A.M.–7 P.M.) where the Formica-and-burger atmosphere is straight from the 1950s. It has good chicken burgers and fries, and even a decent teriyaki.

The **Granite Falls Farmers Marketplace** (360/691-6173) comes to town noon–4 P.M. Sunday late June–September.

Camping

The Forest Service operates 16 campgrounds (518/885-3639 or 877/444-6777, www.recreation.gov, generally open Memorial Day–mid-September, $8–14, $9 extra reservation fee) along the Mountain Loop. Free dispersed camping is allowed on Forest Service lands away from the developed campgrounds.

From Granite Falls, neighboring **Turlo** and **Verlot Campgrounds** are near the Verlot Service Center, while **Gold Basin Campground** is 2.4 miles east of the service center. Gold Basin also features an amphitheater where Saturday night campfire programs are presented in the summer. Across the road is a short, wheelchair-accessible interpretive trail. Continuing on from Verlot, other campsites include **Boardman Creek Campground** (open all year), six miles east; and **Red Bridge Campground,** seven miles east.

From Darrington, Forest Service campsites include **Clear Creek Campground,** four miles south, and **Bedal Campground,** 18 miles south, both open year-round. A mile east of Bedal Campground on Forest Service Road 49 is a quarter-mile path to the base of spectacular **North Fork Sauk Falls,** where the river plunges 45 feet.

From Darrington via Suiattle River Road No. 26, **Buck Creek Campground,** 22 miles northeast of town, features a quiet riverside setting in an old-growth forest. **Sulphur Creek Campground,** 28 miles from Darrington (near the end of Suiattle River Road), is just a mile away from the Glacier Peak Wilderness and is open year-round. A short trail leads from the campground along Sulphur Creek to colorful pools containing rather odoriferous hydrogen sulfide gas. See *Darrington* for other camping options.

Information

Pick up a handful of local brochures at **Granite Falls Town Hall** (206 S Granite Ave., 360/691-6441, http://ci.granite-falls.wa.us).

Getting There and Around

Community Transit (425/353-7433 or 800/562-1375, www.commtrans.org) offers daily bus service throughout Snohomish County.

DARRINGTON

Darrington, once the home of the Sauk-Suiattle Nation, would later be caught up in the mini-gold rush of 1898, when the town began life as an outpost with the colorful name "Starve-Out." Even though the gold mining never really panned out, Darrington did just fine. Loggers started cutting the old-growth trees

OF APPLES AND ARROWS

Every summer, the whole town of Darrington gets together and prepares for folks to come from around the country, aiming to shoot up the joint. This woodsy town is the home to the **National Outdoor Field Championships,** an annual chance for archers to compete against each other and show off their bowmanship. Darington has the dual distinction of being the country's only world-class competition archery field that is open year-round, and the only fully Americans with Disabilities Act (ADA)-accessible range in the United States. The facility relies almost entirely on volunteers as the workhorses of the many events that happen during the year. RV and tent camping is available for participants. Call 360/436-0282 if you think you might be interested in participating, volunteering, or just spectating.

for sale instead of using them to build fly-by-night mining shacks. Loggers arrived from all over, especially Sweden and North Carolina. Many current residents proudly trace their ancestry to those North Carolinian pioneers and celebrate with the bluegrass music of their Tarheel heritage.

Festivals and Events

The last weekend in June brings the **Timber Bowl Rodeo** to the rodeo grounds four miles west of town. Darrington's three-day **Bluegrass Festival and Street Fair** in mid-July is one of the most popular musical events in the Puget Sound Basin, in part because the area has developed some of the best bluegrass musicians outside of Kentucky and North Carolina.

Accommodations

Darrington Motor Inn (1100 Seaman St.,

360/436-1776, $59 s or d) is an attractive, small motel with rooms offering mountain views.

The closest Forest Service campground is the **Clear Creek Campground** (four mi. south of town on Forest Service Road 20, 518/885-3639 or 877/444-6777, www.recreation.gov, $12, $9 extra reservation fee). Not all sites have views of the river, but it will sing you to sleep no matter what. **Squire Creek County Park** (41415 S.R. 530 in Arlington, four miles west of Darrington, 360/435-3441, $18) offers year-round camping amid old-growth Douglas fir and cedar trees. There's no dump station or any hookups, but the spaces will accommodate RVs as well as tents.

Food

Situated in a red-roofed diner with mountain views, **Glacier Peak Café** (1215 Hwy. 530 NE, 360/436-0602) is an ideal spot to sip on a cup of joe over some eggs before a hike or gulp down some soda with a salmon burger afterward.

For something a bit speedier, stop at the **Whitehorse Store** (five mi. west of Darrington on Hwy. 530) for old-fashioned ice-cream cones.

Information

For up-to-date information on trail conditions, campgrounds, fishing, and other outdoor activities, contact the **Darrington Ranger Station** (1405 Emens Ave. N, 0.5 mile north of town, 360/436-1155, www.fs.fed.us/r6/mbs).

Getting There and Around

Community Transit (425/353-7433 or 800/562-1375, www.commtrans.org) offers daily bus service throughout Snohomish County.

North Cascades Highway

The North Cascades Highway—State Route 20—begins in the Skagit River Valley alongside the river, and then crests 5,477-foot Washington Pass before descending into Methow Valley on the east side of the Cascade Range. Along the way, the road passes the small towns of Sedro-Woolley, Concrete, Rockport, and Marblemount before entering North Cascades National Park and Okanogan National Forest lands. This is the mountain country for which Washington is famous, full of striking scenery and outdoor recreation opportunities. This description of the North Cascades Highway starts on the eastern end at Sedro-Woolley and follows the road over the mountains into the Methow Valley.

History

The earliest white man to explore the North Cascades was Alexander Ross and his party, who crossed today's southern park boundary at Cascade Pass in 1814. In 1859, Henry Custer of the International Boundary Commission marveled at the "strange, fantastic, dauntless and startling outlines" of the mountain peaks visible in every direction. Between 1880 and 1910, miners labored at removing gold, platinum, lead, and zinc from this forbidding terrain, but logistic concerns made it scarcely worth it.

On the west side of the mountains, the hydroelectric potential of the roaring Skagit River wasn't harnessed until the George Dam was built in 1924. Ross Dam and Diablo Dam followed over the next several years. The three dams are among the most functional entries in the National Register of Historic Places. This rugged area was preserved as the North Cascades National Park Service Complex in 1968, incorporating the Ross Lake and Lake Chelan National Recreation Areas with access provided by a wide dirt road, itself a former wagon route. By 1979, that dusty trail had

NORTH CASCADES

become the beautiful paved North Cascades Scenic Highway.

Climate

Summer weather in the North Cascades is a product of the so-called "rain-shadow effect" in which the mountains block moisture-laden clouds drifting from the sea, causing sometimes heavy downpours. That leaves little rain passing over the range, making for a cooler, wetter west side and a warm, dry east side. Puget Sounders love the Methow Valley, in part for offering them the opposite of their usual climate—hot sunny summers and crisp, cold winters featuring lots of powdery snow that skiers love most.

Highway 20

Don't expect any gas stations, restaurants, or other facilities (except restrooms at Washington

Pass) along the 75 miles of Highway 20 between Ross Dam and Mazama, so fill up when you leave I-5 (Sedro-Woolley is cheapest if you get lots of miles per tank). No bus service goes along this route either; the closest you'll get is Mount Vernon on the west and Pateros and Okanogan on the east.

The middle section of Highway 20 closes for the winter after the first major snowfall because of avalanche danger. It is usually gated in late November and doesn't open again until late April, sometimes nearly June, depending on the amount of snow. In midwinter, snow depths can exceed 15 feet at the summit. Parts of the highway remain open to snowmobile traffic from Colonial Creek Campground on the west side to Early Winters Campground near Mazama. Lower-elevation hiking trails, such as those along Ross Lake, are generally accessible from April through mid-October; at higher elevations, trails are usually snow-free from mid-July through September.

SEEING THE CASCADES BY MOTORCYCLE

The North Cascades is a great place to tour by car or bicycle, but some roads are best experienced on two wheels of motorized fury. One of the premier rides starts in Marblemount and runs State Route 20 for as long as you want to take it east, all the way to Tiger, 280 miles away. You'll cruise windy roads that cut old-growth forests, a handful of tunnels, views of unbelievably tall dams, and go through a 30-degree temperature change as you cross the Cascades into the Methow Valley. Small towns pop up frequently, many of which are very biker-friendly. Just keep it to summer if you want to avoid snow and ice. If you like light traffic and lots of sweepers, try the 30-mile stretch between Chiawawa Road and State Route 209 running from Lake Wenatchee State Park to Leavenworth. Expect tight twists, hills, and Leavenworth at the end, which is surprisingly biker-friendly for a little Bavarian town.

Cascade Loop Trips

Highway 20 joins Highway 153 at Twisp, Highway 97 near Pateros, and Highway 2 near Wenatchee to form the northwest portion of the "Cascade Loop." This 400-mile scenic drive winds through the North Cascades, past Lake Chelan, through Leavenworth on its approach to Stevens Pass, and returns to western Washington and Whidbey Island. You'll find free *Cascade Loop* booklets at visitors centers along the way, or ask the **Cascade Loop Association** (509/662-3888, www.cascadeloop .com) in Wenatchee for a copy.

A similar promotional highway route is called the North Cascades Loop. It follows the same route over Highway 20, continues on to the twin towns of Omak and Okanogan, turns north on Highway 97, and goes across into British Columbia's Okanagan (note that Canada and the United States spell the word differently), then heads west on the Trans-Canada Highway to the Vancouver area. Look for free *International Loop* booklets at visitors centers.

NOT EXACTLY SHOVEL READY

The North Cascades Scenic Highway (State Route 20) was originally commissioned in 1893, when state legislators set aside $20,000 for the completion of the Cascade Wagon Route. Over the decades that followed, sections of the road were gradually completed, and by 1968 – the year the national park was established – a rough dirt road crossed the summit. The highway finally opened in 1972, some 79 years after the first shovel of dirt had been dug.

SEDRO-WOOLLEY TO CONCRETE

The riverside town of Sedro-Woolley is a town in transition. The decline of the logging industry in recent years has hit hard, forcing the town to look elsewhere for an economic base. It remains a commercial center for the farmlands that surround it, while becoming an outfitting town for adventurers on their way east into North Cascades National Park. East from Sedro-Woolley, Highway 20 skirts the Skagit River, climbing leisurely toward the first Cascade foothills. The landscape is farms, fields, and forests, with the serrated summit of Sauk Mountain to the east.

The fading town of Concrete was once home to the largest cement plant in the state, making possible the construction of the Grand Coulee, Ross, and Diablo Dams. Whizzing by, you'll know the town by the factory towers labeled plainly, "Welcome to Concrete." The last signs of civilization along State Route 20 until the Methow Valley will hit you shortly after in Marblemount. You'll see signs that warn "Last Gas for 69 Miles" and, more importantly, "Last Tavern for 89 Miles." The little town is a good place to stock up on these—and other—essentials, and to get information and backcountry permits for North Cascades National Park.

Sights

MUSEUMS AND INTERPRETIVE CENTERS

Sedro-Woolley Museum (725 Murdock St., 360/855-2390, http://sedrowoolleymuseum. org, noon–4 P.M. Wed., 11:30 A.M.–3:30 P.M. Thurs., 9 A.M.–4 P.M. Sat., 1–4 P.M. Sun., donations) is a newer museum, even though the "ribbon cutting" involved a chainsaw and a log. The building is full of local historical artifacts, including an HO scale train model of the area and a few interesting old vehicles.

Concrete Heritage Museum (7380 Thompson Ave., 360/853-7042, open weekends in summer, $2) recalls the heyday of Concrete and its successes in logging and concrete production.

The fish trap at **Puget Sound Energy Visitors Center** (46110 E. Main St., Concrete, 360/853-8341) pampers salmon more than most. Instead of a fish ladder, the dam has a fish elevator or "fish taxi" as they call it. The dam is too high for a conventional ladder, so they are trapped and ride an elevator straight to the top; see the salmon here between June and December.

The **Bald Eagle Interpretive Center** (Howard Miller Steelhead Park, 52809 Rockport Park Rd., 360/853-7626, www.skagit eagle.org, 10 A.M.–4 P.M. Sat. and Sun.) is staffed by the intrepid Bald Eagle Awareness Team (SRBEAT). It houses exhibits concerning the ecological challenges faced by eagles and the staff will be happy to tell you how and where it is best to watch eagles.

At the **Marblemount Fish Hatchery** (a mile southeast of town on Fish Hatchery Rd., 8 A.M.–4 P.M. daily), visitors can take a self-guided tour and watch a video describing day to day life at the hatchery. It's a great place to see hawks, eagles, and waterfowl, to say nothing of the thousands of baby salmon wiggling around in pools.

SCENIC DRIVES

Highway 9 north from Sedro-Woolley leads through quiet Nooksack Valley with its aging dairy barns, big bales of hay, and comfortable homesteads. A series of rural towns pop up alongside the road. Towns like **Wickersham, Acme, Clipper, Van Zandt, Deming, Nugents Corner,** and **Nooksack** that are little more than a few street signs and a couple of farmhouses.

Meanwhile, fans of old buildings would do well to take a few minutes off the highway to appreciate the elegant decay of **Concrete.** Although environmental regulations in 1968 closed the outdated, dusty plant that gave the town its name, its concrete tower remains. The 5,537-foot summit of Sauk Mountain rises straight behind Main Street. The city was the setting of author Tobias Wolff's novel *This Boy's Life.* Wolff uses Concrete High School as a setting, renaming it "Chinook High." The book was turned into a movie staring Leonardo DiCaprio and filmed on location, including the original high school at 7830 S. Superior Avenue. You can easily cruise by Concrete's historical buildings on Main Street, many of which were built in the years before World War I. Most are still functioning businesses, although not usually the businesses intended for the structures.

Just east of town is the scenic **Henry Thompson Bridge.** Completed in 1918, it was a critical passage over the Baker River until State Route 20 was rerouted in the 1970s. The bridge's white cement arch set against the dark forest makes a great photo on a sunny day.

Entertainment and Events

In mid-May Sedro-Woolley carves out a niche for itself with **Woodfest,** a celebration of wood-carving and woodworking from creative chain-saw art to intricately hand-carved works. The 4th of July brings the weeklong **Loggerodeo** to Sedro-Woolley—a long-standing event that brings people from all over the region. It's a celebration of local heritage and includes a logging show, bluegrass music, magic, a carnival, and a fun-for-all street dance. **Founders' Day** in mid-September includes a pancake breakfast, a community picnic, and a spirited reenactment of the bank robbery that took place here in 1914.

The premier event in the Concrete area is the **Upper Skagit Bald Eagle Festival** (360/853-8784 or 360/853-7626), a family-friendly event that covers the whole month of January. It is chock-full of guided walks, programs, and tours that, beyond eagles, deal with bears and other elements of the local ecology.

Shopping

Rockport Country Store (50502 Hwy. 20, 360/853-8531, 8 A.M.–8 P.M.) has something you don't see every day, a "self-kicking machine." Great for masochists. **Cascadian Farm Roadside Stand** (55749 Hwy. 20, 360/853-8173, open daily May–Oct.) is a sizable permanent stand, selling chiefly blueberries, but a smattering of other berries, pumpkins, and even a small crop of kiwi fruit. The farm is one of the top organic foods brands in the country and the level of care can be tasted even in its summertime organic ice cream.

Sports and Recreation

CYCLING

If you're an ace cyclist, the country around State Route 20 is full of waterfalls and fresh mountain air, which you will feel you've earned after struggling with the hilly, climbing terrain and spooky tunnels. This area should remind you that life is a journey and not a destination. If possible, take your time here and enjoy as many stops along the way as you can. Be warned that the highway is often closed at times between November and December due to avalanche threats.

RASAR STATE PARK

Settled on a quiet 128-acre site along the Skagit River, Rasar State Park (just off Hwy. 20 along Cape Horn Rd., Concrete, www.parks.wa.gov, $17 for tents or $21 for RVs, no reservations) is a great place for a riverside picnic, and bald eagles are visible early in the year. Several trails lead through the tall second-growth forests, and year-round camping is available.

BAKER LAKE

Baker Lake, a hydroelectric reservoir, is very popular with campers, swimmers, motor boaters, and pack and saddle trekkers. The easiest hike in the area is the half-mile, barrier-free **Shadow of the Sentinels Trail** that winds through an old-growth Douglas fir stand and past interpretive signs. It begins a mile beyond the Koma Kulshan guard station.

An excellent, gentle rain forest hike is up the **Baker River.** To reach the trailhead for this five-mile round-trip hike, drive north on Baker Lake-Grandy Lake Road for 14 miles to the Komo Kulshan Guard Station. Follow the Forest Service road for 11.5 miles, then left a mile, then right on the first side road for half a mile to the start of Trail 606. This level, low-elevation trail affords views of glaciers and beaver ponds on the way to Sulphur Creek, the turnaround point. Because of its low elevation, the trail is snow-free from early spring–late fall.

Another Baker Lake hike takes you to **Park Butte,** a 5,450-foot summit with incredible views of Mount Baker glaciers. This summer-only trek is seven miles round-trip, but with an elevation gain of over 2,200 feet, it'll take a good part of the day to complete. Go north for 12.5 miles on Baker Lake-Grandy Lake Road, then turn left on Loomis-Nooksack Road 12 for 3.5 miles, then turn right onto Road 13 for five miles to the road's end. The trail is west of the road, crossing Sulphur Creek before the switchbacks begin.

ROCKPORT STATE PARK

Covering over 600 acres, Rockport State Park has something amazing—a full forest of ancient, old-growth trees that create a canopy so dense, it chokes almost all light from reaching the forest floor. There are five miles of wooded hiking trails and Skagit River steelhead fishing. Unfortunately, it's those very trees that have closed the campgrounds here indefinitely, as windblown branches falling from 200 feet can spoil a campfire weenie roast in a heartbeat. The paved and wheelchair-accessible **Skagit View Trail** leads right down to the riverbank, providing a great place to look for bald eagles in the winter.

Immediately west of the park is the start of **Sauk Mountain Road,** a 7.5-mile gravel road that takes you to a trailhead most of the way

up this 5,537-foot peak. A steep, switchback-filled trail begins at the parking lot, climbing another 1.5 miles to the summit, where you're treated to views of the northern Cascades and the Skagit and Sauk River Valleys.

FLOAT TRIPS

A number of companies offer scenic bald eagle float trips along the Skagit River in December–February, when the population is at a peak. The river is so gentle that wet suits are not necessary; just wear warm winter clothing. One of the area's top river guides, **Pacific Northwest Float Trips** (360/719-5808, www.pacificnwfloattrips.com) has been taking people to see the eagles for almost 40 years. Seventy-seven dollars gets you a four-hour trip with lunch. Your guide will serve you hot chocolate on a heated boat. What more can you ask for?

Professional fishing guide Wayne Ackerlund operates an eagle-watching float trip on the Skagit through **Ackerlund's Guide Service** (206/218-3362 or 866/675-2448, www.ackerlunds.com, $65), which offers its guests propane-heated boats and comfy seats on its four-hour floats. Ackerlund's is a great firm to go through if you fancy some salmon and steelhead fishing.

And every summer, hundreds of tubing fans take to the Nooksack River, meandering down the chilly South Fork from Saxon to Van Zandt. It's a party on the water, where "cold ones" can refer to your canned beer or your toes.

RIVER RAFTING

In the summer, you can float eight miles of the upper Skagit River through North Cascades National Park, where the water is a bit rougher. Still, nothing over a class III, meaning that it's got a little excitement but is a good beginning river for newcomers and a perfect run to take the little ones ages six and up. Try **Alpine Adventures** (800/723-8386, www.alpineadventures.com, $79) or **Orion Expeditions** (800/553-7466, http://orionexp.com, $79). With either company, all of your equipment is provided and both serve a lunch.

Accommodations

UNDER $100

Three Rivers Motel (210 Ball St., Sedro-Woolley, 360/855-2626 or 800/221-5122, $59–159 s or d) is a bit older, but you'll definitely feel like you've gotten your money's worth. It's rare you get free wireless, an outdoor pool, hot tub, and continental breakfast for under $100. **Skagit Motel** (1862 W S.R. 20 in Sedro-Woolley, 360/856-6001, http://skagitmotel.com, $49 s or $66 d) takes pets, has clean rooms, and provides a microwave in each room as well as a community kitchenette.

Halfway between Rockport and Marblemount is **Totem Trail Motel** (57627 Hwy. 20, Rockport, 360/873-4535, www.totemtrail.com, $50 s), a basic but cute one-story motel good for quick overnight stays. It offers parking directly in front of your room. Plastic chairs in the exterior corridor are perfect for smokers.

Hide away in a quiet little cabin at **Grace Haven** (three miles west of Marblemount, 360/873-4106, http://gracehavenretreat.com, $95–110 s or d). This tranquil property offers clean, traditional cabins, fully furnished and including full kitchens and a charcoal grill out back. After a day of hiking, chill out with a game of horseshoes and relax by the outdoor fire pit or warm up with a board game in your own room and sit by the fireplace.

Three miles west of Marblemount, **Clark's Skagit River Resort** (58468 Clark Cabin Rd., 360/873-2250 or 800/273-2606, www.north cascades.com, $79–139 cabins, $89–99 inn rooms s or d, $20 tents, $30 full hookups) is full of character. And rabbits. The owners started out with three bunnies many years ago, and they've now reached a wild population of just under 200. They attract a wide array of hungry, sharp-toothed wildlife, but so far, no guests have been eaten. When you reserve, you can choose your room by size and number of beds, like usual, or by color scheme with close to 30 options.

$100-150

No matter your personality, you'll probably find a suite that fits at the **Hi-Lo Country Hotel and Café** (45951 Main St., Concrete, 360/853-7946, $120–150). Sporting a shady porch and a log façade, the hotel offers manly suites like the Grizzly Adams and the John Wayne, sensitive suites like the Island Getaway and the Lovers Cottage, plus a specially themed Hog Heaven for the hard-core biker resting from a hard ride across State Route 20. Suites have two rooms, plus a bathroom, fridge, and microwave.

Located on the 600-acre Double O cattle ranch, **(Ovenell's Heritage Inn B&B** (4442 Concrete Sauk Valley Rd., Concrete, 360/853-8494, www.ovnells-inn.com, $120–140 shared-bath inn rooms, $110 guesthouse rooms, $135–145 cabins) is the very picture of country elegance. Rooms are beautifully coordinated and luxuriously comfortable. Innkeepers provide a full breakfast in the morning and a sweet dessert at night.

(Buffalo Run Inn (60117 S.R. 20, 360/873-2103, www.buffaloruninn.com, $70–120) is probably the best place to stay in the Marblemount area. The old 1889 roadhouse was purchased by the owners of the neighboring Buffalo Run restaurant and converted into a very open, very comfortable, and very classy inn with an unmistakable Northwest flair.

CAMPING

Cedar Lane RV & Mobile Home Park (8878 Peavey Rd. in Sedro-Woolley, 360/856-0233, www.cedarlanepark.com, $18 full-hookup) has tent and RV sites in a quiet wooded park-type campground.

Six miles past the Forest Service's Koma Kulshan Guard Station on the west shore of Baker Lake, **Baker Lake Resort** (888/711-3033, $75 for 4–6) has a dozen rustic cabins with full kitchens, camping, and RV sites, boat rentals, a store, and restaurant. There's a two-night minimum on weekends, and the resort is open only from mid-April through October.

Puget Sound Energy maintains the **Kulshan Campground** (near Upper Baker Dam on Baker Lake Rd., $10 summer, free during shoulder season). Free camping (no running water) is available at **Grandy Lake County Park** (four mi. northeast of Hwy. 20 on Baker Lake Hwy.). Keep driving up Baker Lake Road to take your pick from a spate of Forest Service campgrounds (518/885-3639 or 877/444-6777, www.recreation.gov, $9 extra reservation fee), including **Horseshoe Cove** ($16), **Panorama Point** ($14), **Shannon Creek** ($14–16), **Boulder Creek** ($14), and **Park Creek** ($12). There is no drinking water at Boulder Creek or Park Creek. A boat-in or hike-in campground at **Maple Grove** is also available.

Right on Highway 20 is **Wilderness Village RV Park** (5550 Hwy. 20, 360/873-2571, $11 tent, $18 full hookups) offering tent and RV sites. The public launderette here has **showers.**

(**Howard Miller Steelhead Park** (52804 Rockport Park Rd. in Rockport, 360/853-8808, $16 tents, $28 RV electricity and water) is quite a large county park with over 50 campsites between three camping areas. There's a coin-op shower, fishing right on the Skagit, and horse trails. The park is home to the Skagit River Interpretive center and also the Bald Eagle Awareness Team. **Grandy Lake** and **Sauk Park,** all part of the same park system, have primitive sites for $7 per night.

Food
Hal's Drive-In (321 State St., Sedro-Woolley, 360/855-0868, 11 A.M.–8 P.M. daily) is a longtime favorite, with burgers, shakes, corn dogs, and onion rings. **Lorenzo's** (902 W S.R. 20, 360/856-6810, Sedro-Woolley, 11 A.M.–10 P.M. daily) has mouthwatering flautas and enchiladas and also a curious appetizer they call "pork hog wings." This local chain has locations in Bellingham and Mount Vernon, too.

(**Buffalo Run Restaurant** (Marblemount, 360/873-2461, noon–9 P.M. Mon.–Thurs., noon–10 P.M. Fri.–Sun.) promises a very memorable red-meat experience. You could order chicken here, but why do that when the restaurant serves adventuresome entrées that include buffalo T-bone steak, buffalo burgers, and buffalo stroganoff—any of which you will remember and crave long after leaving here. The owners run a buffalo ranch a few miles out of town and they make the best meals in the area using bison they raise themselves. The

home-baked breads, berry pies, hearty soups, and fresh-from-the-garden organic greens are special treats. Dine on the flower-lined patio to make your experience at this little burger joint really feel like a dream.

Over on the premises of Clark's Skagit River Resort, **The Eatery** (58468 Clark Cabin Rd., 360/873-2250 or 800/273-2606, www.north cascades.com, 7 A.M.–9 P.M.) serves all-American fare like steaks, meatloaf, burgers, and grilled trout. At the little museum, you can see a homemade flag sewn by miners to celebrate Washington statehood in 1889 and also learn what a "pig scraper" is.

Information and Services
On Highway 20, just west of Sedro-Woolley, you'll find the **Mount Baker Ranger Station/ North Cascades National Park Service Complex** (810 Hwy. 20, 360/856-5700, www .fs.fed.us/r6/mbs, summer Sun.–Thurs. 8 A.M.– 4:30 P.M., Fri. 8 A.M.–6 P.M., winter Mon.–Fri. 8 A.M.–4:30 P.M.) with a North Cascades relief map, books, and brochures for sale, and information on road conditions.

Follow the signs to the National Park Service's **Wilderness Information Center** (milepost 105.3 on Hwy. 20, 360/854-7245 Sun.–Thurs. 7 A.M.–6 P.M., and Fri.–Sat. 7 A.M.–8 P.M. in July and August, with reduced hours in June and the first half of September, call ahead) in Marblemount. Get **backcountry permits** here for the park. Because there are no advance reservations, weekend campers arrive early to get permits for the most popular sites, especially Cascade Pass, Hidden Lake, Monogram Lake, Ross Lake, and Thornton Lakes. If you're willing to accept alternate destinations, you should be able to get into the backcountry under most circumstances. Behind the Wilderness Office is a greenhouse used to grow plants to revegetate damaged backcountry areas.

Getting There and Around
Skagit Transit (360/757-4433, www.skagit transit.org) offers free daily bus service throughout the county, from Anacortes to Concrete.

NEWHALEM AND EASTWARD

Heading east from Marblemount, Highway 20 enters North Cascades National Park after five miles, then passes Goodell Creek and Newhalem Campgrounds, the turnoff to North Cascades Visitor Center, and **Skagit General Store** (milepost 120, 206/386-4489) in Newhalem. The store, owned by Seattle City Light, sells supplies and handicrafts, plus the absolute best fudge ever produced by a power company.

The little settlement of Newhalem is a quiet company town with only one focus: producing electricity for Seattle at nearby Gorge, Diablo, and Ross Dams. The parklike grounds are surrounded by trim clapboard homes occupied by employees of Seattle City Light. In the town park find **Old Number Six,** a handsomely restored 1920s-era Baldwin steam locomotive that hauled passengers and supplies to the Skagit River dams; today it's a favorite of kids. The small **Seattle City Light Visitor Center** here makes a good restroom stop.

East of Newhalem, Highway 20 begins a serious climb into the forested Cascades, and quickly passes **Ross Lake National Recreation Area,** made up of Gorge, Diablo, and Ross Dams as well as the reservoirs attached to each). Be sure to stop at the **Forge Creek Falls** overlook near milepost 123 for views of the creek plunging into the gorge below. **Colonial Creek Campground** is along the highway near Diablo Lake, and a mile east is an overlook where you can peer down on the emerald green lake waters and across to the jagged summits of Pyramid Peak and Colonial Peak.

Continuing eastward, the highway climbs along Granite Creek before topping two passes—4,855-foot Rainy Pass and 5,447-foot Washington Pass. A short paved trail leads from Washington Pass to over-the-highway viewpoints of 7,720-foot Liberty Bell—the symbol of the North Cascades Highway—and Early Winters Spires. Beyond this, the highway spirals downward to the Methow Valley and the town of Winthrop.

NORTH CASCADES NATIONAL PARK

The half-million-acre North Cascades National Park is one of the wildest in the Lower 48, and an outdoors-lover's paradise. It has 318 glaciers—more than half of the total number outside Alaska. Few roads spoil this pristine wilderness, where rugged peaks, mountain lakes, and waterfalls greet the determined backcountry hiker. Nearly all of the park lies within the **Stephen Mather Wilderness,** and it is surrounded by additional wilderness buffers covering well over a million acres: Liberty Bell Primitive Area, Noisy-Diobsud Wilderness Area, Glacier Peak Wilderness Area, Pasayten Wilderness Area, and Mount Baker Wilderness Area.

North Cascades National Park is split up by Ross Lake National Recreation Area and Lake Chelan National Recreation Area. The resulting three parts are managed by the National Park Service, although some of Ross Lake National Recreation Area is owned and run by Seattle City Light, since that is where the dams are. It's a bit of a patchwork, but still, most everything is wild and undeveloped, providing fantastic opportunities for explorations afoot and afloat.

Slip on your boots and wander the trails of North Cascades National Park.

© ERICKA CHICKOWSKI

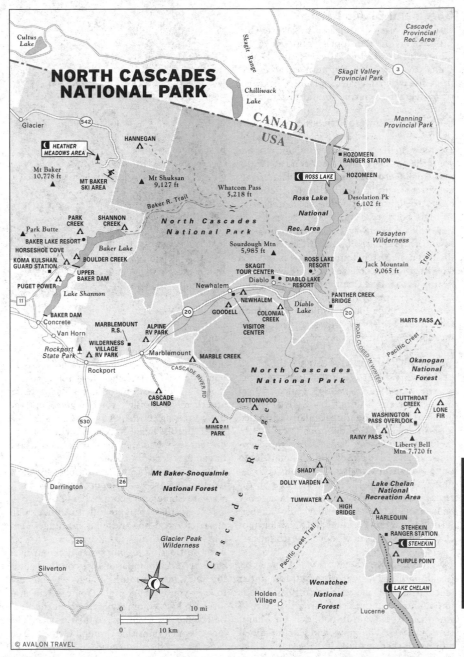

Gorge and Diablo Lakes

Two small reservoirs created by Seattle City Light dams on the upper Skagit River are Gorge Lake, covering 210 acres, and Diablo Lake, covering 910 acres; both are accessible from Highway 20. Diablo and Gorge Lakes get their emerald-green color from fine sediments in the glacial runoff.

The **Gorge Powerhouse** observation lobby (8 A.M.–4 P.M. daily May–Sept.) is accessed by a cable suspension footbridge. Continue beyond the power plant to **Ladder Creek Falls and Rock Gardens.** The colorful flower gardens were first planted here in the 1920s and create a delightful setting for the adjacent falls. At night both are lit up.

A mile off Highway 20 is the tiny company town of **Diablo,** the home of Diablo Power Plant and the Skagit Tour Center. A half dozen free campsites (no potable water) are available at nearby **Gorge Lake Campground,** and a popular (but very steep) five-mile trail leads from here to the 5,985-foot summit of **Sourdough Mountain.** Hikers are treated to lush alpine meadows and panoramic views.

Seattle City Light Tours

Seattle City Light (206/684-3030, www.ci .seattle.wa.us/light/tours, $55 adults, $50 seniors, $45 teens, $40 kids 6–12, free for kids under 6) has been offering regularly scheduled tours of its Skagit facilities since 1928.

Today visitors can cruise across the deep-green Diablo Lake during the 2.5-hour **Diablo Lake Adventure cruise** ($25 adults, $20 seniors, $12 kids 6–12, free under age 5), offered Saturday–Sunday from mid-June–early September, as well as on Fridays July–August. A fuel surcharge of $5 adults and $3 seniors (not charged for kids) is now added to each tour.

(Ross Lake

Reaching down a staggering 540 feet under its calm surface, the eerie green Ross Lake is impoundment of the Skagit River that formed when the Ross Dam impounded the Skagit River in 1949. The snow- and glacier-capped mountains that surround it make you feel like

Ross Lake

© ERICKA CHICKOWSKI

you're in a fantasy world. Unless you want to take an excursion through Canada, there are no launches for nonportable boats. As is, you'll do well to launch kayaks and canoes at Colonial Creek campground on Diablo Lake, and then take a mile's worth of gravel portage before taking on Ross Lake. The glacier-fed waters of Ross Lake almost never rise above 50 degrees, so try to stay in your boat. The lake has an excellent trout fishery.

You'd be hard-pressed to find anything quite like the **(Ross Lake Resort** (206/386-4437, www.rosslakeresort.com, $122–261 d, $10 extra person). Cabins are fully furnished, with electricity and hot and cold running water. The unusual thing is that the cabins are all built on floating log rafts that stick out over the lake. Accommodations are comfy if nothing fancy, but most units do have a woodstove to keep you warm at night. You can rent motorboats, kayaks, or canoes here, but there are no telephones, groceries, or food service. The lodge is open mid-June through October. You can't get here by car. Instead, you can catch the

Seattle City Light boat ($20 round-trip) that leaves the parking lot across Diablo Dam daily at 8:30 A.M. and 3 P.M. The tug takes you to the end of Diablo Lake, where a truck ($8 round-trip) carries you on to Ross Lake.

Ross Lake has waterside campsites and half a dozen trailheads that provide access into adjacent North Cascades National Park. Ross Lake Resort runs a **water taxi** (206/386-4437, 9 A.M.–5 P.M. daily, $50–165 per boat) service, along with boat tours and portages from Diablo Lake for small boats and canoes. The water taxi fares are by the boatload (it can hold six), not per person, so it's best if you can coordinate your travel with other folks to save money. These water-taxi trips are a fun way to reach the backcountry, but be sure to pick up backcountry permits from the Wilderness Information Center in Marblemount before heading out on your hiking or camping adventure.

Hiking
DAY HIKES
More than 300 miles of maintained trails provide ample opportunities to explore North Cascades National Park. Short hikes—some are wheelchair-accessible—abound around Colonial Creek Campground and Newhalem; pick up flyers describing these and others at the visitors centers. Trails below 3,000 feet are generally open by mid-April or May; higher up, you may meet snow in July, so be prepared.

Some of the park's most spectacular scenery can be seen at **Cascade Pass.** Drive to the trailhead at the end of Cascade River Road, a 23-mile mostly gravel road from Marblemount. The first two miles of the seven-mile round-trip hike climb steadily through forest and meadows to the 5,400-foot pass at 3.7 miles. Allow about five hours for this hike.

BACKCOUNTRY TREKS
A free **backcountry permit** is required for all overnight trips into the park, a policy meant to reduce overcrowding and preserve the fragile alpine environment. Pick one up from the Wilderness Information Center in Marblemount or from information or ranger stations in Newhalem, Hozomeen, Sedro-Woolley, Winthrop, Twisp, Chelan, or Stehekin. Some areas fill up on summer weekends, so you may need to go with another option. The North Cascades is among the most rugged ranges in the Lower 48, so plan accordingly: lots of wool clothing, extra food, a waterproof tarp, and a flexible schedule for waiting our storms or resting feet and muscles sore from all the ups and downs.

From June–November, enjoy the 31-mile trip from the East Bank Trailhead (milepost 138) to Hozomeen along Ross Lake's **East Bank Trail.** The trailhead is on Highway 20, eight miles east of the Colonial Creek Campground at the Panther Creek bridge. The trail leads through low forest and along the lakeshore for 18 miles, at which point you have the option of continuing to Hozomeen or taking a side trip up 6,102-foot **Desolation Peak.** The round-trip up the peak is nine miles, almost straight up, with an elevation gain of 4,400 feet; you'll be rewarded with views of Mount Baker, Mount Shuksan, Jack Mountain, and The Pickets. To get right to the peak, skip the first 18 miles of hiking by taking the water taxi to the Desolation Peak trailhead; stay overnight at Lightning Creek Campground, since you probably won't return in time to catch the boat.

The **Pacific Crest Trail** enters the park from the south from Glacier Peak Wilderness Area, crossing Highway 20 at Rainy Pass and heading north through the Liberty Bell Roadless Area and the Pasayten Wilderness Area to the Canadian border.

If you can set up a vehicle shuttle or are willing to hitchhike, an excellent long hike begins at the Colonial Creek Campground, climbs over 6,100-foot **Park Pass** via Thunder Creek and Park Creek trails, and ends at Flat Creek Campground, a total hike of 27 miles. From here, you can catch the shuttle bus to Stehekin and then ride the **Lady of the Lake II** (509/682-4584, www.ladyofthelake.com, $24) down Lake Chelan to the town of Chelan. An alternate ending would be to hike (or catch the shuttle bus) four miles up Stehekin Valley Road and follow **Cascade Pass Trail** over this

5,400-foot pass to the end of Cascade River Road (23 miles south of Marblemount).

If you don't mind a long uphill slog, **Easy Pass** is a nice overnight hike just as long as you don't take "Easy" too literally. The trailhead is six miles west of Rainy Pass on Highway 20 (46 miles east of Marblemount), and Easy Pass Trail climbs steadily for 3.7 miles to this 6,500-foot summit, where you enter North Cascades National Park. The magnificent vista includes knife-edged mountains and active glaciers. From here, you can continue deeper into the wilderness on **Fisher Creek Trail.** Easy Pass Trail is usually open from late July–late September.

Additional hiking trails leading into the park can be accessed from the Mount Baker, Baker Lake, Liberty Bell, Harts Pass, and Stehekin areas.

Pack Trips

Early Winters Outfitters (509/996-2659, www.earlywintersoutfitting.com, $190 per day) is perfect if you want to extend your range a bit by strapping your gear on horses and walking alongside up into the mountains. An experienced chef comes along to keep you well-fed, sometimes with fresh-caught pan-grilled trout.

One of the most ecofriendly tours out there, **Deli Llama** (360/757-4212, www.delillama .com), is a delightful pack company run by a well-traveled husband and wife team who will entertain you with colorful stories over a plate of their gourmet trail food. Meanwhile, the personality-filled llamas bleat and graze nearby. Your gear is carefully strapped to the llamas, who don't seem to mind a bit. The beasts of burden open up a range of backcountry possibilities for those who can't (or just don't wanna) shoulder their own backpacks.

Camping

There are several Park Service campgrounds accessible by car on the North Cascades Highway. **Goodell Creek** (518/885-3639 or 877/444-6777, year-round, $10) has sites sized for tents or RVs and is a good place to put in your kayak. **Newhalem Creek** (518/885-3639 or 877/444-

6777, www.recreation.gov, mid-May–mid-October, $12, $9 extra reservation fee) has a dump station for RVs and flush toilets. It also has a few barrier-free sites. Beautiful **Colonial Creek** (360/854-7200 or 877/444-6777, mid-May–mid-October, $12) does not accept reservations. Camp among the old-growth trees by the shore of Diablo Lake. You can count the glaciers far on Colonial Peak while you sip your morning campfire coffee.

The free **Mineral Park Campground** is also open year-round and especially popular with hunters and anglers. On the east side of the pass, find **Klipchuck Campground,** the largest of State Route 20 campgrounds. The bird-watching opportunities are amazing here, and brushy vegetation makes it a reasonably private campground. The deer are so bold here, they'll snatch the s'mores off your stick if you're not careful.

Information and Services

The elaborate **North Cascades Visitor Center** (milepost 120 on Hwy. 20, 206/386-4495, 9 a.m.–5 p.m. daily April through mid-November, extended to 6 p.m. in July and August, 9 a.m.–4:30 p.m. weekends only Dec.–Mar.) is 14 miles east of Marblemount and a half mile south of Highway 20 in Newhalem. It has a large relief map of the area plus various interpretive exhibits that cover local natural and historical history.

Just 330 feet behind the center, you can find an amazing view of the high, steep, and icy **Picket Range,** a barrier-free trail ideal for listening to bird calls and marveling at the scenery.

LIBERTY BELL ROADLESS AREA

The 141,000-acre Liberty Bell Roadless Area adjoins Highway 20 at Washington Pass and includes a long stretch of the Pacific Crest Trail, as well as some of the most sought-after rock climbing in the Cascades. **Maple Pass** is an outstanding day hike that takes you past two forest-rimmed lakes and over the aforementioned pass. The trail begins right along

Highway 20, from the south parking lot at Rainy Pass (30 miles west of Winthrop). An almost-level paved trail (wheelchair-accessible) leads a mile to **Rainy Lake,** with interpretive signs along the way. The cirque lake is backed by high cliffs with plummeting waterfalls. From here, you can continue up a steeper trail to Maple Pass, and then loop back past **Lake Ann** (good fishing for cutthroat trout) before returning to the parking area, a total distance of approximately six miles. No camping is allowed anywhere along this popular route.

Also popular is an easy trail to **Blue Lake** that leads two miles through subalpine meadows to the emerald waters of this mountain lake. Surrounding it is a trio of spectacular summits: Liberty Bell Mountain, Whistler Mountain, and Cutthroat Peak. The Blue Lake trailhead is a half mile west of Washington Pass.

PASAYTEN WILDERNESS

One of the largest wilderness areas in Washington, the Pasayten (pa-SAY-tin) Wilderness covers 530,000 acres of mountain country. Its northern edge is the U.S./Canadian border, while to the south it extends almost to Methow Valley. The country contains deep canyons, mountains topping 7,500 feet, and an abundance of wildlife that includes a few gray wolves and grizzly bears.

Hiking

The Pasayten Wilderness contains more than 600 miles of trails. One of the quintessential longer day hikes is the 12-mile long **Billy Goat Loop Trail.** To get here, drive nine miles north from Winthrop on West Chewuch Road, and turn left onto Eightmile Creek Road. Continue another 17 miles to the trailhead at the end of the road. The trail climbs through evergreen forests and then over Billy Goat Pass before dropping into the narrow Drake Creek Valley. From here, it circles back around the other side of Billy Goat Mountain and over Eightmile Pass before returning you to the starting point.

The trailhead for a longer loop hike (approximately 30 miles) is 20 miles west of Mazama

---

GRIZZLY BEARS

The Northern Cascades of Washington is home to somewhere between 15 and 30 wild grizzly bears, making them rare but still extremely dangerous. This threatened species can weigh up to 1,800 pounds, run upwards of 30 miles per hour, and stand up to 12 feet on its hind legs. These bears can be brown, black, or reddish, so color is not a good indicator of species. A grizzly bear, unlike the others, has a hump just behind its front legs and has a flat, dish-like face. Trailheads often warn of bear danger, but don't assume you're in the clear if there is no sign. Bear calling-cards include trees with heavily shredded bark, wide tracks with deep claws, and large scat unlike a dog's. Be cautious, but know that there are no recorded fatal grizzly attacks in the state of Washington.

---

at the second switchback above Harts Pass on the way to Slate Peak. Follow the **Buckskin Ridge Trail** (No. 498) from here through high meadows and past Silver Lake to Silver Pass and Buckskin Ridge (7,300 feet) before descending to the Pasayten River. Here you catch trail No. 478 and follow it upriver through old-growth forests to trail No. 498, which takes you back to your starting point. Check out the Green Trails maps or talk with folks at the Winthrop Forest Service office before heading up this interesting but challenging route.

Pack Trips

Several companies lead horse pack trips into the Pasayten, including **Early Winters Outfitters** (509/996-2659 or 800/737-8750, www.earlywintersoutfitting.com), **North Cascade Outfitters** (509/997-1015, www.cowboypoet.com), **Back Country Burro Treks** (509/996-3369), **North Cascade Safari** (509/996-2350), and **Sawtooth Outfitters** (509/923-2548). For a unique experience, **Pasayten Llama Packing** (509/996-2326, www.mtllama.com) leads llama trips into the wilderness.

Methow Valley

To enter the Methow Valley (MET-how) from the west is to step out from under the canopy of ancient trees and cloudy skies tickled by jagged icy mountains and in to a land of golden grasses, rolling hills, and glorious sun. This mellow valley that reminds one of the meandering trout rivers and plains of Montana has a history of farming. For years, the Valley was a choice spot for growing hay, nurturing orchards, and cattle ranching. After State Route 20 was completed and opened to traffic from Seattle and environs, things began to change. Former farmlands became resorts and outfitters and B&Bs. Vacation properties have begun to pop up in the hills. While it is hard for some long-time locals to see the transformation, many more have opened businesses catering to the active tourist who comes to go rafting, fishing, cycling, hunting, or just about any outdoors activity you can imagine. There are still plenty of farms here and on most evenings you can see dozens of deer roaming the fields, grazing and feeling quite at home. To this day, over 75 percent of land in Okanogan Country is publicly owned.

The bustling town of Winthrop is the center of activity in Methow Valley, with its made-over Western theme. Just 13 miles down the road is the town of Mazama, known chiefly for its store that sells gas, groceries, and fishing gear, while 11 miles south is the ranching town called Twisp, named after the Okanogan People's name for the wasps that can be real pests in the summertime. The valley is accessible from all sides during the summer, but Highway 20 closes from late November through April, depending on snowfall.

HARTS PASS AREA

Harts Pass can be a bit daunting. Built by miners in 1893, the gravel road hugs the rock wall, climbing and climbing until it reaches the pass itself, over 6,000 feet in elevation and the highest drivable spot in Washington! If you're not uncomfortable yet, there are no guardrails and the grade is steep enough to overheat an engine in summer. Don't even imagine hauling a trailer up here. Why bother? Well, the view of course. Also, just over the pass, a left turn leads to the ghost towns of Barron and Chancellor, once home to 2,000 miners. Turn right (north) for three steep miles to **Slate Peak Lookout.** A short walk leads to the old lookout tower. Be ready for spectacular 360-degree views of the entire Cascade Range. The road is a great, but tiring, gritty mountain bike ride. The road is not plowed beyond Lost River in the winter. Near Harts Pass, you can camp at two Forest Service campgrounds with gorgeous alpine settings: **Meadows** and **Harts Pass.** What they lack in services they make up for in vistas and cool, clean mountain air. They are usually open mid-July–late September; there is no potable water. Both campgrounds charge $8 per night.

This high-alpine country offers some of the most popular day hiking in this part of the state. **Windy Pass Trail** begins 1.5 miles up Slate Peak Road from Harts Pass and follows the Pacific Crest Trail for 3.5 miles to Windy Pass. The hike begins at 6,800 feet with little additional elevation gain but offers striking views of peaks and meadows all along the route. A second fun hike with little change in elevation begins at Harts Pass and proceeds along the PCT south to **Grasshopper Pass.** The round-trip distance is 11 miles, and the route follows the crest of the mountains to beautiful meadows at Grasshopper Pass. Because of the high elevation, these trails are often covered with snow until late July.

WINTHROP

Located near the junction of the Methow and Chewuch (CHEE-wuk) Rivers, Winthrop began as a mining settlement, settled into middle age as a ranching town, and has re-emerged as a tourist mecca. Home to fewer than 400 year-round residents, Winthrop greets over 600,000 visitors annually. Winthrop's Main

© ERICKA CHICKOWSKI

The Old West town of Winthrop is a favorite summertime vacation spot.

Street buildings have been remodeled with an Old West theme to reflect the town's 1890s mining boom—and to encourage hungry, tired Highway 20 drivers to stop for a meal, gas, and souvenirs. Winthrop also hosts annual festivals and rodeos that reflect the Western mood.

The town of Winthrop goes back to 1891, when an easterner named Guy Waring opened Methow Trading Company to sell goods to the newcomers seeking their fortune in the gold and silver mines. The town was officially incorporated in 1897. Guy Waring's old friend, Owen Wister, came to visit and used some of his experiences in his 1902 novel, *The Virginian*—oft considered to be the first American Western novel.

After the collapse of mining in the area, Winthrop focused on farming, cattle ranching, and supporting the large saw mill in town. And so the town fought its way through fire, flood, and frost in relative obscurity until townsfolk heard the news that the new State Route 20 was going to head directly through town. Hurrying to capitalize on the fact, a group of city leaders stumbled on the idea of renovating the entire length of Main Street in a stylized Western theme. A local benefactor, Kathryn Wagner, widow of a sawmill owner, put up matching funds, and some of the architects that had helped make nearby Leavenworth into a Bavarian wonderland a few years back were brought in to help. By the time the first carloads of tourists crossed Washington Pass in 1972, Winthrop had covered its concrete buildings with false fronts, laid down wooden sidewalks, and added Old West signs and hitching posts. Today the shops are brimming with western wear, hunting and fishing gear, upscale boutiques, books, and, of course, ice cream.

Sights

Winthrop's **Shafer Museum** (285 Castle Ave., 509/996-2712, 10 A.M.–5 P.M. daily summer, 10 A.M.–5 P.M. weekdays May and Sept., donations) is housed in an 1897 log home that is a bit grandiloquently called "The Castle," built by the town's founder, Guy Waring. Displays include pioneer farming and mining tools, bicycles, furniture, an impressive rifle collection, and others. Outside, you'll find a town's worth of buildings, including a general store, print shop, homestead cabin, schoolhouse, and assay office, plus old wagons, mining equipment, and aging farm implements. The 1923 Rickenbacker automobile here is one of just 80 still in existence.

Walk down Riverside (Main Street) to find all sorts of Western shops, most notably **White Buck Trading Co** (509/996-3500), named for a big white buck that was shot nearly 60 years ago. The informal **White Buck Museum** in the rear of the store contains more stuffed critters and a collection of knick-knacks from the past, including—of all things—the first dial phone in Chicago. **Last Trading Post** (509/996-9833) is packed with Old West Americana, from antiques to painted cattle skulls. Downstairs is a museum of sorts, with historic flotsam and jetsam, plus various Native American artifacts.

The Forest Service's **North Cascade Smokejumper Base** (halfway between Winthrop and Twisp along Hwy. 20, 509/997-2031, www.fs.fed.us/r6/oka June–Sept. daily 9 A.M.–5 P.M.) is open for tours during the fire season. The airstrip is one of fewer than a dozen bases for these airborne firefighters who parachute in to forest fires in areas too remote to get to any way else. They are the best of the best. This base happens to be the one at which, in 1939, the Forest Service first played around with the idea of airdropping Forest Service personnel to fight fires.

Entertainment and Events

Three-Fingered Jack's Saloon (176 Riverside Ave., 509/996-2411, 7 A.M.–9 P.M. daily) usually has rock or R&B bands on summer weekends.

The second weekend of May marks the start of Winthrop's festival season with **'49ers Days,** featuring a parade, horse-packing demonstrations, and culminating with the Dollar Watch Cowboy Jamboree—two hours of music, poetry, jokes, magic, and general horseplay. Winthrop hosts the bookend **Methow Valley Rodeo** (509/996-2373, $10 adults, $5 kids 5–12, free kids under 5) which keeps alive the spirit of the small town community rodeo. It's fun to watch local wranglers and junior champs instead of circuit-riders for a change. The Memorial Day rodeo kicks off the summer while the Labor Day festival says a long goodbye.

The three-day-long **Winthrop Rhythm and Blues Festival** in mid-July has quickly become a major blues event, attracting more than 5,000 fans to hear such acts as Charlie Musselwhite, B. B. King, or John Hammond. Locals shake off their cabin fever midway through winter with the downright-silly **Snowshoe Softball Tournament** (888/463-8469), which is a softball game. Played in the snow. In snowshoes. The February event is sponsored by Three-Fingered Jack's, the local tavern. But you probably already guessed that. If you can't make it to Albuquerque's Balloon Fiesta, drift in to the **Winthrop Balloon Roundup** (888/463-8469) in early March. Even if you don't opt for a ride, seeing the multicolored hot-air balloons set against a snow-covered mountain is a sight that will stick with you.

Sports and Recreation
PEARRYGIN LAKE STATE PARK
The 578-acre Pearrygin Lake State Park (five mi. north of Winthrop, www.parks.wa.gov) offers a sandy beach for swimming, plus fishing, camping, a boat launch, store, and boat rentals. This small, spring-fed, glacially carved lake is a delightful break from the dry summer hills of sage and pine that surround it.

MOUNTAIN BIKING
Mountain bikes can be rented from **Winthrop Mountain Sports** (509/996-2886 or 800/719-3826, www.winthropmountainsports.com).

Winthrop is a summer mecca for cyclists, with an incredible range of trails and country roads spreading through the valley and into the surrounding mountains. Pick up descriptions of local routes at the Forest Service visitors center, or call the **Methow Valley Sport Trails Association** (209 Castle Ave.,

509/996-3287 or 800/682-5787, www.mvsta .com) for information and maps. Access the trail system from the Sun Mountain Lodge parking lot. Approximately seven miles of trails are wheelchair-accessible.

One good, though very challenging, ride in the national forest near Winthrop is the **Cedar Creek Trail,** which turns off Highway 20 17 miles northwest of Winthrop. The first three miles of trail are brutally steep and rocky, but past that the next four miles farther up the narrow valley are wonderful and remote. Another popular trail, not as technical as Cedar Creek, is the **Twisp River Valley Trail,** which parallels the clear and cool bubbling waters of the Twisp River. For more details on these and other rides around Winthrop, pick up a copy of *Methow Valley Mountain Bike Routes,* published by the Northwest Interpretive Association and the Forest Service.

RIVER RAFTING

The Methow River is a favorite of white-water enthusiasts, with many access points and a wide range of conditions, from easy float trips to class III–IV white water. Rafters generally float the river from early May till early July, when the river is running hard from spring runoff but the air is warm and dry. The river gets progressively tougher below Winthrop as you follow the Methow to the Columbia, 17 miles downriver. Black Canyon is the pinnacle, with roller-coaster waves and wild action as the river plunges through dozens of rapids.

One of the best ways to experience the long succession of Methow River rapids is to set aside time for an overnight trip. **Orion Expeditions** (800/553-7466, http://orion-exp.com, $150) operates an overnighter, taking care of all rafting equipment and all meals from lunch on day one. Guests can also request tents, though they will need to bring their own sleeping bags.

HIKING

A multitude of hiking trails surround the Methow Valley. For horseback rides and pack trips, contact **Early Winters Outfitters**

(509/996-2659 or 800/737-8750, www.early wintersoutfitting), **Rocking Horse Ranch** (509/996-2768), **Chewack River Riding Stables** (509/996-2497), or **North Cascade Outfitters** (509/997-1015, www.cowboypoet .com).

CLIMBING

The mountains around Methow Valley are becoming increasingly popular with rock climbers. **Mazama Mountaineering** (42 Lost River Rd., Mazama, 503/227-2345, www.mazamas .org) does it all. It teaches one- to seven-day classes, guides rock climbing, backcountry skiing, snowboarding, and mountain biking trips.

GOLF

Winthrop's **Bear Creek Golf Course** (19 Bear Creek Golf Course Rd., 509/996-2284, www .bearcreekgolfcourse.com, $22 weekends, $18 weekdays) lets you play golf in what feels like the middle of nowhere. In a good way. Beyond the boundaries of the course, golden-green grasses sway on a former cattle ranch. Hills stretch to wilderness mountains. This nine-hole course is fun golf, but it makes almost as good of a hike.

HOT AIR BALLOON RIDES

Morning Glory Balloon Tours (509/997-1700, www.balloonwinthrop.com, $195 adult, $150 kids) flies one-hour hot-air balloon rides dust after sunrise year-round. A romantic trip for two with an airborne picnic, flowers, and chocolates will cost you $795 for a couple.

WINTER SPORTS

In winter, Methow Valley often has two or three feet of powdery snow on the ground, making for world-class cross-country skiing. The **Methow Valley Sport Trails Association** (209 Castle Ave, 509/996-3287 or 800/682-5787, www.mvsta.com) maintains four sets of interconnected cross-country ski trails throughout the valley. It grooms 175 kilometers of trails, setting tracks for both classical and skate skis. Even dogs are welcome along several miles of the trail. Fees are $20 for one day or $51 for three days and $35 for dogs. The MVSTA's ski trail systems connect to several local inns and lodges, making it possible to ski right from your front door. A public **warming hut** is located at WolfRidge Resort, and several of the lodges welcome skiers with hot drinks. A **van service** (509/996-8294) provides transport to trailheads throughout the valley.

To get deeper into the backcountry, backcountry skiers may also want to consider hut-to-hut skiing opportunities on the MVSTA-maintained Rendezvous Trail system. A series of five fully equipped cabins (each cabin sleeps eight) are located eight miles apart in the mountains north of Winthrop. Call **Rendezvous Outfitters** (509/996-8100 or 800/257-2452) for details. In addition to lodging, Rendezvous will also provide ski guides or on-trail gear hauling for an extra fee. Reservations are advised.

Rent skis and get cross-country lessons from **Sun Mountain Resort** (509/996-2211 or 800/572-0493, $19 rental, $98 two-hour lesson) where it has its own several-mile trail system and offers plenty of combo lodging & skiing packages. You can also rent your equipment at the **Mazama Country Inn** (509/996-2681 or 800/843-7951), **Jack's Hut at Freestone Inn** (509/996-2752), or **Winthrop Mountain Sports** (509/996-2886 or 800/719-3826).

The nearest slope for alpine skiers and snowboarders is nearby **Loup Loup Ski Bowl** (509/826-2720 or 866/699-5334, www.ski theloup.com, $30–40 adults, $25–32 kids 13–19 and seniors, $20–24 youth 7–12, free for kids under 6), is an unusual nonprofit mountain offering 10 cut runs down its 1,240 vertical-foot mountain. The seldom-crowded slopes have something to keep everyone interested, from rope-tows to a tubing hill to the snowboarding half-pipe.

For those with the bucks, **North Cascade Heli-Skiing** (509/996-3272 or 800/494-4354, www.skisite.com) will take downhillers into untracked powder. A popular three-day trip

that operates out of Mazama guaranteeing at least 21 runs is offered at a mere $2,499 per person. Other packages are as little as $375.

The **Winthrop Ice and Sports Rink** (208 White Ave., 509/996-4199, $3) is an outdoor skate rink which, on a blue-sky day when pillows of snow cover the neighboring roofs, can make for a wonderful and affordable afternoon. You can go tear it up at the **Chewack River Guest Ranch** (588 E Chewuch Rd., 509/996-2497, www.chewackranch.com) astride their rental Yamaha snowmobile. You get the sled plus snowsuit, helmet, and a full tank of gas for $195 per day.

Accommodations

There is some very nice lodging in the area of Winthrop, but like all of Washington, summers book up fast. Plan as far ahead as you can. If you plan to stay at one of the cross-country ski lodges over the Christmas–New Year's holiday, you'll find some of the choicest accommodations full six months in advance. **Methow Valley Central Reservations** (509/996-2148 or 800/422-3048, www.centralreservations .net, 9 A.M.–4:30 P.M. Mon.–Fri.) is a fantastic local resource to help you find vacancies in this surprisingly active little town.

UNDER $100

You'll find several hotels in town to choose from, starting with **Duck Brand Hotel** (509/996-2192 or 800/996-2192, www.methow net.com/duck, $69–79 s or d), which has a very good location in the middle of Main Street.

The pet-friendly **Winthrop Inn** (960 Hwy. 20, 509/996-2217 or 800/444-1972, www .winthropinn.com, $75–135 s or $85–95 d) has clean and comfortable rooms with microwaves and fridges, sharing a small outdoor pool and hot tub. Munch on fresh muffins and coffee each morning while taking advantage of the free wireless Internet. There's even a trailhead just two blocks away.

Snow lovers should also consider a stay at **Chewack River Guest Ranch** (588 E. Chewuch Rd., 509/996-2497, $85 d, $225 up to 6), six miles north of Winthrop. They rent snowmobiles and even lead guided trips in the winter. Chewack is also a great summertime retreat, particularly for horse lovers—guests can board their steeds for free here, and the property sits right next to public land with miles of trails. Choose between several lodge rooms or rent the ranch house with a full kitchen and a wood-burning stove. Finish the day off soaking in the hot tub or cooking up a dinner on the outdoor stone barbecue.

Three-quarters of a mile south of Winthrop, **Winthrop Mountain View Chalets** (1120 S.R. 20, 800/527-3113, www.winthropchalets.com, $55–95 s or d) rents out cute little cabins built for two. They come equipped with kitchenettes and decks and share access to a large hot tub.

Several cozy lodges dot the valley around Winthrop, including **Brown's Farm Inn** (887 Wolf Creek Rd., 509/996-2571, www.methownet.com/brownsfarm, $80–170 d, or $10 per additional guest), nestled into a tranquil corner of the Methow Valley eight miles west of Winthrop. Two of the cabins have kitchenettes and sleep four, while the third has a full kitchen and sleeps up to 10. The family owners will happily point out great hiking, biking, or cross-country skiing destinations within the vicinity.

$100-150

One of the best budget spots in town is **Mt Gardner Inn** (611 Hwy. 20, 509/996-2000, www.mtgardnerinn.com, $69–139 d) a little mom-and-pop place run by a friendly young couple who keep the place in tip-top shape. The furniture is new and rooms are spic-and-span. There are several room options, including pet-friendly rooms and more luxurious rooms with private decks, microwaves, and refrigerators. For a bit more privacy, try the apartment-style suite ($199) that includes a full kitchen, separate bedroom, and a living room with gas fireplace and sleeper couch.

Just south of downtown Winthrop is **Hotel Rio Vista** (285 Riverside, 509/996-3535 or 800/398-0911, www.hotelriovista.com, $100–155 s or d), an Old West–style lodge

with rooms overlooking the Methow River. A path leads from the hotel down to a picnic area along the river.

$150-200

Located right along the Methow River, **WolfRidge Resort** (412-B Wolf Creek Rd., 509/341-4565, www.wolfridge-resort.com, $150–290 d) offers families plenty of fun features, including an outdoor pool, a bubbling hot tub enclosed by a gorgeous river-rock gazebo, a recreation room with a pool table, and over 60 acres of aspen- and pine-forested land to explore. Rooms are in pine cabin–style lodge buildings, ranging from studios up to two-bedroom houses with full kitchens.

Located a half mile west of Winthrop, **River Run Inn** (27 Rader Rd., 509/996-2173 or 800/757-2709, www.riverrun-inn.com) is a small resort that includes private rooms ($100–155 s or d), a six-bedroom house ($450), and cabins ($175–200 for up to four people). Guests will also appreciate the indoor pool, outdoor hot tub, and riverside location. The house and cabin have full kitchens, and kitchenettes are available in some of the rooms.

North Cascades Basecamp (255 Lost River Rd., Mazama, 509/996-2334, www.ncbasecamp.com, $175 d) serves up hearty meals to all its lodge guests. In winter, rates include full room and board, while summertime comes with a hefty breakfast. Guests share bathrooms and very comfortable group areas, including a fireplace living room, a playroom for kids, library, and a hot tub. Families will also enjoy the sledding hill just outside the lodge. Groups seeking a bit more privacy can choose to rent one of Basecamp's cabins for six with a full kitchen ($185–285 up to six), though meals aren't included with this option.

$200-250

For a great stay during any season, visit the **Mazama Country Inn** (15 Country Rd., 509/996-2681, www.mazamacountryinn.com, $95–155 d in summer, $115–260 d in winter). Work up a sweat on the property's tennis court or in the exercise room and then relax those old bones in the sauna and hot tub. The Country Inn almost definitely has the only squash court in the Cascades. The savory restaurant on premises provides a gourmet breakfast for guests and hors d'oeuvres in the evening. A small rental shop can provide snowshoes, cross-country skis, and mountain bikes. Kids are allowed in the summer, but come winter, this is an adults-only place.

Freestone Inn and Early Winters Cabins (17798 Hwy. 20 in Mazama, 509/996-3906 or 800/639-3809, www.freestoneinn.com, $159–235 inn, $235–335 cabins) is set right on the edge of Freestone Lake. Rooms in the modern, elaborate wooden lodge include a light meal served each morning. Or rent cabins with kitchens by the day or the week. The property organizes myriad outdoor activities for guests, such as horse riding, mountain biking, fly-fishing, and more. The on-site helipad is used for heli-skiing or for arriving in your private chopper. Please give advance notice before landing. And if you just want to relax, enjoy the fantastic views out over the lake and surrounding mountains.

OVER $250
Spring Creek Ranch (491 Twin Lakes Rd., 509/996-2495, www.springcreekwinthrop .com, $290 for nine) is a great option for families. This grand 1929 country home is full of understated antique furniture. A separate modern cabin with fireplace sleeps four ($190). The ranch is on 60 acres of land along the Methow River. Bring your horse, dog, cross-country skis, and fishing tackle because you'll get to enjoy them all right here.

Atop a 5,000-foot peak with panoramic views into the North Cascades and the Methow Valley is 【 **Sun Mountain Lodge** (nine miles southwest of Winthrop, 509/996-2211 or 800/572-0493, www.sunmountainlodge.com, $170–405 s or d), one of the premier destination resorts in Washington. Sun Mountain has almost every activity you could want, from fly-fishing lessons and children's programs to the largest string of saddle horses in the region. The impeccable property boasts a swimming pool, exercise room, and three hot tubs. A two-night minimum is required on weekends.

CAMPING
Find rest and repose by the shoreline at **Pearrygin Lake State Park** (five mi. north of Winthrop, 509/996-2370 or 888/226-7688, www.parks.wa.gov, $22 tent, $31 full hookup, $7 extra reservation fee), open mid-April through October. This is the largest lake in the area, with lots of space to fish, swim, boat, and even water-ski.

The Forest Service maintains a dozen campgrounds ($10) within 25 miles of Winthrop, and most other areas are open to free dispersed camping (with the exception of the Highway 20 corridor). Closest are the campgrounds up West Chewuch Road: **Falls Creek** with its beautiful falls just a quarter-mile hike away, and quiet **Buck Lake,** with wood ducks and stands of cattails. Most of these campgrounds are open June–September. Get more information from the Methow Valley Ranger District office (24 W Chewuch Rd., 509/996-4003).

RV campers can also choose to stay at private **Big Twin Lake Campground** (210 Twin Lakes Rd., 509/996-2650, www.methownet .com/bigtwin, $29 full hookups, $23 tent only), right on the 90-acre lake. Rent rowboat for $25 per day, kayaks for $10 per hour, or paddleboats for $5 per hour. The location is perfect for wetting a line.

Food
Because of the town's compact size, it's easy to find a place to eat in Winthrop; just walk the two-block downtown to see what looks good. Downtown's **Duck Brand Hotel & Cantina** (248 Riverside Ave., 509/996-2192 or 800/996-2192, 7 A.M.–9 P.M. daily) serves burgers and backcountry Mexican dishes. There's an outside deck for sunny days, but the restaurant is not ADA-accessible.

The **Arrowleaf Bistro** (253 Riverside St., 509/996-3919, www.arrowheadbistro.com, 5–9 P.M. Thurs.–Tues.) is a community-oriented bistro set in a cute house with a patio. The restaurant is the reply to anyone who's ever said that a town the size of Winthrop can't sustain a small gourmet restaurant. The menu is made up of delectable meals like beef onglet, pork tenderloin, and lamb shank, and a choice of wines for any budget.

Cut that summer heat at **(Sheri's Sweet Shoppe** (at the downtown corner, 509/996-3834, 7:30 A.M.–9 P.M., daily Apr.–Nov., weekends only Nov., Dec.), where you can slurp up over 40 flavors of homemade ice-cream and Italian sodas or munch on favorites like fresh flaky pralines. Enjoy them on the often-sunny deck, and make your friends jealous by using the shop's free wireless to update your Facebook feed. Just the Moosetracks ice cream alone is reason enough to travel to Winthrop—it contains house-made chocolate-peanut butter candies that taste heavenly after a long hike.

The small **Old School House Brewery Company** (155 Riverside, 509/996-3183, www.oldschoolhousebrewery.com, noon–11 P.M. daily) has burgers and home-brewed beer served on its riverside deck.

For pizza, snacks, sandwiches, and ribs, mosey over to **Three-Fingered Jack's**

Saloon (176 Riverside Ave., 509/996-2411, www.3fingeredjacks.com, 7 A.M.–noon, Mon.–Sat.), also downtown. If you're a trivia buff, Jack's is the oldest legal saloon in Washington.

Epicureans will want to hightail it to the **(Sun Mountain Dining Room** (in Sun Mountain Resort, 509/996-2211 or 800/572-0493) just as the sun goes down. This is the best restaurant in the valley, with spectacular views and a superb menu that leans toward Northwest cuisine. Try the award-winning smoked duckling in plum sauce. Definitely make reservations for dinner here.

Mazama Store (50 Lost River Rd., Mazama, 509/996-2855, daily 7 A.M.–6 P.M.) is basically the place you're going to go to if you're in Mazama at lunch time. The deli serves sandwiches, salads, pastas, and espresso.

Information

Local information is available at several Winthrop locales. The downtown **Chamber of Commerce Information Station** (202 Hwy. 20, 509/996-2125 or 888/463-8469,

© ERICKA CHICKOWSKI

Mazama Store

www.winthropwashington.com, mid-Apr.–Sept. daily 10 A.M.–5 P.M., call for hours the rest of the year). The **Methow Valley Visitors Center** (49 Hwy. 20, 509/996-4000, mid-May–mid-Oct. daily 9 A.M.–5 P.M.) is near the can't-miss-it red barn just west of town. Get booklets on mountain biking, scenic drives, and day hikes here.

Getting There

The Methow Valley has no bus service of any kind, and there is no scheduled air service. The nearest commercial airport is in Wenatchee.

TWISP AND VICINITY

Most folks believe that the town was named after the sound made by yellow jacket wasps. If you spend a little time by the water in summer, you might get convinced yourself. Nearby mining, especially gold, put the town on the map in 1898. Of course, the mini–gold rush came and went, leaving the town to give a shot at ranching and farming. The land was good and the ranches thrived, but mother nature had quite a trial in store for the fledgling settlement. A devastating 1924 fire destroyed all but a few of the town's buildings, and a 1948 flood rampaged through, carrying away bridges and buildings, and a bitter freeze in 1968 wiped out local apple orchards.

Twisp rose above it all and today is still buzzing, skimming some of the spillover from nearby Winthrop, but also making do with ranching and logging. The town also has a couple of interesting antique shops, a beautiful B&B, a great brewpub, and several good restaurants.

Recreation

Twisp provides an open-air pool to cool off at its summer-only **Wagner Memorial Swimming Pool** (509/997-5441, $5 adults, $2.25 kids 7–17, free kids under 7) on the northeast edge of town.

To visit a working fire tower with mountain vistas in all directions, take the Alder Creek Road southwest from Twisp to Lookout Mountain. At the end of the road a trail leads 1.3 miles to **Lookout Mountain Lookout.**

Twisp River Road, west of town, provides access to the north side of the 145,667-acre **Lake Chelan-Sawtooth Wilderness,** with a dozen different paths taking off from the valley. A fine loop trip of approximately 15 miles begins just southwest of War Creek Campground on Forest Service Road 4420. The **Eagle Creek Trail** starts at an elevation of 3,000 feet and climbs steadily through Douglas fir forests and meadows, reaching 7,280-foot Eagle Pass after seven miles. Here it meets the **Summit Trail,** with connections to the Stehekin end of Lake Chelan or to other points in the wilderness. To continue the loop hike, follow it south a mile to **Oval Creek Trail.** This path leads back down to the trailhead, passing beautiful West Oval Lake on the way; a two-mile detour climbs to two additional cirque lakes.

Accommodations

Built in 1910, the **Methow Valley Inn B&B** (234 2nd E. Ave., 509/997-2253, www.methow valleyinn.com, $89–149 s or d) is a friendly and homey place, with seven guest rooms and a light healthy breakfast each morning. Four rooms have their own baths, three share a single bathroom. No pets, no kids, but the smart, thoughtful hosts will explain the Inn's "infamous" past. The cross-country skiing trails lead right from the inn.

Blue Spruce Motel (1321 E. Methow Valley Rd., 509/997-8852, $38 s or $45 d, $50 d with kitchenettes) is a no-frills kind of place ideal for the tired hunter or angler. **Idle-A-While Motel** (509/997-3222, $70–110 d motel-style room, $80–125 d cottages) in town is like a campus, with nice little cottages and motel rooms ringing the green. The Inn is dog-friendly, and offers tennis, a hot tub, and sauna.

CAMPING

There are a half dozen Forest Service campgrounds west of town along Twisp River Road. Closest is **War Creek Campground** (late May–early Sept., $8), 15 miles out. There are no hookups in this shady and private camp on the shore of the War Creek River. Pack out your own garbage. While War Creek is a little dicey for all but the smallest RVs, it's best to camp them at **River Bend RV Park** (19961 S.R. 20, two miles north of Twisp on Hwy. 20, 800/686-4498, www.riverbendrv.com, $33–36 full hookups).

Food

The tastiest restaurant in Twisp is 🍷 **Tappi** (201 S. Glover St., 509/997-3345, www.tappi twisp.com, 5:30–9:30 P.M. Fri.–Mon.), which offers smoky, flavorful dishes prepared in its wood-fired ovens, fresh salads, and a fantastic wine selection. Next door is the **Confluence Art Gallery,** which displays changing exhibits of local artists. **Hometown Pizza** (202 Methow Valley Hwy., 509/997-2100, 11:30 A.M.–8 P.M. Mon.–Tues. and Thurs.–Sat., closed Sun. and Wed.) cooks up pizza, calzones, and grinders.

Treat your nose and your taste buds to the smell and flavor of fresh breads and pastries at **Cinnamon Twisp Bakery** (116 N Glover St., 509/997-5030, 6 A.M.–3 P.M. daily summer, 6 A.M.–3 P.M. Mon.–Sat. winter), which bakes up pastries like the namesake Cinnamon Twisps, eclairs, breads and bagels, and toothsome lunchtime sandwiches.

The unofficial town hall in Twisp is inside **Twisp River Pub** (201 N. Methow Valley Hwy., 509/997-6822 or 888/220-3360, www.methowbrewing.com, 11:30 A.M.–8:30 P.M. Wed.–Thurs , 11:30 A.M.–9 P.M. Fri.–Sat., 10 A.M.–8:30 P.M. Sun.), a lively brewhouse that features fresh cookin' and local art and hosts live music on some weekends. If you don't sip a few of its mighty fine brews, at least indulge in one of the decadent homemade desserts. On Sunday, guests are treated to an extended brunch.

The **Glover Street Market** (124 N Glover St., 509/997-1320, 9 A.M.–6 P.M. Mon.–Sat.), where, by its sign's admission, it sells "Pretty Good Groceries." Don't let its false modesty fool you—its fresh and organic food is among the best in the Methow Valley. And it has a pharmacy.

Information

The **Twisp Visitor Information Center** (201 Hwy. 20 S., 509/997-2926, www.twispinfo.com, 8 A.M.–5 P.M. Mon.–Fri.) displays interesting historical school photos on its walls.

The Okanogan National Forest's **Methow Valley Ranger District office** (502 Glover St., 509/997-2131, www.fs.fed.us/r6/oka, 7:45 A.M.–4:30 P.M. Mon.–Fri.) is a good source for trail and camping information.

METHOW AND PATEROS

Scenic Drives

East of Twisp the highway splits; Highway 20 continues east to Okanogan and Omak, and Highway 153 turns south along the Methow River. Highway 20 offers a chance to cruise past old farms and ranches with aging wooden barns, horses grazing in the pastures, and hay piles draped with sky-blue tarps. The road then climbs into Ponderosa pine forests with openings of sage, before topping out in the western larch forests of Okanogan National Forest. These larch trees are especially pretty in the fall when the needles turn a vivid yellow. Near the summit of Loup Loup Pass is Loup Loup Ski Bowl.

Highway 153 is another gorgeous drive, with the cottonwood-lined Methow River bottom surrounded by ranches and rolling hills covered with sage and Ponderosa and lodgepole pines. It leads to the small towns of Methow and Pateros. Methow is the site of a few old buildings and a nice spot to float a raft. **Lightning Pine RV Park** (331 Burma Rd., Methow, 509/923-2572, www.lightningpine.com, $24 full hookups) has a swimming hole, and it will rent you tubes for floating down the river.

Pateros

Five miles south of Methow, at the junction of Highways 97 and 153, is Pateros, which provides access to Alta Lake State Park and Lake Pateros. The surrounding country is packed with fruit orchards and apple processing plants. For a taste, stop at **Rest Awhile Fruit Stand** (53 Hwy. 153, 509/923-2256, www.restawhile fruit.com, just north of town, 509/923-2256, summer daily 7 A.M.–7 P.M., spring and fall 7 A.M.–6 P.M.). It sells some of the most juicy, delicious produce in the whole range. Its apples, cherries, nectarines, plums, and many more are perfect, crop after crop.

Pateros itself consists of a few stores and a pretty waterfront park. It's a popular place to stop and fish or play in the reservoir. Be sure to look up into the hills above town to some of the state's most random public art. Thousands of colorful mosaic reflectors sparkle down from off two old water towers.

South to Chelan

Highway 97 south from Pateros is a busy thoroughfare paralleling the reservoir all the way to Chelan, 17 miles away. **Wells Dam** (seven miles south of Pateros, daily 8 A.M.–6 P.M.) has a viewpoint where you can park and look across the blue lake to the surrounding rocky, arid landscape of grass and sage. There is a rock near the viewpoint that is covered with ancient Native American pictographs, or rock paintings. Visitors are further treated with a viewable fish ladder and a salmon hatchery.

Festivals and Events

The popular and tasty **Apple Pie Jamboree** (253/720-0595 or 509/923-2760, http://paterosapj.com) hits Pateros the third weekend of July and includes a fishing derby, Jet-Ski races, a youth circus with acrobats in training, a quilt show, and several wandering magicians. But people really come for the big pie feed, featuring 500 volunteer-baked apple pies with homemade ice cream. The **Terry Troxel Memorial Regatta** (206/321-3383) takes place on the Columbia River in mid-August is another big attraction. These super-flat boats are often powered with recycled engines from military helicopters, and can rip through the waves at between 135 and 200 mph.

Sports and Recreation

Right in the town of Pateros is **Peninsula**

Park, a verdant green stretch along Lake Pateros. Here are picnic areas, swimming, water-skiing, RV parking, and showers. Sprinklers keep tent campers away.

Popular with the summer crowd is **Alta Lake State Park** (two miles southwest of Pateros off Hwy. 153, 509/923-2473, www.parks.wa.gov). Fish for rainbow trout, swim in the clear waters, or just enjoy the east-of-the-mountains sunshine. A mile-long trail takes you up 900 feet to a scenic plateau overlooking the Columbia River Valley. The campground has tent sites ($22) and RV hookups ($31), and is open April–October, plus weekends and holidays the rest of the year. Individual campsites are reservable April–October at 888/226-7688 or at https://secure.camis.com/WA. In winter, the park is a favorite of cross-country skiers and snowmobilers.

Accommodations

Lodging is available at modern **Lake Pateros Motor Inn** (115 S. Lake Shore Dr., 509/923-2203 or 800/444-1985, www.lakepaterosinn.com, $55 s or $102 d). The motel has an outdoor pool and dock on the Columbia River. It has storage available for boats or snowmobiles.

Two miles from Pateros, **Alta Lake Golf Resort** (140 Alta Lake Rd., 509/923-2359, $80–155 s or d) offers the nicest rooms around, many with kitchenettes. An outdoor pool is here, along with an 18-hole golf course.

Whistlin' Pine Ranch (off Hwy. 153 on the south end of Alta Lake, 509/923-2548, $112 d) is a popular resort for horseback riding and anglers. Tent sites are $22. Rustic cabins ($40 d) and tent cabins ($52 for four persons), deluxe cabins at $112, are also available, as well as RV camping ($30). The outfitter here will arrange horseback riding or hunting trips and lessons.

Chelan and Vicinity

Lake Chelan (sha-LAN) occupies a long, glacially carved valley on the eastern edge of the Cascades. The town of Chelan sits on the southeast shore of the lake; Manson is 7 miles northwest, and tiny Stehekin 55 miles away on the north shore. Stehekin is the only town on the Washington mainland that cannot be reached by road.

Lake Chelan is one of Washington's favorite summer playgrounds, offering resort accommodations, fine restaurants, water-skiing, swimming, and boating, but also delivering magnificent wilderness country just a boat ride away. Over the years the Chelan area has developed into a resort community that has managed to retain its small-town charm. It's still a genuine town with real orchardists, farmers, wilderness outfitters, and forest and park rangers standing in line with you in the grocery checkout line. Your children can meet and play with the children of residents and visitors from all over the world. Few other small towns in Washington have such a wide cross-section of people.

The vast majority of the Lake Chelan watershed is in public ownership and not open to major development. Much of the private land is given over to orchards, although developers have bought up some of this land for condos, resorts, and private homes—a change that doesn't sit well with everyone.

Climate

These statistics will tell you why Chelan is so popular in Puget Sound: only 24 days per year, on average, register temperatures below 32°F, and 33 days are above 90°F. The area sees rainfall on fewer than nine days in an average year, and only 31 days of the year generally get snow, sleet, or hail in excess of an inch. And while no official records are kept, it is sunny a rough estimate of 300 days per year.

Apple Land

Most visitors to Lake Chelan tend to think of it in terms of recreational opportunities, but in agricultural circles, the shores of the lake are much better known for the best apples in the world. Chelan apples are known for their excellent taste, long shelf life, and vivid colors.

Nobody is quite sure why Chelan apples are so much better than those grown only a few miles away. The rich soil, glacier-fed waters, mild climate, cold irrigation water, or any combination of the above are all possible suspects. Scattered among the apple orchards are smaller plots of cherries, pears, apricots, and peaches.

SIGHTS
◖ Lake Chelan

On the north shore of Lake Chelan, drive the 12-mile scenic loop from downtown Manson along the shore of Lake Chelan, up into apple orchards, and past smaller lakes in the foothills, with striking views all along the way. From Manson, drive west on Lakeshore Drive and Summit Boulevard, north on Loop Avenue and Manson Boulevard, east on Wapato Lake Road, then south on the Chelan-Manson Highway back to Manson.

Another scenic drive is on the south shore

LAKE CHELAN BY THE NUMBERS

The crystal clear Lake Chelan is Washington's deepest and longest lake. Carved by Ice Age glaciers that slid down surrounding mountain peaks, this fingerlike lake is 55 miles long but seldom more than two miles wide. Motor to the middle and you're likely to find your anchor chain a bit short – at its deepest point Chelan plunges down 1,486 feet. The only two deeper lakes in America are Oregon's Crater Lake (1,962 feet) and California and Nevada's Lake Tahoe (1,645 feet).

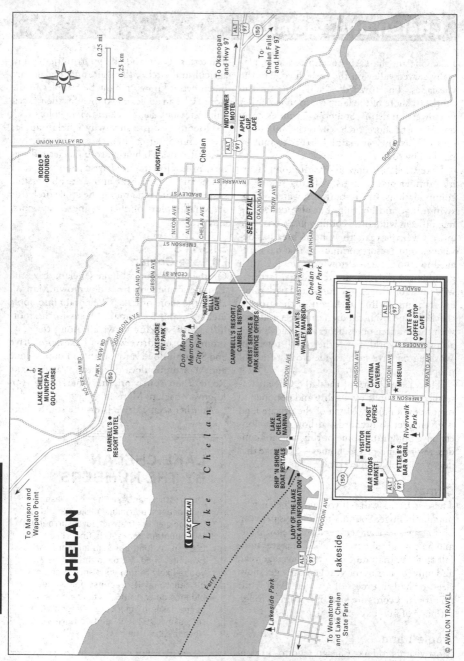

CHELAN

To Okanogan and Hwy 97

To Chelan Falls and Hwy 97

ALT 97 150

MIDTOWNER MOTEL

APPLE CUP CAFÉ

ALT 97

UNION VALLEY RD

RODEO GROUNDS

HOSPITAL

Chelan

NAVARRE ST

BRADLEY ST

DAM

GORGE RD

NIXON AVE

ALLAN AVE

CHELAN AVE

OKANOGAN AVE

TROW AVE

EMERSON ST

SEE DETAIL

HIGHLAND AVE

GIBSON AVE

CEDAR ST

FARNHAM

Chelan River Park

WEBSTER AVE

HUNGRY BELLY CAFÉ

LAKESHORE RV PARK

Don Morse Memorial City Park

CAMPBELL'S RESORT/ CAMBELL BISTRO

FOREST SERVICE & PARK SERVICE OFFICES

MARY KAY'S WHALEY MANSION B&B

WOODIN AVE

JOHNSON AVE

PARK VIEW RD

NO-SEE-UM RD

LAKE CHELAN MUNICIPAL GOLF COURSE

150

DARNELL'S RESORT MOTEL

L a k e   C h e l a n

LAKE CHELAN

LAKE CHELAN MARINA

SHIP 'N SHORE BOAT RENTALS

LADY OF THE LAKE DOCK AND INFORMATION

WOODIN AVE

ALT 97

To Manson and Wapato Point

Ferry

Lakeside Park

Lakeside

To Wenatchee and Lake Chelan State Park

0   0.25 mi

0   0.25 km

Detail inset:

BRADLEY ST

LIBRARY

ALT 97

LATTE DA COFFEE STOP CAFE

SANDERS ST

JOHNSON AVE

WOODIN AVE

WAPATO AVE

CANTINA CAVERNA

MUSEUM

EMERSON ST

VISITOR CENTER

POST OFFICE

Riverwalk Park

PETER B'S BAR & GRILL

BEAR FOODS MARKET

150

ALT 97

of the lake; follow Highway 97 to the **Chelan Butte Lookout** sign across the street from the Park Lake Motel. The road curves upward for seven miles, with pullouts for photos of the lake and surrounding hills, the Columbia River almost directly below, the wheat fields of eastern Washington, and acres of apple orchards. The 3,892-foot butte is also one of the state's best launching pads for hang gliders.

Stormy Mountain has views across Lake Chelan, into the North Cascades, and over into the arid wheat country. You reach it by driving up Lake Chelan's South Shore Road to its end at Twenty-Five Mile Creek State Park, then take Forest Service Road 2805 to its end at Windy Camp. The view here is wonderful; a half-mile hike to the summit of 7,198-foot Stormy Mountain is even better.

Downtown Chelan

The most interesting building in Chelan is **St. Andrew's Episcopal Church** (Woodin Avenue), a charming log structure completed in 1899. The architect remains in dispute, though there is evidence that it may have been Stanford White, the designer of New York's Madison Square Garden. A carillon rings out the hours daily. Also of interest downtown is the **Ruby Theater,** built in 1913. The blocky building is the oldest continually running movie theater in Washington and still has its horseshoe balcony and pressed tin roof. It has showings of three different movies at any given time.

State Parks

Two state parks provide camping and other attractions along the south shore of Lake Chelan. **Lake Chelan State Park** (360/902-8844, www.parks.wa.gov) is right on the lake, nine miles west of Chelan, with an underwater park, a boat launch, and concession stand. **Twenty-Five Mile Creek State Park** (20530 S Lakeshore Rd., 360/902-8844) has a swimming pool for campers and a boat launch.

Apple Tours

Trout Blue Chelan (509/682-2591, www.chelan valley.com) gives free tours of its huge apple warehouses and packing sheds on the road to Chelan Falls. Call ahead to schedule a tour (not offered during the hectic September–Octber harvest period). **Sunshine Fruit Market** (just west of town at the junction of Hwy. 97A and South Lakeshore, 509/682-5695) has a roadside fruit stand open every day during daylight hours in the summer.

ENTERTAINMENT AND EVENTS

Located on land owned by the Colville Tribe and staffed in part by workers who commute all the way from the reservation, **Mill Bay Casino** (455 Wapato Lake Rd., 509/687-6911 or 800/648-2946, www.millbaycasino.com) is a mile southeast of Manson. The little casino presents slot machines, craps, blackjack, roulette, pai gow, and poker.

The year begins with January's **Lake Chelan Winterfest** (800/424-3526) featuring sleigh rides, a cross-country ski race, snow-sculpting contest, talented ice carvers, snowmobile events, Christmas tree bonfire, ski lessons, belly-warming Soupfest, wine walks, magic, and lots of live music. Arts and crafts, a carnival, live music, and food fill the streets on the fourth weekend of June, for the annual **Taste of Chelan Street Fair.** See a popular PRCA rodeo and watch the crowning of the rodeo queen at **Lake Chelan Western Days,** the fourth weekend in July.

The nine-day **Lake Chelan Bach Fest** comes to town each July with concerts in the Performing Arts Center, local churches, and parks. The music ranges from chamber music to requiem masses all the way to selections from classic Broadway musicals.

Neighboring Manson's **Apple Blossom Festival** (509/888-5253) is held the second weekend in May in Manson, with a parade, car shows, and a chicken-noodle dinner at the American Legion Hall. The festival has been going on since just after WWI. The third weekend of May brings a **Chinook Salmon Derby,** with $5,000 for the biggest fish. Manson's **Fourth of July** brings fireworks,

NORTH CASCADES

an arts and crafts fair, a spare-rib barbecue, and a watermelon-seed-spitting contest.

If you like wine, but find traditional wine tours a bit pretentious, strap in, shut up, and get ready for your **Winery Assault Vehicle Excursion** (Chelan Valley Tours, 509/682-2386), or WAVE. One hundred eighty-five dollars gets you and up to eight friends a tour of four or five wineries of your choice. You'll be traveling in style in the backseat of a vintage olive-drab Swiss Pinzgauer military utility vehicle. Snobs need not apply. Chelan Valley Tours also leads several different off-road backcountry trips throughout the season.

SHOPPING

Chelan and Manson have a number of interesting specialty shops. **The Harvest Tree** (109 E. Woodin Ave., 509/682-3618) is what folks out here think of when they hear "Apple Store." It offers gift baskets of several varieties of apples, along with other local goods and produce.

The father-and-son operated **Main Street Gallery** (208 E. Woodin, Chelan, 509/682-9262, www.mainstreetgallerychelan.com) is a wide variety of oils, sculpture, glass, and even clothing. Its batik collection is the best in the area. For menswear ranging from the very formal to the very casual, visit **Company 107** (107 E Woodin Ave., 509/682-4311, www.chelanscompany107.com, 9:30 A.M.–6 P.M. Mon.–Sat., 11 A.M.–4 P.M. Sun.). It's the perfect place if you misjudged the weather at the time of your trip.

SPORTS AND RECREATION
Hiking

The entire Chelan Valley is user-friendly for walkers and runners because the heaviest vehicle traffic is limited to the main routes—Highway 97A, the Chelan-Manson Highway, and the south shore route. Several day hikes are available in the Twenty-Five Mile Creek area. For some face-to-face advice on choosing an area hike, visit the **Chelan Ranger Station** (428 W. Woodin Ave., 509/682-4900, 7:45 A.M.–4:30 P.M. Mon.–Fri.) run by the U.S. Forest Service.

If you're just out for a walk and want to enjoy the scenery, one of the nicest paths is at **Riverwalk Park.** It runs a mile along the Chelan River from the Woodin Avenue bridge to the next bridge downstream and just above the dam. The park has restrooms, a picnic area, and boat launch.

A steep but brief climb is up the cross-topped hill overlooking town, nearby apple orchards, and the lake. The path begins at the intersection of South Saunders Street and East Iowa Avenue.

Hang Gliding and Paragliding

Chelan has an international reputation as an excellent place to hang glide or paraglide. The best place for launching (or watching) is the summit of 3,892-foot **Chelan Butte,** where the hot winds blowing in from the Columbia River Basin give enormous lift. The flying is so good, in fact, that it isn't unusual for a hang glider to launch here and go nonstop to Spokane or into Idaho. Craft can also be launched to the west over the town and lake, with a choice of several landing sites along the lakeshore.

The local hang gliding and paragliding club is the **Chelan Flyers** (www.chelanflyers.com). While it doesn't offer tandem rides or lessons, it can provide you with recommendations for the best local instructors. Newcomers to the sport can get lessons from **Sky Brothers** (612/280-9850) in Chelan. Be advised that learning to fly takes several days, and even then, it's usually necessary to wait a bit until the weather is just right.

Golf

The **Lake Chelan Municipal Golf Course** (509/682-8026, $34–40) has one of the most beautiful settings of any course in the region, full of views of the lake and surrounding mountains. The 18-hole course rents clubs and offers affordable lessons. The destination **Desert Canyon Resort** (509/682-2697 or 800/258-4173, www.desertcanyon.com, $89) is about fourteen miles south of Chelan. This tough target-style course is well-maintained, carts have GPS, and a full pro-shop rents clubs.

Swimming

The lower end of **Lake Chelan** is lined with sandy beaches just right for swimming in the clean, cool waters. By late summer the water at the lower end of the lake is a bearable 70°F. Most public parks have popular swimming beaches, including Lake Chelan State Park, Chelan City Park, Manson Bay Park, Old Mill Park, Chelan Riverwalk Park, Chelan Falls Park, and Beebe Bridge Park.

Fishing

Lake Chelan is a very popular fishing spot, with world-record trout and solid salmon fisheries as well. Nearby, on the Columbia River and in mountain lakes, you will find smallmouth bass and rainbow, cutthroat, brown, and eastern brook trout, as well as other game fish. **Darrell and Dad's Family Guide Service** (231 Division St. in Manson, 509/966-8678, www.darrellanddads.com, $175 full day per adult, two-adult minimum) is a family-oriented outfit that will take you out to stalk trout and salmon and will even smoke your catch for an additional fee. Terry Allan of **Allan's Fishing Guide Service** (509/687-3084, $200 per adult for full day, $100 half day) is a bit of a local celebrity. The last two Washington state-record lake trout were caught aboard his boat. Maybe you'll be the next record-holder.

Boats and Personal Watercraft

Whatever kind of boating activity you like, you'll find it at Lake Chelan. You can bring your own craft or rent personal watercraft, sailboats, canoes, and water-ski boats from several local companies. For kayaks, paddle boards, and other human-powered boats, talk to the folks at **Lakerider Sports** (Don Morse Park in Chelan, 509/885-4767, www.lakeridersports.com). Mount a personal watercraft and make some noise on the water at **Jet Skis Ahoy** (Ship N' Shore Marina, 1230 W Woodlin Ave., 509/682-5125, www.jetskisahoy.com) which will get you set up with Yamaha Waverunners for $125 per half-day. **Chelan Parasail & Watercraft** (509/687-

7245) will give you an exciting parasail flight behind a speeding boat in the summer. For the ultimate experience on the lake, stop by **Sharkey's Watercraft Rental** (509/687-2312, www.lakechelan.com/sharkeys). It will rent you a 21-foot tower boat complete with skis and lifejackets. Wakeboards cost a little extra.

Play Centers and Parks

Water park **Slidewaters at Lake Chelan** (102 Waterslide Dr., 509/682-5751, www.slidewaters.com, Memorial Day–Labor Day daily 10 A.M.–7 P.M., $17 over 4 ft. tall, $14 under 4 ft.), one of Chelan's most popular places for children, is a short walk from the downtown area. Ten water slides overlook the town and lake, plus kiddie slides, a 60-person hot tub, swimming, inner tube ride, and video game arcade.

Lakeshore Bumper Boats in **Don Morse Memorial City Park** (Park Rd. and Nixon, 509/793-2126, Memorial Day–Labor Day daily 10 A.M.–10 P.M.) lets the kids take out some aggression aboard durable little boats. Paddleboats, miniature golf, and go-karts can also be found in Don Morse Park.

Cycling

The popularity of mountain biking has made the Lake Chelan area a particular favorite with bike riders. All sorts of scenic loop trips are possible, covering a wide diversity of terrain. Both highways that go up-lake from Chelan are popular, as are several roads with lighter traffic such as the Manson Loop, the Echo Ridge cross-country ski trails, and numerous Forest Service roads and trails open to mountain bikes. Check with the Chelan Ranger District for information and maps on roads and trails. The Forest Service road winding out past Twenty-Five Mile Creek Campground, up a steep mountainside, is a good workout, offering fantastic views out of the upper reaches of Lake Chelan. Trails can be found branching off into the mountains from this road, which eventually comes out again at Entiat. Get a whole day's ride out of hybrids ($50), beach cruisers ($35) or road bikes ($50) at **Lakerider Sports** (Don Morse Park,

509/885-4767, www.lakeridersports.com), which can also fix and tune a bike or even deliver your equipment right to your door.

Winter Sports

The Lake Chelan Valley is a heavily skied area. In Echo Valley, 12 miles northwest of Chelan, **Echo Valley Ski Area** (1700 Cooper Gulch Rd., 509/682-4002, www.echovalley.org, mid-Dec.–late Feb. Sat.–Sun. 10 A.M.–4 P.M., $20) has day and night downhill skiing on 3,000-foot Echo Mountain. Other facilities here include ice-skating and snowmobile trails. Get to Echo Valley aboard the free Link buses connecting Chelan with Manson; ski racks are on all the buses.

The **Echo Ridge** (trailhead parking on Cooper Gulch Rd., www.lakechelannordic.org, $5) is a project of the Lake Chelan Nordic Ski Club, which hosts 25 miles of groomed cross-country ski trails for every level of ability. Vistas from the summit are extraordinary, encompassing Lake Chelan, the Cascades, and the Columbia River Valley. These other Chelan-area Nordic ski trails include three miles of groomed runs at **Lake Chelan Golf Course** ($5), and another three miles of groomed trails plus plenty of backcountry touring at Stehekin. Get ski trail maps from the chamber of commerce.

Rent cross-country and downhill ski equipment from **Lake Chelan Sports** (137 E. Woodin Ave., 509/682-2629, www.lakechelansports.com, Mon.–Sat. 9 A.M.–6 P.M., Sun. 10 A.M.–4 P.M.).

Snowmobilers will enjoy the 125 miles of trails on both sides of Lake Chelan, accessible from three Sno-Parks. For information contact the Lake Chelan Ranger Station (509/682-2576).

Ice-skaters will find outdoor rinks at Don Morse Memorial Park in Chelan, Echo Valley Ski Area, and Roses, Wapato, and Dry Lakes in Manson.

ACCOMMODATIONS

Make midsummer reservations as early as possible; many of the rooms book up six months ahead of time for weekends in July and August. Winter rates are often 30 percent lower than the listed summer rates. In addition to the places listed here, the Chelan area has many private vacation homes available. The Lake Chelan Chamber of Commerce keeps a complete list and also keeps track of motel availability in the summer.

Under $100

Many people stay at **Holden Village B&B** (509/687-9695, www.holdenvillage.org, $45) en route to Holden Village. The Lady of the Lake stops at nearby Fields Point. This quiet little pit stop is 25 miles west of Chelan, with mountain and lake vistas. It has six guest rooms with shared baths, plus a small dormitory.

Midtowner Motel (721 E. Woodin Ave., 509/682-4051, www.midtowner.com, $85–119 s or d) features rooms with kitchenettes, plus an outdoor pool, hot tub, and sauna. **Mountain View Lodge** (25 Wapato Point Pkwy., Manson, 509/687-9505 or 800/967-8105, www.mountainviewlakechelan.com, $91–130 s or d) also offers an outdoor pool and hot tub. Kitchenettes are available.

$100–150

Wapato Point Village Inn (Wapato Point, Manson, 509/687-2500 or 800/771-5300, www.wpvillageinn.com, $115–125 s or d) has rooms with microwaves and fridges.

A true hidden gem, the **Well Made Bed and Breakfast** (324 W. Highland Ave., 509/670-4127, www.thewellmadebedandbreakfast.com, $100) has all of the cozy, romantic elegance of the B&B before most people even knew what B&B stood for. The rooms are beautifully designed and the omelette breakfast is hearty and delicious.

$150–200

Relax in old-timey splendor at the romantic **Mary Kay's Whaley Mansion B&B** (415 3rd St., 509/682-5735 or 800/729-2408, $155–165 s or d), an elegantly restored 1911 home. It has six guest rooms with private baths.

$200–250

Watson's Harverene Resort (7750 S.

Lake Chelan State Park is a popular camping spot.

a private beach, heated pool, hot tub, sauna, exercise room, lighted tennis courts, putting greens, rowboats, bicycles, moorage, and kids' play area. A four-night minimum is required in midsummer.

Camping

Right in town, the **City of Chelan Lakeshore RV Park** (509/682-8023, full hookups, $44) has both tent sites and RV spaces, along with showers, public swimming, and picnic areas. Rates are lower in the off-season.

Lake Chelan State Park (7544 S Lakeshore Rd, 509/687-3710 or 888/226-7688, www .parks.wa.gov, $22 tents, $31 full hookups, $7 extra reservation fee) is 12 miles up-lake from Chelan along the south shore and offers swimming, tent sites, and RV sites. The park is open daily April–October, and on weekends and holidays the rest of the year. This is the largest and most popular park in the area, with a swimming beach, boat ramp, docks, and summertime campfire programs.

Lakeshore Rd. #2, 10 miles west of Chelan, 509/687-3720 or 800/697-3720, www.watsons resort.com, $200–305 up to six) is made up of family-oriented beachfront cottages that share a private beach, outdoor pool, and hot tub.

Kelly's Resort (12800 South Lakeshore Rd., 509/687-3220, www.kellysresort.com, $210–225 s or d) is a friendly and quiet family resort 13 miles west of Chelan. Shoreside cottages have kitchens, fireplaces, boat moorage, and lake swimming. Choose between cottages in the woods or lakeside units.

Over $250

The longest-running and best resort on Lake Chelan, **Campbell's Resort** (104 W. Woodin Ave., 509/682-2561 or 800/553-8225, www.campbellsresort.com, $210–330 s or d, $320–450 suites) is right in town and offers 150 rooms, plus two pools, hot tubs, boat moorage, and a 1,200-foot sandy beach.

Darnell's Resort Motel (901 Spader Bay Rd., 509/682-2015 or 800/967-8149, http:// darnellsresort.com, $210–446 for up to four) features luxury family accommodations with

The pleasant, wooded **Twenty-Five Mile Creek State Park** (20530 S Lakeshore Rd., 509/687-3610 or 888/226-7688, www .parks.wa.gov, open May–Sept., $22 tents, $31 full hookups, $7 extra reservation fee) is 22 miles west of Chelan at the end of S. Lakeshore Drive, and 10 miles beyond Lake Chelan State Park. It's a favorite place for boaters who use the launch ramp here and purchase supplies at the marina store. It's also a good overnight spot for those about to catch the morning *Lady of the Lake* boat ride from Fields Point.

Tiny **Daroga State Park** (509/664-6381, www.parks.wa.gov, open late Mar.–late Oct., $22 primitive sites, $31 full hookups) is 22 miles southeast of Chelan on the east bank of the Columbia River and just off Highway 97. Be ready for towering high-voltage power lines right next to the campground.

The shore of Lake Chelan is dotted with 14 boat-in campgrounds, accessible by private boat or from the *Lady of the Lake II*. Check with the Forest Service Ranger Station (428 W. Woodin, 509/682-2576, 7:45 A.M.–4:30 P.M. Mon.–Fri. year-round, plus 7:45 A.M.–4:30 P.M.

NORTH CASCADES

Sat.–Sun. late June–early Sept.) for specifics. Several other campgrounds are on the road system, including Antilon Lake Campground, north of Manson.

Beebe Bridge Park (509/663-8121, mid-Apr.–Oct., $28) is a large park along the Columbia River across from the town of Chelan Falls. It has tent and RV sites along with showers, a swimming area, play fields, and a dump station.

FOOD

Chelan has a large number of restaurants from which to choose. They tend to change quite frequently, and new owners or chefs can dramatically improve (or worsen) the reputation, so ask around to see what's hot, or simply take a look inside to see if it looks interesting.

Cafés and Diners

❰ **Apple Cup Café** (804 E. Woodin Ave., 509/682-2933, 6 A.M.–9 P.M. Mon.–Thurs., 6 A.M.–10 P.M. Fri.–Sun., 6 A.M.–9 P.M. Sun.) is a family-type place with very good breakfasts and great cheese blintzes in a lunch-counter-like setting. Head to **Latte Da Coffee Stop Café** (303 E. Wapato Ave., 509/682-4196, 6:30 A.M.–6 P.M. Sun.–Thurs., 6:30 A.M.–6 P.M. Fri.–Sat.) for the best local espressos, plus light breakfasts and lunches in a cozy atmosphere.

For some solid Mexican food served up by a family from Jalisco, check out **Cantina Caverna** downtown (114 N. Emerson, 509/682-5553, daily 11 A.M.–2 P.M. and 5–8:30 P.M.). Try the *enchiladas cangrejo,* done with Dungeness crab, or for more standard fare, a heaping plate of nachos or a burrito.

Steak and Seafood

Peter B's Bar & Grill (116 E. Woodin Ave., 509/682-1031, daily 10:30 A.M.–9 P.M.) sits right along the Chelan River, with a diverse menu of steaks, burgers, pastas, chicken, and seafood. Good food, reasonable prices, and a busy, convivial atmosphere.

❰ **The Campbell Bistro** (104 W. Woodin Ave., 509/682-2561, reservations required) in Campbell's Resort is the old standby, offering elegant dining and a continental menu full of interesting salmon, duck, and beef options. Prices are moderate to expensive. The patio is popular on summer evenings.

Markets

Bear Foods Market (125 E. Woodin Ave., 509/682-5535, Mon.–Sat. 10 A.M.–4 P.M., closed Sun.) is a spacious natural-foods store with a big selection of organic produce and other goods.

The **Chelan Farmers Market** (Emerson St. between River Walk Park and River Walk Inn Hotel) comes to town June–mid-October 4–7 P.M. Thursdays. Manson also has a **farmers market,** held Saturday mornings during the summer and early fall at the Manson Grange.

INFORMATION

For maps or other information, contact the **Lake Chelan Chamber of Commerce** (102 E. Johnson, 509/682-3503 or 800/424-3526, www.lakechelan.com, 9 A.M.–5 P.M. Mon.–Sat., 10 A.M.–3 P.M. Sun.).

The combined Forest Service/National Park Service **Chelan Ranger District Office** (428 W. Woodin, 509/682-2576, 7:45 A.M.–4:30 P.M. Mon.–Sat. summer, 7:45 A.M.–4:30 P.M. Mon.–Fri. Labor Day-Memorial Day.) dispenses information on all forms of outdoor recreation, including many places to camp, picnic, or just have a look around.

GETTING THERE AND AROUND
By Bus

Link (509/662-1155 or 800/851-5465, www.linktransit.com, Mon.–Fri., $1.25 to Wenatchee, $2.50 to Leavenworth) has bus routes covering Chelan and Douglas Counties, including the towns of Chelan, Manson, Wenatchee, and Leavenworth. You can put your skis on the bus in Chelan and ride to Wenatchee, then change to Route 40 and ski at Mission Ridge. Or put your bicycle on the special racks and ride anywhere one-way and pedal back.

No long distance bus service operates to

Chelan, but you can catch the Link bus to Wenatchee for connections to Northwest Trailways and Amtrak.

By Air

Chelan Seaplanes (509/682-5555, www .chelanairways.com) offers daily seaplane service to Stehekin, Domke Lake, and other up-lake destinations, plus sightseeing flights over Lake Chelan and Stehekin Valley. The nearest airport with air service to larger cities is in Wenatchee.

◖ STEHEKIN

Stehekin (ste-HEE-kin) sits at the northwest end of Lake Chelan and can be reached only by boat, floatplane, or foot; thousands of visitors take the boat trip up-lake from Chelan for lunch or an overnight stay at one of Stehekin's resorts. The town is also a launching point for treks into the heart of North Cascades National Park, or beyond into Lake Chelan-Sawtooth Wilderness and Glacier Peak Wilderness.

© ERICKA CHICKOWSKI

dockside at Stehekin

The name Stehekin, a Native American term meaning "the way through," fits this mountain gateway well. The town began in the late 1880s when prospectors came here in search of gold and silver. They found the minerals, but not in sufficient quantity to establish a large mine, and Stehekin has never been connected to the outside world by road. Today it is home to fewer than 100 permanent residents but has all the basics, including a post office, grocery store, restaurant, and grade school. A summer-only outdoor supply shop and bakery are also in town.

Holden Village

Like Stehekin, the old copper and gold mining town of Holden is off the main road system. The *Lady of the Lake II* stops at Lucerne, and a bus takes you 12 miles uphill to Holden (509/687-3644, www.holdenvillage.org, $30 per person). The mine closed in 1957, but the historic buildings remain, now run as a friendly Lutheran retreat that is especially popular with families. There are classes of all sorts, plus sessions on theology, the environment, and interpersonal issues. It's a spectacular mountain-rimmed setting, and many fine trails surround Holden, becoming ski trails in winter. You don't have to be religious or a member of any church to stay here. Guests stay in simple but comfortable lodges, and three healthy meals are included in the rate. A sauna, hot tub, pool room, bowling alley, and snack bar are also in the village. The Lake Chelan Boat Company's vessels stop here daily.

Sports and Recreation

The center for outdoor recreation options is the **Courtney Log Office** (150 yards past the post office along the lake). Here you can set up wagon and horseback rides, as well as week-long guided hikes, through **Stehekin Outfitters** (509/682-7742, www.courtney country.com).

Book an easy raft trip down the Stehekin River through **Stehekin Valley Ranch** (800/536-0745, $50 adults, $40 kids, $10 reservation fee), or rent mountain bikes from

Discovery Bikes (509/686-3014, www.stehekin discoverybikes.com, $4 per hour, $20 daily). Discovery also offers a guided ranch breakfast ride each morning ($30).

HIKING
The Stehekin area is a favorite of hikers of all levels—trails wander in all directions. The National Park Service shuttle buses make it easy to get to the trailheads or back to Stehekin. Keep your eyes open when you walk, since the area has a fair number of rattlesnakes.

A short 0.75-mile loop hike—the **Imus Creek Nature Trail**—begins behind the visitors center and climbs a nearby hill overlooking the lake. Spectacular **Rainbow Falls**—a towering cataract of water that plummets 312 feet—is just off the road amid tall western red cedar trees. Get there by walking (or catching the shuttle) 3.5 miles up the road.

Take the shuttle to High Bridge for a beautiful day hike to **Coon Lake.** The 1.2-mile trail leads uphill to this scenic lake, with excellent views of Agnes Mountain and good bird-watching. Those with more energy can continue another seven miles to the 8,122-foot summit of **McGregor Mountain,** a tortuous climb up countless switchbacks.

One of the most rewarding and family-friendly backpacking hikes to Stehekin takes a bit of advance planning. The **Lakeshore Trail** sidles along the northeast shore of the lake for some amazing views of the pristine water from piney forests and bluffs. Get *Lady of the Lake II* to drop you off 17 miles southeast of Stehekin at Prince Creek Campground and plan at least an overnight hike to get back to Stehekin.

Prince Creek Campground is a great departure point for a fine day hike up **Prince Creek Trail.** The route switchbacks through pine forests and then follows the creek into the high country around Cub Lake (a good place to camp). You'll discover dramatic vistas of the high Cascades from here. The Prince Creek Trail can also be used as part of a 38-mile loop trip that leaves Prince Creek Campground, climbs to the **Summit Trail,** and follows it along the ridge before dropping down to

Stehekin. This hike features lots of ups and downs through forests and alpine meadows, and striking views of surrounding mountains. Much of the Summit Trail passes through the **Lake Chelan-Sawtooth Wilderness** with side trails leading north into the Twisp River drainage.

Additional boat-accessible hikes start from Holden Village, providing access to the Glacier Peak Wilderness. One of the most popular is the **Hart/Lyman Lakes Trail** (No. 1256). From Holden it follows Railroad Creek for 3.5 miles to Hart Lake before switchbacking up to Crown Point Falls and Lyman Lake and on to Cloudy Pass (10.5 miles), where it meets the Pacific Crest Trail. This trail gets a lot of use in midsummer, so don't expect solitude, and bears can be a problem in campsites along Railroad Creek. Showers and campsites are available in Holden Village.

Accommodations
Stehekin is a wonderful place to relax and enjoy the wilderness splendor without interference from TVs or phones. As with all places in the Lake Chelan area, advance reservations are a must in the summer. **Stehekin Landing Resort** (509/682-4494, www.stehekinlanding .com, $139–185 s or d) has lodge rooms and housekeeping units. Amenities include a restaurant, bar, bike and boat rentals, a marina, gas, and groceries. During the winter, the Park Service and the resort jointly maintain 19 kilometers of free **cross-country ski trails.** Rent skis in Chelan or bring your own. The resort has snowshoes for rent.

At **Stehekin Valley Ranch** (509/682-4677 or 800/536-0745, http://stehekinvalley-ranch.com, open mid-June–early Oct., $85–95 per person), nine miles up from Stehekin, your lodging, three hearty meals, and local transportation are included in the price of your cabin. Most are primitive tent cabins with no running water or electricity, and kerosene lamps for light. Showers are nearby. They also have several nicer cabins with private baths.

Several other Stehekin-area houses and cabins are also available for rent by the day or week.

These include **Silver Bay Inn at Stehekin** (509/682-2212 or 800/555-7781, www.silver bayinn.com, $145–299), **Stehekin Log Cabin** (509/682-7742, www.courtneycountry.com, $150–200), and **Flick Creek House** (888/841-3556, www.stehekinvalley.com, $600), which runs off of private hydro power and is secluded enough to have two bathtubs on an open-air balcony.

CAMPING

Purple Point Campground is just a third of a mile from the boat landing in Stehekin. Campers can also ride the shuttle bus from Stehekin to **Harlequin, Bullion, High Bridge, Tumwater, Dolly Varden, Shady, Bridge Creek, Park Creek,** and **Flat Creek** campgrounds along the Stehekin River. **Weaver Point Campground** is a very popular boat access campground at the north end of the lake across from Stehekin. The old Weaver homestead here was the site where *The Courage of Lassie* was filmed in 1944, starring none other than Elizabeth Taylor (and Lassie, of course). All of these campgrounds are free; obtain a camping permit at Golden West Lodge Information Center. All boat-access campgrounds on Lake Chelan do not require a camping permit but do require a dock site pass ($5 per day or $40 for a season pass).

Food

Stehekin Valley Ranch Restaurant (509/682-4677, June–Sept.) serves a menu that includes steaks, burgers, salad bar, and homemade desserts—all of which will taste pretty good after a week of backcountry travel or a long day in the saddle. Reservations are required unless you're staying at the ranch. The restaurant is nine miles up the valley from Stehekin, but free transportation is provided. Two miles up from the boat dock is **Stehekin Pastry Company** (509/682-7742, open summers only), which offers delicious baked goods, ice cream, breakfasts, and espresso.

Information and Services

The National Park Service–run **Golden West**

Visitor Center (360/856-7365, ext. 14, www.nps.gov/noca, year-round Mon.–Fri. 8 A.M.–4:30 P.M., mid-May–mid-Sept. daily 8:30 A.M.–5 P.M.) in Stehekin is the place to go for information on hiking and camping in the area. Talks and evening programs are offered during the summer.

Nearby are **The House That Jack Built**, selling locally made crafts, and **McGregor Mountain Outdoor Supply**. The only public phone in the Stehekin area is next to the coin-operated laundry and shower facility, 200 yards up-lake from the Stehekin landing.

Getting There

A longtime favorite of visitors to Lake Chelan is the 55-mile voyage from Chelan or Manson to Stehekin. **Lake Chelan Boat Company** (1319 W. Woodin Ave., 509/682-2224 or 888/682-4584, www.ladyofthelake.com) has been operating boats along this route for more than 65 years and runs two vessels: the 350-passenger *Lady of the Lake II* ($39), which takes four hours to reach Stehekin, and the 65-foot-long *Lady Express* ($59), which gets there in two hours. Food is available on both boats, and onboard Forest Service interpreters give talks on the human and natural history of the area. Only the *Lady Express* operates November–April, and there is no winter boat service on Tuesday and Thursday.

In addition to Chelan and Manson, the boats stop at Field's Point (accessible by car along the south shore), Lucerne (with access to Holden), and Stehekin. The *Lady II* also makes flag stops at any Forest Service campsite upon request during the summer season. Service changes through the year; pick up a copy of the schedule at visitors centers or from the Lake Chelan Boat Company at the southwest end of Chelan. A separate service provides weekly barge trips up the lake carrying vehicles, fuel, groceries, and supplies to Stehekin. Mix and match the boat schedules for day trips to Stehekin. You can also carry bikes, canoes, or kayaks aboard the boats for an extra charge.

Chelan Seaplanes (509/682-5555, www .chelanairways.com) offers daily seaplane

NORTH CASCADES

service to Stehekin and flightseeing over the Stehekin Valley. You may wish to fly one-way and take a boat in the other direction.

Getting Around
The National Park Service and Stehekin Adventure Company combine to offer daily van or bus transportation from the dock at Stehekin to Flat Creek, 20 miles into the mountains. This service is offered from late May through mid-October and costs $5 one-way to High Bridge, or $12 one-way to Flat Creek. Both buses carry backpacks, and the Stehekin Adventure bus also carries bikes. Contact the Park Service's Golden West Visitor Center in Stehekin for details or reservations (360/856-7365 ext. 14, www.nps.gov/noca, year-round Mon.–Fri.

8 A.M.–4:30 P.M., mid-May–mid-Sept. daily 8:30 A.M.–5 P.M.) or stop by its visitors centers in Stehekin or Chelan. Reservations are not needed for the larger Stehekin Adventures buses. Passengers on both services are given a narrated tour along the way, and you can get on or off at any point along the route.

In the summer, **Stehekin Landing Resort** (509/682-4494) offers daily trips to Rainbow Falls. Its bus meets the *Lady Express* and *Lady of the Lake II* boats when they arrive in Stehekin and provides a narrated 45-minute tour ($7). They also offer bus tours ($20) that include a picnic lunch at High Bridge and a visit to Rainbow Falls and Buckner Orchard, home to the oldest strain of Common Delicious apples in the United States.

Cashmere

Tucked between Wenatchee and Leavenworth, tiny Cashmere (pop. 3,000) has long featured a Colonial American theme on its buildings. Highway 2 between Leavenworth and Cashmere is lined with fruit orchards that grow the best D'Anjou pears in America. Fruit stands sell fresh apples, pears, cherries, apricots, peaches, plums, and berries in season. Because of this fruit production, Cashmere was a logical place to establish a business that produces a confection made from fruit juice, walnuts, and powdered sugar—the treats known as Aplets and Cotlets.

SIGHTS
Candy Town
If you have a sweet tooth, be certain to stop at **Liberty Orchards** (117 Mission St., 509/782-2191, www.libertyorchards.com, Apr.–Dec. Mon.–Fri. 8 A.M.–5:30 P.M., Sat.–Sun. 10 A.M.–4 P.M., Jan.–Mar. Mon.–Fri. 8:30 A.M.–4:30 P.M.), the home of Aplets and Cotlets. These all-natural confections are made of fruit juices and walnuts and are coated with powdered sugar. Tours take 15 minutes or so and end back in the gift shop, where you can

sample a number of different candies and purchase gift boxes.

Chelan County Historic Museum and Pioneer Village
The Chelan County Historical Museum (600 Cotlets Ave., 509/782-3230, www.cashmere museum.org, Tues 10:30 A.M.–4:30 P.M. daily, summer, closed Nov.–March, $5.50 adults, $4.50 seniors $4 students, $3 ages 6–12) has moved and restored 20 of the oldest buildings from the early days of Cashmere and assembled them on a green. Pioneer town necessities like the saloon, the jail, and a mine portal are available to tour. The museum houses Native American baskets, carvings, and beaded clothing, along with natural history and pioneer exhibits.

FESTIVALS AND EVENTS
Cashmere is home to the **Chelan County Fair,** held the second week in September, highlighted by rodeos, musical entertainment, a carnival, the region's top magicians, and exhibits. The first weekend in October brings **Cashmere Apple Days** (509/782-3513) at

© ERICKA CHICKOWSKI

downtown Cashmere

the Pioneer Village. Costumed re-enactors lead the fun, including rides in horse-drawn wagons, exciting mock Wild West shoot-outs, an apple pie–baking contest, music, and dogs impressing the crowd pulling heavy weighted sleds.

ACCOMMODATIONS

Cashmere has two comfortable places to lay your head. **La Toscana Bed and Breakfast** (9020 Foster Rd., 509/548-5448, $110 s or d), between Cashmere and Peshastin, offers elegantly decorated rooms in a lodge on the grounds of a small winery. On a less grand scale, **Village Inn Motel** (229 Cottage Ave., 509/782-3522 or 800/793-3522, www.cash merevillageinn.com, $59 s, $99 d) offers humble motel rooms in its two-story roadside property.

Camping

No tent sites, but plenty of RV spaces ($30 with full hookups, $24 with water and electricity only) with showers are available at **Wenatchee River County Park** (just west of town, 509/662-2525, open Apr.–late Oct.). The park has free Wi-Fi and a sand volleyball court. No reservations are accepted.

FOOD

Far from being a one-trick pony, **Brian's Bulldog Pizza** (107 Cottage Ave., 509/782-1505, www.briansbulldogpizza.com, 11 A.M.–10 P.M. daily) has lots going for it, including a baked potato bar, lasagna, and other goodies to go along with the pizza. Follow your nose to tasty baked goods just down the street at **Sure to Rise Bakery** (115 Cottage Ave., 509/782-2424, Tues.–Sat. 7:30 A.M.–6 P.M., closed Mon.).

GETTING THERE AND AROUND

Catch an inexpensive **Link bus** (800/851-5465, www.linktransit.com, $1.25-2.50) for connections from Cashmere to other parts of Chelan and Douglas Counties, including Leavenworth, Wenatchee, and Lake Chelan.

NORTH CASCADES

Leavenworth

This fanciful Bavarian village, complete with authentic architecture, hand-carved benches, and flower-bedecked streets, female clerks in Bavarian dirndl dresses and waiters in lederhosen, all backdropped by peaks of the Cascades is a natural draw for visitors. People come from all over the country to see the spectacle—so many that the little town has built up 100 lodgings and dozens of restaurants and shops.

History

At one time or another, Leavenworth experimented with every frontier industry out there. Hudson's Bay Company fur traders passed through in the early-19th-century summers, the railroad came teasingly close at the turn of the 20th century, and it took its turn with lumber and farming. But by the 1960s, it was clear that Leavenworth needed to something bold if it was to avoid economic oblivion. City leaders took a look at the impressive mountain backdrop and decided that they'd take a shot at something crazy—remaking the town into an authentic German alpine village. The

renovation gained worldwide attention for the attention to detail, aggressive promotion, and bootstrap efforts. The transformation was hugely successful, turning a struggling town into a daring lesson in community improvement.

SIGHTS
◖ The Bavarian Village

Start your tour of the Bavarian Village in the heart of town, on Front Street. Shops, restaurants, taverns, and hotels are side by side, all beautifully decorated with carved wood, flower boxes, and murals.

Front Street Park (sandwiched between Hwy. 2 and the shops of Front St.) is a relaxing, sunny spot to relax and read a book, or take a break in the central gazebo. It's also the place to see street dances, art exhibits, and other public events, or to stop at the public restrooms. Across Highway 2 is the Chamber of Commerce Visitor Center, and the city hall/library building.

Waterfront Park (8th St. and Commercial

the Bavarian-themed town of Leavenworth

© ERICKA CHICKOWSKI

St.) on the cottonwood-shaded banks of the Wenatchee River, has walkways over and around the river, benches for a respite from shopping, and views of the peaks surrounding Icicle Canyon. You can cross-country ski from here to the golf course during the winter.

Leavenworth National Fish Hatchery

The Leavenworth National Fish Hatchery (two mi. out Icicle Rd., 509/548-7641, daily 8 A.M.–4 P.M.) cranks out some 2.5 million salmon each year. Stop by to watch the steelhead trout and chinook salmon in the raceways (favorite spots for dive-bombing belted kingfishers), or step inside to see displays and educational videos. The real attraction here is an "outdoor aquarium" where you can watch rainbow trout in the eye-level concrete "stream."

Blewett Pass

Highway 97 heads south from the Leavenworth area, connecting Highway 2 with I-90. The road climbs 21 miles to 4,102-foot Blewett Pass, a popular area for hiking, skiing, and snowmobiling. **Blewett Pass Interpretive Trail** offers a three-mile loop through high-country forests. Several nearby Forest Service campgrounds such as Swauk and Mineral Springs have campsites for $12 or less. For more adventure, take the slightly shorter but significantly steeper and more serpentine old highway over Blewett Pass.

The **Swauk Forest Discovery Trail** is an easy three-mile path at the summit of Swauk/Blewett Pass. The trail passes through both old-growth forests and clear-cuts, and educational signs are scattered along the way.

Blue Creek Road (Forest Service Road 9738) leads from the Mineral Springs area west approximately seven miles to an old fire lookout on Red Top Mountain, providing vistas in all directions. This is a popular area to search for blue agates and geodes.

Also nearby is **Mineral Springs Resort** (509/857-2361, $10 with electric hookups, $8 without), which has RV spaces and good meals. Come winter, this area is popular with snow-mobilers and cross-country skiers. Sno-Parks at Swauk Campground and Pipe Creek provide skier-only access to many miles of cross-country trails. For details, contact the Forest Service's Cle Elum Ranger Station (509/852-1100).

ENTERTAINMENT AND EVENTS
The Arts

Leavenworth's **Icicle Creek Center for the Arts** has a series of diverse musical perfor-mances, including jazz, chamber music, blue-grass, symphonies, and string quartets. These are held at Canyon Wren Recital Hall (7409 Icicle Rd., 509/548-6347 or 800/574-2123, www.icicle.org).

The **Leavenworth Summer Theater** (509/548-2000, www.leavenworthsummer theater.org) presents very popular all-ages mu-sical productions of such classics as *The Sound of Music, Carousel,* and *Heidi* at the Ski Hill outdoor stage.

On a less stuffy level, accordion-playing mu-sicians and polka-dancin' fools can be found weekend evenings at **Andreas Keller** (829 Front St., downstairs, 509/548-6000) and **King Ludwig's Restaurant** (921 Front St., 509/548-6625).

Festivals and Events

Leavenworth always finds something to cel-ebrate—festivals and fairs fill the calendar. Contact the chamber of commerce (509/548-5807) for more information. January brings **Bavarian Ice Festival** and its snowshoe and cross-country ski races, dogsled pulls, a tug of war, and fireworks in midmonth. Smaller festi-vals fill the months until the big **Maifest**, held on Mother's Day weekend, when costumed Bavarian dancers circle the Maypole, strutting Bernese Mountain Dogs, and concerts, a parade, and Saturday night street dance are accompa-nied by oompah music from the bandstand and the chiming of bells from the Marlin Handbell

Ringers. Maifest also marks the start of **Village Art in the Park,** featuring area artists every weekend May–October in Front Street Park.

July's **Kinderfest** brings entertainment for children including face painting, a petting zoo, bike parade, and German *magie.* **Leavenworth International Accordion Celebration** in early August brings performances by top musicians, workshops, and competitions. The **Washington State Autumn Leaf Festival** is Leavenworth's longest-running festival and takes place the last weekend of September and the first weekend of October, with a grand parade featuring doz-ens of marching bands. It also includes polka music, street dances, a pumpkin pie–eating contest, clowns, and a pretzel-tossing contest. It would take quite the fool to forget about **Octoberfest** in this little Bavarian village. Covering three weekends, the festival features music, beer, dancing, beer, family activities, and beer. Also noteworthy is the beer.

Christmas is Leavenworth's most festive hol-iday. The **Christmas Lighting Festival** is held the first and second Saturday in December, when all the Christmas lights go on simulta-neously at dusk and Mr. and Mrs. Claus ap-pear in their house in the park. Caroling, sleigh rides, concerts, and food booths add to the hol-iday festivities. The lights stay lit till February, so there's no need to hurry to see them.

SHOPPING

Front Street in Leavenworth is all about shop-ping. Here, you'll find several delightful choc-olate makers, German-themed ornaments, steins, and gifts, and a surprising variety of hats, clothing, books, and music. You'll be surprised at the variety beyond Bavarian gifts. There are culinary stores without a hint of weisswurst and a pet shop utterly bereft of dog-gie lederhosen. **A Matter of Taste** (647 Front St., 509/548-6949 or 800/497-3995, www .amatteroftasteinc.com, 9 A.M.–9 P.M. daily) lets you savor all sorts of unusual culinary treats like sassafras tea coffee jelly and BBQ sauce that comes with a little cowboy hat on the bottle. It also carries humorous gifts. Tromp up the stairs to wander through **Jubilee Global**

Gifts (723 Front St., 509/548-3508, daily 10 A.M.–5 P.M.) with handmade gifts from Africa, Asia, and South and Central America. Much of its profit goes to support charities that help alleviate poverty world-wide.

A few doors down (and past the Danish Bakery, if you can make it beyond the luscious pastries without being enticed inside) is **Nussknacker Haus** (735 Front St., 509/548-4708, www.nussknackerhaus.com, daily 9:30 A.M.–5:30 P.M.), showcasing imported collectibles and hundreds of German nutcrackers for sale. For an even more impressive collection, head upstairs to the **Nutcracker Museum** (735 Front St., 509/548-4708 or 800/892-3989, 2–5 P.M. daily May–Oct., weekends the rest of the year, $2.50 adults, $1 ages 5–16), with a greater variety of styles and designs than you'd ever dreamt possible. It's enough to drive Tchaikovsky nuts.

Next comes **Der Market Platz** (801 Front St., 509/548-7422, daily 9:30 A.M.–6 P.M.), which has an extraordinary stein collection, European crystal, Hummel figurines, and even Bavarian polka CDs. Continue down the block and down the basement stairs to **Die Musik Box** (933 Front St., 800/288-5883, www.musicboxshop.com), where 5,000 intricate music boxes from around the globe create a chorus of whimsical sounds.

SPORTS AND RECREATION
State Parks
Lake Wenatchee State Park (23 mi. north on Hwy. 207, www.parks.wa.gov, $17 no hookups) boasts 12,000 feet of waterfront, set against a backdrop of majestic snow-covered peaks. The fun is year-round with cross-country skiing in winter, plus swimming, fishing, and canoeing in summer. Horseback rides are available in summer from **Icicle Outfitters and Guides** (509/679-1703 or 800/497-3912).

Eight miles east of Leavenworth on Highway 2 is **Peshastin Pinnacles State Park,** where a series of sandstone spires jut out of an arid hillside, making for a rock-climbing mecca across 35 acres. Climbing difficulty generally ranges from 5.6–5.11, with many routes bolted. This is a great spot for beginners still learning how to lead climb with the use of bolts. Several spots make for good

bouldering. Nonclimbers can stop to photograph the dramatic pinnacles, walk the short trails, or watch the more adventurous folks.

Cross-Country Skiing
Leavenworth offers 16 miles of groomed trails within minutes of downtown. Three ski areas are maintained by the Leavenworth Winter Sports Club with both classical and skate-skiing lanes. The most accessible of these is **Waterfront Park,** just a block from downtown and covering almost two miles along the Wenatchee River. It's also the one place in the system where you can ski with your dog. These trails connect with the five-mile **Leavenworth Golf Course Trail. Icicle River Trail,** one mile from Leavenworth on Icicle Road, has five miles of level tracks at the mouth of Icicle Canyon, through meadows and forests above the fish hatchery. **Ski Hill Trail** has a three-mile track, with just over a mile lighted for night skiing (till 9 P.M.) that rolls over the hills adjacent to the downhill ski area. Here you get the added benefit of a lodge and weekend food service. Trail fees are $15 per day for adults, $10 ages 7–17, seniors over 70 and children under 6 free. For more information, contact the **Leavenworth Winter Sports Club** (509/548-5477, winter only, www.skileavenworth.com). Rent cross-country and skate skis at **Der Sportsmann** (837 Front St., 509/548-5623, www.dersportsmann.com, 9 A.M.–6 P.M. daily) or **Leavenworth Ski & Sports** (940 Hwy. 2, next to the Chevron station in the middle of town, 509/548-7864).

Lake Wenatchee State Park, 23 miles northwest of Leavenworth, has 10 kilometers of maintained free trails in the park and on surrounding land, but you'll need a Sno-Park permit (www.parks.wa.gov) to park here. Pick one up in Leavenworth. Cross-country ski lessons and rentals are available nearby at **Leavenworth Outfitters** (25 Division, 509/548-0368, www.leavenworthoutfitters.com) next to Parkside Grocery.

Contact the **Wenatchee River Ranger District office** (509/548-2250) for more details about skiing options over ungroomed

NORTH CASCADES

wilderness trails and logging roads around Blewett Pass in Wenatchee National Forest or Lake Wenatchee. Skiers need a Sno-Park permit to park here.

Backcountry Skiing

For overnight cross-country skiing (17 miles of ski trails), snowshoeing, and snowboarding, plus some of the best Telemark skiing in the high Cascades, stay in rustic luxury at **Scottish Lakes High Camp** (509/884-2000 or 800/909-9916, www.scottishlakes.com, $40 d). Eight cozy cabins come equipped with woodstoves, mattresses, propane stoves, kerosene lamps, and cooking utensils. From the parking area near Coles Corner (16 miles northwest of Leavenworth), the cabins are 8.5 miles away and 3,000 feet higher in elevation. Most folks choose to ride up and back aboard the lodging's 12-passenger Sno-Cat or snowmobile, but they will haul your gear (extra charge) if you have the energy to ski up and back yourself. The cabins are generally open Thanksgiving through April, plus mid-October–mid-November for fall hikers.

Downhill Skiing

Leavenworth has its own tiny ski area, **Leavenworth Ski Hill** (10701 Ski Hill Dr., 509/548-5477, $15 adult day pass), with two rope tows providing uphill transportation for the handful of runs. There's also a snowboard half-pipe. The ski season here is generally shorter than at the bigger areas because of the lower elevation.

Two larger ski areas are close by: **Stevens Pass,** 35 miles to the west on Highway 2, and **Mission Ridge,** 35 miles in the other direction near Wenatchee. Mission Ridge is a favorite of locals because of the dry snow and less-crowded slopes.

Other Winter Recreation

A few local outfits provide old-fashioned sleigh rides. **Red-Tail Canyon Farm** (11780 Freund Canyon Rd., 509/548-4512 or 800/678-4512, www.redtailcanyonfarmleavenworth.com, $17 adults, $8.75 ages 3–12, free 2 and under) has champion Belgian draft horses that pull

you through scenic Red-Tail Canyon. **Eagle Creek Ranch** (509/548-7798, www.eaglecreek.ws, $14.82 adults, ages 3–12 $12, free 2 and under) offers sleigh rides over the meadows and through the woods surrounding the ranch, two miles north of town off Highway 209. For $32 per person, they will run a romantic two-person cutter through the woods. **Mountain Springs Lodge** (14 miles north of Leavenworth, 509/763-2713 or 800/858-2276, www.mtsprings.com) ups the ante by serving a prime-rib dinner before the ride ($65 adult, inclusive; $37 age 3–12) and offers a breakfast ride where they serve you a buffet and then you serve the horses hay and carrots as you ride ($35 adult, $20 child).

See the Cascades and the Leavenworth valley from a unique perspective aboard a dogsled from **Enchanted Mountain Tours** (509/763-2975) or **Alaska Dreamin' Sled Dog Company** (509/763-8017).

Mountain Spring Lodge (509/763-3483 or 800/858-2276, www.mtsprings.com, $65–235) runs snowmobile tours out of Plain that range from 1–5 hours and have a trip for every level of excitement-tolerance. Valid driver's license is required to drive the snowmobile.

River Rafting

The rivers of the central Cascades support many rafting outfitters, but the Wenatchee is easily the most popular river in the state. Above Leavenworth, the Wenatchee drops through rugged Tumwater Canyon, with several intense class VI stretches before calming down to more manageable beginner-level class III rapids below town. Leavenworth is the most common put-in point, and white-water trips cover 16–24 miles. Conditions change through the year; high spring runoff creates excellent white-water conditions from April–mid-July (and often longer). Gentler float trips begin at Lake Wenatchee and cover the stretch of easy water before the river enters Tumwater Canyon near Tumwater Campground (the take-out point). These are especially popular when flow levels drop during August and September. Inner tubers often float down slower parts of the Icicle and Wenatchee Rivers to

Blackbird Island near Leavenworth's Waterfront Park. Rent inner tubes at **Leavenworth Sports Center** (940 Hwy. 2, 509/548-7864), next to the Chevron station, or rent kayaks and canoes at Lake Wenatchee from **Osprey Rafting** (800/743-6269) or **Leavenworth Outfitters** (325 Division, 509/548-0368).

For half-day rafting excursions, expect to pay $50 for white-water trips or scenic float trips. Most companies include guides, wet suits, booties, meals, and shuttle bus service. Contact one of the following companies for more information, or look for their brochures in the visitors center: **All Rivers Adventures** (800/743-5628, www.allrivers.com), **Blue Sky Outfitters** (800/228-7238, www.blueskyoutfitters.com), **Leavenworth Outfitters** (800/347-7934, www.thrillmakers.com), and **Orion River Expeditions** (800/553-7466, http://orionexp.com).

Mountain Biking

Cyclists love the back roads around Leavenworth, including an almost-level seven-mile loop through Icicle Valley. A more adventuresome ride climbs the dirt road up Tumwater Mountain, just north of town, and offers vistas into Tumwater Canyon and the Wenatchee Valley far below. Stop by the local Forest Service offices for descriptions of other mountain biking trails.

Rent mountain bikes from **Leavenworth Mountain Sports** (220 Hwy. 2, next to Chevron, 509/548-7864, www.shoplms.com, daily 10 A.M.–6 P.M.) or **Der Sportsmann** (837 Front St., 509/548-5623, www.dersportsmann.com, daily 10 A.M.–6 P.M., $25 mountain bike with front suspension per day, $40 mountain bike with full suspension).

Hiking

The **Alpine Lakes Wilderness Area,** one of the most popular and scenic hiking destinations in Washington, lies just a few miles west of Leavenworth. Stop by the Wenatchee National Forest's **Wenatchee River Ranger District** (600 Sherbourne, 509/548-2250, www.fs.fed.us/r6/wenatchee) for a brochure on nearby day hikes and a detailed trail guide to longer treks.

The **Lake Wenatchee** area at the north end of Highway 207 has an extensive system of hiking trails. Popular with hikers and photographers is the **Dirtyface Trail,** a steep 4.5-mile one-way hike from the Lake Wenatchee Ranger Station to the Dirtyface Lookout at 6,000 feet, with views of the lake and surrounding scenery. Backpackers may want to try the **Nason Ridge Trail,** a 22-mile one-way scenic trail along the length of the Nason Ridge, starting at South Shore Road off Highway 207. A number of other one-day or longer hikes start from various points along a complicated network of numbered Forest Service roads. Your best bet is to check at the ranger station for detailed maps and printed trail descriptions. This is black bear country—hikers and campers should use standard bear precautions.

The upper Chiwawa River drainage north of Lake Wenatchee is one of the most popular access points for the Glacier Peak Wilderness. Several trails take off near the end of this road, including the heavily used **Phelps Creek Trail,** which follows the creek for five miles to mountain-rimmed Spider Meadows inside the wilderness.

Horseback Riding

During the summer months, **Eagle Creek Ranch** (509/548-7798 or 800/221-7433, www.eaglecreek.ws, $29–40)—a 580-acre ranch surrounded by Wenatchee National Forest—offers horseback rides, wagon rides, and barbecue dinners. More horseplay at the **Mountain Springs Lodge** (19115 Chiwawa Loop Rd, 800/858-2276, www.mtsprings.com, $25–225), where you can do a one-mile instructional ride for $42 or a 10-mile mountain-view ride for $125. Longer custom rides can be arranged.

For something more leisurely, hop on one of the horse-drawn carriages offered by **Alpine Carriage** (509/630-4203) that roll through Leavenworth all summer long.

Play Centers

Icicle Junction (565 Hwy. 2, 888/462-4242) is the local fun park, with miniature golf, bumper-boat rides, video games, and a miniature train. Adults can kick back with a frosty beer and a basket of chicken while watching the game on its 7.5-foot-tall TV.

Golf

For a history-laden round of golf, play the course at **Leavenworth Golf Club** (9101 Icicle Rd. along the Wenatchee River, 509/548-7267, www.leavenworthgolf.com, $24–46) originally laid out in 1926. It's been updated a little bit since then and now plays 5,711 yards as a par 71. **Kahler Glen Golf Course** (near Lake Wenatchee, 509/763-4025, www.kahlerglen .com, $29–40) is a tough slope 122 course providing a challenge with its tight fairways and handful of water features. There is a bar and grill adjacent to the pro-shop to catch some 19th-hole refreshment.

ACCOMMODATIONS

As a favorite vacation spot in both winter and summer, Leavenworth is jam-packed with accommodations options. If you're arriving on a weekend or in the peak summer or winter holiday seasons, try to book your lodging as early as possible, since rooms fill up early.

The **Leavenworth Chamber of Commerce** (509/548-5807, www.leavenworth.org) has brochures describing local lodging places and keeps a list of those with vacancies.

Under $100

At the low end, you won't go wrong at ☖ **Mrs. Anderson's Lodging House** (917 Commercial St., 509/548-6984 or 800/253-8990, www .quiltersheaven.com, $61–121 d) is a proudly Christian establishment offering nine small but comfortable rooms (one has a balcony) in a historic lodging house. Light breakfast is included and there is a well-stocked quilt shop on premise.

Another reasonably priced lodge downtown is the **Evergreen Inn** (1117 Front St., 509/548-5515 or 800/327-7212, evergreeninn. com, $79–139 d), with continental breakfast included. Pets are welcome.

It is adults only at **Blue Grouse Lodge**

(19944 Hwy. 207 near Lake Wenatchee, 509/763-0108 or 800/883-2611, www.blue grouse.com, $95 s or d), which lets out four rooms with access to a sauna and a common room with fireplace.

$100-150

More standard motel-style accommodations can be found downtown at the **Obertal Village Motor Inn** (922 Commercial St., 509/548-5204 or 800/537-9382, www.obertal.com, $85–299 s or d). More expensive suites are available with hot tub and fireplace ($159–179). The Inn is pet-friendly.

Or stay in a rambling, three-story wooden chalet outside of town at **Haus Rohrbach Pension** (12882 Ranger Rd., 509/548-7074 or 800/548-4477, www.hausrohrbach.com, $105–200 s or d), with 10 rooms. Many rooms have decks and great views of the surrounding mountains. The owners also offer Austrian gourmet cooking classes.

The cozy, quiet **Hotel Pension Anna** (926 Commercial St., 509/548-6273 or 800/509-2662, www.pensionanna.com, $150–155 d) also offers a bit of authentic Austrian flair, with furnishings imported from Europe by the owner. It provides a custom iPhone app as a "personal concierge," mating old world with new.

AlpenRose Inn (500 Alpine Pl., 509/548-3000 or 800/582-2474, www.alpenroseinn .com, $130–350 s or d) is located in a quiet area just outside of town, near Icicle Road. Guests are offered access to an outdoor pool, hot tub, and exercise room. Some rooms have a deck and fireplace.

Autumn Pond B&B (10388 Titus Rd., 509/548-4482 or 800/222-9661, www.autumn pond.com, $119–169 s or d) sits along a pond on three acres of land and has a hot tub and six guest rooms with private baths.

The creekside lodge ☖ **Alpine Rivers Inn** (1505 Alpensee Strausse, 509/548-8888 or 800/873-3960, www.alpineriversinn.com, $89–169 d) is only about a 10-minute walk from city center's shops and restaurants. Enjoy an outdoor pool and a complimentary round of putting at Enzian Falls Championship Putting Course in the summer, or borrow Nordic ski gear in the winter. Rooms include kitchenettes, and a European breakfast is served each morning.

$150-200

Head to **Enzian Inn** (590 Hwy. 2, 509/548-5269 or 800/223-8511, www.enzianinn.com, $150–375 d) which is the most authentically furnished in town. Rooms are decorated with Bavarian crafts and furniture, and the owner even plays an alpenhorn from the top floor each morning! The hotel has large indoor and outdoor pools, hot tubs, and an exercise facility.

Bosch Garten B&B (9846 Dye Rd., 509/548-6900 or 800/535-0069, www.bosch garten.com, $139–176 d) has tall windows facing the mountains and three guest rooms with private baths. The attractive grounds include a Japanese-style garden with an enclosed hot tub.

Abendblume Pension (12570 Ranger Rd., 509/548-4059 or 800/669-7634, www.abend blume.com, $158–298) offers elegant rooms with fireplaces in a luxurious small inn; there's a two-night minimum. Breakfast is lavish and includes meat, cheese, muesli, and Danish *ableskivers.*

$200-250

All Seasons River Inn (8751 Icicle Rd., 509/548-1425 or 800/254-0555, www.all seasonsriverinn.com, $225–430 s or d) presents guests with beautifully decorated antique-furnished rooms, some with fireplaces, in a large contemporary chalet-style home. Breakfast is served on the riverfront deck. There's a two-night minimum on weekends. Complimentary items include mountain bikes, snow shoes, wireless Internet, and cold drinks.

Over $250

Tucked away in the hillsides, the luxurious ◖ **Mountain Springs Lodge** (19115 Chiwawa Loop Rd., 18 mi. NW of Leavenworth, 509/763-2713 or 800/858-2276, www .mtsprings.com, $250–350 d) has large and airy cabins with kitchens and private hot tubs. Suites have marvelous freestone fireplaces,

kitchenettes, and spa tubs. There's a two-night minimum on weekends. There is an outfitter on the property, so plan on taking a horseback ride in summer, or going on a sleigh ride or snowmobile adventure during the winter.

Run of the River (9308 E. Leavenworth Rd., 509/548-7171 or 800/288-6491, www .runoftheriver.com, $230–425 d) is one of the most splendid local B&Bs, a luxurious log home along Icicle Creek with a flower-filled yard, outside deck, and hot tub. The six guest rooms have private baths and are decorated with knotty-pine furnishings and whimsically rustic decor. Rooms include whirlpool baths surrounded by river rock, bathrooms with rain showers, Egyptian cotton linens, and private decks with mountain views. Rooms also include old-style manual typewriters and the invitation to type a new page for the guestbook. Be sure to leave the kids behind, as this one is adults only.

The premier **Mountain Home Lodge** (9799 Mountain Home Rd. call for directions—GPS gets confused here, 509/548-7077 or 800/414-2378, www.mthome.com, $150–360 s or d in summer, $300–530 d in winter) has a view the likes of which most people will never see and offers a full breakfast, outdoor pool, hot tub, and tennis in the summer. In wintertime, it grooms 40 miles of private cross-country trails and lays out three gourmet meals for guests each day. Guests also can take advantage of cross-country skis, snowshoes, and toboggans on the property. During the winter, guests are taken to the hotel by a private Sno-Cat. Of course, there are robes for guest use in every room. Its policy on kids is: no kids.

Camping

Wenatchee National Forest campgrounds near Leavenworth are generally open May–late October and charge $8–12. Get there very early on summer weekends or all the spaces may be gone! The closest to Leavenworth is **Eightmile Campground** (eight miles up Icicle Rd.). Six more Forest Service campgrounds are within 20 miles of Leavenworth along Icicle Road.

Another very popular Forest Service tenting

spot, **Tumwater Campground** is 10 miles northwest from Leavenworth along Highway 2. Farther afield (16 miles northwest) is Lake Wenatchee, where you can pitch a tent at the Forest Service's **Nason Creek** and **Glacier View Campgrounds.** Four more Forest Service campgrounds lie northwest of the lake. Other, free campsites (with a Northwest Forest Pass) can be found driving from Lake Wenatchee up Chiwawa Valley Road, past Fish Lake to where the road turns to dirt. Unimproved campsites out this way along the Chiwawa River include **Finner Creek, Riverbend,** and **Rock Creek,** among others.

Showers are available at **Oxbow Trading Post** (16 miles northwest of Leavenworth) in Cole Corner. Hikers and campers can also find hot showers and washing machines at **Die Wascherei** (1317 Front St., daily 7 A.M.–9:30 P.M.).

FOOD

Leavenworth village has a number of restaurants, all very Bavarian from the outside but often more diverse on the inside. Even the local McDonald's features German-style architecture, but there is, sadly, no bratwurst or *leberkäse* on the menu.

Cafés and Diners

Leavenworth is not especially known for its breakfasts. Your two main picks are **Sandy's Waffle & Dinner Haus** (894 U.S. Hwy. 2, 509/548-6779, 7 A.M.–2 P.M. daily), which has all the old breakfast standbys and the **Renaissance Café** (217 8th St., 509/548-6725, www.the renaissancecafe.com, Mon.–Thurs. 7 A.M.– 3 P.M., Fri.–Sat. 7 A.M.–9 P.M., Sun. 7 A.M.– 7 P.M.), which goes off the chart a bit with a tofu scramble, huevos rancheros, toad-in-the-hole, and options from the simple to the decadent.

For lunch, **Uncle Uli's Pub Restaurant** (9th and Front, 509/548-7262, daily 11 A.M.–10 P.M.), has a menu including soups, salads, great sandwiches, and at least one pasta.

Be sure to give your waitstaff a hearty "Willkommen, amigos!" when you walk into **Los Camperos** (200 8th St., 509/548-3314,

Sun.–Thurs. 11 A.M.–9:30 P.M., Fri.–Sat. 11 A.M.–10:30 P.M.). It can set you up with a sausage-filled chorizo burrito or a beans and rice vegetarian burrito—or one of a dozen other dishes. A good spot for pizzas is **Leavenworth Pizza Co.** (894 Hwy. 2, 509/548-7766, 4–9 P.M. Mon–Thurs., 4–10 P.M. Fri., 11 A.M.–10 P.M. Sat., 11 A.M.–9 P.M. Sun.).

Bavarian

Several eateries dish out the starchy, meaty, and thoroughly delicious German fare one expects to find in a Bavarian village. Dine in a Bavarian restaurant that is elegant without being dreary at **Café Mozart** (829 Front St., 509/548-0600, daily 11:30 A.M.–9 P.M.) including *leberkäse,* knackwurst, and *kassler kottlets.* Consider ordering from among its "Symphony of Schnitzels."

King Ludwig's Restaurant (921 Front St., 509/548-6625, Sun.–Thurs. 11 A.M.–8:30 P.M., Fri.–Sat. 11:30 A.M.–10 P.M., www.king ludwigs.com) features German and Hungarian dishes. The specialty of the house is the *schweinshax'n*—roasted pork hock. Several platters are served family-style, for that additional European touch.

Bakeries and Markets

Leavenworth's bake shops provide something for all tastes. **The Gingerbread Factory** (828 Commercial St., 509/548-6592 or 800/296-7097, www.gingerbreadfactory.com, 8:30 A.M.–8 P.M. Thurs.–Mon.) is housed in what could be a giant gingerbread house. The bakery is known for its wonderful soft gingerbread cookies and constructions. The lunchtime deli here is a local favorite for salads, sandwiches, and espresso.

The Danish Bakery (731 Front St., 509/548-7514, daily 9 A.M.–6 P.M.) opened up before the Bavarian transformation and is the longest-running business in town. The Danish pastries make a good break from German chocolate and cookies.

Bavarian Bakery (1330 U.S. Hwy. 2., 509/548-2244) bakes up signature sourdough rye, from-scratch German pastries, and special traditional holiday treats.

Leavenworth Farmers Market (509/667-8654, www.leavenworthfarmersmarket.com) takes place 7 A.M.–11 A.M. Sat. May–Oct., 3 P.M.–6 P.M. May–Sept. at Haymarket Square at 7th and Cherokee.

INFORMATION AND SERVICES

For maps, brochures, and additional information, stop by the **Leavenworth Chamber of Commerce Visitor Center** (220 9th St., 509/548-5807, www.leavenworth.org, Mon.–Sat. 8:30 A.M.–6 P.M., Sun. 10 A.M.–4 P.M.).

Hikers and campers can chat up the rangers at Wenatchee National Forest **Wenatchee River Ranger District** (600 Sherbourne St., 509/548-2550, www.fs.fed.us/r6/Wenatchee, daily 7:45 A.M.–4:30 P.M. mid-June–mid-Oct., Mon.–Fri. 7:45 A.M.–4:30 P.M. the rest of the year).

The **Leavenworth Public Library** (700 U.S. Hwy. 2, 509/548-7923) is right across from Front Street Park. Its periodicals room has a fireplace and stunning mountain vistas. Story time is 11:30 A.M. every Friday.

GETTING THERE AND AROUND

The nearest commercial airport is **Pangborn Memorial Airport,** with service by Alaska Airlines. For Amtrak, the Empire Builder serves the station at Kittitas and South Columbia Street, also in Wenatchee, approximately 30 miles east of Leavenworth.

By Car

Driving to Leavenworth in the winter over Stevens Pass has been described as "driving through a Christmas card." Rocky, snow-covered peaks surround the highway as you approach the 4,061-foot pass; closer to Leavenworth, the Wenatchee River rushes alongside the road through high, rocky walls. The trip from Seattle is about 125 miles. From late fall to early spring, check out the Department of Transportation's **Mountain Pass Report** (206/434-7277, www.wsdot .wa.gov/traffic/passes) for up-to-date info. Have your chains ready! As an alternate route, take I-90 over Snoqualmie Pass to Highway 97 north over Sauk Pass; these passes are generally drier and snow-free earlier than Stevens.

By Bus

Inexpensive local **Link** (800/851-5465, www .linktransit.com, $1.25-2.50) buses connect Leavenworth with other parts of Chelan and Douglas Counties, including Lake Wenatchee, Cashmere, Wenatchee, and the popular tourist destinations of Lake Chelan and the Mission Ridge Ski Area. Buses run Monday–Saturday and can carry bikes in the summer or skis in the winter.

Northwest Trailways (800/992-4618, www.trailways.com) stops in Leavenworth at the Park & Ride near Safeway, with service east to Spokane and west to Everett.

Stevens Pass and Skykomish Valley

U.S. Highway 2 is one of the state's most beautiful drives, and the western end of a transcontinental two-lane route that runs eastward all the way to Maine. Heading west from Leavenworth, the highway enters spectacular Tumwater Canyon, with the roiling Wenatchee River. The road eventually tops out at 4,061-foot **Stevens Pass.**

On the western side of the pass, Highway 2 drops quickly—2,000 feet in 14 miles—to the little town of Skykomish. As you switchback down from the summit, the Burlington Northern railroad tracks emerge from seven-mile-long **Cascade Railroad Tunnel,** one of the longest in the western hemisphere. The drive downhill takes you past rugged snow-covered peaks, plunging waterfalls, popular campgrounds, fishing holes in the Skykomish River, and nature trails to explore along the way. Finally, the grade lessens in the wide

Skykomish Valley (aka "Sky Valley"), as the highway slips through a chain of small towns before emerging into the flat farmland and spreading suburbia near Monroe.

STEVENS PASS

At Stevens Pass you'll find popular downhill and cross-country ski areas, and a jumping-off point for the **Pacific Crest Trail.** Serious backpackers can hook up with the Pacific Crest Trail and hike clear up to Canada or down to Mexico or just a short chunk of the trail. Two wilderness areas on either side of the pass— Henry M. Jackson Wilderness and Alpine Lakes Wilderness—contain striking natural features, from glaciers and alpine meadows to dense forests intersected by clear, clean rivers. Much of the area's beauty can be seen through your car windows and from short roadside paths, but hundreds of miles of hiking trails let you experience its splendor at close range.

Sights and Recreation
◖ **ALPINE LAKES WILDERNESS AREA**
The spectacular Alpine Lakes Wilderness covers over 390,000 acres of high Cascades country, a diverse landscape ranging in elevation from 1,000-foot valleys to towering 9,000-foot mountain spires. Much of the area is high alpine country filled with some 700 crystalline lakes, ponds, and tarns.

Because of its proximity to Seattle and the dramatic alpine-and-lake scenery, this is one of the most heavily used wilderness areas in Washington. The Forest Service has instituted a wilderness permit system that limits the number of hikers in the Enchantment area near Leavenworth. Call the Mount Baker-Snoqualmie National Forest Headquarters (206/775-9702 or 800/627-0062) before heading out. Permits are required throughout the wilderness June 15–October 15. In most areas of the wilderness, free, self-issued permits can be obtained at the trailheads. In the Enchantments, lottery-based permits (www.recreation.gov, $5 per person per day) are required for overnight camping, typically available the first two weeks of March. Midsummer

weekends fill up fast, so apply right away for your best chances. Day use is free in the Enchantments, but you'll need to fill out a permit at the trailhead.

Heading south from Highway 2, the **Pacific Crest Trail** climbs past the downhill ski area and Lake Susan Jane before reaching Josephine Lake on the wilderness boundary (4.5 miles from the highway). From here, you enter a web of trails that covers the high alpine land, opening up many loop-trip possibilities. Two fun and very popular trails (wilderness permits required) begin from the Foss River Road (Forest Service Road 68, two miles east of Skykomish). One of these, the **Necklace Valley Trail** (No. 1062) starts up an old narrow-gauge railroad bed before entering a tight canyon and ascending quickly to a cluster of lakes in upper Necklace Valley. The one-way length is 7.5 miles, with a gain of 3,140 feet in elevation. A second excellent short hike is to follow **West Fork Foss River Trail** to Trout Lake, and then on to a chain of half a dozen jewel-like lakes. The one-way distance is seven miles, with an elevation gain of 2,900 feet.

Many popular trails lead into the Enchantment portion of the wilderness, including the seven-mile **Snow Lake Trail,** which starts from Icicle Road out of Leavenworth. Backpackers often use Snow Lake as a base area and day hike into the rugged and spectacular **Enchantment Lakes.**

HENRY M. JACKSON WILDERNESS AREA
This 103,591-acre mountain wilderness is accessible from the Stevens Pass, Skykomish, Lake Wenatchee, and Darrington areas. The glacier-carved landscape has a Swiss-Alps quality, with numerous alpine lakes, prominent knife-edged ridges, and deep U-shaped valleys. Dozens of backcountry hikes are possible, and ambitious backpackers could continue on into the adjacent Glacier Peak Wilderness Area. The **Pacific Crest Trail** passes through the center of Henry M. Jackson Wilderness before crossing Highway 2 and continuing on southward into the Alpine Lakes Wilderness.

An interesting and scenic 18-mile loop trek can be made by following the **Beckler River**

Road (Forest Service Road 65) from the town of Skykomish to Jack Pass and continuing another mile to Forest Service Road 63. Turn right here, and proceed to the trailhead at the end of the road. The **North Fork Trail** (No. 1051) climbs into high-mountain country from here, through masses of hillside wildflowers in midsummer, eventually emerging into the alpine after five miles or so. It meets the Pacific Crest Trail at Dishpan Gap. Turn right and follow the PCT past Lake Sally and then back around 6,368-foot Skykomish Peak to the Pass Creek Trail, which will take you back to your starting point. Another option is to turn left at Dishpan Gap and follow **Bald Eagle Mountain Trail** (No. 650) back to trail No. 1050, which leads back to the road.

Contact the **Skykomish Ranger District** (74920 NE Stevens Pass, 360/677-2414) for current conditions, use restrictions, and trail descriptions.

DOWNHILL SKIING

About halfway between Skykomish and Lake Wenatchee is **Stevens Pass Ski Area** (206/812-4510 for snow conditions, www.stevenspass.com, $62 adult, $42 kids and seniors, $15 over age 70, $8 under age 6) one of the most popular Alpine ski areas among Seattleites. With a base elevation of 3,821 feet and a summit elevation of 5,845 feet, it features 10 lifts that cover 1,125 acres of beginner through expert terrain. Stevens Pass is generally open mid-November through late April, offering night skiing, ski and snowboard rentals and lessons, a ski shop, restaurant, cafeteria, and cocktail lounges. Many different ski and snowboard schools operate out of Stevens Pass; contact the ski area for a listing. A tubing and sledding area is adjacent to the ski hill.

Lodging is not available at Stevens Pass, although RVs can park in the lot (no hookups). The nearest overnight accommodations are in Skykomish (16 miles west) and Leavenworth (35 miles east).

CROSS-COUNTRY SKIING

Rent cross country skis at **Stevens Pass**

Nordic Center (five miles east of the Stevens Pass downhill area, 360/973-2441, open Fri.–Sun. and on winter holidays, $30 adults, $18 youth), which offers 19 miles of groomed trails. The main route climbs uphill for 4.6 miles, gaining over 700 feet along the way. Once you work up an appetite, head back to the trailhead, where there's a snack bar with hot food.

RIVER RAFTING

The **Skykomish River** is an extremely popular place for rafting during the peak snowmelt period from mid-March–mid-July. The upper portion of the "Sky" from Skykomish to Baring and the South Fork from Skykomish to Index are *not* for beginners. The famous "Boulder Drop" section is class IV-plus water, and there are many other deep plunges and vertical drops of class IV. Trips are available on most early summer weekends, with fewer weekday runs. Some companies restrict Skykomish rafting to those at least 16 years old.

Based in Index, **Chinook Expeditions** (360/793-3451 or 800/241-3451, www.chinook expeditions.com) runs excellent float and whitewater trips, including a six-day Cascade loop trip (May–July, $865) that includes runs down the Skagit, Skykomish, Methow, and Wenatchee Rivers. Chinook also offers Skykomish trips ($79) in the fall months when conditions are fast and wild. **Wave Trek** (425/883-9039 or 800/282-4043, www.wavetrek.com, $85) is an Index-based rafting and kayaking company with trips down both the main fork of the Sky, and the wild North Fork. They also teach multiday kayaking classes for those who want to take a bigger step into river-running.

For a do-it-yourself trip, the lower Skykomish is a peaceful river to raft or kayak, with a few small, generally avoidable, rapids above Sultan. It's rated class II-plus from Big Eddy State Park (aka Sky River State Scenic Park, two miles east of Gold Bar where Highway 2 crosses the river) to Sultan, and class I from Sultan to Monroe.

WATERFALLS

As a beautiful reminder that the forces that formed this area are still at work, several raging waterfalls are right along the roadside as you travel U.S. Highway 2. The easternmost natural roadside attraction is **Deception Falls,** right along the highway approximately seven miles west of Stevens Pass. A short paved path crosses the Tye River and continues to a cascading torrent of water, but much more interesting is the half-mile nature trail that drops down along the river. Educational plaques describe the forest and river, leading to two more impressive cataracts, both backdropped by the deep green rain forest. **Deception Creek Trail** starts on the south side of Highway 2 and provides a humbling old-growth forest hike. The trail climbs 10 miles (gaining almost 2,500 feet along the way) to Deception Pass in the Alpine Lakes Wilderness Area, where you can join up with the Pacific Crest Trail.

About 1.5 miles farther west, **Alpine Falls** drops 50 feet into the Tye River below; park on the south side of the highway and follow the can't-miss path. **Bridal Veil Falls,** a quarter mile east of the Index junction, vary with the season; summer brings two distinctive "veils," while winter freezes the falls into a glistening sheet of ice. Scenic **Eagle Falls** on the South Fork Skykomish River is a favorite place for summertime swimmers who play in the big jade-green plunge pool. Be careful if you join in the fun, since there are more falls just downstream. The falls are 11 miles west of Skykomish and right along Highway 2.

Camping

Forest Service campgrounds provide in-the-woods lodging options in the Skykomish vicinity. **Beckler River** and **Money Creek** (541/338-7869 or 877/444-6777, www.recreation.gov, $16, $9 extra reservation fee) are open late May through September. Beckler River is two miles north of Skykomish on Forest Service Road 65. Money Creek is four miles west of Skykomish and right along Highway 2. Two other, more primitive sites—**Troublesome Creek** and **San Juan Campgrounds**—are near Jack Pass.

Getting There and Around

Stevens Pass is often a challenge to traverse and is sometimes closed by winter storms. If you're heading up to ski at Stevens Pass or continuing east to Leavenworth or Wenatchee, get travel info by dialing 5-1-1.

Northwestern Trailways (800/366-6975, www.trailways.com) stops at Stevens Pass, with service east to Spokane and west to Everett and Seattle.

SKY VALLEY

As you head down from the Cascades into the Skykomish ("Sky") Valley, several towns pop up along Highway 2, each a little larger than the last, till you reach the edge of Seattle's sprawl at fast-growing Monroe. The historic railroad town of Skykomish (sky-KOH-mish) is primarily a resting point on the way into or out of the mountains. You'll pass the tiny mining and logging town of Index, just across the clear waters of the Skykomish River. There are plenty of hiking, rock climbing, steelhead fishing, and mountain biking options in the area. The road continues on to Monroe and back to recognizable, if duller, civilization.

Scenic Drives

For a fascinating 26-mile side trip away from busy Highway 2, head up Beckler River Road, which starts a half mile east of Skykomish. The road (Forest Service Road 65) climbs 13 miles up—the last five are dusty gravel—along the river into Mount Baker-Snoqualmie National Forest before switchbacking over Jack Pass and down the Galena Road.

A forest lookout tower atop **Evergreen Mountain** can be reached via a 1.5-mile one-way hike from the end of Evergreen Mountain Road 6554. The road takes off to the right (east) from Beckler River Road just before you reach Jack Pass. The trail gains 1,300 feet in elevation, but on a clear day the 360-degree view includes Glacier Peak and Mount Rainier. The lookout tower is available for rent at $40 per night (877/444-6777).

Two miles down Galena Road, you can find **Troublesome Creek Nature Trail,** a delightful half-mile path through rain forest and canyon that starts out from Troublesome Creek

Campground. Beyond the campground, Galena Road parallels the North Fork Skykomish River for 10 miles—paved the entire way—ending at Highway 2 near the town of Index.

For a shorter road less traveled, the **Maloney-Sobieski Mountain Road** provides views of Glacier Peak and deep valleys. To get there, head east from the Skykomish Ranger Station for a half mile, then turn left onto Foss River Road (Forest Service Road 68). Drive about 5.5 miles to the intersection of Forest Service Roads 68 and 6835; go right onto 6835. When you reach the next fork, stay to the right onto Forest Service Road 6846 until the next fork; then go left to Sobieski Mountain or right to Maloney Mountain, with spectacular views on either route.

Index

Tiny Index (pop. 150) lies a mile off Highway 2 and just across the clear waters of the Skykomish River. This quaint old mining, logging, and quarrying camp has tidy homes, a delightful old lodge, and an almost-encircling Cascade Range backdrop that features the extremely impressive spire of Mount Index. There are plenty of hiking, rock climbing, steelhead fishing, and mountain biking options in the area. Directly behind town rises **Index Town Wall**, a 400-foot granite cliff that's a favorite of Seattle-area rock climbers. A steep path leads much of the way up the slope for those who aren't climbers; ask at the Bush House for directions.

For a short day hike near Index, try the one-mile one-way hike from Highway 2 just east of town to **Heybrook Lookout**. This Forest Service fire tower provides views of Mount Index, Baring Mountain, and the Skykomish Valley. Slightly longer (2.2 miles one-way) but with little elevation gain is the **Barclay Lake Trail**, which follows the course of Barclay Creek to the lake with a nice view of Baring Mountain. To get to the trailhead, take Barclay Creek Road 6024 for four miles.

◖ Wallace Falls State Park

Located two miles northeast of Gold Bar, this 678-acre park (360/793-0420, www.parks .wa.gov, daily in the summer, Wed.–Sun. Oct.–mid-Apr.) is famous for its towering 265-foot cataract (visible from Highway 2). Two routes lead to Wallace Falls, an easy path along an old railroad grade that's open to mountain bikes, and a steeper route (Woody Trail) that follows closer to the river. The two trails join for the last 1.5 miles, with several viewpoints along the way, including one atop the falls. The hike to the falls is six miles round-trip via Woody Trail and eight miles round-trip via the old railroad grade.

Reptile Serpentarium

Located along Highway 2 a mile east of Monroe, the Reptile Serpentarium (22715-B U.S. Hwy. 2, 360/668-8204, www.reptileman .com, daily 10 A.M.–6 P.M., $6 adult, $5 kids) has a huge collection of reptiles, including deadly cobras, rattlers, mambas, and a water moccasin. Other curiosities unique in the Northwest are an albino alligator and a two-headed turtle. Visitors are invited to handle a number of nonvenomous snakes, if they dare.

Entertainment and Events

On the west end of Monroe sits the enormous **Evergreen State Fair complex** (14405 179th Ave. SE, 360/794-7832 or 360/794-4344, www.evergreenfair.org). The fairgrounds is the site of major equestrian shows all year long, including the **Washington Hunter/Jumper Spring Nationals** in April, the **Pacific Northwest Quarter Horse Shows** in May and September, along with a diversity of other events.

But the biggest event of the year is, by far, the **Evergreen State Fair,** the largest fair in Washington. This fair will get your heart pumping. Yes, you can watch with bated breath as they award the blue ribbon to the finest dairy goat in the county, but be sure you follow up with the demolition derby, ride the Ghost Pirate at the carnival, or take in some A-list musical entertainment. Quarter horses come to perform right next door to a Tokyo-drift style auto race. Better yet, sit in the stands for bubble-blowing contests, a texting contest, or the baby diaper derby. The fair lasts for 11 days, from the last full week in August through Labor Day weekend.

Also at the fairgrounds is the **Evergreen Speedway** (360/794-7711, www.evergreen speedway.com), where you can watch NASCAR auto racing, demolition derbies, and other contests of bravado late March–mid-September.

Accommodations

The historic **Cascadia Inn and Café** (210 Railroad Ave. E, 360/677-2477, www.historic cascadia.com, $40–85 d) in Index has also long been a favorite among Stevens Pass skiers. The 1922 lodge has just over a dozen rooms, nine of which share a bath. The hotel was constructed in 1905, and the back room was popular with card-playing railroad crews. The old depot still stands next to the tracks here.

The nicest local motel in the area is in Monroe. **Best Western Baron Inn** (19233 U.S. Hwy. 2, in Monroe, 360/794-3111 or 877/794-3111, www.bestwestern.com, $89 s or $135 d), features an outdoor pool, hot tub, exercise room, and continental breakfast, plus free wireless Internet. Also in Monroe, the **GuestHouse Inn & Suites** (19103 Hwy. 2, 360/863-1900, in Monroe, $94 s or $127 d) has clean rooms and a friendly staff, although the railroad tracks are fairly close, as a heads-up to those light sleepers.

CAMPING

A couple of miles away from Jack Pass on Galena Road, find **Troublesome Creek Campground** (518/885-3639 or 877/444-6777, www.recreation.gov, $16, $9 extra reservation fee). You can also camp for free anywhere on Forest Service land here. Just look for the side roads heading into the woods.

The closest public campsites to Monroe ($12 tents, $17 RVs) are in two county parks: **Flowing Lake Park** (10 mi. north of Monroe, 360/568-2274, open year-round, no water in the winter months) and **Lake Roesiger Park**

(12 mi. north of Monroe, 360/568-5836, open mid-May through September). Both of these parks have popular swimming beaches, and Flowing Lake has ranger-led nature hikes, along with Saturday-night amphitheater programs in the summer.

Park RVs ($10) or pitch tents ($5) during events at **Evergreen State Fairgrounds** (360/794-4344).

Food

For a friendly family-owned grill on the way from Leavenworth to Monroe, go to Gold Bar's **Mount Index Café** (49315 U.S. Hwy. 2, 360/799-1133) which specializes in country-style comfort foods like biscuits and gravy. Its strong coffee is guaranteed to cut the cold.

The **Hitchin Post Café** (107 W. Main St., 360/805-5495, www.hitchinpostcafe.com) is a popular family spot downtown for breakfast and lunch, with interesting murals painted all through the interior. **Sky River Bakery** (117 W. Main, 360/794-7434, http://skyriv erbakery.com, Tues.–Fri. 7 A.M.–5 P.M., Sat. 7 A.M.–4 P.M., closed Sun.–Mon.) serves sweets, pies, quiche, and signature muffins.

Information

The **Monroe Chamber of Commerce** (211 E. Main St., 360/794-5488, chamber.monroe.net, Mon.–Fri. 9:30 A.M.–4 P.M.) offers brochures about the area.

Skykomish Ranger Station (74920 NE Stevens Pass Hwy., 360/677-2414, daily 8 A.M.–4:30 P.M. Memorial Day–Labor Day, and Mon.–Fri. 8 A.M.–4:30 P.M. the rest of the year) offers recreation tips and topographic maps, books, and current information on trails and campgrounds.

Getting There and Around

Community Transit (425/353-7433 or 800/562-1375, www.commtrans.org) has daily bus service from Monroe to other parts of Snohomish County.

SOUTH CASCADES

Washington's identity is inextricably tied to the breathtaking beauty of Washington's tallest and best-known peak, the perennially snowcapped Mount Rainier. To the residents of Puget Sound, it is simply "the Mountain," a singular peak towering above all others in the Cascades.

A pilgrimage to its base (and for some, its summit) is a must for any Washington traveler, who will be dazzled by surrounding alpine meadows, thundering waterfalls, up-close encounters with glaciers and wildlife, and—if the mountain chooses to peek out from under the clouds—a neck-crick-inducing view of the peak that is more impressive than the postcards imply.

But Mount Rainier isn't nearly the only volcanic wonder in the vast recreational playground of the South Cascades. Temperamental and denuded Mount St. Helens and remote and wild Mount Adams beg to be explored as well. Surrounding all of it are untouched tracts of wilderness, hiking trails galore, ski summits and cross country trails, chilly glacier lakes full of trout, and gurgling creeks meant to be paired with a pitched tent and a crackling fire.

PLANNING YOUR TIME

Recreation junkies can spend a whole summer or a lifetime wandering the trails and peaks of the South Cascades. When you've got limited time, the big draws are Mount Rainier and Mount St. Helens. They're only a couple of hours apart from each other, so Seattle visitors

HIGHLIGHTS

🌙 **Snoqualmie Falls:** Made famous by David Lynch in his eerie 1990s classic *Twin Peaks*, this is the most easily accessible and picturesque waterfall in the state (page 544).

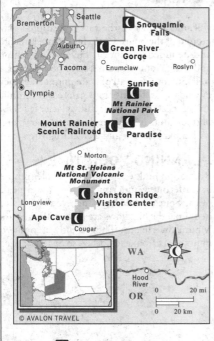

© AVALON TRAVEL

🌙 **Green River Gorge:** The emerald banks of this white-water retreat are bookended by two fabulous state parks (page 555).

🌙 **Mount Rainier Scenic Railroad:** You'll get enough snapshot opportunities to fill a photo album aboard the open-air car chugging along this line (page 558).

🌙 **Paradise:** The first European settlers gave the flower-filled subalpine valley beneath Rainier its heavenly name the moment they set foot there. No one's argued with their assessment ever since (page 566).

🌙 **Sunrise:** The highest point you can reach by automobile in the entire Mount Rainier National Park, this spot offers the most stunning views of the mountain and dozens of trails for exploration (page 569).

🌙 **Johnston Ridge Visitor Center:** Even 30 years after Mount Saint Helens blew its top, the surrounding blast zone is an awesome sight. See the toothpick-like timbers strewn in Spirit Lake, the remnants of mudflows, and the mountain itself from a perch on this ridge (page 593).

🌙 **Ape Cave:** Formed when Mount St. Helens erupted 1,900 years ago, these lava tubes were carved out when a lava flow cooled on the surface but magma continued to ooze below ground for a short time (page 593).

LOOK FOR 🌙 TO FIND RECOMMENDED SIGHTS, ACTIVITIES, DINING, AND LODGING.

could conceivably drive by both in a single day. Just so long as you don't mind not getting out of the car much. Ideally, plan a week at minimum to get out on the trails.

The ideal time for summer exploration is between snowmelt and first snowfall, usually between July and September. Visitors need to be aware of weather conditions prior to heading out. This area of the Cascades typically sees heavy snowfall from as early as October until as late as May, which can be a good or a bad thing depending on your perspective. Certain roads and attractions are closed, but others open up to a whole new dimension of recreational activity only possible when snowdrifts are present.

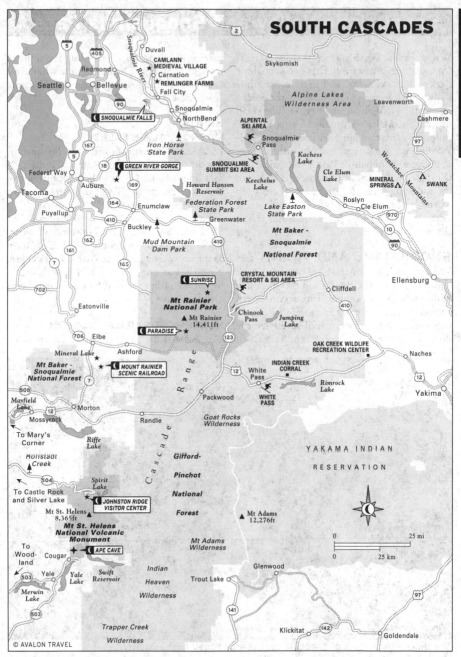

SOUTH CASCADES

Duvall

CAMLANN MEDIEVAL VILLAGE
Redmond
Carnation
REMLINGER FARMS
Fall City

Seattle — Bellevue

Snoqualmie River

Skykomish

Alpine Lakes Wilderness Area

Leavenworth

Cashmere

Snoqualmie
NorthBend

(**SNOQUALMIE FALLS**

ALPENTAL SKI AREA

Snoqualmie
Pass

Kachess Lake

Wenatchee Mountains

97

Iron Horse State Park

SNOQUALMIE SUMMIT SKI AREA

Cle Elum
Lake

MINERAL SPRINGS

Cle Elum Lake

SWANK

Federal Way

(**GREEN RIVER GORGE**

Auburn

169

Howard Hanson Reservoir

Keechelus
Lake

Roslyn

Cle Elum

Tacoma

164

Enumclaw

Federation Forest State Park

Lake Easton State Park

970

10

Puyallup

410

Buckley

Greenwater

Mud Mountain Dam Park

410

Mt Baker - Snoqualmie National Forest

161

165

702

Eatonville

(**SUNRISE**

★

Mt Rainier National Park

CRYSTAL MOUNTAIN RESORT & SKI AREA

Cliffdell

Ellensburg

706

Elbe

(**PARADISE** ★

▲ Mt Rainier
14,411 ft

123

Chinook
Pass

Jumping Lake

410

OAK CREEK WILDLIFE RECREATION CENTER

Naches

Mineral Lake

Mt Baker - Snoqualmie National Forest

(**MOUNT RAINIER SCENIC RAILROAD**

Ashford

12

White
Pass

INDIAN CREEK CORRAL

Rimrock Lake

12

508

Mayfield Lake

12

Morton

Packwood

WHITE PASS

Yakima

Mossyrock

Randle

Goat Rocks Wilderness

To Mary's Corner

Riffe Lake

YAKAMA INDIAN RESERVATION

Hofisladt Creek

504

To Castle Rock and Silver Lake

Spirit Lake

Gifford- Pinchot National Forest

(**JOHNSTON RIDGE VISITOR CENTER**

Mt St. Helens
8,365 ft ▲

Mt St. Helens National Volcanic Monument

To Wood- land

Cougar

(**APE CAVE**

▲ Mt Adams
12,276 ft

Mt Adams Wilderness

25 mi

25 km

503

Yale

Yale Lake

Swift Reservoir

Indian Heaven Wilderness

Trout Lake

Glenwood

Merwin Lake

503

97

141

142

Trapper Creek Wilderness

Klickitat

Goldendale

© AVALON TRAVEL

Snoqualmie Valley and Snoqualmie Pass

When most Washington residents hear "Snoqualmie," they think first of Snoqualmie Pass and its ski areas, and then Snoqualmie Falls, which looked so ominous in the credits of the 1990 TV show *Twin Peaks*. The small town of Snoqualmie is usually an afterthought, unless you live there or have come to appreciate the great restaurants and beautiful scenery of the area. Snoqualmie Pass is the easiest way through the Cascades in winter; it has both the widest highway (I-90) and lowest elevation of any of the mountain passes. The ski areas at the summit bring a lot of vehicular traffic through the region.

SNOQUALMIE AND VICINITY

The quaint little town of Snoqualmie, with about two blocks of civilization on either side of the tracks, has a number of attractions worth a look, including nearby Snoqualmie Falls. As you approach the town, you'll surely see the dozens of aging train engines and railcars in varying states of repair crowding the railroad tracks. They're a silent and somewhat eerie testament to the logging history of the entire Northwest.

Sights
◖ SNOQUALMIE FALLS
Located a mile north of the town of Snoqualmie just off Washington State Route 202, the 270-foot Snoqualmie Falls has been inspiring awe since the last ice age. Two hydroelectric plants on the river are each over 100 years old.

Stop at the falls (close to 6501 Railroad Ave. SE, open dawn–dusk, free) to stand in awe on the nonacrophobic-friendly viewing platform as the noisy river plummets to the rocks below. Near the parking area, a gift shop sells souvenirs and a rather rough espresso. Leashed pets are allowed.

NORTHWEST RAILWAY MUSEUM
The beautifully restored 1890 Snoqualmie

The thundering waters of Snoqualmie Falls are at their best in winter.

© ERICKA CHICKOWSKI

Railroad Depot contains the small **Northwest Railway Museum** (38625 SE King St., 425/888-3030, www.trainmuseum.org, $12 adults, $10 seniors, $8 ages 2–12, free under 3), highlighted by the **Snoqualmie Valley Railroad.** These diesel locomotives take 65-minute to 75-minute excursions around town on weekends late May–October.

TOLT MCDONALD PARK
While away an afternoon at a Snoqualmie Indian wintering camp turned King County campground at Tolt McDonald Park (31020 NE 40th St. in Carnation, 206/205-5434, open year-round), a 574-acre county park just west of Carnation where the Tolt and Snoqualmie Rivers flow together. This secret little stunner provides spots for fly-fishing action in the shadow of a handsome old foot-traffic-only suspension bridge over the Snoqualmie. Camping is available here as well (tents $25, RVs $30 with water and power hookup).

CAMLANN MEDIEVAL VILLAGE
A visit to a certain part of Carnation might make you think the city is a little behind the times. Roughly 600 years behind the times, in fact. Camlann Medieval Village (10320 Kelly Rd. NE, 425/788-8624, www.camlann.org) is a reproduction 15th-century English town complete with costumed re-enactors. Food and drink at the Bors Hede Inn taste the best in the company of knights in armor, minstrels, and maidens. Dramatic productions, medieval magicians, and crafts and food can be enjoyed year-round. Special programs are offered throughout the year.

REMLINGER FARMS
Remlinger Farms (32610 NE 32nd in Carnation, 425/333-4135, $11 ages 1–64, $9 seniors and persons with disabilities) probably has more breadth of U-pick options west of the Cascades. Sure, there are strawberries, but how about pumpkins, too? Goats, miniature horses, llamas, bunnies, and other furry pals are there for the petting, but kept elsewhere so as not to compete with you for berries.

Entertainment and Events
Set among towering evergreens at the foot of the falls, the **Snoqualmie Falls Forest Theater** (36800 SE David Powell Rd., 425/222-7044, www.foresttheater.org) stages musical theater back in the woods Fri.–Sun. in July and August. Tickets run around $18, and reservations are required for the shows, which are often coupled with a huge BBQ dinner. Or course, there are vegetarian options, too.

The **Casino Snoqualmie** (37500 SE North Bend Way, www.casinosnoqualmie.com) puts a distinctly Northwest spin on Vegas-style gambling. The log-and-lodgepole architecture, the 24-hour espresso stand, and the forested setting make this casino as "Seattle" as a well-worn raincoat. Complete with five dining options, two entertainment stages, over 1,600 slot machines, craps, roulette, blackjack, and a 17-table poker area, there are lots of options for an exciting time.

Accommodations
The **℃ Salish Lodge** (6501 Railroad Ave., 425/888-2556 or 800/272-5474, www.salish lodge.com, $299–499 s or d), atop Snoqualmie Falls, is easily the most luxurious hotel in the area, featuring a fireplace, hot tub, feather bed with goose-down comforter in every room, plus a balcony in most. Further treats include a fully equipped exercise room, sauna and steam room, hydrotherapy pools, tanning booths, massage rooms, library, and one of the best restaurants in the area. This is a great place for a honeymoon or a getaway weekend; plunk down $849 for a particularly sweet suite.

A strange and wonderful stay is guaranteed at **Bethabara Farms Bed and Breakfast** (35909 SE 94th St., 425/888-2549, http://bethabarafarms.blogspot.com/, $95 s or $125 d), also known as the House in the Trees. This eclectic structure resembles not so much an inn as a stamp mill, but don't be fooled. The unusual design is brilliantly complemented by the comfortable rooms, the wide and flowery grounds, and the delicious country breakfast served each morning. **Tolt MacDonald Park** (31020 NE 40th St.)

just outside of town has tent sites for $15 per night, RV sites with hookups for $30 per night, or yurts for $50 per night.

Food
The ⟨(**Salish Lodge Restaurant** (6501 Railroad Ave., 425/888-2556) atop Snoqualmie Falls has run continuously since 1916. The dinner menu features seafood and game entrées at around the price-point you'd expect for such lavish digs. The farm-style four-course Sunday brunch remains a regional favorite. The homey lodge atmosphere complete with overstuffed chairs surrounding a warm fire in the lounge is worth the price of admission. Reservations are required, especially if you want a window seat.

Opened in 1997 by a group of local beer connoisseurs, the **Snoqualmie Falls Brewing Company** (8032 Falls Ave., 425/831-2357, www.fallsbrew.com, 11 A.M.–10 P.M. Mon.–Thurs., 11 A.M.–11 P.M., Fri.–Sat., 11 A.M.–9 P.M. Sun.) has fast been racking up awards and loyal fans with its excellent Wildcat IPA, Copperhead Pale Ale, Snoqualmie ESB, Steam Train Porter, and several seasonal beers. Pick any and pair it with a bit of satisfying pub grub served up in the brewery's taproom.

Getting There and Around
Seattle's **Metro** (206/447-4800, metro.kingcounty.gov, $2.25 one-way) bus routes 209 and 214 serve Snoqualmie Falls, Snoqualmie, and North Bend.

NORTH BEND
Located at the foot of Mount Si, the settlement of North Bend (pop. 4,000) is the last Snoqualmie River town before I-90 climbs into the Cascade Range. This sleepy little burg provides many people with bottled water, gas, and beef jerky before they tackle the nearby mountain. Locals consider Si a "conditioning mountain" before they try the "real" trails in the backcountry.

Sights
The **Snoqualmie Valley Museum** (320 Bendigo Blvd. South, 425/888-3200, www

.snoqualmievalleymuseum.org, 1–5 P.M. Thurs.–Sun. Apr.–Oct., donation) has permanent displays of Native American artifacts and pioneer and logging history. The gift shop sells books about local history and souvenir T-shirts.

Shopping
Hikers with family members who could take or leave the great outdoors will thank their lucky stars for the **North Bend Premium Outlets** (461 South Fork Ave. SW, 425/888-4505, Mon.–Sat. 10 A.M.–8 P.M., Sun. 10 A.M.–5 P.M.). This sprawling collection of brand-name outlets such as Adidas, Nine West, and Van Heusen is one of the best and closest to Seattle, and a good excuse to get the non-trekkers out to North Bend.

Sports and Recreation
MOUNT SI AND LITTLE SI
The 4,167-foot-tall Mount Si is a classic area hike, running about eight miles round-trip. The 3,100-foot elevation gain makes the trail a popular off-season training-ground for locals, so don't come here expecting solitude. On a clear day, the views at the summit can be worth the considerable physical effort. To reach the trailhead, turn left on 432nd SE (Mount Si Road) about a mile from the east edge of North Bend. After you cross the Middle Fork of the Snoqualmie River, go right at the first intersection, then drive 2.5 miles to the parking lot, trailhead, and picnic area. The trail is generally snow-free April–November.

An easier alternative to Mount Si is Little Si, offering views across Snoqualmie Valley. The trail is 2.5 miles each way and offers a still-considerable 1,574-foot gain. Get to the trailhead by following North Bend Way a half mile southeast from the Forest Service Ranger Station to Mount Si Road; then turn left and go a half mile to a bridge. Park at the gravel lot here across the bridge, and walk downhill to the signed trailhead just past the fifth house on the right.

TWIN FALLS
Just a short distance from busy I-90, at **Olallie**

NIGHT SKIING

More and more skiers are being attracted to nighttime at the mountain. Lower-priced lift tickets, smaller crowds, plus a major coolness factor have driven many of Washington's premier ski resorts to stay open a few hours after darkness falls. It can be a great comfort, especially when this northern-latitude state starts getting dark outside well before 5 P.M.

Most of the ski areas at **Summit at Snoqualmie** are open until 10 P.M. Tuesday through Sunday. Even the tubing park is open until 9 P.M. on Friday and Saturday.

White Pass near Mount Rainier offers a $25 deal for night skiing, or do it in the dark for free if you bought a daytime pass.

Wenatchee's **Mission Ridge** offers a night-skiing lift pass for $15, lasting 4–9 P.M.

State Park (www.parks.wa.gov), the South Fork of the Snoqualmie River drops 300 feet over a stunning series of cataracts. The park is accessible from exit 34 (five miles east of North Bend). After exiting, turn right on Edgewick Road, and then left onto SE 159th St. Continue a half mile to the park. A 1.3-mile path leads to Twin Falls, and from there, you can cross a footbridge and continue uphill another 1.6 miles to a second trailhead near exit 38. The park is day use only, and no mountain bikes or horses are allowed on the trails. Olallie State Park continues eastward along the river above Twin Falls, with several good spots for catching hatchery trout.

The 113-mile-long **Iron Horse State Park** trail (www.parks.wa.gov) also starts from Olallie State Park and follows a gentle old railroad grade over Snoqualmie Pass and all the way down to the Columbia River, 113 miles later.

RATTLESNAKE MOUNTAIN SCENIC AREA
Peak-baggers who don't feel up to taking on Mount Si for the day are quite fond of the 1.5-mile walk up Rattlesnake Mountain to the 2,079-foot **Rattlesnake Ledge,** with amazing views of the Snoqualmie Valley, Mount Si, and **Rattlesnake Lake** below. Munch on a lunch on the flat rock ledge or wait to head down and picnic on the lake, watching anglers spin and fly-cast for the regularly stocked trout swimming in the chilly water. To get to the lake and the trailhead, take exit 32 off I-90, go south on 436th Avenue SE and drive 3.1 miles to the parking area.

Accommodations
Lodging isn't fancy in North Bend, but the motels here do make a cheap stop for those heading west over the pass toward Seattle. **Edgewick Inn** (14600 468th Ave. SE, 425/888-9000, $75 s or $85 d) is one of a few options. There is a microwave and a fridge in the lobby available for guest use.

The Roaring River at North Bend B&B (46715 SE 129th St., 425/888-4834 or 877/627-4647, www.theroaringriver.com, $119–235 d, no kids) offers views of the Middle Fork of the Snoqualmie River. Most of the five rooms have private entrances and baths, gas fireplaces, and decks. A warm breakfast basket is delivered to your door.

CAMPING
Pitch your tent or park your RV at one the convenient Forest Service campgrounds in the Mount Baker-Snoqualmie National Forest. Situated along the South Fork of the Snoqualmie River, **Tinkham Campground** (exit 42 off I-90, drive east on Tinkham Rd. 55 for 1.5 mi., 541/338-7869, www.recreation.gov, $14–16) is a favorite among local Scout troops who'd like to get out in the woods but don't want to get *too* far from civilization. Same goes for **Denny Creek Campground** (exit 47 off I-90, take left and go under freeway then follow signs to campground 3 mi. away, 541/338-7869, www.recreation.gov, $20 tent, $25 RV), which sits in a valley under the I-90 overpass high above. Tinkham welcomes small RVs but has no hookups, and Denny Creek has electric-only hookups. Both sites are

located near a bunch of great trailheads, including the Denny Creek Trail, which leads to some fun natural water slides only a mile away from the campground. Both sites also offer a couple of barrier-free campsites. Both are open May–September.

Food

George's Bakery (127 W. North Bend Way, 425/888-0632, 7 A.M.–5 P.M. Tues.–Sun.) really draws locals for its sweets, fresh-baked breads, sandwiches, and salads.

Boxley's (101 W North Bend Way, 425/292-9307, www.boxleysplace.com, 4–10:30 P.M. daily, brunch 11 A.M.–4 P.M. Sun.) is exactly the kind of restaurant you wouldn't expect to find in North Bend. Understated elegance and nightly live jazz are the main draws, but the expertly prepared, creative meals practically guarantee a return trip. It is a nonprofit that works to fund music education in the area.

Information and Services

The **North Bend Ranger Station** (42404 SE North Bend Way, 425/888-1421, Mon.–Sat. 8 A.M.–4:30 P.M.), a half mile east of town, has information on local trails, mountain bike routes, and campgrounds. The Snoqualmie Valley Chamber of Commerce has a small **visitors center** (38767 SE River St., 425/888-6362, www.snovalley.org) at the North Bend Train Depot, where they will be glad to provide you with maps, brochures, and other information.

Getting There and Around

King County **Metro Transit** (206/553-3000) operates buses that serve North Bend and surrounding communities. **Greyhound** (800/231-2222, www.greyhound.com) stops in North Bend at the corner of 219 Main Ave. S, with connections throughout the nation.

SNOQUALMIE PASS
Sports and Recreation
SKIING

Located 53 miles from downtown Seattle, and right along I-90's Snoqualmie Pass is

The Summit at Snoqualmie (425/434-7669, www.summitatsnoqualmie.com, $35–55), Washington's oldest and largest downhill ski area. The four separate areas, **Alpental, Summit West, Summit Central,** and **Summit East,** range from beginner trails to backcountry and advanced slopes.

Snoqualmie's **Summit Nordic Center** (425/434-6778) is a cross-country playground with over 31 miles of groomed and tracked trails, and the weekends-only **Summit Tubing Area** (SE corner of the Summit Central main parking lot, 425/434-6791, $12–17) rents inner tubes and offers lighted rope tows. Summit at Snoqualmie services include ski shops, equipment rentals, ski schools, day lodges, food service, child care, and bus service to the area.

ALPINE LAKES WILDERNESS

Snoqualmie Pass is one of the most accessible portals into the Alpine Lakes Wilderness, which stretches between I-90 and Highway 2 at Stevens Pass and Leavenworth. You'll find a number of classic Northwest treks including the breathtaking **Kendal Katwalk** (Pacific Crest Trail trailhead at exit 53 westbound and 52 eastbound off I-90), an exhilarating strip of trail that clings to the granite mountainside, seemingly floating amid a colorful display of wildflowers in spring and summer. You can make it to the Katwalk and back (10.5 miles) in a long day, but many adventurous backpackers prefer to extend the trip to a 33-mile round-trip through meadows and alpine forests to the 6,700-foot pinnacle of aptly named Spectacle Point. Just beware of snow—under no circumstances should you attempt to cross the precarious Katwalk when the white stuff is on the ground.

Accommodations

The **Summit Lodge at Snoqualmie Pass** (603 S.R. 906, 425/434-6300, www.snoqualmiesummitlodge.com, $89–259) pretty much has the corner on the lodging market up by the Snoqualmie slopes. Rooms are decent and clean and the property has an indoor pool, hot tub, sauna, and a restaurant. If you're coming with

BIGFOOT IN WASHINGTON?

Washington State is home to the Cascade Mountains, one of the widest expanses of primordial forest in the Lower 48. Hundreds of thousands of acres are trackless and closed to all vehicles. It is this dense wilderness that many believe is home to a thriving community of Sasquatches, more commonly known as bigfoots.

Bigfoot is no Johnny-come-lately. Northwestern American Indians such as the Coast Salish people have passed along legends about Sasquatch for centuries, and a superhuman beast appears frequently in their artwork. Early white settlers sometimes reported spotting apelike hominids roaming the forest, and reports still trickle in today.

Zoologists don't buy the stories, though,

tending to think that what excitable hikers have actually seen is a bear standing on its hind legs or something less spectacular. True or not, Sasquatch has captivated the imaginations of Washingtonians. One of the largest regional publishers is known as Sasquatch Books. With spring comes the annual Sasquatch! Music Festival, held at the Gorge Amphitheatre. And closing out the fair and carnival season is late August's Bigfoot Daze conference and fair held at Bigfoot Park in Carson. Despite the hoopla and doubters, many "cryptid-hunters" still quietly and humbly go about their business stalking the mythical beast through the woods and mountains of Washington's Cascade Range.

---

a group and want to have room for all your snowy gear, consider renting the three-storey **Snoqualmie Rental Cabin at the Slopes** (West Summit of Snoqualmie Pass, 404/861-0804, www.snoquamierental.com, $335–300 nightly with three-night minimum). The cabin sleeps up to six, who can enjoy jetted tubs, a one-car covered garage, a fire pit, and a full kitchen. You can walk to Summit West and Summit Central or take a shuttle to Alpental, Summit Central, and Summit East.

CAMPING

RV parking is permitted at the summit parking lots, but no hookups are available.

In the summertime, camp at **Kachess Lake Campground** (exit 62, then Forest Service Road 49 approximately 5 mi. to campground, 509/649-3744, www.reserveamerica.com, mid-May–mid-Sept., $20–40), which has tent sites and can accommodate RVs up to 35 feet, although there are no hookups. The blue-green lake offers swimming, boating, picnicking, and a nature trail. The campground is under private management and can get a little rowdy on weekends. It is very popular and reservations are highly, highly recommended.

Crystal Springs Campground (exit 62,

then right on Forest Service Road 54 for 0.5 mi., 509/852-1100, mid-May–mid-Sept., $14) is another favorite base camp retreat for Seattleites with just a spare weekend to get outside. Smaller than Kachess, the grounds tend to be quieter and all sites are first-come, first-served.

Food

Atop Snoqualmie Pass, **Summit Pancake House** (425/434-6249, 7 A.M.–9 P.M. daily) at the Summit Inn serves hearty meals in front of their enormous fireplace. Have some fluffy pancakes and coffee and let your parka dry off. Food is also available at all four ski areas in the winter.

Information and Services

The Forest Service **Snoqualmie Pass Visitor Center** (at Snoqualmie Summit, 425/434-6111, Memorial Day–Labor Day Thurs.–Mon. 8:30 A.M.–3:30 P.M., Jan.–Mar. Fri.–Sun. 8:30 A.M.–3:30 P.M.) has information and issues wilderness permits. This is also the meeting point for Forest Service ranger-led snowshoe hikes in the winter. Hikes are held Friday–Sunday for $15 including snowshoes and poles.

Getting There and Around

Although Snoqualmie Pass is generally the easiest way to traverse the Cascades, it does get snowy and sometimes closes during heavy storms. Contact the Department of Transportation for the **Mountain Pass Report** (888/766-4636, www.wsdot.wa.gov/traffic/passes/snoqualmie). The website includes a webcam showing current conditions at Snoqualmie Pass.

Cle Elum and Vicinity

The towns of Cle Elum and Roslyn provide interesting side trips or starting points for hiking or horseback treks into the magnificent Cascade mountain country just to the north and west. Access is easy, with I-90 cutting down from Snoqualmie Pass along the upper Yakima River Valley, passing fields, farms, and stream-laced valleys as you descend.

CLE ELUM

Cle Elum (KLEE-ell-UM, a Kittitas Indian name meaning "swift water") was first settled in 1870. The town's growth was slow until geologists working for the Northern Pacific Railroad discovered coal in 1884, making Cle Elum quite prosperous for a short time. Today the town is a jumping-off point for hiking, fishing, and other recreational activities in the Wenatchee National Forest.

Sights

CLE ELUM HISTORICAL TELEPHONE MUSEUM

Cle Elum was the last city in America to use a manually operated switchboard. The old telephone exchange building was eventually transformed into the Cle Elum Historical Telephone Museum (221 E. 1st St., 509/674-5702, noon–4 P.M. Sat.–Sun. Memorial Day–Labor Day, and by appointment the rest of the year, $2) and now houses switchboard exhibits, photographs of early Cle Elum, and other memorabilia. Be sure to try the "coal" candy.

CARPENTER HOUSE MUSEUM

The spacious Carpenter House Museum (302 W. 3rd St., 509/674-5702, noon–4 P.M. Sat.–Sun. Memorial Day–Labor Day, free) was built by a local banker and one-time Cle Elum mayor in 1914. It is still decorated with many original furnishings including Tiffany lamps and stunning handcrafted wooden furniture.

Festivals and Events

Cle Elum's big event is **Pioneer Days** (509/674-5958) on the 4th of July, which features family-friendly activities such as a street fair, parade, softball and boccie ball tournaments, and fireworks.

Sports and Recreation

IRON HORSE STATE PARK

This is Washington's most unusual state park (509/656-2230, www.parks.wa.gov), a 113-mile long trail that starts near North Bend, crosses the Cascades, and continues all the way to the Columbia River. A centerpiece of the state's rails-to-trails program, the park is open to hikers, skiers, mountain bikers, and horseback riders but closed to motorized vehicles. The trail begins at Olallie State Park (I-90 exit 34), climbs up the west slope of the Cascades to Snoqualmie Pass, and then descends past Cle Elum and Ellensburg (there is a short gap near here) before ending near Vantage along the Columbia River. The gravel trail is gentle, with a maximum 2 percent grade. It crosses 30 substantial trestles and goes through four tunnels, including the 2.3-mile Snoqualmie Pass tunnel; bring flashlights and warm clothes. No overnight camping is allowed. Trailhead access points can be found near many I-90 exits along the way, including Olallie State Park, Snoqualmie Pass, Easton, South Cle Elum, and Thorp.

LAKE EASTON STATE PARK

About 15 miles west of Cle Elum just off I-90, Lake Easton State Park encompasses 518 forested acres on the west and north sides of Lake Easton and is a popular camping spot (if you can ignore the traffic noise). The mile-long reservoir is good for swimming, boating, trout fishing, and water-skiing. The water level changes through the year in this reservoir, and it is drained each winter to provide irrigation water for eastern Washington farms. Hiking, cross-country skiing, and snowmobiling are popular dry-land sports. Kids enjoy the big-toy playground.

HIKING

The **Cle Elum Ranger District** (803 W 2nd St. in Cle Elum, west end of 2nd St., 509/664-9200, www.fs.fed.us/r6/wenatchee, Mon.–Fri. 7:45 A.M.–5 P.M. and Sat. 8 A.M.–2 P.M.) office of the Wenatchee National Forest has information on more than 750 miles of hiking trails in the area. Stop by their office for maps, a detailed trail guide, and information on camping, cross-country skiing, and snowmobiling information.

CROSS-COUNTRY SKIING

The area offers choice cross-country skiing at **Cabin Creek Nordic Ski Area,** a groomed "sno-park" at exit 63 off I-90, and west of Lake Easton State Park. Permits for day-use will cost you $20 and are available at any ranger station, REI store, or a variety of other retailers.

OUTFITTERS

For horseback trips into the backcountry, contact **Three Peaks Outfitter/Guide Service** (1150 Masterson Rd., 509/674-9661, www.3peaksoutfitters.com) for day rides or multiple-day pack rides. They even provide guided fishing and hunting trips.

Accommodations

Sleep in a converted railway caboose without having to share it with hobos at the **Iron Horse Inn Bed and Breakfast** (526 Marie Ave., 509/674-5939 or 800/228-9246, www .ironhorseinnbb.com, $80–145 s or d). The main building here was built in 1909 by the Chicago, Milwaukee, Pacific, and St. Paul Railroads to house railroad workers. The 10 rooms are all photo- and memorabilia-rich lessons in railroad history. And comfortable, too! A hot tub on the deck is utterly relaxing. Some rooms have private baths; others share. The four cabooses are beautifully appointed and all have private baths. Iron Horse State Park Trail is just a few feet from here, so this is an excellent night's rest for cross-country skiers or cyclists. Two-night minimum on holiday weekends.

Adventuresome cowpokes will find something more their speed at **Flying Horseshoe Ranch** (3190 Red Bridge Rd., 509/674-2366, www.flyinghorseshoeranch.com), a sprawling property that is like summer camp for families. There's just about every kind of rustic lodging under the sun (and snow) available: teepees ($90 for four), platform tents ($90 d), sleeping bunkhouses ($100 for eight), and better-appointed wrangler cabins ($115 for four), all with two shared shower houses and cookhouses for cookin' and cleanin'. There's also two private cabins, one larger one with kitchen and bath ($270 for six) and a smaller honeymooner cabin ($165 d) with just a private bath. The grounds include a stable where you can ride horses, a playfield and ball house with tons of outdoors equipment free for use, and an outdoor pool.

Closer in to town, Cle Elum has a spate of cheap hotels good for those just passing through town along I-90. One of the cleanest and most affordable is **Aster Inn** (521 E. 1st St., 509/674-2551, www.asterinn.com, $55–95 s or d), a quaint little rambler of a motel with individual rooms all decorated uniquely, from Western to floral. Some rooms have kitchenettes, others whirlpool tubs.

CAMPING

About 15 miles west of Cle Elum and just off I-90, **Lake Easton State Park** (509/656-2586 or 888/226-7688, www.parks.wa.gov, $22 for tents, $31 RV hookups, $7 reservation fee, late Apr.–mid-Oct.) has additional camping.

Sun Country Golf Resort (841 St. Andrews Dr., 509/674-2226, www.golfsuncountry.com, full hookups $29 weekdays, $34 weekends, $150 per week), six miles west of Cle Elum, has an RV park and a nine-hole golf course.

Food

Get cinnamon rolls and espresso for the road, or a crusty loaf of Dutch crunch bread fresh from the brick oven (in use since 1906) at **Cle Elum Bakery** (501 E. 1st St., 509/674-2233, Mon.–Sat. 7 A.M.–5:30 P.M., Sun. 7 A.M.–2 P.M.).

Ma Ma Vallone's Steak House and Inn (302 W. 1st St., 509/674-5174, daily 4:30–8 P.M.) serves a large selection of steaks, as well as Italian dishes with homemade pasta. A country buffet is offered on Sunday. **El Caporal** (105 W. 1st St., 509/674-4284, daily 11 A.M.–10 P.M.) has quite good Mexican meals and margaritas.

Information

For local information, stop by the **Cle Elum/ Roslyn Chamber of Commerce** (401 West 1st St., 509/674-5958, Mon.–Fri. 8 A.M.–4 P.M.).

Getting There and Around

Kittitas County Connector (509/674-2251) has bus service to Ellensburg, Thorp, Roslyn, and Vantage.

ROSLYN

Known best for its role as the quirky small-town backdrop for the 1990s show *Northern Exposure,* the old mining depot of Roslyn has for decades drawn in tourists seeking that quintessential mountain hamlet experience. They've come for years to enjoy the town's historic district, fascinating cemetery, and rough-around-the-edges atmosphere borne out of sitting at the boundary of so much of the Cascades' backcountry. Roslyn has managed to maintain its unique flavor even as it attracts a new generation of visitors brought in droves to the mega-resort Suncadia, right on its doorstep just a few miles south. Built on a huge chunk of serene Cascade foothills that were formerly the site of the coal mines that made Roslyn

what it is today, the resort offers some of the best lodging, dining, and recreation opportunities in the state.

Sights

Roslyn's main attraction is its Old West false-fronted buildings, many of which appeared in the 1990s television hit *Northern Exposure,* including the famous Roslyn Café sign. **Central Sundries** (509/649-2210) was the location of "Ruth-Anne's General Store."

The **Roslyn Museum** (203 Pennsylvania Ave., 509/649-2776, daily 1–4 P.M.), next to the Roslyn Café, houses an interesting combination of mining equipment and *Northern Exposure* memorabilia.

Goths, genealogists, and those with morbid temperaments are drawn to Roslyn's **town cemetery.** Actually an amalgamation of 25 cemeteries—quite a few, considering the city's population was never higher than 4,000—the spot was split up to accommodate the wide variety of ethnic groups, religions, and fraternal brotherhoods that thrived here during the town's early coal mining days.

Entertainment and Events

Set in downtown Roslyn, **Brick Tavern** is the oldest licensed tavern in Washington. It opened in 1889 and is famous for the 23-foot-long running water spittoon that still washes away patrons' tobacco juice. A popular stop for motorcyclists, the bar frequently sports a long line of gleaming hogs parked out front.

For those with slightly more refined tastes, **Swiftwater Cellars** (www.swiftwatercellars.com) is set up right at the site of the Roslyn No. 9 Coal Mine over at Suncadia Resort. The elegant bar serves some fantastic wines created by a local family with a long history in Northwest winemaking.

Moosefest in mid-July is a *Northern Exposure* fan-fest, sometimes complete with a parade, dinner, theater, and live music. It's not uncommon for former cast members to drop in on the fun. Roslyn's **Coal Miner Days Festival** over Labor Day weekend includes coal-shoveling contests, performers, a street fair, and the coronation of King Coal. The town hosts many other quirky events throughout the year, such as a **sled run** in mid-January and March's **Running Water Spittoon Race,** in which tiny boats face off at the Brick for a purse of up to $200.

Sports and Recreation
HIKING AND MOUNTAIN BIKING
Take Highway 903 from Cle Elum northwest and right through Roslyn and the tiny town of Ronald to the recreational playground around Cle Elum Lake. At the lake, the road turns into Salmon la Sac Road, with a number of Forest Service roads branching off of it to head to backcountry hiking trails, including access to the south end of Alpine Lakes Wilderness Area. From the north end of the lake, take Forest Service roads 4308 and 4312 to the Thorp Creek trailhead for a 3.1-mile hike to tiny **Thorp Lake** and **Kachess Ridge.**

A six-mile one-way hike on Trail 1307 leaves Salmon la Sac Campground and follows a ridge to an excellent view atop **Jolly Mountain.**

With miles of paths on its extensive property open to the public for exploration at **Suncadia Resort** (3600 Suncadia Trail, 509/649-6400

or 866/904-6301, www.suncadiaresort.com) you don't have to stay there to enjoy the scenery. During the summer the resort rents bikes for $15–20 for two hours or $20–25 for overnight rentals.

GOLF
Suncadia Resort's two championship golf courses, **Prospector** and **Rope Rider** (3600 Suncadia Trail, 509/649-6400 or 866/904-6301, www.suncadiaresort.com, $60–100), have both gained a considerable reputation for scenery and challenging terrain. Seasoned golfers will particularly appreciate Prospector's 7,000-yard course, crafted by the Palmer Course Design Company and featuring more than its fair share of bunkers and water features. Meanwhile Rope Rider offers a course made for long drives and those with appreciation for history. Built directly on the site of the historic Roslyn Mines, it's designed around Tipple Hill, a 120-foot coal tailings now taken over by natural vegetation.

Accommodations
The sprawling **◖ Suncadia Resort** offers some of the most sumptuous mountain digs in

© ERICKA CHICKOWSKI

The Lodge at Suncadia

Washington, if not the entire West. Built on a 6,400-acre tract of mining land that was set aside for years after the shafts were sealed off, the resort offers an unparalleled Cascadian setting. Most guests experience the resort from **The Lodge at Suncadia** (3600 Suncadia Trail, 509/649-6400 or 866/904-6301, www.suncadiaresort.com), a enormous brick and faux-timber hotel that features luxurious rooms ranging from the standard hotel room to two-bedroom units with full kitchens sporting granite counters and the full complement of pots, plates, and utensils. The view rooms offer gorgeous mountain scenery and many rooms offer patios, gas fireplaces, and deep soaking tubs. The outdoor pool and spa overlook the Cascades, and loads of recreational opportunities await literally out the front door.

For a little of that homey, small-town atmosphere, **Huckleberry House** (301 W. Pennsylvania, 509/649-2900, www.huckleberryhouse.com, $95–150 d), a block from downtown on a small hill, lets out four lovely rooms decorated with antiques in a beautifully restored early-century-old house.

CAMPING

The camping here is heavenly, with many options to choose from. Closest to Cle Elum is 34-site **Wish Poosh Campground** (eight mi. northwest of Cle Elum on the eastern shore of Cle Elum Lake, $14–28). Continue up Cle Elum Valley Road to find three more campgrounds. The 23-site **Cle Elum River** (Cle Elum Valley Road #903, 15 mi. north of Cle Elum, $11–22) has potable water, but pit-toilet facilities raise the level of adventure here. **Red Mountain** (Cle Elum Valley Road #903, 16 mi. north of Cle Elum, $13) is even a little rougher—its 10 sites have vault toilets and you must pack your own drinking water. Your compensation is the cheap nightly rate. At the end of the line is **Salmon la Sac** (518/885-3639 or 877/444-6777, www.reserveusa.com, $19–36, $7 reservation fee), a 99-site megacampground,

complete with flush toilets, shared kitchens, public horse corrals, and a guard station.

Food

For such a small town, Roslyn has surprisingly good food. Very good breakfasts at **Roslyn Café** (201 W Pennsylvania Ave., 509/649-2763, www.roslyncafe.com, Mon.–Sat. 11 A.M.–8 P.M., Sun. 9 A.M.–2 P.M.) best known for its colorful mural (altered to say "Roslyn's" for the television show).

For more than 80 years, people have been coming to **Carek's Meat Market** (501 E. 1st St., 509/649-2930, daily 10 A.M.–5 P.M.) to purchase fresh and smoked meats. Today, folks make the pilgrimage all the way from Seattle for the Polish sausages, beef jerky, and pepperoni.

The Brick Tavern (100 W. Pennsylvania Ave., 509/649-2643, Sun.–Thurs. 11:30 A.M.–9 P.M., Fri.–Sat. 11 A.M.–9 P.M.) features live music and dancing on weekends—generally the bar stays open until at least 11 P.M., sometimes until 2 A.M. on busy weekends. **Roslyn Brewing Company** (208 Pennsylvania Ave., 509/649-2232, www.roslynbrewery.com, 11:30 A.M.–8:30 P.M., 11:30 A.M.–7:30 P.M.) brews two beers and their dark and delicious #9 root beer.

Located at the Lodge at Suncadia, **Portals** (3600 Suncadia Trail, 509/649-6400 or 866/904-6301, www.suncadiaresort.com) offers locally sourced, gourmet meals in a dining room overlooking serene mountain vistas. Being a resort dining room, you can sup on breakfast and lunch menus, but the real culinary fireworks come during dinner hours. Check out the Suncadia site for special event dinners held throughout the year.

Information

For local information, stop by the **Cle Elum/Roslyn Chamber of Commerce** (401 West 1st St., 509/674-5958, Mon.–Fri. 8 A.M.–4 P.M.).

Enumclaw and Vicinity

Enumclaw occupies a low plateau surrounded by dairy farms. The views of Mount Rainier are outstanding from just about anywhere in town. Situated along Highway 410, Enumclaw is a portal for summer approaches to Mount Rainier's Sunrise area, as well as a jumping-off point to the remote northeastern corner of the park near Carbon River.

SIGHTS
Mud Mountain Dam Park

Mud Mountain Dam Park (seven mi. southeast of Enumclaw off S.R. 410, 360/825-3211) contains one of the nation's highest earth-and-rock flood-control dams. The park is a fun place to take the young kids to toddle. There is a wading pool, playground, picnic areas, and scenic overlooks. Older kids with more stamina will appreciate a scramble over at least part of the 10 miles of hiking trails that unravel on the grounds.

Federation Forest State Park

Federation Forest State Park (18 mi. west of Enumclaw on S.R. 410, 360/663-2207, www .parks.wa.gov) has 619 acres of old-growth forest along the White River. Amid the virgin timber, an interpretive center (summer Wed. Sun. 9 A.M.–4 P.M., closed winters) houses displays on plants and animals in the forest. The park contains 11 miles of hiking trails, including two short interpretive paths and remnants of the historic Naches Trail, a pioneer trail that connected eastern Washington with Puget Sound. Federation Forest is also popular for fishing and picnicking. There's no camping in the park.

Green River Gorge

A dozen miles northeast of Enumclaw on Highway 169, Green River Gorge Conservation Area is a 14-mile-long protected area that includes narrow gorges, white-water rapids, wildflowers, fossils, and caves along the Green River. Several state parks have been developed along the river, the most dramatic being the **Hanging Gardens Area** (access is via SE 386th St./Franklin-Enumclaw Rd., ask rangers at Flaming Geyser State Park for specific directions), where a trail leads to the fern-covered cliffs lining the river.

Flaming Geyser State Park (SE Green Valley Rd. and SE Flaming Geyser Rd., www .parks.wa.gov) occupies several big bends in the Green River four miles southeast of Black Diamond on Flaming Geyser Road. Old coal-mining test holes produced two geysers, one burning an eight-inch flame and the other sending methane gas bubbling up through a stream. Enjoy hiking, picnicking, fishing, boating, and a playground. This is a take-out point for kayakers and rafters floating the Green River Gorge, and the quiet waters below here (at least in the summer) are popular with inner tubers.

Kanaskat-Palmer State Park (11 mi. northeast of Enumclaw on Farman Rd., www .parks.wa.gov) is another popular play area on the Green River, with fishing (especially for steelhead in the winter), camping, and trails through the riverside forests. Several access points in the park are used by river rafters and kayakers heading down the gorge. Because of several Class III–IV stretches, this part of the river is not for beginners.

Nolte State Park (six mi. northeast of Enumclaw, www.parks.wa.gov, open mid-Apr.–Sept.) is a favorite hangout for picnicking, swimming, and fishing. The main attraction is Deep Lake and the 1.4-mile trail that offers a pleasant stroll around this 39-acre lake.

ENTERTAINMENT AND EVENTS

The oldest county fair in the state, **King County Fair** (360/825-7777, www.kingcounty fair.com) is held the second and third week of July at the Enumclaw Expo Center fairgrounds. A rodeo, top-billed live music acts, 4-H exhibits, food, crafts, racing pigs, and a logging show highlight this popular event.

See loggers in action at the **Buckley Log Show** on the last full weekend of June (www .buckleylogshow.org). Another big summertime activity at the fairgrounds is the **Pacific Northwest Highland Games** (45224 284th Ave. SE., www.sshga.org) held the last weekend in July. In addition to the tests of brute strength that are the main attraction, the games include bagpipe and dance competitions, animal exhibits, and vendors selling Scottish crafts, clothing, and foods. That same weekend brings the **Enumclaw Street Fair,** also dubbed "the Ice Cream and Pickle Festival," with a children's art festival, street dancing, and a food court.

In August, in the little nearby town of Wilkeson, the **National Handcar Races** (509/674-5958) are held in mid-July each year. In addition to the railroad handcar races, a parade, antique show, and arts and crafts festival provide diversions.

SHOPPING

Stop by **MacRae's Indian Bookstore** (1605 Cole St., 360/825-3737, www.macraesindian books.com, Tues.–Sat. 10 A.M.–5 P.M., daily), where you'll find a remarkable collection of books on the original inhabitants of this land, covering both local and nationwide tribes. The store's founder strove to carry literally every title about American Indians available, and that thoroughness is still in evidence today.

SPORTS AND RECREATION

The Mount Baker-Snoqualmie National Forest's **White River Ranger District** (450 Roosevelt Ave. E in Enumclaw, 360/825-6585, www.fs.fed.us.r6/mbs, Mon.–Fri. 8 A.M.–4:30 P.M. year-round, plus Sat. 8 A.M.–4:15 P.M. in summer) will gladly point you to nearby hiking trails, suggest campgrounds, or provide general forest information.

Rent bikes and skis or just gear up for a hike at **Enumclaw Ski and Mountain Company** (240 Roosevelt E, 360/825-6910, skiand-bicycle.com, 7:30 A.M.–6 P.M. Mon.–Fri., 7 A.M.–6 P.M. Sat.–Sun.).

It's not exactly Augusta, but the municipal

Enumclaw Golf Course (45220 288th Ave. SE, 360/825-2827, www.ci.enumclaw.wa.us, $20–24) is a fun slope 65.9 course that plays fast on the front nine, but will take a pretty drive to negotiate the salmon-filled creek that runs through after the turn.

The Green River Gorge is a 14-mile stretch of river north of Enumclaw rated Class III–IV, including many well-known rapids with names like Nozzle, Pipeline, and Ledge Drop. The river has a short spring season, generally March and April, since a dam holds the water back for Tacoma's water supply the rest of the year. Catch a ride aboard the guided tours offered by **River Recreation** (800/464-5899, www .riverrecreation.com), which offers 12-mile trips down the gorge from Kanasket-Palmer State Park to Flaming Geyser State Park, plus a riverside lunch spread.

ACCOMMODATIONS

Stop in at **Best Western Park Center Hotel** (1000 Griffin Ave., 360/825-4490 or 877/467-6553, www.parkcenterhotelenumclaw.com) before or after your Mount Rainier jaunt to unwind in the hot tub or clean up hike-muddied clothes in the laundry room. The Park Center also has a restaurant, exercise room, and lots of parking space for RVs and boat trailers. The property is a bit run-down but clean, and you'll get free breakfast and Wi-Fi. Plus you can bring Rover with you.

Over in Buckley, stay at the **Econo Lodge** (29405 S.R. 410 E, 360/829-1100 or 800/582-4111, $70–130 d). Many rooms are pet-friendly and all have refrigerators and a writing desk. The property has an outdoor pool, hot tub, and outdoor spa, plus a continental breakfast.

Camping

Pound in your tent stakes ($21) or hook up the RV ($31) along the Green River at **Kanaskat-Palmer State Park** (11 mi. northeast of Enumclaw on Farman Rd., 360/886-0148). Then you are ready to hop in a rental boat to explore the river. It's open all year, but with limited winter facilities. Make reservations ($7 extra) at 888/226-7688 or www.parks.wa.gov.

FOOD

Carb up before that long wilderness sojourn at Enumclaw's long-running breakfast favorite, **❰ The Kettle** (1666 Garrett St., 360/825-7033, 5 A.M.–2 P.M. Tues.–Sun.). You can't go wrong with the house specialty omelettes, biscuits and gravy, or a towering stack of flapjacks. All servings are enough to stuff an elephant, so don't be afraid to split a plate.

The funky painted redbrick and green trim exterior draws you into the lively din at **The Mint Alehouse** (1608 Cole St., 360/825-8361, Mon.–Thurs. 11 A.M.–11 P.M., Fri.–Sat. 11 A.M.–midnight, Sun. noon–10 P.M.), a local watering hole and eatery guaranteed to fill you up. The menu is big on pizzas, salads, and sandwiches, with a few nacho and quesadilla options thrown into the mix as well. Beer connoisseurs will appreciate the 31 different brews on tap, as well as the proudly displayed tap handle collection, prized for its diversity.

If you're hankering for real old-fashioned burgers and fries, keep driving south past Enumclaw into Buckley and swing into **Wally's White River Drive-In** (282 S.R. 410 N, 360/829-0871, Sun.–Thurs. 8 A.M.–9 P.M., Fri.–Sat. 8 A.M.–10 P.M.). They serve up the best hunks o' beef in the area.

INFORMATION

The **Enumclaw Visitors Center** (1421 Cole St., 360/825-7666, www.enumclawchamber.com) is open Monday–Friday 9 A.M.–5 P.M., Saturday 10 A.M.–2 P.M., and is closed on Sundays.

GETTING THERE

Metro Transit (425/447-4800 or 800/542-7876, metro.kingcounty.gov, $2.25 one-way) runs two routes in Enumclaw. Route 912 motors to Covington, while route 915 travels to Auburn station, which offers connections to Seattle via Sounder light rail.

Eatonville and Elbe

EATONVILLE

Rural Eatonville is located in farming and logging country in the foothills 25 miles west of Mount Rainier. In recent years, Eatonville has attracted a number of artists and craftspeople, and several small galleries dot downtown.

Sights and Recreation
NORTHWEST TREK WILDLIFE PARK

One of the region's biggest attractions is Northwest Trek Wildlife Park (360/832-6116, www.nwtrek.org, $18 adults, $16.50 seniors, $16 military and Pierce Cty, $12 children ages 5–12, $9 children ages 3–4, children under 3 free). Located on Highway 161 near Eatonville, this 600-acre wildlife park is a refuge for grizzly and black bears, wolves, mountain goats, moose, bighorn sheep, elk, and even a herd of bison. Take the one-hour tour of the park or hike its five miles of nature trails. The park opens at 9:30 A.M. daily Feb.–Oct. and on weekends the rest of the year. Closing times

vary between 3 P.M. and 6 P.M. The trams leave hourly beginning at 10 A.M.

PIONEER FARM MUSEUM AND OHOP INDIAN VILLAGE

Experience what pioneer life was really like as you grind grain, churn butter, and milk a cow at the Pioneer Farm Museum and Ohop Indian Village (three miles north of Eatonville, between Highways 7 and 161, 360/832-6300, www.pioneerfarmmuseum .org, closed Thanksgiving through February, $7.50 adults, $6.50 seniors and kids). Ninety-minute guided tours are available daily 11 A.M.–4 P.M. in the summer, with reduced hours in the spring and fall. The farm is also home to a replica Native American village where you can learn about traditional hunting and fishing, tool making, and foods. Hour-long tours of the village are available only on summer weekends at 1 and 2:30 P.M. and cost an additional $7 for adults and $6 for kids. A trading post sells old-fashioned candy, books, and rabbit skins.

PACK EXPERIMENTAL FOREST

Pack Experimental Forest (9010 453rd St. E., 360/832-6534, www.packforest.org) is on University of Washington land just west of Eatonville. The roads across Pack Forest are open weekdays only, but hiking trails are open daily. Short hiking trails crisscross the forest, taking you through stands of trees of varying ages, including a 42-acre preserve of old-growth Douglas fir, cedar, and hemlock.

Festivals and Events

The biggest local events in this little town are the **Fourth of July** with all the fun of a small-town festival, and the very popular **Eatonville Arts Festival,** held in mid-August.

Accommodations

Stay at the spacious and modern **Mill Village Motel** (210 Center St., 360/832-3200 or 800/832-3248, $80–100 s or d). Rooms come with fridges, microwaves, coffee pots, and TVs with satellite service. Continental breakfast is included.

CAMPING

Camp at **Alder Lake Park** (seven miles south of Eatonville, 360/569-2778, www.tacoma power.com), where both tent sites ($22) and RV spaces ($31 full hookups) are available, along with showers. The seven-mile-long lake was created by a dam that produces hydroelectric power for Tacoma City Light. Reservations are advised for summer weekends. The lake also has a popular sandy beach for sunbathing and swimming.

Food

Dining options are limited in Eatonville, but there are a couple of little eateries worth a pit stop before tackling Rainier. **Cruiser Café** (106 Washington Ave. S., 360/832-8646,http:// cruisercafe.biz, 6 A.M.–8 P.M. daily) grills up slow food fast, preparing tasty sandwiches, burgers with freshly formed patties, and fish and chips dipped in homemade batter. Eat in the dining room within the old converted house, or ask them to box it up so you can get to the park more quickly.

Or you can enjoy chips and salsa, yummy tacos, and other good Mexican food at **Puerto Vallarta** (220 Center St. E, 360/832-4033, 11 A.M.–9 P.M. Mon.–Thurs., 11 A.M.–10 P.M.).

The **Eatonville Farmers Market** (104 Washington St., Washington and Center Sts., May–early Oct. 10 A.M.–2 P.M. Sat.) features fresh produce, flowers, and local crafts.

Information

For more information about the town, visit the **Eatonville Chamber of Commerce** (220 Center St. E, 360/832-4000, www .eatonville.com, Mon.–Fri. 9 A.M.–5 P.M., Sat. 10 A.M.–2 P.M.).

ELBE

Fourteen miles from Mount Rainier National Park, Elbe is a wide spot in the road and a pleasant place to enjoy the foothill sights with a dose of railroad memorabilia. Visitors can eat dinner aboard the Cascadian Dinner Train, spend a night in a caboose at Hobo Inn, or peek inside Elbe's **Evangelische Lutherische Kirche,** a tiny white clapboard church measuring just 18 by 24 feet.

Sights and Recreation

◖ MOUNT RAINIER SCENIC RAILROAD

One way to view the area west of Mount Rainier is from the Mount Rainier Scenic Railroad (49 Mineral Creek Rd., 360/492-5588, www.mrsr .com, $12–73). Buy tickets for the vintage steam train at Elbe Station or at Mineral Lake station, where the 90-minute tour has been departing since massive floods in 2006 washed out a few key bridges along the old line. You'll still get to run through forests and over impressive bridges while being regaled with folksy live music and impressive views—especially when the mountain is out. The train runs twice daily in July and August, and on weekends from Memorial Day to early July and in September.

© ERICKA CHICKOWSKI

Kids are fascinated by the steam engines running on the Mount Rainier Scenic Railroad.

MINERAL LAKE

Rumor has it that oft-lucky trout anglers at Mineral Lake (three mi. south of Elbe on Mineral Hill Rd.) regularly hook enormous 10-pound rainbows and brownies. This hidden glacial lake offers some impressive views of the mountain when it decides to peek out from under its pillow of clouds. Rent boats, fishing poles, and crayfish traps at **Mineral Lake Resort** (148 Mineral Hill Rd., 360/492-5367, www.minerallakeresort.com). Zip around in a pontoon ($125 full day, $75 half day) or slowly paddle yourself around in a rowboat ($10 hourly). Or just fish from the dock for $6; poles can be had for $5 daily. Nonanglers can also play in the water in a paddleboat ($7 per hour).

Accommodations

Elbe's most unusual accommodations are at the **Hobo Inn** (360/569-2500, www.rrdiner .com, $115 s). You can set your bindles down in one of eight antique cabooses—some date back to 1916—that have been completely reconditioned, with beds and bathrooms added. One even features a hot tub. Rates include breakfast at the Mt. Rainier Railroad Dining Company right next door. Make reservations a month ahead in the summer to be assured of your own caboose—there are no stowaways allowed on this train.

You can make Mineral Lake your home base for Rainier expeditions and lazy fishing days from one of two spots along the lake. Families will dig the summer camp vibes at **Mineral Lake Resort** (148 Mineral Hill Rd., 360/492-5367, www.minerallakeresort.com), where they can borrow boats to explore the waters. Guests can either camp in their RVs or cozy up in one of the cabins on the property. The rustic studio cabins ($90–100) sleep up to six and include kitchenettes, outside barbeques and fire pits, and patios. The only catch is that you'll have to share the central bathrooms with the campers and there are no showers on the property. For a bit more space and comfort, the bunkhouse ($180) can fit up to eight, includes all of the amenities of the studio cabins, and has a full bathroom.

Couples in search of a romantic getaway may prefer the historic **◖ Mineral Lake Lodge** (195 Mineral Hill Rd., 360/492-5253, www.minerallakelodge.com, $115–145 s or d), a three-story log lodge built in 1906. The property has over 200 feet of grassy waterfront with the best view of Rainier on the whole lake. There's a bonfire area, private sauna, sunroom with a view, and an inviting porch swing all on the premises. Rooms are done up in themed Americana decor, and continental breakfast is served each morning.

Food

If you don't sleep in a caboose, at least eat in one. Right next door to the Hobo Inn, the **◖ Mt. Rainier Railroad Dining Company** (54106 Hwy. 7 E., 360/569-2505) is known for hearty breakfasts and finger-lickin' barbecue. Try the smoky, hearty servings of homemade stew served in bread bowls. This house specialty is made from leftovers from the barbecue.

© ERICKA CHICKOWSKI

Housed in an old truck weigh station, Scale Shack Burger is a favorite stop on the way to Paradise.

The other old standard in Elbe is across the street. **Scale Shack Burger** (54109 Hwy. 7, 360/569-2247, daily 10 A.M. to 7 P.M.) flips its enormous "scaleburgers" from a converted truckers' weigh station shack. Sit out on one of the picnic tables clustered around the shack and enjoy the colorful tractor tire flowerpots while you munch on behemoth burgers and crispy fries. Be sure to bring cash.

Ashford

Ashford is your last chance for food, lodging, and gas before you enter Mount Rainier National Park from the most popular Nisqually entrance. Rather than being a "last resort," some of the hotels, cabins, and restaurants here are as good as or better than park facilities. Established in 1891, Ashford began as an end-of-the-line town where tourists stepped off the Tacoma Eastern Railroad to enter the park.

For incredible views of Mount Rainier, head north from Ashford on Copper Creek Road (Forest Service Road 59). The road also provides access to the Glacier View Wilderness.

HIKING
Mount Tahoma Trails
Halfway between Elbe and Ashford is the Mount Tahoma Trails Association (www .skimtta.com), featuring 75 miles of groomed cross-country skiing in the winter, and mountain biking, horseback riding, and hiking on the trails in the summer. A series of three huts and a yurt provide overnight accommodations for six people (up to 14 in some of these), making it possible to ski or hike from hut to hut. There's no charge to stay in the huts, but a $25 per-person per-night damage deposit is required in advance, and you'll need a Sno-Park

permit ($20) to park your vehicle. Buy one at Ashford Valley Grocery (29716 Hwy. 706 E, 360/569-2560, 6 A.M.–10 P.M.).

Other Trails

The **Puyallup Trail** (No. 248) ascends from Forest Service Road 59 for 2.5 miles to the park boundary, continuing eastward an equal distance to the park's Westside Road. A side route climbs 5,485-foot **Gobbler's Knob** for a grand view of Mount Rainier. Reach the trailhead by taking State Route 706 east for three miles past Ashford, take a left on 305th Avenue East, follow that for 2.7 miles, take another left on Forest Service Road 037, go 1.5 miles and hang a left on Forest Service Road 59, which you'll follow to its end almost four miles later.

ACCOMMODATIONS

Ashford has quite a few comfortable cabins, B&Bs, and lodges. Because of their popularity, reserve space at least two weeks ahead for midsummer.

Under $100

Built in 1912 as loggers' quarters, **⟨ Whittaker's Bunkhouse** (30205 Hwy. 706 E., 360/569-2439, www.whittakersbunkhouse.com, dorm bed $35 s, motel $95–115 s or d) is a favorite among climbers seeking affordable lodging and comfortable camaraderie in the cozy shared dorm rooms here. The recently renovated private motel rooms also make a great launch pad for active families with little ones who don't quite feel up for camping. Warm up in the hot tub, or head to the espresso shop for a cup of java or to check your email.

Another affordable option is **Nisqually Lodge** (31609 Hwy. S.R. 706 E., 360/569-8804 or 888/674-3554, $95–105 s or d), which has large motel rooms and a hot tub. Rate includes continental breakfast.

$100-150

Literally a stone's throw from the park entrance, **Stone Creek Lodge** (38624 S.R. 706 E., 360/569-2355 or 800/678819-3942, www.stonecreeklodge.net, $110–140) offers some of the best bargain cabins in Ashford. You can't beat the location, and the cabins themselves are modern, hip-roofed cedar cottages with kitchenettes and fireplaces on lightly wooded grounds.

Also near the park entrance, but not nearly as nice, **Gateway Inn Motel** (38820 S.R. 706 E, 360/569-2506, www.gatewayinnonline.com, $129–149) works for those in a pinch during the high season or just stopping over for the night. The cabin interiors are spacious and clean, but dated—in a late 1960s kind of way. But they all have fireplaces and the staff is friendly.

$150-200

A mile west of the park entrance, **Alexander's Country Inn** (37515 S.R. 706 E., 360/569-2300 or 800/654-7615, www.alexanderscountryinn.com, $130–179) is the mainstay of elegant Rainier lodging. Constructed in 1912, the inn was visited by Presidents Theodore Roosevelt and William Howard Taft. Guests will enjoy antique furnishings, fireplaces, stained-glass windows, and the modern addition of a hot tub. A full breakfast is served at the gourmet restaurant on-site—roundly lauded as Ashford's best.

Those who would prefer to focus their chi would likely better appreciate **⟨ Wellspring Spa & Retreat** (54922 Kernahan Rd. E., 360/569-2514, www.wellspringspa.com, $99–147 s or d). This attractive forested property hidden from the main road welcomes guests to cozy up inside its various log cabins. The property is host to a hot tub amidst a beautifully maintained zen garden with a running stream and two spa treatment rooms with their own wood-fired saunas, all of which are available on an hourly basis along with massage therapy. The cabins all come loaded with fridges, microwaves, and wood-burning stoves. Some also have kitchens. More adventurous guests can also choose to stay in the well-appointed platform tents open during the summer months.

Choose from a dozen different classic chalets with private hot tubs at **Jasmer's B&B and Cabins** (30005 S.R. 706 E, 360/569-2682, www.jasmers.com, $150–250). These retreats also come with kitchens, patios, barbecues, fire pits, and picnic tables. Some are pet-friendly and include laundry facilities. Jasmer's also offers fireplace rooms in the main guesthouse that include continental breakfast and a shared hot tub.

A classic old 1910 home, **Mountain Meadows Inn B&B** (28912 Hwy. 706 E, 360/569-2788, www.mountainmeadowsinn.com, $149–169) opens the doors to six spacious guest rooms with private baths in a lovely country setting. Breakfast is a scrumptious sit-down affair perfect for exchanging stories about the great outdoors. Be sure to ask the innkeepers for their own stories—they've traveled all over the world. They'll also be happy to show you their extensive collection of John Muir memorabilia. The inn also has a sauna, fishing pond, and nature trails.

$200-250

The pinnacle of Rainier luxury can be found three miles from the park entrance in **Stormking Spa and Cabins** (37311 S.R. 706 E, 360/569-2964, www.stormkingspa.com, $190–205, no kids). This cluster of four cabins all offer private hot tubs and secluded privacy that make them a favorite among honeymooners. Three of the four are uniquely constructed round cabins with 16-sided walls, and all of them have unique walk-in showers—one made with impressive slate stonework, two with river rock, and one two-person greenhouse shower. On site is a luxury spa offering massage, aromatherapy soaks, and time to sweat in the sauna.

Camping

Avoid driving the camper on the busy national park roads and instead opt to park at the peaceful **Mounthaven Resort** (38210 Hwy. 706 E, 360/569-2594, www.mounthaven.com, $32 full hookup), which offers pretty sites under tall cedars, some near a gurgling creek. Mounthaven offers coin-op laundry facilities,

pay phones, showers, and restrooms, and it is pet-friendly.

Food

Your best option in the Mount Rainier area is served at (**Alexander's Country Inn** (37515 Hwy. 706 E., 360/569-2300, www.alexanderscountryinn.com, noon–3 P.M. lunch, 4–9 P.M. dinner daily in summer, weekends only in winter), where specialties include salmon, trout caught fresh from the backyard pond), home-baked bread, and famous wild blackberry pie. It also offers a large wine list.

Rainier Overland Lodge (31811 S.R. 706, 360/352-8984, rainieroverland.net) serves big family-style breakfasts, a good chicken BLT sandwich, and a choice of all-American faves.

Get espresso coffees and sweets at **Whittaker's Bunkhouse** (30205 S.R. 706 E, 360/569-2439, www.whittakersbunkhouse.com).

The Highlander Steakhouse and Lounge (30319 Hwy. 706 E, right in the center of Ashford, 360/569-2953) will do for a plate of hot food and cup of coffee after a long hike or climb.

Information and Services

Get maps, current weather conditions, and lodging information from **Whittaker Mountaineering** (360/569-2451, Wed.–Sun. 9 A.M.–5 P.M.).

After a weekend of hiking in the park, head to **Wellspring** (360/569-2514) or **Stormking Spa and Cabins** (360/569-2964) for a relaxing massage, sauna, and hot tub.

Summit Haus (30027 S.R. 206 E next to Whittaker, 360/569-2227, www.rmiguides.com) sells and rents a wide range of camping and outdoor clothing and gear. This is also home to Rainier's longest-running climbing guide service, **RMI Guides.**

Highlander Tavern and Laundry (360/569-2953) offers an unusual mix: suds on tap, suds in the launderette, and showers to suds up after a backcountry trip.

Mount Rainier National Park

With 300 miles of hiking trails covering terrain from the lowland forests all the way to the ice-topped summit at 14,411 feet, Mount Rainier is a recreational paradise. More than two million people visit Mount Rainier National Park annually, soaking up towering waterfalls vistas from the winding mountain roads, strolling through flower-filled mountain meadows at Paradise, camping beneath old-growth Douglas fir forests, climbing the mountain's glacier-clad slopes, listening to the bugling of elk on a fall evening, and skiing backcountry trails in the winter.

History

Several Northwestern American Indian tribes made seasonal fishing, hunting, and berry-picking forays into the foothills around Mount Rainier, avoiding the mountain itself. It's unknown if their skittishness was out of reverence for the majestic mountain or because of the weather, which can be both unpredictable and severe. The Lushootseed Indian Tribe called the peak "Ta-ho-ma," meaning "mother of waters" or "white sentinel." The city of Tacoma gained its name from the mountain that rises so tall behind it. In 1792, British explorer Capt. George Vancouver rechristened the mountain after his friend, Rear Adm. Rainier, a man who never did see the American mountain.

In 1883, James Longmire—who had guided climbers to the base of Mount Rainier for many years—discovered a mineral springs near the Nisqually River and staked a mining claim on the site. Longmire recognized the land had much higher value, however. The wild beauty and grand mountain views quickly turned his mind away from mining and toward tourism. His Longmire Springs Resort was built in 1906 and drew hundreds of visitors. The resort is long gone, but the area now qualifies as the national park's oldest developed area and bears the name Longmire in honor of its first settler.

Mount Rainier might never have became the enormous unspoiled national park it is had it not been for a lumber deal made by the shareholders of a wealthy railroad concern. In the early 1800s, the federal government gave away land in a sort of checkerboard pattern to encourage companies to build an intercontinental railroad. Shareholders of the Northern Pacific Railroad took a look at their Mount Rainer land holdings and saw that their land was not much by way of timber. So they struck a bargain with the government. They would exchange their parcels ringing the mountain for government land that was farther away but rich in old-growth trees. The railroad made a fortune, not just from logging but from fares charged to bring visitors to the park they helped create. Not a bad business deal! The

RAINIER'S GLACIERS

Approaching Mount Rainier, most people are struck by the eerie-blue lakes, the snowy cap of the mountain, and its round shape. All three features are caused by our slow, icy friend, the glacier.

Glaciers form when snow and sleet build up on top of a mountain. Pressure from gravity plus thawing and refreezing causes the snow to become a massive sheet of ice. The process can take hundreds of years. Meanwhile the glacier is creeping down the mountain, rearranging rock, smoothing rough edges, and feeding lakes with sediment. Geologists believe that, at the peak of the last ice age, Rainier's glaciers may have stretched up to 30 miles away from the peak!

Even now, Mount Rainier has an amazing collection of glaciers. There are 40 unique glaciers, many of which are viewable from the national park. Since the 1930s, the glaciers have been shrinking a little at a time. There are many theories, but no one is quite sure why.

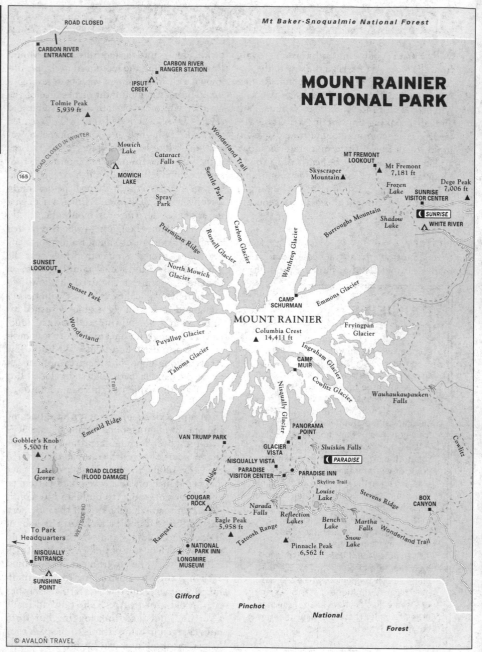

ROAD CLOSED

CARBON RIVER
ENTRANCE

Mt Baker-Snoqualmie National Forest

CARBON RIVER
RANGER STATION

IPSUT
CREEK

Tolmie Peak
5,939 ft

MOUNT RAINIER
NATIONAL PARK

Wonderland Trail

MT FREMONT
LOOKOUT

Mowich
Lake

Cataract
Falls

Skyscraper
Mountain

Mt Fremont
7,181 ft

Dege Peak
7,006 ft

MOWICH
LAKE

165

Seattle Park

Frozen
Lake

SUNRISE
VISITOR CENTER

Spray
Park

SUNRISE

Burroughs Mountain

Shadow
Lake

WHITE RIVER

ROAD CLOSED IN WINTER

Ptarmigan Ridge

Carbon Glacier

Russell Glacier

Winthrop Glacier

SUNSET
LOOKOUT

North Mowich
Glacier

Sunset Park

Emmons Glacier

CAMP
SCHURMAN

Wonderland

MOUNT RAINIER

Columbia Crest
14,411 ft

Fryingpan
Glacier

Puyallup Glacier

CAMP
MUIR

Ingraham Glacier

Trail

Tahoma Glacier

Cowlitz Glacier

Wauhaukaupauken
Falls

Nisqually Glacier

Emerald Ridge

PANORAMA
POINT

Cowlitz

Gobbler's Knob
5,500 ft

VAN TRUMP PARK

GLACIER
VISTA

Sluiskin Falls

Lake
George

ROAD CLOSED
(FLOOD DAMAGE)

NISQUALLY VISTA

PARADISE

PARADISE
VISITOR CENTER

PARADISE INN

Skyline Trail

Ridge

COUGAR
ROCK

Louise
Lake

Stevens Ridge

BOX
CANYON

To Park
Headquarters

WESTSIDE RD

Narada
Falls

Reflection
Lakes

Bench
Lake

Martha
Falls

Wonderland Trail

NISQUALLY
ENTRANCE

NATIONAL
PARK INN

Eagle Peak
5,958 ft

Ramcart

Tatoosh Range

Snow
Lake

SUNSHINE
POINT

LONGMIRE
MUSEUM

Pinnacle Peak
6,562 ft

Gifford

Pinchot

National

Forest

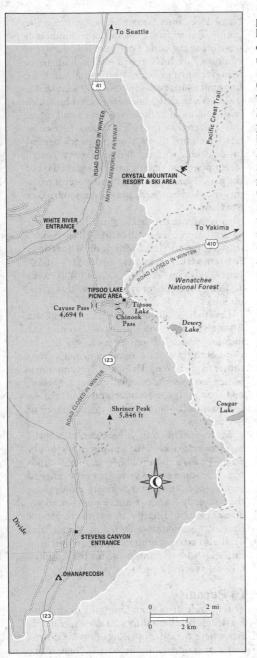

park went on to become our country's fifth-largest national park, and the awesome beauty of this sleeping volcano has been drawing visitors ever since.

Geology

The 14,411 foot volcanic summit of Mount Rainier is estimated to be nearly one million years old. The history of the mountain has been full of shrinking and growing land mass. Layer after layer of ash, lava, and other materials gradually build the mountain up while glaciers slowly carve away at it. And rarely, a volcanic event like an explosive eruption or a mudflow or collapse can change the face of the volcano in an instant. That's what happened about 5,000 years ago when an earthquake or other event caused a portion of the mountain to collapse, sending a slurry of melted glacier, mud, and debris racing at over 60 miles per hour ultimately covering an area of 130 square miles. When the dust cleared on what came to be called the Osceola lahar, Rainier had lost an estimated 2,000 feet of height from her top. A lahar, or volcanic mudflow, is different than an eruption in one significant way. Eruptions can be roughly predicted by watching earthquake activity, steam vents, and the shape of the mountain. Lahars happen almost without warning. The cities of Kent, Orting, Sumner, and Enumclaw are all built on the leftover material from the Osceola event and would be in serious danger during another mudflow. The mountain hasn't erupted since sometime between 1820 and 1854, but was still selected as a "Decade Volcano," meaning that, of all the world's volcanoes, it is one of 16 with the highest potential for destruction of property and loss of life. For now, this majestic giant that most of Washington refers to as "the" mountain will remain a symbol of fair, sunny days and the most recognizable image of all Washington State.

Climate

Because of its incredible height, Rainier creates its own weather by interrupting the air flow around it and causing wet air blowing off the Pacific Ocean to release its moisture. This produces massive amounts of snowfall on the western slopes of the mountain. The mountain's height also accounts for its lenticular clouds—the upside-down-saucer-shaped clouds that obscure or hover just above the summit on otherwise clear days.

Although it can rain or snow any month of the year on Rainier, most precipitation is between October and early May, much of it snow. July and August are the driest and sunniest months. At Paradise (5,400 feet in elevation), the snowpack often tops 15 feet by late March, remaining on the ground until early July. Down the mountain at Longmire (2,761 feet in elevation), snow averages four feet deep in midwinter and is generally gone by the beginning of May.

Throughout most of the park, temperatures are not much different from those around Puget Sound except for wintertime. The average summer day at Longmire is in the 70s, with nights dipping into the high 40s. Temperatures at Paradise are commonly around 10°F cooler than this during the summer. Spring and fall are the times to be careful; rain at Longmire can very often translate to snow at Paradise. But fall weather also means fewer people and the brilliant yellow and red leaves of cottonwoods, vine maples, bigleaf maples, Sitka mountain ash, and blueberry bushes.

SIGHTS

Driving through Mount Rainier National Park provides numerous sightseeing and photographic opportunities; the surrounding mountains, waterfalls, forests, and canyons alone justify the trip. Several amazing places don't require a lengthy backpacking trip, easily seen by just about anyone looking to see Washington's beauty up close and personal. The following descriptive tour begins in the southwest corner of the park and follows the main roads to the northeast corner.

Longmire Area

Longmire is seven miles from the Nisqually entrance in the southwest corner of the park.

Named for James Longmire, whose Longmire Springs Resort first attracted large numbers of travelers to the park, Longmire is home to the National Park Inn (housed in an old Longmire Mineral Springs Resort building), and the **Longmire Museum** (360/569-2211 ext. 3314, 9 A.M.–5 P.M. daily) one of the oldest museums in the National Park service. The small museum—located in the original park headquarters—contains displays on the park's natural history, along with exhibits of basketry, a small totem pole, and photos from the early days of the park. Nearby is a small transportation history museum inside the historic **Longmire Gas Station.**

Several nearby hiking trails cover the gamut, from easy strolls through the woods to steep mountain climbs. The **Wilderness Information Center** (360/569-6650, June–mid-Sept. daily 7:30 A.M.–4:30 P.M.) at Longmire can provide you with all the options.

Less than a mile in length, the **Trail of the Shadows** takes you on a stroll around the meadow where Longmire's resort stood, with views of the mountain. A longer loop hike continues from here up Rampart Ridge to a majestic view over the Nisqually River far below, and then joins the **Wonderland Trail.** Follow this back to Longmire for a total distance of five miles.

More adventurous hikers can climb the many switchbacks to the summit of 5,958-foot **Eagle Peak,** a distance of seven miles roundtrip. The route passes through a wide range of vegetation, from dense old-growth stands along the Nisqually River to flowery alpine meadows offering extraordinary vistas across to Mount Rainier. The mountain-encircling Wonderland Trail also passes through Longmire, making this a favorite starting point for backcountry hikes of varying lengths.

◖ Paradise

The 13-mile drive from Longmire to Paradise is a delightful climb through tall evergreen forests where periodic openings provide down-valley and up-mountain vistas. Three miles

PEAK-A-BOO

picture perfect Narada Falls

One day as I rolled up the windy hill to Paradise, I stopped at a viewpoint for a moment to take in the view of the Tatoosh Range that had opened up in the clouds. As I stood there, a car with out-of-state plates rolled in and a family clambered out and looked around quizzically. The teenaged son approached me.

"So . . . where's the mountain?"

I pointed to the mass of fog and clouds that had been at my back. "That-a-way."

The youngster was noticeably bummed. Unfortunately, those are the breaks in the Pacific Northwest, particularly around the damp country that surrounds Mount Rainier. Many tourists who come to see the monumental peak fail to understand that Mount Rainier spends a lot of time under the clouds – those blue-sky photographs of her in all her glory are so remarkable because they're hard to line up. Sometimes Rainier might be under the weather even when everywhere else is clear.

The mountain is so big that it creates its own weather system.

The trick is to stay flexible – sometimes weather might be better on one side of the mountain while the other side is socked in – and appreciate the park for what it is. Sure, you might come for the mountain, but Mount Rainier National Park has countless trails, meadows, and riversides that would wow you if you could just let go of the weather disappointment.

Here are just a few of my favorite spots to chase away the cloud-cover blues:

- Box Canyon
- Grove of the Patriarchs Trail
- Narada Falls
- Ohanapecosh
- Paradise Visitor Center
- Tipsoo Lake

before you reach Paradise is a pullout overlooking **Narada Falls,** where a steep trail leads to the plunge pool at its base.

But that's just a prelude to the beauty of Paradise Valley. At an elevation of 5,400 feet, the valley's alpine meadows erupt in a riot wildflowers in the short Rainier summer, the colorful display a contrast against the snowy summit that towers above. Get here in late July and August to see the peak of the floral display. Paradise is easily the most popular area of the park, with an abundance of short and long hiking trails, grand scenery, and ample winter recreation opportunities.

Built in 1917, **Paradise Inn** offers mountain-vista accommodations and meals mid-May through September only. Paradise visitors should do themselves a favor and take a peek inside before tromping away on a hike. The lobby hall and its massive fireplaces surrounded by rustic furniture are the best part of the inn.

A spiderweb of trails spins out over the subalpine forests and high-country meadows at Paradise; see the visitors center for a detailed map. The **Nisqually Vista Trail,** is the easiest with a 1.2-mile loop hike that leads through flowery high-country meadows west of the visitors center. Almost everyone in decent physical condition takes the oft-crowded **Skyline Trail,** a five-mile romp above the tree line to Glacier Vista and Panorama Point. Needless to say, the views are extraordinary. Be sure to carry water and stay on the path. Far too many folks wander off, creating damage to the meadows that takes years to restore.

Heading east from Paradise toward Stevens Canyon, the road passes **Reflection Lakes,** where on a calm and clear day the mirror-like surface reflects Mount Rainier and a rim of forest. The **Pinnacle Peak Trail** starts at the Reflection Lakes parking lot; hike this 1.5-mile trail to the saddle between Pinnacle and Plummer Peaks for Mount Rainier vistas. You'll be gaining 1,100 feet in elevation along the way.

An easier trail takes you uphill to **Bench and Snow Lakes.** The trailhead is a mile east of Reflection Lakes on Stevens Canyon Road, and the path goes 1.25 miles each way, through late-summer meadows filled with bear grass and flowers.

To gather suggestions on other hikes, visit **Paradise Visitor Center** (360/569-2211, ext. 2328, daily 9 A.M.–7 P.M. in the summer, and 10 A.M.–6 P.M. in spring and fall, open weekends and holidays only Oct. 15–early May), a gorgeous new facility that matches the steep-roofed, stone-and-shingle architecture of Paradise Inn, while offering visitors up-to-date multimedia presentations, museum displays, and access to park rangers who are ready to answer questions and suggest hikes. During the summer, naturalists lead walks and give talks on a daily basis, and in winter they lead weekend snowshoe treks.

Stevens Canyon/ Ohanapecosh Area

East of Paradise, the road passes 100-foot-high **Martha Falls** and cuts across the slopes of Stevens Canyon as it follows Stevens Creek downhill. At **Box Canyon** a short trail leads to a footbridge spanning the deep but narrow gorge created by the Muddy Fork of the Cowlitz River. By the time you reach the junction with Highway 123, the road is deep within old-growth forests of Douglas fir and western hemlock at an elevation of just 2,200 feet.

The **Ohanapecosh Visitor Center** (360/569-6581, 9 A.M.–6 P.M. daily late June through Sept., and 9 A.M.–5 P.M. daily Sept.–Oct., closed mid-Oct.–late May). Rangers lead two-hour walks several times a week during the summer months.

The **Grove of the Patriarchs Trail** starts just west of the Stevens Canyon entrance station and covers 1.5 miles of virgin forest terrain. This easy loop trail circles an island in the crystalline Ohanapecosh (oh-HAH-na-pee-kahsh) River, passing thousand-year-old Douglas firs, western hemlocks, and western red cedars that tower over a verdant fern-filled understory.

A longer hike, the **Silver Falls Trail,** follows the river in a three-mile loop that takes you to the 75-foot cataract of Silver Falls, passing a side trail to the site of Ohanapecosh Hot Springs Resort along the way. It's illegal to enter the shallow springs here. The trail begins at the Ohanapecosh Campground.

The **Shriner Peak Trail** starts from Highway 123, 3.5 miles north of the Stevens Canyon entrance; park on the west side of the road about a half mile from the Panther Creek bridge. This eight-mile hike—about five hours round-trip—is almost completely devoid of shade and ends up at a lookout/ranger station at Shriner Peak (5,846 feet).

Cayuse Pass

North from Ohanapecosh, Highway 123 follows the Ohanapecosh River and Chinook Creek upstream, reaching 4,694 feet at Cayuse Pass, 11 miles from the Stevens Canyon entrance station. Here the road meets Highway 410, which continues north past the White River entrance and east over Chinook Pass, where Tipsoo Lake creates a picture-postcard image. Yakima is another 64 miles to the east.

(Sunrise

The Sunrise area occupies a high subalpine plateau showcasing the northeast side of Mount Rainier. Getting here is half the fun; a long series of switchbacks takes you 11 miles up from Highway 410, past the White River entrance station and through tall evergreen forests along the river before finally emerging into subalpine meadows offering all-encompassing vistas. Because of the rain-shadow effect, this side of Mount Rainier gets far less precipitation than the western side, and the vegetation reflects this. Green and tawny grasses and even whitebark pine are common here. The Sunrise area is home to large numbers of elk during the summer and fall. Elk are not native to the park but were brought here from Yellowstone and other parts of the West between 1903 and 1933; around 1,500 of them now inhabit the park.

Located at 6,400 feet, the log cabin **Sunrise Visitor Center** (360/663-2425, 10 A.M.–6 P.M. daily July–early Sept., 10:30 A.M.–4 P.M. mid-Sept. only) houses natural history displays and

© ERICKA CHICKOWSKI

Rainier peeks from under the trees at Longmire.

has viewing telescopes where you can check out Mount Rainier's glaciers, including massive Emmons Glacier, largest in the Lower 48. The interpretive staff leads daily nature walks; stop by the information desk for times and destinations. Not far away is **Sunrise Lodge** (July–Sept. only) with food and gifts, but no lodging.

Many trails head out from the Sunrise area, including sections of the Wonderland Trail and shorter hikes to nearby lakes and mountains. The **White River Hiker Information Center** (at the entrance station, daily late May–Sept.) has backcountry and climbing permits, along with maps and other information. **Shadow Lake Trail** is one of the most popular, a three-mile jaunt that departs from Sunrise parking lot, drops to a rim overlooking the White River Valley, and then follows that ridge to Shadow Lake. Return via Frozen Lake and Sourdough Ridge.

To get to **Mount Fremont Lookout** from the Sunrise parking lot, follow the trails to Sourdough Ridge and Frozen Lake, then branch off to the north. The mountain is 7,181 feet high, a gain of 1,200 feet. This well-marked six-mile path takes about three hours round-trip.

For **Dege Peak,** start between Sunshine Point and the Sunrise parking area; this one-mile trail climbs 7,006-foot Dege Peak in the Sourdough Mountains.

Carbon River Area

In the far northwest corner of the park, Carbon River sees far fewer visitors than other better-known destinations. The region is best known today for its magnificent temperate rain forest. Access is via Highway 165 south from Enumclaw and Buckley. The Carbon River Road was destroyed in 2006 and is in the process of being converted to trail. Access is still permitted up to the **Carbon River Ranger Station** (360/829-9639) where many trails begin, including the one to Ipsut Creek Campground.

The alternative, a gravel road, enters the park south of here and climbs to Mowich Lake, located in a high bowl-shaped cirque glacier. Get details at the **information center** (360/829-5127) in the town of Wilkeson.

The Carbon River Road is still open to hikers and bikers, so consider schlepping your stuff into the Ipsut Creek Campground and exploring via day hikes. From the campground, take the quarter-mile **Carbon River Rain Forest Trail** for a quick taste of Mount Rainier's only true rain forest. The **Carbon Glacier** extends northwest from Mount Rainier, reaching just 1,100 feet in elevation. A section of the Wonderland Trail leads from Ipsut Creek Campground to the snout of the glacier, 3.5 miles each way. Just to be on the safe side, be mindful of rocks that may fall from the glacier.

From Mowich Lake, hike the three-mile trail past pretty Eunice Lake and on to the historic **Tolmie Peak** fire lookout at 5,939 feet in elevation.

SPORTS AND RECREATION

Backcountry Hiking

Rainier's hiking season is quite short, with trails snow-free from mid-July–mid-October, though trails at the lower elevations may open earlier and remain snow-free later in the year. It's always advisable to dress in layers for *all* seasons when hiking in the Cascades, choosing cool synthetics, wool, and rain gear. About 300 miles of hiking trails crisscross the park, many miles of which are suitable for day hikes. The park has a helpful *Wilderness Trip Planner* available by mail; get a copy from the park's backcountry desk (360/569-2211, ext. 3317). A number of companies lead guided hikes in the park, including **REI Adventures** (800/622-2236, www.rei.com). Contact the park for other concessionaires with similar services.

BACKCOUNTRY REGULATIONS

Backcountry permits are required for all overnight trips in the park throughout the year and are available for free if you wait until 24 hours before leaving on your trip, or $20 to reserve the permit ahead of time. Get them from the wilderness information centers and ranger stations in Longmire, White River, Wilkeson, Ohanapecosh, and Paradise, or print out a reservation from the Web (www.nps.gov/mora) and send it in with the fee. Permits are available up to 24 hours before you depart. If you're heading into a popular area on a busy weekend, your first choice may be full. Sunday–Thursday nights are far less crowded, so head out on these days if possible.

Fires are not allowed in the backcountry, so bring a stove along. Be sure to filter or otherwise treat any drinking water, since the protozoan Giardia and other harmful microorganisms may be present. Always practice no-trace camping and haul out any garbage. Hikers in backcountry meadows should stay on the trails at all times; plants here have only a brief growing season, and damaged areas take a long time to recover. Pets are not allowed on any park trails.

There are three types of backcountry camps within the park. **Trailside camps** are located every 3–7 miles along backcountry trails, including the mountain-circling Wonderland Trail. Trailside camps all contain a nearby water source and pit toilet, and five people (in two tents) are allowed at an individual campsite. The vast majority of hikers use these established campsites. If you choose to camp away from these sites, you'll need to stay at **cross-country camps**, hiker-chosen sites located a quarter mile away from the trail and other camps and at least 100 feet from water sources. Hikers are not allowed to establish cross country camps along the Wonderland. Climbers generally curl up in **alpine camps**, in areas above 6,000 feet. The rule here is that tents must only be set on permanent snow or ice or on bare-ground areas previously used as a campsite. Don't clear new tent sites or build windbreaks on rocky areas. The rocks you pull up could be protecting fragile alpine plant root systems.

WONDERLAND TRAIL

The Wonderland Trail is a backpacker's dream: 93 miles of passes, forests, streams, and alpine meadows that completely encircle the mountain. The trail has lots of ups and downs, including 3,500-foot changes in elevation in several stretches of the route. Allow 10–14 days for the entire trip. Food (but not fuel) can be cached at ranger stations along the way by mailing packages to yourself; contact the Park Service (360/569-2211) for addresses and other specifics.

You can start your Wonderland hike almost anywhere—Mowich Lake, Longmire, White River, Box Canyon, or Ipsut Creek among the possibilities. A wide range of shorter one-way and loop hikes are also possible along the Wonderland Trail.

Also for marathon packers, the **Pacific Crest Trail** touches the east edge of the park at Tipsoo Lake on Highway 410, continuing north to British Columbia and south to Mexico.

OTHER TRAILS

The **Mother Mountain Loop** is a rewarding two- or three-night trip in the northwest section of the park. Begin at the Ipsut Creek Campground, making sure to allow time to hike in and out 4.8 miles each way along the washed-out Carbon River Road to this trailhead. Then follow the Wonderland Trail up the Carbon River, and then turn onto the **Spray Park Trail**. The trail approaches Cataract Falls (a quick side trip) and crosses Marmot Creek. Camping is permitted about one mile below Seattle Park in Cataract Valley with a permit. Hike across a permanent snowfield into Spray Park (where avalanche lilies carpet the meadows late in the summer), and continue to Mowich Lake, turning northeast to follow the Wonderland Trail down Ipsut Creek and back to your starting point. It's about 16 miles round-trip.

Another good overnighter, though not a circular route, is **Indian Bar.** This hike starts at Box Canyon on Stevens Canyon Road, crosses Nickel Creek, then turns left to follow the Cowlitz Divide. At Indian Bar, the Ohanapecosh River divides a meadow; the shelter is on the west side, just above Wauhaukaupauken Falls. Return by the same route for a total of 15 miles.

Gobbler's Knob is a fire lookout (5,500 feet) that can be reached from Round Pass on Westside Road near the Nisqually entrance. This 2.5-mile trail passes Lake George. Westside Road is closed at Fish Creek, three miles up, due to recurring floods that have washed out the road, so you may need to wade across (sometimes this is not safe). The area is always prone to floods and mudflows. Bikes are allowed on the road (but not off the road) beyond here, but be sure to get current conditions from the Park Service before heading up. The lookout is also accessible from outside the park via the tiny Glacier View Wilderness.

Climbing

Because of its many glaciers and rocky faces, Mount Rainier has long been one of the premier training peaks for American climbers. More than 4,500 people reach Mount Rainier's summit every year—of some 9,000 who attempt it. Two days are usually required for the trek: the first day involves a four- to five-hour hike over trails and snowfields to **Camp Muir,** the south-side base camp at 10,000 feet, or **Camp Schurman,** on the northeast side at 9,500 feet. The second day starts early (about 2 A.M.) for the summit climb and the return to the Paradise starting point. Reservations are not accepted for the high camps, so be prepared to camp outside: Muir's 25-person capacity is frequently filled, and Schurman has no public shelter—your only luxury is a pit toilet.

All climbers must be in top physical condition before heading out, and experience in glacier travel is highly recommended. Rainier is a difficult climb, and before heading up, you need to undertake a rigorous conditioning program. Above the high camps climbers are roped, using ice axes and crampons to inch their way over glaciers to the summit. All climbers must register and get a **climbing card** ($30 annually) at a hiker information center, visitors center, or ranger station before their climb. Solo climbers need the park superintendent's approval. Climbers can reserve camping privileges on the mountain for an additional $20 fee.

GUIDED CLIMBS

Even inexperienced climbers can conquer the mountain if they are in excellent physical condition. Currently three park-sanctioned guide companies operate on Rainier.

Each service offers a number of guided climb routes, from the most accessible Camp Muir route to the path over the vast white Emmons Glacier on up to the extremely challenging Liberty Ridge route.

Founded in part by famed Everest climber Louis Whittaker and his twin brother, Jim, in 1968, **Rainier Mountaineering, Inc.** (summer 360/569-2227, winter 253/627-6242, www.rmiguides.com) offers guided treks up Mount Rainier, along with snow- and ice-climbing seminars for climbers of all skill levels ($187 one-day snow- and ice-climbing school, no reservations necessary). Most popular is the four-day summit climb package ($970). RMI also offers crevasse rescue seminars, private lessons, and six-day winter mountaineering seminars ($1,930). Some of the required equipment—including boots, crampons, ice ax, and pack—is available for rent at the Guide House in Paradise.

Some beginners may appreciate the personal attention offered by either **Alpine Ascents** (206/378-1927, www.alpineascents.com) or **International Mountain Guides** (360/569-2609, http://mountainguides.com); both run slightly more expensive than RMI but have a maximum 2:1 climber-to-guide ratio on their expeditions through Camp Muir. Alpine Ascents runs three-day summit climb packages for $1,280, which includes round-trip transportation from Seattle, a helpful benefit for out-of-towners wishing to avoid renting a car to get up to base camp. International Mountain Guides runs a longer, 4.5-day Muir summit that is the least-rushed guided climb up the mountain offered by any company. Similar to RMI, both companies also offer more challenging route options and a range of clinics and classes to improve climbing skills. Climbing programs operate from late May–late September.

Other Summer Recreation

Fishing is generally disappointing at Rainier

FIRST TO THE TOP

Climbing a 14,411-foot volcano that has completely unpredictable weather and is snowy year-long takes a certain kind of person. Local Salish tribes kept a respectful distance, sticking to the lowlands surrounding the mountain for hunting and gathering berries. Once white settlers arrived in the area, however, the mountain that dominated the entire Puget Sound was an irresistible challenge. The first documented peak-bagger was Union Civil War veteran Gen. Hazard Stevens, a Congressional Medal of Honor recipient who was fearless or crazy or both. His party included the secretary to the governor of Washington territory, a painter, a farmer, and a young local Native American named Sluiskin. In 1870, they set out at the warmest point of summer and found the goings easy...at first. Farmer James Longmire,

at 2,600 feet, decided that perhaps he'd left his iron on and should go check on it. Edward T. Coleman, the painter, had seen enough after day one and turned back himself. Even intrepid Sluiskin faltered before the peak, made camp, and waited to see whether Stevens and the government secretary, P. B. Van Trump, would return victorious or end up in a frosty crevasse somewhere. Van Trump and Stevens soldiered on, catching some sleep at the true peak and returning, to the astonishment of Sluiskin. Today, their names are written in the record books, and also in the names of various peaks, meadows, streams, and lakes in the Rainier area. Climbing the mountain, even in winter, is still a popular pastime. And still a serious challenge – even today, many who go up never come down.

(www.nps.gov/mora); the fish, if you wrangle any, are small. Or, as the Park Service notes, "anglers' success is often less than anticipated."

The fish in park lakes are non-native—all here are survivors of previous stocking efforts that have long since subsided. As a result, there are no limits or restrictions to what you catch on the lakes, with the exception of Frozen, Reflection, Shadow, and Tipsoo Lakes, which are all closed water. Within park streams, park officials ask that you use barbless hooks to protect native fish. Fishing for bull or Dolly Varden trout and chinook salmon is prohibited, and there's a six-pound limit for all other fish, not to exceed 12 fish. No fishing is allowed on Klickitat Creek above the White River entrance supply intake, Ipsut Creek above the campground water intake, Edith Creek basin above the Paradise water supply intake, and Laughingwater Creek above the Ohanapecosh intake. Only fly-fishing is allowed on Ohanapecosh and its tributaries.

No fishing license is required. The park's lakes and ponds are ice-free from July–October; rivers, streams, and beaver ponds are usually fishable from late May through late October.

Nonmotorized **boating** is allowed on all park lakes except Frozen Lake, Reflection Lakes, Ghost Lake, and Tipsoo Lake; canoes are a great way to view the wildlife.

Horses are allowed on 100 miles of horse-trails; contact the Park Service for a horse-trail map.

Cyclists find Mount Rainier's roads to be steep, winding, and narrow—a prescription for trouble due to the heavy automobile traffic. Use extreme caution when **cycling** in the park, since RVers have a reputation for not always knowing the width of their vehicles. None of the backcountry trails in the park are open to mountain bikes, although nearby Forest Service land has hundreds of miles of such trails.

Cross-Country Skiing

Mount Rainier is famous for its abundant backcountry, where the snow seems to reach out forever, and the Telemark skiing is unmatched in Washington. Many beginners head to the Paradise parking lot to ski up the unplowed road, or out the trails to Nisqually Vista, Narada Falls, or Reflection Lakes. None of these are groomed, but it generally doesn't take long for other folks to set down tracks in the new snow. The area gets an incredible 630 inches of snow in a typical year!

The east-side roads provide other skiing options, including, of course, the groomed slopes at **Crystal Mountain Ski Area,** just a few miles outside the park's northeast corner. For a quieter experience, the Ohanapecosh area is a good bet. Park near the ranger station and ski up the roads toward Cayuse Pass or Box Canyon if you are ambitious, but be sure to check about avalanche dangers before heading up. Easier skiing can be found in the unplowed Ohanapecosh Campground loops.

Rent skis, avalanche beacons, snowshoes, and other winter gear from the **Longmire** store (360/526-2411). It also provides ski lessons and tours. Ski rentals are not available at Paradise. If you plan to overnight in the backcountry, be sure to get a permit before heading out; they are required year-round (but free in winter). Call 360/569-2211 ext. 3314 for current avalanche conditions, or talk with Park Service folks in Longmire before heading up the hill.

Facilities are open for winter sports at Paradise from December–April. The park constructs a supervised snow play area here in early December. The area is very popular for inner tubes, saucers, or other soft sliding toys (no wooden toboggans or sleds with metal runners are allowed), but bring your own, since they are not available for rent.

Ranger-led **snowshoe walks** are offered at the Paradise Visitor Center on winter weekends and holidays. Snowshoes are free to use during these walks and can be rented from the lodge gift shop or the Longmire Store at other times.

ACCOMMODATIONS

There are two inns within the park itself; both are run by the park concessionaire, **Mount Rainier Guest Services** (360/569-2275, www.guestservices.com/rainier). Each has a storied history and offers unparalleled access to the park, but for real comfort and relaxation the cabins and B&Bs in Ashford really are the way to go. Prices at both inns within the park are through the roof, and neither can quite shake that bit of institutionalized dreariness

that lingers around many lodges within the national park system.

The **National Park Inn** ($112–190 s or d) at Longmire is open daily year-round. This inn has a central stone fireplace and decent rooms with shared or private baths. Built in 1917, **Paradise Inn** ($109–197 s or d) is an imposing wooden lodge with high ceilings, stone fireplaces, and unsurpassed mountain views from its elevation of 5,400 feet. The lodge underwent a $22 million renovation in 2008, but even after that the units are still not exactly up to luxury levels. The lodge is open daily from late May through September; rooms have shared or private baths.

Camping

There are hundreds of sites to pitch a tent or park an RV within Mount Rainier National Park's campgrounds (800/365-2267, http://reservations.nps.gov), all with running water and flush or pit toilets but no RV hookups. Coin-op showers are available at the Paradise Visitor Center when it is open, but you'll need to head to Ashford or other towns for laundry facilities. Gathering firewood is prohibited in the park, but it can be purchased at the Cougar Rock and Ohanapecosh campgrounds, as well as the Longmire General Store.

Easier places to stake the tent or roll up the camper are **Cougar Rock Campground** (2.5 miles northeast of Longmire, $12–15) or **Ohanapecosh Campground** (near the southeast entrance on Highway 123, $12–15). Both are open late May–mid-October and can accommodate RVs up to 32 feet. Both also feature drinking water, flush toilets, and dump stations for RVs. Reservations are highly recommended from July 1–Labor Day at these two grounds.

Those making the sojourn up to Sunrise and hikers planning on bivouacking up at Camp Schurman before an Emmons Glacier attempt like to stop in at **White River Campground** (on the east side in the Sunrise area, open late June–late Sept., $10).

The road is bumpy leading to the free **Mowich Lake Campground** (open June–Oct.) walk-in sites, the facilities are primitive, and

Even if you don't stay the night, take a few minutes to tour the lobby at Paradise Inn.

© ERICKA CHICKOWSKI

there's no running water. But you'll be rewarded for your trouble by smaller crowds and pretty lakefront spots. Camping is not permitted in the Paradise area or along park roads in the summer, but winter camping is allowed at Paradise once the snow depth tops five feet. Get permits and details on locating your camp from the visitors center.

FOOD

Longmire has a sit-down restaurant inside the **National Park Inn** (360/569-2411, open year-round). The dining room at **Paradise Inn** (360/569-2413, late May–Sept.) serves three meals a day and a big Sunday brunch during its season of operation. For something less formal, the **Paradise Visitor Center** (open daily May–early Oct., weekends and holidays year-round) operates a snack bar with typical fast food.

The cafeteria at **Sunrise Lodge** operates only between late June and early September. Limited groceries are available year-round at Longmire General Store and during the summer at Sunrise.

Call ahead, as hours vary from month to month at all of these venues.

INFORMATION AND SERVICES
Admission

Entrance to Mount Rainier National Park is $15 per vehicle, and $5 per person for folks arriving by foot and on bikes, motorcycles, buses, or horses. Your entrance fee is good for seven days. If you plan to visit several parks, or surrounding national forests or other federal recreation lands, get an $80 America the Beautiful National Parks and Federal Recreational Lands Annual Pass. Seniors over age 62 can pay a one-time fee of $10 for a lifetime version of this pass, and disabled visitors can obtain one for free at the park's entrance.

Information

Information and assorted publications are available at visitors centers in Longmire, Paradise, Ohanapecosh, and Sunrise, and from the various entrance stations. The park's quarterly newspaper, *Tahoma,* is packed with up-to-date details on park activities, camping, hiking, climbing, and facilities. Request a copy in advance of your visit, along with a park map and other brochures, from the Park Service (360/569-2211). The **Northwest Interpretive Association** (877/874-6775, www.discovernw.org) sends out a mail-order catalog of publications and topographic maps. **Park headquarters** (360/569-2211, www.nps .gov/mora) are located nine miles outside the park in Ashford's Tahoma Woods area.

Services

Gift shops are found at Sunrise, Paradise, and Longmire. Camping supplies are limited in the park; it's better to bring yours in from the outside. Climbing supplies—including boots, crampons, ice axes, and packs—can be rented from the RMI Guide House at Paradise or Summit Haus in Ashford.

Park **post offices** are in Paradise Inn (summer) and Longmire's National Park Inn (all year). Short on cash? The closest **ATM** is located in Ashford at Ashford Valley Grocery (29716 Hwy. 706 E).

Interpretive Programs

The National Park Service schedules nature walks, campfire programs, and children's activities from July–late September. Program schedules are posted at visitors centers and campgrounds, as well as in the park newspaper, *Tahoma*. Come winter, naturalists offer snowshoe walks at Paradise.

GETTING THERE AND AROUND
By Car

In 1911, the first automobile to reach Mount Rainier National Park was a touring car carrying none other than President William H. Taft. Maybe because of his weight, maybe because of the wet dirt roads, he got bogged down and had to be pulled the rest of the way by a team of mules. Since then, the roads have improved somewhat and should provide less worry, although neither mule-teams nor gasoline are available in the park. Be sure to fill your tank in one of the surrounding towns.

Winter snow closes most of Mount Rainier's roads, with the exception of the section between the Nisqually entrance and Paradise. This road closes each night and reopens in the morning after the plows have cleared any new-fallen snow. Tire chains are frequently required and you should always have them when touring the mountains during any season. The road between Paradise and Ohanapecosh

is generally open Memorial Day–early November, while State Route 123 and State Route 410 over Cayuse Pass usually open in late April and remain open till the first heavy snowfall (November). Chinook Pass is open from early June–November, and the road to Sunrise generally opens by the first of July and closes once the snow gets too deep, frequently in early October. Early snows can close any of these, so be sure to call the National Park (360/569-2211) to see which roads are open. The Longmire store sells tire chains, in case you've set out without them.

Bus Tours

Unfortunately, there are no bus or van shuttle services operating from Sea-Tac Airport to Mount Rainier—those looking for longer explorations must at least make it by car to Ashford.

In recent years the parks service has started experimenting with a free summertime passenger shuttle running between Paradise and Longmire every half hour 9 A.M.–5 P.M. Friday–Sunday, with extended service to Ashford Saturday and Sunday. Contact the Longmire visitors station for info.

Gray Line (206/626-5208 or 800/426-7532, www.graylineofseattle.com, $85 adults, $65 kids) leads 10-hour day trips to the park from Seattle, which is a lot of ground to cover in that short a time. **Tours Northwest** (888/293-1404, www.seattlecitytours.com, $99.27) runs similar tours that depart from Seattle and take you to Mount Rainier and back in 10 hours.

Chinook Pass and Highway 410

From Enumclaw, the winding route of Highway 410 cuts through the northeast corner of the park until it hooks east at Crystal Mountain, threading through Chinook Pass over to Naches and the Yakima Valley on the eastern side of the mountains. Highway 410 southeast of Crystal is a fair-weather route, closed in winter and often dusted with snow as late as June.

CRYSTAL MOUNTAIN AND GREENWATER
Sports and Recreation
CRYSTAL MOUNTAIN SKI AREA

Most Washington skiers will agree that nothing makes their hearts pitter-patter like standing in front of bluebird skies and freshly fallen powder at Crystal Mountain (33914 Crystal Mountain

Rd. in Crystal Mountain, 360/663-2265, snow conditions 888/754-6199, www.crystalmoun tainresort.com, lifts open daily 9 A.M.–4 P.M. mid-Nov.–mid-Apr.). This is Washington's largest and highest-elevation ski area, with some of the nicest lifts and lodges in the Northwest. On clear days you can take in views of Mount Rainier while carving up the slopes, no matter what your skill level—there's everything from bunny slopes to double-black-diamond routes to get the old ticker pounding. Even cross-country skiers can get into the act on miles of groomed trails.

Adult lift tickets are $65 all day. Youth age 11–17 cost $60 all day. Kids 0–10 years old can wriggle their legs over the chairlift all day for $5. Seniors over 70 can buy lift tickets for $40 all day. And beginners of any age can pick up a lift ticket good only for the bunny slope for $37.

Other services at Crystal Mountain include rentals, ski and snowboard schools, day care, and several restaurants.

Crystal Mountain is 76 miles from Seattle. The **Crystal Mountain Express** (800/665-2122) provides bus service from Seattle, Bellevue, and Tacoma on weekends and holidays late December–February. The cost is $89 adult round-trip, including an all-day lift ticket.

HIKING

Several popular hiking trails lead from the Crystal Mountain area to the **Pacific Crest Trail** in the nearby Norse Peak Wilderness Area, including the **Silver Creek Trail** (No. 1192) and **Bullion Basin Trail** (No. 1156), both of which reach the PCT in a bit over two miles of hiking. The PCT itself climbs across the backbone of these ridges for approximately 27 miles from Government Meadow (accessible via Forest Service Road 70) on the north end, to Highway 410 near Chinook Pass on the south end. Along the way it cruises over high ridges, including two that top 6,400 feet; a popular side path leads to the summit of 6,856-foot Norse Peak for extraordinary views across to Mount Rainier.

Another long favorite is the **Crystal Mountain Trail** (No. 1163), a 12-mile loop hike (or mountain bike ride) that follows a ridge along Crystal Mountain. Unfortunately,

the resort does not run a summer lift prog so you'll have to crank it out on your own.

For a short hike with excellent views of Mot Rainier, head 32 miles east from Enumclaw o Highway 410 to Corral Pass Road (No. 7174), and follow it seven miles to a parking area just before the Corral Pass Campground. From here, the appropriately named **Rainier View Trail** climbs for a mile to a 6,080-foot ridge overlooking the mountain. This is a popular place to camp, but carry water since none is available at the ridge. The trail continues beyond this, connecting with the Castle Mountain Trail, 2.2 miles from your starting point. An additional five miles of hiking brings you to the Pacific Crest Trail near Martinson Gap. Check with the Forest Service for the condition of Castle Mountain Trail; at last check it was difficult to follow.

Located off State Route 410 at Forest Service Road 74, **Carbon Trail** (No. 1179) cuts across Clearwater Wilderness for 9.4 miles, with a mile-long spur to the summit of 6,089-foot Bearhead Mountain, which provides views across the alpine meadows to still-wild Mount Rainier and the heavily logged slopes of adjacent private and Forest Service lands. To reach the trailhead, you must turn up Forest Service Road 7450 from Forest Service Road 74 and follow 7450 to its end. High-clearance vehicles are suggested.

Accommodations

Crystal Mountain Lodging Suites (33000 Crystal Mountain Blvd., 360/663-2558 or 888/668-4368, www.crystalmountainlodging .com, $275–545 for four) has one- and two-bedroom condos within walking distance of the lifts. All condos have kitchens; some have fireplaces and share an outdoor heated pool. Save considerably on weekdays, in summer, or with ski-package deals.

Crystal Mountain Hotels (33818 Crystal Mountain Blvd., 360/663-2262 or 888/754-6400, www.crystalhotels.com) has rooms at the Village Inn ($170–225 d), the Austrian-style Alpine Inn ($195–250 d), and the cycle-friendly Quicksilver Lodge ($195–250) near the base of the mountain.

Just five minutes away from the turnoff to the

ate River entrance to the national park and the steep ascent to Sunrise, (**Alta Crystal Resort** (68317 S.R. 410 E, 360/663-2500 or 800/277-6475, www.altacrystalresort.com, $219–269 d) is one of the more popular year-round lodging picks near Crystal. The property features a hot tub and swimming pool, plus hiking and Nordic skiing trails. Kids love the nightly bonfires in the summer. Choose between one- and two-bedroom condo units in the central lodge or a luxurious honeymoon cabin.

CAMPING

Get regional camping and hiking information from the **Naches Ranger District** (509/653-1400). The Forest Service operates many popular campgrounds along Highway 410 between Enumclaw and Crystal Mountain, including **The Dalles Campground** (26 miles southeast of Enumclaw on S.R. 410, 518/885-3639 or 877/444-6777, www.reserveusa.com, $14). The short and easy **Dalles River Trail** leaves from the campground and follows the White River. The main attraction here is a Douglas fir tree that reaches almost 10 feet in diameter. Also along the highway is **Silver Springs Campground** (35 miles southeast of Enumclaw on S.R. 410, 518/885-3639 or 877/444-6777, www.reserveusa.com, $14), near the turnoff to Crystal Mountain Resort on Highway 410. Both of these are open mid-May–mid-October.

Food

Food of all types is available at on-the-mountain and base eateries. The highlight among them is **Summit House** (33914 Crystal Mountain Rd., 360/663-2265). Accessible only by chairlift, this is the highest restaurant in the state and offers a phenomenal view of Mount Rainier; watch for climbers approaching the summit. Open for lunch and dinner, the Summit House is a favorite place to watch the sunset over Mount Rainier. Reservations are strongly recommended on weekends. In the summer, Crystal Mountain serves a special sunset dinner at Summit House. For $85 per person you'll be whisked up the chairlift before twilight and served a choice of soup or salad, an entrée, dessert, and a nonalcoholic beverage as the sun fades over the mountain.

As you're headed back toward Enumclaw after a day of skiing, do as the locals do and stop at **Naches Tavern** (58411 S.R. 410 E, 360/663-2267, daily 11 A.M.–2 A.M., closes early in shoulder seasons, call for hours) in the tiny village of Greenwater. The cozy lounge has a country feel, a friendly atmosphere, and good food served in large quantities. Order up an entrée or buy a hot dog and roast it over the crackling fire in their fireplace.

CHINOOK PASS

The highest of the Cascade mountain passes, Chinook Pass rises more than a mile above sea level on Highway 410. Just west of the pass, the highway enters Mount Rainier National Park, passing **Tipsoo Lake,** one of the most beautiful and easily accessed Cascade alpine lakes. Enjoy a picnic lunch here against a striking Mount Rainier backdrop. More adventurous folks will enjoy the **Naches Peak Loop,** a 3.5-mile hike that skirts the lakeshore and then circles this mountain. Part of this loop follows the Pacific Crest Trail.

Boulder Cave is up a Forest Service road just west of the little settlement of Cliffdell on State Route 410. Take a flashlight to explore this tunnel-like cavern.

For an interesting loop backpacking trip that includes a section of the PCT, take Bumping River Road past Bumping Lake, and turn onto Road 18 to its end, where the **Bumping Lake Trail** (No. 971) climbs the headwaters of the Bumping River to Fish Lake. Here you turn north on the PCT, follow it to the **American Ridge Trail** (No. 958), and then hike two miles to the **Swamp Lake Trail** (No. 970), where you turn again to reach your starting point. The round-trip distance of this loop hike is approximately 27 miles.

Accommodations

(**Whistlin' Jack Lodge** (20800 S.R. 410 in Cliffdell, 25 miles northwest of Naches on Highway 410, 509/658-2433 or 800/827-2299, www.whistlinjacklodge.com) is on the sunny side of the mountains, with just 15 inches of precipitation annually and over 300 days of sunshine. Open year-round, the lodge includes a motel ($110), cabins ($160–265), restaurant, lounge with live music on weekends, gas, and groceries. If you are already hungry heading over Chinook Pass, be sure to stop at the diner here—it is a long haul to Yakima on an empty stomach and the choices in Naches are sparse.

Choose between classic motel rooms or cabins with fireplaces and kitchens at **Squaw Rock Resort & RV Park** (15070 S.R. 419, 20 miles northwest of Naches on S.R. 410, 509/658-2926, www.squawrockresort.net, $110–160 s or d). Situated along the Naches River, this resort has a heated pool, hot tub, restaurant, store, and public showers.

Closer in to Naches and Yakima, **Apple Country Inn B&B** (4561 Old Naches Hwy.,

509/664-0400, $85–120 d) is a remodeled 1911 farm house and working ranch positioned perfectly between Rainier and wine country in the Yakima Valley. Two guest rooms have private baths, a continental breakfast is served, and kids are welcome.

More than a dozen Forest Service campgrounds can be found just off Highway 410 between the national park and the town of Naches. Some are free; others charge $8–12. These are only available on a first-come, first-camp basis.

Bumping Lake Road leads past eight Forest Service campgrounds, the little settlement of Goose Prairie, and Bumping Lake. Boats can be rented and RV spaces are available at **Bumping Lake Marina** (509/575-0417). **Goose Prairie Inn** (509/837-3767) has a restaurant and cabin rentals, but these are generally only available in the fall and winter.

White Pass Scenic Byway

Winding its way east from I-5 through farmland, old-growth forests and one of the state's prettiest alpine passes, White Pass Scenic Byway (U.S. 12) runs between Mount Rainier and Mount St. Helens. This makes it an ideal route for wanderlust-filled wayfarers hoping to spend a week or two exploring the state's two biggest volcanic attractions and the vast stretches of wilderness areas that span between them.

MOSSYROCK AND VICINITY

Mossyrock occupies farming country along the Cowlitz River northwest of Mount St. Helens and east of Chehalis. The primary crops raised here are tulips, blueberries, and Christmas trees. Two dams have created nearby Riffe and Mayfield Lakes, choice territory for anglers, boaters, and picnickers.

Sights
MARYS CORNER
AND JACKSON HIGHWAY
Twenty miles west of Mossyrock on Highway 12 and just three miles east from I-5 is the

crossroads called Marys Corner. Just south of the intersection on Jackson Highway is the **John R. Jackson House,** a log cabin built in 1845 that was a popular stopover for travelers on the Oregon Trail.

Two miles south of Marys Corner, the road passes **Lewis and Clark State Park** (4583 Jackson Hwy. in Winlock, 360/864-2643), which preserves a proudly standing grove of old-growth evergreen. Several short trails provide loop hikes through the tall Douglas fir, western red cedar, western hemlock, and grand fir trees. The west side of Lewis and Clark State Park emphasizes horseback use.

A pullout four miles east of Mossyrock along the highway leads to a viewpoint offering a glimpse—on clear days—of Mount St. Helens, 24 miles to the south.

Sports and Recreation
There is no question that the Mossyrock area's greatest draw is its position almost exactly between Mount Rainier and Mount St. Helens. Cyclists, hikers and climbers, especially those

traveling in RVs, might well find themselves accidentally in the little town of Mossyrock. But for anglers, it is a top-notch destination of its own. The nearby lakes and ponds are chock-full of trout, bass, catfish, panfish, salmon, and perch. And the Cowlitz River is legendary for its steelhead catch. Best of all, you don't have to have a boat to get out there and start catching. On the west side of town, fish **Mayfield Lake Park** (180 Beach Rd., 360/985-2364) for trout, bass, and coho salmon. **Mossyrock Park** (202 Ajlune Rd., 360/983-3900) to the east opens up Riffe Lake, home to trophies in just about all species. Both parks also have fee-based boat launches. For some peace, quiet, and fighty largemouth, visit Swofford Pond, just slightly south of Riffe Lake. It is closed to all gas-powered engines and fully stocked with legal sized trout. All three require a valid Washington fishing license and knowledge of state limits and regulations.

ccommodations

rawling along the southern shores of the ke, **Lake Mayfield Resort and Marina** 50 Hadaller Rd. in Mossyrock, 360/985- ,357, www.lakemayfield.com) offers a spate of lodging options at its full-service property. The waterfront resort is ideal for boat-owners, with a marina that includes a boat ramp and eight docks. This sportsman's special does not offer daily housekeeping service, but you can choose between one- and two-bedroom condo units ($149–199), all with full kitchens, satellite television, and air conditioning. "Luxury" is in the eye of the beholder. For tent campers, the log-built bungalows ($59–79) seem heavenly with their rigid-framed beds, wooden roof, and porch-swing. Bathrooms are nearby and there are coin-op showers.

Seven miles west of Mossyrock in Salkum, **The Shepherd's Inn B&B** (168 Autumn Heights Dr., 360/985-2434 or 800/985-2434, www.theshepherdsinn.com, $90–125 d) is an attractive, quiet, country home with five guest rooms (shared or private baths), including an indoor hot tub and full breakfast. Salkum's **Country Cabins Motel and RV Park** (2527

U.S. 12 in Salkum, 360/985-2737, $53 s or d) is an attractive wood-faced motel block with cozy and super clean rooms with kitchenettes and benches in front of the room for relaxing after a hard day of fishing.

CAMPING

To reach **Mossyrock Park** (202 Ajlune Rd., 360/983-3900), turn south at the Mossyrock flashing light and follow the signs three miles east. Here you'll find walk-in tent sites ($21), RV sites with no hookups ($19), electric-only RV spots ($23), and full RV hookups ($30). Picnic tables dot the lakeshore and boat launches are the best way of getting out on green-blue Riffe Lake. More properly called a reservoir, it bears the name of the little community that was drowned under 225 feet of water as part of the construction of the Mossyrock Dam in 1968.

If you turn north at the Mossyrock light, you'll eventually get to **Ike Kinswa State Park** (360/983-3402), about three miles off the highway. This 454-acre park is open year-round for trout fishing on Mayfield Lake, with swimming, picnicking, lakeside campsites ($22), and RV sites ($28). In the winter, look for bald eagles on the trees along the shore. Make reservations ($7 extra) at 888/226-7688 or www.parks.wa.gov. Another place for RVs on the road to Ike Kinswa Park, two miles north of the highway, is **Harmony Lakeside RV** (563 S.R. 122, 360/983-3804, $38–49 with full hookups).

In addition to its enclosed cabin and condo units, **Lake Mayfield Marina and Fishing Resort** (350 Hadaller Rd. in Mossyrock, 360/985-2357) also offers camping. RV owners can roll in ($38–58), and campers can unfurl their tents onto sites with water ($39) or the primitive sites at the resort's secluded Adventure Island ($29).

For a little more solitude, **Barrier Dam Campground** (273 Fuller Rd. in Salkum, 360/985-2495) offers wooded tent ($18) and RV sites with full hookups ($28). The property also has a convenience and tackle store. If you're here for the fishing, this is one of the best locations you can pick.

MORTON TO PACKWOOD

Passing the glinting waters of Riffe Lake, you're likely to see timber-burdened semis zooming in either direction as you approach a string of small logging towns framed with a checkered mix of freshly cut and second-growth forested slopes. Among these hamlets is Randle, which sits at the Highway 12 junction with Forest Service Road 25, the northeastern gateway to Mount St. Helens. Here too is where the highway begins banking north toward Rainier's southeastern corner. As you travel on through Packwood, you may realize that you've reached the center of several amazing wilderness areas and a perfect launching-point for either Rainier or St. Helens. Mountain bikers, hikers, snowmobilers, and anglers will find themselves in the middle of a forested public playground.

Sights

The pride of Morton is the 1910 **Morton Train Depot** (downtown, 360/496-0070), which was recently featured on the History Channel show *Mega Movers* as it chugged to its present home along the Tacoma Eastern line. The interior is still being restored, but the exterior is as sharp as it was over 100 years ago. Three miles west of Morton on Short Road is a great binocular-view of Mount St. Helens' crater and lava dome.

Festivals and Events

The **Morton Loggers Jubilee,** held the second weekend in August, is one of the largest timber carnivals in Washington. In addition to the standard ax throwing, log rolling, and other contests, you'll discover a riding lawnmower race, parades, barbecues, and dancing, along with an arts and crafts fair. Memorial Day tends to pack the local hotels and campgrounds. Not just because it is the kick-off for summer, but because Randle, Packwood, and Cascade Peaks Campground hold a gigantic **Swap Meet and Flea Market** (360/983-3778). Even if it doesn't interest you, be mindful because it really does fill local lodging.

Sports and Recreation

HIKING

The **Woods Creek Watchable Wildlife Trail** is an easy 1.5-mile path through mixed forests, a meadow, and past several beaver ponds. It leaves from the Woods Creek Information Station. Also nearby—at the end of a quarter-mile path—is beautiful 60-foot **Iron Creek Falls**.

One of the quintessential hikes around this area is up **Packwood Lake Trail** (trail No. 78, from trailhead at end of Forest Service Road 1260) to the titular lake. This gentle climb starts in a few harvested forest areas before hitting the Goat Rocks Wilderness area. It might not be pretty to walk through, but the Forest Service is in the business of managing our timber resources—how else are we going to build roofs over our heads? Besides, in this instance the clearings offer a great peek at Rainier on clear days. Once you hit the wilderness boundary you'll be surrounded by plenty of old-growth forest all the way until the trail meets trail No. 81, when Packwood Lake Trail leads just outside the wilderness boundary down to the lake (4.2 miles from trailhead), which provides good summertime fishing. You can continue up in elevation along the trail past Packwood Lake to Mosquito Lake and Lost Lake until it ends 9.6 miles later. Because this trail does lead through the wilderness area, mountain bikes are not allowed, but horses are. Bikers should consider the parallel **Pipeline Trail** (trail No. 74, from trailhead at end of Forest Service Road 1260), which runs 4.5 miles up to the lake.

The nine-mile **Tatoosh Trail** (No. 161) is a strenuous forest and alpine hike but has outstanding views, especially if you take the side route to the 6,310-foot mountain that was formerly topped by Tatoosh Lookout. Another enjoyable side trail leads a half mile to Tatoosh Lakes. Get to the trailhead by turning off Highway 12 at the Packwood Ranger Station and following Forest Service Road 52 to Road 5270, which takes you to the trailhead, 11 miles from the Ranger Station.

FISHING

Packwood Lake reflects Mount Rainier on clear days and is home to a thriving rainbow trout fishery that anglers can take a crack at by shore or float tube. This is one of the best fishing holes around Packwood, but far from the only—other favorites include Dog Lake, Leech Lake for fly fishers, and Skate Creek, accessible from the small and virtually unknown **Packwood State Park** (www.parks.wa.gov). This park has tall trees and decent fishing, but no facilities. Access is via Forest Service Road 52 across the Cowlitz River.

WINTER SPORTS

Packwood is also great fun in the winter. Cross-country skiers and snowmobilers flock to the **Packwood Winter Recreation Area** to slip and slide on the white stuff. Go about seven miles southwest of Packwood on Forest Service Road 21 to reach **Johnson Creek Sno-Park,** from which miles of groomed trails extend. You must have a Sno-Park Pass to access the park. Get one at Tatoosh Food Mart (13053 U.S. 12, 360/494-7001).

Accommodations

The Seasons Motel (200 Westlake, 360/496-6835, $90 s or $100 d) has a friendly staff and serves a warm breakfast each morning.

The liveliest spot in Randle is **Tall Timber Motel** (10023 U.S. 12, one mile east of Randle on U.S. 12, 360/497-2991, www.talltimbers restaurantloungemotel.com, $65–105 s or d), which plays host to a homespun diner and a lounge that attracts local barflies, as well as a collection of comfortable motel rooms. Cozy and friendly, **Hotel Packwood** (104 Main St., 360/494-5431, www.packwoodwa.com) is a renovated 1912 hotel that sends its guests back in time with its big veranda and lobby featuring a brick fireplace and antique piano. Stay in modest rooms with shared ($35 s or d) or private ($50) baths. Or opt for the Roosevelt Suite, which hosted T. R. back in the hotel's heyday.

Crest Trail Lodge (12729 U.S. 12, 360/494-4944 or 800/477-5339, www.cresttraillodge .com, $70 90 s or d) is updated, clean, and pet-friendly. There is free wireless in the rooms and a hot breakfast in the morning—hard to find at this price. The **Inn of Packwood** (13032

U.S. 12, 360/494-5500, www.innofpackwood .com, $50 s or d) is great for getting in out of the elements. It also sports an outdoor pool and hot tub. The inn has kitchenette units available for $145 for up to six people and some rooms have a staggering view of the south side of Mount Rainier.

CAMPING

The nearest public campground to Randle is the **Iron Creek Campground** (12 miles south on Forest Service Road 25, 518/885-3639 or 877/444-6777, www.reserveusa.com, open mid-May–late October, $20 for tents, $36 for RVs). Campfire programs are given at Iron Creek Friday and Saturday evenings in the summer. **Tower Rock Campground** (open mid-May–late Sept., $18–20) is six miles east of Iron Creek on Forest Service Road 76. Nearer to Packwood is **La Wis Wis Campground** ($20–38 tents, $41 RVs), seven miles northeast of town on U.S. 12. One of the big plusses here is the covered picnic benches, in case you get caught camping in the rain. If you're not too fussy, the six free but primitive sites at **Summit Creek Campground** beckon. They are 12 miles north of town, and just east of the Highway 12 and Highway 123 junction on Forest Service Road 2160. You'll still need a $5 National Forest pass for the Gifford Pinchot National Forest. There is no free lunch, even if it's cooked over a campfire.

RV pilots have some pretty good options in the area. Families can break out the fishing poles at **Tower Rock U-Fish RV Park** (137 Cispus Rd. in Randall, 360/497-7680 or 888/830-7089, www.towerrockrv.com, $22 with full hookups, $20 electric), has a stocked trout pond that you can fish without a license. The store rents fishing tackle and bait. Tent sites are also available for $16. The U-Fish is definitely a little place with a lot of character.

You can choose instead to hook up at **Packwood RV Park** (12985 U.S. 12, 360/494-5145, $30). This mostly wooded property is very close to Packwood, has on-site laundry and showers and is occasionally host to passing elk.

Food

This is a stretch that folks visit for jaw-dropping scenery, not mouth-watering food. It's not quite bad to the point where you'll need to hunt down an elk, but you could easily do worse than catching and grilling your own trout. In Randle, check out **Cliff Droppers** (12968 U.S. 12, 360/494-2055, 11:30 A.M.–10:30 P.M. Tues.–Sun.) for a familiar sort of burger and milkshake joint. In Packwood, your best option is **Cruisers Pizza** (13028 U.S. 12 in Packwood, 360/494-5400, 11 A.M.–9 P.M. daily), which serves an unusual assortment of toppings along with the old standbys. Have a beer or glass of wine to reward yourself for your active day or long drive.

Information

The **Morton Chamber of Commerce** (2nd and Westlake, 360/496-6086, http://morton-chamber.lewiscounty.com) operates a summer-only log cabin visitors center. Randle's **Cowlitz Valley Ranger Station** (10024 U.S. 12, three mi. east of town, 360/497-1100, May–Sept. daily 8 A.M.–4:30 P.M., Oct.–Apr., Mon.–Fri. 8 A.M.–4:30 P.M.) has detailed information on local hiking and mountain biking trails. Get information on nearby Gifford Pinchot National Forest from **Packwood Work Center** (13068 U.S. 12, 360/494-0600, www.fs.fed.us/gpnf).

WHITE PASS

U.S. Highway 12 between Yakima and Mount Rainier traverses 4,500-foot White Pass. The route climbs westward along the Tieton River through heavily forested areas with a few clear views of Rainier along the way.

The **Pacific Crest Trail** intersects White Pass as it continues north to Chinook Pass and south through the Goat Rocks Wilderness on its long path to Canada and Mexico. The PCT follows the crest of the Cascades for 36 miles through the Goat Rocks Wilderness, passing through some alpine meadows but generally following rough terrain 4,200–7,500 feet in elevation. The two miles between Elk Pass and Packwood Glacier are the most hazardous, but

the scenery here is also the most spectacular. The trail is usually snow-free from late July–mid-September, but even in late August you can expect to cross snowfields up to a half mile across, so bring your ice ax and warm clothing—several hikers have died from hypothermia on these exposed ridges.

A beautiful 13-mile loop trip begins at the Berry Patch trailhead near Chambers Lake Campground at the end of Forest Service Road 2150 on the southwest side of the wilderness. The **Snowgrass Trail** (No. 96) that climbs past high meadows near Snowgrass Flat is well known for its summertime wildflowers. From here, you can connect with the PCT, or follow **Lily Basin Trail** (No. 86) along the ridge, and then return via exposed **Goat Ridge Trail** (No. 95) to your starting point.

White Pass Ski Area

Located off Highway 12 about 55 miles west of Yakima, and 12 miles southeast of Mount Rainier National Park, White Pass Ski Area (48935 U.S. 12, 509/672-3101, www.skiwhitepass.com, weekend full-day lift tickets are $57 adults, $37 kids and seniors) offers a 1,500-foot vertical drop and 650 acres of skiing, served by five chairlifts (including a high-speed quad chair) and two Poma tows. The base elevation is 4,500 feet. Amenities include ski and snowboard lessons and rentals, child care, cafeteria, and bar. The resort also operates a small Nordic ski center; you can rent cross-country skis and get a pass for $16.

Near the ski area, **White Pass Village Inn** (48933 U.S. 12, 509/672-3131, www.whitepassvillageinn.com, $140–178 d in winter) has condos of various sizes, with a winter-only heated outdoor pool. Nearby, find a store, gas station, and the **Summit House Restaurant** (509/672-3111, open in winter only).

Eight miles east of White Pass Ski Area on U.S. Highway 12, **Indian Creek Corral** (40911 U.S. 12, 509/672-2400, www.indiancreekcorral.com) offers two-hour ($50), overnight ($250, two-person minimum) and multiday horseback rides in the summer. Hikers can also take advantage of their drop-camp service.

Rimrock Lake Area

Traveling along Highway 12, you can't miss **Rimrock Lake,** just a few miles east of White Pass. This massive blue-green lake was created in 1927 by what was then one of the largest earth-filled dams in the country. Today Rimrock is popular with anglers in search of good-sized silvers mid-May–late June, and with boaters, swimmers, and campers. **Silver Beach Resort** (40350 U.S. 12, 509/672-2500, www.campingatsilverbeach.com) has rustic cabins with kitchenettes ($80, sleeps four), RV hookups ($25 full hookups), and a boat dock.

Tieton River-Rafting

In September, when most of the rivers in Washington have slowed to a trickle, river rats from around the Pacific Northwest gather around the normally quiet Tieton River for the big yearly event they call the "flip flop." That's when the engineers over at Rimrock Dam push a button and unleash a torrent of water that drains through the Tieton out to the greater Yakima River drainage area to provide Yakima Valley farmers valuable irrigation supplies. Rafters reap the benefits with an exciting class III (intermediate) ride that starts high in the mountains and descends at a rapid 50-feet-per-mile pace down through basalt canyons and into the dry valley on the east side of the Cascades, where the Tieton meets Naches River. The flip-flop only lasts about a month, but some rafting companies will still take you out through October.

There are dozens of rafting companies with encampments up and down the river. Get the most bang for your buck from **Blue Sky Outfitters** (800/228-7238, www.blueskyoutfitters.com), which paddles an epic 21-mile run along the river—longest among all guide services out there. Blue Sky also serves up a generous gourmet barbecue dinner after

---

ROLLING ON THE RIVER

Washington's river-rafting opportunities range from the slow, smooth, and scenic to the breathless, churning whitewater runs for only the most adventurous. Rafting trips are rated based on skill and thrill level, so it's pretty important to know what you're getting yourself into, especially as a beginner.

- Class I: sit back and enjoy the ride. You won't even touch a paddle. Example: The Skagit River from Marblemount.

- Class II: a little bumpier. You'll be paddling and there might be some rolling rough patches, but nothing crazier than driving Seattle streets. Example: Upper stretches of the Methow River.

- Class III: a tiny bit of danger, but you'll be helping to paddle away from rocks. You'll probably feel the bottom drop out as you run little falls of 3-5 feet. Example: The Wenatchee River starting around Leavenworth.

- Class IV: gets you into the lower rungs of the major league. Water can be unpredictable and tight maneuvering is a must. You might find yourself going over a considerable drop. Example: The Methow River from Winthrop and down.

- Class V: you'd better be in good shape, because taking a breather with the paddling puts everyone at risk. Your mental endurance is going to be more important, too, as you shoot through long stretches of white water. If you get dunked, your best rescue equipment is prayer. Example: The Skykomish from Index.

- Class VI: hidden dangers, huge waves, and zero margin of error. Professionals think twice, as getting tossed from the raft carries an overwhelming chance of death. As extreme as you can undertake and have the possibility of coming home. Example: If you have a chance of surviving these runs, then you already know where they are.

all is said and done aboard the rafts. Other respected services include **Downstream River Runners** (800/234-4644, www.riverpeople .com, $75), which employs some of the most experienced guides on the Tieton and provides snacks before and after your trip, and **Alpine Adventures** (800/723-8386, www.alpine adventures.com, $84), which has arranged special weekend packages with Yakima innkeepers.

Elk and Bighorn Sheep

During most winters, the large White Pass elk population and a small herd of bighorn sheep are fed at the **Oak Creek Wildlife Recreation Area** (two mi. west of the intersection of Highways 410 and 12, and 17 mi. west of Yakima, 509/575-2740). Best times to see them are early morning or late afternoon, when the animals are most active.

Approaching Mount St. Helens

CASTLE ROCK AND SPIRIT LAKE MEMORIAL HIGHWAY

The west side of Mount St. Helens offers the quickest access and has some of the finest views and the most developed facilities. Nearly 900,000 visitors take this route each year. Most visitors find the easiest, most breathtaking views at one of five elaborate visitors centers. The main access route to the west side is Highway 504, the **Spirit Lake Memorial Highway.** Starting from the town of Castle Rock (exit 49 from I-5), Highway 504 offers a 54-mile scenic climb right to the heart of the volcanic destruction that resulted from the 1980 eruption. A secondary access is S.R. 505, which cuts east from I-5 at the tiny town of **Toledo** (exit 60) and joins S.R. 504 after 16 miles near the town of **Toutle** (TOOT-ul). The route below follows Spirit Lake Memorial Highway from I-5 to its terminus inside the national monument.

Castle Rock

Castle Rock lies just west of I-5 along the Cowlitz River. The town is named for a 150-foot-high rocky knob that can be climbed by an easy-to-find path. The town was hit hard by the eruption of Mount St. Helens in 1980, when mud flows turned the Cowlitz into a raging torrent that washed out bridges and damaged or destroyed more than 200 homes. In town is a memorial to Harry Truman, the oldtimer who died at his Spirit Lake home when the volcano erupted and buried the lake in hundreds of feet of debris.

SIGHTS

The **Castle Rock Exhibit Hall and Visitor Information Center** (147 Front Ave. SW, 360/274-6603, 9 A.M.–6 P.M. daily summer, free) details the town and its connection to the Cowlitz River, the importance of the timber industry to the economy, and the impact of the 1980 eruption of Mount St. Helens.

FESTIVALS AND EVENTS

The **Castle Rock Fair** on the fourth weekend of July is the big annual event, with a parade, stage shows, games, and carnival. The Mount St. Helens Motorcycle Club sponsors **Pro-Am TT Motorcycle Races** (www.mshmc.org) all summer at Castle Rock racetrack.

ACCOMMODATIONS

Castle Rock has the best options for Mount St. Helens–area lodging. The **7 West Motel** (864 Walsh Ave. NE, 360/274-7526, www.7westmotel.com, $48 s or $55 d) has the cheapest rooms in Castle Rock and isn't fancy, but neither is it shabby. **Timberland Inn & Suites** (1271 Mt. St. Helens Way, 360/274-6002 or 800/900-6335, www.timberland-inn .com, $79 s or $89 d), is single-floor with parking right in front of the room, and heavily insulated rooms to block out the neighbors and the neighboring highway. And to take a step up in price and quality, try the **Blue Heron Inn** (2846 Spirit Lake Hwy, 360/274-9595, www.blue heroninn.com, $170 s or d, $215 whirlpool tub suite, both with breakfast), a charmer from top to bottom. Its highly polished wooden floors, its views of Mount St. Helens, and free wireless Internet make it worth the extra dough.

Silver Lake

Your first big stop should be the comprehensive **Silver Lake Visitor Center** (five mi. from I-5 on Spirit Lake Memorial Hwy., 360/274-2100, 9 A.M.–5 P.M. May–Sept. daily, 9 A.M.–5 P.M., Oct.–Apr. daily, $5), where the creative and insightful exhibits interpret the eruption and its heavy impact on the region. The mountain is 30 miles from here, but on a clear day, you can see it through the spotting scopes outside. In addition to maps, books, and current trail and road information, the center offers daily educational programs throughout the year.

ACCOMMODATIONS

Silver Lake Resort (3201 Spirit Lake Hwy., 360/274-6141, www.silverlake-resort.com, $80–115 s or d) has motel rooms with a balcony over the water and full kitchens, rustic two-bedroom cabins with full kitchens, and RV and tent sites. They also rent fishing boats.

Five miles up from I-5, the spacious **Blue Heron Inn B&B** (2846 Spirit Lake Hwy., 360/274-9595, www.blueheroninn.com, $170 s or d, $215 d for the hot tub suite) has seven guest rooms, all with private baths. A full breakfast and dinner are served. Not suitable for kids under five.

Seaquest State Park (888/226-7688, www.parks.wa.gov, $22 tents, $31 RVs) is right next to the visitors center, within a beautiful stand of gigantic old-growth Douglas firs and hemlocks. Camping is available here year-round. Silver Lake is one of the best bass fishing lakes in the state, and a public boat ramp is a mile east of the park. RV owners can also stop by **Mount St. Helens RV Park** (167 Schaffran Rd., 360/274-8522, www.mtsthelensrvpark .com, $37 for full hookups).

Hoffstadt Bluffs and Creek

As you continue east on Spirit Lake Highway from Silver Lake, the road slips past the trailer homes of Toutle at the juncture of the South and North Fork of the Toutle River, and then up along the North Fork into the mountains.

© ERICKA CHICKOWSKI

Mount St. Helens over Silver Lake

Much of the route is on private timberland, with Weyerhaeuser tree plantations lining both sides of the road. A few miles west, signs point to the famous buried A-frame, a home that was newly build just before the eruption. The river of melted glacier that came roaring down the mountain partially buried it, but the top floor still stands surrounded by grass. Continue east through the Weyerhaeuser tree farms to **Hoffstadt Bluffs Visitor Center** (15000 Spirit Lake Hwy., 360/274-7750 or 800/752-8439, www.hoffstadtbluffs.com, May–Oct. daily 10 A.M.–6 P.M.) at milepost 27. Owned by Cowlitz County, this timber-frame building houses two gift shops, a demonstration glass-blowing studio, and a restaurant (June and Sept. daily 11 A.M.–6 P.M., July–Aug. 11:30 A.M.–6 P.M.) whose menu lists burgers among its other treats. Eat inside and enjoy the picture-window panorama, or outside on the patio overlooking the North Toutle Valley and Mount St. Helens. A picnic area is also available, with telescopes to watch the several hundred elk below and the mountain above.

Eco Park Adventure Trails (360/274-7007, $60 for a two-hour trip) offers horseback adventures within the blast zone around the bluffs.

ACCOMMODATIONS AND FOOD

Stay as close to the mountain as you can get from the west side at ▌ **Eco Park at Mount St. Helens** (just past mile marker 24, 360/274-7007). It's owned by the same family who once ran the Spirit Lake Lodge, which was destroyed in the 1980 eruption. Eco Park offers the only accommodations inside the blast zone. The resort has summertime basic cabins ($100–110 d), yurts ($75 d), and campsites ($18) in a remote area on the northeast side. RVs are accepted on the site, but there are no hookups.

Toutle Diner and RV Park (5037 Spirit Lake Memorial Hwy., Toutle, 360/274-6208) offers full hookups ($21), some sites with cable TV. The diner (Sun.–Thurs. 8 A.M.–9 P.M., Fri.–Sat. 8 A.M.–10 P.M.) offers typical roadhouse fare, along with espresso and free Wi-Fi. The property also has shower and laundry facilities.

Upper Toutle Valley

From here eastward, Spirit Lake Memorial Highway climbs steadily uphill, with wide shoulders for bikes and numerous turnouts to take in the scenery. RVers should park at Hoffstadt Bluffs and those towing trailers should leave them there, since the road has some 7 percent grades ahead.

Next stop is the **Hoffstadt Creek Bridge,** one of 14 bridges that had to be reconstructed on Highway 504 after the eruption. The new bridge rises 370 feet above the canyon and stands near the edge of the blast zone—an incredible 14.8 miles from the crater. Everything from here on was killed by the heat of the explosion. Also, from here on you can see a sharp contrast between what private companies did after the eruption and what took place on Forest Service land. Weyerhaeuser salvage-logged its lands and immediately replanted millions of trees. With fertilization, the new stands are coming back surprisingly fast; some trees are already 40 feet tall! As a public agency, the Forest Service had a rather different mandate, and no logging or replanting took place within the national volcanic monument. Instead, the area has become a natural laboratory where scientists can study the recovery process, and where visitors can marvel at the power of nature. (Salvage logging and replanting were, however, done on Forest Service lands outside the monument boundaries.)

Today the upper Toutle River Valley is home to over 500 Roosevelt elk, many of which are visible by hiking two miles down Road 3100 near the Hoffstadt Creek Bridge. Despite harsh conditions, the elk survive on the nutritious grasses and clover that were planted in the mudflow following the eruption.

North Fork Ridge

The **Forest Learning Center** (Spirit Lake Memorial Hwy. milepost 33, 360/274-7750, 10 A.M.–4 P.M. Fri.–Sun. May–Sept., closed in winter, free) highlights some of the differences between public management and that of Weyerhaeuser Company, with emphasis on Weyerhaeuser's salvage and recovery efforts after the eruption. The center sits on a 2,700-foot-high bluff over the North Fork of the Toutle River. Elaborate exhibits take you through a diorama of the forest prior to the 1980 eruption, an "eruption chamber" where a you-are-there multimedia program surrounds you, and then past additional exhibits extolling the salvage, reforestation, and recovery efforts, plus the benefits of private forestry practices and conservation. The Forest Learning Center is especially popular with families; kids can climb aboard a toy helicopter or play in the seven-foot-high rubber volcano outside. Telescopes provide a chance to watch elk in the valley below, and a one-mile trail descends into the valley. Other facilities include a gift shop and picnic area.

Be sure to stop at the **Elk Rock Viewpoint** at the entrance to the Mount St. Helens National Monument for magnificent views of the crater to the south and the deep river valley below, filled with a 700-foot-deep layer of rock, ash, and debris. Don't forget to look below for Roosevelt elk.

WOODLAND TO COUGAR
Woodland
Woodland acts as the southern gateway to Mount St. Helens, with Highway 503 heading northeast to the volcano. The area was first settled in the 1840s, and the town was incorporated in 1906. A 32-mile scenic climb into the hills along the highway cuts through second-growth forests, with periodic glimpses of Lake Merwin and Yale Lake—reservoirs that were created by dams on the Lewis River.

SIGHTS
There isn't a lot to the town of Woodland, but be sure to follow the signs to **Hulda Klager Lilac Gardens** (115 S Pekin Rd. in Woodland, 360/225-8996, www.lilacgardens.com, $2) where you'll discover an 1889 farmhouse surrounded by three acres of grounds filled with colorful flowers and trees of all descriptions. Hulda Klager began hybridizing lilacs in 1903 and developed more than 250 new varieties, including 10 that can be found in the gardens here.

The gardens are open year-round, and lilac starts (rooted lilac cuttings) are available weekdays, but the lovely Victorian-era home is open only for Lilac Week (the week preceding Mother's Day).

The **Cedar Creek Grist Mill** (10 miles east of Woodland off NE Cedar Creek Rd., 360/225-5832, www.cedarcreekgristmill.com, 1–4 P.M. Sat., 2–4 P.M. Sun., donation requested) is a postcard-perfect mid-19th-century mill that was built to grind grain using the power of the Cedar Creek. A small museum charts the history of the little mill. And even if history is not your thing, the wooded banks and swift running creek are just too beautiful to miss. At the end of October, you can come help press 8,000 pounds of apples and walk away with a free bottle of cider for your effort.

FESTIVALS AND EVENTS
The third weekend in June brings the **Planter's Days** (360/225-9888) celebration, billed as the state's oldest continuously running community festival. The four-day event celebrates the building of dikes to prevent flooding of Woodland and includes a carnival, fun run, pancake breakfast, firemen's barbecue, frog-jumping contest, and car show.

SPORTS AND RECREATION
The lilac gardens border pretty **Horseshoe Lake.** The lake is a popular fishing hole for trout and largemouth bass. Anglers may also want to stop at the Lake Merwin and Lake Speelyai. Merwin is known for some large tiger muskies, while Speelyai attracts fishing poles with its kokanee population. Both lakes make for pleasant relaxing and swimming, as does the Yale Park Recreation Area on Yale Lake.

Paradise Point State Park (five miles southeast of Woodland just off I-5, 360/263-2350 or 888/226-7688, www.parks.wa.gov) is a long stretch of riparian shoreline, inviting fishing, boating, and swimming in the East Fork Lewis River, as well as a two-mile hiking trail.

ACCOMMODATIONS
There are several lodging choices in the Woodland

area. Formerly the Cedar Inn, **Motel 6 Woodland** (1500 Atlantic Ave., 360/225-6548, $54–79) is simple but comfortable. There's an indoor heated pool and their parking lot can handle RVs and semi-tractor trailers. The wireless Internet is free in all rooms, but be sure to ask for a microwave and fridge room if you want them.

The **Lewis River Inn** (1100 Lewis River Rd., 800/543-4344, http://lewisriverinn. com, $77–97 s or d) is, true to form, right on the Lewis River. Some rooms offer nice views of the cold, flowing waters. To step up a bit in comfort and price, book with the **Lewis River B&B** (2339 Lewis River Rd., 360/225-8630, $125 s or $150 d), a bright, airy property with green lawns and a gorgeous deck overlooking the river. And if you're heading out early to outwit those fish, your hosts will do their best to get you a full, hot breakfast before you go.

Paradise Point State Park (five miles southeast of Woodland just off I-5, 360/263-2350 or 888/226-7688, www.parks.wa.gov, $21 tent, $7 reservation fee) is open for camping April–September, plus weekends and holidays the rest of the year. Because of its location right along I-5, this isn't a particularly quiet place to spend a night, but at least the highway makes for easy access.

More camping is available at **Woodland Special Campground** (NW 389th St., 800/527-3305, mid-May–mid-Oct., free) in dense forests three miles east of Woodland, run by the Department of Natural Resources.

Private grounds worth a look include **Columbia Riverfront RV Park** (1881 Dike Rd., 360/225-8051, $35–42 full hookups), which affords river views from some of its sites, and **Woodland Shores RV Park** (1090 A St., 360/225-2222, $35, $50 electric deposit required) which also has a little gift shop in the office selling cute handmade knitted and crocheted goods.

FOOD
Woodland is full of good old-fashioned

hearty American food and the kind of coffee shop frequented by loggers and truckers instead of compulsive Mac users. Case in point, **America's Family Diner** (1447 Goerig St., 360/225-3962) is actually family-run and mixes truly personal customer service with truly satisfying meals. **Rosie's Restaurant** (1245 Lewis River Rd., 360/225-9800, 6:30 A.M.–8 P.M. daily) serves breakfast all day and runs dinner specials every night. There's mac and cheese for the kids, liver and onions for great-grandpa, and something to please everyone else in between.

Cougar
The highway eventually leads you to the hamlet of Cougar, which serves as a jumping-off point for access to the southern and eastern sides of Mount St. Helens National Volcanic Monument.

ACCOMMODATIONS
Stay at the comfortable, kid-friendly **Monfort's B&B** (132 Cougars Loop Rd., 360/238-5229, $60–90 s or d) with two guest rooms, private baths, and full breakfasts. The biggest property around Cougar is **Lone Fir Resort** (16806 Lewis River Rd., 360/238-5210, www.lonefirresort.com, $60–75 s or d), which offers motel rooms and a cabin in a wooded location with an outdoor pool. RV spaces are also available here ($27 full hookup).

Another good choice is **Cougar RV Park** (16730 Lewis River Rd., 360/238-5224), an eight-acre property staffed by a friendly bunch of folks. You'll find RV hookups ($25) and rustic camping cabins ($30 for up to five), basic shelters and beds on which to unroll the ol' sleeping sacks.

Information
A small trailer at Lakeshore Drive and Goerig Street houses the **Woodland Chamber of Commerce Information Center** (360/225-9552, 9:30 A.M.–4:30 P.M. daily year-round, and until 7 P.M. Fri.–Mon. Apr.–Oct.).

SOUTH CASCADES

Mount St. Helens National Volcanic Monument

Prior to May 18, 1980, Mount St. Helens had the most perfectly shaped cone in the Pacific Northwest volcanic chain. The momentous plume of pumice and smoke Mount St. Helens spewed that day transformed a quiet and beautiful landscape into a moonscape wasteland. Today plants and animals are returning to the land as it recovers, but lingering fields of devastation continue to amaze and astound visitors. Mount St. Helens has become one of Washington's must-see sights. Several visitor facilities, access roads, and trails have been built since the eruption and now offer ample opportunities to learn about the power of this active volcano.

Visiting Mount St. Helens

In 1982, the 110,000-acre **Mount St. Helens National Volcanic Monument** was created, and the area has been gradually opened to visitors as roads, bridges, visitors centers, and trails are built. The government still keeps parts of it off-limits to serve as a natural laboratory for scientists. They have learned one basic fact so far: nature heals itself more quickly than anyone expected. Plant and animal life is returning quite rapidly considering the extent of the destruction.

The Forest Service has imposed stringent regulations on activity within the National Monument, both to protect visitors from potential hazards and to protect the area as a natural laboratory of ecological change. Visitors must stay away from certain areas and not venture off trails; a minimum $100 fine, stringently enforced, awaits those who travel off-trail.

Roads approach Mount St. Helens from the east and west sides, offering dramatic views into its center, while more adventurous visitors can climb to the summit from the south side. The vast majority of visitors arrive from the west, turning off I-5 and following Spirit

ERUPTION!

At 8:32 A.M. on May 18, 1980, Mount St. Helens blew her top in an eruption that had the explosive power of several atomic bombs. An otherwise forgettable small earthquake was just enough to cause the already-bulging mountain to cut loose a massive slurry of rock, snow, and ice that rampaged down the north slope at 200 mph, boiling picture-postcard Spirit Lake and filling it with snapped-off ruins of ancient fir and cedar trees. The next avalanche blasted down the North Fork of the Toutle River, turning it into an unbridled destructive force, sweeping away bridges and burying homes.

The landslides were just the beginning. When the true eruption began, clouds of ash and hot gasses rushed in a broad arc to the northeast, choking all life and searing the landscape at temperatures greater than 900°F. Speeding at the rate of a modern jetliner, the cloud, or pyroclastic flow, was impossible to

outrun. The most poignant demonstration of the inescapable deadliness of the flow was Dr. David Johnston, a young volcanologist manning the station six miles from the mountain during the explosion. As he watched the flow approach, he excitedly reported to the Vancouver, Washington, station, "Vancouver, Vancouver – this is it!" just before his observation post was obliterated.

When the rage of the mountain had ended, 57 people were dead, millions of dollars of homes, agriculture, and infrastructure were destroyed, and all the wildlife in a 15-mile stretch of virgin forest was killed. Ash choked auto carburetors from the Pacific east to Idaho. St. Helens's ash was detectable across one third of the country. It still holds the unhappy record of being the worst, most fatal, most costly volcanic eruption in American history.

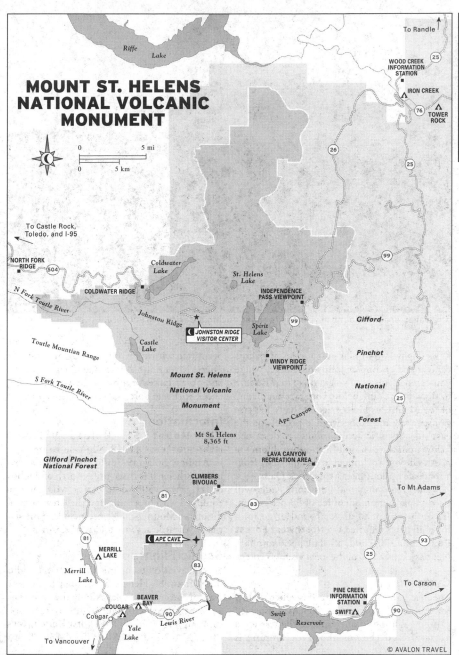

MOUNT ST. HELENS NATIONAL VOLCANIC MONUMENT

0   5 mi
0   5 km

To Randle

WOOD CREEK
INFORMATION
STATION

IRON CREEK

TOWER
ROCK

To Castle Rock,
Toledo, and I-95

NORTH FORK
RIDGE

Coldwater
Lake

St. Helens
Lake

INDEPENDENCE
PASS VIEWPOINT

N Fork Toutle River

COLDWATER RIDGE

Johnston Ridge

JOHNSTON RIDGE
VISITOR CENTER

Spirit
Lake

Gifford-

Toutle Mountian Range

Castle
Lake

Pinchot

S Fork Toutle River

WINDY RIDGE
VIEWPOINT

Mount St. Helens

National Volcanic

National

Monument

Ape Canyon

Forest

Mt St. Helens
8,365 ft

Gifford Pinchot
National Forest

LAVA CANYON
RECREATION AREA

CLIMBERS
BIVOUAC

To Mt Adams

APE CAVE

MERRILL
LAKE

Merrill
Lake

BEAVER
BAY

To Carson

PINE CREEK
INFORMATION
STATION

COUGAR

Cougar

Yale
Lake

Lewis River

Swift
Reservoir

SWIFT

To Vancouver

Riffe   Lake

© AVALON TRAVEL

© ROBERT BROWN/123RF.COM

The valley around Mount St. Helens is experiencing a period of recovery.

Lake Highway 54 miles past a series of visitors centers and ending at Johnston Ridge, where you can peer into the volcano's crater. Be sure to fill your gas tank before you start out on any of the Mount St. Helens access roads; gas stations are few and far between, especially on the east side. Specific access routes are described below from the east, south, and west. From the north side you are limited to distant views from a roadside pullout near Mossyrock Dam.

Visitors stopping in at Johnston's Ridge will need to pay a monument fee of $8 per person. If you just want to drive around or go for a hike, all that's required is a **Northwest Forest Pass** (800/270-7504, $5 daily, $30 annual). Get passes from any of the local visitors centers.

Camping

Specific campgrounds are described below for each side of Mount St. Helens. Dispersed camping is allowed only outside the restricted areas around the volcano. No camping is

permitted within the upper North Fork of the Toutle River drainage, around Coldwater Lake and Spirit Lake, or around the volcano itself; check with the Forest Service for specifics.

Information

The **Mount St. Helens Volcanic Headquarters** (42218 NE Yale Bridge Rd. in Amboy, 360/449-7800, www.fs.usda.gov/mountsthelens) is three miles north of Amboy on Highway 503. The office will get you equipped with brochures and the latest on conditions at Mount St. Helens, including the status of volcanic activity and trail closures.

Scenic Flights

Several aviation companies offer scenic flights over Mount St. Helens, affording passengers a view of the crater and lava dome that you can't get otherwise. Helicopter flights over the volcano are provided by **Hillsboro Helicopters** (360/274-7750 or 800/752-8439, www

.hillsboro-aviation.com, $165) from Hoffstadt Bluffs and **Applebee Aviation** (503/647-0404, 30 minutes for $249 pp, up to three passengers) from Eco Park Resort.

WEST SIDE ACCESS
Coldwater Ridge

Once the home of St. Helens' premier man-made attraction, Coldwater Ridge Visitor Center shuttered its doors in late 2007. Mountain oglers should still stop here to get a good look at the peak from the quarter-mile **Winds of Change Interpretive Trail**, just outside the closed visitors center. For another short hike, head two miles downhill to five-mile-long Coldwater Lake, where the quarter-mile **Birth of a Lake Trail** takes you by boardwalk past the debris avalanche left behind by the eruption. The lake is known for excellent rainbow and cutthroat trout fishing, with a minimum size of 16 inches for keepers. Rafts or float tubes are recommended to lessen the damage from bankside anglers, and gasoline-powered motorboats are prohibited. There's no camping, and be sure to stay on the trails or risk a $100 fine.

◖ Johnston Ridge Visitor Center

Spirit Lake Memorial Highway ends eight miles uphill from Coldwater Lake at the 4,300-foot level and the Johnston Ridge Visitor Center (24000 Spirit Lake Hwy. in Toutle, 360/274-2140, 10 A.M.–6 P.M. daily mid-May through Sept., 10 A.M.–4 P.M. daily the rest of the year). This facility emphasizes the geology of Mount St. Helens and ongoing scientific research work and is named for Dr. David Johnston, the geologist who was working here in 1980 when the volcano erupted. His last radio transmission, sent out as the mountain gave way, still haunts anyone who hears it: "Vancouver, Vancouver, this is it!" This visitors facility peers directly into the lava dome—just three miles away—that formed after the eruption (encased in clouds 200 days each year). Step inside to find a large model of the volcano that shows how the eruption progressed, geological monitoring

equipment, and displays on the landscape both before and after the explosion. The highlight is a 16-minute film that re-creates the eruption in gripping, wide-screen detail. A half-mile **Eruption Trail** loops past a marker commemorating the 57 people killed by the 1980 blast.

Hiking and Camping

For a spectacular hike with commanding views into Spirit Lake, begin at the Johnston Ridge Observatory and follow **Boundary Trail** four miles to Harry's Ridge. For an overnight hike, continue along this path to the summit of Mount Margaret and down before returning via the 5.5-mile **Lakes Trail.** You can camp at several small high-country lakes here (permit required). This is a research area, and scientists are attempting to keep human impacts to a minimum, so hikers need to stick within 10 feet of the trails.

There are no developed campsites within Mount St. Helens National Volcanic Monument. Camping is prohibited along the Spirit Lake Memorial Highway inside the monument boundaries.

SOUTH SIDE ACCESS

The south side of Mount St. Helens was not impacted nearly as much by the 1980 eruption and is best known as the access route to climb the summit, for Ape Cave, and for various hiking trails, including the Loowit System that circles the mountain. These sites are all accessible from Cougar.

◖ Ape Cave

This 12,810-foot lava tube is one of the longest such caves in the nation, and one of the most popular visitor attractions at Mount St. Helens. The cave is 10 miles northeast of Cougar at the junction of Forest Service Roads 83 and 90 and is open all the time. From the entrance a staircase leads down to a chamber where the route splits. The downhill arm ends after an easy 0.75-mile walk, while the uphill route is more difficult and rocky, continuing 1.5 miles to an exit where an above-ground trail leads back to the starting point. Forest Service interpreters lead half-hour tours of Ape Cave twice a day in the summer. Be sure to bring drinking water and two flashlights and extra batteries (or rent a lantern for $2). Wear hiking boots, gloves, and warm clothes (the air is a steady 42°F all year). A small **visitors center** (10 A.M.–5:30 P.M. daily mid-June through Labor Day) can provide assistance, publications, and lantern rentals. A Northwest Forest Pass ($5) is required for access to the cave. The road is plowed to the Trail of Two Forests, a half mile away, in the winter.

Climbing Mount St. Helens

Mount St. Helens is the second-most-climbed peak on the planet, exceeded only by Japan's Mount Fuji. Its popularity stems from the fact that in the summer the ascent is more of a tough hike and scramble than a true technical climb.

Even though the climb is not technically difficult, don't underestimate the steep slopes and severe weather. The first stretch ascends through the forest at a gradual pace, but above the 4,800-foot level the pole-marked route is a scramble over boulder fields, volcanic pumice, ash, and snowfields that are often present through mid-July. The crater itself is off-limits to the general public because steam explosions can create extremely dangerous conditions. Avoid the edge of the crater when snow tops the peak, since you may be stepping on a cornice that could give way.

Most folks take around eight hours for the nine-mile round-trip trek. Some climbers prefer to get a head start the night before, camping three miles up at the 4,800-foot level, where you'll find a composting toilet. Camping is not allowed above this point.

All climbing routes up Mount St. Helens are from the south side of the peak, and a permit is required for everyone climbing above the 4,800-foot level. These permits are sold online by advance purchase only at www.msh institute.org. Make reservations as early as possible after February 1, since most summer

weekends are reserved by late March. A permit costs $23 between Nov. and Oct. and is free the rest of the year. Check with the monument (360/247-3900, 360/247-3961 for a recorded message) before planning a climb. Remember that St. Helens is an active volcano, and all climbs will be cancelled in case of volcanic hazards or eruptive activity. It can also snow any time of year. Call 503/808-2400 for the latest weather forecast. Listen to the report for Mount Hood, as the weather on the two mountains is invariably similar.

Hiking

A very easy path is the **Trail of Two Forests,** a brief boardwalk that takes you past the molds left when trees were immersed in lava flows 2,000 years ago. You can even crawl through two of these ancient impressions. The trail is right across from Ape Cave on Forest Service Road 8303.

One of the most interesting hikes on the south end of Mount St. Helens is the 2.5-mile **Lava Canyon Trail,** which drops 1,400 feet along the Muddy River. This canyon was scoured out by a mudflow during the 1980 eruption, revealing sharp cliffs and five tall waterfalls. Although the upper end is wheelchair-accessible, the lower part crosses a long suspension bridge and then descends a cliff face by a steel ladder. Great for the adventurous, not fun if you have a case of acrophobia. Get to the trail by following Forest Service Road 83 nine miles (paved the entire way) beyond Ape Cave to the trailhead.

The **Loowit System** (No. 216) is a difficult 29-mile trail that circles Mount St. Helens and is accessible from trailheads on all sides of the mountain. Plan on three days to get all the way around, and be prepared for lots of up-and-down hiking and faint trails in places. Camping is available at various points along the way, but contact the Forest Service for specifics since some areas are off-limits.

For an enjoyable loop hike, head to the end of Forest Service Road 8123 on the southwest side of the mountain and the start of **Sheep**

Canyon Trail (No. 240). This path climbs through old-growth forests and drainages that were ravaged by volcanic mudflows and into a flower-filled alpine meadow along the Loowit Trail before returning downhill on the Toutle Trail (No. 238), which connects to the Sheep Canyon Trail and your starting point. Total distance is approximately seven miles.

The **Lewis River Trail** (No. 31) follows along this beautiful river from the Curly Creek Falls to Lower Falls (a fun swimming hole), a distance of more than 10 miles. Between Curly Creek Falls and Lower Falls on Road 99 is **Big Creek Falls,** plummeting 125 feet into a pool that is popular for summer dips. Above Lower Falls, you can follow the road to a series of roadside falls, including the scenic Middle Falls and Upper Falls.

Winter Sports

Forest Service Road 83's two Sno-Parks offer a wide area for winter activities, including cross-country skiing, snowshoeing, and snowmobiling. Most popular is the **Marble Mountain Sno-Park,** located seven miles east of Cougar on Forest Service Road 90, and another six miles up Road 83. Get a Sno-Park permit ($11) and ski trail maps at **Cougar Store** (16842 Lewis River Rd., 360/238-5228, winter 6 A.M.–8 P.M. Sun.–Thurs., 6 A.M.–9 P.M. Fri.–Sat.). Snowmobilers must also purchase an additional $30 annual permit. A large log **warming shelter** is open here in the winter months and includes a woodstove. Rent it as a summertime cabin (June–Oct., $100 for up to 10 people) from the Forest Service (360/247-3900).

Camping

The Forest Service's **Lower Falls Campground** (15 miles east of the Pine Creek Information Station on Forest Service Road 90, 518/885-3639 or 877/444-6777, www.reserveusa.com, mid-May–mid-Oct., $18 tents, $35 RVs, $5 extra for reservations) is a nice place for camping, with views of three large falls along the Lewis River and a hiking trail that heads downriver for 10 miles.

Several other non–Forest Service public campgrounds provide camping on the south side of Mount St. Helens. Near the town of Cougar, **Cougar Campground** and **Beaver Bay Campground** offer tent camping ($12) and showers on the Yale Reservoir along Forest Service Road 90. Go north on Road 8100 to **Merrill Lake Campground,** a free Department of Natural Resources camping area May–Sept., or head east on Road 90 to **Swift Campground** (just south of the Pine Creek Information Station, $17). Reserve a spot through Pacific Power and Light (503/464-5035). They also have very popular summer-only campgrounds at **Cresap Bay Park** (seven miles north of Amboy on Hwy. 503, $17) and **Saddle Dam Park** (near the Yale Lake dam on Frasier Rd., $17). Cresap Bay and Swift Campgrounds have campfire programs on Friday and Saturday nights June–August.

Information

Three miles north of Amboy on Highway 503, **Mount St. Helens Volcanic Headquarters** (42218 NE Yale Bridge Rd., 360/247-7800) is open Monday–Friday 7:30 A.M.–5 P.M. year-round. The Forest Service's **Pine Creek Information Station** (17 miles east of Cougar on Forest Service Road 90) is open daily 9 A.M.–6 P.M. from mid-June through September.

EAST SIDE ACCESS

Unlike the west side, where a wide, new highway passes four visitors centers that seem to compete with each other to see which one can offer the most wows per minute, visitors to Mount St. Helens's eastern flanks will discover narrow, winding one-lane routes, simple information stations, and more basic facilities. This is the wild side of the mountain, where the crowds are fewer and you're allowed to draw your own conclusions without being inundated with flashy multimedia shows and elaborate computer animations. Information, maps, and monument passes ($3–6) are available at the **Woods Creek Information Station** (approximately seven miles south of Randle) and the **Pine Creek Information Station** on the east end of Swift Reservoir (20 miles east of Cougar).

The east side of Mount St. Helens is accessed by Forest Service Road 25, which heads south from the town of Randle. This paved but steep one-lane road (with turnouts) continues all the way to Pine Creek Ranger Station on Swift Creek Reservoir, south of the mountain. It is closed due to snow from late October–Memorial Day weekend and is not recommended for trailers or RVs. For easier driving, drop off your trailer at the Woods Creek Information Station or Iron Creek Picnic Site on Forest Service Road 25 if traveling from the north, or at the Pine Creek Information Station if you're coming from the south.

To Windy Ridge

Forest Service Roads 25, 26, and 99 provide access to the east side of Mount St. Helens. The primary destination on the east side is Windy Ridge, where you can see Spirit Lake and a magnificent up-close view of the volcano. Take Roads 25 and 99 to reach the viewpoint. Forest Service Road 26 turns south from Iron Creek Campground and leads to **Quartz Creek Big Trees** area, where a half-mile path takes you through old-growth Douglas firs that escaped the eruption. Just a mile away is the edge of the zone where trees were flattened in the blast (trees in this area were salvaged after the eruption). From here on, everything was destroyed by the force of the eruption. Road 26 is blocked south of here due to washouts.

At **Ryan Lake** another short trail provides views of the lake filled with downed trees. This area is usually accessible year-round, with open, flat areas for cross-country skiing. **Meta Lake**—at the junction of Forest Service Roads 26 and 99—has a paved trail and the famous **Miner's Car,** destroyed in the blast. Three people had driven here the night before the volcano gave way on May 18, 1980 and were

killed in a nearby cabin by the superheated explosion. Meta Lake is coming back surprisingly fast from the destruction, in part because ice and snow protected fish and other animals from the heat. Nature walks are offered here daily during the summer months.

Windy Ridge stands at the end of Road 99, 4,000 feet above sea level and 34 miles southwest of Randle. It is just five miles from the crater itself. Climb the 361 steps for an incredible view into the volcano, across the devastated pumice plain, and over log-choked Spirit Lake. Forest Service interpretive personnel are here daily May–October, providing frequent talks about the volcano from the amphitheater.

There are no improved campgrounds along Forest Service Roads 25 or 99 between Iron Creek Campground in Randle and Cougar.

Hiking

For something strenuous, follow the 2.5-mile **Norway Pass Trail** (No. 1) through blown-down forests to the 4,500-foot pass, gaining 900 feet in elevation along the way. You can continue beyond to the Coldwater Lake area, return the same way you came, or return to Independence Pass along Road 99 via **Independence Pass Trail** (No. 227), with extraordinary views over Spirit Lake. The round-trip distance for this is six miles. The Norway Pass Trailhead is just a mile north of Meta Lake; a water pump is also here.

Harmony Trail drops 570 feet in just a mile, offering the only legal access to the shore of Spirit Lake. Most living things were killed when pyroclastic flows filled it in 1980, causing water temperatures to reach almost 1000°F. The trailhead is halfway between the Independence Pass trailhead and Windy Ridge.

At Windy Ridge you can hike the six-mile **Truman Trail** (No. 207) for up-close-and-personal views of the lava dome inside the crater, and to connect with the round-the-mountain **Loowit Trail** (No. 216). A spur of this (216 E) leads to Loowit Falls, where 100°F water pours out of the crater (no swimming).

Norway Pass

Information

Get information on Mount St. Helens at the Forest Service's **Woods Creek Information Station** (six mi. south of Randle on Forest Rd. 25, daily 9 A.M.–5 P.M. mid-May–Sept.)—they even offer drive-through service! **Cowlitz Valley Ranger Station** (three miles east of Randle on U.S. 12, 360/497-1100) is open daily 8 A.M.– 4:30 P.M. Memorial Day through September, and weekdays the rest of the year. **Pine Creek Information Station** (17 miles east of Cougar on Forest Service Road 90 and 45 miles south of Randle, 9 A.M.–6 P.M. daily mid-May–Sept.) has information for the southeast side of St. Helens.

Mount Adams and Gifford-Pinchot

If it stood alone, 12,276-foot Mount Adams would be a prime recreation site, silhouetted on license plates and key chains. But from a Seattle viewpoint, Adams is geographically behind and below its limelight-hogging neighbors. The distance from main towns and roads make Mount Adams an ideal spot to escape civilization.

is of volcanic origins; unlike its neighbors, the mountain is believed to have been formed by a congregation of volcanic cones instead of a single large one. The mountain has been relatively quiescent for 10,000 years, and large glaciers crown its summit, including the Klickitat Glacier, second biggest of all Cascadian glaciers.

Geology

Like its more active neighbors, Mount Adams

Getting There

There are two ways to approach Mount

Hikers survey Mount Adams.

Adams: from Seattle, take I-5 south to I-205 near Vancouver, then follow I-205 to U.S. 14 and head east. At Underwood, take State Route 141 north to Trout Lake. An alternative is to take I-5 south past Chehalis, then east on U.S. 12 to Randle and take the Randle Road (Forest Service Road 23) south for 56 miles to Trout Lake. This isolated road is definitely the scenic route, and the entire length is paved. Approaching from the east, you can drive down U.S. 97 to Goldendale and west on SR 142 to Klickitat and take the Glenwood-Trout Lake Road, or follow S.R. 14 from Maryhill to Underwood and drive north. The roads into the Mount Adams area are closed each winter due to heavy snowfall.

MOUNT ADAMS WILDERNESS

This 42,280-acre wilderness covers the summit of Mount Adams, along with the entire eastern and northern flanks. The east side of the peak lies within the Yakama Reservation and is termed "Tract D." Trails—including the Pacific Crest Trail—provide a semicircular path through the heart of the wilderness. A new backcountry permit system is being discussed for Mount Adams Wilderness; check with Mount Adams Ranger District in Trout Lake (2455 S.R. 141, 509/395-3400) for details.

Climbing Mount Adams

Mount Adams is one of the easiest Northwest alpine peaks to climb; in fact, it's often used as a first climb by area mountaineering clubs. Before you begin, be sure to register with the Mount Adams Ranger Station in Trout Lake (509/395-2501, June 1–Sept. 30 Mon.–Thurs. $10, Fri.–Sun. $15). The south slope route is least difficult: it begins at 6,000 feet at the end of Forest Service Roads 8040 and 500 at Cold Springs Camp, climbing up the old road for several miles, then ascending **South Climb Trail** (No. 183), crossing snowfields and zigzagging up pumice to the peak. Climbers should carry an ice ax, rope, crampons, warm clothing, sunglasses, and other basic supplies.

Hiking

The most heavily used trail in the Mount Adams Wilderness is **South Climb,** a 2.2-mile trail from Cold Springs Campground to timberline, where climbers depart for routes to the summit. Those who prefer to stay low can follow the **Around the Mountain Trail** (No. 9) northwest for about six miles to the **Pacific Crest Trail** (PCT).

The 21 miles of the PCT that pass through Mount Adams Wilderness are accessible from Forest Service Road 23, near its intersection with Forest Service Road 8810, on the south; on the north, the PCT crosses Forest Service Road 5603 near Potato Hill. Subalpine meadows, glacial streams, dense forest, wildflowers, and scenic viewpoints reward the adventurous hiker.

Beginning at Morrison Creek Horse Camp on the south side of Mount Adams, 2.7-mile **Crofton Butte Trail** (No. 73) follows the mountain's lower slopes for scenic views of the butte. Take Forest Service Roads 80 and 8040 for about 10 miles from Trout Lake. The southeastern portion of the wilderness lies within the Yakama Reservation (509/865-5121), and hikers will need a separate camping permit.

Camping

The Mount Adams Ranger District has 17 developed campgrounds on the south side of Mount Adams. Most are free, but there is a $17 fee at the larger campgrounds, including **Moss Creek** and **Peterson Prairie.** The historic **Peterson Prairie Guard Station,** west of Trout Lake, can be rented (Dec.–Apr., $59 d) and is popular with skiers, snowshoers, and snowmobilers. Contact the Mount Adams Ranger Station in Trout Lake (509/395-3400) for reservations.

Other Forest Service campgrounds line Forest Service Road 23, the route that connects the town of Randle with the northwest side of Mount Adams. These are managed by the Cowlitz Valley Ranger District in Randle (360/497-1100) and range from free to $17 a night. Best among them is **Takhlakh Lake Campground,** which affords a gorgeous view of Mount Adams.

TRAPPER CREEK WILDERNESS

Located halfway between Mount St. Helens and the Columbia River and covering just 6,050 acres, this is one of the smaller wilderness areas in Washington. It is also one of the few places in this part of the state where the forests have been spared from logging. Several trails provide access; longest is the **Observation Trail** (No. 132), which takes you through dense old-growth stands of timber, across a ridge, and to a spur trail that edges up 4,207-foot Observation Peak for panoramic views. From here, you can continue down to the junction with **Trapper Creek Trail** (No. 192), which takes you back along this pretty creek to your starting point. This loop hike is approximately 12 miles long. Call the Mount Adams Ranger District (509/395-3400) for details.

INDIAN HEAVEN WILDERNESS

The 20,960-acre Indian Heaven Wilderness offers miles of little-used hiking trails; you won't find Mount Rainier's crowds here because the average day hiker isn't willing to drive this far into the woods on beat-up Forest Service roads. The wilderness covers a high plateau that is split through by the Pacific Crest Trail and dotted with small ponds, evergreen forests, meadows, and mosquitoes. It is located due west of Trout Lake and north of Carson. Call the Mount Adams Ranger District (509/395-3400) in Trout Lake for details.

Hiking

Thomas Lake Trail is a well-used 3.3-mile path that starts on the west side of the wilderness from Forest Service Road 65 and passes Dee, Thomas, Naha, Umtux, and Sahalee Tyee lakes before intersecting with the Pacific Crest Trail near Blue Lake. Head north on the main road from Carson, then turn right onto Forest Service Road 65 for about 17 miles to the trailhead.

The Pacific Crest Trail traverses Indian Heaven Wilderness from south to north. Start at Crest Horse Camp, just south of the wilderness boundary on Forest Service Road 60 (right off Forest Service Road 65); the trail passes lakes, meadows, and forest for 17 miles through the wilderness area, then connects with Forest Service Road 24 near Surprise Lakes on the north side.

TROUT LAKE AND GLENWOOD

Trout Lake is a tiny agricultural settlement with dairy farms and horse and alpaca ranches. Trout Lake is mostly known for being the main access point for the Mount Adams area and being the site of the Forest Service's **Mount Adams Ranger Station** (509/395-3400, year-round Mon.–Fri. 8 A.M.–4:30 P.M.). Stop in for maps, camping information, and current trail conditions. Mountain climbers must register here to climb Mount Adams (June 1–Sept. 30, Mon.–Thurs. $10, Fri.–Sun. $15).

Sights

Approaching Trout Lake from the south on S.R. 141, the **Indian Sacred Viewpoint** provides a spectacular view of Mount Adams. For a closer look, take Forest Service Road 23—the main Mount Adams access road—about eight miles north from Trout Lake. Just before the pavement gives way to gravel, you'll have an inspiring view of the mountain to the east.

Festivals and Events

The main local events are Glenwood's **Ketchum Kalf Rodeo** on the third weekend of July, and the community-oriented **Trout Lake Fair and Dairy Show** (509/493-3630) on the first weekend of August. In mid-July, the **Trout Lake Festival of the Arts** (509/395-2488) attracts local artists of all types.

Sports and Recreation

GULER ICE CAVE

Ancient volcanic activity formed this 650-foot-long, four-section lava tube cave, which during pioneer times supplied ice for the towns of The Dalles and Hood River. Accessible from Ice Caves Campground, six miles west of Trout Lake, the cave entrance is a collapsed

sink, 15 feet across and 14 feet deep, connected to three other collapsed sinks by passageways. Wear warm clothing and sturdy boots, as it does get slippery down there. Bring at least two dependable flashlights, and a helmet certainly wouldn't hurt, either. The cave is managed by the Forest Service.

MOUNTAIN BIKING

The areas of the Gifford Pinchot National Forest north and west of Trout Lake, toward Mount St. Helens and Mount Rainier, are criss-crossed with hundreds of dirt roads and single-track trails, a veritable paradise for adventurous mountain bikers. One great ride is up **Table Mountain,** located on Forest Service Road 90, three miles southwest of the intersection with Forest Service Road 23. Bikers can either bite the bullet and slog up the steep trail, or take the easier logging road to the top and bomb down the trail. Either way, a round-trip ride will take 3–4 hours. If you're up for a 19-mile ride that will fully test your skills, the **Blue Lake Trail** is one of the best in Washington. It branches off Forest Service Road 23 approximately three miles south of the North Fork Campground. A second trail reaches Blue Lake leaving Forest Service Road 23 just south of North Fork Campground, meaning bikers can take a longer loop ride if time permits. For information on these and other rides, ask at the Mount Adams Ranger Station in Trout Lake or at the Randle Ranger Station in Randle.

Accommodations and Food

Kelly's Trout Creek Inn Bed and Breakfast (25 Mt. Adams Rd., Forest Service Road 23 just past the Chevron in Trout Lake, 509/395-2769, www.kellysbnb.com, $75–100 s or d) offers comfortable accommodations in a 1940s farmhouse, with excellent breakfasts. You can also rent the entire house for $230.

But why go through the trouble if you're just taking a rest before your "alpine start" at Mount Adams? The **Trout Lake Valley Inn** (2300 S.R. 141, 509/395-2300, $90–110) is a cozy type of unfinished-wood-and-buffalo-head-on-the-wall stopover that's perfect for a place in the shadow of a mountain. Also in Trout Lake is **Serenity's** (2291 Hwy. 141, 509/395-2500 or 800/276-7993, www.serenitys.com, $89–259 d), with cabins with kitchenettes and hot tubs; there is a two-night minimum. The restaurant here serves BBQ to die for.

Glenwood's 80-acre ◖ **Mt. Adams Lodge at Flying L Ranch** (25 Flying L Ln., 509/364-3488 or 888/682-3267, www.mt-adams.com, $95–150 d) sits in a secluded valley on the eastern slope of the Cascades, with a spectacular skyline dominated by Mount Adams. The lodge is a favorite venue for family reunions and other groups, but there are also more private cabins. All include a full breakfast. Guests enjoy the hot tub and one-mile hiking trail.

The Forest Service maintains several fee campsites in the area around Trout Lake, including **Takhlakh Lake** ($17) and **Ollalie Lake** ($14). The section of the Gifford Pinchot National Forest surrounding Trout Lake, roughly between Mount Adams, Mount St. Helens, and Mount Rainier, is dotted with all manner of great spots for dispersed camping. Forest Service Roads 23, 25, and 90 are good places to begin looking.

Right next to the Chevron gas station in Trout Lake is **KJ's Bear Creek Café** (2376 S.R. 141, 509/395-2525, summer daily 6 A.M.–9 P.M., fall and spring 6:30 A.M.–8 P.M., winter 6 A.M.–7 P.M.), serving up tasty breakfasts like huckleberry pancakes, when they're in season, and standard lunches and dinners to hungry hikers and travelers out of a small dining room. This is Trout Lake's only eatery, so gobble that food while it is hot.

Trout Lake has a popular **Saturday market** (Trout Lake Grange, 509/493-3630) in July and August, with fresh produce, arts and crafts, and baked treats.

EASTERN WASHINGTON

Once you cross the Columbia River on I-90 headed toward Spokane, you witness the open spaces of the Great American Desert, running from Washington all the way down to Mexico. The trees of the Spokane area and the Okanogan Highlands provide the fir lining of the desert's fringe. The Columbia River's serpentine curve cutting across the state defines the desert's northern and western boundaries.

This land of extremes freezes in the winter and sizzles in the summer, and rarely drinks up rains. You might think that a region seeing just 10 inches of rain per year, 300 sunny days, and a dry dusty wind would be an uninhabitable wasteland. But much of the landscape changed practically overnight with the completion of a string of dams and reservoirs that created

hundreds of ponds, lakes for recreation, and most important to the region, arable farmland. For water-logged western Washingtonians, the sun-soaked land of reservoirs and lakes can be just the thing to help them dry off—or at very least, get wet by choice.

You would never guess that this desert used to be a lake, but that's exactly the case. During the last ice age, a natural dam trapped enough water to create an enormous lake covering more than 3,000 square miles. Marks from its shoreline can still be seen along the mountains above the basin.

Eventually, the ice dam melted, sending all that water on a geological rampage, radically changing the look of the region over no more than two or three days. Should you pass

© ERICKA CHICKOWSKI

HIGHLIGHTS

◖ Riverfront Park: Downtown Spokane's centerpiece park, the site of Expo '74, ambles along the Spokane River, with numerous attractions, including a dramatic gondola ride over the Spokane Falls (page 608).

◖ Ginkgo Petrified Forest State Park: Come see this forest made of stone and you'll understand why petrified wood is the official state gem (page 619).

◖ Gorge Amphitheatre: The view over the Columbia River is enough to upstage the world-class bands that play this renowned stage throughout the summer (page 624).

◖ Ohme Gardens: A green oasis sitting high above the hard-scrabbled dry land east of Wenatchee, this garden sanctuary features rock terraces, alpine vegetation, soothing waterfalls, and quiet ponds (page 631).

◖ Sun Lakes State Park and Dry Falls: Turbulent waters carved the cliffsides here during the ice age, when, for a time, this was a waterfall four times the size of Niagara Falls (page 641).

◖ Grand Coulee Dam: America's crowning engineering achievement, the largest concrete dam in the country (page 644).

◖ Omak Stampede and Suicide Race: Athletes and horses train for years in this traditional Native American competition, where riders hoof pell-mell down a steep embankment and over the Okanogan River (page 651).

◖ Stonerose Interpretive Center: Kids and adults alike get a kick out of digging for fossils at this Eocene-era fossil bed (page 654).

◖ Steptoe Butte State Park: Enjoy views of the low-slung Palouse hills atop what local Native Americans once called "power mountain" (page 666).

◖ Palouse Falls State Park: Peer over the basaltic edge as the waters thunder down the state's most dramatic falls (page 677).

LOOK FOR **◖** TO FIND RECOMMENDED SIGHTS, ACTIVITIES, DINING, AND LODGING.

through the middle of eastern Washington, see how the rock features in the **Channeled Scablands** shaped like enormous ships, their bows all pointing toward the source of the flood. One particularly good example of this phenomenon, Steamboat Rock in Banks Lake, even sports a nautical name.

INFORMATION

A **Northwest Forest Pass** ($5 daily, $30 annual) is required for trailhead parking in Colville, Okanogan, Umatilla, and other Washington National Forests.

© MARY HATHAWAY/123RF.COM

the clocktower in Spokane's Riverfront Park

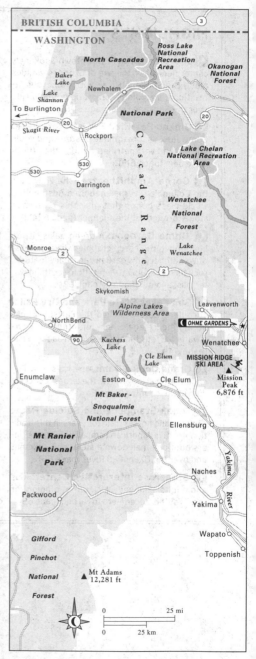

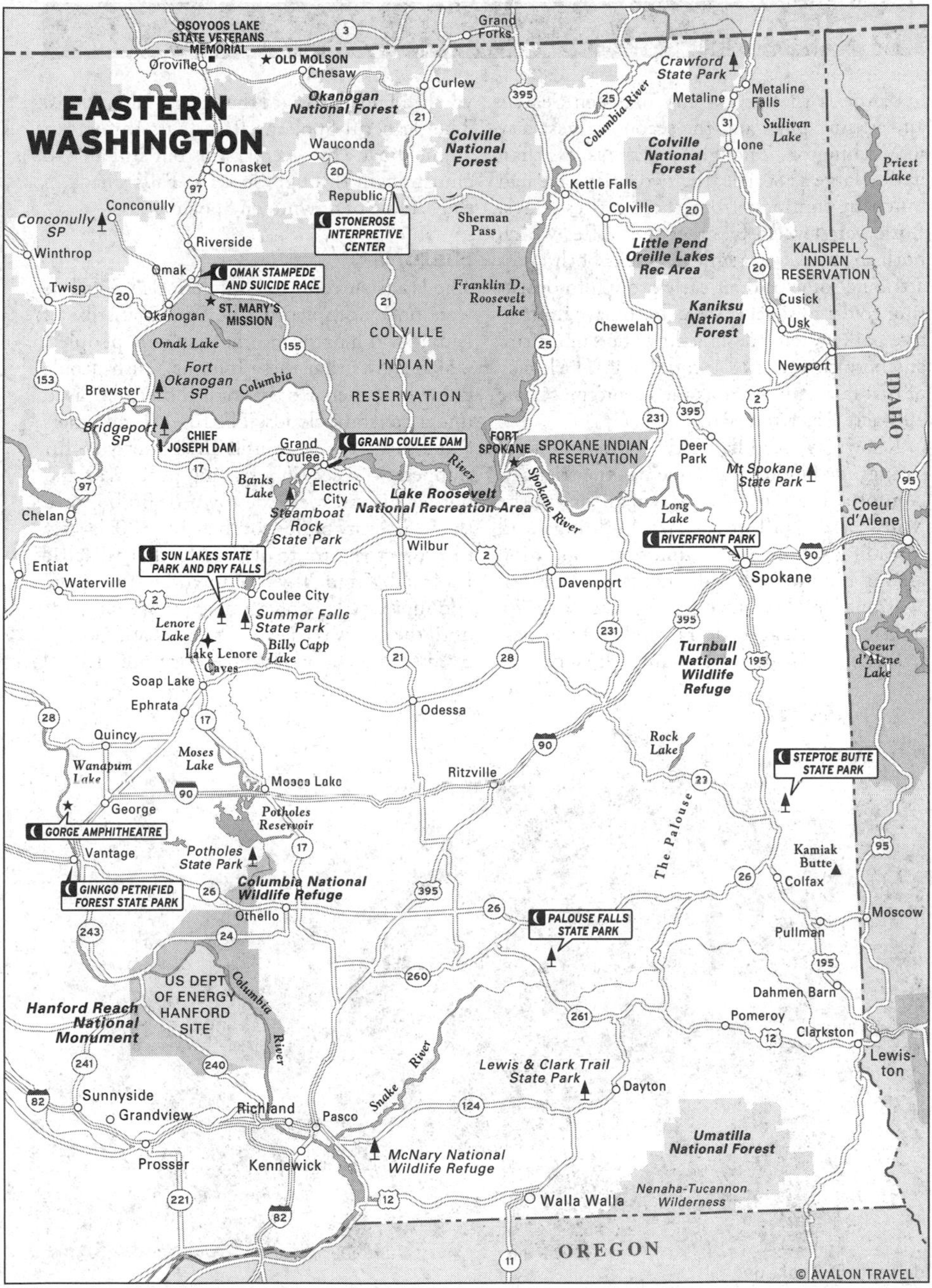

EASTERN WASHINGTON

OSOYOOS LAKE STATE VETERANS MEMORIAL

Oroville
★ OLD MOLSON
Chesaw
Curlew
Grand Forks
3
395
Crawford State Park
Metaline
25
Columbia River
Metaline Falls
Sullivan Lake
31
Ione
Priest Lake

Okanogan National Forest
21
Wauconda
20
Colville National Forest
Tonasket
97
Republic
Colville National Forest
Kettle Falls
Priest Lake

Conconully
Conconully SP
Riverside
Winthrop
Omak
Twisp
20
Okanogan
ST. MARY'S MISSION
STONEROSE INTERPRETIVE CENTER
Sherman Pass
Colville
20
Little Pend Oreille Lakes Rec Area
20
KALISPELL INDIAN RESERVATION
Cusick
Usk

OMAK STAMPEDE AND SUICIDE RACE
21
Franklin D. Roosevelt Lake
Kaniksu National Forest
Chewelah

Omak Lake
155
Fort Okanogan SP
Columbia
153
Brewster
COLVILLE INDIAN RESERVATION
25
Newport
2

Bridgeport SP
CHIEF JOSEPH DAM
17
Grand Coulee
GRAND COULEE DAM
FORT SPOKANE
SPOKANE INDIAN RESERVATION
Deer Park
231
395
Mt Spokane State Park
95

97
Banks Lake
Electric City
Steamboat Rock State Park
Lake Roosevelt National Recreation Area
Spokane River
Long Lake
Coeur d'Alene

Chelan
SUN LAKES STATE PARK AND DRY FALLS
Wilbur
2
RIVERFRONT PARK
90

Entiat
Waterville
2
Coulee City
Davenport
Spokane

Lenore Lake
Summer Falls State Park
Billy Capp Lake
231
395
Coeur d'Alene Lake

Lake Lenore Caves
Soap Lake
Ephrata
17
21
28
Odessa
Turnbull National Wildlife Refuge
195

Quincy
Moses Lake
90
Ritzville
Rock Lake
90
STEPTOE BUTTE STATE PARK

Wanapum Lake
28
George
Moses Lake
Potholes Reservoir
The Palouse
95

GORGE AMPHITHEATRE
Vantage
Potholes State Park
17
Kamiak Butte
26
Colfax
26

GINKGO PETRIFIED FOREST STATE PARK
26
Columbia National Wildlife Refuge
395
26
PALOUSE FALLS STATE PARK
Moscow

243
Othello
24
Pullman
195

US DEPT OF ENERGY HANFORD SITE
260
261
Dahmen Barn
Pomeroy
Clarkston
12
Lewiston

Hanford Reach National Monument
241
240
Columbia River
Snake River
Lewis & Clark Trail State Park
Dayton
124
Umatilla National Forest

82
Sunnyside
Grandview
Richland
Pasco
Kennewick
McNary National Wildlife Refuge
Nenaha-Tucannon Wilderness

Prosser
221
82
12
Walla Walla

OREGON
11

IDAHO

EASTERN WASHINGTON

© AVALON TRAVEL

EASTERN WASHINGTON

Spokane

Spokane is the largest city between Seattle and Minneapolis and the second-largest city in Washington. Though Spokane is less than half as large as Seattle, the two cities have had much in common from their earliest days: Both were leveled by great fires, after which both towns were rebuilt in brick; both cities attribute some of their early growth to outfitting gold and silver miners; both have impressive park systems designed by the same firm; and both cities hosted a world's fair. The legacy of that fair remains Spokane's centerpiece: the 100-acre Riverfront Park.

Known as the "Lilac City" for its bountiful springtime blooms, Spokane has the friendly, comfortable atmosphere of a small city in the Midwest. Its tall downtown buildings and spreading suburbs seem almost an apparition among the undeveloped landscape of eastern Washington. The surrounding landscape is a mixture of rich agricultural lands with its perfect circular fields, and rolling, piney hills as you head north toward the Selkirk Mountains. The peaceful Spokane River cuts through it all, held back by several dams but still able to churn down through Spokane Falls smack in the middle of downtown Spokane,

History

The lands surrounding modern-day Spokane were once occupied by the Spokane Tribe of Indians. Their name means "sun people," which shows that these Interior Salish people knew how their Coastal Salish brethren lived under constant clouds. The first white settlers came to this area around 1810 and were fur trappers who set up a trading post. War and border disputes left the town in limbo until the U.S. Army built a fort here in 1880, largely to protect the route of the Northern Pacific Railroad. Gradually, the town became more and more settled and attracted more railroads until the city was a nexus for goods of all kinds. Even the obligatory 19th-century fire in 1889

downtown Spokane

© ERICKA CHICKOWSKI

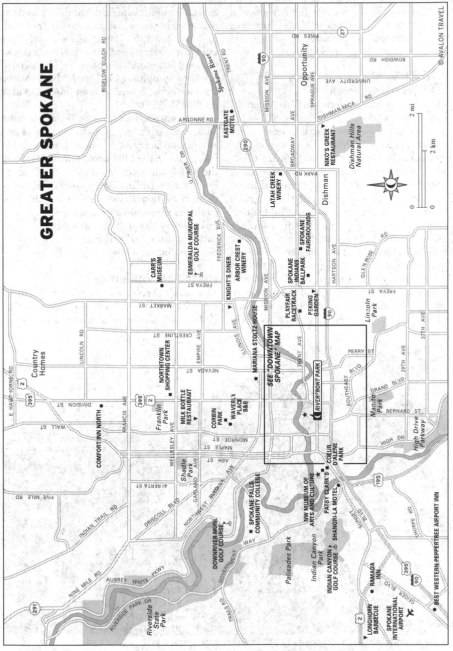

GREATER SPOKANE

2 mi

2 km

Country Homes

Dishman Hills Natural Area

Dishman

Opportunity

Lincoln Park

Manito Park

High Drive Parkway

Riverside State Park

Riverside Park Dr

Indian Canyon Park

Palisades Park

Franklin Park

Shadle Park

Shanti-La Motel

Spokane International Airport

NIKO'S GREEK RESTAURANT

EASTGATE MOTEL

CARR'S MUSEUM

ESMERALDA MUNICIPAL GOLF COURSE

KNIGHT'S DINER

ARBOR CREST WINERY

LATAH CREEK WINERY

SPOKANE INDIANS BALLPARK

SPOKANE FAIRGROUNDS

PLAYFAIR RACETRACK

PEKING GARDEN

MARIANA STOLTZ HOUSE

NORTHTOWN SHOPPING CENTER

MILK BOTTLE RESTAURANT

CORBIN PARK

WAVERLY PLACE B&B

COMFORT INN NORTH

SPOKANE FALLS COMMUNITY COLLEGE

DOWNRIVER MUN GOLF COURSE

NW MUSEUM OF ARTS AND CULTURE

PATSY CLARK'S

INDIAN CANYON GOLF COURSE

RIVERFRONT PARK

COEUR D'ALENE PARK

RAMADA INN

LONGHORN BARBECUE

BEST WESTERN PEPPERTREE AIRPORT INN

SEE "DOWNTOWN SPOKANE" MAP

seemed to pave the way for further growth. Wheat, sawmills, and nearby finds of precious metals kept Spokane alive during periods that put an end to similar developments.

SIGHTS
◖ Riverfront Park
Spokane may have been the smallest American city to host a World's Fair, but the 1974 centerpiece of the event is still testament to Spokane's successful effort. This one-of-a-kind city park (507-N Howard St., 509/625-6601, http://spokaneriverfrontpark.com) covers over 100 downtown acres. If it's a pastoral interlude you're looking for, stroll the fragrant, flower-lined paths, and walk the bridge that rises over the upper falls and ends at Canada Island, where the falls split, leaving a patch of land in the middle. Take the gentle rocking gondola over the churning foam of **Spokane Falls,** illuminated at night. A 155-foot clock tower rises alongside the river, a reminder of a long-demolished Great Northern Railroad depot. It's still wound by hand once per week.

Several sculptures are scattered throughout the park, ranging from historical, to metaphorical, to downright silly. The silliest are a 12-foot-tall Radio Flyer wagon and a mechanical goat that will "eat" small bits of trash. The home of Spokane Symphony Orchestra, the **Spokane Opera House,** is here, as is an **IMAX Theater** (509/625-6686).

For a more active tour, stop by the **Pavilion** amusement park, featuring daring rides as well as tamer attractions for young kids. Be sure to take a spin on the 1909 **Looff Carousel** ($2) on the park's south side, each chair hand-carved by master craftsman Charles Looff. The jungle-themed **mini-golf** ($4) is fun for kids and adults, as is the 30-minute narrated park tour train. From October through February, the park opens up the Ice Palace, offering lessons, theme nights, and just plain ice skating.

Historical Buildings
You can't miss the **Spokane County Courthouse** (W. Broadway at Jefferson St.). Built in 1895 and modeled after a pair of French

Take a gondola ride over Spokane Falls in Riverfront Park.

© ERICKA CHICKOWSKI

EASTERN WASHINGTON

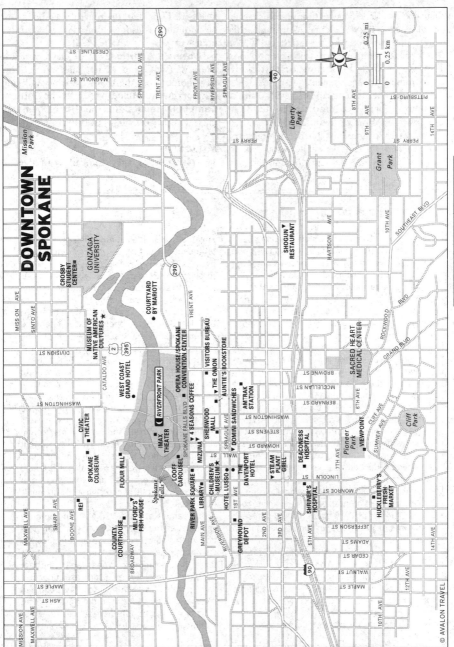

DOWNTOWN SPOKANE

GONZAGA UNIVERSITY

CROSBY STUDENT CENTER■

Mission Park

MISSION AVE
MAXWELL AVE
SHARP AVE
BOONE AVE
SINTO AVE
MISS ON AVE

CRESTLINE ST
MAGNOLIA ST
SPRINGFIELD AVE
TRENT AVE
FRONT AVE
RIVERSIDE AVE
SPRAGUE AVE

290

90

Liberty Park

PERRY ST
PITTSBURG ST
8TH AVE
9TH AVE
14TH AVE
PERRY ST

Grant Park

10TH AVE
HARTSON AVE
SOUTHEAST BLVD

ROCKWOOD BLVD
GRAND BLVD

SHOGUN ▼ RESTAURANT

SACRED HEART MEDICAL CENTER

290

TRENT AVE

MUSEUM OF NATIVE AMERICAN CULTURES ★

COURTYARD BY MARRIOTT ●

CATALDO AVE
DIVISION ST
2
395

WEST COAST GRAND HOTEL ■

RIVERFRONT PARK ★

OPERA HOUSE/SPOKANE CONVENTION CENTER

VISITORS BUREAU ▼
AUNTIE'S BOOKSTORE ■
▼ THE ONION

BROWNE ST
MCCLELLAN ST
BERNARD ST
WASHINGTON ST
STEVENS ST
HOWARD ST
8TH AVE

AMTRAK STATION ■

SPOKANE FALLS BLVD
4 SEASONS COFFEE ●
SHERWOOD MALL ■
MIZUNA ▼
SPRAGUE AVE
WALL ST
DOMINI SANDWICHES ▼

IMAX THEATER ◀
RIVER PARK SQUARE ■
LIBRARY ▼
CHILDREN'S MUSEUM ■
HOTEL LUSSO ■
THE DAVENPORT HOTEL ▼
STEAM PLANT GRILL ▼

DEACONESS HOSPITAL ■

Pioneer Park
VIEWPOINT ▼
SUMNER AVE
CLIFF AVE
Cliff Park

CIVIC THEATER ■
SPOKANE COLISEUM ■
FLOUR MILL ■
LOOFF CAROUSEL ■
Spokane Falls
MILFORD'S FISH HOUSE ■
COUNTY COURTHOUSE ■
REI ■

SHRINER'S HOSPITAL ■
MONROE ST
LINCOLN ST
HUCKLEBERRY'S FRESH MARKET ■

GREYHOUND DEPOT ■

RIVERSIDE AVE
MAIN AVE
1ST AVE
2ND AVE
3RD AVE
6TH AVE
7TH AVE
JEFFERSON ST
ADAMS ST
CEDAR ST
WALNUT ST
MAPLE ST
ASH ST
BROADWAY
MAXWELL AVE

90

12TH AVE
10TH AVE
14TH AVE

MAPLE ST
WASHINGTON ST

0.25 mi
0.25 km
N

© AVALON TRAVEL

châteaux, the castlelike courthouse seems rather out of place in busy Spokane. Amazingly, this ornate masterpiece was designed by W. A. Ritchie, a 29-year-old man with no previous design experience; his architectural training came from a correspondence course.

Visit the magnificent sandstone **St. John's Cathedral** (1125 S. Grand Blvd., 509/838-4277, www.stjohns-cathedral.org, free) to see an impressive example of gothic architecture, complete with stained-glass windows and stone carvings. Forty-nine-bell carillon concerts are held here Thursday at noon. Take a guided tour on Monday, Tuesday, Thursday, or Saturday noon–3 P.M.

Browne's Addition, on the city's west side along W. Pacific and W. 1st, boasts some of the city's homes from the 1890s. Nearby you'll find the **Northwest Museum of Arts and Culture, Campbell House,** and the **Glover Mansion** (321 W. 8th Ave., 509/459-0000).

Museums

The **Museum of Arts and Culture** (2316 W.

THE NEZ PERCE WAR

American settlers to what later became Eastern Washington were not particularly good neighbors to the native Nez Perce people. Constant conflict sprung up over Americans digging up camas fields, stealing Indian livestock, and pushing the boundaries of the tribe's reservation to suit their needs for farming, grazing, and mining. The two groups swapped abuses until the issue came to a head in 1877, when the U.S. Army and the Nez Perce people fought a brutal battle for access to rich lands in the Wallowa Valley.

In that year, the U.S. government tried to persuade Chief Joseph and his men to return to the 1863 reservation from which they had gradually drifted away. The commanding general gave Chief Joseph an ultimatum to move back within 30 days. He accepted, sadly aware that a fight would lead to the destruction of his people. Conflicts are almost always started by a small, senseless act in an atmosphere of blinding tension, and so it was here. Three Indians attacked a group of settlers, killing four men. The next day, a group of Indians killed upwards of 14 settlers, including women and children.

It was impossible for the army to not act swiftly at this point. Their first meeting at White Bird Canyon proved to be a disaster, however, with the outnumbered Nez Perce forcing the U.S. cavalry into retreat. Chief Looking Glass and Chief White Bird proved to be capable tacticians and fearsome enemies, and managed to hold their own against a thousand U.S. troops, many of whom were battle-tested Civil War vets. As American reinforcements seemed to be arriving daily, it was clear to the Nez Perce leaders that something drastic was necessary.

In a move that was to become legendary, 800 Nez Perce and their livestock began a rapid retreat, fighting skirmishes and staving off rear-action attacks as they went, through Idaho, Montana, down toward Yellowstone, and back to Montana. They then appealed to the Crow Nation, who turned out not to have any interest in tangling with American cavalry just then. Fast losing hope, they turned toward Canada, but their 1,500 mile trek, heavy losses of men and materiel, and frosty winter conditions had taken a hard toll. The army caught up with them near Bear's Paw Mountain. Here, the Nez Perce fought a valiant but doomed defensive battle before an exhausted Chief Joseph was left little choice but to surrender his forces.

The same Nez Perce tribe which had once replenished the stores of Lewis and Clark was now marched off to reservations in faraway Oklahoma and Kansas. Many, many years later, the respected and peaceable Chief Joseph made the journey back west, moved to the Colville Reservation near the beautiful river and placid lake, and died in the same Northwest his people had called home for millennia.

1st Avenue, 509/456-3931, www.northwest museum.org, 10 A.M.–5 P.M. Tues.–Sun., $7 adults, $5 seniors) is heavy on painting and textile arts, as well as eco-exhibits and a few local historical pieces. A tour of the neighboring early 1900s Tudor Campbell home is included in your museum entrance fee.

Spokane is justifiably proud of local **Gonzaga University** (Hamilton St. at Centennial Trail, www.gonzaga.edu). The Jesuit liberal-arts school is home to the **Jundt Art Center** (509/328-4220) with changing exhibits, along with an extraordinary glass chandelier by Dale Chihuly.

MOBIUS Kids (110 N. Post St., 509/624-5437, www.childrensmuseum.net, Tues.–Sat. 10 A.M.–5 P.M., $5.75 for kids or adults, $4.75 seniors and military) is a great place for some pint-sized exercise of both the mental and physical varieties. Tiny ones can crawl through a primordial rain forest while older kids can interact with live insects and play with scaled down industrial equipment.

Finding some time on his hands, a retired railroad switchman decided to build a shrine to all things unusual at **Carr's One of a Kind in the World Museum** (5225 N. Freya, 509/489-8859, Sat.–Sun. 1–4 P.M., $5 adults, children under 10 free. The eccentric collector has put together a collection like no other. Full of taxidermy squirrels and bears, handmade replicas of Chinese junks and Egyptian antiquities, the museum also houses limos owned by JFK, Jackie Gleason, and Elvis Presley. And you are invited to sit behind the wheel of whichever you choose. Mr. Carr has put together a museum of things that amuse him and they amuse him greatly. Maybe they'll amuse you, too.

Mount Spokane State Park

This sprawling park (www.parks.wa.gov) 30 miles northeast of the city on Highway 206 encompasses 5,881-foot Mount Spokane and 5,306-foot Mount Kit Carson. Enjoy hiking, mountain biking, and camping in the summer, downhill or cross-country skiing in the winter. A narrow, winding road (no RVs) climbs to the summit of Mount Spokane, where you can stop for a peek at the incredible 360-degree vista, which encompasses parts of Idaho, Montana, British Columbia, and Alberta. Dirt roads lead to other areas, and trails crisscross the park offering day hikes for all levels of ability.

Other Gardens and Parks

Manito Park and Gardens (4 W. 21st Ave., 509/456-8038, daily 8 A.M.–dusk) is a city park with floral and botanical displays, a conservatory full of tropical plants, and a pretty duck pond. A formal English garden, a Japanese garden, and a rose garden create a beautiful setting for an afternoon outing.

Stroll through the **John A. Finch Arboretum** (3404 Woodland Blvd., 509/624-4832, daily dawn–dark, free) is the lushly landscaped home to dozens of species of maples, rhododendrons, and ornamental trees along quiet-flowing Garden Springs Creek.

Cat Tales Zoological Training Center (17020 N. Newport Hwy., 509/238-4126, www.cattales.org, 10 A.M.–6 P.M. Tues.–Sun. May–Sept., 10 A.M.–4 P.M. Tues.–Sun. Oct.–Apr., $8 for adults, $6 for seniors, and $5 for kids under 12) is a nonprofit that homes and protects endangered big cats, grizzly bears, and a variety of other threatened animals. It offers a more intimate tour than most zoos are capable of doing.

Wineries

Many wineries in the greater Spokane area import grapes from nearby Yakima and produce small batches of wine.

Washington's largest producer of merlot wines, **Latah Creek Wine Cellars** (I-90 exit 289 at E. 13030 Indiana Ave., 509/926-0164, www.latahcreek.com, 9 A.M.–5 P.M. daily) is an attractive Spanish mission–style winery that features tours, tastings, an art gallery, and a grassy courtyard.

Arbor Crest Wine Cellars (4705 N. Fruit Hill Rd., 509/927-9463, www.arborcrest .com, noon–5 P.M. Mon.–Sun.) also has a tasting room and gift shop. The building, Cliff House, is a National Historic Site with a magnificent view and parklike grounds. To use

EASTERN WASHINGTON

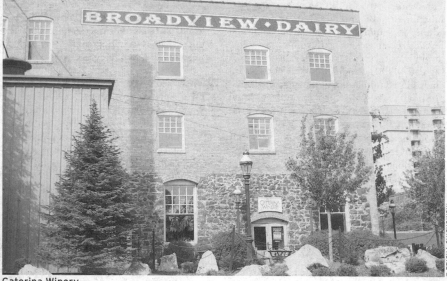

© ERICKA CHICKOWSKI

Caterina Winery

the word "eclectic" when describing the estate building does a disservice both to the word and the building. It operates a separate **tasting room** (808 W. Main, 3rd floor, 509/747-3903, 11 A.M.–9 P.M. Mon.–Thurs., 11 A.M.–10 P.M. Fri.–Sat., noon–5 P.M. Sun.).

The small **Caterina Winery** (905 N. Washington, 509/328-5069, www.caterina .com, noon–6 P.M. Wed.–Sun.) is downtown in the historic Broadview Dairy Building. Its affordable wines are made to be more main-stream-accessible than some other small vintners.

ENTERTAINMENT AND EVENTS
Nightlife

Spokane city nightlife is fairly typical for a midsized town surrounded by colleges. Larger concerts and events tend to pass the city by on their way west to Seattle and Portland, but there is a bustling local music scene hoping to put Spokane on the map. Until then, there are plenty of drinking and dancing picks for just about any taste. Pick up a free copy of *The*

Inlander (www.inlander.com) newspaper for information on upcoming events.

Downtown's **A Club** (416 W. Sprague Ave., 509/624-3629, www.aclubspokane.com) is a lively spot for all-ages shows and 21-plus shows. Alcohol is served during 21-plus shows only and even on off nights, there is pinball and pool. **The Spot Light Lounge & Night Club** (321 W. Sprague Ave., 509/624-0722) is one of the hottest gay hotspots in town. There is a full menu and bar, along with two dance floors for DJ-fueled dancing.

Gonzaga kids eat and put back pints at **Jack & Dan's Tavern** (1226 N Hamilton St., 509/487-6546), a decades-old classic owned by the dad of John Stockton, the former National Basketball Association (NBA) star and a Gonzaga alum. At **Mootsy's Tavern** (406 W. Sprague, 509/838-1570), the concerts and po-etry readings often pack the house.

O'Doherty's Irish Grille (W. 525 Spokane Falls Blvd., 509/747-0322) does a great job at not taking itself too seriously. Its keg is full of Guinness, its calendar is full of live music, and there is even a "Theology on Tap" series, which features a brief talk from a local Catholic priest followed by a Q&A session.

The Arts

Riverfront Park (509/625-6685 or 800/336-7275, www.spokaneriverfrontpark.com) is the site of concerts and other entertainment during the summer.

The time-tested **Spokane Symphony** presents classical, pops, and chamber concerts, plus annual performances of *The Nutcracker*. Concerts are held at the Martin Woldson Theater at the Fox, a 1931 venue that will give the art-deco architecture lover endless goosebumps.

The **Spokane Civic Theater** (1020 N. Howard, 509/325-2507, www.spokanecivic theatre.com) is a community theater that tends toward big-name musicals, with some unique song-filled adaptations of nonmusical material.

Festivals and Events

The **Lilac Bloomsday Run** (509/838-1579, www.bloomsdayrun.org) held the first Sunday in May, tends to attract around 50,000 runners with a downtown 12K course. Spokane hosts one of America's largest fitness and running trade shows to coincide with the event.

After Bloomsday, Spokane blossoms with the two week **Lilac Festival** (509/535-4554, www.spokanelilacfestival.org), featuring lilac floats, royalty, magic, and parties. The event is solemnly dedicated to our men and women in uniform, making it no surprise that the culmination is the Armed Forces Day Torchlight Parade on the third Saturday of May.

Ballers from all over the country come together in groups of three to compete in **Hoopfest** (509/624-2414, www.hoopfest.org) the biggest three-on-three tournament in the world. More than 7,000 teams pick-and-roll their way into town in June. Competitors range from third-graders to college heroes. Even if you don't play, the finals for the 3BA Elite Division is probably some of the tightest, most competitive ball you'll ever see.

On the fourth Saturday in July Allegro Baroque and Beyond holds its **Royal Fireworks Festival** (509/455-6865, www.allegrobaroque .org), a celebration of baroque music in open-air and historic-building venues. Fireworks follow the music. **Pig Out in the Park,** on the week before Labor Day, is a free festival giving local restaurants and musicians a chance to reach an enormous audience in Riverfront Park. The **Spokane Interstate Fair** (509/477-1766, www.spokanecounty.org/fair), held for nine days in mid-September, has a little something for everyone. Carnival rides, mutton bustin', butter churning, hypnotists and top magicians, a demolition derby, and the unforgettable racing pigs. The pro rodeo features riding, roping, and running clowns.

In late November, the Spokane Symphony puts on its **Christmas Tree Elegance** program, featuring a tree lighting and viewing, music, a black-tie dinner dance, carolers, carriages, and a grand raffle.

SHOPPING

Downtown, a two-block section of Wall Street (between Riverside Avenue and Spokane Falls Boulevard) is a popular pedestrian mall. Head to Crescent Court (Main and Wall) for a food court offering a range of quick meals. Hop aboard one of the frequent trolleys to cruise up Wall Street and along Spokane Falls Boulevard, before circling the Riverfront Park area. Skywalks crisscross Wall Street and other parts of downtown Spokane, linking 14 blocks above street level. The late 19th century brick **Flour Mill** (621 W. Mallon) is now home to over a dozen specialty retailers and restaurants. The selection is much more colorful than the average mall.

Book lovers will get a warm welcome at **Auntie's Bookstore** (402 W. Main, 509/838-0206, www.auntiesbooks.com, 9 A.M.–6 P.M. Mon., 9 A.M.–9 P.M. Tues.–Sat., 11 A.M.–6 P.M. Sun.). Big for an indie bookstore, Auntie's uses its extra space for frequent book signings and events, sets aside a good bit of space for local titles and gifts.

SPORTS AND RECREATION

Drive a few miles in any direction from Spokane and you run the risk of stumbling into an opportunity for recreation. Located just 33 miles from Spokane is **Coeur d'Alene Lake,** one of the most beautiful in the mountain west with the world's longest floating boardwalk and an 18-hole shoreline golf course with a floating green. Immediately north of Spokane are the **Selkirk Mountains,** where you'll find all sorts of wild country and a string of small towns along the Pend Oreille River. To the south are the wide-open spaces of the Palouse farmlands; to the west lies a massive desert in the Columbia Basin, along with famous Grand Coulee Dam.

Riverside State Park

Not to be confused with Riverfront Park downtown, Riverside Park (9711 W. Charles Rd., www.parks.wa.gov) is six miles northwest of town, a large and varied park canopied by ponderosa. As the name suggests, it sits along the Spokane River. Access is from Nine Mile Road on the north side of the river or along Government Way on the south shore. The 7,655-acre park is a popular place for camping, hiking, horseback, bird-watching, and there are 600 acres of land for off-road vehicles—dirt bikes in summer and snowmobiles in winter.

The premier hiking trail in the park is the **Centennial Trail** which passes most of the signature sights of the park. The 37 mile path is mostly level, with a few climbs to keep things interesting. It passes a military cemetery, curious rock formations, and stunning views of the river. Bald eagles, coyotes, and deer are frequent companions along the way. Best access is from the Nine Mile Day Use area on the north end of the park or the Wilber Trailhead on the west side of the park.

A favorite hiking destination is the **"Bowl and Pitcher"** area, where a trail leaves the campground and crosses a suspension bridge to connect with a network of enjoyable paths. These unusual volcanic formations stand along the fast-flowing river and are visible from a dramatic overlook; the resemblance to a bowl and pitcher is vague. Get here by heading northwest from town on Highway 291 (Nine Mile Road) and turning left onto Rifle Club Road, then

left again on Aubrey L. White Parkway after a half mile. The park entrance and the Bowl and Pitcher are on the right after 1.7 miles.

Another feature of Riverside State Park is the **Spokane House Interpretive Center** (12 mi. northwest of Spokane on Hwy. 291, 509/466-4747 Wed.–Sun. 10 A.M.–6 P.M. summers only, free) on the site of the first structure built by white men in the Pacific Northwest. Erected in 1810 by the Northwest Fur Company, this fur-trading post sat at the confluence of the Spokane and Little Spokane Rivers. After 16 years of use, the post was moved to a better site at Kettle Falls. No evidence remains of the trading post, but the interpretive center relates its history in a diorama, exhibits, and artifacts. It is located a half mile north of the bridge (on the northeast bank).

Spectator Sports

The Northwest League's **Spokane Indians** (www.spokaneindiansbaseball.com) play Class-A Short Season baseball at the Interstate Fairgrounds Stadium on Havana Street. The large stadium is the classiest ballpark in the league and follows a handful of games with a fireworks show. In the winter, the junior ice hockey team, the **Spokane Chiefs** (700 W. Mallon Ave., 509/535-7825, www.spokanechiefs.com), slap the puck around in the Spokane Veterans Memorial Arena, competing in the Western Hockey League. The Veterans Memorial Arena also plays host to concerts, ice shows, rodeos, circuses, and other major events.

Shake off the traffic and get ready for speed at the **Spokane County Raceway** (509/244-3333, www.spokaneracewaypark.com). Drag racing, funny cars, midgets, bikes, jet cars, and an F1 road course that is sure to satisfy the high-velocity aficionado in you. Races are held year-round.

Skiing

Thirty miles northeast of town on Highway 206 at Mount Spokane State Park, **Mt. Spokane Ski & Snowboard Park** (29500 N. Spokane Park Dr., tickets 509/238-2220, snow report 509/443-1397, www.mtspokane

.com, $45 adult, $38 college and military, $35 youth) offers alpine skiing and snowboarding, including five chairlifts, and a 2,000-foot vertical drop. It's uncrowded and friendly, with a small-town atmosphere. Night skiing draws the crowds here, as does the dry snow and 360-degree view of the Cascade, Selkirk, and Rocky Mountains. Other features include ski and snowboard school and rentals, restaurant, and bar, but no child care. Bus transportation from Spokane is available on weekends.

Some 15 miles of groomed **cross-country ski trails** are adjacent to the downhill area. Get Sno-Park permits at local sporting goods stores before heading up to ski. The 10K **Langlauf Cross-Country Ski Race** (509/922-6080, www.spokanelandlauf.org) takes place here in early February, which is always well-attended.

Other nearby ski areas include **49° North** (509/935-6649, www.ski49n.com) near Chewelah, along with two Idaho resorts: **Schweitzer Mountain Resort** (800/831-8810, www.schweitzer.com) and **Silver Mountain** (800/204-6428, www.silvermt.com).

Golf
Spokane is considered to be one of the five best golfing cities in America. More than a dozen good courses can be found in the area, including municipal **Indian Canyon** (S. Assembly and West Dr., 509/747-5353, http://spokane golf.org), one of the top public courses in the United States and host to the Rosauers Open Professional Gold Association (PGA) tournament. Golfers who love the sport for its outdoorsy aspects will also appreciate **The Creek at Qualchan Golf Course** (301 E. Meadow Lane, 509/448-9317), which boasts its own bird and wildlife sanctuary, along with ponds, creeks, and tricky protected greens. For a quick, fun round, tee off at **Pine Acres Par 3** course (11924 N Division St., 509/466-9984, $8 for 9 holes) or drop $7.50 on a bucket of range balls and drive away your stress.

Rafting
Contact **Wiley E. Waters White Water**

Rafting (888/502-1900, www.riverrafting .net) for white-water rafting opportunities on the Spokane River, including a stretch called the Devil's Toenail. The launch point is very convenient to downtown.

Climbing
Wild Walls Climbing Gym (202 W. Sprague, 509/455-9596) has an indoor rock-climbing wall with instruction and gear rentals. A day pass costs $15 and requires belay certification.

Outfitters
The local Spokane **REI** (1125 N. Monroe, 509/328-9900, 10 A.M.–9 P.M. Mon.–Fri., 9:30 A.M.–7 P.M. Sat., 10 A.M.–6 P.M. Sun.) has all sorts of classes and guided trips throughout the year. It also rents camping and other outdoor gear.

ACCOMMODATIONS
Spokane has accommodations for nearly every taste and budget, from urbane boutiques to cozy country inns to one-night cheap hotels. During major summer events, such as the Lilac Bloomsday Run in May and Hoopfest in June, travelers should make reservations well in advance.

Under $100
Road-dogs hightailing it along I-90 can save some scratch by stopping at **Shangri-La Motel** (2922 W. Government Way, 509/747-2066, $45), a bare-bones but clean and safe crash pad perfect for a night or two's rest. For slightly more comfortable budget digs, try **Comfort Inn North** (7111 N. Division, 509/467-7111 $75 d), one of the better chain motels in town. This place is immaculate, it's got a little "library loft" over the lobby for borrowing, and you'll be greeted with fresh cookies upon check-in.

Or for a little touch of home, stay at ◖ **Marianna Stoltz House** (427 E. Indiana, 509/483-4316 or 800/978-6587, www.marian nastoltzhouse.com, $89–109 s). Set in a classic American foursquare home built in 1908, this affordable bed-and-breakfast stands on a tree-lined street near Gonzaga University. A wide veranda, spacious parlor, and antique furnishings add to the allure. The four antique-furnished guest rooms have private baths.

$100-150

Families with active kids are in for a treat at the ◖ **Ramada Inn** (next to Spokane International Airport, 509/838-5211www.theramada.com, $112 d) near the airport. You can let the little fishes loose on the inn's fantastic water park with four indoor pools and a giant twisty, turny water slide. There's a hot tub for the adults, too. The hotel also offers a free hotel shuttle. Rooms come equipped with high-speed Internet, but you've got to pay for it.

Within walking distance of the Spokane River and Riverside Park, **Courtyard by Marriott** (401 N. Riverpoint Blvd., 509/456-7600 or 800/321-2211, www.courtyard.com, $179 s or d) features an on-site bistro, hot tub, and exercise room.

Waverly Place B&B (709 W. Waverly Place, 509/328-1856, www.waverlyplace.com, $105-150 d) is a Victorian-era home on Corbin Park. Built in 1902, this gorgeous B&B features hardwood floors, gas chandeliers, a wraparound porch, and an outdoor swimming pool. The four guest rooms have private or shared baths, and kids are welcome. A gourmet breakfast is served each morning.

$150-200

◖ **The Davenport Hotel** (10 S. Post St., 509/455-8888 or 800/899-1482, www.the davenporthotel.com, $169-209 d, suites $349-599 d) will spoil you to the point where you'll feel like Robin Leach should be nipping at your heels. The lobby says it all, with an interior chiseled in marble and a skylight ceiling accented with amazingly ornate and gilded crown moldings. It is decorated with luxe sofas, a trickling water fountain, and a baby grand piano. It just keeps getting better once you check in and dive into your plush bed. Rooms in the main hotel building are decorated with antique-style furnishings and floral linens, while rooms in the new tower feature hipper modern decor, including suede bedspreads and leopard-print chairs. All rooms come with marble walk-in showers, ultra-comfortable mattresses, and big flat-screen TVs. Housekeeping offers turndown service each night, leaving behind the hotel's signature soft peanut butter brittle. Wander the property and you'll find a fitness center, business center, indoor pool, and hot tub. It is also a pet-friendly establishment, and they'll even walk your dog for you.

For a more urbane, but equally luxurious option, head out of downtown to ◖ **Northern Quest Resort and Casino** (100 N. Hayford Rd., 877/871-6772, www.northernquest .com, $149-209, suites $239-579) in nearby Airway Heights. Its hip neo-Mod Squad stylings are dominated by a rich palette of chocolate, beige and aqua. With super soft beds, a pillow menu, and huge bathrooms featuring a body spray shower that will have you thinking about redesigning your own place back home, the rooms offer every opportunity for comfort. All of the little extras add up. Each room comes equipped with a Keurig coffee maker, wireless Internet is included in the room fee, there are plenty of outlets to plug in phones, laptops, and other charger batteries without unplugging lights, and even the desk chairs are very comfy. Downstairs the property features a luxe spa with steam room, sauna, and whirlpool, a sports bar that has the largest HD plasma screen in production by Panasonic, a cigar bar, a number of dining options, and, of course, a Vegas-style casino with enough slots and table games to keep the excitement rolling all day. The resort also offers complimentary shuttle service to the airport and downtown Spokane in its fleet of Cadillac Escalades.

Hotel Lusso (808 W. Sprague Ave., 509/747-9750 or 800/426-0670, www.hotel lusso.com, $149-159 d, suites $179-295) is another snazzy alternative for those with refined tastes. Built in 1890, this luxury boutique hotel offers elegantly classic rooms, though the standard queen rooms are on the smallish size. All rooms come with deep soaking tubs, big desks, and free wireless Internet. The hotel bar is everything it should be, with dark wood paneling and a denlike atmosphere perfect for nursing a drink with some pals after a long day sightseeing or making sales calls. There's also a fitness center on property.

Camping

The closest public campgrounds are in **Riverside State Park** (509/456-3964, www.parks.wa.gov, $22 tents, $31 RVs with utility hookup and onsite dump station) six miles northwest of town. **Mt. Spokane State Park** (509/238-4258, www.parks.wa.gov, $22), 30 miles northeast of Spokane, has tent sites among old-growth timber and granite outcroppings and is open May–October.

Private RV parks in the area are a bit limited. **Alderwood RV Resort** (14007 N. Newport Hwy., 509/467-5320 or 888/847-0500, www.alderwoodrv.com, $30–37) is considered one of Eastern Washington's most quiet and pretty RV campgrounds. Pull-through sites will handle rigs up to 70 feet. Take a dip in the pool, play some chip-and-putt golf, or just enjoy the gardenlike setting. The **Spokane County Fair and Expo Center** (404 N. Havana St. Ste. 1, 509/477-2784) also allows onsite camping, and while it's not a wooded wonderland, it generally offers some solitude.

FOOD
Cafés and Diners

For all-American breakfast comfort food served in an old yet elegant railroad car, don't miss (**Knight's Diner** (2909 N. Market, 509/484-0015, www.knightsdiner.com, 6:30 A.M.–2 P.M. Tues.–Sat., 7 A.M.–2 P.M. Sun., closed Mon.), a Spokane landmark for over 40 years. Sit at the long mahogany counter to watch the chef working a mountain of hash browns and catch the banter slung by the speedy waitresses. You'll find a cross-section of Spokane folks at this popular morning eatery any day of the week.

The (**Milk Bottle Restaurant** (802 W. Garland Ave., 509/325-1772, Mon.–Sat. 11 A.M.–4 P.M., closed Sun.) has been around since 1932 and is locally famous for burgers, shakes, and homemade ice cream. Just look for, well, the giant milk bottle.

Domini Sandwiches (703 W. Sprague Ave., 509/747-2324, www.dominispokane.com, Mon.–Fri. 6:30 A.M.–5 P.M., Sat. 8:30 A.M.–3:30 P.M., closed Sun.) has been serving happiness on a bun for over 90 years. This family-run shop has a great chaotic atmosphere and huge sandwiches with thick slices of meat.

Also well worth a visit for pastas, sandwiches, salads, desserts, and espresso is **Lindaman's Gourmet-to-Go** (1235 S. Grand Blvd., 509/838-3000, www.lindamans.com, Mon.–Sat. 8 A.M.–9 P.M., closed Sun).

The Onion (302 W. Riverside, 509/747-3852, open at 11 A.M. daily) is a Spokane institution with fast and friendly service, and gourmet burgers dripping with goodness. Huckleberry milk shakes are another favorite, and the beer selection offers something for everyone. True to form, the restaurant has killer onion rings.

Not to be confused with the national chain, the **Longhorn Barbecue** (7611 W. Sunset Hwy., 509/838-8372, Sun.–Thurs. 6 A.M.–9 P.M., Fri.–Sat. 6 A.M.–8 P.M.) was founded by immigrants from Texas in the 1940s, who brought their frontier talents to a hungry Eastern Washington. This down-home restaurant serves up a variety of ribs, steaks, and smoky pork in a relaxed setting.

Find good atmosphere, along with tasty muffins, cookies, scones, and espresso at **Rocket Bakery** (1325 W. 1st Ave., 509/747-1834, 6 A.M.–6 P.M. daily).

Contemporary Northwest

Stacks at Steam Plant (159 S. Lincoln, 509/777-3900, www.steamplantgrill.com, Sun.–Thurs. 3–10 P.M., Fri.–Sat. 3– 10 P.M.) is worth a visit even if you're not hungry. The restaurant is built inside an old steam plant, treating diners to an 80-foot ceiling, two 225-foot smokestacks and catwalks throughout. Also, their 28-ounce ribeye is really good.

The moody lighting and architecture pay homage to the Kalispell Indians' revered

Manresa Grotto at 🌙 **Masselow's Restaurant** (100 N. Hayford Rd., 509/481-6020, www.northernquest.com, 6–11 A.M. and 4–10 P.M. Mon.–Fri., 8 A.M.–noon and 4–10 P.M. Sat.–Sun.), located inside the tribe's glitzy Northern Quest Resort and Casino. The restaurant also tips its hat to the tribe with the Indian fry bread and huckleberry sauce served once you're seated, but the best tribute is the food. The sophisticated menu presents an array of dishes featuring fresh Northwest ingredients, heavy on the salmon, buffalo, and greens grown nearby. Everything is marvelously presented, a great mix of wine pairings are available to complement the wine and service is charmingly attentive.

Mizuna (214 N. Howard, 509/747-2004, www.mizuna.com, 11 A.M.–10 P.M. Mon.–Sat., 4–10 P.M. Sun.), a classy enclave with exposed brick walls, wood floors, and marble tables, serves up beautifully presented dishes that feature fresh seasonal ingredients.

Luna (5620 S Perry St., 509/448-2383, www.lunaspokane.com, 8 A.M.–2 P.M. and 5–9 P.M., daily) is a delightful and trendy little bistro serving Northwest classics made with fresh, local ingredients whenever possible. Scallops and salmon share the menu with delicacies like rabbit ravioli.

Asian

For Japanese teppanyaki-style food grilled right in front of you, visit the tastefully dark **Shogun Restaurant** (821 E. 3rd Ave., 509/534-7777, daily 5–9 P.M.). You can always just have the sushi instead.

Peking Garden (3420 E. Sprague Ave., 509/534-2525, Mon.–Thurs. 11 A.M.–10 P.M., Fri.–Sat. 11 A.M.–11 P.M., closed Sun.) has been run by the same owners since before the 1974 Expo. Its large menu is full of great, affordable options and there is karaoke on the weekends.

Taste of India (3110 N. Division St., 509/327-7313, Mon.–Thurs. 11 A.M.–9:30 P.M., Fri.–Sat. 11 A.M.–10 P.M., Sun. 11 A.M.–9 P.M.) has very good Indian food, but if you like it hot, you'd better emphasize to the wait staff that you want it really, really hot. Afterwards, don't deny yourself a chai tea. They brew it up right.

Italian

For pizza, pastas, calzones, and desserts in a comfortable downtown setting, head to **Europa Pizzeria and Bakery** (125 S. Wall St., 509/455-4051, http://europapizzaria.com, daily 11 A.M.–midnight). The train runs directly above the building, which, strangely enough, is charming instead of hopelessly irritating.

An Italian place with great specials, including a smoked salmon lasagna, is **Luigi's** (245 W. Main, 509/624-5226, www.luigis-spokane.com, Tues.–Fri. 11 A.M.–10 P.M., Sat.–Mon. 4–11 P.M.). It also has a three-course prix fixe offering between 4 P.M. and 9 P.M. daily. **Rock City** (808 W. Main St., 509/455-4400, www.rockcitygrill.com, Sun.–Thurs. 11:15 A.M.–9 P.M., Fri.–Sat. 11:15 A.M.–9:30 P.M.) serves Italian favorites with a haute cuisine twist. The menu is full of creative, upscale takes on burgers, calzones, and pizzas.

Steak and Seafood

Milford's Fish House (719 N. Monroe St., 509/326-7251, www.milfordsfishhouse.com, Tues.–Sat. 5–10 P.M.) will bring out the early 19th-century dandy in you with its oak, mahogany, and tin ceiling. Its beautiful seafood, steaks, oysters, and friendly service make Milford's a top spot in Spokane.

In the Old Flour Mill near Riverfront Park, **Clinkerdagger** (621 W. Mallon Ave., 509/328-5965, http://clinkerdagger.com, daily 9 A.M.–2:30 P.M. and 4:30–10:30 P.M.) is the best place to dine while overlooking Spokane Falls. Get a stomach-satisfying overview of its offerings with the Grand Tasting Sampler, a presentation of Dungeness crab, teriyaki tenderloins, tiger prawns, scallops, and tuna tartare.

Markets

For upscale grocery shopping at its best, head to **Huckleberry's Fresh Market** (926 S. Monroe St., 509/624-1349, 7 A.M.–10 P.M. daily), and an excellent place to get produce, healthy foods, and wine. The deli features salads, soups, sandwiches, sushi, and baked goods. Of course, the goal is groceries that are free-range, minimally packaged, sustainably farmed, free-trade certified, non–animal tested, organic, no hormone, and when appropriate, gluten-free.

The **Spokane Farmers Market** (Division and 5th Ave., 509/995-0182, www.spokane farmersmarket.com) takes place 8 A.M.–1 P.M. Saturday and Wednesday mid-May through October.

INFORMATION AND SERVICES

Visit the **Spokane Regional Convention and Visitors Bureau** (201 W. Main, 509/747-3230 or 888/776-5263, www.visitspokane.com, 9 A.M.–5 P.M. daily) for maps, brochures, and other information.

Check your email for free on the computers at the main **Spokane Public Library** (906 W. Main, 509/444-5300, www.spokanelibrary .org). It is open Monday through Saturday and is filled with public art and a lovely gallery of paintings.

GETTING THERE AND AROUND
By Air
Spokane International Airport (www

.spokaneairports.net), just west of town, is served by several major airlines, including Delta, Alaska, Frontier, Southwest, United, and US Airways.

By Train
Amtrak's *Empire Builder* (221 W. 1st Ave., 509/624-5144 or 800/872-724, www.amtrak .com) has daily service to Spokane from Chicago and Minneapolis, continuing west to Ephrata, Wenatchee, Everett, Edmonds, and Seattle or southwest to Pasco, Wishram, Bingen, Vancouver, and Portland.

By Bus
Spokane Transit (509/328-7433, www.spokane transit.com, $1.50) serves downtown Spokane and the Cheney area.

Greyhound (221 W. 1st Ave., 509/624-5251 or 800/231-2222, www.greyhound .com) provides nationwide connections from the Spokane bus terminal (221 W. 1st Ave.), as does **Northwestern Trailways** (509/838-5262 or 800/366-6975, www.nwadv.com/northw).

I-90 Corridor

Blasting past the passes and into the heart of eastern Washington's farmland along the speedy I-90 corridor is the preferred method of travel across this part of the state. While most people are headed to a specific spot, be it Ellensburg for the rodeo, the Gorge for a concert, or one of many sun-drenched lakes on the way to Spokane, there are plenty of other quirky little stops on this route to keep curious road-trippers busy.

ELLENSBURG TO GEORGE
Most folks in Washington know Ellensburg for one thing only: the rodeo. While the town is host to the best rodeo arena in the country and one of the oldest rodeos anywhere, visitors are usually surprised that the local feel is more that of a sleepy college town than a Wild West main street. That's because once the dust has settled

on the Labor Day rodeo, kids start rolling in to Central Washington University, annually increasing the local population by about 10,000. The town also provides a great stopover for Western Washingtonians who, for whatever reason, don't quite feel up to the long drive home after taking in a concert at the amazing Gorge Amphitheater in nearby George.

Sights
(GINKGO PETRIFIED FOREST STATE PARK
Eastern Washington hasn't always been the dusty stretch of highway it is today. Once upon a time—20 million years ago, give or take a few millennia—dense forests covered the rolling hills and bordered the twisty rivers. But it was quite a bit less peaceful than it sounds. Huge cracks in the earth's crust blasted out massive

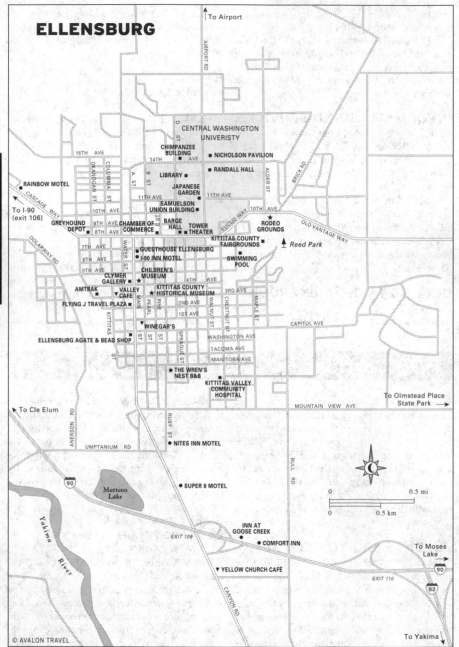

ELLENSBURG

To Airport

CENTRAL WASHINGTON
UNIVERISTY

CHIMPANZEE
BUILDING
NICHOLSON PAVILION
RANDALL HALL
LIBRARY
JAPANESE
GARDEN
SAMUELSON
UNION BUILDING
BARGE
HALL
TOWER
THEATER
CHAMBER OF
COMMERCE
RODEO
GROUNDS
KITTITAS COUNTY
FAIRGROUNDS
Reed Park
GUESTHOUSE ELLENSBURG
I-90 INN MOTEL
SWIMMING
POOL
CLYMER
GALLERY
CHILDREN'S
MUSEUM
AMTRAK
VALLEY
CAFE
KITTITAS COUNTY
HISTORICAL MUSEUM
FLYING J TRAVEL PLAZA
WINEGAR'S
ELLENSBURG AGATE & BEAD SHOP
THE WREN'S
NEST B&B
KITTITAS VALLEY
COMMUNITY
HOSPITAL
To Olmstead Place
State Park
To Cle Elum
NITES INN MOTEL
SUPER 8 MOTEL
Mattoon
Lake
INN AT
GOOSE CREEK
EXIT 109
COMFORT INN
To Moses
Lake
YELLOW CHURCH CAFÉ
EXIT 110
To Yakima

RAINBOW MOTEL

To I-90
(exit 106)

GREYHOUND
DEPOT

AIRPORT RD

BRICK RD

OLD VANTAGE WAY

CASCADE WAY

DOLARWAY RD

ANERSON RD

UMPTANIUM RD

Yakima River

MOUNTAIN VIEW AVE

BULL RD

CANYON RD

15TH AVE
14TH AVE
11TH AVE
10TH AVE
9TH AVE
8TH AVE
7TH AVE
6TH AVE
5TH AVE
4TH AVE
3RD AVE
2ND AVE
1ST AVE
WASHINGTON AVE
TACOMA AVE
MANITOBA AVE
CAPITOL AVE

OKANOGAN ST
COLUMBIA ST
A ST
B ST
D ST
ALDER ST
EUCLID WAY
WATER ST
MAIN ST
PEARL ST
PINE ST
SPRAGUE ST
KITTITAS ST
WALNUT ST
CHESTNUT ST
MAPLE ST
RUBY ST

0   0.5 mi
0   0.5 km

© AVALON TRAVEL

ELLENSBURG BLUE AGATE

Formed millennia ago and deposited in the glacier till surrounding the Ellensburg mountainsides, the rare and beautiful Ellensburg Blue Agate has captivated local people for only a blink of an eye compared to the length of its existence.

Also known simply as **E-blue,** this precious gem comes in a range of colors from sky blue to a deep purplish color, though prized above all is a vibrant cornflower blue. According to local legend, Native American tribes valued these blue stones for their beauty, so much so that only tribal chiefs were allowed to wear them.

For several decades tourists came up to Ellensburg just to root around the soil for E-blue. The famed New York jeweler Tiffany & Co. even used the gem in some of its jewelry. By 1940 or so the most productive agate beds were depleted, making finds rare. Most of the existing beds are on private land, and even those who do get a chance to scour them consider a single small find pretty good for a whole day's work. All things considered, your time is probably best spent scouring local jewelry stores who sell raw, polished, and set stones at a wide price range.

Petroglyphs in the area have been shown to be over 10,000 years old.

CLYMER MUSEUM

The Clymer Museum (416 N. Pearl St., 509/962-6416, www.clymermuseum.com, 10 A.M.–5 P.M. Mon.–Fri., noon–5 P.M. Sat.–Sun., donations accepted) honors John Ford Clymer, who was born in Ellensburg in 1907 and went on to fame for his nature illustrations and paintings of the Old West. Art galleries and interpretive exhibits fill this historic building.

THORP MILL

The Thorp Mill (11640 N. Thorp Hwy., Thorp, 509/964-9640, www.thorp.org, 11 A.M.–3 P.M. Thurs.–Sun. late May–Sept.), eight miles northwest of Ellensburg, is a restored 1883 mill originally restored by local High School students. Work is still in progress, but the long boxy building makes for a nice picture.

THE BULL

A bull on a bench? Find the locally notorious aluminum sculpture *The Bull* taking it easy on a park bench on 4th and Pearl, legs crossed. A strategically placed cowboy hat preserves modesty and keeps you guessing whether the old fellow is a bull or a steer. It was created by noted sculptor Richard Beyer.

OLMSTEAD PLACE STATE PARK

See a working pioneer farm at Olmstead Place State Park (509/925-1943, www.parks.wa.gov, dawn–dusk daily Memorial Day–Labor Day, by appointment the rest of the year). Tours are available noon–4 P.M. Saturday–Sunday.

CENTRAL WASHINGTON UNIVERSITY

Central Washington University campus (400 E. University Way, 509/963-1262, www .cw.edu) has some pleasing options for a lazy afternoon. A **Japanese Garden** and the **Sarah Spurgeon Art Gallery** (509/963-2665, www .cwu.edu/~art) showing student and alumni art are tucked away on campus.

The **Chimpanzee & Human Communication**

lava flows that swept the trees into nearby lakes. From there, the wood was replaced by minerals little by little until they became, essentially, trees of stone. These days, as you explore the park, you're bound to find dozens of tree species preserved in this unique way.

An **interpretive center** (4511 Huntzinger Rd. in Vantage, 509/856-2700, www.parks .wa.gov, 10 A.M.–6 P.M. daily mid-May–Aug.) about 30 miles east of Ellensburg (exit 136 of I-90) shows off several choice specimens of petrified wood and shows a short film explaining why gingkoes are so special. As proof that people have found this spot interesting for years and years, you can also find here several Wanapum rock engravings or petroglyphs.

EASTERN WASHINGTON

Vantage Bridge over the Columbia River

© LIJUAN GUO/123RF.COM

Institute (509/963-2244, www.cwu.edu/~cwuchci) is home to three chimpanzees who are being taught American Sign Language. The doors open to the public for hour-long educational **Chimposiums** ($11 adults, $8.50 students) on the weekends.

SCENIC DRIVES

For a beautiful country drive, head west from the interpretive center along the **Vantage Highway** that connects Vantage to Ellensburg. This is the back way and makes a good bike ride (narrow shoulders, alas). Sagebrush, rugged land, cattle, and ranches give this a Western appeal. Tune in the AM radio for cowboy or Mexican music to fit the mood. If you're a fan of back roads, take the Vantage Highway, which parallels I-90 for much of this area. Two miles west on Vantage Highway are several interpretive trails that lead uphill past more examples of petrified trees. A 2.5-mile trail leads across the dry, windblown hills past an assortment of scrappy wildflowers, sagebrush, and broad views. Watch for bald eagles, hawks, deer, elk, coyote, and a variety of lizards and snakes, including the poisonous northern Pacific rattlesnake.

For a look at one of the more unusual geologic features in the area, take exit 143 (six miles southwest of George) from I-90, and follow Old Vantage Road west down Frenchman Coulee to the basaltic rock **Pillars,** a favorite rock-climbing spot.

Entertainment and Events

NIGHTLIFE

Ellensburg is simultaneously a rodeo town, a college town, and in the middle of nowhere. Expect the 'Burg to be a little light on dancing and music but heavy on bars that are heavy on beer.

The **Starlight Lounge** (402 N. Pearl St., 509/962-6100) is a lounge that attracts quite a few Central Washington students on the weekends, not just for drinks but for the great dinner menu as well. For a more local-friendly atmosphere, check **The Tav** (117 W. 4th Ave., 509/925-3939), a low-lit place with pool tables where people drink Pabst Blue Ribbon without

SHOOT THE BULL WITH LOCAL COWPOKES

If you find yourself in Eastern Washington during the summertime, you've gone and got yourself caught up in rodeo season. Rodeos can be an exciting way to be a part of local culture, but you'd better be prepared with a working knowledge of terms, lest you identify yourself as "not from 'round here."

PRCA – The Professional Rodeo Cowboys Association, which sanctions rodeos and venues nationwide.

All-Around – award given to the cowboy who showed the most grit in two or more events.

Bareback Riding – event in which a cowboy jumps on the back of an enraged horse, called a bronc or bronco, without a saddle or proper reins, and tries to stay on for eight seconds. If he makes it, both he and the horse are rated on a scale of 0–50.

Steer Wrestling – also called bulldogging, features a mounted cowboy running down a steer, jumping off, and wrestling the steer to the ground.

Team Roping – two mounted competitors ride after a steer, which they then catch in a lariat. Team roping is unusual in that men and women compete evenly, either mixed or single-sex.

Saddle Bronc Riding – similar to bareback riding, only with a saddle.

Tie-Down Roping – based on an actual ranch necessity, a mounted cowboy tries to rope a calf, jump down, and restrain the animal as quickly as possible.

Steer Roping – a mounted cowboy chases a running steer, lassos its horns, then cranks his horse in the other direction, flipping the steer, at which point the cowboy jumps down and ties up the steer.

Barrel Racing – an event mainly for cowgirls, it is a high-speed run through a cloverleaf pattern of barrels.

Bull Riding – the king of rodeo events, bull riding involves busting out of a shoot aboard an enraged bull and trying to stay on for eight seconds that feel like an eternity. Should the cowboy make eight seconds without being trampled or gored, he and the bull are both rated on a 0–50 scale.

a trace of irony. For the most part. There's outdoor seating, a jukebox, and a good pub menu. And the **Iron Horse Brewery** (1000 Prospect St., 509/933-3134, www.ironhorse brewery.com) is closed by 9 P.M. or 10 P.M. every night, but if you can drink fast, you can get good and loaded with interesting brews like 509 Style, Double Rainbow, Light Rail Ale, and local favorite Irish Death.

ELLENSBURG RODEO

Labor Day weekend's Ellensburg Rodeo (509/962-7639 or 800/426-5340, www .ellensburgrodeo.com) is one of the venerable few rodeos that is long-running enough to be known as an "Old Rodeo," for its size, integrity, and dedication to the form. Expect to see the standards: calf roping, wild horse races, barrel races, cowboys on enormous Brahma bulls, and saddle broncs during this four-day event. Expect the unexpected, too, like dog-

assisted buffalo herding in the main ring, and the upper-echelons of America's rodeo clowns. At the same time, the **Kittitas County Fair** enters full swing, with music, rides, and food. Rodeo tickets include admission to the fair and you can order up to a year in advance—helpful since nearly all the tickets are gone for weekend events by early August.

ELLENSBURG NATIONAL ART SHOW AND AUCTION

Visit the Ellensburg National Art Show and Auction (509/962-2934, www.westernartassoci ation.org) the third weekend in May. More than 200 artists display their work. Demonstrations include the "Quick Draw," where artists each create a work of art in 45 minutes.

ANNUAL THRESHING BEE AND ANTIQUE EQUIPMENT SHOW

Held the second weekend following Labor

EASTERN WASHINGTON

Day at Olmstead Place State Park, the Annual Threshing Bee and Antique Equipment Show (509/925-3137) is really just wholesome hometown fun. The Kittitas Valley Early Iron Club sponsors this old-timey event with pancake breakfasts and homemade ice-cream and a daily tractor parade. Every year has a featured line of tractor chassis and engines. It makes for a great antidote to big-city cynicism.

☾ GORGE AMPHITHEATRE

There are just not many venues in the entire world that approach the beauty and scope of the Gorge Amphitheatre (754 Silica Rd. NW in George, 206/464-2000, www.live nation.com). On the grassy hill facing the stage at a daylight show, the view of the Columbia River Gorge is absolutely guaranteed to upstage the performer, no matter who it is. The same hill provides unexpected acoustics and the wide lawn has plenty of room for lying on an old blanket or dancing wildly, however you happen to swing. The generally crisp blue sky gives way to an umbrella of stars only visible on the edges of civilization, sort of like this remarkable place. The outside venue makes a great fit for mellow and jam acts like Jack Johnson, Massive Attack, and frequent guest Dave Matthews Band. Rock 'n' roll acts like Tom Petty and David Bowie have managed to light up the stage, too. It takes an act with real confidence to play here. With a capacity of over 20,000, shows fill motels as far away as Wenatchee and Moses Lake. Plan ahead. Camping and RV spaces are available on adjacent grounds, and a concessionaire sells food.

FOURTH OF JULY

It doesn't take much pondering to figure out how the founders of the city of George, Washington, came up with the name. On the 4th of July, the city hosts a celebration out of proportion to its little population. The **George Washington Celebration** starts with the **Cherry Bomb Fun Run** (509/787-5632, http://georgecoffeehouse.com), a 10k race and a two-mile race. Choose based on your fitness level and your preference for standard or metric

measures. Every year, townsfolk work to create a staggering half-ton cherry pie. Have an enormous piece while watching the evening fireworks. Entertainment lasts all day and often features the very talented Wenatchee Youth Circus.

Shopping

The Ellensburg Blue agate, a 1930s favorite of Tiffany & Co., is the hometown secret treasure. This stone, found only here, can be purchased at a few shops in town, uncut, finished, or mounted in jewelry. **Ellensburg Agate & Bead Shop** (201 S. Main St., 509/925-4998, 9 A.M.–5 P.M. Mon.–Sat., until 6 P.M. in summer) carries gemstones, beads, and lapidary equipment. **Art of Jewelry** (709 South Main St., 509/925-9560) specializes in Ellensburg Blue jewelry.

There are dozens of other cute boutiques and galleries around these jewelry shops on both Pearl and Main Streets). **Gallery One** (408½ N. Pearl, 509/925-2670, www.gallery-one. org) is a big, multifunction gallery featuring

downtown Ellensburg

THE CATASTROPHIST

The Channeled Scablands are just about as strange as they sound. Unlike regular river valleys in the area, this entire system of dry channels features rounded bottoms and flows out of Spokane before fanning out into the Columbia River. Nineteenth- and early-20th-century geology held it as a general law that geological changes happened gradually and uniformly, and so most visitors believed that the channels were the result of slow erosion.

University of Chicago professor J Harlen Bretz was just not buying it, however. He became obsessed with the feature after visiting in the 1920s. Glaciers and other usual suspects just didn't make sense. There were high-water marks on cliffs. Boulders had been carried far from their source. The only thing that would fit the evidence was a catastrophic flood. Or maybe multiple floods. His work brought him ridicule with colleagues branding him as a "catastrophist" rather than a uniformitarian, like them. Ivy Leaguers trashed University of Chicago as a "Western trade school." His research brought him a level of disgrace difficult to understand outside of academic circles. Still, he persisted.

Finally, after many painstaking years, Bretz came up with the theory that an enormous dam made of ice had backed up a lake that was maybe half the volume of Lake Michigan. When the Ice Age ended and the dam melted and crumbled, all that water came tearing down through present-day Montana, Idaho, and Washington; a flood so epic that it might have lasted for weeks. Along the way, it gouged lakes, steepened canyons, and made a certain series of wiggly channels that seemed otherwise impossible to explain.

It would take Bretz and his supporters another 40 years before his theories would be recognized as the most probable explanation of the Channeled Scablands. Ultimately it would take a chartered bus trip leading all the way from Montana to Eastern Washington, where his opponents could see, step by step, the way things might have played out. Redeemed, Bretz was finally honored with the prestigious Penrose Medal from the Geological Society of America. It proved the wisdom of one of his supporters, proclaiming of his colleagues that now "we are all catastrophists!"

As you drive along the Columbia River, take a moment to glance at these little traces in the dirt and think about how they alone set off one of the greatest geological debates of the entire 20th century.

showings of works by some of the best regional artists as well as offering gifts and hosting classes. **Pearl Street Books** (421 N. Pearl, 509/925-5678) is a cozy bookshop where you can easily browse away the afternoon. Quilters will find a sense of purpose in Ellensburg at **Quilts by Dezine** (422 N. Pine St., 509/925-4122, 10 A.M.–5:30 P.M. Mon.–Fri., 10 A.M.–4:30 P.M. Sat.) where you'll find trunk shows, classes, and plenty of supplies.

Sports and Recreation
IRON HORSE TRAIL
The Ellensburg area is beribboned with backcountry roads for bike or horse. The best among them is Iron Horse Trail, alternately known as John Wayne Trail, which stretches 110 miles across the state. The trail runs parallel to the Yakima River, with several trailheads in and around Ellensburg.

For horseback rides, contact **Happy Trails Horse Adventures** (Eaton, 509/656-2634, www.happytrailsateastonwa.com). It offers horseback rides with an extra dose of excitement—instead of staring at a bobbing tail in front of you, some rides let you ford rivers, peek at elk, climb a mountain, and visit a secret lake, all of them at least partially on the Iron Horse. Prices start at $90 and will be quoted out for a fully customized overnight catered ride.

The 0.75-mile **Altapes Creek Trail** is a short hike that leads from the red early-pioneer barn to the little Seaton Cabin Schoolhouse. The 217-acre Olmstead Place Park also offers some relaxing seasonal fishing in the Coleman Creek.

WATER SPORTS

The **Yakima River** is a favorite place for tubing during the summer, and a great place to cool off when temperatures top 100°F. Much of the 40-mile stretch between Cle Elum and Roza Dam is a relaxing float. The most popular run is the five- to six-hour 15 miles from Teanaway Bridge (below Cle Elum) to the diversion dam.

Rent rafts and kayaks in Thorp, or schedule a guided tour at **Rill Adventures** (509/964-2520, www.rillsonline.com). Try its magical Full Moon Floats on the "Yak" with snacks and light beverages ($40).

The river is also a productive fly-fishing spot for beautiful, fat rainbow trout, and few can get you outfitted more thoroughly than the delightfully named **Worley-Bugger Fly Co.** (306 S. Main St. #3, 888/950-3474, www.worley buggerflyco.com). The experienced guides offer full-day and half-day tours starting at $300.

ROCK HUNTING

Rockhounds know that Kittitas County is the only place on earth you'll find the Ellensburg Blue agate. Try your luck at the **Rock N Tomahawk Ranch** (2590 Upper Green Canyon Rd., 509/962-2403, $5). The owners here will give you a brief orientation about finding Ellensburg blue and then set you loose on their 160-acre spread to see what you can find. Hunt for free at Dry Creek on Highway 97, or along Horse Canyon Road. Just remember that these lands allow surface hunting only. Also, for your safety, don't cross on to private property, and whatever you do, don't anger the grazing cows.

WILDLIFE-WATCHING

Winter wildlife lovers can watch hundreds of elk share a hay picnic at the Washington Department of Wildlife's feeding station in Watt Canyon, 15 miles west of Ellensburg. Get here by heading west on I-90 to exit 101, then across the freeway and uphill a quarter mile. Turn right on Old Thorp Cemetery Road and follow it to Watt Canyon Road, where you turn left and continue a mile to the elk-feeding site.

OUTFITTERS

Mountain Hard Wear (105 E. 4th Ave., Ellensburg, 509/925-4626, www.mountain hardwear.com) rents mountain bikes, in-line skates, tents, climbing shoes, skis, backpacks, and other outdoor gear.

Accommodations

Lodging is nearly impossible without a long-established reservation during the Ellensburg Rodeo in early September, the Western Art show in May, and Gorge Concerts on summer weekends.

The **Inn at Goose Creek** (1720 Canyon Rd., 509/962-8030 or 800/533-0822, www .inn-at-goose-creek.com, $119 s or d) is different. Very different. The 10 rooms all have different motifs, ranging from a room in which it's Christmas all year long, to the All-Star Sports Fan room, complete with basketball hoop table. Each room includes a fridge and whirlpool tub, and a continental breakfast is served.

A favorite among parents visiting their kids at CWU, **GuestHouse Ellensburg** (606 N. Main St., 509/962-3706 or 888/699-0123, $135 d) is an easy four-block walk from campus and close to the shops of the historic downtown. The Victorian home situates guests in one of two suites done up with the best of the old and the new: English antiques and big flat-screen TVs. Wine lovers will be pleased to find Ellensburg WineWorks operating beneath them on the first floor.

Rainbow Motel (1025 Cascade Way, 509/933-7100, $57–105 s or d) has standard rooms; kitchenettes are also available. **I-90 Inn Motel** (1390 Dolarway Rd., exit 106 off I-90, 509/925-9844, $62 s or $72 d) has lakeside rooms with continental breakfast; pets are welcome.

Super 8 Motel (1500 Canyon Rd., 509/928-4888 or, www.super8.com, $81 s or $94 d) has an indoor pool and hot tub. **Quality Inn** (1700 Canyon Rd., 509/925-9800 $95 s or $99 d) has an indoor pool, sauna, and hot tubs.

For an eye-opening building with an unreal view of the Columbia River, visit the █ **Cave B Inn & Spa** (344 Sillica Rd. NW., Quincy, 509/785-2283, www.sagecliffe.com, starting at $200). The resort is styled in graceful curves and basalt-amalgam walls so as to blend in with the scenery organically. Relax and gaze at the surrounding vineyard from the outdoor pool. Standalone "Cliffehouses" are essentially standalone suites, "Cavern Rooms" make you feel you've gone to ground with the cavelike stone room entrances, and the inn rooms are high-ceiling, two-person-shower, bright and airy hiding places. Plan ahead. All rooms book up early year-round.

Concert-goers seeking a crash pad generally find **Vantage Riverstone Resort** (551 Main St., 509/856-2800, www.vantagewa .com, $120–150) offers a good balance between economy and convenience. Located under 30 minutes from the Gorge, this nothing-but-the-basics motel is a good option for those who don't want to rough it at the amphitheater's campground. Be fair warned, though, the party atmosphere on concert nights can keep the beats going pretty late into the night. Light sleepers should probably bring ear plugs.

CAMPING

The nearest public campground to Ellensburg is 27 miles east at **Wanapum State Recreation Area** (4511 Huntzinger St. in Vantage, 509/856-2700, $22 tents, $31 RVs with full hookups) in the Columbia Basin. Closer to Ellensburg, RV spaces are available at the **Kittitas Valley Event Center** (800/426-5340, www.co.kittitas .wa.us) during the summer months. **Yakima River RV Park** (791 Ringer Loop, 509/925-4734, www.yakimarv.com, $20–30) campground is on a working ranch with three stalls available to guests traveling with horses. Guests can fly fish for free on the property. The campground is super pet-friendly.

And it's impossible to overlook the highest-demand camping in the area, **The Gorge Campground** (754 Silica Rd. NW, www.livenation.com, $60–150) available during shows at the amphitheater and at other times, too. Food is available for purchase and the venue provides security. And don't expect a wilderness experience. Sites are noisy and close together, security is active, no pets of any kind are allowed, and for a site that frequently hosts the band Phish, enforcement can be remarkably tough on users of illicit substances.

Food
ELLENSBURG

The Valley Café (103 W. 3rd Ave., 509/925-3050, 11 A.M.–9 P.M. daily) is a European-style bistro where you won't go wrong any meal of the day. Dinner highlights include innovative takes on Northwest meats and seafood like ahi tuna katsu. Great salads, curries, risottos, and pasta round out the diverse menu.

Originally the sanctum of a Lutheran church, **Yellow Church Café** (111 South Pearl St., 509/933-2233, www.yellowchurchcafe.com, 11 A.M.–9 P.M. Mon.–Fri., 8:30 A.M.–9 P.M. Sat.–Sun.) has a heavenly spread of kobe burgers, ahi tuna, salmon, and other dishes made with high-quality ingredients.

Ellensburg's hot summer days and the silky ice creams of **Winegar's** (1013 E. University Way, or 608 N. Main St., 509/933-1823 and 509/933-1821 respectively, 6 A.M.–5:30 P.M. Mon.–Fri., 7 A.M.–5 P.M. Sat., 8 A.M.–5 P.M. Sun.) were made for each other. There is a stableful of inventive flavors, including its delicious maple ice cream.

The **Kittitas County Farmers Market** (on 4th St. between Pearl and Pine, 509/925-1776, www.kcfarmersmarket.com, 9 A.M.–1 P.M. Sat. May–Oct.) brings fresh produce, baked goods, and arts, seafood, and specialty pet products. The annual schedule usually includes performances by musicians, local magicians, and dance troupes.

If Ellensburg is a gateway to wine country, then **Ellensburg Wine Works** (606 N. Main St., 509/962-8463, www.ellensburgwineworks .com, noon–7 P.M. Tues.–Sat.) is your ticket puncher. This quaint emporium of all things vinous is tucked away in the bottom floor of a charming bed-and-breakfast. The owners pride themselves on their eclectic and sometimes obscure selection of local wines. Taste their hand-picked vintages all day on Friday and Saturday.

VANTAGE
The windy point that is Vantage doubtlessly inspired **Blustery's** (301 Main St., 509/856-2434). It's a good stopover if you're heading west toward Seattle and could really use a burger and milkshake.

Information and Services
The **Kittitas County Chamber of Commerce** (609 N. Main St., 509/962-6148, www.kittitas countychamber.com, 8 A.M.–5 P.M. Mon.–Fri. year-round) can give you info on smaller local events.

The **Ellensburg Public Library** (501 N. Anderson St., 509/962-7204, www.ci .ellensburg.wa.us) invites you to curl up by one of its cute stained-glass windows and check your email or change your Facebook status.

GETTING THERE AND AROUND
Ellensburg and Kittitas county does not operate busses or other public transit. Call **Rodeo Town Taxi** (407 N Walnut St., 509/929-4222) for local cab rides. **Greyhound** (1512 Hwy. 97, 509/925-1177 or 800/231-2222, www.grey hound.com) can get you out of town from its depot in Ellensburg.

The nearest commercial airport is **McAllister Field** in Yakima, which is served by Alaska Airlines.

MOSES LAKE TO RITZVILLE
The small city of Moses Lake, named for Chief Moses of the Sinkiuse Tribe, is a quiet settlement beside the bank of the eponymous lake. The main reason most folks visit Moses Lake is the opportunity for water sports on the lake or nearby Potholes Reservoir, but it does draw its share of travelers headed to or from concerts at

the Gorge Amphitheater in George. The area usually gets no more than eight inches of rainfall and can boast some of the state's highest summer temperatures. This area was, as you'd expect, a parched desert when early white settlers showed up at the end of the 19th century. The construction of the Grand Coulee Dam and its irrigation channels in the 1930s miraculously turned the hardscrabble land into some of the most fertile farmland in the country. Moses Lake has one of the largest airports in the country, but chances are, you'll never take off or land there. It is a training and testing facility for the U.S. military, the Boeing Company, and National Aeronautics and Space Administration (NASA).

Moving east through amber waves of grain, you'll pass through the town of Ritzville. Make sure you pass through slowly, as the town government seems to be largely funded by speeding tickets issued to I-90 travelers. Ritzville was once a major railroad hub for the shipping of grain and flour. The endless fields are carved by endless roads, almost hypnotizing the cross-state traveler.

Sights
COLUMBIA NATIONAL WILDLIFE REFUGE
The Columbia National Wildlife Refuge (headquarters at 44 S. 8th St., Othello, 509/488-2668, http://pacific.fws.gov) contains a changing landscape of cliffs, wide-open sagebrush grasslands, eroded canyons, and a scattering of more than 50 lakes and ponds. The refuge is home to more than 100,000 birds each fall and is a vital winter resting area for mallards and Canada geese. Although the refuge is closed to public entry during the peak season for the protection of the birds, it is open for bird-watching, hiking, camping, and fishing in the spring and summer.

MUSEUMS
Moses Lake Museum and Art Center (401 S. Balsom St., 509/764-3830, www.mlrec.com, Tues.–Sat. 11 A.M.–5 P.M., free) displays fossils, geological specimens, and a full-sized sculpture of an ancient mammoth.

Armed forces buffs may want to check out the small **Schiffner Military and Police Museum** (4840 Westshore Dr., 509/765-6374, open by appointment) with over a hundred uniforms, tons of medals, and tools used by servicemen and women on display.

Entertainment and Events

Centennial Theater along Moses Lake is the home to free concerts throughout the summer.

The Memorial Day weekend **Spring Festival** features a carnival, jugglers, parades, restored rods and low-riders, fireworks, lip-synch contest, and a 10K run.

A popular rodeo is the highlight of the **Grant County Fair** (off Hwy. 17, 509/765-3581, www.grantcountyfair.com) held the third week of August at the fairgrounds just north of town.

Sports and Recreation

WATER SPORTS

Located at the southwest end of O'Sullivan Dam, **Potholes State Park** (O'Sullivan Dam Rd., 509/765-7271 or 888/226-7688, www.parks.wa.gov) is a popular spot for fishing and sunbathing. Irrigation waters from the O'Sullivan Dam made their way south and filled dozens of geological pockmarks with water. Now the park is a haven for water-skiers, picnickers, and swimmers. Birdwatchers also have the opportunity to scope the thousands of migratory waterfowl who take a breather in this unexpected oasis.

Moses Lake's city-run **Cascade Park** (Valley Rd., 509/766-9240, mid-April through mid-October) at the city's eponymous body of water is chiefly a boat-launch that also has public showers.

WATER PARKS

Surf 'n Slide Water Park in McCosh Park (401 W. 4th Ave., 509/764-3842, www.mlrec .com, open mid-May through mid-Sept., $9 adults, $7 kids 5–12, free under 4) runs a high-octane surfing simulator, two 200-foot water slides that tower over the crowd, a tube slide,

sand volleyball courts, food, and lots of green space to relax. You can also cool off on those blistering summer days at **Ritzville Water Park** (105 E. 10th Ave, 509/659-1003, www .ritzville.com, $4 adults, $3 ages 4–14, $3.50 over 55), a park with two pools, a water slide, and food concessions.

SAND DUNES

Hike, slide, or ride your off-road vehicle over 3,000 acres of sand dunes south of the city of Moses Lake. Go four miles south on Division St., or take exit 174 off of I-90, then follow the signs as they lead you south. Dry primitive camping is permitted.

GOLF

Play golf in the sunshine at **The Links at Moses Pointe** (4524 Westshore Dr., 866/764-2275, www.mosespointe.com, $35), a beauty of a course overlooking the lake. The lush fairways and especially sticky rough are a good day out for a deep-driver. The 130-slope course should give your skills a workout.

Accommodations

If you're going to take in a concert at the Gorge, book your room as soon as you buy your ticket. Hotels get slammed in Moses Lake during any big show.

Sunland Motor Inn (309 E. 3rd Ave., 877/765-1170, www.sunlandinn.com, $43–60 d) has good, clean rooms and free wireless Internet.

Centrally located **Lakeshore Resort Motel** (3206 W. Lakeshore Ct., 509/765-9201, $65 s or $68 d) has cottages, cabins, and an outdoor heated swimming pool right on Moses Lake.

Inn at Moses Lake (1741 E. Kittleson Rd., 509/766-7000 or www.innatmoseslake.com, $90 d) is just off the freeway and has in-room coffee and free wireless Internet.

Holiday Inn Express (1735 E. Kittleson, 509/766-2000, www.hiexpress.com, $150 d) is the contractor or business-traveler's choice with a large copy, print, and fax center, meeting rooms, and free wireless Internet. An in-room mini-fridge, microwave, and work desk with lamp make for a great office on the road. Plus there are cinnamon buns.

Best Western Lake Front Hotel (3000 Marina Dr., 509/765-9211 or 800/235-4255, $119 s or $129 d) is a nicely redecorated resort right on the lake. Amenities include an outdoor pool, hot tub, health spa, exercise facility, and tennis courts. Pets are allowed by prior arrangement. In Ritzville, **Cedars Inn Ritzville** (1513 S. Smitty's Blvd., 509/659-1007, $70) is the closest you're getting to the Ritz in town. The motel-style rooms aren't fancy, but they are clean and comfortable. The Inn is pet-friendly and has an open area for cooped-up animals to decompress and rip around like crazy. There's an outdoor pool and free nighttime snacks. The property is Americans with Disabilities Act (ADA)–accessible.

CAMPING

Potholes State Park (at the west end of O'Sullivan Dam, 509/765-7271) has tent sites ($21) and RV spaces ($31); open year-round. Make reservations ($7 extra) at 888/226-7688 or www.parks.wa.gov.

Public campsites are also available in **Scooteney Park** (11 mi. south of Othello along Hwy. 17, 509/234-0527, $8 no hookups) and at **Soda Lake Campground** within Columbia National Wildlife Refuge.

Suncrest Resort (303 Hansen Rd., 509/765-0355, $30–40) is the place to park your rig and unwind with some horseshoes, volleyball, video games, or a dip in the big asterisk-shaped pool. The **Cedars Inn & RV Park Ritzville** (1513 S. Smitty's Blvd., 509/659-1007, $30) has pull-through spots for RVs up to 60 feet. There's laundry, showers, and you can register 24 hours a day.

Food

Michael's on the Lake (910 W. Broadway Ave., 509/765-1611, www.michaelsonthelake .com, 11 A.M.–10 P.M. daily) serves clever entrées that mix Northwest favorites with international flavors on a deck overlooking Moses Lake.

For Chinese cooking in a range of styles, head to **Eddie's Restaurant** (801 N. Stratford Rd., 509/765-5334, Tues.–Sun. 4–9 P.M., closed Mon.).

Chico's Pizza (Vista Village Shopping Center, 509/765-4589, Sun.–Thurs. 4–9:30 P.M., Fri.–Sat. 4–10:30 P.M.) serves pizza pies with enough toppings to leave you pleasantly confused. For spicy Mexican food, cross the border. That being the border from Grant County into Adams County for Ritzville's **Casuela's Grill** (214 W Main St., 509/659-4431, 11 A.M.–9 P.M. Mon.–Thurs., 11 A.M.–10 P.M. Fri.–Sat., 11 A.M.–8 P.M. Sun.). Fat burritos and tasty salsa make this a good rest stop.

The **Moses Lake Farmers Market** (McCosh Park on the Dogwood St. side, 509/750-7831, 7:30 A.M.–1 P.M. Sat. May through Nov., 2–6 P.M. June through Oct.) invites you to "Get Fresh With the Locals" and pick some fresh produce from an area known for agriculture.

Information

For local information, contact the **Moses Lake Chamber of Commerce** (324 S. Pioneer Way, 509/765-7888 or 800/992-6234, www.moses lake.com, 8 A.M.–5 P.M. Mon.–Fri.). Moses Lake is a helpful stopover on a long trip.

Getting There

Both **Greyhound** (509/765-6441 or 800/231-2222, www.greyhound.com) and **Northwestern Trailways** (509/624-9863 or 800/366-3830, www.nwadv.com) have bus service throughout the Northwest from Shilo Inn (1819 E. Kittleson Rd.). The nearest **Amtrak** station is in Ephrata.

Wenatchee

Set on the northern reaches of the Columbia just east of the North Cascades, Wenatchee is a thriving place with an abundance of shops, museums, and restaurants, plus a fun riverside path and many great places to explore nearby. The name Wenatchee comes from a Native American term meaning "water flowing out." Philip Miller was Wenatchee's pioneer apple grower and one of the first white settlers. In 1872, Miller took squatter's rights on a parcel of land in the Wenatchee Valley and planted a handful of apple seedlings that eventually grew to make Wenatchee what it is today.

Wenatchee gets over 300 sunny days and only 10–15 inches of rain per year. The warm, sunny days, cool nights, and volcanic ash soil combine to provide ideal conditions for apples, pears, cherries, peaches, and other fruits in the mountain valleys.

SIGHTS
⟨ Ohme Gardens

Once the private joy of the Ohme family, these highly acclaimed gardens (3327 Ohme Rd., junction of Highways 2 and 97, 509/662-5785, www.ohmegardens.com, 9 A.M.–7 P.M. daily Apr. 15–Oct. 15, 9 A.M.–6 P.M. daily the rest of the year, $7 adults, $3.50 ages 7–17, free for kids under 7) just north of Wenatchee were purchased by the state in 1991. Now covering nine acres, the gardens resemble natural alpine scenery: evergreens, grass, ponds, and waterfalls blend with the existing rock—a cool reprieve from the scorching Wenatchee sunshine. A lookout from the gardens' highest point provides broad views of the valley, Cascades, and Columbia River. Steep drop-offs in some sections make this a hazardous place for toddlers. Please leave your pets at home.

Rocky Reach Dam

If you're not already all dammed-out, take a stretch break at Rocky Reach Dam (509/663-8121, www.chelanpud.org, 8 A.M.–6 P.M. daily Memorial Day–Labor Day, 8 A.M.–4 P.M. daily in the spring and fall, closed Jan.–mid-Feb). The 4,800-foot-long dam and nicely landscaped surroundings offer boating, fishing, picnicking, a museum, interpretive center, and viewable fish ladder.

EASTERN WASHINGTON

© ERICKA CHICKOWSKI

Ohme Gardens

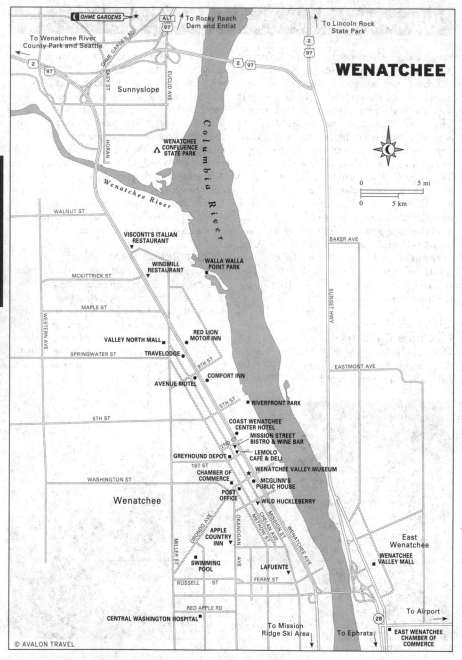

WENATCHEE

OHME GARDENS

To Rocky Reach Dam and Entiat

To Lincoln Rock State Park

To Wenatchee River County Park and Seattle

OHME GARDEN RD

EASY ST

Sunnyslope

EUCLID AVE

HORAN

Columbia River

WENATCHEE CONFLUENCE STATE PARK

Wenatchee River

WALNUT ST

VISCONTI'S ITALIAN RESTAURANT

WINDMILL RESTAURANT

WALLA WALLA POINT PARK

BAKER AVE

MCKITTRICK ST

MAPLE ST

WESTERN AVE

RED LION MOTOR INN

VALLEY NORTH MALL

TRAVELODGE

9TH ST

SUNSET HWY

SPRINGWATER ST

COMFORT INN

AVENUE MOTEL

EASTMONT AVE

5TH ST

5TH ST

RIVERFRONT PARK

COAST WENATCHEE CENTER HOTEL

MISSION STREET BISTRO & WINE BAR

2ND ST

GREYHOUND DEPOT

LEMOLO CAFE & DELI

1ST ST

WENATCHEE VALLEY MUSEUM

CHAMBER OF COMMERCE

MCGLINN'S PUBLIC HOUSE

WASHINGTON ST

Wenatchee

POST OFFICE

WILD HUCKLEBERRY

ORONDO AVE

OKANOGAN

MISSION ST

METHOW ST

CHELAN AVE

WENATCHEE AVE

APPLE COUNTRY INN

MILLER ST

AVE

East Wenatchee

WENATCHEE VALLEY MALL

SWIMMING POOL

LAFUENTE

RUSSELL   ST

FERRY ST

RED APPLE RD

To Airport

CENTRAL WASHINGTON HOSPITAL

To Mission Ridge Ski Area

To Ephrata

28

EAST WENATCHEE CHAMBER OF COMMERCE

0   5 mi

0   5 km

Museums

Wenatchee Valley Museum and Cultural Center (127 S. Mission St., 509/888-6256, www.wenatcheewa.gov, 10 A.M.–4 P.M. Tues.–Sat., closed Sun.–Mon. and holidays, $5 adults, $4 seniors and students, $1 ages 6–12, free for kids under 5) is one of the most charming museums in the state, housing a large collection exploring Wenatchee history from its Native American roots through the pioneer days up to modern agricultural displays. Upstairs, you'll discover an impressive Great Northern-inspired model railroad.

Apple-Picking

To get out under the orchards and see the area's

TAKE A BITE OUT OF WENATCHEE

Washington apples are famous throughout the world for their diversity and crispness. The city of Wenatchee calls itself "The Apple Capital of the World." Dating back to 1872, this city, the county seat of Chelan County, has been obsessed with apples. Apples are plastered across store signs, churches, sports teams, to say nothing of the thousands of trees bearing the genuine article.

- **Braeburn** – This crisp, juicy red apple is a transplant from New Zealand. They start coming to market in mid-October.

- **Cameo** – A great cooking apple and a Washington State discovery, the cameo resists browning and works great in salads.

- **Fuji** – These reddish-pink apples store well and taste sweet. They grow in Washington between late September and early November.

- **Gala** – Red dappled with yellow, the gala is small but perfect for snacking. Look for them in early fall.

- **Gingergold** – A rare treat, the gingergold is a transplant from the East Coast and grows just a few short weeks at the end of summer.

- **Golden Delicious** – Great for cooking or eating raw, the golden delicious is just the ticket for perfect cider.

- **Granny Smith** – The firm, slightly sour apple appears in mid-October and makes a bang-up pie. Try slicing these green gems and sprinkling them with a tiny bit of salt.

- **Jonagold** – These delicious, bright red apples are perfect for dessert. Enjoy them in the fall, since they are not available year-round in stores.

- **Pink Lady** – This blushing beauty is delightfully sweet and nuanced. A newer favorite, this apple is available from fall through early spring.

- **Rome** – These apples can taste a little mealy when eaten fresh but are absolutely ideal for cooking. Look for them from fall through early winter.

- **Red Delicious** – Who isn't familiar with the red delicious? This firm, succulent apple is number one for a reason. Tasty and with undeniable eye-appeal, the red delicious tastes best when icy cold.

Pick up fresh apples in Wenatchee.

prized crop in all its deliciousness, try a tour from **Washington Apple Country** (866/459-9614, www.appleorchardtours.com, $24–59), which offers everything from orchard hay rides and U-pick tours to specialty dining tours that blend orchard and vineyard visits.

The **Washington State Apple Commission Visitor Center** (2900 Euclid Ave., 866/459-9614, www.appleorchardtours.com, 8 A.M.–5 P.M. Mon.–Fri., 9 A.M.–5 P.M. Sat., 10 A.M.–4 P.M. Sun. May–Dec., 8 A.M.–5 P.M. Mon.–Fri. the rest of the year) present information about apples and apple juice and provides refreshing samples.

ENTERTAINMENT AND EVENTS
Nightlife
On many Friday and Saturday nights **Caffé Mela** (17 N. Wenatchee Ave., 509/888-0374, www.caffemela.com, 7 A.M.–7 P.M. Mon.–Fri., 8 A.M.–7 P.M. Sat.) hosts a parade of talented locals on its intimate stage, keeping the doors open until at least 10 P.M.

Prepare to be serenaded *en Español* at **Grizzly's Lounge** (1225 N. Wenatchee Ave., 509/663-0711, 4–11 P.M. Sun.–Thurs., 4 P.M.–1:30 A.M. Fri.–Sat.), which hosts an array of musicians on Friday nights, focusing especially on Spanish music.

A DJ spins rock and pop music most nights at the **Wenatchee Roaster & Ale House** (201 N. Wenatchee Ave., 509/662-1234). Situated inside the Wenatchee Center Hotel, the Roaster is a lively place to take a date for a late-night bite to eat in the lounge, where the kitchen is open until midnight. Music plays 9 P.M.–12:30 A.M. Tuesday–Thursday and 9 P.M.–1:30 A.M. Friday–Saturday.

For a casual game of pool and a bit of flirty conversation, head over to **Willie's Sports Bar** (921 Valley Mall Pkwy., 509/884-7917) in East Wenatchee. Outfitted with big-screen TVs and big pitchers of brew, this is a bustling spot for the just-turned-21 set.

Or for a classier evening, sip and swirl local vintages at the mood-lit lounge in **Shakti's** (218 N Mission St., 509/662-3321, www .shantisfinedining.com, 4:30–8:30 P.M. daily),

which also serves a mean martini and lots of inventive appetizers.

The Arts
Wenatchee is home to a thriving performing arts scene that seems to support many more performances than one would expect from a town of its size. The focal point of this community is the 550-seat **Pacific Arts Center Wenatchee** (123 N. Wenatchee Ave., 509/663-2787, www.pacwen.org), that hosts traveling performances from troupes such as the Moscow ballet, the Seattle Symphony string quartet, and the Seattle Opera Young Artists program.

Complementing the PAC is the **Music Theatre of Wenatchee** (233 B N. Wenatchee Ave., 509/662-7814, www.mtow.org), where local performers run regular musical theater shows throughout the year.

Perhaps the most unique venue in town is the **Press Room Theatre** (14 N. Mission, 509/670-8233), a cozy little performance hall built in the old printing press room the local *Wenatchee World* left empty after building new print facilities. The building proved an extremely apt theatre venue due to the acoustic panels installed during the press days to dampen printing noise and prevent it from bothering workers in the rest of the building. Press Room Theatre is home to the local **Mission Creek Players** (www.ncwtheater .com), which also puts on performances at the Music Theatre. This is also home to cabaret-style improv comedy acts on Friday nights at 8 P.M. Admission costs $5.

Festivals and Events
The "Apple Capital of the World" is the only proper place to hold the annual **Apple Blossom Festival** (509/662-3616, www.appleblossom .org), which blooms in the beginning of May. This grand 11-day event features parades and music, crowning of royalty, and the awarding of the "Apple Citizen of the Year" to the individual who has best furthered the interests of the local orchard community. The apple pie–eating contest is thankfully placed some time after the Apple Blossom Run.

The **Wenatchee Youth Circus** (509/662-0722, www.wenatcheeyouthcircus.com), is commonly called "The Biggest Little Circus in the World." Local youth train throughout the year in such skills as trapeze, juggling, high wire, and clowning. Come summer, they take their show on the road to venues throughout Washington. The circus is regarded as one of the absolute top nonprofessional circus troupes in the country.

SHOPPING

Macy's, Sears, and Ross Dress for Less anchor the mid-sized **Wenatchee Valley Mall** (511 Valley Mall Parkway, 509/884-6645, www.wenatcheevalleymall.com) in East Wenatchee. Downtown has a wide selection of boutiques. **Amanda's Book Store** (11 Palouse St., 509/630-8085, www.amandas bookstore.com) is a cute little bookstore with a chairs facing a big, bright window for test-driving your purchases before buying. **Colyar Jewelry** (23 S. Wenatchee Ave., Ste. 102, 509/662-3116, 9:30 A.M.–5:30 P.M. Tues.–Fri., 9:30 A.M.–4 P.M. Sat.) has created several in-house lines of jewelry that you'll find nowhere else. **The Guilded Lily** (2 N. Wenatchee Ave., 509/663-1733, 10 A.M.–5:30 P.M. Mon.–Sat.) dominates the gift market downtown. You'll find flatware, bath and body goods, purses, and whatever else you might need to add that last touch of flair to your home, or send back east for the holidays. For the strictly functional, head up Wenatchee Avenue to find all the big chains such as Wal-Mart.

SPORTS AND RECREATION
Spectator Sports
The new **Town Toyota Center** (1300 Walla Walla Ave., 509/667-7847, www.towntoyota center.com) puts on ice skating, North American Hockey League hockey, and big concerts and exhibitions.

Racing fans have plenty to get their hearts pounding at the **Wenatchee Valley Super Oval** (3385 Fancher Field Rd., 509/884-8592, www.wvso.com) on Fancher Heights above East Wenatchee. The April–September schedule features stock cars, sprints, monster trucks, and even a bus race! Leave your video equipment at home, as it is strictly prohibited. But do bring cash, as they don't accept credit or debit cards.

Apple Capital Recreation Loop
The Apple Capital Recreation Loop Trail is more than 13 miles of paved trail perfect for a stroll, bike ride, run, or skate session. During the winter months, you may even find cross-country skiers getting in shape here.

For $18 a day, you can rent a bike to cruise the loop trail from **The Second Wind Bicycle and Nordic Shop** (85 NE 9th St., 509/884-0821) in East Wenatchee. Come winter you can also pick up a pair of cross-country skis for $20 per day.

Several parks provide restroom facilities, picnic grounds, and play areas along the loop. The trail follows both sides of the Columbia River, connecting parks such as **Wenatchee Confluence State Park,** where you can swim in a roped-off area in the summer and **Riverfront Park** (509/661-4551), with an ice rink and mini-railroad available for special events. Near where the Columbia and Wenatchee Rivers meet, **Walla Walla Point Park** (509/661-4551) also has a swimming beach and provides areas for soccer, softball, swimming, tennis, volleyball, and horseshoes. There is even a handicapped-accessible fishing pier.

On the south end, the trail crosses the river on a footbridge to East Wenatchee. One path heads north through Porter's Pond Nature Area and back over the Odabashian Bridge, and a second continues south to tiny **View Point Park,** a great place to watch sunsets. Two miles farther south is **Rock Island Hydro Park,** another riverside park with paths, a boat ramp, and a swimming area.

Skiing
Just 12 miles from Wenatchee, **Mission Ridge Ski Area** (7500 Mission Ridge Rd., 509/626-5208, www.missionridge.com, lift tickets run $51 adults, $35 seniors, $45 ages 13–17, $35

ages 7–12, $9 kids age 6 and under) is the area's largest slope and Washington's east-side secret, with drier powder and more sun than other Cascade ski areas. It has 36 runs, a snowboard half-pipe, a restaurant, lounge, ski and snowboard rental shop, ski school, and child-care facility. Mission Ridge is generally open Thanksgiving–early April. A SkiLink bus (509/663-6543, www.linktransit.com, $3 round-trip) shuttles skiers and skis from Wenatchee, Leavenworth, or Chelan.

Golf

Golfers will enjoy playing the par-69 **Three Lakes Golf Club** (2695 Golf Dr. off the Wenatchee-Malaga Hwy., 509/663-5448, $25–30). The straight-and-narrow links-style course offers views of the river and mountains.

The Jack Frei–designed **Desert Canyon Golf Resort** (1201 Desert Canyon Blvd., Orando, 800/258-4173, www.desertcanyon.com), north of East Wenatchee offers a beautifully groomed course. Greens fees are $89 in summer, $69 in spring and fall. The 134 slope should provide a good challenge for most weekend players.

Water Sports

BlueSky Outfitters (800/228-7238, www.blueskyoutfitters.com) offers half-day ($74), full-day ($92), and overnight ($249) rafting trips on the Wenatchee River, considered one of the top 10 rafting runs in the United States. Trips put in at Riverside Park.

If you can't wait to get wet, check out **Riverside Recreation** (509/670-6457, www.riversiderecreation.net) to rent personal watercraft or full-sized boats for some river fun. Tow and launch yourself or opt for their delivery service. Jet Skis are $200 for six hours while a 20-foot Openbow will run you around $330 per day.

Horseback Riding

If you prefer your locomotion drier and four-legged, take a horseback trail ride at the **Lake Wenatchee State Park Riding Stable** (Lake Wenatchee State Park, 509/763-3647,

May–Sept.). Guided rides run from $23 for a two-mile ride up to $130 for a full-day ride.

Skating

Skaters can shred one of Washington's best skateboard parks, **Pioneer Skate Park** (220 Fuller St., dawn–10 P.M. daily) The park is lit at night. Safety equipment is a must.

ACCOMMODATIONS

The **Wenatchee Area Chamber of Commerce** (2 S. Mission St., 509/662-2116, www.wenatchee.org) keeps track of room availability and can transfer you to local motels and B&Bs that are chamber members. Many of the motels offer ski package deals in the winter.

Under $100

Out on bustling Wenatchee Avenue, you'll find a number of affordable lodging choices. **Motel 6 Wenatchee** (610 N. Wenatchee Ave., 509/663-8167 or 800/722-0852, $50 s or $65 d) is one of the best deals in town, with an outdoor pool, hot tub, and sauna. **Avenue Motel** (720 N. Wenatchee Ave., 509/663-7161 or 800/733-8981, www.avenuemotel.com, $55 s or $65 d) also includes an outdoor pool, hot tub, and kitchenettes, plus has a different look than your standard motel. Pets are allowed.

A cozy inn along the big bend of the Columbia is **Travelodge** (1004 N. Wenatchee Ave., 509/662-8165 or 800/578-7878, www.travelodge.com, $53 s or $90 d), with an outdoor pool, hot tub, and sauna.

$100-150

Set within a beautiful 1920 Craftsman home, **Apple Country Inn** (524 Okanogan Ave., 509/664-0400, www.applecountryinn.com, $85–120) welcomes guests with a wraparound porch and a comfortable living room for lounging. Rooms are cozy, with comfy beds and the choice between shared or private bath arrangements. Families can book a separate carriage house on property for a bit more space and a full kitchen. Breakfasts include a hearty warm dish complemented by seasonal fruit grown by the owners on their off-site farm.

Located on a peaceful 10-acre riverside spread, **Warm Springs Inn** (1611 Love Ln., 509/662-8365 or 800/543-3645, www.warm springsinn.com, $115–140 s or d) is a sprawling 1917 ivy-covered mansion. The three guest rooms and suite all have private baths and full breakfasts. Maybe it's the pretty property or the fact that it's on Love Lane, but the B&B is a popular wedding venue.

Red Lion Hotel (1225 N. Wenatchee Ave., 509/663-0711, www.redlion.com, $135–155 s or d) has free wireless, a pool and hot tub, and laundry valet service.

For a deluxe stay, try the **Coast Wenatchee Center Hotel** (201 N. Wenatchee Ave., 509/662-1234 or 800/716-6199, www.wenatcheecenter.com, $130–165 s or d). This hotel has a great view of the river and mountains, and the Wenatchee Roaster and Ale House is conveniently located on the 9th floor. Ask about special golf or romance packages.

Camping

Wenatchee Confluence State Park (509/664-6373, open year-round) sits at the juncture of the Wenatchee and Columbia Rivers, just north of town, and has a pedestrian bridge across the Wenatchee River to marshes on the south side. Tent sites are $21, and RV hookups cost $31. Neatniks should bring some change, as there are coin-operated showers on-site. Make reservations for Wenatchee-area state parks ($7 extra) at 888/226-7688 or www.parks.wa.gov.

Six miles west of Wenatchee on Highway 2, **Wenatchee River County Park** (509/662-2525, Apr.–Sept.) has playgrounds, cookout areas, and camping for tents ($20) and RVs ($30).

Some say that the geologic feature across the river from **Lincoln Rock State Park** (509/884-8702, www.parks.wa.gov, mid-Mar.–Oct.) looks like old Abe's profile. The park is seven miles north of East Wenatchee on Highway 2 and sports a day-use area that has a swimming beach on the Columbia River, boat moorage, and tennis courts. The park has tent sites ($21) and full-hookup RV spaces ($31). Interpretive programs are offered at the amphitheater on summer evenings.

FOOD

Hard economic times have taken their toll on Wenatchee, as other neighboring cities. Many great restaurants have closed their doors, but many seem to be getting by all right with the help of locals and travelers.

Cafés and Diners

Start the day with delicious breakfasts and espresso at **Wild Huckleberry Bakery & Breakfast House** (302 S. Mission, 509/663-1013, 8 A.M.–2 P.M. Sun.–Mon., 7 A.M.–3 P.M. and 5–9 P.M. Tues.–Sat.).

Set inside a historic building, ◖ **McGlinn's Public House** (111 Orondo Ave., 509/663-9073, www.mcglinns.com, 11 A.M.–10 P.M. Mon.–Thurs., 11 A.M.–10:30 P.M. Fri.–Sat., 11 A.M.–9 P.M. Sun.) offers beautifully plated and scrumptious meals at unpretentious prices. The wood-fired oven here produces some amazing steaks, roasted chicken, and pizzas and all of the veggies and salads are sourced locally. Pair them up with local brews or vino and enjoy the scenery—the redbrick walls, colorful hanging glass lights, and the antique skis "jumping" from the top of the bar all complete the atmosphere in this family-friendly eatery.

For more of a deli-sandwich kind of menu, see the **Lemolo Café & Deli** (114 N. Wenatchee Ave., 509/664-6576, 10 A.M.–4 P.M. daily). The colorful-as-a-playroom café serves soups, salad, and pizzas. It does quite a lunch business.

Steak

Warm wood paneling, cozy booths, and red vinyl pay homage to the roadhouse past of **The Windmill** (1501 N. Wenatchee Ave., 509/665-9529, www.thewindmillrestaurant.com, 5–9 P.M. daily). The giant windmill outside, not so much. Wenatchee's nicest steakhouse lays out thick, juicy cuts of beef, accompanied by home-cooked apple pies. Leave a few bites on your dinner plate to justify one of the rich dessert pies. In the summer, the signature berry cream cheese pie is not to be missed.

International

Woo someone special with the house specialty

crepes at the candlelit **Mission Street Bistro & Wine Bar** (202 N Mission St., 509/665-2406, www.missionstreetbistro.com, 9 A.M.–10 P.M. Mon.–Sat., 11 A.M.–3 P.M. Sun.) served with a wide array of fillings and paired with any number of local wines from Mission's amply stocked cellar.

Visconti's Italian Restaurant (1737 N. Wenatchee, 509/662-5013, www.viscontis.com, 11 A.M.–9:30 P.M. Mon.–Fri., 5–10 P.M. Sat.–Sun.) serves quite good Northern Italian food in a white-linen setting. It corks both local and Italian wines to complement the great food.

Tacos and nachos extraordinaire get cooked up at **Lafuente** (816 S. Mission, 509/664-1910, 11 A.M.–10 P.M. daily).

Wok-About Grill (110 N. Wenatchee Ave., 509/662-1154, 11 A.M.–9 P.M. Mon.–Sat. in summer, 11 A.M.–8 P.M. Mon.–Thurs., 11 A.M.–9 P.M. Fri.–Sat. in winter, closed Sun.) is a Mongolian barbecue with a big grill in the center of the room and quick service. It's great for filling bellies on a budget.

Markets

The Wenatchee area is filled with fruit stands selling fresh apples, apricots, cherries, peaches, and pears in season. **Stemilt Growers** (3615 Hwy. 97 Alt., 509/662-9667, www.stemilt.com) is a large local apple, cherry, and pear grower with tours and a retail shop.

The **Wenatchee Valley Farmers Market** (South Chelan Ave., 509/668-0497, www.wenatcheefarmersmarket.com, 10 A.M.–3 P.M. Sun. June–Sept.) takes place in Memorial Park. Other Wenatchee farmers markets take place on Columbia Street (at Palouse St., 8 A.M.–1 P.M. Sat. May–Oct. and 8 A.M.–1 P.M. Wed. late June–Oct.), and Methow Park (corner of Spokane St. and Methow St., 3–7 P.M. Thurs. July–Oct.).

INFORMATION AND SERVICES

For maps, brochures, or specific information on the Wenatchee area, contact the **Wenatchee Valley Convention and Visitor Center** (5 S Wenatchee Ave., 800/572-7753, www.wenatcheevalley.org).

Get camping and hiking information from the **Okanogan-Wenatchee National Forest** headquarters (215 Melody Lane, junction of Highways 2 and 97, 509/664-9200, www.fs.fed.us/r6/wenatchee).

Emergency medical services can be obtained at **Central Washington Hospital** (1201 S. Miller St., 509/662-1511, www.cwhs.com).

Hurt animal companions are cheerfully healed at the **Animal Hospital of Wenatchee** (10 N. Chelan Ave., 509/663-8845, www.animalhospitalofwenatchee, 8:30 A.M.–5 P.M. Mon.–Fri.).

GETTING THERE
By Air

Pangborn Memorial Airport (1 Pangborn Ave., 509/884-2924, www.pangbornairport.com) serves the region's aeronautical needs. **Alaska Airlines** (800/252-7522, www.alaskaair.com) operates a number of flights between Pangborn Field and Seattle.

Wings of Wenatchee (3764 Airport Way, 509/886-0233, www.wowgofly.com) offers charter and flightseeing trips out of Pangborn. A 30-minute zoom over the area runs $89 for up to three people, or a 60-minute for $160.

By Bus and Train

Columbia Station (at Wenatchee and Kittitas) is Wenatchee's downtown transportation center. Amtrak trains, Link buses, and Northwest Trailways all stop here, providing convenient connections for travelers.

Link (509/662-1155, www.linktransit.com) has bus service throughout Chelan and Douglas counties, including Wenatchee, Chelan, Leavenworth, and to Mission Ridge Ski Area. The buses also carry bicycles. **Northwestern Trailways** (800/366-3830, www.northwesterntrailways.com) offers bus service east to Spokane and west to Everett and Seattle.

Amtrak's (800/872-7245, www.amtrak.com) *Empire Builder* train serves Wenatchee, with daily service east to Spokane and Chicago, and west to Seattle.

U.S. Route 2 and State Route 28

From Wenatchee, take either U.S. 2 or State Route 28 for the scenic route across the state to Spokane. These roads are quiet, used mainly to get produce to market. You'll see quite a bit of that produce on either side of the road as Columbia-irrigated farmlands sprout up gently waving stalks of wheat and hay, broken by the occasional ranch. Long ago, this region saw massive volcanic eruptions, floods that would raise Noah's eyebrows, ice ages that ground away at the land, and the scorching high temperatures that have continued into the present. You can see evidence of nature's hissy fits in the coulees (deep channels made by glacial melt), craters, and mounds that dot the land, particularly along the stretch of State Route 17 that links the two parallel byways together.

QUINCY TO ODESSA
Once desert, this area is now the breadbasket of Washington thanks to the West Canal, which feeds water from the Columbia River and irrigates these fields.

Sights
EPHRATA
The **Grant County Historical Museum and Pioneer Village** (742 N. Basin St., Ephrata, 509/754-3334, May–Sept. Mon., Tues., and Thurs.–Sat. 10 A.M.–5 P.M. and Sun. 1–4 P.M., closed Wed. Oct.–Apr., $3.50 for adults, $2.50 for ages 6–15, and free for kids under 6) houses displays pertaining to early settlers, Native Americans, and extensive genealogy information. The pioneer village is made up of 30 buildings, including a Catholic church, a saloon, a jail, and a blacksmith.

ODESSA
Odessa was settled by Volga Germans, ethnic Germans who first emigrated to Russia before coming to Eastern Washington in the late 19th century. More than three quarters of the town's residents still claim descent from the original pioneers. The wide main street (1st Avenue) passes neat small homes of brick and wood, along with a handful of German-style buildings, including city hall. The **Odessa Historisches Museum** (4th and Elm St. in Odessa, 509/982-2539, 2–4 P.M. Sun. summers) has exhibits on the tightly knit Volga German community. On display is a replica of a barn from early Odessa. Nine miles west of Odessa off Highway 28 is the ghost town of **Irby,** where the 90-year-old Irby Hotel stands surrounded by desolate desert country. South of town are several growing Hutterite colonies, communal and pacifist Anabaptists who practice the old ways, like the Amish or Mennonites. For tours, call **Schoonover Farms** (509/982-2257).

SOAP LAKE
Located five miles northeast of Ephrata, Soap Lake is a small body of salty, highly alkaline water surrounded by the deserts of the Columbia Basin. People have raved about the medicinal properties of the foamy lake for centuries and come from all over to "take the cure" for ailments such as psoriasis and arthritis, now as then. The city of the same name was once a bustling resort area and home to the Soap Lake Sanitorium, which capitalized on the lake's legendary qualities. The 17 natural minerals and oils in the water give it a soft soapy feel, hence the name. It's said that the water is a match for the legendary waters of Baden Baden, Germany. Drought and the Great Depression of 1933 meant the end of the mineral spa for decades, although the New Age crowd has rediscovered its many and varied benefits and can be spotted on the beach in summertime caked in mud from head to toe.

LAKE LENORE CAVES
Approximately nine miles south of Sun Lakes State Park, Highway 17 passes a series of four shallow caves, located high up the coulee cliffs. A trail leads from an information sign to several of these rock openings, once occupied by

prehistoric nomadic peoples. Across the highway is a sign describing the Lahontan cutthroat trout that have been stocked in the creek.

Entertainment and Events

The main local event is Quincy's **Farmer Consumer Awareness Day** (509/787-2140, www.quincyfarmerconsumer.com) on the second Saturday of September in Quincy. It includes the usual community fair trappings, plus geological walks and tours of farms and food plants.

Demonstrations of pioneer crafts are given in Ephrata during both the **Living Museum** on the second weekend of June and **Pioneer Day,** the last weekend of September. During these events, Pioneer Village comes alive with costumed participants in every building—from apple pressing to wool spinning and cowboy poetry.

Hard times have seen the end of many of Soap Lake's festivals, but the king of them all, **Smokiam Days** (509/246-1821) is the town's 4th of July fest, featuring the usual salmon BBQ and fireworks, but you get a full music festival by the shores of the lake and a super-competitive horseshoes tournament that can get pretty heated at times.

Odessa's Germanic heritage comes out in **Deutschesfest** on the third weekend of September. The festival includes a parade, homemade German food, arts and crafts, a carnival, and fun run, but the main attraction is a *biergarten* with polka, country and western, and bluegrass music from the Oom Pas and Mas band.

Sports and Recreation

East Beach has play equipment, lake access, and restrooms. The Soap Lake Chamber of Commerce is also here, if you need maps or directions. **West Beach** is on the other side of town and makes for some good splashing around in the mineral-rich waters. One warning: swim in loose-fitting suits to avoid chafing that can be aggravated by the highly alkaline water. Also be careful to rinse off at the showers and to put on sunscreen after bathing since the minerals in the water act to increase tanning and burning.

Odessa Golf Club (13080 28th St., 509/982-0093) is a nine-hole course on the west end of town and has space for RV hookups.

Accommodations

Country Cabin (711 2nd Ave. SW, Quincy, 509/787-3515, $60 d) is an interesting spot that looks like a single-family log cabin. The motel rooms are around the side and all allow you to drive directly to your door. It seems custom-built to suit Gorge Amphitheatre travelers. The **Crescent Hotel** (710 10th Ave. SW., 509/797-7001, $119) makes for a good night's sleep. The king- and queen-sized suites have microwaves, fridges, and adequate TVs. A continental breakfast is served in the morning. **Lacollage Inn** (609 E. First Ave. in Odessa, 509/982-2412, www.lacollage inn.com, $50–60 s or d), a kitschy hotel featuring themed rooms with artfully done murals splashing the walls from floor to ceiling. Ephrata has a couple of decent chain motels, including **Travelodge** (31 Basin St. SW, 509/754-4651 or 800/255-3050, www.travelodge .com, $50 s or $55 d), which has a heated pool, and **Best Western Ephrata** (1257 Basin SW, 509/754-7111, $115 d), with rooms featuring microwaves and fridges, plus some with full kitchen units ($160 d).

Creative types will prefer ◖ **Ivy Chapel Inn B&B** (164 D St. SW, in Ephrata, 509/754-0629, www.theivychapelinn.com, $85–110 d). Originally a Presbyterian Church, it is now a distinctive and friendly B&B. The ivy-covered redbrick building contains six guest rooms with private baths and full breakfasts. Kids under 10 are not allowed. For a more private Soap Lake soak, try **Notaras Lodge** (231 Main St., 509/246-0462, www.notaraslodge.com, $75–108 d) where the more expensive units featuring in-room whirlpools with Soap Lake water piped in, bathroom phones, skylights, and balconies.

◖ **The Inn at Soap Lake** (226 Main Ave. E, 509/246-1132, www.innsoaplake.com, $59–125 d) was built in 1905 from rounded river stones. Rooms are nicely furnished with antiques and have kitchenettes and mineral water soaking tubs. Rates include a continental breakfast. Canoe and paddleboat rentals are available here.

CAMPING

Pitch tents or park RVs at about a mile south of Ephrata at **Oasis RV Park & Golf Course** (a mile south of town, 877/754-5102, www.oasis rvandgolfresort.com, $30 full hookups, $20 tents) is pet friendly, has cable TV as part of its hookup, and some nice big shade trees.

Soap Lake's municipally run **Smokiam Campground** (509/246-1211, open Apr.–Oct., $10 tents, $20 RVs) has waterfront camping. Well, it is actually just a gravel lot sandwiched between the lake and the highway. Another option is the **Soap Lake RV Resort** (22818 Hwy. 17 N., 509/246-0413, www.soaplakervresort .com, $20 tents, $30 full hookups), a wooded site with a striking view of the lake.

Eight miles west of Quincy off Highway 28, **Crescent Bar Resort** (509/787-1511, www .crescentbarresort.com, $100–210 d condo, $34 tent, $40 RV) on Wanapum Reservoir offers a restaurant, condos, and camping, plus a wide choice of recreation, from swimming to golf.

Food

Downtown Ephrata is no bustling commercial hub, but you can get sandwiches and pies from **The Country Deli** (245 Basin St. NW, 509/754-3143, Tues.–Sat. 6:30 A.M.–8 P.M., Sun.–Mon. 6:30 A.M.–3 P.M.) or pizzas from **Time Out Pizza** (1095 Basin St. SW, 509/754-1111, daily 11 A.M.–9 P.M.).

For a taste of the area's German heritage, visit Odessa's **Voise Sausage** (7 S. 1st St., 509/982-2956, www.germansausage.com), where the sausage, bratwurst, and bologna are all made on the premises.

In Soap Lake, **Don's Steak House** (14 Canna St. across from Notaras Lodge, 509/246-1217, Mon.–Thurs. 11 A.M.–9:30 P.M., Fri. 11 A.M.–10 P.M., Sat. 4–10 P.M., Sun. noon–8 P.M.) specializes in delicious steak, seafood, and Greek dishes.

Information and Services

In Odessa, contact the **Odessa Chamber of Commerce** (509/982-0049, www.odessa chamber.com); in Quincy, the **Quincy Valley Chamber of Commerce** (119 F St. SE, 509/787-2140, www.quincyvalley.org); the summer-only **Soap Lake Chamber of Commerce** (509/246-1821, www.soaplakecoc.org); or **Ephrata Chamber of Commerce** (90 Alder St. NW, 509/754-4656, www.ephratawachamber .com, Mon.–Fri. 9 A.M.–4 P.M.), which also has a visitor's pamphlet lobby open all weekend.

WATERVILLE TO DAVENPORT

As you leave Wenatchee, you'll get a better look at the homes and businesses tucked along the river. Take a good look, because from here, you'll be cruising through agricultural fields that seem to stretch out from the purple mountains' majesty to infinity. Unlike the more central areas of states, no city looms on the horizon for miles. Here, cities sneak up on you, and such is the case with Waterville. The town seems ripped from the past with its wide streets, historic homes, and patent medicine ads. Passing further through the carpet of green and gold, you'll pass long, thin Banks Lake, which irrigates all of the farmland you see around you. Nearly two hours out of Waterville, you'll encounter Davenport, a farm and ranching city and Lincoln County seat.

Sights

WATERVILLE

Waterville is also home to the **Douglas County Historical Museum** (509/745-8435, 11 A.M.–5 P.M. Tues.–Sun. May 20–mid-Oct., admission by donation), where the kooky collection includes a 73-pound meteorite, a two-headed calf, and the old Winthrop post office.

◖ SUN LAKES STATE PARK AND DRY FALLS

Sun Lakes State Park (seven mi. southwest of Coulee City on Hwy. 17, 888/226-7688, www .parks.wa.gov, $21 tent, $31 full hookups, $7 extra reservation fees) is famous for its "dry

© ERICKA CHICKOWSKI

Dry Falls Lake

falls," an ancient waterfall of enormous proportions that has dried out to become a rocky cliff. The main part of Sun Lakes Park boasts horse trails, boating, swimming, and rainbow trout-fishing. Concessions offer snacks, fishing supplies, horse rentals, and groceries. A road leads east from Park Lake along the basalt cliff walls lining Meadow Creek to Deep Lake, and hiking trails provide access to other parts of this fascinating park.

Dry Falls Interpretive Center (four mi. north of the main park entrance along Hwy. 17, 509/632-5583, mid-May–mid-Sept. daily 10 A.M.–6 P.M.) describes the incredible geologic history of this area. Outside, the cliff-edge viewpoints look out on a cluster of lakes far below, bordered by green plants and set against stark basalt cliffs. There is a certain savage beauty about this place, especially at dusk. A steep path leads a half mile down from the overlook to Dry Falls Lake.

Watching the Columbia River flow, you'd never guess the size of the cataclysm that it caused and the changes it made to the landscape. During one of the last ice ages, the river got dammed by ice and sediment. That caused the creation of an unimaginably large reservoir that eventually broke through, sending a 2,000-foot-high raging torrent of water that gouged the coulees and caused instant erosion on many rock formations in the area. The Lower Grand Coulee is a dry watercourse that probably helped to hold all that water.

DAVENPORT
About 35 miles west of Spokane you'll experience your first taste of civilization after so many miles of farmland in Davenport. It's the seat for Lincoln County and a minor farming and ranching center. There you can find the **Lincoln County Historical Museum** (Park and 7th Streets, 509/725-6711 or 800/326-8148, Mon.–Sat. 9 A.M.–5 P.M. May–Sept., plus Sun. 1–4 P.M. June–Aug.) for local memorabilia and a collection of agricultural equipment in the back building. The strangest sight here is the death mask of the outlaw Harry Tracy, a member of the Hole-in-the-Wall Gang

who lived in Spokane for a couple of years and then committed suicide after being cornered by lawmen nearby. The museum also serves as the local visitors center. Bird-watchers will want to ask where burrowing owls can be seen right in town.

Sports and Recreation

Banks Lake, which lies outside Lake Roosevelt National Recreation Area on the southwest side of the Grand Coulee Dam, is a 27-mile-long, clear-blue beauty surrounded by the deep sides of the coulee. In the early '50s, the coulee was dammed on both ends and filled with water from the Columbia. To get here, the water must be pumped 280 feet uphill miles southwest of Coulee City. **Badger Mountain** (509/745-8273), six miles south of Waterville, is a small area with three rope tows and a 1,500-foot drop—a family place for downhill and cross-country skiing and snowboarding.

SUMMER FALLS STATE PARK

Nine miles south of Coulee City on Pinto Ridge Road, Summer Falls State Park (www

.parks.wa.gov) is an appropriately named park, since the falls created by the irrigation project exist only in the summer when irrigation water is needed. (The water reaches here from Banks Lake via an irrigation canal.) This is a cool spot for a picnic or fishing, but there's no camping. Pay attention to sirens, they'll warn of sudden flow increases that make it very dangerous to swim.

Accommodations

In Waterville, the choice is fairly clear. The **Waterville Historic Hotel** (102 E. Park St., 509/745-8695 or 888/509-8180, www.water villehotel.com, $55–99 s or $69–112 d) was built in 1903, and rooms have antique furnishings, private or shared baths, and there are deluxe suites available.

Most Coulee City accommodations lack much for glamour. But clean rooms can be found at a good price, which is especially perfect for someone headed to the water or woods before sunrise. **Sun Lakes Park Resort** (seven mi. south of Coulee City, 509/632-5291, www .sunlakesresort.com, $90–169 d) rents cabins

the Waterville Historic Hotel

and mobile homes on its lakeshore property. Splash in the lake or in the pool on property, or rent a rowboat to go farther adrift. The resort is open mid-April–mid-October. **Ala Cozy Motel** (509/632-5703, $52 s or $62 d) is a little less elaborate and half as expensive. Kids can still enjoy the outdoor pool in the summer. Kitchenettes are available. **Banks Lake Lodge** (109 N. 6th St., 509/632-5596, $35–75

d, 10 percent military discount) also has lakefront rentals. Choose between standard units or those with full kitchens. All units have a microwave and fridge.

Camp RVs at **Coulee Lodge Resort** (509/632-5565, Apr.–Sept., $25), which also offers cabins ($60–85 d) and mobile homes ($80–120 d), six miles south along Blue Lake.

Grand Coulee Dam and Vicinity

If you've been driving through the desert country of central Washington, Grand Coulee Dam comes as quite a surprise. Instead of barren sage, grass, and rock, you're suddenly in a cluster of small towns with lush green lawns and split-level suburban homes. This oasis in the desert is the result of one of the largest construction projects ever undertaken, the Grand Coulee Dam hydroelectric project. The Grand Coulee is a 50-mile-long gorge carved in part by the cataclysmic Spokane Floods thousands of years ago.

SIGHTS
◖ Grand Coulee Dam

Massive Grand Coulee Dam Twice as high as Niagara Falls and nearly a mile long. It's one of the world's greatest producers of hydroelectricity. The dam stands 550 feet above bedrock, is taller than the Washington Monument, and has a 1,650-foot-wide spillway. Its 12 million cubic yards of concrete and steel are enough to build a six-foot sidewalk all the way around the equator.

Just west of the dam, the gigantic pipes called penstocks pump water 280 feet uphill into Banks Lake. From there, the water feeds into a series of canals and irrigates a half-million acres of farmland in the Columbia Basin.

Even though the area was bone dry, it was strongly suspected that the soil was very fertile. In the throes of the Depression, while farms were failing everywhere, Congress and FDR pushed through a massive $60 million

appropriation bill to test the theory. The first concrete was poured in 1935 and continued steadily until 1942. Work continued even after the outbreak of WWII, since power generation certainly qualified as a strategic need. Seventy-seven men died during this dangerous endeavor, but contrary to persistent rumors, not a single one of them is entombed in the concrete wall of the dam.

Regrettably, the effects of the dam went beyond fruit pies and farmer's markets. The new water flow wiped out the salmon fishing grounds that the Colville Tribe, among others,

DAM'S THE FACTS

- Year completed: 1951

- Number of Construction Deaths: 77 men

- Amount of Concrete Used: 11,975,521 cubic yards

- Cost of Construction (2011 dollars): $970,000,000

- Length: 5,223 feet

- Height: 550 feet

- Spillway Width: 1,650 feet

- Number of Generators: 33

- Power Capacity: 6,480 megawatts

- Land Irrigated by Dam: 500,000 acres

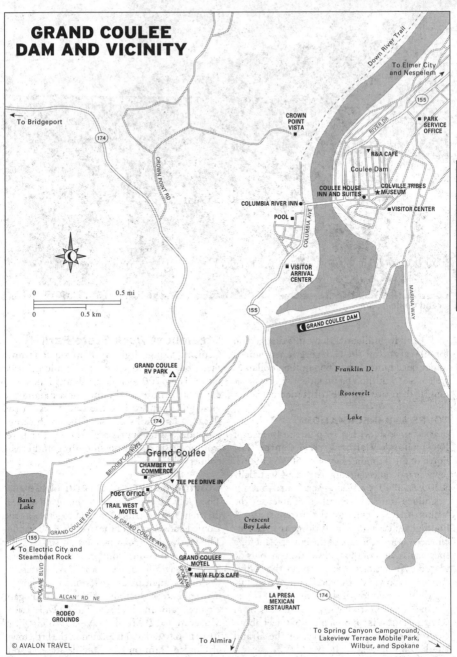

GRAND COULEE DAM AND VICINITY

To Elmer City and Nespelem

Down River Trail

155

To Bridgeport

174

CROWN POINT RD

CROWN POINT VISTA

RIVER DR

PARK SERVICE OFFICE

R&A CAFÉ

Coulee Dam

COULEE HOUSE INN AND SUITES

COLVILLE TRIBES MUSEUM

COLUMBIA RIVER INN

VISITOR CENTER

POOL

COLUMBIA AVE

VISITOR ARRIVAL CENTER

MARINA WAY

| 0 | | 0.5 mi |

| 0 | | 0.5 km |

155

GRAND COULEE DAM

GRAND COULEE RV PARK

Franklin D.

Roosevelt

Lake

174

BRIDGEPORT HWY

Grand Coulee

CHAMBER OF COMMERCE

TEE PEE DRIVE IN

POST OFFICE

TRAIL WEST MOTEL

Banks Lake

GRAND COULEE AVE

155

To Electric City and Steamboat Rock

W. GRAND COULEE AVE

Crescent Bay Lake

SPOKANE BLVD

GRAND COULEE MOTEL

SPOKANE WAY

NEW FLO'S CAFÉ

ALCAN RD NE

RODEO GROUNDS

LA PRESA MEXICAN RESTAURANT

174

To Almira

To Spring Canyon Campground, Lakeview Terrace Mobile Park, Wilbur, and Spokane

EASTERN WASHINGTON

© VALERIE GARNE/123RF.COM

Grand Coulee Dam

had fished for millennia. Lawsuits dragged on for 40 years before the U.S. government agreed to pay out a lump sum of $53 million dollars as well as a $15 million payment every year for as long as there are Colville tribal members.

TOURS AND INFORMATION

Start your visit with a stop at the Bureau of Reclamation's **Visitor Arrival Center** (just north of the dam on Hwy. 155, 509/633-9265, www.grandcouleedam.org, late May–Sept. daily 8:30 A.M.–9:30 P.M., Oct.–Apr. 9 A.M.–5 P.M.).

Guided tours are usually available; see the Visitor Arrival Center for the current status. A highlight of the dam tour is riding the glass incline elevator to the face of the power plant for a spectacular view of the spillway from an outside balcony. An artifact room displays the Native American tools and arrowheads uncovered during the construction of the dam.

One of the best views of the dam is from **Crown Point Vista,** on a bluff 626 feet above the river, and two miles west of the Grand Coulee on Highway 174.

Steamboat Rock State Park

Cruising along Highway 155, you can't miss Steamboat Rock State Park, a scenic volcanic butte rising 700 feet above Banks Lake. You can hike a mile to the top for a panoramic view and then explore the 640 acres on the flat top. The trail starts near the north campground. Winter sports are also popular here, from ice fishing to snowmobiling and cross-country skiing.

Colville Reservation and Museum

The Colville Reservation is home to several different Indian tribes grouped together as the Confederated Tribes of the Colville Reservation. The Native American peoples on the Colville subsist on income from various tribal businesses: a sawmill, grocery stores, fish hatchery, wood treatment plant, government support, a marina, and prosperous casinos in Okanogan, Coulee Dam, and Manson. The Colville Tribal Museum (512 Mead Way, 509/633-0751, 10 A.M.–6 P.M. daily) is located in the little town of Coulee Dam on the Colville Reservation.

One of the highlights of the museum is a medal passed from Lewis and Clark to the Nez Perce people. In Nespelem, Chief Joseph of the Nez Perce lies buried along with 150 other tribal members. The cemetery is on the north end of town. Follow 10th St. uphill to reach the simple white obelisk marking his grave.

South of Nespelem is the **Colville Indian Agency** (509/634-2200, www.colvilletribes .com), headquarters for the reservation. Local beadwork is sold in the nearby **Trading Post Store** (509/634-2700).

SCENIC DRIVES

There are two very scenic drives through this land of rivers and desert: **Highway 21** between Keller and Republic, and **Bridge Creek/ Twin Lakes Road** connecting Inchelium to Highway 21. The latter of these climbs west from Inchelium into remote hills covered with ponderosa pine and other evergreens on mile-wide North Twin Lake. West of the lake, the narrow, winding road climbs through rounded mountains dense with trees. It eventually descends into rolling hills covered in grass and sage as you reach the Nespelem area.

ST. MARY'S MISSION

This Jesuit mission (509/826-2097, open daily) was founded in 1896 in order to bring Catholicism to the Okanogan and Chelan Indians. The mission building began as a log cabin and gradually grew until two fires destroyed nearly everything early in the 20th century.

A new church was completed in 1915, with local settlers and Native Americans cooperating in the building of the altarpiece. Today the mission contains a mix of old and new buildings, including the Colville-run Indian School. Up the hill behind the church, you'll find a cemetery and a carved wooden burro.

To reach the mission, take Highway 155 east of Omak for four miles, then go 1.5 miles south.

Entertainment and Events

Each summer evening brings a most unusual and immensely popular event to Grand Coulee Dam: an elaborate high-tech **laser light show** (509/633-9265 at 10 P.M. Memorial Day–July, 9:30 P.M. in August, 8:30 P.M. in September) that paints 300-foot figures on the face of the dam and tells the history of the Columbia River, of the Native American people who first lived here, and of the dam and how it transformed the desert land.

This program packs the house, even though the "house" can sit on surrounding hillsides or in their vehicles. Best vantage points are from the Visitor Arrival Center, from the parking lot just below here, from the park at the east end of the bridge in Coulee Dam, and from Crown Point Vista (farther away, but overlooking the entire area).

The second weekend in May, the **Colorama Festival** brings a rodeo, parade, flea market, and carnival to the Coulee Dam area. Also in mid-May, the **Sunbanks Resort Rhythm & Blues Festival** (509/633-3786) includes three full days of live music. The **Memorial Day Festival** (800/268-5332) features arts and crafts, music, food, a fun run, and the grand opening of the laser light show followed by a big fireworks display off the top of the dam.

Bring some coin for the slots and the blackjack tables at **Coulee Dam Casino** (515 Birch St., Coulee Dam, 800/556-7492, www.coulee casino.com).

Across the highway from the tribal offices is the Nespelem Community Center and a powwow circle that comes to life during the **4th of July Nespelem Powwow and All-Indian Rodeo,** a 10-day event with dance competitions—some involving full regalia—along with drumming, "stick" gambling, and delicious fry bread. The compound is bordered with dozens of tepees during the festivities. Do not enter the dance circle or take photos without asking. Other powwows are held in Nespelem on Veteran's Day and New Year's Day.

SPORTS AND RECREATION
Lake Roosevelt

Enormous Lake Roosevelt—stretching more than 150 miles from the dam almost to the

Canadian border—is popular with boaters, water-skiers, swimmers, anglers, and campers.

Much of Lake Roosevelt (named after Franklin Delano Roosevelt) falls in **Lake Roosevelt National Recreation Area** (1008 Crest Dr., 509/633-9441, www.nps.gov/laro). The dry, sunny climate is perfect for lake activities; summer temperatures range from the mid-70s–100°F, with evenings cooling off to the 50s or 60s. Winter visitors often come for cross-country skiing, ice fishing, and snowmobiling. More than 1.8 million folks pass through this area each year.

No lifeguards on the lake, but popular swimming beaches are found at **Spring Canyon** and **Keller Ferry** in lower Lake Roosevelt, and at **Fort Spokane** and **Porcupine Bay** on the Spokane River arm. The water in the Spokane River arm tends to be 5–8 degrees warmer than the rest of the lake, where it averages in the 60s in June, rising to the 70s in August. If you're swimming outside a protected area, keep an eye out for boats!

Twenty-three public boat launches line Lake Roosevelt. All boats must have a launch permit ($6 for a permit covering seven consecutive days). Call the Park Service (509/633-9441) for more info regarding annual permits. From April through June only a few of the launches are usable because the lake is lowered about 100 feet to accommodate the spring runoff. Call the reservoir hotline (800/824-4916) for an estimate of current and future water levels. Be sure to steer clear of protected swimming beaches and the waters near the dam.

A state fishing license is required to fish in the recreation area; you can pick one up—along with current fishing regulations—at most area hardware or sporting goods stores or marinas. The 30-plus species of fish inhabiting these waters include walleye, rainbow trout, and enormous white sturgeon, averaging 100–300 pounds but known to be as much as 1,800 pounds. Other residents include the kokanee salmon, yellow perch, bass, cutthroat trout, perch, and pike. Popular fishing spots are where rivers and streams meet the lake—the Sanpoil River, Wilmont Creek, Hunters

Creek, Kettle River, and others—or the waters near high shoreline cliffs, such as those near Keller Ferry.

DAM TRAILS

Several local paths provide a chance to get away from the dam and explore. The **Candy Point Trail** begins from a trailhead 300 feet down the hill behind the Coulee Dam Credit Union in the town of Coulee Dam and climbs steeply to Crown Point overlook, then over Candy Point, before returning to the river near Coulee Dam City Hall.

The **Down River Trail** is a gentle 6.5-mile path along the river north from the bridge, with several tree-lined rest areas. A less developed trail heads south from the dam to the towns of Grand Coulee and Electric City.

Accommodations

One of the best ways to explore the reaches of Lake Roosevelt is aboard a rented houseboat. Houseboats are upwards of 62 feet long, and come equipped with a variety of amenities, such as full kitchens, gas grills, hot tubs and more. Most can sleep up to 13. Rates start at around $1,000 per night, almost always at least a two-night minimum. For more information, contact **Lake Roosevelt Resort and Marina** (509/738-6121 or 800/635-7585, www.lake roosevelt.com).

Lodging is mostly unpretentious in the Coulee area. Advance reservations are a good idea for the busy summer weekends; one or two months ahead should get you weekend lodging at the better motels. Winter rates can really plummet.

Overlooking the dam, the pet-friendly **Coulee House Inn and Suites** (110 Roosevelt Way in Coulee Dam, 509/633-1101 or 800/715-7767, www.couleehouse.com, $99–170 d) has nice facilities that include an outdoor pool, hot tub, sauna, and exercise room. Watch the laser show from the property. **Columbia River Inn** (10 Lincoln Ave. in Coulee Dam, 509/633-2100 or 800/633-6421, www.columbia riverinn.com, $105 d) is has recently renovated rooms, an outdoor pool, and hot tub.

The rooms provide views of the laser light show on summer evenings.

Sky Deck Motel (138 Miller Ave., Electric City, 509/633-0290, $65–165 d) is an attractive motel directly on Banks Lake with an outdoor pool and hot tub.

The rooms at **Grand Coulee Motel** (Spokane Way in Grand Coulee, 509/633-0770, www .grandcouleemotel.com, $55–145 d) have a fridge and coffeemaker, and most are designed with a little more flair than your average motel room.

Campers can stay at one of 35 campgrounds (10 of these are accessible only by boat) that line both sides of Lake Roosevelt and the Spokane River arm. None of the campgrounds offer hookups, showers, or reservations, but all have restrooms and most have running water. A $10 fee is charged for all but the boat-accessible campsites, which are free. Summer **campfire programs** are offered Friday and Saturday evenings at Evans, Fort Spokane, Spring Canyon, Kettle Falls, Keller Ferry, and Porcupine Bay campgrounds. Most campgrounds are open year-round; Porcupine Bay is open May–October. There is a 14-day camping limit.

The best camping on Banks Lake is at **Steamboat Rock State Park** (eight mi. southwest of the dam on Hwy. 155, 888/226-7688, www.parks.wa.gov, $12 primitive, $17 standard tent, $23 full hookups, $7 extra reservation fee). Pull up an RV or throw a tent down on a grassy loop site, or hike a little less than a mile to a primitive and private spot right by the lake. These primitive sites can also be accessed by boat. If you stay, be sure to hike to the top of the rock over the steep but short trail that offers windswept vistas of the coulees.

The region is awash in private RV parks, with top honors split between **Coulee Playland Resort** (Banks Lake in Electric City, 509/633-2671, www.couleeplayland.com, $28–34 full hookups) and **Sunbanks Resort** (on Banks Lake just south of Electric City, 509/633-3786 or 888/822-7195, $22 tent or RV with water and electric, ask for sewer). Coulee Playland has the nicer waterfront and campsites, with a fully stocked marine and fishing store that is mighty convenient for those prone to losing

tackle. Meanwhile, Sunbanks offers a nice restaurant, recreational rentals, a miniature golf course, espresso shop, and even an art gallery.

Food

The Coulee Dam area is not for gourmands, but you will find good food, generous portions, and friendly service. **New Flo's Café** (316 Spokane Way, Grand Coulee, 509/633-3216, 5:30 A.M.–1 P.M. daily, closed Mon. in winter) serves big solid American breakfasts and lunches for a reasonable price. It's a great place to meet some townies.

R & A Café (514 Birch St., Coulee Dam, 509/633-2233, 6 A.M.–2 P.M. Mon.–Sat., closed Sun.) serves generous portions of family-style home cooking for breakfast and lunch.

La Presa Mexican Restaurant (515 E. Grand Coulee Ave., Coulee Dam, 509/633-3173, 11 A.M.–10 P.M. daily) has great-tasting Mexican food and the star of the menu, *campechana*—octopus scallops and prawns over chopped vegetables and served in a glass—definitely deserves a try.

Information and Services

The best place for information is the **Grand Coulee Dam Visitor Arrival Center** (at the dam, 509/633-9265, www.grandcouleedam .org). Stop by the **Lake Roosevelt National Recreation Area Headquarters** (1008 Crest Dr. in Coulee Dam, 509/633-9441, www. nps.gov/ laro, Mon.–Fri. 7:30 A.M.–4 P.M.) for additional details. Ranger stations are in Kettle Falls and Fort Spokane, and chamber of commerce visitors centers are in Grand Coulee and Coulee City.

There are small stores with **groceries and supplies** at Daisy Station, and in the marinas at McCoys, Seven Bays, Keller Ferry, and Kettle Falls. The surrounding towns of Kettle Falls, Coulee Dam, Grand Coulee, Colville, and Northport have food, lodging, and other services. Rent boats at **Keller Ferry Marina** (509/647-2253), **Seven Bays Marina** (509/633-0201 or 800/648-5253) or **Kettle Falls Marina** (509/738-6121 or 800/635-7585).

For information on the surrounding area, contact the **Grand Coulee Dam Area Chamber**

of Commerce (306 Midway in Grand Coulee, 509/633-3074 or 800/268-5332, www.grand couleedam.org, summer Mon.–Sat. 8 A.M.– 8 P.M., fall–spring Mon.–Fri. 8 A.M.– 5 P.M.). A summer-only **visitors center** (509/632-5713) is located in Mason City Park (just uphill from the grocery store) in Coulee City. The Bureau of Reclamation's big **Visitor Arrival Center** is just north of the dam on Highway 155.

Getting There and Around

Two ferries cross Lake Roosevelt year-round: the **Keller Ferry** (daily 6 A.M.–11 P.M., free) connects with Highway 21 in the south part of the recreation area, and farther north, the **Gifford Ferry** (6 A.M.–9:30 P.M. in summer, free) joins Highway 25 near Inchelium. Both ferries carry passengers and vehicles and take about 15 minutes for the crossing.

Okanogan Valley and Highlands

A dry area surrounded by mountains, ranches, and orchards full of apples, pears, peaches, and cherries, Okanogan Valley is bisected by the serpentine Okanogan River, with Highway 97 generally running its course south to north all the way up into Canada. The highway cuts through most of the valley's major towns— Okanogan, Omak, Tonasket, and Oroville— before entering Canada. East of here lies the Okanogan Highlands, a low range of mountains and hills covered with forests and rangeland. Sparsely populated and with few services, the Highlands offer scenic back roads, plenty of grounds for outdoorsy activities and even a place to hunt fossils.

OKANOGAN VALLEY
Sights
CHIEF JOSEPH DAM

The Chief Joseph Dam spans over a mile across the Columbia River and supplies the electrical needs of 1.5 million people throughout the West. Water backed up behind the dam forms Rufus Woods Lake. The dam itself was named after Chief Joseph, famous leader of the Nez Perce in the 1870s, who is buried on the nearby Colville Reservation.

Dam tours (509/686-5501, 10 A.M., noon, 2 P.M. Memorial Day–Labor Day) are available for free in summer.

FORT OKANOGAN STATE PARK

Twenty-one miles south of Okanogan on Highway 97 near the intersection with State Route 17, Fort Okanogan State Park (509/923-2473, www.parks.wa.gov, open daily 10 A.M.–6 P.M. mid-May–Sept.) marks the site of an 1811 fur-trading post. The **interpretive center** (10 A.M.–5 P.M.) is filled with interesting artifacts, displays, and dioramas of this historic fort. The fort sites were excavated by archaeologists in the 1950s and early '60s, prior to the area being inundated by construction of the Wells Dam.

OKANOGAN AND OMAK

Check out displays depicting pioneer life in the area at **Okanogan County Historical Museum** (1410 2nd N in Okanogan, 509/422-4272, www.okanoganhistory.org, Memorial Day– Labor Day daily 10 A.M.–4 P.M., donation). Outside, find a replica of an Old West village, along with a replica of the old firehall.

Built in 1915, the **Okanogan County Courthouse** (3rd and Oak in Okanogan) has a Mediterranean-style red-tile roof and a gothic exterior with a central tower. A **mural** on the side of Main Street Market features a painting of the Suicide Race. A **walking trail**—marked by big horseshoes denoting past Suicide Race winners—leads from downtown Omak to East Side Park.

SCENIC DRIVES

As you continue to drive along east on State Route 20 from the North Cascades, it crosses the Okanogan River, and takes a decidedly northern drift, joining up with Highway 97.

This was once a route into Canada's Cariboo gold fields, later a cattle-droving route, and ultimately an auto highway. Mountains, orchards, and farmlands continue to be your companion as you cruise along next to the river. You'll pass little towns like Riverside and Tonasket, mostly settled in the late 1800s, mostly farm-oriented, and mostly charming with their historic buildings and midsummer parades. The signs announcing the city of Oroville should inform you also that you are but one lake away from the Canadian border.

The pretty little burg of Conconully is 22 miles northwest of Omak and sits at an elevation of 2,300 feet, making for summertime temperatures much cooler than in the steamy Okanogan Valley. Conconully has a couple of stores and restaurants, along with several popular lakeside resorts.

Conconully sits between the natural Conconully Lake and the unnatural Conconully Reservoir. Built in 1910, the latter was the first Bureau of Reclamation irrigation project in America.

Entertainment and Events

The Omak Performing Arts Center is the site of all sorts of events through the year, including concerts by **Okanogan Valley Orchestra and Chorus** (http://ovocinfo.com, 509/422-2456). The **Breadline Café** (102 S. Ash in Omak, 509/826-5836) has folk, jazz, rock, or R&B most nights. For country music, head to **Cariboo Inn** (233 Queen St. in Okanogan, 509/422-6109) or **The Western Restaurant** (1930 N. 2nd Ave. in Okanogan, 509/422-6769). Get in on some high-stakes bingo at **Okanogan Bingo Casino** (Hwy. 97, 800/559-4646) to play some live poker, or just camp in front of your favorite slot machine.

◖ OMAK STAMPEDE AND SUICIDE RACE

Omak is world-famous for its annual Stampede and Suicide Race (509/826-1983 or 800/933-6625, www.omakstampede. org), held the second weekend in August at East Side Park. Festivities include two parades, a big Western art show, carnival, and a major professional rodeo. During the week of the Stampede, at least pass by the **Indian Encampment** in East Side Park, temporary home to hundreds of Native Americans from various tribes who demonstrate traditional living.

The main event is a thrilling horse race in which riders blast down a 200 foot 62-degree slope before fording the Okanogan River and entering the arena full of cheering fans. Quite a few of the participants in the race come from the nearby Confederated Tribes of the Colville Reservation, many of whom feel that the event is a personal spiritual connection to their mounted-warrior heritage. A shuttle bus provides service between Omak and Okanogan during the Stampede.

OKANOGAN DAYS

Okanogan Days, on the first weekend of May, features a parade and music. **Art in the Park** in the downtown park on the third weekend in June brings together artists and craftspeople, along with tasty snacks at food booths. The **Okanogan County Fair** (509/422-1621, www .okanogancountyfair.org) at the fairgrounds in Omak brings more rodeo action, horse racing, a livestock auction, and musical entertainment in early September.

SNOW DOG SUPER MUSH RACE

The Snow Dog Super Mush Race (509/826-3226, www.conconullysupermush.com) in January is one of the biggest sled dog races in the Northwest and has events for dog teams from 12 dogs to 2 dogs. In between heats, kids can ride the sleds slowly around the spectator's area.

OROVILLE MAY FESTIVAL

The second weekend of May means Oroville May Festival (509/476-2739), a two-day party featuring a Special Royalty tea and dance, a bass tournament, and a parade of bikers with engines roaring and jackets patched.

TONASKET FOUNDERS DAY RODEO

Tonasket Founders Day Rodeo (509/486-4643)

the first weekend of June includes a big Professional Rodeo Cowboys Association (PRCA)–sanctioned rodeo, parade, fun run, and cowboy breakfast.

Sports and Recreation

The Okanogan River is a popular place for tubing in the summer months. **The Bike Shop** (137 S. 2nd Ave. in Okanogan, 509/422-0710) rents bikes.

Play golf at family-friendly **Okanogan Valley Golf Club** (105 Dankar Cutoff Rd., 509/826-6937, www.okanoganvalleygolf.com, $23) just west of town.

Loup Loup Ski Bowl (www.skitheloup.com) in the Methow Valley between Okanogan and Twisp on Highway 20 offers Alpine skiing on a 1,250-foot vertical drop.

BRIDGEPORT STATE PARK

Three miles northeast of Bridgeport on Rufus Woods Lake, Bridgeport State Park (509/686-7231, www.parks.wa.gov) offers boating, fishing, swimming, campsites ($14 for tents, $20 for RVs), and showers. The 750-acre park is an oasis of cottonwood and aspen trees surrounded by dark, beehive-shaped volcanic formations. Keep your eyes open for rattlesnakes. The park is open April–October and includes the nine-hole **Lakewood Golf Course** within its boundaries. During the summer, Army Corps of Engineers rangers give Saturday night campfire programs.

CONCONULLY STATE PARK

Conconully State Park (509/826-7408, www.parks.wa.gov) sits along the shore of Conconully Reservoir and contains a log cabin and a sod-roofed replica of the first Okanogan County courthouse; Conconully was the county seat from 1889–1914. The reservoir is a popular place for boating, fishing, and swimming. Trees surround spacious grassy lawns that make fine picnicking spots; take the half-mile nature trail for a relaxing stroll. Cozy campsites are $14 (no RV hookups); open mid-April through October, and on weekends and holidays the rest of the year.

OSOYOOS LAKE

A mile north of Oroville on Highway 97, **Osoyoos Lake State Veterans Memorial Park** offers fishing, swimming, waterskiing, and concessions on a natural lake shared with our Canadian neighbors. The east side of Osoyoos Lake has apple and pear trees planted in the early 1860s by Hiram F. "Okanogan" Smith, the first permanent white resident of the area. Smith brought his trees in from Fort Hope, British Columbia, by backpack. Several of the 135-plus-year-old trees are still bearing fruit.

WINTER SPORTS

Palmer Lake, 18 miles west of Oroville, a popular spot with ice-fishermen, is managed by the Bureau of Land Management; a boat launch and picnic area are at the south end of the lake.

About 12 miles northeast of Tonasket, **Sitzmark** (509/486-1027 or 509/486-2700, Wed.–Sun. and winter holidays) is a family slope with a 680-foot vertical drop. Enjoy also nearly four miles of groomed cross-country trails. The area generally opens just after Christmas. The snow can be marginal at times, so be sure to call ahead. **Highland Park Sno-Park** (10 mi. northeast of Tonasket) has around seven and a half miles of groomed cross-country trails.

Accommodations

Be sure to make motel reservations far in advance if you plan to attend the Omak Stampede and Suicide Race in August.

Camaray Motel (1320 Main St. in Oroville, 509/476-3684, $65–105 s or d) has comfortable rooms and an outdoor pool and a mini-fridge/microwave unit, as does **Red Apple Inn** (20 Whitcomb Ave. S. in Tonasket, 509/486-2119, $46 s or $49 d), which features clean rooms with a hand-painted mural in every unit. Microwaves and refrigerators are helpful should you choose to take a lunch down to the river.

Start the day with a complimentary hot breakfast at **Rodeway Inn** (122 N. Main in Omak, 509/826-0400, www.rodeway.com,

$64–89 s or $59–64 d), which features no-frills, dog-friendly motel rooms right in town and a swimming pool on premises. Or try **Motel Nicholas** (a half mile north of Omak on Hwy. 215, 509/826-4611, $45 s or $85 d), a cute little family owned motel with fridges, microwaves, and free Wi-Fi. It is within walking distance of a Wal-Mart store.

Okanogan Inn and Suites (11B Appleway Rd., the junction of Highways 97 and 20, Okanogan, 509/422-6431, www.okanogan inn.com, $65 d) features a room-service menu, satellite TV, and round-the-clock coffee in the lobby. There's an outdoor pool, plus a modest workout room.

Get the family outdoors at **Sun Cove Resort** (93 E. Wannacut Ln. in Oroville, 509/476-2223, http://thesuncoveresort.com,, April–Oct,, $80 d) on two-mile-long Wannacut Lake. Cozy cabins near to hiking, swimming, and fishing, plus tent and RV spaces. Enjoy a swimming pool, guided horse-trail rides, and boat, kayak, and canoe rentals.

Spectacle Lake Resort (10 McCammon Rd. in Tonasket, 12 mi. northwest of Tonasket on Loomis Hwy., 509/223-3433, www.spectacle lakeresort.com, $65–200 d) has rustic cabins, motel rooms, and a three-bedroom house.

There are two comfortable cabin resorts around Conconully: **Liar's Cove Resort** (509/826-1288, www.liarscoveresort.com, $85–105 d) rents full-sized cabins on the water, all with bathrooms and kitchens. **Shady Pines Resort** (509/826-2287, www.shadypinesresort .com, $79–150 d) has waterfront cabins, as well, also with private baths and kitchens.

If you'll be using deer musk instead of lavender soap, **Kozy Kabins & RV Park** (509/826-6780 or 888/502-2246, $22 RV with full hookups, $42 d), is ideal, with bare-bones huts with fridges and stoves. Bring your own cooking gear. There are shared bathrooms and showers, plus a community fire pit. Hunting dogs and other hounds are welcome.

CAMPING

Riverside camping ($3) and RV hookups ($12) are available at Okanogan's **Legion Park** (509/422-3600) on the north end of town and at **East Side Park** (509/826-1170) in Omak, next to the visitors center. Both are open all year. The **Okanogan Fairgrounds** (175 Rodeo Trail, 509/422-1621, $30) has full-hookup sites, but be aware that pets are strictly prohibited.

Five free Forest Service campgrounds are within nine miles of Conconully; closest is **Cottonwood Campground,** just two miles out on Forest Service Road 38. The others are **Sugarloaf, Oriole, Kerr,** and **Salmon Meadows.**

RV slots can be found at **Orchard RV Park, Eisen's RV Park,** or the parking lot at **Prince's Center.** Tent campers will do much better at **Osoyoos Lake State Veterans Memorial Park** (509/476-3321 or 888/226-7688, www .parks.wa.gov, $12, $7 extra reservation fee) a mile north of town, with tent sites but no RV hookups. Open April through October, plus weekends and holidays the rest of the year. The campground is often full all summer long.

Food

Omak's ◖ **Breadline Café** (102 S. Ash St., 509/826-5836, Tues.–Sat. 11 A.M.–9 P.M., closed Sun.–Mon.) is *the* place for lunch in the area, with soups, salads, sandwiches, and espresso. The restaurant is also popular for dinner, offering pastas, meats, and cocktails. The decor in this old soda pop–bottling warehouse is funky mismatched chairs and tables, aging signs, and painted exposed beams.

American Legion Park in Okanogan has a **farmers market** (509/826-1259) May–mid-October on Saturday 9 A.M.–1 P.M.

Sample freshly brewed German beer with smoked and barbecued entrées at **Alpine Brewing Company** (821 14th Ave. in Oroville, 509/476-9662).

Get fresh local fruits and juices from the cooler at **Golddigger Apples** (1220 Ironwood, 509/476-3646, Mon.–Fri. 8 A.M.–5 P.M.).

Oroville also has a **farmers market** across from the visitors center in the city park on Saturday 9 A.M.–noon, May through August.

Information and Services

The **Washington State Information Center**

(509/476-2739, www.orovillewashington .com) is along Highway 97 on the north end of Oroville and is open daily in the summer, with reduced hours the rest of the year.

The **Omak Visitor Information Center** (401 Omak Ave., 509/826-4218 or 800/225-6625, www.omakchamber.com, Mon.–Fri. 9 A.M.–5 P.M. year-round, plus Sat.–Sun. 10 A.M.–1 P.M. in the summer) has a ton of local information. The Okanogan National Forest **Supervisors Office** (1240 S. 2nd Ave. in Okanogan, 509/684-7000, www.fs.fed .us/r6/oka, Mon.–Fri. 7:45 A.M.–4:30 P.M.) has hiking and camping information for the Okanogan Valley and Highland country.

Highland Stage Company (509/486-4699) has two- and five-day stagecoach rides over the Okanogan Highlands.

OKANOGAN HIGHLANDS

East from Highway 97, the high elevation forests of the Okanogan Highlands carpet the hillsides all the way past Kettle River and Lake Roosevelt. Included within these boundaries are vast reaches of ponderosa pine, Douglas fir, and western larch forests, reaching up to numerous peaks topping 7,000 feet. They grow in both the Okanogan and Colville National Forests, both of which checkerboard the region. The huge chunks of public lands here offer a plethora of recreational activities, including 1,600 miles of hiking trails, dozens of campgrounds, and hundreds of miles of cross-country skiing and mountain biking trails.

Sights
SCENIC DRIVES
The **Oroville-Toroda Creek Road** cuts east from Oroville to Chesaw, climbing a canyon and emerging into open rolling grass hills with caps of western larch, Douglas fir, and ponderosa pine. Scattered ranch houses dot these hills.

Tiny Chesaw consists of something like 30 people in a smattering of homes, along with a store, tavern, and loads of nostalgically aging abandoned buildings.

After eight miles, a side road leads five miles north to Molson, Washington's best known

almost–ghost town, a delightful place in a wildly remote setting. Only a handful of folks still live here, surrounded by pieces of the past and the expansive land. Photography fans with a penchant for snapping pictures of civilization being reclaimed by nature will adore this route.

Meanwhile, on **State Route 20** the drive from Republic climbs easily into Colville National Forest through mixed forests of western larch, Douglas fir, ponderosa pine, lodgepole pine, and aspen. The ascent tops out at **Sherman Pass**, the state's highest at 5,575 feet. In spite of the elevation, you won't see dramatic snowcapped peaks, just thousands of acres of forested hills. A 10-minute hike from the parking lot at the pass leads to views of lands to the east. This drive is particularly beautiful in the fall when the larch and aspen show their colors.

OLD MOLSON
Old Molson town consists of eight weathered log and clapboard structures from the early 1900s, including a false-fronted bank, shingle mill, homestead cabin, and assay office. Inside are collections of antiques and historic photos from the area; outside are old wagons, threshers, and aging farm equipment.

Molson Museum (http://okanoganhistory.org, Memorial Day–Labor Day daily 10 A.M.–5 P.M.) is housed in a three-story brick schoolhouse a quarter mile up the road. Inside, find antique hand tools, historic photos, and a collection of artifacts from the area's rich mining history. Volunteers serve cookies and tea and will tell you about the area's rich past.

◀ STONEROSE INTERPRETIVE CENTER
The Stonerose Interpretive Center (15-1 N. Kean St. in Republic, 509/775-2295, www .stonerosefossil.org, May–Oct. Tues.–Sat. 10 A.M.–5 P.M., also Sundays mid-June–mid-Sept.) is named after the fossil of a long-extinct variety of rose found on the center's site. The ground also yielded up fossils of many other plants, fish, and insects that have been found here and are now on display, along with literature on fossils and paleontology.

© ERICKA CHICKOWSKI

Fossil hunting at Stonerose Interpretive Center

The public is invited to dig fossils at the **Boot Hill Fossil Site** ($3 adults, $2 ages 12–18 and seniors, free for children under 12) on the northern edge of town. You must get permission through the Stonerose Center and can only keep three fossils. Hammers and chisels may be rented for $3.

KETTLE FALLS

A town that initially had its roots as a Hudson's Bay Company outpost in the mid-19th century, Kettle Falls' namesake water feature was destroyed when the Grand Coulee Dam was built, but the plucky residents moved their town site to another set of falls and renamed them for consistency's sake.

But the old falls aren't forgotten. The small **St. Paul's Mission,** in a grove of tall pines near old Kettle Falls, was built by Jesuits in 1847. Missionaries held services here for the Native Americans who often fished for salmon in these waters. The Catholic chapel was closed 1858–1862, but it briefly reopened

for the summer salmon runs in the 1870s. The structure was turned over to the National Park Service in 1974.

Not far away is the **Kettle Falls Historical Center** (509/738-6627, weekends in May and Wed.–Sun. 11 A.M.–5 P.M. June 1–Labor Day, closed winters, donation), a small building that houses murals, artifacts, and exhibits portraying the old ways of life.

Meyers Falls is a small dam that has been producing electrical power here since 1903. The **Meyers Falls Interpretive Center** gives some perspective. The cascades are a few feet distant, dropping 20 feet into a pretty plunge pool below

Entertainment and Events

If you wander the northern backroads of the Highlands, be sure to stop at the false fronted **Chesaw Tavern,** a friendly watering hole that draws the good ol' girls and boys from the remote homesteads in the hills around this outpost. The ceiling is bedecked with thousands of dollar bills posted by bikers, hikers, and other travelers who've had a brew or two here and the bar is lined with stools made from the seats of old tractors.

Prospector's Days, held the second weekend of June, is the main event in Republic, with a parade, golf tournament, crafts show, pancake feed, rodeo, stock car races, and even a cattle drive.

Town & Country Days is the big summer event in Kettle Falls, arriving the first weekend of June and featuring a parade, fun run, and local arts and crafts. This is also when the town grouch is chosen. The **Governor's Cup Walleye Tournament** on the third weekend of June is followed by the **Lake Roosevelt Regatta** on the second weekend of July.

Kettle Falls' **Woodland Theatre** (120 W. 3rd Ave., 509/738-6430) features plays, concerts, and musicals throughout the year.

Sports and Recreation

HIKING

Big Tree Botanical Area is a mile northeast of Lost Lake Campground (seven miles south of

EASTERN WASHINGTON

Chesaw) and includes enormous western larch (tamarack) trees. A short interpretive trail leads through the forest.

The Colville National Forest **Republic Ranger District** (180 N. Jefferson, 509/775-3305, www.fs.fed.us/r6/colville) office has detailed brochures on hiking and mountain biking routes in the area, including the popular **Lakes Area Mountain Bike Loop** south of town and the Sherman Pass area to the east. Ask here about the "Mystery Man Trees" on North Namankin Creek, images of a man emblazoned on trees.

For an easy and very scenic walk, take the half-mile hike to **Nine Mile Falls.** The trailhead is southeast of Republic; get directions from the Forest Service.

At Sherman Pass, a side road leads to a trailhead for the **Kettle Crest Trail,** an excellent 30-mile-long hike that cuts north over the summit of the Kettle River Range. The area is popular with backcountry skiers in the winter.

Two miles up the Kettle Crest Trail is a spur to the top of 6,782-foot Columbia Mountain. Take this Forest Service path—**Columbia Mountain Trail**—for a wonderful short (but steep) climb to the summit, where you'll find a decrepit Civilian Conservation Corps (CCC) lookout cabin and wide-angle vistas. It's a bit over five miles round-trip from the trailhead to the top of the mountain, making a fine chance to stretch your legs and enjoy the quiet, forested land and the ravens playing in the thermals. Water is available from a spring along the trail.

CYCLING

East of Chesaw, quiet country roads take you along bucolic Toroda Creek and Kettle River lined with tall riparian forests and populated by hunters each fall. The land is marked with country homes and farmsteads, irrigated pastures, hilltop pine trees, open meadows, and grazing cattle. It's a fantastic place for bike riding, especially in the fall when leaves turn a brilliant yellow. During Prohibition, this part of Washington was a major center for smuggling Canadian liquor across the border.

© ERICKA CHICKOWSKI

Curlew Lake

WATER SPORTS

Located on the eastern shore of Curlew Lake, halfway between Curlew and Republic, **Curlew Lake State Park** is a pretty little park offering shady picnic spots, along with good fishing and swimming.

Fishing is a favorite activity in Lake Roosevelt. A net pen project near Kettle Falls produces rainbow trout, and the **Sherman Creek Hatchery** (four mi. west of Kettle Falls, 800/824-4916) raises kokanee salmon for Lake Roosevelt. Call for the current lake elevation.

Lake Roosevelt is a feeding area for more than 200 bald eagles during the winter months, particularly the stretch from Kettle Falls south to Gifford Ferry. Best time to see these birds is late November–mid-February.

Accommodations
REPUBLIC AND CURLEW

Northern Inn (852 S. Clark, 509/775-3371 or 888/801-1068, $66 s or $74 d) is an attractive place with clean and comfortable rooms. Kitchenettes are also available, as is wireless

Internet for an extra charge. **Klondike Motel** (150 N. Clark Ave., 509/775-3555, $44–68 d) offers standard motel units, as well as kitchenette rooms. The **Prospector Inn** (979 S. Clark Ave., 509/775-3361, www.theprospectorinn.com, $51 or $64 d) is a clean little motel with the added amenities of a sauna and hot tub.

Ride horses all day long at **K-Diamond-K Ranch** (509/775-3536, www.kdiamondk.com, $180 per person), a friendly, family-owned cattle ranch on 30,000 acres where guests go on horseback rides and hikes or just enjoy being outdoors. Stay in four large rooms with shared bath and savor three hearty meals a day. Meals, lodging, and rides are all included in the rate.

Slightly northeast of Republic, Lake Curlew is a favorite cabin and RV resort getaway in the Highlands to stay around these parts. For a roof over your head, check out the duplex and cabin units at **Black Beach Resort** (80 Black Beach Rd., Republic, 509/775-3989, $55–91 d). Or stay underneath the Milky Way at the attractive, shady campsites at **Curlew Lake State Park** (509/775-3592, www.parks.wa.gov, Apr.–Oct., $17 for tents, $20 for RVs), with good fishing and swimming.

For something a little closer to Curlew proper, hit **Wolfgang's Riverview Inn** (509/779-4252, www.televar.com/wolfgang, $45–60 d), two miles north of town center. This Bavarian-style lodge is a favorite among hunters and anglers and offers guided fly-fishing tours.

Bonaparte Lake Resort (509/486-2828, www.bonaparte-lake-resort.com, $45–65 d) features rustic cabins, as well as RV and tent camping. Get to the lake by heading three miles west from Wauconda on Highway 20, and then six miles north on Forest Service Road 32. Bring your own linens, towels, and kitchen utensils. The restaurant here makes the finest steaks in the area.

CHESAW

Four Forest Service campgrounds—**Beth Lake, Lost Lake, Bonaparte,** and **Beaver Lake**—are located south of Chesaw on the back way to Wauconda. They are open mid-May–mid-September and cost $8.

KETTLE FALLS

Grandview Inn Motel (978 Hwy. 395, 509/738-6733, $52 d, $60 d for kitchenette) has a delightful woodsy location overlooking Lake Roosevelt and comfortable rooms, some with kitchenettes. A more homey option is **Blue Moose Cabin Rentals** (five mi. west of Kettle Falls, 509/738-6950, www.bluemoosecabins.com, $65 d), which has three cabins with kitchenettes.

The National Park Service operates the wonderful **Kettle Falls Campground** (two mi. south of Hwy. 395/20 on Boise Rd., 509/738-6266, www.nps.gov/laro, year-round, $10, no RV hookups) in tall ponderosa pines along Lake Roosevelt. Campfire programs take place most summer evenings; check at the Ranger Station for offerings. No reservations, so get here early for summer holiday weekends. Take showers at the Chevron station on the west end of town.

The Park Service maintains a very popular campground, boat ramp, and swimming beach (no lifeguard) along the shore of Lake Roosevelt just south of Highway 395/20.

Private RV parks around Kettle Falls include **Circle Up RV Park** (on Boise Rd. south of the Park Service office, 509/738-6617, $22 full hookups), **Grandview Inn and RV Park** ($25), and **North Lake Roosevelt Resort** (Roosevelt Road, 509/738-2593, $13 tent, $21 RV).

Food

Dine on big steaks, prime rib, and sweet desserts at the **Riverside** (6 River Street, 509/779-4813, 4–8 P.M. Fri.–Sun.). Curlew's best eatery, it's open for dinners only. It's also a popular resting place for road-weary bikers and road-trippers.

Join the locals at a table in the **Wauconda Café** (509/486-4010, 9 A.M.–7 P.M. Mon.–Sat., 9 A.M.–5 P.M. Sun. in summer, call for winter hours), a small dining room overlooking the valley below. Surprisingly good food is served three meals a day, including burgers, shakes, steaks, prime rib, and even Chinese meals on weekends.

Little Gallea (345 W. 3rd, Kettle Falls, 509/738-6776, Mon.–Sat. 5 A.M.–2 P.M., 5–11 P.M., closed Sun.) is the local breakfast and lunch joint with well-prepared and inexpensive American food. For good steaks and seafood, stop by **Hudson Bay Co.** (2 Columbia Dr., 509/738-6164, daily 11 A.M.–9 P.M.).

More than a dozen local orchards produce cherries, apricots, peaches, pears, apples, and other fruits. Many of these operate fruit stands or have U-pick operations near the site of old Kettle Falls along Lake Roosevelt. Get a brochure from the chamber of commerce, or just head down Peachcrest Road for a self-guided tasting adventure.

China Bend Vineyards & Winery (3751 Vineyard Way, Kettle Falls, 509/732-6123 or 800/700-6123, www.chinabend.com) offers tastings of its organic wines and salsas.

The grounds are gorgeous and right on the Columbia River. They also have a popular 4th of July celebration here each summer.

Information and Services

Republic's **visitors center** (509/775-3387, Tues.–Sat. 10 A.M.–4 P.M. mid-Apr. through Oct.) is next to the Stonerose Center.

East of here is the **Danville Port of Entry** (8 A.M.–midnight daily), where a single building is occupied by both U.S. and Canadian customs agents.

Find restaurant and lodging information at the **Kettle Falls Area Chamber of Commerce** (downtown along Hwy. 395/20, 509/738-2300, www.kettle-falls.com, daily 1–3 P.M. in summer). Hours are hit or miss in the off-season.

Get Colville National Forest information at **Colville National Forest District** (255 765 S. Main St. in Colville, 509/684-7000, www .fs.fed.us/r6/colville).

The Northeast Corner

Washington's northeast corner is dominated by Stevens and Pend Oreille (pon-der-RAY) Counties. The region is a paradise of good fishing, all-season recreation from swimming to snow skiing, an abundance of wildlife, and very few people. This corner of the state isn't on the way to anywhere else in Washington, so only a determination to escape civilization or a strong exploratory drive brings visitors out here.

Several small towns serve the area: Kettle Falls, Colville, Chewelah, Ione, Metaline Falls, and Newport. They are unpretentious and friendly places and, although all have overnight accommodations and places to eat, most things of interest to visitors are out in the forests and along the rivers and lakes. Except for a bus that connects Colville with Spokane, there are no buses, trains, or planes servicing this part of Washington.

Pend Oreille River is one of just two rivers in North America that flow northward;

it enters Canada north of Metaline Falls before circling back south to join the Columbia River near the town of Boundary. Small lakes are scattered throughout northeast Washington. Many are encircled by summer cabins, modest year-round homes, or resorts and RV parks.

COLVILLE NATIONAL FOREST

Colville National Forest spreads over 1.1 million acres in half a dozen scattered puzzle pieces, reaching from Metaline Falls to Wauconda, 67 air-miles away. Abutting it on both sides are additional public lands: Okanogan National Forest to the west and Kaniksu National Forest reaching eastward into Idaho. The eastern portions of the Colville are capped by the Selkirk Mountains, one of the last places in the Lower 48 still home to fearsome grizzly bears. The forests are a mixture of evergreen and deciduous species, with grand fir, subalpine fir, lodgepole pine, aspen, Douglas fir, western white pine, western red cedar, western larch, birch, and cottonwood trees.

Hiking and Camping

Contact any Colville National Forest ranger station for a map and detailed descriptions of day hikes and longer treks. This is bear country, so make noise, store your food safely, and choose another route if you encounter bears, bear tracks, or droppings.

Abercrombie Mountain Trail is a three-mile one-way hike to a ridge top with panoramic views of the Pend Oreille and Columbia River Valleys from 7,300 feet. From Colville, take Aladdin Highway north for 23 miles to Deep Creek Road, turn north onto Deep Creek Road for seven miles, then turn right on Silver Creek Road 4720 to the junction with Road 7078. Take 7078 north to Road 300, then follow it to the road's end where the trail begins. Most of the three miles is wooded, crossing several streams and huckleberry bushes on the way to the ridge. This trail is also popular with hunters—an orange vest wouldn't hurt, especially in the early mornings.

Information

For more specific information on hiking, camping, and other recreational activities in the Colville National Forest, contact **Colville National Forest Headquarters** (765 S. Main, 509/684-7000, www.fs.fed.us/r6/colville). District offices are in Colville, Kettle Falls, Sullivan Lake, and Newport.

COLVILLE

Like many of its neighbors in this part of Washington, Colville depends on timber, mining, farming, and tourism to survive. There are still three sawmills in Colville fed by timber from Colville National Forest and private lands. Downtown Colville is a prosperous slice of middle America, and the surrounding area shows even more evidence: a sparkling new high school on the edge of town and the only Wal-Mart in this corner of the state.

Sights

Stevens County Historical Museum (700 N. Wynne St., 509/684-5968, June–Aug. daily 10 A.M.–4 P.M., May and Sept. daily 1–4 P.M., donation) contains items from Fort Colville, along with Native American artifacts.

Outside the museum you'll find the three-story **Keller House,** completed in 1912 and essentially unchanged today.

Entertainment and Events

The PRCA **Colville Panorama Rodeo** (509/684-4849, www.colvillepanoramarodeo.com) comes to town on Father's Day weekend. **Colville Rendezvous Days** (509/684-5973, www.colvillerendezvous.org) on the first weekend of August features a kung-fu exhibition and a battle of the bands. Early August or September brings the **Northeast Washington Fair** (509/684-2585) with a parade, animal judging, carnival, and live music. Colville is one of the few places that still has a drive-in movie theater; it's three miles west of town.

Sports and Recreation

Golfers can enjoy **Colville Elks Golf Course** (509/684-5508), an 18-hole course.

Nine miles east of Chewelah, **49° North** (509/935-6649, www.ski49n.com, $28 adults) has day and night skiing on 1,900 vertical feet of slope from four chairlifts. Terrain is set aside for powder skiing on weekends. Be sure to drive to the ski area from Highway 395 on the Chewelah (west) side; the road in from Highway 20 on the east is a narrow gravel road, impassable in winter and no fun the rest of the year.

Accommodations

Bennie's Colville Inn (915 S Main St., 509/684-2517, www.colvilleinn.com, $48–102 s) is pet-friendly with an indoor pool, hot tub, and a fitness center pass. The brick-faced **Comfort Inn** (166 NE Canning Dr., 509/684-2010, www.comfortinn.com, $89 d) has an indoor pool and hot tub and serves a continental breakfast.

Tent camping and RV spaces are available at

the **Northeast Washington Fairgrounds** on Columbia Street. Four Forest Service campgrounds are located in **Little Pend Oreille Lakes Recreation Area,** 25 miles northeast of Colville along Highway 20. Several more remote campgrounds are free, including **Big Meadow Lake Campground** (27 mi. northeast of Colville on Meadow Creek Road). Here you'll find three miles of hiking trails (partly wheelchair-accessible), a replica of a homestead cabin, and a 35-foot wildlife-viewing tower where you may see moose, beavers, ospreys, or even black bears.

Food

Talk 'N' Coffee (119 E. Astor, 509/684-2373, Mon.–Fri. 7 A.M.–4:30 P.M., closed Sat.–Sun.) next to the chamber office has homemade scones and good espresso.

Barman's Country Store (230 S. Main, 509/684-9710, Mon.–Sat. 10 A.M.–6 P.M., Sun. 11 A.M.–5 P.M.) has an old-fashioned soda fountain with sandwiches and homemade ice cream floats.

Colville has **farmers markets** (509/684-2326) on Wednesday noon–6 P.M. May–October at the corner of Hawthorne and Elm, and Saturday 8:30 A.M.–1 P.M. at 3rd and Main.

Information

Ask for info at the **Colville Chamber of Commerce Visitor Information Center** (121 E. Astor, 509/684-5973, www.colville.com, Mon.–Fri. 10 A.M.–noon and 1–4 P.M.).

For Forest Service information, visit the **Colville Ranger District** (755 S. Main, 509/684-7000, www.fs.fed.us/r6/colville, Mon.–Fri. 7:30 A.M.–4:30 P.M.) behind the Federal Building.

LITTLE PEND OREILLE LAKES RECREATION AREA

Heading east from Colville on Highway 20, the road cuts through beautiful mixed forests. Be sure to stop at **Crystal Falls,** 12 miles east of Colville, where the waters of Little Pend Oreille River drop over a 30-foot cascade.

Approximately 25 miles northeast of Colville on Highway 20 is the Little Pend Oreille chain of eight lakes, offering more than 75 miles of multiuse trails open to hiking, motorcycles, mountain bikes, and horses. In winter, the Forest Service maintains 15 miles of groomed cross-country ski trails. The lakes themselves are popular for swimming, sailing, boating, fishing, and canoeing. The country around here is a mix of open meadows and dense forests with plenty of larch trees that change colors brilliantly in the autumn.

Recreation

The Little Pend Oreille trail system has seven trails to satisfy all hikers and cross-country skiers alike. A popular 2.4-mile loop, the historic interpretive **Springboard Trail** begins at the east end of the Gillette Campground.

Frater Lake Trail has three ski/hike loops that start at Frater Lake on the east end of the recreation area. The two-mile **Tiger Loop** cuts through Douglas fir close to the lake on gentle terrain. The longer and steeper Coyote Rock Loop crosses a stream and meadow and has a viewpoint from Coyote Rock. Across on the south side of Highway 20 is the 2.6-mile **Lake Leo Trail,** popular with beginning cross-country skiers because of its gentle terrain.

Accommodations

Beaver Lodge Resort (2430 Hwy. 20 E. in Colville, 509/684-5657, www.beaverlodge resort.com, $55 d) is a fun family property on Lake Gillette, with comfortable cabins, tent ($20) and RV ($30 full hookups) spaces, and boat and canoe rentals. There's also a store, deli, and laundry.

You'll find four Forest Service campgrounds in the Little Pend Oreille Lakes area ($10). **Lake Leo, Lake Thomas, Gillette,** and **Lake Gillette** campgrounds are open Memorial Day to Labor Day (Lake Leo is open until the snow falls).

IONE

Ione is a lumber and tourism town along the Pend Oreille River 35 miles north of Usk.

© GREGORY JOHNSTON/123RF.COM

Relax by Pend Oreille River in Ione.

Steamboats plied the Pend Oreille River in the 1880s; today nearby Box Canyon Dam backs up the river to create a popular place to water ski and fish. The Vaagen Brothers sawmill is Ione's main employer.

Sights and Recreation

Three miles north of Ione is **Box Canyon Dam.** Stop at the **visitors center** (509/447-6700, open daily in summer) for summer tours. The small pond here (complete with float) makes a great swimming hole and picnic area.

The U.S. Forest Service's **Edgewater Campground** ($6–10; open mid-May through Sept.) sits across the Pend Oreille River and two miles north up Box Canyon-LeClerc Road (County Road 3669).

Accommodations and Food

The friendly and clean **Ione Motel and RV Park** (509/442-3213, $40–85 s or d) is right on the river and has rooms with microwaves and fridges, as well as RV hookups available.

On Highway 20 between Cusick and Ione,

Outpost Resort (509/445-1531, $45–150 d, $25 hookups, $15 tent) has rooms, a restaurant, groceries, boat launch, and camping. They also offer pontoon boat tours of the Pend Oreille River.

Box Canyon Resort (five mi. north of Ione, 509/442-3728 or 800/676-8883, $50 s or $55 d, $72 d kitchenettes) offers simple accommodations near Ione.

Information

To get information on Ione, Metaline, and Metaline Falls, call the **Pend Oreille County office** (509/447-1900, Mon.–Fri. 9 A.M.–5 P.M.).

Getting There and Around

The North Pend Oreille Valley Lions Club **Excursion Train** (877/525-5226, $12) chugs between Ione and Metaline Falls, crossing Box Canyon Dam along the way. Trains leave Ione at 11 A.M., 1 P.M., and 3 P.M., with a stop in Metaline Falls before returning. They generally run six weekends each summer from mid-June–mid-October. Call for reservations.

EASTERN WASHINGTON

METALINE AND METALINE FALLS

The twin towns of Metaline and Metaline Falls—jointly home to 500 people—sit across the Pend Oreille River from each other and just 10 miles from Canada. Metaline Falls is a delightful little burg with quiet streets and small frame homes with neatly trimmed lawns. Stop at **Metaline City Park** where the spacious lawns provide a place to picnic, toss a Frisbee, or just hang out by the water.

Crawford State Park

You can tour one of the largest limestone caves in the state, **Gardner Cave** (12 mi. northwest of Metaline Falls off Hwy. 31, 509/446-406, www.parks.wa.gov), at Crawford State Park. The cave is open late May–mid-September, with free guided tours Thursday–Monday between 10 A.M. and 4 P.M. Tours take you almost 500 feet into this 1,055-foot cavern, past oddly shaped stalactites, stalagmites, and columns. Dress warmly, as it's always cold inside. As you drive up to the cave, a sharp eye might spot **mountain goats** in the far distance from a marked pullout along Flume Creek near the park. Bring your binoculars.

Entertainment and Events

All summer long, the historic **Cutter Theatre** (509/446-4108) in Metaline Falls features plays, lectures, and concerts year-round. For first-run films in a small town, head down the block to the **Showhouse.**

The North Pend Oreille Valley Lions Club **Excursion Train** (509/442-5466, $12) rolls into Metaline Falls from Ione between mid-June and mid-October.

On Labor Day Weekend, **Affair on Main Street** brings arts and crafts, music, magic, and fun.

Accommodations and Food

Built in 1910, the historic **Washington Hotel** (509/446-4415, $40 d) is home to 18 restored rooms with handmade quilts, original furnishings, and bath down the hall. A studio and gallery include the innkeeper's works in progress.

Circle Motel & Sporting Goods Store (15802 Hwy. 31, two mi. north of Metaline Falls on Hwy. 31, 509/446-4343, www.circlemotel.com, $63–83) has rooms with microwaves, fridges, and satellite TV.

Next to the Washington Hotel is **Cathy's Café** (221 E. 5th Ave., 509/446-2447, Mon.–Fri. 5:30 A.M.–2 P.M., Sat.–Sun. 7 A.M.–2 P.M.), a down-home eatery, perfect for a nice cold sundae.

Information

Find information in the summer at the **Metaline Falls Visitor Center** (www.povn.com/cutter, daily 10 A.M.–5 P.M. Memorial Day to Labor Day only); stop by the Washington Hotel at other times.

SULLIVAN LAKE AREA

Four-mile-long Sullivan Lake anchors a large section of Forest Service land within Colville National Forest, providing outstanding camping and hiking opportunities. A feeding station at the south end of Sullivan Lake is a good place to look for **bighorn sheep** in the winter. The pristine Salmo-Priest Wilderness and the Grassy Top Roadless Area provide a slice of the real wilds of Washington. The Forest Service's **Sullivan Lake Ranger District office** (509/446-7500, www.fs.fed.us/r6/colville) is at the north end of the lake.

Hiking

Sullivan Lake Trail is a four-mile, one-way hike along the eastern shore of Sullivan Lake through forested areas, connecting Sullivan Lake Campground with Noisy Creek Campground. The clear blue lake is the main attraction, but watch for bighorn sheep, black bear, and white-tailed deer. This is a very nice hike, especially in the fall.

Salmo-Priest Wilderness

One of Washington's least-known wilderness areas, the 39,937-acre Salmo-Priest Wilderness sits in the northeastern-most corner of the state, bordering Idaho and Canada. Dense old-growth western red cedar, Douglas fir, grand fir, and western larch forests cover the forest floor with deep shadows. This is not the best place for woodland novices, but a number of trails provide hiking opportunities for the adventurous. The weather is fickle and often wet, so bring your rain gear. Best times to hike are mid-July–mid-August. No backcountry permits are required.

The Salmo-Priest Wilderness is home to a number of endangered animals, including gray wolves, grizzly bears, black bears, and the last woodland caribou in the Lower 48 states. For your safety, pick up free food storage containers from the Sullivan Lake Forest Service office before heading out, and be sure you know how to stay safe in bear country!

A loop trip begins from the east end of Forest Service Road 2220 that leaves Forest Service Road 9345 just north of Sullivan Lake. The **Salmo Basin Trail** climbs up through virgin evergreen forests and crosses into Idaho (and almost into Canada) before joining the **Shedroof Divide Trail** near 7,572-foot Snowy Top (a rough but rewarding side trip). Follow Shedroof Divide Trail back across into Washington and its junction with **Salmo Divide Trail,** which will take you back to your starting point, a total distance of approximately 19 miles. Much of the trail is at 6,000 feet in elevation. Breathe deeply!

USK, CUSICK, AND KALISPEL LANDS

As you pass the little paper mill town of Usk, realize that you are just one river and a deep forest away from both Idaho and British Columbia. The beautiful wild country continues along through Cusick, where you might catch a glimpse of the country fairgrounds and a few rusty pickups and well-treated working dogs.

Sights

Manresa Grotto is a 70-foot-wide cavern on Kalispel Tribal lands, right along LeClerc Creek Road and five miles north of the Pend Oreille River bridge at Usk. This spacious rock grotto was used by Father Jean Pierre DeSmet in the 1840s as a combination home and church to preach to local Native Americans. A stone altar and pews (of a sort) are still inside, and mass is held in mid-September every year. Osprey nest near here along the shore of the lake.

The Kalispel Tribal offices and the **Our Lady of Sorrows** church (built in 1914) are two miles south of here. Stop off to visit with the herd of 100 buffalo grazing immediately south of the office. Behind here is the powwow grounds used for the Salish Fairs.

Festivals and Events

The first weekend of August brings the unusual **Salish Fair** at the Kalispel powwow grounds. It includes a buffalo barbecue, arts and crafts, stick games (gambling), war dancing, and a baseball tournament. Also enjoyable are the **Salish Barter Fairs** held here in August, where you can purchase or trade Native American crafts and other works. The **Pend Oreille County Fair & Rodeo** comes to Cusick in late August.

Accommodations and Food

Blueslide Resort (400041 Hwy. 20, Cusick, 509/445-1327, $45 d motel, $70–80 four-person cabin) is a nice family-oriented place with a motel and cabins, along with tent camping and RV spots on the Pend Oreille River. Facilities include a boat ramp and dock, swimming pool, and store, but no TVs. This is the only place where boaters can buy fuel along the river.

Just south of Usk at the junction of Highways 211 and 20 is **Crossroads Café** (509/445-1515, daily 6 A.M.–8 P.M.), a large bar and all-American eatery with live music on weekends. The **Usk Bar & Grill** makes good burgers.

Camping

Four Forest Service campgrounds are along the shore of Sullivan Lake and nearby Mill Pond: **Sullivan Lake East, Sullivan Lake West, Mill Pond,** and **Noisy Creek.** All are open Memorial Day–Labor Day. Find good swimming beaches at Noisy Creek and the two Sullivan Lake campgrounds. All can also be reserved (518/885-3639 or 877/444-6777, www.recreation.gov, $10, $9 extra reservation fee).

NEWPORT AND VICINITY

The town of Newport is the Pend Oreille County seat and the largest settlement in these parts. It sits along the Pend Oreille River.

Sights

The **County Historical Society Museum** (Washington and 4th, 509/447-5388, mid-May–Sept. daily 10 A.M.–4 P.M., voluntary donation) is built in an old Idaho & Washington depot, the museum hosts exhibits of various items, historical and sentimental.

Just two miles east of Newport in Idaho is the **Albeni Falls Dam** (208/437-3133), where tours are given daily in the summer.

Festivals and Events

Start the summer at **American Heritage Days** in early May at the fairgrounds. Events include old-timey demonstrations, dancing, food, and crafts. The **Newport Rodeo** in late June includes a parade, carnival, cowboy breakfast, food and craft booths, and the main attraction, a PRCA-sanctioned rodeo.

The annual **Poker Paddle,** held the third weekend in July, consists of a 40-mile canoe trip down the Pend Oreille River; participants collect poker cards at various stops along the two-day route.

Sports and Recreation

The wheelchair-accessible **Pioneer Park Heritage Trail** begins at the Pioneer Park Campground and leads past interpretive signs that detail the life of the Kalispel Tribe. **Lower Wolf Trail,** a short loop trail beginning from the north edge of town, passes through forest and wildflowers, affording views of Ashenfelder Bay. To reach it, turn north on Warren Avenue at its junction with Highway 20, continuing about a mile to the trailhead. The path is actually a series of short loops totaling 1.5 miles; half of them are wheelchair-accessible (but graveled).

The **Upper Wolf Trail System** consists of 2.5 miles of loop trails located just north of Newport off Laurel-Hurst Street. The trail system is popular with mountain bikers in the summer and cross-country skiers in winter.

A longer ski/bike/hike trail is the **Geophysical Trail System,** located approximately nine miles northwest of town on Indian Creek Road. In the winter, the Forest Service grooms six miles of trails. You'll need a Sno-Park permit to park here for skiing. The **Geophysical Observatory** was originally used for earthquake monitoring but now serves to detect the detonation of nuclear weapons. It is one of three such sites in America. It's closed to the public; the instruments are too sensitive!

Four Forest Service campgrounds are close to Newport: **Brown's Lake, South Skookum Lake, Pioneer Park,** and **Panhandle.** They charge $10 and are open Memorial Day–September. Pioneer Park Campground is two miles north of town on LeClerc Road; cross the bridge over the Pend Oreille River, and turn left. Campsites are also available two miles east at the Priest River Recreation Area in Idaho.

Accommodations and Food

Your best local lodging option is **Golden Spur Motor Inn** (924 W. Hwy. 2, 509/447-3823, $50 s or $60 d).

Set along a crystal-clear mountain lake deep in the country, **Marshall Lake Resort** (seven mi. north of Newport on Leclerc Rd., 509/447-4158, $35–70 d) is a favorite with hunters, anglers, and city-crazed stress-balls looking to unwind under the stars. The property offers rustic trailer cabins, as well as tent campsites ($15) and RV hookups ($18 electric). Cabins include kitchens and everyone shares restrooms with showers. Rent a variety of boats and canoes to explore the lake or ply its waters for fat cutthroat trout, or explore trails on more than 1,000 private acres.

Owen's Grocery and Deli (4th and Washington) has a deli and old-fashioned soda fountain with malts and banana splits. Get fresh produce and handicrafts at Newport's **Earth Market** on summer Saturdays 9 A.M.–1 P.M.

Information

The museum at the old depot houses the **Newport Visitor Center** (509/447-5812, summer daily 9 A.M.–5 P.M., fall–spring Mon.–Fri.,

9 A.M.–noon). Stop by the **Newport Ranger District** (315 N. Warren Ave., 509/447-7300) for brochures on local trails and campgrounds. Ask here for directions to the South Baldy Lookout and the Roosevelt Grove of Ancient Cedars.

HUCKLEBERRY MOUNTAIN AND THE SPOKANE RIVER AREA

For a beautiful country drive, head west from Chewelah along the paved road connecting the one-store towns of Bluecreek and Cedonia. It takes you through lush valleys with big old dairy barns in varying stages of disrepair, and over gentle Huckleberry Mountain, covered with forests of ponderosa pine and western larch.

Highway 25 is another delightful drive, following the shore of Lake Roosevelt from Northport all the way to Fort Spokane, 90 miles to the south. The dark blue lake waters contrast sharply with hills of pine and grass. Numerous campsites line this shore (see *Lake Roosevelt* for specifics).

Gifford Ferry (6:30 A.M.–9:30 P.M.) crosses the reservoir every day, taking you to the town of Inchelium on the Colville Reservation.

Spokane Reservation

South of the tiny town called Fruitland, Highway 25 heads away from Lake Roosevelt and across the Spokane Reservation to Fort Spokane and Davenport. **Wellpinit,** the only settlement on the reservation, has a community store, post office, and big high school with "Wellpinit Redskins" emblazoned on the front. The essentially undeveloped reservation is scenic, hilly land covered in open ponderosa pine, large sections of which have been logged.

Fort Spokane

From 1880–1898, the U.S. Army post at Fort Spokane served to keep the peace between the Native Americans on the forested Colville Reservation to the north and the white settlers on the grassy plains to the south. Not much ever happened, and so it was shut down in 1898, except for a brief stint as the HQ for the Colville Agency, and later as a tuberculosis hospital. In 1960, the National Park Service restored the remaining structures and added some relics and artifacts.

Take a walking tour through the grounds to see four of the original buildings. Trailside displays relate the fort's history, and the brick guardhouse (1892) has a **visitors center** (509/725-2715, daily 9:30 A.M.–5:30 P.M. from mid-May–early Sept.).

The Park Service maintains a nearby swimming beach, campgrounds ($10), and amphitheater for Saturday campfire programs from mid-June–early September. Across the river on reservation land you'll find the **Two Rivers Casino** (800/722-4031), with roulette, craps, and blackjack; RV hookups are also available. Heading south toward Davenport, Highway 25 passes through an open landscape of rolling wheat fields with scattered old red barns and two-story white houses. Side roads off the highway provide access to **Seven Bays Marina** and **Porcupine Bay,** popular camping, fishing, swimming, and boating areas within Lake Roosevelt National Recreation Area.

Long Lake Area

Long Lake Dam spans the Spokane River near the east edge of the Spokane Reservation. The grounds here offer a pleasant spot for contemplation beneath ponderosa pines; free lakeside summer-only campsites are available at **Long Lake Camp,** five miles east on Long Lake Dam Road.

Approximately five miles east of the junction between Highways 291 and 231 are a couple of large boulders surrounded by a chain-link fence. Behind the fence are several red-painted figures of unknown age, the **Long Lake petroglyphs.** East from here on Highway 291 the road follows the beautiful shore of Long Lake for quite a few miles. Forested hills climb away from the blue lake waters. The road continues past Riverside State Park and then on to Spokane, 35 miles from the junction with Highway 231.

Palouse Country and Pullman

A broad area of gently rolling hills that un-folds just south of Spokane and runs all the way down to the Snake River and the Blue Mountains, Palouse Country stands as the breadbasket of the state. The rich, loamy soil and hot summer days of the Palouse are an ideal combination that have made it one of the most productive wheat growing areas in the world for generations. A summer's drive on the region's quiet byways will motor you along acres and acres of golden fields that seem to merge into eternity over the horizon.

Though mostly rural, there are signs of life out here. The Palouse is home to the state's second-largest educational institution, Washington State University. The surround-ing town of Pullman bleeds WSU crimson and gray. A quintessential college burg, Pullman's known as the "crossroads of the Palouse" and visitors will be greeted here by a prosperous and tidy downtown full of redbrick buildings and friendly mom-and-pop establishments.

SIGHTS
Turnbull National Wildlife Refuge
Just south of Cheney, 17,000-acre Turnbull National Wildlife Refuge (509/235-4723, www.r1.fws.gov) has miles of trails and roads for walking, cross-country skiing, horseback riding, mountain biking, or driving through the protected lake area. This refuge, unlike oth-ers in eastern Washington, is not open to hunt-ing; this is strictly an observation-only area, and nature lovers will be rewarded with sight-ings of grebes, hawks, shorebirds, deer, coyotes, owls, badgers, herons, and an occasional bald eagle or peregrine falcon. The refuge is open every day during daylight hours, and a $3 per vehicle fee is charged March–October.

◖ Steptoe Butte State Park
Follow the signs from Highway 195 and drive to the top of Steptoe Butte State Park (509/549-3551, www.parks.wa.gov), about 50 miles south of Spokane, for panoramic views of the Palouse

Rural Palouse Country is one of the most productive wheat-growing areas in the world.

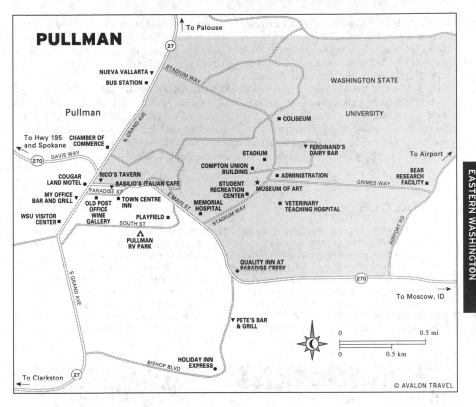

PULLMAN

To Palouse

27

NUEVA VALLARTA ▼
BUS STATION ■

STADIUM WAY

WASHINGTON STATE

Pullman

N GRAND AVE

COLISEUM

UNIVERSITY

To Hwy 195   CHAMBER OF
and Spokane   COMMERCE ■

DAVIS WAY

270

STADIUM ■

▼ FERDINAND'S
   DAIRY BAR

To Airport ↗

COMPTON UNION
BUILDING ■

COUGAR
LAND MOTEL ●   RICO'S TAVERN
               ▼
               BASILIO'S ITALIAN CAFE

MY OFFICE   PARADISE ST
BAR AND GRILL ▼ OLD POST   TOWN CENTRE
               OFFICE ■   INN ●

WSU VISITOR   WINE
CENTER ■   GALLERY

STUDENT
RECREATION
CENTER ■

E MAIN ST

MEMORIAL
HOSPITAL ■

SOUTH ST

PLAYFIELD ■

STADIUM WAY

■ ADMINISTRATION

★ MUSEUM OF ART

GRIMES WAY

BEAR
RESEARCH
FACILITY ■

■ VETERINARY
  TEACHING HOSPITAL

AIRPORT RD

Λ
PULLMAN
RV PARK

QUALITY INN AT
PARADISE CREEK ●

270

To Moscow, ID

S GRAND AVE

▼ PETE'S BAR
  & GRILL

0   0.5 mi
0   0.5 km

BISHOP BLVD   HOLIDAY INN
              EXPRESS ●

To Clarkston 27

© AVALON TRAVEL

River farmland and Idaho's mountains to the east. Almost a perfect pyramid—its original name was Pyramid Peak—it is also a popular place for kite flyers because of the almost-constant wind.

The state park has a day-use area at the foot of the peak with a well and picnic tables (open year-round). The best time to visit Steptoe Butte is early in the morning and late in the evening, when the low sunlight defines the rolling Palouse hills and you can see far into Idaho, south to the Blue Mountains of Washington and Oregon, west to the Cascade Range, and north past Spokane into Canada.

The park is east of Highway 195 on Hume Road. Follow the signs from the town of Steptoe if you're coming from Spokane; if you're driving north from Colfax and Pullman,

the signs for the butte and Hume Road are a short distance south of Steptoe.

Washington State University

Washington State University has a student body of more than 17,000 distributed throughout one graduate school and seven undergraduate colleges offering more than 100 major fields of study. The school is well known as an agricultural research center, but facilities also include an Electron Microscopy Center, Nuclear Radiation Center, Water Research Center, and an International Marketing Program for Agricultural Commodities.

The **Museum of Anthropology** (on the first floor of College Hall, 509/335-3441, Mon.–Thurs. 9 A.M.–4 P.M., Friday 9 A.M.–3 P.M.) has traveling exhibits from all over the globe and

Northwest Native American artifacts. Certainly the most unusual items are the plaster casts of what are purportedly Sasquatch footprints.

My favorite WSU museum is the **Jacklin Collection** (inside the Physical Sciences Building, 8 A.M.–5 P.M. weekdays). Here you'll discover the largest petrified wood collection in the western states, many pieces of which have been beautifully polished. In the entryway are several fun (and maybe even educational) science exhibits to play with.

Connors Museum of Zoology (in the Science Building, open by appointment only) claims the largest public collection of animals and birds in the Pacific Northwest.

FERDINAND'S DAIRY BAR

The Food Quality Building is home to Ferdinand's (509/335-2141 or 800/457-5442, www.wsu.edu/creamery, Mon.–Fri. 9:30 A.M.–4:30 P.M., and on special event weekends, including home football games), a soda fountain

A PALOUSEY

The Palouse River begins just south of Spokane and runs south all the way to the Snake River and the Blue Mountains. It is bounded on the east by the Selkirk Mountains in western Idaho, and on the west by the Channeled Scablands.

Early French fur traders probably encountered the Palus tribe, which sounded quite a bit like their word for green grassland, *pelouse*. The name was contagious, and before long, the land, local Indians, and the river were all Palouses. The Nez Perce rode a particular type of sturdy, fast, leopard-spotted horse, a descendant of those ridden by the Conquistadores, that was the envy of the basin. White settlers dubbed them "Palouse" or "palousey" horses and the phrase "a palousey" was further morphed into "Appaloosa." Today, the national headquarters of the Appaloosa Horse Club is right across the Washington line in Moscow, Idaho.

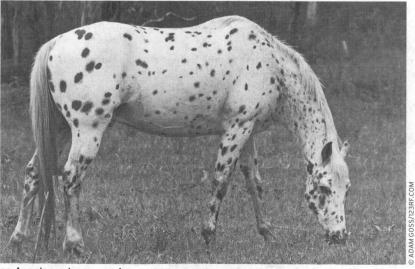

an Appaloosa horse grazing

© ADAM GOSS/123RF.COM

run by the university's agricultural school, and the most popular tourist attraction on campus. As part of its agricultural research work, the university has maintained a dairy herd for more than 70 years; today, most of the milk produced goes into cheeses and ice cream.

The most famous product at Ferdinand's is **Cougar Gold,** a delicious cheddarlike cheese that is only sold in hefty 30-ounce tin cans. The cheeses are aged for up to a year to develop the proper flavor and texture.

MUSEUM OF ART

The Museum of Art (509/335-1910 or 509/335-6607, www.wsu.edu/artmuse, Tue. 10 A.M.–10 P.M., Mon. and Wed.–Fri. 10 A.M.–4 P.M., Sat.–Sun. 1–5 P.M.) in the Fine Arts Center houses Washington's finest arts exhibition space east of the Cascades, with changing exhibits throughout the year. Also here is a permanent collection of works by well-known 19th- and 20th-century American and European painters, from Goya to Warhol. Some of these works are always on display during the summer. Student art galleries on campus can be found elsewhere in the Fine Arts Center.

BEAR RESEARCH FACILITY

Don't miss the bear research facility along Airport Road on the east edge of campus. The WSU Bear Research Center (509/332-1511, www.natural-resources.wsu.edu) is the only place where adult grizzlies are housed for nutritional, physiological, and ecological research by graduate students and visiting scientists. They are visible behind a stout fence. The resident bears were orphaned as cubs and would not have otherwise survived. In the winter, they hibernate in special temperature-controlled dens. Tours are available by reservation.

Dahmen Barn

Tiny Uniontown, a dozen miles south of Pullman, was first settled by German immigrants in the 1880s. Today, agriculture is the main support, as evidenced by the big grain elevator on the north side of town and the rolling farmland all around. Constructed in 1904,

St. Boniface Church is Washington's oldest consecrated Catholic church.

The most distinctive feature—it's pretty hard to miss—is Steve Dahmen's old barn surrounded by an ever-expanding (600 feet at last measuring) fence of **iron wheels.** The wheels came from steam engines, threshing machines, hay rakes, tractors, wagons, and even sewing machines. Stop by to talk to the fence's friendly creator and to sign his guest book.

Moscow, Idaho

Although it's across the state line, the town of Moscow, Idaho, is a twin to Pullman. Moscow is just 10 miles away and has a number of attractions worth visiting: the **University of Idaho,** the **Appaloosa Museum and Heritage Center,** and many historic structures, including the **McConnell Mansion.** The country around here rises quickly into forested mountains, quite a change from the rolling grasslands of the Palouse.

ENTERTAINMENT AND EVENTS

Nightlife

The best dancing and boozin' bars are in nearby Moscow, Idaho, but Pullman has a couple of options. **Rico's Public House** (200 E. Main St., 509/332-6566, Sat.–Fri. 11:30 A.M.–2 A.M., Sun. 1 P.M.–2 A.M.) is a great rockin' place with blues and jazz bands, imported beers, and homemade wine coolers.

The college co-eds and jocks flock to **Cougar Cottage** (900 NE Colorado St., 509/332-1265), a divey joint with cheap brew and a definite frat vibe—no surprise considering its proximity to Greek Row.

If that scene isn't your thing, mingle with the locals, grad students, and professors at **My Office Bar and Grill** (215 S. Grand Ave., 509/334-1202, www.myofficepullman.com, 11 A.M.–2 A.M. Mon.–Fri.), or take in a little handcrafted beer at **Paradise Creek Brewery** (245 SE Paradise, 509/338-9463, www.opo wines.com).

Festivals and Events

Cheney's mid-July **Rodeo Days** (509/235-

8480 or 509/235-4848, www.cheneyrodeo .com) features bronc- and bull-riding, calf roping, and a parade at one of the largest amateur rodeos in the Northwest.

Colfax Summer Festival on the second weekend of July includes a parade, car show, fun run, basketball tournament, and live music. The Palouse Empire Fairground near Colfax has rodeos, horse shows, and fairs all summer long. The main event is the four-day **Palouse Empire Fair** beginning the weekend after Labor Day. It features a rodeo, demonstrations of antique harvesting equipment, a carnival, and all the standard country fair activities.

Pullman's annual **Fourth of July** celebration actually covers three towns. It begins in Johnson, 10 miles south of Pullman, with music and a parade. Then it's on to Albion, six miles north of Pullman, for a big potluck meal at Community Hall. In the afternoon, head back to Pullman for a barbecue, live music, and after-dark fireworks show.

Pack your bottle of Beano for Pullman's main event in late August, the venerable **National Lentil Festival** (800/365-694, www .lentilfest.com). Over 200 gallons of lentil chili is simmered and served at the event, which also features a street fair, big parade, arts and crafts fair, live entertainment, a kids fishing derby, and a cook-off with such specialties as lentil pizza and even lentil ice cream.

The big **Holiday Arts and Crafts Show** comes to WSU's Beasley Coliseum in late October and is followed by the **Downtown Holiday Celebration,** complete with carolers and Santa Claus on the first Saturday of December.

The **Lionel Hampton Jazz Festival** (208/885-6765, www.jazz.uidaho.edu) in nearby Moscow is one of the biggest area events. Held the third weekend in February, it features many of the greats in jazz.

The Arts

The university's 12,000-seat **Beasley Performing Arts Coliseum** (information 509/335-1514, tickets 800/325-7328, http://

beasley.wsu.edu) stages events from rock concerts to comedy shows. The university has theaters in Daggy Hall (509/335-7236) where you can attend Shakespearean plays and student productions. Many other musical recitals and theatrical performances (509/335-8525) take place on campus all year.

Established in 1969, the **Washington-Idaho Symphony** (509/332-3408, www.washington idahosymphony.org) puts on a number of productions a year. You can also hear free **summer outdoor concerts** at Reaney Park on Wednesday evenings from the third weekend of June through July.

SPORTS AND RECREATION
Spectator Sports

The **WSU Cougars** (509/335-9626 or 800/462-6847, www.wsucougars.com) field teams in football, basketball, baseball, gymnastics, and track and field. The 40,000-seat **Martin Stadium** really rocks in even-numbered years when the Cougars play the archrival University of Washington Huskies in the annual Apple Cup.

Parks

Lawson Gardens (Derby St. near Dilke St.) covers 11 acres of land and features a formal rose and flower garden with a reflecting pool and gazebo. On the west side of town, **Sunnyside Park** has hiking trails, picnic areas, tennis and basketball courts, and playgrounds; this is the site of Pullman's annual 4th of July picnic and fireworks. **Reaney Park** on Reaney Way and Gray Lane has a swimming pool, gazebo, and playground.

The paved **Bill Chipman Palouse Trail** follows a gentle old railroad grade for eight miles, connecting Pullman with Moscow, Idaho. It's a great place for in-line skating or bike riding. The trail starts next to Quality Inn at the intersection of Highway 270 and Bishop Boulevard.

Outdoor Recreation Center

Located in the university's Hollingberry Field House, the Outdoor Recreation Center

(509/335-2651) offers excellent noncredit classes in kayaking, cross-country skiing, rock climbing, wilderness survival, backpacking, and other subjects. Most of these are open to the public for a fee. It also has a **climbing wall** and rents a wide range of equipment to both students and the public, including backpacks, tents, rafts, canoes, skis, and snowboards.

Student Recreation Center

The Student Recreation Center (next to coliseum, 509/335-8732, http://urec.wsu.edu, $8 day pass) is a modern facility with lots to offer: a swimming pool, a 50-person hot tub, indoor hockey rink, basketball court, elevated track, Olympic weight room, and racquetball courts.

ACCOMMODATIONS

If you're planning to be in town for WSU football games or graduation, reserve several months, and maybe a year, ahead of time. The busiest time is when the Apple Cup Game (against archrival University of Washington) comes to Pullman. Late folks end up staying in Clarkston and "commuting" to the game.

Tucked into a gleaming white 1908 farm home, **Hazelton House** (210 NW Olsen St., 509/334-0408, www.hazeltonhousebb.com, $120–170) offers all of the special touches one expects of a cozy bed-and-breakfast. Wake up to a big hearty breakfast, relax over a cup of coffee on the deck when the weather warms up, and munch on cookies in the afternoon. This comfortable establishment is popular with visiting professors and families coming for special events such as graduation.

The following local motels are arranged by price. **Cougar Land Motel** (120 W. Main, 509/334-3535 or 800/334-3574, $50 s or $60 d) offers access to an outdoor pool. One of the nicest motels in town, **The Manor Lodge** (445 SE Paradise St., 509/334-2511, www.thetowncentreinn.com, $97–113 d) is a two-story, outdoor-entry motel with renovated rooms that all include refrigerators and microwaves, plus free Internet access. For $5 more, rent a

unit with a dining room table and equipped kitchen. Families with large pets or small children and limited-mobility guests should ask for a ground floor room, as the spiral staircases are a bit difficult to navigate.

The **Hilltop Inn & Restaurant** (928 NW Olson St., 509/332-0928 or 800/527-1133, www.hotelonthehill.com, $149 s or $159 d) has an indoor pool, hot tub, sauna, exercise room, and hot buffet breakfast. Plus, Porky's Pit BBQ restaurant is right on-site.

Facilities include an outdoor pool, sauna, hot tub, fitness center, and breakfast buffet at **Quality Inn Paradise Creek** (1400 SE Bishop Blvd., 509/332-0500 or 800/669-3212, www.qualityinn.com, $124–164 d). **Holiday Inn Express** (1190 SE Bishop Blvd., 509/334-4437 or 800/465-4329, www.hiexpress.com, $84 s or d) has an indoor pool, hot tub, fitness center, and continental breakfast.

The **Churchyard Inn B&B** (206 St. Boniface St., Uniontown, 509/229-3200, www.churchyardinn.com, $95–103 d) contains seven guest rooms with private baths in a gorgeous brick 1905 inn, originally built as a convent serving next-door St. Boniface Church. No kids are allowed.

Premier Alpaca Ranch & Guest Home (401 S. Railroad Ave., Uniontown, 509/229-3655, www.premieralpacas.com, $100 d, $130 for four) is a restored century-old home with a guesthouse, plus an indoor lap pool. Guests will love to touch the alpacas.

Camping

Campers can stay at the tiny city-run **Pullman RV Park** (509/334-4555, Apr.–Nov., $20 full hookups, $6 tents) next to the city playfield at South and Riverview Streets. Visitors can also find camping at **Kamiak Butte County Park** (13 mi. northeast of Pullman on Hwy. 27, 509/397-6238, $15 tent and RV, no hookups), which offers more natural digs, including a 3.5-mile trail through a wooded setting, but it isn't as convenient to the university.

Near Cheney are more than a dozen small recreation lakes, many with resorts. You can also park RVs or pitch tents at **Peaceful Pines**

Campground (a mile southwest of Cheney on Hwy. 904, 509/235-4966). Several small resorts in the area have cabins, camping, RV parking, boat rentals, and fishing: **Klink's Williams Lake Resort** (18617 W. Williams Lake Rd., 509/235-2391), and **Four Seasons Campground & Fishing Resort** (on Sprague Lake, 509/257-2332, www.fourseasons campground.com). **Palouse Lions Park** also has riverside campsites.

Three-hundred-acre **Kamiak Butte County Park** (four mi. southwest of Palouse along Hwy. 27, 509/397-6238) has camping and picnicking. A steep, one-mile hiking trail leads through evergreen forests to the top of this 3,641-foot butte, providing views of the Palouse Hills.

FOOD
Cafés and Delis

The cheapest eats are found on campus at the **Compton Union Building** (http://cub.wsu.edu). Find five different eateries here, from cafeteria fare to sit-down comestibles. Also be sure to check out the ever-popular **Ferdinand's Dairy Bar** at WSU for ice cream, milkshakes, and cheeses. **Dissmore's IGA** (1205 N. Grand Ave., 509/332-1393, 24 hours daily) has a good deli.

American

The Hilltop Restaurant (Colfax Hwy., 509/334-2555, Sun.–Thurs. 4–9 P.M., Fri. 4–10 P.M., Sat. 5–10 P.M.) features a panoramic city view, decent steaks, and a popular Sunday brunch.

Swilly's Café (200 NE Kamiaken, 509/334-3395, www.swillys.com, Mon.–Fri. 11 A.M.–3 P.M. and 5–9:30 P.M., Sat. 5–9:30 P.M.) is a popular yuppified bistro with excellent lunches and dinners made from the freshest produce, baked goods, seafood, and meats. Riverside outdoor seating adds to the charm. Dinner reservations are recommended.

International

You won't go wrong at **Basilio's Italian Café** (337 E. Main St., 509/334-7663, www .basilios.net, Sun.–Thurs. 11 A.M.–9 P.M., Fri.–Sat. 11 A.M.–10 P.M.), a big brick-walled space where you order at the counter. Quick service and reasonable prices mean it's popular with local students. The best local place for pizzas is **Sella's Calzones & Pizza** (1115 E. Main St., 509/334-1895, Tues.–Sat. 11 A.M.–10 P.M., Sun.–Mon. 11 A.M.–9 P.M.).

Enjoy authentic Mexican cuisine at **Nuevo Vallarta** (1110 N. Grand Ave., 509/334-4689, daily 11 A.M.–10:30 P.M.) and good Chinese food at **The Emerald** (1140 N. Grand Ave., 509/334-5427, daily 10:30 A.M.–11 P.M.).

INFORMATION AND SERVICES

Start your campus visit at the very helpful **WSU Visitor Center** (Hwy. 270 and Grand Ave., 509/335-8633, http://visitor.wsu.edy, Mon.–Fri. 7 A.M.–4 P.M., plus some Saturdays) in the historic train depot. Football and other sports tickets are sold in the visitors center.

Public parking is available at a number of lots around campus. Get a parking day-pass from the visitors center or on campus at the Public Safety Building.

Free **campus tours** (509/335-8633, Mon.–Fri. at 10:30 A.M. and 1 P.M.) depart the University Relations Office in Room 370 of the Lighty Student Service Building. These hour-long walking tours are offered year-round.

The **Pullman Chamber of Commerce** (415 N. Grand Ave., 509/334-3565 or 800/365-6948, www.pullmanchamber.com, Mon.–Fri. 9 A.M.–5 P.M.) has all sorts of local brochures, including a walking tour of historic buildings.

Brused Books (235 E. Main St., 509/334-7898, 11 A.M.–6 P.M. daily) is a fun place to browse for used books. The store's name came to the owner in a dream. Really.

GETTING THERE AND AROUND
By Air

Moscow-Pullman Airport (3200 Airport Complex N., Pullman, 509/338-3223) provides only general aviation support for private and freight aircraft.

By Bus

Pullman Transit (509/332-6535, www.pull mantransit.com, Mon.–Fri.) provides bus service throughout town.

Northwestern Trailways (1002 Nye St., 509/334-1412 or 800/366-6975, www.nwadv .com/northw) has bus service north to Spokane, and south to Boise, Idaho.

Clarkston and Vicinity

Clarkston is tucked into the southeast corner of Washington along the Snake River, and right across the bridge from its larger neighbor, Lewiston, Idaho. The names reflect the time Lewis and Clark camped nearby in 1805. The first white settlers were cattle ranchers, and late-19th-century irrigation projects made it possible to branch out into farming. Clarkston is Washington's most inland seaport, more than 450 miles east of the Pacific via the Columbia River and its chief branch, the Snake. International shipping began to add to the local economy in the 1970s, and now the region ships paper products and other goods to East Asia. Clarkston winkingly refers to itself as the "Gateway to Hell's Canyon."

SIGHTS AND RECREATION
Hells Canyon Recreation

Quite a few local companies offer float trips and jetboat excursions through the deepest river gorge in North America, the Snake River's Hells Canyon, separating Oregon and Idaho.

Approximately 68 miles of the river—from Hells Canyon Dam in Oregon to the Washington border—is a National Wild and Scenic River. The Snake River features class II through IV rapids passing ancient petroglyphs, an ancient lava flow, abundant wildlife, and rugged canyon scenery.

For a complete list of commercial guides and outfitters, contact the Forest Service's **Hells Canyon Office** (three mi. south of Clarkston on Hwy. 129, 509/758-0616, www .fs.fed.us/r6/w-w, Mon.–Fri. 7:30–11:30 A.M. and 12:30–4:30 P.M. year-round, plus summer weekends). The **Clarkston Chamber of Commerce** (502 Bridge St., 509/758-7712 or 800/933-2128, www.clarkstonchamber.org)

also has information on local river-running companies.

Scenic Drives

To reach Pullman and other points north, you need to cross into Lewiston, Idaho, and traverse the Clearwater River bridge. From here, you can follow the heavily trafficked Highway 95, which connects into Highway 195, or follow the **Old Spiral Highway** instead. The latter road, which has been repaved, switchbacks and corkscrews its way up a shorter and considerably more interesting route, with spectacular views into Washington, Idaho, and Oregon from the 2,750-foot summit. A less extraordinary but still very scenic drive is along Highway 129 south from Clarkston to the Oregon border.

Asotin

The pretty little town of Asotin is six miles south of Clarkston along the Snake River. Visit the **Asotin County Historical Museum** (3rd and Filmore, 509/243-4659, Mon.–Sat. 1–5 P.M. in summer, Sat. 1–5 in winter, no charge) to see early artifacts and buildings and one of the largest collections of branding irons in existence. Ask here for directions to several petroglyphs visible south of Asotin.

Parks and Trails

Five miles south of Clarkston, **Chief Looking Glass Park** provides boat access to the Snake River, with launch ramps, docks, and moorage, plus picnic tables and a playground. The paved 16-mile **Clearwater and Snake River National Recreation Trail** starts here and follows the levees north to Clarkston, over the bridge to Lewiston, and then back south along the river to

Hells Gate State Park (which has a big swimming beach). The trail is a favorite bike riding, in-line skating, and walking route. South of Clarkston, the path cuts through **Swallows Park,** where a basalt rock is crowded with cliff swallow nests each spring. Swallows Park has river access for boating, swimming, and picnicking.

Eight miles west of town on Highway 12, **Chief Timothy State Park** (www.parks .wa.gov) sits on Silcott Island in the middle of Lower Granite Lake (the dammed-up Snake River). The park was named for a Nez Perce chief who befriended early white settlers. He is buried in Clarkston's Beachview Park. The area's history and geology are depicted at the small **Alpowai Interpretive Center** (intermittent hours). Also here are campsites, a boat launch, playground, swimming beach, and summertime concession stand.

A more interesting destination is **Fields Spring State Park** (4.5 mi. past Anatone on Hwy. 129, 509/256-3332, www.parks .wa.gov). This 445-acre park centers on 4,500-foot **Puffer Butte,** where the ridge-top vistas stretch over three states, down the deep gorge of Grand Ronde Canyon, and across the Wallowa Mountains. Get to the top on a mile-long trail from the day-use parking lot, passing summertime fields of wildflowers, and forests of ponderosa pine and other evergreens. Campsites are available, and winter visitors will enjoy the miles of cross-country ski trails and a lighted sledding hill.

Water Sports

Several local parks offer Snake River swimming, and the Clearwater River—just over the Idaho border—is a popular summertime inner-tubing spot. Nearby reservoirs offer a variety of boating opportunities, including windsurfing. The Snake River is famous for its rainbow trout, bass, steelhead, salmon, and monster sturgeon.

ENTERTAINMENT AND EVENTS
The Arts
The best place for live music (rock and pop

tunes) is **Boomer's** (301 2nd St. in Lewiston, 509/746-2005).

Valley Art Center (842 6th St., 509/758-8331) features rotating exhibits and sales and also offers workshops and classes in all media.

Festivals and Events
The **Asotin County Fair,** held the last weekend in April, features a rodeo, parade, and stock show and sale. Also in late April, Lewiston's **Dogwood Festival** celebrates spring's flowering dogwoods with a major regatta, an all-breed dog show, a quilters exhibition, art, music, and jugglers. **Lewis and Clark Days** is a celebration of history and adventure, including canoe carving, held in Clarkston in mid-October.

ACCOMMODATIONS
Clarkston offers a handful of budget motels. The **Motel 6** (222 Bridge St., 509/758-1631 or 800/466-8356, www.motel6.com, $46) is clean and uniformly decorated, with an outdoor pool. Pets are allowed by prior arrangement.

The **Best Western RiverTree Inn** (1257 Bridge St., 509/758-9551, www.bestwestern .com, $110 d) has clean, updated rooms with comfortable furnishings and wireless Internet. You'll also find amenities such as an outdoor pool and an indoor hot tub.

Camping
The closest public campground is across the bridge in Idaho and three miles south of Lewiston along the Snake River at **Hells Gate State Park** (www.idahoparks.org/parks, 208/799-5015, $12–18).

Eight miles west of town on Highway 12, **Chief Timothy State Park** (eight mi. west of Clarkston on U.S. 12, 509/758-9580 or 888/226-7688, www.parks.wa.gov, $21 tents, $31 full hookups, $7 extra reservation fee) also has campsites with coin-operated showers. Open March–early December. **Fields Spring State Park** (30 mi. south of Clarkston on Hwy. 129, 509/256-3332, $12 primitive, $17 standard tenting) has campsites with showers and is open all year. No reservations. Because it is at 4,000 feet in elevation, Fields Spring offers a cool break on hot summer days.

RV campers will probably be happiest at **Granite Lake RV Resort** (306 Granite Lake Dr., 509/751-1635 or 800/989-4578, $29–42), a grassy lakeside resort that offers fancy touches such as paved sites, satellite TV, wireless Internet, and complimentary continental breakfast and newspapers served to your door each morning. The pet-friendly property also has laundry facilities and showers. In addition to the lake, there is also an adjacent 18-hole putting golf course and a 16-mile walking path along the Snake River.

FOOD

Sit down for a coffee and big breakfast with the Clarkston locals at **Come Inn Café** (508 Diagonal St., 509/758-2884).

Fazzari's (1281 Bridge St., 509/758-3386, 4–10 P.M. Mon.–Fri., 11 A.M.–10 P.M. Sat.–Sun.) features very good pizza, spaghetti, and sandwiches. **Rooster's Landing** (1550 Port Dr., 509/751-0155, Sun.–Thurs. 11 A.M.–9 P.M., Fri.–Sat. 11 A.M.–10 P.M.) seems almost too big for Clarkston and has a big patio right on the river, a menu of steaks, seafood, burgers, and a fun atmosphere.

INFORMATION

For maps or other information, contact the **Clarkston Chamber of Commerce** (502 Bridge St., 509/758-7712 or 800/933-2128, www .clarkstonchamber.org, Mon.–Fri. 9 A.M.–5 P.M.) or the **Lewiston Chamber of Commerce** (111 Main St., 208/743-3531 or 800/473-3543, www .lewistonchamber.com). Although Clarkston and Lewiston have different area codes, it's a local call from Clarkston to Lewiston, and you don't need to dial the area code for these calls.

GETTING THERE

Alaska Airlines (800/547-9308, www.alaska air.com) has service from Lewiston Airport to Seattle, Spokane, Boise, and Portland. **Skywest Airlines** (800/221-1212, www .delta.com) also serves this area. **Northwestern Trailways** (509/624-9863 or 800/366-3830, www.nwadv.com/northw) has bus connections north to Pullman and Spokane and south to Boise, Idaho, from the bus stop at Don's Chevron in Lewiston.

Snake River and Blue Mountains Country

As you drive Highway 12 from Clarkston to Walla Walla, the country offers up a hilly palette of grassland, sage, and strip-cropped wheat fields. Harvesting these rolling fields requires special self-leveling combines. The wide, easy highway sails over Alpowa Summit and then drops slowly down to the town of Pomeroy on the western side. The Selkirk Mountains of Washington and Idaho are visible to the northeast, and the Blue Mountains of Washington and Oregon occupy the southern horizon.

WENAHA-TUCANNON WILDERNESS

This 177,000-acre wilderness straddles the Washington/Oregon border within Umatilla National Forest. The rugged terrain consists of deep canyons, narrow basaltic ridges, and mountains covered with lodgepole pine and other conifers. Some 200 miles of maintained trails cross the wilderness, with access from all sides, but the area is primarily used by elk hunters.

Hiking

The fun-sounding **Mount Misery Trail** (No. 3113) starts from the end of Diamond Peak Road (42 miles south of Pomeroy) off Forest Service Road 40, at an elevation of 5,900 feet. This 16-mile-long trail follows Horse Ridge for several miles, providing dramatic vistas into the wilderness and good camping spots with nearby springs. A number of loop trips of varying lengths are possible from this trail, or you can simply hike out as far as you want and return back down this relatively easy route. Snow is likely to cover the trails until mid-June.

A popular lower-elevation path is the five-mile-long **Panjab Trail** (No. 3127) that begins at the end of Forest Service Road 4713, approximately 60 miles south of Dayton. Starting at 2,900 feet in elevation, this path climbs 5.6 miles to the Indian Corral area at an elevation of 5,600 feet. It ends on a ridge top offering breathtaking vistas, and from here you can continue deeper into the wilderness on several other trails. Because of the lower elevation, this trail is accessible earlier in the summer.

A lovely day hike begins from the Teepee Campground, 32 miles south of Dayton at the end of Forest Service Road 4608. The **Oregon Butte Trail** (No. 3134) climbs for three miles into the wilderness—gaining 900 feet as you go—and ends at an old fire lookout. There's a good campsite on the ridge and a cold spring down the hill a short distance.

LOWER SNAKE RIVER AREA
Reservoir Recreation

The once-mighty Snake River through southeastern Washington is now just a series of placid reservoirs behind massive dams built in the 1960s and '70s. The lakes are popular with boaters, and locks make it possible for barge traffic to travel from the mouth of the Columbia all the way to Clarkston. Farthest east of these in Washington is Lower Granite Dam, which creates Lower Granite Lake. Downstream from here, Lake Bryan, Lake Herbert G. West, and Lake Sacajawea provide additional recreation opportunities.

A number of parks and boat launches provide year-round recreation on these reservoirs. **Wawawai County Park** (509/397-6238 or www.whitmancounty.org) has camping ($10), picnic areas, a playground, rock climbing, and hiking trails. Get here by heading north from Clarkston on Highway 195 to tiny Colton, and turning left on Wawawai Road. Follow the road approximately 15 miles to the park. The last stretch is called Wawawai Grade Road. Just south of the park, **Wawawai Landing** has a launch ramp and dock on Lower Granite Lake.

Lower Granite Dam and reservoir are accessible by driving 25 miles north from Pomeroy. The dam has a visitors center and a fish ladder with underwater windows. The locks are a good place to watch barges loaded with wheat heading downriver for Portland.

Just west of this dam on Lake Bryan is **Boyer Park and Marina** (509/397-3208, www.portwhitman.com) with launch ramps, moorage, docks, swimming beach and bathhouse, picnic area, and camping.

Central Ferry State Park (Hwy. 127 about 12 mi. north of Dodge, 509/549-3551 or 888/226-7688, www.parks.wa.gov, $12 primitive, $23 full hookups, $7 extra reservation fee) features a swimming area with lifeguards, boat launches and docks, bass and catfish fishing, a picnic area, snack bar, camping, and showers. The park is open mid-March–mid-November.

The **Lower Monumental Dam,** about six miles from Kahlotus on Devils Canyon Road, has a visitors center, fish ladder, picnic area, and boat dock. **Windust Park,** three miles downstream of the dam on the north shore, has free primitive campsites (open all year), swimming, a picnic area, and boat launch facilities.

Little Goose Dam, the creator of Lake Bryan, is about a mile west of Starbuck on Highway 261. Facilities here include a boat dock, fish-viewing area, and visitors center.

Lyons Ferry State Park

Located in remote and desolate country at the confluence of the Snake and Palouse Rivers, this popular park (509/646-3252, www.parks.wa.gov) has fishing, swimming, and boating. It's eight miles northwest of Starbuck on Highway 261. The campground has out-in-the-sun primitive ($8) and standard ($13) sites; open April–mid-November.

In 1968, Washington State University researchers discovered human bones shown to be at least 10,000 years old, making this one of the earliest known human occupation sites in North America. Unfortunately, the Lower Monumental Dam inundated this site, but the graves were moved to a nearby hill. A 0.75-

mile trail leads from the campground to the new gravesite.

The Army Corps of Engineers has free dispersed camping along the reservoir, approximately two miles north of Starbuck. Near the state park is **Lyons Ferry Hatchery** (509/549-3551), where self-guided tours are available. **Lyons Ferry Marina** (509/399-2001) has additional campsites, a launch ramp for the Snake River, and a small store.

Palouse Falls State Park

About six miles north of Lyons Ferry and another two miles in along a gravel road is Palouse Falls (www.parks.wa.gov), one of the most incredible waterfalls in Washington. It's particularly impressive in the spring when the flow reaches its peak. Acrophobics should stay away from the cliff-top overlook that affords views of the pool far below.

The state park has picnic tables and on-the-lawn campsites ($8; open mid-March–early October). Primitive, unmaintained trails lead to the top of the falls and down into the gorge

below. Watch your step if you take these steep and sometimes dangerous paths.

DAYTON

Home to some 2,500 people, the small farming town of Dayton is full of landmark buildings all set against the great view of the Blue Mountain range Lewis and Clark passed through in this land in 1806, by which time the Cayuse Indians had long established a dirt racetrack for their war horses, a track which has since become Dayton's Main Street. The town also lives in the shadow of the ruin of a Green Giant plant, once the source of a third of the world's canned asparagus. The company packed off for Peru in 2005.

Sights
DEPOT MUSEUM
Built in 1881, Dayton's Stick-Eastlake train depot is now the town museum (222 E. Commercial St., 509/382-2026, www.daytonhistoricdepot .org, Nov.–Apr. Wed.–Sat. 11 A.M.–4 P.M., May–Oct. Wed.–Sat. 10 A.M.–noon and

© LIJUAN GUO/123RF.COM

Palouse Falls State Park

EASTERN WASHINGTON

1–5 P.M., Sun. 1–4 P.M., $5 adults, free 12 and under). The museum contains the original depot furnishings and woodstove downstairs, and various exhibits describing the town's history.

HISTORIC BUILDINGS

Dayton's impressive **Columbia County Courthouse** was built in 1887, making it the oldest continually functioning courthouse in the state of Washington. The stout Italianate-style courthouse is one of more than 80 local buildings listed on the National Register of Historic Places. Pick up a walking tour brochure of the others from the Depot Museum.

The **Boldman House Museum** (410 N. First St., 509/382-2026, 1–4 P.M. Fri. and Sat.) is a Queen Anne home decked out exclusively with furnishings used on-site by the Boldman family. Pretty gardens surround the building.

LEWIS AND CLARK TRAIL STATE PARK

Five miles west of Dayton, Lewis and Clark Trail State Park (36149 Hwy. 12, 509/337-6457, www.parks.wa.gov) was a stopping point for Lewis and Clark's Corps of Discovery in 1806. The park's tall old-growth trees and the cooling fish-filled waters of the Touchet River are a welcome break from the sizzling summer heat of the encircling wheat fields. There is a mile-long nature trail to help you appreciate the park.

Festivals and Events

Little Dayton is a town that lives for off-beat and one-of-a-kind events. Celebrate long-eared stubbornness at **Mule Mania** (Columbia County Fairgrounds on N. Pine and Commercial St., 800/862-6299, http://mulemaniadayton.com). There are mules galore as well as a chuck wagon cook-off, a Western collectables show, and the signature Fat Ass Express Relay Race. **Dayton Days** (509/382-4825, www.historicdayton.com) on Memorial Day weekend, includes three days of pari-mutuel horse racing, a rodeo, parade, arts and crafts displays, and food. Fathers Day weekend's **All Wheels Weekend** (800/882-6299, www.allwheelsweekend.com) celebrates everything dadlike: car shows, demolition derbies, and the

liberating feel of a nice satin dress. It seems at some point, there was some confusion about the nature of "drag races." Local men actually do pretty themselves up for a tricycle duel, followed by a hirsute "beauty contest."

Sports and Recreation

The town has an Olympic-size outdoor **swimming pool** open summers in the city park, as well as a nine-hole **golf course.**

Ski Bluewood (262 E. Main St., 509/382-4725, www.bluewood.com, $42 adult, $38 kids, $33 seniors), 22 miles southeast of Dayton and 52 miles from Walla Walla, offers downhill skiing on 1,125 vertical feet in the Umatilla National Forest. Because Bluewood is over 300 miles from the coast, conditions here are generally drier than on most Washington slopes. Slopes cover a spectrum from beginner through expert terrain.

Accommodations

There are a surprising number of lodging choices in Dayton. Least expensive is **Blue Mountain Motel** (414 W. Main St., 509/382-3040, www.bluemountainmotel.net, $44–99 d), popular for its country-style rooms. The pet-friendly property offers free wireless Internet, and guests can munch on complimentary cookies in the lobby throughout the day. The **Weinhard Hotel** (235 E. Main St., 509/382-4032, www.weinhard.com, $155–210 d) offers upscale Victorian accommodations. Beautifully restored and furnished with antiques, the hotel drips with elegance.

(The Purple House B&B (415 E. Clay St., 509/382-3159 or 800/486-2574, www.purplehousebnb.com, $95–135 d) is in a white-trimmed, lavender Queen Anne home. It has four guest rooms with private or shared baths, plus a separate carriage house. Lounge by the outdoor pool in the summer or curl up with a book in the library. Guests with disabilities will be happy to note that the home has wheelchair access.

CAMPING

The closest public campsites are in **Lewis**

and Clark Trail State Park (36149 Hwy. 12, 509/337-6457, www.parks.wa.gov, $21–31, no hookups). A campground here has space for tents and vehicles and is open early May–mid-September. In the off-season you can camp in the day-use area. Coin-operated showers are available as is an RV dump station.

The Umatilla National Forest's **Godman Campground** (25 miles southeast of Dayton on Forest Service Road 26) offers high-country camping up at an elevation of 6,050 feet. This free site has no running water and remains open until closed by snow. At the campground is a trailhead for the West Butte Creek Trail into Wenaha-Tucannon Wilderness Area.

Food

Dayton's claim to fame is **(Patit Creek Restaurant** (725 E. Main St., 509/382-2625, Wed.–Thurs. 11:30 A.M.–1 P.M. and 4:30–6:30 P.M., Fri. 11:30 A.M.–1 P.M. and 4:30–7:30 P.M., Sat. 4:30–7:30 P.M., closed Sun.–Tues.), the only four-star French restaurant east of the Cascades. The decor is simple, but the changing menu features regional dishes made from fresh local ingredients. Reservations are strongly advised.

Information

The **Dayton Chamber of Commerce** (166 E. Main St., 509/382-4825 or 800/882-6299, www.historicdayton.com) offers local information.

EASTERN WASHINGTON

BACKGROUND

Washington is whatever you want it to be. Here, you can snuggle up in a coffee shop, sip the country's top espresso, and listen to jazz in Seattle, or you can roll out a sleeping bag on the side of snowy Mount Baker and see no one for days. Go skiing if that's your thing, or bounce over sand dunes in the desert if you'd rather. You can gape at an enormous snow-capped volcano at Mount Rainier or look down hundreds of feet into the Columbia Gorge. The state offers the top salmon, best apples, and top-quality wines when compared with anywhere else. It's a state with so many extremes, so many different ways to travel, and sights that range from ancient trees and 19th-century mines to the enormous Boeing aircraft factory. You choose what you want Washington to be. It's all here for you.

Like most of the country, Washington is a place in transition. Much of what helped to build this community—logging, mining, fishing—have dried up and blown away. Many of the towns left in industry's wake have tried to turn to tourism for support, but in tough times, fewer people are willing to travel to remote places in the heart of the state. While major cities are bound to land on their feet, some smaller communities in eastern and central Washington are becoming virtual ghost towns, just like the 19th-century mining ghost towns that molder not far away from them. Still, Seattle remains hugely popular among Asian tourists, especially from Japan, many of whom have an appreciation for much of what makes western Washington work—high technology and fresh fish.

© ERICKA CHICKOWSKI

The Land

GEOGRAPHY AND CLIMATE
A State Divided

Of course, when most people think of Washington State, they imagine Seattle with its nearly relentless gray skies and drizzle. Or maybe they think of deep, primitive rain forests cut only by racing rivers or snowcapped mountains. And that, certainly, is a big part of the story. But the Cascade Mountain range that runs from British Columbia south past the Oregon border has a special effect on the other two-thirds of the state. Easterly winds blow dark clouds full of rain across Western Washington, leaving a doused green landscape in their path. But as they hit the Cascades, the mountains slow those clouds down until they've dumped their moisture in the surrounding forests. Only then can they pass. What you're left with is a dry desert-like terrain, wheat-covered plains, and gorges of several hundred feet cut by snaky rivers over millions of years. Washington may be the "Evergreen State," but the motto does a great disservice to the beautiful, less populated side of the state.

The Olympic Mountain range is another state feature that too often gets short shrift. Washington's Mount Rainier—said to be the most recognizable mountain in America—makes every other range seem neglected by contrast. The spectacular Olympic range—a wall of granite, snowcapped for most of the year—is the centerpiece of one of the wildest parts of the state. These mountains, too, wrestle with the wet winds coming off the Pacific, protecting the nearby San Juan Islands, Port Angeles, and Whidbey Island from too much rainfall. Meanwhile, Olympic National Park and surrounding areas can take as much as a truly unbelievable 150 inches of rain per year. The upside is that all that rain creates something wonderful. The primordial rain forests that grow here are something out of high fantasy. The emerald mosses and red cedars, the peaceful rivers with wide freestone banks, the soft loamy trails are dreamlike, especially if you're out early enough to spot a Roosevelt elk in the mist—a species that lives only here.

Western Washington

Some might tell you that Seattle is not quite what you've heard. That the rainfall, really, is no more than Chicago or New York. And while Seattle's paltry 37 inches of annual rainfall is comparable to other cities, it's not "how much" but rather "how often" that sets the city apart. With a whopping 200-plus cloudy days per year, few cities outside of dreary Alaska can come close to matching the weather here. Thunderstorms are rare; tornados nearly nonexistent. Western Washington's winter temperatures remain mild, dropping below freezing only rarely. Flatland snowfall is very rare, and anything that sticks means a day off of school. It's a sensible policy, since some downtown Seattle roads have a dizzying 22-degree grade that is not very fun to drive when dry, let alone when covered with ice or snow. The western Cascades and Mount Rainier usually get several feet of snow over most of the year, so head south or east for the white stuff.

IT'S WHAT TIME, NOW?

If you've never lived in or visited the northern latitudes, you could be in for a surprise. Around the time of the summer solstice – around the end of June – days get long. Really long. Most of the state sees the sun come up just after 5 A.M. and not set until after 9 P.M.! The northern border of the state has an even more exaggerated schedule. That's a lot of time for recreation. But come wintertime, prepare yourself for a punishingly short eight-hour day, most of which is probably cloudy anyway.

LIGHTS, CAMERA, ACTION

Washington makes a great background for movies and TV programs, and quite a few of both have filmed here. The most popular show filmed in Washington was *Northern Exposure*, a lighthearted fish-out-of-water story that followed a New York doctor's move to harsh, slow-paced Alaska. The show was filmed in the lovely little town of Roslyn, and fans of the show can still find many familiar sights there. Fans of the films *Sleepless in Seattle* and *Singles* will also recognize plenty of scenery from these love stories as they explore the Seattle area.

It's not all young love and cuteness, though. David Lynch's mind-twisting murder mystery series *Twin Peaks* also affords Washington a star-turn, with Snoqualmie and North Bend especially prominent and including an unforgettable shot of Snoqualmie Falls and the Salish Lodge. The 1999 film adaptation of local author David Gunderson's *Snow Falling on Cedars* uses the Puget Sound islands on which it was based as backdrop, and Stephen King's 2002 miniseries *Rose Red* uses Thornwood Castle in Steilacoom as its setting. Notching up the creepiness factor just a bit more, blockbuster show *The X Files* frequently did shoots in northern Washington, and who could forget the bleak and drizzly Seattle of the 2002 U.S. version of Japanese horror flick *The Ring*?

Other western Washington backdrops include a role for Port Angeles in *The Hunt for Red October*, extensive shooting in Forks for the *Twilight* series of movies, and even more for *An Officer and a Gentleman* in Port Townsend, Fort Worden, and Bremerton.

In the central and eastern portions of the state, things take a turn for the bleak. The hunting scenes in 1978's *The Deer Hunter* were shot not in Pennsylvania, but at Nooksack Falls near Glacier, Washington. And if you saw Kevin Costner's apocalyptic epic *The Postman*, you'll recognize Boundary Dam in Metaline Falls as the site of Bridge City. Probably, you'll just have to take my word on that last one.

If pressed to guess the weather outside in Seattle, just say "55 degrees and cloudy" and you've got an excellent chance of being right. Come July, though, when skies clear and temperatures climb, locals develop seasonal amnesia, wondering why the whole world doesn't move to this paradise. Temperatures usually run from the upper 70s through the upper 80s July–September. Locals begin to complain bitterly when the mercury reaches 82 or so. Best to just smile and zip up your jacket when asked if it's hot enough for ya.

Eastern Washington

The vast expanses of Eastern Washington share a climate with Idaho and Montana, although they are bit more mild in the winter. Temperatures here often break the 100° F mark in summer and can drop below 20°. The burnt-yellow grasses testify to the fact that Eastern Washington gets, on average, 7–15 inches of rainfall annually. The area is the northern end of the Great American Desert, although huge lakes behind dams on the Snake and Columbia Rivers and the irrigation they provide might well trick you into not believing it. The waving strands of wheat give you an inkling of the fact that these are some of the most productive farms in the country. Hot weather and dry vegetation can lead to summer wildfires that spread as fast as the wind will take them.

Toward the eastern fringes of the state, the flat landscape starts to get cooler and geographically choppier. The northeast and southeast corners of the state draw five times the amount of rainfall as most of the rest of the eastern portion, but like the rest of the region, they get 10–35 inches of wintertime snow.

Flora and Fauna

Washington has a widely varied assortment of flora and fauna that reflects its richly diverse climate and geography. The Pacific Ocean and Puget Sound, the Olympic rain forest, the mountainous regions of the Cascades and Olympics, and the arid land of Eastern Washington each support a unique population of birds, animals, and plants.

THE FORESTS

Washington's state tree, the western hemlock, is widely used in the forest industry as a pulpwood species, and it and Douglas fir are two of the most abundant low-elevation trees in the state. Above 3,000 feet in elevation, Pacific silver fir and mountain hemlock take over. Bigleaf maples are distinguished by—you got it—their enormous leaves, up to a foot across. The Pacific madrona is found along the coast and characterized by waxy, evergreen leaves and peeling reddish bark that exposes a smooth under-skin. Other common trees are the western red cedar, Sitka spruce, grand fir, black cottonwood, red alder, and vine maple. Northeast Washington and parts of the Cascades have other species, including lodgepole pine, western larch, western white pine, ponderosa pine, and Engelmann spruce.

Olympic Rain Forest

At Olympic National Park, the Hoh, Queets, and Quinault River Valleys constitute the better part of the Olympic Rain Forest, an area unlike any other in the world. The largest known western hemlock and Sitka spruce grow in the Quinault Valley, the largest Douglas fir is in Queets, and the largest red alder is in the Hoh Rain Forest. The four major species here—the Sitka spruce, western red cedar, Douglas fir, and western hemlock—all grow very tall: trees average 200 feet, with many topping 300 feet.

The height of the trees isn't the only fascinating aspect of the rain forest. The area is strikingly green and seems untouched.

Chainsaws and axes never disturbed this forest, leaving a landscape that is really and truly prehistoric. Soft and dripping ferns and mosses cover rocks, logs, and anything that doesn't move out of their way. Table-sized shelf-lichens jut from the trunks of trees as if installed by human hands. Even when the rain isn't falling, ocean fog and residual humidity will still keep that sense of uncanny damp. Someone so disposed could spend a lifetime enjoying the plants and animals that call this special place home.

Old-Growth Forests

Old-growth forests are at least 250 years old, although there are trees here that could date back to the medieval period of Europe. Because these massive trees moderate temperatures and hold much of the snow, original forests keep their environment a little more stable, which adds to the comfort level and sustainability of wildlife populations. The trees, bushes, and herbs that grow in this sheltered place can help as well. Standing dead trees—called snags—provide nesting sites for birds, flying squirrels, and other animals, while the fallen trees create nutrient-rich mulch as they decay. In many old-growth forests, these fallen giants become "nursery logs," with new trees sprouting in a straight line along the trunk.

FLOWERS

Washington's state flower—the coast rhododendron—is found from British Columbia south to northern California and east to the foothills of the Cascades. About 500 natural species grow here, along with several hundred more greenhouse varieties, not to mention countless hybrids.

Rhodies are standard fare in Western Washington gardens, relatively easy to grow, and beautiful to behold, in colors from yellows to pinks to bright reds and whites. The best-known rhododendron gardens are on Whidbey Island, Bainbridge Island, and in the towns of

© ERICKA CHICKOWSKI

alpine wildflowers in summer

Federal Way and Brinnon. Visit in spring and early summer to enjoy them at their peak.

MARINELIFE
Killer Whales (Orcas)

The orca, or killer whale, is the largest member of the family Delphinidae, a classification that includes toothed whales and dolphins. Named "killer whales" because they take warm-blooded prey, these opportunistic cetaceans eat anything from seals to birds, otters, dolphins, fish, and squid, depending on the local food supply. In Puget Sound, they generally eat salmon, rockfish, and cod.

Orcas are highly social, traveling in packs or "pods" of up to 40 individual whales. Families stay together, protecting the young and mourning their dead. There are three resident pods in Puget Sound and along the Washington coast, with a total of about 75 members. Transient pods occasionally swim into the area but don't usually stay long. The most frequent sightings are around the San Juan Islands, especially at Lime Kiln State Park on the west side

of San Juan Island. Get the latest at the San Juan Island–based **Whale Museum** website (www.whale-museum.org).

Gray Whales

Every spring, tour boats leave the docks at Westport and a few other coastal towns for a close-up look at the migrating California gray whales. These enormous whales—up to 42 feet in length and upward of 30 tons—migrate from the Bering and Chukchi seas to the warm breeding lagoons off Baja California in winter, passing the Washington coast southbound in November and December and northbound from April–June. Occasionally a group of gray whales will come into Puget Sound, seemingly by accident. Most, however, follow the outer coastline. In 1998, the coastal Makah Tribe was restored the right to harvest whales given them in the 1855 Treaty of Neah Bay. While they hunted for two years, dogged by protestors at every step, the right was again suspended and has lingered in bureaucratic and legal purgatory for years.

Gray whales are easily identified by their gray color, the absence of a dorsal fin, and bumpy ridges on their backs; their faces are generally covered with patches of barnacles and orange whale lice. Unconcerned with their appearance, gray whales often lift their faces out of the water up to about eye level in a motion referred to as spyhopping.

Porpoises

Commonly seen in the Strait of Juan de Fuca alongside the ferry *Coho* from Port Angeles to Victoria, B.C., **Dall's porpoises** frequently travel south through the Admiralty Inlet and, on rare occasions, as far south as Tacoma. Dall's porpoises reach lengths of 6.5 feet and can weigh up to 330 pounds; they feed primarily on squid and small fish.

In summer and early fall, schools of up to 100 **Pacific white-sided dolphins** enter the Strait of Juan de Fuca, traveling as far inshore as Port Angeles but rarely any farther east. Reaching up to seven feet in length and 200 pounds, they have black backs, white shoulders and bellies, and hourglass-shaped streaks that run from their foreheads to their tails. Like the Dall's porpoise, white-sided dolphins enjoy riding bow waves and often leap full-length out of the water alongside a boat.

Seals and Sea Lions

Harbor seals are numerous throughout Puget

SALMON

Few things represent the Northwest as recognizably as the noble salmon. For thousands of years, coastal Native Americans such as the Salish people have relied heavily on these fish for their livelihood. The fact that salmon are born in rivers, spend much of their lives in saltwater, then return to rivers to spawn in a regular rhythm make them the perfect focus of seasonal Native rituals and ceremonies. Traveling through Washington, you're bound to spot many representations of these hook-billed fish in Native paintings, art, and totem poles.

When white settlers arrived, salmon made up a large part of their diet and economy, as well. Over fishing, pollution, and damming rivers that were critical to salmon reproduction caused a huge drop in their population. The drop has completely destroyed the traditional way of life for many Native American tribes throughout the state. The problem hardly stops with humans. Bears, eagles, orcas, harbor seals, and porpoises absolutely rely on salmon for their survival.

Thankfully, government agencies, environmental groups, sport fishermen, power companies, and tribal governments have come together to help fix the problem. Strict pollution standards have been put in place, dams have been breached along spawning routes, huge fish hatcheries release millions of fry every year, and dams have been equipped with fish ladders that help them get over the towering dams. Things are looking up for the salmon, but there's still a long way to go.

SALMON SPECIES IN WASHINGTON

• Chinook – also called king salmon, this largest of the local salmon can reach 130 pounds.

• Chum – an endangered species, these salmon have the least commercial value. They are named after a Chinook Indian word meaning "spotted."

• Coho – the ultimate game fish and the best salmon for eating. Most fish markets offer orange-colored coho meat, either wild-caught or farmed.

• Pink – usually canned or smoked, these pink-meat salmon have an unusual hump on their backs.

• Sockeye – these salmon are silver while living in the ocean, but turn a bright red as they head back upriver to spawn. Some spawn in lakes and are called kokanee salmon.

SLUGS

If members of the Washington government were asked to pick an official invertebrate, it would certainly end up being the common slug. Looking like little green or brown squirts of slime with eye stalks, slugs populate Western Washington pretty much year-long. The cool, damp climate is slug Shangri-la, and the slippery fellows can be found in the deep woods as easily as on your front doorknob. Slugs can curl up into a ball to protect themselves, or flatten and elongate themselves to squeeze into tight places, although not squishing them on the trail takes vigilance. Known as pseudopods, or false-footed creatures, they glide along on sticky mucus that leaves trails wherever they go. The pride of native slugs, the **banana slug,** is quite a little beast, looking light green or yellowish with dark spots and growing up to six inches long. It now competes for room with the transplant **black slug,** which is more common on neighborhood sidewalks these days.

Slugs are known for munching up garden plants, although some are actually predators, feeding off of insects or earthworms. Slugs are persistent pests. They can be killed by sprinkling a bit of table salt on them. A small dish of beer put out in the garden helps, too – they're attracted to the stuff not knowing that it will desiccate them to death. Budweiser should do fine, except in Redmond, Bellevue, and Woodinville, where they will turn their slimy noses up at all but quality microbrew.

© ERICKA CHICKOWSKI

Washington's favorite gastropod, the banana slug

Sound and the Strait of Juan de Fuca. They can be seen at low tide sunning themselves on rocks. Though they appear clumsy on land, these 100- to 200-pound seals are poetry in motion underwater and can stay underwater for as long as 20 minutes.

The **California sea lion** is a seasonal visitor to the Strait of Juan de Fuca and northern Puget Sound, though on some mornings in winter and early spring their barking can be heard in shoreline communities as far south as Tacoma. A large group of them collects just offshore from Everett, where a commercial tour boat takes visitors out for a closer look.

The lighter-colored **Steller sea lions** are more numerous in the Puget Sound area, numbering up to several hundred in winter, primarily around Sucia Island in the northern sound. The males of the species are much larger than the females, growing to almost 10 feet in length and weighing over a ton, while the females are a dainty six feet long and 600 pounds. They are almost white when wet, but the male has a yellow mane.

Other Marine Creatures

Puget Sound is home to the largest species of **octopus** in the world. Though it grows to 12 feet across the arms and weighs 25–30 or more pounds, it's not dangerous, and in fact, often plays with divers.

Another peculiar Puget Sound inhabitant is the **geoduck** (pronounced GOOEY-duck, from the Lushootseed *gweduck,* meaning "dig deep"). These large clams can burrow as deep as five feet and weigh in at four or five pounds, with reports of some clams exceeding 15 pounds. The fleshy part of the body is so large that neither the entire body nor the siphon can be completely withdrawn into the shell. Geoducks are generally cut up and used in chowder, but some quality restaurants serve them as regular menu items or specials.

The **horse clam** is the second-largest Pacific Northwest clam, weighing up to five pounds. Horse clams only dig about two feet deep, so they're much easier to gather and can be found in Cultus and Useless Bays at the south end of Whidbey Island. Both geoducks and horse clams prefer sandy or sand-gravel beaches.

Combing the shoreline for wild clams is a popular activity in Western Washington. Seasons and regulations can be complex, and periodic algae blooms make the clams dangerous to eat. Call the **Washington Department of Fish and Wildlife** (360/902-2500 or 866/880-5431) before gunning for shellfish.

LAND ANIMALS

Washington has one of the most diverse wildlife profiles in the country, owing to careful management by the state and federal governments. Sensible hunting laws and abundant wild areas maintain the much-cherished diversity of animal life in the state.

Mule deer, the rare Columbian white-tailed deer, black bears, cougars, marmots, beavers, rabbits, and squirrels are fairly common in Washington, and with directed effort, you should be able to spot any one of them. More reclusive are Rocky Mountain and Roosevelt elk, bighorn sheep, mountain goats, badgers, muskrats, nutria, woodland caribou, and wolves can be found usually only by naturalists or the very lucky. The North Cascades is home to about 30 grizzly bears, which you should rather hope you don't see.

Columbian White-Tailed Deer

Lewis and Clark wrote about this particular type of deer, which are smaller and have a slightly longer tail than mule and whitetail deer. The little fellow is on the endangered species list, although populations are increasing. Find them at the **Julia Butler Hansen National Wildlife Refuge** (just west of Cathlamet on Hwy. 4, 360/795-3915, www.r1.fws.gov).

Roosevelt Elk

The Roosevelt elk live only on the Olympic Peninsula, mostly inside the boundaries of Olympic National Park, which was formed, in part, to protect them. Roosevelt elk are named for president and conservationist Theodore Roosevelt, who was instrumental in their preservation.

Cougars

Call them cougars, panthers, catamounts, mountain lions, or pumas, but any way you call them, they mean trouble. They are smooth, silent-moving, high-jumping predators who call even fairly urban forests home. They will stalk for an hour or more if necessary, hiding behind trees and boulders. These buff-colored cats weigh around 115 pounds and can sprint at 40 mph. Cougars prefer elk and deer or rabbits and marmots, but they are opportunistic hunters. They are shy and will generally escape long before a human approaches, but attacks and even fatalities are not unheard of. In cougar country, it's best not to hike alone, and those with pets or small children should be especially vigilant.

Attitudes toward these big cats have changed dramatically over the years. Cougar populations are increasing in Washington at the same time as human developments push homes and people onto land that was previously wild. This combination has led to an increase in cougar attacks throughout the West; of 14 fatal cougar attacks in the last century, four took place in the last decade. None of the fatalities occurred in Washington, but brazen attacks have taken place in recent years, particularly on small children. If you come face to face with a mountain lion, maintain eye contact while backing slowly away. Try to appear larger than you are by raising your arms or by spreading a jacket or shirt. If you have children with you, pick them up. Talk loudly. But never, never run. Wildlife officials say compressed-air horns and pepper spray may ward off cougar attacks, and cougars are less likely to attack more than one person traveling together. The North Cascades National Park website (www.nps.gov/noca/naturescience/cougars.htm) has additional safety tips for travel in mountain lion country.

Bears

Black bears are fairly widespread in Washington, with large populations on the Olympic Peninsula and in the northeast corner of the state. All of the black bears on the Olympic Peninsula are black, but they may be black, brown, or honey-colored in other areas. They'll eat anything, from carpenter ants to berries to dead elk to salmon, plus anything you fail to protect at your campsite.

Grizzly bears are rare in Washington, but there are a couple dozen in the North Cascades and in the Selkirk Mountains. These 500-plus pound bears are relentless killers and have an endlessly cranky disposition. It can be very difficult for a nonexpert to identify a grizzly, as they might look more brown or black than expected. While they pose a threat in the Cascades, no clear grizzly deaths have been reported in Washington since the times of early settlers.

OUR MAJESTIC CAD

Which Northwest native did Ben Franklin refer to as one of "bad moral character [who] does not get his living honestly"? One that is "like those among men who live by sharping and robbing, he is generally poor and very lousy"? Of course, Franklin's "rank coward" is better known to us as the bald eagle.

Watching an eagle sit on a 12-foot nest, or hang in the sky forever without flapping a wing, or crashing purposely after a trout in a glacial lake makes one guess that Franklin was probably kidding. Seeing your first bald eagle in the wild is an experience you'll always remember. Seeing dozens lined up along the Skagit River each winter, waiting to snatch up some salmon, is an almost surreal experience.

Bald eagles can have up to a seven-foot wingspan and can weigh up to 20 pounds. They can hit up to 100 mph while diving for fish or four-footed prey. Their population is quite healthy in Washington at the moment. They can be found all across the state, although they prefer the tall trees and ocean view of the western reaches, especially the San Juan Islands.

BIRDS

The Washington state office of the **National Audubon Society** (360/786-8020, www.wa.audubon.org) has detailed information on birds and bird-watching in the state.

Eagles

Approximately 300 pairs of bald eagles make their year-round home in Washington, primarily west of the Cascades. In winter that number swells to over 1,600 birds, drawn to rivers throughout the state by the carcasses of spawned-out salmon. Several outfitters in the Skagit River area offer eagle-spotting boat trips in winter.

The adult bald eagle's distinctive white head

and tail make it easy to spot. Their large nests, sometimes measuring over 8 feet wide and 12 feet high, are often found in old-growth spruce and fir snags.

San Juan Islands hosts the largest bald eagle population in the state, where the birds enjoy the warm updrafts around Mount Constitution on Orcas Island and Mount Findlayson and Mount Dallas on San Juan Island, and along the Strait of Juan de Fuca. The annual salmon-spawn brings the birds to the inland Skagit, Sauk, Nooksack, and Stillaguamish Rivers.

Owls

Washington's most famous nighttime aerial hunter is the **northern spotted owl,** which nests in old-growth forests along the Pacific Coast. The snags and broken trees within provide ideal nesting spots and smaller, sheltered trees for young owls who can't yet fly properly and must use their feet to climb from tree to tree. These forests are full of spotted-owl food: flying squirrels, snowshoe hares, and wood rats. Spotted owls are big eaters and quite territorial; 2,200 acres of old-growth forest will support but a single pair of owls. Because suitable forest is being greatly reduced by logging, the spotted owls' numbers are diminishing—only an estimated 2,500 pairs remain in the Pacific Northwest's old-growth forests, though the population appears to have stabilized somewhat in recent years.

Other Birds

There are quite a few other interesting birds in Western Washington, including great blue herons, a frequent sight standing near lakes or winging along, long legs hanging. The belted kingfisher is a common year-round resident of Puget Sound and the Strait of Juan de Fuca. Red-tailed hawks are often perched along I-5 and other highways, waiting for a meal. Noisy Steller's jays, blue with a black head, are also called "robber jays" because they will quite literally steal food off of your plate at a picnic.

In the Cascades and east of the mountains, the beautiful mountain bluebird is sometimes spotted in snags in open areas, and the town of Bickleton in southern Washington is known as the "Bluebird Capital of the World" for the thousands of birdhouses built by local residents. East of the mountains, striking black-and-white long-tailed magpies are frequently seen flitting over the highway.

THE SPOTTED OWL VS. THE TIMBER INDUSTRY

The northern spotted owl is a Pacific Northwest forest dweller that lives only in tall, dense, old growth forests. More than a century of logging in Western Washington has taken a major toll on the habitat for these owls, and in the late 1980s and early 1990s, environmental groups successfully petitioned the U.S. Fish and Wildlife Service to list the owl as a threatened species. As a result, loggers are required to leave 40 percent of old-growth forest intact within 1.3 miles of any reported spotted owl activity or nesting. Since then, the region has lost thousands of jobs in the logging industry, although some studies suggest that other forces are at least partially to blame. Ironically, spotted owl populations have also continued to decline, perhaps because the barred owl, a fierce competitor, has begun invading the territory of the spotted owl. Loggers and their allies tend to regard the whole episode as part of a leftist agenda that puts the survival of a largely insignificant species over the economic livelihood of people. Environmentalists see the plight of the owl as a microcosm for the environment as a whole and a call to reform and conserve. The Forest Service is considering a program to destroy part of the barred owl population to ease pressure on the spotted owl. Despite the heated controversy that rages on below, the unassuming spotted owl seems pretty well personally disinterested in all of the fuss surrounding it.

History

PREHISTORY

Although Washington is one of the more recent additions to the United States, archaeological evidence suggests that the Pacific Northwest was one of the first populated areas in North America. In recent years, animal and human remains as much as 13,000 years old have been found across the state. The finds suggest that Washington has been occupied by man for longer than just about anywhere else in the country.

The Washington archeological community was astonished when, in 1970, a powerful sea tide uncovered a nearly complete Makah Indian village on the coast. Probably covered by a mudslide in the early 1700s, the find yielded tens of thousands of artifacts now on display on the Makah Reservation in Neah Bay.

One of the most fascinating discoveries occurred in 1977, when Emanuel Manis, retired on a farm outside of Sequim, was digging a pond on a back corner of his land and found two enormous tusks. A Washington State University archaeological team, led by zoologist Carl Gustafson, concluded that these were 12,000-year-old mastodon tusks. The group discovered other mastodon bones, including a rib that contained the bone point of some prehistoric weapon used to kill the animal. These bones are now on display at the Sequim-Dungeness Museum in Sequim.

Native Americans

It's thought that, in ancient times, the ancestors of modern-day Native Americans arrived on the continent, having moved east across a bridge of land that once spanned the Bering Strait. Washington then would have made an

WASHINGTON NATIVE AMERICAN TRIBES

• Cathlamet	• Hoh	• Palouse	• Snohomish
• Cathlapotle	• Humptulips	• Pshwanwapam	• Snoqualmie
• Cayuse	• Kalispel Klickitat	• Puyallup	• Spokan
• Chehalis	• Kwaiailk	• Queets	• Squaxon
• Chelan	• Kwalhioqua	• Quileute	• Suquamish
• Chilluckittequaw	• Lummi	• Quinault	• Swinomish
• Chimakum	• Makah	• Sahehwamish	• Taidnapam
• Chinook	• Methow	• Samish	• Twana
• Clackamas	• Mical	• Sanpoil	• Wallawalla
• Clallam	• Muckleshoot	• Satsop	• Wanapam
• Clalskanie	• Nez Perce	• Semiahmoo	• Watlala
• Columbia	• Nisqually	• Senijextee	• Wenatchee
• Colville	• Nooksack	• Sinkaietk	• Wishram
• Copalis	• Ntlakyapamuk	• Sinkakaius	• Yakama
• Cowlitz	• Okanagon	• Skagit	
• Duwamish	• Ozette	• Skilloot	

early stop after entering the Americas. They spread throughout Washington, adopting different lifestyles and establishing different identities as they did so. Western tribes utilized the ample hardwoods for canoes and shelter, and developed a diet of salmon, whales, and shellfish. Not strictly saltwater mariners, they also traveled up the Columbia well east of the Cascades.

Eastern tribes relied on the salmon that navigated the rivers to spawn, and also deer, elk, bear, and squirrel for their diet. They moved around quite a bit more than their western counterparts. In the 18th century, members of these tribes adapted to horseback riding, making hunting and fighting more effective.

The Europeans' arrival was met with reactions ranging from tolerant acceptance to swift murder. Relations between the races are still divided over the interpretation of 160-year old peace treaties, property, water, and especially fishing rights. Twenty-two reservations are scattered throughout Washington, although most Washington Native Americans live elsewhere.

A NEW WORLD

The first foreigners to land on Washington's shores were probably Chinese and Japanese fishermen who arrived weeks or months after they were blown off course. None of the Asian nations was interested in expanding across the Pacific in those days, and nobody particularly cared about the land to the east. Records, if any, were skimpy and ignored. That was definitely not the case in southern Europe.

Spanish Explorers

In 1592, exactly a century after Columbus made his landfall in the Caribbean, a Greek explorer using the Spanish name Juan de Fuca sailed along Washington's coast and claimed to have discovered the fabled "Northwest Passage," an inland waterway crossing North America from the Pacific to the Atlantic.

Spain, hoping to regain some of its diminishing power and wealth, sent an expedition in the 1700s to explore the Northwest Coast.

WHAT'S IN A NAME?

Many place names in Washington are based on American Indian words and can be difficult to pronounce for the uninitiated. Here are correct pronunciations of a few of the trickiest for travelers.

- Anacortes – anna-CORT-ess
- Bingen – BIN-jin
- Chehalis – chuh-HAY-less
- Cle Elum – clee-EL-uhm
- Chelan – SHELL-an
- Dosewallips – DOSE-wallops
- Duvall – DU-vall
- Enumclaw – EE-nuhm-claw
- Issaquah – IS-ah-qwah
- Hyak – HI-yak
- Methow – MET-how
- Mukilteo – muck-ill-TEE-oh
- Puyallup – pyoo-ALL-up
- Queets – kweets
- Sammamish – suh-MAM-ish
- Sequim – skwim
- Skagit – SKA-jiht
- Snoqualmie – snow-QUAL-mee
- Toutle – tootle
- Tyee – TIE-e
- Washougal – wah-SHOO-guhl
- Wenatchee – wuh-NACH-ee
- Yakima – YAK-i-maw

In 1774, Juan Perez explored as far north as the Queen Charlotte Islands off Vancouver Island, and was the first European to describe the Pacific Northwest coastline and Olympic Mountains, before he was forced to turn back by sickness and storms.

In 1775, a larger Spanish expedition set out, led by Bruno de Heceta and Juan Francisco de la Bodega y Quadra. Heceta went ashore at Point Grenville, just north of Moclips on the Washington coast, and claimed all of the Northwest for Spain. Farther south, Bodega y Quadra sent seven men ashore in a small metal craft for wood and water who were quickly killed in what became the first European encounter with coastal Native Americans. The two ships sailed away without further incident. Quadra named the island Isla de Dolores (Isle of Sorrows), today's Destruction Island.

Russian Voyages

Russian exploration of the Pacific Northwest began in the mid-1700s, when Vitus Bering led two expeditions to determine whether a land bridge connected Russia with North America. Bering sailed as far south as the Columbia River before turning back. The abundance of sea otters and beavers led Russian fur traders to establish posts from Alaska to northern California, which posed a serious threat to other nations hoping to stake a claim.

Early English and American Exploration

England was the force to be reckoned with in the battle for the Northwest. In 1787, Charles Barkley and his wife, Frances, explored and named the Strait of Juan de Fuca. In 1788, John Meares named Mount Olympus and other features of the Olympic Peninsula.

An American, Robert Gray, sailed out of Boston to explore and trade along the Northwest Coast in 1792. Stopping first at Nootka Sound—the hot spot to trade on Vancouver Island—Gray worked his way south and spent three days anchored in today's Grays Harbor. Continuing south, Gray discovered the mouth of the Columbia River and traded there with the Chinook people before heading home.

Best known today, however, is the expedition led by George Vancouver in 1792. His goal was to explore the inland waters and make one last attempt at finding the Northwest Passage. The names of Vancouver's lieutenants and crew are a list of Washington place-names: Baker, Rainier, Whidbey, Puget. The expedition carefully charted and thoroughly described all navigable waterways and named every prominent feature.

Lewis and Clark Expedition

The best-known overland expedition began in St. Louis in 1804, led by Meriwether Lewis and William Clark.

Lewis and Clark's Corps of Discovery faced one hardship after another before crossing the Rocky Mountains and eventually finding the Columbia River. The party got a rather rushed tour, sailing toward the mouth of the Pacific Ocean, finally arriving at what was to be Fort Clatsop in Astoria, Oregon, directly along the Washington border. Captain Clark, a better navigator than speller, wrote "Ocian in View! O! the Joy!" on finally seeing the Pacific.

The First White Settlers

During the time between the early exploration and the permanent settlement of the Northwest, British and American trading posts emerged to take advantage of the area's abundant supply of beaver and sea-otter pelts. Two English companies, the North West Company and Hudson's Bay Company, merged in 1821; American fur-trading outfits included many small, independent companies as well as John Astor's Pacific Fur Company and the Rocky Mountain Fur Company.

The most influential of them, the Hudson's Bay Company, built its temporary headquarters on the north side of the Columbia, 100 miles inland at Fort Vancouver, across the river from its confluence with the Willamette.

The settlers planted crops (including the apples and wheat that are so important to Washington's economy today), raised livestock, and made the fort as self-sufficient as possible. At its peak, 500 people lived at or near the fort. Fort Vancouver served as a model for other Hudson's Bay Company posts at Spokane, Okanogan, and Nisqually. When settlers began arriving in droves and the beaver population diminished in the late 1840s, the Hudson's Bay Company was crowded out and moved its headquarters elsewhere.

Missions were another important method of establishing white settlements in the Washington Territory. The first missionary, Jason Lee, was sent by the Methodist Church in 1834 to introduce Christianity to the native peoples. Instead he spent much of his time and resources ministering to whites at Fort Vancouver.

The promise of free land under the Organic Act of 1843 and the Donation Land Law of 1850 fueled the "Great Migration" of 1843, in which almost 900 settlers traveled to the Oregon Country, six times the number of the previous year. More pioneers followed: 1,500 in 1844 and 3,000 in 1845. Most settlers came by way of the Oregon Trail from St. Joseph, Missouri, along the North Platte River, through southern Wyoming and southern Idaho into Oregon, then north to the Columbia River. Soon the route looked like a cleared road. Traces of it can still be seen where the wagon tires dug ruts in stone and where wheels packed the ground so hard that grass still cannot grow. Washington's early settlers congregated around five fledgling cities: Seattle, Port Townsend, Oysterville, Centralia, and Walla Walla; other smaller communities developed at Tumwater, Steilacoom, Olympia, and Fairhaven, now part of Bellingham. In eastern Washington the major communities were Spokane and Walla Walla.

Settling the Claims

By 1846, only the United States and England retained claims to the Oregon Country— Spain and Russia had sold or lost their North American possessions. Negotiators brought the

THE WHITMAN MASSACRE

One young man, feeling the call of God to Christianize the Western Native Americans, failed at his task. But in sacrificing his life, he changed the entire course of history of the state of Washington and the nation as a whole.

Medical missionary and New Yorker Marcus Whitman believed he had a calling: to set up missions in the Northwest and teach the Flathead and Nez Perce Indians about Christ and the Bible. In 1836, he, his wife, and a few more missionaries struck out for the West, eventually settling by the Blue Mountains and near present-day Walla Walla. This was no mean feat – Whitman and his crew blazed the trail that, only a decade later, would become the Oregon Trail, traveled by thousands.

Whitman established several missions in this nameless land, but found to his deep unhappiness that the Cayuse and Nez Perce refused to be Christianized. They were, however, very interested in his skills as a doctor, and Whitman was often called upon to minister to Indians and passing settlers as well.

The Cayuse were generally peaceable, although taken to raid the occasional wagon train and rustle cattle or horses. Their unhappiness began to grow as more and more wagon trains began to pass through, and whites brought diseases for which they had no immunity. A measles outbreak in 1847 was especially serious, and Whitman was forced to dedicate all his time to treating the disease.

Indians watched as their people died in droves, yet whites, with some immunity to the disease, often recovered. That, coupled with pre-existing tension and the tradition that healers were to be held responsible for their patient's health, caused things to quickly get out of hand. In November of 1847, a group of Cayuse rode through the mission, murdering Whitman, his wife, several other missionaries, and two young female orphans the Whitmans had adopted. Fifty other settlers were captured and later ransomed off.

In the ensuing outcry, the Oregon Trail was firmly established as an emigration route and the U.S. government officially established Oregon Territory, the first governing body west of the Rockies. Three years later, five Cayuse warriors were captured and accused of participating in the raid. They were fed, baptized, given Christian names, and then hanged, a brutal yet efficient end.

U.S. and England to agreement on a division at the 49th parallel from the Rockies to the main channel between Vancouver Island and the mainland, running through the center of the Strait of Juan de Fuca to the Pacific Ocean.

The unspecified "main channel" was viewed to be either the Rosario Strait or the Haro Strait, leaving the San Juan Islands in the middle of the disputed waterway. Both nations claimed the islands. The British maintained a Hudson's Bay Company fort, but American settlers began moving in and establishing farms. In 1859, an American shot and killed a British-owned pig that had repeatedly rooted in his garden, and the resulting uproar nearly started a war. The British demanded payment for the pig, the American refused, and soon both sides began bringing in soldiers and heavy weapons. Within three months the English had a force of 2,140 troops, five warships, and 167 heavy guns arrayed against the American army's 461 soldiers and 14 cannons. Fortunately, calmer heads prevailed, and no further shots were fired in the "Pig War." Soldiers of both nations remained on the islands for the next 13 years, and in 1872, Germany's Kaiser Wilhelm was chosen to conduct arbitration. He awarded the islands to the Americans and pronounced the Haro Strait the dividing channel.

In spite of all this arbitration, one small piece of real estate managed to be overlooked. A peninsula hung down from the Canadian mainland into the Strait of Georgia south of the 49th parallel, making it American land. Rather than settling the matter when it was discovered, the appendix still dangles there and is known as Point Roberts, a bit of America attached to Canada.

Growth of a New State

In 1848, President James Polk designated the region Oregon Territory. Settlers gradually spread out and moved farther away from the territorial capital. Finding themselves without influence while living in the northern section of the territory, settlers decided to separate from Oregon in 1852. Washington Territory was created soon after and included much

THE MERCER GIRLS

In the 1860s, Seattle faced a major crisis. As was the case with many still-rough frontier towns, the nascent city just wasn't attracting many single women. In 1864, Asa Mercer emerged as a leader who sought to fix that ticklish problem. After collecting money from townsfolk, he set out to the East Coast, approaching Civil War widows, school teachers, and other unattached ladies. The first trip netted a haul of 11 prospective brides. The next expedition in the following year did a bit better, bringing almost 100 women. While Mercer himself took a bride and split for Wyoming, all but one of the women married. Today, ritzy Mercer Island carries his name, and several present-day Seattleites consider it a strong source of pride to be descended from the original Mercer Girls.

of present-day Idaho and Montana. In 1863, Idaho Territory was carved off the whole, followed by Montana Territory in 1864, giving the territories much the same boundaries that the states now occupy.

When Washington became a territory, its population was under 4,000 people; by 1880 it had grown to over 125,000 and was considered a serious candidate for statehood. Washington was admitted as the 42nd state in 1889, with Olympia as its capital and a growing population of over 173,000.

Into the 20th Century

The rest of the Victorian era saw the growth of timber, mining, commercial fishing, and the arrival of railroads that made it all possible. The railroad was like a human artery—it brought life to every place it touched. Cities were born and died based on the reports of geologists and the influence of big money. Even towns on the line weren't guaranteed success, though. Crippling fires tore through Spokane, Ellensburg, and Seattle in the 1880s. In each case, the city was able to rebuild in brick, but the national Panic of 1893 put a halt to progress for some time. The year 1896 brought an unexpected boon to Seattle when prospectors struck gold in what would become known as the Klondike Gold Rush. For a few short years, early Seattleites made the only real money of the rush, selling picks, shovels, and even some questionable sled-dogs to the eager miners.

The first and second World Wars changed Washington's economy from one based largely on mining, farming, logging, and fishing to manufacturing and ship and airplane building. Locally born company Boeing would ultimately get contracts for over 13,000 B-17 Flying Fortresses over the course of World War II. Boeing continues to be a major employer in Western Washington.

In 1962, Seattle's world-famous Space Needle would first puncture the skyline as the centerpiece of the 1962 World's Fair. It drew almost 10 million people during its six-month run and created a permanent addition to the city's culture with the Seattle Center. Spokane followed suit 12 years later with Expo '74, emphasizing environmental concerns and cleaning up its own Spokane River in the process.

Industry and Economy

Washington's earliest industries were based exclusively on exploiting the state's natural resources. Logging and fishing were mostly shut down over environmental concerns, while mining never really produced profitable fruit for the state. Farming remains the basis for much of Washington's economy, and hydroelectric power creates jobs and low electricity costs from the state's plentiful resources. Over the years, though, manufacturing, shipping, and other industries have become increasingly important to the state's economy, particularly the trio of Boeing, Microsoft, and Weyerhaeuser.

MINING

Coal was first discovered east of Bellingham in 1849, and mining began in 1855. Discoveries of coal in the Cascades in the late 1800s gave rise to a number of small mining towns (such as Black Diamond, Carbonado, Wilkeson, Newcastle, Cle Elum, and Roslyn) on both sides of the Cascades. Though coal was plentiful—geologists today believe there are 6–65 billion tons in the state—it was soft and therefore limited in its uses. Often found in steep ravines or streams, it was also difficult to extract and transport. Underground explosions and other accidents gave Washington more mining fatalities per number of miners than any other state for several years in the late 1800s. By the turn of the 20th century, coal from the Rocky Mountains had become a cheaper and more practical fuel source, and by 1930 coal mining had virtually disappeared.

Other minerals begat industries that met with varying degrees of success. Discoveries of gold and silver in the mountains of Washington's northeastern corner caused short-lived rushes—and Indian wars, as whites crossed onto reservation lands. A successful silver, gold, and lead refinery in Tacoma was started in 1890 by William R. Rust; he later sold the plant to the American Smelting and Refining Company (ASARCO) for processing copper.

A gold mine still operates in Republic, but Washington's most valuable minerals are the least exotic: 60 percent of the money made from mineral production is derived from cement, stone, and gravel pits in the western half of the state.

LUMBER

The Pacific Northwest states of Washington, Oregon, and Idaho supply about half of the total lumber in the United States. Wood and wood products have been a vital part of Washington's economy ever since the coastal Native Americans first began using cedar for longhouses, totem poles, and canoes. British explorer John Meares was the first to ship lumber

© ONUR ERSIN/123RF.COM

The lumber industry is a vital part of Washington's economy.

to the Orient in 1788. Seattle's founding fathers depended on lumber sales to San Francisco for much of their income. The lumber business boomed with the cheaper transportation provided by the arrival of the railroads in Puget Sound in the late 1880s and 1890s.

In 1900, Frederick Weyerhaeuser purchased 900,000 acres of prime forest land from the Northern Pacific Railroad for $6 an acre, later increasing his holdings to over two million acres by 1913. With over six million acres today, the Weyerhaeuser Corporation is the largest lumber company in the country.

Forests cover over 23 million Washington acres, 18 million of which are commercial forests. It's difficult to look at the shaved hillsides of the Cascades and not think it offensive, but all of us use wood, the trees are replanted, and logging and wood products still employ a substantial number of Washington's workers.

FARMING

Since prehistoric times, agriculture has been profitable in Washington. Railroads and refrigeration gave local farms a big boost, but it wasn't until the Columbia Basin Irrigation Project opened up a half million parched acres for farming in 1952 that the state turned into a true farming powerhouse. Today, Washington farmers and ranchers produce crops worth billions of dollars annually. The biggest money crop is wheat, grown on three million acres in eastern Washington, and generally shipped overseas to Asian markets. Other important crops are hay, potatoes, apples, pears, cherries, grapes, onions, and other fruits and vegetables. Washington is one of the few states that grows cranberries, in bogs near Willapa Bay.

Washington is probably best known for its apples, some 10 *billion* of which are grown annually, approximately 40 percent of the nation's total apple production. A majority of the apples grown in Washington are of the red delicious variety, though other varieties such as gala, braeburn, and fuji have gained in popularity within the last few years.

One of the state's fastest-growing crops is wine grapes. In 1972, Washington had just six wineries. Today there are more than 250, and visitors come to tour the Columbia and Yakima Valleys much as they would California's wine-producing regions. Washington is now recognized as one of the prime wine producers in the country, with many award-winning wines and 10 official wine-growing regions. Washington boosters point out that these valleys lie at the same latitude as France's Burgundy and Bordeaux regions. The state's largest producer of wines is Chateau Ste. Michelle, with wineries in both the Yakima Valley and Woodinville.

FISHING

Full of rivers, lakes, and seashore, Washington was long heaven for subsistence, commercial, and sport fishermen. Until the 1980s, the Pacific Northwest salmon industry harvested more than 250,000 pounds of salmon annually. In the 1990s, the runs collapsed due to a combination of warm oceanic currents, the destruction of spawning habitat by dams and logging, overfishing, and droughts. Ocean fishing was banned off the coast of Washington and Oregon, and except for certain tribal fisheries and a few short openings, it has remained closed.

SHIPPING

From the time Seattle's earliest settlers dropped a horseshoe on a clothesline into Elliott Bay to determine its depth, shipping has played an important role in the development of Puget Sound communities. Today, Seattle and Tacoma are among the most important seaports in the world.

The first goods shipped from Seattle were logs that would be used as dock pilings in San Francisco. Lumber and wood products still account for a good portion of the area's exports, particularly from smaller ports such as Everett, Port Gamble, Port Angeles, Hoquiam, Olympia, and Bellingham. Seattle and Tacoma are important containerized shipping ports, where bulk and manufactured goods from airplanes to wheat are exported to Japan, China, Taiwan, Canada, and Australia. Both the ports of Tacoma and Seattle continue to be national trade leaders, and the future for containerized shipping in Washington looks bright. Oil tankers also arrive from Alaska to supply four oil refineries in Anacortes and Ferndale.

While Seattle and Tacoma get most of the shipping attention, Columbia River ports have been doing very well, thank you, especially the deep water ports of Portland, Vancouver, Longview, and Kalama, which do a big business as terminals for wheat, corn, soda ash, logs, and other materials coming down the Columbia River bound for Pacific Rim nations. These same ports import massive amounts of alumina from Australia, limestone from Canada, and cement from China, along with countless other products.

ESSENTIALS

Getting There

The **Washington State Department of Transportation's** website (www.wsdot.wa.gov) is one-stop shopping for links to the various auto, ferry, bus, air, bike, and train options around the state.

BY AIR
Washington's two major airports are **Seattle-Tacoma International (Sea-Tac)** and **Spokane International,** served by nearly all the major carriers and a handful of smaller airlines. Alaska Airlines (800/252-7522, www.alaskaairlines.com) connects many Washington cities including Seattle,

Spokane, Bellingham, Lewiston, Pasco, Port Angeles, Pullman, Walla Walla, Wenatchee, and Yakima.

BY TRAIN
Amtrak (800/872-7245, www.amtrak.com) serves Washington with two routes. The north–south route along the West Coast is aboard the *Coast Starlight,* which has service several times a day to Seattle, Tacoma, Olympia/Lacey, Centralia, Longview/Kelso, Vancouver, Portland, and south to Los Angeles. The modern and stylish *Cascades* provides daily train connections north to

Vancouver, B.C., via Edmonds, Everett, Mount Vernon, and Bellingham. The east–west route to Chicago is on the *Empire Builder*, which has daily service to Spokane, then turns southwest to Portland with stops at Pasco, Wishram, Bingen/White Salmon, and Vancouver, or to Seattle via Ephrata, Wenatchee, Everett, and Edmonds.

Note that Amtrak requires advance reservations. You can't just go down to the station and climb aboard.

BY CAR

Highways and roads are generally well maintained in Washington. The main approaches to Washington are I-5 from the north or south in the coastal area, I-90 from parts east, and I-84 from eastern Oregon.

Getting Around

BY CAR
Car Rentals

All the major car rental agencies operate at or near Seattle's Sea-Tac Airport, and any of them can be reached via their toll-free numbers or online. Many car rental agencies give discounts to active-duty military, and members of AARP, AAA, or Costco, so don't forget to mention it when booking. The best deals are sometimes from locations away from the airport where the taxes are lower, but you'll need to get there from the airport and that can add to your costs. I've found that **Thrifty Car Rental** (800/847-4389, www.thrifty.com) often has some of the lowest rates; it's a good starting point for price comparisons. For wheelchair-friendly van rentals, contact **Wheelchair Getaways** (425/788-7318 or 800/642-2042, www.wheelchairgetaways.com).

Safety on the Road

From late fall to early spring, expect snow at I-90's Snoqualmie Pass (between North Bend and Cle Elum in central Washington), Stevens Pass on U.S. Highway 2, and White Pass on State Highway 12. Closures often affect Cayuse Pass on State Highway 410 and Rainy and Washington Passes on State Highway 20 (the North Cascades Highway) after the first snowfall each winter.

Snow tires or chains are frequently required on the passes, but even when they're not, it's always a good idea to carry a set of chains and emergency equipment (flares, shovel, blankets, food, and cell phone). Before you set out, call the Department of Transportation's **Mountain** Pass Report (511, www.wsdot.wa.gov/traffic/passes); it gives road and weather conditions for all of the Cascade passes from October 15 through April 15. The website also has live cameras showing current conditions at a dozen passes in the Cascades and elsewhere.

BY BUS
Intercity Buses

Greyhound (206/628-5526 or 800/231-2222, www.greyhound.com) serves most major cities in Washington, providing nationwide connections. Its main routes are along I-5 from Canada to Oregon, along I-90 from Seattle to Spokane, and I-82 from Ellensburg to Pendleton, Oregon.

Public Transit Buses

Washington's public buses (866/936-8246) offer a comprehensive system, with low-priced service throughout all of western Washington. The coverage is less complete east of the Cascades, but still good. Many buses have bike racks. On the Web, visit www.wsdot.wa.gov/transit/for a complete listing of buses, trains, and other travel options.

Bus Tours

A number of companies offer multiday motor coach tours throughout the Pacific Northwest. The largest is **Gray Line of Seattle** (206/626-5208 or 800/426-7532, www.graylineofseattle.com).

BY FERRY
Washington State Ferries

The Washington State Ferry System

(206/464-6400, www.wsdot.wa.gov/ferries) is the largest mass transit system in the state, carrying more than 26 million passengers and 11 million vehicles each year. This is the most scenic way to see the Sound, but the system also serves many commuters who ride the ferry to work each day in Seattle, Tacoma, or Everett. Ferries operate every day, including holidays.

The best sightseeing is on the Anacortes–San Juan Islands route, which once a day continues to Sidney, British Columbia. Ferries also connect Port Townsend with Keystone (Whidbey Island); Clinton (Whidbey Island) with Mukilteo (southwest of Everett); Edmonds with Kingston (on the Kitsap Peninsula); Seattle with Winslow (Bainbridge Island) and Bremerton; Fauntleroy (southwest Seattle) with Southworth (southeast of Bremerton) and Vashon Island; and Tacoma (at Point Defiance) with Tahlequah (at the south end of Vashon Island).

The ferry system operates on a first-come, first-served basis, with reservations available only for the international routes from Anacortes to Sidney, B.C., and from Orcas Island or San Juan Island to Sidney. Foot passengers never need to wait, but those in vehicles may find themselves watching several ferries come and go before they can get onboard at peak hours.

The larger ferries have food service—beer, wine and snack-food vending machines. The smaller boats have vending machines only. Pets on leashes are allowed on the car decks or in carrying containers on passenger decks. Bikes, kayaks, and canoes are also allowed onboard for a small surcharge.

Other Ferries

A number of small Washington ferries provide service around the state, including service to Anderson Island, Guemes Island, and Lummi Island within Puget Sound, along with three Columbia River ferries.

Several private companies offer ferry connections to Vancouver Island. BlackBall Ferry Line runs the **MV Coho** (360/457-4491, www .cohoferry.com) from Port Angeles to Victoria,

B.C., across the Strait of Juan de Fuca. From Seattle, the **Victoria Clipper** (800/888-2535, www.clippervacations.com) has passenger-only service to Victoria daily in summer.

Independent tour and charter boat companies in Seattle, Tacoma, Everett, Bellingham, the San Juan Islands, Westport, and other coastal cities offer sight-seeing, fishing, and whale-watching tours throughout the year.

BY BICYCLE

Something about cycling makes a visit seem so much more intimate than just breezing through in a car. If you're willing to make the effort, Washington offers almost limitless rewards for the two-wheeled. Whidbey Island, for example, offers miles of under-traveled roads, sunnier weather than Seattle, and great state parks where you can rest. Many of the other Puget Sound islands, such as the San Juans, Vashon, Bainbridge, Mercer, and Camano Islands, are also easy to get to, are as challenging a ride as you choose to tackle, and have little automobile traffic.

Even the more populated city centers strive for bike friendliness, perhaps best embodied by Seattle's **Burke-Gilman Trail.** The 14-mile paved path runs from the scenic industrial ruins at Gasworks Park all the way to Kenmore at the north end of Lake Washington. There, it hooks up with the Sammamish River Trail, which goes right past Woodinville's Chateau Ste. Michelle and Columbia wineries—great places to stop for lunch with a bottle of wine.

In West Seattle, the road and bike path from Alki Beach to Lincoln Park is a popular 12-mile loop. Five Mile Drive in Tacoma's Point Defiance Park is open to cars as well, but cyclists are given a wide berth. The road passes through an impressive old-growth forest.

The **Washington State Department of Transportation** (360/705-7000, www.wsdot .wa.gov) publishes bicycle maps and guidelines, including a very helpful statewide map showing traffic data and road widths to help determine which roads are the safest.

Sports and Recreation

The beauty of Washington is that you can surf on a Westport beach one day, go horseback riding the next, and be on the edge of a Mount Rainier glacier the following day. The Pacific Coast has long beaches for playing in the sand, fishing, or beachcombing; the various national parks and forests offer backcountry hiking at its finest in the Olympics, Cascades, and northeast Washington; Puget Sound is a haven for sea kayaking and sailing; Columbia Gorge offers some of the finest windsurfing on the planet; anglers love the countless lakes, reservoirs, and rivers; river rafters and kayakers head down the state's white-water rivers throughout the summer; and cyclists discover roads and trails of every description. In the winter, the options shift to snow sports, and Washington has 'em all, including skiing of all types, snowboarding, sledding, skating, and snowmobiling.

ORGANIZATIONS
The Mountaineers

Established in 1906, The Mountaineers (bookstore at 7700 Sand Point Way NE, Seattle, 206/521-6002, www.mountaineers.org) is an organization of outdoor enthusiasts with a strong environmental bent. Based in Seattle, the club organizes hiking, climbing, cycling, skiing, snowshoeing, sea kayaking, and many other activities and events throughout the year. They even have a singles group where you can meet others with similar interests. Membership costs $73 per year, and members receive *The Mountaineer,* a bimonthly magazine listing local activities, along with 20 percent discounts on their many excellent books.

Washington Department of Fish and Wildlife

This state agency (360/902-2200, www.wdfw

DOG PARKS

Washington is a tremendously dog-friendly state, with its open trails, pet-friendly hotels, and millions of birds and squirrels to chase. You and your best friend never have to go far to have an adventure — Washington is full of truly excellent dog parks.

Marymoor Park is the premier pooch park west of the Cascades, featuring 40 leash-free acres of canine recreation. Play fetch in the grassy fields or splash around in the mellow Sammamish Slough. This well-landscaped and flawlessly maintained park is sure to set tails wagging.

I-5 Colonnade Dog Park is near downtown Seattle. This unique park is nestled underneath a lofty I-5 overpass, although it's easy to forget about the hustle and bustle a hundred feet over your head. This long, terraced park is a great place for socializing or fetch, and even provides complete shelter from the rain.

The **SCRAPS Dog Park** in Spokane is the first off-leash park in Spokane County. A repurposed rest area, the park is a three-acre dog party by the East's big city.

Fort Steilacoom Park in Lakewood near Tacoma hosts a great park, divided into sections for big dogs and little dogs. Near the former site of a historic mental hospital, the park features open areas for running as well as shady groves and sniff-tastic brush.

When in Yakima, check out the **Norman & Nellie Byrd Off-Leash Dog Park** along the Yakima Greenway Path. It can seem a bit deserted at times, so be sure to bring a few toys if you go.

The city of **Vancouver** has a fascinating policy on off-leash dogs, featuring over 30 parks and areas that have off-leash hours at least part of the day. From beaches to fields, there is something for any sort of dog here. Check www.cityofvancouver.us/parks-recreation/parks_trails/parks/off_leash.asp for the latest hours and locations.

.wa.gov) is in charge of fishing, hunting, and clamming in Washington. Contact them for current game fish regulations, or pick up the fat *Fishing in Washington* booklet at sporting goods or other stores that sell fishing licenses.

PUBLIC LANDS

Almost 45 percent of Washington's 42.6 million acres are publicly held. The rules, regulations, permit requirements, and fees on public lands change constantly, especially Forest Service and Park Service lands, so check with a local ranger station before heading out, or purchase *Washington's Backcountry Access Guide,* an excellent booklet that explains regulations in each area. Buy it online at www.mountaineers.org.

National Parks

Washington's three major national parks attract millions of visitors each year and offer must-see sights. **North Cascades National Park** (www.nps.gov/noca) covers a half million acres of wild mountain country that includes more than 300 glaciers, hundreds of miles of hiking trails, and the 55-mile-long Lake Chelan. **Mount Rainier National Park** (www.nps.gov/mora) contains the state's tallest and best summit: 14,411-foot Mount Rainier. Hiking trails encircle the peak, and scenic mountain roads provide lingering views of the mountain meadows, subalpine forests, and glaciers that make this one of the nation's crown jewels. **Olympic National Park** (www.nps.gov/olym) is famous for the lush west-side rain forests with enormous old-growth trees, but it also has dramatic mountainous country and the incomparable Pacific coastline.

Forest Service Lands

United States Forest Service lands cover more than nine million acres in Washington State within seven national forests. These forests are managed for multiple uses, maintaining a balance between recreational use, habitat stewardship, and responsible timber harvesting. The national forests of Washington also contain 24 wilderness areas that cover more than 2.5 million acres. Over half of the total acreage falls within the three largest: Glacier Peak Wilderness (576,900 acres), Pasaytan Wilderness (530,000 acres), and Alpine Lakes Wilderness (393,360 acres). The Forest Service also manages Mount St. Helens National

FIND EASTERN WASHINGTON, FIND A BOX, FIND YOURSELF

If I told you that the birthplace of geocaching was the Northwest, would you be remotely surprised? While Dave Ulmer, father of the sport, was an Oregonian, he recognized that the wild open spaces and thick forests of the region were ideal for hiding stuff for others to find. Since then, caches have been left from Washington's eastern border to the sea, making the state a playground for enthusiasts.

Geocaching, for those living under a rock, is a sport in which folks copy down global positioning system (GPS) coordinates online and then use them and a GPS receiver to locate boxes or tubes, wherever they might be. Sounds simple, but the mild inaccuracy of commercial GPS units and the fact that the cache could be buried, stuck in a tree, or in someone's desk drawer adds the challenge. And in Washington, it's not impossible for a geocache to be thousands of feet up at the peak of a mountain. Eastern Washington is especially full of treasures waiting to be found due to the rocky, remote locations available for sadistic cachers to leave their containers. Just be mindful of rattlesnakes, which can easily be found without any special equipment.

The best places to get started are www.geocaching.com and www.groundspeak.com. You might not even need equipment – many modern phones have a GPS built right in.

FOREST SERVICE ROAD NUMBERING SYSTEM

The way the Forest Service numbers its roads can seem inscrutable to outsiders, who might find it a bit esoteric. Here's all you need to know: If you see a road with two numbers, say Forest Service Road 25, that is a main arterial. These are typically well maintained, either paved or very level gravel roads that are passable to passenger vehicles. A road with a four- or three-digit number is a collector or local road. These are the more rugged roads that you would typically think of when you imagine a Forest Service road. Try these only with high-clearance and four-wheel-drive vehicles. And be careful! There aren't usually any guardrails on Forest Service roads.

Volcanic Monument and the Columbia River Gorge National Scenic Area, two of the state's most interesting natural areas.

Many Forest Service trailheads now charge user fees. Day use is generally $5 per vehicle per day, or pay $30 for an annual **Northwest Forest Pass** (877/874-6775, www.discovernw .org), which can be used in most national forests in Washington. The plus side is that 80 percent of this money is used to maintain local recreation areas and trails. For details on recreation in the forests, contact the headquarters offices below or stop by a local ranger station.

Colville National Forest (765 S Main St., Colville, 509/684-7000, www.fs.usda.gov)

Gifford Pinchot National Forest (10600 NE 51st Circle, Vancouver, 360/891-5003, www.fs.fed.us/gpnf)

Columbia River Gorge National Scenic Area (902 Wasco St., Hood River, Oregon, 541/308-1700, www.fs.usda.gov/crgnsa)

Mount St. Helens National Volcanic Monument (42218 NE Yale Bridge Rd., Amboy, 360/449-7800, www.fs.usda.gov/ mountsthelens)

Mount Baker/Snoqualmie National Forest (Mountlake Terrace, 425/775-9702 or 800/627-0062, www.fs.usda.gov/mbs)

Okanogan National Forest (1240 S. 2nd Ave., Okanogan, 509/826-3275, www.fs.usda .gov/okawen/)

Olympic National Forest (1835 Black Lake Blvd., Olympia, 360/956-2402, www. fs.usda .gov/olympic)

Wenatchee National Forest (215 Melody Ln., Wenatchee, 509/664-9200, www.fs.usda .gov/okawen)

Umatilla National Forest (2517 SW Hailey Ave., Pendleton, 541/278-3716, www.fs.usda .gov/umatilla)

State Parks

The state of Washington manages 125 state parks covering over 230,000 acres. State park facilities are surprisingly diverse, including several historic forts (Fort Townsend, Fort Flagler, Fort Ebey, Fort Worden, and others), many miles of sandy ocean beaches (including Grayland Beach, Fort Canby, Long Beach, Ocean City, and Pacific Beach), one of the largest public telescopes in the region (Goldendale Observatory), a park devoted to whale-watching (Lime Kiln), a campground where Lewis and Clark spent a night (Lewis and Clark Trail), and an incredible waterfall surrounded by desolate eastern Washington land (Palouse Falls). In addition, the state park system includes numerous historic sites, environmental learning centers for schoolkids, and 40 marine parks, many of which are accessible only by boat.

For the freshest info on Washington State parks, visit www.parks.wa.gov or call 360/902-8500.

WINTER SPORTS
Downhill Skiing and Snowboarding

Washington's best ski and snowboard areas are stretched along the Cascades from Mount Baker to Mount Rainier. Snow on the western slopes of the Cascades is usually wet and heavy, but some ski areas on the eastern slopes, such as Mission Ridge, have powdery snow.

Visitors centers carry the *Washington State Winter Recreation Guide.*

Cross-Country Skiing

Cross-country, or Nordic, skiing is particularly popular on the eastern slopes of the mountains, in part because the snow is more powdery and the weather is usually sunny and clear. Some of the best cross-country skiing is in the Methow Valley, with close to 100 miles of trail marked, the majority of which are groomed. The **Methow Valley Sports Trail Association** (509/996-3287, www.mvsta.com) provides a hotline for ski-touring information and a brochure showing the major trails. Other popular cross-country skiing areas include Mount Tahoma Trails (near Mount Rainier National Park), Echo Valley (near Lake Chelan), Hurricane Ridge (Olympic National Park), Leavenworth Winter Sports Club, Stevens Pass Nordic Center, White Pass Nordic Center, and Summit Nordic Center. Most of these areas groom trails for both traditional and skate-skiing.

The state maintains more than 40 **Sno-Parks** in the Cascades and eastern mountains, with nearby skiing trails that are sometimes groomed, sometimes not. The permits required to park at these plowed areas are available from retail outlets throughout the state. The cost is $20 for a one-day pass, or $40 for the entire winter season, with the money helping to pay for plowing, signs, trail grooming, and maintenance. The **State Parks and Recreation Commission** (360/902-8844, www.parks.wa.gov/winter) sells Sno-Park permits and has maps and brochures of groomed cross-country ski trails and other ski areas.

For the current snow avalanche danger in the backcountry, contact the **Forest Service** (206/526-6677) or the **Northwest Weather and Avalanche Center** (www.nwac.noaa.gov).

Snowmobiling

The state maintains over 2,200 miles of groomed snowmobile trails, primarily in the Cascades and northeast corner of the state. For a map showing snowmobile trails and a publication on snowmobile use in the state, contact **Washington State Park Recreation Division** (360/902-8844, www.parks.wa.gov/winter).

CAMPING
State Parks

Washington maintains more than 80 state parks with campgrounds, offering clean and scenic accommodations across the state. Tent sites are around $21, RV hookups (not available in all campgrounds) cost around $31. Some state parks also offer more primitive campsites for $9 that attract hikers and cyclists. Most park sites include a picnic table, barbecue grill, nearby running water, garbage removal, a flush toilet, and coin-operated hot showers. Many state parks are closed October–March; those that remain open often have limited winter camping facilities. Most campground gates close at 10 P.M., so don't roll in too late.

Campground reservations (888/226-7688, www.parks.wa.gov) can be made for nearly half of the state parks and are available as little as two days in advance, or as much as 11 months ahead of time. A $6.50 reservation fee is charged in addition to the first night's campground fee and can be paid online by credit card. You can choose a specific site from a provided map. The general state parks phone number is 360/902-8844.

The state also maintains 40 or so marine state parks in the San Juan Islands and around Puget Sound. Moorage occupancy is limited to 72 hours and cannot be reserved in advance. The **Cascadia Marine Trail System** includes more than 35 campsites around Puget Sound available to sea kayakers and users of other small human-powered or sailing vessels. Get maps and information from the **Washington Water Trails Association** (206/545-9161, www.wwta.org).

Other Public Campgrounds

Campsites at national forests and parks are scattered across Washington. Some sites are free, but most campgrounds charge $8–20. Most of these campgrounds are reservable for an extra fee of $6. Call **ReserveUSA** (877/444-6777) or make reservations on the Web at www.recreation.gov.

Washington's **Department of Natural Resources (DNR)** (800/527-3305, www.dnr.wa.gov) manages millions of acres of public lands in the state, primarily on a multiple-use basis. Campsites can be found at DNR forests throughout the state; DNR produces a helpful map showing more than 80 free public campgrounds on its land, available online.

Private RV Parks
Every town of any size has at least one private RV park. These private campgrounds generally charge $3–5 for showers if you're not camping there. People traveling in RVs often find that they prefer private parks to state and national parks, since they have better amenities. General rates can range from $20 per night up to $60.

Accommodations and Food

ACCOMMODATIONS
Lodging in Washington covers the complete spectrum, from five-star luxury accommodations where a king would feel pampered all the way down to seedy motels so tawdry that even the roaches think twice. The law of supply and demand holds fairly true when it comes to motel rates. You'll pay the least at motels in rural areas away from the main tourist track, and the most at popular destinations in peak season. This is especially true on midsummer weekends for such places as the San Juan Islands, Chelan, Leavenworth, Whidbey Island, or Long Beach, and for Seattle and vicinity year-round. At many of the resort towns, you may need to reserve months ahead of time for the peak season, and a minimum stay of two or more nights may be required. It always pays to call ahead.

Listed rates do not include state tax (8 percent) and local taxes, which can sometimes be substantial. Also, the rate listed generally reflects what you can expect during festivals or in the peak of the summer season. Winter rates are almost always considerably lower.

For an exhaustive listing of motels, hotels, and bed-and-breakfasts in Washington, request a copy of the free **Washington State Visitors Guide** (877/906-1001, www.stayinwashington.com) or pick it up at larger visitors centers around the state.

Hostels
Hostels offer the cheapest lodging options in Washington, with bunk-bed accommodations for just $15–30 per person. They are a good choice for single travelers on a budget, or anyone who wants to meet other travelers of all ages. **Hostelling International** (also known as AYH) run a sort-of accredited or vetted hostels, with statewide headquarters at the Seattle hostel (206/281-7306, www.hiayh.org). You'll need to bring your own sleeping bag or linens, and an annual membership fee is required. Another downside is that many hostels kick you out around 10 A.M. and remain closed till 5 P.M. or so, and no alcohol is allowed. Some also have a curfew. Most have a few spaces for couples who want their own room, but you may need to reserve these in advance.

Private hostels range all over the place, from the rambling old school hostel at Bingen that is now a destination for windsurfers to the funky Doe Bay Village Resort where the clothing-optional hot tub is full most evenings.

Motels and Hotels
The largest cities—Seattle, Spokane, Tacoma, Bellevue, Olympia—obviously have the greatest range of accommodations. All of these cities, without exception, have reasonably priced lodging just outside city limits, so you can stay a half hour or less away and spend the extra money having fun. If you're staying at the pricier chains, be sure to ask about discounts such as AAA member rates, senior discounts, corporate or government rates, business travel fares, military rates, or other special deals.

In Seattle or Spokane, you can stay at the budget chains near the airport. In Tacoma, stay up the road in Fife. Make reservations ahead of time whenever possible, as the least expensive rooms fill up fast. Finding a room—any room—can be extremely difficult in summer (even on weekdays) at popular resort areas such as Lake Chelan, the San Juan Islands, the national parks, or along the ocean. Again, staying a half hour from the action can better your chances of finding a room as well as saving you money—try the motels in Wenatchee when Lake Chelan is filled up, or stay in Forks or Port Angeles instead of at Olympic National Park lodges.

Bed-and-Breakfasts

More than 500 bed-and-breakfasts are scattered around the state of Washington. Some parts of the state, particularly Port Townsend, are filled with restored turn-of-the-20th-century Victorian homes that have been converted to B&Bs. Other B&Bs are old farmhouses, lodges, cottages, or modern homes with private entrances. In most cases, a room at a B&B will cost as much as one of the better motel rooms. You may miss the cable TV and room service, but you'll get a filling breakfast, probably some good conversation when you want and peace and quiet when you don't.

Many B&Bs don't allow kids or pets, and almost none allow smoking; probably a third of the rooms won't have a private bath although the shared bath is usually just a few steps away. A bed-and-breakfast is one of the better ways to get acquainted with a new area and a good choice for people traveling alone, since you'll have opportunities to meet other travelers over the sideboard.

The **Washington Bed and Breakfast Guild** (800/647-2918, www.wbbg.com) produces a brochure describing the accommodations and amenities of its member properties. **Seattle B&B Association** (206/547-1020 or 800/348-5630, www.seattlebandbs.com) also has a brochure, and you'll find links to many of Seattle's better places at its website. **A Pacific Reservation Service** (206/439-7677 or 800/684-2932, www.seattlebedandbreakfast .com) offers reservations at hundreds of B&Bs, houses, cottages, houseboats, condos, and lodges throughout the Pacific Northwest.

FOOD AND DRINK

Over the years, local produce and preferences have come to define "Northwest cuisine." Fresh salmon is popular and can be found on virtually every restaurant's menu. Red snapper, halibut, and cod are also served fresh almost everywhere in Western Washington. Less common are the local Olympia oysters and geoduck clams. As you head east, dinner starts to come on the hoof, with delicious beef and quite a bit of bison as well. The fresh produce from the east is unbeatable.

Farm Fresh

Western Washington is also known for its strawberries, blackberries, and various other berries. For a detailed directory of organic farms, natural foods grocers, and organic restaurants, and a complete listing of 70 or so farmers markets, contact the **Washington State Farmers Market Association** (206/706-5198, www .wafarmersmarkets.com). The many farms around Puget Sound are listed in a free *Farm Fresh Guide* available in local visitors centers or online at www.pugetsoundfresh.org.

Eastern Washington is the place to go for fresh fruit and produce. Washington apples are mostly of the red and golden delicious, gala, braeburn, fuji, and granny smith varieties. Many other kinds of fruit are grown along the central corridor—cherries, peaches, and apricots. The Walla Walla sweet onion is mild enough to bite into raw, like an apple, and it is sold in gift packs. Asparagus, pears, and berries of all kinds are also big Eastern Washington crops.

Beer and Wine

Washington is home to several microbreweries. The larger ones, such as the Redhook Ale Brewery in Woodinville, offer tours and tasting.

Washington wines have become world-class

in the last decade or so, winning awards and gaining in popularity across the country. Most of Washington's wine grapes come from vineyards in Yakima Valley and Columbia River Valley, and wineries line the highway between Yakima and the Tri-Cities and into Walla Walla.

For details on the state's wineries, see the Touring the Washington Wine Country booklet, available in visitors centers around the state or directly from the **Washington Wine Commission** (206/667-9463, www.washingtonwine.org).

PLATE AND BARREL

Don't just *see* Washington, *taste* it, too! The Evergreen State is bountiful with culinary delights. It's enough to bring tears to a foodie's eyes. Here are some of the best culinary experiences across the state.

VINEYARD TOURS
In the center of the state, **Yakima Valley** has the most variety of wineries, vineyards, tasting rooms, and cellars in a 50-mile stretch.

BLAKE ISLAND SALMON DINNER
Hop aboard the **Tillicum Village** tour boat for a ticket to cedar-plank cooked salmon accompanied by tribal dance.

ORCHARD TOURS
Wenatchee is the self-professed Apple Capital of the World. Stretch your legs under the shade of the area orchards and taste a few unique heirloom varieties.

COUNTRYSIDE TOUR
The cloistered **San Juan Islands** still live by their own produce, dairy, and meat. Taste farm-fresh food sold at countryside stands, and get the freshest stuff at the bed-and-breakfasts and restaurants that support their neighbors.

PIKE PLACE MARKET TOUR
Stop for an espresso at the very first **Starbucks** and then hit up **Seattle Food Tours** (www.seattlefoodtours.com) for a journey of the taste buds through the Emerald City's hub of all things culinary.

DIM SUM
Take a chance in the **International District,** and grab a few dishes you don't recognize from the carts those nice waiters push by your table.

DINNER AT HERBFARM
The ultimate multi-course dining experience is tucked away near the **Woodinville** wineries.

SLURPING UP OYSTERS
Washingtonians love their shellfish, especially the kind known for love. The oyster beds along Chuckanut Drive supply two of the finest purveyors of oysters on the half shell in the state, **The Oyster Bar** and **Chuckanut Manor.**

CAMPFIRE-FRIED TROUT
Nothing beats fresh-caught trout cooked over open coals. The wooded expanse of the **Okanogan and Colville National Forests** offer some of the best mountain lakes and streams, with plenty of campsites nearby to build the fire.

MUNCHING FRESH-PICKED BERRIES
Western Washington is redolent with the scent of blackberries and blueberries in late summer. You have to work harder for the blueberries – they typically grow alongside mountain trails around July and August. But blackberries are everywhere around the Puget Sound in August. Try **Discovery Park** in Seattle for a surefire picking spot.

Tips for Travelers

ACCESS FOR TRAVELERS WITH DISABILITIES

In existence since 1977, the nonprofit **Alliance of People with disAbilities** (206/545-7055 or 877/539-0212, www.disability pride.org) works to provide advocacy, education, and other assistance for people with significant disabilities. The **Washington Department of Transportation's** website (www.wsdot.wa.gov/choices) has details on accessible transportation choices. **Wheelchair Getaways** (888/376-1500, www.wheelchair getaways.com) rents wheelchair-friendly vans in Seattle.

Washington is a leader in developing barrier-free recreation sites on federal and state lands, and the state publishes a detailed **Accessible Outdoor Recreation Guide.** Find it at visitors centers, by calling 360/902-3000, or on the Web at www.parks.wa.gov/ada-rec. See also **Accessible Trails in Washington's Backcountry,** published by The Mountaineers (www.mountaineers.org).

GAY AND LESBIAN TRAVELERS

Gay and lesbian travelers will find Washington as open-minded as it is beautiful. It's home to a populous lesbian, gay, bisexual, and transgender (LGBT) community, particularly in the Seattle metropolitan area. Even in most rural parts of the state, gays and lesbians will feel safe and accepted by Washingtonians.

While there's not really any kind of "lavender line" in Seattle, much of the LGBT nightlife and cultural pulse is centered around the colorful Capitol Hill neighborhood. Here you'll find a wide variety of bars catering to the LGBT community.

Seattle is also home to one of the largest Pride (www.seattlepride.org) parades in the West. Held each June, the parade typically winds through downtown along 4th Avenue.

TRAVELING WITH PETS

With its wide open spaces, mountainous trails, and temperate weather, Washington is a rewarding place to travel with your furry companions. Where appropriate, I've tried to include information about pet-friendly lodging, parks, and trails. In Seattle, I'd have to say my personal favorite pet-friendly lodging is at the attentive **Alexis Hotel,** which not only accepts pups with open paws but also offers pet sitting.

As you venture further afield, you'll find that the state is fairly liberal about its wilderness pet policies when compared to other western states, such as California. Leashed dogs are allowed at campgrounds and trails within the state park system and banned only from designated swimming areas at those parks. You can also bring your leashed dog throughout all national forest land except designated wilderness areas.

Though leashed dogs can visit Mount

Washington's recreational opportunities are best enjoyed with a furry pal.

© ERICKA CHICKOWSKI

Rainier, Olympic, and North Cascades National Parks, they are only allowed in paved areas and developed campgrounds, not on trails. The sole exception is along the Pacific Crest Trail, which allows dogs on leashes no longer than six feet.

Health and Safety

GIARDIA

Although Washington's backcountry lakes and streams may appear clean, you could be risking a debilitating sickness by drinking untreated water. The protozoan *Giardia lamblia* is found throughout the state, spread by both humans and animals (including beaver, hence the nickname "Beaver Fever"). This parasite usually takes up to a week after contact to present itself, and the cramping, nausea, and diarrhea can last up to 25 days.

The disease is curable with drugs, but it's always best to carry safe drinking water on any trip, or to boil any water taken from creeks or lakes. Bringing water to a full boil is sufficient to kill Giardia and other harmful organisms. The most popular option is to use a water filter of the sort widely available in camping stores. Note, however, that these may not filter out other organisms such as *Campylobacter jejuni,* bacteria that are just 0.2 microns in size. Chlorine and iodine are not always reliable, taste foul, and can be unhealthy.

If you think you have picked up Giardia, be sure to see a medical professional immediately. It's seldom life-threatening, but can cause long-term health damage if left untreated.

HYPOTHERMIA

Anyone who has spent time in the outdoors knows the dangers of exposure to cold, wet, and windy conditions. Even at temperatures well above freezing, hypothermia—the reduction of the body's inner core temperature—can prove fatal. The ailment can strike during the summer as well, so always be prepared. In the higher elevations of the Cascades and Olympics the weather is unpredictable, and the temperature can drop dramatically in a matter of hours or even minutes.

In the early stages, hypothermia causes uncontrollable shivering, followed by a loss of coordination, slurred speech, and then a rapid descent into unconsciousness and death. Always travel prepared for sudden changes in the weather. Wear clothing that insulates well and that holds its heat when wet. Wool and polypropylene are far better than cotton, and clothes should be worn in layers to provide better trapping of heat and a chance to adjust to conditions more easily. Always carry a wool hat, since your head loses more heat than any other part of the body. Bring a waterproof shell to cut the wind. Put on rain gear *before* it starts raining; head back or set up camp when the weather looks threatening; eat candy bars, keep active, or snuggle with a friend in a down bag to generate warmth.

If someone in your party begins to show signs of hypothermia, don't take any chances, even if the person denies needing help. Get the victim out of the wind, strip off his clothes, and put him in a dry sleeping bag on an insulating pad. Skin-to-skin contact of the torso is advised for serious cases of hypothermia, and that means you and optimally one other person should partially strip and climb in the sleeping bag. Do not give the victim alcohol or hot drinks, and do not try to warm the person too quickly since it could lead to heart failure. At this point, try to get medical help as soon as possible. Ideally, you're far better off keeping close tabs on everyone in the group and seeking shelter *before* exhaustion and hypothermia set in.

TICKS

Ticks can be an annoyance in parts of Washington, particularly lower-elevation brushy and grassy areas in the spring and early summer. They drop onto unsuspecting humans and other animals to suck blood and can spread Lyme disease or relapsing fever, although this is rare in Washington.

When hiking, avoid ticks by tucking pant legs into boots and shirts into pants, using insect repellents containing DEET, and carefully inspecting your clothes while outside. Light-colored clothing (easier to see the ticks) and broad hats may also help. Check your body while hiking and immediately after the trip. If possible, remove ticks before they

BEAR SAFETY

Bears generally try to steer clear of humans, unless you manage to surprise them. While there is no certain way of avoiding serious injury or death in a bear encounter, being smart and prepared can lend a lot of protection. The Washington Department of Fish and Wildlife's website (www.wa.gov/wdfw) has additional safety tips for travel in bear country.

- Carry a bell and consider investing in a large can of pepper spray sold as "bear spray." Some hikers carry a small air horn available at sporting goods and boating stores to make a lot of noise and confuse the bear.

- If you walk with the wind, any bears ahead will smell you out, and probably move off.

- If you can't see 50 yards on any side, make some noise by talking, singing, clapping your hands, rattling a can of pebbles, wearing a bell, or dragging a stick.

- Avoid hiking alone, as bears rarely trouble groups.

- Absolutely don't let your dog off leash in the wilderness! It may sniff out a bear and lead it back to you, to say nothing of the danger of falling or encountering a snake, cougar, or bobcat.

- When camping in bear country, store all food, soap, garbage, and clothes worn while cooking in a sack hung from a tree branch at least 10 feet up and 4 feet out from the tree trunk.

- In an established campground, keep the

above items in your car's trunk or in bear-proof canisters that are often provided.

- Don't sleep where you cooked dinner, and keep sleeping bags and gear away from cooking odors.

- In a primitive site, move far away from camp to do your bathroom duties or even brush your teeth.

- If you do encounter a bear, you'll probably not have a lot of bandwidth to dedicate toward identifying it, but different bears require different approaches. A grizzly's color can't be used for identification. Look for the grizzly's shoulder hump and a dish-face profile from its eyes to the end of its nose. The snout is shorter and broader than other bears.

- Slowly move out of the bear's path and stay upwind so the bear will know you're there.

- Don't turn your back and do not run – even pro sprinters can't match a bear's charge.

- Should the bear approach, try to spot a climbable tree, but don't climb unless as an absolute last resort, as even grizzlies can climb and often can reach 10 feet high just by standing on hind legs.

- Sometimes dropping an item such as a hat or pack will distract the bear, and the sound of talking might help in convincing bears you're not a tasty threat.

- If the bear sniffs the air or stands on its hind legs, don't panic. It is probably just curious at the moment and there's a good chance it will take off after it figures you out.

become embedded in your skin. If one does become attached, use tweezers to gently remove the tick with a slight twist, being sure to remove the head. Try not to crush the body since this may release more bacteria. Apply a triple antibiotic ointment such as Neosporin to the area, and monitor the bite area for two weeks. You may want to save the tick in a jar with some damp tissue paper for later identification.

BACKCOUNTRY SAFETY TIPS

The most important part of safely enjoying the backcountry is to be prepared. Know where you're going: get maps, camping information, and weather and trail conditions from

- The bear might huff and posture, but don't panic. Most bear charges are a bluff and the bear will often stop short and amble off.
- Keep retreating!
- If attacked by a black bear, aggressively fighting back is the approach advised by experts.
- If attacked by a grizzly bear, victims seem to have equal success with fighting and play-ing dead. These massive animals are very unpredictable.
- Sometimes, although rarely, a bear will assault a tent in the middle of the night. Defend yourself *very* aggressively. Never play dead. Be sure to have a flashlight and pepper spray handy. If someone is attacked in a tent near you, yelling, throwing rocks, using your air horn, or honking a car horn may help.

© ERICKA CHICKOWSKI

Don't kid yourself, bears are out there. Always exercise caution in the wilderness.

DRIVING IN DEER COUNTRY

Mule deer, white-tailed deer, and black-tailed deer thrive throughout Washington, from the woods of Western Washington to the deserts of the East. Even neighborhoods within the city of Seattle sometimes see a deer or two. Driving through deer country requires certain precautions, as even low-speed collisions can be expensive and potentially deadly.

• Be attentive during dawn and dusk. That's when deer are most active.

• Pay attention to "Deer Crossing" signs.

• Watch the driver ahead of you. When his brake lights come on, it could be because he's spotted a deer.

• Deer are prone to leaping out of roadside swales into the road.

• When you see one deer, be cautious – others are usually nearby.

• If you do hit a deer, try to move the carcass off of the road. If the deer was merely injured, call the nonemergency police number for your locality.

a ranger or sporting goods store before setting out. Don't hike alone. Bring more than enough food so hunger won't cause you to continue when weather conditions say stop. Tell someone where you're going and when you'll be back.

Always carry the **10 essentials:** map, compass and/or GPS, water bottle, first-aid kit, flashlight, matches (or lighter) and fire starter, knife, extra clothing (a full set, in case you fall in a stream) including rain gear, food, and sunglasses—especially if you're hiking on snow. In addition,

sage advice for hikers

© ERICKA CHICKOWSKI

many hikers now carry cell phones, although a signal in the backcountry is mighty rare.

Check your ego at the trailhead; stop for the night when the weather gets bad—even if it's 2 P.M.—or head back. Don't press on when you're exhausted—tired hikers are sloppy hikers, and even a small injury can be disastrous in the woods.

Information and Services

MONEY

Foreign currency can be changed for a small fee at Sea-Tac Airport or in downtown Seattle exchange bureaus. ATMs are available virtually everywhere, debit cards are generally accepted without surcharge, and the major credit cards will serve you well in most places. Few merchants will accept an out-of-state check, however. In rural areas, even gas stations might accept cash only, so it is best to carry a little cash when leaving the cities, but doesn't hurt even in downtown Seattle. Olympia, for instance, is locally famous for its cash-only bars and restaurants. With all the politicians in town, who can blame them?

COMMUNICATIONS AND MEDIA
Telephone
Washington is broken up into five distinct area codes. Numbers within Seattle bear 206 prefixes, while those in the Eastside and Seattle's surrounding suburbs use the 425 area code. In and around Tacoma and Olympia, numbers start with 253. The rest of Western Washington bears the catchall 360 area code, while Eastern Washington numbers use the 509 prefix.

Currently the state only requires 10-digit dialing between area codes, not within them. When placing a long distance call, be sure to dial a 1 first. Otherwise, as is the case when calling between Seattle and the Eastside, simply dial the 10 digits and you'll be patched through.

Internet
Washington is an extremely technologically savvy state, so finding an open Internet connection in your travels should be a fairly easy task. Most hotels, motels, and bed-and-breakfasts offer some sort of Internet connectivity, though many still charge for the privilege. The luxury hotels in Seattle are particularly guilty of doing so, which is funny considering most chain motels offer Wi-Fi at no extra cost.

Similarly, most coffee shops and many restaurants in town also offer Wi-Fi gratis, though it will usually set you back at least the cost of a latte. If you're pinching pennies or if you're traveling without a computer, lean on the local library systems, many of which across the state provide free Wi-Fi connectivity or the use of an Internet-enabled PC for noncardholders.

The city of Seattle also provides free Wi-Fi connectivity in limited areas of town as part of an ongoing pilot project. One can access the free network, which is named "seattlewifi" in the SSID, from the U District and Columbia City neighborhoods, and within City Hall, Occidental Park in Pioneer Square, Westlake Park downtown, and Victor Steinbrueck Park near the Market.

Frequent ferry travelers can also find Wi-Fi aboard Washington State Ferries, though there is a fee for the service (www.boingo.com/ferrywifi, $7.95 per connection).

Newspapers and Magazines
Maybe it's the rain, but Seattleites and Washingtonians in general are big readers. As a result, you'll likely encounter a full spectrum of newspapers, magazines, pamphlets, and newsletters in your travels.

In Seattle, the paper of record is the *Seattle Times* (http://seattletimes.nwsource.com). Alternative papers the *Stranger* (www.thestranger.com) and *Seattle Weekly* (www.seattleweekly.com) give their mainstream journalism sisters and brothers hell with a more edgy breed of features and a pretty robust rundown of entertainment happenings.

Seattle is also home to not one, but two slick city glossies, *Seattle Magazine* (www.seattle mag.com) and *Seattle Met Magazine* (www.seattle met.com), the latter of which I prefer for its quirky storytelling and imaginative photography and art direction.

In Tacoma, the locals are informed by the *News Tribune* (www.thenewstribune.com), while in Olympia they read the *Olympian* (www.theolympian.com).

Across the mountains, the *Spokane Spokesman Review* (www.spokesman.com) is the biggest name in media, along with the *Yakima Herald* (www.yakima-herald.com).

The state is also home to numerous other hometown weeklies. To get the scoop on which towns produce a paper, visit www.usnpl.com/wanews.php for a cheat sheet.

MAPS AND TOURIST INFORMATION

For a free travel packet that includes the very helpful *Washington State Visitors Guide,* contact Washington State Tourism (800/544-1800, www.experiencewashington.com). Its website provides comprehensive details and links on Washington travel. You can also pick up maps and brochures in person at the larger visitors centers around Washington.

For details on Washington's federal lands, visit the **Outdoor Recreation Information Center** inside the Seattle REI store (222 Yale Ave. N, 206/470-4060, www.nps.gov/ccso/oric .htm). It is staffed by National Park Service and Forest Service personnel who can answer your questions about hiking trails, campgrounds, and backcountry access. Ranger stations at the national parks and forests can sell you forest and topographic maps and provide campground and trail information and other printed material.

RESOURCES

Suggested Reading

FOOD AND WINE

Calcott, Katy. *The Food Lover's Guide to Seattle*. Seattle: Sasquatch Books, 2004. A comprehensive look at the city's rich crop of greengrocers, bakeries, cheese shops, wine specialists, and much more.

Gregutt, Paul. *Washington Wines and Wineries: The Essential Guide*. Berkeley: University of California Press, 2010. A refreshing primer on the state's favorite libation, with details on varietals, growers, and tasting rooms.

Rex-Johnson, Braiden, and Jackie Johnston. *Pacific Northwest Wining and Dining*. Indianapolis: Wiley, 2007. A storytelling cookbook featuring regional recipes, stories about area dining institutions, and a collection of photos that will satisfy the eyes if not the stomach.

HISTORY AND CULTURE

Clark, Ella. *Indian Legends of the Pacific Northwest*. Berkeley: University of California Press, 2003. Learn the folktales of regional natives.

Hayes, Derek. *Historical Atlas of the Pacific Northwest*. Seattle: Sasquatch Books, 2002. Very informative atlas depicting the many faces of the Northwest in map form, from the earliest explorers to the present day.

Kirk, Ruth, and Carmela Alexander. *Exploring Washington's Past: A Road Guide to History*. Seattle: University of Washington Press, 1996. A town-by-town description of hundreds of historical sights around the state.

Speidel, William. *Sons of the Profits*. Seattle: Nettle Creek Publishing Co., 2005. Written by the quirky founder of the Seattle Underground Tour, this is an offbeat look at the colorful characters of Seattle's past.

Swan, James G. *The Northwest Coast, Or Three Years' Residence in Washington Territory. 1857*. Seattle: University of Washington Press, 1992. The personal account of a 19th-century Indian Agent to the Makah people, describing settler and Indian life of the time.

NATURAL SCIENCES

Alt, David D., and Donald W. Hyndman. *Roadside Geology of Washington*. Missoula, MT: Mountain Press Publishing Co., 1984. Easy-to-understand book on volcanoes, glaciers, floods, and how they created Washington's particular features.

Kozloff, Eugene N. *Plants and Animals of the Pacific Northwest*. Seattle: University of Washington Press, 2003. It may be older than this author, but still the most thorough book of its kind.

Sept, Duane J. *The Beachcomber's Guide to Seashore Life in the Pacific Northwest (Revised)*. Vancouver, British Columbia: Harbour Publishing, 2009. Identify shells, rocks, and other seaside finds with this handy reference.

Whitney, Stephen, and Rob Sandelin. *Field Guide to the Cascades & Olympics.* Seattle: The Mountaineers, 2004. An easily -packable, waterproof guide to flora and fauna perfect for long hikes and camping trips.

HIKING AND CLIMBING

Beckey, Fred. *Cascade Alpine Guide: Climbing and High Routes.* Seattle: The Mountaineers Books, 2000-2009. Four volumes of very detailed Cascade climbing routes, plus historical information and photos.

Burton, Joan, and Ira Spring. *Best Hikes with Kids: Western Washington and the Cascades.* Seattle: The Mountaineers Books, 2006. Having kids doesn't have to mean the end of your days on the trail. A guide to short hikes, all featuring lakes, waterfalls, views, or other points of interest that will motivate kids of all ages.

Copeland, Craig, and Kathy Copeland. *Hiking from Here to Wow North Cascades.* Berkeley: Wilderness Press, 2007. Skip the standard hikes and go straight to the ones that make you say "Wow" by perusing the lineup in this guide.

Landers, Rich. *100 Hikes in the Inland Northwest: Eastern Washington, Northern Rockies, Wallowas.* Seattle: The Mountaineers Books, 2003. Descriptions, photos, and maps of hikes in eastern Washington plus parts of Idaho, Montana, and Oregon.

Manning, Harvey, and Penny Manning. *Walks & Hikes in the Foothills and Lowlands Around Puget Sound.* Seattle: The Mountaineers Books, 1995. The legendary trail guide Harvey Manning passed away several years ago, but his cranky yet endearing guides endure. Manning was an extremely active member of The Mountaineers, a tireless wilderness advocate, and was responsible for naming countless trails and natural features in western Washington.

Molvar, Erik. *Hiking Olympic National Park.* Helena, MT: Falcon Press, 2008. A popular guide to the trails winding through the Olympic National Park.

Wood, Robert L. *Olympic Mountains Trail Guide.* Seattle: The Mountaineers Books, 2000. Detailed trail descriptions, maps, and photos of national park and national forest trails on the Olympic Peninsula.

OTHER OUTDOOR RECREATION

Brandvold, Dan. *Wingshooter's Guide to Washington.* Belgrade, MT: Wilderness Adventures Press, 2001. Everything you need to know to hunt Washington's dozens of species of game birds.

Landers, Rich, Dan Hensen, Vern Huser, and Doug North. *Paddling Washington: 100 Flatwater and Whitewater Routes in Washington State and the Inland Northwest.* Seattle: The Mountaineers Books, 2008. Whether you're looking for a quiet canoe trip or a roaring raft ride, this volume is for you.

Mueller, Marge, and Ted Mueller. *Exploring Washington's Wild Areas.* Seattle: The Mountaineers Books, 2002. This book provides an overview of Washington's wilderness areas and national parks, with brief descriptions of hiking and climbing in each. An excellent introduction to these wild places.

Mueller, Marge, and Ted Mueller. *North Puget Sound: Afoot & Afloat.* Seattle: The Mountaineers Books, 2006. Painstakingly detailed guide to North Puget Sound, from Point Roberts to Whidbey Island and west to Neah Bay, helpful to both boaters and landlubbers. Boat launches, parks, points of interest, plus photos and maps.

Poffenbarger, Amy, and Mark Poffenbarger. *Mountain Biking Washington: A Guide to Washington's Greatest Off-Road Bicycle Rides.* Guilford, CT: Globe Pequot, 2006.

Romaine, Garret. *Gem Trails of Washington.* Upland, CA: Gem Guide Books, 2007. The perfect guide for rockhounds on the road. Includes GPS coordinates for better finding hunting grounds in the middle of nowhere.

Spring, Vicky, and Tom Kirkendall. *100 Best Cross Country Ski Trails in Washington.* Seattle: The Mountaineers Books, 2002.

Stienstra, Tom. *Moon Washington Camping.* Berkeley: Avalon Travel, 2006. The authoritative guide to public and private campgrounds around the state.

Trudell, Steve, and Joe Ammirati. *Mushrooms of the Pacific Northwest: Timber Press Pocket Guide.* Portland: Timber Press. 2009. A guide to one of Washington's most peaceful yet dangerous outdoor activities. Features hundreds of indigenous mushrooms and advice on their edibility.

SEATTLE IN-DEPTH

Dwyer, Jeff. *Ghost Hunter's Guide to Seattle and Puget Sound.* Gretna, LA: Pelican Publishing Company, 2008. Hang around Seattle's best haunts with help from this eccentric book.

Elenga, Maureen. *Seattle Architecture: A Walking Guide to Downtown.* Seattle: Seattle Architecture Foundation, 2008. Architecture buffs and urban explorers are sure to enjoy the various site histories and descriptions detailed here.

Fischer, Monica. *Best Places Seattle.* Seattle: Sasquatch Books, 2008. The list format can be a bit wearing, but this book offers a very comprehensive compendium of Seattle dining choices.

Lucas, Eric. *Seattle Survival Guide.* Seattle: Sasquatch Books, 2005. Crucial guide to hitting the ground running after transplanting to Seattle.

Moon Metro Seattle. Berkeley: Avalon Travel, 2005. A handy map-based guide offering tips on Seattle's hotspots.

ONWARD TRAVEL

The following is an invitation to check out other Moon books in which Washington visitors may be interested. All of these are authoritative guides for their respective regions. Find out more on the web at www.moon.com.

Hempstead, Andrew. *Moon British Columbia.* Berkeley: Avalon Travel, 2008.

Jewell, Judy, and W.C. McRae. *Moon Coastal Oregon.* Berkeley: Avalon Travel, 2012.

Jewell, Judy, and W.C. McRae,. *Moon Oregon.* Berkeley: Avalon Travel, 2012.

Pitcher, Don. *Moon San Juan Islands.* Berkeley: Avalon Travel, 2012.

Kelly, James P. *Moon Idaho.* Berkeley: Avalon Travel, 2011.

Burlingame, Jeff. *Moon Olympic Peninsula.* Berkeley: Avalon Travel, 2012.

Internet Resources

ABOUT WASHINGTON
State of Washington
www.access.wa.gov
The official Washington website is a great starting point, with links to state, local, and federal agencies. You'll find everything from public libraries to the Cemetery Board here.

Washington Chambers of Commerce
www.wcce.org
Features links to regional and local chambers of commerce websites.

Washington State Department of Transportation
www.wsdot.wa.gov

This site contains links to the public ferry, bus, air, bike, and train options around the state.

TRAVEL
The Map Company
www.wamaps.com

This site features detailed maps from all over the state, available to view for free online or for purchase.

Seattle B&B Association
www.seattlebandbs.com

Member-based organization featuring a directory of associated B&Bs.

Seattle/King County Convention & Visitors Bureau
www.seeseattle.org

Head to this website for updates on local events and some information on restaurants and lodging.

Washington Bed and Breakfast Guild
www.wbbg.com

The state B&B association's website has links to homepages run by its many members.

Washington State Hotel and Lodging Association
www.stayinwashington.com

This private association has list-style directories of hundreds of member hotels, motels, and B&Bs. It also produces a free visitors guide available in most visitors centers.

Washington State Tourism
www.experiencewashington.com

This is the state's tourism department site, and should get at least a look-see from anyone planning to visit.

OUTDOOR RECREATION
The Mountaineers
www.mountaineers.org

Established in 1906, this is the preeminent Seattle-based environmental and outdoor activity organization, which sponsors thousands of outdoor trips and events throughout the year, publishes books, and is generally friendly and inviting.

National Park Service
www.nps.gov

Washington is home to nine different national parks, from the minuscule Klondike Gold Rush National Historical Park in downtown Seattle to the half-million acres of land within North Cascades National Park. Learn about them at the official Park Service homepage.

Outdoor Recreation Information Center
www.nps.gov/ccso/oric.htm

This REI-store-based kiosk is perfect for learning about outdoor recreational opportunities on federal and state lands around Washington. Their information desk is inside the big Seattle REI store.

Recreation.gov
www.recreation.gov

Reserve campsites at public campsites in Washington national parks and national forests.

Ski Washington
www.skiwashington.com

Nine of the state's largest downhill ski areas are accessible through this Web portal that also gives condition reports across the state.

U.S. Forest Service Pacific Northwest Region
www.fs.fed.us/r6/r6nf.htm

This site contains links to national forests throughout the Pacific Northwest.

Washington Department of Fish and Wildlife
http://wdfw.wa.gov/

Not always easy to navigate, this site contains information about fishing permits and seasons, shellfishing regulations, hunting permits, and tons of wildlife and legislation concerns. You can purchase your fishing license online.

Washington State Accessible Outdoor Recreation Guide
www.parks.wa.gov/ada-rec
This site has details on barrier-free recreation sites on federal and state lands.

Washington State Parks and Recreation Commission
www.parks.wa.gov
Filled with details on Washington's excellent state parks. You can also make campground reservations.

NEWS AND EVENTS

Art Guide Northwest
www.artguidenw.com
This is the online version of a free publication that details gallery openings and exhibits throughout the Pacific Northwest.

Hometown News
www.hometownnews.com/wa.htm
This site contains links to websites for virtually all of Washington's newspapers.

Saturdaymarkets.com
www.saturdaymarkets.com
This site lists information on farmers markets around Washington.

Washington Festivals and Events Association
www.wfea.org
An online source for upcoming activities of all types.

Washington State Fairs
www.wastatefairs.com
Want to learn more about the dozens of county, regional, and state fairs and rodeos around Washington? This is a great place to start your search.

Index

T

List of Maps